The 1995 Good Weekend Guide

Edited by Alisdair Aird

Deputy Editor: Fiona May

Associate Editors: Robert Unsworth, Karen Fick

Walks Consultant: Tim Locke

BCA

LONDON   NEW YORK   SYDNEY   TORONTO

This edition published in 1995 by BCA by arrangement with Vermilion,
an imprint of Ebury Press

CN 1933

Typeset from author's disks by Textype Typesetters, Cambridge
Printed and bound by Clays Ltd, St Ives plc.

CONTENTS

INTRODUCTION

Despite the recession, places such as historic houses, gardens, wildlife centres and the like have reported a general rise in the number of people visiting them. Rather fewer people seem to be going to museums and galleries. Yet, with great advances in presentation techniques, it's in the museums' field that some of the most exciting finds are now to be made – you just have to know where to look for them.

London is, of course, a special case, packed with museums and galleries of the highest international standing, many right at the forefront of presentation technology. Out of London, though, there's an immense variety of fascinating collections. Tyneside, Glasgow and Edinburgh stand out for a magnificent range of mainly free museums and galleries, full of life and interest. And there are the great out-of-London treasure-houses of the arts, notably the Fitzwilliam in Cambridge, the Walker Gallery in Liverpool, the Bowes Museum in Barnard Castle (Northumbria), the Ashmolean in Oxford, the Burrell Collection in Glasgow, the National Gallery of Scotland in Edinburgh and the National Museum of Wales in Cardiff.

The most widely appealing 'museums' today are those which display not so much things as experiences – how people used to live or work. Often, these are spread over enough ground to house a large village or small town, and show whole communities in action, real people in period dress. Or they may pack similar effects into a much smaller area, using dark rides or other relatively advanced technology, even with relevant smells and vibrations as well as sights and sounds.

Currently the best of these living museums is the North of England Open-Air Museum, Beamish, Northumbria, with large-scale competitors in the Welsh Folk Museum, St Fagans; the Blists Hill Open-Air Museum, which is part of the wonderful collection of Ironbridge Gorge Museums, Shopshire; and the Black Country Museum, Dudley, Midlands. Also outstanding in this field, if mostly on a smaller scale, are Norton Priory, Runcorn, Cheshire (medieval monastic life); Morwellham Quay, Devon (Victorian); Canterbury Heritage Museum, Kent; White Cliffs Experience, Dover, Kent; Wigan Pier, Lancs (early 1900s); Bede's World, Jarrow, Northumbria (Dark Ages); Museum of East Anglian Life, Stowmarket, Suffolk; Chalk Pits Museum, Amberley, Sussex (active traditional workshops); and Weald & Downland Open-Air Museum, Singleton, Sussex (traditional buildings). The most interesting countryside collection is Reading University's Museum of English Rural Life, Berkshire; the Castle Museum in York has the most fascinating collection relating to everyday life since the 1600s.

Although one would think that escaping from transport was an essential ingredient of an enjoyable break, transport museums enthrall many people. The most enjoyable of these is the Tram Museum at Crich, Derbys. Also outstanding are Duxford Airfield, Cambs (Europe's best aircraft museum), the National Waterways Museum in Gloucester, the Heritage Motor Centre at Gaydon, Midlands, and the National Railway Museum in York.

The most entertaining science or industry museum is now Manchester's Museum of Science and Technology. The Yorkshire Mining Museum, Middletown, Rhondda Heritage Park in Porth and Swansea's Maritime and Industrial Museum (both Wales) are also quite enthralling.

Other great museums which fascinate people of all ages, even if they're not specially interested in the subject, are the Robert Opie Collection, Gloucester (advertising and packaging); H M Naval Base, Portsmouth (HMS *Victory*, *Mary Rose* and more); the remarkable Walter Rothschild Zoological Museum, Tring, Herts; Quex House, Birchington, Kent (extraordinarily eclectic, the museum we've most enjoyed finding this year); the Gallery of English Costume, Rusholme, Manchester; the vastly intriguing ethnology collection at the Pitt-Rivers Museum, Oxford; and the wide-ranging very interactive Newcastle Discovery, Northumbria. The museum which currently stands out as the most interesting in Britain is the National Museum of Photography, Film and Television in Bradford, Yorks.

A great many other relatively specialised museums turn out in practice to be of far wider appeal than expected – there's so much enthusiasm behind them that they have a vigour which more general collections can't match. Here, we list the 50 most enjoyable specialised places outside London – some awesomely large, some very small indeed:

Cowper and Newton Museum, Olney, Bucks
Peterborough Museum, Cambs (models by Napoleonic prisoners-of-war)
Goonhilly Satellite Station, Cornwall
Dock Museum, Barrow-in-Furness, Cumbria
Bovington Tank Museum, Dorset
Colchester Castle, Essex (Roman)
Toy Museum, Stansted, Essex
D-Day Museum, Portsmouth, Hants
Sammy Miller Motorcycle Museum, New Milton, Hants
Royal Marines Museum, Southsea, Hants
Museum of Army Flying, Middle Wallop, Hants
Butser Ancient Farm, Chalton, Hants
Button Museum, Ross on Wye, Hereford & Worcs
Avoncroft Museum of Buildings, Bromsgrove, Hereford & Worcs
Verulamium Museum, St Albans, Herts (Roman)
Docks Museum, Hull, Humberside
National Fishing Heritage Centre, Grimsby, Humberside
Historic Dockyard, Chatham, Kent
Western Approaches, Liverpool (WWII command bunker)
Customs & Excise Museum (part of Maritime Museum), Liverpool
Historic Warships, Birkenhead, Lancs
Helmshore Textile Museum, Lancs
British Lawnmower Museum, Southport, Lancs
National Cycle Museum, Lincoln
Museum of Entertainment, Spalding, Lincs
Discovery Centre (jewellery), Birmingham
Bradfield House Glass Museum, Kingswinford, Midlands
Cogges Farm Museum, Witney, Oxon (Victorian farm life)
Pendon Museum of Miniature Landscape, Long Wittenham, Oxon (1930s
    model railway and landscape, in progress)
British Folk Art Museum, Bath
American Museum, Bath
Fleet Air Arm Museum, Yeovilton, Somerset
Derby Day Experience, Epsom, Surrey
Finchcocks, Goudhurst, Sussex (keyboard instruments)
Rejectamenta Nostalgia, East Wittering, Sussex (20th-c bric-a-brac)
Underground Quarry, Corsham, Wilts
Bedwyn Stone Museum, Great Bedwyn, Wilts
Great Western Railway Museum, Swindon, Wilts
Museum of Automata, York
Colne Valley Museum, Golcar, Yorks
Shibden Hall Folk Museum, Halifax, Yorks
Millenium, Scarborough, Yorks (the town since 1000)
Eden Camp, nr Malton, Yorks (WWII)
People's Palace, Glasgow (social history)
Teddy Melrose, Melrose, Scotland (teddy bears)
New Lanark Visitor Centre, Scotland
Inveraray Jail, Inveraray, Scotland
Golf Museum, St Andrews, Scotland

Nelson Museum, Monmouth, Wales
Llancaiach Fawr, Nelson, Wales (Elizabethan life)

All these places have moved with the times (to see just how far they've moved, visit the meticulously entertaining re-creation of a Victorian natural history display at the Ipswich Museum in Suffolk). However, it's sadly true that many museums have themselves become museum pieces. That traditional rainy-day standby of the holidaymaker, the local museum, now runs a serious risk of being outclassed by local competition. In many towns, there are now much more interesting places to visit nearby. We have dropped quite a number of local museums from this edition for that reason. That's not to say they have entirely outlived their usefulness, as in most cases they still meet an important local need, being valuable repositories of local information and history. However, as there are some fine local museums to prove that spirited and lively displays give a real sense of enjoyment and discovery, it seems a wasted opportunity that so many others seem content to live back in the days when a row of murky glass cases with fading hand-written cards would do.

On the whole, prices at all types of tourist attraction this year are very similar to last year's, with few major increases; and we have been struck by the number of tourist attractions which without charging extra have been adding to what they offer visitors. So, given the static prices, visitors are in general getting better value for money than before.

You'd perhaps expect the few places where prices have sharply increased to be swamped with visitors. As we've said above, the general trend has been for tourist attractions to report increased numbers of visitors. Not all have, though. We have carried out a survey of prices in 277 major paid-entrance tourist attractions (historic houses, monuments, museums, galleries, wildlife attractions and the like) which have reported a fall in visitor numbers in 1993, the most recent full year for which figures were available as we went to press. (We did not include any National Trust properties – see below.)

How many of these, to improve their value-for-money rating, gave us a lower price for this year's *Guide* than for last year's? Only 3%! The most striking and most praiseworthy price reduction is at Bristol's Industrial Museum, where the local authority has cut the admission price by half.

Only 39% of these places facing falling visitor numbers have held their prices steady. Most have actually increased their prices; 8% have put them up by an amount roughly equivalent to the current low level of general price inflation. However, 49% have evidently decided that the right answer to falling visitor numbers is a significant hike in prices – well over the retail price index. A quarter of these price-hikers have pushed up their prices by 20% or more. This is deplorable. As an answer to sagging popularity, it seems an almost insulting disregard for giving good value.

100 years old and going strong

The National Trust celebrates its centenary this year. It has been the indispensable power behind the preservation of much of the best English and Welsh countryside and really worthwhile houses. It is now coming up with what we believe to be the right answer to overcrowding in its most popular properties – selling a limited number of timed-admission tickets for them, instead of eliminating publicity for them as before. The National Trust is giving particular value this centenary year, both in generally holding down admission prices, and in a series of special events such as music-and-firework spectaculars which should be well worth watching out for. See **Using the Guide** for how to join – which brings you free admission to hundreds of Britain's most enjoyable properties.

Tourism in Britain is extremely important to the national economy: excluding day trips, British people spend a total of about £10 billion a year on short breaks or longer holidays here, and foreign visitors bring in about as much again. Even so, spending on holidays here has grown more slowly than spending by British people on holidays abroad, so that there is in effect a deficit approaching £4 billion a year in the 'holidays balance of payments'.

The national Tourist Boards, and British Tourist Authority (responsible for promoting holidays in Britain abroad), have brought great professionalism to tourism market research, promotion and support. But it seems to us that for over 20 years they have spent too much energy on what is now surely a lost cause: trying to resuscitate Mudbury on Sea, Great Yawnmouth and those other moribund seaside resorts which have no real style of their own and can never hope to compete with Lyme Regis, Scarborough, Torquay, Broadstairs, Eastbourne, Brighton, Blackpool, Tenby or Llandudno, say – let alone all those foreign beaches with their guaranteed warmth and sunshine. In contrast, their promotion of some areas for summer holidays has been almost too successful: the Peak District now has to ban motorists from some areas on summer weekends, and the Lake District, Dartmoor and Exmoor, the Yorkshire Dales and Moors, the New Forest, and in Wales the Brecon Beacons and Pembrokeshire coast, all have parts that are far too heavily trampled in summer.

There is one unique strength in Britain's holiday appeal which it seems to us deserves much more attention instead. That is the astonishing variety of attractive and highly individual places to stay in, well sited in areas of real interest – often these are the smaller hotels and inns, and the more characterful B&B places. Only people who buy and read books such as this find out how rich a choice there is of these. Yet they should surely be the basis of many more people's voyages of discovery into Britain. For that, what's needed is efficient collaborative regional book-a-bed-ahead schemes using a head-hunter approach to select participating establishments on a merit basis. People could trust the schemes to find them establishments with some character, style and individuality (rather than the all too anonymous places which can apply to join existing tourist board listings). And, for touring, once people were booked into one establishment, that place would be able to book them on for the next night into somewhere of the same sort of standing, further along their route. This would turn what's now a scattered myriad of individual establishments cut off from one another into a powerful network that people could rely on to find their way through the best parts of undiscovered Britain in comfort and style. Surely that's a better horse for the tourist boards to back than those steady losers, the failing seaside resorts – let alone flogging to death last year's winners (the Lakes, Dartmoor and the other overvisited National Parks).

Working on this book, we've always been struck by the way that in almost every small area of Great Britain there is a whole range of interesting places to visit. In many areas local tourist boards do a great deal to publicise them, and this year it seems that more local tourist information centres (TICs) are including in their leaflets money-off coupons to encourage visits (so it's certainly worth calling in at a TIC to see what's on offer). Also, there is the embryonic beginning of a move to collaborative ticketing: well priced joint tickets admitting to several attractions in the same area, as we've found for example in Ironbridge (Shrops), Greenwich (London) and Biggar (Scotland). There's surely a great deal more which could be done on these and related lines: green passport tickets to all the gardens in an area, for instance, or special-offer tickets which, once you visit one attraction, then give you cut-price admission to a wide range of other unrelated attractions in the same area.

The best areas

If you can get away outside high summer and thus avoid the crowds, the areas with the widest appeal are Cumbria, Devon, the Yorkshire Dales, the Cotswolds in Gloucestershire, and Derbyshire. Even at peak times these do have at least some unspoilt parts where you can escape the crowds, and some marvellous attractions that most people don't know about. Other areas full of interest, with lovely scenery, include Northumbria, Somerset, Lancashire (these three all have particularly energetic local tourist organisations); Shropshire, Herefordshire, west Dorset, the Isle of Wight; much of Cheshire, Cornwall, Northamptonshire and Sussex; parts of Norfolk, Suffolk and Wiltshire; most of Scotland and Wales. East Kent is excellent for family breaks; West Yorkshire stands out for a tremendous range of unusual sightseeing possibilities.

York is ideal for a city break, and London is superb for shows, shopping, eating out and above all museums, galleries, cultural events and sightseeing. Other excellent cities for visitors are Edinburgh, Bath and Chester. We'd also strongly recommend Cambridge, Oxford, Durham, Salisbury, Exeter, and perhaps Norwich, Lincoln and Shrewsbury. Rye in Sussex is the most charming smaller town for a short break.

Two hot tips, both in Kent

For people who like getting there ahead of the crowds, Godinton Park near Ashford is a really charming relatively 'undiscovered' stately home, and the gardens of Groombridge Place, until recently kept private, are quite spectacular. They won't be open till spring.

Ugly parking

Our big grouse this year is about those stately homes which ruin a grand façade by planting an ugly car park right in front of it. In brochures what you see is a memorable masterpiece of architecture beautifully set off by a sweep of majestic courtyard; in real life, it's hidden sadly behind a brash clutter of parked cars. What next: coaches in the forecourt of Buckingham Palace?

Future *Guides*

This is the third edition of the *Guide*. It already draws greatly on the knowledge and experience of hundreds of readers, and we hope that future editions will gain more strength and of course new entries from readers' reports. (We estimate that this edition includes nearly 20% more detail than the last.) The more people tell us about their own experiences and ideas, the better the book will become. So please write to us about hotels, farmhouses or whatever you've enjoyed for short or longer holiday stays, about restaurants and other good places to eat in, about interesting events, and about the things you've enjoyed doing and places you've enjoyed visiting. (And tell us about the bad times, too!) You can use the tear-out card in the middle of the book, report forms at the back of the book, or just write on ordinary paper. For letters posted in Britain you don't need a stamp: the address is *The Good Weekend Guide*, FREEPOST TN1569, WADHURST, E Sussex TN5 7BR.

Alisdair Aird

USING THE GUIDE

The Counties

England has been split alphabetically into county chapters. Occasionally, counties have been grouped together into a single chapter, and metropolitan areas have been included in the counties around them – for example, Merseyside in Lancashire. This follows the pattern which we have found works well in the companion *Good Pub Guide*, and allows people who have both books to cross-refer easily. If in doubt, check the Contents.

Scotland and Wales have each been covered in single chapters, and London appears immediately before them at the end of England.

We have subdivided most chapters into smaller areas, each of which could form the basis of a weekend break or short holiday. So Devon, for instance, has five areas, Yorkshire seven.

Where to stay

In each section, hotels, inns and other places to stay such as farmhouses are listed in price order, starting with the most expensive. The price we show is the total for two people sharing a double or twin-bedded room with its own bathroom, for one night in high season. It includes full English breakfast (unless only continental is available, in which case we say so), VAT and any automatic service charge that we know about. So the price is the total price for a room for two people. We say if dinner is included in this total price. It is included in some of the more remote places, especially in Scotland and Wales, and may also be in some other places where the quality of the food is a main attraction; in these cases, the establishment concerned does not normally offer B&B on its own. In some of the places we list, some or occasionally even all the bedrooms share bathrooms; we say if this is the case.

An asterisk beside the price means that the establishment concerned assured us that that price would hold until the end of summer 1995. Many establishments were unable to give us this assurance; this last year, bedroom prices have been holding very steady, but to be on the safe side it might be prudent to allow for an increase of around 5% by then.

A few hotels will do a bargain break price at weekends even if you're staying for just one night. If so, that's the price we give, and we show this with a **w** beside the price. Many more hotels have very good value short break prices, especially out of season, if you stay a minimum of at least two nights; if you plan to stay in one area rather than tour around, it's well worth asking if there's a special price for short breaks when you book. In the present economic climate, many hotels also offer short-notice bargains which don't appear on their tariffs if they are underbooked on a particular night, so as to fill their rooms even at a discount. So, especially if you are not booking in advance, ask what price they can quote you for that particular night.

If there's a choice of rooms at different prices, we always give the cheapest, and if we know that maybe the back rooms are the quietest or the front ones have the best views or the ones in the new extension are more spacious then we say so. If you want a room with a sea view or whatever, you should always ask specifically for this, and check whether it costs extra.

If the hotel closes for any day or part of the year, we say so. But, especially in outlying areas, hotels have been known to close at other times if their business is very slack. And this last year or two we've found some go out of business altogether. So don't head off into an area where there are no nearby alternatives without checking by telephone first.

We always mention a restaurant if we know the inn or hotel has one. Note that we always commend food if we have information supporting a positive recommendation. So a bare mention that food is served shouldn't be taken to imply a recommendation of the food.

Where to eat

Restaurants are listed in rough price order, starting with the most expensive. The price in **bold type** is for one person having a typical three-course restaurant meal with half a bottle of wine, including any automatic service charge. So double it to get a meal for two. Prices in normal type are for more informal meals. The second price, after the |, is for a lunchtime sandwich or similar snack if the establishment offers one. The last price, after the /, is for a single-dish meal.

We list any scheduled closing dates. We have found quite a few instances of unscheduled closures in the last year or two, and recommend booking if your plans would be thrown into turmoil by finding a place unexpectedly closed. Moreover, many of the restaurants we list are very popular, and without a booking you may find there's no room for you.

If you want a good meal out in any area, look at the places to stay as well as the restaurants, especially in country areas. When we praise a hotel or inn for its food, that means it's well worth consideration as a place for a good meal out. In some parts of the country, it's in these hotel restaurants that you'll find the best food.

Our brief mentions of places to eat in the text of the **To see and do** sections are based on our own inspections or on firm recommendations from readers.

Children

We asked all hotels, restaurants and other places to stay in and eat at which have full entries in the *Guide* whether they allow children. If the entry doesn't mention children, that means the establishment has told us that it welcomes them, with no restrictions. If there are restrictions (either an age limit, or segregated early evening meals for them), we spell these out. We have found that very occasionally establishments turn out in practice to be more restrictive about children than they claim. And of course managements change, and so do their policies. If you are travelling with children, to avoid misunderstandings it's always worth checking ahead that there will be no problem. Please let us know if you find any difference from what we say. Obviously too you should bear in mind the character of the hotel or restaurant, as described, and in relation to your own children. While some children might fit perfectly into the atmosphere of a dignified and old-fashioned country house, others might be fractiously ill at ease there – no fun for you, or for the other guests.

Locations

As far as possible, we list places to see (and hotels and restaurants) under the name of the nearest village or town. We use **bold type** to name the locality, and SMALL CAPITAL LETTERS to name the establishment. If the village is so small that you probably wouldn't find it on a road map, we've listed it under the name of the nearest sizeable village or town instead.

The maps use the same locality name as the text. We include places in their true geographical locations – so if a village is actually in Buckinghamshire that's where we list it, even if its postal address is via some town in Oxfordshire.

Prices and other factual details

Information about opening times and so forth is for 1995. In some cases establishments were uncertain about these when the *Guide* went to press in 1994; if so, we say in the text. (And of course there's always the risk of changed plans and unexpected closures.) When we say 'cl Nov–Mar' we mean closed from the beginning of November to the end of March, inclusive; however when we say 'cl Nov–Easter' we mean that the establishment reopens for Easter.

Where establishments were able to guarantee a price for 1995, we have marked this with an asterisk. In many cases establishments could not rule out an unscheduled price increase, and in these cases – ie, no asterisk against the price – it's probably prudent to allow for a 10% increase in around April 1995. If you find a significantly different price from that shown, *please let us know*.

National Trust

NT after price details means that the property is owned by the National Trust, and that for members of the Trust admission is free. There is a similar arrangement for properties owned by the National Trust for Scotland (NTS); the two Trusts have a reciprocal arrangement, so that members of one may visit the properties of the other free. Membership is therefore well worth while if you are likely to visit more than a very few properties in the year – quite apart from its benefit to the Trusts' valuable work. Details from National Trust, PO Box 39, Bromley, Kent BR1 1NH (0181-464 1111); or National Trust for Scotland, 5 Charlotte Sq, Edinburgh EH2 4DU (0131-226 5922).

Telephone numbers

We give telephone numbers (including the new extra 1 in the dialling code – which already works for all numbers) for all places recommended in the **Where to stay** and **Where to eat** sections. This year for the first time we have also included them in the **To see and do** sections for most places which are not run by large organisations such as local authorities, the National Trust or English Heritage (or their equivalents in Scotland and Wales); and for the organisers of events recommended in the Calendars.

Disabled access

We always ask establishments if they can deal well with disabled people. We mention disabled access if a cautious view of their answers suggests that this is reasonable, though to be on the safe side anyone with a serious mobility problem would be well advised to ask ahead (many establishments made clear that this helped them to make any special arrangements needed). There may well be at least some access even when we or the establishment concerned have not felt it safe to make a blanket recommendation – again, well worth checking ahead. There are, of course, many places where we can't easily make this sort of assessment – particularly the less formal 'attractions' such as churches, bird reserves, waterside walks, and viewpoints. In such cases (which should be obvious from the context) the absence of any statement about disabled access doesn't mean that a visit is out of the question, it simply means we have no information about that aspect. We're always grateful to hear of readers' own experiences. An important incidental point: many places told us that they would give free admission to a wheelchair user and companion.

Recommenders

At the end of each chapter we include the names of people who have given us help with that chapter for this new edition. Besides people who have written to us with information specifically for this book, some writing to us about the companion *Good Pub Guide* have given us information which has proved useful for this book too. Where this has been a real help to the chapter concerned, we have in acknowledgement printed their names too.

Special interest lists

Lists at the back of the book pick out hotels and other places to stay which are by the waterside, which have good walks right on their doorstep, which are placed right by lots of other things to do, which have food that's good enough to count as a definite part of their appeal, which have under their roof or in their own grounds enough for you to be happy staying put for the day, and which are tucked away in really quiet spots.

Changes during the year – please tell us

Changes are inevitable during the course of the year. Managements change, and so do their policies. We very much hope that you will find everything just as we say. But if you find anything different, please let us know, using the report card in the middle of the book, the forms at the end of the book, or just a letter. For letters posted in Britain you don't need a stamp: the address is *The Good Weekend Guide*, FREEPOST TN1569, WADHURST, E Sussex TN5 7BR.

Reports

This *Guide* depends very heavily indeed on readers reporting back to it. In that sense it's very much a collaborative venture: and the more people that send us reports, the better the book will be. So please do help us by telling us about places you think should be added to the book, or removed from it, or even just confirming that places still deserve their entry. We try to answer all letters (though there may be a delay – and between the end of May and October we put all letters aside until after the end of the hectic editorial rush). People who help us do get a special offer discount price on the next edition. There's a note on the sort of information we need at the back of the book, with report forms; and a tear-out report card in the middle of the book.

Map references

Most place names are given four-figure map references, looking like this: NT4892. The NT means it's in the square labelled NT on the map for that area. The first figure, 4, tells you to look along the grid at the top and bottom of the NT square for the figure 4. The *third* figure, 9, tells you to look down the grid at the side of the square to find the figure 9. Imaginary lines drawn down and across the square from these figures should intersect near the locality itself.

The second and fourth figures, the 8 and the 2, are for more precise pin-pointing, and are really for use with larger-scale maps such as road atlases or the Ordnance Survey 1:50,000 maps, which use exactly the same map reference system. On the relevant Ordnance Survey map, instead of finding the 4 marker on the top grid you'd find the 48 one; instead of the 9 on the side grid you'd look for the 92 marker. This makes it very easy to locate even the smallest village.

Symbols

We have used the same symbols in the text and on the maps to pick out all the main types of places to visit. Though you don't need to pay any attention to the symbols, you can if you like use them to scan the text or a map quickly, to see what castles, say, or gardens a particular area has. These are what we have used the symbols to denote:

★ Attractive village or town

🏠 Interesting house – anything from an intimate cottage to the stateliest of stately homes

🏰 Castle, ruined abbey or other romantic ruin

🏛 More or less archaeological site such as Roman remains, neolithic stone circles, early medieval mazes, Iron Age hill forts

✝ Church, cathedral, minster, inhabited abbey

✲ Nature conservation, including wildlife reserves

➹ Bird reserve, bird centre (including falconry)

🐘 Zoo, safari park, anywhere keeping exotic animals

🐄 Farm animals, farm park, country centre, farm museum, even vineyard

🐟 Anything to do with fish, including both fishing and aquariums

🦋 Butterfly park or farm

❀ Garden, plant centre, arboretum, landscaped park

🌳 Wood, forest

❈ Place or feature of great natural beauty

❀ Viewpoints

🍎 Orchards, fruit farms, pick-your-own

☊ Cave, cavern

🏺 Museum

🖼 Art gallery, sculpture park

⚓ Boat museum

✈ Air museum

🚗 Motor museum

⚒ Open-air museum (including industrial museums)

♭ Heritage centre such as Jorvik Centre in York

🚂 Steam locomotives, railway

🚣 Boat trip

☺ Amusement park, theme park, leisure park, permanent funfair

☢ Craft centre or craft workshop: potters, glassblowers, weavers etc

🏭 Factory visit (including power station visits)

✗ Windmill or other type of mill

! Something exciting like hot-air balloon trips or somewhere with hands-on experience.

Some places embrace all sorts of different attractions in just the one locality. With these, instead of cluttering the maps with all sorts of different symbols, we show a ✪ on the map.

On the maps, a bed symbol indicates recommended places to stay; a knife-and-fork symbol indicates recommended places to eat. A boot symbol shows the start of a walk mentioned in the **Walks** sections.

BERKSHIRE

Berkshire's best possibilities for a short break or a quiet weekend away are in the west – rolling downland countryside, civilised small villages linked by pleasant minor roads, and comfortable and attractive places to stay.

Although East Berkshire has less scope for a short holiday, it does have two outstanding attractions for a day away: Windsor, and the finest stretch of the Thames, either for towpath sauntering or for boating.

EAST BERKSHIRE

Days-out country rather than somewhere for a short break: Windsor is exceptional for a day's sightseeing; the most beautiful stretch of the Thames flows through this area, and there are charming gentle walks.

Strolls by the Thames, in Windsor Great Park, the Savill Garden or Valley Gardens can be very rewarding, and the river between Marlow and Henley is idyllic on a bright, early summer or autumn afternoon (in holiday time the Thames does get very busy). There are several quietly attractive villages to explore. Windsor Castle is an immensely powerful draw for visitors, and the town has plenty to fill a day's or more sightseeing. Elsewhere, Dorney Court is a fine ancient building with the deep charm of a proper family home.

Where to stay

Windsor SU9676 OAKLEY COURT Windsor Rd, Water Oakley, Windsor SL4 5UR (01628) 74141 **£99w**; 94 rms. Splendid and beautifully restored Victor–ian country-house hotel set in 35 acres of grounds by the Thames and used in the *St Trinians* films (among others); spacious, comfortable lounges with many original features, open fires, fine food in oak-panelled restaurant, lovely views; 9-hole golf course, croquet lawn, fishing and boating.

Hurley SU8283 OLDE BELL Hurley, Maidenhead SL6 5LX (01628) 825881 **£76**; 36 elegant rms. Civilised and old-fashioned timbered inn with traces of its origins as a Norman monastic guesthouse; oak-panelled restaurant, beamed bar with open fire, friendly service, peaceful garden.

Windsor SU9676 MELROSE HOUSE 53 Frances Rd, Windsor SL4 3AQ (01753) 865328 **£42**; 9 rms. B & B in a Victorian house close to city centre, with cheer-ful welcome, big breakfast room and snug lounge.

Holyport SU9176 MOOR FARM Holyport, Maidenhead SL6 2HY (01628) 33761 *****£38**; 3 rms (no smoking). B & B in wing of timber-framed medieval house with beams, antiques, and flower-filled garden; no evening meals (vil-lage pubs nearby); also self-catering cottages (one suitable for the disabled); Suffolk sheep, horses, stabling, riding and tuition by arrangement.

Please let us know what you think of places in the *Guide*. Use the report forms at the back of the book or simply send a letter.

To see and do

Windsor SU9676 By far the greatest magnet for visitors in the east of the county; if you've never been, or not been for a long time, it's well worth an expedition. Besides the obvious tourist attractions, there's plenty to interest quieter tastes. The town is, of course, dominated by its famous castle, the largest inhabited one in the world. The little streets to the south of it have many pretty timber-framed or Georgian-fronted houses and shops. The High St, by contrast, is wide and busy. You can walk by the Thames (for example, from Home Park, beyond the station); or across to Eton – see below. There's also a good evening racecourse (and theatre). The Royal Oak opposite the Riverside station is now the most useful pub here for lunch, though the Donkey House (Thames St) is hard to beat for its riverside position; the Union is the best pub in the quieter nearby Thames-side village of Old Windsor.

🏰 ❀ 🏠 ✝ ☕ ! CASTLE Originally a wooden fort built by William the Conqueror, this is still the official residence of the monarch today. A mass of towers, ramparts and pinnacles, it's an impressive place to wander round. Henry II constructed the first stone buildings, inc the familiar Round Tower, from the top of which, on a good day, you can see 12 counties. It's a shame you can no longer stroll freely through the precincts as you used to be able to, or even just pay to visit certain parts; you now have to pay a cover-all charge to get into the grounds. The entry ticket takes in all the main previously separate features of the castle, inc what for many is the highlight – the magnificent ST GEORGE'S CHAPEL, a splendid example of Perpendicular architecture, with intricate carvings on the choir stalls, fine ironwork, an amazing fan-vaulted ceiling and the arms and pennants of every knight entered into the Order of the Knights of the Garter. It is generally closed Sun mornings and occasional other dates, often at short notice – best to check on the tel number given below.

Similarly, the STATE APARTMENTS are closed whenever the Queen is in residence. It was in these private quarters that the 1992 fire did its

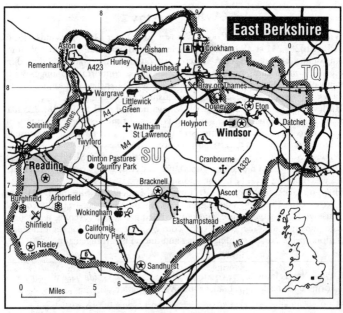

worst, though only two of the 16 rooms were destroyed. Currently, Perspex covers let you see the extent of the damage, and it's hoped that these will stay in place to show the restoration work's progress. Other rooms are decorated with carvings by Grinling Gibbons and ceilings by Verrio, and are full of superb paintings (which change from time to time) from the Royal Collection, inc notable Rembrandts and Van Dycks, porcelain, armour, and exceptionally fine furniture. Shop, disabled access; (01753) 831118 for details of opening times; *£8, or £5 on days when the Chapel or State Apartments are closed. The guards generally change on alternate days only, at 11am – again, tel for exact dates.

Separate charges still apply for the following two parts of the castle: the money from the first goes to charity. QUEEN MARY'S DOLL'S HOUSE An exquisite creation by Edwin Lutyens, built for Queen Mary in the 1920s, with perfectly scaled furniture and decoration. Opening hours as State Apartments; £1.50. ROYAL CARRIAGES AND QUEEN'S PRESENTS A regularly changing display of gifts from foreign governments to the Queen, with some oddities, as well as the beautifully kept carriages – homely as well as stately. Hours as State Apartments; £1.70.

❀ SAVILL GARDEN The range of colours here is often quite dazzling and it really is an outstanding place to visit. The 35 peaceful acres take in woodland, formal rose garden, rock plants, herbaceous borders and so forth, and are punctuated with a number of rare trees, shrubs and plants. Perhaps best in spring, but good at any time of the year. This spring should see the opening of a new temperate house. Meals, snacks, good shop with plant sales, disabled access; cl 25–26 Dec; (01753) 860222; £3.20.

❀ ♤ ❋ VALLEY GARDENS A lovely place for a relaxing stroll, with over 400 acres of woodland – 50 of which are devoted to rhododendrons, making this the largest planting of the species in the world. Also an outstanding collection of trees and shrubs, heather garden, waterfowl

lakes, and attractive landscaping. It's free for pedestrians, and a £2.60 fee admits cars by a gate at Englefield Green. Both this and the previous garden are on the edge of Windsor Great Park.

🏠 FROGMORE HOUSE (Home Park) Generally forgotten former royal residence, now rarely open but well worth a look when it is. An impressive list of former tenants includes Queen Charlotte, Queen Victoria and Queen Mary. It's a beautiful place, built in 1618, with 19 magnificent rooms to explore; amongst the watercolours and drawings are some youthful works by Queen Victoria. Open wknds in Aug and early Sept, and a couple of dates in May; (01753) 868286; £3.50.

♿ CROWN JEWELS OF THE WORLD (Beascod St) Authentic, glittering recreations of the crowns, regalia and other jewels of a dozen or so different countries. Even though nothing is real it's quite a dazzling display. Shop; cl Nov–Mar exc by appointment, maybe limited hours Sun; (01753) 833773; *£3.50.

♿ HOUSEHOLD CAVALRY MUSEUM (Combermere Barracks, St Leonards Rd) Fine and comprehensive display of weapons, armour, uniforms, and horse tack used from 1600 to present day. Shop, disabled access; cl 12.30–2, all wknds and bank hols; (01753) 868222; free.

! BRASS RUBBING CENTRE (St John the Baptist Church, Windsor High St); cl Sun, Nov–Easter; free to go in; rubbings from 95p.

! Work is well advanced on the new LEGOLAND in Windsor Great Park which it's hoped will be ready by Easter 1996.

★ 🏠 ✝ ♿ 🖼 Eton SU9678 (so close it's pretty much part of Windsor) has a restrained and decorous High St with a mix of interesting old shops and houses. Its glory is the COLLEGE, the famous public school, whose stately Tudor and later buildings in graceful precincts are marvellously calm during the school's holidays. The CHAPEL is an outstanding late Gothic building in the Perpendicular style. THE MUSEUM OF ETON LIFE tells the story of the school from its foundation in 1440 up to the present, with fascinating videos showing what it's like to be educated here today. The various historical documents turn up some bizarre information – for example the fact that in the 17th c smoking was compulsory for all scholars as a protection against bubonic plague. The BREWHOUSE GALLERY has some good watercolour drawings and changing exhibitions, and next door there's an unusually

exhaustive collection of Egyptian antiquities. They do long or short tours of the school; shop, some disabled access; cl am in term-time and all Oct–Mar; (01753) 671177; from £2.20. The College runs residential courses in the summer with topics as diverse as rowing and choral singing.

In the town, the Waterman's Arms and Hogshead are useful pubs for lunch.

Other things to see and do

⛵ **Boating on the Thames** This is a lovely stretch of the river (though busy in summer), flowing through lively towns and villages, past grand houses in imposing grounds to idyllic reaches by steep quiet woodland – with islets where you can picnic. A particularly pretty trip is from Wargrave to Henley to Medmenham Abbey to Hambleden, Hurley and Marlow Reach. A good shorter stretch is Cliveden Reach (the two miles between Cookham and Boulter's Lock). As well as motor launches, you can now hire very attractive (not to mention silent and quite environmentally friendly) electric launches, though for the purists, and the energetic, only a rowing boat will do. IPG Marine in Marlow, (01494) 882210, have five centres; rowing boats start at £8 an hour, outboard motorboats £20 an hour, or electric launches (up to eight people) at £75 for a half-day (£120 all day). Bray Boats in Maidenhead, (01628) 37880, have small boats/motor launches ranging from £14 an hour to around £80 a day; they also run half-hour or two-hour trips.
❀ **Arborfield** SU7567 HENRY STREET GARDEN CENTRE Specialist rose and bedding plant grower, with a well stocked garden centre. From July–Sept you can wander through the fragrant rose fields; they rotate these on a seven-year cycle, and this year are back to the beginning, so the walk to look at the flowers is at its shortest. Guided tours by appointment, snacks,

shop; free. The Walter Arms over at Sindlesham is good for lunch.
Ascot SU9268 ROYAL ASCOT Probably the most famous racecourse in the world, though most visitors tend to spend as much time watching the people as the horses. It was founded by Queen Anne in 1714 and the four-day Royal Meeting in June is still one of the highlights of the English season; to try for admission to the Royal Enclosure, British citizens should apply to Ascot Races (Royal Enclosure and Members' Stand), St James's Palace, London SW1; foreign citizens to their embassy. For the other stands, contact the racecourse itself; tickets must be booked in advance and are available from 1 Jan. There are plenty of other top-class races throughout the year, when ticket prices range from £4–£24 depending on which enclosure you head for (the Silver Ring is the cheapest), and on non-race days there are guided tours. Meals, snacks, shop, disabled access; (01344) 22211 for dates. In town, EMPEROR HOUSE has one of the country's most extensive displays of antique and modern timepieces, with some wonderful longcase clocks; cl Sun; (01344) 873121. The Duke of Edinburgh at Woodside SU9270 is a good place for lunch.
✝ **Bisham** SU8485 The CHURCH is worth a look, and sitting on a bench in the churchyard by the Thames on a fine evening is rather special. The Bull is a decent pub here.

✔ ♄ ♈ ❀ ☺ **Bracknell** SU8769 Few will find much to delight them in the town itself, but it's worth tracking down THE LOOK OUT, a countryside and heritage centre that's the starting point for 2,600 acres of woodland. The forest consists mainly of conifer plantations but is full of nature trails and wildlife (as well as an Iron Age hill fort), while the visitor centre has various changing exhibitions and displays. As its name suggests there's an elevated platform with good views of the surrounding area. A very full timetable of events goes from orienteering and hedge-laying to pond-dipping and other particularly well organised children's activities; Snacks, shop, disabled access; cl 25-26 Dec; (01344) 868222; grounds free, 75p for exhibitions.

The town does have some reasonable leisure facilities, and the Old Manor is a good new pub for lunch.

❀ **Burghfield** SU6668 OLD RECTORY Plantsman's garden with oriental rarities and cottage-garden plants. Snacks, plant centre selling plants from other gardens in the area; disabled access to most of garden; open last Weds of month exc Nov–Jan; £1. If you write to them you may be able to arrange a visit at other times. The Hatch Gate here is a friendly pub for lunch.

★ ▣ **Cookham** SU8884 The village, leading down to the Thames, is attractive, and has several decent pubs of which the very smart Bel & the Dragon and Uncle Tom's Cabin up on Cookham Dean Common are the current pick. STANLEY SPENCER GALLERY (King's Hall) Spencer really made his mark on Cookham – it was his birthplace and he spent most of his working life here, so this rewarding little gallery, housed in a former Methodist chapel, has lots of personal items as well as a good range of his unique work. Highlights include *The Last Supper* and the curious *Christ Preaching at Cookham Regatta*. Shop, disabled access; cl wkdys Nov–Easter; (01628) 520890; *50p.

▥ ♣ **Dorney** SU9278 DORNEY COURT Engaging, partly 15th-c, timber-framed manor house with pleasant gardens and some very fine furniture, as well as the Elizabethan Palmer Needlework tapestry. The same family have lived here for over 450 years, and you can trace the different generations through the many portraits. In the 16th c the first pineapple raised in England was grown here – they still have pick-your-own fruit and vegetables every day in season (usually Jun–Aug). Also a new plant centre, with plants from Blooms of Bressingham. Teas, shop; open Easter and bank hols in May, then pm Sun, Mon and Tues Jun–Sept; (01628) 604638; *£4. The Pickwick over at Eton Wick is useful for lunch.

☛ **Littlewick Green** SU8379 COURAGE SHIRE HORSE CENTRE (A4, 2 miles W of Maidenhead) A friendly place that's stayed simple and relatively uncommercialised. You can go right up to the horses, and watch them being groomed and plaited up; also a display of harnesses and rosettes, guided tours, audio-visual presentation, picnic area, and working forge. Meals, snacks, shop, disabled access; cl Nov–Feb (though may be open half-term and part of Christmas school hols); (01628) 824848; £3.

♠ ♣ ! **Reading** SU7272 Now Berkshire's sprawling county town, it is largely 19th-c red brick and not a tourist centre; but the three main museums are worth visiting. MUSEUM OF ENGLISH RURAL LIFE (University of Reading, Whiteknights Park; 2m SE on A327, so you don't have to go into the busy centre) Probably the best exploration of life in the English countryside over the last couple of hundred years or so that we know of, taking in farm tools, rural crafts, and domestic room settings; there's a fine collection of waggons, and interesting studies of social change. Shop, disabled access; cl 1–2, Sun, Mon, 25 Dec–1 Jan; (01734) 318663; *£1. The university also has small museums devoted to natural history and Greek archaeology. BLAKE'S LOCK MUSEUM (Gasworks Rd) Very well-organised museum concentrating on Reading's waterways, trades and industries; the several galleries feature a reconstructed bakery (the town was well known for biscuit-making), barber's shop and printer's workshop, and various changing exhibitions. Shop, disabled access; cl am wknds and bank hols, all Mon (exc bank hols); (01734) 390918; free. READING MUSEUM AND ART GALLERY (Blagrave St) More varied local history, in a showy neo-Gothic building, with lots of hands-on displays and exhibitions about the town and its people, and a Victorian copy of the Bayeux Tapestry. Meals, snacks, shop, disabled access; cl am Sun and bank hols, all Mon (exc bank hols); free. In West St, Vicars & Sons is an old-fashioned game butcher's, established in the 19th c – an interesting shop with good food.

If you're feeling in an extravagant mood a BALLOON TRIP gives a very different view of Berkshire; lift off from town centre parks every day in summer and wknds in winter, dawn and dusk; 0181-840 0108; £95. Sweeney & Todd in Castle St is the best place here for lunch, and the canalside Fisherman's Cottage (Kennet Side) is also very popular.

✚ ☛ ⚘ ※ ⛺ ♨ ♪ **Riseley** SU7263 WELLINGTON COUNTRY PARK AND NATIONAL DAIRY MUSEUM (off B3349 Reading–Basingstoke) Plenty to do in this huge country park, its meadows, woodland and lakes stretching over 350 acres; marked nature trails, miniature steam railway, deer park, collection of small domestic animals, and adventure playground. The museum covers the history of the dairy industry with attractive copper, pewter and wooden tools, and milk delivery vehicles. You can fish, sail, windsurf or row on the lake, and there are one-day starter courses; booking is essential. Meals, snacks, shop; cl wkdys Nov–Feb; (01734) 326505; £2.95.

❀ ⚘ ♪ 🐄 **Sandhurst** SU8361 TRILAKES COUNTRY PARK AND FISHERY Not just for fishermen, these attractive lakes and surrounding park and woodland have lots of animals and birds wandering round, some of which you can feed. Shetland pony rides for children between 3–4 on summer Suns, while in spring you can bottle-feed the lambs. Also model railway, and birds of prey some bank hols. Meals, snacks (not after 2 in winter), shop, limited disabled access; cl wkdys Nov–mid Mar; (01252) 873191; £1.80, fishing £6.50.

☛ **Twyford** SU7876 THAMES VALLEY VINEYARD (Stanlake Park) English wines made by a pioneering blend of tradition and technology; pre-booked tours only inc tasting. Meals by appointment, shop, disabled access by appointment; cl am Sun, 25 Dec–1 Jan; (01734) 340176; £4.95. The Land's End is useful for lunch. Just off the A4, ROCKS COUNTRY WINES produce a range of country wines, liqueurs and mead, with tastings and a walled herb garden; cl am Sun; (01734) 342344, free. The Bull at Wargrave SU7878 nearby is useful for lunch.

★ ✝ **Waltham St Lawrence** SU8276 Attractive quiet village with ancient centre, chiefly notable for the magnificent 14th-c SHOTTESBROOKE CHURCH, in a pleasant park just E. The Bell here is an appealing old place for lunch.

🎨 🍴 **Wokingham** SU8068 HOLME GRANGE CRAFT CENTRE (Heathlands Rd) Paintings, sculpture, models, fish, etc, even circus shop. Meals, snacks, disabled access; cl 25 Dec–2 Jan; free. Heathlands Rd has a couple of farm shops and pick-your-own plots.

✝ The **churches** at Cranbourne SU9372 and Easthampstead SU8667 are worth seeing if you pass, for their fine stained glass by William Morris, Edward Burne-Jones and others.

For **children to let off steam**, ❀ ⚘ CALIFORNIA COUNTRY PARK SU7864 (S of Wokingham on B3016, turning right at Wick Hill opposite B3430) has woods to run around in, lots of sand, and a vast paddling place; very popular locally.

❀ ☺ DINTON PASTURES COUNTRY PARK SU7872 (off B3030 S of Hurst – which has decent pubs) has rather more for older children, inc windsurfing and canoeing.

★ **Other attractive villages** worth looking at if you're near, and all with decent pubs and pleasant local walks, include Aston SU7884, Bray SU9079, Cookham SU8884, Datchet SU9876, Holyport SU8977, Hurley SU8283, Sonning/Sonning Lock SU7575 (nice stroll through churchyard and along the Thames), Wargrave SU7878.

Walks

There's plenty of opportunity for pleasant strolling here. In particular, the **Thames'** nostalgic qualities of boating and Edwardian England are seen to full effect from leisurely strolls along the towpath, kept very well nowadays. A very fine stretch extends from **Maidenhead** SU8783 to **Henley** SU7882, sharing the river with Bucks and Oxon. There are lovely Thames walks from **Remenham** SU7683 ◻-1 in either direction. This reach is the course of the Henley Regatta; you can instead start from Henley itself (coming back over the bridge – see Oxon chapter) or **Aston** SU7884; (the Flower Pots here is a useful halt). Another good starting point for river walks is **Boulter's Lock** SU9082 ◻-2 (head upstream).

There are few bridges across the river, and much of the hinterland is developed, but opportunities for round walks abound around **Cookham Dean** SU8785 and **Cookham** SU8884 ◻-3, with great views from the chalk escarpment of **Winter Hill** SU8786. Paths in this area are very well kept, and it is hard to lose the way seriously, although woodland walking sometimes means you have to keep your eyes skinned for arrow markers painted on trees.

Windsor Great Park ◻-4 has miles of well kept parkland, so sensitively landscaped that it takes the occasional surprising find (statues, even a totem pole) to remind you that it's not natural. It's the only real prospect in this part of the county for walks that'll get you decidedly exercised. **Virginia Water** SU9768 ◻-5 is very beautiful, particularly in autumn; and the Long Walk gives glorious perspectives of Windsor Castle. Best access via Valley Gardens or Savill Garden car parks.

Finchampstead Ridges SU8063 ◻-6 is a steepish chunk of heather and pinewood, not big but with a good natural character, fine views and sheltered picnic spots. The editor found a meteorite here when he was 11. Not far off, the much broader stretches of pinewoods ◻-7 between **Crowthorne** SU8464 and **Bracknell** SU8769 offer much longer but less varied walks, with many tracks inc some based on Roman roads; parking off the A3095/B3430, the best start is the well organised and informative Look Out Point, off the B3430 at SU8766.

Maidenhead Thicket SU8581 ◻-8 (mixed old woodland and common) has easy access from the A423 and A4.

Driving

This area is not really worth thinking about for pleasure driving. In the main, roads here are for traffic not scenery (though the B3348 W of Crowthorne takes you down a magnificent wellingtonia avenue, with good views, before you turn back towards Wokingham on the B3016).

Where to eat

Shinfield SU7368 L'Ortolan (01734) 883783 Luxurious and innovative French cooking in Victorian rectory with conservatory extensions; delicious puddings, fine cheeseboard, classic wine list inc French regional wines; disabled access; cl pm Sun, Mon, 2 wks end Aug, ditto Feb. **£41.25**.

Bray-on-Thames SU9079 Waterside (01628) 20691 Carefully and prettily refurbished restaurant with big windows overlooking the Thames; superb French cooking, fine French cheeses, lovely wines, and a smart but surprisingly relaxed atmosphere; small terrace, little electric launch for private hire; bedrooms; cl 26 Dec for 5 wks, Mon, am Tues pm Sun from 3rd wknd Oct–mid Apr; no children under 12; disabled access. **£36**.

Remenham SU7683 Little Angel (01491) 574165 Intimate little restaurant with good seafood, tasty bar snacks, fine wines and well kept beer; cl 25–26 Dec. **£18|£2.75/4.95**.

WEST BERKSHIRE

Civilised comfort, good food, bracing downland walks.

This has good scope for a relaxing short break, with a fair choice of comfortable and civilised places to stay, and no shortage of decent food. There is a reasonable amount to see, but scattered about so that you'd reckon on spending at least some time driving around, exploring; for the most part, roads are good and there are some fine downland drives with wide views. This is also quite a good area for walking in attractive countryside, with a range of possibilities from gentle strolls to long hikes. Particularly for families, the Beale Wildlife Gardens at Lower Basildon are very rewarding, and on a nice day a horse-drawn barge trip from Kintbury is tempting; our pick of places for older people to visit here would be Basildon Park, with Wyld Court Rainforest at Hampstead Norreys increasingly alluring for plant-lovers.

Where to stay

Streatley SU5980 SWAN DIPLOMAT High St, Streatley, Reading RG8 9HR (01491) 873737 *£134; 46 comfortable, well-equipped rms (many overlooking the water). Well run and attractive riverside hotel with relaxed, airy lounges, waterside restaurant and cosy lunch room; restored Magdalen College barge, popular leisure club, and flower-filled garden; disabled access.

Pangbourne SU6376 COPPER Church Rd, Pangbourne, Reading RG8 7AR (01734) 842244 £92 (inc dinner); 22 rms, most overlooking gardens. Timbered and creeper-covered coaching inn with beamed bar, comfortable sitting room, smart lounge, charming restaurant; good, often unusual, food and some fine wines; disabled access.

Hungerford SU3368 BEAR Charnham St, Hungerford RG17 0EL (01488) 682512 £72w; 41 comfortable, attractive rms with antiques and beams in older ones. Civilised hotel bar with fresh flowers, open fires, and stuffed bear; restaurant has decent food and very good wines.

Hamstead Marshall SU4165 WHITE HART Hamstead Marshall, Newbury RG15 0HW (01488) 58201 *£60; 6 beamed, comfortable rms in converted barn. Civilised Georgian country inn in quiet village with good food inc Italian dishes and popular puddings; log fire in pleasant bar, friendly service, and interesting walled garden; cl Sun, and 25–26 Dec.

Yattendon SU5574 ROYAL OAK The Square, Yattendon, Newbury RG16 0UF (01635) 201325 £50; 6 rms, mostly with bath. Elegant and comfortable old inn in peaceful village, with very good, sophisticated food and, excellent wines; prettily decorated, panelled bar, pleasant service, and lovely garden; cl 25 Dec; disabled access in restaurant (not bedrooms).

Kintbury SU3866 DUNDAS ARMS Kintbury, Newbury RG15 0UT (01488) 58263 £50; 5 rms in old stable block overlooking River Kennet. Old-fashioned pub by canal (lots of ducks and daffodils), with honest cooking using fresh ingredients in restaurant; good bar food too and decent range of wines, (especially clarets); good breakfasts, pleasant service; cl Christmas–New Year; disabled access.

Hungerford SU3368 MARSHGATE COTTAGE Marsh Lane, Hungerford RG17 0QX (01488) 682307 £48.50; 9 individually decorated rms, mostly with bath. Friendly little family-run hotel backing on to Kennet & Avon Canal with seats overlooking water and marsh and more in sheltered courtyard; mountain bikes for hire; cl Christmas; children over 5, disabled access.

East Ilsley SU4981 CROWN & HORNS East Ilsley, Newbury RG16 0LH (01635) 281205 £38; 10 rms, some in converted stable block. Lively and friendly old pub in horse-training country (and used as the Dog & Gun in the BBC series *Trainer*); interesting beamed rooms, pretty paved stable yard, decent bar and restaurant food, and lots of whiskies; skittle alley.

To see and do

🏠 ❀ **Basildon** SU6078 BASILDON PARK Lovely Bath stone Palladian mansion with grand rooms full of fine pictures and furniture, and delicate plasterwork on ceilings and walls; also an unusual seashell collection in the Shell Room. Outside are old-fashioned roses, a pretty terrace, and grounds beyond. The classical frontage is particularly impressive. Summer teas, light lunches wknds and bank hols, shop, disabled access; open pm Weds–Sat and bank hols Apr–Oct, cl Weds after a bank hol; £3.50, £2.50 grounds only; NT. The Red Lion at Upper Basildon is good for lunch.

🐏 🐖 **Bucklebury** SU5570 BUCKLEBURY FARM PARK The best way of seeing the herd of red deer and the other traditional farm animals in this 60-acre park is by taking the free tractor trailer ride, but it is worth exploring on foot as well. You can feed the geese and ducks and there are plenty of seasonal events such as lambing, shearing and even strawberry picking

in summer. Snacks, shop, limited disabled access; cl Mon–Thurs exc bank hols and school hols, all Oct–Easter; (01734) 714002; *£1.80. The Blade Bone is useful for lunch.

🌴 **Hampstead Norreys** SU5376 WYLD COURT RAINFOREST Unusual and quite fascinating tropical rainforest reconstructed under glass, with thousands of weird-looking plants currently in danger of extinction; particularly strange are the giant 8-ft lily pads (best from Jun–Oct), which start life the size of a pea. The orchid collection is exceptional. Three different areas, Lowland Tropical, Amazonica and Cloudforest, each with its own climate and atmosphere. The centre is developing quite quickly: they already have a good few plants you won't see anywhere else in Europe and hope to propagate most of these. Teas, shop (with good plants for sale), disabled access; cl 25–26 Dec; (01635) 200221; *£3.50. The Red Lion over at Compton is good value for lunch.

West Berkshire

★ ♣ **Hungerford** SU1612 Attractive large village or small town with some interesting shops (inc a notable wine merchant), and wknd afternoon CANAL TRIPS from the wharf Easter–Oct (also pm Weds in July and Aug); from £3. There are a good number of ANTIQUE SHOPS, some general, others specialising in items as diverse as fireplaces, kitchen furnishings and billiard tables.

♣ **Kintbury** HORSE-DRAWN BARGE TRIPS Round trip on restored Kennet & Avon Canal lasting 1½ hrs; cl end Sept–Easter; (01635) 44154; £3.50.

! 🏛 † **Lambourn** SU3278 Quiet, streamside racehorse-training village below the downs. LAMBOURN TRAINERS' ASSOCIATION (Windsor House) Guided tours around successful racehorse training centre; you can watch the horses being put through their paces on the downland gallops, as well as see their stables and meet individual horses. Wear suitable shoes, and you must make an appointment. Snacks, shop, disabled access; cl pm, all Sun and bank hols; (01488) 71347; £5 plus VAT. Up on the downs (OS Sheet 174 SU329828) SEVEN BARROWS is a Bronze Age cemetery with at least 32 barrows – a spectacle even for the uninitiated. CHURCH OF ST MICHAEL AND ALL ANGELS A fine parish church, originally Norman, with Perpendicular additions. The George is useful for lunch.

💘 🐦 �} ♣ 🏚 ❀ **Lower Basildon** SU6078 BEALE WILDLIFE GARDENS (Church Farm, Lower Basildon) Good and informative nature park, with a range of birds and mammals – game birds, waterfowl, owls and parrots, Highland cattle, rare breeds of sheep, a deer park, pets' corner, tropical house and a good variety of plants and insects. Very conservation-minded – they do plenty of breeding and just about all their animals were born here, in conditions as near as possible to the wild. The surroundings well deserve their listing as an Area of Outstanding Beauty; also Thames trips, narrow-gauge railway, the National Centre for Model Ships and Boats, and children's playground. Meals, snacks, shop, disabled access;

usually cl late Dec–Feb but worth checking; (01734) 845172; £4. In summer a boat trip operates to the park from Reading.

† ♣ 🍴 🏚 🗑 **Newbury** SU4666 A busy shopping town, but there are some nice old parts, with interesting older buildings among the High Street shops. ST NICOLAS is a fine early 16th-c Perpendicular church with a magnificent pulpit. By here, West Mills (st) is the best evocation of the town's 18th-c prosperity, and leads to the attractively restored canal. BOAT TRIPS may run some days from the old wharf, beyond the market square on the other side of the High St; the Kennet & Avon Canal Trust information centre should have details. The NEWBURY DISTRICT MUSEUM (The Wharf) is especially good on the Civil War battles fought here and on the development of ballooning. Shop, disabled access ground floor only; cl am Sun , bank hols; free. There are picturesque buildings in Argyll Rd and Newtown Rd, beyond the end of the High St S of the railway. The town has an excellent racecourse, with mid-week and weekend races all year; (01344) 22211. Just N off B4494 is DONNINGTON CASTLE, a tall medieval ruined castle – actually the gatehouse of a much larger fortress destroyed in the Civil War. W of the town, the Water Rat at Marsh Benham is good for lunch; in the town itself the Lock Stock & Barrel is well placed on the canal.

🍴 † **Padworth** SU6166 KENNET & AVON CANAL VISITOR CENTRE (Aldermaston Wharf) Set in a nice little house beside the canal, with exhibitions on the canal's history and information on its use; also good trails and walks. They have details of boat trips along the canal's various stretches – see also Hungerford and Newbury. Snacks (in picnic garden), shop, some disabled access; cl am Sun, all Nov–Easter; (01734) 7122868; free. CHURCH Quietly situated, and feels very ancient and peaceful. The Round Oak is useful for lunch.

💘 **Pangbourne** SU6376 PANGBOURNE MEADOW Traditional meadow by the Thames, scythed after flowering and seeding to preserve a wide range of wild flowers. The riverside Swan is pleasant for lunch, and the village has some decent shops; it was the home of Kenneth Grahame, who perhaps found inspiration around here for *The Wind in the Willows*.

🏕 ❀ ✔ 🏚 **Theale** SU6371 ENGLEFIELD HOUSE (A340) Attractive woodland with interesting trees, water and formal gardens, and deer park. Shop,

limited disabled access; open Mon all year, plus Tues–Thurs Apr–Jun; *£1. The house is open by appointment, (01734) 302221. The recently re-opened Volunteer is useful for lunch.

★ **Other attractive villages**, all with decent pubs, include Aldworth SU5579, Bagnor SU4569, Chaddleworth SU4177, Standford Dingley SU5771, and Yattendon SU5574.

Walks

Around **Streatley** SU5980 ⌂-1 there are walks along the Thames and contrasting paths up on the downs (the long-distance Ridgeway Path, one of the oldest tracks in England, follows surfaced farm roads in places hereabouts, but also takes in some quiet countryside). More dramatic is the high escarpment ⌂-2 of **Inkpen Beacon** SU3562 and **Walbury Hill** SU3761, reached from a minor road S of Inkpen SU3564 (where the Swan is good for lunch). The gibbet on top of the hill is a macabre relic from the days of highwaymen. Immediately S lie some lovely rolling downlands laced with gentle and mostly well-marked tracks, field paths and woodland paths overlapping into Hants and Wilts. Other paths tap quickly into sections of the Ridgeway with good views from **Aldworth** SU5579 and **West Ilsley** SU4782 (both have good pubs).

Thatcham Moor SU5166 ⌂-3 is said to be the largest area of inland freshwater reed beds in England; lots of birds (some rare), moths, and marshland and aquatic plants. Car park S of A4.

The Kennet & Avon Canal ⌂-4 has been well restored in the last few years, and is now very pleasant to stroll or cycle along, from Thatcham SU5167, Aldermaston Wharf SU6067, Hungerford SU3368, Kintbury SU3866, Marsh Benham SU4267 or Woolhampton SU5767 (in addition to the Dundas Arms at Kintbury and the Water Rat at Marsh Benham, the Bear in Hungerford and the Rowbarge at Woolhampton have decent food in civilised surroundings).

Driving

The Lambourn Valley is one of the prettiest drives here – from Newbury, out past Woodspeen, go through the pretty villages of Boxford, East Garston and Eastbury to Lambourn itself. The B4001 up over Lambourn Downs, into Oxon via Wantage, takes you back over the downs on the B4494 to Newbury. Other good quiet scenic routes include the B4009 Streatley–Newbury; and the back road Pangbourne–Upper Basildon–Aldworth, then left on the B4009 and right towards Compton–the Ilsleys–Farnborough (lovely Georgian ex-rectory on right), then left on the B4494 towards Newbury.

For long-distance travel the A4 is quite a pleasant alternative to the M4.

Where to eat

Marsh Benham SU4267 WATER RAT (01635) 582017 Comfortable, thatched restaurant with nice 'Wind in the Willows' paintings around the walls; some interesting dishes, also light meals in stylish bar; good service; disabled access. £21.50|£2.50/£7.50.

Inkpen SU3564 SWAN (01488) 668326 Rambling, beamed country inn in quiet village, with popular Singaporean food as well as western dishes. £17.50|£3.25/£3.75.

Stanford Dingley SU5771 BULL (01734) 744409 Very friendly country pub with good, often unusual, food in comfortable bars, well kept beer, and quick service. £15|£2.50/£6.

West Ilsley SU4782 HARROW (01635) 281260 White-tiled village inn over-looking duck pond and green; friendly, lively atmosphere, and good bar food like local wild rabbit or game pie; no-smoking dining room at lunch-time; notable children's play area with lots of animals; disabled access. £14.75|£2/£4.85.

East Ilsley SU4981 SWAN (01635) 281238 Well refurbished, 16th-c coaching inn with good-value bar food, pretty back terrace, and sheltered lawn with play area. £14|£2.95/£5.

Help this year from: HNJ, PEJ, Neil Franklin, Jill Knox, Susan and John Douglas, Pippa Bob-bett, Margaret Dyke, DAV, Martin and Karen Wake, R C Morgan, Brian and Anna Marsden, Mayur Shah, TBB, DK, Julie and Mike Taylor, Peter and Lynn Brueton, D and J Johnson, Gor-don, Bill and Jane Rees, Rob and Helen Townsend, Colin Pearson, D G Clarke, S R Jordan, JCW, Ralf Zeyssig, Dayl Gallacher, S C Collett-Jones, K R Waters, W L G Watkins, Dr and Mrs R E S Tanner, Mr and Mrs G D Amos, Dave and Carole Jones, Amanda Hodges, Rona Mur-doch, G Atkinson, Jim Penman, JRS, A E and P McCully, Paul and Janet Giles.

BERKSHIRE CALENDAR

Some of these dates were provisional as we went to press.

FEBRUARY

25 **Reading** Maidenhead and District Dog Show at Rivermead Leisure Complex (01734) 470851

MARCH

4 **Didcot** Railway Centre, Thomas the Tank Engine – *till Sun 5* (01235) 817200

APRIL

14 **Lambourn** Lambourn Trainers Open Day – racing stables open to the public (01488) 71347

16 **Riseley** Grand Easter Egg Hunt – food, crafts and falconry display at Wellington Country Park – *till Mon 17* (01734) 326444

30 **Taplow** Horse Show and Country Fair (01628) 603179

MAY

3 **Windsor** Frogmore Gardens and House open – *till Thurs 4* (01483) 211535

6 **Chieveley** Newbury Steam Funtasia at Newbury Showground – *till Mon 8* (01663) 732750; **Newbury** Spring Festival – *till Sat 20* (01635) 32421

10 **Windsor** Royal Windsor Horse Show at Home Park – *till Sun 14* (01753) 860633

13 **Windsor** Savill Garden Spring Plant Fair at Windsor Great Park (01753) 860222

21 **Burchetts Green** (nr Maidenhead) Berkshire College of Agriculture Country Fayre and Open Day (01628) 824444; **Reading** Children's Festival – *till 3 Jun*

25 **Windsor** Windsor International Horse Trials at Great Windsor Park – *till Sun 28* (01962) 779715

BERKSHIRE CALENDAR

MAY cont

27 **nr Reading** Craft Fair in grounds of Stratfield Saye House – *till Mon 29* (01256) 882882

28 **Knowl Hill** Berkshire Country Fair (01628) 21160

29 **Sandhurst** Donkey Derby at Memorial Hall (01252) 879060

JUNE

4 **Windsor** Queen's Cup polo at Windsor Great Park (01784) 434212

12 **Windsor** Garter Ceremony at St George's Chapel after procession from Windsor Castle *(limited tickets in advance for the Castle grounds from the Lord Chamberlain's Office, St James's Palace, London SW1)*

13 **Ascot** Royal Ascot races – *till Fri 16* (01344) 22211

24 **Chieveley** Garden and Leisure Show at Newbury Showground – *till Sun 25* (01491) 247111; **Hurst** Horse Show and Country Fair – *till Sun 25* (01734) 345253; **Reading** Waterfest (01734) 390373

30 **Windsor** Royal Windsor Rose and Horticultural Show at Windsor Castle (follow Home Park Private signs) – *till Sun 2 July* (01753) 852352

JULY

1 **Bracknell** Festival – *till Sun 2* (01344) 427272

9 **Sandhurst** Carnival (01252) 878848

12 **Reading** WOMAD Festival at Rivermead – *till Sun 23* (01734) 504343

15 **Woodcote** Steam Fair – *till Sun 16* (01491) 680573

16 **Didcot** Railway Centre, Children's Steamday (01235) 817200

20 **Reading** Real Ale and Jazz Festival – *till Sat 22* (01734) 390358

AUGUST

12 **Knowl Hill** Steam Fair – *till Sun 13* (01628) 823393

25 **Reading** Rock Festival – *till Sun 27*

26 **Windsor** Savill Garden Autumn Plant Fair, Windsor Great Park (01753) 860222

27 **Spencers Wood** Swallowfield Horticultural Show – *till Mon 28* (01734) 883575

SEPTEMBER

2 **Cookham** Regatta (01628) 810550

3 **Spencers Wood** Wokingham and Reading Agricultural Show (01734) 732232

9 **Didcot** Railway Centre, Thomas the Tank Engine – *till Sun 10* (01235) 817200

16 **Chieveley** Newbury and Royal County of Berkshire Show at Newbury Showground – *till Sun 17* (01635) 24711

BUCKINGHAMSHIRE

The most beautiful scenery here is unquestionably in the southern part of the county. One of Britain's most luxurious hotels heads a list of very attractive places in which to stay, handy both for the beechwoods of the Chiltern Hills and for the finest stretch of the Thames (shared with Berkshire on the right bank). This area of the Thames and Chilterns rates highly as a place for a short break, with charming walks, some lovely villages, and plenty of good places for meals – from attractive old pubs to grand hotel restaurants. Though there are interesting places to visit here, it's the north and west of the county – off the usual tourist map – which have a remarkable collection of magnificent houses and estates open to the public.

THAMES AND CHILTERNS

Fine places to stay in attractive surroundings, good eating out and the best walking near London

There are some good, well run attractions here, including several to keep a young family happy, but the main appeal is the countryside – especially the partly wooded Chiltern Hills, with their charming quiet valleys, tucked-away villages with pretty brick-and-flint houses, and endless possibilities for rewarding strolls and longer walks in lovely surroundings. Almost any season is nice here, but spring and autumn through to November show the beechwoods at their most beautiful. There's an extensive choice of relatively informal places in which to eat, well suiting the area's character as good walking territory, though less choice for a spectacular evening out. The Thames here is best seen from a boat, but there are also a few pleasant places to stroll along. A decent range of interesting places to stay includes Cliveden, one of England's grandest National Trust properties and now an extremely well run hotel – very special if you can afford it. Our short-list of top attractions here would include Cliveden's gardens, the Bekonscot Model Village in Beaconsfield, West Wycombe Park, the Chilterns Open-Air Museum at Chalfont St Giles, and Chenies Manor House.

Where to stay

Taplow SU9082 CLIVEDEN Taplow, Maidenhead SL6 0JF (01628) 668561 *£223; 37 luxurious, individual rms with maid unpacking service and a butler's tray. Superb Grade I listed stately home with gracious, comfortable public rooms, fresh flowers, and a surprisingly unstuffy atmosphere; imaginative food in several restaurants, marvellous wines, friendly breakfasts around a huge table, and impeccable, bright staff; lovely views over the magnificent NT Thames-side parkland and formal gardens (open to the public); pavilion with indoor and outdoor swimming pools, Turkish and spa baths, and beauty treatments; tennis, squash, croquet, riding, coarse fishing, boating; disabled access.

Marlow SU8586 COMPLEAT ANGLER Marlow Bridge, Marlow SL7 1RG (01628) 484444 **£165**; 62 pretty, individually furnished rms overlooking garden or river. Famous Thames-side hotel with comfortable panelled lounge, balconied bar, and spacious beamed restaurant with marvellous view; imaginative food, friendly, prompt service; tennis, croquet, coarse fishing; disabled access.

Aston Clinton SP8712 BELL London Rd, Aston Clinton, Aylesbury HP22 5HP (01296) 630252 **£89**; 21 comfortable rms, some in main building with antiques, some (more modern but spacious) in converted stables around a flower-filled courtyard; dogs by arrangement – staff will supply dog bowl/blanket. Early 17th-c coaching inn with elegant panelled drawing room, flagstoned smoking room, restaurant with attractive murals and excellent, modern French cooking; formal but kind service; pretty, mature gardens; disabled access.

Cadmore End SU7892 BLUE FLAG Cadmore End, High Wycombe HP14 3PS (01494) 881183 **£75w**; 16 rms in little modern hotel by traditional pub. Several comfortable beamed areas with standing timbers and partitions, attractive small restaurant with wide choice of well prepared food served by efficient, uniformed staff; cl 25–26 Dec; no children.

Fawley SU7586 WALNUT TREE Fawley, Henley-on-Thames, Oxon RG9 6JE (01491) 638360 *£50; 2 rms with showers. Popular dining pub in lovely spot with Chilterns all around; pleasantly furnished bars, imaginative food, good wines, and no-smoking conservatory; children over 5.

Hambleden SU7886 STAG & HUNTSMAN Hambleden, Henley-on-Thames, Oxon RG9 6RP (01491) 571227 *£48.50; 3 good rms. Little country pub surrounded by Chilterns beechwoods with compact lounge, attractively simple public bar, good food, and pretty garden; cl 25 Dec; no children.

To see and do

! Beaconsfield SU9490 BEKONSCOT MODEL VILLAGE The oldest model village in the world, with scaled-down churches, castles, zoo and even a racecourse, as well as a gauge-1 model railway. Snacks, shop, disabled access; cl Nov–mid Feb; (01494) 672919; *£3. The Old Hare is good for lunch.

✝ Booker SU8391 BLUE MAX COLLECTION (Wycombe Air Park) The 15 or so aircraft here, inc a 1917 Sopwith Camel and 1940 Battle of Britain Spitfire, are all veterans of films or TV, from *Indiana Jones* to *Poirot*; every month they have an open evening when several of them are flown. Snacks, shop; cl Nov–Easter; (01494) 529432; £2.50. There are lots of good pubs nearby for lunch: besides those shown on the map, we'd mention the Prince Albert at Frieth.

★ Bradenham SU8297 is a pretty village surrounded by ancient woodland. The Rose & Crown at nearby Saunderton is useful for lunch.

↥ ♟ ➤ Chalfont St Giles SU9993 CHILTERN OPEN-AIR MUSEUM (Newland Park, Gorelands Lane) A good number of traditional Chilterns buildings that would otherwise have been demolished have found their way here in the last 20 years, painstakingly dismantled and rebuilt again piece by piece. Dotted about the 45 acres are structures as diverse as an Iron Age house, a Victorian farmyard, an Edwardian public convenience and a 1940s prefab, several containing displays on their original use; also a nature trail through the parklands and adventure playground. Lots of events throughout the year, inc an open-air theatre. Snacks, shop, disabled access; cl until 2, all day Mon (exc bank hols) and Tues, Nov–Mar; (01494) 871117; £3.

MILTON'S COTTAGE (Deanway) The writer completed *Paradise Lost* and began *Paradise Regained* at this

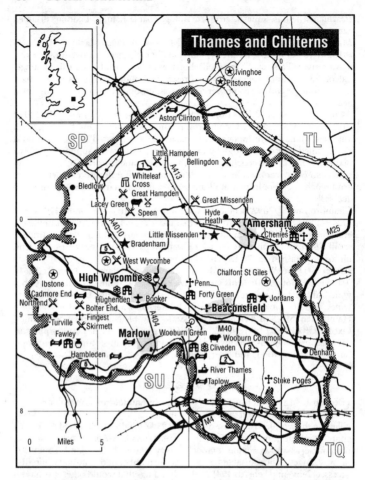

Thames and Chilterns

timber-framed, 16th-c cottage; first editions of these are among the rare books and memorabilia on display, and there's a charming cottage garden, full of plants and flowers mentioned by Milton in his poetry. Shop, disabled access; cl 1–2, am Sun, all day Mon (exc bank hols) and Tues, Nov–Feb; (01494) 872313; *£2.

CHALFONT SHIRE CENTRE Home to several handsome working horses, some of which children can ride on. Impressive collections of carriages and heavy harnesses. Snacks, shop, disabled access; cl Oct–mid-Mar; (01494) 872304; £2.60. The Pheasant is useful for lunch, as is the Greyhound over in Chalfont St Peter.
⋔ ✝ **Chenies** TQ0198 MANOR HOUSE

Rewarding little 15th-c house with Tudor rooms, doll collection, tapestries, priests' hole and a 13th-c crypt; the gardens include a physic garden, herbs, and a maze. Snacks, shop; open pm Weds, Thurs and bank hols Apr–Oct; (01494) 762888; *£3.80 house and garden, *£1.90 garden only. ST MICHAEL'S CHURCH has the rich family monuments of the Bedfords (viewed through a glass panel), 15th-c brasses and a Norman font. The Red Lion is good for lunch.
✿ ⋔ **Cliveden** SU9185 CLIVEDEN GARDENS Nearly 400 acres of lovely formal gardens, woodland and parkland overlooking the Thames. The magnificent house used to belong to the Astors and is now a luxury hotel

(a splendid place for lunch if you can afford it), although visitors can see three of the rooms with their family portraits, elegant furnishings and beautiful decor. Meals and snacks (not Mon or Tues), shop, very good disabled access; gardens cl Dec–Mar, house open only Thurs and Sun Apr–Oct from 3–6; £3.50, house £1 extra; NT.

🏠⚲ **Fawley** SU7586 FAWLEY COURT Looks like a typical English stately home, but though it does boast some fine Wyatt interiors and an elaborate ceiling by Grinling Gibbons, it's now owned by a Polish religious group, and has a unique museum dedicated to their homeland. Particularly strong on Polish military history with plenty of armour and weaponry, along with manuscripts and portraits of Polish kings. The grounds (landscaped by Capability Brown) run down to the river, and you can stay here, B & B or half and full board; limited disabled access; open Weds, Thurs and pm Sun Mar–Nov, cl wk after Easter and Whit Sun; (01491) 574917; £2. The Walnut Tree is good for lunch.

🏠 **Forty Green** SU9292 The Royal Standard of England pub stands out as a quite remarkable old building: and is full of interesting furniture – crowded at weekends, it's well worth a quiet prowl during the week.

⚲❋ **High Wycombe** SU8593 is a sprawling, suburban-looking town which grew around the furniture industry, starting with chair-making using beech wood from the Chilterns. The 18th-c building which houses the CHAIR MUSEUM (Castle Hill House) has a comprehensive collection of the various styles produced nearby. Displays too on other regional crafts and local history, along with pretty landscaped gardens. Shop; cl 1–2 Sat, all Sun and bank hols; free; (01494) 421895.

🏠❋ **Hughenden** SU8695 HUGHENDEN MANOR The home of Benjamin Disraeli until his death in 1881, this imposing old house still has many of the former Prime Minister's books and other possessions, as well as related memorabilia, portraits of friends and formal gardens. Shop, some disabled access; cl am, Mon (exc

bank hols) and Tues, Good Fri, Nov–Mar; £3.50; (01494) 432580; NT. The Le De Spencer on the common at nearby Downley is quite useful for lunch.

❋❄🏠 **Ivinghoe** SP9416 is a pleasant old village with the 18th-c FORD END WATERMILL, the only remaining working watermill in the county. An unusual feature is the sheep wash, a special pool into which sheep were dropped and washed by a jet of water from the mill pool, so that they would fetch a better price when sold. Shop; open pm Sun and bank hols May–Sept, with milling 3–5pm on bank hols and second Sun in Jun, July and Sept; *70p. The village gives its name to a 760-ft-high beacon, with good views and an Iron Age earthwork on top. This area is almost encircled by Hertfordshire, so see that chapter for nearby attractions. The Old Swan down at Cheddington or the Red Lion at Marsworth are quite handy for lunch.

★🏠 **Jordans** SU9791 is interesting as a quiet tree-filled village built mainly this century in honour of the first, 17th-c, Quaker meeting-place here – a simple, evocative building. The nearby Mayflower Barn was built with timbers from the famous ship. The Greyhound at Chalfont St Peter is quite handy for lunch.

❋▬ **Lacey Green** SU8299 SMOCK MILL The oldest surviving smock mill in the country, and indeed the third oldest windmill of any type, was built in 1650 at Chesham and moved here in 1821. It's been well restored after a period of neglect; open pm Sun Apr–Oct; 50p. Nearby is a HOME OF REST FOR HORSES, and Rupert Brooke's old favourite, the Pink & Lily, is good for lunch. Other well restored windmills can be seen at Pitstone (see below), **Loosley Row** SP8100, and **Ibstone** SU7593, unusual for having 12 sides.

★† **Little Missenden** SU9298 The CHURCH of this pretty village has some wall paintings from the 12th c and some pre-Norman traces; and the village itself has attractive old timbered and tiled houses. The Crown is good for a sandwich.

⚲†❋♣ **Pitstone** SP9415 As well as a

decent little agricultural museum and an interesting old church, this small village has the oldest windmill in the country, built in 1627. Shop; *£1. You can hire canal boats for a week or just a day from the wharf (over the B489), and there are pleasant canal walks from there to the Red Lion or White Lion at Marsworth.

★ ⌂ ❀ ! † ❋ **West Wycombe** SU8394 was bought by the NT in its entirety in 1929 when it was threatened with road-widening. It's still beleaguered by traffic, and you risk getting run over as you step back to admire the architecture along the village street – all the sites we mention are just off this street. WEST WYCOMBE PARK 300 acres of beautifully laid-out parkland surround this splendid 18th-c Palladian house, unaltered since its completion. The magnificent rooms have a good collection of tapestries, furniture and paintings, and the Italianate painted ceilings are particularly notable. Disabled access to grounds only; cl am, Fri, Sat, Sept–May; £4, £2.50 grounds only; (01494) 524411 NT.

HELL FIRE CAVES Great fun, these spooky old caves were extended in the 1750s by Sir Francis Dashwood to provide work for the unemployed. Legend has it that the Hell Fire Club (founded by Dashwood) met in the tunnels for drinking, whoring and sorcery, and you can well believe it as you head down through the atmospheric Gothic entrance. The tunnels extend for about a third of a mile underground, and are filled with colourful models and tableaux, some representing famous friends of Sir Francis. Snacks, shop; cl am and all Sat during Mar, Apr and winter, wkdys Nov–Mar; £2.50; (01494) 524411.

The interesting CHURCH OF ST LAWRENCE on the site of an Iron Age fort was again adapted by Dashwood, and crowned with a golden ball so big that it too served as a meeting-place for the Hell Fire Club. The view from the top of the tower is impressive, and the church's interior has a number of unusual features; tower £2. The George & Dragon is good for lunch.

⌂ **Whiteleaf Cross** SP8203 is a large, ancient hill cross dug out of the chalk on the Chilterns escarpment, above which is a Neolithic barrow. The Red Lion below is good for lunch.

🐄 **Wooburn Common** SU9387 ODDS FARM PARK Well liked by readers, this is a good working farm with rare breeds of cattle, pigs, sheep and poultry; not an enormous place but friendly and interesting. Children can feed the lambs and other baby animals and there's a pets' corner with rabbits and guinea pigs. Meals, snacks, shop, disabled access; cl Nov-Easter; (01628) 520188; £2.75. The Royal Standard and the Chequers Hotel are useful for lunch.

🎨 **Wooburn Green** SU9188 GLASS CRAFT Glass-craft centre in 300-year-old converted barn, with demonstrations of glass-blowing and production of stained glass; they do one-day courses. Snacks, shop, limited disabled access; cl Mon, Christmas; (01494) 671033; *£2.

⚓ **Boating on the Thames** Marlow Reach is lively and attractive, and a good centre for trips in either direction: IPG Marine here, (01494) 882210, hire rowing boats from £8 an hour, outboard motorboats £20 an hour, or silent electric launches (up to eight people) at £75 for a half-day (£120 all day). If you don't want to picnic on the boat, the Compleat Angler, right by the river, is a fine place for lunch, and the Hare & Hounds out towards Henley is a good bet.

† **Interesting churches** can be seen at Fingest SU7791 – famous for its huge Norman tower with a twin saddleback roof (the Chequers is nice for lunch); at Stoke Poges SU9983 where the churchyard inspired Thomas Gray's poem (he's buried here), and which has 17th-c stained heraldic glass in the 16th-c chapel; and at Chalfont St Giles SU9993 where there are retouched 14th-c wall paintings (the Greyhound is useful for lunch).

★ **Other attractive villages**, all with decent pubs, include Bledlow SP7702 (where there's also a Norman church with early wall paintings), Denham TQ0386, Great Missenden SP8901,

Hambleden SU7886, Hyde Heath SU9399, Ibstone SU7593, Little Hampden SP8503, Marlow SU8586, Northend SU7392, Penn SU9193 (interesting church), Speen SU8399, Taplow SU9082 and Turville SU7690 (in perhaps the most lovely valley of all here).

Walks

Some would put this part of Buckinghamshire at the top of their personal list of favourite places for walks.

The well wooded Chilterns, of which the finest tracts lie in Bucks, offer plenty of easy-going walks, with a good scattering of rural pubs and pretty villages, though sometimes you have to plan walks carefully to avoid the numerous suburban developments. The escarpment where the hills drop sharply down to the plain gives some very distant views, for instance from above Bledlow SP7702 (good pub). The signposted Ridgeway takes in the most dramatic features, including **Coombe Hill** SP8506 ⌂-1, the highest point in the Chilterns, with its Boer War Memorial on top (an excellent place for views – and for kite-flying). Wendover Woods with some well marked nature trails are adjacent. The town of Wendover SP8607 (the Red Lion here is walker-friendly) gives nearby access, or you can follow paths from Ellesborough SP8306, and sneak views of Chequers, the Prime Minister's country retreat (emphatically private); an alternative path in is from Dunsmore SP8605 (decent pub).

Burnham Beeches SU9585 ⌂-2 is a supreme example of a Chilterns beechwood, splendid in spring and autumn colours, and with maybe a glimpse of deer; maps are posted throughout the forest, but it is quite easy to lose one's bearings; the main starting-point is at East Burnham Common car park SU9584, opposite the W end of Beeches Rd at Farnham Common. Among several pubs dotted around the forest, one of the nicest for lunch is the Blackwood Arms on Littleworth Common SU9386.

Church Wood Nature Reserve on the edge of the immaculate village of Hedgerley SU9787 ⌂-3 is managed by the RSPB, with over 80 species of birds in 34 acres. Hodgemoor Woods SU9693 W of Chalfont St Giles is an ancient woodland with three colour-coded nature trails.

The **Chess Valley** TQ0098 ⌂-4 shared with Herts is miniature and unspoilt, and accessible even without a car from Chalfont & Latimer station on the Metropolitan Underground line; Chenies, Latimer and, just over the Herts border, Sarratt are the villages to head for.

A visit to the caves and village at **West Wycombe** SU8394 ⌂-5 can be easily combined with a walk into the beechwoods just N; the pretty village of Bradenham SU8297 makes a good objective for longer circular walks.

Other places to start a Chilterns walk from (or finish at – all these have decent pubs) include Bolter End SU7992, Botley SP9702, Bryants Bottom SU8599, Fawley SU7586, Fingest SU7791, Frieth SU7990, Hampden Common SP8401, Hawridge Common SP9505, Lower Cadsden SP8204, Penn Street SU9295, Prestwood SP8700, Skirmett SU7790, Wheelerend Common (SU8093; best for shortish potters) and Whiteleaf SP8104.

There's a good footpath along much of the Thames here (on either this bank or the opposite Berks one), and work is afoot to fill in the gaps. The footbridge over the weir at Hambleden SU7886 is attractive and the best starting-point, and besides Marlow itself you can also get down to the river from Bourne End SU8985 (where the Chequers is prettily placed) and Taplow SU9082 (the Oak & Saw is a useful pub here).

Driving

The byroads that take you through any of the villages mentioned above as attractive are worth while. The country lanes leading NW out of Chesham are all pretty. There are some good views from the B474 N of Beaconsfield (worth stopping in Penn for these). High Wycombe is best avoided.

Where to eat

For a special meal out, the three hotels heading the list of places in the **Where to stay** section at the beginning of this chapter are (in order, and at a price) the first choice.

Speen SU8399 OLD PLOW (01494) 488300 Charmingly cottagey place offering a wide choice of good food in beamed rooms with log fires, decent wines, and pleasant welcoming staff; cl pm Sun, Mon; partial disabled access. £32|£4.95/£6.95.

Amersham SU9597 HEDDON'S FRENCH CAFÉ (01494) 431491 Unlicensed restaurant with good atmosphere and food; cl 25 Dec. £22|£3.25/£6.50.

Skirmett SU7790 OLD CROWN (01491) 638435 Delightfully unspoilt village pub with imaginative food, relaxed atmosphere, log fires, no-smoking tap room, and pretty garden; cl Mon exc bank hols; no children under 10. £20|£4.50/£9.

Little Hampden SP8503 RISING SUN (01494) 488393 Imaginative food in secluded upmarket dining pub with attractive terrace and good surrounding walking country; cl pm Sun, Mon. £19.50|£3.50/£6.95.

Bellingdon SP9405 BULL (01494) 758163 Attractive cottagey dining pub with good food in beamed bar; pretty garden; cl pm Sun, 25 Dec; disabled access. £18/£6.

West Wycombe SU8394 GEORGE & DRAGON (01494) 464414 Striking, partly Tudor inn in handsome NT village, with lots of character, good bar food, big garden, and bedrooms; near many places of interest. £18|£2/£6.

Great Missenden SO8900 GEORGE (01494) 862084 Attractive old place originally built as a hospice for the nearby abbey; beams, alcoves, big log fire, popular, good-value food, large secluded terrace; bedrooms; cl pm 25–26 Dec; disabled access. £17|£2.25/£6.50.

Northend SU7392 WHITE HART Cosy little 16th-c pub with good, popular food, friendly owners, log fires, and lovely garden. £15.50|£2/£6.

Bolter End SU7992 PEACOCK (01494) 881417 Rambling bar with friendly atmosphere, welcoming log fire, and good food using the best produce; no children. £15|£3/£6.

Great Hampden SP8401 HAMPDEN ARMS (01494) 488255 Comfortable, little two-room country pub by cricket green, with good choice of well presented food, and friendly, efficient young licensees; good for walks; disabled access. £15|£5.25.

NORTH AND WEST BUCKINGHAMSHIRE

Some splendid stately homes and landscape gardens, though the countryside itself is not special; and there's little for younger people or families.

Off the main tourist track, this area has splendid landscaping around several great houses which make it rewarding for people who enjoy stately homes; Ascott at Wing and Waddesdon Manor are both grand examples of the Rothschild family's remarkable combination of great taste with great wealth, and Stowe Landscape Gardens are among the world's finest. Claydon House at Middle Claydon and Chicheley Hall are also well worth visiting. There's a bit of walking – enough to keep strollers happy. The choice of places to eat out at and to stay in is reasonable though not outstanding.

Where to stay

Aylesbury SP8213 HARTWELL HOUSE Oxford Rd, Aylesbury HP17 8NL (01296) 747444 *£165; 47 lovely rms, some with four-posters and fine panelling, inc 10 secluded suites in separate building with its own private garden. Elegant, historic, Grade I listed building with Jacobean and Georgian façades, wonderful decorative plasterwork and panelling, fine paintings and antiques, marvellous Gothic central staircase, and splendid morning room, library and dining room (excellent food); 90 acres of parkland with ruined church, lake and statues, and fine spa with indoor swimming pool, saunas, gym and so forth, as well as an informal restaurant; woodland path leads to walled garden and two tennis courts; croquet, game fishing; children over 8; good disabled access.

Winslow SP7627 BELL Market Sq, Winslow, Buckingham MK18 3AB (01296) 714091 £39.50; 19 rms. Elegant, black and white timbered inn with comfortable hotel bar, all-day coffee lounge, log fires, and good food in bar and restaurant; pleasant inner courtyard; disabled access.

To see and do

⚬**Aylesbury** SP8213
BUCKINGHAMSHIRE COUNTY MUSEUM (St Mary's Sq, Church St) They've been working hard to improve and update the displays and exhibitions here, and though several rooms are still under wraps, it should all be complete by Oct 1995; new features include a lively Roald Dahl gallery and plenty of regional art. Snacks, shop, disabled access; cl 1.30–2, Sun, bank hols; (01296) 696012; free. The Aristocrat (Wendover Rd) is useful for a snack from lunchtime onwards, and the Bottle & Glass (out on the A418 at Gibraltar) has good food, but probably the best local place is currently the Chequers at Weston Turville.

! ⚬ **Boarstall** SP6214 DUCK DECOY Displays and working demonstrations of one of only three remaining 18th-c working duck decoys. Don't worry, ducks today are lured into the pipes and ringed for migration information rather than to be eaten; also woodland walks and nature trail. Best to tel (01844) 237488 for opening times, usually wknds and bank hols,

plus 4–7 Weds, Apr–Aug; £2; NT. Brill (see below) is the nearest useful place we know of for lunch.

✗ ❀ ★ The windmill at **Brill** SP6513 is in a magnificent position right on the edge of the Chilterns, with distant views across Oxford (and places to picnic and a good pub nearby); there's been a mill on this site for over 700 years. The village itself is quietly attractive, too, and there's a decent walk along the ridge and down to Boarstall (see above). The Pheasant is good for lunch, with a view of the windmill; and the Sun here is useful too.

★ ⚬ **Buckingham** SP6934 itself has quite a lot of attractive early 18th-c brick buildings, and much of the nostalgic charm of a once-important town that has been eclipsed by rivals (in this case Aylesbury and Milton Keynes). OLD GAOL MUSEUM Small local history museum in extraordinary, early Gothic-Revival fort, with good audio-visual show in an intact original cell; they hope to expand the displays over the next few years. Shop; cl Thurs, all Oct and Jan-Mar; *£1.

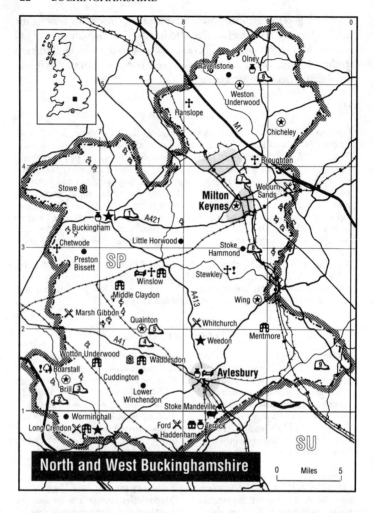

North and West Buckinghamshire

0   Miles   5

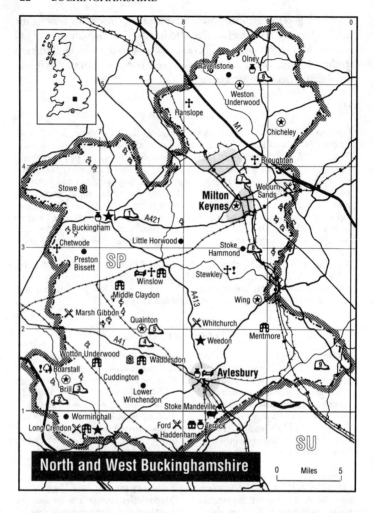 **Chicheley** SP9045 CHICHELEY HALL Particularly fine Georgian house with lovely plasterwork, panelling, and carving; also a naval museum (especially sea paintings), and gardens with 18th-c dovecot. Snacks, shop, limited disabled access; opening hours for 1995 haven't been finalised and there's a chance it will be open only for pre-booked parties – check first; (01234) 391252; £3. The Chester Arms is useful for lunch.

★ 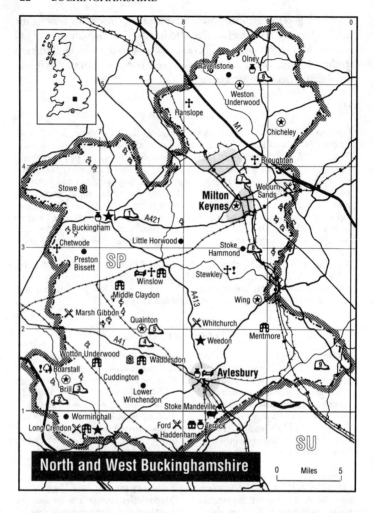 **Long Crendon** SP6808 The cottages in the High St are very pretty, some little changed since the village was a rich wool centre in the 15th c. A particularly lovely timber-framed building is the early 15th-c COURTHOUSE, probably built as a wool store; open pm Weds, Sat, Sun and bank hols Apr–Sept; £1; NT. There are snacks in the nearby church house, and two decent pubs; the Mole & Chicken out at Easington does good food.

 Mentmore SP9019 MENTMORE TOWERS An astonishingly grand mansion built in 1855 for Baron de Rothschild, its breathtaking grandeur giving a good idea of the family's wealth and power at the time; it looks like a cross between an Italian palazzo and Versailles. All the original contents were sold in 1977, and though the rooms are still dramatically opulent you can't help feeling its glory days are over. In Sept there's a fireworks concert in the grounds; open Sun only, with guided tours at 2.30 and 3.15; (01296) 662183; *£3. The Stag, built for the Rothschilds' estate, is a civilised place for lunch.

Middle Claydon SP7125 CLAYDON HOUSE The wonderfully over the top rococo decor is the prime attraction of this mainly 18th-c house – quite a surprise given the classical simplicity of the exterior. Highlights are the carvings by Luke Lightfoot, and the fantastic walls, ceilings and overmantels, though there are also a number of interesting portraits by the likes of Lely and Van Dyck, inc one of Charles I. The original owner found his tastes were considerably richer than his pocket, and his ambitious plans eventually bankrupted him; his family still live here. They have a number of possessions of Florence Nightingale, a frequent visitor. A new room has recently been opened. Snacks, disabled access; cl am, Tues and Thurs, Nov–Mar; £3.50; NT. The Verney Arms at Verney Junction, towards Winslow, is a pleasant place for lunch.

Milton Keynes SP8938 is Britain's largest new town, with roads well laid out to keep traffic moving easily and well away from pedestrians, and a lot of greenery – not to mention the famous concrete cows in a field on the N side of the H3 road (Monks Way, or A422) near the A5 junction. There's a very swish shopping centre at Midsummer Boulevard, named for its alignment with the summer solstice. For those interested in the new town development, CITY DISCOVERY CENTRE (Bradwell, SP8339), in a 16th-c farmhouse in the 17-acre grounds of a former abbey, shows the history and growth of Milton Keynes, inc 4,000 slides chronicling the town's construction, and lots of old maps and photographs. Local readers say it's got a lot going for it; there's also a 14th-c barn and chapel, medieval fishponds, herb gardens, and a nature trail. Best of all are the various fun events, inc after-dark walks to see the bats, and pond-dipping. Snacks, shop, disabled access; cl wknds (exc last Sun in month in summer), bank hols and Christmas–New Year – best to book yourself in on (01908) 227229 or (01908) 312332; free.

MUSEUM OF INDUSTRY AND RURAL LIFE (Stacey Hill Farm, Wolverton, SP8141) Collection of agricultural, industrial and domestic items reflecting the history of the area over the last couple of centuries; snacks, shop, disabled access; cl am, all day Mon (exc bank hols when they have extra exhibits and events), Tues, Nov–Apr; (01908) 316222; £1.25.

Tucked around the city are various villagey corners, and the Swan (Broughton Rd in the Old Village) and Cross Keys (Woodstone), both of which are thatched, the canalside Black Horse at Great Linford and Olde Swan at Woughton on the Green are all pleasant retreats for lunch.

Olney SP8851 This pleasant, stone-built extended village has the enthusiastically run COWPER AND NEWTON MUSEUM, home from 1768–1786 of hymn-writer William Cowper, and now displaying various of his personal possessions, manuscripts and poems, and some belonging to his friend John Newton, curate of Olney and composer of *Amazing Grace*. Also fine lace exhibition, costume gallery, and summerhouse in two small gardens; they plan to introduce a shoemaker's workshop. You'd never guess it now but in the 18th c this elegant house was reckoned to be in the seedier part of town. Shop; cl 1–2, Mon (exc bank hols), mid-Dec–Jan; (01234) 711516; *£1.50. See section on walks for a good riverside stroll to or from Olney. The Bull, HQ for the town's famous Shrove Tuesday pancake race, is useful for lunch.

Quainton SP7521 BUCKS RAILWAY CENTRE Recently celebrating its silver jubilee, this is one of the largest collections of engines and rolling stock we know of, with examples from all over the world attractively displayed in a restored country station; also vintage steamtrain rides, workshops, miniature railway and museum with local railway exhibits. Snacks, shop, disabled access; steamdays Sun and bank hols Apr–Oct as well as Weds in Jun, July and Aug; static days Sun Jan–Mar and Dec, and Sat Apr–Oct; (01296) 655450; £4. The recently restored QUAINTON TOWER MILL is the tallest tower mill in Bucks; open am Sun; (01296) 655348. Waddesdon [SP7417] (see below) is the closest good place for lunch.

☛ **Stoke Mandeville** SP8310 BUCKS GOAT CENTRE Goats galore as well as pigs, poultry, sheep, donkeys and pets; you can feed the animals, and they often have kids (of the capricorn kind) and other small animals for sale. Also a furniture showroom and nursery. Snacks, shop, disabled access; cl Mon (exc bank hols); (01296) 613063; *£2. The Chequers over at Weston Turville is good for lunch.

❀ **Stowe** SP6837 STOWE LANDSCAPE GARDENS Restoration continues apace at these stunning gardens, stretching over a staggering 580 acres, and first laid out between 1713 and 1725. In particular, the statues and buildings are being returned to their full glory, and the water gardens will before too long once again provide a home for exotic waterfowl. Modestly named Capability Brown was head gardener for 10 years, and the monuments and temples that adorn the grounds are by the likes of James Gibb, Sir John Vanbrugh and William Kent. Several suitably grand events throughout the year, but at any time this is a spectacular place to visit – the scale of its artistry really rather staggering. Snacks, shop, disabled access (inc electric-powered cars at no extra charge); open daily during school hols (inc over Christmas) and Mon, Weds, Fri and Sun from late Mar–end of October – best to tel (01280) 813164 for full details; £3.60; NT. Since 1923 a public school, the house is very elegant from the outside, but once inside you may feel it's outclassed by its surroundings; open pm daily exc Sat during the Easter hols (exc Easter wk) and summer hols (exc bank hol wknd); £2. The Bull & Butcher at

Akeley has a good-value buffet lunch.

⚙☕ **Terrick** SP8308 CHILTERN BREWERY (B4009, nr Wendover) Friendly little family-run brewery producing excellent, characterful beers. The tours (with tastings) are generally open only to groups of a dozen or so people, but the good shop is open all the time; disabled access; cl Sun; (01296) 613647; brewery and museum £1; conducted tours Sat £2.50.

🏠❀ **Waddesdon** SP7417 WADDESDON MANOR Reopened after a glittering restoration, this late 19th-c, Renaissance-style château is the most spectacular of the mansions built for Baron Ferdinand de Rothschild. Plenty of rooms to see, each of them astonishingly as lavish as the last, and filled with a dazzling array of furnishings, porcelain, portraits, and other *objets*; there are a good few works by Reynolds and Gainsborough among the picture collection. On our last visit the upstairs rooms were not completed, but these should be ready by Easter. The late Victorian formal gardens surrounding the house are quite splendid, and there's also a cast-iron rococo aviary (still in use). They've recently opened up the fabled wine cellars, where as well as huge vintage bottles they keep a collection of labels designed or painted by some of the century's greatest artists. A really excellent place to visit, but it does get busy; try and get there early, they operate a timed ticket system for the house, and if you arrive too late it's possible you won't get in at all. Good snacks, shop, disabled access; open pm Thurs–Sun and bank hols Mar–Oct (though grounds open at 11am), plus pm Weds in July and Aug; (01296) 651211; prices have been £3 to get in the grounds, with an extra £4 (£5 Sun and bank hols) for the house, though as we went to press they were considering having separate charges for each floor; NT. The Five Arrows is good for lunch (and has some good Rothschild wines in all price ranges).

★ **Weedon** SP8118 is a lovely little village with 17th- and 18th-c houses; the White Swan in nearby Whitchurch is a decent stop for lunch.

♆ ♞ ❀ Weston Underwood SP8650
FLAMINGO GARDENS AND ZOOLOGICAL
PARK Notable collection of rare and
endangered birds from all over the
world, with unusual pink-backed
pelicans, vultures, cockatoos, and
toucans as well as flamingos. Also
mammals such as bison, llamas and
white wallabies. William Cowper
wrote many of his poems in the area
now patrolled by peacocks and
cranes, and extracts appear on several
of the statues and urns. Shop, disabled
access; cl am Mon (exc bank hols),
Tues and Fri (exc in July and Aug),
Oct–Easter; £3.50. The Cowper's Oak
is a pleasant place for lunch.

♞ ❀ † Wing SP8822 ASCOTT Another
of the Rothschild mansions, its black
and white timbers and jutting gables
quite a contrast to the luxuriant
opulence of nearby Waddesdon. Once
again it's crammed full of treasures,
but this is perhaps more like a home
and less like a museum; indeed it's still
lived in. Ming and K'ang Hsi
porcelain, paintings by Hogarth,
Rubens and Gainsborough, Dutch art
by Hobbema, Cuyp and others, and
French and Chippendale furniture.
The 260-acre grounds have extensive
gardens with many rare trees and
shrubs. Some disabled access; house
open pm Apr–mid-May and Sept exc
Mon; gardens open pm Weds and last
Sun of month Apr–Sept; *£5, *£3
garden only; NT. ALL SAINTS CHURCH
has a fine monument to Sir Robert
Dormer (died 1552), a 10th-c apse,
crypt and nave, and 12th-c font.
Mentmore is just to the south.

♞ Winslow SP7627 WINSLOW HALL
Striking house almost certainly
designed by Wren, and unusually has
survived without any major structural
changes. A modest but friendly place,
with a collection of Chinese art; open
pm Weds and Thurs in July and Aug,
and bank hol wknds, or by
appointment; (01296) 712323; £4.
The Bell is useful for lunch.

♞ Wotton Underwood SP6815
WOTTON HOUSE Restored 18th-c
house built to the same design as

Buckingham Palace, with the park
redesigned by Capability Brown. The
guided tours here have been well liked
for their informality, but as we went
to press they weren't sure whether
they would be opening in 1995; best
to check with Aylesbury tourist
information on (01296) 382308. The
Red Lion at Ashendon and Bull &
Butcher at Ludgershall are both useful
for lunch.

† Interesting churches include the one
at STEWKLEY SP8525 which has good
examples of late Norman work (two
decent pubs here), BROUGHTON
SP8940 for its retouched 14th- and
15th-c wall paintings, CHETWODE
SP6429 where there's some fine early
glass and Early English windows, and
at HANSLOPE SP8046 where the spire is
higher than most in the county. A less
traditional place of worship is KEACH'S
MEETING HOUSE, WINSLOW SP7627,
the oldest non-conformist chapel in
the county.

For **children to let off steam** ☺ MOUNT
FARM LANE has a lakeside children's
play area, pitch and putt course,
tennis courts, and wildfowl. ❀ ♞
WILLEN LAKESIDE PARK SP8241
(Brickhill St, Milton Keynes) actually
has two lakes – one with water sports,
hotel and restaurant, and the other
for birdwatching. There's also a
Japanese peace pagoda built by
Buddhist monks, a turf maze, and
nature trail.

You can book hour-long ! BALLOON
TRIPS over the whole county from
Stewkley SP8526; they cost £110 and
only two people can go up at a time.

★ **Attractive villages** include Lower
Winchendon SP7312, a secluded old
place with carefully restored houses
and a charming, simple church. The
walk over the hill to Upper
Winchendon gives interesting views.
Others, all with decent pubs, are:
Cuddington SP7311, Haddenham
SP7408, Little Horwood SP7930,
Preston Bissett SP6529, Ravenstone
SP8450, Stoke Hammond SP8829,
Weston Underwood SP8650 and
Worminghall SP6308.

Walks

Mildly undulating at best, this is not vintage walking territory, but there are pockets of minor interest for gentle strolling. Bucks County Council publish a series of circular walks (free from information centres, or from the County Hall, tel [01296] 382845). These include a 4½-mile route from **Thornborough Bridge** SP7233 ◌-1 on the A421, taking in a mill, the site of a medieval village, and the Buckingham Arm Canal.

Shabbington Wood SP6210 ◌-2 nr Oakley over on the W of the county has been designated a Site of Special Scientific Interest because of its rich butterfly habitats; a special butterfly trail has been created to help you spot some of the 40-odd species here.

There is reasonable scope for village-to-village walks such as those around **Brill** SP6513 ◌-3, **Waddesdon** SP7417 ◌-4 and **Quainton** SP7420 ◌-5. The last two are on the 30-mile North Bucks Way from Chequers Knap above Great Kimble SP8205 to Wolverton SP8140 in Milton Keynes; this includes the prominent viewpoint of Quainton Hill SP7521.

Milton Keynes SP8938 has several walks with local beauty spots and points of historical interest; leaflets available locally. There are good footpaths to nearby lakes from the Swan pub in the Old Village.

The **riverside** walk ◌-6 to Olney SP8851 from the Robin Hood pub at Clifton Reynes SP9051 (or vice versa) is short but attractive, passing an old mill.

Several decent **canalside** walks ◌-7, ◌-8 include ones between Great Linford SP8542 (good family pub) and New Bradwell SP8341 (another pleasant pub); or at Marsworth SP9114, where there's an imposing flight of locks, and a family pub at Startops End SP9214; or near Stoke Hammond SP8829 (lockside pub).

Ivinghoe Beacon SP9617 ◌-9 is discussed in the Herts chapter.

Driving

This part of the county has a fair variety of different landscapes, with modestly hilly country and some fine views along the quiet country road NW from Aylesbury, through Quainton and Edgcott to Marsh Gibbon (where there's a good pub); and off the A41 just E of Waddesdon, turning S through Upper Winchendon to Long Crendon then right along the B4011, turning right off it to Brill and then back up to the A41 via Ludgershall. The B4033 S from Stony Stratford through Great Horwood to the pleasant, small market town of Winslow is also a decent drive. Milton Keynes itself is beginning to mature and, as it's been so thoughtfully laid out with concern for its surrounding landscape, is surprisingly pleasant to drive around – certainly not a place to avoid if your route looks like passing that way.

Where to eat

Woburn Sands SP9235 SPOONERS 61 High St (01908) 584385 Smart, pretty restaurant with good-value French and English cooking, and welcoming atmosphere; worthwhile snacks downstairs; cl Sun, Mon, Christmas wknd, 1 wk summer; disabled access. £28|£2.75|£5.

Long Crendon SP6908 ANGEL Bicester Rd (01844) 208268 Friendly dining pub with cheerful staff serving fresh, well prepared food – especially fish dishes; cl pm Sun. £20|£4.50|£6.

Ford SP7709 DINTON HERMIT (01296) 748379 Cosy, tucked away little stone pub, with good home-made bar food and more elaborate evening menu; no food Sun, Mon; disabled access. £19|£2|£5.

Marsh Gibbon SP6423 GREYHOUND (01869) 277365 Friendly, old stone pub serving good Thai food and well kept beers in pleasant, traditional bars; nice garden. £17|£3|£7.

Whitchurch SO8020 WHITE SWAN (01296) 641228 Homely, partly thatched, old pub with very cheerful atmosphere, friendly service, and a wide choice of good bar food; big garden. Fairly handy for both Waddesdon and Quainton; cl pm Sun; partial disabled access. **£11.50**/£2.50/£4.50.

Help this year from: Barbara Hatfield, Jenny and Michael Back, S J Patrick, Peter Plumridge, P Saville, DJW, Chris Warne, Mr and Mrs T F Marshall, Cindy and Chris Crow, Nigel Norman, Clifford Payton, A M Pickup, Paul and Maggie Baker, Graham and Kaern Oddey, Janet Pickles, H Hazzard, Ron and Val Broom, Mike Tucker, Mike Pugh, Michael Sargent, George Atkinson, S J Collett-Jones, Mr and Mrs M J Martin, S T Whitaker, Rhoda and Jeff Collins, Neil and Anita Christopher, John C Baker.

BUCKINGHAMSHIRE CALENDAR

Some of these dates were provisional as we went to press.

FEBRUARY

4 **Aylesbury** Chess Congress at the Civic Centre – *till Sun 5* (01296) 555187

28 **Olney** Pancake Race (since 1455)

MARCH

18 **Aylesbury** Festival of the Arts – *till 22 April*, with closing concert on 30 April (01296) 555219

APRIL

29 **High Wycombe** Arts Festival – *till 28 May* (01494) 528226

MAY

7 **High Wycombe** Carnival (01494) 421892

8 **Quainton** May Day Fair (01296) 655348

14 **Ivinghoe** National Mills Day at Ford End Watermill, Ford End Farm (01582) 600391

18 **High Wycombe** Mayor-Making and procession (01494) 461000 (mayor's secretary)

JUNE

4 **Buckingham** Children's Day at Stowe Landscape Gardens (01280) 823334

10 **Chalfont St Giles** Woodcraft Weekend at Chiltern Open-Air Museum – *till Sun 11* (01494) 871117

17 **Marlow** Regatta (01491) 575478

18 **Halton** RAF Halton Air Show (01296) 623535

28 **Taplow** Cliveden Open-Air Theatre Festival – *till 8 July* (01628) 605069

JULY

1 **Prestwood** Chiltern Traction Engine Steam Rally at the Hangings – *till Sun 2* (01923) 262845

7 **West Wycombe** Battle of Trafalgar at West Wycombe Park (01494) 524411

8 **Buckingham** Summer Festival – *till Fri 14* (01280) 814385

BUCKINGHAMSHIRE CALENDAR

JULY cont

15 **Burnham** Carnival (01628) 605772

16 **Cox Green** Fun Day (01628) 605772

AUGUST

27 **Chalfont St Giles** Children's Days at Chiltern Open-Air Museum – *till Mon 28* (01494) 871117

28 **Winslow** Horticultural Show at the Public Hall

SEPTEMBER

2 **High Wycombe** Wycombe and District Show at Wycombe Rye – *till 3 Sept* (01494) 463463

7 **Weedon** Buckinghamshire County Show at the County Showground (01296) 83734

21 **Thame** Agricultural Show at the Showground (01844) 212737

23 **Wooburn Green, Marlow, High Wycombe, Bourne End** Wooburn Festival – *till 14 Oct* (01628) 524243

24 **Aylesbury** Charter Day – a Stuart day (01296) 87592

OCTOBER

7 **Chalfont St Giles** Harvest Celebration at Chiltern Open-Air Museum – *till Sun 8* (01494) 871117

14 **Buckingham** Charter Fair – *till Sun 22, also Sat 28 – till Sun 29* (01280) 823020

NOVEMBER

5 **Downley** Torchlight Procession and Bonfire

11 **Fenny Statford** Firing the Poppers on St Martin's Day – celebration held since 1730 in honour of St Martin, the patron saint of the church. Poppers are quart-size metal vessels filled with 'shilling powder' and fired with a hot rod (01908) 372825

CAMBRIDGESHIRE AND BEDFORDSHIRE

The city of Cambridge itself is the predominant reason for most people coming to this area, and is a charming place for a short break (we have found quite a few new places to stay in and eat at here this year). Woburn Abbey and Whipsnade also stand out as rewarding places for a day out. Elsewhere there are some worthwhile places to visit, and as they are not heavily exploited as tourist attractions they are not overrun with visitors.

There are several very pretty villages – and many more where a patient stroller with an eye for detail can pick out quite a lot of interest. In general, the countryside is too flat for great scenic appeal. The best of it is up on the Dunstable Downs in Bedfordshire, though other parts are refreshing, such as the quiet beauty of Wicken Fen in Cambridgeshire. There's a melancholy, open-sky grandeur about the dead level open fen country in the north of the area, especially in autumn or the chill of winter.

We find Tourist Information Centres in this area are among the best – very helpful with information, maps and trails.

CAMBRIDGE AND THE SOUTH

Arguably Britain's most attractive, ancient university city, with some good places for family excursions outside.

The city's pulse really quickens when the centre is filled with students during the university terms, and is most worth seeing when students outnumber tourists. In the summer, when it is host to foreign students, its popularity with coach tours means that particular places can suddenly be flooded with herds of visitors, so perhaps the best time of all is spring or autumn. In winter it often has a damp, fenny chill.

Outside the city, the zoo at Lynton, the remarkable collection of aircraft and other fighting equipment at Duxford, and the stately Wimpole Hall are the pick of the area's attractions, and the M11 makes them good destinations for family outings from London. Older visitors might well find plenty of other things to fill a quiet weekend.

Where to stay

Six Mile Bottom TL5757 SWYNFORD PADDOCKS Six Mile Bottom, Newmarket, Suffolk CB8 0UE (0163 870) 234 £107; 15 individually furnished rms with good bthrms. Gabled mansion in neat grounds, with carefully furnished panelled rooms, log fire, relaxed atmosphere, and friendly service; tennis, putting, croquet; cl 3 dys between Christmas and New Year.
Duxford TL4745 DUXFORD LODGE Ickleton Rd, Duxford CB2 4RU (01223) 836444 £67.50; 15 rms. Carefully run Victorian hotel in an acre of neatly kept

gardens; with good food in airy restaurant, cosy bar, and relaxed atmosphere; disabled access.

Cambridge TL4658 CAMBRIDGE LODGE Huntingdon Rd, Cambridge CB3 0DQ (01223) 352833 £65; 11 rms, most with own bthrm. Edwardian house with open fire in relaxed and comfortable lounge; friendly service, and good, freshly prepared food in popular restaurant; cl 27–30 Dec; disabled access.

Cambridge TL4658 ARUNDEL HOUSE 53 Chesterton Rd, Cambridge CB4 3AN (01223) 67701 £53.50; 105 comfortable rms, 6 without bthrm. Carefully preserved terrace of fine, early Victorian houses overlooking the River Cam and parkland; comfortable plush bar, airy lounge with open fire, elegant restaurant, and seats in the pleasant garden; cl 25–26 Dec.

Cambridge TL4658 KIRKWOOD HOUSE 172 Chesterton Rd, Cambridge CB4 1DA (01223) 313874 £46; 5 rms, some with own bthrm. B & B in small Edwardian house close to the river and a short walk to the town centre; good breakfasts (packed lunches on request); children over 7; cl mid-Dec–mid-Feb.

Little Gransden TL2754 GRANSDEN LODGE FARM Little Gransden, Sandy, Beds SG19 3EB (01767) 677365 £34; 6 rms. Working farm of 860 acres with pedigree Gelbwieh cattle; big lounge, dining room, friendly atmosphere; and gardens with fish ponds; no evening meals (plenty of pubs and restaurants locally).

To see and do

Cambridge TL4658 Ancient and graceful university buildings dominate the centre, now largely pedestrianised. Though the colleges look private, you can usually wander into the courtyards (not at exam time); some have a small charge for admission. The dining halls and chapels are worth seeking out in some colleges. The Fitzwilliam Museum is very special. Though there's quite a bit of mostly hi-tech light industry towards the outskirts, the centre seems almost untouched by the outside world. It has the character of a small, old-fashioned market town (with an excellent market in Market Hill – emphatically not a hill even by fenland standards), and is a lot quieter and generally prettier than Oxford – you do get a real sense of centuries of study. Moreover, compared with Oxford, the architecture has a striking diversity. Another essential ingredient is the river and its associated tracts of greenery known collectively as The Backs, with charming lawns, trees, college gardens, paths snaking in and out of the colleges, and punts gliding past the weeping willows. In term-time, there are countless events (and the West Rd concert hall has outstanding acoustics); any college notice-board will show what's on.

🏠 ❀ ✝ COLLEGES The finest is Trinity, where the imposing Great Court is open to the public (the porters may intervene if you go into pretty Nevilles Court or New Court without looking as though you belong; the river's just beyond). Kings is probably the best known, with its magnificent chapel (see below); pleasant to walk through and over the bridge. Gonville & Caius (pronounced `keys') is small and snooty but very pretty. Queens has a half-timbered courtyard and an eye-catchingly gaudy painted hall, as well as the famous Mathematical Bridge (built without any bolts or fastenings, until curiosity got the better of some engineers who dismantled it and

found they couldn't put it back together in the same way). Peterhouse is the oldest, founded in 1284; the buildings carry their years very gracefully and it has a park. St Johns has the very photographed Bridge of Sighs. Jesus, a bit off the main beat, is huge and grandly impressive, and Emmanuel has notable gardens. Two charming smaller colleges are Clare and Trinity Hall, next to each other by The Backs.

Tourism isn't exactly welcomed by the dons (they can get terribly agitated if you even look at the grass let alone accidentally step on it) and, in an effort to keep the crowds down, some of the colleges charge about £1 for admission. In particular, you'll now have to pay £2 to enter KINGS COLLEGE CHAPEL, but it' worth it; at any time the fan-vaulted ceiling and Rubens' *Adoration of the Magi* are breathtaking, but they seem even more special if you're lucky enough to visit while the choir is practising. There's a useful exhibition too; disabled access.

Almost any stroll through the central streets will give you numerous other things to look at. Between the colleges and university buildings are numerous less imposing but attractive old buildings, often grouped together quite picturesquely – a row of old-fashioned shops perhaps, or a cluster of very varied but harmonious houses. Quite a few shops are that bit different and worth popping into.

Don't try to drive around; there really is no parking, and apart from the pedestrianised centre there's a frustrating tangle of one-way streets. Head for one of the big NCPs. If you don't plan to take a car at all, it's worth noting that the bus station's a good deal more central than the train station. For a first-time visit, the TOUR BUS is good (about an hour), and goes along The Backs, too. Walking tours set off from the TOURIST INFORMATION CENTRE (Wheeler St) five times a day in summer.

🖼 FITZWILLIAM MUSEUM (Trumpington St) Times have changed since the early days of this venerable institution, when its collections were open only to those members of the public considered properly dressed. Very grand and impressive, it's a wonderful place, crammed with more dazzling treasures than you could hope to examine in one visit. In fact, unless you're planning to spend the whole day there you might not be able to see everything anyway – on wkdys the upper and lower galleries are each only open half the day, downstairs from 10–2, upstairs 2–5. If you're short of time the best thing to do is try to visit around lunchtime so you can see both, or go at the wknd when both galleries are open at the same time. Among the downstairs collections are Greek, Egyptian, and Roman antiquities, European ceramics, English glass, carvings, and armour, while upstairs are paintings inc works by Titian, Canaletto and the French Impressionists. Decent café, shop, recently improved disabled access; cl am Sun, all Mon, 24 Dec–1 Jan, Good Fri, and galleries as described above; (01223) 332900; free.

�» UNIVERSITY BOTANIC GARDEN (Cory Lodge, Bateman St) The site has grown since the garden's foundation in 1762, and now covers 40 acres with some marvellous mature trees, a geographic rock garden, a scented garden, water and winter gardens, and many rare plants inc several national collections. Rarely crowded, so it's pleasant to stroll through. Snacks, shop, disabled access; cl 25–26 Dec; garden and glasshouses cl 12.30–2; (01223) 336265; £1.50.

🖼 CAMBRIDGE & COUNTY FOLK MUSEUM (2–3 Castle St) Handsome 16th-c building near the river, once an inn, now a useful exploration of the everyday life of people in the region over the last few centuries, with displays of items from tools through toys to tea caddies. Regular craft days; shop, disabled access to ground floor only; cl am Sun, winter Mon, 24 Dec–2 Jan, Good Fri; (01223) 355159; free.

🖼 KETTLE'S YARD (Castle St) Refurbishment and extensions complete, the gallery has now reopened and displays various temporary exhibitions, while the house still has its fascinating 20th-c paintings and sculptures, lovely 18th-c furniture and oriental carpets, and collections of shells and stones. There are interesting St Ives connections. Snacks, shop, disabled access; cl am, Mon, 24 Dec–2 Jan; (01223) 352124; free.

🖼 MUSEUM OF CLASSICAL ARCHAEOLOGY (Sidgwick Ave) One of the few surviving collections of casts of Greek and Roman sculpture. Shop, disabled access; cl wknds, Easter, Christmas; free.

🖼 UNIVERSITY MUSEUM OF ARCHAEOLOGY & ANTHROPOLOGY (Downing St) Recently totally refurbished, there's a variety of interesting displays looking at man's

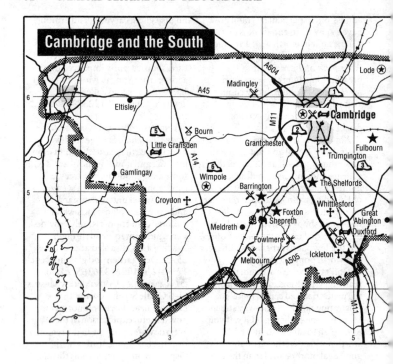

development through the ages; some emphasis on local and British archaeology, and a new exhibition on changing traditions. Shop, disabled access; cl am exc Sat, pm Sat, Sun, 24 Dec–2 Jan, Easter wk, Aug bank hol – they hope to extend the opening hours over the summer, so it's worth checking first; (01223) 333516; free.

☐ WHIPPLE MUSEUM OF SCIENCE (Free School Lane) Diverse collection of scientific instruments and apparatus from the 16th c onwards. Interesting even even if science isn't your thing, with plenty to make you thankful we no longer need to rely on sundials and abacuses. Disabled access by appointment; cl am, wknds, maybe other dates; (01223) 334540; free, though £2 charge for special exhibitions.

☐ SCOTT POLAR RESEARCH INSTITUTE (Lensfield Rd) The international centre for polar studies, with Arctic and Antarctic expedition displays (an emphasis on Captain Scott), Eskimo arts and crafts, and wildlife displays. Shop, disabled access; open 2.30–4 only, cl Sun, some bank hols, Fri before Christmas–2 Jan; (01223) 336540; free.

☐ SEDGWICK MUSEUM (Downing St) The university geology museum, with one of the world's best collections of fossils, and rocks from Darwin's journey in HMS *Beagle*. Shop, some disabled access; cl 1–2pm, pm Sat, all Sun; free. Down the same street is the University Museum of Zoology; cl am and all wknds; free.

✝ ✹ Of many free churches here, it's worth noting ST BENET'S, one of the city's oldest, the popular HOLY SEPULCHRE or Round Church, and GREAT ST MARY'S with its fine roof and good city views from the tower. Another place with good views is Castle Mound, beyond Bridge Street, which has an indicator to pick out the sights.

There are lots of secondhand bookshops worth a look. HEFFERS (Trinity Street) is particularly good,

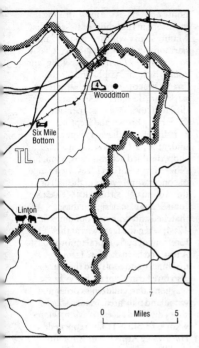

and the general bookshops are as fine as you'd expect from this university town. On the first Sat of the month there's a CRAFT FAIR on St Johns Green.

⚓ PUNTING is the only way to travel, though if your skills in this department were picked up in Oxford you'll find they do things a little back to front here. You can punt right along The Backs, and even down to Grantchester, a pleasant little village still much as described in Rupert Brooke's poem of the same name, with the civilised Orchard Tea Gardens (lovely in summer) and three pubs. You can hire punts from Scudamores on Mill Lane or other stations along the water; prices generally start at around £4 an hour. Bumps races (several rowing eights start off in a line and have to catch up with the one in front) take place on the river in Feb, Jun and July.

Cyclists will enjoy the towpaths here; nettle-free, and safe if you have children with you.

Other things to see and do

⚒ **Bourn** TL3256 The WINDMILL here is thought to be the oldest trestle post mill in the country; open pm last Sun of month (or the Mon if that Sun is a bank hol wknd) Apr–Oct – may be best to check first; (01223) 243830; £1; small car park.

✚ 🐂 ☺ ☕ ! **Duxford** TL4846 DUXFORD AIRFIELD A branch of the Imperial War Museum, this is probably Europe's best collection of military and civil aircraft, with over 130 flying machines from flimsy-looking biplanes to state-of-the-art Gulf War jets; they often fly some so you may be lucky enough to see, say, a Spitfire in action. They have tanks and other vehicles too, several set in dramatic battle-zone tableaux, and an extremely hi-tech simulator (they prefer the more dramatic name of dynamic motion theatre), as well as the prototype Concorde, naval exhibits (inc a midget submarine), a summer narrow-gauge railway,

pleasure flights, and an adventure playground. The Second World War Operations Museum has sound effects to make it seem like you're caught up in a bombing raid. Easily enough to fill up most of a day, and don't worry about the weather – most exhibits are under cover. Meals, snacks, shop, disabled access; cl 24–26 Dec; (01223) 835000; £5.95. The John Barleycorn is good for lunch.

🐾 **Linton** TL5646 ZOOLOGICAL GARDENS (Hadstock Rd) Well liked by readers, a family-run zoo with the emphasis firmly on conservation and breeding; a number of birds and animals are born here each year, so there's always something different to see. Current residents include giant tortoises, snow leopards, Sumatran tigers, tarantula spiders, snakes and other unusual threatened species from around the world – all housed in enclosures as close to their natural habitats as possible. Just as we went to press they told us of the birth of a baby tapir, which, when fully grown, will look like a cross between a pig and an elephant. Snacks, shop, disabled access; cl 25 Dec; (01223) 891037; £3.75. The picturesque Bell is useful for lunch.

Not far from here towards Balsham is the ❧ CHILFORD HUNDRED VINEYARD, a friendly 18-acre winery with interesting old buildings and tours on the hour; cl Oct–Apr; (01223) 892641; £3.50 (inc two tastings and a little souvenir glass).

❋ ☖ 🏠 ✕ Lode TL5362 ANGLESEY ABBEY The lovely gardens that surround this handsome 17th-c house were quite a recent addition, laid out in Georgian style from 1926 by the first Lord Fairhaven; the gardener who looks after them has just celebrated his 50th year here. All that remains of the original priory is a medieval undercroft, but the house has an eclectic collection of furnishings and paintings; not all engage the attention for very long but it's definitely worth pausing at Constable's view of the Thames and the landscapes by Claude. The bookshelves in the library are made from Rennie's Waterloo Bridge. The grounds also have a WATERMILL, restored to working condition and once again milling flour. Meals, snacks, shop, disabled access; cl Mon and Tues, mid-Oct–Mar; £3; NT. The Red Lion at Swaffham Prior is fairly handy for lunch.

🐾 ❋ Shepreth TL3947 WILLERS MILL WILD ANIMAL SANCTUARY Genuine little wildlife rescue centre with all sorts of unwanted or injured animals and birds. They also have a fish farm where the koi will feed right out of your hand; meals and snacks (in elevated tree-top café), disabled access; cl 25 Dec ; (01763) 262226; £3.50, slightly more Sun and bank hols. Worth a visit nearby are the tranquil gardens of DOCWRA MANOR, at their best Apr–Jun but always with a variety of unusual plants grown and for sale. Lovely intimate walled garden; (01763) 261557; £1.50. The Plough is useful for lunch.

🏠 ❋ 🏛 ❧ Wimpole TL3351 WIMPOLE HALL Probably the county's biggest house and one of the most striking mansions in the whole of East Anglia. Mainly 18th c with an imposing and harmonious Georgian façade, it has a lovely *trompe l'oeil* chapel ceiling, and rooms by James Gibbs and Sir John Soane. Best of all are the 360 acres of parkland, designed by several different notable landscapers inc Capability Brown and Repton; the remains of a medieval village are under the pasture. Meals, snacks, shop, disabled access; cl am, Mon, Fri, Nov–Mar; £4.50. NT. A varied range of concerts and events in the hall or the grounds. WIMPOLE HOME FARM Sir John Soane also designed these thatched and timbered buildings in 1794, when the farm was at the forefront of agricultural innovations. A restored barn displays farm machinery and tools and there are also rare farm animals, heavy horse waggon rides, children's corner and woodland play area. Meals, snacks, shop, disabled access; cl Mon, winter wkdys; £3.50; NT. The reopened Hardwicke Arms is handy for lunch.

★ **Villages** worth stopping at include Barrington TL3949, with its superb village green, pretty timbered houses, interesting church and a good pub, and nearby Foxton TL4148 is especially interesting if you've brought *The Common Stream* by Rowland Parker as weekend reading (an intricate account of the village through the ages). Fulbourn TL5156 is an attractive, largely thatched village, with a windmill on the Cambridge rd, a good farm shop with pick-your-own fruit, and a pretty church; a path E takes you to the wooded line of the Fleam Dyke, a miles-long, Dark Age defence earthwork. Ickleton TL4943 has a fine church, with Roman columns as bases for its arches, and interestingly carved pews. The churchyard is lovely, and around the church and small green are several beautiful old houses – often a good deal older, in fact, than their Georgian refacing suggests. The Shelfords TL4652 will reward a slow stroll for those with an eye for architectural detail, and even a quick drive through will show up several delightful timbered houses.

Other attractive villages include Linton TL5646, Madingley TL3960, Meldreth TL3746, and (all with decent pubs) Eltisley TL2659, Gamlingay TL2452, Great Abington TL5348, Great Chishill TL4239 (well restored windmill), and Woodditton TL6659.

✝ **Churches** worth visiting include the quiet little country one at Croydon TL3149, and those at Trumpington TL4455 where there's the second oldest brass in England, and Whittlesford TL4748 (a rich interior; the Tickell Arms a little way off is a most unusual pub).

Walks

From Magdalene Bridge in the city of Cambridge there's a pleasant **towpath walk** ⌂-1 out into the meadows – tranquil, with only punts as far as the lock. Beyond that, you could walk as far as Ely, with oarsmen setting an altogether more vigorous tone – though the Plough at Fen Ditton TL4860 would probably weaken your resolve. Another pleasant stroll out from Cambridge is the walk from Mill Lane along the meadow towpath to **Grantchester** TL4455 ⌂-2. The various quaintly named parks in the town are all OK for strolling, and you can at least sit on the grass there.

The surrounding countryside is not really distinguished for walking, but there are some possibilities. The **Gog Magog Hills** TL4954 ⌂-3 S of Cambridge are worth a passing visit; among tall trees you can trace the main rampart and ditch of Wandlebury Iron Age fort, and there are good views of the city's distant towers and spires.

The miles-long ancient embankment known as the **Devil's Ditch** ⌂-4 E of the city lets you fuel a walk with thoughts of whether it was built to fight off the Romans, or some centuries later to protect the riches of East Anglia from Midlands warlords. A good start would be from the B1061 N of Dullingham TL6357 (where there's a good pub; there's another at nearby Woodditton TL6659). It's not much of a topographical feature, and is crossed by one or two busy roads.

Hayley Wood TL2952 ⌂-5 near Little Gransden TL2755 has a huge variety of wildlife; its hedges, trees and other plants have been little disturbed since the 13th c if not earlier.

One of the best pockets of scenery hereabouts is around **Wimpole Hall** TL3351 ⌂-6, which has ready-made farm and folly trails.

Driving

The M11 and the A45 are generally fast and trouble free. The A11 can have long queues and is not a pleasant road. On the whole the countryside here is too flat for interesting pleasure drives. There are one or two bright spots, such as the long-winded A14, an old coaching road on Roman foundations which carries little traffic now; and the A1304 towards Newmarket, passing handsome rolling gallops and the immaculate paddocks of top stud farms.

Where to eat

Melbourn TL3844 PINK GERANIUM Station Rd (01763) 260215 Pretty, 16th-c thatched cottage with good sophisticated cooking, a homely, relaxed atmosphere, and pretty little garden; cookery courses too; cl am Sat, Mon; disabled access. £41.90.

Cambridge TL4658 MIDSUMMER HOUSE Midsummer Common (01223) 69299 Close to the river, with several small attractively furnished eating areas; imaginative French cooking, good wines; cl 1 Jan, am Sat, Mon, pm Sun. £39/£15 (2-course lunch).

Cambridge TL4658 Twenty Two Chesterton Rd (01223) 351880 Simple and pretty evening restaurant with good modern cooking, lovely puddings, fine wine list and friendly service; cl Sun, Mon, 1 wk over Christmas; children over 10. £25.

Madingley TL3960 Three Horseshoes (01954) 210221 Smart, thatched dining pub with nicely decorated small dining area, attractive conservatory, and good, well presented food (popular summer buffet); pleasant village; restaurant cl pm Sun. £23|£3.50/£6.50.

Fowlmere TL4245 Chequers (01763) 208369 Civilised old coaching inn with smartly dressed waiters, ambitious food in galleried restaurant, good puddings, excellent wines; log fire in bar; also a conservatory and attractive garden; cl 25 Dec; disabled access. £17.75 lunch|£3.50/£6.

Duxford TL4745 John Barleycorn (01223) 832699 Pretty, early 17th-c thatched country pub; attractively furnished with quietly chatty bar, popular, good food, and courteous service; fine hanging baskets and flower-filled back garden; no children. £16|£3.90/£7.

Barrington TL3949 Royal Oak (01223) 870791 Marvellous choice of interesting vegetarian dishes in firmly run thatched and timbered pub. £15|£3/£6.

Cambridge has many attractive snack places inc Clowns (King St, off Sidney St), Roof Garden (top floor of Arts Theatre – side entrance in St Edwards Passage, opposite Kings), Boards (down a floor), the tiny Little Tea Room (All Saints Green), Copper Kettle (Kings Parade), Kings Pantry (Kings Parade), and Browns (Trumpington St).

Decent Riverside Pubs include the Anchor (Silver St Bridge), Boathouse (Chesterton Rd), Fort St George (Midsummer Common), Mill (Mill Lane) and Pike & Eel (Water St, Chesterton). The best pub away from the river is the smoke-free Free Press (Prospect Row); the Eagle (Benet St) has a good deal of atmosphere.

NORTH CAMBRIDGESHIRE

Civilised old hotels and inns, good food, some fine old buildings, but the countryside is generally very flat with little for young people.

A break in this part of the county might suit older people best, with some very civilised places in which to stay, decent food readily available, and cathedrals, churches and other fine buildings to look at. The fen country has a lot to offer bird watchers, who would also enjoy the waterfowl gardens at Peakirk. Otherwise, the flat silt fens and huge working fields reclaimed from the marshes make much of the countryside rather monotonous – though some people love its misty bleakness in autumn, say. To the west, the land is drier and more rolling, with stonebuilt villages reminiscent of Leicestershire.

Ely with its graceful cathedral is the area's gem, though Wisbech also has much to repay a visit. The area can be very chill in winter.

Where to stay

Huntingdon TL2371 George George St, Huntingdon PE18 6AB (01480) 432444 £102.90; 24 well equipped rms. Fine galleried courtyard in old posting house; quietly elegant, with comfortable lounge and good food.

Huntingdon TL2371 Old Bridge 1 High St, Huntingdon PE18 6TQ (01480) 52681 *£89.50; 26 excellent rms. Creeper-covered Georgian hotel with attractively decorated lounge and log fire in panelled bar; imaginative food and extensive wine list in restaurant and more informal lunchtime room (pretty murals); quick, courteous service; riverside gardens.

Wansford TL0799 HAYCOCK Wansford, Peterborough PE8 6JA (01780) 782223 £89w; 51 attractively decorated rms. Old-fashioned, character-filled, golden stone inn with comfortable, carefully furnished lounges and pubby bar; pretty lunchtime café; smart restaurant with good food, excellent wines and efficient, friendly service; garden with boules, fishing and cricket; disabled access. The little village it dominates is attractive, with a fine bridge over the Nene, and a good antique shop.

Ely TL5380 LAMB 2 Lynn Rd, Ely CB7 4EJ (01353) 663574 *£85; 32 comfortably modern rms. Former coaching inn opposite cathedral, with pleasant small lounge and popular bar.

Needingworth TL3472 PIKE & EEL Needingworth, St Ives, Huntingdon PE17 3TW (01480) 463336 £55; 6 rms. Very peaceful riverside spot, with spacious lawns and marina; roomy, plush bar, big open fire and easy chairs in a smaller room, and a glass-walled restaurant; good breakfasts, friendly staff.

Stilton TL1689 BELL High St, Stilton, Peterborough PE7 3RA (01733) 241066 *£50w; 19 rms. Elegant, carefully restored coaching inn with attractive rambling bars, big log fire, and pleasant courtyard. Stilton cheese originates from here and is still on the interesting menu; cl 25–26 Dec.

To see and do

🏠🏭✿ ★ **Buckden** TL1967 BUCKDEN TOWERS For centuries these grand old buildings constituted the palace of the Bishops of Lincoln, and were a regular stopping point for other notable personages on their travels (inc, albeit unwillingly, Catherine of Aragon, imprisoned here in 1533). Now returned to ecclesiastical hands, it's being carefully restored, and the 15th-c Great Tower and Gatehouse are particularly worth a look, as are the gardens, undergoing a reconstruction along 16th–17th-c lines. Shop, disabled access; cl Mon, Tues; (01480) 810344; donations appreciated. The rest of the village is attractive too. The Montagu Arms out at Grafham is useful for lunch.

🏠✿ **Elton** TL0893 ELTON HALL From the back a glorious Gothic fantasy, a fascinating lived-in house dating back to Tudor times, with splendid furnishings, porcelain and paintings, inc works by 15th-c old masters, Gainsborough and Constable. The library has a prayer book that belonged to Henry VIII, with his writing inside, and the gardens are very pleasant, especially in summer when the roses are in bloom. Snacks; open pm bank hol Sun and Mon, Weds and Sun July and Aug, also Thurs in Aug; (01832) 280454; £3.80. The Black Horse is very handy for lunch.

★ † ☗ ✿ 🏠 **Ely** TL5380 is a busy little market town with good shops and some lovely old buildings – well worth a leisurely stroll around. After the Norman Conquest it was a centre of Anglo-Saxon resistance under Hereward the Wake. The main attraction is the CATHEDRAL, one of England's most striking, its distinctive towers dominating the skyline for miles; especially good views coming in on the Soham rd. Completed by the late 12th c, it was restored in a surprisingly sympathetic manner mainly in the mid-19th c. The façade, covered in blind arcading, is fantastic, but most remarkable perhaps is the Octagonal Tower – over 400 tons suspended in space without any visible means of support; it looks especially atmospheric from inside, the bright light that streams down it contrasting sharply with the rest of the dimly lit interior. The Lady Chapel (England's biggest) has the widest medieval vault in the country, and there's a splendid Norman nave, seeming even longer than it really is because it's so narrow. Also not to be missed are a couple of elaborately sculpted medieval doors – and see if

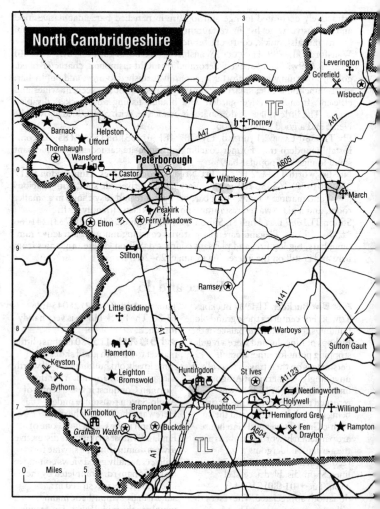

North Cambridgeshire

you can spot the railwayman's epitaph, with its unique imagery. Meals, snacks, shop, disabled access; (01353) 667735; £2.80. The STAINED GLASS MUSEUM here cares for fine medieval and more modern stained glass rescued from redundant buildings and churches. Various styles are shown, and models illustrate how the windows are made – a process that can only be described as 'panestaking'. Well worth a visit – a bonus is the unusual views it gives of the cathedral. Snacks, shop; cl am Sun, wkdys Nov–Feb exc some school hols; (01353) 667735; *£1.80.

The good ELY MUSEUM in the High St has interesting displays on the history of the city and its people, inc an exhibition on Hereward the Wake, some vintage racing bicycles and a video with fascinating early footage. Shop; cl 1-2.15, all Mon, Christmas wk, some summer wkdys; (01353) 666655; £1. THE TOURIST INFORMATION CENTRE (St Mary's St) is in a fine old house that from 1636 belonged to Oliver Cromwell and his family, and several rooms are furnished in period style. There's also a video on the draining of the fens. Cl winter Sun, 25–26 Dec, 1 Jan; £1.50

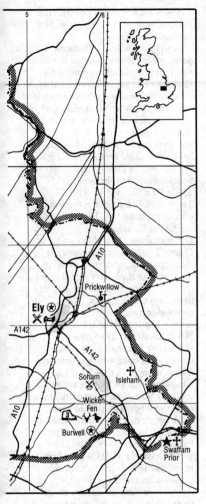

only breeding group of two-toed sloths in the country; if you don't see what you want first time, keep wandering around – the animals pop in and out all the time. They're constantly adding new things to see. Snacks, shop, disabled access; cl 25 Dec; (01832) 293362; *£3.50.

★ † **Hemingford Grey** TL2970 is a charming village with a peaceful view of the church over the willow-bordered river (the odd church tower is the result of its spire being lopped off by an 18th-c storm); one stone house among the thatched brick ones is Norman and said to be England's oldest. Nearby Hemingford Abbots is also pretty, and the Axe & Compass here is useful for lunch.

Huntingdon TL2371 has grown considerably in recent years, but one of its finer buildings is The George, a particularly handsome Georgian coaching inn. CROMWELL MUSEUM (Grammar School Walk) Huntingdon has had two MPs that can claim to have run the country, and this restored Norman building commemorates the first. It's actually where the future Lord Protector went to school (as did Pepys), and many of his possessions are on display. Shop; cl 1–2, all Mon, am winter wkdys, 24–26 Dec; (01480) 425830; free. The Old Bridge is a civilised place for lunch, and the humbler Victoria is useful too.

Kimbolton TL0968 KIMBOLTON CASTLE Catherine of Aragon lived here until her death, but the current building dates mainly from the later Stuart period. Now a school, its splendid wall paintings and frescos are well worth a look if you're in the area, and there's some interesting work by Vanbrugh, Hawksmoor and Robert Adam. Open pm Sun and Mon bank hol wknds from Easter, also pm Sun mid-July to Aug; (01480) 860505; *60p. The recently reopened New Sun is good for lunch.

† **March** TL4197 is pleasant, and a good base for exploring the fens (the Three Horseshoes at The Turves over on the far side of West Fen has good seafood). The church, with its wonderful angel roof, was described by Betjeman as being 'worth cycling 40 miles in a headwind to see'.

for exhibitions. They have details here of a route around the area called the Cromwell Trail, taking in a number of other places in the county with Cromwell connections. The Cutter, out at Annesdale off the A10, is an attractively placed riverside pub.

✦ **Hamerton** TL1379 HAMERTON WILDLIFE CENTRE A favourite of several of our correspondents – an expanding centre providing sanctuary for over 120 different kinds of animal, some of which are extinct in the wild. Enclosures of meerkats, wallabies, marmosets, gibbons and many more, most of them in family groups, inc the

Peakirk TF1606 PEAKIRK WATERFOWL GARDENS As just about all the birds here were reared in captivity they're very tame and can be fed by hand – always fun; they sell corn in the gatehouse but the birds seem to prefer bread, so if you have any spare do take it along. The gardens have over 100 different species of waterfowl inc rare and unusual breeds, all in a lovely setting; a good outing even if you're not exactly a twitcher, fascinating if you are, especially in spring when there are lots of baby birds. It's a particular favourite with several readers. Snacks, shop, disabled access; cl 24–25 Dec; (0733) 252271; £2.50. The Ruddy Duck is useful for lunch, and other decent places in the area are the Golden Pheasant at Etton and the Fitzwilliam Arms at Marholm.

Peterborough TL1999 has preserved much of its long history and fine old buildings, though it expanded hugely in the mid-1970s and is now a thriving industrial town (with a good pedestrianised shopping centre). The CATHEDRAL is one of the most dramatic in the country, its extraordinary west front a medieval masterpiece, with a trio of huge arches. Despite the damage inflicted inside by Cromwell (he is said to have looked on approvingly as prayer books were torn up and the organ smashed), the richly Romanesque interior has preserved its original fabric to a remarkable degree; especially worth a look are the elaborately vaulted retro-choir and the fine, early 13th-c painted wooden nave – though you'll probably need good light and glasses to see this at its best. Snacks, shop, disabled access; free.

CITY MUSEUM AND ART GALLERY (Priestgate) Standing out from the usual local history, industry and wildlife are detailed models made by Napoleonic prisoners of war held at Norman Cross prison camp, the largest such display in existence. Also various changing exhibitions. Shop, disabled access; cl Sun, Mon; free.

ST MARGARET'S CHURCH, in the suburb of Fletton, has some exceptionally fine little Anglo-Saxon sculptures, and just W of the centre LONGTHORPE TOWER (Thorpe Rd) is a 13th–14th-c fortified house with rare wall paintings. Cl winter wkdys, and 25–26 Dec, 1 Jan; £1.20.

FLAG FEN (2 miles E) The latest development at this Iron Age site is a new building to display some of the finds the excavations have turned up, inc the only Bronze Age timber visible in Europe. They're still digging, and in summer you may be able to watch archaeologists painstakingly uncovering more secrets. They also have a re-created Bronze Age farm so you can put the discoveries in context. Snacks, shop, disabled access; cl 25–26 Dec; (01733) 313414; £2.80. The best place for lunch is some miles outside the town – the Haycock, along the A47 at Wansford.

Prickwillow TL5892 PRICKWILLOW ENGINE TRUST MUSEUM The story of water, pumping and fen drainage in the area since the last Ice Age; a major redevelopment should result in quite a lively exhibition. Snacks, shop, disabled access; best to check for times and prices (01353) 88230.

Ramsey TL2885 ABBEY GATEHOUSE The ruins of an ornate Gothic gatehouse with buttresses and friezes, along with the 13th-c Lady Chapel (all that's left of the abbey itself); cl Nov–Mar. Some of the stone from the abbey is thought to have made up the nearby RAMSEY MUSEUM; open pm Thurs and Sun Apr–Sept, or by appointment; (01487) 813285; free.

St Ives TL3171 Pleasant little town, with graceful church, small local museum, and walks by the curving river. There's an unusual tiny chapel on the old bridge, rising straight out of the water; key from museum. The riverside Pike & Eel out at Needingworth is pleasant for lunch.

Thornhaugh TF0600 SACREWELL FARM AND COUNTRY CENTRE Pleasantly simple and undeveloped, this friendly place is very well liked by visitors. Based around an old working watermill, it tells the story of farming and country life over the last few generations, with demonstrations and displays of rural crafts, tools and machinery, as well as gardens, maze and nature trails, lots of animals and pick-your-own fruit in season. They seem very organised as far as children are concerned. Snacks, shop, disabled access; (01780) 782222; *£2. The Haycock at Wansford is good for lunch.

✝ ⚭ **Thorney** TF2804 rises from the flatlands like an island – which it was, when this was all half-submerged marsh. Much older than most villages in the area, it has a Norman-modified Saxon church on its green, and some interesting yellow-brick workers' houses put up by the Duke of Bedford. The friendly HERITAGE CENTRE has good displays covering Thorney's long history, and organises tours of the village and abbey. Shop, some disabled access; open pm wknds Apr–Oct and pm Weds Jun–Sept, or by appointment; (01733) 270006; the heritage centre is free, tours are £1. The Rose & Crown is good for lunch.

🚂 ⚙ **Wansford** TL0799 NENE VALLEY RAILWAY 15-mile round trip on steamtrains through delightful countryside, on all that's left of the first railway line to reach Peterborough. Also a fine collection of steam locomotives and rolling stock, small museum, and special events. If the station looks familiar, it's because the site is a favourite with film-makers. Meals, snacks, shop, disabled access; best to phone for train times, (01780) 782854; £1 site admission, £6 for the train. The Haycock is particularly good for lunch.

🐝 **Warboys** TL3080 GRAYS HONEY FARM (5 miles NE, off A141) A buzzing little place with all you ever wanted to know about the industrious honey bee; there are bees at work in observation hives, and an ingenious model railway explains how they talk to each other – you can even make your own beeswax candle. Snacks, shop (with all kinds of honey-based products), disabled access; cl Sun, and 24 Dec–Apr, though the shop is usually open then; (01354) 693798; *90p.

🌿 🦢 **Wicken** TL5670 WICKEN FEN represents the best scenery in north Cambs, and is outstanding for birdwatching (there is a hide). It is the oldest nature reserve in the country, originally safeguarded in 1899 as the villagers wanted somewhere to cut reeds for thatching: a surprising marshy and wooded semi-wilderness, beautiful

at all times of year, home to a wide variety of plants, birds and other wildlife. It has some good trails, and the last Fenland windpump (moved here from elsewhere). Shop, disabled access; cl 25 Dec; £2.50; NT. The Lazy Otter over on the A10 S of Stretham is a useful riverside family dining pub.

🏠 ▣ 🌼 ⚭ ★ **Wisbech** TF4609 PECKOVER HOUSE Lovely early 18th-c house with rococo decoration, contemporary art exhibitions, and a two-acre Victorian garden with kitchen garden and greenhouses – where orange trees are still fruiting after 250 years. Afternoon tea; house open pm Weds, Sun and bank hols, garden open pm Sat–Weds, both cl Nov–Mar; (01945) 583463; £2.40, £1 garden only. WISBECH & FENLAND MUSEUM has a good collection of ceramics, parish registers and lots of books inc early manuscripts, with a new display on slavery and the slave trade. Shop; cl Sun, Mon, Christmas; free. The North Brink along the River Nene has handsome Georgian houses (the Red Lion and the Rose among them are both decent pubs).

★ **Other attractive towns and villages** worth stopping at include Barnack TF0704, which has interesting dotted-about clusters of stone-built houses, a windmill, a part-Saxon church and a fine pub (the Millstone); Brampton TL2170 (decent pub in converted watermill, and nearby woods to explore), Burwell TL5866, Fen Drayton TL3368, Helpston TF1205 (John Clare's village), Holywell TL3370, Leighton Bromswold TL1175 (decent pub too), Elton TL0893, Rampton TL4268, Swaffham Prior TL5764 (two churches sharing same churchyard; decent pub), Ufford TF0904, and Whittlesey TL2797 (decent pubs). ✂ This part of the country is particularly rich in **windmills and watermills**, and, apart from the ones already mentioned, fine examples can be found at Burwell TL5866, Houghton TL2871 (lovely building in a pretty setting; the Jolly Butchers nearby is a decent family pub), and Soham TL5973, one of very few English villages where two mills still survive – you can buy flour ground here.

✝ Some **interesting churches** include those at Burwell TL5866 (handsome, airy building with fine oak roof), Castor TL1298 (two pleasant old thatched pubs here), Isleham TL6474 (wonderful roof), Leverington TF4411 (the tower and its spire are noteworthy, as is the two-storey 14th-c porch), Little Gidding TL1382 (if closed ask at the farmhouse), and Willingham TL4070 (fine tower and spire, many early wall paintings, and some fine early screens).

Bike riding is a popular activity around here as the ground is so flat, and some safe places to ride with young children are at Ferry Meadows TL1497 and from St Ives to Houghton TL2872. Other places for **children to let off steam** include the ❀ ♨ ✝ ⚙ ☺ FERRY MEADOWS COUNTRY PARK (4m W of Peterborough off A605), 500 acres with children's play areas, two big lakes with watersports and boat trips, bird reserves, pony and trap rides, miniature railway, two golf courses and pitch and putt (open to all), and ♪ ✔ ✝ GRAFHAM WATER TL1468 which has fishing and sailing (you can hire boats by the day – (01223 235235), nature reserve with birdwatching hides and trails, and good disabled access.

Walks

The overall impression of flatness is redeemed by one or two good features. The **River Ouse** ◁-1 between St Ives TL3171 and Hemingford Grey TL2970 is a popular weekend stamping-ground, with Houghton Mill TL2872 as a charming set piece. **Grafham Water** TL1468 ◁-2, the huge reservoir NW of St Neots, has an attractive waterside path along its northern shore.

Wicken Fen TL5075 ◁-3 (NT) has a remarkable range of plants and insects, with lovely nature trails (one for wheelchairs); it has been carefully preserved as an example of what the fens were like before they were turned over to intensive agriculture – see entry in **To see and do** section, above. From near **Whittlesey** TL2799 ◁-4 you can walk along the Hereward Way (the Dog in a Doublet pub on B1040 is good).

Monks Wood at Woodwalton TL2180 ◁-5 has quite a variety of moths and butterflies. The ancient woods such as **Knapwell Wood** TL3367 and **Papworth Wood** TL3362 ◁-6 have lovely spring flowers (a decent pub at Elsworth TL3163 is handy for both).

There are pleasant riverside walks from the Anchor at Sutton Gault TL4279 – see entry in **Where to eat** section at the end of this chapter.

Driving

Several former coaching villages, such as Stilton and Buckden, strung along beside the A1 make quietly interesting diversions from it now that they've been bypassed. From Buckden, the byroad to the Offords and then Papworth St Agnes is worth the short detour. The A1 itself carries a lot of traffic without many holdups, as does the A604. The B660 N of Kimbolton (starting with a passing look at Kimbolton and Stonely) is a very old coaching road taking you through gently rolling riding country and past some attractive, ancient, timbered and plastered buildings. It's pleasantly traffic-free, like many of the area's B roads. In the flat fens, distant villages make themselves known with a spire or church tower peeking up over a clump of trees on the horizon – there are often several in sight at a time. The straight but narrow byroads look temptingly fast on the map, but you do tend to find yourself trundling along behind tractors from time to time – and fenland roads have a nasty habit, very pronounced on rainy nights, of planting a sudden and unexpected right-angled bend in your tracks.

Where to eat

Bythorn TL0575 WHITE HART (01832) 710226 Relaxed, stylish inn with a variety of comfortable styles and furnishings, very friendly; good set menu in no-smoking restaurant; cl pm Sun, Mon; disabled access. £27/£5.95.

Keyston TL0475 PHEASANT (01832) 710241 Civilised and pretty, thatched former smithy with no-smoking room; a wide choice of imaginative cooking, fine wines, and friendly service; cl pm 25–26 Dec. £25/£8.50.

Ely TL5380 Old Fire Engine House (01353) 662582 Former fire engine station next to the cathedral, with good seasonal English cooking, nice puddings and interesting wine list; large walled garden; also has an art gallery; cl pm Sun, bank hols, 2 wks after Christmas; disabled access. £20.50l£3.50/£12.

Sutton Gault TL4279 ANCHOR (01353) 778537 Delicious food in stylish, heavily timbered dining pub with candles and gas lighting; good real ales and wines, and waterside tables – delightful setting; cl pm winter Sun. £19l£3/£7.50.

Fen Drayton TL3368 THREE TUNS (01954) 30242 Friendly thatched inn on banks of a stream in a pretty village; full of Tudor beams and timbers, two inglenook fireplaces, and good bar food; disabled access. £13l£1.25/£4.50.

Gorefield TF4111 WOODMANS COTTAGE (01945) 870669 A pudding lovers' paradise with over a dozen – and up to three dozen on Sat evenings; very popular restaurant, happy atmosphere, and helpful service. £12.50l£1.75/£5.25.

BEDFORDSHIRE

Two outstanding family attractions – Woburn Abbey and Whipsnade.

Woburn Abbey has a remarkable variety of interest for people of any age, and enough space to absorb lots of visitors without getting overcrowded. Visiting both it and Whipsnade could fill a long, happy and exhausting family weekend. There's quite a wide range of other things to see and do, most notably gorgeous Luton Hoo, and the interesting collection of veteran aircraft at Old Warden.

Dunstable Downs offer decent walking and remarkable views, though otherwise the county's scenery is generally not memorable. The brick-making which has so scarred the countryside south-west of Bedford has had its positive side – many towns and villages which might otherwise not be at all special have a sort of friendly glow from their warmly attractive masonry.

Where to stay

Flitwick TL0335 FLITWICK MANOR Church Rd, Flitwick, Bedford MK45 1AE (01525) 712242 *£125; 15 comfortable, thoughtfully decorated rms. 17th-c country house surrounded by interesting gardens, with log fire in entrance hall, comfortable lounge and library, and smart restaurant with fine French wines and delicious food using lots of fresh fish, home-grown and local produce; tennis, putting, croquet.

Leighton Buzzard SP9225 SWAN High St, Leighton Buzzard LU7 7EA (01525) 372148 £56w; 38 rms. Handsome coaching inn with pleasant lounge, relaxed bars, and attractive restaurant with English cooking.

Woburn SP9433 BELL Woburn, Milton Keynes, Bucks MK17 9QD (01525)

290280 *£55w; 25 attractively decorated rms, some with antiques. Lovely old inn, carefully restored, with beamed restaurant, popular bar, and good food; also, residents' own lounge and bar; cl 25–30 Dec.

Sandy TL1651 HIGHFIELD FARM, Sandy SG19 2AQ (01767) 682332 *£36; 6 rms, 1 with shared bthrm. Peace and quiet in comfortable farmhouse on 300-acre arable farm, with log fire in residents' sitting room.

To see and do

❀ ▣ ☕ Ψ **Bedford** TL0449 itself has decent riverside gardens and a few nice buildings, but despite its long history is really a straightforward modern town. The Bedford River Festival around the spring bank hol is always a lively time to visit. CECIL HIGGINS ART GALLERY & MUSEUM (Castle Close) A very rewarding place to visit, with the kind of paintings most other museums can only dream about; great works by Turner, Constable, Rembrandt, Matisse, Picasso, Dali and many others. The Victorian mansion's beautifully furnished rooms make it look like the family living there have popped out, as while it's clear that lots of thought has gone into the displays, nothing seems at all out of place. An award-winning extension has excellent collections of local lace, glass and ceramics. Shop, disabled access; cl am Sun, all Mon (exc pm bank hols); (01234) 211222; free. The BEDFORD MUSEUM (Castle Lane) next door is more traditional, but there are a few oddities among the local history, geology and wildlife, as well as various room reconstructions. Shop, disabled access; cl Mon (exc pm bank hols), am Sun, 25 Dec, Good Fri; free. John Bunyan lived around here for most of his life, and there's a little musem, as well as a trail around related sites. On the way out of town PRIORY COUNTRY PARK has an interesting mix of wildlife. The Foresters Arms (Union St) is a decent pub, and the Three Tuns at Biddenham is in easy reach.

! 🏛 **Dunstable Downs** TL0019 (see **Walks** section of this chapter) You can watch GLIDERS being towed up by planes and returning on their own, at wknds or in summer; two car parks and lots of space to run around. And FIVE KNOLLS here is an important Bronze Age burial mound, excavated by Agatha Christie's husband Sir Mortimer Wheeler, and Gerald Dunning. See Whipsnade below for lunch places.

★ 🏛 † **Elstow** TL0546 Perhaps the county's finest village, with a very attractive core of old timbered houses by the green, inc the MOOT HALL, an outstanding brick and timber, medieval market house with a collection of John Bunyan's works (he was born nearby), a reconstruction of his writing room with fine 17th-c furniture and other items related to him. Shop; cl am, Mon (exc bank hols), Fri, Nov–Easter; 60p. The attractive church with its unusual detached tower has a 'Pilgrim's Progress' window.

🚂 **Leighton Buzzard** SP9225 LEIGHTON BUZZARD RAILWAY Good collection of over 50 locomotives from around the world, with a fleet of 11 steamtrains to whisk you through gently varied countryside. This year they plan several further industrial heritage displays at the Stonehenge Works terminus. Snacks, shop, disabled access; open Sun and bank hols Easter–end Sept, also some summer wkdys and wknds up to Christmas – best to phone for details on (01525) 373888; £4.

🏛 ❀ ☕ Ψ 🐾 **Luton** TL0921 is a big, relatively modern industrial town; so it's quite a surprise to find here, neatly tucked between the M1 and Luton Airport, a magnificent country mansion in 1,500 acres of parkland – LUTON HOO, started by Robert Adam, and grandly remodelled early this century for Sir Julius Wernher. There was a recent much-reported robbery, but it still has Wernher's rich collection of furniture, Fabergé jewellery, tapestries, English porcelain, Russian royal robes, and paintings. The grounds were landscaped by Capability Brown. Meals, snacks, shop, disabled access;

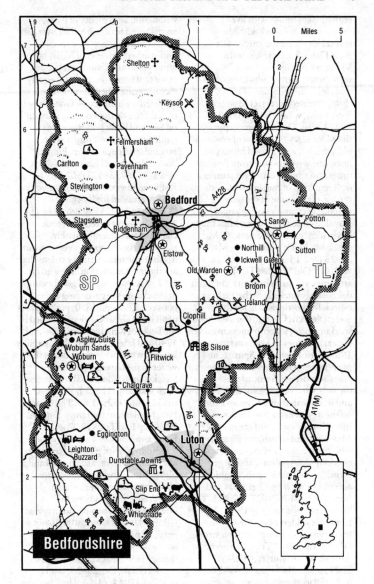

Bedfordshire

cl Mon (exc bank hols), Oct–Easter; (01582) 22955; £5, garden only £2.50.

You have to penetrate the town itself for LUTON MUSEUM & ART GALLERY (Wardown Park, Old Bedford Rd), a small Victorian mansion in pleasant grounds, with displays on local history and archaeology, local lace and hat-making. Snacks, shop, disabled access; cl 25–26 Dec, 1 Jan.

STOCKWOOD CRAFT MUSEUM AND GARDENS (Stockwood Park, Farley Hill) Ideal for a restrained and uncomplicated day out, with plenty to see; the museum part is next to a number of traditional working craftsmen's studios with live demonstrations at wknds. Also several lovely period garden settings, inc a 17th-c knot garden and a Victorian cottage garden, a refreshingly witty sculpture garden and children's play area. Snacks, shop, disabled access; cl Mon (exc bank hols), wkdys Nov–Mar; (01582) 38714; free. The centre incorporates the MOSSMAN COLLECTION of restored old vehicles, with a good history of horse-drawn transport from Roman times and vintage cars representing a different kind of horsepower; perhaps the highlight is one of the only remaining examples of a genuine Royal Mail coach. Some wknds they have rides through the park. Cl Mon (exc bank hols); wkdys Nov–Mar; 25–26 Dec, 1 Jan.

★ ♣ ♥ ⚘ ♰ **Old Warden** TL1343 An attractive village in its own right, built deliberately quaintly in the 19th c, but especially worth visiting for the SHUTTLEWORTH COLLECTION: nearly 40 working historic aeroplanes covering the early history of aviation from a 1909 Blériot to a 1941 Spitfire, in purpose-built hangars on a classic grass aerodrome. Some of these are the only surviving ones of their type, and it is worth trying to go up in one on the days when a few are flown (usually the first Sun of the month, May-Sept, but worth checking first). Also great airship relics, veteran cars, children's playground, and large picnic area. Snacks, shop, disabled access; cl a wk over Christmas and New Year; (01767) 627288; *£5. The SWISS GARDEN is an early 19th-c, romantic wilderness garden, with pretty vistas – a nice place for a stroll. Disabled access; cl Tues, and every day exc Sun in winter; (01234) 228330; £2. The village has a decent pub, and its church has a number of European wood carvings, inc some from the private chapel of Henry VIII's wife Anne of Cleves. The Hare & Hounds is good for lunch.

♱ ♥ ⚘ ♖ **Sandy** TL1749 THE LODGE The elegant, 19th-c, Tudor-style house is the headquarters of the RSPB and isn't open to the public, but it's surrounded by a nature reserve covering 106 acres of heath, lake and woodland, with plenty of birds, animals and trails spread all over. It's perfect for watching rare species undisturbed, but even if birdspotting is not your thing, this is a relaxing place to wander through, especially nice in spring when the woods are carpeted with bluebells. Good range of activities throughout the year, and on Sun and bank hols there are pm guided tours. Don't forget your binoculars. Snacks, shop, limited disabled access; cl Christmas–New Year; (01767) 680551; £2, free for RSPB members. The Locomotive nearby is useful for lunch.

♠ ⚘ **Silsoe** TL0835 WREST PARK The 19th-c house inspired by French châteaux has several ornately plastered rooms open to visitors, but it's the enormous formal gardens that are the main attraction. They go on for 150 acres and give a good example of the changes in gardening styles between 1700 and 1850; perhaps best of all is the Great Garden, designed by the Duke of Kent between 1706 and 1740 and later modified by Capability Brown, with lovely views down the water to the baroque pavilion. Snacks, shop, some disabled access; open wknds and bank hols Apr–Oct; (01525) 860152; £1.80. The George Hotel is pleasant for family lunches.

♖ ♥ **Slip End** TL0818 WOODSIDE FARM AND WILDLIFE PARK Very good for children, with plenty of friendly and feedable farmyard animals and a playground; a new indoor centre allows you to handle rabbits and collect eggs straight from the hen house. Also rare breeds, poultry and wildfowl, and a farm shop. They sell pets and poultry, along with all the accessories you'll need to look after them. Meals, snacks, shop, disabled access; cl Sun, Dec 25–26, Jan 1; (0582) 841044; £1.50. The Chequers at Caddington is useful for lunch.

♖ ♞ **Whipsnade** TL0117 WHIPSNADE WILD ANIMAL PARK Just when you think this enormous place can't get any bigger they add something new; the most recent additions are enclosures for dwarf crocodiles, cheetahs and the black rhino. Altogether there are over 2,500 rare and endangered animals in big open paddocks, many of whom were born here. A steam railway takes you round (or you can take your own car), and as well as the usual animals there are daily demonstrations of birds from around the world and sealions and elephants at work; there's a very good children's zoo too and it's all in a lovely downland setting. Meals, snacks, shop, disabled access; cl 25 Dec; (01582) 872171; £6.95. Tucked just off the village road is the Tree Cathedral, trees now mature planted in the plan of a cathedral in the 1930s, as a war memorial. The Old Hunters Lodge is good for lunch; the Red Lion at Studham is also quite close (with a common to stroll on).

★ 🏠🖼️🌱🐂🐖🐘☺ **Woburn** SP9433 Some lovely 18th-c houses (and decent pubs – not to mention antique shops) in the village, but what really draws the crowds are the two top-class attractions, especially Woburn Abbey & Deer Park. On the site of a Cistercian abbey, this magnificent mainly 18th-c mansion has been the home of the Dukes of Bedford for over 350 years, and has a sumptuous collection of art inc paintings by Rembrandt, Van Dyck and Gainsborough, lovely English and French 18th-c furniture and fine porcelain and ceramics. The 3,000 acres of surrounding parkland were landscaped by Humphrey Repton, and today are populated by several varieties of deer, one of which was saved from extinction here. There's also a bird sanctuary, big antique centre, pottery and mature trees. Meals, snacks, shop, disabled access by arrangement; cl Nov–Dec and wkdys Jan–Mar; (01525) 290666; £6.50 (the antique centre is 20p extra). Woburn Safari Park There's always something exciting about coming here – you can almost imagine you really are driving through the African plains, with lions and tigers (if you're lucky) just on the other side of the windscreen. The 300 acres of abbey parkland also feature bears and monkeys, sealion, parrot and elephant shows, a pets corner, fairground attractions, cable railway and a boating lake, as well as a lively new centre Wild World, with plenty of activities to help children find out more about the animals. Particularly good fun is Penguin World, another recent addition, which has an underwater viewing area. Meals, snacks, shop, disabled access; cl winter wkdys; (01525) 290407; £7.50. The Bell is useful for lunch.

★ **Interesting villages** include Shelton TL0368, where the pretty little cottages, Hall, and rectory are grouped around the quite delightful church, with 13th-c work inside, wall paintings, and a 14th-c font on seven legs. Felmersham SP9857 has a lovely church by a medieval tithe barn, and some other attractive old houses, with the river below. Nearby Pavenham SP9955 is also pretty, with a stroll down to the river. Sutton TL2247 is notable for its picturesque, steeply humped packhorse bridge, looking more like a part of Devon or Derbyshire; ironically, cars have to use a more ancient crossing, the shallow ford beside it. A decent pub nearby is named after John o' Gaunt, the village's former owner.

Other attractive villages include Aspley Guise SP9335, spacious Biddenham TL0249 (nice 12th-c church), Broom TL1743 and Northill TL1446 (all with good pubs), as well as Carlton SP9555, Clophill TL0837, Eggington SP9525 and, straddling the county boundary, Woburn Sands SP9235, with good wooded walks nearby. Ickwell Green TL1545 nr Northill is well worth a look, too, with its colourful thatched houses around a broad green; Stagsden SP9849 is pleasant, with a good few thatched houses, and strolls in the woods nearby. Stevington SP9853 has a handsomely restored windmill, and a holy well opposite the handsome church.

✝ Some **other churches** worth investigating include Chalgrave TL0027 and Potton TL2449 (it's the gravestones that are worth the visit).

Walks

The **Dunstable Downs** TL0019 ◠-1 have arguably the finest walk in Beds or Cambs, with great views from a spectacular escarpment path which can be linked in to a circuit incorporating Whipsnade village TL0018 and the nearby Tree Cathedral. Elsewhere, the predominant interest for walkers is in the greensand country, with the long-distance Greensand Ridge Walk taking in **Woburn Abbey** SP9632 ◠-2 (a right of way crosses the park) and **Ampthill Park** TL0337 ◠-3 (surprisingly heathy but landscaped by Capability Brown, with lovely trees and a water-lily lake). The **Harrold-Odell Country Park** SP9657 ◠-4 also has a lake, with waterfowl (especially in winter), a nature reserve, and quite a few paths; decent pubs in both nearby villages. Summer is the best time to visit **Chicksands Wood** TL1439 ◠-5 for its butterflies, Chinese muntjac deer and varied flora. The ancient **Maulden Wood** TL0538 ◠-6 has a picnic site, marked walks, and more muntjac deer. **Sundon Country Park** TL0428 ◠-7 is sheep-cropped downland with good views and marked walks (some quite steep).

Other after-lunchish walks are near **Eaton Bray** SP9620 ◠-8 (part of the Icknield Way Long Distance Footpath), nr **Sharpenhoe** TL0630 ◠-9, and nr **Shillington** (Aspley End) TL1232 ◠-10; all three places have decent pubs. The Globe in Linslade SP9225 is a decent pub with a leaflet showing pleasant nearby walks.

Driving

The road along Dunstable Downs and then through Totternhoe, Stanbridge and Egginton gives some fine views and is pretty, especially when the apple trees are in blossom. The public roads through Woburn Park are very pleasant. Nowadays the A5 is a reasonably attractive alternative to the M1.

Where to eat

Woburn SP9433 Paris House (01525) 290692 Half-timbered house on the Woburn estate (deer wandering about and lawns on which to enjoy aperitifs); French cooking (good fish), decent wines, and relaxed, friendly atmosphere; cl pm Sun, all Mon, Feb. **£22.50 lunch, £37 evening/£14.**
Ireland TL1341 Black Horse (01462) 811398 Busy, attractively refurbished beamed pub with interesting and generous daily changing food inc good fish dishes pm Thurs, Fri and Sat; nice restaurant, popular at wknds, so book; cl Mon; disabled access. £18|£1.40/£4.75.
Keysoe TL0762 Chequers (01234) 708678 Attractive and friendly pub with comfortably modernised beamed bars; consistently good, interesting food and well kept beer; cl Tues, 25–26 Dec. £13.50|£1.80/£6.30.
Broom TL1743 Cock (01767) 314411 Unspoilt 17th-c village inn with no bar counter and beers straight from the cask; decent lunchtime bar food includes especially good cheeses, evening dishes more elaborate; no food pm Sun. £12|£1.30/£5.

Help this year from: John Wooll, Jenny and Michael Back, David Unsworth, Tom Evans, Bob and Maggie Atherton, Mr and Mrs Powell, R Martin, Martin Copeman, CW, JW, Keith Symons, Tom Smith, Paul Cartledge, BJSM, Dr and Mrs P J S Crawshaw, George Atkinson, Mr and Mrs McDougal, L Priest, N Law, P and D Carpenter, Dr Paul Kitchener, Nigel and Sara Walker, Rita Horridge, Bill Sykes, Bill and Lydia Ryan, J N Child, J E Brown, Stephen Brown, Mrs J M Day, the Sandy family, David Shillitoe.

CAMBRIDGESHIRE AND
BEDFORDSHIRE CALENDAR

Some of these dates were provisional as we went to press.

JANUARY

6 **Whittlesey** Straw Bear Festival, ancient and picturesque – *till Sat 7*

FEBRUARY

19 **Peterborough** Community Dance Festival at Key Theatre (01733) 237073

25 **Bedford** Bedfordshire Music Festival at the Corn Exchange – *till Sat 4* (01234) 708566

28 **Toddington** Shrove Tuesday Ceremony: *just before midday* children gather on Conger Hill, with ears to the ground listening for the witch frying her pancakes

MARCH

12 **Woburn** Dolls Fair at Woburn Abbey (01480) 216372

17 **Luton** Antique fair at Luton Hoo – *till Sun 19* (01582) 22955

18 **Alwalton** National Shire Horse Show at the East of England Showground (01733) 234451

APRIL

1 **Thriplow** Daffodil Weekend – *till Sun 2* (01763) 208132

9 **Huntingdon** Dolls Fair at Hinchingbrooke House (01480) 216372

MAY

6 **Arrington** Country Skills and Working Craft Fair at Wimpole Hall and Home Farm – *till Mon 8* (01263) 734711

7 **Alwalton** Truck Fest at the East of England Showground – *till Mon 8* (01733) 234451

8 **Ickwell** May Festival on the Green (01767) 317481; **Stilton** Cheese Rolling Contest, stalls and May Day celebrations (01480) 425831

13 **Bedford** Regatta (01234) 341171

21 **Alwalton** BMF Rally at the East of England Showground (01733) 234451

28 **Linton** Dolls Fair at Chilford Hall (01480) 216372

JUNE

3 **Alwalton** Steam and Vintage Spectacular at the East of England Showground – *till Sun 4* (01733) 234451; **Cambridge** Strawberry Fair

4 **Woburn** Beds & Bucks Stationary Engine Club Rally at Woburn Abbey (01525) 290666

10 **Woburn** Garden Show at Woburn Abbey – *till Sun 11* (01525) 290666

11 **Woburn** Large Models Association at Woburn Abbey (01525) 290666

24 **Ampthill** Festival Gala Day (01525) 402402; **Lewsey** Festival (01582) 696355

28 **Wisbech** Rose Fair at St Peter's Parish Church – *till 2 July* (01945) 583086

JULY

2 **Ely** Riverside Gala and Raft Race at Willow Walk; **Woburn** Corvette Club National Car Rally at Woburn Abbey (01525) 290666

CAMBRIDGESHIRE AND BEDFORDSHIRE CALENDAR

JULY cont

8 **Witcham** World Pea-Shooting Championships; **Woburn** National Riley Car Club Rally Weekend – *till Sun 9* at Woburn Abbey (01525) 290666

13 **Cambridge** Film Festival – *till Sun 30* (01223) 352001

16 **Woburn** Sheepdog Trials at Woburn Abbey (01525) 290666

18 **Alwalton** East of England Show at East of England Showground – *till Thurs 20* (01733) 234451

28 **Cambridge** Folk Festival at Cherry Hinton Hall grounds – *till Sun 30* (01223) 358977

29 **Alwalton** Faith 95, a gathering of all religious denominations – till 5 Aug (01733) 234451

AUGUST

17 **Alwalton** Ponies UK at the East of England Showground – *till Sun 20* (01733) 234451

19 **Woburn** De Havilland Moth Club Annual Fly-in at Woburn Abbey – *till Sun 20* (01525) 290666

20 **Woburn** Commercial Vehicle Rally and Road Run at Woburn Abbey (01525) 290666

26 **Ely and District** Horticultural Society Great Autumn Show at Paradise Sports Hall – *till Sun 27* (01353) 664004; **Silsoe** National Craft Festival at Wrest Park House and Gardens – *till Mon 28* (01525) 860152

27 **Alwalton** American Spectacular at the East of England Showground – *till Mon 28* (01733) 234451

28 **Kempston** Fun Day at Addison Howard Park (01234) 857566

31 **Alwalton** British Show Ponies Society at the East of England Showground – *till 2 Sept* (01733) 234451

SEPTEMBER

3 **Dunstable** Countryside Day on Dunstable Downs, nr B4541 (01234) 228336; **Linton** Dolls Fair at Chilford Hall (01480) 216372

8 **Toddington** South Bedfordshire County Show at the South Bedfordshire County Showground – *till Sun 9* (01525) 875170

9 **Haddenham** Steam Rally – *till Sun 10* (01487) 841893

15 **Luton** British Craft Show at Luton Hoo – *till Sun 17*

19 **Ely** County Brass Band Championship

OCTOBER

22 **Woburn** Dolls Fair at Woburn Abbey (01480) 216372

NOVEMBER

18 **Arrington** Wimpole Christmas at Wimpole Home Farm – *till Sun 19* (01263) 734711

19 **Huntingdon** Dolls Fair at Hinchingbrooke House (01480) 216372

CHESHIRE

This county has a great deal to offer, with attractive scenery, a thoroughly civilised feel, and a good many interesting places to explore, including some very impressive stately homes and other marvellous buildings. Away from the wild steep moors of the east, Cheshire's towns, villages and countryside leave a deep impression of well-tended, solid comfort. The central plain of rich farmland is pleasantly broken up by woods and hedges, with splendid black and white timbered buildings and a profusion of meres or lakes. There is a range of fine sandstone hills in the west. Chester itself is a glorious city to visit, full of interest: it's in the west of the county, and on the whole that part has most for visitors to enjoy, and the widest choice of good places to stay.

In the east, though, there is also much to discover. Former silk- and cotton-mill towns such as Macclesfield and Bollington show off their past proudly, with no sense of the stress or decay that's often marked such manufacturing changes elsewhere.

Throughout the county, an intricate network of canals takes in some of the most interesting scenery, with well kept towpaths. The modern industrial heartland is largely concentrated within a fairly self-contained and therefore easily avoidable area by the Mersey, with chemical works at Northwich and engineering around Crewe.

CHESTER AND THE WEST

Chester is a rewarding and richly preserved showpiece; it is surrounded by attractive countryside studded with lovely villages, interesting places to visit, rather good walking, and nice places to stay.

Chester itself is exceptional, with whole areas of beautifully restored and preserved timbered buildings within its partly Roman/medieval city wall – and yet plenty of up-to-date life. Its zoo is exemplary. Out in the country, narrow-boat canals and leafy lanes wind through pastures grazed by plump black and white cows or glossy-coated horses, villages have thatched black and white cottages, and romantic castles crown craggy wooded hills. Outside Chester, some of the most interesting places to visit include Britain's most spectacular garden centre at Bridgemere, the boat museum at Ellesmere Port, a vivid re-creation of medieval monastic life in Runcorn, the botanic gardens at Neston, Arley Hall at Northwich, and romantic Peckforton Castle. Tabley Hall, new to this edition of the guide, is very splendid. We have expanded the range of places to stay in the Chester area (including a nice guesthouse, new to us, right in the centre).

Where to stay

Chester SJ4166 CHESTER GROSVENOR Eastgate St Chester CH1 1LT (01244) 324024 £209.90; 86 individually furnished, very comfortable rms. Imposing half-timbered hotel with sumptuously furnished day rooms, imaginative food in stylish restaurant and more informal brasserie, as well as exemplary service; sauna, gym, solarium; cl 25–26 Dec; disabled access.

Sandiway SJ6071 NUNSMERE HALL Tarporley Rd, Sandiway, Northwich CW8 2ES (01606) 889100 £123; 32 attractive rms. Luxurious lakeside hotel on wooded peninsula, with elegantly furnished lounge and library and wood-panelled cocktail bar; very good modern cooking, and a warm welcome from courteous staff; disabled access.

Chester SJ4166 CRABWALL MANOR Parkgate Rd, Mollington, Chester CH1 6NE (01244) 851666 £100w; 48 very comfortable, individually decorated rms. Partly castellated, comfortable hotel in landscaped grounds; restful, attractive day rooms, open fires, very good modern British cooking, and friendly service; disabled access.

Worleston SJ6556 ROOKERY HALL Worleston, Nantwich CW5 6DQ (01270) 610016 £95; 45 individually decorated rms. Fine early 19th-c hotel in lovely parkland; elegant lounges, log fires, intimate restaurant with enjoyable food, and friendly service; cl 26–30 Dec; disabled access.

Rowton SJ4564 ROWTON HALL Whitchurch Rd, Rowton, Chester CH3 6AD (01244) 335262 £88; 42 rms; 18th-c country house in eight acres of award-winning gardens, with conservatory lounge, comfortable bar, log fires and a relaxed atmosphere; leisure club with swimming pool, gym, sauna and solarium; cl 25–26 Dec; disabled access.

Fullers Moor SJ4166 FROGG MANOR Nantwich Rd, Fullers Moor, Broxton, Tattenhall, Chester CH3 9JH (01829) 782629 £63; 6 lavishly decorated rms. Enjoyable Georgian manor house full of ornamental frogs and antique furniture; open fires, restful upstairs sitting room, little bar, old-time music, and an elegant dining room leading to the conservatory which overlooks the garden.

Hoole SJ4368 HOOLE HALL Warrington Rd, Hoole, Chester CH2 3PD (01244) 350011 £61; 99 rms, some no smoking. Extended and attractively refurbished 18th-c hall with good food in two restaurants, and friendly service; good disabled access.

Higher Burwardsley SJ5256 PHEASANT Higher Burwardsley, Chester CH3 9PF (01829) 70434 *£60; 8 rms in comfortably converted, sandstone-built barn. Pretty, half-timbered, 17th-c inn on top of Peckforton Hills with marvellous views; interesting decorations and a huge fireplace in the attractive old-fashioned bar, no-smoking conservatory, good food, and friendly staff; lots of walks nearby; disabled access.

Crewe SJ7056 CREWE ARMS Nantwich Rd, Crewe CW1 1DW (01270) 213204 £60; 53 spacious rms. Sympathetically refurbished hotel with comfortable bar and lounge, and a spacious restaurant; close to station.

Sandbach SJ7661 OLD HALL Newcastle Rd, Sandbach CW11 0AL (01270) 761221 £50w; 15 rms. 17th-c hotel with lots of panelling, friendly welcome, and popular restaurant; disabled access.

Cotebrook SJ5765 ALVANLEY ARMS Cotebrook, Tarporley CW6 9DS (01829) 760200 *£50; 2 rms. Handsome, 16th-c, creeper-covered farmhouse with pleasant beamed bars, a chintzy little hall, good food, and a garden with pond and geese; no children.

Weston SJ7352 WHITE LION Main Rd, Weston, Crewe CW2 5NA (01270) 500303 £47w; 17 comfortable rms. Pretty 17th-c timbered inn with low-beamed rooms, friendly service and relaxed atmosphere, no-smoking areas, and a wide range of popular food; own bowling green; cl Christmas wk.

Bickley Moss SJ5549 CHOLMONDELEY ARMS Bickley Moss, Malpas SY14 8BT (01892) 720300 £46; 4 rms with showers. Airy, converted Victorian school-house close to castle and gardens, with lots of atmosphere, interesting furnishings, open fire, imaginative bar food (especially puddings) and a very good choice of wines; disabled access.

Chester SJ4166 CASTLE HOUSE 23 Castle St, Chester CH1 2DS (01244) 350354 **£42**; 5 comfortable rms, most with own bthrm. Small, family-run, carefully preserved 16th-c guesthouse in the middle of the city, with helpful, friendly owners, and fine breakfasts.

Wettenhall SJ6261 BOOT & SLIPPER Wettenhall, Winsford CW7 4DN (0127 073) 238 **£40**; 5 attractive rms with showers. Cosily refurbished 16th-c coaching inn on small country lane, with low beams and open fires in quiet bars, and a relaxed, friendly atmosphere; good breakfasts.

Higher Wych SJ4943 MILL HOUSE Higher Wych, Malpas SY14 7JR (01948) 73362 *£32**; 2 rms, 1 with shared bthrm. Very welcoming and friendly B & B in a former farmhouse, with relaxed atmosphere and good breakfasts – evening meals if requested; cl Christmas.

To see and do

Chester SJ4166 Many people rate Chester as one of the most rewarding cities to visit in the whole country. It was the site of an important fort in Roman times (when it was known as Deva), and later plentiful river traffic kept it rich. The old centre is ringed by a medieval TOWN WALL that's more complete than any other in Britain and incorporates much of the original Roman one. You can walk the whole way round, enjoying marvellous views. Partly because of the constraining influence of the wall, the centre of town is an easy place to get around, not too big, and with the main streets pretty much free of cars (there may be a few buses). If you're driving in, you'll be shunted round to one of the big car parks, and at certain times you may have to queue a while to get a space.

🏠 THE ROWS, which give the city's heart a magnificently Elizabethan look, are sets of ornamentally timbered, two-storey shops – with open upper arcaded galleries – radiating from the central Cross. A particular charm of The Rows is that, besides being attractive to look at and charming to walk through, they include good shops (and a useful pub, the Boot, on Eastgate Row N). Some of Chester's most glorious timber-framed buildings are to be found in Watergate. There are more fine buildings jettied out over the pavement in Lower Bridge St (for instance, the late 17th-c Falcon, once a house used by the Duke of Westminster's ancestors, but now a good pub), and in St Werbergh St, off Eastgate (despite their Elizabethan look, built in the 1890s; Eastgate's striking clock was constructed for Queen Victoria's diamond jubilee).
✝ The CATHEDRAL looks not unlike an ordinary church at first glance, but is far more impressive inside, with some marvellous medieval carving in and above the choir stalls and some fine vaulting. Unusually, at the Reformation its new dean (previously the abbot of the Benedictine abbey which the cathedral replaced) managed to preserve many of the former abbey buildings, so the precincts still include peaceful, arcaded, flagstoned cloisters, an unusual medieval chapter house, and older Norman parts inc a refectory – fittingly brought back into use as a café. Meals, snacks, shop, disabled access; free. There are quiet cobbled Georgian lanes around Abbey Square, behind the cathedral a little way down Northgate.
🏛 ROMAN REMAINS include some broken Roman columns in a neat and peaceful garden running along the town wall by the gate at the bottom of Pepper St. Nearby is the excavated part of a very large Roman amphitheatre – probably big enough to seat nearly 10,000 people.
🏠 DEVA ROMAN EXPERIENCE (Pierpoint Lane, off Bridge St) Lively new exploration of Chester's Roman heyday, with the sights, sounds and smells of streets, fortresses, markets

and even bathhouses. Good fun – it starts off as though you're on board a Roman galley. At the end there's an exhibition of Roman, Saxon and medieval relics found on the site, based around a live archaeological dig, with plenty of hands-on displays. Snacks, shop, disabled access; cl Dec 25–26; (01244) 343407; £3.80.

⌂ ▣ ♭ The GROSVENOR MUSEUM (Grosvenor St) as you might expect has an exceptionally well displayed Roman collection, with plenty of household items giving a good idea of domestic life in Roman times. Look out too for the huge ancient tombstones. A passage from here leads to a Georgian house with restored Georgian and Victorian rooms, as well as an art gallery, and good displays of silver and furniture. They've recently added a natural history gallery. Shop; cl am Sun, Good Fri, Dec 25–26; (01244) 321616; free. They also have a little outpost, the CHESTER HERITAGE CENTRE, in a former church on Bridge St Row, concentrating on the city's history. Cl am Sun; £1, free if you're a Chester resident; (01244) 317948.

♭ The city's VISITOR CENTRE (Vicars Lane) has more history, with videos and exhibitions and a re-created Victorian street. Also tourist information desk and regular guided tours of the city. Meals, snacks, shop, disabled access to ground floor only; free.

✿ Attractive VIEWPOINTS include the tree-shaded Groves looking out to the medieval bridge over the River Dee; and the bridge at the N end of Northgate, which gives a close view of the so-called Bridge of Sighs over the canal far below.

🏰 The CASTLE is now largely moated by car parks, but has some impressive buildings, both medieval and grandiose late 18th c.

Besides places mentioned in **Where to eat**, the Albion (Park St) is currently the city's best pub; Watergates (Watergate St) has good food in a lovely medieval crypt; the Falcon (Lower Bridge St), Custom House (Watergate St), canalside Old Harhers Arms (Russell St) and Telfords Warehouse (Raymond St) are all useful for lunch, while the Boot is excellently placed in Eastgate Row N.

🐄🐖 CHESTER ZOO out on the city's N edge is the biggest in Britain, set in 110 acres of glorious gardens filled with rare animals in near-natural enclosures. Tropical house, chimpanzee island, penguin pool with underwater viewing panels, waterbus, a new overhead train zipping round the grounds, and children's farm. In summer there may be other attractions such as puppet shows and brass rubbings for children – a visit can easily last all day. Meals, snacks, shop, disabled access; cl 25 Dec; *£7.

Other things to see and do

! **Anderton** SJ6475 has a unique BOAT LIFT. Nearly 120 years old, this remarkable construction can simultaneously raise and lower two pairs of narrow boats in gigantic water tanks, bridging the 50-ft drop between the Trent & Mersey Canal and the Weaver Navigation Canal.

🏰 ✿ **Beeston** SJ5459 BEESTON CASTLE Legend has it that Richard III left buried treasure at this now-ruined 13th-c fortress, perched atop dramatically rising crags, with wonderful views of the surrounding countryside. Good exhibition; shop; cl 25–26 Dec; (01829) 260464; *£2.

The pub of the same name, handy for the canal, is useful for lunch.

✿ **Bridgemere** SJ6352 BRIDGEMERE GARDEN WORLD is a garden-lover's paradise – 25 acres of gardens (inc the Women's Institute cottage garden), plants, glasshouses, and garden furniture, with more plants in more varieties than anywhere else in Britain (indoor and outdoor), and professional help on hand for any sort of query. Best to visit in the morning before the coach parties arrive. Good meals and snacks, excellent shop, disabled access; cl 25–26 Dec; (01270) 520381; free exc for garden kingdom, £1. Several contributors rate this as among the most worthwhile places to visit in the whole country.

✗ ★ **Bunbury** SJ5758 WATERMILL Mid-19th-c mill that was worked until 1960; it was well restored in 1977 and now once again produces flour. Open pm wknds and bank hols Easter–Sept; £1.20. The village itself is attractive, with pretty cottages around the 14th-c church. There's another good watermill at Stretton (see entry below). The Dysart Arms is useful for lunch.

✿ **Burwardsley** SJ5156 CHESHIRE CANDLE WORKSHOPS Demonstrations of candle-making and now other crafts too, as well as a big craftshop. Meals, snacks, disabled access; cl Mon and Fri for around six wks in the New Year; (01829) 70401; free. The Pheasant in Higher Burwardsley is good for lunch.

✿ ∀ † **Cholmondeley** SJ5351 is famously pronounced Chumly. CHOLMONDELEY CASTLE GARDENS A very pretty place to stroll through, with acres of colourful ornamental gardens around elegant castle buildings (not open); fine woodland and lakeside walks as well as rare breeds of animals inc llamas and an ancient private chapel. Snacks, shop and plant centre, disabled access; open pm Sun, Weds, Thurs and bank hols Apr–Sept; (01829) 720383; £2.50. The Cholmondeley Arms is excellent for lunch.

🚂 **Crewe** SJ7056, a 19th-c railway town, has smartened up a lot in the last decade or two, with bargains (especially china) in the market, a pedestrianised centre, colourful Queens Park and a useful foyer restaurant in the Victorian theatre. RAILWAY AGE (Vernon Way) Rapidly developing exhibition with the widest selection of preserved electric and diesel locomotives in the country, along with models, miniature and standard-gauge railways and other displays. They organise unusual courses in subjects such as signalling training. Snacks, shop, disabled access; ring to check opening times (01270) 212130; £3, £2.50 wknds, more for special events. The Crewe Arms is good value for lunch.

† **Daresbury** SJ5983 The CHURCH, attractive enough in other ways, draws many visitors for its ALICE IN WONDERLAND stained-glass window commemorating Lewis Carroll, who was born here; pleasant strolls by the canal. The Ring o' Bells is useful for lunch.

✿ ♣ ✿ **Ellesmere Port** SJ4077 BOAT MUSEUM Nicely set in a historic dock complex, the world's largest floating collection of canal boats, as well as steam engines, a blacksmith's forge, workers' cottages, stables, big indoor exhibitions, and boat trips; also displays on canals and canal horses, lots of events, and regular craft fairs. Meals, snacks, shop, disabled access; cl winter Thurs and Fri; (0151) 355 5017; £4.50.

✿ **Little Budworth** SJ5965 CHESHIRE HERBS Award-winning, specialist herb nursery growing and selling over 200 different varieties from agrimony to yellow melilot; they hold regular talks and summer courses. Shop, disabled access is possible though not ideal; cl 24 Dec–2 Jan; (01829) 760578; free. The Alvanley Arms at Cotebrook is quite handy for lunch.

† ★ ✿ ✿ **Nantwich** SJ6552 has a pedestrian-only centre around the splendid 14th-c CHURCH, with its exceptional carved choir stalls; look out for the devil forcing open a nun's mouth, and the wife threatening her husband with a ladle. Much of the town, destroyed by a firestorm in 1583, was rebuilt then in intricate black and white timbering, and with countless window-boxes in flower in spring and summer is a fine sight especially around the centre. There are quite a few decent antique shops, and the central Lamb Hotel is good for lunch. (As most of south Cheshire's roads seem to intersect at the town, traffic can be a problem.) Off the A51 about a mile SE, STAPELEY WATER GARDENS is the world's largest watergarden centre with display pools, fountains, waterfalls, gardens, coldwater and tropical fish, and a huge heated glasshouse full of palms, piranhas, giant water lilies, sharks, and parrots. They sell plenty of other gifts as well as plants (chocolates, crafts, etc) and they have a collection

of early 20th-c memorabilia; regular special events. Meals, snacks, shop, disabled access; gardens free, palm house £2.90. FIRS POTTERY (Aston; on the A530, about 5 miles from Whitchurch) Friendly place organising one-day pottery workshops (half-days for children), so you can try your hand at being a craftsman; a true case of pot luck. Booking essential; (01270) 780345; £18 for a day course, inc lunch and tea and coffee (£7 children, Tues am during school hols). There's a good shop, sellings all sorts of useful pots. The Bhurtpore is good for lunch.

🏵 **Neston** SJ2978 LIVERPOOL UNIVERSITY BOTANIC GARDENS (NESS GARDENS) Extensive collection of specimen trees and shrubs, herbaceous plants, renowned heather, rock, rose and water gardens, with a slide show and other exhibitions; good children's adventure playground, and picnic area. Lots of events and lectures. Meals, snacks, shop, disabled access; cl 25 Dec; (0151) 336 7769; £3. Parkgate (see **The Wirral** entry below) is handy for lunch.

🏠🏵✝🏵☕⛴🏛 **Northwich** SJ6674 ARLEY HALL & GARDENS The dramatic-looking house is Victorian Jacobean, but the same family have lived on the estate for over 500 years, so there are a few older furnishings and mementoes on display. Outside, the award-winning grounds include walled, scented, and herb gardens, a shrub rose collection, a more informal woodland area, and craft workshops (furniture, garden furniture, masonry, china); there's also an interesting private chapel. Meals, snacks, shop and new nursery, disabled access; cl am Mon (exc bank hols), Oct–Mar; £4.40, £2.80 gardens only. From the car park, tractor and trailer rides take you to nearby STOCKLEY FARM, a friendly little working farm that's ideal for children. Open Weds, Sat, Sun and bank hols Apr–Sept, every day exc Mon in Aug; £2.50. SALT MUSEUM (London Rd) Cheshire is the only British county to produce salt on a large scale, and this place has audio-visual displays, reconstructions and objects going back to Roman times to explain how it's done, why we need it

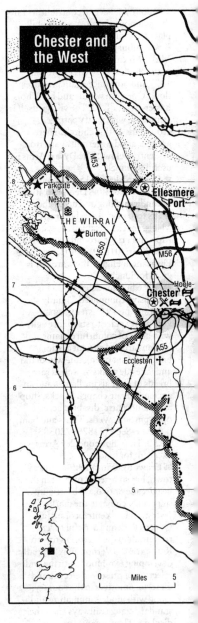

Chester and the West

and how the salt mines changed the county's landscape and social life. A new gallery has microscopes allowing you to see the intricacy of each crystal. Snacks, shop; cl am wknds, all Mon (exc bank hols and in Aug), 25–26

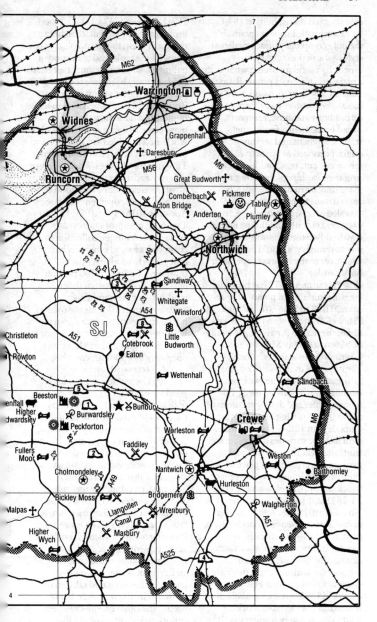

Dec, Good Fri; (01606) 41331; £1.
Northwich was one of the main salt
towns, and you can follow the SALT
HERITAGE TRAIL around some of the
other buildings. From the quay there
are cruises down the river. The trip

out to Comberbach SJ6477 is well
worthwhile for lunch at the Spinner &
Bergamot.

Peckforton SJ5356 PECKFORTON
CASTLE It seems bizarre to talk about a
medieval Victorian castle, but that's

exactly what this is, built in 1840 using authentic medieval plans. It's the only completely intact medieval-style castle in the country, so is especially useful for seeing what such a place was like in its prime. Rising majestically from its wooded hilltop it has all the features you'd expect – forbidding gatehouse, ramparts, broad battlements, fine chapel, stables, kitchens and servants' quarters, as well as attractive labourers' cottages, and fine views over the Cheshire plain. Bringing the place fully up to date are hi-tech animatronic tour guides. Snacks, disabled access; cl mid-Sept–Easter; (01829) 260930; £2.50. The Beeston Castle at Beeston is handiest for lunch, though you could perhaps walk over to the Pheasant at Higher Burwardsley.

⚓☺ PICKMERE SJ6877 has boat hire, lakeside funfair and plenty of open space. The Red Lion is useful for lunch.

🏠♠⚓🐾❄ RUNCORN SJ5183 is a new town; the reason for visiting it would be NORTON PRIORY MUSEUM & GARDENS (Manor Park), a lovely 12th-c priory that developed into a Georgian stately home, with prize-winning exhibitions on medieval monastic life, and demonstrations of tile-making, carving and sculpture. Outside is an 18th-c walled garden with historic varieties of flowers and fruit, and beautiful woodland gardens. An enchanting place to explore, with lots of special events. Snacks, shop, disabled access; cl am, 24-26 Dec, 1 Jan, walled garden cl Nov–Feb; (01928) 569895; inclusive price £2.40, museum/grounds £1.70, garden 60p. More centrally, the Sunday-afternoon MINIATURE TRAIN RIDES in the park on Stockham Lane are popular with children; there are views from the ruins of HALTON CASTLE SJ5382 up on its grassy hill.

✗ Stretton SJ4553 has a working WATERMILL in lovely countryside. The wooden mill machinery is the oldest in the county, its two ancient wheels still producing corn. Shop; cl am, Mon, wkdays Oct and Mar, all Nov–Feb; (01606) 41331; £1. The Cock o' Barton up on the A534 is quite useful for lunch.

🏠▣! Tabley SJ7378 TABLEY HOUSE Probably the finest Palladian house in the north-west, this grand place is best known for its splendid collection of paintings. Sir John Fleming Leicester (whose family lived here for over 800 years) was the first great collector of British art, and he hoped to turn his home into a national gallery. His plans came to nothing, but most of the works he assembled are still here, inc pictures by Turner, Reynolds, Henry Thompson and James Ward amongst others. Readers recommend this quite highly. Snacks, shop, very good disabled access; open pm Thurs–Sun Apr–Oct; (01565) 750151; *£3.50. TABLEY OLD SCHOOL CUCKOO CLOCK COLLECTION A unique collection of cuckoo clocks and other mechanical timepieces from all over the world. At the moment there are 400 rare and beautiful clocks, most of them working, but the number is constantly increasing, as the owners nip off to Europe to track down more. Because of this (and as it takes time to get them all going) the exhibition is open only by appointment. Shop, disabled access; (01565 633039); *£3.50. The Smoker at Plumley is good for lunch.

🐾 Walgherton SJ6949 DAGFIELDS CRAFT CENTRE All sorts of crafts and goods made and sold in picturesque country barns, inc toys, model farms, oak garden furniture, dried flowers, leather, woollens, etc. Meals, snacks, shop, disabled access (but no facilities); free, but 50p for animals and pets' corner; (01270) 841336. The Boars Head is useful for lunch.

♿▣ Warrington SJ6188 is not an inspiring town for visitors, but has a very lively MUSEUM & ART GALLERY Decorated skulls and shrunken heads, an Egyptian mummy and a toy-packed nursery, an odd tableau of stuffed animals, and a number of beetles and other creepy-crawlies; enthusiastic displays of wildlife, history and art. Snacks, shop, disabled access; cl Sun and bank hols; free. The Ferry at Fiddlers Ferry, down by the Mersey off the A562 at Penketh SJ5688, is prettily placed for lunch.

⬇T! ❄ Widnes SJ5185 is another place not in itself alluring to visitors, but its

CATALYST is a thriving centre exploring the chemical industry and how it affects our lives, full of lively hands-on exhibits, computer games and demonstrations presented in a really enjoyable and entertaining way; children should get a lot out of it. Last year saw the completion of the first phase of an extension (dramatically changing the look of the building) and a new permanent exhibition is due to open early this year. The views from the Observatory are splendid, with glass floors, ceilings and walls creating quite a bizarre feeling. Meals, snacks, shop, disabled access; cl Mon (exc bank hols), 24–26 Dec, 1 Jan; (0151) 420 1121; *£3.

★ **The Wirral** is much built up, with extensive dormitory villages as well as more industrial areas. Much of it, inc Port Sunlight, is in Merseyside now, so is included in our Lancashire chapter. Its Cheshire parts include the charming unspoilt village of Burton SJ3274 (strolls in a wood of handsome old Scots pines just N), and nearby Parkgate SJ2878. This interesting village is the country's only inland seaside resort, the Dee estuary having retreated since its palmy days at the end of the 18th and early 19th c. Before that, it was a more important port than Liverpool, and there's an eerie charm in sitting in the Boathouse or Red Lion on the 'Promenade', looking out over the marshes to the distant waters and the Welsh hills on the far side, and remembering those times of silk ships, and of long-gone kings, admirals and poets (and even Handel) who took ship here. A similar sense of stranded time can be had at the Harp by the ruined marshside quay near Little Neston SJ2976.

Delightful villages – all with decent civilised pubs that we can vouch for – are Barthomley SJ7752 (thatch, black and white timbering, up and down lanes, fine church); Christleton SJ4465 (village green, pond, almshouses, medieval packhorse bridges); Grappenhall SJ6386 (ancient grinning cat on church tower, canal strolls); Great Budworth SJ6778 (charming – imposing church and many pretty cottages); Marbury SJ5645 (attractive church, lake and wood surroundings); and Malpas SJ4947 (extraordinarily uplifting ceiling in the 14th-c hilltop church near fragmentary castle ruin, pretty cottages and some grander buildings).

Other charming villages include Eaton SJ5762 (unassuming picture-postcard combinations of thatch, stone and timbering); Eccleston SJ4163 (romantically eclectic, 19th-c estate village built for the Duke of Westminster, with richly expansive sandstone church that's a culmination of Victorian ecclesiastical architecture); and Whitegate SJ6369 (thatch, village green, fragmentary remains of the biggest English Cistercian monastery opposite the church, lakeside walk on nearby derelict railway).

☛ Visits to WORKING DAIRY FARMS that make their own **ice-creams** have become popular, especially Snugbury's (Park Farm) at Hurleston nr Nantwich SJ6552 and Cheshire Ice-cream Farm (Drumlan Hall Farm) nr Tattenhall SJ4858 – at both you can sample various flavours and see the cows being milked.

Walks

The 30-mile **Sandstone Trail** follows the romantically wooded sandstone ridges, crags and outcrops stretching right across this area from Overton SJ5276 in the N (the church here is pretty, and the Ring o' Bells is a most attractive pub, with Mersey views) to the Shropshire border S of Malpas SJ5645 (the ancient Bell o' the Hill pub nr Tushingham SJ5346 down there is a useful stop). The scenery is very varied, and this trail offers the best walking hereabouts. One particularly fine section is around the **Peckforton Hills** ᑌ-1, with splendid views of real and real-looking romantic castles, and good pubs usefully placed at Bulkeley (SJ5052) and Higher Burwardsley (SJ5256). From the A534 nr **Harthill** SJ5055 ⌂-2, the trail ascends Raw Head, the most spectacular natural feature of the central Cheshire ridge, with sandstone cliffs weathered into bizarre shapes, and a cave to explore.

The trail passes through another very popular area for walks, the **Delamere Forest** ⌂-3. Here there are several square miles of mainly coniferous plantation, with some older oak and other woodland, inc plenty of open stretches and picnic places, and some small stretches of reedy water. There's good access from several places inc Delamere SJ5669 and Hatchmere SJ5672, with decent, prettily placed pubs in both villages.

The Shropshire Union Canal threads in various directions through the area, with interesting stretches for strolls, inc the flight of over a dozen locks nr **Audlem Wharf** (SJ6543) ⌂-4, the charming section through the richly wooded farming country below Beeston Castle at **Wharton's Lock** W of Tiverton SJ5360 ⌂-5, and the pretty **Llangollen Branch** ⌂-6, with good access from Marbury SJ5645 and Wrenbury SJ5948 (there are decent pubs in all these places, and the Dusty Miller at Wrenbury has an interesting lifting bridge by it). There are canal walks from the Nag's Head at Wheelock SJ7559.

Marbury Country Park ⌂-7 has some quiet short walks, and gives on to the extensive Budworth Mere, with sailing, and herons, ducks, grebes and coots pottering around the rushes; good pubs nearby at Comberbach (pronounced Comberbatch) SJ6477 and Great Budworth SJ6778.

Little Budworth Country Park SJ5965 ⌂-8 provides a strong contrast to most of this area's richly manicured countryside: poor, wild heath with young bogs and scrawny birch woods.

Several more or less isolated pubs make useful start or finish points for country walks: the Cock at Barton (SJ4554, nr the attractive village of Farndon – where you can get down to the River Dee); the Copper Mine at Fullers Moor (SJ4954), the Tiger's Head at Norley SJ6772 (Pytchleys Hollow), and the Fiddle i' th' Bag up nr Penketh SJ5686 (Alder Lane off the A49; an unexpectedly remote-feeling spot between the disused St Helen's Canal and the broad River Mersey).

Driving

Any of the roads that link villages we've mentioned as attractive are worth taking, especially for instance the circular route linking Norbury, Marbury and Wrenbury in the S. Another interesting backroads drive is along the narrow lanes around Bickerton Hill, and then from Bulkeley on the A534 through Peckforton and Beeston, turning right there and going across to Bunbury. The B5152, from the A51 S of Tarporley up to Overton, is a nice drive. Especially on a spring or summer evening, the A41, A49 and A51 can be surprisingly quick and pleasant. The A534 W of Nantwich is a good road with interesting views.

Where to eat

Chester SJ4166 GARDEN HOUSE 1 Rufus Court, off Northgate St (01244) 313251 First-floor restaurant in handsome Georgian building, with interesting good food; cl Sun. **£22** (though they do a cheaper house menu) £2.50/£7.
Plumley SJ7175 SMOKER (01565) 722338 Popular thatched 16th-c pub, very handy for the M6; relaxed atmosphere despite its popularity, interesting old prints, wide range of good food, decent wines, and big garden; disabled access. **£20|£2/£5.**
Acton Bridge SJ5975 RHEINGOLD RIVERSIDE RESTAURANT (01606) 852310 A favourite of local contributors; disabled access. **£19.50|£2.50/£4.**
Bickley Moss SJ5549 CHOLMONDELEY ARMS (01829) 720300 Carefully converted Victorian schoolhouse; excellent food, very good wine list, well

kept beers, a lively atmosphere and with interestingly furnished rooms. £19|£3.65/£6.25.

Comberbach SJ6477 SPINNER & BERGAMOT (01606) 891307 Welcoming, pebble-dashed pub with bowling green and lots of animals in garden; very cosy in winter, very good-value bar lunches and good evening food, popular Sun lunches and vegetarian meals; cl pm 25 Dec; children over 14; disabled access. £17.50|£2/£5.

Chester SJ4166 FRANCS 14 Cuppin St (01244) 317952 Cheerful, timbered brasserie with very fine French country food; disabled access. £16/£5.

Cotebrook SJ5765 ALVANLEY ARMS (01829) 760200 Handsome, old, creeper-covered farmhouse, with generous helpings of good, promptly served food; nice garden with country views. £15.50|£2/£6.

Faddiley SJ5953 TOLLEMACHE ARMS (01270) 74223 Friendly, timbered 15th-c pub in an unexpectedly quiet country setting; cosy cottagey feel, decent, good-value bar lunches, tasty puddings, and agreeable to children, providing special menu and a Wendy house with toys in the garden; cl Mon exc bank hols. £13|£2.60/£5.

Marbury SJ5645 SWAN (01948) 3715 Friendly pub in an attractive village, with good walks to Llangollen Canal, appetising home cooking inc good puddings. £1.85/£5.

EAST CHESHIRE

Interestingly preserved mill towns and villages, Pennine-edge moorland, striking stately homes and other buildings, good walking.

Macclesfield and Bollington have made the most of their mill-town past, with good walkways past their surprisingly handsome, heritage industrial buildings set into tortuously steep hillsides; the smaller Styal has been particularly well restored. The pick of the area's great houses include Tatton Park at Knutsford, Lyme Park near Disley, Little Moreton Hall at Scholar Green, and Gawsworth Hall. The best of this area's scenery is in the east and north-east, with some terrific views and fine walks; small, steep, stone-walled pastures, shaggy sheep, deep twisty valleys, austere moorland. But even the flatter countryside of the Cheshire Plain is interestingly varied, with fine trees, rich parkland, leafy lanes and delightful, hidden-away villages.

The eastern part is in the Peak District National Park, which also includes parts of Derbyshire and Staffordshire.

Where to stay

Macclesfield SJ9271 SUTTON HALL Bullocks Lane, Sutton, Macclesfield SK11 0HE (01260) 253211 £85; 9 marvellous rms. Welcoming and secluded, historic baronial hall, full of character – stylish rooms with tall black beams, stone fireplaces, suits of armour and so forth; friendly service and good food; can arrange clay-pigeon shooting/golf/fishing.

Lymm SJ6787 DINGLE Rectory Lane, Lymm WA13 0AH (01925) 752297 £58; 30 rms. Comfortably modernised 18th-c building, attractively situated above the sandstone ravine, and close to the village centre; sauna, solarium, etc, 9-hole putting green, and free mountain bikes; cl 25 Dec–1 Jan.

Knutsford SJ7578 LONG VIEW 51–55 Manchester Rd, Knutsford WA16 0LX (01565) 632119 *£55; 23 attractive rms. Friendly Victorian hotel with period and reproduction furnishings, and original fireplaces; pleasant cellar bar, good, well presented food; cl 24 Dec– 2 Jan.

Holmes Chapel SJ7667 OLD VICARAGE Knutsford Rd, Holmes Chapel, Crewe CW4 8EF (01477) 532041 £48w; 25 comfortable rms. Very friendly hotel with attractively spacious lounge and bar, and reasonably priced, good food in the brasserie; disabled access.

Brereton Green SJ7864 BEARS HEAD Brereton Green, Sandbach CW11 9RS (01477) 535251 £39.60w; 24 comfortable rms in attached modern block, with others in an older part leading off a courtyard. Run by the same family for 50 years, this civilised, timber-framed, old pub has traditional beamed bars, good food in the bar and candlelit restaurant, decent Italian wines, courteous Italian staff, and summer barbecues.

To see and do

🏠 ✿ **Adlington** SJ9180 ADLINGTON HALL The exterior of this imposing 16th-c manor house is quite a mixture – it's rather a shock to walk round the corner from the lovely, timber-framed east wing to the altogether plainer brick, north front, and the elegant south front is different again. Inside, the highlight is the fantastic Great Hall (dating back slightly earlier to 1480), its hammer-beamed roof patrolled by finely carved angels, and the walls adorned with richly painted murals – rediscovered by accident when a game of shuttlecock damaged the plaster that had hidden them. The centrepiece is a magnificent 17th-c organ, unrivalled in size and style, reputed to have been played by Handel. There's a fine yew walk and lime avenue in the landscaped gardens; antique/craft fairs held regularly. Snacks, shop, some disabled access; open pm Sun and bank hols from Good Fri–end Sept; (01260) 272018; house £2.70, garden £1. The Ash Tree at Butley Town is useful for lunch.

🏠 † ✿ 🐿 **Capesthorne** SJ8472 CAPESTHORNE HALL 18th-c family home of the Bromley-Davenports, who have lived on the site since the time of the Domesday Book. Fine paintings include Lowry's unusual interpretation of the house's striking exterior, there's a good collection of Roman and Greek busts and vases, and some American-colonial furnishings. Also a lovely Georgian chapel and 60 acres of gardens and woodland, with a nature trail and arboretum. Snacks, shop, disabled access; open pm Sun and bank hols Apr–Sept, also Weds from May, and Tues and Thurs in Jun and July; (01625) 861221; £4, £2.25 garden only. The Mill at Withington is fairly handy for lunch, if you don't want the longer trip to the Dog over at Peover Heath.

🏠 ✿ 🍺 ✿ **Disley** SJ9784 Outside this pleasant hillside village is LYME PARK, a wonderful country estate, the great hall at its centre a magnificent blend of Elizabethan, Georgian and Regency architecture and styles. They no longer do guided tours except for groups, so you can take your time looking at the various treasures, which include intricate carvings, lovely tapestries, paintings and furniture, a particularly grand staircase, and a fine collection of English clocks. Around the house are 17 acres of Victorian gardens with an orangery, sunken Dutch garden and wilderness garden, and a sprawling ancient park with herds of red deer, nature trails, and Countryside Centre. From the top of the park's former hunting tower, the Cage, you can – on a good day – see six counties; there's a pleasant walk down to the canal, and the long-distance Gritstone Way (see **Walks** section) starts here. Meals, snacks, shop, disabled access; house and gardens cl Oct-Mar (exc gardens open pm wknds Nov and Dec), house also cl am and all Thurs and Fri; the park is open all year; £3 per car to go into the park, then £3 house and garden, £1 garden only; NT. The Devonshire Arms over at Mellor (Gtr Manchester) and the Lantern Pike at Little Hayfield (Derbys) are the best, reasonably handy places for lunch.

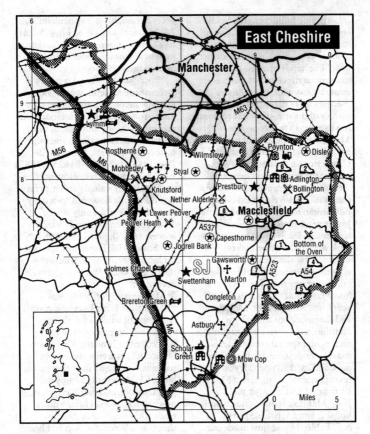

★ † ⌂ ❀ **Gawsworth** SJ8969 has fine
houses in parkland, ponds, an
interesting church, and an unusual,
unspoilt farm pub. Its pride is
GAWSWORTH HALL, a very pretty
timbered manor house dating back to
Norman times and the former home
of Mary Fitton, possibly the 'dark
lady' of Shakespeare's sonnets. Inside
is plenty of fine furniture, stained
glass, pictures and sculptures, while in
summer the grounds have an open-air
theatre with an appealingly varied
range of concerts and plays; gardens
and park. Snacks, shop; cl am,
Oct–Mar; (01260) 223456; £3.40.
The Sutton Hall Hotel over at Sutton
Lane Ends is quite handy for lunch.
⌘ ! ⌂ **Jodrell Bank** SJ7970 JODRELL
BANK SCIENCE CENTRE AND ARBORETUM
Plenty to do at this lively place, which
has developed quite a lot over the last

few years. The centrepiece is still the
huge radio telescope, the second
largest in the world and as big as the
dome of St Paul's, but they also have
the fun science centre, with displays
and exhibitions examining subjects as
diverse as plants, prisms and planets,
all in a pleasingly down-to-earth way.
Outside is an arboretum with 2,500
types of tree, as well as nature trails,
picnic spots, and an Environmental
Discovery Centre. Regular shows in
the planetarium. Meals, snacks, shop,
disabled access; cl Nov–mid-Mar exc
pm wknds and school hols; (01477)
571339; £3.50. The Red Lion at Lower
Withington is quite handy for lunch.
★ ⌂ ❀ ♪ ⌷ **Knutsford** SJ7578,
despite its obvious present-day
prosperity and some rather heavy
traffic, has a pleasantly old-world feel,
with lots of striking Georgian and

other period buildings. (It quickly conjures up schoolday memories of reading Mrs Gaskell's *Cranford*, its alias). TATTON PARK is on its northern edge. The handsome neo-classical mansion at the centre of this busy estate is Georgian, but the more modest Old Hall hints at the long history of the site – they like to boast it has its roots in the Stone Age. Magnificent collection of furnishings, porcelain and paintings (inc two Canalettos) in the opulent state rooms; the restored kitchens and servants' quarters providing quite a contrast. The lovely grounds boast an Edwardian rose garden, Italian and Japanese gardens, an orangery and fern house, leading to a big country park with mature trees, lakes, signposted walks, deer and waterfowl; you can fish, hire bikes, or take a carriage ride. There's also a home farm that works as it did 60 years ago, with vintage machinery and rare breeds of animals; in addition, a children's playground, and regular special events. Meals, snacks, shop, some disabled access; park and gardens open all year (except winter Mon), rest cl Mon (exc bank hols), Oct wkdays, and Nov–Mar (exc farm open Sun), plus house cl am; £6; (01565) 654822; NT. Tabley House (just inside our West Cheshire section) is just outside the town, over the M6.

🐾⛾ ❀ **Macclesfield** SJ9273 Away from the modern shopping streets are plenty of fine old buildings associated with the early Industrial Revolution and the silk industry, and a more ancient core with quaint little cobbled alleys. The SILK MUSEUM (Roe St) has a notable audio-visual programme covering the history of silk and its uses, room settings, exhibitions, textiles and garments. Meals, snacks, shop, disabled access; cl am Sun, Good Fri, 24–26 Dec, 1 Jan; (01625) 613210; *£2. PARADISE MILL (Park Lane) Good fun; helpful guides (many of whom are former silk workers) demonstrate the silk production process on the mill's restored handlooms, and room settings give a good idea of working conditions in the 1930s. Shop, good disabled access; cl am, Mon (exc bank hols), 24–26 Dec, 1 Jan, Good Fri; (01625) 618228; £2. For £3.40 you can get a joint ticket for the above two attractions.

WEST PARK MUSEUM (Prestbury Rd) Decent little museum with a wide range of decorative arts, some interesting Egyptian antiquities, 19th- and early 20th-c paintings inc fine bird and animal pictures, and local history. Shop; cl am, Mon, 24–26 Dec, 1 Jan, Good Fri; (01625) 619831 free. HARE HILL Acres of lovely parkland with walled garden, pergola and fine spring flowers. Open daily mid-May-Jun, then only Weds, Thurs, Sat, Sun until end Oct, cl winter; *£2.50; (01625) 828981; NT. The Sutton Hall Hotel, just S, is best for lunch, but the moorland pubs mentioned under **Walks** are in fairly easy reach.

🐦 **Mobberley** SJ7879 HILLSIDE ORNAMENTAL FOWL Excellent private collection of wildfowl with rare species like magpie geese, white-headed stifftail and the Abyssinian black duck, as well as aviaries of softbills, flamingos and other exotic birds. Children should enjoy the penguin pool, and they have a family of white wallabies. This is a place readers like very much. Snacks, shop; open Weds, Sat, Sun and bank hols Easter–Oct; (01565) 873282; £2.50. The Bird in Hand, Church Inn and Roebuck are all useful for lunch.

❀ 🏠 **Mow Cop** SJ8557 Right on the Staffs border is a shaggy steep hill with a castellated folly on top, and a rock pinnacle left by former quarrying. Rich views over Cheshire (and the village just behind, which is in Staffs, somehow by contrast underlines the essential richness and grace of Cheshire itself). Worth a look if passing.

✗ **Nether Alderley** SJ8476 NETHER ALDERLEY MILL Interesting 15th-c watermill with carefully preserved atmosphere, and restored working waterwheels which have Elizabethan timber work and Victorian machinery. It looks lovely as you approach, with its long roof sloping down almost to the ground. They still grind flour for demonstration purposes. Open pm Weds, Sun and bank hols from Apr–Oct, also Tues, Thurs, Fri and Sat Jun–Sept; £1.80; NT.

🐚 ❀ **Poynton** SJ9283 BROOKSIDE GARDEN CENTRE has a splendid miniature railway, chuffing its way through an authentically detailed circuit in a pretty garden setting. The replica West Country station is packed with railway memorabilia. Parking is not always easy. Meals, snacks, shop, disabled access; railway runs Weds and Sun Apr–Sept, plus Tues and Thurs in July and Aug, Sun only in Oct and cl Nov–Apr; 40p.

★ ❀ † **Rostherne** SJ7484 is a quiet little village worth pausing at. It has charming brick cottages along a cobbled pavement, and offers a lovely view over one of the county's broadest meres from the graveyard of the attractive timbered church. The Swan With Two Nicks over at Little Bollington is pleasantly placed for lunch.

🏚 ⚓ **Scholar Green** SJ8356 LITTLE MORETON HALL One of the best-preserved half-timbered buildings in Britain, its splendid black and white exterior covered with such a profusion of lines the effect is almost dizzying; it's remained pretty much unchanged since it was built in 1580. The inside, though largely unfurnished, has some interesting features too, especially the wainscoted Long Gallery, Great Hall and chapel. You can see the original gatehouse and moat, and there's a re-creation of a typical 17th-c knot garden. Regular open-air theatre and concert performances. Meals, snacks, shop, disabled access to ground floor only; cl am, all Mon and Tues, Nov–Mar; £2.80 wkdys, £3.60 wknds; NT. Nearby, HERITAGE NARROW BOATS at Kent Green have silent, electric narrow boats to hire by the day (01782) 785700; cl Nov–Easter; £38 wkdys for 1–3 people, £48 wknds. The Rising Sun, doing well under new management, is good for lunch.

↧T 🏚 ❀ 🚤 **Styal** SJ8383 QUARRY BANK MILL AND COUNTRY PARK One of the best and most extensive places in the country to get to grips with the Industrial Revolution. The 18th-c cotton mill that's the centrepiece here still produces cloth, with demonstrations of spinning and weaving, and lively exhibitions on factory conditions and life for the mill workers and their bosses. The village was built by the mill owners, and has carefully preserved workers' cottages, chapels and shops, inc the house where the young pauper apprentices lived, while around it the lovely park has good woodland or riverside walks. You can buy the cloth woven here, and there are lots of events throughout the year. Meals, snacks, shop, disabled access (recently improved through the park); cl Mon Oct–Mar; apprentice house only £2.50, mill only £3.50, mill and apprentice house £4.50; NT. The Old Ship is pleasant for lunch. The PEACOCK FARM SHOP nearby is a notable family-run business, very welcoming too, thanks to the hundreds of colourful daffodils they've planted on the roadside; meat and greengrocery as well as the farm produce, and their pony and donkey are extremely family-friendly.

† **Churches** of note include Astbury SJ8461 (graceful detached spire, spectacular roofing, rich carving; the village is very attractive, too), Marton SJ8568 (simple, 14th-c, shingle-roofed with black and white timbering, in unpromising surroundings) and Mobberley SJ7879 (magnificently carved Tudor rood screen).

★ **Attractive villages,** all with nice pubs, include Lower Peover SJ7474 (many people's Cheshire favourite: cobbled lanes, glorious, 14th-c black and white timbered church, quiet watermeadows); Lymm SJ6787 (pretty cottages in the Dingle, boat trips on Bridgewater Canal (092575) 4900, strolls to the lake at Lymm Dam); Prestbury SJ9077 (very prosperous air now, with good shops, the Legh Arms and the homelier Admiral Rodney; pleasant riverside walks to the S, along the Bollin); and Swettenham SJ8067 (rich paddocks with wrought-iron fences, daffodils in spring in a dell by an old mill).

Walks

The hilly eastern edge of the county forms part of the Peak District, and offers some grand views westwards towards North Wales. **Teggs Nose Country Park** SJ9573 ◻-1 has a useful summer information centre, and good walks with far views, punctuated by relics of the former quarrying here. By the turn off the A537, the Setter Dog is a good pub. From the park, a well-marked track heads off S into Macclesfield Forest, with steep, deep-green pine plantations around neatly walled small reservoirs; on the far side of this, the isolated Leather's Smithy (E of Langley SJ9471) is a warmly welcoming moorside refuge, and the Stanley Arms at Bottom of the Oven SJ9872 has been good.

This track is actually part of the long-distance **Gritstone Way**, which is well marked and offers a few days' walking of the highest quality. It runs along these western flanks of the Peak District from **Lyme Park** SJ9682 ◻-2 (itself laced with gentle paths), to join the Staffordshire Way at Rushton Spencer SJ9462 (where the Crown is good for lunch). Further N, the Way can be picked up to track across high stone-walled pastures at either Pott Shrigley SJ9478 (the Cheshire Hunt in Spurley Lane is a good pub here) or, with fine views, at Rainow SJ9576 (the Highwayman, a mile above the village, is a distinctive old pub). **Kerridge Hill** SJ9475 ◻-3 above Bollington (SJ9377) is topped by the curious folly known as White Nancy. Bollington is itself certainly worth a stroll: handsome stone mill town buildings, grand canal viaducts, attractive perspectives of the surrounding villages, and useful pubs such as the Church House and Vale.

These hills and moors SE of Macclesfield SJ9273 have many other good walks. A particular delight is that so many can be based around good, civilised, country pubs with decent food: the Crag, in its untypically leafy, sheltered valley at **Wildboarclough** SJ9868 ◻-4, fits well with a walk to the Three Shires Head and the summit of Shutlingsloe, and the Ship at **Danebridge** SJ9665 ◻-5, nr Wincle, is ideal for walks into the Dane Valley and along the exhilarating moorland tops of the Roaches (which are just over the Staffs border). Another well-placed pub in this popular walking area is the Hanging Gate at Higher Sutton SJ9569, nr Langley.

The **Middlewood Way** ◻-6 is a sort of linear country park between Macclesfield and the N border, along a former railway. It is attractively bordered with wild flowers and trees, with tracks for cyclists (bicycle hire at Lyme Park or Bollington) and horse rides (can also be hired by the hour, about £10); several decent pubs in Bollington SJ9377, one at Whiteley Green SJ9278. The pleasant stretches around the Poynton inclines SJ9283 are underrated, and the Boar's Head here is a good-value refreshment stop.

The **Macclesfield Canal** ◻-7 meanders through fine high countryside from the N border nr Disley [SJ9784], to pass Bollington, Macclesfield and Congleton SJ8663, with plenty of access points; S of the A54 and just W of its junction with the A523, a staggering flight of 10 locks leads down to a sturdily elegant iron aqueduct.

Alderley Edge SJ8677 ◻-8 (not to be confused with the straggling suburban settlement named after it to the W) rises high out of the plain, with good walks through woodland and fine views of the higher hills to the E. The local caving club members are working towards opening some of the former copper mines which honeycomb the area.

The **Cloud** SJ9063 ◻-9 has a craggy summit and drops steeply to the plain, with grand views; the Coach & Horses at Timbersbrook is a useful nearby pub.

Driving

There are quite magnificent views from the A537 E of Macclesfield, and good ones from the A5002 NE. A quiet and pleasant country drive is that along the lanes through the rich parkland around Goostrey, Peover Heath and Over Peover N of Holmes Chapel. There are pleasant hill drives around Macclesfield – for instance, through Sutton Lane Ends, Langley, the Macclesfield Forest and on up to the A537; or S from Sutton Lane Ends to Wincle and Danebridge. From off the A537, between Walker Barn and the Cat & Fiddle Inn (the second highest in England), an excellent moorland road heads N past the big reservoir, into fine empty countryside. Going across country, Congleton can be quite a bottleneck, and the A523 and A6 tend to be slow. In contrast, the A50, made virtually redundant by the M6, is a good fast road.

Where to eat

Knutsford SJ7578 LA BELLE EPOQUE 60 King St (01565) 633060 Popular Art Nouveau restaurant with elaborate food and helpful, friendly staff; cl am Sat, Sun, first wk Jan; children over 10. £27.50/£16.50.

Bollington SJ9377 MAURO'S 88 Palmerston St (01625) 573898 Friendly Italian restaurant with excellent fresh fish and lovely puddings; cl am Sat, last 3 Suns of month, 3 wks in summer; disabled access. £23/£4.95.

Bottom of the Oven SJ9872 STANLEY ARMS (01260) 252414 Unspoilt, isolated moorland pub close to Macclesfield Forest; very friendly, and has had good ambitious food, but tenants may be changing; cl 25 Dec; disabled access. £16|£1.95/£3.95.

Peover Heath SJ7973 DOG (01625) 861421 Busy pub in a quiet lane, with big helpings of interesting food, open fires, and a relaxing series of small enclaves around the central bar. £16.50|£3.85/£6.30.

Help this year from: Roy Smylie, Pauline Crossland, Dave Cawley, E G Parish, Miss P A Hedley, Dilys Unsworth, S R and A I Ashcroft, Gill and Keith Croxton, Sue Holland, Dave Webster, Mr and Mrs R J Phillips, Ian Phillips, Andy Petersen, Tony and Lynne Stark, Terry Buckland, A Lomas, Nigel Woolliscroft, Andrew Wilson, Mrs H Jack, A F C Young, Andrew and Ruth Triggs, M A Cameron, Paul Noble, Andrew Stephenson, Lynn Sharpless, Bob Eardley, C H and P Stride, Julie Peters, W C M Jones, G E Stait, J and P Maloney, David Shillitoe, Mr and Mrs J H Adam, Susan Bertschinger, Sue Badel, Maeve and Peter Thompson.

CHESHIRE CALENDAR

Some of these dates were provisional as we went to press.

JANUARY

28 **Nantwich** Holly Holy Day, celebration of the battle of Namptwyche (01270) 610983

MARCH

17 **Northwich** Antiques Fair at Arley Hall – *till Sun 19* (01565) 777353

APRIL

14 **Ellesmere Port** Traditional Boat Gathering at the Boat Museum – *till Mon 17* (0151) 355 5017

17 **Runcorn** Fun and Games for Easter at Norton Priory (01928) 569895

23 **Sandbach** Transport Through the Ages – veteran cars, lorries, buses in the town centre (01270) 763376

MAY

6 **Knutsford** Royal May Day: before the processions and activities, the pavements are carpeted with sands of different colours to form elaborate patterns (01565) 632611

8 **Runcorn** May Day at Norton Priory (01928) 569895; **Sandbach** Elizabethan Market (01270) 763231

13 **Chester** Lord Mayor's Show and Festival of Transport in the town centre and at the Roodee – *till Sun 14* (01244) 317962; **Marbury** Merry Days – *till Sun 14* (01948) 663758

19 **Chester** Beating the Retreat, colourful traditional military ceremony in the Castle Square (01244) 352427

20 **nr Nantwich** Reaseheath College of Agriculture Open Day – *till Sun 21* (01270) 625131

27 **Ellesmere Port** Festival of Boats at the Boat Museum – *till Mon 29* (0151) 355 5017

29 **Northwich** Regatta (01606) 862862

JUNE

1 **Neston** Ladies Day – afternoon procession in period costume (0151) 336 3104

10 **Siddington** Fireworks and Laser Concert at Capesthorne Hall – *till Sun 11* (01625) 861221

16 **Middlewich** Folk and Boat Festival – *till Sun 18* (01606) 833946

17 **Appleton Thorn** Bawming the Thorn: traditional procession and festivities during which children 'bawm' (dance round) a hawthorn tree – originated when a crusading knight planted an offshoot of the Glastonbury Thorn here (01925) 444400

18 **Runcorn** Midsummer Festival at Norton Priory (01928) 569895

20 **Tabley** (nr Knutsford) Cheshire County Show at the County Showground – *till Weds 21* (01829) 760020

24 **Willaston** World Worm Charming Championships (01270) 661528

CHESHIRE CALENDAR

JULY

1 **Runcorn** Carnival (01928) 580366

2 **Chester** River Carnival and Raft Race (01244) 324888; **Northwich** Carnival (01606) 862862

7 **Warrington** Walking Day – popular northern tradition originally to draw people away from the races: long processions wind round the town (01925) 442180

8 **Northwich** Garden Craft Fair at Arley Hall – *till Sun 9* (01565) 777353

15 **Widnes** Halton Show at Spike Island – *till Sun 16* (0151) 424 2061 ext 4661

21 **Chester** Summer Music Festival – *till Sat 29* (01244) 320722

26 **Nantwich** and South Cheshire Show at Dorfold Hall Park (01270) 780306

30 **Ellesmere Port** Vintage and Classic Car Show at the Boat Museum (0151) 355 5017

AUGUST

13 **Macclesfield** Rushbearing Ceremony at Macclesfield Forest Chapel (01625) 504114

20 **Macclesfield** Family Fun Day at West Park – entirely free day for all the family (01625) 504115

26 **Crewe** and Nantwich Carnival at Queen's Park – *till Sun 27* (01270) 610983; **Poynton** Show at Poynton Park (01625) 872065

27 **Ellesmere Port** Model Boat Extravaganza at the Boat Museum – *till Mon 28* (0151) 355 5017

SEPTEMBER

8 **Crewe and Nantwich** Folk Festival – *till Sun 10* (01270) 663120

9 **Malpas** Yesteryear Rally – *till Sun 10* (01978) 780749; **Runcorn** Archaeological Extravaganza at Norton Priory (01928) 569895

16 **Winsford** Vale Royal Show at the Civic Hall (01606) 863026

17 **Runcorn** Walled Garden Horticultural Show at Norton Priory (01928) 569895

23 **Siddington** Craft Fair at Capesthorne Hall – *till Sun 24* (01625) 861221

26 **Chester** National Waterways Festival (01203) 407070

OCTOBER

7 **Ellesmere Port** Tugs, Pushes and Steam Event at the Boat Museum – *till Sun 8* (0151) 355 5017

13 **Northwich** Antiques Fair at Arley Hall – *till Sun 15* (01565) 777353

CORNWALL

Cornwall takes so long to get to that for most people, especially in the summer holidays, it's hardly worth thinking about as a place for a short break: journey times which fade into the edges of a longer holiday dominate and overshadow a short one. Out of high season, though, when there's much less competition for road space, Cornwall offers very substantial rewards to those prepared to spend the time getting there: attractive prices, lots to do, and a very relaxed pace of life. Except in the south-east, it's virtually treeless, mainly rolling pasture and moorland, with stupendous coastal scenery, and spooky tin-mining ruins and leftovers peppering the landscape. It's not strong on great architecture, though there are some delightful, unspoilt country churches and, particularly in the east, small stately homes.

Cornwall's long been on the tourist circuit, with resort development, theme parks, gift shops and an enormous number of family attractions – this year we've added quite a few small rare-breed farms and animal centres. Escapists can always find solitude by walking a few miles along the coast. There are 500 miles of coastal walks here, much of the land owned and beautifully preserved by the National Trust.

It's not a good area for car touring or cycling: roads don't usually follow the coast and tend to be shut in by very high hedges. From London, you should allow about five hours' driving out of season to get well into the county; it's about three hours from Bristol – across just a couple of counties.

South-east Cornwall's chief charm is the relatively sheltered coast, with plenty of interesting villages and little coves. Virtually every harbour advertises boat and fishing trips, or sharking trips (you watch sharks being caught). Mid-Cornwall has much the same type of appeal, though there's a more dramatic coast (and fewer fishing-village coves); it has the best choice of fine gardens to visit, and its bigger towns are appealing. West Cornwall, again, has some charming, little, sheltered sea villages, but also a much wilder side. It's exceptionally rich in archaeology – Bronze Age burial chambers and standing stones, Iron Age hill forts and village sites, ancient stone crosses. Penzance has some good features, and St Ives wears its popularity very well indeed. The Isles of Scilly are ideal for a really relaxing break, with Penzance the quickest jumping-off point. North Cornwall's coast is divided between the long stretch of well equipped sandy beach resorts at one end and great tracts of little-visited wild cliffs at the other; windswept Bodmin Moor is the county's most untouched inland area. Generally, good places to eat are most easily found in the south, rarest in the west.

All four areas are within fairly quick reach of each other; so, staying in one, you can easily visit something that appeals in another.

Late May and early June is an ideal time for a break here, with the scenery at its best and relatively few other visitors. In the summer holidays the most popular places do get very busy indeed, with frustrating traffic jams and parking problems. September and October is seal-pup time.

SOUTH-EAST CORNWALL

Intricately varied coast dotted with picturesque fishing villages and sheltered coves; a fine choice of places to stay, plenty of walking.

There are some dramatic headlands and stretches of cliff for bracing walks, but it's the abundance of sheltered little bays, creeks and pretty villages tucked between them which makes this area so picturesque, and so attractive to families. It's ideal for pottering about in boats. The area has Cornwall's most lovely house, Cotehele, near Calstock; Lanhydrock House, and Antony House, at Torpoint, are also well worth visiting, as are Trewithen Gardens, near Probus, and the Lost Gardens of Heligan, near Mevagissey. Dobwalls Adventure Park is a family favourite. There's an excellent choice of distinctive places to stay, with decent if not outstanding food, including plenty of genuinely fresh local fish.

Where to stay

Calstock SX4368 DANESCOMBE VALLEY Lower Kelly, Calstock PL18 9RY (01822) 832414 *£130; 5 lovely rms. Very attractive, small Georgian house with first-floor verandah and fine views over a wooded bend on the River Tamar; warm and friendly owners, quiet, relaxing atmosphere, open fires, flowers, books (no TV), and delicious food using fresh local produce; Cotehele House (NT) is just 15 minutes' walk; cl Nov–Mar; children over 12.

Carne Beach SW9038 NARE Carne Beach, Par TR2 5PF (01872) 501279 £120; 36 lovely rms to suit all tastes – some stylish ones overlook the garden and out to sea. Attractively decorated and furnished hotel on a magnificent clifftop site, with secluded gardens and outdoor swimming pool; antiques, fresh flowers and log fires in the airy, spacious day rooms, excellent food inc wonderful breakfasts, and run by staff who really care; very good for quiet family hols, with safe sandy beach below; cl 6 wks from 3 Jan; disabled access.

Portloe SW9339 LUGGER Portloe, Truro TR2 5RD (01872) 501322 *£108; 19 rms. Friendly, family-run smuggling inn right by the sea, with excellent views; smart, comfortable furnishings, and good food at sensible prices; fine nearby walks; cl 21 Nov–10 Feb; children over 12.

St Keyne SX2460 WELL HOUSE St Keyne, Liskeard PL14 4RN (01579) 342001 £105; 7 attractive rms with lovely views. Light and airy Victorian country house in three acres of gardens, with hard tennis court, swimming pool and croquet lawn; particularly good food and fine wines in dining room overlooking the terrace and lawns; children over 8 at dinner (high tea available).

Gerrans Bay SW8937 PENDOWER BEACH HOUSE Gerrans Bay, Portscatho, Truro TR2 5LW (01872) 501241 £100 inc dinner; 11 rms, most with own bthrm. Carefully modernised, 16th-c hotel in own grounds on the edge of a lovely sandy beach, with superb sea and coastal views; relaxed atmosphere in homely rooms, and tempting fish dishes (cold lobster on the terrace is special); tennis court; cl Nov–Mar; disabled access.

Golant SX1155 CORMORANT Golant, Fowey PL23 1LL (01726) 833426 *£92; 10 rms with lovely views. Friendly hotel in pretty riverside setting; log fire and big picture windows in the lounge, candlelit dining room with imaginative food inc fresh fish, home-made breads, cakes and jams; heated swimming pool; cl Jan; children over 12; disabled access.

Looe SX2652 TALLAND BAY Talland, Looe PL13 2JB (01503) 72667 £90; 22 rms with sea or country views. Country house in lovely gardens above the sea; comfortable lounges and bar with relaxed atmosphere, courteous service, pretty oak-panelled dining room; heated outdoor swimming pool, putting, croquet, snooker, sauna and solarium; cl Jan; children over 6 in restaurant (high tea for younger ones); disabled access.

Fowey SX1252 FOWEY HOTEL The Esplanade, Fowey PL23 1HX (01726) 832551 *£82; 30 rms, most with bthrm. Pleasant large hotel with an informal atmosphere in the homely rooms, enjoyable restaurant, and wonderful views from the bar; good disabled access.

Bodinnick SX1352 OLD FERRY Bodinnick, Fowey PL23 1LX (01726) 870237 £74; 12 rms, mostly with bthrm. Ancient inn in a lovely position on the edge of Fowey estuary, with splendid views; simple furnishings, tasty breakfasts, decent evening meals (not winter), and a games room hewn into the rock; handy for walks; no accommodation Nov–Mar.

Portscatho SW8735 ROSELAND HOUSE Portscatho, Truro TR2 5EW (01872) 580644 £56; 18 pleasant rms. Clean, well kept and comfortably furnished hotel in six acres of grounds, with wooded path down to a private beach; welcoming, helpful staff, tasty home-made food using local produce, and lots of clifftop walks; a good centre for exploring the area; disabled access.

Pelynt SX2055 JUBILEE Pelynt, Looe PL13 2JZ (01503) 220312 £56; 15 rms. Smart but relaxing pub with Queen Victoria mementoes, comfortable furnishings; good waitress-served bar food, and well equipped children's play area; partial disabled access.

St Mawes SW8433 RISING SUN St Mawes, Truro TR2 5DJ (01326) 270233 £55; 11 rms. Small, attractive hotel in popular, picturesque waterside village with harbourside views; quiet lounge and cocktail bar, lively locals' bar and airy conservatory.

Fowey SX1252 MARINA The Esplanade, Fowey PL23 1HY (01726) 833315 *£54; 11 rms, several with lovely views (some with balcony). Elegant, homely hotel over-looking the water where there are moorings for guests; comfortable lounge, dining room and sheltered gardens that share the fine view; helpful, friendly service, and good food (especially fish); cl Nov–Feb; children over 6 in restaurant.

Pillaton SX3664 WEARY FRIAR Pillaton, Saltash PL12 6QS (01579) 50238 *£50; 13 rms. Pretty 12th-c inn by the church (Tues evening bell-ringing) in a pleasantly remote village; lots of charm and character, attractive furnishings, and good food.

Polperro SX2051 LANDAVIDDY MANOR Landaviddy Lane, Polperro, Looe PL13 2RT (01503) 72210 £48; 8 rms, 4 with shared bthrm. Attractive, 18th-c manor house with fine views over the two acres of peaceful gardens and over the bay beyond; comfortably furnished lounges, open fire, a relaxed atmosphere and candlelit dining room; Nov–Jan; children over 10.

St Keyne SX2564 OLD RECTORY St Keyne, Liskeard PL14 4RL (01579) 342617 £40; 8 comfortable rms, 1 with shared bthrm. Friendly hotel in three acres of grounds; comfortably furnished lounge with open fire, help-yourself bar, and nice homely atmosphere; cl wk over Christmas; children over 12.

St Hilary SW5531 ENNYS St Hilary, Penzance TR20 9BZ (01736) 740252 £40; 5 thoughtfully decorated rms. Lovely, secluded, 17th-c manor house on a small working farm, with grass tennis court and swimming pool in the pretty garden, log fire in the comfortable sitting room, enjoyable food using home-grown and local produce, and a relaxed friendly atmosphere; cl Christmas.

Crafthole SX3654 FINNYGOOK Crafthole, Torpoint PL11 3BQ (01503) 30338 £40; 4 small but very warm and comfortable rms. Friendly inn with broad sea views from the residents' lounge; also a spacious, modernised lounge bar, pleasant restaurant, and good-value food; disabled access.

Watergate SX2354 HARESCOMBE LODGE Watergate, Looe PL13 2NE (01503) 263158 *£40; 4 rms. Friendly and carefully modernised, 18th-c house, with waterfalls and old stone bridges in the quiet garden; half-an-hour's walk along the river path into Looe; no children.

Lanhydrock SX0763 TREFFRY FARM Lanhydrock, Bodmin PL30 5AF (01208) 74405 *£37; 3 pretty rms. Friendly farmhouse with wood-panelled lounge, fine breakfasts, and evening meals using home-grown veg and fruit; calves to feed, cows to milk, and free-range hens; Lanhydrock stately home (NT) is 300 yds away; cl Nov–Easter; children over 6.

Fowey SX1252 SHIP PL23 1AZ (01726) 832230 £37; 6 nicely old-fashioned rms (some oak-panelled), mostly with shared bthrm. Attractive old inn with some nautical touches in the comfortable bar, coal fire, and a family dining room with a big stained-glass window; good mix of locals and visitors.

St Martin SX2655 BUCKLAWREN FARM St Martin, Looe PL13 1NZ (015034) 738; £36; 5 rms. Spacious farmhouse on 500-acre dairy and arable working farm, with croquet and putting in the big garden; large homely lounge, sun lounge, and farmhouse cooking using home-grown and local produce; cl Nov–March.

To see and do

★ **Attractive seaside villages and towns** are the highlight of this area. Tucked into the rocky coast, they are often really lovely, with friendly local people. Generally well sheltered, they're often pleasantly mild when other parts of the West Country are cold. In summer they manage to keep their charm, as the strolling crowds never overshadow the natural local character. Favourites include Fowey, Mevagissey, Polperro, Portscatho and St Mawes and are described below. Others with nothing specific to see but immensely appealing in their own way are: Kingsand/Cawsand SX4350 (higgledy-piggledy charm, nr great cliff walks; the Halfway House and Rising Sun both have good, fresh fish), Portloe SW9339 (tiny, unspoilt village wedged into a precipitous cove; good teashop/small restaurant, as well as the Lugger – see **Where to stay** section above), Porthallow SX2251 (snug, little fishing harbour; the Five Pilchards is beautifully set) and Polkerris SX0952 (terrific view – almost even better in winter – across St Austell bay from well restored ancient quay). All these have decent pubs, as does Cargreen SX4362, prettily sited on the Tamar.

🏠 ❀ ✕ ⌔ ❇ **Calstock** SX4167
COTEHELE Tucked away in a network of twisting roads high above the Tamar, this rambling granite house has hardly changed since it was built defensively around its courtyard in the late 15th c; there's no electricity, so the dark and atmospheric rooms can have quite an authentically medieval feel. Fine furniture, armour, tapestries and embroideries, with fascinating period workshops outside; lovely terraced gardens, a medieval dovecot, restored watermill in the valley, and lovely woods to walk in many directions. It is over-visited (indeed, the National Trust is doing all it can not to encourage further visits), so except out of season you might well decide not to swell the crowds yourself. Down at Cotehele Quay a NATIONAL MARITIME MUSEUM outpost shows the quay's

history, and the last of the Tamar ketch-rigged barges has been restored here. Meals, snacks (tearoom in pleasant riverside setting, with good cream teas), shop; cl Fri and Nov–Apr, house cl am; £5; NT. Pleasant walks along the Tamar from the village. The Carpenter's Arms at Lower Metherell and the unusual Who'd Have Thought It at St Dominick also good for lunch.
! **Callington** SX3669 is not in itself remarkable, but off the A388 S is DUPATH HOLY WELL, the best-preserved of Cornwall's many holy wells – its unappetising water is said to cure whooping cough; free.
❇ **Charlestown** SX0351 is an interesting, working china-clay port, with tall ships as well as modern cargo boats; it's been much used as a film/TV setting (eg for *Poldark*). SHIPWRECK & HERITAGE CENTRE Large

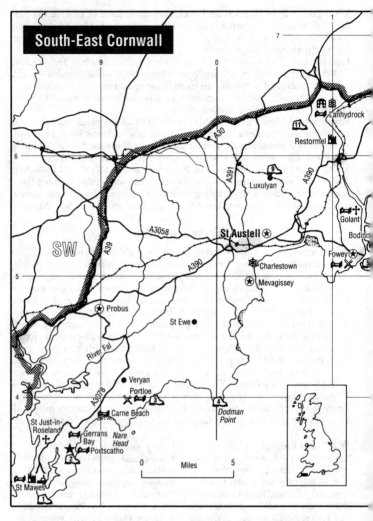

South-East Cornwall

collection of shipwreck items and other local history exhibits, along with a diving display, audio-visual show, lifeboat, and life-sized tableaux. Meals, snacks, shop, disabled access; cl Nov–Feb; (01726) 69897; *£2.95. There are always at least two out of a fleet of five tall ships in the harbour, and most of these offer tours by costumed guides. Several were built in the 18th c, but perhaps the most interesting is a reconstruction of Columbus's *Santa Maria*. The harbourside Rashleigh Arms is useful for lunch.

☺ **Dobwalls** SX2165 ADVENTURE PARK Good theme park with lively attractions, inc steam and diesel train-rides along a two-mile stretch of miniature American-style railroads, aerial cableways, and super slides. Also an excellent and highly unusual wildlife gallery, with period artwork brought vividly to life by atmospheric, interactive tableaux. Great for children. Meals, snacks, shop, disabled access; cl wkdys Nov–Mar exc half-term; (01579) 20578; £6.50. The Highway is useful for lunch.

Calstock

Cotehele House

A38

Dobwalls

SX

Braddock

St Keyne

A390

A388

A38

A387

St Germans

Pillaton

Torpoint

Trecangate

reath

Pelynt

St Martin

Crafthole

A374

Lanteglos Highway

Looe

Lansallos

The Long Sands

Polperro

ENGLISH CHANNEL

★ Fowey SX1252 (pronounced 'Foy'), is steep, lively and bustling, has an exceptional riverside position, with pretty views from up the hill on either side, and some interesting shops in its maze of quaint alleys and tiny lanes. All manner of boats in the harbour, from yachts to ocean-going ships; car ferry to Bodinnick SX1352 and foot ferry to Polruan SX1251, the similarly steep little harbourside hamlet opposite – less interesting, but with lovely views of Fowey (both have decent pubs); also other boat trips. St Catherine's Castle is a ruined stronghold built by Henry

VIII, restored in the mid-19th c.
Lanhydrock SX0863
Lanhydrock A huge place, this fine old house has over 30 rooms on three floors open to the public, inc the servants' quarters – quite a contrast to the grand 'upstairs' rooms. The highlight has to be the Long Gallery, with its magnificently illustrated Old Testament scenes – it's one of the few original 16th-c parts left, as a disastrous fire in the 19th c resulted in major changes and refurbishments. Pretty, formal GARDENS. Good meals and snacks, shop, disabled access; house

cl Mon (exc bank hols), both house and gardens cl Nov–Mar; £5, £2.60 grounds only; NT. The Crown down at Lanlivery is very pleasant for lunch.

† ♨ **Lanreath** SX1757 is a pleasant village with some remarkable woodwork in its exceptional medieval CHURCH. The FOLK MUSEUM here has an absorbing and far-ranging collection of redundant bits and pieces, with a good taped commentary.

★ ♥ ♨ **Looe** SX2756 is a seaside resort, packed with tourist shops, teashops and pubs, but has a nice, easy-going atmosphere even in high season. The old fishing village, with its picturesque harbour and narrow little backstreets, is now immersed in tourism, and is the main shark-fishing place. MONKEY SANCTUARY at Murrayton, just E. Fascinating, protected breeding colony (the world's first in captivity) of Amazon woolly monkeys in wooded grounds – you can get right up to the animals; useful indoor exhibition and talks. Meals, snacks, shop, limited disabled access; cl Fri, Sat, Oct–Easter; (01503) 262532; £3.50. LIVING FROM THE SEA Cornwall's fishing history, from Tudor times to the present day, with a lobster and shellfish aquarium and an exhibition about sharks – in summer it often displays a locally caught shark in ice. Shop, disabled access; cl Mon Apr–May, and all Nov–Easter; £1.20. Summer BOAT TRIPS from here, inc out to nearby St George's Island.

★ ✿ ♨ ♨ **Mevagissey** SX0145 is a bustling place, a picturesque fishing village much expanded into quite a commercialised resort, but fun, with hillside cottages, narrow streets, gift shops, and a busy working harbour. The Ship is the best pub here. LOST GARDENS OF HELIGAN Forgotten and neglected between 1914 and 1991, these splendid gardens are now undergoing an enormous restoration – probably the biggest of its kind in Europe. Some very fine mature trees, Victorian walled gardens, lots of rhododendrons, lakes, and a big collection of tree ferns, bamboos, palms and nursery. It's a friendly place, and they're more than happy to talk about their work. Readers rate it very highly. Meals, snacks, shop,

partly disabled access; (01726) 844157; cl 25 Dec; *£2.80. The Llawnroc Inn at Gorran Haven is handy for lunch. WORLD OF RAILWAYS (Meadow St) Over 2,000 model trains trundling through a realistic little world that takes in Cornish china-clay pits, ski resorts, fairgrounds, towns and country. Shop, some disabled access, no parking; cl Oct–May exc Easter; £2.25. FOLK MUSEUM (East Quay) 18th-c boat-builder's shed with fishing equipment and china-clay industry displays. Small shop, disabled access ground floor only; cl am Sun and Oct–Easter; 30p.

★ **Polperro** SX2051 is almost unbelievably pretty – tiny streets around a very quaint, sheltered fishing harbour and little cottages perched on rocks. Once a busy smuggling place, it now has some quite decent craft shops tucked away and one or two tourist attractions, inc oddities like the shell-encrusted Shell House; the Blue Peter and Three Pilchards are unspoilt harbourside locals. Very busy in summer.

★ **Portscatho** SW8735, very sheltered, has a picturesque little harbour, lovely clifftop walks, and some fine nearby beaches – excellent for families. The Plume of Feathers is popular for lunch.

✿ ♨ † **Probus** SW8947 TREWITHEN (A390 between Probus and Grampound) Justly famous landscaped gardens, with many rare trees and shrubs and nurseries. The early 18th-c house is often a little unfairly overshadowed by what's outside, and is an interesting, obviously lived-in family home. Snacks, rare plants for sale, disabled access; house open pm Mon and Tues Apr–July and Aug bank hol Mon, gardens open Mar–Sept, cl Sun; (01726) 882763; house £2.80, gardens £2 July–Sept, £2.20 Mar–Jun. The nearby PROBUS GARDENS are quite interesting, on a much humbler scale: how to choose the right plants/layout for your individual garden, propagation displays, herb, vegetable and fruit trials, historical plant collection, some outside sculpture. Probably best between Jun and Sept, but good for ideas at any time of the year. Snacks, shop, disabled access; cl winter wknds, 25–26 Dec; (01726) 882597; *£2.35. The CHURCH has the tallest tower in Cornwall, but is not special inside. The Hawkins Arms is useful for lunch.

⛨ Restormel SX1060 CASTLE Very well preserved, dating from the 13th c, with fine views over Fowey Valley, and a notable round keep. Snacks, shop; cl winter Mon, 24–26 Dec, 1 Jan and some other winter dates, best to phone first (01208) 872687; £1.25. The Royal Oak in Lostwithiel is good for lunch.

✝ ⛴ ❀ ▦ St Austell SX0252 is the centre of the china-clay industry and a busy modern shopping town; its Holy Trinity CHURCH has a fine tower and interesting font. The area N is a strange bleak moonscape of whitish spoil heaps with metallic blue lakes dotted among them. Up here off the A391 (so you don't have to go into the town) is the WHEAL MARTYN MUSEUM, an interestingly restored 19th-c clayworks showing the 200-year history of china-clay production; working waterwheels and other equipment, horse-drawn waggons, steam locomotives, working pottery, audio-visual show, nature trails with a spectacular viewpoint over a huge clay pit, and children's adventure trail. Snacks, shop; cl Nov–Mar; (01726) 850362; £3.90. AUTOMOBILIA (about 4 miles W of town) Over 50 cars, motorcycles and other vehicles from 1904 to the 1960s, inc a vintage Bentley, Rolls-Royce and Aston Martin, with a permanent auto-jumble that vintage-car owners may find useful. Snacks, shop, disabled access; cl Nov–Mar; (01726) 823092; *£3.

✝ St Germans SX3557 CHURCH has a wonderful Norman doorway and a particularly fine east window; worth a look if you're passing this waterside village. There's a good view towards Port Eliot, a stately home designed by John Soane (not open).

✝ St Just-in-Roseland SW8435 CHURCH is in an idyllic creekside spot and its steep graveyard is like a lost subtropical garden – well worth a visit on a quiet sunny day, or in spring, with the baby rooks blethering and the smell of wild garlic. The words on the inscribed stones by the path seem quite fitting.

⚓ ⛨ St Mawes SW8433 has very pretty harbourside and estuary views, a long waterfront to stroll along, a foot-passenger ferry to Falmouth and other boat trips (full of yachtsmen and others in summer, lots of guesthouses). The 16th-c FORTRESS is blessed with a trouble-free history, and so remarkably well preserved. Shop, some disabled access – check first; cl Mon and Tues in winter, 24–26 Dec, 1 Jan; (01326) 270526; £1.35. The Idle Rocks and Rising Sun are useful for lunch.

🏰 ❀ Torpoint SX4355 ANTONY HOUSE The finest classical house in Cornwall, little changed since the early 18th c, with interesting contents and paintings in its panelled rooms; also older stables and outhouses, riverside gardens redesigned by Humphrey Repton, and a dovecot. Snacks, shop, disabled access to ground floor only; open pm Tues–Thurs Apr–Oct, as well as Sun Jun–Aug, and bank hols; £3.40; NT. MOUNT EDGCUMBE out here is rated very highly by readers, a mansion reconstructed after WWII bombing, with period furniture and (the main attraction) acres of lovely gardens and parkland. Snacks, shop, disabled access; house cl winter (but park and gardens open then, free); (01752) 822236; £3.

🐾 Trecangate SX1757 PORFELL ANIMAL LAND Unspoilt and friendly place with deer, wallabies, goats, ducks and chickens among 15 acres of sloping fields and woodland. New enclosures for raccoons and coati. Snacks, shop, disabled access; cl Nov–Easter; (01503) 220211; *£3. The Ship over at Lerryn is fairly handy for lunch; the stepping stones over the river there are a hit with children.

★ Attractive inland villages with decent pubs include St Ewe SW9746 and Veryan SW9139 (famous for its five devil-proof thatched round houses; also a watergarden sheltered by holm oaks).

✝ Other interesting churches include Braddock SX1662 (wood carvings), Golant SX1155 (complete 15th-c fittings; waterside village), Lansallos SX1751 (carved bench ends) and Lanteglos Highway SX1543 (Perpendicular but not – subsidence has left the arches at drunken angles).

Walks

The best walks here are along the coastal cliffs, much of the land owned by the NT. **St Anthony Head** SW8431 ⌂-1 on the E side of the Fal estuary has superb views, and easy walks along low, level cliffs; parking at the head itself, SW8431, or near Porth Farm on the way down). Virtually the whole of **Gerrans Bay** SW8937 ⌂-2 is good easy walking, from Portscatho SW8735 or Pendower Beach SW8938 (a good sandy stretch). **Portloe** SW9339 ⌂-3 has more rugged scenery, with stiffish climbs on to Nare Head SW9137. **Dodman Point** SX0039 ⌂-4 (reached from Gorran Haven SX0141, or one of the closer car parks – for instance, at Hemmick Beach) lends itself to a round walk with three-quarters of the route being along cliff-tops.

From **Fowey** SX1251 ⌂-5 a popular circular route is one where you go across on the Bodinnick car ferry, take the path through the steep creekside woods round to Polruan SX1251, and come back on the other foot ferry. **Talland Bay** SX2251 ⌂-6 provides an easy one-mile walk along the coast to enter Polperro's harbour (SX2051) the best way – a sensible alternative to sweating out summer traffic jams in Polperro village itself. **Rame Head** SX4148 ⌂-7 at the E end of Whitsand Bay juts far out and is capped by a primitive hermitage chapel – a worthwhile walk from the pretty village of Kingsand SX4350. Close by is the **Mount Edgecumbe Country Park** SX4552 ⌂-8, with woodland and parkland walks and some striking waterside views of Plymouth SX4475.

Inland, from **Luxulyan** SX0558 ⌂-9 (which has a pleasant church) you can walk along the lush wooded valley to the S, strewn with huge granite boulders and crossed by an impressive viaduct; if you feel adventurous you can climb up the valley to the top of the viaduct. Though the **Tamar Valley** ⌂-10 is short on good circular walks, there are woodland paths close by Cotehele SX4268.

The rock at **Roche** SW9860 ⌂-11 is worth the short walk from the B3274, with a 14th-c, ruined ivy-covered chapel built into it, and a ladder up (decent pub nearby off past the station).

Driving

Most roads here twist so much that what looks a short distance on the map works out much longer in practice. Overtaking is rarely feasible, and unclassified roads are often single-track, which slows things down even more – you have to keep backing up to a passing place.

In spring and early summer, the tall, roadside hedged banks which block the view from many byroads compensate by being virtual walls of wild flowers.

In this part of Cornwall, getting up on to the A30 is generally a quicker, even if longer, way of driving any distance than trying to wriggle about cross-country. The A390 is much slower.

An unusually good unclassified road in this area is the one running almost due S from off the A39 just SW of Indian Queens, down through Grampound Road, past the back entrance to Trewithen, and on to Tregony.

The B3279 from St Stephen to Nanpean gives some of the best views over the strange china-clay moonscape.

The narrow lanes from St Blazey (off the A390 SW of Lostwithiel), along the Luxulyan Valley past Luxulyan and then north towards Lanivet take you through a former granite-producing area and past Helman Tor – there's a short path to this fine, signposted viewpoint.

The King Harry chain-drawn car ferry, on the B3269 N of St Mawes, is a quaint way from this area through to Mid-Cornwall – a favourite family crossing.

Where to eat

Several of the hotels and inns recommended in the **Where to stay** section are also good for diners eating out – see beginning of this chapter.

Fowey SX1252 FOOD FOR THOUGHT Town Quay (0172 683) 2221 Generous helpings of carefully presented food in quayside evening restaurant – fine fish and some simple as well as other more elaborate dishes, lovely puddings; cl Sun, Jan, Feb; children over 10. £27.

Polperro SX2051 KITCHEN The Coombes (01503) 72780 Cottagey, informal evening restaurant with interesting food inc vegetarian and fresh fish – local lobster and crab are especially wonderful; cl Sun, Mon; children over 10. £20.

Portloe SW9339 TREGAIN TEA ROOMS Small restaurant serving interesting, well cooked food and specialising in local fish (lovely crab) and locally produced smoked fish, pasties, cider and ice-creams; 2 bedrooms; cl pm Sun. £20l£2/£4.

MID-CORNWALL

Good mix of coastal scenery, comfortable places to stay, very enjoyable walks, great gardens and other interesting attractions.

The lush almost subtropical gardens at Trelissick and Mawnan Smith, spectacular in spring, are rewarding at any time. Flambards leisure park near Helston is one of Britain's best family attractions, and the Poldark Mine Centre at Wendron is well thought out. Goonhilly, a new addition to the guide, makes for an unusual visit. The eastern part of the coastline is intricately cut into estuaries and hidden creeks, rich in bird life, with some beautifully placed pubs – good for leisurely exploration by car, better on foot, best of all for pottering about in a boat. Further west are some fine, long sandy beaches. Walking can be very enjoyable, with some memorable highlights. Falmouth, with its huge harbour, is a sizeable town with a great deal of appeal to visitors.

Inland, the defunct mining industry has left central Cornwall with a surprising industrial face: the linked towns of Redruth, Pool and St Agnes are reminiscent of some towns in the industrial north.

There's a good choice of places to stay on or near the south coast.

Where to stay

Mullion SW6719 POLURRIAN Mullion, Helston TR12 7EN (01326) 240421 £132 inc dinner; 39 rms, some with memorable sea view. White, clifftop hotel with path down to a sheltered, private cove below; civilised modern comfort, good breakfasts, leisure club with heated swimming pool, and heated outdoor pool, badminton, tennis, mini-golf, squash and croquet; good with children; cl Nov, Jan–Feb; disabled access.

Mawnan Smith SW7728 MEUDON Mawnan Smith, Falmouth TR11 5HT (01326) 250541 £130; 32 well equipped, comfortable rms in separate wing. Family-run, old stone mansion with newer wing in a beautiful subtropical garden laid out by Capability Brown; fine views from the dining room, carefully refurbished lounge with log fire, and helpful, friendly service; free golf at Falmouth (those on weekend breaks pay £12 per round); cl Jan–Feb; children over 5; dogs by arrangement (not in public rooms); limited disabled access.

Mawnan Smith SW7728 NANSIDWELL COUNTRY HOUSE Mawnan Smith, Falmouth TR11 5HU (01326) 250340 £90; 12 individually decorated rms. Comfortable, creeper-covered granite house in wonderful woodland garden, with sea views and direct access to a good beach; comfortably elegant rooms with log fires, fresh flowers, books, and fine food inc home-grown produce, home-made jams and breads in the excellent restaurant; hard-working, enthusiastic owners; popular with older people; many gardens to visit nearby; cl Jan; children over 7 in restaurant in evening (though they do high tea); disabled access.

Mithian SW7450 ROSE-IN-VALE COUNTRY HOUSE Mithian, St Agnes TR5 0QD (01872) 552202 £67.50; 17 rms. Secluded and quietly set Georgian house with 2 acres of neatly kept gardens, outdoor swimming pool, badminton and croquet; undergoing careful major refurbishment and the introduction of a more adventurous menu; very relaxed friendly atmosphere, and helpful, local service; good with children; disabled access.

Gillan SW6527 TREGILDRY Gillan, Helston TR12 6HG (01326) 231378 *£63; 10 good rms with fine views over Falmouth Bay. Quiet and comfortable, family-run hotel in four acres of grounds with private access to the cove below; local fish dishes, and helpful service; cl Nov–Feb.

Lizard SW7712 HOUSEL BAY Housel Cove, The Lizard, Helston TR12 7PG (01326) 290417 £60; 23 rms, many with sea views. Clifftop hotel with marvellous views and path down to a sandy beach; plush lounges, thatched bar, and friendly owners; cl Jan–early Feb.

Treleigh SW7043 INN FOR ALL SEASONS Treleigh, Redruth TR16 4AP (01209) 219511 £50; 12 rms. Spacious, stylishly modern inn with restful atmosphere, carefully chosen muted colours in comfortable lounge, good, interesting food, and helpful service.

Gunwalloe SW6522 HALZEPHRON Gunwalloe, Helston TR12 7QB (01326) 240406 £50; 2 cosy rms. 500-year-old ex-smugglers inn run by knowledgeable and friendly Cornish couple, good food in bar areas and bistro-style restaurant, open fire, and fine views of Mount's Bay; lots of walks, nearby beaches, golf and boating; cl 24–28 Dec; children over 12.

To see and do

† **Carharrack** CHURCH SW7341 has an exhibition on Cornish Methodism and John Wesley, who preached at the chapel that used to stand here. Disabled access; open am Mon–Thurs during school terms and other times by appointment; (01209) 820381; free. Wesley preached more regularly at nearby Gwennap SW7440, where GWENNAP PIT, the amphitheatre he used, still has services (2.30 summer Sun), and there's also a visitor centre with exhibitions. Centre cl 12–2, pm Sat, all Sun; free. The peaceful theatre itself is open all the time. The Fox & Hounds at Lanner is useful for lunch.

🏠 **Come-to-Good** SW8140 QUAKER MEETING HOUSE Lovely, thatched, green-shuttered building of 1710, timeless simplicity inside.

★ ⚓ 🔭 ❀ **Falmouth** SW8032, the county's biggest town, is worth a morning or afternoon visit. It has a huge natural harbour full of sailing boats of every description – big sea-going ships, passenger ferries (to St Mawes and Truro – great fun) and boat trips; it's also a busy but pleasant shopping centre with some nice old-fashioned streets, ships' chandlers and a good bustling atmosphere, though surprisingly few sea views. The spiky-leaved dracaena trees away from the centre give it a quite foreign feel. PENDENNIS CASTLE One of Henry VIII's chain of coastal defences, with later 16th-c fortifications and superb views. Summer snacks, shop, disabled access to lower gun deck, shop and coffee shop; cl 24–26 Dec, 1 Jan; (01326) 316954; *£2.10. A MARITIME MUSEUM opposite Marks & Spencer has a big exhibition of packet ships and is densely packed with local history; it has a steam tug open to the public down in the little inner harbour. The Quayside,

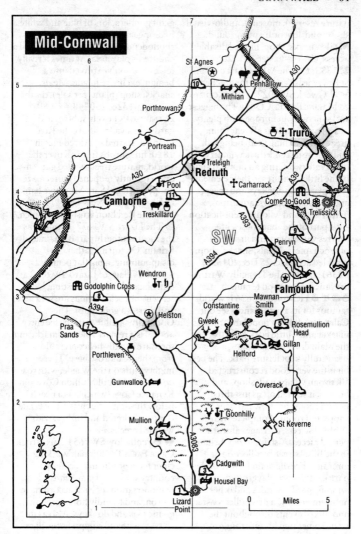

Mid-Cornwall

and Seahorse on Maenporth Beach, both waterside, are useful for lunch.

Godolphin Cross SW6031
GODOLPHIN HOUSE 15th-c house of the Earls of Godolphin, well known for its colonnaded front, and the painting of one of the three Arab stallion ancestors of all British bloodstock. In the stables is an exhibition of old maps and documents, as well as a number of old farm waggons. Teas, shop (plants and herbs for sale), disabled access to ground floor and garden only; open pm Thurs

May–Sept (all day in Aug), as well as pm Tues July–Sept and bank hols; (01736) 762409; £3.

Goonhilly Downs SW7221
SATELLITE EARTH STATION A refreshing change from Cornwall's multitude of leisure parks, a fascinating look at one of the planet's foremost telecommunications centres. The vast aerials rising out of the heath are an awesome sight, and the visitor centre gives you a chance to operate one of the tracking dishes yourself. Also a bus tour round the site (which is a

nature reserve), museum, audio-visual show, and adventure playground. Meals, snacks, shop, limited disabled access; cl Nov–Easter; (01326) 221333; £3. The White Hart over at St Keverne is very good for lunch.

✛ ✒ **Gweek** SW7027 SEAL SANCTUARY & MARINE RESCUE CENTRE The biggest seal sanctuary in Europe with plenty of seals and sealions all year round; great fun watching them being fed, and they've just added a new underwater observatory offering an unusual view of the little creatures in their element. Also penguins, donkeys and sheep, audio-visual displays, aquarium, nature trail and wildlife identification – it's part of the chain of sea life centres we recommend in several other chapters. Meals, snacks, shop, disabled access; cl 25 Dec; (01326) 22361; £4.25. The Trengilly Wartha at Nancenoy is good for lunch.

♨☺✝❀ **Helston** SW6626 is world-famous for its Furry Dance (see our **Calendar**). It has a popular Saturday market and a little FOLK MUSEUM, but the main draw is FLAMBARDS, a beautifully kept leisure park. The best bit is the very good reconstructed Victorian village with shops and houses; it started off as just three period rooms but now has over 50 shops and rooms, complete with cobbled streets, carriages and other period pieces. Also life-sized 'Britain in the Blitz' street, a collection of aircraft (once the main feature of the park), adventure playground, award-winning gardens, rides and other amusements (inc a new rollercoaster), and lots of events throughout the year. Something for most age groups, and rather better than the average theme park – you could easily spend most of a day here. Meals, snacks, shop, disabled access; cl Nov–Easter; (01326) 564093; *£7.95. The simple Blue Anchor pub has a 15th-c working brewhouse which you can usually look around at lunchtime.

❀ **Mawnan Smith** SW7727 TREBAH GARDEN This steeply wooded ravine garden, widely reckoned to be one of the finest in the world, falls from the 18th-c house down to a peaceful private beach on the River Helford; huge subtropical tree ferns and palms, giant gunnera, lots of blue and white hydrangeas, 100-year-old rhododendrons, some fine trees, and a children's play area. At times it really looks like you've strayed into a benign, exclusive jungle. Meals, snacks, shop (plants for sale), disabled access; (01326) 250448; *£2.80.

GLENDURGAN Lovely subtropical garden in a valley above the River Helford, started by Alfred Fox in 1820; fine shrubs from all over the world, mature trees, walled garden and a recently reopened laurel maze. Shop, snacks; cl Sun, Mon (exc bank hols), Good Fri, Nov–Feb; *£2.60; NT. The Red Lion is useful for lunch.

❀ **The Lizard** SW1177 is famous as the most southerly part of mainland Britain. On top it's rather disappointing, a big flat peninsula, with the village of Lizard SW7012 a dull place (though interesting, local serpentine rock carvings are sold here, and there's a good pub). The Goonhilly satellite station (see entry above) is a remarkable landmark, and there are usually helicopters aloft from their Culdrose base. There are mighty cliffs on the W side, with roads down to beautiful Mullion Cove and Kynance Cove (which has a beach below the dramatic cliffs). The E side is more sheltered and lusher, with wooded creeks.

🐄♨ **Penhallow** SW7651 CALLESTOCK CIDER FARM Traditional, working cider farm producing scrumpy, country wines and jam, with demonstrations of each according to season, and friendly horses, rabbits, goats, pigs and donkeys. Also a CIDER MUSEUM with old equipment such as ancient presses, and hives of the bees needed for pollination. Summer snacks, shop (with samples of everything they make); cl Sun (exc shop 12-3 pm), Sat Nov–Dec, and all Jan–Easter; (01872) 573356; free, small charge for museum, which also includes a tractor ride.

⬇ **Pool** SW6641 CORNISH ENGINES Two big beam engines originally used for pumping water from tin and copper mines, and also for lifting this former mining settlement's men and ore from 1,700 ft below ground. Shop; cl Nov–Mar; *£2.20; NT.

♉**Porthleven** SW6225 SHIPWRECK CENTRE MUSEUM Aptly sited on the rocks that brought so many sailors to their doom, a good collection of objects salvaged from wrecked ships, as well as a history of the harbour and the local lifeboat. Shop; cl Nov–Easter; (01326) 565724; £1.20. The prettily placed Ship is good for lunch.

★ ♣☺! **St Agnes** SW7150 is a former mining town, now with a holiday role; some attractive, steeply terraced cottages, and fine cliff scenery nearby. PRESINGOLL BARNS (Penwinnick Rd) New craft centre with demonstrations of pottery, candle and fudge-making, good picnic areas; (01872) 553007; free, small charge for pottery tuition. ST AGNES LEISURE PARK Mature landscaped gardens with well known Cornish buildings in miniature, dinosaur replicas, an animated circus and haunted house and fairyland; floodlit at night. Meals, snacks, shop, disabled access; cl Nov–Mar; £4.10. The Railway is an interesting pub for lunch.

❀❋ **Trelissick** SW8339 TRELISSICK GARDEN Woodland park with beautifully kept gardens of camellias, magnolias and hydrangeas, also a subtropical garden and other unusual plants; wonderful views of the King Harry Passage and over to Pendennis Castle. Meals, snacks, shop, disabled access; cl am Sun, garden cl Nov–Mar, but park, shop, gallery, restaurant open until 22 Dec; £3; NT. The Punch Bowl & Ladle at Penelewey is good for lunch.

🐂♉**Treskillard** SW6739 SHIRE HORSE FARM & CARRIAGE MUSEUM (Lower Gryllis Farm) The horses here aren't just for show, they still work the land; also working blacksmith's and wheelwright's shops and a good display of horse-drawn models, farm implements and carriages. Snacks, shop, disabled access; cl Sat and Nov–Whitsun; £2.75.

♉✝ **Truro** SW8244 is a busy town with good shops (market day Weds); Lemon St is a particularly fine Georgian street, and Boscawen St is cobbled. ROYAL CORNWALL MUSEUM (River St) Comprehensive coverage of Cornish history inc tales of local characters like Black John of Tetcott, an 18th-c dwarf whose favourite trick was apparently tying mice together by their tails, swallowing them and pulling them up again. Also a notable assemblage of minerals, new Egyptian gallery and some fine paintings and drawings. Meals, snacks, shop, disabled access; cl Sun, bank hols, 25–26 Dec, 1 Jan; (01872) 72205; *£1. The CATHEDRAL is one of the newer Anglican ones, designed in 1880 in Early English style and finished in 1910; the twin spires of the west front are handsome, and pop up dramatically from behind shops and houses. The Wig & Pen, Globe and William IV are all good for lunch.

⬇↑ **Wendron** SW6731 POLDARK MINE AND HERITAGE CENTRE A fun feature of this old tin mine is its underground post box, the deepest in Britain – a popular box to send postcards from. More serious attractions include a tour of the mine (longer this year), an 18th-c village, a film on the history of Cornish mining, old cottages, big collection of working beam engines and other antiquities, and plenty of children's amusements. Varied enough to interest widely differing age groups. Meals, snacks, shop; cl Nov–Easter; (01326) 563166; £5.25.

★ **Attractive coastal villages** with decent pubs include Cadgwith SW7214 (fish stores, thatched cottages, pretty cove), Coverack SW7818 (good walks and view of The Manacle rocks), Mullion SW6719 (carved into a fiercely craggy coast), Penryn SW7834 (pretty houses dropping down to the river), Porthtowan SW6948, Portreath SW6545, and St Keverne SW7821. Constantine SW7229 is an attractive inland village with a good pub.

Waterside pubs in delightful settings include the Royal Standard at Flushing SW8033, Pandora on Restronguet Creek past Mylor Bridge (SW8036; the best location of any Cornish pub – you can park in Mylor Bridge for a leisurely two-mile waterside walk there and back, or drive all the way), Shipwright's Arms at Helford SW7526 ('Frenchman's Creek' walk from here), Ferryboat at Helford Passage SW7627, Heron at Malpas SW8442 and New Inn at Manaccan SW7625.

Walks

The most southerly point in England, **Lizard Point** SW1177 ⌂-1 (in itself not that special) is a good start for bracing cliff walks in either direction, with good views. Lizard village SW7012 (even less special) is well placed for longer walks encompassing Church Cove to the E and Kynance Cove to the W. Inland, the Lizard is largely flat and not really worth extended walks. Dramatic **Mullion Cove** SW6617 ⌂-2 is best reached by a there-and-back walk along the cliff from Porth Mellin SW6618; the extension S to Kynance Cove is outstanding. A rewarding short stroll on the coastal path from picturesque **Cadgwith** SW7114 ⌂-3 leads S to Chynhalls Point SW7817, past the aptly named Devil's Frying Pan, where the waves foam into a spectacular collapsed cavern. The NE part of the Lizard around **Helford** SW7526 and **Dennis Head** SW7825 ⌂-4 is appreciably leafier, and has some intricate coves and an undemanding coastal path.

At **Rosemullion Head** SW7927 ⌂-5 (from Mawnan SW7827, or Maenporth SW7929), there's a sheltered sandy cove with a decent modern pub/restaurant). From **Coverack** SW7818 ⌂-6 you can walk S to **Black Head** SW7716 and maybe beyond, and NE to **Lowland Point** SW8019 (also reached from Porthoustock SW8021 or St Keverne), for dramatic views of The Manacles. At **Rinsey** SW5927 ⌂-7, the coastal path passes two magnificently sited, ruined tin and copper mine buildings – Wheal Prosper and Wheal Trewavas – both now maintained as landmarks by the NT. A few miles inland, **Tregonning Hill** SW6029, ⌂-8 although it takes only a few minutes to climb, has an impressive view; here in 1746 William Cookworthy made the first discovery of china clay in England, and went on to make porcelain. A pleasant short walk with a good finish is the stroll round from **Mylor Bridge** SW8036 ⌂-9 to the pub at Restronguet Passage.

Almost any stretch of the **coast path** in the north gives long, bracing, clifftop walks (a good base is Portreath SW6545, which has a decent pub); **Wheal Coates** SW6949 ⌂-10 is one of the most photogenic mine ruins on the Cornish coast, and the diversion up St Agnes Beacon SW7150 is well worth it for the commanding views.

A good inland viewpoint is Carn Brea SW6840 ⌂-11.

There's a particularly fine beach at Kynance Cove on the Lizard peninsula; it's a long walk down from the car park but well worth it – strange rock formations, caves and sandy coves (lovely views from the cliff walk S). Praa Sands SW5727 is a popular family beach, and the long stretch of rocky beach S of Porthleven SW6225 (good pubs in the village) is a pleasant walk if the surf's not beating in too fiercely.

Driving

The B3293 S from Helston and the A3083 down to the Lizard, and the byroad that runs between them across Goonhilly Downs, are unusual for the area in being relatively straight and high, giving quite distant views. Otherwise, roads near the coast tend to give few decent views – though in spring the massive banks and hedges that shut you in are delightfully colourful. In the north, there are some sea views from the B3301. The A39 between Falmouth and Truro can be tiresomely slow at almost any time of year.

A mighty inland viewpoint is Carn Brea, above the industrial towns of Redruth and Camborne; a strange mock-medieval castle near the moorland summit is a restaurant/tearoom now; turn off the byroad S of Redruth at Carnkie.

Where to eat

Helford SW7526 RIVERSIDE (01326) 231443 Cosy, creekside evening restaurant with carefully kept garden and terrace for aperitifs and meals; daily changing, carefully cooked imaginative food with an emphasis on fish and shellfish; cl Nov–Mar; disabled access. £28/£8.

St Keverne SW7921 WHITE HART (01326) 280325 Friendly pub with a fine choice of fresh fish chalked up on a board – lovely scallops and delicious crab salad; chatty atmosphere, pleasant furnishings. £16|£2/£7.

Mithian SW7450 MINERS ARMS (0187 255) 2375 Secluded Tudor pub with lots of character, fine old furnishings, reliable good food and real ale; disabled access. £12|£2.75/£5.25.

WEST CORNWALL

Decidedly different and remote, with some wild coast, fine bracing walks and a good choice of places to stay.

West Cornwall's strongest appeal is to people who love the outdoors. Though in winter it's milder than most places, with violets out along the cliffs even in January, at any time of year the winds can be fierce. The landscape is austere: wild coastline with challenging clifftop walks and some magnificent scenery, small rather withdrawn-looking granite villages and farmsteads, wind-beaten pastures. Past the age of seven or so, children appreciate and enjoy the wildness, but there are fewer paid-for family outings here than in other parts of Cornwall: among them the fairy-tale castle on St Michael's Mount is well worth the visit from Marazion, and Paradise Park at Hayle is popular, while Trengwainton Garden at Madron is excellent for quieter tastes. No first-time visit to this part of Cornwall would be complete without a look at St Ives. There is a very visible abundance of prehistoric remains, in addition to the remarkable prehistoric villages near Madron and Sancreed.

The area does have a noticeably separatist sense of its own identity, almost like the more nationalistic parts of Wales; but though visitors are clearly seen as outsiders, the locals are far from unfriendly.

Where to stay

St Ives SW5140 GARRACK Burthallon Lane, St Ives TR26 3AA (01736) 796199 £96; 18 rms, some in more modern wing. Friendly hotel in two acres of gardens, with wonderful sea views; cosy lounges with books and open fires, family room, restaurant serving good food inc fresh shellfish, helpful staff, and indoor leisure centre; no children under 4 in evening dining room; disabled access.

Penzance SW4730 ABBEY HOTEL Abbey St, Penzance TR18 4AR (01736) 66906 *£85; 7 charming rms. Stylish little 17th-c house, close to the harbour, with marvellous views; relaxed atmosphere in the comfortable drawing room full of flowers, fine paintings and antiques, pretty garden, and good set menu in the small restaurant; cl 3 dys over Christmas; children over 2.

Newlyn SW4628 HIGHER FAUGAN Newlyn, Penzance TR18 5NS (01736) 62076 £76; 12 rms. Country house in 10 acres of quiet gardens and grounds, with outdoor swimming pool, tennis, and putting green; pleasantly old-fashioned sitting room, helpful owners, and good home-made food using local fish and veg; disabled access.

Sennen SW3425 LAND'S END HOTEL Sennen, Land's End, Penzance TR19 7AA (01736) 871844 £75; 34 elegant airy rms, many with splendid sea views.

Comfortable, refurbished hotel right on the clifftop, with fine views; good food in pretty conservatory-style restaurant, informal bar with lots of malt whiskies, and helpful staff; disabled access.

St Ives SW5140 SKIDDEN HOUSE Skidden Hill, St Ives TR26 2DU (01736) 796899 £66; 7 rms. Small, 16th-c, warmly welcoming hotel nr the beach; carefully cooked food in the cosy dining room, comfortable lounge and bar; dogs welcome by prior arrangement; cl part Nov/Dec; disabled access.

Carbis Bay SW5239 HOWARDS St Ives Rd, Carbis Bay, St Ives TR26 2SB (01736) 795651 £58; 26 rms, some with shared bthrm. Neatly kept modernised hotel with sea views, heated swimming pool, cheerful lounge and dining room, and good food.

Lamorna Cove SW4524 LAMORNA COVE Lamorna Cove, Penzance TR19 6XH (01736) 731411 £52; 15 well furnished rms, most with cove views. Comfortable, beautifully situated hotel overlooking gardens to the sea; with homely rooms, light airy restaurant using fresh local food (especially seafood), very good, attentive service, and outdoor heated swimming pool; marvellous walks; cl Jan–2nd wk Feb.

Sennen SW3425 OLD SUCCESS Sennen, Penzance TR19 7DG (01736) 871232 *£50; 12 light and airy rms, a few with shared bthrm. Magnificent views from friendly, modernised, old fisherman's inn with attractive bar, comfortable lounge, and popular food in neat dining room; small, well behaved dogs welcome.

St Ives SW5140 KANDAHAR 11 The Warren, St Ives TR26 2EA (01736) 796183 *£40; 5 rms, some with shared bthrm. B & B in a house overlooking the harbour and up the coast to Newquay; comfortable old-fashioned lounge and good breakfasts; cl Christmas and New Year.

Pendeen SW3834 TREWELLARD MANOR FARM Pendeen, Penzance TR19 7SU (01736) 788526 *£36; 3 rms, 1 without bthrm. Victorian house in lovely coastal spot with log fire in lounge, outdoor summer swimming pool, and fine walks all round; cl Christmas.

Buryas Bridge SW4429 ROSE FARM Buryas Bridge, Penzance TR19 6AN (01736) 731808 £35; 3 delightfully furnished rms. Relaxed, informal, friendly farmhouse tucked away down a remote country lane; excellent breakfasts around a big wooden table; can see animals (working farm); children love it; cl 25–26 Dec.

Botallack SW3633 MANOR FARM Botallack, St Just-in-Penwith, Penzance TR19 7QG (01736) 788525 £34; 3 rms. Blissfully quiet and friendly, 17th-c, local granite farmhouse on a working farm, with medley of furnishings in the comfortable lounge; good breakfasts with home-baked bread, and safe walled garden; no pets; marvellous walks along cliffs, lots of ruined mines, and small coves.

To see and do

✦ ❀ ❦ 🐄 🐾☺ **Hayle** SW5537 PARADISE PARK Exotic and endangered bird species from all over the world, from humming birds to eagles, with successful breeding, too. The Victorian gardens also house the Cornish Otter Sanctuary, the World Parrot Trust, a lively falconry display, rare farm animals, miniature railway and amusement centre. Lively, enjoyable, and good for children, who can claim a free badge by completing a wildlife quiz sheet. Meals, snacks (they brew their own ales), shop, disabled access; (01736) 753365; £4.95.

🐾 **Lamorna** SW4424 The cove is pretty, with good walks along the coastal path. LAMORNA POTTERY In school hols children can try their hands at the wheel here, and the rest of the time, as well as the pottery, there's a boutique selling locally made clothes and jewellery and a garden with acclaimed cream teas. Meals, snacks, shop, disabled access; cl Nov–Feb; free. The Lamorna Wink is useful for lunch.

❀ ☺ ♫ **Land's End** SW3425 The most westerly point of England, with wild and blustery walks along dramatic clifftops, and on a clear day, views out as far as the Scilly Isles. You may not be able to stand and contemplate it on

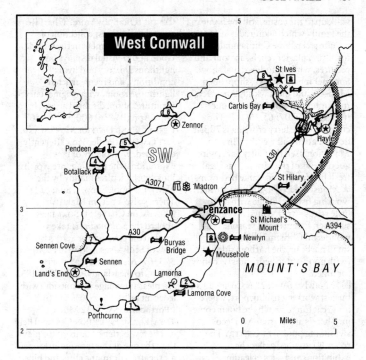

West Cornwall

St Ives

Carbis Bay

Hayle

Zennor

SW

Pendeen

Botallack

A3071   Madron

Penzance

St Hilary

A30

St Michael's Mount

A394

Newlyn

Sennen Cove

A30   Buryas Bridge

Mousehole

MOUNT'S BAY

Sennen

Land's End   Lamorna

Porthcurno   Lamorna Cove

0   Miles   5

your own – the 200-acre site has been extensively developed for families in the last few years, and it's become almost like a theme park, with 'multi-sensory experiences', gift shops, craft centres, farm animals and burger bars. Don't let this put you off – the lively EXHIBITIONS and hi-tech displays are done with some panache, and give useful introductions to the history and folklore of the area. Lots for the whole family, and as it's so big, you can usually find relatively peaceful spots away from the crowds. An RSPB observation hide has information on the coastline's wildlife. Meals, snacks, neat shopping arcade, good disabled access; cl 25 Dec; (01736) 871812; *£5.50.

✿ **Madron** SW4532 TRENGWAINTON GARDEN The name in Cornish means 'Farm of the Spring' and it does always seems to be spring at this lovely place, the favourable climate allowing the growth of plants that are not usually found outdoors in England. Magnolias, azaleas, rhododendrons, walled gardens, lovely tree-fern grotto, and good

views to Mounts Bay. Snacks, shop; cl Mon, Tues, Sun, Nov–Feb; cream teas, disabled access, interesting plant sales; £2.50; NT.

🏛 **nr Madron** SW4734 CHYSAUSTER ANCIENT VILLAGE You can get a good impression of village life 2,000 years ago at these remains of eight courtyard houses (the oldest identifiable street in the country), with little terraced gardens, wall-bases of workshops and stables, and even the remains of sleeping benches. On a windy hillside overlooking the coast, the site is also notable for its large untreated meadow, popular with wild birds and, depending on the season, bright with bluebells, heather or unusual orchids. Shop; cl Nov–Mar; (01736) 61889; *£1.35.

🏰 **Marazion** SW5130 ST MICHAEL'S MOUNT There's something particularly awe-inspiring about this medieval castle, rising up majestically from the sea. On gloomy or stormy days the picturesque silhouette seems even more dramatic. The little island is reached by ferry or by foot along a causeway at low tide; once there, the walk up to the castle, still the home of the family which acquired it in 1660, is quite steep. Fine Chippendale furniture, plaster reliefs, armour and pictures, with an audio-visual show. Summer meals, snacks, shop; open Mon–Fri and most wknds Apr–Oct; for winter opening best to phone (01736) 710507; £3.20; NT. The charge for the ferry crossing is 70p; it doesn't go in bad weather. In Marazion itself the Cutty Sark, with good views of the Mount, has local fresh fish (and good-value bedrooms).

★ **Mousehole** SW4726 is an attractive working fishing village with steep little roads – very visited in high summer, lovely out of season; wonderful Christmas lights in the small harbour; the harbourside Ship (with good-value bedrooms) is handy for lunch.

▣ ❋ **Newlyn** SW4628 is Cornwall's busiest working fishing port, where it's great fun to watch the boats come in. There's an unusual Art Deco swimming pool. ART GALLERY The recently extended gallery has exhibitions and sales of leading, contemporary local, national and international art; various special events and lectures. It's in a lovely coastal setting with fine views. Shop, disabled access; cl Sun; (01736) 63715; free. At Christmas, the fishermen decorate the harbour and its boats with spectacular lights. The Dolphin (towards Penzance SW4730) is useful for lunch.

↓т **Pendeen** SW3834 LEVANT MINE An unusual mine beneath the sea, powered by the oldest steam engine in Cornwall. It stopped working in 1930, but is operating for visitors after a vigorous restoration campaign. Shop, disabled access (but no facilities); open Sun–Fri July–Sept, and Fri Jan–Jun; £2; NT. The nearby Pendeen Watch lighthouse is worth a look, and the Radjel is good for lunch.

🎪🐎▣❋⚓ **Penzance** SW4730 is a nice, relaxed town by the sea, and a major shopping centre for the area. The prettiest part is Chapel St, where the extravagantly designed, early 19th-c Egyptian House deserves a passing look, and the Turk's Head is a good pub. Spruced up with a fresh coat of paint, the NATIONAL LIGHTHOUSE CENTRE (Old Buoy Store, Wharf Rd) is probably the finest collection of lighthouse equipment in the world. Good audio-visual displays on lighthouse history and living conditions, and reconstructed lighthouse room, with original curved furniture. Shop, disabled access; cl Nov–Apr; (01736) 60077; *£2.50. PENZANCE AND DISTRICT MUSEUM AND ART GALLERY (Penlee Park) Recently extended, with plenty of new exhibitions; the paintings are worth a look, with pictures mainly by the Newlyn school. Shop; cl Sun; *£1. There's also a decent MARITIME MUSEUM on Chapel St. BOAT TRIPS aboard the *Scillonian III* take you around the coastline or across to the Isles of Scilly – see below; (01800) 373307. Also regular HELICOPTER FLIGHTS to the islands. Gulval SW4832 is a pleasant village just outside (with a decent pub).

! Porthcurno SW3822 MINACK THEATRE AND EXHIBITION CENTRE There can be few better backdrops for plays than the one at this famous little open-air theatre – dramatic cliffs and blue sea stretching far off into the distance. Varied 17-week summer season, and an exhibition on the life of Rowena Cade, the remarkable woman who built the theatre with her own hands. Snacks, shop, disabled access; cl Nov–Mar, and exhibition cl during matinees; (01736) 810181; shows £5, exhibition £1.50. Porthcurno's lovely silver sands – generally reckoned to be one of Cornwall's best beaches – recently became the property of the National Trust, along with so much of the coastline round here. The Logan Rock at Treen is good for lunch.

★ ▣ **St Ives** SW5140 A charming place, despite the summer crowds, with its attractive working harbour, narrow streets and alleys (cobbled Fore St is the prettiest); there are good, wide beaches. Its popularity with artists is best explored at the TATE GALLERY ST IVES, specialising in Cornish art. Works by the familiar St Ives-school names are regularly joined by new displays of 20th-c art with a Cornish connection. It's an impressive building, outside and in, fully exploiting its spectacular cliffside setting – views are best from the café. Meals, snacks, shop, disabled access; (01736) 796226; cl Mon Sept–May. The *£2.50 admission charge also covers entrance to the BARBARA HEPWORTH MUSEUM & SCULPTURE GARDEN devoted to her work and life, with sculptures in the house, studio and subtropical garden, as well as photographs and letters. A tranquil escape from the holiday hordes. Besides the Pig 'n' Fish (see **Where to eat** section), the Castle is useful for lunch. 🏛 **Sancreed** SW4229 CARN EUNY ANCIENT VILLAGE Dating from the 1st

c, the substantial traces of a little village of stone courtyard houses, and a 66-ft underground passage leading to a circular chamber. ♨ ✗ ✝ **Zennor** SW4538 WAYSIDE MUSEUM Decent little local history museum; the adjacent watermill has been fully restored and you should be able to see the wheel gently turning. Teas, shop (specialising in Cornish books and crafts); cl Nov–Easter; (01736) 796945; £1.75. The CHURCH is best seen in its granite landscape from the hills above. The Tinners Arms is useful for lunch.

ISLES OF SCILLY

The islands, about 30 miles west of Land's End, are charmingly unspoilt and a great place for a really relaxing short stay if you're close enough for the travelling not to be a serious obstacle. They have beautiful scenery, an almost subtropical climate, and a variety of shorelines giving excellent coastal walks. The largest, St Mary's, which is just six square miles, can be comfortably circled in a day. Tresco and St Agnes are the other main populated ones; there are over 100 in all, some just strange-shaped rocks jutting out of the sea, their only visitors seals, dolphins and puffins.

You can get there from Penzance by ferry (from £29 return) or more spectacularly by helicopter, a 20-minute ride with really beautiful views of the Cornish coast and the approach to the islands (return fares start at £53). The islands also have their own little airline Skybus which leaves from Land's End, Newquay or Exeter several times a day. The trip from Land's End is the quickest and cheapest (from £50 return), and there may be cheaper standby flights available on the day (no flights Sun). They also do packages in conjunction with Intercity, tel (01736) 787017 for full details.

Where to stay

Tresco SV8915 ISLAND Tresco, Isles of Scilly TR24 0PU (01720) 22883 £180 inc dinner; 40 rms, many with balcony and terrace overlooking the superb grounds or sea. Tiny private island, renowned for its wonderful subtropical Abbey Gardens and reached by helicopter or boat – the hotel's tractor-drawn bus (no cars allowed, though bike hire available) takes you to this spacious, very friendly modern hotel; colonial-style bar, library, fine food, panoramic views, swimming pool, and private beach; cl end Oct–end Feb; disabled access. **Hugh Town** SV9010 TREGARTHENS Hugh Town, St Mary's, Isles of Scilly TR21 0PP (01720) 22540; £110 inc dinner; 29 rms, most with sea views. Magnificent views over the harbour and outer islands of Samson, Bryher and Tresco from this extended and modernised hotel, first opened in 1848; neatly kept rooms, good food and pleasant service; cl 26 Oct–24 Mar; children over 5; no dogs. **Pelistry Bay** SV9311 CARNWETHERS COUNTRY HOUSE Pelistry Bay, St Mary's, Isles of Scilly TR21 0NX (01720) 22415 £76 inc dinner; 10 rms. Well run country guesthouse nr a very fine beach, with an acre of lovely gardens, heated swimming pool, and croquet; lounge with helpful books about the islands, well stocked bar, good, freshly cooked, set 4-course dinner using local produce, and a sound wine list; also a and games room with pool table and table tennis; sauna; lots of coastal walks; cl Nov–Mar; children over 7.

To see and do

As each of the islands is so small, few apart from Tresco have many specific attractions – visitors mainly come in order to 'get away from it all'. The total population of the islands is just 2,000, so there really can be a refreshing feeling of complete isolation. By far the best activity on all the islands is walking – there are plenty of white sandy beaches to stroll along, or unusual plants and birds to track down. Hiring bikes is another good way of exploring and enjoying the scenery. Thanks to the climate, flowers come out early, and spring and autumn sunsets can be particularly beautiful. A good plan is to island-hop – there are regular ferries between the larger islands, though it can prove expensive. Every Fri evening and some Weds in summer you can watch the racing of the traditional six-oar gigs that used to dash out to shipwrecks.

♨ ✈ ♿ ♜ 🏠 ✿ 🏛 **St Mary's** SV9010
The hub of Scilly Isles life, though its centre, Hugh Town, is little more than a village by mainland standards. Most ferries and planes arrive here, and you can get a number of PLEASURE CRUISES from the Old Quay out to the bird and seal colonies on the outer islets and islands; there are fishing trips from here too. The MUSEUM is a good introduction to the area's geology and natural history, with a collection of shipwrecked treasures. The LONGSTONE HERITAGE CENTRE concentrates on the ecology and maritime history of the islands. Up in the north, at Bants Carn, there's a burial chamber and ancient village. Back down south, walk out to Peninnis Head for good views of the Wolf and Bishop's Rock lighthouses. Just along the coast is STAR CASTLE.

✿ ♿ 🏛 **Tresco** SV8915 The highlight here is the amazing SUBTROPICAL GARDEN around the grounds of the abbey, begun in 1834, which, despite storms, contains a magnificent collection of exotic plants, even bananas. Also in these grounds is VALHALLA, a collection of carved figureheads from wrecked ships, many dating back to the 17th c. Helicopters from Penzance land just outside the garden gate, so it's possible (though not cheap) to come here for just a day. The southern parts of the island are mainly sandy, but in the north it's more wild and rugged, with the remains of castles of both Charles I and Oliver Cromwell, and a cave known as Piper's Hole. Cycling and walking here are real pleasures.

✿ **St Agnes** SV8807 has the most south-westerly community in the British Isles, and is joined to a smaller island called Gugh by a sandbar, awash at high tide. The sheltered cove here is especially popular. The 17th-c lighthouse is the second-oldest in Britain. The views from here out to the rocks and islets are very atmospheric – especially when you remember more ships have been wrecked here than anywhere comparable in the world.

Bryher SV8715 is a tiny quiet place, even by Scilly standards. The south bay has lots of wild flowers.

St Martin's SV9215 is a narrow rocky ridge with flowers stretching down to the main attraction – the extensive beaches, very popular for picnics.

Where to eat

The hotels listed above are good, and on St Mary's, the simple Atlantic in Hugh Town is a local favourite. Also:
St Agnes SW7150 TURKS HEAD The Quay, Isles of Scilly (01720) 22434 Idyllically placed pub overlooking a sweeping bay and with outstanding views; good food inc plenty of fresh fish, cream cakes/ices all afternoon, evening barbecues; can take food down to the beach; has one twin bedroom; disabled access. **£13.50|£1.75/£4.50.**

Walks

Most of the coastline is marvellous for clifftop walks – a lot harder work than those along the rest of the S coast to the E, and bracing winds too. At **Treen** SW3923 ⌂-1 you can walk from the Logan Rock pub (good food) to the Logan Rock peninsula SW3922 (extraordinarily balanced boulder), and away along the NT cliffs to the magical open-air Minack Theatre, cut into the steep cliffs. When there isn't a performance on, you can wander around it (and then clamber down to the wonderful silver-sand Porthcurno beach SW3822 – at low tide you can walk round to the other side, but watch you don't get cut off). **Lamorna Cove** SW4520 ⌂-2 (where there's another decent pub, a bit up the lane) also has some splendid cliff walks in both directions.

From **Land's End** SW3425 ⌂-3 there are fine cliff walks in both directions – the one to Sennen SW3425 is lovely, and the cove there is worth looking around. On a wild day **Botallack** SW3632 ⌂-4, with its ruined engine house right down by the sea, is very dramatic, and there are fine steep walks all around. The moors nearly reach the sea around **Morvah** SW4035 ⌂-5, and within a few miles from here you can take in the cliff path, the moors close to the ruin of Ding Dong Mine, the prehistoric stone hoop of Men an Tol and the Iron Age hill fort of Chûn Castle (close by Chûn Quoit, a Bronze Age burial chamber). Around Zennor SW4538 ⌂-6 (decent pub), you can walk for miles without seeing another soul; nr Treen SW4337 (not to be confused with the one on the S coast), Gurnards Head SW4338 juts dramatically into the Atlantic.

Beaches to walk along include the long one below the cliffs at **Whitesand Bay** SW3527 ⌂-7, stretching away N of Sennen Cove SW3524 (very popular with surfers), and (out of season, when the caravan and camp sites are empty) the magnificent sands around **St Ives Bay** SW5440 ⌂-8, with good cliff walks W.

Driving

As elsewhere in Cornwall, the byroads do wiggle about quite sharply and tend to be narrow. But the largely unfenced B3306 from St Ives to Land's End is a fine drive with good coast and moorland views, and the B3301 between Hayle and Portreath also has some long sea views. The B3315 SW of Penzance has a view of the Merry Maidens stone circle, S of the road nr Lamorna (maidens turned to stone for dancing on the Sabbath; the two pipers, also petrified, are on the opposite side of the road).

The minor road from Madron, NW of Penzance, to Morvah passes Lanyon Quoit, a magnificent, exposed Bronze Age burial chamber with a huge capstone; and by a telephone box further on, a side turn leads to a farm by Chûn Castle – an impressive Iron Age hill fort with visible masonry in the ramparts, and a great view over the coast. On the opposite side of the road at that telephone box is a signed path to Men an Tol, a mysterious, upright Bronze Age stone hoop. The similar, blustery moorland road from Badgers Cross nr Gulval, to Treen on the N coast takes you right by Chysauster ancient village (see entry in **To see and do** section).

Where to eat

St Ives SW5140 PIG 'N' FISH Norway Lane (01736) 794204 Simply decorated restaurant serving interesting, very fresh fish dishes; cl Sun, Mon, Nov–mid-Mar. £25.

NORTH CORNWALL

Majestic coastal scenery in the north; extensive family resort developments and safe, sandy beaches between Newquay and Padstow; lively family attractions, some fine places to stay.

The northern part of this long coast is exposed and rugged, with Cornwall's highest cliffs, dramatic surfing beaches and much completely unspoilt seaboard – no development, little car access, just wildlife, wind, waves and the occasional walker. Port Isaac and Boscastle are the pick of this area's few settlements. Tintagel is over-commercialised, but its castle is one of the most romantic places in the West Country. The coast from Padstow southwards is a marked contrast, developed this century as an almost continuous line of family resorts, with plenty of good, safe, sandy beaches. Padstow itself is a fetching combination of fishing port and resort; Newquay is Cornwall's biggest seaside resort, a lively holiday centre.

There are plenty of family attractions in this part of Cornwall, notably the intriguing World in Miniature at Goonhavern, the otter park at North Petherwin, other animal centres at Bolventor, Tredinnick and Launceston, and steamtrains from Bodmin, Launceston and Newlyn East. For quieter tastes there are attractive houses to visit at Trerice, Bodmin and Padstow, and some interesting prehistoric remains, especially at St Neot, Minions and St Cleer. Inland, the windswept, rather inhospitable Bodmin Moor, though not so good for walkers as Dartmoor, has its own bleak character, with strange tors, prehistoric traces, rarely seen black panthers, wind-bent trees, granite walls and lonely lakes.

Though there's a very good choice of places to stay, those for eating out are thinner on the ground.

Where to stay

Constantine Bay SW8574 TREGLOS Constantine Bay, Padstow PL28 8JH (01841) 520727 **£134 inc dinner**; 44 light rms, some with balcony. Quiet and relaxed seaside hotel close to a good sandy beach; with comfortable traditional furnishings, log fires, imaginative food in the refurbished restaurant, and friendly, helpful staff; sheltered garden and indoor swimming pool; lovely nearby walks; also, 4 self-catering apartments; discounts at 8 local golf courses; cl 5 Nov–16 Mar; disabled access.

Port Isaac SX0080 PORT GAVERNE, Port Isaac PL29 3SQ (01208) 8802441 **£86**; 19 comfortable rms (sound of the sea). Particularly lovely place to stay and an excellent base for this area (dramatic coves, good clifftop walks, and lots of birds); big log fires in well kept bars, relaxed lounges, decent bar food, very good restaurant food, and fine wines; also, restored, 18th-c, self-catering cottages; cl mid-Jan for 6 wks.

Padstow SW9175 OLD CUSTOM HOUSE South Quay, Padstow PL28 8ED (01841) 532359 **£76**; 26 attractive rms. Attractively refurbished hotel overlooking the harbour, with conservatory and spacious bar, and a good restaurant with lots of fish dishes.

St Wenn SW9665 WENN MANOR St Wenn, Bodmin PL30 5PS (01726) 890240

£60; 3 rms. Carefully restored restaurant, tucked away in rolling hills in 4 acres of wooded grounds; panelled bar with inglenook fireplace, candlelit dining room with 2 open log fires, and good food; croquet.

Trenale SX0688 TREBREA LODGE Trenale, Tintagel PL34 0HR (01840) 770410 **£58**; 7 rms with views across fields to the sea. Handsome manor house with log fire and honesty bar in a comfortable smoking room, an elegant first-floor drawing room, and good set dinner in the oak-panelled dining room; children over 5; lots of walks.

Crackington Haven SX1396 MANOR FARM Crackington Haven, Bude EX23 0JW (018403) 304 *£56; 5 pretty rms. Lovely, Domesday-listed manor surrounded by 25 acres of farmland and 2 acres of landscaped garden; house-party atmosphere, antiques in 4 lounges, log fire, games room, and a fine 4-course dinner; no smoking; no children. The village is a minute seaside settlement.

Little Petherick SW9172 OLD MILL COUNTRY HOUSE Little Petherick, Wadebridge, Cornwall PL27 7QT (01841) 540388 £53; 6 rms, 1 with shared bthrm. 16th-c corn mill in lovely riverside gardens with waterwheel and other original features; beamed sitting/dining room, lounges, and attentive service; cl Nov–Feb; no children.

Trelights SW9979 LONG CROSS Trelights, Port Isaac PL29 3TF (01208) 880243 **£44**; 10 rms, some with sea view. Well modernised Victorian house with interesting, period 'garden of secrets' – attractive plants in carefully restored, interlocking hedged enclosures snugged down against the winds; disabled access.

Maxworthy SX2592 WHEATLEY FARM Maxworthy, Launceston PL15 8LY (01566) 781232 *£38; 4 rms. In the same family for 5 generations, this working sheep and dairy farm has comfortable, pretty furnishings, log fires, a games room with table tennis and toys, animals to visit, pony rides, and a safe play area for children; cl Oct–Mar; self-catering cottages, too.

Quintrell Downs SW8560 MANUELS FARM Quintrell Downs, Newquay TR8 4NY (01637) 873577 £36; 3 rms, 2 with shared bthrm. Comfortable and relaxed 17th-c farmhouse with log fires, candlelit dinners, and pretty garden; good for children – bottle-feed calves, collect eggs and so forth (free baby-sitting, too); cl Christmas.

Tregadillett SX2983 ELIOT ARMS Tregadillett, Launceston TL15 7EU (01566) 772051 *£40; 2 rms, shared bthrm. Friendly, creeper-covered, old house with lots to look at (like 66 antique clocks inc seven grandfathers), and very good food with plenty of fish and interesting daily specials; cl 25 Dec.

Tregaswith SW8963 TREGASWITH FARMHOUSE Tregaswith, Newquay TR8 4HY (01637) 881181 £40; 4 pretty, homely rms. 18th-c house with beams and antiques on a smallholding breeding horses (pony rides) and rare poultry; dogs welcome by arrangement.

Crackington Haven SX1396 TREWORGIE BARTON Crackington Haven, Bude EX23 0NL (01840) 230233 *£34; 5 attractive, no-smoking rms. Traditional 16th-c farmhouse on a small working farm in quiet, rolling countryside and run by friendly owners who've been here for 20 years; very good food using local produce, open fires; cl Oct, Dec, Jan.

To see and do

✝ 🏠 **Altarnun** SX2281 CHURCH has an enchanting set of 16th-c, carved bench ends – much humanity and humour. The Rising Sun, just N is useful for lunch. Nearby, WESLEY'S COTTAGE – just off the A30 at Trewint – is the world's smallest Methodist place of worship, and has a primitive, little, time-warp room used by Wesley in 1744.

🏠 ✳ ⚘ 🏛 🐾 ♣ **Bodmin** SX0360 PENCARROW Notable 18th-c house with fine paintings and furniture, a rococo ceiling in the music room and, perhaps the highlight, 50 acres of lovely formal and woodland gardens with over 600 different rhododendrons and an acclaimed conifer collection. Also marked trails, a children's play area, pets' corner,

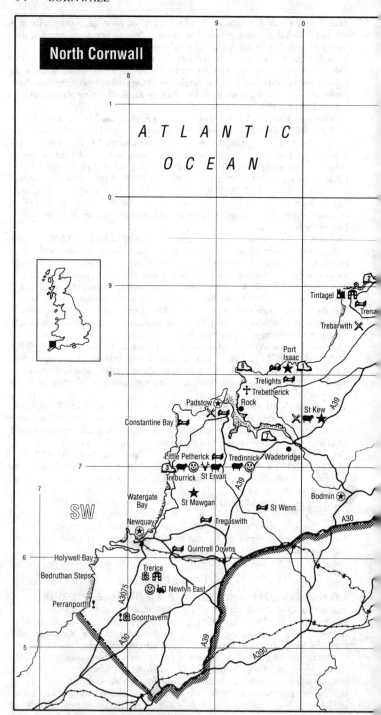

North Cornwall

ATLANTIC

OCEAN

Tintagel

Trena

Trebarwith

Port
Isaac

Trelights

Trebetherick

Padstow   Rock

Constantine Bay   St Kew

Little Petherick   Tredinnick   Wadebridge

Treburrick   St Ervan

Watergate
Bay   St Mawgan   St Wenn

SW   Newquay   Bodmin

Tregaswith

Holywell Bay   Quintrell Downs

Bedruthan Steps   Trerice

Newlyn East

Perranporth

Goonhavern

A3075   A30   A39   A390   A39   A30

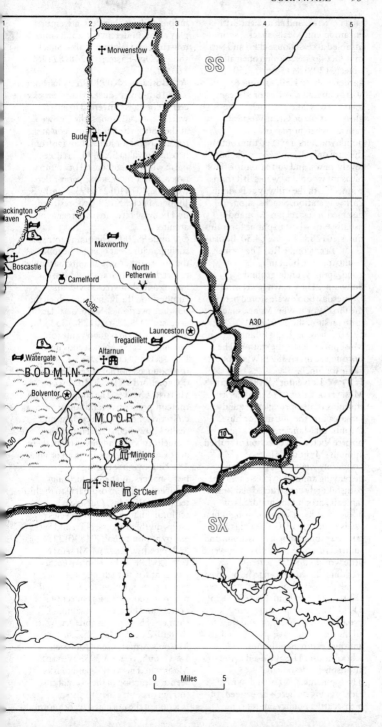

CRAFT CENTRE, and an ancient British encampment. Meals, snacks, shop, disabled access; house cl Fri and Sat, mid-Oct–Easter, garden open all the time; (01208) 841369; *£3.50, garden only *£1.50. BODMIN & WENFORD RAILWAY Restored steam locomotives take you back to the glory days of the Great Western railway when hordes of holidaymakers travelled this route to the sun; only 3½ miles of track, but lovely views, and you can stop off for pleasant woodland walks. BR trains connect with the railway at Bodmin Parkway station. Snacks, shop, disabled access; cl Jan–Mar and usually Nov – best to phone for train times; (01208) 73666; £4.50. BODMIN GAOL (Berrycombe Rd) The former county prison, built in 1778, with good, spooky, underground dungeons. The Crown Jewels and Domesday Book were stored here in the First World War. Meals, snacks (pub on site), shop; (01208) 76292; £2.80. There's a Light Infantry Museum opposite the station. The Borough Arms (A389 NW) is good value for lunch.

! ⌂ ❦ 🐄 Bolventor SX1876 POTTER'S MUSEUM OF CURIOSITY Set in the little complex that's sprung up around Jamaica Inn, the pub immortalised by Daphne du Maurier, this is a quite bizarre Victorian collection of stuffed animals. Mr Potter's love of taxidermy went far beyond simply displaying animals in glass cases – he painstakingly constructed elaborate tableaux around the hundreds of bodies that local farmers brought him as his fame spread. Guinea pigs play cricket, rabbits sit in a classroom, and squirrels carouse in a pub in this weird little world – and the 'kittens' wedding' has to be seen to be believed. Meals, snacks, shop, disabled access; cl 24–25 Dec and Jan; (01566) 86250; £1.95. The current owners are expanding the collection and the site all the time, and have also opened an antiques centre in Bolventor's old school house. The pub itself is still atmospheric despite the developments. COLLIFORD LAKE PARK Plenty going on here – rare breeds of birds, cattle, poultry, and sheep,

indoor and outdoor pets, adventure play areas, undercover assault course, museum, and lakeside walks. Snacks, shop; cl Oct–Easter; (01208) 821469; *£3.50.

★ ✝ Boscastle SX0990 Pretty harbour with 16th-c pier squeezed into a rocky creek, cottages converted from warehouses, gift shops; the Cobweb at the bottom and the Napoleon at the top are useful for lunch. Not far from here at Trevalga SX0690, Tredole Farm will arrange coastal or country HORSE AND PONY TREKKING; non-riders welcome; (01840) 250495. Nearby St Juliot CHURCH SX1290 was restored by Thomas Hardy in his career as an architect.

♻ ✝ Bude SS2006 The main centre for surfing, with great beaches beyond the dunes; otherwise an unremarkable resort. BUDE AND STRATTON MUSEUM Sailing and shipwrecks, with an emphasis on the Bude canal which the building overlooks. Shop, disabled access; cl Oct–Mar; (01288) 353576; 50p. The Falcon is good value for lunch. The carved bench ends up at POUGHILL CHURCH SS2207 (pronounced poffle) are entertaining.

♻ Camelford SX1083 MUSEUM OF HISTORIC CYCLING The couple who run this comprehensive (and still growing) collection met through cycling, and really know their stuff. Housed in Camelford's old railway station, there are over 200 bicycles, from an original 1819 hobbyhorse through boneshakers and penny-farthings (properly called an ordinary) to the hi-tech bikes of today. Outside is a sculpture made up of old bicycles. Shop, disabled access; cl Fri and Sat exc by appointment; (01840) 212811; *£2. NORTH CORNWALL MUSEUM & GALLERY Life in the region over the past century, with displays of cider-making and farming, reconstructed moorland cottage, and collections of pottery and even early vacuum cleaners. Shop; cl Sun and Oct–Mar; (01840) 212954; *£1.25. The Mason's Arms is useful for lunch.

! ❀ Goonhavern SW7953 WORLD IN MINIATURE The world's landmarks seen at a fraction of the normal cost – though of course they're also a fraction of the normal size. Beautiful gardens with thousands of plants, lots for children, and a special cinema. Meals, snacks, shop, disabled access; cl Nov–Feb; £4.

★ ⛺🐂🎣🚂☺ **Launceston** SX3384 on its hillside is the most attractive inland town in Cornwall, with winding old streets and an untouristy feel. STEAM RAILWAY Two-ft-gauge line on the trackbed of the old North Cornwall Railway, running through two miles of scenic valley – on sunny days in an open carriage; also engine displays, model railway, and car and motorcycle museum. Meals, snacks, shop, disabled access; open Good Fri–Easter Mon, then Sun and Tues only until Whitsun, then daily (exc Sat) to Sept, with some trains Dec wknds; (01566) 775665 for exact dates and times; *£4.25. For a while Launceston was Cornwall's capital, and the museum in Georgian LAWRENCE HOUSE has displays and artefacts on the town's past; cl wknds, bank hols and Oct–Mar; free. The 12th- and 13th-c hilltop CASTLE is substantial and commanding, though ruined – it was captured four times during the Civil War. Shop, some disabled access; cl Nov–Mar; £1.25. Good walks and trails round here. TRETHORNE LEISURE FARM (Kennards House, 3m W) 140-acre working dairy farm ideal for children, who can milk Daisy the cow, walk the miniature ponies, play with the rabbits, bottle-feed the lambs or just look at the animals and poultry in their paddocks. Also birds of prey centre, golf course and very big play area. Meals, snacks, shop, disabled access; cl Sun (exc golf); £3.50, golf £8 a round.

✝ **Morwenstow** SS2015 CHURCH has Norman arches and 16th-c bench ends, with shipwrecked sailors' headstones in the graveyard. A driftwood shack, built for contemplation by a Victorian parson over the impressive cliffs, is preserved by the NT. The Bush is an interesting old pub, and the NT tearoom is delightful.

⛺☺ **Newlyn East** SW8356 LAPPA VALLEY STEAM RAILWAY AND LEISURE PARK 15-inch gauge, steamtrain trips through pretty countryside to an old lead mine, currently being restored;

there's a film on its history and the disaster that struck in 1846. It's surrounded by parkland with lakes, woodland walk, a maze, crazy golf and play areas. Meals, snacks, shop, some disabled access; cl Nov–Mar, and Mon in Oct – best to check train times; (01872) 510317; *£4.50, covers fare and all attractions.

🐷☺🎣🐂♪ **Newquay** SW8756 is a thorough-going seaside resort with excellent, safe golden beaches below fine cliffs, no shortage of souvenir shops, an alcohol-free zone declared on the streets, theme parks on the edge. There are older houses around the harbour. ANIMAL WORLD (Trenance Leisure Park) Formerly Newquay Zoo, the emphasis here is very much on conservation, with carefully designed enclosures of monkeys, penguins, lions and now tortoises, as well as a maze, gardens, and activity parks. In the summer hols they have daily 'animal encounter sessions' where you can meet some of the creatures close up. Meals, snacks, shop, disabled access; cl 25 Dec; (01637) 873342; £4. You can get a joint ticket that includes entrance to WATER WORLD, a lively fun pool on the same site. DAIRYLAND Bustling dairy farm, its showpiece the daily milking sessions when cows step aboard a bizarre merry-go-round milking machine and are milked to the strains of classical music. Also informative farm-life exhibitions, very good and well labelled nature trails, museum of rural bygones, farm park and plenty of activities for children. Meals, snacks, shop, disabled access; cl Nov–Mar; (01872) 510246; £4.50. SEA-LIFE CENTRE (Towan Promenade) Latest in the reliable chain – an incredible see-through tunnel creates the illusion of walking along the seabed, and lots of bubble windows bring you face to face with fish, eels and even sharks. Meals, snacks, shop, some disabled access; cl 25 Dec; (01637) 872822; £4.25. Active children should enjoy the HOLYWELL BAY LEISURE PARK with rides, golf and pony-trekking (not Sat); cl Oct–Apr; (01637) 830095; park free (charges for some attractions).

❦ **North Petherwin** SX2889 Tamar Otter Park The number of otters has declined alarmingly over the last decade – this friendly place breeds them and releases them into the wild to make sure they don't disappear altogether; the attractive, Asian, short-clawed otters bred here are fun to watch playing. Three species of deer roam free, and there are waterfowl lakes, wallabies, and nature trails. Snacks, shop, disabled access; cl Nov–Mar; (01566) 785646; £3.80.

★ 🎡🔔 **Padstow** SW9175 has quaint streets, old buildings clustered around the working fishing harbour, and attractive slate houses. The Camel estuary is popular for sailing: gentle dreamy scenery with lots of little boats. Prideaux Place Still a lived-in family home, this fine old house has been very well restored over the last few years. Not much has changed since it was built in the late 16th c, and highlights include the elegant ceilings, atmospheric library and the intricate biblical tableaux in the Great Chamber. Notable concerts and special events in the grounds. Snacks, shop, disabled access to ground floor only; cl am, Fri and Sat, Oct–Easter; (01841) 532411; £3.50. Shipwreck Museum Not far from the town's little harbour, a collection of relics and tales of the plentiful shipwrecks along this coast. Shop, disabled access; cl Nov–Mar; (01841) 532663; £1. The London Inn, Golden Lion and Old Custom House are useful for lunch.

❗ **Perranporth** SW7554 has glider flights under instruction from Trevellas Airfield; (01726) 842798.

★ **Port Isaac** SW9980 Delightful, steep, fishing village, a favourite with many: tiny streets, houses hanging high over the pretty harbour; the Golden Lion here is a good pub. Park at the top and walk down. Just up the coast Port Gaverne is a beautiful NT cove.

❦ 🐄 **St Ervan** SW8970 Trenouth Farm Rare Breeds Centre Good, unspoilt, working farm with all sorts of rare breeds of animals and poultry; lots of pigs (the piglets may even race up to greet you) – even Iron Age pigs crossed with wild boar. A friendly place, never busy with tourists, and as

it's so uncommercialised, children really get a lot out of it. Teas, shop, mostly disabled access (but no facilities); cl Oct–Easter; (01841) 540606; £2.95. The Ring o' Bells over at St Issey is useful for lunch.

★ 🐄 **St Kew** SX0276 Delightful quiet leafy village with old-fashioned feel. Donkey and Pony Sanctuary Agreeably low-key little centre with rescued donkeys, baby farm animals (feeding times 11.30 and 3), cart rides, adventure playground, picnic area and bike hire; (01208) 841710 for 1995 dates and prices. The St Kew inn is a nice place for lunch.

✝ 🏛 **St Neot** SX1867 The village church is well known for its early stained glass, and also has an unusual stone vault in the south porch. Nearby ancient remains include the five impressive Brown Gelly Barrows and some hut circles. Carnglaze Slate Caverns are big, long-abandoned mining chambers, with a lake at the far end of one; guided tours. The London Inn is good for lunch.

🏰 🎡 **Tintagel** SX0588 has been a tourist trap since the 19th c, but is well worth penetrating for Tintagel Castle Forgetting the myths and legends, these dramatic 12th- and 13th-c ruins have a spectacular setting and unrivalled views. On sunny days, archaeologists work on the site and it's busy with tourists; try and come out of season, when the crowds are fewer and the mist and crashing waves create an appropriately mysterious atmosphere. There's quite a lot of climbing involved, and the often steep steps among the crags can be slippery in wet weather, so do come prepared. As for King Arthur, latest theories suggest he came from Shropshire, but a small exhibition puts forward the Cornish case. Shop; cl 24–26 Dec, 1 Jan; (01840) 770328; £2. A Land Rover service can ferry you to the site from the village at regular intervals throughout the day. Old Post Office Small, saggy-roofed, 14th-c manor used in the 19th c as a post office. Shop; cl Nov–Mar; £1.90; NT. The Tintagel Arms is useful for lunch.

✝ **nr Trebetherick** SW9377 St Endoc's church is tucked well away from the roads under a seaside hill, looking out to Padstow Bay; a nice stroll from the village. The Carpenter's Arms is useful for lunch.

🐾 ☺ **Treburrick** SW8670 TAMARISK LEISURE PARK Small place based around a farm with tame animals and rare breeds; various activities inc archery and scrumpy-tasting. Younger children will love feeding the lambs – older ones may prefer the free computer games; (01841) 540829; £3.50. The Farmer's Arms in St Merryn is useful for lunch.

🐾 ☺ **Tredinnick** SW9270 SHIRE HORSE ADVENTURE PARK There's far more to this busy complex than just the magnificent horses. An owl sanctuary demonstrates night-time flight, there's a children's farm, an exhibition of carts, waggons and rural equipment, a watermill, photography display, nature trails, working craftsmen and a big adventure playground. The shire horses themselves are displayed in an indoor arena, and you can see them being groomed in their stables, along with rather less powerful Shetland ponies. Lots for all ages, but ideal for children, and a visit can take up most of the day. Meals, snacks, shop, disabled access; cl Nov–Easter; (0841) 540276; *£4.50. The Ring o' Bells at St Issey is handy for lunch.

🏠 ❀ **Trerice** SW8457 TRERICE Pretty Elizabethan house with unusual gables and elaborate plasterwork ceilings in the magnificent Hall and Great Chamber. Fine furnishings

from the 17th and 18th c, notable paintings inc several by John Opie, early embroideries, Oriental and English porcelain, and in the grounds a rather unusual collection of lawnmowers; lovely colourful gardens with Cornish fruit trees. Snacks, shop, very good disabled access; cl Tues and Nov–Mar; £3.60; NT. The Two Clomes at Quintrell Downs is quite handy for lunch.

🏛 This part of Cornwall is full of interesting **prehistoric monuments**. Nr Minions SX2671, the HURLERS STONE CIRCLES SX2571 is made up of three Bronze Age circles – the central one still has 14 stones standing. Close by is the famous RILLATON BARROW where the lovely Rillaton gold cup (now in the British Museum) was found, along with other interesting relics. Not far off at St Cleer is TRETHEVY QUOIT SX2568, a very photogenic megalithic tomb. The Crow's Nest SX2669, down nr Darite, is handy for lunch. The strange CHEESEWRING **SX2572** on Bodmin Moor, another appealing camera subject, is made up of several improbably overhanging granite slabs. Also see St Neot entry, above.

★ St Mawgan SW8765 is an inland **attractive village** with a good pub, the Falcon.

John Betjeman was very fond of this area; the local tourist board do a good trail of sites connected with him, as well as one for sites associated with Daphne du Maurier.

Walks

Some particularly fine stretches of cliffs for walking are around **Port Isaac** SW9980 ᗡ-1. A good start for **Tintagel** SX0588 ᗡ-2 is from Rocky Valley, a craggy valley leading from the B3263 to the sea. The **Bedruthan Steps** SW8469 ᗡ-3, off the B3276 Newquay–Padstow rd, are really special with their dramatic rock pinnacles, cliffs and lovely sandy coves. Further N, **Boscastle** SX0990 ᗡ-4 has fascinating clifftop views, and from **Crackington Haven** SX1396 ᗡ-5 is a good walk to High Cliff, Cornwall's highest.

On the E side of the Camel estuary SW9376 ᗡ-6, sand dunes suddenly give way to a rocky headland, Rumps Point, which can be walked round in an hour or so.

Along the **disused railway** ᗡ-7 from Wadebridge SW9872 to Padstow SW9175 – a level six miles along the edge of the Camel estuary, with banks of wild flowers, birds, and lovely views between cuttings – you can walk or cycle (bike hire at either end), or picnic on the small beaches at low tide. Those with less energy could park at Wadebridge, walk to Padstow, have lunch and get the bus back (2.30pm from the old station). You might then walk on through scenic countryside beyond Bodmin SX0360 (worth stopping at Helland pottery, just by the path at Helland Bridge).

Bodmin Moor is not as richly endowed as Dartmoor for walking, and much is boggy and rough. For a taste of its bleak grandeur, start at Minions SX2671 ⌂-8 and explore the Hurlers stone circles SX2571 and the Cheesewring **SX2572** (see **To see and do** Section, above); there is a clear track between them. The nearby track from Sharptor SX2573 to Kilmar Tor SX2574 affords fine views. The summit of **Rough Tor** (pronounced Roe Tor) SX1480 ⌂-9, reached from a signed car park off the A39 nr Camelford, gives views of Brown Willy, the highest point in Cornwall. **Kit Hill** ⌂-10, off the A390 N of Callington SX3669, with a huge chimney stack and mine shafts, gives impressive views across to Dartmoor.

Riding is popular on the moor, and quite a few stables on or around it cater for all levels of riding ability.

Driving

The best views of Bodmin Moor are from the A30 rather than the minor roads, which tend to hug its valleys. The B3276 from Newquay to Padstow has some good sea views, and the B3254, an old coach road from Launceston up to Kilkhampton, gives good views of the contrasting North Cornish farming country. The B3266 S from Boscastle down towards Bodmin is a good road, fast by Cornish standards, and though the A39 is slow in summer it's an excellent road at other times.

Where to eat

Padstow SW9175 SEAFOOD (01841) 532485 Wonderfully fresh seafood straight from the boats, in a busy, airy, quayside restaurant; good puddings, and long, interesting and fairly priced wine list; conservatory for aperitifs; bedrooms; cl Sun, 1 May, late Dec/Jan. **£22 lunch, £33 dinner**|£5.75/£14.
Padstow SW9175 TASTE BUD AND RAFTERS (01841) 532565 Two eating places under one roof. Taste Bud is a charming, friendly little restaurant, £20, and Rafters is a bistro offering lighter meals, £13.50|£2.25/£5; both places are served by the same kitchen; cl Sun (exc summer hols), and end Oct–March.
Trebarwith SX0585 PORT WILLIAM (01840) 770230 Fresh fish from local fishermen (and tiddlers from the landlord) in this marvellously placed old harbourmaster's house; other good food too, nautical decor, tables out by the water, lovely sunsets. **£16**|£2/£7.
St Kew SX0276 ST KEW (01208) 84259 Good, popular food in this rather grand-looking stone pub, with friendly service, nice old-fashioned furnishings, and a peaceful garden; children over 6 in evenings. **£14**|£1.50/£5.95.

Help this year from: D J Underwood, Brian Websdale, Maj Gen R M Jerran, Anna Sanderson, Norma and Keith Bloomfield, B and K Hypher, David and Michelle Hedges, Margaret Cadney, Jo Rees, Mike and Heather Barnes, Ann and Bob Westbrook, GA, PA, P and J Shapley, A E and P McCully, Basil Minson, R L Turnham, Gerry Hollington, Richard Dolphin, Bronwen and Steve Wrigley, M W Edwards, Margaret Cadney, R L Turnham, John Wooll, Nigel Woolliscroft, Adrian Acton, Martin and Penny Fletcher, Mr and Mrs W J A Timpson, Lynn Sharpless, Bob Eardley, Don Kellaway, Angie Coles, Peter and Lynn Brueton, P and M Rudlin, C J Parsons, Jeff Davies, Sue Holland, Dave Webster, Richard Bamford, Nick Wikeley, Mr and Mrs W J A Timpson.

CORNWALL CALENDAR

Some of these dates were provisional as we went to press.

JANUARY

Marazion Charter Anniversary – *till Dec*

Newlyn A series of major exhibitions to mark the centennial year of Newlyn Art Gallery – *till Dec*

1 **Mawnan Smith** Trebah Icicle Charity Swim at Trebah Garden (01326) 250448

FEBRUARY

6 **St Ives** Hurling of the Silver Ball and Feast Monday Celebrations throughout the town: a ball is thrown from the wall of the parish church by the mayor into the waiting crowd and then passed from one person to another until midday, when the person last holding the ball takes it to the mayor at the Guildhall (01736) 797840

28 **St Ives** Hurling of the Silver Ball (as above)

MARCH

4 **Lostwithiel** St Piran's Day Celebrations in the town centre (01872) 74057; **Truro** Cornwall Brass Band Association Annual Contest in the City Hall (01726) 61042

APRIL

Cornwall Gardens Festival, over 70 gardens open to the public – *till 31 May* (01872) 74057

1 **Falmouth** Spring Flower Show in the town centre – *till Sun 2* (01872) 74057

9 **St Endellion** Easter Festival at St Endellion Church – *till Sun 16* (01208) 850463

15 **Land's End** Trial at the Custom House (01359) 70954

28 **Boscastle** Beer Festival – *till 1 May* (01872) 74057; **Newquay** Great Cornwall Balloon Festival on the sea front – *till 1 May* (01637) 872211

29 **Camborne** Trevithick Day, a celebration of the town's history in the Industrial Revolution (01209) 712941; **Saltash** May Fair (01872) 74057

30 **Land's End** Duchy Marathon, starts and finishes at the Custom House

MAY

1 **Padstow** Obby Oss Celebrations, ancient May Day celebration in the town centre (01872) 74057

6 **Helston** Furry Dance, ancient spring street festival celebrating the passing of winter (01326) 572082

8 **Helston** VE Day Celebrations at Flambards Village Theme Park, Culdrose Manor (01326) 574549

10 **St Mellion** International Open at St Mellion Golf and Country Club – *till Sun 14* (01932) 859777

13 **Stratton** Re-enactment of the Battle of Stamford Hill at Stratton Junior School – *till Sun 14* (01872) 74057

CORNWALL CALENDAR

MAY cont

20 **Tintagel** Festival of Music and the Arts – *till Mon 29* (01208) 74121

26 **Redruth** Murdoch Weekend, annual commemoration of William Murdoch's gaslight invention – *till Sun 28* (01209) 210038

27 **Bude** World Open Skittles – *till Mon 29* (01872) 74057; **Porth** Custom Car Rally at Trevelgue Holiday Park – Mon 29 (01872) 74057

28 **Launceston** Steam Engine Rally (01566) 772333

29 **Porthcurno** Minack Theatre Summer Festival – *till 16 Sept* (01736) 810694

JUNE

2 **Bude** Folk Arts and Cider Festival at Parkhouse Centre and Castle Grounds – *till Sun 4* (01288) 356888

4 **Land's End** Cornwall Vintage Vehicle Rally at the Custom House (01736) 871501

8 **Wadebridge** Royal Cornwall Show – *till Sat 10* at the Royal Cornwall Showground (01208) 812183

10 **Saltash** Sailing Regatta on the River Tamar – *till Sun 11* (01872) 74057

11 **Helston** Vintage Car Club Rally at Flambards Village Theme Park, Culdrose Manor (01326) 574549

12 **Penzance** Golowan Week – *till Sun 25*, inc Sea and Sail Festival from Fri 23 and Mazey Day on Sat 24 (01736) 332211

17 **Land's End** Steam Rally at the Custom House – *till Sun 18* (01736) 871501

19 **St Day** Feast Week – *till Mon 26* (01872) 74057

23 **Callington** Midsummer's Eve Bonfire at Kit Hill Country Park (01872) 74057; **Truro** Three Spires Festival at Truro Cathedral – *till Sat 8 July* (01872) 863346

25 **Mevagissey** Feast Week – *till 1 July* (01872) 784057

JULY

2 **Newquay** 1900 Week: Victorian events – *till Fri 7* (01637) 872519

8 **Merrymeet** Liskeard Country Show at Trengrove Farm (01579) 343125

9 **Lostwithiel** Carnival Week – *till Sat 15* (01872) 740577

15 **Camborne** Show at the Showground (01209) 717038

17 **Stithians** Show, traditional agricultural show and an evening concert at Kennal Farm

20 **Launceston** Agricultural Show (01566) 772333

23 **Stratton** Festival – *till Sun 30* (01872) 74057; **Washaway** Game and Country Fair at Pencarrow House (01208) 841369

24 **Penzance** International 505 Sailing Championships at Mounts Bay – *till 4 Aug* (01872) 74057

AUGUST

1 **St Endellion** 37th Summer Festival – *till Fri 11* (01208) 850463

CORNWALL CALENDAR

AUGUST cont

2 **Land's End** Air Day at the Custom House (01736) 871501; **St Keverne** Ox Roast (01326) 280487

4 **Falmouth** Classic Boats – *till Sun 6* (01326) 211555

5 **Launceston** Garden Society Show (01566) 772333; **(Tredinnick** nr St Issey) Cornish Traction Preservation Club Steam and Vintage Working Rally at Tredinnick Farm, off the A39 – *till Sun 6* (01208) 831293

6 **Falmouth** Regatta Week — *till Sat 12* (01326) 211555

9 **Camelford** Agricultural Show (01840) 212954

19 **Bude** Carnival Day (01288) 355100

20 **Fowey** Royal Regatta and Carnival — *till Sat 26* (01726) 833217; **Bude and Holsworthy** Two Counties Road Race (01288) 354240

25 **Wadebridge** Cornwall Folk Festival — *till Mon 28* (01208) 813100

26 **Bude** Jazz Festival – *till 2 Sept* (01684) 566956

27 **Stithians** Cornish Game and Country Fayre at the Showground, Kennal Farm (01209) 73366

28 **Bude** Horticultural Show (01288) 354240; **Newlyn** Fish Festival at the Harbour Complex (01736) 63499; **Ruan Minor** Kennack Sands Horse Show and Gymkhana (01326) 290824

SEPTEMBER

2 **Helston** Harvest Fair – *till Mon 4* (01326) 563357; **Newquay** Festival – *till Sat 9* (01872) 74057

16 **Lostwithiel** Garden Society Annual Produce Show at the Community Centre (01208) 872207

29 **Morwenstow** Harvest Arts Festival – *till 1 Oct* (01872) 74057

OCTOBER

4 **Callington** Honey Fair, ancient charter street fair, various exhibitions and demonstrations (01579) 50230

28 **Helston** Firework Show at Flambards Village Theme Park, Culdrose Manor (01326) 574549

DECEMBER

14 **Lostwithiel** Christmas Pageant (01208) 872207

18 **Saltash** Christmas Carol Service and Torchlight Procession

CUMBRIA

This is England's most beautiful area, including the amazingly varied Lake District, with England's highest mountains, as well as the coast and the Eden Valley. It's the best county for walks, from lazy waterside strolls to serious hill walks. The hills themselves vary greatly in character, as do the lakes: Buttermere, Crummock Water, Ullswater and Wast Water approach the grandeur of Scottish lochs, while Derwent Water wavers between highland and lowland in flavour, and Windermere, the longest, is dotted with villas built by Victorian magnates.

There are lots of interesting places to visit, particularly in the Southern Lakes, fewer in the west and the Pennines. There's an excellent choice of places to stay, many of which serve really good food. For lunch, there are plenty of decent, civilised pubs (allowing children) in town and country alike, and most tourist attractions, as well as all the main centres, have refreshments.

Out of season, we'd suggest that the areas to consider first are the Northern and Southern Lakes. But in the summer holidays and at other holiday peak times, these parts attract so many people that traffic does clog the steep, narrow lanes to some favourite spots. Though the pressure of visitors can put some strain on the more accessible of even the wilder places at these times, in high summer you've more chance of finding real peace in the west (quieter, but with marvellous fell walks around Wast Water), or over in the Pennines east of the M6. The coast is a mild disappointment in comparison, but does have some good places; the best coastal scenery is around Morecambe Bay.

For a weekend visit to central Lakeland, May (sheets of wild flowers on the hills) and June are ideal: more sun, far less crowded. The views are often clearest (and the ground firm and dry for walkers) in October and November, though afternoons are short then. The weather here is notoriously unreliable and often very wet indeed, but in fact, in a typical year, three out of four Cumbrian weekends are dry and sunny.

For all but the hardiest, expert outdoorsmen, winter up here is too bleak for pleasure – unless you plan to stay indoors.

Public transport in the Lakes is good and useful for round-trip, long walks; information service (01228) 812812. Local information leaflets offer plenty of choice of well guided walks; information too from National Park visitor services (0153 94) 46601, and from the flourishing Cumbria Wildlife Trust (0153 94) 32476, which controls many reserves. Bicycles can be hired by the day in the main towns (considering the scenic grandeur, you can cycle for a surprisingly long way, at least in the central area, without having to struggle up steep hills). Many places offer riding: around £10 an hour for adults, £8 for children.

The National Trust controls over 25 per cent of the entire area of the Lake District National Park. In addition to many of the most interesting houses and gardens, it owns or controls most of the high central fell country, the whole of Loweswater, Crummock Water, Buttermere and Wast Water and their shores, much of Windermere, Derwent Water, Ennerdale Water, Grasmere Lake and Rydal Water. So preservation of and access to the countryside here is outstanding. And this is an area where membership of the Trust does particularly pay off.

SOUTHERN LAKES

Gloriously varied scenery, excellent places to stay in, a great many interesting things to see and do; best visited out of season.

This region concentrates more scenic beauty into a smaller central area than any other part of the Lakes, with exceptionally good walking. So its heart around Ambleside and Windermere is very busy indeed in summer. The places we recommend to stay in do in themselves give considerable insulation against the summer crowds, but the area comes into its own at quieter times of year – you really do need a degree of peace and quiet to enjoy the beauty of its glorious central area between Grasmere and Windermere.

The choice of places to stay here is very good indeed, with a splendid range of styles and prices (the cheaper places are naturally a good deal humbler than the most expensive ones). The Langdales, particularly Great Langdale, are outstanding for a quiet break, with plenty of walking on your doorstep.

The area has lots to see and do, apart from walking and enjoying the scenery; it offers more than any other part of Cumbria. Ambleside and Windermere are both quite intensively developed for visitors. Kendal, a genuine country town, has much of interest but, being outside the Lakes proper, is not a good base for them. We'd recommend a look at Hawkshead, Troutbeck and Cartmel, and among the many other places of interest, the great houses and impressive gardens of Holker Hall at Cark-in-Cartmel, Levens Hall and Sizergh Castle probably take the pick. The Wordsworth trail at Grasmere and Rydal is heavily trodden in summer, but very rewarding at quieter times.

Where to stay

Windermere SD4109 MILLER HOWE Rayrigg Rd, Windermere LA23 1EY (0153 94) 42536 **£168.75 inc dinner**; 13 very comfortable rms, many with fine views. Peaceful and very relaxing individual hotel high over the lake, with splendid views from the day rooms, conservatory and sloping garden; there's an expectant theatricality about the excellent evening meals which adds to the special-event feel of eating here; remarkably wide-ranging New World wine list with helpful tasting notes; no-smoking dining room; also, light lunches; children over 8; cl Dec–Feb.

Grasmere NY3406 MICHAEL'S NOOK Grasmere, Ambleside LA22 9RP (0153 94) 35496 **£168 inc dinner**; 12 lovely rms, 2 suites. Beautifully furnished hotel with fine antiques, paintings and rugs (the owner is a former antique dealer); lovely flowers, comfortable sofas by open fires in the cosy bar or elegant drawing room, fine food, and good walks; also, Great Danes and exotic cats; free use of indoor pool and health facilities at nearby Wordsworth Hotel (under the same ownership, and listed below); children by arrangement.

Rydal Water NY3606 WHITE MOSS HOUSE Rydal Water, Grasmere, Ambleside LA22 9SE (0153 94) 35295 *£158 inc dinner; 5 thoughtfully furnished rms in main house, plus separate cottage let as one unit with 2 rms. Attractive, stripped-stone small country house in charming, mature grounds overlooking the lake – and once owned by Wordsworth; comfortable lounge, fine, no-choice, 5-course meals in a pretty, no-smoking dining room and excellent wine list; free use of hotel rowing boat, free fishing and free use of local leisure club; cl Dec–Feb; not suitable for toddlers.

Langdale NY2807 LANGDALE Langdale, Ambleside LA22 0PN (0153 94) 37302 £130; 65 very comfortable rms in various Lakeland stone blocks and cottages spread through 35 acres of woodland (best bedrooms in Edwardian house £30 extra). Self-contained estate with cocktail bar and lounge, good food in the smart restaurant, and extensive leisure facilities inc a big indoor swimming pool; great walks nearby.

Ambleside NY3804 WATEREDGE Borrans Rd LA22 0EP (0153 94) 32332 *£122 inc dinner; 23 good, comfortable rms. Beautifully placed, welcoming hotel with neat gardens running down to Lake Windermere; light, airy lounges, good meals in a cosy, beamed, no-smoking dining room, and excellent service; children over 7; cl mid-Dec–early Feb.

Windermere SD4199 HOLBECK GHYLL COUNTRY HOUSE Holbeck Lane, Windermere LA23 1LU (0153 94) 32375 *£120 inc dinner; 14 individual rms, many with fine views. Charming, warm and friendly country house in mature, landscaped gardens overlooking Lake Windermere; 5 acres of woodland, tennis court, comfortable lounges, billiard room, and very good food in the oak-panelled restaurant; children over 8 in restaurant.

Grasmere NY3406 WORDSWORTH Grasmere, Ambleside LA22 9SW (0153 94) 35592 £116; 37 comfortable and attractive rms. Well run hotel, right in the village, with stylish lounges and an airy restaurant overlooking the landscaped gardens; relaxed conservatory and popular pubby bar, friendly service; also, a heated indoor pool, mini-gym, and sauna; good disabled access.

Grasmere NY3406 SWAN Grasmere, Ambleside LA22 9RF (0153 94) 35551 £115.90; 36 rms (many newly refurbished) and most with fine views. Smart and friendly 17th-c inn in beautiful fell-foot surroundings, with beams and inglenooks, an elegant, no-smoking dining room, and attractive garden; lovely walks; partial disabled access.

Ambleside NY3804 ROTHAY MANOR Rothay Bridge (Coniston Rd), Ambleside LA22 0EH (0153 94) 33605 *£112; 18 attractive rms, many overlooking the garden. Family-run, Regency-style country house in mature grounds, with log fires and fresh flowers in quietly civilised and deeply comfortable day rooms, and good English food in the no-smoking dining room; windsurfing/waterskiing etc close by and free use of nearby leisure club; cl 3 Jan–10 Feb; good disabled access.

Witherslack SD4384 OLD VICARAGE Witherslack, Grange-over-Sands LA11 6RS (0153 95) 52381 £90; 15 rms, many with antiques. Very friendly, comfortable Georgian house well away from the tourist bustle, with Victoriana in the day rooms, excellent food, and good nearby walks.

Crook SD4695 WILD BOAR Crook, Windermere LA23 3NF (0153 94) 45225 *£84; 36 rms. Comfortable, well run, extended hotel with period furnishings and log fires in its ancient core, attentive service, and good food in the no-smoking dining room; free access to nearby leisure club and discounts on watersports.

Windermere SD4199 LANGDALE CHASE, Windermere LA23 1LW (0153 94) 32201 £84; 31 rms, many with marvellous lake views. Welcoming, family-run hotel in a lovely position on the edge of Lake Windermere, with waterskiing and bathing from the hotel jetty; tennis, croquet, putting and rowing, afternoon tea on the terraces, gracious, oak-panelled rooms with antiques, paintings, fresh flowers and open fires; very good food inc huge breakfasts, and friendly service; disabled access.

Cartmel SD3879 UPLANDS Haggs Lane, Cartmel, Grange-over-Sands LA11 6HD (0153 95) 36248 *£80; 5 pretty rms. Comfortable Edwardian house in 2 acres of garden with sea views, attractively decorated rooms, and helpful service; the main draw is undoubtedly the richly imaginative food in the no-smoking dining room; cl 1 Jan–25 Feb; children over 8.

Bowness SD4097 BURN HOW GARDEN HOUSE Bowness, Windermere LA23 3HH (0153 94) 46226 £76; 26 pretty rms, some in chalets in lovely grounds. Extended, family-run Victorian house with good food in the light and airy no-smoking restaurant; free use of nearby leisure club; good disabled access.

Rydal NY3706 GLEN ROTHAY Rydal, Ambleside LA22 9LR (0153 94) 32524 *£72; 11 comfortable, individual rms. Friendly, small hotel at the foot of a steep slope near Rydal Water; with armchairs by the log fire in a beamed and panelled lounge, plush bar, and relaxed atmosphere; cl 1st 2 wks Jan.

Grizedale SD3494 GRIZEDALE LODGE Hawkshead Hill, Grizedale, Ambleside LA22 0QL (0153 94) 36532 £70; 9 no-smoking rms. Friendly and comfortable hotel in the middle of the magnificent Grizedale Forest – lots of walks from the front door; log fire in the lounge bar, and imaginative, fresh food in the attractive restaurant; cl 2 Jan–mid-Feb; children under 5 provided with high tea at 5.30; disabled access.

Hawkshead SD3598 DRUNKEN DUCK Barngates, Hawkshead, Ambleside LA22 0NG (0153 94) 36347 £69; 10 rms. Very well run, happy inn – alone in 60 hillside acres – with several cosy rooms, good fires, and views of Lake Windermere in the distance; fine, interesting food inc tasty puddings; fishing in a private tarn; cl 25 Dec; limited disabled access.

Little Langdale NY3204 THREE SHIRES Little Langdale, Ambleside LA22 9NZ (0153 94) 37215 £68; 10 rms. Stone-built country inn with beautiful views, comfortably old-fashioned residents' part, separate walkers' bar, and pretty gardens; open wknds only in Dec, cl Jan.

Elterwater NY3305 BRITANNIA INN Elterwater, Ambleside LA22 9HP (0153 94) 37210 £66; 13 rms, most with shower. Simple, charmingly traditional pub in fine surroundings opposite the village green, with happy, friendly atmosphere and hearty home cooking; pleasant walks; cl Christmas.

Hawkshead SD3598 HIGHFIELD HOUSE Hawkshead Hill, Hawkshead, Ambleside LA22 0PN (0153 94) 36344 *£62; 11 good rms. Welcoming, Victorian country house in a spacious woodland garden with fine views (good walks from the door), open fire in the comfortable lounge, cosy bar, and generous food inc packed lunches and children's high tea; cl 23–25 Dec, 4–26 Jan.

Lowick Bridge SD2986 BRIDGEFIELD HOUSE Spark Bridge, Ulverston LA12 8DA (01229) 885239 £60; 5 rms. Small, quiet, Victorian country house in wooded grounds, with good, imaginative food in the no-smoking dining room, open fire in the drawing room, and friendly, helpful service; good with children; well disciplined dogs welcome.

Torver SD2894 OLD RECTORY Torver, Coniston LA21 8AX (0153 94) 41353 £56; 8 well equipped rms. Quiet, tastefully furnished, family-run hotel in NT farmland, with elegant lounge, imaginatively served food and superb views from the dining room; pleasant walks from the doorstep, packed lunches; disabled access.

Hawkshead SD3598 KINGS ARMS Hawkshead, Ambleside LA22 0NZ (0153 94) 36372 £54; 9 rms, most with own bthrm. Picturesque old inn overlooking the square, with friendly and traditional rooms, popular food, and a lovely terrace; cl 25 Dec.

Far Sawrey SD3893 SAWREY Far Sawrey, Ambleside LA22 0LQ (0153 94) 43425 £51; 17 rms, most with bthrm (5 new rms to be added soon). Friendly hotel well placed at the foot of Claife Heights; simple pubby and smarter bars, friendly staff, good straightforward food, and seats on a pleasant lawn with fine views of Lake Windermere; cl 18–30 Dec; kind to children, dogs allowed; limited disabled access.

Windermere SD4199 FIR TREES Lake Rd LA23 2EQ (0153 94) 42272 *£51; 7

attractive, spotless rms, inc 2 big family ones. Well run, comfortable Victorian house with informal, relaxed atmosphere; antiques in the attractive lounge, fine staircase, warmly helpful service (detailed suggestions of what to do), and hearty breakfast.

Kendal SD5293 Low Jock Scar Selside (6 miles from Kendal), Kendal LA8 9LE (01539) 823259 *£50; 5 rms, most with own bthrm. Relaxed and friendly little country guesthouse in 6 acres of garden and woodland; with residents' own lounge, and good home cooking; no smoking; cl Nov–Feb; children at owners' discretion.

Langdale NY2906 Old Dungeon Ghyll Great Langdale, Ambleside LA22 9JY (0153 94) 37272 £50; 14 rms, some with shared bthrm. Friendly and simple, walkers' and climbers' inn dramatically surrounded by fells, wonderful views and terrific walks; popular food – best to book for dinner if not a resident.

Bowland Bridge SD4289 Hare & Hounds Bowland Bridge, Grange-over-Sands LA11 6NN (0153 95) 68333 *£50; 16 attractive rms, mostly with own bthrm. Friendly, extended village inn below the fells, with a welcoming landlord (ex-international soccer player); log fires, beams and stone walls in the lounge bar, cosy residents' lounge, open fires, and a sheltered garden.

Windermere SD4199 Archway 13 College Rd, Windermere LA23 1BU (0153 94) 45613 *£48; 5 pretty rms. Neatly kept and cosy Victorian, no-smoking guesthouse with antiques, books and interesting paintings in the lounge; attentive, helpful owners, and imaginative food inc marvellous breakfasts; children over 10.

Hawkshead SD3598 Summer Hill Country House Hawkshead Hill, Hawkshead, Ambleside LA22 0PP (0153 94) 36311 £42; 5 immaculate, tasteful rms. Tranquil, no-smoking, 17th-c house in a lovely setting overlooking the village and mountains, with friendly discreet owners; cosy log fire and comfortable furnishings in the residents' lounge, and good breakfasts inc homemade bread and scones; tables in the garden for afternoon tea; children over 7; cl Nov–Jan.

Torver SD2894 Church House Torver, Coniston LA21 8AZ (0153 94) 41282 *£39; 5 spacious, airy rms, 2 with shared bthrm. Tidy, 14th-c inn with splendid views over the surrounding hills; big fires, two bars, residents' lounge, fine food, and a sizeable garden; good walks abound; no accommodation at Christmas.

Burneside SD5095 Garnett House Farm Burneside, Kendal LA9 5SF (01539) 724542 £30; 5 rms, 2 with shared bthrm. Homely lounges and dining room in a farmhouse on a large dairy/sheep farm; log fires, and decent food; self-catering cottages, too; cl 25 Dec, 1 Jan.

To see and do

Ambleside Just N of the lake NY3804, this has a busy, holiday-oriented shopping centre inc excellent outdoor equipment shops strung along its central one-way system, with probably the quaintest information centre in the Lakes – the little National Trust shop in the tiny, stone Bridge House over Stock Ghyll by the main car park. In the side lanes above here are one or two attractive older buildings. Traditional glass blowing at Adrian Sankey, Rydal Rd; good demonstrations and shop, but no pressure to buy. Hayes Garden World (Lake Rd) is a big garden centre in landscaped gardens; café, disabled access. The Queen's Hotel is good value for lunch, and the short cut up to the Kirkstone Pass Inn on the A592 is enjoyable.

❀ ⌂ Stagshaw (just S, Waterhead) is a hillside woodland garden with lovely lake views, mature camellias, rhododendrons, magnolias and heathers; best in spring. Open daily Apr–Jun, then by appointment Jul–Oct; (0153 94) 35599; *£1 NT. There's little left of the Roman fort in nearby Borrans Park NY3703. ⌂ ❀ Brockhole (A591 S, or launch from town pier) Exemplary National Park information centre in a country house with well landscaped gardens and attractive lakeshore grounds; also audio-visual show, displays and exhibitions and adventure play area.

Special talks and events throughout the year. Meals, snacks, shop, disabled access; visitor centre cl Nov–Mar, gardens and grounds open all year; (0153 94) 46601; free, but £2.20 for parking.

Kendal SD5293 is a real town as opposed to a tourist centre – busy, with hectic traffic, but lots of small closes leading off the busy main street, some of them attractively restored to give a feel of what the place was like in the 18th c hey-day of the wool-weaving industry. The Globe and Phoenix are cheap for lunch.

🏠 🖼 ♄ ABBOT HALL (Kirkland) Beautifully restored Georgian house with period furniture, silver, china and glass. The impressive art collection reflects Kendal's importance in the 18th c as the centre of an artists' school, and includes works by Ruskin, Turner, Constable, and especially George Romney, along with an enjoyable collection of 20th-c British art. Good craft shop, disabled access; cl am Sun, am Sat Nov–Apr, 23 Dec–mid-Feb; (01539) 722464 to check; *£2.50. The entrance cost now includes admission to the MUSEUM OF LAKELAND LIFE & INDUSTRY behind, which has lovingly re-created period rooms, shops and workshops and any number of items on every aspect of life in the area. There's an almost palpable feel of the past, and subjects as diverse as shoemaking, Arthur Ransome and Postman Pat; some disabled access; open as above.

♨ THE KENDAL MUSEUM (Station Rd) specialises in Lakeland natural history and archaeology, with lots of realistically mounted stuffed animals, Roman antiquities, local geology and natural history, as well as a gallery devoted to the work of Alfred Wainwright. Shop, disabled access; cl

am Sun, 25–26 Dec, 1 Jan; £2.50. A ticket to all three museums described above is available.

🐎 ❋ 🏠 The ruined CASTLE on a small hill on the E edge was the birthplace of Henry VIII's wife Catherine Parr. There's little more now than parts of the outer wall with some towers – but children enjoy it, and there are fine views. A humble building associated with it is the CASTLE DAIRY (Wildman St), an unspoiled Tudor house with some period furniture. Open pm Weds only, Apr–Oct; one of the best-value old houses in the book, still just *5p.

🖼 BREWERY ARTS CENTRE (Highgate) handsomely restored, imposing old building with good changing events and exhibitions, café, bar and landscaped garden. Cl Sun, best to check in advance what's on; (01539) 725133.

🏭 ⚓ K SHOES have a big factory shop at Netherfield; café; cl Sun. LAKELAND CANOES (Hollins Lane, Burneside) hire them by the day, and will take them to and fro for you. WEBBS GARDEN CENTRE (Burneside Rd) is big, with lots of plants – where that wonderful lettuce came from; decent café, disabled access.

Windermere SD4199/**Bowness** SD4097 An extensive, largely Victorian development of guesthouses and small hotels spreads up between the older village of Bowness and the hillside station. It has a touristy feel right through the year, especially around the main street down to the steamer piers. In Bowness itself, there is an inner core of narrower, much older streets and buildings – one of the most ancient is the engaging Hole in t' Wall pub.

❋ ⚓ STEAMBOAT MUSEUM (Rayrigg Rd) Nearly three dozen gleamingly restored, graceful antique steamboats, inc the 1850 *S.L. Dolly*, the oldest

mechanically powered steamboat in the world, and the famous record-breaker *Miss Windermere IV*; weather permitting, there are launch trips out on

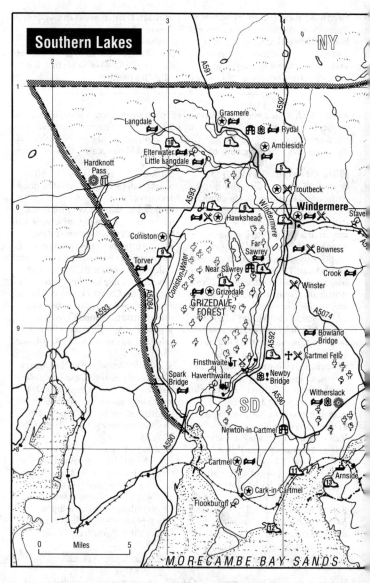

Southern Lakes

the lake (£3.75, 50-minute trip). Also a few boats that comfortably predate steam, and various special events such as vintage-boat rallies and model-boat regattas. Snacks, shop, disabled access; cl Nov–Mar; (0153 94) 45565; £2.80. ♿ ! WORLD OF BEATRIX POTTER (Old Laundry, Crag Brow, Bowness) Of all the Beatrix Potter exhibitions around Lakeland this is probably the one that will appeal to young children the most, with astonishingly detailed walk-in sets peopled by all the characters from the books. New for 1995 will be a rather jolly sounding clock, from which familiar faces will emerge every hour; each year they also have a special display focusing on one of the books – this time it should be the turn of that industrious washer-

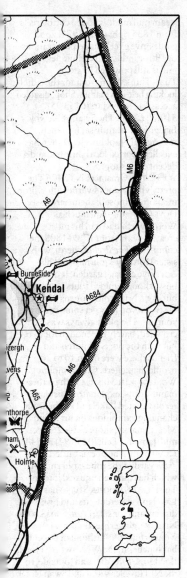

woman Mrs Tiggy-Winkle. Also big-screen video of Miss Potter's life etc. Meals, snacks, shop, disabled access; cl 25 Dec; (0153 94) 88444; £2.85. RIDING, short or long, can be arranged from Wynlass Beck Stables (bottom of Patterdale rd). The Birdcage, College Rd, is a good ANTIQUE SHOP – mostly small things, especially lamps; cl Thurs, Sun.

Other things to see and do

🕭 **Arnside** SD4678 is a good start for the 20-minute BR train trip along the N shore of Morecambe Bay to Ulverston: long viaducts, stupendous views. The Ship at nearby Sandside also has glorious views.

✗ 🕭 **Beetham** SD5079 HERON CORNMILL AND MUSEUM OF PAPERMAKING Well organised, working watermill with a history dating back to 1096, though the currrent building is 18th c. The big paperworks next door has paper-making displays and a growing exhibition. Shop, disabled access; cl Mon exc bank hols, Oct–Easter; (0153 95) 63363; £1.25. Beetham itself is attractive, and the Wheatsheaf is good for lunch.

🏠 ❀ ✔ 🖾 **Cark-in-Cartmel** SD3776 HOLKER HALL Opulently built and furnished, mainly Victorian mansion with appealingly unstuffy and unregimented feel despite the beauty. The glorious, 25-acre formal and woodland GARDENS are often said to be among the best gardens in the country, with spectacular water features, rose garden, rhododendron and azalea arboretum, rare plants and shrubs. Also a deer park, unusual kitchen museum, entertaining MOTOR MUSEUM, adventure playground and new toy and teddy exhibition, so lots to see. Snacks, shop, disabled access; cl Sat, Nov–Mar; (0153 95) 58838; £3 gardens, grounds and exhibitions; Hall and motor museum extra. The nearby Engine is good for lunch.

★ ✝ ✗ **Cartmel** SD3879 Picturesque little alleys lead off the delightfully harmonious central square – especially the one out through the former PRIORY GATEHOUSE. The PRIORY CHURCH, which towers massively over the village, is an interesting mix of architectural grandeur from the 12th to the 16th c, inc fine carving. Lots of arts and crafts in the village. CRAFT WORKSHOPS at Broughton Lodge Farm (N towards A590), inc demonstrations. A vegetarianish café, with home-baking; cl Mon and Tues exc bank hols, and Nov–mid-Apr. The Cavendish Arms and the King's Arms are good for lunch.

✝ **Cartmel Fell** SD4288 CHURCH in a

wonderful, tucked-away country location has interesting early pews and a fine triple-decker pulpit. The Mason's Arms is deservedly very popular indeed for lunch (and has bedrooms).

🏠 ❀ ❀ ♣ **Coniston** SD3195 is an unpretentious village at the foot of its mountain, the Old Man. Decent lunches in the beautifully set Sun (bedrooms), the Black Bull and Yewdale Hotel. BRANTWOOD on the opposite shore of the lake was Ruskin's rambling Victorian house. It still has lots of his furniture, books and paintings, but the real attraction of the site is the surroundings and setting, especially the very extensive, informal, hillside woodland gardens (best in late May/ Jun). Until fairly recently the grounds were a wilderness of overgrown rhododendrons, but they're in the middle of a restoration programme and now have all sorts of interesting and old-fashioned plants and features. Good hour's walk on the nature trail, and mouth-watering views of lake and fells. Snacks, good shop, disabled access (grounds steep in places); cl Mon and Tues mid-Nov–mid-Mar; (0153 94) 41296; *£3.

BOAT TRIPS on Coniston Water are a quiet joy in the opulent Victorian steam yacht which sails daily end Mar–Oct, from Coniston Pier, Brantwood and Park-a-Moor; (0153 94) 41288 for times – best to ring between 9 and 10.30am or you're likely to get the answerphone. Or hire rowing or other boats from the boating centre run by the National Parks (cl Nov–Apr), 15 minutes' walk from the village; rowing boats from £4 per hour, with £1 per extra person; motorboats from £11.50, electric boats £14.50. PONY TREKKING on the fells above, short or long rides, from Spoon Hall; cl Nov–Easter.

🐟 **Elterwater** village NY3305 is idyllically placed in Langdale, with lake views. BARNHOWE CRAFT CENTRE Restored barn with interesting yarns, weaving and spinning equipment, demonstrations and lessons. Cl Sun and Dec–Easter. The Britannia is very popular for lunch.

✗ ⬆T **Finsthwaite** SD3788 STOTT PARK BOBBIN MILL Set in coppiced woodland, this former water-and-steam mill made wooden cotton reels from 1835 right up to 1971; good guides give excellent demonstrations of 19th-c industrial techniques. The mill is still powered by steam Tues–Thurs. Watch out for the lethal-looking belt-drive lathes. Shop, disabled access; cl Nov–Mar; (0153 95) 31087; £2.20. The Swan at Newby Bridge is pleasantly set for lunch.

🐟 Peaceful **Flookburgh** SD3676 has excellent potted local shrimps, and a decent craft shop.

★ 🏠 ⬡ † 🅰 **Grasmere** NY3406 The pretty village does swarm with visitors in summer, most of them here to see DOVE COTTAGE – still much as Wordsworth had it in his most creative years from 1799–1808 (he completed *The Prelude* here), with sister Dorothy's journals and his extensive cottage garden. It does get busy (though guided tours cope well), but in early morning (opens 9.30) out of season you may get some space to yourself. The place always was crowded; barely big enough for two, but with the poets' children and friends there were often 10 to 20 people living here. Good adjoining WORDSWORTH MUSEUM with pictures, manuscripts, explanatory displays, reconstructed Lakeland kitchen, and changing exhibitions on his friends. Meals, snacks, shop; cl 24–26 Dec, mid-Jan–mid-Feb; (0153 94) 35544; £3.90 both. The poet is buried in the graveyard of the robust old church, which has quite an unusual interior. The HEATON COOPER STUDIO has Lakeland watercolours and prints on display and for sale; cl am Sun. SARAH NELSON's gingerbread shop is wonderfully old-fashioned. Decent bar lunches in the Wordsworth Hotel, Red Lion, Tweedies and (outside, to the N) Traveller's Rest and Swan Hotel.

🐴 🐟 ✔ **Grizedale** SD3494 FOREST PARK Woodland trails from short strolls to half-day walks, punctuated by often hard-to-spot timber and rock sculptures. Lots of other activities too, with a CRAFT CENTRE, good information centre (cl winter), bookable, deer observation hides, orienteering, adventure play area, and even a theatre/ concert arena. In all, six or seven square miles of mainly coniferous hillside timber to get lost in. Some disabled access; (0229) 860373; parking £1. The Eagle's Head at Satterthwaite is the handiest place for lunch.

🏛❋ **Hardknott Pass** NY2101 HARDKNOTT ROMAN FORT Quite well preserved and very interestingly restored, but most notable for its staggering lonely position high in the mountains; magnificent views to the sea. The drive here is daunting (see **Driving** section below), and the site can be hazardous in winter.

🐮🐾 **Haverthwaite** SD3484 LAKESIDE & HAVERTHWAITE RAILWAY Short steam trip connecting with cruise boats (Lakeside is the stop at the S end of the lake for the Windermere lake steamers – a good combined trip); small collection of steam and diesel locomotives. Meals, snacks, shop, disabled access; no trains Nov–Mar; (0153 95) 31594 for times; £3 return. Artcrystal (Low Wood) have demonstrations of CRYSTAL ENGRAVING by hand.

★ 🖼🏠✝†⚓ **Hawkshead** SD3598 is a must: a virtually unchanged Elizabethan Lakeland village with sturdy outside walls, and sheltered, flower-filled inner courtyards. Though very popular with summer visitors, even at its busiest it has a pleasantly foreign 'different' feel, and the fact that cars are kept out helps a lot. The BEATRIX POTTER GALLERY, in the former offices of the author's husband, has a generous, annually changing selection of the original illustrations of Peter Rabbit and other favourites, as well as rather different, more acutely (almost acidly) observed drawings. A timed ticket system operates to keep it uncrowded, so during peak holiday periods you may have to wait to get in. Shop; cl wknds, Nov–Mar; *£2.60; NT. The OLD GRAMMAR SCHOOL, now a museum, is worth poking your nose into, if only to see where Wordsworth carved his name on a desk (he attended 1779–83). The church has some eye-catching, early 18th-c murals. The best pubs for lunch in the village are the Queen's Head and King's Arms, though on the outskirts, the Outgate Inn and the beautifully placed Drunken Duck are well worth a visit. Trout FISHING and BOAT HIRE are

available on nearby Esthwaite Water, the largest stocked lake in the region. 🐾 **Holme** SD5278 (the one SE of Milnthorpe, off the B6384) The Dales of Bank House Farm, Holme Mills, make unusual chess sets and nursery furniture; cl wknds; (01524) 781646.

🏠❋🐮 **Levens** SD4985 LEVENS HALL Impressive Elizabethan mansion based around an older core, with fine, carved oak chimney pieces, ceiling plasterwork, Spanish leather panelling, period furnishings and interesting paintings. The magnificent topiary GARDENS in their original layout of 1692 are perhaps the highlight of a visit, the fantastic shapes really standing out against the ancient grey stone of the house; a new fountain garden commemorates the garden's recent tercentenary. Also model and other STEAM ENGINES (pm only; in steam, bank hol Mons, some summer Suns – maybe children's rides), play area, grand beech trees, and deer park. Snacks, plant sales, shop, disabled access to grounds; cl Fri and Sat, all Oct–Mar; (0153 95) 60321; £3.90, £2.50 grounds only. The Hare & Hounds is good for lunch.

🐴🦋 **Milnthorpe** SD4981 LAKELAND WILDLIFE OASIS (A6 S) Millions of years of evolution flash before your eyes at this lively jungle house, a fascinating cross between a zoo and museum. Action models and interactive displays explain how we got to where we are today, and there are lots of brightly coloured and unusual fish, birds and animals. One hall has exotic butterflies and insects and the tropical hall offers a chance to design your own mammal. Snacks, shop, disabled access; cl 25 Dec; (0153 95) 63027; *£2.85. The Wheatsheaf at Beetham and Blue Bell at Heversham are both good for lunch.

🏠 **Near Sawrey** SD3796 HILL TOP Small, remote 17th-c farmhouse, kept exactly as it was when owned by Beatrix Potter, who wrote many of her stories here; no longer included in tourist board leaflets as NT (great beneficiaries of her generosity) feel too many people come already, and to reduce the pressure you may decide not to join the queuing crowds yourself. Shop; cl Thurs and Fri, all

Nov–Mar; £3.30. NT. The old-fashioned, NT-owned Tower Bank Arms is a good pub with nicely furnished bedrooms.

❀ ! **Newby Bridge** SD3786 GRAYTHWAITE HALL GARDENS Well kept, late Victorian garden, strong on rhododendrons and late spring flowering shrubs; open Apr–Jun only; (0153 95) 31248; *£2. From outside the well set Swan Hotel, the Windermere Balloon Company run BALLOON TRIPS over the whole of this area (weather permitting); (01229) 581779; £120. They sometimes take off from other places too.

🏠 **Newton-in-Cartmel** SD4083 WRS ARCHITECTURAL ANTIQUES (Yew Tree Barn, on the A590) Sometimes bizarre collection of house and garden furnishings – the showrooms are crammed with period fireplaces, bathrooms, beams and doors. Meals and snacks, shop; free. The Lindale Inn just S is useful for lunch.

🏠 ❀ **Rydal** NY3706 RYDAL MOUNT Wordsworth and his family lived at Rydal longer than at any of their other homes; moving here from Grasmere, the poet's sister Dorothy described it as 'a paradise', and they stayed for the rest of their lives. The house itself is rather modest, with family portraits and period furniture, but it's what's outside that really stands out – the good-sized garden is still much as the poet laid it out, consciously picturesque, with original ideas that people are still rediscovering today. The setting is lovely, overlooking mountains and lakes, and they often have readings of the poetry it inspired. Shop; cl Tues in winter, and all the last 3 weeks of Jan; (0153 94) 33002; £2. Decent campsites nearby. The Glen Rothay Hotel does decent lunches.

🏠 ❀ 🍴 **Sizergh** SD4987 CASTLE Originally just a tall and sturdy 14th-c tower, this lovely lakeside house has been harmoniously extended over the centuries by the family who have lived here for generations. Fine Tudor and Elizabethan carving, panelling and furniture, Jacobite relics, and terraced gardens surrounding a grand flight of steps to the water. Lots to interest a gardener, inc an enormous rock garden, Japanese maples, water-garden, wild flowers, and daffodils in the crab-apple orchard; the autumn colours are lovely. Snacks, shop, disabled access to garden; cl am, all Fri and Sat, Nov–Mar; £3.30, £1.70 garden only; NT. THE BARN SHOP (Low Sizergh Farm) Recommended by several of our correspondents – plenty of fresh farm foods such as cheese, meat, ice-cream, sausage and bread, and other local produce inc Morecambe Bay shrimps, with a craft shop and pick-your-own strawberries in season. The tearoom overlooks the milking parlour. Cl Mon Jan–Mar; (0153 95) 60426; free. The Strickland Arms, owned by the NT, is useful for lunch.

🖋 **Staveley** SD4798 (the one N of Kendal) Peter Hall is a CABINET-MAKER, and at his shop you can see furniture being made or restored, and woodturners at work. Shop, disabled access; cl Sun, and Sat and bank hols exc showroom and shop. The Eagle & Child is good value for lunch.

★ 🏠 ❀ ❋ **Troutbeck** NY3926 is a delightful settlement of ancient farms strung along a steep valley below high fells. TOWNEND is an excellent example of one of these – the perfectly preserved home of the same comfortably off, very traditional farming family for 300 years till the 1940s, showing little change over all that time. Solid, simple, unshowy comfort, and a sensible, down-to-earth and entirely self-sufficient layout. Cl am, all Mon (exc bank hols) and Sat, Nov–Mar; £2.50; NT. The beautifully placed hillside village has several more such 'statesmen's' farms. HOLEHIRD (off the A592, S) is the Lakeland Horticultural Society's hillside garden, covering five acres with a wide variety of well growing plants, inc the national collections of hydrangeas and some other families; lovely views. Disabled access; cl mid-Nov–mid-Mar by arrangement, (0153 94) 46008; £1. The quaint Queen's Head is good for lunch, and the beautifully set Mortal Man is popular.

❀ ❋ **Witherslack** SD4384 HALECAT GARDEN Good example of modern landscaping, with fine views from the mainly herbaceous garden; plants for sale (especially hydrangeas). Cl am Sun and Sat; (0144) 852229; free.

Boating on Windermere

The silent steam launch *Osprey* does a stately 45-minute tour of the lake, and if it's running – tel (0153 94) 45565 – is the pick of the sightseeing boat trips; £3.95. Lots of other launches, of all sorts of shapes and sizes, run cruises of varying lengths from Bowness Bay, Ambleside, Waterhead and (not Nov–Mar) Newby Bridge. The Lakeside pier at the S end is the terminus for the Haverthwaite steam railway.

Rowing boats can be hired from the Bowness Bay Boating Company; from £3 per hour, £2 per extra person. They also have motorboats, a number of launches and so on – at least one of which is equipped to take disabled people; ring (0153 94) 43360 to check. Lake Holidays Afloat do motorboats too; around £49 for a full day. A pleasant place to hire rowing boats (not Nov–Easter) is Fell Foot Park nr Newby Bridge, an 18-acre park with plenty of room for lakeside picnics; café and shop (cl Nov–Easter), some disabled access; parking £2.50; NT. They can also provide details of boating and fishing on other NT waters, tel (0153 95) 31273.

Lakeland Sailing at Ferry Nab, Bowness, do day, weekend or longer cruises and courses on large sailing yachts; from £50 a day. Windsurfing or waterskiing can be arranged at Low Wood Water Sports Centre, Windermere; windsurfing, canoeing or dinghy sailing from Mar–Oct, at Windermere Sailing Centre, Leigh Groves Building, Rayrigg Rd, Windermere.

The chain ferry linking the ferry road below Bowness with the Hawkshead road below Far Sawrey is a utilitarian way of taking to the water; but though it runs every 20 minutes and saves miles of driving, queues mean that it saves time only out of season.

Walks

Many of the recommended places to stay here have grand walks right from their doorsteps. The area has a tremendous choice of other walks, short and long: the following suggestions would keep anyone busy for quite a long stay, but really only scratch this magnificent surface.

Grasmere Water ⌂-1, **Rydal Water** and **Elterwater** are famous for their lovely settings, and there are pleasant walks all around; you can even link all three together in a long afternoon's walk filled with glorious views. The walk up the good track to Easedale Tarn from Grasmere quickly gets you away from the crowds and into a fine valley; the lake itself is romantically set below rocks.

From Windermere (opposite the station) the short, steep walk (half-hour each way) up to **Orrest Head** SD4199 ⌂-2 gives spectacular views over the lake and the Pennines; lovely at sunset. For another fine view, the hill of **Gummer's How** SD3988 ⌂-3, further S from Windermere, is an easy 20-minute climb from the road. There are also good views over the lake from the walk up wooded **Claife Heights** SD3797 ⌂-4, above the ferry at Far Sawrey SD3893; or, more undemandingly, from the track along the shore N from there. Windermere is surprisingly short on lakeside paths – there are short ones at Bowness **SD4906** (to Biskey Howe) and along parts of the wooded western shore.

From Ambleside NY3804, a path leads up to **Wansfell Pike** NY3904 ⌂-5, toy-like in size compared with the bigger fells, but the view is as good as many. An even smaller protuberance is **Latterbarrow** SD3699 ⌂-6 nr Hawkshead SD3598, but it is elevated enough above a relatively low-lying area to give views over Windermere and Langdale NY2807. **Tarn Hows** SD3299 ⌂-7, an easy hour's walk from Hawkshead SD3598, is a gorgeously photogenic small lake; particularly beautiful on a still clear autumn day. The sculpture trail in **Grizedale Forest** SD3494 ⌂-8 (see entry in **To see and do** section) enlivens the forest plantations, making a good rainy-day activity; the sculptures are set in various spots throughout the forest. The visitor centre issues a map showing where to find them.

Coniston Water SD3195 ◇-9 has a lovely path on its W side, S of Coniston; you can combine this walk with one on a higher-level route along the Walna Scar 'road' (an ancient, hard track closed to through traffic) which lies beneath the Old Man of Coniston SD2797, the outstanding viewpoint of the vicinity. Climb the Old Man from Coniston, go up past the remains of copper mines, and return down the Walna Scar road.

Great Langdale NY2906 ◇-10, dominated by the awesome Langdale Pikes, is the area's main centre for more serious fell-walking in grand scenery. One very popular shorter walk here is up the good track to Stickle Tarn, from the car park by the Stickle Barn (useful for refreshments), and Bow Fell and Crinkle Crags are two longer fell walks. Wainwrights, in the not specially graceful settlement of Chapel Stile off the B5343, another useful refreshment place, is particularly popular with many of our contributors as a base for walks along here.

The sedately old-fashioned resort of Grange-over-Sands SD4077 ◇-11 is the start for summer guided walks over **Morecambe Bay Sands**, oddly otherworldly: glistening tidal flats, quick-stepping patrols of wading birds, distant hills, grisly tales of people and horses sucked under; tel (053 95) 34026 for times, which depend on tides. From here, there's also a pleasant walk up through the woods to **Hampsfield Fell** SD3979 ◇-12 for terrific views over the bay. Further stunning views of the bay are from **Humphrey Head Point** SD3973, a ¼-mile-long headland protruding into the sea, and from **Arnside Knott** SD4577 ◇-13, nr Arnside, which looks across to the Southern Lakeland fells.

Driving

In summer, this area is decidedly not a place for the impatient driver, as its more beautiful parts tend to choke with slow queues of scenery-watchers.

The B5343 into Great Langdale is the least taxing road into this area's mountain scenery, an austere valley surrounded by awesome hills; you can keep on a poorer steeper road to go up and over, passing nr pretty Blea Tarn, and coming back down through the gentler Little Langdale.

From Little Langdale the very steeply twisting back road up over Wrynose Pass gives exhilarating views; you can then either fork left down the glorious Duddon Valley past Seathwaite and Ulpha, or keep on over the breathlessly steep Hardknott Pass (you can see the Isle of Man on a clear day). Stop for Hardknott Fort (see entry in **To see and do** section) over the summit.

The road along the Winster Valley, turning off the A5074 S of Bowness at Winster and running down through Bowland Bridge and Cartmel Fell to Lindale, is very pretty (and passes nr the Mason's Arms on Cartmel Fell, an outstanding pub).

The back roads through Grizedale Forest, S of Hawkshead, are usually quiet; we've seen deer on them on autumn and winter evenings.

The B5282 from Milnthorpe has quiet views across the Kent estuary.

It's worth knowing that the M6 (and its now much less heavily trafficked elder sister the A6) has splendid distant fell and Pennine views. Incidentally, heading N from junction 38, the Tebay service area, locally owned and run, is unusually pleasant – much more personal-seeming than most; and heading S from junction 37, the Killington Lake service area does have a gorgeous lakeside setting.

Where to eat

Bowness SD4097 PORTHOLE 3 Ash St (0153 94) 44793 Long-established, bustling bistro with consistently good evening meals, some Italian and some very English dishes; a genuine personal touch to the service and olde-worlde surroundings; decent wine; a reliably enjoyable evening out; cl Tues, mid-Dec–mid-Feb; disabled access. £26.50.
Windermere SD4199 ROGERS 4 High St (0153 94) 44954 Beautifully presented

and individualistic, French-based cooking in an intimate evening restaurant, lovely and cosy; helpful service; cl Sun exc bank hols, 1 wk summer, 1 wk winter; partial disabled access. £20.

Cartmel Fell SD4288 MASONS ARMS (0153 95) 68486. Old-fashioned building in an unrivalled setting with wonderful views; superb range of beers inc own brew and interesting continental real ales, and very popular food – 50 per cent vegetarian; cl 25 Dec. £18|£3/£7.25.

Hawkshead SD3598 DRUNKEN DUCK (0153 94) 36347 Marvellous choice of varied vegetarian dishes (and some meaty ones, too) in an exceptionally popular pub in walking country; cheery service, well kept beers, and cosy and traditionally pubby rooms. £16|£2/£6.

Troutbeck NY4103 QUEENS HEAD (0153 94) 32174 Gabled 17th-c inn with rambling bar, some fine antique carving, and very good, imaginative bar food; bedrooms; cl 25 Dec. £14.50|£3.50/£6.

Winster SD4293 BROWN HORSE (0153 94) 43443 Excellent food in a carefully refurbished pub, with interesting European dishes (and English ones, too), fine puddings, thoughtful wine list and well kept beers; cheerful, helpful service. £14|£2/£5.50.

NORTHERN LAKES

This area closely rivals the Southern Lakes for beauty; it is less crowded in summer, more mountainous (though with great variety of scenery), with fine gardens and excellent places to stay.

Ullswater and Derwent Water both have great beauty: Ullswater has some of the best (if most expensive) places to stay right by the lake shore; Derwent Water, with its islands and its handier proportions, is perhaps even more pleasant for idle boating. Borrowdale is splendid for a quiet break (perhaps at Seatoller House – if you can get in), with an almost endless variety of interesting walks from the simplest to the most challenging. Virtually all the other places we recommend to stay in are also well placed for walkers.

Keswick, the area's holiday heart, has plenty going on for all ages. Penrith is more of a genuine market town. Outside, Dalemain House at Dacre, Lingholm Gardens at Portinscale, Mirehouse near Bassenthwaite, Hutton-in-the-Forest at Skelton, and possibly the small town of Cockermouth are the pick of the places to visit. There are also quite a few very attractive little villages. Lowther Leisure Park at Hackthorpe has a lot to keep families occupied.

Where to stay

Pooley Bridge NY4724 SHARROW BAY Pooley Bridge, Penrith CA10 2LZ (0176 84) 86301 *£250 inc dinner; 28 lovely rms with antiques, books, and games, mostly with own bthrm. Country-house hotel in quiet, idyllic spot by Ullswater; lovely views of lake and mountains and legendary for the years of loving care the owners have put into the distinctive style, furnishings and decor; perfect, unobtrusively attentive service, particularly good, richly worked-out English cooking – a vast choice (and two contrasting dining rooms of great character); cl Dec–Feb; children over 13; disabled access.

Watermillock NY4522 LEEMING HOUSE Watermillock, Penrith CA11 0JJ (0176 84) 86622 £128; 39 cosseting rms, many with beautiful views. Well run, extended hotel in 20 acres of quiet lakeside grounds, with log fires in comfortable lounges, a cosy panelled bar, fine food in the lovely, no-smoking dining room, and good, courteous service; boating; good provision for the disabled.

Mungrisdale NY3731 MILL HOTEL Mungrisdale, Penrith CA11 0XR (0176 87) 79659 *£105 inc dinner; 9 rms, most with own bthrm. Very friendly, small streamside hotel, beautifully situated in a lovely valley hamlet hidden away below Blencathra; an open fire in the cosy and comfortable sitting room, and good, imaginative, 5-course meals; cl Nov–Feb; disabled access.

Watermillock NY4522 OLD CHURCH Watermillock, Penrith CA11 0JN (0176 84) 86204 £90; 10 rms, some with lovely Ullswater view. Attractive, 18th-c Lakeland house, peacefully located in waterside gardens; log fires and individual furnishings in attractive and civilised day rooms, kind service, and excellent English dinners at 8pm in the no-smoking dining room; rowing/windsurfing boats; cl Nov–Mar.

Bassenthwaite Lake NY1930 PHEASANT Bassenthwaite Lake, Cockermouth CA13 9YE (0176 87) 76234 £88; 20 rms. Civilised hotel with delightfully old-fashioned pubby bar, restful lounges with open fires, comfortable old armchairs, antiques and fresh flowers; interesting gardens merge into surrounding fellside woodlands; cl 24-25 Dec; disabled access.

Derwent Water NY2618 LODORE SWISS Derwentwater, Keswick CA12 5UX (0176 87) 77285 £75; 70 well equipped rms. Long-standing but well updated, big holiday hotel, with lots of facilities in 40 acres of lakeside gardens and woodland, inc swimming, tennis and other games; open fires in comfortable day rooms, an elegant restaurant, and particularly good with children (nursery with NNEB nannies, baby-sitting, baby-listening service); now a Stakis hotel.

Ireby NY2439 OVERWATER HALL Ireby, Carlisle CA5 1HH (0176 87) 76566 £72; 13 rms. Relaxed and friendly, family-run hotel in 18 acres of gardens and woodland; with a log fire in the elegant and comfortable drawing room, good, imaginative food in the cosy dining room; lots of walks; children over 7 in restaurant (high tea 5pm); well behaved dogs welcome.

Lorton NY1525 NEW HOUSE FARM Lorton, Cockermouth CA13 9UU (01900) 85404 *£70 inc dinner; 3 rms with wonderful hillside views. Friendly 17th-c house (not a working farm) with beams, flagstones, open fires, and two residents' lounges; very good food inc game and fish caught by the owner, and home-made scones and preserves; lots of walks; no smoking; cl winter; children over 12.

Buttermere Valley NY1622 PICKETT HOWE Buttermere Valley, Brackenthwaite, Cockermouth CA13 9UY (01900) 85444 *£70; 4 rms with thoughtful extras like home-made biscuits and torch. At the end of its own track and surrounded by stunning mountain scenery stands this 17th-c longhouse with its friendly, relaxed atmosphere, lovely antiques, log fires, beams and slate floors; fine food in the candlelit dining room, very sound wine list, and wonderful breakfasts inc home-made oatcakes, jam, marmalade and so forth; no smoking; cl Dec–end Mar; children over 10.

Underskiddaw NY2624 RED HOUSE Underskiddaw, Keswick CA12 4QA (0176 87) 72211 £68*; 20 rms. Friendly and comfortable, Victorian country house in 8 acres of wooded grounds with wonderful views, where visitors are treated as house-guests; spacious day rooms with a log fire in the lounge hall, play area for children, and putting; house-party groups welcomed; cl 2 wks leading up to Christmas and 3 wks after New Year; disabled access.

Thirlmere NY3116 DALE HEAD HALL Thirlmere, Keswick CA12 4TN (0176 87) 72478 £61; 9 pretty rms, most with lake views. Peaceful, partly 16th-c country house in lovely lakeside grounds, with comfortable lounges, log fire, friendly owners, and home-cooked food using produce grown in own walled garden; children over 10.

Brandlingill NY1626 LOW HALL Brandlingill, Cockermouth CA11 0RE (01900) 826654 £50; 5 pleasant rms. Beautifully sited, partly 17th-c farmhouse below Whinlatter Pass and close to Cockermouth; with big peaceful garden, good home cooking in the beamed dining room, and log fires and books in the lounges; no smoking; cl Nov–Feb; children over 10.

Dockray NY3921 ROYAL ULLSWATER Dockray, Ullswater CA11 0JV (0176 84) 82356 £48; 10 rms. Friendly and homely, family-run hotel with open fires in the spacious bars, and good-value, hearty meals; in a fine spot between the hills and lake, with walks from the doorstep; limited disabled access.

Keswick NY2624 GEORGE St John's St, Keswick CA12 5AZ (0176 87) 72076 £40; 17 unpretentiously comfortable rms, shared bthrms. Bustling inn with beams and flagstones downstairs, a little panelled bar with log fire and Wordsworth associations, and a smart restaurant; trout fishing.

Seatoller NY2413 SEATOLLER HOUSE Seatoller, Keswick CA12 5XN (0176 87) 77218 *£46; 9 rms. Friendly, house-party atmosphere in a 17th-c house that has been a guesthouse for over 100 yrs, with self-service drinks and board games in the comfortable lounges, and a good, no-choice, fixed-time hearty dinner (not Tues) where all the guests sit together at big tables; packed lunches; many walks from the doorstep as the house is at the foot of Honister Pass; cl Nov–mid-Mar; children over 5.

Cockermouth NY1231 **High Stanger Farm** Lorton Valley, Cockermouth CA13 9TS (01900) 8223875 *£30; 2 rms, shared bthrm. 17th-c farmhouse in a quiet spot with wonderful views, log fire in the comfortable lounge, and friendly owners.

To see and do

Keswick NY2624 is the tourist centre of the Northern Lakes, with lots of Victorian villas (many of them now guesthouses and small hotels) outside quite a traditional centre, with small cobbled closes running off the main streets. It's full of breeches, boots and knapsacks in high season, with useful outdoor equipment shops, and is a routine stop on coach tours. The lively Dog & Gun is very popular for lunch, with the Pheasant out towards Crosthwaite also worthwhile. The Wild Strawberry is a quaint tearoom with an upstairs gallery; cl Tues and Weds. Lakeside Tea Gardens (Lake Rd) has home-baking, lots for children, pleasant modern furniture and crockery inside and a garden with trees and chaffinches; cl about 5pm. George Fisher (Borrowdale Rd) is a good, big, outdoors shop.

📷 CARS OF THE STARS (Standish St) An unusual collection of cars from film and television dating back to Laurel & Hardy's Model T Ford, taking in Chitty Chitty Bang Bang, the Batmobile and cars belonging to James Bond and Postman Pat along the way. Shop, disabled access; cl wkdys Dec and Jan; (0176 87) 73757; £2.50.

👶 THE PENCIL MUSEUM (Southey Works) is surprisingly interesting, with a good audio-visual presentation, and some unexpected exhibits. Shop, disabled access; cl 25–26 Dec, 1 Jan; (0176 87) 73626; £2.

🕯 BEATRIX POTTER'S LAKE DISTRICT (Packhorse Court) The focus here is on the life of the writer herself, and particularly the farms, land and scenery that she used so much of her money to preserve; a multi-media show brings it all to life, and there's a related exhibition. Shop, disabled access; cl wkdys Nov–Mar; £2.50; NT.

👶 The town also has a thoroughly traditional local MUSEUM (Fitzpark, Station Rd), where the Poets' Corner stands out. Shop, disabled access; cl Nov–Mar; £1.

✿ From the boat pier, a short stroll takes you up to Friar's Crag for a fine lake view; the car park on the B5289 just S gives access to another great lake viewpoint, Castle **Head**.

🏛 The Castlerigg Neolithic STONE CIRCLE NY2923, just E, is well preserved and gives photogenic perspectives of the mountains (the best times for pictures are morning and evening); take a map to identify the peaks it aligns with. The site is owned by the National Trust, and there's a brief explanation of the stones' history.

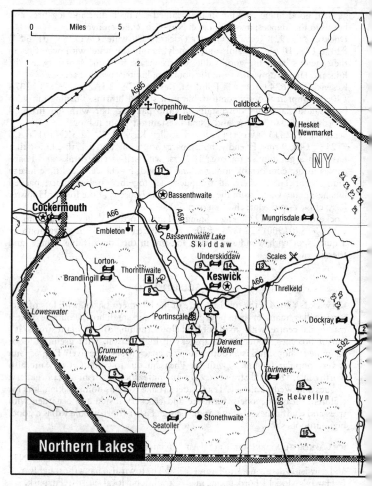

Northern Lakes

Penrith NY5130 is a real locals' rather than tourists' town, and the biggest in Lakeland. It is very much a northern country town, with solid stone streets, an unreconstructed traffic problem, farmers from far and wide descending on its Skirsgill agricultural market (Tues, sometimes Fri too in late summer/autumn), and genuinely traditional Lakeland shops selling real fudge and toffee, rich cakes (Birketts), local cheeses (Grahams), prize Cumberland sausages (Cranstons), local antiquarian books, and cheap and sturdy country clothes. John Norris (21 Victoria Rd) is the outstanding fishing/outdoor wear shop, with something for everyone; good prices. The George and Agricultural Hotel both have decent-value food.

▨ CASTLE Built in the 14th c as a defence against Scottish raids, and the home of Richard III when he was Duke of Gloucester; now in ruins and surrounded by a park; free.
▨ ❋ ⚲ ⌂ BROUGHAM CASTLE NY5329 (off the A6, S) is a sturdy Norman ruin on steep lawns above riverside sheep pastures; you can climb to the top of the keep to really appreciate the view. Traces of Roman remains too, with a small exhibition of tombstones. Snacks, shop; cl Nov–Mar; (01768) 62488; £1.25. BROUGHAM HALL CRAFT CENTRE nearby has many crafts inc woodturning, silver and metal work,

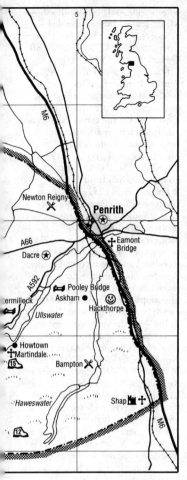

snacks, shop, disabled access; (01768) 892733; *£3.

🎵 MUSEUM (Middlegate) A useful introduction to Penrith and the surrounding area; cl Sun exc pm in summer; free.

Other things to see and do

★ † 🏠 🌸 **Bassenthwaite** NY2228 Attractive, close-set little village – the 12th-c parish church is three miles S; the Sun is a decent pub. MIREHOUSE (off the A591, S) The family that still lives in this modest 17th-c house once had excellent literary connections, so the fine rooms have a number of mementoes of Wordsworth, Carlyle and Tennyson among others, as well a few good pictures. There are sometimes piano recitals in the music room, and on Weds in Jun, July and Sept they usually have displays of lace-making. Outside is an interesting garden (bee/butterfly plants), as well as peaceful lakeshore grounds, lakeside church, and woods with well thought-out adventure play areas. Lots to do, with a surprising number of activities for children. Good home cooking in ex-mill tearoom, shop, disabled access; house open pm Sun, Weds and bank hols Apr–Oct, also Fri in Aug, other times by appointment, grounds open daily; (0176 87) 72287; £3, garden only £1. There's escorted RIDING through woodland from Armathwaite Hall Equestrian Centre, Coalbeck Farm. Readers tell us they know of few nicer sites for a caravan than the one at Englethwaite Hall nr here.

🎵 🎵 🗙 † **Caldbeck** NY3240 Riverside restaurant, craft shops and small mining MUSEUM in restored watermill. Cl Mon exc bank hols, Tues and Weds Oct–Nov, and all Dec–mid-Mar. John Peel's grave is in the nearby churchyard, and the Oddfellows Arms is useful for food.

★ 🏠 🏚 🎵 **Cockermouth** NY1231 Quietly attractive riverside town. WORDSWORTH HOUSE The poet's happy childhood home, a handsome, restored, 18th-c town house with fine furniture, pictures by friends and contemporaries, good original panelling, plasterwork and walled

---

stonemasonry and a smokehouse, all in the attractive stone courtyard of a 15th-c hall. The house and grounds have been undergoing a massive restoration and there's plenty to see. Meals, snacks, shop, disabled access; phone for opening times; (01768) 68184; free, though invite £1 donation. 🎵 🎵 WETHERIGGS POTTERY (Clifton Dykes NY5326, signed off the A6, further S) Interesting working pottery – one of the oldest in the country – with 19th-c steam engine and equipment and smallish museum; children can try their hands at the wheel. They've been closed for renovations, but should be open again by Easter – best to check first. Meals,

garden above the river. Well worth a visit in its own right as well as for its Wordsworth associations, and interesting to see how different it is to the places he lived in later on. Meals, snacks, shop; cl Sat exc on bank hol wknds (or in July and Aug), Sun and Nov–Mar; £2.40; NT. The Norham opposite is a good teashop, and the comfortable Trout does good food. JENNINGS BREWERY Tours of traditional Castle Brewery, where the water for brewing is still drawn from the well that supplied the castle at the time of the Norman Conquest. Shop; tours Mar–Oct, 10.30am and 2pm wkdys, 11am Sat – booking advisable; (01900) 823214; no children under 12; £2.50. CASTLEGATE HOUSE GALLERY (Castlegate) Friendly, lived-in, Georgian house opposite the castle, with walled garden, Adam ceiling and sales of paintings and crafts. Cl Thurs, Sun, and all Jan and Feb; (01900) 822149; free. TOY AND MODEL MUSEUM Mainly British toys from the last century. Cl Dec and Jan exc by appointment; (01900) 827606; *£1.80. ⌂⌂❋✝ **Dacre** NY4626 DALEMAIN HOUSE Despite the Norman façade this fine old house is largely Elizabethan, and has a number of features even older, so there's an appealing variety of periods and style. Some rooms are grand, others are charming, with splendid furnishings and paintings and a good deal for children to enjoy. Particularly interesting is the Chinese room, its hand-painted wallpaper and intricate fittings the height of fashion in their time . The Norman peel tower houses a regimental museum, and the courtyard has rural bygones in the barn; also an adventure playground, and deer in the carefully landscaped PARK with lake and mountain views. Atmospheric restaurant, shop, disabled access; cl Fri and Sat and Oct–Easter; (0176 84) 86450; £4, £3 grounds only. The village CHURCH has pre-Norman sculpture, and quaint medieval stone bears in the graveyard. The King's Arms in Stainton is good for lunch. ↓✝ **Embleton** NY1731 WYTHOP MILL Unusual little museum with well displayed, vintage woodworking tools and machinery powered by a waterwheel; also a Victorian kitchen,

wheelwright and blacksmith's shops. Meals, snacks, limited disabled access; cl Mon (exc bank hols), 6 wks from Jan; (0176 87) 76394; *£1.80. ☺**Hackthorpe** NY5423 LOWTHER LEISURE PARK (signed off the A6, S of Penrith) Lots for families – funfair, safe boating, miniature train rides, challenging play areas, putting, kiosks, circus, and events like jousting – all in attractive parkland. Meals, snacks, shop, disabled access; check for winter opening times; (01931) 712523; £5.50. Askham with its two good pubs is handy for lunch. ❋**Portinscale** NY2523 LINGHOLM GARDENS Beatrix Potter wrote *The Tale of Squirrel Nutkin* here, probably inspired by the other members of his family that you'll still see scampering through the extensive woodland and lovely formal gardens. Rare trees and shrubs especially rhododendrons, Himalayan meconopsis and primulas, fine lake views; best at daffodil time, late May or Jun, or in the autumn when the leaves have begun to turn. Snacks, good plant sales, disabled access; cl Nov–Mar; (0176 87) 72003; £2.60. ⌂✝**Shap** NY5415 ABBEY (left towards Keld, off the A6 going N out of village) The best feature is the unspoilt and undeveloped riverside seclusion; the abbey itself is very ruined, but it's possible to trace the 13th-c layout in some detail. Nearby KELD CHAPEL is a lonely, untouched shepherds' church in a riverside hamlet. The Greyhound is good value for lunch. ⌂✿**Thornthwaite** NY2225 THORNTHWAITE GALLERIES have fine art, pottery and other unusual examples of craftsmanship, as well as teas, summer try-your-hand-at-it demonstrations, and a play area. Snacks, shop, disabled access (but no facilities); cl Tues and Dec–Feb; (0176 87) 78248; free. The Coledale Inn at Braithwaite is good for lunch. **Ullswater** NY4020 AIRA FORCE is a 65-ft waterfall in lovely NT land overlooking the lake – see also **Walks** section; restaurant and shop. It looks its best after rain or on a misty morning. The good Royal Hotel at Dockray NY3921 is handy for lunch. ✝**Country churches** are generally simple here, though candlelit St Wilfred's (B6262 E of Eamont Bridge) NY5328 is an exception for its magnificent furnishings inc continental treasures; others worth stopping at include Watermillock NY4522 for its evocative photographs of all its 1930s parishioners; Torpenhow NY2039 (formidably Norman, inc some Roman masonry); and Martindale NY4419 (attractive primitive stonework).

★ Other attractive villages in fine scenery include Askham NY5123 (two greens – each with a good pub), Hesket Newmarket NY3438 (interesting old inn brews its own beer), Stonethwaite NY2613 (the Langstrath is a good stop for thirsty walkers) and Threlkeld NY3325 (the Salutation is useful). The comfortable Kirkstile Inn at Loweswater NY1222 deserves a mention for its glorious setting.

Boating

On Ullswater, elegant Victorian steamers converted to diesel run between Pooley Bridge, Howtown and Glenridding; disabled access, cl Dec–Mar. Sailing dinghies can be hired by competent sailors from Ullswater Marina at Watermillock or the sailing school at Glenridding (cl winter). Rowing and other boats can be hired from Tindals in Glenridding; rowing boats from £4 per hour, motorboats from £9.50.

Regular Derwent Water launches run all year from Keswick to half a dozen points around the lake. Rowing boats and launches can be hired in Keswick; from £3 per hour.

You can also hire rowing boats on Buttermere and Crummock Water.

Walks

Head in practically any direction here and you can walk for minutes or hours. All the out-of-town places to stay that we have listed can recommend fine walks straight from their door.

Ullswater's NY4020 eastern shore ⌂-1 is outstanding; there are very many differing views, with a rewarding combination of waterside stretches and higher ground – from which to see more sweeping vistas. On the best and most popular stretch, Howtown–Patterdale–Glenridding, you will meet quite a few other people in summer (when it can be combined with the steamer for a round trip; best to take the steamer on the way out in case the service is cancelled). The Howtown Hotel is a good break in a stunning setting, and Hallin Fell NY4319 nearby gives an aerial view of the lake. The main road runs along the western side, but over here there's a pleasant if more populated stroll from the car park on the A592, just NE of the A5091 junction, through lakeshore woods to the Aira Force waterfalls NY3920 ⌂-2 and the 'gothick' folly of Lyulphs Tower, with Wordsworth's daffodils a bonus in spring; above here, Gowbarrow Park NY4021 has the best lake views on this side.

Derwent Water NY2618, too, has gorgeous lakeside scenery, romantic little islets, ancient woodland and a variety of mountain backdrops. A boat service connects several points on the lake. From Keswick, the walk S to Friar's Crag NY2622 ⌂-3 and up to Castlehead Wood has exquisite views. Walla Crag above Great Wood NY2721 (often teeming with red squirrels) gains loftier heights, though the view is not that different; a moorland path heads to the photogenic Ashness Bridge NY2719, from where a rewarding return walk is one down to the shore and back again. Walks along the west shore ⌂-4, best reached from car parks off the back road between Grange NY2517 and Swinside NY2421, can be combined with the more demanding walk up Cat Bells NY2419 for the best views of the lake.

Buttermere lake shore ⌂-5 offers a splendid, varied, flat walk, with glorious views, plenty of safe opportunities for children aged six or more to let off steam, and even a tunnel; weather has to be really savage to spoil it. Parking at Gatescarth NY1915 is £2. The Bridge Hotel in the little village is handy for lunch. The walk from this village up Low Bank to Rannerdale Knotts NY1618, above nearby Crummock Water gives good views, and another rather more challenging but rewarding walk is up Hay Stacks NY1913 and Fleetwith Pike NY2014. You can walk round **Crummock Water** ⌂-6, best from the car park by Lanthwaite Wood NY1520 off the B5289 towards Loweswater NY1222 at the N end; the scenery is less rewarding than around Buttermere, but there's a pretty view from the hill above the wood.

Borrowdale ⌂-7 is many people's favourite Lakeland base for walks, with good paths along or just above the River Derwent, especially from Grange. Other prized walks all giving or leading to fine views include mossy Johnny Wood (from Rosthwaite NY2514 or Seatoller NY2413), the two famous waterfalls, both best after rain – Taylorgill Force NY2210 (above Seathwaite) and Lodore Falls NY2618 (behind Swiss Lodore Hotel) – and a walk up to the lovely 'lost village' of Watendlath NY2716 (for instance, from Rosthwaite). More challenging walks with grand views include the path winding up the back of impregnable-looking Castle Crag NY2415 (terrific lake views) from Grange. From the summit of Honister Pass NY2213 you can tackle Brandreth NY2111, and perhaps head on via Windy Gap for the least taxing ascent of Great Gable NY2110. Determined fell-walkers enjoy the unspoilt packhorse track from Seathwaite over Styhead Pass NY2210 down into Wasdale, and the summit of the pass is a start point for a fiercely dramatic route up Scafell Pike NY2107. The Scafell at Rosthwaite is a fine walkers' local.

Walks through the **Thornthwaite Forest** ⌂-8, the first-ever Forestry Commission plantation, and up to the fells above it (with lake and mountain views) are best started with a visit to the Whinlatter Visitor Centre NY1924 (B5292 above Braithwaite); good explanatory forestry displays, shop, forest maps, teas.

Dodd Wood NY2427 ⌂-9 (off the A591 N of Keswick) has marked walks through the woods, or on open hillside, with Bassenthwaite views.

The northern part of the area is less interesting for walkers, though there's a pleasant stroll from **Caldbeck** NY3239 ⌂-10 to a peaceful spot with a waterfall called the Howk NY3139. **Binsey** NY2235 ⌂-11, a pathless lump of a hill, has splendid views by virtue of its geographical isolation.

The area's great fell-walks include **High Street** NY4411 ⌂-12 (a Roman ridge road), reached best from Haweswater Reservoir (where there's a useful hotel); **Blencathra** NY3227 ⌂-13; **Skiddaw** NY2629 ⌂-14 (quite an easy haul up from Applethwaite, for far views); the walk up Martindale to Dalehead NY4316 from **Howtown** ⌂-15, then up over the fells to Bedafell Knott NY4216 and down into Patterdale (gorgeous views, Herdwick sheep, buzzards, ring ouzels); **Fairfield** NY3511 ⌂-16, climbed by a horseshoe layout of ridges from Rydal. The green slaty fells N of Buttermere offer superlative routes along high ridges ⌂-17: Whiteless Pike NY1818, Causey Pike NY2120, Crag Hill NY1920 and Grasmoor NY1720 are among the most exciting points. **Helvellyn** NY3415 ⌂-18 is most easily tackled from Thirlmere NY3116, but much more exciting when reached from Glenridding NY3817 and Striding Edge NY3415, where the path follows a narrow rocky edge (mild scrambling needed – best ascended rather than descended) above a great post-glacial corrie; it's a day's severe walking, for perhaps the grandest and certainly the most popular of all Lakeland panoramas, with dramatic ridges leading off for miles.

Driving

Even in high summer the area N of the A66 is much less heavily trafficked than the central Lakes area. Up here, the Mungrisdale–Hesket/Newmarket–Caldbeck road, signed off the A66, a mile W of the A5091 Windermere turn-off, takes you through lovely, quiet scenery.

The A66 itself is a good road for covering a lot of ground quickly at any time of the year; all other A roads here can be tiresomely slow.

The B5289 along Derwent Water, then up Borrowdale and over the Honister Pass has a fairly steady stream of traffic in summer – it's understandably popular for the enchanting lake views, the picturesquely wooded crags of riverside Borrowdale itself, and then the more austere high pass and the forbidding screes beyond; one or two craft shops, and tea breaks at Grange, Stonethwaite (signed off to the left) and Seatoller (inc a National Park base in a converted barn; cl Oct–Easter). On this road, a stop by the river above Grange Bridge gives a romantic view of Maiden Moor; and on a clear autumn day the Ashness Bridge just up the Watendlath single-track turn-off is memorably photogenic. The full detour to Watendlath itself is recommended only for the most serenely patient summer driver, but is well worthwhile out of season; the little hamlet is very photogenic, and does have a café.

Among other good scenic roads are the Keswick–Grange road, inc a detour through the richly leafy lanes below Swinside, and then, in clear weather, on up the gauntly formidable Keskadale Pass; the Swindale road (gated), signed off the Bampton–Shap road nr Rosgill; the B5322 Threlkeld–Thirlmere (there's a very photogenic view of Clough Head from the Brigham/Keswick side road turning off just past Yew Tree Farm; one of the prettiest views of Thirlmere itself is back down on the A591, from the lakeside car park).

Where to eat

Scales NY3427 WHITE HORSE (0176 87) 79241 Cosy and isolated farmhouse inn, in dramatic setting under Blencathra, a perfect haven after walks; best to book as generously served food, using fresh local produce, is very popular. £17.50|£2.20/£4.50.

Newton Reigny NY4832 SUN (01768) 67055 Small, welcoming village pub with good, original food, using fresh ingredients, and well kept real ales; bedrooms; disabled access. £12|£2/£6.

Bampton NY5118 ST PATRICKS WELL (01931) 713244. Imaginative food in unpretentious surroundings (also simple, good-value bedrooms); no children later in the evening; cl winter Mon lunch; £12|£1.50/£5.50.

CUMBRIAN COAST AND WEST LAKES

Some grand austere scenery and unfrequented beaches; much less to do than in Central Lakeland, and a much narrower choice of places to stay.

This area has some of the most impressive scenery and walking in the county. It doesn't have anything to equal the delicious charm of the famous lakes, but has the austere grandeur of Wasdale, with awesome, towering screes plunging dauntingly into Wast Water, England's deepest lake, overlooked by England's highest mountain, Scafell Pike, among other tremendous peaks that made this the birthplace of British rock-climbing. It is altogether quieter than the Central Lake District, and largely separated from it by high ridges with tortuous roads over the few passes. The choice of places to stay and things to do is very much more restricted. Eskdale is an attractive area for walks, with a fine steam railway, Muncaster Castle (a most enjoyable stately home), and Boot (steam railway terminus, and centuries-old, working watermill); Furness Abbey near Barrow is impressive, and Maryport and Ulverston deserve a look. Sellafield at Seascale has an exciting visitor centre. The coast is untouristy, with miles of unfrequented beaches (as well as some run-down-looking places and the big nuclear power plant).

If you've never been to any other part of the Lakes, this is not the best place to start an acquaintance with them. But if you have – or are looking for somewhere really rather out of the usual run – then this area has a lot to recommend it.

Where to stay

Silloth NY1153 SKINBURNESS Silloth, Carlisle CA5 4QY (0169 73) 32332 **£60**; 25 comfortable rms. Well equipped, Victorian seaside holiday hotel away from town, overlooking the sea and Scotland; good provision for the disabled.
Wasdale Head NY1808 WASDALE HEAD Wasdale Head, Seascale CA20 1EX (0194 67) 26229 **£58**; 6 simple but warmly comfortable, pine-clad rms. Old, flagstoned and gabled, walkers' and climbers' inn, in magnificent setting surrounded by steep fells; popular home cooking for 7.30pm dinner, huge breakfasts, civilised day rooms, cheerfully busy public bar; self-catering cottages.
Eskdale Green NY1400 BOWER HOUSE Eskdale Green, Holmbrook CA19 1TD (0194 67) 23244 **£53.50**; 24 comfortable rms, some in annexe. Relaxed and pleasantly isolated old stone inn, with nicely tended, sheltered garden; log fires in a warren of rooms, comfortable separate lounge, popular good-value food inc wonderful puddings, and friendly staff.

To see and do

† **Abbey Town** NY1750 HOLME CULTRAM (on B5302 Wigtown–Silloth) is the remains of a once formidably rich Cistercian abbey – extraordinarily grand for this quiet village.
🐾❋† **Barrow** SD2069 is a run-down, industrial shipbuilding town with high unemployment. The BR RAILWAY from here to Whitehaven hugs the coast and has good views, missed by the road. DOCK MUSEUM (North Rd) Rather futuristic-looking new museum focusing on how Barrow developed from a tiny hamlet to the biggest iron and steel centre in the world, before becoming renowned for shipbuilding; displays range from simple fishing boats to Trident submarines. Meals, snacks, shop, good disabled access; cl Mon, and Sun and Tues in winter; (01229) 870871; free. FURNESS ABBEY (off the A590, N) Impressive, warm sandstone, Norman remains of the one-time second-richest monastery in England, with

lovely arched cloisters, peaceful lawns, and views of the pretty valley. Small museum; disabled access; cl Mon Oct–Mar, 24–26 Dec, 1 Jan; *£2.
✗🐾 **Boot** NY1801 The steam railway (see entry for **Ravenglass**) ends here, at Dalegarth station. ESKDALE WATERMILL Attractively set, working two-wheeled mill dating back to 1578; milling machinery and exhibition, with a picnic area nr woodland waterfalls. Snacks, shop; cl Mon exc bank hols and all Oct–Mar; *£1.25. The Burnmoor Inn, very well placed for walkers, is good for lunch, as are the Bower House and King George IV further down Eskdale at Eskdale Green.
🏚▣ **Egremont** NY0111 is dominated by its very ruined Norman CASTLE (as so often, the gatehouse is the best preserved part) in a public park. LOWES COURT GALLERY Georgian house with local arts and crafts for

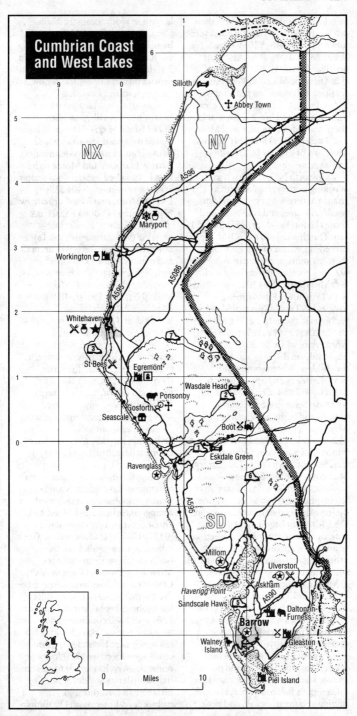

**Cumbrian Coast
and West Lakes**

NX

NY

Silloth

Abbey Town

A596

Maryport

Workington

A5086

A595

Whitehaven

St Bees

Egremont

7

Wasdale Head

2

Ponsonby

Gosforth

Seascale

Boot

4

Ravenglass

Eskdale Green

6

A595

SD

Millom

Ulverston

Haverigg Point

4

Askham

Sandscale Haws

5

A590

Dalton-in-
Furness

Barrow

Walney Island

Gleaston

Piel Island

0   Miles   10

sale. Cl pm wkdys Jan and Feb, then pm Weds the rest of the year and some lunchtimes; (0946) 820693; free. The White Mare down at Beckermet is good for lunch.

✗ 🏭 **Gleaston** SD2671 Well restored working WATER MILL in peaceful surroundings, with displays of corn milling and rural life. Meals, snacks, shop, some disabled access; cl Mon and Tues; (01229) 869224; *£1.50. The ruins of a partly built medieval castle are nearby.

🌣 † **Gosforth** NY0703 POTTERY Working pottery, maybe with a chance to throw a pot; they also do residential weekend courses. Good shop; cl Mon Jan–Mar, 25–26 Dec, 1 Jan. The churchyard has a 10th-c carved CROSS, one of Britain's finest; there are more ancient, carved hogback tombstones in the church.

❀ ♨ **Maryport** NY0436 is a small port with 18th- and 19th-c streets. STEAMSHIPS Two fully restored old tugboats in the harbour; the *Flying Buzzard* has enthusiastic tours of the whole ship, while the adjacent *Vic 96* has hands-on displays and activities for children. Cl am wknds, all Nov–Easter exc by appointment; (01900) 815954; £1.60. MARITIME MUSEUM (Senhouse St) Pictures, models and paintings illustrating Maryport's maritime heritage. Cl 1–2pm Fri and Sat (and every day in winter), all Sun exc pm in summer; free. SENHOUSE MUSEUM (The Battery, Sea Brows) Impressive collection of well displayed Roman military altar stones and inscriptions, mainly dug up from the former fort next door in the 18th c, but begun in the 1570s, making it one of the oldest collections of antiquities in the country; also other artefacts inc a Celtic serpent stone. Snacks, shop, disabled access; cl Mon (exc bank hols), Weds Oct–Jun and Tues and Thurs Nov–Mar; (01900) 816168; £1.50.

† 🏭 ♨ ✦ **Millom** SD1780, though not much of a town, has an interesting CHURCH and RUINED CASTLE around what's now a farm (ask at the house for permission to look round the ruins). The decent little FOLK MUSEUM (St George's Rd) has displays of local mining and farm history, and period

home and work reconstructions. Shop, disabled access; cl Sun (exc bank hol wknds) and Oct–Whitsun exc bank hols; (01229) 772555; 75p. S of the town, a broad lagoon built to protect former mineworks is now a bird reserve, the loneliness exaggerated out of season when the nearby holiday village is deserted.

🏭 **Piel Island** SD2364 is a small island, shared by a basic inn and a grand 14th-c, ruined fortress commanding Barrow Harbour and Morecambe Bay. It's reached by ferry (not winter exc by arrangement – (01229) 833609) from Roa Island nr Barrow.

🐗 **Ponsonby** NY0605 FARM PARK (Cumrey Kitchen) Rewarding working dairy farm, with local and other friendly rare breeds of animals and poultry, traditional farm activities, and a pets' corner. Snacks, shop, disabled access; cl Mon (exc bank hols), Oct–Easter; (01946) 841426; £2.20.

🛏🍷🏰❀✦✗🏛 **Ravenglass** SD0996, situated by the well sheltered Esk estuary, has a pretty sailing harbour; in summer, a local fishing boat sells freshly caught fish on the shore. RAVENGLASS & ESKDALE RAILWAY England's oldest, narrow-gauge steamtrains, lovingly preserved and with open carriages chugging through 7 miles of unspoilt valley to Dalegarth; they like to boast that it's the most beautiful train journey in England, and it's certainly well in the running. Cafés each end, and a small museum at Ravenglass. Meals, snacks, disabled access (advisable to arrange ahead); cl 22–25 Dec, best to phone for train times and dates; (01229) 717171; £5.60 return. Good 3-hour summer walk back from Boot (walks booklets from stations). MUNCASTER CASTLE, GARDENS & OWL CENTRE (1m E) The same family have lived in this grand old house since King John granted them the land in 1208 – and will continue to do so as long as a magical glass drinking bowl remains intact. Extended over the centuries (especially 19th) from the original tower, its elegant rooms have rich furnishings and decor, inc fine Elizabethan furniture and embroidery. Entertaining Walkman tour, and glorious Esk and mountain views from the terrace. The lovely 77-acre grounds are particularly rich in species rhododendrons, also unusual trees, nature trail, adventure play area and lots of owls and other rescued birds of prey (you can adopt one to help this rehabilitation work). Closed-circuit TV of nesting owls, along with talks and displays every afternoon at 2.30 – the birds fly, weather permitting. Meals, snacks, shop and plant centre, disabled access; house cl am, Mon exc bank hols, Nov–Mar; garden and owl centre open all year; (01229) 717614; £4.90, just garden and owl centre £3. A well restored working WATERMILL A595 NE, has Victorian machinery, a pets' corner, and flour for sale. Cl Sat, Nov–Mar; (01229) 717232; *£1.25. The so-called WALLS CASTLE, just outside the village, is actually a Roman bath-house, but its walls stand taller than any other building of its age so far north.

☎ **Seascale** NY0401 SELLAFIELD By Easter 1995 they hope to have concluded a massive multi-million-pound redevelopment of the visitor attractions here, with the introduction of Disney-style rides and hi-tech displays about nuclear power. Not all the details were finalised when we went to press, and it will be interesting to see what they're up to. They may be closed until redevelopment is complete, so best to ring first. Meals, snacks, shop, disabled access; cl 25 Dec; (019467) 27027; free. Seascale itself has a pleasant beach, and a singularly scenic golf course, where every hole offers views of the sea or the mountains; the third tee ironically puts Sellafield into the same scene as a ring of prehistoric stones. The Scawfell Hotel, overlooking the sea, is comfortable for lunch.

🏠 ☎ ♂ ⚔ ♫ ♌ **Ulverston** SD2978 SWARTHMOOR HALL (A590, SW) Lovingly restored Elizabethan manor with period furnishings, the birthplace of Quakerism after George Fox was sheltered here in 1652; it has his portable four-poster among other mementoes. Guided tours twice a day, at 10am and 2pm. Shop; cl Thurs and Sun (exc by appointment), Fri, mid-Oct–mid-Mar; (01229) 583204;

donations appreciated (run by the Society of Friends). You can visit the factory of CUMBRIA CRYSTAL, and on weekdays watch the craftsmen blowing, cutting and (Mon–Thurs) engraving; £1. The factory shop (also open pm Sun Jun–Sept) is good value, with cheap seconds. The PORK PIE SHOP at the N end of Market Place is perhaps England's best, while the Doll's House Man (Furness Galleries, Theatre St) makes DOLLS' HOUSES, farms, wooden animals and so on, and usually has examples on display. Cl Sun and Mon; (01229) 587657. Lots more local crafts at ULVERSTON POINT, a converted granary by the old watermill (not Sun). LAUREL & HARDY MUSEUM (Upper Brook St) The only exhibition of its kind, fittingly in Stan Laurel's home town, with mementoes and all-day films. The owner (a former mayor) really knows his subject. Shop, disabled access; cl 25 Dec; (01229) 582292; *£2. The HERITAGE CENTRE on Lower Brook St has local history displays. Cl Sun, and Weds from Christmas–Easter. The Bay Horse out at Canal Foot is excellent for lunch.

🦆 **Walney Island** SD1868, over the bridge from Barrow, has some long roads of low houses, but is mostly a windswept sweep of duney grass – a very offshore-feeling; excellent birdwatching at both ends – both are nature reserves, with interesting plants. The Queen's Arms is useful for lunch.

★ ♂ **Whitehaven** NX9718 Interesting, planned as an 18th-c industrial town and major port, now being restored after decline. The harbour is attractive at high tide (a bit dirty at low tide). The local small MUSEUM (Civic Hall, Lowther St; cl Sun, bank hols) sets the context well. Michael Moon BOOKSHOP has vast and rewarding secondhand stock, the best in the Lakes; cl Sun, bank hols. Some other interesting shops in the side streets. The Richmond (Hensingham) is useful for lunch.

♂🏛 **Workington** NX9928 HELENA THOMPSON MUSEUM (Park End Rd) has some antique and Georgian costumes, as well as pottery, silver, furniture and local history, in period surroundings. Cl Sun; (01900) 62598; free. Cobbled Portland Square is pretty.

WORKINGTON HALL (Curwen Park, N) Former mansion, now a ruinous hulk around the Norman tower, in a public park – odd conjunction. A famous letter by Mary Queen of Scots to her cousin Elizabeth I was written here. Shop; cl 1–2pm, am wknds, Mon (exc bank hols), Nov–Easter; (01900) 735408; 70p. The Alamin Indian restaurant (Jane St) is good.

Walks

Eskdale ⌂-1 is excellent for walks, especially around Boot NY1801, to the Stanley Ghyll Force waterfall SD1799, or up towards the open fells (the landlord of the Burnmoor Inn is helpful with route suggestions); or for good views up Muncaster Fell, above the castle and the mill. There is a nature trail in the grounds of Muncaster Castle. You can use the Ravenglass & Eskdale railway as part of a round trip.

Wasdale ⌂-2 is the start for many magnificent fell-walks, inc the ascents of Great Gable NY2110 and Scafell Pike NY2207; one less taxing walk is straight up the head of the valley to the summit of Black Sail Pass NY1811 and back. Apart from around the interesting churchyard, it's not so good for gentle strolls, and parking at Wasdale Head NY1808 can be a problem in summer or at holiday times. As well as the Wasdale Head Hotel, the Strands lower down is a useful stop for food.

The coast has one particular lure for walkers and birdwatchers: the **cliff path** ⌂-3 between Whitehaven NX9718 and St Bees NX9512 – each town has a railway station. From the beach car park NW of St Bees, an easy walk takes you up the nature reserve, sandstone headland, famous for its bird life, and with magnificent sea and hill views.

There are lots of long beaches, deserted except in high season, from Ravenglass SD0996 down to Hodbarrow Point SD1878 good for breezy seaside walks; one of the nicest spots on this entire coast is the huge stretch of impressive dunes on **Haverigg Point** SD1378 ⌂-4, nr Millom. The dunes at **Sandscale Haws** SD2075 ⌂-5, nr Barrow, are protected as a nature reserve.

The **Duddon Valley** ⌂-6 is a favourite starting point for rather more demanding walks, either by the river or up into the heights, with the Newfield Inn at Seathwaite SD2396 a good base.

The Fox & Hounds in the quiet village of Ennerdale Bridge NY0716 is handy for walks around **Ennerdale Water** ⌂-7.

Driving

The daunting Hardknott Pass and the back road up the Duddon Valley from Ulpha, which joins it, both give magnificent mountain views – best in good weather out of season. For coastal views, the A5087 long way round between Ulverston and Barrow has fine views across Morecambe Bay and carries little traffic; up in the north, the B5300 coast road N of Maryport, looking across the sea to Scotland, is virtually deserted except in high summer. Traffic is generally relatively light throughout this area, though don't reckon on quick journey times along the A595 – which does have views of both hills and sea on many stretches.

Where to eat

Ulverston SD2978 BAY HORSE (01229) 53972 Beautifully presented and very innovative food, inc interesting vegetarian choices and an emphasis on fresh fish dishes; nicely placed inn overlooking Morecambe Bay; bedrooms; cl am Mon; children over 12. £30|£1.35/£7.50.
Whitehaven NY9718 BRUNOS 10 Church St (01946) 65270 Candlelit Italian

bistro in small tasteful rooms of a Georgian house; bedrooms; cl Sun–Tues lunch. £20|£2.45/£3.75.

Askham SD2177 PUNCH BOWL (01931) 712443 Relaxed and friendly pub with big helpings of interesting bar food, well kept beers, civilised furnishings, and a warm log fire. £17|£2.50/£6.50.

St Bees NX9712 SEACOTE HOTEL Beach Rd (01946) 822777 Lovely views and headland walks, with decent food in a pleasant, roomy bar or restaurant; welcoming to children. £14.50|1.60/£3.

CUMBRIAN PENNINES AND THE NORTH

Unspoilt even in summer, this area has quiet river valleys below desolate moors; attractive prices.

This part of Cumbria is one of England's least-known areas. Yet, though there are few set-piece tourist attractions here, there are a good many places of interest worth tracking down. Alston, Kirkby Lonsdale and Appleby are distinctive small towns of considerable character. Talkin Tarn, the Acorn Bank Garden at Temple Sowerby, and Birdoswald Roman fort near Gilsland are all worth visiting, and Brampton has an interesting priory and castle. Even the city of Carlisle has some unexpected treasures.

For most people, the chief attraction is the appealing mixture of quiet river valleys with more awesome open country and high moors. Much of the high country is too bleak and boggy for most walkers, but drivers have the joy of fine views from roads that see relatively little traffic. The railway crossing the moors between Carlisle and Settle is perhaps the best way of all of seeing this unusual part of England.

The Lakes themselves are of course within easy reach.

Where to stay

Brampton NY5361 FARLAM HALL Brampton, Hallbankgate (A689, S) CA8 2NG (0169 77) 46234 *£184 inc dinner; 12 comfortable rms. Charmingly Victorian (though parts are much older) and very civilised country house with log fires, excellent, attentive service, and a good 4-course dinner; peaceful, spacious grounds with a croquet lawn and small, pretty lake; cl Christmas; children over 5; dogs welcome.

Alston NY7246 LOVELADY SHIELD Nenthead Rd CA9 3LF (01434) 381203 £95; 12 rms. Wonderfully located country house with the River Nene running along the bottom of the garden; tranquil atmosphere, courteous staff, log fires in comfortable rooms, and very good food inc fine breakfasts; cl Jan; children over 5 in restaurant for dinner (high tea available).

Crosby-on-Eden NY4559 CROSBY LODGE High Crosby, Crosby-on-Eden, Carlisle CA6 4QZ (01228) 573618 *£88; 9 spacious rms with 2 more in a stable conversion. Imposing and carefully converted country house in attractive mature grounds, with comfortable and appealingly individual furnishings, interesting food, and friendly, long-standing owners; nice countryside; cl 24 Dec for one month; disabled access.

Faugh NY5155 STRING OF HORSES Faugh, Carlisle CA4 9EG (01228) 70297 *£68; 14 newly decorated rms. Attractive and friendly 17th-c coaching inn in pleasant surroundings, with interesting carved furniture in cosy communicating rooms, popular food, pleasant service, and a piano player in the re-styled restaurant; outdoor heated swimming pool and indoor leisure centre; cl 24–25 Dec.

Barbon SD6383 BARBON INN Barbon, Carnforth LA6 2LJ (0152 42) 76233 £55; 10 simple but comfortable rms, some with own bthrm. Small, friendly village inn, in a quiet spot below the fells, with a relaxing bar, armchair lounge, good meals in the candlelit dining room, and helpful service.

Casterton SD6379 PHEASANT Casterton, Carnforth LA6 2RX (0152 42) 71230 £55; 10 comfortable rms, most with countryside views. Small, civilised inn with pleasant atmosphere, good food in the panelled dining room, cosy residents' lounge, no-smoking garden lounge, and cheerful staff; small but sound wine list; disabled access.

Ravenstonedale NY7204 FAT LAMB Cross Bank, Ravenstonedale, Kirkby Stephen CA17 4LL (0153 96) 23242 *£54; 12 comfortable rms. Welcoming moorland inn, in beautiful open countryside, with a log fire in the cheerfully modernised, 2-room bar, and own 5-acre nature reserve; disabled access.

Sedbergh SD6692 DALESMAN Main St LA10 5BN (0153 96) 21183 *£50; 6 comfortable and cheerful rms, most with bthrm. Friendly and nicely modernised, old village pub, popular with walkers, and with a wide choice of good food.

Brampton NY5361 KIRBY MOOR Longtown Rd CA8 2AB (0169 77) 3893 £44; 6 comfortable rms. Beautifully furnished, Victorian country house in attractive surroundings, with open fires, conservatory, good, home-cooked fresh food, and fine views; cl 25–26 Dec.

Hadrian's Wall NY6967 HOLMHEAD Hadrian's Wall, Greenhead, Carlisle CA6 7HY (0169 77) 47402 *£43; 4 rms. Friendly old house in a sheltered valley; comfortably if simply furnished, with plenty of games for children and decent, freshly prepared food using local produce and served around a big, candlelit, oak table; no smoking; also, a separate cottage with good disabled facilities; special wknds with lectures/slides for 'Wall' enthusiasts.

Maulds Meaburn NY6217 MEABURN HILL FARM Maulds Meaburn, Penrith CA10 3HN (01931) 715205 *£42; 3 rms. 16th-c longhouse on a 200-acre suckler beef and sheep farm, with beams, antiques and open fires in the comfortable rooms, a well stocked library, and farmhouse breakfasts; also a large garden, orchard, and fine views; cl Jan–Easter.

Talkin NY5557 HULLERBANK Talkin, Brampton CA8 1LB (0169 77) 46668 *£38; 3 rms. Comfortable and very friendly Georgian farmhouse in unspoilt countryside, with a relaxed atmosphere and fine food using home-grown and local produce inc home-produced lamb; no smoking; cl 25 Dec, 1 Jan; children over 10.

Kirkcambeck NY5269 CRACROP FARM Kirkcambeck, Brampton CA8 2BW (0169 77) 48245 *£36; 3 rms. Friendly Victorian farmhouse on 425 acres with stock animals and very good, marked farm trails (they are keen on conservation); comfortable and homely rooms, good food; also a games room and sauna; no smoking; cl Christmas.

Alston NY7246 MIDDLE BAYLES FARM CA9 3BS (01434) 381383 *£35; 2 cosy rms. Traditional, 17th-c stone farmhouse in a lovely spot with fine views and walks, cattle and Swaledale sheep; good, home-made food and open fires; no smoking; cl Christmas, April (lambing time).

Dent SD7187 SPORTSMANS Cowgill, Dent, Sedbergh LA10 5RG (01539) 625282 £34; 6 rms with shared bthrm. Unassuming, comfortable pub, notable for its wonderful position in Dentdale by the River Dee, with the viaduct of the old Settle–Carlisle railway close by, and walks in all directions; open log fires and good-value, home-made food; cl 25 Dec.

Garrigill NY7441 GEORGE & DRAGON Garrigill, Alston CA9 3DS (01434) 381293 £30; 4 small rms, shared bthrm, but clean and comfortable. Friendly 17th-c pub on a dead-end road in beautiful walking countryside, with an informal flagstoned bar, stone-and-panelled dining room, and log fire in a smashing fireplace; good service; children over 12.

Winton NY7810 BAY HORSE Winton, Kirkby Stephen CA17 4HS (0176 83) 71451 £30; 3 clean, good-value rms. Well kept, unpretentious moorland pub in a lovely setting, with welcoming, low-ceilinged rooms, and good, generous home cooking; children over 5.

See also Appleby entry, under **Where to eat** section.

To see and do

★ ⚒ ❀ 🖼 **Alston** NY7246 Interesting little Pennine town with a surprising number of pubs up and down its very steep, cobbled main st (the Angel and Turk's Head are best), also a craft shop with locally produced foods too, and home-baked teas, fresh coffee (cl Jan–mid-Feb). The chief attraction here is the SOUTH TYNEDALE RAILWAY, with steam or diesel, vintage narrow-gauge train trips along a lovely winding valley. From this year they plan to run a service up to Kirkhaugh in Northumberland. Teas, shop; limited service on Mon and Fri in Jun, Sept and Oct, and all Nov–Apr – best to check dates and times; (01434) 381696; £2.60 return. HARTSIDE NURSERY (A686, W) is a beautifully situated alpine nursery with a small streamside garden and rare plants for sale; it's quite a draw for birds and wildlife. They hope to establish a woodland walk soon. Shop, some disabled access with notice; cl am Sun, Nov–Feb (exc by appointment); (01434) 381372; free. GOSSIPGATE GALLERY (The Butts) Local arts and crafts, with various changing exhibitions and a good, big shop. Their annual sheep show (spotlighting wool products) in Sept and Oct is popular. Snacks, disabled access (though no facilities); cl Jan–mid-Feb; (01434) 381806; free. The Angel is useful for lunch.

★ 🏰 ❀ 🏚 ❀ 🐦 **Appleby** NY6921 is an appealing riverside town; the main street, rising from the harmonious 12th-c church to the castle, is still a grand sight despite the cars, with a good few attractive buildings inc a lovely courtyard of almshouses; there are pleasant strolls by the Eden. APPLEBY CASTLE CONSERVATION CENTRE The castle itself is in remarkable shape for a partly 11th-c building, with one of the best-preserved keeps in the country; terrific views from the ramparts at the top. The Clifford

family lived here for nearly 700 years, though they moved later to the grander house next door – the Great Hall – which has antiques, paintings and Chinese porcelain on display. The main feature of the attractive grounds is the big collection of birds, waterfowl and rare farm animals in a lovely setting above the river. Meals, snacks, shop, limited disabled access; cl Oct–Easter; (0176 83) 51402; £3.50. The National School of Falconry has recently moved here, and has displays throughout the year; (0176 83) 51783. The Royal Oak is most enjoyable for lunch.

★ **Barbon** SD6383 is an unpretentious village given appeal by its fine setting, just below the fells. The Barbon Inn is good.

✝ **Brampton** NY5361 LANERCOST PRIORY Impressive and extensive remains of a Norman priory, built with stone recycled from Hadrian's Wall. A lovely riverside setting, with the entrance arch picturesquely framing the nave, restored in the 18th c as a red sandstone church and with stained glass by William Morris and Burne-Jones; Sun services by candlelight. Shop, some disabled access; cl during services; free. The attractive Abbey Bridge Inn attached to the New Bridge Hotel, nr the priory, is good for lunch.

🏰 ❀ ⚒ **Brough** NY7915 CASTLE Classic ruined Norman fortress, in a romantic setting on the moors above the village, with great views; free. Coffee shop with home-baking (not Nov–Easter) in CLIFFORD HOUSE CRAFT SHOP (good for handmade jewellery), in the village. The Golden Fleece is useful for lunch.

♮ ✝ 🏰 ❀ 🍺 🏚 ⚒ **Carlisle** NY4056 is a sizeable town, not an obvious weekend destination, but does have plenty to interest the visitor, with several quietly attractive old buildings (and a very helpful visitor centre in

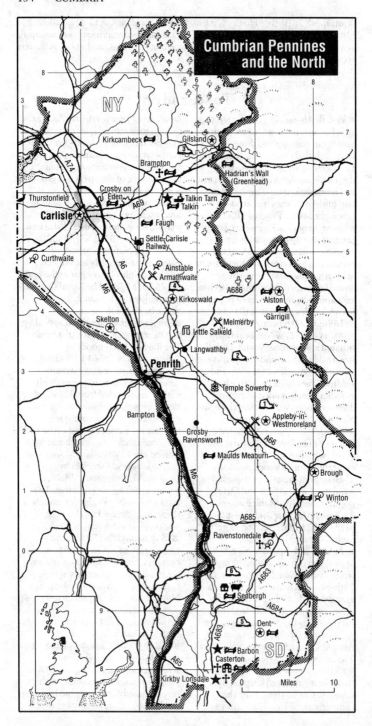

Cumbrian Pennines and the North

one of them, the Old Town Hall, Green Market). TULLIE HOUSE (Castle St) Lively displays of Border history, using state-of-the-art techniques of sight, sound and smell to really get you involved. Children especially will find lots to do, from exploring mine tunnels to trying out a Roman crossbow. Dramatic, evocative and great fun – with a particularly interesting look at the notorious Reiver families. The ground floor has a more conventional (and free) art gallery/museum. Meals, snacks, shop, disabled access; cl am Sun, 25 Dec; (01228) 34781; *£3.30 (get there between 10 and 11am and it's half-price). The unpretentious little CATHEDRAL, founded in 1122 and severely damaged in the Civil War, has fine examples of stained glass among its treasures; try to go on a bright morning when the sunlight comes streaming colourfully through the east window. Also medieval carvings inc the Brougham Triptych, painted panels and stonework and crypt treasury. Meals, snacks, shop, disabled access (exc to restaurant); free. The extensive medieval CASTLE, rather gaunt and forbidding, is surprisingly well kept considering its violent history. You can still see the dungeon with its centuries of prisoners' carved graffiti, interesting period furnished rooms, a portcullised gatehouse, and lots of staircases and passages; climb to the top for good views from the ramparts. It also has a regimental museum (cl Sun am winter) with battle models, weapons and videos. Snacks, shop; cl 24–26 Dec, 1 Jan; (01228) 591922; £2. The GUILDHALL in Greenmarket is a handsomely restored, medieval timbered hall; worth a look inside if passing – some displays; 50p. ST CUTHBERT'S CHURCH is remarkable for its mobile pulpit.

The racecourse attractively placed out at Durdar has meetings every month exc Aug; (01228) 22973 for dates. The **Settle–Carlisle** railway, up Ribbledale and into the Cumbrian Pennines, stopping at Dent Station, Garsdale Head, Kirkby Stephen, Appleby, Langwathby and other Eden Valley villages, is a memorable 70

miles of grand scenery, best from Appleby to Settle; (01228) 44711 for times and fares – they have occasional steam runs. The Howard Arms (Lowther St) is useful for lunch.

⌂ † Casterton SD6379 has the CASTERTON SCHOOL of Brontë fame, and the CHURCH has some attractive pre-Raphaelite stained glass and paintings. The Pheasant pub is good.

🐾 📷 Dalton-in-Furness SD2374 SOUTH LAKES WILD ANIMAL PARK Recently opened 14-acre wildlife centre, well placed for fine views of the entire Furness peninsula. Plenty of animals such as wallabies, antelope, raccoons, coatis and porcupines, and a 4-acre section with pheasants and ducks wandering free and waiting to be fed; also a nature trail, lakeside walls and pets' corner. Snacks, shop, some disabled access; cl 25–26 Dec, 1 Jan; (01229) 466086; £2.75. The village also has a rather austere square CASTLE.

★ † 🎨 Dent SD7187 has some modern outskirts but centrally is a delightful, steep cobbled village, a rewarding end to an attractive drive – though now on the tourist trail, so busy in summer; the Sun, an attractive and welcoming inn, brews its own beer, and the church is well worth a look. E of the village, towards Denthead, Colin Gardner (Stone House, Cowgill; also gun cabinets; cl wknds) and Little Oak Furniture (Bridge End, Denthead) both make TRADITIONAL FURNITURE.

🏠 ✳ 🐾 Gilsland NY6166 BIRDOSWALD ROMAN FORT (off the B6318, W) Big fortress, still being excavated, on well preserved stretch of Hadrian's Wall, in fine countryside above River Irthing; commanding views and good display centre. Snacks, shop, disabled access; centre cl Nov–late Mar; £1.75. The GOAT FARM at Holme View nearby sells prize-winning traditional cheeses.

★ † Kirkby Lonsdale SD6278 is a small and usually quiet town of considerable character, with interesting old yards and ginnels, good country shops, enjoyable pubs, and a fine CHURCH. It's more lively on Thurs country-market day. Just below the town there's a pretty stretch of the River Lune, good for walking or just lazing about – or even swimming if it's hot. The Lune Valley is appealing countryside, little visited by tourists.

🏰 ❀ ★ **Kirkoswald** NY5641 Ruins of a 13th-c CASTLE, with the remains of three towers and a gatehouse and fine views towards the Pennines. The village is attractive, and has a decent pub. The Joiner's Arms at Lazonby is useful for lunch.

🏛 **Little Salkeld** NY5736 gives access off the lane N to the quaintly named STONE CIRCLE Long Meg and her Daughters NY5737.

✝ ⚒ **Ravenstonedale** NY7203 The village is notable more for its pleasant riverside scenery than for its buildings – apart from the unspoilt CHURCH which escaped Victorian refitting: longitudinal pews, three-decker pulpit, steeply pitched gallery (steep stairs up), fine E window memorial to the Fothergill family (one was the last female Protestant martyr to be burned at the stake); choose a bright day for the best light. Beckside Gallery makes hardwood TRADITIONAL FURNITURE. The Black Swan is good for lunch.

🐏 🐄 **Sedbergh** SD6692, at the foot of the Howgill Fells (see **Walks** section), has a helpful Yorkshire Dales National Park Centre on Main St (cl Dec–Easter), concentrating on this area. HOLME FARM 2pm tours of traditional hill farm, with plenty of young animals and a nature trail. They also do occasional evening tours with badger watch; cl Oct–mid-Mar; (05396) 20654; *£2. PENNINE TWEEDS (Farfield Mill) is a factory shop for the riverside Victorian mill using 1930s looms. Cl Sun Nov–Mar (05396) 20654. The Dalesman is good for lunch.

🏚 ❀ 🐟 **Skelton** NY4435 HUTTON-IN-THE-FOREST Legend has it that this formidable mansion was the castle of the Green Knight of Arthurian legend. Grandly extended in the 17th c from its 14th-c peel tower core, then castellated more recently, it's crowded with interesting period furniture, tapestries and antiques, with a magnificent panelled gallery. Outside, a terraced garden runs down to the lake, and there's an 18th-c walled formal garden, and a more romantic Victorian garden with grand trees, 17th-c dovecot and woodland nature walk. Snacks, shop; house open pm Thurs, Fri and Sun May–Sept, plus Easter wknd, Weds in August, and all bank hols, garden open every day exc Sat; (0176 84) 84449; £3, £1.50 garden only. The Clickham at Blencow is good for lunch.

⛵ ★ **Talkin Tarn** NY5458 Lovely lake with partly wooded shores, peaceful mountain views, plenty of space for strolling, and a nature trail. Disabled access, teas. You can hire rowing boats (from £4.40 an hour) and mountain-bikes. The village is pretty; the Blacksmith's Arms is popular for food.

❀ **Temple Sowerby** NY6127 ACORN BANK Richly planted terraced and walled garden with 250 varieties of medicinal and culinary herbs, clematis, unusual old fruit trees, and herbaceous borders; the steep wild garden drops down to the stream. Shop, disabled access; cl Nov–Mar; *£1.60; NT.

🎣 **Thurstonfield** NY3257 Trout-FISHING on a well stocked, sizeable lake set in peaceful woodland at Lough Fishery; tackle and boat hire, inc one for disabled anglers. Cl Oct–mid-Mar.

⚒ We've already mentioned a good few local craftsmen. Others can be found at **Curthwaite** NY3249, where Ian Laval of Meadow Bank Farm is a very traditional CABINET-MAKER (cl wknds), and Michael King at Oakleigh, Todd Close, nearby makes silver and gold JEWELLERY (cl Sun, Mon); and at **Ainstable** NY5346, where Jim Malone has a traditional WORKING POTTERY. Another good pottery at **Winton** NY7810 is the long-established LANGRIGG POTTERY; best to ring first as it's not always open – (0176 83) 71542; the Bay Horse here is useful for lunch. **Other attractive villages**, all with decent pubs, include Armathwaite NY5146, Bampton NY5118, Crosby Ravensworth NY6215 (Maulds Meaburn NY6217 is also pretty), Langwathby NY5734 and Garrigill NY7441.

Walks

There are decent walks close to or even right from the door of all the places we suggest to stay in.

The high Pennines have few walking routes over them and are extremely bleak: this is the reserve of the dedicated peat-bog enthusiast. But **High Cup Nick** NY7426 △-1, a great scoop in the ridge, is one of the most dramatic features in the whole of the Pennine range. An easy way to get an idea of the remoteness of these hills is to walk from Dufton NY6825 along paths encircling Dufton Pike. The hill roads mentioned in the **Driving** section below give access to several worthwhile tracks. The back road from Langwathby NY5733 (on the A686) through Skirwith to Kirkland, leads to a **Roman track** △-2 which plunges northwards into the Pennines. There are other walks from the clusters of sheep farms along the foot of the Pennines between here and Appleby NY6921.

Surviving traces of **Hadrian's Wall** △-3, not the famous bits, can be reached on well signed paths from the lanes between the A69 and the B6318 N of Brampton NY5361.

The **Nunnery Walks** △-4 at Staffield NY5443 are private paths through old woodland, inc the lovely Eden Valley river gorge with waterfalls and quiet pools; teas; 50p. There are other good free walks in this delightfully wooded, sheltered valley, for instance from Armathwaite NY5146 and Wetheral NY4654. The valley has the reputation of staying dry when it's pouring over in Lakeland.

Dentdale and the Howgill Fells are part of the Yorkshire Dales that somehow ended up in modern Cumbria. **Dentdale** △-5 has easy to middling walks from Dent SD7187, in the shadow of Whernside. The **Howgills** △-6 are bold 2,000-footers, empty and tough going; the easiest walks into them are up Winder from Sedbergh SD6692, and from the A683 N of Sedbergh to majestic Cautley Spout waterfall.

Driving

Many roads here are very rewarding for country drives. The A683 Kirkby Lonsdale–Sedbergh–Kirkby Stephen passes through fine countryside, and the B6260 to Appleby has good views. The back road through the Lyent Valley, N of Orton, takes you through very unspoilt, quiet farmland and villages. N of Temple Sowerby, the B6412 to Lazenby and then the back road through the Eden Valley to Armathwaite and on up to Wetheral affords delicious peaceful views. The B6413 Lazonby–Brampton takes in some commanding high ground, and the A689 Brampton–Alston has very varied views. The road up Barbondale from Barbon and then on past Dent to Denthead and the splendid railway viaduct, or perhaps round into Deepdale, reaches deep into the hills.

On the trunk roads, queues can build up on the A65 heading down into Yorkshire, and on parts of the A66 (though it's being improved). The A686 carries far less traffic, but is more twisting. All three roads have fine views.

Where to eat

Appleby NY6921 ROYAL OAK (0176 83) 51463 Warm and friendly, partly 14th-c coaching inn with extremely good, interesting food, huge breakfasts, fine range of beers, and fine wines; comfortable bedrooms. **£18.90|£2.20/£8.40.**

Melmerby NY6237 SHEPHERDS (01768) 881217 Welcoming place in an unspoilt sandstone village, with popular home-made food inc a marvellous range of cheeses, delicious puddings, and lots of daily specials using only local produce; quick, amicable table service; cl 25 Dec; partial disabled access. **£16|£1.25/£6.50.**

Armathwaite NY5146 DUKES HEAD (0169 92) 226. Comfortable and friendly pub/restaurant in an attractive village, with good home cooking, decent wines; bedrooms. **£14.50|£1.80/£6.**

CUMBRIA CALENDAR

Some of these dates were provisional as we went to press.

Rushbearing ceremonies here date from medieval times, when church floors were covered with straw and sweet-smelling herbs. Special days were set aside for renewing the coverings, attended by merrymaking and thanksgiving. Rushes are carried into the church by a procession.

JANUARY

1 **Kirkby Stephen** Nine Standards Fell Race

FEBRUARY

5 **Grasmere** Wordsworth Winter School at Dove Cottage – *till Fri 10* (0153 94) 35544

24 **Grasmere** Wordsworth Book Collectors Weekend at Dove Cottage – *till Sun 26* (0153 94) 35544

MARCH

20 **Kendal** Mary Wakefield Westmorland Music Festival – *till Sat 25* (01539) 824696

APRIL

7 **Casterton** Folk Dance Weekend – *till Sun 9* (01539) 725215

15 **Whittington** Point to Point (0152 42) 21175

21 **Kendal** Northern International Festival of Mime, Dance and Visual Theatre at the Brewery Arts Centre – *till 1 May* (01539) 725133

MAY

6 **Carlisle** and Borders Spring Show at Victoria Park (01228) 810208 – *till Mon 8*

19 **Keswick** Jazz Festival – *till Sun 21* (01900) 602122

28 **Calderbridge** Country Field Day (0194 67) 25340

29 **Kendal** Medieval Market (01539) 721154

JUNE

8 **Appleby** Horse Fair: gypsies gather from all over Europe on Fair Hill for this 300-year-old event with fortune-telling, camp fires and spectacular horse, carriage and van sales – *till Weds 14* (0176 83) 51177

18 **Kirkby Lonsdale** Brass Band Contest (0152 42) 71422

19 **Brough** Hound and Terrier Show (0176 83) 51921

25 **Endmoor** Country Fayre (0153 95) 60054

29 **Warcop** Rushbearing (0176 83) 41379

JULY

1 **Ambleside** Rushbearing (0153 94) 33205; **Musgrave** Rushbearing (0176 83) 41355

6 **Bowness-on-Windermere** Lake Windermere Festival – *till Sun 9* (0153 94) 382273

8 **Appleby** Carnival (0176 83) 51177; **Maryport** Carnival (01900) 815954

15 **Carlisle** Cumberland Show (01228) 560364

22 **Penrith** Agricultural Show at Brougham Hall Farm (01931) 713325

28 **Flookburgh** Cumbria Steam Gathering – *till Sun 30* (0152 42) 71584

CUMBRIA CALENDAR

AUGUST

2 **Ambleside** Lake District Summer Music Festival (01629) 823733 – *till Weds 16*

4 **Bowness-on-Windermere** Classic Motorboat Rally at Windermere Steamboat Museum – *till Sun 6*, with public viewing on *Sat 5 Aug* (0153 94) 45565; **Lowther** Horse Driving Trials and Country Fair – *till Sun 6* (01931) 712378

5 **Cockermouth** Show (01946) 66344

8 **Kirkby Lonsdale** Lunesdale Show (0152 42) 71437

9 **Cartmel** Show (0153 95) 34905

10 **Appleby** Agricultural Show (01931) 714571; **Ings** Lake District Sheepdog Trials at Hill Top Farm (0153 94) 32468

16 **Gosforth** Agricultural Show (0194 67) 24652

17 **Grasmere** Traditional Sports inc Lakeland wrestling (0153 94) 32127; **Rydal** Sheepdog Trials

19 **Skelton** Show (01768) 62953

22 **Hawkshead** Show (0153 94) 36609

23 **Threlkeld** Sheepdog Trials (0176 87) 79260

25 **Kendal** Folk Festival at the Brewery Arts Centre – *till Sun 27* (01539) 725133

26 **Dufton** Agricultural Show and Sheepdog Trials (0176 83) 62015; **Patterdale** Dog Day (Sheepdog Trials) (0176 84) 82370

27 **Grange-over-Sands** MG Rally at Holker Hall (0153 95) 58328

30 **Ennerdale** Show (01946) 861391

SEPTEMBER

3 **Hesket Newmarket** Agricultural Show (0169 74) 78663

14 **Crooklands** Westmorland County Show at Lane Farm (01539) 567804

16 **Egremont** Crab Fair inc world gurning (face-pulling) championships (01946) 820376

24 **Urswick** Rushbearing (01229) 869402

OCTOBER

14 **Wasdale** Show (0194 67) 25340; **Wasdale** Cumbria Brass Band Association Contest (01946) 61955

21 **Buttermere** Show (01900) 85210

NOVEMBER

3 **Kendal** Jazz and Blues Festival at the Brewery Arts Centre – *till Sun 19* (01539) 725133

16 **Santon Bridge** Biggest Liar in the World Competition in the town, with the highest mountain, deepest lake, smallest church and biggest liar (01946) 67575

DECEMBER

2 **Kirkby Lonsdale** Christmas Fair (0152 42) 71437

3 **Keswick** Victorian Fair (0176 87) 72698

Help this year from: J Roy Smylie, M D Hare, David Moss, Mr and Mrs C Roberts, Lucy James, N H and A H Harries, H K Dyson, Peter and Lynn Brueton, Peter and Pat Frogley, Julie and Andy Hawkins, David Eberlin, Neil and Elaine Piper, G W Lindley, David Heath, Andy and Jill Kassube, John Allsopp, Graham and Lynn Mason, David and Margaret Bloomfield, Paul and Ursula Roberts, LM, Mr and Mrs S Ashcroft, Bronwen and Steve Wrigley, Michael and Harriet Robinson, Paul and Maggie Baker, WAH, Mike and Ann Beiley, Malcolm Phillips, Nick Cox, Derek and Margaret Underwood, Philip Saxon, Philip Vernon, Kim Maidment, Jan and Dave Booth, CW, JW, Dave Lands, B M Eldridge, J B Neame, S and D Shaw, Sara Geyer, Mick Whelton, D J and P M Taylor, David and Margaret Bloomfield, Nigel Woolliscroft, Joe and Carol Pattison, Sue Holland, David Webster, Irene Shuttleworth, John Oddey.

DERBYSHIRE AND STAFFORDSHIRE

This area includes much of the Peak District National Park, and some grand stately homes. Mid-Derbyshire has a most appealing mix of beautiful scenery with interesting places to visit. It has the best choice of places to stay in the area, and is very good walking country. There is enjoyable walking in other parts of the county, too – particularly in the bleaker north, though Dove Dale, shared between the south of the county and Staffordshire, is a real honeypot for walkers. The south of Derbyshire also has some very rewarding attractions, from stately homes to restored survivals of early industry. Staffordshire, though not an obvious choice for a weekend break, has some surprising delights and is well worth considering – especially if you've already spent some time in Derbyshire.

MID-DERBYSHIRE

Magnificent houses and other interesting buildings, delightful dales scenery; very civilised.

The beautiful dales country, which spreads into the southern area and the fringes of Staffordshire, is very rewarding both for walkers and for drivers, and is punctuated by charming villages. Our short list of outstanding places to visit in the area would start with Chatsworth, Hardwick Hall and Haddon Hall at Over Haddon, with Matlock/Matlock Bath being well worth a visit (the Riber Castle wildlife park is enjoyable); Lea Gardens is gorgeous in late spring, and Bolsover Castle and Eyam Hall are very attractive too. Poole's Cavern in Buxton is the county's best show cave. There's a very good choice of places to stay; eating out is rather civilised, too. In summer, the most lovely dales do have almost a crocodile of walkers snaking along them, though even then you can find quiet areas; as with other popular areas, this is perhaps ideally suited to short breaks out of season – autumn and particularly late spring are good times.

Where to stay

Baslow SK2572 CAVENDISH Baslow, Bakewell DE45 1SP (01246) 582311 £116.30; 23 spotlessly kept, comfortable and individually furnished rms (varying in size) with fine views. Charming hotel on the edge of Chatsworth Park, with most attractive, well furnished day rooms (some furnishings come from Chatsworth House), open fires, fine food in the two restaurants, and very courteous staff; disabled access.

Bakewell SK2272 HASSOP HALL Hassop, Bakewell DE45 1NS (01629) 640488 *£98; 13 gracious rms. Mentioned in the Domesday Book and in lovely parklands surrounded by fine scenery, this handsome hotel has antiques and oil paintings, an elegant drawing room, oak-panelled bar, good food, and friendly service; tennis; cl 24-26 Dec; disabled access.

Baslow SK2572 FISCHER'S BASLOW HALL Calver Rd, Baslow, Bakewell DE4 1RR (01246) 583259 *£95; 6 comfortable, individual rms. Handsome manor house with lots of antiques and paintings, bold fabrics, open fires and fresh flowers; beautifully presented food in the airy dining room or in the lunchtime Café Max, and courteous, attentive service; cl 25–26 Dec.

Matlock SK3060 RIBER HALL DE4 5JU (01629) 582795 £92; 11 lovely, characterful rms with antiques, chocolates and baskets of fruit. 15th and 16th-c manor house in peaceful countryside, with pretty garden, heavily beamed rooms full of period furniture and fresh flowers; also, a popular, elegant restaurant with ambitious food and fine wines; extensive grounds with tennis, clay-pigeon shooting; children over 10.

Rowsley SK2566 PEACOCK Rowsley, Matlock DE4 2EB (01629) 733518 £86.50; 14 comfortable rms. Handsome, early 17th-c hotel by a lovely trout river (private fishing in season), with well kept gardens, friendly staff, antiques, and a good, very popular restaurant.

Ashford in the Water SK1969 **Riverside Country House** Fennel St, Ashford in the Water, Bakewell DE4 1QF (01629) 814275 £80; 15 individually decorated, pretty rms. Creeper-covered Georgian house in a delightful village with lovely, river-fronted gardens; a quiet, relaxed atmosphere, antiques and log fires in the cosy day rooms, imaginative food (served all day) in the two dining rooms – using silver and cut crystal – and good service.

Ashford in the Water SK1969 ASHFORD HOTEL 1 Church St, Ashford in the Water, Bakewell DE45 1QB (01629) 812725 £70; 7 decent rms. Small, traditional hotel with oak beams, open fires, bar, and residents' lounge overlooking the garden; good food in the country restaurant.

Monsal Head SK1871 MONSAL HEAD HOTEL Monsal Head, Bakewell DE4 1NL (01629) 640250 *£70; 8 very good rms, most with own bthrm. Comfortable and enjoyable small hotel in an exceptional setting high above the River Wye; with a horsey theme in the bar (converted from old stables), Victorian-style restaurant, well prepared decent food, and good service; cl 25 Dec.

Grindleford SK2478 MAYNARD ARMS Main Rd, Grindleford, Sheffield S30 1HP (01433) 630321 £59.50; 13 rms. Comfortable first-floor lounge with a log fire and good views over the Peak National Park, smart, welcoming hotel bar, a good choice of food, and particularly attentive service; limited disabled access.

Biggin-by-Hartington SK0673 BIGGIN HALL Biggin-by-Hartington, Buxton SK17 0DH (01298) 84451 £56; 15 spacious rms with antiques, some in a converted 18th-c stone building and bothy. Lovely, carefully renovated, 17th-c house in quiet grounds, with two comfortable sitting rooms, log fires, and imaginative food using free-range produce and seasonal veg; children over 12; limited disabled access.

Winster SK2460 DOWER HOUSE Winster, Matlock DE4 2DH (01629) 650213 £55; 3 rms. Elizabethan country house with excellent standards, a homely atmosphere, and good breakfasts (home-made preserves) eaten with the family; packed lunches if required; lots to do nearby.

Buxton SK0673 WESTMINSTER HOTEL 21 Broad Walk, Buxton SK17 6JR (01298) 23929 £40; 12 rms. Neatly kept, modest and friendly hotel overlooking Pavilion Gardens, with a pleasant dining room (they do an early supper for opera/concert goers), lounge and bar, excellent breakfasts, and prompt, courteous service; cl Dec–Jan.

Rowland SK2072 HOLLY COTTAGE Rowland, Bakewell DE45 1NR (01629) 640624 *£38; 2 rms, shared bthrm. 200-year-old cottage on a quiet lane and surrounded by peaceful rolling countryside; with open fire in the large lounge, an attractive dining room, excellent breakfasts with home-made rolls and bread, and lovely gardens; cl Nov–Dec.

Great Longstone SK2071 BARN Main St, Great Longstone, Bakewell DE4 1TZ (01629) 640335 *£32; 2 warm, very comfortable and spotlessly clean, ground-floor rms, shared bthrm. Converted barn on the main street of an attractive village; with an upstairs open-plan lounge and dining room; no smoking; cl Christmas wk; children over 10.

To see and do

✝☗⇊⊤ **Bakewell** SK2168 is unfortunately traffic-ridden, but a civilised small town away from the traffic, especially around the CHURCH (itself graced with a fine set of memorials). You can still get those raspberry tarts here, from the Bakewell Pudding Shop in the main square where they were first made in 1860. OLD HOUSE MUSEUM 16th-c former home of revolutionary industrialist Richard Arkwright, still with its original wattle-and-daub interior walls and open-timbered chambers. A little folk museum has 19th-c costumes, children's toys, lacework, craftsman's tools and farm implements. Cl am, Nov–Mar; (01629) 812231; £1.80. MAGPIE MINE Last worked in 1958 and stabilised in the 1970s, these surface remains give a good idea of a 19th-c lead mine. Disabled access; free. The Castle Hotel and Stitch's Wine Bar are good for lunch.

🏰 **Bolsover** SK4770 The original ruined CASTLE on this site dates back to the 12th c, but it was rebuilt in 1613 as a spectacular mock castle – about 200 years ahead of this fashion. Battlements and turrets adorn the outside, while inside are allegorical frescoes, fine panelling and ornate fireplaces; also a 350-year-old indoor riding school used for riding by the disabled. Snacks, shop, some disabled access; cl winter Mon and Tues, 24–26 Dec, 1 Jan; (01246) 823349; £2.10.

★!☗♋️❀ BUXTON SK0673 has changed a lot over the years but does have some handsome buildings dating from its days as a flourishing spa resort, with Georgian terraces (the Crescent is a noble example of a Georgian streetscape) and a restored Edwardian opera house. Its annual festival injects life back into those grand buildings and is very good indeed. MICRARIUM In the former Victorian pump room of the spa, the wonders of nature are magnified through lots of push-button microscopes and displays. Shop, disabled access; cl Oct–Mar; (01298) 78662; *£2.50. The MUSEUM & ART GALLERY has lots of local and Peak District interest. POOLE'S CAVERN (Buxton Country Park) The best show cave in the Peak District and the longest in Britain, a spectacular natural limestone cavern in 100 acres of woodland, with well lit stalactites and stalagmites, a video show and exhibitions on caves, woodland and the Romans. As in other caverns, wrap up well. Snacks, shop, disabled access into cavern; cl Nov-Easter; (01298) 26978; £3.20. GRIN LOW WOODS, just S of the town, are well landscaped with mature woodland and the Victorian folly of Solomon's Temple (fine views from the top); there's a useful information centre, though it's not always open. The Railway (Bridge St) is good for lunch, and the Old Clubhouse (opposite the opera house) is useful too.

🏠❀🐦★ **Chatsworth** SK2669 CHATSWORTH Famously splendid home of the Duke and Duchess of Devonshire on the banks of the River Derwent. Sumptuously furnished and decorated, it's one of the grandest country houses in England, with a superb collection of fine and decorative arts. The rooms aren't exactly what you'd call cosy, but what they lack in charm is made up for by the breathtaking treasures on display, inc paintings by Rembrandt and Van Dyck among others, and an intriguing *trompe l'oeil* violin that looks like it's hanging on the back of a door. The lovely gardens cover over 100 acres and are full of surprises, while the surrounding park was landscaped by Capability Brown; also a farmyard and adventure playground. Meals, snacks, shops (inc perhaps the best farm shop in the country, towards Pilsley), garden centre, disabled access to garden only; house and garden cl Nov–Mar, farmyard and adventure playground cl Oct–Mar; (01246) 582204; house and garden £5.50, garden only £3, adventure playground and farmyard £2. The estate village of Edensor SK2469, opposite the main gate, is a marvellous mix of styles, with fine views from the lane leading up out of

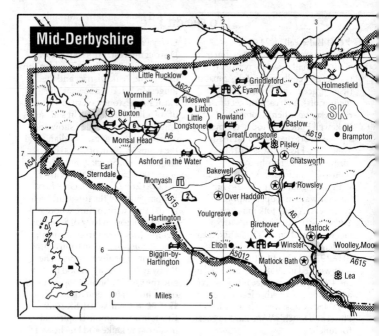

Mid-Derbyshire

it. Joseph Paxton, responsible for much of Chatsworth's gardens and co-designer of the village, is buried here. Around Chatsworth are two more most attractive, small estate villages, both with good pubs for lunch: Baslow SK2572 and Beeley SK2667.

✝ 🔥 ❀ **Chesterfield** SK3871 is not a tourist town, but its largely 14th-c CHURCH has a really striking leaning spire, and is a rich building inside. The town MUSEUM has the story behind it (cl Weds and Sun; free). The Victorian market hall has flourishing markets every day exc Tues and Sun (junk on Thurs, street entertainment summer Sats). Nearby GRASSMOOR COUNTRY PARK is a pleasant place to stroll through, and an example of reclaimed land put to good use. The Derby Tup out on Whittington Moor is an enjoyable ale house with good-value, simple food.

🎫 🚗 **Clay Cross** SK3963 COUNTRYSIDE CENTRE Changing exhibitions of art and photography with a country-related theme, and plenty of details and advice for walks and nature trails. Shop, disabled access; best to check opening times

(01246) 866960; free. The Plough at Brackenfield SK5658 is a prettily set country pub nr here.

★ 🏠 **Eyam** SK2276 is an attractive secluded village. During the Great Plague, infected villagers stayed here for fear of infecting people outside: plaques record who died where, and stones on the village edge mark where money was disinfected. EYAM HALL Sturdy looking 17th-c manor house, still very much a family home, with furniture, portraits and tapestries, fine Jacobean staircase and impressive stone-flagged hall. They've recently opened up the old washhouse. Snacks, shop, disabled access to ground floor only; open Weds, Thurs, Sun and bank hols Easter–Oct; (01433) 631976; £3.25. A timed ticket system is in operation. The Miner's Arms is very good for lunch.

🏠 ❀ ✕ **Hardwick Hall** SK4463 HARDWICK HALL The marriages of the redoubtable Bess of Hardwick couldn't necessarily be described as happy but she certainly did very well out of them, the fourth leaving her enough money to build this triumphant, Elizabethan prodigy

Snacks (home-baking), shop and garden centre, some disabled access; cl 17 July 1995–20 Mar 1996; (01629) 534380; *£2.50. The Tavern at Tansley is handy for lunch.

✔ 🏠 ❀ **Matlock** SK3060 RIBER CASTLE WILDLIFE PARK Specialising in rare breeds and endangered species of birds and animals, a 25-acre park set high up on Riber Hill in the grounds of ruined Riber Castle; excellent views. Snacks, shop, disabled facilities; cl 25 Dec; (01629) 582073; £3.80. The Three Stags is useful for lunch.

🏠 ⬇ ☺ ✔ 🏠 **Matlock Bath** SK2958 has a spectacular wooded cliff looking across the lower roadside town to pastures by the Derwent; up the side of the gorge, quiet lanes climb steeply with some 18th- and 19th-c villas. A pleasantly busy place, with lots to do. HEIGHTS OF ABRAHAM A dramatic cable car ride takes you from the Derwent Valley to the summit of this 60-acre country park, and perhaps just as thrilling are the two show caverns, one telling the story of 17th-c lead miners, the other introduced by a multi-vision programme. Also a nature trail, play area and picnic sites. Meals, snacks, shop, disabled access; cl Nov–Easter exc wknds from mid-Feb; (01629) 582365; £5.30. PEAK DISTRICT MINING MUSEUM AND TEMPLE MINE Static and moving exhibits explaining the history of the industry from Roman times, with an early 19th-c, water-pressure pumping engine (unique in Britain), and a new interactive display, the Tunnel of Death, looking at the dangers of working in a mine. Also tours of the old Temple Mine workings, and the chance to pan for minerals – they found a tiny amount of gold last year. Snacks, shop, disabled access; cl 25 Dec; (01629) 583834; *£2. GULLIVER'S KINGDOM AND ROYAL CAVE Growing family theme park with hectic rides and chair lift, cave tour, cowboy town and ghost town. Meals, snacks, shops; cl wkdys mid-Sept–end of Oct, all Nov–Mar; £4.50. If you're staying round here, other useful family attractions include the AQUARIUM AND HOLOGRAM GALLERY (the big tank used to be a swimming pool), and the

house. The beautifully symmetrical towers are modestly crowned with her monogram ES and there's an amazing expanse of glass (some say to help her failing sight). The house and contents have both remained largely unchanged, with fine tapestries and needlework, inc some by Mary, Queen of Scots. Large park, and gardens laid out in a walled courtyard. Meals, snacks, shop, limited disabled access; house cl am, all Mon (exc bank hols), Tues and Fri, and Nov–Mar, garden also cl Nov–Mar; house and garden £5.50, garden only £2; NT. Not far from this 'new' house is the shell of Hardwick Old Hall, the first house Bess built here, in a rather less impressive state than its successor; £1.55 – a joint ticket for both houses is available. Also on the estate is a WATERMILL recently restored by the NT. The Hardwick Inn at the end of the park, also NT-owned, is useful for lunch, and much of the park is open free at all times – attractive for walks.

❀ **Lea** SK3257 LEA GARDENS Beautiful woodland gardens, with rhododendrons inc rare species and cultivars, azaleas and rock plants.

MODEL RAILWAY MUSEUM attached to a model shop, with a scale working model of Mellorsdale as it was in 1906; best to check wknd and winter opening; (01629) 583993.

🏛 **Monyash** SK1566 has some mysterious ancient monuments, the ARBOR LOW STONE CIRCLE and the GIB HILL BARROW. The Bull is good for lunch.

🏠 **Old Whittington** SK3874 REVOLUTION HOUSE Innocuous-looking, old thatched cottage, 300 years ago the birthplace of what came to be known as the Glorious Revolution. The whole story is told on an audio-visual display and there are period rooms and furniture. Shop, disabled access to ground floor only; cl Nov–Easter exc 17–24 Dec and 27 Dec–2 Jan; (01246) 453554; free. The White Horse is good value for lunch.

🏠 ❀ ✿ **Over Haddon** SK2066 HADDON HALL For some this is the most perfectly preserved, medieval manor house in England, still with its 12th-c painted chapel, 14th-c kitchen and banqueting hall with minstrels' gallery. The house has barely changed in 400 years, partly because the Dukes of Rutland, who owned it, preferred to spend more time at Belvoir Castle. Some of the rooms can seem a little bare, and there aren't that many furnishings or pictures, though a highlight is Rex Whistler's painting of the house in the beautiful silver-panelled long gallery. Outside are long terraced rose gardens. Meals, snacks, shop; cl Mon (exc bank hols), Sun during July and Aug, all Oct–Mar; (01629) 812855; £4.

LATHKILL DALE CRAFT CENTRE (Manor Farm) Plenty of crafts and demonstrations, from stained glass to barometer and clock workshops. Meals, snacks, shops, disabled access; cl 25 Dec. The Lathkil Hotel is good for lunch.

❀ ★ **Pilsley** SK2471 THE HERB GARDEN Big main garden with lots of herbs and old English roses, as well as smaller gardens specialising in rare medicinal herbs, pot-pourri or lavender. Teas, shop; cl Oct–Mar exc by arrangement; (01246) 854268; free. Pilsley itself is nice, and the

Devonshire Arms has food using fresh Chatsworth ingredients.

✕ ✿ 🏛 **Rowsley** SK2566 CAUDWELL'S MILL AND CRAFT CENTRE 19th-c working flour mill, powered by water turbines, with crafts such as glass-blowing and woodturning. Meals, snacks, shop, disabled access; cl wkdys Jan and Feb and 24–26 Dec; (01629) 734374; site free, mill £1.50. Rowsley also has an interesting STONE CIRCLE called the Nine Ladies. The Peacock is a civilised place for lunch, and the Grouse & Claret here is useful too.

★ 🏠 **Winster** SK2460, once a bustling market town but now just a village, with the 17th-c MARKET HOUSE as a reminder of those days; it was one of the earliest properties acquired by the National Trust, for whom it's now an information centre. Cl winter wkdys. The Miner's Standard is nice for lunch.

🐴 **Wormhill** SK1274 DONKEY VILLAGE Farm and picnic area surrounded by friendly donkeys. It's run by a trust which rescues donkeys and gives handicapped or disabled children a day out with them; no charge, but donations (and sponsors) very welcome – you can also book children's birthday parties, with rides etc. The Angler's Rest in Miller's Dale is good value for lunch.

★ **Attractive villages** with decent pubs include Ashford in the Water SK1969, Earl Sterndale SK0967, Elton SK2261, Hartington SK1360 (good cheese shop inc local stilton), Little Hucklow SK1678, Litton SK1675, Little Longstone SK1971 (Great Longstone SK2071 nearby is charming, too), Old Brampton SK3372 (count the minutes between one and two o'clock on its church clock), Over Haddon SK2066, Pilsley SK2471, Tideswell SK1575 (spacious 14th-c church known as the Cathedral of the Peak). The church at Youlgreave SK2164 is also interesting.

Cycling is good on the Monsal Trail (see **Walks**, below). You can hire bicycles by the half-day or day from Parsley Hay Cycle Hire, Parsley Hay SK1463. Charges are around £6 a day for an ordinary bicycle to £12 for a mountain bike.

Walks

The **White Peak** area has high, flat pastures with neat fields of rich grassland enclosed by silvery stone walls, clusters of often very photogenic farm buildings, small old-fashioned villages and, cutting through the limestone, the intricate channels of the dales. It gives an abundance of generally gentle walking.

Winding **Monsal Dale** ◁-1 is the outstanding valley in this central area, its pastoral quality emphasised by the disused limestone cotton mills along the way. It's especially lovely in May and June, with wild flowers enriching the pastures along the broader stretches. Don't expect to have it to yourself. There's good access from the A6, a couple of miles towards Buxton from Ashford in the Water SK1969; and from Monsal Head SK1452, where the hotel has pleasant refreshment facilities and where a disused railway viaduct adds to the interest. This viaduct forms part of the Monsal Trail – see below. The B6049, N off the A6 SE of Buxton, gives access to Miller's Dale SK1573, just past the little village of that name (where the Angler's Rest is a decent pub). Upstream of Monsal Dale is rather less visited but also lovely – as is its continuation Chee Dale SK1273.

Lathkill Dale SK1865 ◁-2 has a charming combination of woods, steep pastures and more well weathered signs of old mines; its short tributary Bradford Dale is also very attractive.

The **River Derwent** ◁-3 has pleasant stretches where Izaak Walton fished, either upstream from Rowsley SK2566, or from the B6012 N of there, at the Calton Lees car park SK2568 – there's open access to Chatsworth Park on this W side of the river, which is particularly lovely.

The well wooded **Goyt Valley** SK0177 ◁-4 with its three miles of reservoirs is a man-made landscape, but nonetheless charming, and very peaceful even though popular on fine weekends; reached off the A54 W of Buxton SK0673. Shining Tor SK1454 is a breezy but undemanding moorland walk from the summit of a minor road.

The E edges of the **Dark Peak** ◁-5 include the abrupt ramparts of Curbar Edge SK2575 and Froggatt Edge SK2476, popular with rock-climbers and easily accessible from the road. Birchen Edge SK2772 and Wellington's Monument SK2673 are obvious objectives from the Robin Hood inn at Curbar SK2574.

The **Monsal Trail** ◁-6 outshines the other former railway-track walks in the Peak District, though like them it is in parts more exposed to the winds than walks down in the dales. It runs from Wye Dale SK1072, E of Buxton, to Coombs Road viaduct SK2274, S of Bakewell. W of Miller's Dale Station SK1573, the trail leaves the old railway and takes a stepping-stone route along the river beneath the towering cliffs of Chee Tor SK1273 before rejoining the railway track.

Further E, well out of the Peak District, **Cresswell Crags** SK5374 ◁-7, beside Crags Pond, form the basis of a short but attractive there-and-back walk through woodland.

A particular virtue of the area is the large number of decent **country pubs** that seem as though they have been perfectly positioned for walkers. These include the Miner's Arms at Milltown, Ashover SK3561 (despite quarrying), the Robin Hood at Baslow SK2572 (handy for the ridge of Baslow Edge), the King's Head at Bonsall SK2858 (very child-friendly, by the Limestone Way), the Druid at Birchover SK2462 (handy for Stanton Moor, and the odd little Row Tor just behind the pub), the Barrel on the ridge at Bretton SK2077, the Chequers just below Froggatt Edge SK2476, the Maynard Arms and Sir William at Grindleford SK2478, the Robin Hood at Lydgate nr Holmesfield SK3177 (for the Cordwell Valley), the Bull at Monyash SK1566, the unfashionably basic New Napoleon by Ogston Reservoir SK3761, the Lathkil at Over Haddon SK2066 (for Lathkill Dale), and the Bull's Head at Wardlow SK1874 (for well wooded Cressbrook Dale).

Driving

Roads here give plenty of attractive views, though not usually very distant ones. Any route off the main roads W of a line drawn straight down through Chatsworth is likely to be enjoyable, with particular favourites inc the B6012 past Chatsworth itself (busy in summer), the high roads above Lathkill Dale, the back road from Baslow through Hassop, the Longstones, Cressbrook and Litton to Tideswell, and the B6049 from Tideswell across Miller's Dale. The A615 E of Matlock runs through some lovely scenery, and W of the town the B5056 and B5057 are good.

Where to eat

Holmesfield SK3277 ROBIN HOOD (01742) 890360 Rambling ex-farmhouse with consistently fine food, inc interesting daily specials; open all day Sun for food; good nearby walks. £20|£2.50/£7.50.

Eyam SK2276 MINERS ARMS Water Lane (01433) 630853 Good, restful dining pub in a small village, with lovely home-made food and decent wines; bedrooms; cl pm Sun, Mon, 1st 2 wks Jan. £20|£1.95/£4.75.

Birchover SK2462 DRUID (01629) 650302 Pleasantly remote, creeper-covered house with a huge choice of very popular, often unusual food, and good, friendly service; cl 25 Dec; children under 5 must leave by 8.15pm; partial disabled access. £17|£3.60/£8.

Buxton SK0673 DANDELION DAYS 5 Bridge St (01298) 22843 Very good, generous helpings of vegetarian food in a restaurant above a health-food shop; pleasant and prompt service; cl Mon. £7.50|£1/£2.50.

Woolley Moor SK3661 WHITE HORSE (01246) 590319 Old dining pub run by very friendly people – and popular with locals; very good food using the best local produce, lots of daily specials, decent wines and beers; lovely views, nice children's play area. £14.50|£2.70/£5.50.

SOUTH DERBYSHIRE

Dove Dale here is matchless; also great houses, interesting, well restored industrial remains, superb tramway museum

The tramway museum at Crich is one of Britain's most interesting places to visit even if you have no enthusiasm for trams themselves, and Sudbury Hall, Calke Abbey and Kedleston Hall are all splendid. Cromford is a fascinating survivor of the earliest days of the Industrial Revolution. The dales country in the north-west part of the area is particularly appealing, with pale stone buildings and walling underlining the natural beauty.

Where to stay

Dove Dale SK1452 PEVERIL OF THE PEAK Dove Dale, Ashbourne DE6 2AW (0133 529) 333 £102; 47 rms, with sherry and chocolates provided. Relaxing hotel in a pretty village, with comfortable sofas and log fire in the lounge, and a modern bar overlooking the garden; tennis; wonderful walking nearby.

Ashbourne SK1846 CALLOW HALL Mappleton Rd DE6 2AA (01335) 343403 £90; 16 lovely, well furnished rms and excellent bthrms. Friendly and relaxed Victorian mansion up a long drive through grounds with fine trees; comfortable drawing room with open fire, fresh flowers and period furniture, and very good food in the popular and elegant restaurant (they have their own pâtis-serie, and the meat is hung and butchered on the premises), inc breakfasts with home-made sausages and freshly squeezed orange juice; private fishing; cl 25–26 Dec; disabled access.

Shottle SK3149 DANNAH FARM Bowmans Lane, Shottle, Belper DE56 3DR (01773) 550273 £58; 9 rms with old pine and antiques. Pretty and carefully restored Georgian farmhouse with two comfortable sitting rooms, and popu-lar, imaginative cooking, inc home-made bread, in the attractive, no-smoking dining room; calves, ducks, hens, lambs in spring, Vietnamese pot-bellied pigs, farm dogs and cats.

Hopton SK2553 HENMORE GRANGE Hopton, Wirksworth DE4 4DF (0162 985) 420 £55; 12 rms. Friendly and carefully modernised, stone-built farm-house and renovated farm buildings with lots of original features; old-fash-ioned hospitality, and a garden designed to attract butterflies; disabled access.

Kirk Ireton SK2650 BARLEY MOW Kirk Ireton, Ashbourne DE6 3JP (01335) 370306 £35.75; 5 rms. 17th-c building with lots of woodwork in the very old-fashioned series of interconnecting bar rooms; close to Carsington Reservoir with its watersports and fishing; cl Christmas wk.

To see and do

🐄 **Alkmonton** SK1838 BENTLEY FIELDS OPEN FARM Unspoilt and traditional livestock farm stretching over 245 acres; they milk their cows at 1 and 4pm. Lots of different breeds of sheep, pig and poultry, and in spring if you're lucky you may see calving or lambing – or chicks pecking their way out of their eggs. All 450 sheep are usually sheared on the early May bank holiday, weather permitting. Teas, shop, some disabled access; open every bank hol Sun and Mon, plus Easter wk, and Sun in July and Aug; (01335) 330240; *£1.50. The Crown over at Marston Montgomery is quite handy for lunch.

★ ✝ 🏛 **Ashbourne** SK1846 has quite a good few interesting Georgian buildings in the streets off the hillside market place, especially leading to its elegantly proportioned CHURCH, which has a famous white marble statue of a sleeping child. DERWENT CRYSTAL CENTRE (Shaw Croft) Quality glassworks and engravers, with demonstrations and factory shop. Disabled access; cl Sun, 25–26 Dec, 1 Jan; free. The Gingerbread Shop sells the town's long-standing speciality. Smith's Tavern is good for lunch.

🏠 ❀ **Calke** SK3722 CALKE ABBEY One of the most rewarding NT properties in the whole country, an unusual baroque mansion still in pretty much the same state as it was when the last baronet died here in 1924.

Restoration slowly proceeds, and part of the interest is the well explained restoration process itself. Splendidly decorated rooms with fascinating displays and treasures (inc an extensive natural history collection), but also more dilapidated corridors and rooms where family possessions were just bundled together in heaps. Not the kind of thing you usually see in a place like this, and it gives you a better appreciation of how for a long time the abbey was a much-loved family home. One of the most striking objects is the Chinese silk state bed, presented by the royal family in 1734 and then left by the eccentric family in its original packaging, only to be found by chance in 1985. Also carriages in the stable block, extensive wooded parkland and walled gardens. Meals, snacks, shop, disabled access; cl Thurs and Fri, Nov–Mar, house cl am; £4.50, garden only £2; NT. The house has a timed ticket entry system. The White Swan in Melbourne and Holly Bush at Breedon on the Hill are both quite handy for lunch.

🚋 **Crich** SK3554 NATIONAL TRAMWAY MUSEUM A favourite of many correspondents: lovingly restored vintage trams from all over the British Isles, many of them in working order and running along a one-mile period street overlooking the Derwent Valley. Unlimited rides on the

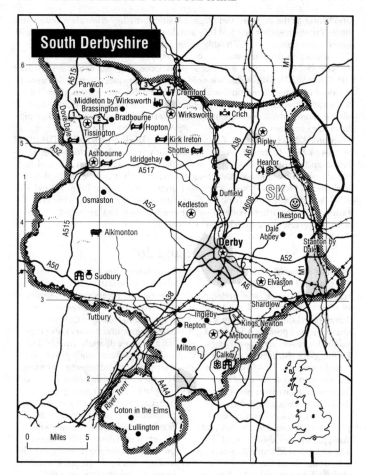

South Derbyshire

vehicles, and very good indoor museums, exhibitions and displays, inc a lively audio-visual show on the history of trams. The vehicles look especially good lit up – try and go on a Dec afternoon just before it starts to go dark. Meals, snacks, shop, disabled access (but not on to trams); cl Fri in May and Sept, wkdys during first 2 wks in Oct, Nov–Mar exc Santa specials; (01773) 852565; £4.50. The Yew Tree at Holloway is handy for lunch. The village is pronounced 'Cry', not 'Critch'.

Cromford SK2956 is a good example of an 18th-c cotton milling village, little developed after its original building, and rewarding to stroll through. Carefully preserved,

North St (1777) is the first true industrial street in the world. CROMFORD MILL Richard Arkwright established the world's first successful, water-powered cotton mill here in 1771, giving it a strong claim to be one of the birthplaces of the Industrial Revolution; it's currently being restored, and there are several craft shops. Meals and snacks in wholefood restaurant, shop, disabled access; cl 25 Dec; (01629) 825776; £1.50 for guided tour. The nearby restored CANAL is a quiet and attractive, early Industrial Revolution setting with a restored steam-powered pumping house and a fine aqueduct over the river; pleasant walks along here, and horse-drawn barge trips in summer. The HIGH PEAK JUNCTION WORKSHOPS out here have exhibitions and a film; cl winter wkdys. The Boat is useful for lunch.

✝ ❀ ⚓ 🖼 🍴 🏠 ♫ Derby SK3536 is a big busy city, but not too daunting for a visitor to penetrate, and has several things worth visiting; it's got far more open spaces than you'd expect. The 16th-c tower of the CATHEDRAL is the second-highest in the country; the rest of the building was replaced in the 18th c. Bess of Hardwick is buried in the vaults beneath the elaborate monument she ordered for herself, and there's a delightful early Georgian screen. Shop, disabled access; cl one Fri and Sat in Jun for arts festival; they open the tower a couple of days each year (good views), and have bell-ringing demonstrations then; (01332) 381685 for dates. INDUSTRIAL MUSEUM (Full St) Restored early 18th-c silk mill and adjacent flour mill, with among its comprehensive displays probably the world's finest collection of Rolls-Royce aero engines, starting with the Eagle of 1915; they should this year have opened a new Power Gallery with lots of buttons and hands-on displays. Shop, disabled access; cl am Sun and bank hols, 25–26 Dec; (01332) 255308; 30p, free on Sun. DERBY MUSEUM AND ART GALLERY (The Strand) Important collections of porcelain and the paintings of local artist Joseph Wright, as well as other antiquities, natural history, militaria, and geology. Shop, disabled access; cl am Sun and bank hols, 25–27 Dec; free. PICKFORDS HOUSE MUSEUM (Friargate) Built in 1770 as a combined workplace and family home, now Derby's biggest museum showing domestic life in the 18th and 19th c. Temporary exhibitions, and Georgian garden. Shop, limited disabled access; cl am Sun and bank hols, 25–27 Dec; *30p.

ROYAL CROWN DERBY (Osmaston Rd) Displays and tours of bone-china factory, with museum tracing the industry's development from 1748; tours by arrangement. Snacks, shop; cl 12.30–2 pm, wknds (though shop open Sat), 25 Dec; (01332) 712800; tour £2.50 – no children under 10. A Tudor grammar school in St Peter's Churchyard is now a HERITAGE CENTRE with displays on Derby's history and an audio-visual show. Snacks, shop; cl Sun and bank hols; free. Walking tours leave here most Mon afternoons; (01332) 299321 to check; £3.50 inc tea. Two interesting places for a lunchtime snack are the Brunswick nr the station (brewing its own beers), and the Abbey Inn, Darley St – all that's left of an 11th-c abbey.

❀ ♣ ♫ ♿ Elvaston SK4132 ELVASTON CASTLE COUNTRY PARK 200 acres of lovely 19th-c landscaped parkland, with formal and Old English gardens, wooded walks, and wildfowl on the ornamental lake. Also restored estate workshops with traditional crafts, and nature trails. Snacks, shop, disabled access; museum cl am, Mon and Tues and Nov–Mar, visitor centre cl wkdys Nov–Mar; gardens and grounds free (though there is a 60p car parking charge, more at wknds), museum £1.20. Shardlow is convenient for lunch.

❀ ♣ Heanor SK4346 SHIPLEY COUNTRY PARK Medieval estate developed and landscaped in the 18th c, now with 600 acres of woodland, lakes and fields. A pleasant place to wander, with the former railway lines transformed into leafy walkways; you can hire bikes (daily Easter and Jun–early Sept, wknds only rest of the year, £3.50 for three hours) and decent cycle routes are available from the visitor centre. Snacks, shop, disabled access; visitor centre cl am winter wkdys.

☺ Ilkeston SK4642 AMERICAN ADVENTURE THEME PARK Fully themed park over 200 acres, with hugely varied rides involving many of the different facets of that continent. Meals, snacks, shop, disabled facilities; cl some wkdys in Mar, Sept and Oct, and all Nov–Feb; (01733) 531521; £10.99.

🏠 ♿ ❀ Kedleston SK3041 KEDLESTON HALL Palladian mansion built in the 18th c and thought by many to be the finest example of Robert Adam's work in the country – it's certainly the least altered. Interesting *objets d'art*, original furnishings and a good collection of paintings, as well as a museum of items collected by Lord Curzon when he was Viceroy of India. Extensive formal gardens with marvellous rhododendrons and long woodland walks. Adam also designed a charming boathouse and bridge in the park. Meals, snacks, shop, some disabled access (best to phone in advance); house and shop open pm Sat–Weds Apr–Oct, grounds open daily in season; (01332) 842191); £4.20; NT. The nearest place we can suggest for lunch is the Three Horseshoes at Lees, beyond the A52.

★ † ⌂ ❀ ♘ **Melbourne** SK3825 is a pleasant small town, with a good, relaxed feel and villagey lanes; the White Swan and Railway Hotel are useful for lunch. The CHURCH of St Michael and St Mary is impressive, more like a cathedral than an ordinary parish church. MELBOURNE HALL Behind its 18th-c façade, this grandly extended house dates back in part to the 13th c, and during its illustrious history has twice been the home of British prime ministers; fine pictures and furnishings. Glorious formal gardens with fountains, pools, and famous yew tunnel; interesting craft centre. Meals, snacks, shop, disabled access; gardens open pm Weds, Sat, Sun and bank hols Apr–Sept, house open pm only in Aug (but cl first three Mons); (01332) 862502; *£3.50, *£2.50 for house or garden only.

♘ **Middleton** SK2756 MIDDLETON TOP ENGINE HOUSE Beam engine built in 1829 and used to haul waggons up the Middleton incline on the Cromford & High Peak Railway, the story of which is told in the visitor centre. Snacks, shop, disabled access; open every Sun Easter–Oct (engine static), and first wknd each month (engine in motion); (01629) 823204; static engine *35p, in motion *60p, visitor centre free. See also Wirksworth entry, below.

♘ ⌁ ⌂ ♨ **Ripley** SK3950 MIDLAND RAILWAY CENTRE Regular steamtrain passenger service through country park, and developing industrial museum looking at the golden days of the Midland Railway. Meal, snacks, shop, disabled access; cl 25 Dec; best to ring for train timetable, (01773) 570140; £5.95. DENBY POTTERY

VISITOR CENTRE Guided factory tours (not pm Fri or wknds) show the intricate skills of potters and craftsmen; it's a more laborious process than you might think, with over 30 pairs of hands touching every teacup during its manufacture. Also museum, large factory shop and children's play area. Snacks, shop; (01773) 743644; tours £2.99, craftroom £1.99. The Excavator on the A610 out at Buckland Hollow is useful for lunch (all afternoon, Sun).

⌂ ♨ **Sudbury** SK1632 SUDBURY HALL Individual but attractive Stuart mansion with elaborate carving, frescoes, murals and plasterwork inside the splendidly elegant rooms. Also here is the very good NATIONAL TRUST MUSEUM OF CHILDHOOD, with a chimney climb for sweep-sized children. Meals, snacks, shop; cl am, Mon (exc bank hols), Tues, Good Fri, Nov–Mar; £4.40 for everything, or £3.20 house and grounds, £1 grounds only, £2.20 museum only; NT. The Boar's Head Hotel is useful for lunch.

★ † ♘ **Tissington** SK1752 is the most beautiful village in the Peak District. Its broad main street is wonderfully harmonious, with wide grass verges, and handsome stone houses inc a Jacobean hall (not open) and an interesting church. The grey-stone gardener's cottage is familiar from many calendars; craft centre, garden centre, decent homely café.

⌁ ♘ ♭ **Wirksworth** SK2854 Since 1978 the Civic Trust and local authorities have restored many old buildings here, and the town is beginning to be well worth a visit. The Knockerdown inn out on the B5035 is pleasant for lunch, and the Carsington Reservoir, also out that way, is beginning to tone into the landscape. NATIONAL STONE CENTRE The main features of the site are the 330 million-year-old tropical lagoons and limestone fossil reefs, though there's also the Story of Stone exhibition, guided nature trails, and activities like gem-panning or fossil-rubbing. Snacks, shop, some disabled access; cl 25 Dec; (01629) 824833; *£1.80. WIRKSWORTH HERITAGE CENTRE Old silk and velvet mill, with displays inc explanations of local customs like well-dressing and clypping the church. Meals, snacks, shop; cl am Sun, Mon (exc bank hols and from Aug–mid-Sept), Tues (exc from Aug–mid-Sept), and late Dec–early Feb; (01629) 825225; 85p. See also Middleton entry, above.

★ **Particularly appealing villages** are a strong attraction here, and, besides those already mentioned, include Bradbourne SK2152 (with an ancient Saxon cross outside its Norman church), Brassington SK2354 (the Olde Gate here is a lovely old pub), Coton in the Elms SK2415, Dale Abbey SK4338 (the Carpenter's Arms at Ilkeston SK4642 is handy, and it's sited nr the Hermit's Cave and remarkable All Saints Church, part of which was formerly the village inn), Duffield SK3443, Idridgehay SK2849, Kirk Ireton SK2650 (the interesting old Barley Mow is good), Lullington SK2513 (the Colvile Arms is a nice unspoilt pub), Milton SK3126 (the Swan is good), Stanton by Dale SK4638 (the Stanhope Arms is useful), Osmaston SK1944 (pleasant path through lakeside park), Parwich SK1854 and Repton SK3026.

The RIVER TRENT impresses with its silent power; Ingleby SK3426 is one good access point – for example, from the big garden of the John Thompson pub, which brews its own beer.

The **Shardlow** SK4330 CANAL BASIN is attractive, with some handsome, former wharf buildings – one now an antiques warehouse, another the Hoskins Wharf pub/restaurant; the Crown and the Malt Shovel are good pubs here.

This really is a splendid area for CYCLING, particularly on the Tissington Trail (see **Walks** section, below). You can hire bicycles by the half-day or day from Ashbourne Cycle Hire, Mapleton Lane, Ashbourne SK1846, and Middleton Top SK2756, nr Cromford . Charges are around £6 a day for an ordinary bicycle to £12 for a mountain bike. As these centres generally replace their stock each year, you can often pick up a bargain when they sell off the old bikes in Dec.

Walks

Dove Dale ⌂-1, shared with Staffs (the River Dove marks the boundary), is the most popular of all the dales. Partly wooded, it has a beautifully varied mixture of water, trees and pastures, and is lined with crags and curiously shaped out-crops of rock. To see fewer people, head for the upstream sections: the barer pastures and steep hillsides of Milldale SK1354, the wooded peace of Beresford Dale SK1259, or Wolfscote Dale SK1357, with its dramatic rocky gorge and still trout-pools (best reached from Hartington SK1260, where the Jug & Glass up on the main road is useful for lunch). Other handy nearby refreshment places are the Okeover Arms at Mapleton SK1648 and (to be found on the Staffs side) the Izaak Walton Hotel, nr Ilam (cosier inside than it looks from out), Watts Russell Arms at Hopedale and the George at Alstonefield.

The **Tissington Trail** ⌂-2 follows a disused railway track from Ashbourne SK1846 up to Parsley Hay SK1463 on the A515, where it joins the similar High Peak Trail from Buxton SK0673 to nr Cromford SK2956. This has a particularly interesting finale from Middleton Top engine house SK2756 to High Peak Junction, dipping down a great incline past old engine houses to reach the **Cromford Canal** ⌂-3, along which it's a short walk to Cromford. Earlier, branching off at Roystone Grange is an archaeological trail.

Driving

Many of the minor roads W of the A6 wind attractively through silver-walled pastures and past quiet farming hamlets. Of the main roads, the B5056 N of Ashbourne up towards Bakewell, the B5053 Ashbourne–Wirksworth and A5012 Cromford–Grangemill give a good feel of the character of the dales.

Where to eat

Melbourne SK3825 BAY TREE 4 Potter St (01332) 863358 Small, family-run, cottagey restaurant with beams and simple furnishings; carefully presented, popular food (Sun lunch is booked up weeks ahead), and thoughtful, relaxed service; cl pm Sun, Mon, all Jan. £32|£3.20/£10;

Tutbury SK2028 OLDE DOG & PARTRIDGE (01283) 813030 Excellent carvery in half-timbered inn with stylish rooms, well kept beers, good wines, and friendly service. £17|£2/£6.15.

Kings Newton SK3826 HARDINGE ARMS (01332) 813808 Good, quickly served roasts, fish, salads and other food in a comfortable, interesting, beamed and timbered 17th-c inn; cl pm Mon; disabled access. £12|£2.50/£5.

NORTH DERBYSHIRE: THE HIGH PEAK

More austere than other parts of the county; most appeal for serious walkers, but striking drives too.

Castleton has most of the area's relatively few visitor attractions clustered around it, chiefly the various underground show caverns. It also has the most varied walks in the area; the further north you head into the High Peak, the bleaker it becomes – territory for the really serious long-distance walker. The whole area can be forbidding in winter, and at any time of year has a more austere appeal than the rest of the county.

Where to stay

Hathersage SK2381 GEORGE Hathersage, Sheffield S30 1BB (01433) 650436 £77; 18 pretty rms (the back ones are quietest). Substantial and comfortably modernised old inn with a neat, flagstoned back terrace by the rose garden; cosy, traditionally furnished bars, and popular food; a good base for walks; children under 16 free if sharing room with parents.

Castleton SK1583 CASTLE Castleton, Sheffield S30 2WG (01433) 620578 £59; 9 well equipped rms. Comfortable hotel with handsome flagstones, beams and stripped stonework in the plush bars, decent bar and restaurant food, and open fires; cl 25 Dec.

Castleton SK1582 OLDE NAGS HEAD Castleton, Sheffield S30 2WH (01433) 620248 £52; 8 warm, comfortable rms. Village hotel renovated to preserve its character, with an open fire, antique furniture, small bar, well presented traditional bar food, and a decent restaurant.

Hathersage SK2381 HIGHLOW HALL S30 1AX (014336) 50393 *£50; 6 quiet, well equipped rms, 3 with own bthrm. B & B in a big, 16th-c manor house in lovely countryside, with a newly refurbished lounge and dining room, and excellent breakfasts (evening meals by arrangement); can walk into village.

Hope SK1783 POACHERS ARMS Hope, Castleton S30 2RD (01433) 620380 *£50; 6 rms. Friendly village pub with several interconnecting bars, efficient service, and generous helpings of interesting and varied well cooked food.

To see and do

★ 🏰 ☀ ♋ ⚓ **Castleton** SK1583 has attractive, dark stone buildings (one of the most impressive now a youth hostel), and is dominated by the ruins of PEVERIL CASTLE, built in the 12th c for Henry II, high above the village and with magnificent views. Shop; cl 24–26 Dec; (0433) 620613; *£1.25. The village is very much geared to visitors, and fills with walkers and cavers in

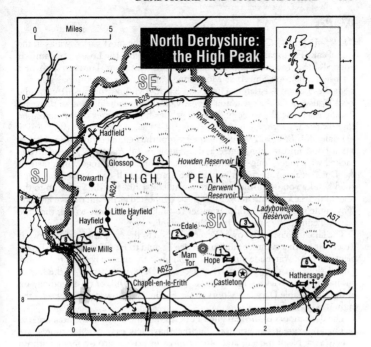

North Derbyshire:
the High Peak

summer; plenty of cafés, and shops selling polished pieces of the Blue John fluorspar that's found only in the nearby mine workings. PEAK CAVERN, actually in the village, is the biggest natural cavern in the county and really does seem huge – the entrance hall is so large it used to house an entire village. From there it's a half-mile walk along electrically lit subterranean passageways to the Great Cave, 150 ft wide and 90 feet long. By the time you finish the tour in the Devil's Dining Room you'll be 450 ft underground. Snacks, shop; cl Nov–Easter; (01433) 620285; *£3. BLUE JOHN CAVERN Containing eight of the 14 known veins of Blue John, this has been the main source of the mineral for nearly 300 years. It's an impressive example of a water-worn cave, over a third of a mile long, with chambers 200 ft high. Snacks, shop; cl 25 Dec only, though check first in winter; (01433) 620638; £4. SPEEDWELL CAVERN, a lead mine until 1790, is very atmospheric, with a long flight of steps down to a half-mile underground boat trip along floodlit passages, finishing up in a cathedral of a cavern with an impressive 'bottomless pit' – great fun.

The subterranean canal you drift along took 11 years to construct. Snacks, shop; cl 25 Dec; (01433) 620512; *£4.50. TREAK CLIFF CAVERN Very good, informative tours of Blue John mine-working since 1750, with rich veins of the mineral and quite staggering stalactites and stalagmites. Well positioned lights create spooky shapes and atmospheric shadows. The entrance is very narrow, and it's quite steep. Snacks, shop; cl 25 Dec only, though check first in winter; (01433) 620571; *£3.50. The Castle and Olde Nag's Head are good for lunch, and in the pretty nearby village of Hope SK1783, the Cheshire Cheese, Poachers Arms and Woodroffe Arms are all useful.

† **Hathersage** SK2381 has connections with Charlotte Brontë, who wrote *Jane Eyre* here. The CHURCH is the legendary site of Little John's grave. It's a good village for walkers and climbers, and in addition to the George, the Scotsman's Pack is useful for lunch.

At **Hayfield** SK0387 you can hire bikes to take along the Sett Valley Trail, about which there's also an information centre here.

Walks

Castleton SK1583 ⌂-1 and Hope SK1783 have the most varied walks in the High Peak. The great walk here is to take in Castleton, the Lose Hill/Mam Tor ridge SK1383, the caves and Winnats Pass SK1382; Mam Tor is so shaly that it's been called the Shivering Mountain. Cave Dale is an optional side trip from the back of Castleton. Quarrying has had an unfortunate effect on the local landscape in the area, and limits walks further afield, though there are some pleasant walks to be had in the gentler high pastures of the limestone country to the south.

Edale SK1285 ⌂-2, famous as the start of the Pennine Way into Scotland, has a good information centre and a couple of hikers' pubs. It tends to be packed with eager, long-distance walkers on Sunday mornings. For a taste of the Dark Peak proper, this can be the start for half-day walks that quite quickly take you up through the stone-walled pastures of the valley on to the edge of the dark plateau above. The track signposted as the alternative Pennine Way route up Jacob's Ladder is easier to find, and has more to see, than the official Pennine Way plod across a huge blanket bog.

The lane up past **Ladybower Reservoir** ⌂-3 to the car park by the Derwent Reservoir (with a summer minibus service beyond to Howden Reservoir) gives plenty of easy, waterside-cum-forest walking on the relatively sheltered, stone-walled slopes of the upper parts of Derwent Dale, with access to the higher moors for better views – for example, up on to Win Hill, or on a kind day on to the formidable Derwent Moors to the E. The Ladybower pub down on the main road is useful.

The dark moors of the real **High Peak** ⌂-4 in the north of the area are one of England's great wildernesses. But they have few easy circular routes, are largely very bleak indeed, and often consist of private grouse moor with no rights of public access. The car park at the top of Snake Pass (on A57 Glossop–Hathersage) is nr the centre of the biggest of the National Trust's moorland holdings here, giving free access to the miles of misnamed Hope Woodlands SK1091 (there aren't many trees on these high moors).

The moorland village of **Hayfield** SK0387 ⌂-5 and its attractive, nearby smaller sister Little Hayfield have good walks around them, both up towards Kinder Scout SK0888 and to the Lantern Pike viewpoint SK0288 in the opposite direction. There's also a popular walk along a hillside former railway to New Mills SK0085, looking down on the mill buildings by the River Sett. The Lantern Pike inn in Little Hayfield could hardly be more welcoming.

There are worthwhile walks in the countryside around **Hathersage** SK2381 ⌂-6 – for example, in the pleasant moorland, pastures and woodland making up Longshaw SK2678, nr the Fox House inn up on the Sheffield road; or, closer and gentler, down along the River Derwent towards Grindleford SK2478.

Torrs Riverside Park SJ9985 ⌂-7, a deep gorge below New Mills, is a good place to potter among the ivy-covered remains of former mills and other industrial relics; the canal basin over at Buxworth SK0282 is interesting, with a useful pub.

The **Goyt Way** ⌂-8 between Buxworth and Marple, partly following the Peak Forest Canal, is a pretty walk.

Though it has to be approached from outside this area (off the A626 Glossop–Marple), the Little Mill, nr Rowarth SK0189, is well placed in off-the-beaten-track walking country, with a good walk up to Lantern Pike SK0288.

Driving

The High Peak is very rewarding for drivers – a car may be an easy way out, but it is certainly the quickest and least strenuous way of getting a good visual impression of the magnificent scenery. An advantage is that there's rarely the traffic congestion which mars other such areas. The A6024, A628 (rather slow), A57, A624 and A625 all have some outstanding views. Particularly pleasing back roads include the circuit through Edale from Hope; the B6061 from the A625 to Sparrowpit (where the Wanted Inn is an increasingly popular stop); and the B6001 S of Hathersage.

Where to eat

Hadfield SK0296 OLD HOUSE Woodhead Rd (01457) 854009 Old farmhouse with stone walls and views of the reservoir in the valley; friendly, prompt staff and good food from a constantly changing menu; vegetarian dishes, decent puddings and wines; cl Mon; £16|£2.50/£6.50

STAFFORDSHIRE

A county with unexpected pleasures: pockets of excellent scenery, an interesting industrial past.

The north-east, sharing Dove Dale with Derbyshire, and with its own charming Manifold Valley and Churnet Valley, is part of the Peak District, with some fine walking and pleasing drives. Just outside this area, the garden of Biddulph Grange is notable. Further south and west, there's a good deal of industry: on the face of it less appealing, though the Potteries, and to an extent Burton-on-Trent, have some engaging industrial museums. There are also some splendid open spaces down here, especially the park of Shugborough Hall, and Cannock Chase. The canal network has some particularly lovely stretches, and the county has a good many attractive villages, as well as quite a few other places worth visiting – Alton Towers is a very popular family destination. Prices here are on the low side, so Staffordshire is good value for a weekend with a difference.

Where to stay

Rolleston-on-Dove SK2427 BROOKHOUSE HOTEL Brookside, Rolleston-on-Dove, Burton-on-Trent DE13 9AA (01283) 814188 £85; 21 comfortable rms with Victorian brass or four-poster beds. Handsome, William and Mary brick building in 5 acres of lovely gardens, with comfortable, antique-filled rooms, and good food in the elegant little dining room; children over 12; disabled access.

Butterton SK0756 BLACK LION Butterton, Leek ST13 7SP (01538) 304 232 £47; 3 rms. Unspoilt, 18th-c stone inn in lovely walking country; homely, rambling rooms, good log fire, good food, and a parakeet called Sergeant Bilko; not far from interesting places to visit; plus plenty of opportunities to enjoy various country sports.

Alrewas SK1715 CLAYMAR HOTEL 118A Main St, Alrewas, Burton-upon-Trent DE13 7AE (01283) 791281 £45; 20 rms. Spotlessly clean and comfortable hotel with a pleasantly decorated bar, fine food inc an excellent Sunday lunch, and very good cheerful service; disabled access.

Greendale SK0343 OLD FURNACE FARM Greendale, Cheadle, Stoke-on-Trent ST10 3AP (01538) 702442 £40; 2 big, comfortable rms with good bthrms. B & B in a modernised farmhouse set in lovely surrounding countryside; homely, relaxed atmosphere, large, tasty breakfasts, and very friendly, efficient service.

Betley SJ7549 ADDERLEY GREEN FARM Heighley Castle Lane, Betley, Crewe CW3 9BA (01270) 820203 £36; 3 rms, 1 with bthrm. Georgian farmhouse on a big dairy farm with large garden; fishing; cl Christmas/New Year; children over 5.

Oakamoor SK0544 TENEMENT FARM Three Lows, Ribden, Oakamoor, Stoke-on-Trent ST10 3BW (01538) 702333 £35; 4 rms with showers. B & B on a traditional farm breeding beef cattle (sheep also), with fine countryside all round; also self-catering cottage; cl Nov–Mar.

Warslow SK0858 GREYHOUND Warslow, Buxton SK17 0JN (01298) 84249 *£34; 4 clean and comfortable rms with shared bthrms. Warm, welcoming atmosphere in a plain-slated stone building, with generous helpings of home-made food inc hearty breakfasts, and handy for many of the Peak District features; children over 10.

To see and do

☺ ❀ **Alton** SK0742 ALTON TOWERS They've added a couple of new rides here recently, the horrendous-looking Nemesis and the altogether gentler Toyland Tours. The first whisks you round unfeasible angles at breakneck speeds, the second takes you to an enchanted toy factory; perhaps perversely, it is of course the former that is currently drawing huge queues, but the existence of the latter shows what a wide-ranging place this giant among theme parks is. Mixed up among the 125 rides are a number of more sedate activities and attractions for all ages, with lovely extensive gardens and a less daredevil section for younger children. Theme park fans will love it, others may be pleasantly surprised. Meals, snacks, shops, disabled access (for most rides too); cl early Nov–mid-March; (01538) 702200; £15, a little less Mar–May and the public footpaths through the Capability Brown parkland are free. The Talbot in the village is good for lunch.

❀ **Biddulph** SJ8858 BIDDULPH GRANGE GARDEN Extensively restored high Victorian garden, divided by its founder into a number of smaller themed gardens to house specimens from all over the world. A very interesting and quite rare survival. Snacks, shop; cl am wkdys, Mon, Tues, Nov–Mar (exc wknds Nov–mid-Dec); £3.90; NT. The Coach & Horses up at Timbersbrook, off the A527 towards Congleton, is pleasant for lunch.

🝊 🏠 🚋 **Burton-on-Trent** SK2423 is dominated by its connections with the brewing industry, and the BASS MUSEUM, VISITOR CENTRE AND SHIRE HORSE STABLES is a fine museum devoted to this topic – with of course an emphasis on Bass and the company's shire horses (who can take you on a ride of the town). The minimum age for brewery tours is 13. Outside are larger exhibits such as a Daimler van in the shape of a bottle of IPA. Special events throughout summer and a brass-band concert every fourth Sun lunchtime. Meals, snacks, shop, disabled access; (01283) 511000; £3.45. The nearby Cooper's Tavern – selling the beer of a different brewer – is a fine example of what pubs were like 50 years or more ago, and in the same town down by the river, the little Burton Bridge Brewery shows brewing at the very opposite end of the scale. The Queen's Hotel is a comfortable place for lunch, as is the Marquis Suite carvery at the New Talbot Hotel on Anglesey Rd; the Boat House at Stapenhill has river and wetland views, and the Horseshoe out at Tatenhill is always good value. Nearby Rangemore SK1722 has a GARDEN CENTRE well liked by readers, with farm animals for children.

🔩 🏚 ❀ **Cannock Chase** SK0017 Miles of lovely countryside and woodland; dotted around the 17,000 acres are Iron Age hill forts, nature trails, streams, pools and springs, and lovely spots for picnics or dramatic views. There's an information centre at Marquis Drive, and decent campsites. Readers tell us Brindley Heath is particularly interesting to stroll around. See also **Walks** section

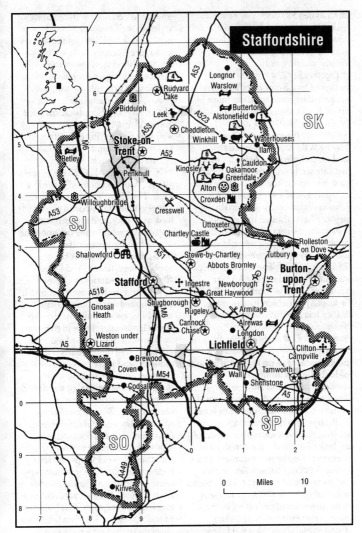

below. The Moat House at Acton Trussell SJ9318 does good food and is fairly handy.

! Cauldon SK0749 is notable for its pub, the YEW TREE; a very unpretentious place packed with an extraordinary and delightfully higgledy-piggledy collection of remarkable bygones, especially more or less musical ones such as polyphons and grandfather clocks.

Chartley Castle SK0128 (just over 6 miles W of Uttoxeter) is a fine old ruin, with good views.

Cheddleton SJ9752 FLINT MILL 17th- and 18th-c fully preserved watermills, with a little museum. Shop; closed am wknds; free. RAILWAY CENTRE Small steam locomotive museum in a Victorian station building, with occasional short steam runs in summer. Snacks, shop; open only pm Sun Apr–Oct, and some dates in Dec; (01538) 360522; £2. The Boat down by the canal is interesting for lunch.

† Clifton Campville SK2510 CHURCH is lovely – practically perfect, and the Green Man nearby is a useful lunch stop.

🏛 **Croxden** SK0639 ABBEY ruins in quiet surroundings, with some towering arches surviving. The Raddle at Hollington is a decent, family, country pub.

✝ **Ingestre** SJ9724 CHURCH was designed by Christopher Wren and is reckoned by some to be the finest small 17th-c church outside London.

✠ **Kingsley** SK0147 WILDLIFE SANCTUARY International charity Care for the Wild recently named this dedicated little place Britain's best wildlife welfare centre, and over the past few years they've saved the lives of hundreds of animals and birds. Conservation really is the main priority here, though there's still plenty for visitors to see and do. Snacks, shop; guided tours 11am and 2.30pm, by appointment; (01538) 754784; *£2.25. The Cross in scenic surroundings, along the A52, at Cauldon Lowe is good for lunch.

🐟 **Leek** SJ9856 Nearby Coombe Valley has an RSPB BIRD RESERVE. Shop, disabled access; free.

★ ✝ 🍴 🍷 🎭 🏛 🌳 **Lichfield** has an attractive centre, largely pedestrianised, with many 18th-c and older buildings among the more modern shops (and antique shops). The CATHEDRAL, with its three graceful spires and close surrounded by lovely buildings, is magnificent inside, and its west front is memorable, especially at dusk or in the dark when shadows seem to bring the profusion of statues to life. SAMUEL JOHNSON BIRTHPLACE MUSEUM (Breadmarket St) Dr Johnson was born here in 1709; the house is now furnished in period-style, with many mementoes of him and an audio-visual show. Shop; cl Christmas and New Year; *£1. HERITAGE EXHIBITION AND TREASURY Sympathetically restored, old chapel site with an audio-visual exhibition on Lichfield's history and a display of ceremonial silver and old documents. Meals, snacks, shop, disabled access; cl 25–26 Dec, 1 Jan; (01543) 256611; £1.25. By prior arrangement you can go up to the viewing platform in the spire, from where there are splendid views of the surrounding countryside. HANCH HALL (4 miles NW) is an interesting little mansion with an unusual mixture of architectural styles, as well as collections of needlework, old dolls and costumes and a rare Regency bed used by Shelley. Good views from the observation tower, and the partly landscaped grounds are fun, with peacocks and pheasants wandering about. Snacks, shop, some disabled access; cl am, Oct–Apr; (01543) 490308; £3. The Pig & Truffle (Tamworth St) and Scales (Market St) are useful for lunch.

✤ **Newborough** SK1325 is a peaceful village, with decent food in the Red Lion. The PIANO WORKSHOP (Yoxall Lane) usually has 40 or so pianos to look at or play, and you can watch restoration work going on; good for secondhand instruments or spare parts; open Weds, Sat or by appointment, (01283) 75433.

🏛 🍷 📷 **The Potteries** (Stoke-on-Trent SJ8745 and the five towns around it) These linked towns cling to small steep hills, giving some memorable urban landscapes. Pride in their past (and present) has focused museum attention well on the Staffs pottery industry, and you can visit several factories, ancient and modern – there's still a great deal of hand work in china production, inc modelling and painting. GLADSTONE POTTERY MUSEUM (Uttoxeter Rd, Longton) Good museum in a restored 'potbank', complete with old warehouses, workshops and four huge bottle kilns. Daily pottery demonstrations, and a gallery. Meals, snacks, shop, disabled access; cl over Christmas; (01782) 319232; £3. MINTON MUSEUM (London Rd, Stoke) Displays of the factory's products from 1800 to the present. Shop; open 10.30–12 and 2–3.30 or by arrangement, cl factory holidays – usually around end of Jun; (01782) 744766; free. SIR HENRY DOULTON GALLERY (Nile St, Burslem) Pottery treasures from the famous company covering 150 years, along with archive material; tours of factory available. Meals, snacks, shop, disabled access to shop only; cl wknds and factory and bank hols – best to check first; (01782) 575454; museum free, tours £2.50. SPODE (Church St,

Stoke) The birthplace of fine bone china, this is the oldest manufacturing ceramic factory in the Potteries – the techniques shown on the tour haven't changed much since the 18th c; a museum has lots of rare and precious pieces. Meals, snacks, factory shop, disabled access; no tours pm Fri or wknds, though shop is open Sat; tours by appointment, (01782) 744011; free. WEDGWOOD VISITOR CENTRE (Barlaston) The story of that favourite item on wedding lists; art gallery, museum and a reconstruction of Wedgwood's original 18th-c Etruria workshops. Snacks, shop, disabled access; cl Sun Oct–Easter, Christmas, 1 Jan; (01782) 204141; £2.95. CITY MUSEUM AND ART GALLERY (Bethesda St, Hanley) Good coverage of all aspects of regional life, inc a magnificent collection of pottery and porcelain. Meals, snacks, shop, disabled access; cl am Sun, 25 Dec–1 Jan; (01782) 202173; free. The New Inn (Derby St, Hanley) is useful for lunch.

♣ ⚑ ♥ **Rudyard Lake** SJ9558 is reckoned by some of our readers to be one of the most beautiful sights in Staffs; you can hire a boat, there's a miniature railway (Mar–Oct) and the muddy marshland provides a haven for wading birds; the meadows and forested slopes above are pleasant for walks and picnics. The Crown (Congleton road, off the A523 at Ryecroft Gate) has decent Greek and other food.

🏠 ☉ **Shallowford** SJ8729 IZAAK WALTON COTTAGE Recently rethatched and refurbished home of the author of *The Compleat Angler*, with displays on his life and the development of angling over the last 400 years. Also herb garden and picnic orchard. Cl Mon, Nov–Mar; (01785) 760278; £1.15. The Worston Mill at Little Bridgeford is attractive for lunch.

🏠 ☉ ☞ **Shugborough** SJ9922 SHUGBOROUGH HALL AND COUNTY MUSEUM Imposing ancestral home of the Earls of Lichfield, begun in the late 17th c and enlarged in the 18th; magnificent state rooms with fine glass, silverware and art, and restored working kitchens, laundry, pantry and brewhouse. Also interesting marionettes transferred from the former Puppet Theatre Museum at Abbots Bromley. The park has a variety of unusual neo-classical monuments, a working rare-breeds farm, an agricultural museum and restored corn mill. Meals, snacks, shop, disabled access; cl Oct–Mar; entry to estate *£1.50, museum *£3.50, house *£3.50, farm *£3.50, combined ticket *£7.50; NT.

🏠 ⚑ ▣ **Stafford** SJ9223 Greengate St has what's said to be the biggest TIMBER-FRAMED HOUSE in the country, built with local oak in 1595; period room settings and an information centre. Just to the SW of town, the remains of the CASTLE are worth a look. The Norman fortress was rebuilt in the Gothic Revival style in the early 19th c, then allowed to fall into disrepair. There's a visitor centre with good displays, and a medieval herb garden. Weekend teas, shop, disabled access to visitor centre only; (01785) 57698; £1.10. SHIRE HALL ART GALLERY Temporary exhibitions of contemporary art, craft and photography, with a shop selling British crafts. Cl Mon, Sun; (01785) 278345; free. The Malt & Hops (A34/A449 roundabout) and the Sun (Lichfield Rd) are useful for lunch.

🐄 ⚘ ♥ ⚑ **Stowe by Chartley** SK0027 AMERTON WORKING FARM Working dairy farm with milking at 4pm, farm shop, trails, garden centre, craft workshops, Wildlife Rescue Centre and little steam railway (Sun and bank hols only). Cl 25–26 Dec; (01889) 270294; farm free, wildlife centre £1, train 60p. The Cock is useful for lunch.

🏰 🏠 † **Tamworth** SK2004 TAMWORTH CASTLE Glorious mixture of architectural styles from the original Norman motte and bailey walls, through the Elizabethan timbered hall, to the fine Jacobean state apartments. Lots to see and do, and the haunted bedroom and talking knight are good for children. Shop; cl am Sun; (01827) 63563; *£3. Tamworth also has a decent town trail, as well as the country's only indoor ski slope with real snow. St Editha's CHURCH has windows by William Morris.

🏛 **Wall** SK0906 ROMAN SITE Known to its former inhabitants as Letocetum, this Roman fort was an important military base from around AD 50; excavations began in the 19th c and revealed one of the most complete Roman bath-houses in the country. Also a furnace room, exercise hall and various finds from this site and others nearby. The good audio-tour seems to bring it all back to life. Shop; cl 1–2pm, Nov–Mar; (01543) 480768; £1.25. The Black Bull at Shenstone is useful for lunch.

🏛 📷 ❀ **Weston under Lizard** SJ8010 WESTON PARK Particularly striking and richly decorated 17th-c stately home, with a fine collection of furnishings, tapestries, porcelain and paintings, inc works by Van Dyck, Rubens, Gainsborough and Constable, and a number of letters from Disraeli. The deer park and grounds were landscaped by Capability Brown, and have a restored 18th-c terrace garden, brightly planted broderie garden, and interesting trees and shrubs. Also pets' corner, adventure playground and miniature railway. Meals and snacks, shop, some disabled access; open wknds Apr–mid-Sept, daily in school hols (exc Mon and Fri mid-June–July); (0195276) 207; £4.50, park and gardens only £3. The Bell at Tong in Shrops is good for lunch.

❀ **Willoughbridge** SJ7540 DOROTHY CLIVE GARDEN Woodland gardens created by the late Col Harry Clive in memory of his wife; at their best perhaps in spring and early summer, but lovely all year. Rhododendrons, azaleas, old roses, water garden, rock garden. Snacks, disabled access; cl Nov–Mar; (01630) 647237; £2. The Falcon in Woore is good for lunch.

🐦 🐄 **Winkhill** SK0651 BLACKBROOK WORLD OF BIRDS Unusual species and aviaries, as well as a collection of waterfowl and children's farm. Cl Nov–Mar; (01538) 308293; £2.50.

★ Quietly **attractive villages**, all with decent pubs, include Abbots Bromley SK0724, Alstonefield SK1355, Butterton SK0756, Coven SJ9006, Kinver SO8483 (the one right over in the W; some of Britain's only rock houses are nearby, still lived in 30 years ago; there are good views from the Iron Age fort on top of the ridge), Longdon SK0714, Penkhull SJ8644, Rugeley SK0418 (with a beautiful 12th-c church), Shenstone SK1004, Tutbury SK2028 (the Norman church has a notable west doorway and elaborate carvings; there's also a glass factory and an attractive ruined castle with good views, and in addition to the Olde Dog & Partridge, the Castle at Hatton is useful), and Waterhouses SK0851. Longnor SK0965 is more of a small town, but despite its grand church has a pleasantly villagey feel (and a good craft centre). Brewood SJ8808 is another small charming town. Codsall SJ8602 is notable in summer for its profusion of lupins (Moors Farm has a decent farm shop and small country restaurant), and Ilam SK1350 is an attractive estate village (no pub).

Walks

Dove Dale ◠-1, perhaps the finest of all the dales, is shared with South Derbys (and described in the **Walks** section of that county).

There are also many worthwhile walks in the **Manifold Valley** ◠-2. Although it has fewer of the sensational rock features that abound in Dove Dale, there is plenty of charm – more or less steep riverside pastures, ancient woodland in the narrower steeper gorges, waterside caves; there's good access to the hills above it, such as Wetton Hill SK1056, which have attractive views. The best viewpoint of all, not to be missed, is Thor's Cave SK0954, high above the dale. Wooded Ilam Park SK1351 shows the Manifold Valley at its most sheltered. The branch off up Hamps Dale SK0654 is also extremely pretty. There are good pubs nearby at Warslow, Wetton and Hulme End.

The **Churnet Valley** ◠-3 offers very pleasant walks from Alton SK0742 or Oakamoor SK0544; the best goes through Hawksmoor and Greendale to pass the broad fishponds in wooded Dimmings Dale and comes back down to the river past an old smelting mill – and a good café called the Ramblers' Retreat (cl Mon). Hawksmoor Wood SK0344 is itself an attractive nature reserve, and the Talbot in Alton is useful for lunch.

There are **moorland walks** ⌂-4 from the side roads off the A53 N of Leek, and up here The Roaches SK0062 form an impressive western barrier at the edge of the Dark Peak; exhilarating walks atop.

Cannock Chase SK0017 ⌂-5 is the breathing space for the county's more industrial area: miles of forest and rolling heath, with fallow deer often seen. The large Castle Ring hill fort SJ0412 has fine views over the woods to the Trent Valley, and there are good views W towards the Welsh borders from the heights N of Broadhurst Green SJ9815.

The county is liberally laced with canals, and their towpaths give many miles of good walks. The **Caldon Canal** ⌂-6 and the Staffordshire & Worcester Canal have the best scenery. There's usually something happening at the Froghall Wharf SK0247 canal terminus (maybe horse-drawn barge trips, tel (0538) 266486), with an interesting walk along the canal to Consallforge SK0049 (unusual remote pub here). The nearby Nature Park continues this strange, lost-valley scenery. There's also good canal access at Gnosall Heath SJ8220 and Great Haywood SJ9922 (nr the longest packhorse bridge in the country), and from the decent pubs at Amington SK2304 (the Gate), Armitage SK0816, Cheddleton SJ9651, Denford SJ9553 nr Leek, High Offley SJ7826 (Bridge 42 on the Shropshire Union – unusual pub), Norbury Junction SJ7922, Filiance Bridge in Penkridge SJ9214 and Shebden SJ7626. The Trent & Mersey Canal has little towpath here, but Fradley Junction SK1414, with a nice waterside pub, is an attractive place for a stroll, with lots happening on the water.

Driving

The NE corner has the county's most interesting roads. The A53 high moorland road N of Leek has good views, and again up in this part of the county, the B5053 (with a very pretty stop at the riverside Jervis Arms at Onecote SK0555, friendly to children) gives an excellent impression of the dales country. The B5417 and B5032 E of Cheadle are both appealing roads. You can drive through Cannock Chase on quiet side roads.

Where to eat

Waterhouses SK0850 OLD BEAMS Leek Rd (01538) 308254 Very pretty cottage surrounded by flowers and creepers, with oak beams, antique furniture, a cosy, friendly atmosphere, excellent, carefully cooked food, and good service; bedrooms; cl am Sat, pm Sun, Mon; disabled access. **£26.45 lunch, £40.45 dinner**/2-course meal £10.95.
Armitage SK0816 OLD FARMHOUSE (01543) 490353 Pleasant restaurant with good, very popular food, and friendly service; cl pm Sun, Mon, am Sat, 1st 2 wks Jan, last 2 wks Aug; disabled access. **£17.50/£7.95**.
Cresswell SJ9739 IZAAK WALTON (01782) 392265 Very neatly kept, upmarket dining pub with good, impressive food and pretty, country furnishings; cl 25–26 Dec; disabled access. **£16/£1.95/£4.50**.

Help this year from: Barbara Hatfield, Jenny and Michael Back, Roger Huggins, B M Eldridge, Dr Keith Bloomfield, Nigel Wooliscroft, J F M West, Ann and Colin Hunt, Geoffrey and Irene Lindley, Michel Hooper-Immins, Nigel Hopkins, Dr and Mrs J H Hills, W H and E Thomas, JJW, CMW, Geoffrey and Irene Lindley, John Cadnam, Mayur Shah, G A Clark, Sue Demont, Tim Barrow, P Corris, Dorothee and Dennis Glover, GA, PA, Phil and Heidi Cook, Sandra Iles, John Beeken, L W Baal, Mike and Wendy Proctor, C Findell, Pat and Tony Young, Alan Woolley, Peter Yearsley, Richard Lewis, David and Shelia, Stephen and Julie Brown, Mark and Mary Fairman, Jenny and Roger Bell, M G Hart, Dr Paul Kitchener, Margaret and Paul Digby, Tony Short, Sarah and Steve de Mellow, S Howe, D W Gray.

DERBYSHIRE AND STAFFORDSHIRE CALENDAR

Some of these dates were provisional as we went to press.

In summer, many Derbyshire villages decorate their wells and springs with flowers and flower petal pictures in their annual festive well dressings. Originally a pagan water-worshipping ceremony, this is now part of the Christian calendar. A procession led by the clergy, and a blessing of the wells usually initiates a week of village celebrations. To avoid the crowds, go a day or two before the actual ceremony and get a good, close view of the elaborate flower pictures which should stay fresh for almost a week. Some of the best are at Eyam, Tissington and Ashford in the Water.

FEBRUARY

4 **Hanley** L S Lowry The Man and His Art at City Museum and Art Gallery – *till 19 March* (01782) 205033

28 Shrove Tuesday **Ashbourne** Shrovetide Football Game: a free-for-all between an unlimited number of Up'ards and Down'ards (from above and below Henmore Brook) who compete to get the ball to goals which are 3 miles apart along the brook (01335) 43666; **Lichfield** Shrovetide Fair with colourful civic procession from the Guildhall to the Market Sq (01543) 257503; **Winster** Pancake Races

MARCH

26 **Elvaston** Doll Fair at Elvaston Castle (01480) 216372

APRIL

1 **Milford** Flowers in the House at Shugborough Estate – *till Sun 2* (01889) 881388

8 **Milford** Gamekeepers Fair at Shugborough Estate – *till Sun 9* (01889) 881388

16 **Tamworth** Easter at Tamworth Castle – *till Mon 17* (01827) 63563; **Weston under Lizard** Festival of Transport at Weston Park – *till Mon 17* (0195 276) 201

19 **Burton-Upon-Trent** Competitive Festival of Music and Drama – *till Sat 22* (01283) 652973

22 **Milford** Lambing Weekend at Shugborough Estate – *till Sun 23* (01889) 881388

23 **Lichfield** St George's Day Court at the Guildhall (01543) 257503

29 **Weston under Lizard** Point to Point at Weston Park (0195 276) 201

MAY

2 **Newborough** Well Dressing (01246) 207777

6 **Weston under Lizard** Craft Fair – *till Mon 8* at Weston Park (0195 276) 201

7 **Milford** Classic Car Event at Shugborough Estate – *till Mon 8* (01889) 881388

13 **Chatsworth** Angling Fair (01328) 830367; **Milford** Shearing Weekend at Shugborough Estate – *till Sun 14* (01889) 881388; **Weston under Lizard** Horse Trials – *till Sun 14* at Weston Park (0195 276) 201

21 **Milford** 1940s Event in the Museum at Shugborough Estate (01889) 881388

DERBYSHIRE AND STAFFORDSHIRE CALENDAR

MAY cont

24 **Stafford** County Show at the County Showground – *till Thurs 25* (01785) 58060

25 **Tissington** Well Dressing – *till Wed 31* (01246) 207777

27 **Endon, Brackenfield, Chester Green, Wirksworth, Monyash, Middleton** (nr Youlgreave) Well Dressings in all these towns (01785) 277336

28 **Weston under Lizard** Spring Spectacular Family Day – *till Mon 29* at Weston Park (0195 276) 201

29 **Castleton** Garland Ceremony commemorating the escape of Charles II from the Roundheads. A mass of flowers and oak foliage in the shape of an old-fashioned beehive is placed on the head of the 'king'. *At 18.30* he makes his way through the village on horseback to the churchyard and the garland is placed on top of the church tower; **Elvaston** Derbyshire County Show at Elvaston Castle (01602) 324653; **Lichfield** Court of Arraye and Bowers Procession, inc crowning the Bower Queen, sports and a market at the Guildhall and city centre

JUNE

4 **Milford** Donkey Day at Shugborough Estate (01889) 881388; **Uttoxeter** Midland Counties Show at the Racecourse (01889) 562561

9 **Lichfield** Jazz Festival at Lichfield Arts Centre – *till Sun 11* (01543) 262223

10 **Ashford in the Water** Well Dressing (01246) 207777

11 **Milford** Victorian Street Market at Shugborough Estate (01889) 881388

16 **Lichfield** Folk Festival at Lichfield Arts Centre – *till Sun 18* June (01543) 262223

17 **Derby** Festival – *till Sun 25* (01332) 255507; **Milford** Afternoon of Scottish Dance at Shugborough Estate (01889) 881388

18 **Hanley** Exhibition at the City Museum and Art Gallery to mark the bicentenary of the death of Josiah Wedgwood – *till 1 Oct* (01782) 202173

22 **Lichfield** Real Ale, Jazz and Blues Festival at Lichfield Arts Centre – *till Sun 25* (01543) 262223; **Milford** Viennese Evening at Shugborough Estate (01889) 881388

24 **Hope** Wakes and Well Dressing (01246) 207777; **Weston under Lizard** German Shepherd Dog Show – *till Sun 25* at Weston Park (0195 276) 201

JULY

1 **Weston under Lizard** National Hovercraft Rally – *till Sun 2* at Weston Park (0195 276) 201

2 **Milford** Transtar Motoring Pageant at Shugborough Estate (01889) 881388

5 **Stafford** Festival *till Sun 16* (01785) 53595

7 **Lichfield** Festival and Fringe at Lichfield Arts Centre – *till Sun 16* (01543) 257298; **Newton Solney** Summer Festival of Music and Art at the Newton Park Hotel – *till Sun 9* (01283) 703568

9 **Elvaston** Doll Fair at Elvaston Castle (01480) 216372; **Milford** Doll and Teddybear Fair at Shugborough Estate (01889) 881388

12 **Buxton** Well Dressing and carnival (01298) 25106; **Buxton** Festival – *till Sun 30* (01298) 70395

DERBYSHIRE AND STAFFORDSHIRE CALENDAR

JULY cont

15 **Milford** Gardening Event at Shugborough – *till Sun 16* (01889) 881388

16 **Ashbourne** Highland Gathering (01335) 29415

22 **Milford** Firework and Laser Concert at Shugborough Estate (01889) 881388

23 **Milford** Goose Fair at Shugborough Estate (01889) 881388

AUGUST

2 **Bakewell** Show at the Showground – *till Thurs 3* (01629) 812736

9 **Ashover** Agricultural and Horticultural Show (01246) 863412

16 **Barlow** Well Dressing (01246) 207777

19 **Osmaston** Ashbourne Show at the Pologround (01335) 330552

22 **Weston under Lizard** National Pony Club Championships – *till Thurs 24* at Weston Park (0195 276) 201

26 **Eyam** Well Dressings (01246) 207777; **Wormhill** Well Dressings (01246) 207777

27 **Eyam** Plague Sunday Service at Cucklett Dell *at 15.30*; **Weston under Lizard** Town and Country Fair – *till Thurs 24* at Weston Park (0195 276) 201

28 **Chesterfield** Evening Fireworks (01246) 207777; **Matlock Bath** Illuminations Grand Switch-on, events include parading of illuminated boats every weekend, concerts, clifftop fireworks – *till last Sat in Oct* (0629) 55082

SEPTEMBER

2 **Chatsworth** Country Fair – *till Sun 3* (01328) 830367; **Glossop** Victorian Weekend – *till Sun 3* (01457) 855920

9 **Lichfield** Sheriff's Ride (01543) 250011

10 **Worksworth** Festival of Music and Art – *till Sun 24* (01629) 823408

11 **Abbots Bromley** Ancient Horn Dance in the village streets, probably a fertility dance. *At 7.45* the dancers collect the horns from St Nicholas Church. Dancers include 6 men, Maid Marion, a boy with bow and arrow, a hobby horse and a jester

16 **Milford** Steam Fair at Shugborough Estate – *till Sun 17* (01889) 881388; **Weston under Lizard** Midland Game and Country Sports Fair – *till Sun 17* at Weston Park (0195 276) 201

17 **Elvaston** Doll Fair at Elvaston Castle (01480) 216372

OCTOBER

12 **Ilkeston** Charter Fair

22 **Milford** Apple Day – *till Sun 17* at Shugborough Estate Farm (01889) 881388

NOVEMBER

4 **Milford** Bonfire Night at Shugborough Estate (01889) 881388

27 **Derby** Bonnie Prince Charlie 250th Anniversary – *till 10 Dec* (01332) 299659

DECEMBER

5 **Milford** Christmas Evenings – *till Fri 8* at Shugborough Estate Farm (01889) 881388

DEVON

O ne of Britain's finest areas for a short holiday, Devon has a tremendous variety of scenery, a relaxed pace of life, and plenty to see and do. It has a lot to please everyone – including children. There are lovely gardens, pretty, thatched villages clustered around ancient churches and equally ancient pubs, glorious vistas of coast and moor, some decidedly unstuffy museums, all sorts of rustic pursuits, and vintage steamtrains puffing through gorgeous river valleys. There is a splendid range of places to stay, and some very decent food.

The sheltered seaside villages of the south coast have a lot going on and a delightful hinterland: ideal for a relaxing weekend. This coast stays relatively mild even in winter – when other parts of the county can be very bleak.

Dartmoor and its surroundings probably have more to offer the first-time visitor than Exmoor. Exeter is a charming small city and a useful base – good roads get you quickly to the coast and to Dartmoor.

Devon is best visited in spring, early summer or autumn: no hold-ups on the roads, even richer colours in the countryside – a real sense of space and peace.

Some of the best views here are from trains; besides the steam lines, the BR Devon Rail Rover is a good deal – £25 adult for any three days out of seven, or £35 for a week of unlimited journeys.

EXETER AND EAST DEVON

Exeter is a very good base for a short break; the area has interesting places to visit, and an attractive coast.

Devon's east coast is very popular for family summer holidays, and there are four old-fashioned resorts. Exmouth is the liveliest and largest, a family beach resort doubling as a working port. Seaton, quieter, is a more typical family resort, with much less of a beach. Budleigh Salterton, the quietest, is rather retiring and genteel. Sidmouth is slightly busier, with a good deal of character as well as plenty for families – for most people, it's the most appealing of the four for a short break. The prettiest place on the coast here is Branscombe, a series of largely unspoilt, thatched hamlets strung along a lovely seaside valley.

Inland, coastal downs give a gently varied landscape of charming wooded valleys with views and high pastures between, and several attractive villages. North of the A30/A35 is more self-contained farm-land, mainly well hedged traditional stock and dairy farms.

Exeter itself is a good choice for a short break. With the M5 so close and with fast trains, it's easy to reach from a long way away. A quietly handsome city in its own right, it has a lot to see; all its museums are interesting and particularly well organised. There are worthwhile places to visit close by, and good roads which bring the other parts of Devon within comfortable reach for a day out. Very quiet at weekends, during the week Exeter is active without being crowded or noisy.

Elsewhere, some of the most enjoyable places to visit include Killerton, the working mill museum at Uffculme, Bicton Park gardens, Farway countryside park and the village of Ottery St Mary.

There is much better walking in other parts of the county, but the coastal path here has some fine moments.

Where to stay

Hawkchurch ST3400 FAIRWATER HEAD COUNTRY HOUSE Hawkchurch, Axminster EX13 5TX (01297) 678349 £120; 21 rms (the garden wing ones are best). Family-run country house overlooking the picturesque Axe valley; log fire, pleasantly old-fashioned rooms; good, traditional, home-made food using fresh local produce; friendly, helpful staff, and a lovely garden; cl Dec–Feb.

Gittisham SY1398 COMBE HOUSE Gittisham, Honiton EX14 0AD (01404) 42756 *£97; 15 individually decorated, pretty rms. Peaceful, Elizabethan country hotel in gardens with lawns and shrubbery; elegant day rooms furnished with antiques, family portraits, and fresh flowers; a happy, relaxed atmosphere, good food using some home-grown produce, and fine wines; cl 26 Jan–10 Feb.

Whimple SY0497 WOODHAYES Whimple, Exeter EX5 2TD (01404) 822237 *£90; 6 lovely spacious rms. Big Georgian country house in neat grounds, with comfortable, quietly decorated lounges, a small library, open fires, a flagstoned bar and pretty dining room; fine food inc excellent breakfasts; children over 12.

Branscombe SY1988 LOOK OUT Branscombe, Seaton EX12 3DP (0129 780) 262 £84; 6 pretty rms. Early 19th-c, very atttactively converted coastguards' cottages with lots of beams, antiques and flagstones; good food using local produce, secluded cottage garden and marvellous views; fine walks along the beach or cliffs; cl 4 days over Christmas; children over 8.

Exeter SX9292 ROYAL CLARENCE Cathedral Yard, Exeter EX1 1HB (01392) 58464 £79w; 56 rms in Victorian, Georgian or Tudor style. Handsome 14th-c hotel with a Georgian façade facing the cathedral; lots of character and original features, an oak-panelled restaurant, quiet lounge, and popular bar.

Exeter SX9292 ST OLAVES COURT Mary Arches St, Exeter EX4 3AZ (01392) 217736 £76w; 15 well equipped rms. Homely, stone-built house in its own walled garden, with comfortable rooms, old-fashioned service, and imaginative food in the candlelit restaurant; 400 yds from the cathedral; disabled access.

Higher Bulstone SY1988 BULSTONE Higher Bulstone, Branscombe, Sidmouth EX12 3BL (0129 780) 446 £72; 13 rms, 7 with own bthrm. Set in over 3 acres and surrounded by fields, this is a super place for family holidays – with both parents' and children's needs catered for; lots of facilities and warm, friendly, personal staff; cl Dec–Jan; children under 5 free; limited disabled access.

Weston ST1200 DEER PARK Weston, Honiton EX14 0PG (01404) 41266 £70; 26 rms. Georgian mansion in 30 acres of parkland, with warm and friendly, relaxed atmosphere, pleasantly old-fashioned rooms, good traditional cooking using home-grown veg and fruit, fine wines; 5 miles of private fishing, croquet, 18-hole putting green, games room and swimming pool; disabled access.

Rousdon SY2990 DOWER HOUSE Rousdon, Lyme Regis DT7 3RB (01297) 21047 £66; 9 rms. Family-run hotel in lovely grounds, with log fires in the hall and lounge, good bar and restaurant food (especially fish dishes), big breakfasts, and efficient but unobtrusive service; indoor swimming pool; high tea for children over 7; cl Nov.

Axminster SY2998 GOODMANS HOUSE Furley, Membury, Axminster EX13 7TU (01404) 88690 *£46; 6 rms. Friendly 16th/17th-c house in 12 acres with fine views, walled kitchen garden and fruit trees (the organically grown food is used in their good home cooking); an attractive, candlelit dining room with an inglenook at each end, and a Georgian-style conservatory; cl last wk Nov–mid-Feb (though open Christmas/New Year for houseparties); self-catering cottages.

Exeter SX9292 WHITE HART 66 South St, Exeter EX1 1EE (01392) 79897 **£46**; 59 decent rms. Rather splendid, well run 14th-c inn with lots of different eating areas (wine-bar type as well as a proper restaurant); a marvellous, atmospheric bar, open fires, beams, antiques, an excellent range of wines, and friendly service; no accommodation 24–26 Dec.

Chardstock ST3004 GEORGE Chardstock, Axminster EX13 7BX (01460) 20241 **£42.50**; 4 rms. Neatly thatched, old village inn with character furnishings, beams and old gas lamps, a quietly chatty feel, good food in the bar and restaurant, and close to good walks; children over 12.

Exeter SX9292 EDWARDIAN 30–32 Heavitree Rd, Exeter EX1 2LQ (01392) 76102 **£40**; 13 rms, 11 with own bthrm. Popular guesthouse close to the city centre with cosy lounge, attractive dining rooms, and warm, friendly, resident owners; cl Christmas.

Tipton St John SY0991 GOLDEN LION Tipton St John, Sidmouth EX10 0AA (01404) 812881 **£38.60**; 2 rms. Bustling village local with lots of fresh flowers in the softly lit bar, a small no-smoking restaurant, good food, and decent wines; several golf courses nearby; cl 25–26 Dec; children over 7.

Sidford SY1390 BLUE BALL Sidford, Sidmouth EX10 9QL (01395) 514062 **£36**; 3 rms with nice touches like free papers, fruit and fresh flowers; shared bthrm. Welcoming, thatched, 14th-c inn run by the same family since 1912; very friendly service, and decent food inc hearty breakfasts.

Cullompton ST0107 OBURNFORD FARM, Cullompton EX15 1LZ (01884) 32292 **£34**; 6 rms. Working farm with Channel Island dairy cows (lovely clotted cream), beef cattle and some cereal crops (guests can help feed the calves); an attractive lounge and dining room, log fires, and good food using home-grown produce.

Stockland ST2404 KINGS ARMS Stockland, Honiton EX14 9BS (01404) 881361 **£30**; 3 rms. Cream-faced, thatched pub in a pleasant village setting, elegant rooms, very good bar lunches and evening restaurant food (especially fish), interesting wine list; skittle alley, live music pm Sun; cl pm 25 Dec; well behaved children only.

To see and do

Exeter This has a good, relaxed atmosphere, buoyed up by the thriving university. Though large parts of the centre were devastated by WWII bombing, some choice streets and buildings survive, with pretty, partly Tudor narrow lanes leading from the mainly pedestrianised High St into the serene, tree-shaded cathedral Close, with one or two Tudor buildings among the gracious Georgian ones. In the centre, modern shops are integrated into the old layout very discreetly indeed. With many smaller churches, decent book- and other shops, pubs and so forth nearby, this is a very pleasant part for browsing around. Particularly attractive streets include Southernhay at the end of The Close, and Stepcote Hill, a picturesque detour from Fore Street.

The Quay, beyond the streams of fast traffic on the ring road (there are quiet underpasses), has become lively and entertaining. It has handsomely restored buildings, resurgent cafés and pubs (the Prospect is good), and a growing number of craft shops and the like. There are boat trips down the ship canal to Exminster; or you can walk down, passing the Double Locks (a favourite pub) and ending at the Turf Hotel looking out over the estuary.

✝ The CATHEDRAL is well worth visiting: England's finest example of decorated Gothic architecture, with its magnificent nave soaring to the fan-vaulted roof, and intricately carved choir stalls. It also boasts the longest Gothic vault in Europe – superbly atmospheric. Snacks, shop, disabled access; guided tours 11am and 2.30pm wkdys, just 11 Sat;

voluntary donations. The Well House has an unrivalled view over The Close. 🏛 The medieval GUILDHALL (High St) with its ornately colonnaded, Elizabethan façade is one of the oldest municipal buildings still in use; the roof timbers rest on bosses of bears holding staves, and within there are paintings and civic silver and regalia. Shop; cl pm Sat, all Sun and bank hols, and during civic functions; free.

! A rather more unusual medieval attraction is the network of UNDERGROUND PASSAGES (entrance via Boots Arcade in High St), built in the 13th c to bring water into the city. There's an introductory exhibition and video, then you're taken on a guided tour of the tunnels themselves, still much as they were centuries ago. Flat shoes are recommended. On Sat, they do longer tours for those who want to go into the more creepy and constricted parts – great fun, but be prepared to get muddy then. Shop; cl Sun, am winter wkdys, all day winter Mon; £2.10.

✝ 🏛 ST NICHOLAS'S PRIORY (Mint Lane) 11th-c Benedictine monastery housing an unusual Norman undercroft, Tudor room and a 15th-c kitchen. Occasional historical days with costumed characters. Shop, disabled access to ground floor only; cl 1–2pm, am Sat, Sun, Nov–Easter; £1.

🏛 🏯 ! CONNECTIONS DISCOVERY CENTRE (Castle St) Elegant Regency building in the grounds of the city's former Norman castle, with lively, hands-on exhibits, games and displays on subjects like the Romans, ancient Egypt, Victorian life and the Second World War; it's mainly open only to schools, though there are selected days (usually school hols) when anyone can have a go – best to tel (01392) 265858 to check. Snacks, shop; £1. Part of the castle's formidable, very early gateway still survives.

♨ ROYAL ALBERT MEMORIAL MUSEUM (Queen St) Wonderful Gothic exterior, and inside notable displays of regional silver, African woodcarvings, archaeology, paintings and natural history. Until the end of Feb 1995 they should still have the exhibition Dinosaurs from China, with huge skeletons and full-size, moving and roaring animatronic models (£3), then from Jun–Sept they plan a major exhibition looking at how British artists have responded to the Devon landscape. Snacks, shop, limited but gradually improving disabled access; cl Sun; free. ✵ MARITIME MUSEUM (The Haven) Excellent and exhaustive collection of boats from all over the world – gondolas to steam dredgers to African dug-out canoes. A great thing about this museum has been the way they positively encourage children to clamber over the boats, but just as we were going to press they told us they may be moving elsewhere; best to check with the tourist information centre before setting off, on (01392) 265700.

Apart from the White Hart, decent pubs in fine buildings nr the cathedral are the Ship (Martins Lane) and Well House (The Close); down on The Quay, the Prospect is good. The Cowick Barton out on Cowick Lane is worth knowing, too.

Other things to see and do

🏊 ✤ Beer ST2389 A rather cottagey resort village, still with some fishing boats pulled up on the shingle beach. PECORAMA PLEASURE GARDENS Fun for railway lovers, with the house containing models and train collections, and outside a miniature steam and diesel passenger line with stunning views of the bay. Also putting green, aviary, and children's play area with a maze and an assault course. Meals, snacks, shop, disabled access; cl pm Sat, Sun (exc Jun–Sept), outdoor features cl Oct–Easter (exc half-term); (01297) 21542; £2.85. The village was famous from Roman times for its cavernous whitestone quarries, which can be visited. The waterside Anchor has good, fresh, local fish.

✵ 🏊 ♘ Bicton SY0684 BICTON PARK GARDENS Busy place centred around 50 acres of lovely gardens, shrubs, lakes and woodland, with a rather jolly railway through the grounds to keep children amused. A futuristic-looking glass palm house turns out to have been built in the early part of the reign of Queen Victoria, and has a fine collection of tropical trees and plants; also fuschia, geranium and orchid houses, bird garden, pinetum, crazy golf and adventure playground, and magnificent Italian gardens, Meals, snacks, shop and plant centre, disabled access; cl Nov–Feb; (01395) 568465; £3.75. Nearby, the entirely separate gardens of BICTON COLLEGE OF AGRICULTURE are of great if more specialised appeal; long, monkey-puzzle avenue through parkland, a rich collection of magnolias, camellias and flowering cherries, a national pittosporum and agapanthus collection, many other plants, and a 17-acre arboretum with woodland garden. Snacks, plant centre; open all year (though shop may be cl winter wknds); (01395) 568353; *£2.

★ † **Broadclyst** SX9897 is a pretty, thatch and cob village, with a marvellous old church – photogenic outside, interesting in. The New Inn and Red Lion are decent pubs.

🐑 ☺ **Clyst St Mary** SX9790 CREALY COUNTRY Ideal for children – a bustling complex with acres of activities inc go-karts, archery, a farm where you can milk the cows, slides and boats, pony rides, adventure playgrounds and lakeside walks. Special events each Sun in season, from car rallies to conker championships. Meals, snacks, shop, disabled access; cl wkdys Nov and Dec and all Jan–mid-Feb; (01395) 233200; £3.85.

❀ ❀ **Dalwood** SY2499 BURROW FARM GARDENS Part of this 5-acre site has been created from an ancient Roman clay pit, and there are spacious lawns, borders and unusual shrubs and trees; also, a woodland garden, pergola walk with old-fashioned roses, and super views. Cream teas Sun, Weds and bank hols, nursery; cl am, all Oct–Mar; (01404) 831285; *£2. The pretty Tuckers' Arms is good for lunch, and the King's Arms at Otterton is also handy.

★ † **East Budleigh** ST0684, an attractive and quietly placed cob and thatch village, has a pleasant CHURCH with fascinating Jacobean carved pew ends, some grotesque, some hilarious, some frankly rude.

† ♨ ! 🐄 🐑 ☺ **Exmouth** SY0080 More of a family seaside holiday place than somewhere for a short break, this is still worth a visit for its lively working docks area, its long sandy beach and its stately church; summer boat trips. A LA RONDE Extraordinary 16-sided house, built around 1795 and decorated in part with feathers, seashells, seaweed and sand. A charmingly whimsical place, the outside looking not entirely unlike a giant biscuit barrel. Snacks, shop; cl Fri and Sat, all Nov–Easter; £3; NT. WONDERFUL WORLD OF MINIATURE Home of the world's biggest OO model railway, 7,500 ft of track indoors with another 1,800 outside. Some of the detail is amazing, right down to the birds in the trees. Shop; cl Nov–Easter; (01395) 278383; £2. WORLD OF COUNTRY LIFE 40 acres of good, family-based activities, with friendly animals in the pets' corner, an adventure playground and safari rides through the paddocks of deer and llamas; also a reconstructed Victorian street, classic motorcycle collection, crafts, and steam engines. Meals, snacks, shop, disabled access; cl Nov–Easter; (01395) 274533; £4. The Nutwell Lodge at Lympstone and Salterton Arms in Budleigh Salterton are the best nearby places for lunch, though the seafront Deer Leap is useful.

🐑 **Farway** SY1895 FARWAY COUNTRYSIDE PARK Traditional and modern breeds of farm animals on over 108 acres of beautiful countryside, along with pony and donkey-cart rides, trekking, nature trails, and a tropical house with iguanas, tree frogs and chameleons. Meals, snacks, shop, disabled access; cl Oct–Easter; (01404) 87379; £3.

🏰 **Hemyock** ST1313 CASTLE Friendly, low-key castle where the family that run it really take care with the guided tours. It was used as a Civil War prison for Royalists, and the site's 700-year history is well illustrated by life-size tableaux in the visitor centre; they've recently re-erected an old cider press and apple mill. Shop, disabled access; open pm Sun and bank hols Easter–Sept, plus pm Tues and Thurs in July and Aug, or by appointment; (01823) 680745; *£1. The Catherine Wheel is useful for lunch.

🏛⛪ Honiton ST1500 This country town has some handsome Georgian buildings along its long high st, and some interesting shops. The Red Cow (High St) is good value for lunch. ALLHALLOWS MUSEUM 13th-c building with useful displays of Honiton lace, and demonstrations of lace-making in Jun, July and Aug; also exhibits on town's pottery and clock industries. Shop; cl Sun, Nov–Easter; (01404) 44966; *80p.

❀🏛 **Killerton** SS9700 KILLERTON Best of all in spring, 15 acres of beautiful hillside gardens, shrub borders and planted beds, with an impressive avenue of beech trees. The 18th-c house has a costume exhibition covering 300 years of fashion in period furnished rooms, though it's the gardens that really give the place its special appeal. Meals, snacks, shop and plant centre, good disabled access (with buggies round the grounds); house cl Tues, all Nov–Mar; £4.60, £2.80 garden only; NT. The Three Tuns in Silverton is good for lunch.

✂📷★ **Otterton** SY0684 OTTERTON MILL CENTRE Working watermill still grinding flour for the bread, cakes and pies sold on the premises. Also craft workshops, and display of East Devon lace. Meals, snacks, shop and garden centre, some disabled access. Some interesting evening events; cl 25–28 Dec, restaurant cl winter wkdys; (01395) 568521; *£1.75. The village is pretty, and the King's Arms is a decent pub.

✝🏛🎵❀♥ **Ottery St Mary** SY0995 is a restrained small town – or extended village – with some attractive old buildings around its interesting, twin-towered church. The London Inn is useful for lunch. CADHAY Beautiful Tudor and Georgian manor house, with a fine, timbered, 15th-c roof in its great hall, and an unusual court of sovereigns – a pretty courtyard with statues of various monarchs. Disabled access to garden and downstairs; open late May bank hol Sun and Mon, then

pm Tues, Weds and Thurs July–Aug, plus Sun and Mon Aug bank hol; (01404) 812432; *£3. ESCOT AQUATIC CENTRE & GARDENS Tropical and coldwater fish from Koi carp to piranhas, also rabbits and other pets, otters, Victorian walled rose garden, wild boar enclosures, walks, views and parkland. Meals, snacks, shop, disabled access; cl 25–26 Dec; (01404) 822188; £1.95. OTTER NURSERIES AND GARDEN CENTRE (Gosford Rd) Good for trees, shrubs and plants, with an ornamental fish pool and garden areas. Meals, snacks,

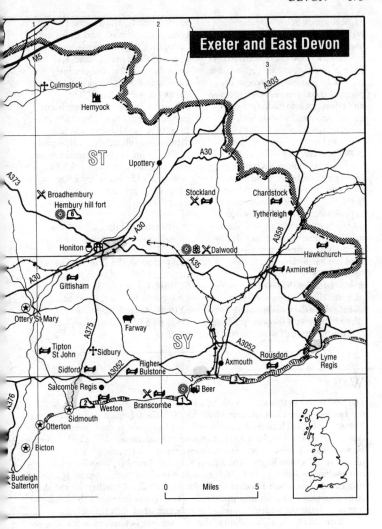

Exeter and East Devon

shop and plant centre, good disabled access; cl 25–26 Dec. The circular TUMBLING WEIR by an 18th-c mill signed off Mill St is unusual, and photogenic. ★ 🐄 🚌 **Sidmouth** SY1287 well repays a visit, with attractive old streets, very 18th c, running back from the seafront, and grander Regency buildings facing the sea. It was a fashionable upper-class resort in the early 19th c, and many of the town's buildings show undoubted architectural verve – there's very little seaside tat. The pebbly beach has fishing boats pulled up on it, and the

town is protected by warm, red sandstone cliffs; it stretches back along the river valley, though away from the sea the buildings are less interesting. The Tudor Rose and Old Ship are good for lunch (the Blue Ball up at Sidford better still). VINTAGE TOY & TRAIN MUSEUM (above Fields department store). Toys, games and children's books from 1925–1975, inc the first and last Dinky toy, Hornby trains and military figures. Snacks, shop; cl Sun, bank hols, Nov–Easter; (01395) 515124; *£1.30. The local history MUSEUM (in a fine Regency house) organises walking tours round the town, Tues and Thurs at 10.15am. DONKEY SANCTUARY 5,500 distressed donkeys have passed through this centre over the last 20 years; it's a dedicated place, and you can really see the care and effort put into making their guests' stay comfortable. Snacks, shop, disabled access; (01395) 579266; free.

★ ❀ **Topsham** SX9687 is an old-world seaside village, its buildings (and large number of good pubs and inns – the Passage is currently the best for food) showing its past importance as a port. Well worth a quiet potter. There's a small, local maritime museum. Just outside, the Bridge Inn on the Clyst St George road has hardly changed in style since the 16th c.

★ ⚓ † **Uffculme** ST0612 is a big but pleasant village above the River Culm, where the COLDHARBOUR MILL WORKING MUSEUM shows every stage in the production of wool, on two working levels; also a weaver's cottage, carpenters' workshops, restoration of a steam engine and other displays. Meals, snacks, shop, limited disabled access; cl winter wknds, and at least a wk at Christmas; (01884) 840960; £3.85. The attractive church has a magnificent carved screen. The Globe at Sampford Peverell is quite handy for lunch.

† **Interesting churches** at Cullompton ST0107 (remarkable painted screen; a busy little town), Culmstock ST1014, Sidbury SY1391 (a pretty village, with a very good pub nearby at Sidford) and Silverton SS9502 (another nice village).

★ **Attractive villages**, all with decent pubs, include seaside Axmouth SY2591, Branscombe SY1988, Lympstone SX9984 and Salcombe Regis SY1488, and Broadhembury ST1004, Butterleigh SS9708, Chardstock ST3004, Otterton SY0684, Tytherleigh ST3103, Upottery ST2007 and Woodbury SY0187.

Walks

The best walks in this area are along the coastal cliffs, for example the walk to the broken white cliffs of **Beer Head** SY2889 △-1 from Beer itself or from Branscombe; the Hooken undercliff here is a tremendous chalk jumble of collapsed clifflands. There's a long stretch of **red sandstone cliffs** △-2 between Sidmouth and Branscombe, reached from either place (or, steeply but very prettily, from Salcombe Regis). The steeply tumbled, brambly, wooded wilderness of **Dowlands Cliffs** SY2889 △-3, E of Axmouth, is interesting, with a lot of small birds. The **High Land of Orcombe** SY0279 △-4, reached by the shore road E out of Exmouth and protected against campsite encroachment by its National Trust ownership, is useful for a shorter stroll with sea views.

Off the B3180, E of Woodbury SY0187, are miles of **heath** △-5 with some pinewoods – a place to get away from people even in high summer (red flags warn if there's firing on one section which is a shooting range). From the highest points, nr the road, there are far views along the coast and to Dartmoor. The wooded hill fort right by the road is worth a look, and it's a bit eerie tracing the ramparts through the beech trees.

Off the A373 NW of Honiton, you can walk up into **Hembury hill fort** ST1103 △-6 for good views.

Driving

Some fine views are to be had from the A375 S of Honiton, as you come over the heath of Gittisham Hill; on the left you can pick out one or two of the Bronze Age burial mounds which dot this area, with many more by the B3174 towards Beer. There are more pleasant views from the B3180 over Woodbury Common, which cuts through a wooded Iron Age hill fort.

The back road forking S of the A30, just SW of its junction with the A303 nr Upottery, is a good ridge road, giving fine views of the surrounding farmland. The remains of the hill fort on the left, a mile or so short of the transmission mast, is worth the short detour.

A quiet and pretty valley drive is the B3397 through Uffculme to Culmstock, and then the back road to Hemyock (which has the ruined remains of a medieval castle, over a stream from the church).

Of the more long-distance roads, the A3052 is good, with attractive scenery virtually all the way along to the Dorset border. Except at busy times it's also quite quick. From it, the detour down through Branscombe is thoroughly worthwhile. The A30 can be rather tedious E of Exeter.

For getting into Exeter, much the quickest way from either the M5 or the A38 is to keep on round to the westbound A30 and go into the city from the Alphington roundabout.

Where to eat

Lympstone SX9984 RIVER HOUSE (01395) 265147 Marvellous river views from big picture windows in the lounge, interesting food (inc fresh fish) in the first-floor restaurant using some home-grown produce; kind, friendly service; cl pm Sun and Mon, Christmas; children over 6; disabled access. £43/£5.75.

Broadhembury ST1004 DREWE ARMS (01404) 84267 Friendly and efficiently run 15th-c pub with excellent, perfectly cooked, very fresh fish dishes, lovely puddings, well kept beers, fine wines, and atmospheric, attractively decorated rooms; disabled access. £25/£4.50/£8.

Exeter SX9292 LAMBS 15 Lower North St (01392) 54269 Cheerfully run by knowledgeable staff, with a well balanced menu using fresh seasonal, local produce and everything – from nibbles to breads and puddings – is totally home-made; thoughtful wine list; cl lunchtimes Sat and bank hols. £20/£8.50.

Topsham SY9688 AMADEUS (01392) 873759 Small, popular restaurant with a cosy, relaxed atmosphere and four little rooms (one is a lounge); generous helpings of good honest food using local produce, and friendly, courteous service; children over 12. £19.50 dinner, £16 lunch.

Dalwood ST2400 TUCKERS ARMS (01404) 881342 Delightful, thatched medieval longhouse with well prepared, enterprising bar food and lots of colourful hanging baskets; bedrooms. £16/£2.95/£8.

Stockland ST2404 KINGS ARMS (01404) 881361 Bustling old inn, very much the heart of the community, with a wide choice of excellent bar food, hearty breakfasts, popular Sunday lunches, theme nights, well kept beers, fine malt whiskies, and good wines. £15/£7.50.

Budleigh Salterton SY0682 SALTERTON ARMS (01395) 445048 Tucked-away but busy little pub, with a wide choice of good food using lots of fresh fish, vegetarian choices too, and enormous salads; disabled access. £15/£1.30/£4.95.

Branscombe SY1988 FOUNTAIN HEAD (0129 780) 359 14th-c inn in lovely sheltered village, with lots of beams, panelling, and log fires; good-value bar food, own-brew beers, quick service, and friendly dog; disabled access. £14.50/£1.60/£4.95.

Butterleigh SS9708 BUTTERLEIGH (01884) 855407 Unpretentious and welcoming, 16th-century village inn with interesting and attractive furnishings, very good bar food, and well kept beers. £12.50/£1.50/£5.

Exeter SX9292 DOUBLE LOCKS Canal Banks, Alphington (01392) 56947 Friendly and very relaxed lockside pub, popular with students, with good, simple bar food (all day, though cl Sun afternoon), summer barbecues, and up to 10 real ales on handpump; disabled access. £1.80/£3.60.

DARTMOOR

**The county's finest inland scenery, varied and intricate;
very interesting places to visit, excellent places to stay.**

The moor itself is a magnificent brooding wilderness, with excellent walking. All sorts of points of interest, especially perhaps its prehistoric remains, make it far from monotonous. Around its edges are many lovely valleys and villages, delightful to explore. Among many other attractions for visitors, front-runners include Morwellham Quay, Castle Drogo at Drewsteignton, Lydford Gorge, Buckland Abbey and the Garden House at Buckland Monachorum, and the rare breeds farm at Bovey Tracey. The steam railway from Buckfastleigh to Totnes is a delightful outing.

Where to stay

Chagford SX7087 GIDLEIGH PARK Chagford, Newton Abbot TQ13 8HH (01647) 432367 **£285 inc dinner**; 15 opulent and individual rms with fruit and flowers provided. Luxurious, Dartmoor-edge, mock-Tudor hotel with a very comfortable drawing room, conservatory overlooking the fine grounds (of which there are 40 acres, with walks straight up on to the moor), log fires, particularly fine cooking and exceptional wine list; caring staff.

Lewdown SX4486 LEWTRENCHARD MANOR Lewdown, Okehampton EX20 4PN (0156 683) 256 *£125; 8 well equipped rms with fresh flowers and period furniture. Lovely 17th-c manor house with dark panelling, ornate ceilings, antiques, fresh flowers, log fires and comfortable seating; friendly welcome and relaxed atmosphere, and a candlelit restaurant with very good food; peaceful estate surrounding the garden, with shooting, fishing and croquet; children over 8 (unless by arrangement); dogs by arrangement.

Haytor SX7677 BEL ALP HOUSE Haytor, Newton Abbot TQ13 9XX (01364) 661217 **£120**; 9 spacious rms. Handsome Edwardian country house with elegant, airy rooms, comfortable furniture, log fires, friendly atmosphere, and fine, careful cooking in the pretty restaurant; wonderful views and attractive garden; disabled access.

Lifton SX3885 ARUNDELL ARMS PL16 0AA (01566) 784666 **£90**; 29 well equipped rms. Carefully renovated old coaching inn with 20 miles of its own waters – fishing is the main thing; comfortable lounge, log fires, very good food in the smart restaurant, decent wines, and kind service; cl 2 days over Christmas.

Bovey Tracey SX8178 EDGEMOOR HOTEL Haytor Rd, Bovey Tracey, Newton Abbot TQ13 9LE (01626) 832466 *£82.50; 12 charming rms. Ivy-covered country house in neatly kept gardens on the edge of Dartmoor; with a comfortable lounge and bar, log fires, good food in the elegant restaurant, and high tea for children under 8; dogs welcome; disabled access.

Sandy Park SX7189 MILL END Sandy Park, Chagford, Newton Abbot TQ13 8JN (01647) 432282 £80; 16 neat rms. Former flour mill with a waterwheel, in neatly kept grounds below Dartmoor; comfortable lounges, interesting food, and good service; cl 6–16 Dec, 9–20 Jan; dogs welcome (not in public rooms).

Moretonhampstead SX7585 WHITE HART Moretonhampstead, Newton Abbot TQ13 8NF (01647) 40406 £63; 20 rms. Former Georgian posting house, well run and comfortable, with interesting furnishings in the civilised lounge bar and hall, lively back bar, good bar food, and a no-smoking restaurant; children over 10.

South Zeal SX6593 OXENHAM ARMS South Zeal, Okehampton EX20 2JT

(01837) 840244 £60; 8 rms. Grandly atmospheric old inn dating back to the 12th c and first licensed in 1477 (Neolithic standing stone still forms part of the wall in the TV room); elegant, beamed and panelled bar with a chatty, relaxed atmosphere and open fire, decent food and wines, charming ex-monastery small garden.

Doddiscombsleigh SX8586 Nobody Doddiscombsleigh, Exeter EX6 7PS (01647) 52394 £53; 7 rms, some in a Georgian manor house 150 yds down the road, and most with own bthrm. Friendly, atmospheric 16th-c pub with beams, heavy wooden furniture, and inglenook fireplace in the attractively furnished two-roomed lounge bar; outstanding cellar running to 800 wines and 250 malts; popular food in the bar and restaurant inc 40 Devon cheeses, and good views from the garden; local church worth visiting for its fine stained glass; cl 25 Dec; no children.

Haytor Vale SX7677 Rock Haytor Vale, Newton Abbot TQ13 9XP (01364) 661305 £50.90; 10 rms, most with own bthrm. Civilised old inn on the edge of Dartmoor National Park, with fine food (inc fresh fish), a good mix of visitors and locals in the two rooms of the panelled bar, open fires, no-smoking restaurant, courteous service, and a big garden; walking, fishing, riding and golf nearby.

Holne SX7069 Church House Holne, Newton Abbot TQ13 7SJ (0136 43) 208 £50; 6 rms. Medieval, Dartmoor-edge inn with a comfortable, atmospheric, pine-panelled lounge bar, freshly prepared food using local produce, restaurant, decent wine list, pleasant service, and lots of good walks close by.

Lydford SX5184 Castle Lydford, Okehampton EX20 4BH (0182 282) 242 £49.90; 8 rms, most with own bthrm. Friendly 16th-c inn in an ancient village, with lots of interesting antiques and furnishings, log fires, beams and flagstones, and good food; nice garden with a new covered terrace, and pets' corner; next to castle and nr attractive gorge.

Moretonhampstead SX7586 Great Sloncombe Farm Moretonhampstead, Newton Abbot TQ13 8QF (01647) 440595 £38; 3 rms – the big double is the favourite. Lovely 13th-c farmhouse on a working dairy and stock farm with friendly owners; carefully polished, old-fashioned furniture, decent food, log fires, a relaxed atmosphere, and good nearby walking and birdwatching; no smoking; dogs welcome.

Gulworthy SX4374 Rubbytown Farm Gulworthy, Tavistock PL19 8PA (01822) 832493 £34; 3 rms. Comfortable and prettily furnished 17th-c farmhouse in the Tamar Valley; no smoking; cl over Christmas; children over 5.

Holne SX7069 Wellpritton Farm Holne, Ashburton TQ13 7RX (0136 43) 273 £34; 4 pretty rms, 3 with own bthrm. Small, very friendly Dartmoor farm keeping sheep and cattle (also, donkeys, goats, rabbits, chickens, dog, cats); with a comfortable sitting room, good, carefully presented food, and a small swimming pool; cl 25–26 Dec; children over 5 (younger by arrangement, out of season).

To see and do

Dartmoor itself is classic moorland, where distant vistas of changing greens and browns fade into the austere grey-blues of far shoulders and edges. The moor is punctuated with all sorts of interesting focal points and features: numerous, easily traceable prehistoric remains; strange, wind-sculpted, eroded granite tors which crown many of the slopes; the little streams that thread over boulders; tamed watercourses where leats or miniature canals (dating back to the 16th c, one was cut by Drake to supply Plymouth) curl carefully around the contours; sheltered valleys folded into the moors, where white houses crouch among sycamores and oaks; occasional higher miniature forests of much more stunted oaks grouped around the rocks; abandoned tin-mine workings with ruined wheelhouses; the shaggy ponies hoping for a hand-out. The villages around it are well worth exploring: typically, thatched and white-plastered stone cottages clustered around an ancient stone church beside its church-house inn. The towns ringing the moor have useful facilities.

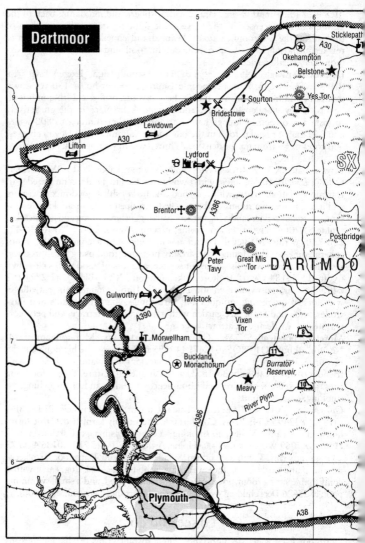

Dartmoor

★ ❀ ♪ **Ashburton** SX7569 is probably the best of the small towns
around the moor, and has distinct
character. RIVER DART COUNTRY PARK
is pleasant for walking or fishing, with
adventure playgrounds for children.
Snacks, shop; cl Oct–Mar; *£3.80.
The London Inn is good.

◑ ◔ **Bickington** SX7972 GORSE
BLOSSOM MINIATURE RAILWAY AND
WOODLAND PARK Unlimited rides on
7¼-inch-gauge steam railway through
35 acres of woodland; also nature

trails and a new outdoor model
railway in Swiss mountain setting.
Meals, snacks, shop, some disabled
access; cl Oct–Easter; (01626)
821361; *£3.50. The Dartmoor
Halfway is useful for lunch.

◑ ♈ ✗ 🏠 **Bovey Tracey** SX8078 is
an unassuming, small, Dartmoor-
edge town; the Riverside Hotel is
handy for lunch. PARKE RARE BREEDS
FARM (B3344, W) Lots of rare breeds
of cattle, sheep and pigs in fields and
stalls, and poultry and waterfowl in a

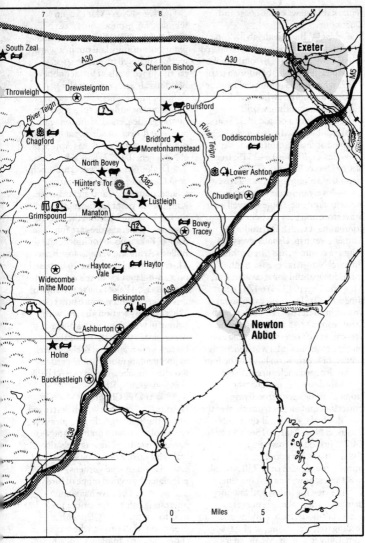

walled garden with pond; also fine walks through extensive NT parkland by a wooded river, and Dartmoor National Park information centre. Meals, snacks, shop; cl Nov–Mar; (01626) 833909; *£3. There's a good, varied CRAFT CENTRE at Bovey Tracey Mill in a former watermill. TEIGN VALLEY GLASS & HOUSE OF MARBLES (Pottery Rd) Glass factory specialising in marbles. You can watch the glass-blowing, and there's a little museum devoted to the tiny round things that so many people seem to lose. Meals, snacks, shop, disabled access; cl Sun Christmas–Easter; (01626) 835358; free. The LOWERDOWN POTTERY (off the B3344) does fine decorated pottery; cl wknds exc summer and maybe other times, check first, (01626) 833408; free.

† ✸ **Brentor** SX4780 CHURCH (above back road Lydford–Tavistock, just S of North Brentor). 12th c and one of England's smallest, it is notable for its lonely position on a hill, with

remarkable views of the coast and Dartmoor.

✝ ⌘ ✚ ✿ 🚂 **Buckfastleigh** SX7367 BUCKFAST ABBEY Originally established in 1018 but after the Dissolution of the Monasteries left abandoned until 1882, when it was refounded by four remarkable monks, who then did most of the rebuilding work themselves over a period of 32 years; good exhibition. Meals, snacks, shop, disabled access; exhibition cl Nov–Easter; (01364) 642519; free. SOUTH DEVON RAILWAY GWR steamtrain along the wooded River Dart – lovely unspoilt scenery. It now stops just outside Totnes as well as at Staverton, and they do tickets combining it with a Dartmouth–Totnes river trip. Usually every 1½ hours in summer, less often other times; cl Nov–Mar exc for Santa trains in Dec, and some days in Apr, May and Oct; (01364) 642338 for times; £5.60. The train can also take you right to the BUTTERFLY PARK AND DARTMOOR OTTER SANCTUARY, where you can watch otters swimming and playing from an underwater viewing tunnel, or see them on land in the four big landscaped enclosures. Also a specially designed, undercover tropical garden with free-flying butterflies and moths from all over the world. Meals, snacks, shop, disabled access; cl Nov–Mar; (01364) 642916; £4.25. Just out of town PENNYWELL FARM CENTRE is a good, friendly and unfussy place, with over 750 animals in 80 acres, as well as lovely scenery, wildlife viewing hides, and falconry demonstrations. Different events every half-hour, from milking and feeding to ferret racing, so always something going on. Meals, snacks, shop, disabled access; cl Jan and Feb; (01364) 642023; £3.95. The White Hart is useful for lunch.

🏠 🚂 ✿ ⌘ **Buckland Monachorum** SX4868 BUCKLAND ABBEY The home of Francis Drake until his death in 1596, and of his family until 1946. A good history of the Sir and the site includes the famous drum said to sound whenever England is in danger; also craft workshops, herb knot garden and good walks. Meals, snacks, shop, disabled access to ground floor only;

cl Thurs, and Nov–Mar exc pm wknds; *£4, grounds only *£2; NT. GARDEN HOUSE Profusion of unusual plants, beautifully laid out in a warm garden sheltered by picturesque, partly ruined walls of former abbey buildings. It's now practically doubled in size with a new 6-acre development adding a spring garden, quarry garden, rhododendron walk and wild flower meadow. Interesting plant sales, snacks and teas Apr–Sept; cl Nov–Feb; (01822) 854769; £2.50. The Drake's Manor is good for lunch.

★ ✿ **Chagford** SX7087 is a large village, quite busy, and an attractive jumping-off point for the moor; even the bank is thatched, and the two old-fashioned general stores are fun. The Ring o' Bells is good for lunch, and the Buller's Arms and very atmospheric Three Crowns Hotel (said to be based on a 13th-c monks' hospice) are useful too. GIDLEIGH PARK Lovely grounds of this luxury country-house hotel (see **Where to stay** section above), with colourful woodland walks and a watergarden using the natural Dartmoor streams and rocks, as well as immaculate more formal gardens. Excellent lunches, cream teas; cl bank hols and wknds; 50p.

★ 🚂 ✿ ✚ ❀ 🏠 **Chudleigh** SX8679 Despite the 1807 fire which destroyed lots of the buildings, this is a pleasant old wool town with pretty cottages in narrow, winding lanes; there's also a little vineyard. ROCK GARDEN AND CAVE 3 acres of wild gardens, populated by a good range of birds and wildlife. The cave has some interesting calcite formations and next to it is the Fairy Glen with a pretty waterfall – from where it's a short walk up Chudleigh Rock for dramatic vistas of the surrounding countryside and moors. Snacks, nursery, disabled access to nursery only; garden and cave cl Oct–Apr; £1.50. UGBROOKE HOUSE is an interesting early example of the work of Robert Adam. Delightfully informal guided tours. Teas, disabled access; open pm Sun, Tues, Weds, Thurs and bank hols mid-July–early Sept; (01626) 852179; £3.80. The Ley Arms just off the A38 up at Kenn is very good for lunch.

★ ▲ ❀ ❉ ♤ ⏚ **Drewsteignton**
SX7390 Above the charming village
(with a delightfully unspoilt pub) is
the impressive, granite CASTLE DROGO,
designed by Lutyens and built earlier
this century as a bizarre and brilliantly
inventive mixture of medieval style
and 20th-c luxury, with cunningly
disguised radiators and amazing
details even in the kitchen and
lavatory. Lovely grounds with yew
hedges forming an outer barbican,
good guided walks through the
surrounding woodland, super views –
it's 900 ft up overlooking the gorge of
the River Teign. Meals, snacks, shop,
limited disabled access; cl
Nov–Easter, castle cl Fri (though
garden, shop and tearoom still open);
*£4.60; NT. A well signposted minor
road W of the village takes you to
SPINSTER'S ROCK, a well preserved
Neolithic burial chamber and the
most easily accessible prehistoric
feature in the area.

★ 🐗 **Dunsford** SX8189 is a peaceful
and unspoilt thatched village.
BRIMBLECOMBE'S FARM CIDER (Farrants
Farm, B3212) produce excellent
scrumpy, which you can try out,
tapped from the barrels on the earth
floor of a barn. Depending on that
year's fruit, they may be open through
the winter – best to check first;
(01392) 811456. The Royal Oak is
good for lunch.

❀ ♤ **Lower Ashton** SX8484
CANONTEIGN FALLS AND COUNTRY PARK
Pleasant country park covering 80
acres of ancient woodland, with a
high waterfall; also lakes, wildfowl,
miniature horses, children's
commando course. Meals, snacks,
shop; cl mid-Nov–Easter; (01647)
52434; £3.25. The Manor pub in the
village is useful for lunch.

🕈 ▲ **Lydford** SX5184 LYDFORD
GORGE Spectacular gorge formed by
the River Lyd cutting into the rock,
causing boulders to scoop out
potholes in the bed of the stream.
Dramatic sights such as the Devil's
Cauldron whirlpool and the White
Lady waterfall; children like it but
need to be watched carefully. Snacks,
shop; most parts cl Nov–Mar, check
first; (0182) 282441; £2.80; NT. The
forbidding CASTLE (also recently taken

over by NT) has a daunting stone keep
dating from 1195; the upper floor was
used originally as a tin-mine law
court, the second as a prison for those
who offended against the fierce
stannary laws ('First hang and draw,
Then hear the cause by Lydford law');
free. The Castle Inn is very good.

⬇ **Morwellham** SX4469
MORWELLHAM QUAY In Victorian
times Morwellham was the greatest
copper port in the Empire; now it
houses a thriving and meticulously
researched open-air museum in lovely
countryside, full of costumed guides
re-creating life in those boom years.
Lots to see, inc restored cottages
complete with pigs in the backyard,
working blacksmith, cooper,
coachmen and quayworkers, rides
into the mines, horse-drawn carriages,
museums and lovely walks. Very
popular in school holidays, and a visit
can easily last all day. Meals, snacks,
shop, some disabled access; cl 24
Dec–2 Jan; (01822) 832766; £6.75
(reduced price and operations in
winter). The Ship (part of the centre)
is good, with period-costumed
waitresses and period drinks.

★ 🐗 **North Bovey** SX7483 is a
delightful, peaceful spot, not usually
invaded by tourists: oak-shaded
green with mounting block, stone
cross, pump, ancient cottages and
church; the Ring of Bells is good.
MINIATURE PONY CENTRE (Wormhill
Farm) Lots of the friendly little
animals, and they don't mind children
riding on them; also bigger horses,
displays and exhibitions, other
animals such as pigs, donkeys,
chipmunks and wildfowl, and an
adventure playground. Meals,
snacks, shop, good disabled access; cl
Fri (exc Easter), Nov–Mar; (01647)
432400; £3.95.

🍴 ✕ ⚘ ▲ **Okehampton** SX5895 is a
straightforward, Dartmoor-edge,
working town. MUSEUM OF DARTMOOR
LIFE (West St) Well converted old
watermill with interactive displays
about life for the people of Dartmoor
from prehistoric times onwards.
Meals, snacks, shop, some disabled
access; cl Sun Oct–May, Sat
Nov–Mar, and Christmas; (01837)
52295; £1.50. Dartmoor Tourist

Information Centre and working craft studios are next door. The CASTLE tower on a steep, grassy mound above the river is remarkable above all for the way it stays standing – a balancing act of ruined masonry zigzagging up into the sky. It's the biggest medieval castle in Devon, with sections dating from the 11th to 14th c; good woodland walks. Snacks, shop; cl 1–2 pm, all Nov–Mar; (01837) 52844; £1.80. The White Hart Hotel generally has a CRAFT FAIR every Weds in summer, and OKEHAMPTON BEARS, down The Arcade, is a display of teddies in a doll's house setting (cl Sun exc some in summer; free).

! Sourton SX5390 The HIGHWAYMAN is an extraordinary pub, one bar recalling a galleon, the other a sort of fairy-tale fantasy, and the garden demonstrates yet more exuberant imagination – all meticulously done by the owners, not some brewery theme pub.

↓⊤ Sticklepath SX6494 MUSEUM OF WATERPOWER AND FINCH FOUNDRY No longer producing the sickles, shovels and tools for which it was known in the 19th c, but the waterwheels and machinery are all still working; also a display of tools, a gallery devoted to water power, and occasional craft days. Snacks, shop; cl Tues, Nov–Mar; (01837) 840046; £2.10. The thatched Devonshire Inn in the village is good value.

★ † 𝕳 Widecombe in the Moor SX7176 is one of the most interesting (and most visited) little villages in the area, immortalised by the trip of Uncle Tom Cobbleigh and all to Widecombe Fair. The granite-carved village sign shows them all crowded on to their old grey mare. The CHURCH is known as the Cathedral of the Moors, and has a distinctive and disproportionately high tower. The adjoining 16th-c CHURCH HOUSE AND SEXTON'S COTTAGE are worth a look; Church House open Tues and Thurs Jun–mid-Sept, adjacent Sexton's Cottage (NT and Dartmoor National Park information centre and gift shop) cl 24 Dec–mid-Feb; free. As well as the little shops, there are several places doing nice cream teas, and clotted-cream ice-cream; the reconstructed Olde Inne in the village is very popular with tourists, but for more of a Tom Cobbleigh flavour, try the Rugglestone Inn just outside.

★One of the most **attractive villages** in the whole of England is Lustleigh SX7881, with charming riverside walks in utterly unspoilt woodland around it, or up to Hunter's Tor on Dartmoor. Primrose Cottage is hotly tipped for cream teas, and the Cleave Inn is good. Other noteworthy ones include Belstone SX6293, Bridestowe SX5189, Bridford SX8186, Holne SX7069, Manaton SX7581 (the Becky Falls private riverside woodland, on the B3344 to Bovey Tracey, is very pretty for family walks; restaurant, shop; cl Dec–Easter; £2.50 per car), Meavy SX5467 (pronounced Mewy locally; the parish still owns the pub), Moretonhampstead SX7585 (less secluded than the others, but more to see), Peter Tavy SX5177, South Zeal SX6593, and Throwleigh SX6690. All these have good pubs or inns.

Walks

Dartmoor is outstanding for walking, but you should be aware that mist can come down very suddenly, and if you venture on to the open moor you must carry a compass. A lot of the moor is a long way from the road, hence rather inaccessible. There are more paths for walkers than the right-of-way network suggests, but don't assume a right of way marked on the OS map will be visible on the ground (the black dashed lines on these maps are generally more reliable). Old mineral railways and cart tracks make for some good walkers' routes. There are plenty of things to head for, to give a moorland walk a sense of purpose – most obviously, one of the many tors of naked rock rising out of the moor (beware: the rounded rocks can be a good deal more slippery than they look).

Among the finest paths is **Dr Blackall's Drive** ⌂-1 (not named on the OS map), from Bel Tor Corner to New Bridge: this specially created carriage drive gives splendid views of the Dart Valley. The fortress-like collection of **Haytor Rocks** SX7577 ⌂-2 makes a striking and popular objective; nearby is an abandoned quarry served by an unusual 19th-c tramway with grooved-granite rails. In this same general area, the majestically monumental Hound Tor SX7478 is usually quieter, with an interesting, excavated, abandoned medieval village nearby. Honeybag Tor SX7278, close by, has marvellous views over Widecombe SX7176 (though not shown on the OS map, there's a path to it along the spine of the ridge). A bit further N is the quaint Bowerman's Nose SX7480 looking snootily out over a patchwork of pastures.

In the W, the **Vixen Tor** SX5474 ⌂-3, towering up from the bracken, looks unclimbable, but is quite easily reached from behind; this area of the Walkham Valley is relatively lush and green, with old railway tracks from mineral lines which once served local quarries.

Nr Lustleigh SX7881, a ridge path to **Hunter's Tor** SX7682 ⌂-4 gives panoramic views of Lustleigh Cleave and the Bovey Valley. Up in the lonelier northern part of the moor, **Yes Tor** SX5890 and **Great Mis Tor** SX5676 ⌂-5 have great views over the moor. This is the highest terrain in southern England though, as throughout this northern area, access is often barred by army firing practice.

Two attractive, popular and easy-to-reach, ancient packhorse **clapper bridges** ⌂-6 are those by the roads at Postbridge SX6478 and Dartmeet SX6773 – good centrepieces for strolling. From the Angler's Rest at **Fingle Bridge** SX7499 ⌂-7, there's a lovely 'Fisherman's Path' by a wooded stretch of the River Teign; you can return at high level on the 'Hunter's Path', passing near Castle Drogo and gaining tremendous views. A path along the gently graded **Devonport Leat** ⌂-8 (a watercourse first engineered 200 years ago to give Devonport a water supply), in the western moors, takes in some remote scenery and makes getting lost quite difficult; it's easily reached off the B3212 NE of Yelverton.

Hundreds of ancient sites exist, but the large majority shown on the OS maps are invisible to all but the most astute archaeologist. The most impressive is by a stream at **Grimspound** SX7080 ⌂-9, with a fine, old, lichened granite cross nearby to mark the way for later medieval travellers. The upper valley of the **River Plym** SX5866 ⌂-10 has numerous visible hut circles, stone rows and cairns.

The **Burrator Reservoir** SX5567 ⌂-11 gives a 5-mile walk in beautiful woodland and moorland surroundings (Sheepstor church on the way has interesting memorials to the Brookes family, former rajahs of Sarawak). **Yarner Wood** SX7778 ⌂-12, nr Bovey Tracey SX8078, is a National Nature Reserve and has a nature trail.

Another approach to walking here is to use a pub or hotel as a start or finishing point. The Peter Tavy Inn SX5177, Elephant's Rest at Horndon SX5280, Forest Hotel at Hexworthy SX6572, East Dart Hotel at Postbridge SX6579, Warren House SX6780 E of there, Plume of Feathers in Princetown SX5873, Dartmoor Inn at Merrivale SX5475 and Two Bridges Hotel at Two Bridges SX6175 are all situated right on the moor; and the Rock at Haytor Vale SX7677, Church House at Holne SX7069, Tavistock at Poundsgate SX7072, Devonshire Inn at Sticklepath SX6494, Highwayman at Sourton SX5390, Tradesman's Arms at Scorriton SX7068, Oxenham Arms Hotel at South Zeal SX6593 and Northmore Arms at Wonson SX6789 are on the edges. Elsewhere, the Church House at Meavy SX5467 and Skylark at Clearbrook SX5265 are both nr the wooded River Meavy.

Driving

A very exciting drive into really wild, bleak scenery can be had at weekends, on every day in Aug and at other times when army training is not going on, from Okehampton Camp; tel (01837) 52939 for recorded information. This army road, potholed in places, takes you up on to the highest land in southern

England. A good, conventional road right across the moor is the B3212 (though very slow going once off the moor to the E, where it becomes virtually impossible to overtake crawlers). The B3357 also gives a good visual impression of the moor, and passes a well defined Bronze Age site just E of Merrivale. The back road off the B3344, just NW of Manaton southwards towards Ashburton, is pleasant. On unfenced Dartmoor roads, pay special attention to straying ponies and sheep.

Where to eat

Gulworthy SX4472 HORN OF PLENTY (on A390, just W of Tavistock) (01822) 832528 Relaxed restaurant in a 17th-c house overlooking the Tamar Valley, with excellent, carefully cooked food inc fresh fish and local meat, lovely puddings and cheeses, fine wine list; friendly service, and vine-covered terrace for aperitifs; good bedrooms; children over 13 (though younger are welcome for Sun lunch); cl am Mon, 25–26 Dec; disabled access. **£25/2 courses £16**.
Bridestowe SX5189 WHITE HART Friendly, 17th-c village inn with consistently good food in the pleasant restaurant, decent bar food too; bedrooms; fishing nearby; no children in bar (allowed in restaurant). **£20|£2/£4.25**.
Lydford SX5184 CASTLE (0182 282) 242 Charming, pink-washed Tudor inn with freshly cooked, very good and imaginative bar food, friendly, helpful staff, and an excellent choice of wines by the glass; interesting furnishings, and big, well kept garden. **£19|£3/£6.50**.
Cheriton Bishop SX7793 OLD THATCH (01647) 24204 Welcoming 16th-c inn with nice bar food from a big menu, interesting puddings, and friendly service; cl 1st 2 wks Nov; no children, disabled access. **£13|£1.85/£4.75**.

SOUTH DEVON

Intimate coastal scenery, attractive seaside towns of considerable character, interesting places to visit; Plymouth is well worth going to – and of course there's Torbay.

Dartmouth has particular charm as a place for a weekend break or short stay at any time of year, and many parts of the coast and countryside here share its intimate, relaxed and unshowy appeal, as does Totnes. By contrast, there are the promenades, low cliffs, bright gardens and palm trees of Torbay and its English Riviera. And at the opposite end of this stretch of coast, busy Plymouth has some interesting and unusual rainy-day attractions.

Inland, the countryside is typified by well hedged hilly pastures, small combes and steeply wooded valleys, and occasional vividly deep-red earth fields. The coast has an intricate mixture of small coves, stretches of cliff, and sheltered creeks and estuaries cut deeply into the coastal hills – very popular in summer with sailors.

Among a good choice of things to do and places to visit, highlights are the steam railway between Buckfastleigh and Totnes (perhaps combined with a river trip), magnificent Saltram near Plympton, Coleton Fishacre garden at Kingswear, Powderham Castle, Paignton Zoo, Overbecks garden near Salcombe, and the shire horse centre at Dunstone. There are some beautifully situated places to stay.

Where to stay

Burgh Island SX6443 BURGH ISLAND Burgh Island, Bigbury-on-Sea TQ7 4AU (01548) 810514 **£174 inc dinner**; 14 Art Deco seaview suites, most with balconies. Cut-off, small island – access by hotel Land Rover (or foot) at low tide, seagoing summer tractor-on-stilts at high tide, 300-yd crossing from Bigbury. Lovingly extravagant, 1930s restoration: domed palm court, sun lounge, classic cocktail bar; tennis, mini gym, snooker, walks, and sea fishing. Island has a romantic 14th-c pub – and summer crowds. No dogs; cl Mon–Thurs Jan–Feb; disabled access.

Salcombe SX7337 TIDES REACH South Sands, Salcombe TQ8 8LJ (01548) 843466 **£144 inc dinner**; 38 rms, many with estuary views. Unusually individual resort hotel run by long-standing owners and set in a pretty wooded cove by the sea; with airy, luxury day rooms, good restaurant food using fresh local produce, and friendly, efficient service; squash, snooker, leisure complex, health area, and big heated pool; windsurfing etc, beach over lane, and lots of coastal walks; cl Nov–Feb; children over 8.

Malborough (2m, S) SX7037 SOAR MILL COVE Malborough, Salcombe TQ7 3DS (01548) 561566 ***£130**; 16 comfortable rms, some leading on to garden. Neatly kept, single-storey building in an idyllic spot by a peaceful and very beautiful cove on NT coast (excellent walks); with lovely views, extensive private grounds (inc a new rose garden), tennis/putting, very warm indoor pool; also, outstanding service, log fires, very good food inc local produce (especially fish), fine wines, and thoughtful, early-evening children's meal; cl Nov–10 Feb; disabled access.

Torquay SX9264 IMPERIAL Park Hill Rd, Torquay TQ1 2DG (01803) 294301 ***£125**; 167 rms. Modern-looking resort hotel in a commanding spot just above the sea, currently undergoing major refurbishment, and set in 5 acres of lovely gardens; health and leisure club, heated indoor and outdoor pools, lots to do, good programme of event weekends; disabled access.

Goveton (just E) SX7546 BUCKLAND-TOUT-SAINTS Goveton, Kingsbridge TQ7 2DS (01548) 853055 **£100**; 12 luxurious period rms. Handsome Queen Anne mansion in well kept grounds with croquet/putting; antiques, panelling, fine plasterwork, imaginative food using good local produce in the no-smoking restaurant, notable wines, and excellent, personal service; children and dogs by arrangement.

Plymouth SX5356 PLYMOUTH MOAT HOUSE Armada Way, The Hoe, Plymouth PL1 2HJ (01752) 662866 **£92**; 212 rms, many with fine views. Well run, modern hotel overlooking Plymouth Sound and the Hoe; light, airy public rooms, good food in the restaurant with panoramic views, leisure club inc indoor swimming pool, gym, sauna and so forth, and very good facilities for children; disabled access.

Dartmouth SX8751 ROYAL CASTLE 11 The Quay, Dartmouth TQ6 9PS (01803) 8330333 **£76**; 25 individually furnished rms. Well restored Georgian hotel (with 16th-c core) overlooking the inner harbour – great views from most rooms; lively and interesting public bar with open fires and beams, quiet library/lounge with antiques, a drawing room overlooking the quayside, winter spit-roasts in the lounge bar, an elegant, upstairs seafood restaurant, decent bar food, and friendly staff.

Ashprington SX8157 WATERMANS ARMS Tuckenhay Rd, Bow Bridge, Ashprington, Totnes TQ9 7EG (01803) 732214 ***£65**; 10 comfortable and attractive rms. Fine old inn over a quiet lane from a tidal creek; with an upstairs residents' lounge, beamed and flagstoned bar, decent bar food, evening restaurant, and caring staff; garden with tables overlooking the river and ducks; pets welcome.

Galmpton SX8754 MAYPOOL PARK HOTEL Maypool, Galmpton, Churston TQ5 0ET (01803) 842442 **£65**; 10 rms. Converted Victorian cottages down a tree-lined quiet lane with marvellous views over the Dart estuary – and steamtrains 200 ft below; comfortable rooms, attentive service, and good food using fresh local produce; no smoking; cl Nov, Jan–Feb.

Ermington SX6353 Ermewood House Totnes Rd, Ermington, Modbury PL21 9NS (01548) 830741 *£60; 12 rms (front ones have river view but some traffic noise, back ones are quieter). Ex-rectory with a fine log fire in the lounge, drinks terrace over the gardens, pleasant dining room, good wines, and amiable service; cl Christmas and New Year; children over 12.

Dartmouth SX8751 Ford House 44 Victoria Rd, Dartmouth TQ6 9DX (01803) 834047 £56; 3 individually decorated rms. Close to the harbour, this Regency town house has an open log fire in the comfortable drawing room, antiques, fine food using fresh local produce and eaten around a big table, helpful service, and a sheltered garden; you can take over the whole house for a weekend party.

Dartington SX7962 Cott Dartington, Totnes TQ9 6HE (01803) 863777 *£50; 6 character rms. Pretty, ancient inn with a fine thatched roof (the longest in southern England), heavy-beamed communicating rooms with open fires and flagstones, good food inc lots of fresh fish and wines (8 by the glass), no-smoking restaurant, and nice nearby walks; cl evening 25 Dec; disabled access.

Totnes SX8060 Old Forge Seymour Pl, Totnes TQ9 5AY (01803) 862174 £50; 10 rms, 8 with own bthrm. Carefully restored 600-year-old building – still a working forge – with a lounge, plentiful breakfasts and vegetarian menu, and a big walled garden; no smoking; good disabled access.

Blackawton SX8050 Normandy Arms Blackawton, Totnes TQ9 7BN (0180 421) 316 £48; 5 pretty rms. Quaint, friendly pub in a quiet village, with a cosy main bar, log fire, some interesting displays on WWII battle gear, and decent, generous food in the bar and restaurant; no accommodation 24–26 Dec.

Staverton SX7964 Sea Trout Staverton, Totnes TQ9 6PA (01803) 762274 *£48; 10 cottagey rms. Comfortable pub in a quiet hamlet nr the River Dart; two relaxed, beamed bars, log fires, popular food in the bar and airy dining conservatory, and a terraced garden with fountains and waterfalls; no accommodation 24–25 Dec.

Frogmore SX7742 Globe Frogmore, Kingsbridge TQ7 2NR (01548) 531351 *£45; 6 rms, most with own bthrm. 18th-c inn with a pleasant atmosphere, comfortable lounge bar, friendly owners, and both bar and restaurant food.

Aveton Gifford SX6947 Court Barton Farmhouse Aveton Gifford, Kingsbridge TQ7 4LE (01548) 550312 £42; 7 rms, 6 with own bthrm. Pretty, creeper-clad, 16th-c farmhouse on 300 acres of arable land, with a cosy, homely lounge, log fires, a warm welcome, and flower-filled garden; cl Christmas.

Preston SX8574 Sampsons Farm Preston, Newton Abbot TQ12 3PP (01626) 54913 £40; 5 rms, 2 with own bthrms. Thatched, 14th-c longhouse with beams, panelling and big open fires in the cosy sitting rooms, a relaxed, welcoming atmosphere, and very good food in the popular restaurant; lots of nearby walks; self-catering too.

Ermington SX6353 Crooked Spire Ermington, Ivybridge PL21 9LP (01548) 830202 £35; 3 decent rms, shared bthrm. Friendly village pub with a neatly kept bar, good local atmosphere, amiable service, and generous fresh food.

Galmpton SX6840 Burton Farm Galmpton, Kingsbridge TQ7 3EY (01548) 561210 £35; 7 rms, most with own bthrm. Welcoming working farm in lovely countryside, with a dairy herd and pedigree sheep (guests are welcome to look around and help); traditional farmhouse cooking using home-produced ingredients; cl Christmas.

Slapton SX6643 Tower Slapton, Kingsbridge TQ7 2PN (01548) 580216 £34; 3 simple rms, shared bthrm. Atmospheric, friendly old pub with low-ceilinged bars, open log fires, lots of real ales, popular food (Italian part-owner) in the bar and small restaurant, and neatly kept garden.

Hazlewood SX7148 Crannacombe Farm Hazlewood, Loddiswell, Kingsbridge TQ7 4DX (01548) 550256 £32; 2 rms. Quietly set and comfortable Georgian farmhouse on a working stock farm in a lovely unspoilt valley; with prize-winning cider, and hearty food; no smoking; babysitting; cl Christmas.

To see and do

Dartmouth SX8751 Charming, waterside, small town with many exceptional buildings, especially around the inner harbour. Though so popular, it's kept its own strong character, and stays very much alive through the winter. Cobbled Bayards Cove, with an old fort and steep, wooded hills behind, is particularly photogenic, as is pedestrianised Foss St. Markets Tues, Fri: the Old Market is picturesque. The Royal Naval College is a striking building. Interesting shops, plenty of waterside seats, lots of action on the river. Parking in summer can be trying; best to use the good park-and-ride on the B3207 Halwell Rd.

♨ RIVER TRIPS up to Totnes pass some of Devon's prettiest scenery that's impossible to walk or drive by; you can combine this with steamtrains (see Buckfastleigh entry in the Dartmoor section) or a connecting bus back – which saves hearing the commentary a second time. You can also go on circular tours of the surrounding area. There may still be boats in winter – tel (01803) 832109 to check; £5.40 return to Totnes. Also quaint car and pedestrian ferries to Kingswear and the A379 (can be a 2-hour car wait at peak summer times).

🏰 ❋ ♨ CASTLE Classic, late 15th-c battlemented fortress, virtually intact, with cannon and later gun batteries, and great views out into the Channel. In summer, you can get a little ferry out to here. Snacks, shop; cl Mon and Tues from Oct–Easter; (01803) 864406; £1.80.

✝ ST SAVIOUR'S Lots of charming detail, well worth a close look, inc altar, pulpit, painted rood screen, brasses on the chancel floor, elaborate 14th-c hinges on the S door.

♂ MUSEUM (The Butterwalk, Duke St) Well restored, 17th-c timbered house with rich panelling and plasterwork; the displays are largely nautical, with lots of ship models. Shop; cl Sun, 25–26 Dec; *80p.

⚙ NEWCOMEN ENGINE HOUSE (Royal Avenue Gdns) Huge steam-powered, atmospheric, beam-engine pump, thought to be the world's oldest, worked from 1720–1913. Shop, disabled access; cl winter Sun, 24–26 Dec; (01803) 834224; 50p.

♂ HENLEY MUSEUM (Anzac St) has a collection of local history and botany, worth a look if passing. Cl Oct–May; 25p.

Paignton SX8960 Down by the sea this is a typical resort, with a long promenade between a good sandy beach and green; but the little harbour is pretty, with working fishing boats as well as yachts. The original inland core has an attractive, red sandstone church with some interesting buildings nearby, especially KIRKHAM HOUSE, a handsome, sandstone, Tudor merchant's house with a lofty hall. Attractive Elberry Cove between here and Brixham is altogether quieter.

🐘🦏! ZOO AND BOTANICAL GARDENS (St Michael's; SX8859) Well run and shown, with over 1,300 animals and birds (many of them breeding) playing and feeding in 75 acres of beautifully planted surroundings; also, summer subtropical lakeside miniature railway, and a splendid hands-on centre for children to enjoy and learn about animals. Meals, snacks, shop, good disabled access; cl 25 Dec; (01803) 557479; £5.75.

🚂 PAIGNTON AND DARTMOUTH STEAM

RAILWAY GWR steamtrains run from here, right by the sea along Tor Bay (halts at Goodrington Beach, which has closer parking, and Churston), then along the Dart estuary to Kingswear. The front Pullman coach is less crowded, and there's a model railway at the Paignton end. You can combine this with a boat from Dartmouth–Totnes, and bus from Totnes–Paignton. Every 45 mins in high summer, less often other times. Snacks, shop, disabled access; cl

Nov–Mar exc some of Dec, and maybe other days out of season, (01803) 555872 for times; £5.80 return. This is easily one of the nicest such steamtrain trips we know of.

✿ 🏛 OLDWAY SX8960 Colourful, formal and subtropical lakeside gardens; also, parts of Singer sewing-machine king's opulent, Versailles-style, colonnaded mansion are open. Summer meals, snacks, disabled access; cl Sun exc pm in summer; free.

Plymouth SX4475 A busy, largely modern city, though there are some interesting escapes from the bustle. In places The Hoe has something of the feel of smaller seaside prome-nades (the Waterfront bar/restaurant is a pleasant stop). A tour bus can take you to the main attractions, though it's perhaps more fun on one of the BOAT TRIPS run by Tamar Cruises from Mayflower Steps, off Madeira Rd, Barbican; 1-hour trips, with commentary, are £3. The ferry over to Torpoint puts Antony House and Mt Edgcumbe in very easy reach – see South-East Cornwall section. Besides places recommended in **Where to eat** (below), the Yard Arm (behind Moat House) and Bank (behind Theatre Royal) are good for lunch.

🏛 BARBICAN Carefully restored since the war, narrow, twisty streets of old buildings W of working Sutton Harbour, photogenic – evocative even in wet weather. New St is its oldest part. The next five attractions are all round here.

🏛 PRYSTEN HOUSE (Finewell St) The city's oldest house, an austere, late 15th-c granite building with a galleried courtyard, in its time used as a priest's house, a wine store and a bacon factory. Unpretentious, but quite atmospheric restored rooms, with displays inc a model of 17th-c Plymouth and several yards of Devon's new ambitious tapestry on American colonisation. Its fine well used to be the local water source. Cl Sun, Nov–Mar; *50p.

✝ ST ANDREW'S (nearby) Bombed but lovingly restored, with John Piper

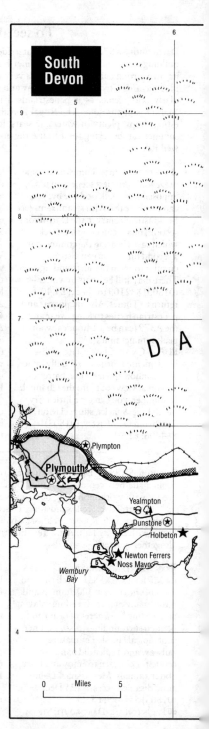

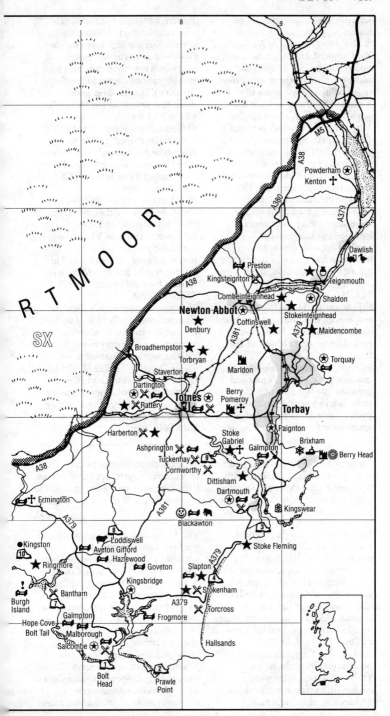

stained glass showing the city's history.

⬤ MERCHANT'S HOUSE (St Andrew's St) Well restored, 16th-c jettied house, now telling the city's day-to-day history in displays themed on tinker, tailor, soldier, sailor; also early Victorian apothecary's shop and schoolroom. Shop; cl 1–2 pm, Sun, Mon (exc bank hols), Oct–Mar; £1.

⬤ BLACK FRIARS DISTILLERY (60 Southside St) Photogenic home of Plymouth Dry Gin, now the only English gin still made in its original distillery, founded in 1793. The building itself dates back much further, and has had periods as a monastery and a prison; tours include demonstrations of production, a film of the town's history and, of course, a sample of the gin itself. Meals, snacks, shop; cl Sun and Oct–Easter; (01752) 665292; *£1.75.

🏠 ELIZABETHAN HOUSE (New St) Now reopened, a splendid, timber-framed, Tudor sea-captain's house, with period furniture. Cl Mon and Tues; £1.

⬤ DOME (The Hoe) State-of-the-art evocation of Plymouth's past and present using feel-part-of-it technology – you can stroll along lively Elizabethan streets, dodge press gangs, meet Drake and the Pilgrim

Fathers, and come bang up to date with satellite and radar monitoring of current harbour action and weather. Good fun as well as interesting, and well worth two hours (you may have trouble parking nearby for longer than that). Snacks, shop, good disabled access; cl 25 Dec; (01752) 603300; £3.40.

🏠❋ SMEATON'S TOWER (The Hoe) Colourfully striped, 18th-c, former Eddystone Rocks lighthouse, moved here 110 years ago, with a good view from the top if you like steps. Cl Nov–Easter; 70p.

🏰❋ ROYAL CITADEL (The Hoe) Unrivalled views of the city and sea from this magnificent 17th-c battlemented fortress. The gateway is particularly striking, and the barracked parade-ground is still in use; tours at 12 and 2pm May–Sept, starting from the Dome; (01752) 775841; £2.50.

🐟 AQUARIUM (just outside Citadel) Comprehensive collection of sea fish, crustaceans etc, run by scientific institution, with plenty to touch and do. Snacks, shop, disabled access; cl 25–26 Dec; (01752) 222772; *£2.

⬤ The CITY MUSEUM (Drake Circus) has well shown collections of mostly West Country interest. Snacks, shop, disabled access; cl Sun, Mon (exc bank hols); free.

Torquay SX9264 Palm trees and rocks, promenades, colourful gardens, decorous guesthouses and huge hotels, broad Victorian streets, apparently recession-proof smooth shops, sheltered red beaches; summer bustle around the attractive harbour with lots of shops (the Hole in the Wall is a useful pub), boat trips, aquarium.

❗🏘 MODEL VILLAGE (Hampton Ave, Babbacombe; SX9265) Hundreds of one-twelfth scale buildings in 4 acres of miniaturised landscape, beautifully done, and perhaps the best of its type. Also, an extensive model railway, sound effects and summer-night lighting. They've recently added a replica of Stonehenge. Snacks, shop, good disabled access; cl 25 Dec; (01803) 328669; £3.50, plus parking. The Cary Arms down by the beach is useful for lunch.

🏴 KENTS CAVERN (Wellswood; SX9264) The oldest directly dated archaeological site in Britain;

excavations are still going on, some of the finds causing scientists to reconsider their earlier theories about prehistoric life. Good guided tours really bring out the mystery of the caves, with reconstructions and dramatisations of life for cave families 30,000 years ago, and colourful stalagmites and stalactites adding to the eerie atmosphere. Very well presented, and definitely worth an hour or so if you're in the area. They occasionally do special themed shows, at Christmas or on summer eves. Summer snacks, shop, disabled access (with prior notice); cl 25 Dec; (01803) 294059; £3.25.

🏛🏠🖼✿ TORRE ABBEY (King's Drive; SX9063) Some of the earlier parts of the abbey remain, inc the medieval sandstone gatehouse, ruined Norman tower, and tithe barn, but they've been eclipsed by the later house with its 17th-, 18th- and 19th-c period rooms. The main feature now is the art gallery, along with a showy garden and palm house, and an Agatha Christie room full of possessions of the author, who was born in Torquay. Snacks, shop; cl Nov–Mar exc by appointment; (01803) 293593; *£2.50.

🏠🔊 BYGONES (Fore St, St Marychurch; SX9166) Enthusiastically reconstructed, life-sized Victorian street, with well stocked period shops and rooms. Also a model railway and WWI walk-in trench experience, with the soldiers' dug-outs and dramatic sound effects. Café, shop; cl 25 Dec;

(01803) 326108; £2.50.

🔊 MUSEUM (529 Babbacombe Rd) One of the most interesting local bygones here is the cannon that turns out to be a clock, designed to fire its charge at midday. Also fascinating finds from the Ice Age and older Devon caves. Shop; cl Sat Oct–Easter, and Sun exc pm July–Sept; (01803) 293975; *£1.75.

★ COCKINGTON SX8963 Winding lanes of olde-worlde thatched cottages and bric-a-brac/craft shops in a sheltered village with millpond etc, well preserved by Torbay Council. The Drum pub (a useful stop) was designed to match by Lutyens in 1934. Frightfully pretty, very touristy in summer, with open horse-drawn carriages.

! 🔊 CLIFF RAILWAY SX9265 Dizzy swoop from Oddicombe Beach to a high wooded clifftop. Disabled access; cl Oct–Easter; 40p each way.

Totnes SX8060 The picturesque Elizabethan area known as THE NARROWS is very atmospheric, especially the High St down to the arch at the top of Fore St, with quaint pillared arcades. Bustling on Tues May–Sept, when many traders wear Elizabethan costume. There may be horse-drawn omnibus rides down at Steamer Quay in summer; fun for children. See Dartmouth entry for excellent river trips; working harbour too. You can walk some way downstream on either side of the River Dart.

🏛✿ CASTLE Part Norman, part 14th-c, these classic circular remains were lucky enough to avoid any battles, so the keep is pretty much intact. There's a tree-shaded inner lawn, and lovely views of the town and down to the river. Shop; cl 1–2 pm, winter Mon and Tues; £1.35.

🏠🔊 BOWDEN HOUSE (Ashprington Rd, S; SX8059) Good spooky tours by costumed guides of handsomely restored, grand Tudor and baroque rooms with weaponry, and separate PHOTOGRAPHY MUSEUM with still and moving pictures (inc cartoons) in attractive grounds. Snacks, disabled access to museum only; open pm Mon–Thurs and bank hol Suns from mid-Mar–Oct, cl other Suns but may be car boot sales then; (01803) 863664; £4.50.

🔊 MUSEUM (70 Fore St) Stately Elizabethan merchant's house with a galleried courtyard, herb garden, local

costumes and oddities, and the inventions of Totnes boy Charles Babbage, creator of one of the earliest computers. Shop; cl lunchtime (exc July, Aug), Sat (exc July, Aug), Sun, Nov–mid-Mar; (01803) 863821; *£1.

🚗 MOTOR MUSEUM (Steamer Quay) Mainly vintage and racing cars and motorcycles, all good runners, even an amphibious Amphicar. Shop, disabled access to ground floor only; cl Nov–Easter; (01803) 862777; £3.50.

🔊 DEVONSHIRE COLLECTION OF PERIOD COSTUME (43 High St) Good collection of period costumes and accessories from the 18th c to the present day, ranging from high fashion to ordinary work clothes, with changing annual exhibitions. Shop; cl Sat, am Sun, Oct–May; *£1.

The SOUTH DEVON RAILWAY is described under Buckfastleigh entry (see Dartmoor section).

Other things to see and do

✱ ▦ **Berry Head** SX9456 has tremendous coast, sea and shipping views from an ex-quarry country park; squat lighthouse and formidable Napoleonic War battlements with cannon (and guardhouse café); a nature trail takes in kittiwakes and guillemots on the cliffs, as well as uncommon plants.

▦ † **Berry Pomeroy** (off the A385, just E of Totnes; keep on past village) SX8362 CASTLE Reputedly Devon's most haunted castle, hidden away on a crag over a quiet wooded valley. Appropriately spooky Norman gatehouse and walls around the ruins of an imposing and unexpected Tudor mansion, with an interesting 15th-c fresco inside. Snacks, shop, disabled access; cl Oct–Mar; (01803) 866618; £1.80. The red sandstone, 15th-c village CHURCH is worth a look on the way; odd monument in Seymour Chapel.

☺ 🐓 **Blackawton** SX8050 WOODLAND LEISURE PARK Parkland with extensive play areas from a toddlers' village to scary mega slides; also a little zoo with wallabies, llamas and foreign birds. Meals, snacks, shop, disabled access; cl 24–26 Dec; £3.50. The Normandy Arms is useful for lunch.

⚓ ✱ **Brixham** SX9256 Busy fishing port, lots of activity (and summer seaside shops and cafés) in the harbour, some pretty, narrow streets on the hill above. Summer boats around Tor Bay. The local history MUSEUM (Bolton Cross) is good, with quite a maritime emphasis. Shop, mostly disabled access; cl Sun, Nov–Easter; £1.20. The quaint Quayside Inn is handy for lunch.

! **Burgh Island** SX6443 Across the broad tidal sands from rather run-down Bigbury-on-Sea, a true island and quite remote-seeming when the tide's in – in summer, an odd, giant tractor-on-stilts wades back and forth with passengers. The Pilchard is a useful sea-view pub.

♫ 🐓 ✱ **Dartington** SX8062 CIDER PRESS CRAFT CENTRE Cluster of 16th- and 17th-c buildings with craft shops, farm foods, herbs and such, and restaurants, inc a good vegetarian

one; the surroundings add a lot to the attraction, with a nearby medieval great hall in a photogenic, lawned courtyard, sculpture gardens, and streamside nature trail. Disabled access; cl Sun, 25–26 Dec, 1 Jan; (01803) 864171; free. The Cott, very good indeed for lunch, is close by.

▶ ▦ **Dawlish** SX9676 is an old-fashioned, small resort with modern developments and camps outside; red sandstone cliffs, good beach, waterside parks with black swans, promenade, pier; the mainline railway cut through the cliffs right by the water is striking. DAWLISH WARREN SX9879 Sandy grassy spit (with golf course) largely blocking up the Exe estuary, with glistening tidal flats full of wading birds, and dunes with some rare plants. In summer get well out to the point, to avoid the seaside tat, crowds and caravan parks at the station end; in winter it's splendidly wild and blowy, with thousands of ducks, brent-geese and waders (even avocets) congregating at high tide to wait till the mudflats show again; spring/autumn migrants. Free, but they do guided summer nature walks for £1; (01626) 863980 for times. The Mount Pleasant is very handy for lunch.

🐎 🦋 ▶ 🐕 **Dunstone** SX5951 NATIONAL SHIRE HORSE CENTRE A good, fine-weather, family outing, with around 40 shire horses and foals, waggon rides, smithy and saddlery, butterfly house, falconry displays (pm only), adventure playground and pets' corner – you can get right up to the animals. Meals, snacks, shop and craft centre, disabled access; cl 24–26 Dec; (01752) 880806; *£5.50, reduced rates in winter as less displays. The Dartmoor Union in Holbeton is quite handy for lunch.

★ ▦ † ⚓ 🏰 🍴 **Kingsbridge** SX7344 Small town of character – pretty cobbled lanes diving off steep Fore St, arcaded shops, pillared market house (market day Weds), interesting monuments in the church, boats on the tidal estuary (and ferry to Salcombe); the waterfront Crabshell is very popular for seafood. COOKWORTHY MUSEUM (Fore St) Good local history museum in a 17th-c grammar school. Shop, disabled access; cl Sun, Oct wknds, all Nov–Mar; (01548) 853235; *£1.60. They have regular craft demonstrations.

❀ **Kingswear** (2m E, off Lower Ferry Rd at Tollhouse) SX9050 COLETON FISHACRE D'Oyly Carte's romantic and lush subtropical garden, with 20 colourful acres dropping down to a pretty cove; formal terraces, walled garden with stream-fed ponds, unusual trees and shrubs, grassy woodland paths. Snacks; cl Mon, Tues, Sat, Nov–Mar (exc pm Sun Mar); £2.60; NT. More ambitious marked paths beyond the gardens take you along the cliffs, showing how wild this part was before the garden was planted. See Paignton entry (above) for the Dart Valley Railway. The Ship is quite useful for lunch.

☛ **Loddiswell** (Lilwell) SX7148 VINEYARD 10 acres, part under polythene, producing award-winning medium wines; tastings and wine-making videos. Snacks, shop with herbs and vines for sale, disabled access; cl am and wknds (exc July and Aug or bank hol Suns), guided tours at 2.15pm and 4pm; (01548) 550221; tours £2.50, walkabouts £1.50. The Loddiswell Inn is good for lunch.

🏰 **Marldon** (1m N, off the A3022; or off the A381 at Ipplepen turnoff) SX8664 COMPTON CASTLE Formidably fortified and rather picturesque 14th- and 16th-c manor around a courtyard with portcullised entrance, particularly interesting for its completeness – galleried great hall, ancient kitchen, chapel and rose garden. Snacks, shop, limited disabled access; cl 12.15–2pm, Tues, Fri–Sun, Nov–Mar; £2.60; NT.

★ Modbury SX6551 has attractive buildings especially in steep Church St, with quite a photogenic church at the top and pretty Exeter Inn at the bottom. Brownston St is quite interesting too, especially the ornate water conduit at the top.

🏠 ❀ ❉ 🏚 NEWTON ABBOT SX8671 is very much a working town. TUCKERS MALTINGS (Teign Rd) One of the few remaining working malthouses in the country, and the only one open to the public – every year they produce enough malt for 15 million pints of beer. The tours show all aspects of malting (you can touch the grain and taste the malt), and they've recently set up their own brewery. Also hands-on displays and a reconstructed old street. Meals, snacks, shop; cl Sat and all Nov–Easter, exc by arrangement; (01626) 334734; *£3.60 (inc sample of beer). PLANT WORLD (St Marychurch Rd) Quite a wacky little garden, built and planted as a giant map of the world, with all the countries containing their correct native plants, trees and flowers – many of them quite rare in this country, but flourishing in the mild Devon climate. Also a good plant centre (with seeds of some of the rarest plants), old-fashioned English garden and fine views from the picnic area. Disabled access to plant centre only; cl Christmas wk; (01803) 872939; £1 for garden. BRADLEY MANOR (off the A381, S) Peaceful 15th-c house nr a stream through extensive wood-fringed grounds; quiet walks. Open pm Wed Apr–Sept; *£2.60; NT. Just N of town at Forches Cross, SX8473 ORCHID PARADISE is a colourful place, with lots of rare and endangered species in elaborate indoor reconstructions of their natural habitats. Good in winter – it's always warm. Snacks, nursery and shop, disabled access (but no facilities); cl 25 Dec; (01626) 52233; £1.50. The Court Farm at Abbotskerswell and the Old Rydon at Kingsteignton both do good food.

★ **Newton Ferrers/Noss Mayo** SX5447 Picturesque twin villages on a very sheltered, rocky, wooded creek of the Yealm estuary; besides some modern development, there are attractive, whitewashed cottages; lots of yachting in summer, fine setting. The Dolphin, Old Ship and Swan are all pleasant places for lunch.

🏚 ❀ ★ **Plympton** (2m W, off the A38/A379 at Marsh Mills roundabout) SX5255 SALTRAM Magnificent, mostly 18th-c mansion still with pretty much all the original contents, and especially notable for its unaltered Robert Adam rooms. George II furnishings, decoration and paintings (strong on Reynolds, who as a regular guest advised on which other pictures to buy), interesting period kitchen, stately garden with orangery, and parkland by the wooded Plym estuary. Meals, snacks, shop, local art/ crafts gallery, disabled access; house cl am, Fri and Sat, Nov–Mar; £5, garden only £2.20, parking may be extra; NT. The old town around St Maurice Church is worth a look if you're here: attractive, partly arcaded streets, very ruined motte and bailey castle.

Powderham SX9683 CASTLE The ancestral home of the Earls of Devon, badly damaged in the Civil War but elaborately restored in the 18th and 19th c, with rich decorations and furnishings. Many of the state rooms were used in the film *The Remains of the Day*, and a new exhibition has photographs of the production. Spectacular rose garden, home to Timothy, the 155-year-old tortoise, and a broad deer park with good views over the Exe estuary. Good guided tours; meals, snacks, shop, some disabled access; cl Sat, Oct–Easter; (01626) 890243; *£3.95. The waterside Anchor and Ship at Cockwood both have good seafood.

★ **Salcombe** SX7337 Steep narrow streets, fishing village full of enjoyable holiday bustle in summer; lots of souvenirs, bric-a-brac and boating shops, as well as teashops and pubs overlooking the sea, nearby beaches and coves. BOAT trips and boat hire. OVERBECKS SX7237 (South Sands; also signed from Malborough) Named after the eccentric research chemist who lived here until 1937, the quaint museum here still has many of his possessions and inventions – notably the Rejuvenator which Overbecks claimed had 'practically renewed' his youth. For many the chief attraction will be the luscious subtropical gardens, with terraced plantings among woodland, many rarities and plenty of palms and citrus fruits; outstanding late May–Jun for the magnolias, but worth a trip any time of the year. Glorious views out to sea. Also a colourful statue garden, picnic belvedere and doll collection. Snacks, shop; cl Sat and Nov–Mar; £3.40; NT.

★ **Shaldon** SX9372 Interesting and colourful mix of seaside houses spanning 200 years of architectural fancy, with some lovely corners, especially down by the water away from the centre, also much older cottages in Crown Sq. High, grassy, sandstone Ness overlooks the sea and Teignmouth, with a tunnel cut by the 19th-c landowner to a sheltered beach; the beautifully sited Ness House up here is useful for food. WILDLIFE TRUST (Ness Drive) Breeding collection of rare and endangered foreign birds, and small mammals inc monkeys; cl 25 Dec; £2.30. The BOTANIC GARDENS here are pleasant, with lots of rare shrubs and trees and nice views; free.

★ **Stoke Gabriel** SX8457 is a steep village above a sheltered side-pool of the Dart estuary, with its 14th-c church (and ancient yew) and Church House (pleasant for lunch) perched prettily on a high cobbled terrace.

★ **Teignmouth** SX9473 is a popular resort for family holidays, with good beaches, windsurfing and so on. Also some handsome 19th-c streets, active docks and a decent local history MUSEUM (French St). The quayside Ship is useful for lunch.

Yealmpton SX5751 KITLEY CAVES Tours of stunning illuminated caves, and above ground, 50 acres of pretty woodland and riverside walks; lots of varieties of plants, shrubs and trees, displays and exhibitions, plus the story of the creator of Old Mother Hubbard and her canine companion. Snacks, shop; cl Nov–Good Fri; £2.90.

Good churches at Ermington SX6353, where there's a crooked 14th-c stone spire above the tower (Victorian rebuilding kept the tilt), and Kenton SX9583, its harmonious, medieval, sandstone masonry photographing well against a blue sky; fine carving inside.

★ **Other attractive villages**, all worth looking at if you're near, and all with decent pubs, include Broadhempston SX8066, Coffinswell SX8968, Combeinteignhead SX9071 (in addition to the Wild Goose in the village, the waterside Coombe Cellars is outstanding for families), Denbury SX8168, Dittisham SX8654,

Harberton SX7758, Holbeton SX6150, Maidencombe SX9268, Rattery SX7461, Ringmore SX6545, Slapton SX8244, Stoke Fleming SX8648, Stokeinteignhead SX9170 (the Green Man is the best pub here), Stokenham SX8042 and Torbryan SX8266.

Walks

The coastal path is the main attraction for walkers. The finest part of Devon's southern seaboard is between Plymouth SX4475 and Brixham SX9256 – much of it quite unspoilt. In summer, ferries cross the rivers (except the River Erme S of Ermington SX6353, which you have to cross at low tide). **Bolt Head/Bolt Tail** ⌂-1 is 6 miles of one of the best coastal path sections, with remote and exposed clifftops, glorious coves, far views and well preserved Iron Age earth ramparts on Bolt Tail; all NT. Best access is via Overbecks SX7237, Soar Mill Cove SX7037 or Hope Cove SX6739. **Prawle Point** SX7735 ⌂-2, further E, also has impressive scenery: wind-blasted gorse, grass and thrift above low but fierce cliffs, lending itself to a round walk, with a useful network of green lanes leading inland to the village of East Prawle SX7836 (where the Pig's Nose is a useful stop). **Dartmouth Castle** and **Compass Cove** SX8849 ⌂-3 make an enjoyable excursion on foot, though the immediate hinterland is unremarkable.

Slapton Sands ⌂-4 are 6 miles of almost straight shingle N of the lighthouse at Start Point SX8337, backed by hills in the S and by road, shingle bank, lake (Slapton Ley nature reserve, with marked nature trail), marsh, and then low cliffs in the N. Good for out-of-season desolation, sheltered from westerly winds, with a storm-ruined village at Hallsands SX8138, and a salvaged tank memorial to US Normandy landings practice at Torcross SX8242; take-away picnics from the Green Dragon at Stoke Fleming SX8648 (A379, N), and the Cricket at Beesands SX8140 is right on the beach.

There are attractive walks by the wooded **Yealm estuary** ⌂-5 from Noss Mayo SX5447, then beyond to Gara Point SX5246 and exposed cliff; largely NT. This can be reached in sections via the Noss Mayo–Holbeton coastal ridge rd. **Wembury Bay** ⌂-6 gives good views, starting from Wembury SX5248, past the church at the start of NT clifftops; woods and pastures on the opposite shore, Plymouth shipping in the distance.

Bantham Sands ⌂-7 allow a gentle walk through the dunes from Bantham SX6643 to the broad stretch of rivermouth sand facing Burgh Island. You can go on above the rocks S, for views of Bolt Tail and the coves between.

Other good places for walks include **Loddiswell** SX7248 ⌂-8 (cross the river by the lane towards Woodsleigh, then a quiet walk upstream by riverside pastures and woods towards Topsham Bridge).

Tuckenhay SX8156 ⌂-9 (a pretty mile E along wooded Bow Creek from Maltsters Arms); **Kingston** SX6347 ⌂-10 (several walks down to unspoilt beach).

Driving

Pretty or interesting stretches of road include parts of the A384 Buckfastleigh–Totnes; A379 Shaldon–Maidencombe (sea views), and Stoke Fleming–Stokenham; B3210 Totnes–Ermington; the B3210 off the A38 S of South Brent, continuing from Avonwick on the back road Diptford–Moreleigh (can link with the next suggestion); back road to Slapton signposted off the A381 a mile or so S of Halwell; coast road along the Kingsbridge estuary, S of South Pool; Ashburton–Woolston Green–Littlehempston–Berry Pomeroy–Stoke Gabriel; coast ridge road Holbeton–Noss Mayo. If you want to do much driving here, come out of season: in summer, negotiating the narrow lanes can be very slow and frustrating.

The A38 is the backbone of getting around here, fast except at the worst summer peaks: it's a pleasant road, too, with good views. The A380 is fairly fast out of season. On other main roads, be prepared for slowish traffic at almost any time of the year, and reckon to go really slowly on most back roads (though the milk tankers seem to use them as race tracks). As an example, allow 50 minutes to an hour to get to Dartmouth from the end of the M5 – longer at peak holiday times. From most places here, you can get well into Dartmoor by car in about an hour or less.

Where to eat

Dartmouth SX8751 CARVED ANGEL 2 South Embankment (01803) 832465 Subtly tuned yet unpretentious combinations of unexpected flavours, with carefully chosen fresh ingredients, make for memorable meals in this outstanding restaurant; smart yet friendly, with a view of the kitchen on one side and the water on the other; fine wines at every price range; cl pm Sun, Mon, 6 wks from early Jan. **£32 lunch, £48 dinner/£9.50.**

Plymouth SX4755 CHEZ NOUS 13 Frankfort Gate (01752) 266793 Informal and friendly French bistro, with careful cooking of fresh local produce, especially fresh fish and fine puddings; some distinguished wines, and friendly atmosphere; cl Sun and Mon, 3 wks Feb, 2 wks Sept; partial disabled access. **£41.**

Tuckenhay SX8156 FLOYDS INN (SOMETIMES) (01803) 732350 Attractively furnished bars and an airy, popular restaurant – overlooking a picturesque creek – with enterprising, if pricey, cooking using first-class ingredients. **£35/£13.**

Kingsteignton SX8773 OLD RYDON (01626) 54626 Cosy old pub with a constantly changing, wide choice of imaginative bar food inc good puddings; big garden; restaurant cl pm Sun (bar food available, then); children under 8 until 8pm. **£22|£2.95/£4.95.**

Dartmouth SX8751 BILLY BUDDS 7 Foss St (01803) 834842 Cheerfully run and popular little restaurant with good, fresh, often interesting food and a sensible wine list; cl Sun and Mon, 3 wks Feb–Mar; children lunchtime, but over 11 in evening. **£20|£2.95/£4.95** (lunch), **£12.50** (dinner).

Dartington SX7762 COTT (01803) 863777 Warm, welcoming and ancient Devon longhouse, with lots of fresh fish dishes and interesting daily specials, fine choice of wines and real ales; traditional, heavy-beamed rooms, and friendly dogs and cats; a good place to stay. **£20/6.50.**

Torcross SX8241 START BAY (01548) 580553 Notable, fresh seafood generously served in a busy, thatched, 14th-c pub overlooking a 3-mile pebble beach; live cider; family room; no food 25 Dec; partial disabled access. **£20|£2/£4.50.**

Salcombe SX7338 SPINNAKERS (01548) 843408 Relaxed waterside restaurant with good, popular food inc fresh local fish and nice puddings; cl pm Sun, Mon (open summer then), winter Tues, mid-Nov–mid-Feb. **£18.25|£3.75/£5.95.**

Cornworthy SX8255 HUNTERS LODGE (01803) 732204 Unpretentious country local, with a cottagey log-fire restaurant and tables on the big lawn, serving a remarkable range of interestingly cooked generous food. **£18|£1.90/£4.25.**

Dartmouth SX8751 CHERUB Higher St (01804) 832571 Interesting seafood specialities in one of Dartmouth's most ancient and picturesque buildings. Children in upstairs restaurant only. **£18|£1.95/£4.25.**

Ashprington SX8156 DURANT ARMS (01803) 732240 Friendly, gable-ended dining pub, very popular for its very good, changing food, well kept beers, and friendly service; family room. **£17.45|£1.50/£3.95.**

Bantham SX6643 SLOOP (01548) 560489 Close to a sandy beach (good for surfing), this 16th-c nautical village inn has sound bar food inc lots of fish, hearty breakfasts, decent beers and wines; they have holiday cottages; cl 25 Dec. **£15|£2/£7.**

Stokenham SX8042 CHURCH HOUSE (01548) 580253 Wide range of well presented food, especially local fish and seafood, in an ancient and friendly rambling pub; nice garden. **£15|£2.20/£5.50.**

Plymouth SX4755 CHINA HOUSE Sutton Harbour (via Sutton Rd, off the A374) (01752) 260930 Well converted, 17th-c waterside warehouse beautifully placed opposite Barbican; very lofty and spacious, with beams, log fire, flagstones and bare slate, nautical decorations, and a first-floor dining area which becomes an evening restaurant; good disabled access. £15|£2.45/£4.95.

Harberton SX7758 CHURCH HOUSE (01803) 863707 Ancient village pub with magnificent medieval panelling, attractive old furnishings, generous helpings of good bar food, well kept beers, and decent wines; cl 25/26 Dec, pm 1 Jan; children in family room. £14|£2.50/£4.95.

Rattery SX7461 CHURCH HOUSE (01364) 42220 One of Britain's oldest pubs – with big open fires, friendly customers and staff; good bar food, decent wines and beers, fine malt whiskies, and nice dog and cats; peaceful setting. £13.25|£2.75/£5.30.

Totnes SX8060 KINGSBRIDGE Leechwell St (01803) 863324 Several unexpected dishes among the more usual bar food in a plushly refurbished but interesting pub – the town's oldest building; cl 25 Dec. £11.25|£1.75/£4.95.

NORTH DEVON

Relatively untouristy away from the few traditional resorts; attractive places to visit, some charming, civilised places to stay in.

Ilfracombe, the main resort, stays active all year; it's a pleasant and distinctive place that has family attractions but doesn't become too trippery in summer. The lower-key beach resorts such as Woolacombe and Westward Ho! go into mothballs when the season's over – without the summer sun-seekers, their marvellous beaches are good for lonely walks, and elsewhere there are fine, bracing cliff walks. Outside the few resorts and the legendary, pretty Clovelly and Combe Martin, this part of Devon is largely untouched by tourism, and there are long stretches of coast which are empty even in summer. Major attractions include Bickleigh (for its castle and Devonshire's Centre), Arlington Court, the woodland gardens at Rosemoor near Torrington and at Knighthayes Court at Bolham, and Hartland Quay.

Where to stay

South Molton SS7125 WHITECHAPEL MANOR, South Molton EX36 3EG (01769) 573377 *£98; 10 pretty rms. Carefully restored, Grade I listed Elizabethan manor in large grounds, with a magnificent Jacobean carved oak screen in the entrance hall, fine panelling, beams and log fires; relaxed atmosphere in the cosy bar and comfortable lounge, excellent, thoughtful service, fine, modern cooking as well as home-made breads, jams and marmalade, and carefully chosen wines; handy also for Exmoor; disabled access.

Chittlehamholt SS6420 HIGHBULLEN Chittlehamholt, Umberleigh EX37 3HD (01769) 540561 £95 inc dinner; 37 comfortable, elegant and often spacious rms in main building and various annexes. Victorian Gothic mansion set in huge wooded parkland and gardens, with 9-hole golf course, indoor tennis court and swimming pool, table tennis, and squash court; consistently good food, an intimate restaurant overlooking the valley, busy little bar, library, and relaxed, informal service (no reception, you ring a bell and wait); children over 8; no dogs.

Morchard Bishop SS7707 WIGHAM Morchard Bishop, Crediton EX17 6RJ (0136 37) 350 £88 inc dinner; 5 rms. Picturesque, thatched longhouse on a 30-acre farm, with house-party atmosphere, two sitting rooms, big log fires, snooker room, dining room with honesty bar and set dinner using home-grown fruit, veg and dairy produce; no smoking and no pets (they have their own); outdoor heated swimming pool; children over 8.

Bishop's Tawton SS5630 HALMPSTONE Bishop's Tawton, Barnstaple EX32 0EA (01271) 830321 *£80; 5 pretty rms. Quietly relaxing, small country hotel with a log fire in the comfortable sitting room, enjoyable food in the panelled dining room, good breakfasts, and caring service; pretty garden, nice views; cl Jan; children over 12.

Clawton SX3599 COURT BARN Clawton, Holsworthy EX22 6PS (0140 927) 219 £66; 8 individually furnished rms. Charming country house in 5 acres of pretty grounds, with croquet, 9-hole putting green, small chip-and-putt course, tennis and badminton courts; comfortable lounges, log fires, library/tv room, good service, imaginative food, and a quiet, relaxed atmosphere; dogs allowed; cl 2–7 Jan.

Sheepwash SS4806 HALF MOON Sheepwash, Beaworthy EX21 5NE (0140 923) 376 £64; 14 rms. Civilised, heart-of-Devon hideaway in a colourful village square, with 10 miles of private salmon-, sea trout- and brown trout-fishing on the River Torridge; a neatly kept, friendly bar, solid old furnishings and a big log fire; good wines, an evening restaurant and lunchtime bar snacks; cl Jan; dogs welcome; disabled access.

East Buckland SS6731 LOWER PITT East Buckland, Barnstaple EX32 0TD (01598) 760243 *£60; 3 comfortable rms. Quiet, pretty stone farmhouse with a log fire in the cosy lounge, good, well presented food using herbs and veg from their own garden and fresh local produce in the simply furnished dining room and attractive conservatory; friendly service; cl 25–26 Dec; children over 12.

Knowstone SS8223 MASONS ARMS Knowstone, South Molton EX36 4RY (01398) 341231 £55; 4 rms. Delightfully unspoilt, 13th-c thatched pub with very individual character, relaxed, friendly service, good, homely bar food, restaurant, decent wines and nice garden; pleasant walks nearby; cl Christmas; limited disabled access.

Croyde SS4439 WHITELEAF Croyde, Braunton EX33 1PN (01271) 890266 *£54; 3 rms. Attractively furnished and thoughtfully run, comfortable guesthouse, with the emphasis on really notable food (menu changes each night), and decent wines; close to both village and beach; dogs welcome; cl Dec–Feb, 2 wks May/July/Oct.

Meeth SS5306 GIFFORDS HELE Meeth, Okehampton EX20 3QN (01837) 810009 £52; 3 cosy rms. Traditional, friendly farmhouse on the banks of the River Torridge (own game and trout-fishing), with 175 acres of award-winning conservation land to walk around, walled garden and children's play area; oak beamed bar, log fire, books and games, attractive dining room with good, seasonal food, and fine indoor swimming pool; self-catering cottages.

West Buckland SS6531 HUXTABLE FARM West Buckland, Barnstaple EX32 0SR (01598) 760254 *£44; 6 rms. 16th-c farmhouse surrounded by carefully converted, listed stone buildings, open fields, fine views, sheep, chickens, rabbits and Squeak the Shetland pony; candlelit dinner with wholesome, home-made food using home-grown produce, home-made wine and bread, and a relaxing sitting room; cl Christmas.

Hatherleigh SS5404 TALLY HO Market St, Hatherleigh, Okehampton EX20 3JN (01837) 810306 £40; 3 rms. Friendly and characterful old inn with genuinely old-fashioned fittings, welcoming Italian licensees, lots of Italian food, no-smoking restaurant, and interesting own-brew beers; landlord will arrange fishing; children over 8.

Buckland Brewer SS4220 COACH & HORSES Buckland Brewer, Bideford EX39 5LU (01237) 451395 £36; 2 rms above bar. Welcoming, well preserved, 13th-c thatched village pub with a cosy beamed bar, log fires in inglenook fireplaces, truly home-made, enjoyable food, dining room, and pleasant garden; children over 10; no dogs.

Oakford SS9121 NEWHOUSE FARM Oakford, Tiverton EX16 9JE (0139 85) 347 £36; 3 rms. 17th-c longhouse on the edge of Exmoor National Park and part of a working farm with beef suckler cows and a small flock of friendly sheep;

cottage sitting room, inglenook fireplace, beams, and country dining room serving home-made food inc good bread, pâtés and puddings; cl Christmas; children over 10; no pets; limited disabled access.

Torrington SS4919 BLACK HORSE High St, Torrington EX38 8HB (01805) 22121 *£28; 3 rms. Pretty twin-gabled inn – reputedly the headquarters of General Fairfax in the Civil War – with oak panelling and beams, good-value bar and restaurant food; handy for RHS Rosemoor garden and Dartington crystal.

To see and do

♠★♂✿ Appledore ST0614 has a pretty centre of narrow, cottagey streets off the quayside road which looks out over the Taw estuary, and ship- and boat-building in the yard just upstream. NORTH DEVON MARITIME MUSEUM Good exploration of Devon's maritime history, with a different topic in each room. Shop; cl 1–2pm, am Easter–May bank hol and during Oct, and all Nov–Easter; £1. The Beaver, Royal George and Seagate Hotel, all with lovely views, are useful for food.

♠♂✿ Arlington SS6140 ARLINGTON COURT From its Victorian heyday up to 1949, Rosalie Chichester filled this early 19th-c house with model ships, stuffed birds, holiday souvenirs – in fact anything she could get her hands on; her assemblages have been watered down since then, but you can still see quite a fascinating medley. Covering 3,500 acres, the grounds have attractive landscaped gardens and a number of Shetland ponies and sheep, along with a Victorian garden and conservatory, woodland and lakeside nature trails, and an unusual collection of carriages and other horse-drawn vehicles, with rides available. Meals, snacks, shop, disabled access; cl Sat (exc bank hol wknds), Nov–Easter; £4.60, garden only £2.40; NT. The Old Station House up the A39 at Blackmoor Gate is good for lunch.

✹★ Ashford SS5335 BUTTERFLY HOUSE AND GARDENS Well looked after collection of tropical butterflies, with plenty of plants and birds, and two acres of landscaped gardens outside. Meals, snacks, shop, disabled access; cl Nov–Easter; (01271) 42880; £2, gardens free. The Ring of Bells at Pilton is useful for lunch.

★✿♂🏠 Barnstaple SS5533 This busy town is the main shopping centre for the area; as big new stores have opened outside the centre and as there's now a bypass, the old part has got its second wind. It has a good deal of unforced charm, with many interesting buildings inc an imposing, 18th-c colonnaded arcade on the Great Quay, a lofty Victorian market hall (market days are Tues and Fri), almshouses behind the church, more off the square by the long, old stone bridge, and some interesting shops. It's still a working port, though in a very small way now. The best nearby pub is the Chichester Arms up in Bishop's Tawton. MARWOOD HILL GARDENS (Marwood; off the A361 towards Braunton) 18 well kept and colourful acres inc rare trees and shrubs, small lakes, extensive bog garden, collections of clematis, camellias, alpines and eucalyptus, and national collections of astilbes and tulbachia. Sat teas, shop and plant centre, some disabled access; cl 25 Dec; *£2. The Muddiford Inn is quite handy for lunch. MUSEUM OF NORTH DEVON (The Square) Rapidly expanding centre becoming more interactive all the time, with a new Tarka exhibition concentrating on the local environment. Shop, disabled access to ground floor only; cl Sun and Mon; (01271) 46747; *£1. They also have an exhibition at St Anne's Chapel nearby, which re-creates the 17th-c school that was here. Cl 1–2pm, Sun and Mon, Oct–Mar; 50p. BRANNAMS (Roundswell Industrial Estate) Guided tours of the big pottery (their terracotta pots are indispensable to many gardeners), with a chance to throw your own pot, and a small museum. Meals, snacks, shop, disabled access; no tours most wknds, but shop open Sat; (01271) 43035; £2.75. On Pilston Causeway there's a good SHEEPSKIN SHOP; you can tour the adjacent factory. In summer,

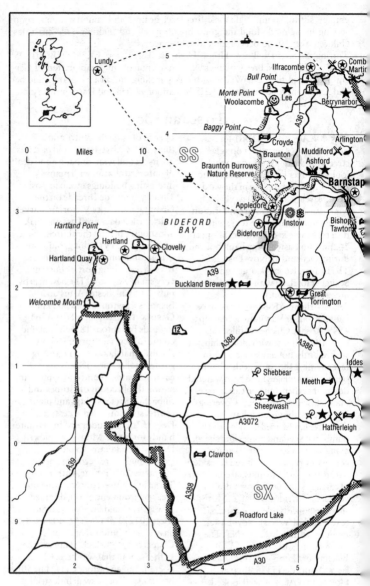

you can generally hire bikes from the main BR station.

🏠✝🎠🚗✕🌳🏚🦽 **Bickleigh** SS9407
BICKLEIGH CASTLE Charming, moated and fortified, manor house, still very much a family home; the 11th-c chapel is said to be Devon's oldest complete building. Also a medieval hall, armoury and guard room, Tudor bedroom, 17th-c farmhouse, museum of 19th-c domestic objects and toys, and exhibitions on maritime history, the Civil War and the man who inspired Ian Fleming's 'Q' character. All done with great enthusiasm, and with plenty to amuse children. Snacks (inc good cream teas), shop, some disabled access; open pm Weds, Sun and bank hols Easter–May, then pm daily to early Oct; (01884) 855363;

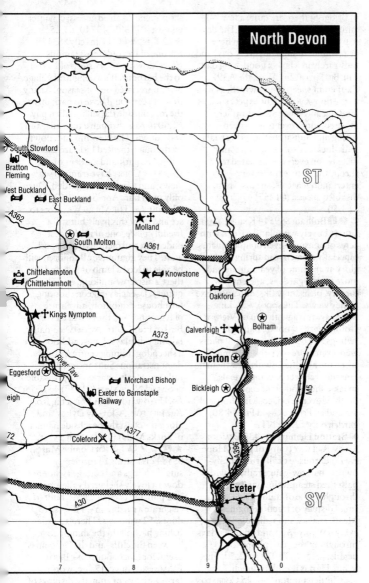

North Devon

South Stowford

Bratton Fleming

West Buckland East Buckland

A362

South Molton A361 Molland

Chittlehampton
Chittlehamholt Knowstone

Oakford

Kings Nympton Calverleigh Bolham

A373

11 Tiverton

Eggesford River Taw

Morchard Bishop Bickleigh

eigh Exeter to Barnstaple
Railway M5

72 A377 A396

Coleford A30

Exeter

A30

7 8 9 0

ST

SY

£3.20. DEVONSHIRE'S CENTRE
Something here to occupy most
people, with a restored working
watermill, unusual breeds, shire
horses, bird area with flamingos and
penguins, agricultural and motor
museums, railway, farm and craft
shops and a notable 'craft' grocer's
shop. Meals, snacks, shops, some
disabled access; cl winter wkdys

Christmas-Easter; £3.50. The pretty
riverside village has two good pubs.
★ ▲ ➤ **Bideford** SS4526 Quiet
hillside town – now bypassed – with a
notable medieval bridge and some
pleasant old streets, partly
pedestrianised, behind the Quay
(where the King's Arms is useful for
lunch). One of the oldest streets is
Bridgeland St, and up towards the top

of Bridge St there are quite a few antique or antiqueish shops. The day-trip boat for Lundy sails from here year round, though not every day, and only rarely in Mar – a good, long day. THE BIG SHEEP (2m W, on the A39) Exuberant sheep centre which, as well as the things you might expect such as lambing and shearing, has rather more eccentric events like sheep-racing and miniature sheepdog trials – with ducks. Also, exhibitions and displays on everything related to sheep, and nature trails; very entertaining. Meals, snacks, shop, disabled access; (01237) 477916; *£3.50.

❀ ❀ 🏛 Bolham SS9514 KNIGHTSHAYES COURT Lovely woodland garden with acres of unusual – even unique – plants, especially attractive in spring but a glory at any time of year; alpine and more formal gardens, ancient yew topiary, pleasant walks, and good Exe Valley views. The spooky-looking house is extravagantly ornate Victorian Gothic, with elaborate painted ceilings and decor. The original plans were even more over-the-top, but when the horrified owner saw them he sent the architect packing. Meals, snacks, shop and plant centre, disabled access; cl Dec–Mar, house cl am and all Fri exc Good Fri; £4.80, garden only £2.80; NT.

🚂 Bratton Fleming SS6437 EXMOOR STEAM RAILWAY (Cape of Good Hope Farm) Enthusiastically run, family-owned, narrow-gauge railway with half-sized steamtrains winding through a mile of countryside, and a small display of traction engines. Meals, snacks, shop, disabled access; every day July–Aug and on other days throughout the year, phone for details; (01598) 710711; £2.50. The White Hart is useful for lunch.

🚗 Chittlehampton SS6325 COBBATON COMBAT COLLECTION Growing private collection of over 50 British and Canadian WWII vehicles, quite tightly packed under cover but looking ready for action; also mock-ups of wartime scenes, weaponry, all sorts of other wartime memorabilia, and play area with a Sherman tank. The owner describes it all as a hobby that got rather out of hand. Summer snacks, shop, some disabled access; cl winter wknds; (01769) 540740; £3.25.

★ ❀ ❀ 🍴 🛤 🏛 Clovelly SS3124 has one of Devon's most famous views, down the very steep old street to the harbour. It's a delightful village, best appreciated out of season. At any time of year you'll have to park up at the top, outside the village, then pay £1.50 to pass through a turnstile, and walk down. The New Inn and, down by the quay, the Red Lion are useful pubs. The parkland gardens of CLOVELLY COURT have tranquil sea views, and a fine walled garden. Open only pm Thurs Apr–Sept; (01237) 431200; £1. THE MILKY WAY Lots to see and do at this lively but still friendly place, one of the biggest undercover attractions in the south west. They guarantee all children will be able to feed a lamb or kid, and there's also cow-milking, a working pottery, laser clay-pigeon shooting, farmhouse exhibition, adventure playground, and the North Devon Bird of Prey Centre, with twice-daily falconry displays. Latest additions are a sheepdog training centre (no demonstrations Sun) and a little railway. Meals, snacks, shop, disabled access; cl Nov–Mar; (01237) 431255; £4. Up towards the A39 is a big Iron Age HILL FORT, Clovelly Dykes, and along the coast the beachside hamlet of Bucks Mills is well worth a visit.

★ 🍴 ☺ ✔ � ! ❀ 🚗 Combe Martin SS5847 is a string of former smallholdings and cottages scattered down a lovely sheltered valley, and an odd pub, the Pack of Cards, built to celebrate a cards win – 4 floors, 13 doors, 52 windows. There's a little fishing harbour in the shingly cove between the cliffs, and the Dolphin is useful for lunch. BODSTONE BARTON FARMWORLD Busy, 17th-c, working farm with lots of animals, displays of old and new agricultural methods, nature trails, a huge adventure playground, tractor and trailer rides, craft displays, and regular special events. Meals, snacks, shop, disabled access; cl Nov–Feb; (01271) 883654; £1.99, small extra charge for some rides. COMBE MARTIN WILDLIFE AND DINOSAUR PARK Good range of animals and birds in over 20 acres of woodland, inc a pair of rare snow leopards and meerkats in a huge desert enclosure. Also meticulously researched, life-size dinosaurs, some of which move and roar – like the 25-ft-high Tyrannosaurus Rex. The gardens have rare and tropical plants. Meals, snacks, shop, disabled access; cl mid-Nov–mid-Mar; (01271) 882486; £4.95. COMBE MARTIN MOTORCYCLE COLLECTION Growing collection of British bikes displayed against old petrol pumps, signs, garage equipment and other motoring nostalgia. Shop, disabled access; cl Oct–May; (01271) 882346; *£2.

† ❀ ✿ **Eggesford** SS6811 is a quiet Taw Valley village with a 14th-c CHURCH, and a garden centre prettily set in the walled garden of a ruined house; refreshments on a terrace with lovely views. The Lymington Arms at Wembworthy is good for lunch.

🏛 ♠ ❀ ♪ **Hartland** SS2624 has HARTLAND ABBEY, a fine old house on the site of an Augustinian abbey, with fine rooms (the drawing room is modelled on the House of Lords), an exhibition of old photography, and woodland walks in the peacock-filled parkland. Snacks, shop; open pm Weds May–Sept, plus Sun July and Aug, and bank hol Mon and Sun from Easter; (01237) 441264; £3, grounds only £1.50. Also in the village, CRAFT SHOPS inc a working pottery and a Windsor-chair-maker (children's sizes too).

❀ ✗ ♨ **Hartland Quay** SS2224 Grand, isolated spot at the foot of a toll road, on a jagged coast which looks like a dramatic cross between illustrations for geology textbooks and ones for a shipwreckers' manual. On the way down, detour to DOCTON MILL, an interestingly planted, largely naturalised, extensive, sheltered streamside garden by an ancient, restored watermill. Snacks; cl Nov–Feb; (01237) 441369; £1.50. They have a couple of bedrooms you can stay in. Down by the sea is a useful inn, and the MUSEUM covers four centuries of shipwrecks – even big ships still go down here – as well as smuggling, trade and natural history. Shop; cl Oct–late May bank hol (exc Easter); (01288) 331353 *50p. Just S at Spekes Mill Mouth, the sea-eroded

valley leaves the river dangling down the cliff in a SEASIDE WATERFALL.

★ ♪ **Hatherleigh** SS5404 is an attractive hillside village – even the church slopes – with fine inns (the Tally Ho, brewing its own beer, and the George) and a good craft POTTERY (20 Market St).

† ♠ 🏛 ❀ ♨ ✗ 🎒 ☺ ! **Ilfracombe** SS5147 has a busy harbour sheltered by high cliffs, with terraces of late Victorian boarding houses and small hotels looking out over it from their perches among the trees of the steep bay. There are period resort buildings and gardens, and even tunnels cut through the rock to a former Victorian bathing place. The 14th-c chapel above the harbour mouth has doubled as a lighthouse for over 450 years; the LIFEBOAT STATION can be visited (donation requested). HOLY TRINITY CHURCH (Church St) is worth a look for its richly carved, 15th-c waggon-roof, one of the most striking in the area. The Coach House (Bicclescombe Park Rd) and Royal Britannia (harbour) are good for lunch. In summer, the paddle steamer *Waverley* or the traditional cruise ship *Balmoral* run cruises from the pier to Lundy, Minehead, and other places – even as far as Swansea. There are day trips to Lundy in summer.

CHAMBERCOMBE MANOR, in a lovely secluded valley just SE, is one of the country's oldest houses, dating from 1066, with eight rooms (one haunted) furnished in period style – from Elizabethan to Victorian. Grisly stories on the guided tour, 11th-c private chapel, gardens and wildfowl ponds and a new natural history museum. Snacks; cl am Sun, all Sat, and Oct–Easter; £3. The Thatched Inn is handy from here. HELE MILL Early 16th-c mill still producing wheatflakes and four grades of wholemeal flour. Shop; cl am Sun, Sat, and Nov–Easter; £1.60. Not far away Bicclescombe Park has a restored 18th-c CORN MILL. WATERMOUTH CASTLE (A339, E) Billed as 'Devon's Happy Castle', this is a fine 19th-c structure overlooking the bay, transformed into a world of gnomes, goblins, trolls and fairy tales, with slides, carousels and a musical water show. Very much a place for families, with young children probably the ones who'll enjoy it most. Meals, snacks, shop, disabled access; cl Sat, plus Fri and poss other times out of main season, and all Nov–Mar – best to check first; (01271) 867474; £4.85. ROLLING FALLS MODEL VILLAGE is an astonishingly realistic scale replica of nearby Clovelly, especially interesting at night. Disabled access; cl Sat, all Oct-Mar; (01271) 864579; *£2.

❀ ❀ **Instow** SS4730 at the mouth of the Torridge estuary has an expanse of tidal sands, with dozens of moored boats stranded on them at low tide. The waterside Quay is useful for lunch. TAPELEY PARK The Italianate garden with rococo features and walled kitchen garden is probably the main draw, though as well as the house there's a pets' corner, play area, and woodland walk. The British Jousting Centre is based here too, and may have demonstrations. Good views down to the sea. Teas and snacks in period dairy, shop, disabled access; cl Sat, and Oct–Easter; (01271) 860528; £3.50 wkdys, £4 Sun, £4.50 bank hols.

🜂 **Muddiford** SS5638 has a working TROUT FARM, good for experts and beginners, with a little pool where you're practically guaranteed a bite; (01271) 44533; 85p.

🜂 **Roadford Lake** SX4291 is a new reservoir, carefully landscaped and recently opened – a peaceful place populated only by brown trout; cl Nov–Mar; £12.50 for a day's permit.

🜀 **Shebbear** SS4409 is a quiet village, notable if you're passing for its odd Devil's Stone by the green; also a working wood-fired POTTERY.

★ 🜀 **Sheepwash** SS4806 is another nice village with cob and thatch houses around the green; the Half Moon is good for lunch. A mile N in Duckpool Cottage, a traditional wood-fired POTTERY.

★ 🐄🖤🍷🏠 **South Molton** SS7125 This country town has an attractive central square and imposing church, and its farming roots show in the Thurs cattle market. The Old Coaching Inn is a comfortable place for lunch. QUINCE HONEY FARM (North Rd) The biggest wild bee farm in the world, with specially designed tunnels between observatories to avoid disturbing the little workers, and observation hives looking right into the centre of their colonies. Snacks, shop with lots of honey and their own beeswax skin and hair care products; cl Nov–Easter (though shop stays open); (01769) 572401; £2.90. The 18th-c Guildhall has a very well displayed local history MUSEUM, and monthly art and craft shows. Shop, disabled access; cl 1–2, pm Weds and Sat, all Fri and Sun and Dec–Feb; free. 3m SW at Clapworthy Mill, HANCOCK'S DEVON CIDER have an exhibition and film showing how they produce their scrumpy. It's a nice spot for a picnic. Snacks, shop; cl 1–2, all Sun, Nov–Easter (but shop open all year); (01769) 572678; £1.75.

🜂🐦❀❀ **South Stowford** SS6541 (off the B3226, N of Bratton Fleming – where the White Hart is handy for lunch) EXMOOR ANIMAL & BIRD GARDENS Good-sized collection of weird and wonderful creatures, most of which breed successfully throughout the year; well landscaped grounds with good views. Feeding time is 3.30. Also an assault course for children. Snacks, shop, disabled access; cl 25 Dec; (015983) 352; £3.

🏰✝🐰🖤🍷🐄🔔 **Tiverton** SS9512 CASTLE Built in 1106 as a royal fortress dominating the River Exe, this handsome place still has its Norman tower and gatehouse, as well as an interesting clock collection and one of the best assemblages of Civil War armour and arms. You can stay in apartments right in the oldest parts of the building. Shop, disabled access; cl am, Fri, Sat, and Oct–Easter (exc by arrangement); (01884) 253200; £3. The nearby ST PETER'S CHURCH is magnificently decorated with rich carving, and there are other grand buildings (inc the Jacobean council offices) in this once prosperous wool town, well worth walking around. A former 19th-c school has a local history MUSEUM with two waterwheels and an excellent railway gallery. Shop, disabled access to ground floor only; cl Sun, Christmas–early Feb; (01884) 256295; *£1. TIVERTON CRAFT CENTRE Four showrooms with the work of over 170 local craftsmen – inc pottery, jewellery, glass, paintings, prints and spinning. Limited disabled access; cl Sun and first 2 wks in Jan; (01884) 258430; free. HIGHFIELD VINEYARDS (Longdrag Hill) Tours of working vineyard with free tastings; shop; cl Sun, 25 Dec–Feb. In summer, there are HORSE-DRAWN BOAT TRIPS along the attractively restored canal from the wharf. Snacks, shop, disabled access (with prior notice); cl Oct–Easter, booking advisable (01884) 253345; £5.65. They do motorboat trips too.

🏠✝☀🐾🏠⚓ **Torrington** SS4919 is a quiet, dairy-farming town on a ridge above the River Torridge, with some attractive buildings inc 14th-c Taddiport Chapel (for a former leper colony), the imposing Palmer House, and a rather grand church built to replace the original blown up in the Civil War. There are good views from the neatly mown hill above the river, and other nearby strolls on the preserved commons surrounding the town. The Black Horse is useful for lunch. RHS Garden ROSEMOOR (off the B3220, just S) A wonderful place, created by Lady Anne Berry and now being developed by the Royal Horticultural Society as a national garden. Marvellous collection of rare trees, shrubs, and other plants in a charmingly landscaped, sheltered woodland setting, rose, stream and bog gardens, foliage and plantsman's garden and a new fruit and vegetable garden. Meals, snacks, shop and garden centre, disabled access; gardens cl 25 Dec, visitor and plant centre and all facilities cl Jan and Feb; (01805) 624067; £2.50. DARTINGTON CRYSTAL Tours of factory, safely showing the craftsmen at work, a permanent exhibition on glass and crystal, well priced goblets and decanters on sale. Meals, snacks, shop, disabled access (prior arrangement); visitor centre/factory cl Sat out of season, and Sun exc July and Aug; £2.20. Another worthwhile garden near here is THE DOWNES (A386 towards Bideford, nr Monkleigh): fine, big, woodland garden with interesting flowering trees and shrubs and lovely

landscaped lawns. Wknd teas, plant sales; cl Oct–Mar, though Jun–Sept is by appointment only; (01805) 622244; £1. You can stay in a self-contained wing of the Georgian house. ☺ **Woolacombe** SS4543 beach is particularly nice, and its Atlantic breakers now draw quite a few surfers. The Mill at Ossaborough is pleasant for lunch. ONCE UPON A TIME Run by the same people as Watermouth Castle at Ilfracombe, this is a super place for children, with lots of rides and other activities; there's a children's driving school which even offers tests. Meals, snacks, shop, disabled access; cl Sat, all Nov–Mar; (01271) 867474; *£2.25 (£4 children).

🚂 The ordinary British Rail EXETER–BARNSTAPLE line (known as the Tarka line), mostly tracking along closer to the River Taw than the road does, is one of the finest of all for scenery.

★ **Other attractive small villages** with decent pubs include Berrynarbor SS5646, Buckland Brewer SS4220, Calverleigh SS9214 (good church), Iddesleigh SS5708, King's Nympton SS6819 (another fine church), Molland SS8028 (yet another), Knowstone SS8223, Lee SS4846 (by the sea) and Winkleigh SS6308.

⚓ The day trip to **Lundy** by boat from Bideford or, in summer, Ilfracombe is difficult to fit into a short stay in Devon, but is well worth considering if you're there for any longer. It's famous for the migrant birds that come here in spring and autumn, but the remoteness and loneliness could also be a powerful draw. Lovely walks along its 7 miles of formidably high cliffs and windswept rough pastures; small church, evocative castle ruins, two lighthouses (one the highest in Britain), freely wandering goats, small Soay sheep and ponies; also, the chance of seeing seals (especially in autumn), the introduced small sika deer – and, of course, puffins. Accommodation can be arranged through the Landmark Trust (01628) 825925. The Marisco Tavern is a good place to eat, at any time of the day. The return boat trip (about 2¼ hours each way) is about £21; (01237) 423365 for sailing times.

Walks

Good spots for wild coast walks include the cliff walks around **Welcombe Mouth** SS2117 △-1 (rather a rough drive down; the prettily set Old Smithy in Welcombe is a good stop); those around **Hartland Quay** SS2224 △-2 and on both sides of Hartland Point SS2326 (toll gates to both); the woods, cliffs and clifftop farmland **W of Clovelly** △-3, reached from the village or from the NT's isolated farmhouses at The Brownshams SS2826; the cliffs between **Ilfracombe** SS5147 **and Lee Bay** △-4 (the Grampus up the sheltered wooded valley in the pretty village of Lee SS4846 is a useful stop); and **Bull Point** SS4646 △-5 and Morte Point SS4545 (the Ship Aground by the church in Mortehoe is a useful start). Baggy Point SS4240, reached from Croyde SS4439 (where the Thatched Barn is a pleasant family pub), has a path good enough for wheelchairs.

Other fine coastal walks include the vast expanse of great swelling dunes at the **Braunton Burrows** Nature Reserve SS4535 △-6 reached from the B3231, W of Braunton (red flags warn if there's shooting on the range here; the Mariner's Arms, in South St, Braunton, is a useful, pleasantly untouristy pub); the dunes, sand slacks and meres behind the pebble ridge at **Northam Burrows** SS4430 △-7, with the Atlantic rollers swinging in along the rock-strewn Saunton Sands beyond – deserted out of season, but popular with families in summer; and the great surfy beach at **Woolacombe** SS4543 △-8, a fine place out of season when the resort has shut down.

The **Tarka Trail** △-9 (see Exmoor section) includes sections on disused railways from Barnstaple SS5533 and Bideford SS4526, which can be walked or cycled (local bicycle hire £5 a day, more for mountain bikes). The best section is the one from Barnstaple through Instow SS4730 and Bideford up to Great Torrington. In autumn and winter particularly, it gives close views of the wading birds massed on the tidal sands of the estuary, and year-round the section up to Great Torrington is very attractive.

The **Old Railway** △-10, above Ilfracombe, is another popular disused railway trail, with a tunnel, interesting plants, and attractive scenery inc the lakes of Slade Reservoirs SS5045. For a one-way walk it's best to do it in reverse – better views – and it's downhill all the way; Red Bus 31 or Filers 303 up from the town to Lee Bridge or Lee Cross (or to the Fortescue Hotel for a preliminary bracer).

Eggesford SS6811 △-11 is a good base for inland walks (and a stop on the Barnstaple–Exeter rail line): in Flashdown Wood, up wooded Hayne Valley to Wembworthy (the Odd Wheel is a decent family pub), or through Heywood Wood, where the mound of the former castle gives good views (and there are picnic-table sets).

Bradworthy SS3214 △-12 is another recommended jumping-off point, with some quiet local strolls on the common, or over by Lake Tamar, a couple of miles SW.

Driving

The A361 North Devon link road from the M5 makes getting into this area much more tolerable than it used to be. Moreover, it has taken enough pressure off several other roads here to make them enjoyable as routes for pleasure drives (eg the old B3221, see below).

The A377 along the Taw Valley has pretty views of this twisty wooded valley, but is not a quick road. The B3217, southwards off it, through High Bickington, Dolton and Monkokehampton is a good, rolling, old coach road. Another of these is the B3220 from Great Torrington through Beaford and Winkleigh. Yet another is the former B3221, now declassified, from South Molton through Ash Mill, Rackenford (with Devon's oldest pub, and a craftsman cabinet-maker at Woodpeckers) and Calverleigh to Tiverton. From all these, the views are of rather reserved rolling farmland. For something wilder,

try the moorland road, NW from Stibb Cross on the A388, to Woolfardis-
worthy and on towards Clovelly.

There are impressive sea views from the B3231 looping through Croyde, W
of Braunton, and more scenically from the back road between Woolacombe
and Mortehoe; the A399 has good views out to sea E of Ilfracombe. The best
coast drive is the Hobby Drive, a toll-road track through the Clovelly woods
below the A39.

Where to eat

Combe Martin SS5847 JUST JOHNSONS King St (01271) 883568 Pleasantly
decorated evening restaurant with good food, friendly service and relaxing
atmosphere; cl Sun/Mon. £20.
Coleford SS7701 NEW INN (01363) 84242 Comfortable thatched inn, six centuries old, with good and often unusual food, fine wines, and an attractive garden
with stream; recently refurbished bedrooms; cl 25–26 Dec. £18.50|£1.95/£4.65.
Hatherleigh SS5404 GEORGE (01837) 810454 Pleasant old pub with huge
beams, vast fireplaces and thick stone walls, decent bar food, well kept beers,
and helpful service. £2/£6.50.
Iddesleigh SS5708 DUKE OF YORK (01837) 810253 Thatched, mainly 14th-c
pub with homely country furnishings and good food. £1.75/£5.

EXMOOR

Outstanding scenery, particularly on the coast.

The moor and especially its steep and interesting coast has excellent
walking – by no means a second-best to Dartmoor in that respect, and
with the virtue of having fewer people around in summer. Where it
drops away sharply to the sea, fast streams and rivers cut deeply into
wooded valleys which can be of outstanding beauty. The moor itself
has in some places been more tamed than Dartmoor, in that it's been
drained and resown with richer-growing grasses for better pasture.
But it's still a wild place, with hawthorns and low oak trees bent and
gnarled by the winds, and (unlike Dartmoor) wild deer.

It is above all the scenery which is the lure here: among the handful
of places to visit, Selworthy, Lynmouth, Allerford (with its farm
park), Winsford, Exford and Dulverton are the pick.

Though part of Exmoor lies in Somerset, we've covered the whole
of the moor area in this chapter (some places, such as Dunster within
the boundary of the National Park but outside the moor itself, are
described in the West Somerset section).

Where to stay

Dulverton SS9127 ASHWICK COUNTRY HOUSE, Dulverton TA22 9QD (01398)
23868 £118 inc dinner; 6 quiet and thoughtfully decorated rms. Small Edwardian
country house in 6 peaceful acres of sweeping lawns, watergardens, and mature
trees; galleried entrance hall warmed by a log fire, comfortable lounge, very good,
careful cooking using fresh local produce, and excellent service; children over 8.
Heddons Mouth SS6549 HEDDONS GATE Heddons Mouth, Parracombe, Barnstaple EX31 4PZ (0159 83) 313 £110 inc dinner; 14 comfortable rms named

for their original use and many with views. Victorian country house hotel in interesting large gardens on the edge of Exmoor, with a marvellously relaxed and friendly atmosphere; Edwardian sitting room with lovely views, pleasant library/Victorian morning room, an attractive dining room, very good home cooking inc 6-course dinners and proper afternoon tea, and helpful service; cl Nov–Easter; children over 10; disabled access.

Countisbury SS7449 Exmoor Sandpiper Countisbury, Lynton EX35 6NE (0159 87) 263 *£90; 16 comfortable rms. Big, low white inn opposite a moorland church, with low-beamed, dimly lit rooms set out for eating; decent food, friendly service, and good nearby walks.

Exford SS8538 White Horse Exford, Minehead TA24 7PY (0164 383) 229 *£90; 19 comfortable rms. Three-storey, Exmoor village inn, with country-kitchen furnishings in an open-plan bar, log fire, good value bar food, real ales, and friendly, efficient staff; disabled access.

Lynton SS7149 Hewitt's The Hoe, North Walk, Lynton EX35 6HJ (01598) 52293 £90; 10 rms. You can walk for miles through this friendly Victorian hotel's wooded 27 acres and on down to the sea, and the formal terraced gardens are being gradually restored; comfortable rooms with fine oak panelling and stained glass, antiques, log fires, and good food in the no-smoking candlelit restaurant; children by arrangement.

Lynmouth SS7249 Rising Sun Mars Hill, Lynmouth EX35 6EQ (01598) 53223 *£79; 16 comfortable and cosy rms. Historic, thatched 14th-c inn with lovely views over the little harbour and out to sea; an oak-panelled dining room, a beamed and panelled bar with uneven oak floors, good food and wines, charming terraced garden, and lots of nearby walks; children over 5.

Dulverton SS9127 Tarr Steps, Dulverton TA22 9PY (0164 385) 293 *£76; 13 rms, 11 with own bthrm. Former Georgian rectory in 8 acres of slightly wild gardens and surrounded by 500 acres of land with rough shooting and trout-filled river, riding, clay-pigeon shooting on Sun mornings; relaxed atmosphere, comfortable sitting room with a log fire, and good food and wines; cl Feb, first 2 wks Mar; well behaved dogs welcome; disabled access.

Lynton SS7149 Lynton Cottage North Walk, Lynton EX35 6ED (01598) 52342 £74; 17 well equipped, comfortable rms, many with sea view. Relaxed and homely, family-run hotel with fine views down over the sea and countryside; a friendly small bar, comfortable lounges with big windows, and good food in the attractive restaurant; cl Jan; children over 10.

Exebridge SS9244 Anchor Exebridge, Dulverton TA22 9AZ (01398) 23433 £60; 7 attractive rms. Peaceful place with a river running past the inn's sheltered lawn; a companionable bar with individually chosen pieces of furniture and warm, woodburning stove, comfortable residents' lounge, a country restaurant, good, simple bar food inc vegetarian dishes, and a decent children's menu.

Withypool SS8435 Westerclose Country House Withypool, Minehead TA24 7QR (0164 383) 302 £58; 10 rms. Family-run, 1920s hunting lodge in 9 acres of gardens and paddocks, with moorland views; comfortable lounges, a relaxed atmosphere, and good food using local produce; cl Jan–Feb; dogs welcome.

Porlock SS8846 West Porlock House Porlock, Minehead, Somerset TA24 8NX (01643) 862880 *£48; 4 rms. Nicely proportioned former manor house in its own gardens and grounds; very good food (evening meals only served at wknds), spacious and carefully furnished rooms, and kind, personal service; no smoking (except in one lounge); cl Dec; children over 10.

Porlock SS8846 Ship Porlock, Minehead TA24 8QT (01643) 862507 £39; 11 rms. 13th-c village inn close to the sea and moor, with a characterful, low-beamed front bar, traditional old benches on the tiled and flagstoned floor, log fires, a candlelit dining room, and simple, popular food; dogs welcome; disabled access.

Dulverton SS9127 Highercombe, Dulverton TA22 9PT (01398) 23451 £38; 3 rms. Imposing country house in 8 acres of fine mature gardens and close to open moorland; with a big lounge, open fire, and fine views; may do evening meals; self-catering also.

Selworthy SS9346 HINDON FARM Selworthy, Minehead TA24 8SH (01643) 705244 *£36; 3 rms, some with own bthrm. Relaxed and friendly working farm with sheep, pigs, calves, goats and horses (you can help if you want to), lots of lovely walks around the farm or further afield, and a large lawn with stream and ducks; attractive sitting room and dining room, log fires, fine breakfasts, and a games barn with snooker, table tennis, darts and fancy dress; can arrange riding or bring your own horse; dogs welcome; self-catering wing also; cl Nov–Feb.

To see and do

There are rather fewer places to visit in this area – the main attraction is the scenery, and there are some lovely little towns and villages worth a look.

★ 🐄 🦃 🐕 🐎 **Allerford** SS9047 is a pretty, stonebuilt village with a lovely packhorse bridge. BOSSINGTON FARM PARK Formerly the Somerset Farm Park, with rare breeds, working heavy horses, baby animals for children to fuss over, and a new birds of prey centre. The Saxon manor house has an exhibition of horse-drawn trade vehicles. Snacks, small shop, some disabled access; cl Sun and Nov–Feb; (01643) 862816; *£2.50. In the village is an enthusiastic, little local history MUSEUM with a reconstructed schoolroom and summer craft demonstrations. Cl Sun, and mid-Oct–Easter; free. The Victory is very popular for lunch.

★ **Dulverton** SS9127, the main town for Exmoor, is a civilised place with a handsome old stone market house and a fine bridge over the river which has cut this steeply wooded valley. The Lion Hotel is useful for lunch.

★ ✝ **Exford** SS8538 is prettily set in a sheltered valley by a small streamside green; the church up the hill a bit is well worth a look. The White Horse is good for lunch, and the staghound kennels are here.

★ ☕ 🦆 **Lynton** SS7149 and its harbourside extension, Lynmouth, down at the bottom of the cliff railway track, is a delightfully situated steep village, tucked into the wooded seaside gorge where the East and West Lyn tumble down to the sea. Lynton itself, the main settlement, clearly shows its origins as a Victorian resort in what was then known as Little Switzerland, with hillside villas now quiet boarding houses, photogenic corners and some older cottages. There are pretty cottages down by the little tidal harbour itself, also craft

shops and so forth. In the old part of the upper village, the LYN AND EXMOOR MUSEUM is in an 18th-c cottage with its kitchen restored to authenticity, and amongst its displays has a scale model of the former Lynton–Barnstaple narrow-gauge railway (you can still walk much of its track bed). Shop; cl 12.30–2pm, Sat, am Sun, Nov–Easter; 70p. GLEN LYN GORGE has been restored after the Lynmouth flood of 1952, with walks and an exhibition on water power. Exhibition cl Nov–Easter, gorge may be closed in bad weather; (01598) 53207; £2. It has decent holiday flats in a peaceful setting. The VALLEY OF ROCKS (see **Walks** section below) is an easy, free walk from the village. WATERSMEET HOUSE (1½ miles E) The 19th-c fishing lodge itself is not particularly remarkable (though it has interesting local wildlife displays), but the estate that surrounds it really is attractive – a perfectly relaxing wooded valley, with the house at the meeting point of the rivers. Just right for an afternoon's pottering, though some of the walks can be steep. Meals, snacks, shop, disabled access by appointment only; cl Nov–Mar; (01598) 53348; free; NT. The Crown, Royal Castle and Olde Cottage Hotel are useful for lunch, and the Rising Sun down by the harbour is good.

♱ **Malmsmead** SS7947 The Exmoor Natural History Society run leisurely strolls through the striking scenery around their NATURAL CENTRE every summer Weds at 2.30pm; Jan Ridd brought his bride Lorna around here in *Lorna Doone*. The Exmoor Sandpiper at Countisbury up towards Lynton is useful for lunch.

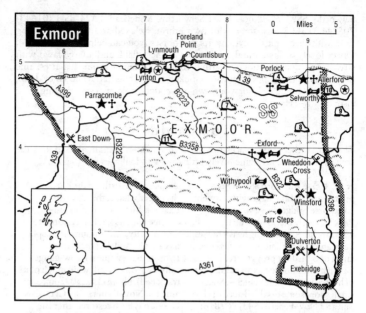

★ † Parracombe SS6644 is a lovely little village worth visiting in its own right, but particularly interesting is ST PETROC'S CHURCH, one of the few churches to have a completely unspoilt medieval fabric with a Georgian interior; cl Nov–Easter but key available from custodian. There's also a scale model of the old Lynton–Barnstaple railway here. The Fox & Goose is useful for lunch.

† Porlock SS8846 has a lot of traffic, but some attractive cottages with distinctive lighthouse-like chimneys and thatched roofs (one is the Ship, good pub); nearby the much quieter harbour of Porlock Weir SS8647 is tucked below the wooded cliffs – long walks along the coast, or through the woods up to the tiny and quite isolated CULBONE CHURCH.

★ † Selworthy SS9246 is a glorious, unspoilt village – rated by a number of our contributors as the most attractive they've ever seen – with groups of white thatched cottages around a prettily planted hillside green looking out over Exmoor, and trees behind. The CHURCH is a gem, with a fine waggon-ceiling with roof bosses.

★ Winsford SS9034 is a quiet and attractive village below high hills, with the River Exe lacing through its countless bridges. The Royal Oak is good for lunch.

Walks

The coast is an enticing mix of upland, plunging wooded river valleys and wild clifftops – ideal for super-varied walks. The cream of it is around **Lynton** SS7149 and **Lynmouth** SS7249 △-1. To the E, paths run along the Lyn River to Watersmeet SS7448, where the Farley Waters tumble down to meet the East Lyn in a series of rocky cascades among steeply picturesque oak woods (there's a discreet NT refreshment pavilion here). There's another scenic path high above the same valley along its S side, and riverside paths head on further upstream, to the prettily set Rockford Inn SS7547 and beyond. Just N of Watersmeet, the Foreland Cliffs SS7551 are the highest in the country – a good walk with dramatic views.

W from Lynton, the **Valley of Rocks** SS7049 △-2 is a great valley bowl, with steep crags and pinnacles of rock dividing it from the sea (and a dreadful unscreened car park smack in the middle). It's reached by an easy coastal path, or by paths over Hollerday Hill SS7149 (wooded, but opens out dramatically on top). Further W are some rugged, moorland hills by the sea, with secretive wooded combes: **Heddons Mouth Cleave** SS6549 △-3 (there's a good walk down from the beautifully placed Hunter's Inn SS6548, W of Martinhoe), and the terraced walkway known as the Ladies Mile SS6448 which runs along a charming valley nr Trentishoe. Heading W from **Porlock Weir** SS8647 △-4 along the shore at the foot of the wooded cliffs, even the most avid pebble-hunter would find all he wanted.

The peaceful countryside of inland Exmoor is perhaps best appreciated from along paths by the rivers. A notable stretch is to be found along the **River Exe** △-5 between Exford SS8538 and Winsford SS9034. The River Barle's most famous feature is the **Tarr Steps** SS8632 △-6, the finest of all the stone and slab clapper bridges for packhorses; the path along the river, which runs between Simonsbath SS7739 and Dulverton SS9127, is uneven and surprisingly slow-going in places. **Badgworthy Water** SS7944 △-7 can be taken in by a path from Malmsmead SS7947, getting into the heart of *Lorna Doone* country – it gets wilder and more remote with every step southwards (the surrounding moors provide a handful of return routes).

Exmoor's great ridge walk is **Dunkery Hill** △-8, with Dunkery Beacon SS8941 as its high point surveying a huge chunk of south-west England and south Wales. It is easily walked from the nearby road; a splendid place to leave the car is Webbers Post SS9043 (which is also good for local pottering). It can also be incorporated into longer walks from Horner Woods SS8944 or Luccombe SS9144. Less well known but also recommended is **Grabbist Hill** SS9844 △-9, which can be climbed from nearby Dunster SS9943. Above Selworthy SS9246, there are walks with excellent views on **Selworthy Beacon** SS9148 △-10.

The Tarka Trail, not yet complete, will eventually run to nearly 200 miles linking Exmoor, Dartmoor and the north Devon coast, following the route of Henry Williamson's *Tarka the Otter* – and is most enjoyable with a copy of the book. One beautiful section in this area is the route around **Pinkworthy Pond** SS7242 △-11 and The Chains SS7342, reached from the car park a couple of miles along the B3358 E of Challacombe (where the Black Venus is good). Others are around Watersmeet and along the coastal path westwards – see above.

Note that some of Exmoor's moorland paths have a disconcerting habit of fizzling out without warning.

Driving

The B roads and the minor roads up over Exmoor (for instance, the one running due N from Exford, or the Yarde Down road out of Simonsbath) all have good views, and except at peak holiday times are usually pretty empty. Some smaller roads particularly worth exploring include the toll roads W of Lynton; the narrow back road on the Exmoor bank of the East Lyn, through Brendon, Malmsmead and Oare; and the road from Wheddon Cross N to Luccombe, over Dunkery Hill (this route is not so good in reverse). Even the main A39 has some outstanding views (and some very steep hills).

Where to eat

Dulverton SS9225 Carnarvon Arms Brushford (01398) 23302 Good bar and restaurant food, and friendly staff in this comfortable sporting hotel with its own stabling, fishing and shooting; bedrooms; disabled access. **£32.06**|£1.35/£4.

Winsford SS9034 ROYAL OAK (0164 385) 455 Prettily placed thatched inn with cosy bars, log fire, and a wide choice of often very good bar and restaurant food; bedrooms. **£22.50|£3/£5.95**.

East Down SS5941 PYNE ARMS (01271) 850207 Popular pub near Arlington Court with interesting old rooms, very decent bar food and reasonable wines; cl 25 Dec; no children; disabled access. **£17|£2/£5.50**.

Wheddon Cross SS9238 REST & BE THANKFUL (01643) 841222 Helpful staff and varied bar food in this comfortably modern, three-room bar, with two log fires and an aquarium; also a restaurant and children's room (though, if staying, must be over 11); disabled access. **£15|£2.75/£5.25**.

Help this year from: B M Eldridge, David Burnett, Donna Lowes, Mr and Mrs M Clifford, John Fazakerley, J Radley, B and K Hypher, C A Williams, J L Jones, S R and A J Ashcroft, Michael and Harriet Robinson, Hugh and Peggy Holman, M V and J Melling, Mr and Mrs J Brown, Harry and Irene Fisher, David Eberlin, Gordon, Michael Butler, Mr and Mrs A K McCully, D Cox, Bill Sharpe, David Lewis, D B Delany, George Atkinson, Tim Brierly, Steve Goodchild, A Plumb, Canon and Mrs M A Bourdeaux, Frank Cummins, A Cull, Nigel and Lindsay Chapman, Mary Reed, A Craig, Rowly Pitcher, Mr and Mrs R Head, Robert and Gladys Flux, Tim and Chris Ford, Mrs J Horsthuis, Nigel and Teresa Brooks, Ted George, John Sanders, Joan and Gordon Edwards, Mayur Shah, J R Williams, Steve Dark, E B Davies, Alan and Brenda Holyer, P R Ferris, Dr and Mrs R E S Tanner, David Holloway, John Wilson, Mr and Mrs David Lee, Pat and John Millward, Howard and Margaret Buchanan, Joy Heatherley, John Wilkinson, Alan and Heather Jacques, Tim and Lynne Crawford, Heather and Howard Parry, June and Tony Baldwin, Dave Braisted, Sue Demont, Tim Barrow, Peter and Audrey Dowsett, Jane Palmer.

DEVON CALENDAR

Some of these dates were provisional as we went to press.

JANUARY

1 **Exeter** Chinese Dinosaurs Exhibition at the Royal Albert Memorial Museum – *till 25 Feb* (01392) 265858

APRIL

7 **Lynton** Jazz Weekend at the Town Hall (01271) 72064 – *till Sun 9*

21 **Newton Abbot** Maltings Beer Festival at Tuckers Maltings (one of the best festivals in the country at Britain's only traditional working malthouse) – *till Sun 23* (01626) 334734

29 **Torquay** Spring Exhibition of the Devon Art Society at Torre Abbey – *till 14 May* (01803) 298797

30 **Clyst St Mary** Toy and Train Collectors Fair at the Westpoint Showground (01392) 444777; **Exeter** Greenfingers Garden Fair at the Royal Livestock Centre (01342) 842345

MAY

1 **Blackawton** Worm Charming (01803) 834224

4 **Great Torrington** May Fair (01805) 622441

6 **Great Torrington** Carnival (01805) 622441

8 **Uffculme** Sheep Show at Coldharbour Mill Working Wool Museum (01884) 840960

11 **Holsworthy** Agricultural Show (01237) 477676

13 **Tiverton** Festival – *till Sun 21* (01884) 257222

18 **Clyst St Mary** Devon County Show at Westpoint Showground – *till Sat 20* (01392) 444777; **Paignton** Festival of Arts and Culture – *till Sun 21* (01803) 296296

19 **Plymouth** Lord Mayor's Day Parade (01752) 668000

22 **Torbay** Festival of Arts and Culture: a celebration of mystery and crime fiction inc film, theatre and murder weekends – *till Sat 27* (01803) 296296

26 **Combe Martin** Hunting of the Earl of Rone, inc a procession during which an effigy of the earl is seated facing backwards on a donkey and then thrown into the sea – *till Mon 29* (01271) 883319

27 **Brixham** Festival of Arts and Culture – *till 4 Jun* (01803) 296296; **Budleigh Salterton** Gala Week – *till 3 Jun*; **Torquay** English Riviera Dance Festival – *till 10 Jun* (01895) 632143

29 **Bickleigh** Street Market (01884) 255480; **Stockland** Country Fair (01404) 881447

JUNE

3 **Clyst St Mary** Devon County Dog Show at Westpoint Showground – *till Sun 4* (01392) 444777; **Crediton** Boniface Festival – *till Weds 14* (01363) 776011; **Crediton** Flower Festival – *till Thurs 8* (01363) 772334

4 **Dawlish** Arts Festival – *till Fri 23* (01626) 865709

7 **Sidmouth** Arts Festival – *till Weds 21* (01395) 516441

10 **Ilfracombe** Victorian Week – *till Sun 18* (01271) 862419

DEVON CALENDAR

JUNE cont

17 **Brixham** International Trawler Race and Quay Festival at New Fish Quay (01803) 882325; **Lynton** Lyn and Exmoor Festival – *till Sun 25* (01271) 76365; **Saltram** Summer Plant Fair at Saltram House (01752) 336546; **Yeoford** Fun Day (01363) 84814

24 **Cullompton** Festival – *till 2 July* (01884) 35522; **Dartmouth** Carnival – *till 1 July* (01803) 834224; **Ottery St Mary** Pixie Day; **Yelverton** Summer Craft Fair at Buckland Abbey – *till Sun 25* (01822) 853607

25 **Holsworthy** Vintage Car Rally (01237) 477676

30 **Exeter** Festival, Best of British – *till 16 July* (01392) 265200

JULY

1 **Kenton** Powderham Horse Trials at Powderham Castle – *till Sun 2* (01626) 890243; **Torbay** Championship Swim (01803) 328616

2 **Ilfracombe** National Youth Arts Festival – *till Fri 7* (01271) 862419

8 **Kenton** Open Air Concert and Historic Vehicle Gathering at Powderham Castle – *till Sun 9* (01626) 890243; **Plymouth** South-West Inter-Federation Philatelic Exhibition at the Guildhall (01398) 331731

12 **Holsworthy** St Peters Fayre (01237) 477676

15 **Yealmpton** Wild West Week at the National Shire Horse Centre – *till Sun 23* (01752) 880268

21 **Yelverton** Jazz in the Great Barn at Buckland Abbey – *till Sat 22* (01822) 612792

22 **Dartington** International Summer School – *till 26 Aug* (01803) 865988; **Tiverton** Mid-Devon Show (01363) 83166

23 **Dartmouth** Town Week – *till Sun 30* (01803) 834224

25 **Holsworthy** Vintage Car Rally (01237) 477676

26 **Lifton** Milford Steam and Vintage Rally at Milford Farm – *till Thurs 27* (01566) 772333

27 **Berry Pomeroy** Totnes and District Show (01803) 863168

29 **Leeford** Country Fair; **Marldon** Apple Pie Fair

31 **Salcombe** Town Regatta – *till 5 Aug* (01548) 843927; **Woolsery** and District Agricultural Show at Thomery Farm (01409) 241273

AUGUST

2 **Landkey** North Devon Show at Plym's Farm (01769) 60205

3 **Honiton** Agricultural Show at the Showground (01404) 891763; **Poughill** Revel and Cuckoo Fayre (01288) 354240

4 **Sidmouth** International Festival of Folk Arts – *till 11 Aug* (01296) 393293

5 **Paignton** Regatta – *till Sun 13* (01803) 550452

10 **Okehampton** Agricultural Show

12 **Yealmpton** Steam and Vintage Rally at the National Shire Horse Centre – *till Sun 13* (01752) 880268

13 **Dawlish** Carnival Week – *till Sat 19* (01626) 864499

DEVON CALENDAR

AUGUST cont

14 **Torbay** Royal Regatta – *till Fri 18* (01803) 299772

19 **Torquay** Summer Exhibition of the Devon Art Society at Torre Abbey – *till 3 Sept* (01803) 298797

24 **Dartmouth** Royal Regatta – *till Sat 26* (01803) 832435

26 **Kenton** West Country Flower Show at Powderham Castle – *till Mon 28* (01626) 890243; **Plymouth** Navy Days at HM Naval Base – *till Mon 28* (01752) 555914; **Yealmpton** Medieval Field of Combat at the National Shire Horse Centre – *till Mon 28* (01752) 880268

28 **Brixham** Fish Market Open Day (01803) 859123; **Dartington** Literature Festival at Dartington Hall Gardens – *till 4 Sept* (01803) 867311

27 **Honiton** Hill Rally: steam engines, veteran cars, main ring parades and demonstrations, fire engines, military and commercial vehicles – *till Mon 28* (01404) 41115

SEPTEMBER

Plymouth 375th Anniversary of the Sailing of the *Mayflower* (01752) 261125

2 **Ilsington** Sheepdog Trials at Halshanger Manor (01364) 661243

3 **Tiverton to Thorverton** Exe River Struggle Raft Race (01884) 234332; **Yealmpton** Classic Car Show at the National Shire Horse Centre (01752) 880268

9 **Bideford** Regatta and Carnival (01237) 474559

12 **Widecombe-in-the-Moor** Fair with traditional games at the Old Field (0136 43) 368

14 **Torquay** Flower Festival at Central Church *till Sun 17* (01803) 328588

16 **Tiverton** Carnival (01884) 234332

20 **Barnstaple** Ancient Chartered Fair *till Sat 23* (01271) 73311

OCTOBER

1 **Buckfastleigh to Totnes** River Dart Raft Race (01803) 863168

7 **Dartmouth** Fishing Festival *till Mon 9* (01803) 834224

14 **Exeter** Carnival – grand illuminated procession

26 **Bampton** Fair (01884) 234332

29 **Clyst St Mary** Toy and Train Collectors Fair at Westpoint Showground (01392) 444777

NOVEMBER

4 **Ottery St Mary** Rolling of the Tar Barrels (01404) 812252

5 **Shebbear** Turning the Devil's Boulder: said to be one of the oldest annual events in Britain. In the evening, the church bell rings and the villagers turn the boulder

18 **Kingsbridge** Extravaganza and Illuminated Carnival (01548) 853195

28 **Ashburton** Court-Leet and Baron at St Lawrence Chapel where the borough court has met for 600 years

DORSET

West Dorset has a very wide appeal, its largely quiet coast backed by a varied hinterland, with secluded valleys, narrow lanes threading through peaceful farmland and tucked-away villages, and some splendid high viewpoints. There are plenty of interesting places to visit in this area, and a good choice of attractive places to stay. Bournemouth is a thoroughly civilised, sedate resort.

BOURNEMOUTH AND EAST DORSET

Well kept resort area, miles of sandy beaches.

The Bournemouth conurbation, stretching for miles along good beaches, dominates the area, with a lot to do and look at – particularly in and around Poole. Away from Poole's busy waterfront, the conurbation is comfortable – civilised and spacious rather than lively. There is an enormous choice of places to stay, from big resort hotels to quiet guesthouses tucked away in the extensive leafy suburbs (we include a very selective shortlist).

Inland, Wimborne Minster has the most interesting places to visit, and there are several other worthwhile attractions in the vicinity – enough, certainly, to fill a weekend. This part of Dorset does not have the county's best scenery, and though there are some pleasant places for a stroll there is little to satisfy the keen walker. We have been surprised to find such a scarcity of really recommendable places to eat at here.

Where to stay

Poole SZ0190 HAVEN Sandbanks, Poole BH13 7QL (01202) 707333 £120; 97 attractive rms, most with fine views. Neatly kept hotel at the entrance to the harbour looking across the water to the Purbeck Hills, Brownsea Island or the Isle of Wight; spacious and comfortable public areas, comprehensive leisure centre with indoor and outdoor swimming pools, private sandy beach, and imaginative food in the two restaurants; disabled access.

Poole SZ0190 MANSION HOUSE Thames St, Poole BH15 1JN (01202) 685666 *£80; 28 cosy rms. Civilised old merchant's townhouse close to the waterfront, with a lovely sweeping staircase, antiques in the elegant residents' lounge, cosy cocktail bar, good food in the attractive restaurant, and courteous, old-fashioned service.

Bournemouth SZ0991 LANGTRY MANOR 26 Derby Rd, Eastcliff, Bournemouth BH1 3QB (01202) 553887 £79; 25 rms, some in the lodge. Built by Edward VII for Lillie Langtry, with lots of memorabilia, relaxed public rooms, and good food inc Edwardian dinner every Sat evening; children over 7; disabled access.

Horton SU0307 NORTHILL HOUSE Horton, Wimborne BH21 7HL (01258) 840407 *£65; 9 comfortable, neatly kept rms. Family-run, 19th-c former farmhouse in 2-acre grounds, with log fires in the lounge and small bar, good English cooking in the attractive conservatory, lovely breakfasts, and helpful, courteous service; good nearby walking; cl 20 Dec–15 Feb; children over 8; good provision for the disabled.

Winton SZ1696 Fishermans Haunt Salisbury Rd, Winkton, Christchurch BH23 7AS (01202) 477283 *£61; 20 comfortable rms, most with own bthrm. Much extended and modernised former fishing inn, with decent food in the riverside restaurant as well as the spacious series of interestingly furnished bar rooms; cl 25 Dec; disabled access.

Farnham ST9515 Museum Farnham, Blandford Forum DT11 8DE (01725) 516261 £60; 4 rms in converted stables. Traditional, civilised, Cromwellian country inn in an attractive thatch and stone village; inglenook fireplace and classical music in the lounge bar, conservatory, decent food inc excellent breakfasts, and a sheltered terrace and garden; cl 25 Dec; disabled access.

Poole SZ0590 Inn in the Park Pinewood Rd, Branksome Chine, Poole BH13 6JS (01202) 761318 *£45; 5 comfortable rms. Small hotel with lots of pine in the residents' area, an attractive dining room, decent small bar, good-value bar food, tables on the sunny terrace, and nice, steep walks down to the sea.

Bournemouth SZ0991 Silver Trees 57 Wimborne Rd BH3 7AL (01202) 556040 *£42; 5 rms. Attractive Victorian house with a pretty dining room looking over the neatly kept wooded gardens, cosy lounge, and helpful owners; children over 5.

Cranborne SU0513 Fleur-de-Lys Cranborne, Wimborne BH21 5PP (01725) 517282 £42; 8 rms, 1 without bthrm. Nicely placed, old creeper-clad pub in *Tess of the d'Urbervilles* country, close to the New Forest; with an attractively modernised oak-panelled lounge bar, simply furnished, beamed public bar, and decent bar food; cl 24–26 Dec.

To see and do

Bournemouth SZ0991 Neatly kept streamside gardens in the centre, a pier that's one of the few to look as fresh as when it was built, long promenades below the low cliff, miles of sandy beach (note dogs aren't allowed in summer); things like a good local orchestra raise the tone well above the usual seaside resort average.

All this, with the mild climate, has made the town expansively popular both as a civilised place to retire to and as a centre for regular development. So behind the resort area is a big, busy town surrounded by suburbs, with tall modern buildings and monumental traffic schemes. But down by the sea you're well insulated from all of that. And the western residential suburbs of Westbourne and particularly Branksome Park (the Inn in the Park, Pinewood Rd, is a good stop here) are quiet, with pinetree valleys winding down to the sea. Besides our single **Where to eat** entry in this section, Botlers Crab & Ale House (Old Christchurch Rd) is useful.

! Dinosaur Safari (Expocentre, Old Christchurch Lane) A family favourite, full of computerised displays, fossils and bones comparing the prehistoric beasts to more familiar mammals, with a daunting-sounding section devoted to building your own dinosaur. Shop; cl 24–26 Dec; (01202) 293544; £3.50. Two other exhibitions in the same building offer a similar mix of fun and education: Mummies and Magic looks at the subject of mummification, and Bournemouth Bears is a new display taking in teddies of all ages, shapes and sizes, with a lively and well presented history of how the little furry creatures have developed over the last century; times and prices as above.

♨ Russell-Cotes Art Gallery and Museum (East Cliff) Good collections of 17th-c to 20th-c paintings, ceramics and furnishings. Snacks, shop, disabled access; cl Mon, 25–26 Dec, Good Fri; (01202) 551009; £1 wkdys, wknds free.

♨ Shelley Rooms (Boscombe Manor) Small museum devoted to the life and work of the poet, especially the last part of his life, with displays of other romantic literature. Cl am, all Mon, 25–26 Dec, Good Fri; (0202) 303571; free.

✈ There may be DC-3 Dakota nostalgia flights in the summer from the airport; check with the tourist information, (01202) 789789.

Poole SZ0190 merges indistinguishably into Bournemouth on the edges, but in its centre is wholly distinct, with a more lively feel, especially around The Quay (where the Portsmouth Hoy is handy for lunch). The broad natural harbour is still busy with the comings and goings of boats and small ships (several decent pubs to watch them from); launch ferries around the harbour, and out to Brownsea Island, tel (01202) 666226. The Custom House is a fine sight, and there are a good many other interesting old buildings along here; the streets behind, some pedestrianised, are well worth strolling through. The harbour view changed dramatically in 1993, when the twin towers of Hamworthy power station were demolished. The Old Harry (High St) is useful for lunch.

🏮🏺🐗🍴🐴🐄🛠️⛵ GUILDHALL (Market St) Fine Georgian building, now a modest local museum; the nearby pub named after it has good, fresh fish. WATERFRONT MUSEUM (High St) Decent local history museum, unusually housed in the medieval town cellars as well as in a later 18th-c mill; sections on smuggling, Scouts and sailing, a reconstructed Victorian street, and changing temporary exhibitions. Teas, shop, disabled access; (01202) 683138; cl 25–26 Dec, 1 Jan, Good Fri. Prices vary according to the time of year, from £2.50 in high season to £1.50 in winter, and include entry to next-door SCAPLEN'S COURT, a well restored medieval merchant's home showing domestic life through the ages (though you can buy a separate ticket for this, from around £1). There's now a craft gallery upstairs. POOLE POTTERY (The Quay) has been producing its distinctive china here since 1873. Good tours of the factory (with Walkman commentary), museum and a film; you can have a go at throwing and decorating your own pot – or, if it all gets too much for you, smash up a few plates. Restaurant with harbour views (open in evening too), shop, disabled access; cl 12.30–1.30, 25 Dec, poss some winter wknds; (01202) 666200; £1.95. STEAMDAYS (Hennings Wharf, The Quay) is a railway museum with an enormous OO gauge model railway, as well as smuggling and space exhibitions, and displays of other models inc boats. Meals, snacks, shop; cl 24–25 Dec; *£2. There's an aquarium in the same building, with snakes as well as fish.

At Sandbanks, by the harbour mouth, there's a chain ferry across to the Studland side (and in summer lots of people waiting for it). 🌺❀ COMPTON ACRES GARDENS (Canford Cliffs) SZ0689 For many people this is Poole's outstanding attraction, with lovely statuary among fine plants landscaped in an eclectic variety of styles – the Japanese garden seems very authentic, and indeed we're told it's the only one of its type in Europe. Good views of the hills and Poole harbour. Meals, snacks (a decent creperie), shop and plant sales, disabled access; cl Nov–Feb; (01202) 700778; £3.70. ⚓🦢❀🌸⛵ **Brownsea Island** SZ0187 is an unspoilt 500-acre island in the middle of the huge natural harbour, most famous perhaps as the site of the first Scout camp in 1907. Lots of birds (inc peacocks), animals and butterflies in heath and woodland, large heronry, nature reserve, and fine views back towards the coast from the beaches. It's a really splendid place to explore. From mid-July to mid-Aug they usually have open-air Shakespeare or opera. Frequent ferries from Poole – though don't forget to check the time of the last one back. Snacks, shop, disabled access; cl Oct–Mar; £2.20; NT.

Christchurch SZ1593 at the opposite end of the Bournemouth complex has attractive Georgian brick buildings in its old centre, a restored watermill, and a quay looking out over the yachting harbour – busy in summer. Hengistbury Head, overlooking the harbour and reached from the Bournemouth side, is a popular place for strollers, with traces of an Iron Age hill fort. On the other

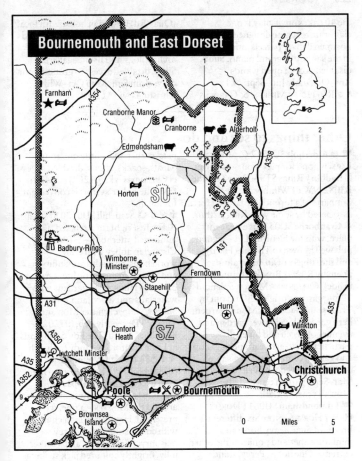

Bournemouth and East Dorset

Farnham
Cranborne Manor
Cranborne
Alderholt
Edmondsham
Horton
SU
Badbury Rings
Wimborne Minster
Ferndown
Stapehill
A31
Hurn
A35
Canford Heath
Winkton
SZ
Lytchett Minster
Christchurch
Poole
Bournemouth
Brownsea Island

0   Miles   5

side of the harbour mouth, long beaches stretch way into Hampshire from the vast Mudeford car park (the Haven House by the sea here is well worth knowing for its unrivalled position, and the Sandpiper is a useful modern, seaside pub); pleasant walking out of season.

✝ ♿ ✳ PRIORY This magnificent, medieval monastic church recently celebrated its 900th anniversary. At well over 300 ft it's the longest parish church in the country, and well repays a good look, interesting outside and very striking inside, with remarkable carving. The 'Miraculous Beam' apparently only fitted in the roof thanks to divine assistance, so prompting the renaming of the borough to Christchurch (it used to be called Twynham). Shop, disabled access; cl 25 Dec exc for services. The church has a little museum open in the summer (cl 12.30–2.30; 50p) and good views from the tower (50p) – though with 176 steps you have to earn them.

🏰 All that remains of the CASTLE is a ruined keep, and the ruins of the NORMAN HOUSE, probably used by the castle constable. It's quite well preserved, with one of the earliest chimneys constructed in this country, and an ancient dung heap by a millstream; free.

♿ TRICYCLE MUSEUM (Quay Rd) Fun little museum of tricycles from Victorian times to the present. Among the 40 trikes on display is one elaborate machine designed to help postmen deliver parcels, and another in the shape of a grand piano. Shop, disabled access; open wknds Apr–Oct, daily Jun–Sept; *£1.

♿ ❀ RED HOUSE MUSEUM & GARDENS

(Quay Rd) Georgian house with local history displays, dolls, costumes and herb garden, as well as new archaeology and fishing galleries. Shop, disabled access to ground floor only; cl am Sun, Mon Oct–Whit, Christmas wk; *£1.

Other things to see and do

🐖 🦆 **Alderholt** SU1212 CRANBORNE FARM is good for pick-your-own fruit. 🏛 **Badbury Rings** ST9602, just off the B3082 NW of Wimborne, are the ramparts of a formidable late hill fort, associated by some with King Arthur. ❀ **Cranborne** SU0513 is a peaceful place, with the Fleur-de-Lys – a good pub well known to Thomas Hardy and the subject of an entertaining poem by Rupert Brooke (framed inside). CRANBORNE MANOR Splendid 17th-c gardens originally laid out by Tradescant; Jacobean Mount garden, herb garden, lovely river garden and avenues of beech and lime; all particularly attractive in spring. Shop and garden centre, limited disabled access; gardens open Weds only Mar–Sept, garden centre daily exc Mon all year; *£2.50.

🐖 **Edmondsham** SU0611 DORSET HEAVY HORSE CENTRE Six different breeds of huge heavy horse and miniature Shetland ponies at the other extreme. One horse, Percy, stands over 19 hands and is a dedicated beer drinker. Snacks, shop, disabled access; cl Mon and Sat Nov–Easter; (01202) 824040; *£3.50, maybe less out of season. The Albion is handy for lunch.

! ❀ 🐖 🦆 **Hurn** SZ1296 ALICE IN WONDERLAND MAZE Maze made up of 5,200 bushes cleverly cut into the shape of Alice characters; also play areas, croquet lawns, herb gardens, farmyard with rare breeds, and pick-your-own fields with berries, beans, potatoes, courgettes and sweetcorn. Snacks, shop; cl Nov–Easter; (01202) 483444; *£2.50. The Avon Causeway is useful for lunch.

🌺 🐎 **Lytchett Minster** SY9593 THE COURTYARD CENTRE (Cottage Farm, Huntick Rd) has a good range of country arts and crafts, along with a

pets' corner and a little museum. Meals, snacks, shops, disabled access; cl Christmas wk; (01202) 623423; free. The Baker's Arms is convenient for lunch.

✝ 🌺 ❀ 🦆 **Stapehill** SU0500 STAPEHILL ABBEY Just right for a relaxed, unhurried afternoon – a 19th-c Cistercian abbey with craft workshops, agriculture exhibition and lessons in monastic life; acres of park and landscaped gardens with waterfalls and woodland walk. Snacks, shop; cl winter Mon and Tues, 23 Dec–early Feb; (01202) 861686; *£4.50. The Fox & Hounds at Little Canford is handy for lunch.

★ ✝ ♿ 🏛 ❀ ✗ 🦆 🏰 **Wimborne Minster** SZ0199 has Georgian houses (and decent antique shops and auctions) in the narrow central streets around the MINSTER – a fine, well preserved, largely Norman church with contrasting red and grey masonry, twin towers, and a rather jolly, brightly coloured jack striking the clock bell every quarter. Interesting things inside include the Norman crypt, a distinctive astronomical clock and the original chained library. Shop, disabled access. Close by is the PRIEST'S HOUSE MUSEUM (High St), an interesting, historic townhouse with a good range of local history in carefully researched period rooms; regular cooking displays in the Victorian kitchen, and a charming walled garden. Summer teas, shop, disabled access to ground floor only; cl Sun exc pm Jun–Sept, Nov–Mar exc 2 wks after Christmas – ring for details; (01202) 882533; £1.50. Dormers (Hanham Rd) and the White Hart (Corn Market) are handy for lunch.

KINGSTON LACY HOUSE, GARDEN & PARK Impressive mansion just W of town, built in the 17th c, then remodelled by Charles Barry in the 19th. Grand Italian marble staircase, superb Venetian ceiling, and outstanding paintings such as the *Judgment of Solomon* by Sebastiano del Piamtino, with others by Titian, Rubens and van Dyck. The enormous grounds have landscaped gardens, and summer concerts and plays. Meals, snacks, shop, disabled access to park and gardens; cl Thurs and Fri and Nov–Mar; £5.20, £2.10 grounds only; NT. KNOLL GARDENS (Stapehill Rd) Rare and exotic collection of plants in various colourfully themed gardens, with well over 4,000 different named species. Meals, snacks, shop and garden centre, disabled access; cl Nov–Feb; (01202) 870842; *£3.45. WALFORD MILL (Stone Lane) Former 18th-c flour mill with exhibitions and lots of local hand-made crafts. Meals, snacks, shop, disabled access; cl Mon Christmas–Mar; free. MERLEY HOUSE & MODEL MUSEUM Fine 18th-c mansion with interesting plaster ceilings and an excellent collection of 5,000 toys inc model cars, aeroplanes, and working model railways. Snacks, shop, disabled access; cl Oct–Easter (except Sun and half-term in Oct); (01202) 886533; £1.65. MERLEY BIRD GARDENS Historic walled gardens with a collection of exotic birds, shrubs and watergardens. Snacks, shop, disabled access; cl 25 Dec; (01202) 883790; £3. Just W of town, at Pamphill, is a good, big farm shop.

Some places to see **snowdrops**, usually at their best in Feb and the first week of Mar, include Kingston Lacy ST9701 (see above, under (**Wimborne Minister** entry) and Wimbourne St Giles SU0312, by the fine church and almshouses, just off the B3078, S. The prehistoric Knowlton Circles SU0209, with a ruined medieval church, is a nice spot nearby.

★ Farnham ST9515 is an **attractive village** with a decent pub.

Walks

This is not generally a good area for the sort of walking that gets your appetite up. Bournemouth SZ0991 is, of course, just a very short drive from the New Forest – see Hampshire chapter. Closer, by far the best place for a stroll is **Hengistbury Head** SZ1790 ⌂-1: not a long walk, but the feeling of space and views are outstanding. From the hill fort of **Badbury Rings** ST9602 ⌂-2, a Roman road lets you strike out for miles northwards. There are pleasant country walks around the Fox & Hounds at Little Canford SZ0499.

Driving

In the hinterland, the B3078 up to Cranborne and, crossing it, the minor road from Three Legged Cross to the Gussages give a good taste of the countryside. Traffic in the Bournemouth conurbation is well managed, but as elsewhere in big urban areas strangers will find the flow a bit baffling and daunting at first. The foolproof way into the centre is the A338.

Where to eat

Bournemouth SZ0991 SOPHISTICATS 43 Charminster Rd (01202) 291019 Consistently good and enjoyable food in a popular restaurant decorated with a cat theme; good-value wines and delicious puddings; cl Sun, 2 wks Feb, 2 wks Nov; disabled access. £27.

DORSET COAST

Grand scenery, a couple of elegant, old seaside towns, charming, small villages, and good places to stay.

There are some very civilised places to stay here, serving fine food, as well as good-value, simpler establishments. This area has the best walking in the county, chiefly along the coast, with some marvellous views; you have to go right down to Cornwall to find anything as good on England's south coast. Outside the traditional resorts which do have the sorts of attractions you'd expect of them (Weymouth has the most to offer for a short stay), the area doesn't abound in places to visit. We'd pick as its most rewarding the gardens and swannery at Abbotsbury, and Corfe Castle. Lulworth Castle has just opened: quite interesting. There are plenty of pretty villages.

The most striking countryside is on the Isle of Purbeck, a mixture of rugged coast with quieter farmland, and attractive villages nestling into folds in the hills. North of the hills, towards Poole Harbour and Studland Bay, the heathland, partly planted with conifers, is a popular roaming ground for nature lovers. West of Weymouth, a pleasantly busy mix of port and resort, there's the tremendous sweep of the Chesil Beach, its pebbles and boulders immaculately graded by millennia of storms: this is emphatically *not* for swimming from – the undertow will suck you straight down. The long lagoon behind is peaceful and of interest to birdwatchers. Lyme Regis is a charming period resort, with high downs inland between here and Bridport.

The flatter heathland west of Wareham has been tank training ground for decades, and is generally not nearly so interesting.

Where to stay

Wareham SU9287 PRIORY Church Green, Wareham BH20 4ND (01929) 551666 £90; 19 very comfortable rms – the best being in the converted boathouse. Beautifully converted medieval buildings set in 4 acres of carefully kept riverside gardens; two elegant lounges furnished with antiques (pianist on Sat evening), delicious English cooking served in the converted abbot's cellar, and genuinely welcoming service.

Corfe Castle SY9681 MORTONS HOUSE Corfe Castle, Wareham BH20 5EE (01929) 480988 *£80; 17 rms. Elizabethan manor house with a comfortable, oak-panelled drawing room, winter log fire and fresh flowers, and an attractive restaurant with very good food and fine wines; pretty walled gardens overlooking the thatched cottages of this lovely village.

West Bexington SY5387 MANOR West Bexington, Dorchester DT2 9DF (01308) 897616 *£78; 13 rms with sherry and decent tea. Handsome and civilised, old stone hotel mentioned in the Domesday Book, and in a pleasant, quiet setting overlooking Chesil Beach; relaxed and informal atmosphere, a comfortable lounge, popular, pubby cellar bar, log fires, good bar food, excellent restaurant food, and friendly service; cl pm 25 Dec.

Osmington Mills SY7381 SMUGGLERS Osmington Mills, Weymouth DT3 6HF (01305) 833125 £55; 6 rms. Best out of season, this much-extended, thatched stone pub – prettily set just above the sea – has cosy corners, log fires, appropriate woodwork and nautical decorations, good-value bar food, and a partly no-smoking restaurant.

Abbotsbury SY5785 ILCHESTER ARMS Abbotsbury, Weymouth DT3 4JR (01305) 871243 £50; 10 comfortable rms – the back ones have sea views. Handsome, old stone inn close to the abbey with famous swannery; rambling beamed bar decorated with hundreds of swan pictures, log fire, breakfasts served in the attractive, no-smoking conservatory, a restaurant, and pleasant staff; plenty of coastal and country walks.

East Knighton SY8185 COUNTRYMAN East Knighton, Dorchester DT2 8LL (01305) 852666 £45; 6 rms. Attractively converted pair of old cottages, with open fires and plenty of character in the main bar, a no-smoking family room, generous food in the carvery restaurant, and courteous staff.

West Lulworth SY8280 CASTLE West Lulworth, Wareham BH20 5RN (01929) 41311 *£41; 14 smallish rms, 12 with own bthrm. Bustling thatched pub nr Lulworth Cove, with good food in both the bar and dining room, a lively flag-stoned bar and quieter, more modern lounge; also, an award-winning garden (Morris dancers in summer); good walking country; disabled access.

Corfe Castle SY9681 KNITSON OLD FARMHOUSE Corfe Castle, Wareham BH20 5JB (01929) 422836 £34; 3 rms. Big, ancient cottage on a working farm with Jersey cows and sheep, and a large garden with hens, pigs and 3 horses; com-fortable sitting room with flagstones and a wood-burning stove, good, evening food (Fri–Mon only), using home-reared pork and lamb and served in the spa-cious kitchen; no smoking; cl Nov–Jan.

To see and do

★ ✦ ♤ ❀ ✝ ♏ ♖ ♩ **Abbotsbury**
SY5785 is a delightful Dorset village with many interesting places to visit, the most famous being the unique SWANNERY, founded by Benedictine monks 600 years ago and still home to the only sizeable colony of swans in the world that can be seen during nesting time; the swan families quite happily come right up to visitors, and during the cygnet season (end of May–Jun) you might see some of the hundreds of eggs hatching right next to you. One day this July, they'll be having their biennial round-up, a sort of swan census when scientists check all the birds' tags, health and weight; an interesting spectacle. Also, the country's oldest working duck decoy, children's activities, and interesting reed-bed walks. Snacks, shop, good disabled access; (01305) 871684; cl Nov–Easter; £3.50. SUBTROPICAL GARDENS 20 acres of beautiful woodland with the very mild coastal climate allowing rare and record-breaking plants and trees to flourish; the central walled garden in spring is a mass of azaleas, camellias and rhododendrons. Also a woodland trail, aviary and play area. Snacks, shop and plant centre, some disabled

access; cl 25–26 Dec; (01305) 871387; £3.50 summer, less in winter. The 14th-c hilltop CHAPEL (not always open), with a bare earth floor, belonged to the abbey, of which there are a few medieval fragments around the church. The abbey also owned the huge, medieval, thatched TITHE BARN, now a country museum with a good show of rural life; craft fairs and dovecot. Disabled access; cl winter exc Sun; (01305) 871817; £2. The village (in the news not so long ago thanks to a local artist's statue of a naked man) also has an OYSTER FARM (cl am winter), and the Ilchester Arms is good for lunch. This is the best place for access to Chesil Beach (see **Walks** section, below).
♖ **Arne** SY9788 WORLD OF TOYS (Arne House) Growing private collection of toys and musical boxes. Snacks, shop, disabled access; cl am (exc July and Aug), Sat and Mon (exc bank hols and Aug), all Oct–Mar; (01929) 552018; £1.95. The little village is relatively undiscovered, with a quiet beach and nature trail. The Half Way, on the A351 at Norden Heath, does good Greek and other food.
♖ ⌂ **Bovington Camp** SY8388 TANK MUSEUM Great fun, even if military

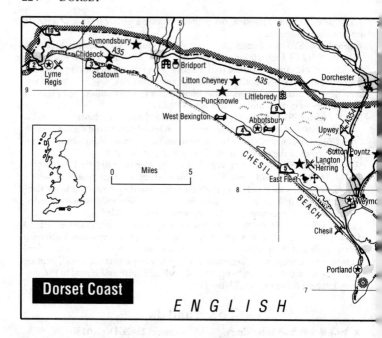

Dorset Coast

ENGLISH

museums don't normally appeal. Over 260 armoured fighting vehicles from 23 countries, some of which you can go inside, as well as tank simulators, costumes, medals, weapons, videos, and special displays, going right up to the Gulf War. Meals, snacks, shop, disabled access; cl 10 days at Christmas; (01929) 403463; £5. CLOUDS HILL Lawrence of Arabia's cottage while he was a private in the tank corps here; his sleeping bag, furniture and other memorabilia can be seen in the three ascetic little rooms on display. Cl am, Mon (exc bank hols), Tues, Sat, and all Nov–Mar; *£2.20; NT. The Countryman at East Knighton is quite handy for lunch. ♿🏭 **Bridport** SY4692 is still the country's main producer of rope, and its old harbour is now the busy fishing port of nearby West Bay, a restrained small resort (where the West Bay Hotel has good local seafood). The old town centre has an interesting local history MUSEUM in a fine Tudor building. Shop; (01308) 22116; cl am Sun, plus Mon, Tues, Thurs and Fri Nov–Mar; *70p. By arrangement they'll open up the CHANTRY, a medieval priest's house with many

original features. The HARBOUR MUSEUM, just S of town, is also worth a look, with rope and net-making displays. Disabled access; cl Oct–Mar; 50p. The George Hotel is a friendly place for lunch.

★ 🏰 ❀ ! 🏵 ♿ **Corfe Castle** SY9681 The CASTLE is the most spectacular ruin in the area, with superb views from its dramatic hilltop position – and itself immeasurably enhancing the outlook from the surrounding countryside. The site is remarkably atmospheric considering how little of the castle is left, and it's great fun clambering over the ancient stones. Meals, snacks, shop; cl wkdys Nov–Jan; £2.90; NT. If you then wonder what the Norman castle looked like before Parliament destroyed it in 1646, the CORFE CASTLE MODEL VILLAGE has a faithful reconstruction set in attractive gardens. Cl Nov–Easter; (01929) 481234; *£1.50. A Tudor building nearby has a decent local history MUSEUM, with dinosaur footprints. Disabled access; cl wkdys Nov–Mar exc some school hols; free. Parking can be a problem in the town in summer. The Greyhound and Fox are

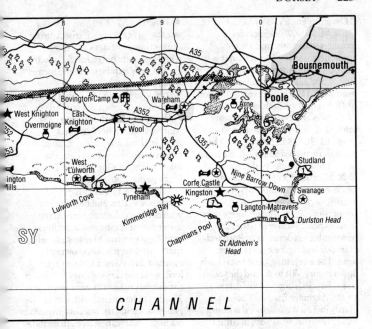

both good old pubs; the Greyhound at Norden Heath (A351 towards Wareham), also decent, may be quieter in summer.

† ⌁ **East Fleet** SY6380 nr Chickerell is interesting, particularly for the former church which was wrecked by a legendary 1824 storm. Swans nest on the nearby Fleet lagoon and can be seen free, and there are pleasant walks in the vicinity. Specially interesting if you've read J M Faulkner's *Moonfleet*. The Elm Tree at Langton Herring is handy for lunch.

Kimmeridge Bay SY9079 has intriguing rock strata, and is a lovely spot – kept quieter than it might be by the toll. The New Inn up at Church Knowle is good for lunch.

⌁ **Langton Matravers** SY9978 The COACH HOUSE MUSEUM looks at the Purbeck stone industry, with an audio-visual show. Cl 12–2pm, all Sun, and Nov–Mar; *60p.

✤ **Littlebredy** SY5889 Bridehead's LAKESIDE GROUNDS, below the church (public path alongside), are lovely – like Stourhead in miniature. The Coach & Horses at Winterbourne Abbas is quite a handy food stop, with an excellent children's play area.

★ ! ⌁ ⌁ **Lyme Regis** SY3492 is an enchanting old seaside town, with rather an elegant, steep main street and interesting side streets; the esplanade is pretty, and there's a lively little fishing and yacht harbour (which masqueraded uncredited as an Isles of Scilly port in the recent TV adaptation of Mary Wesley's *Harnessing Peacocks*). Pleasant coast and valley walks. The Pilot Boat on the front is the best place for lunch; the Royal Standard pub has a lighted terrace leading to the beach. DINOSAURLAND Plenty to entertain and educate children here; there's an excellent collection of fossils, and they do fossil walks along the beach. Snacks, shop, disabled access to ground floor only; cl winter wkdys exc school hols; (01297) 443541; £2.90, guided beach walks £3.50. Right on the historic harbour wall (making nearby parking tricky) is a decent, family-run MARINE AQUARIUM, its inmates constantly changing as local fishermen find different things on the shore or in the sea; cl Nov–Easter; (01297) 443678; £1.10. They also run entertaining scenic BOAT TRIPS around the coast; £3 an hour.

♨ Owermoigne SY7685 MILL HOUSE
CIDER MUSEUM Working cider
museum with 18th- and 19th-c
equipment (during Oct–Dec harvest
season), a video demonstrating how it
works, and sales of the cider
produced. They also have a collection
of 18th- and 19th-c clocks. Cl
Christmas and New Year, no cider
sales 12–3 Sun (thanks to licensing
laws); (01305) 852220; £1.75. The
beautifully placed Sailor's Return at
East Chaldon is good value for lunch.
❀ ⛴ ♨ Portland SY6870 This odd,
much-quarried promontory, with its
narrow neck and long naval
connections, gives tremendous views
from its peak. Nearer at hand, the
remarkable sea defences of Portland
Harbour laid out below are a fine
sight. The interesting CASTLE was built
under Henry VIII to defend the south
coast. Snacks, shop; cl Nov–Mar;
£1.80. A cottage used by Thomas
Hardy in *The Well-Beloved* is now a
local history MUSEUM with maritime
displays. Shop, limited disabled access;
cl 1–1.30pm, Mon Sept–Easter; £1.20.
The Pulpit (handy for a stroll to the
lighthouse and cliffs) and Cove House
(just by the beginning of Chesil Beach)
are useful for lunch.
🐴 ❀ ✌ ❀ Swanage SZ0278 is a fairly
quiet 19th-c resort. SWANAGE RAILWAY
Six-mile steamtrain rides and an
exhibition of old railway memorabilia
include wartime troop and evacuee
trains. Snacks, shop, disabled access;
cl winter wkdys exc school hols;
(01929) 424276 for train times; £4.
DURLSTON COUNTRY PARK 260 acres of
spectacular clifftop scenery and
unspoilt countryside; good spots to
watch seabirds, butterflies or deer,
traditional farming – or pleasant just
for walking. Snacks, shop, good
disabled access (they have a little
buggy for bumpy ground);
information centre cl wkdys
Nov–Mar; (01929) 424443; free,
though parking £1.20 in summer (60p
winter). The beach at nearby
STUDLAND SZ0382 is lovely; there's a
nature reserve behind, a NT visitor
centre with snacks and a shop in
summer, and the Bankes Arms (busy
in summer) has great views and
useful food.

★ Tyneham SY8880 This ABANDONED
VILLAGE on the army's Purbeck firing
ranges (open holidays and most
wknds) is quite poignant; there's an
explanatory exhibition in the former
schoolroom.
✝ ⛪ ✌ Wareham SY9287 is a largely
modern town, but has a few striking
old buildings, inc the CHURCH of St
Martin's, with a finely carved
memorial to Lawrence of Arabia, and
two very traditional old inns, the
Black Bear and King's Arms. The
Quay public house is in a fine
position. BLUE POOL (3 miles S, at
Furzebrook) Peaceful beauty-spot
with curious colour changes in the
water whenever the weather alters,
from light green to blue to suddenly a
rich turquoise; it's bluest on an
overcast day. Also, a little museum
looking at the clay industry for which
the site was originally excavated, and
25 acres of heathland with lots of rare
plants and animals. Snacks (in quaint
tea house celebrating its 60th birthday
on 8 Jun), shop, some disabled access;
facilities and museum cl Oct–Easter,
site cl Dec–Feb; (01929) 551408; £2.
⛴ ❀ ❀ ✝ ♪ West Lulworth SY8280 is a
lovely spot, just above a very beautiful
cove with extraordinary nearby rock
formations; the thatched Castle Inn is
useful for lunch. LULWORTH CASTLE
Recently opened to visitors for the first
time, this 17th-c castle was a lived in
home until a fire in 1929. Restoration
work is still going on, so it's not yet all
open, but the SE tower has splendid
views over the wooded park, and the
formal gardens are a nice spot for a
picnic. Also a Catholic chapel (the first
to be built in England after the
Reformation) and an Anglican church
built in part by Thomas Hardy, about
whom there's an exhibition inside.
Shop; best to check winter opening,
(01929) 400352; *£1.50. LULWORTH
COVE HERITAGE CENTRE Interesting
exhibitions on topics like smuggling,
local plants and wildlife, and country
wines. Shop, disabled access; cl 25 Dec;
(01929) 400587; *£1.50.
★ ⛴ ! ❀ ♪ ♪ ♪ 🎣 ❀ Weymouth
SY6778 has elegant 18th- and 19th-c
terraces along its curving esplanade,
and some older buildings in the
narrower partly pedestrianised streets

behind. The harbour is lively, with big ferries leaving from the outer quay, and the town's inner ring road running one-way around the inner harbour. Overlooking the harbour, the Old Rooms and the Ship are both useful for lunch. On the far side of the harbour, the narrow streets of the old town are worth exploring. The resort has a good beach, and lots of lively family attractions. SEA LIFE PARK (Lodsmoor Country Park) Stunning marine-life displays and an eerie recreation of what it's like to be caught in a sunken wreck at the bottom of the sea. Plenty of creatures to touch, close-up views of sharks from the observatory, blue whale splash pool, children's adventureland, and lakeside picnic area; a reliable family day out, informative and entertaining. Meals, snacks, shop, disabled access; cl 25 Dec; (01305) 788255; £4.50. DEEP SEA ADVENTURE & TITANIC STORY (Custom House Quay) The search for buried treasure brought vividly to life, with good interactive displays on underwater exploration and shipwrecks, a collection of Titanic signals, and summer diving displays. Shop, disabled access; cl 24–26 Dec; (01305) 760690; *£3.35. BREWER'S QUAY Skilful conversion of harbourside Victorian brewery into a shopping and leisure complex: particularly worth a look here are the TIMEWALK, with imaginative recreations of scenes from the town's history (limited disabled access), the DEVENISH SHIRE

HORSE STABLES, and DISCOVERY, a new, hands-on science centre. They also have a new co-operative craft centre, and run ferry and boat trips across the bay; cl last 2 wks Jan, 25–26 Dec; (01305) 777622; £3.50. NOTHE FORT Interesting armed Victorian fort on three levels, with an enormous amount of things to see – spread over a staggering 70 rooms. Children can clamber over some of the vehicles and guns, and there are fine views of the harbour and coast. Snacks, shop, disabled access; open daily mid-May–Sept, pm Sun only in winter; (01305) 787243; £2. Good views too from the garden of the Nothe Tavern (with tasty fresh fish), and from the pleasant nearby Nothe Gardens.

✔ **Wool** SY8486 in Hardy's Wessex was the ancient seat of the d'Urbervilles. MONKEY WORLD Rescue centre for apes and chimps, allowing them to roam free in big enclosures; also children's obstacle course and play areas. Snacks, shop, disabled access; *£3.75. The Countryman at East Knighton is the best nearby place for lunch.

★ **Attractive villages,** all with decent pubs, include Burton Bradstock SY4889, Chideock SY4292 (sadly ripped in half by the A35; nearby Seatown occupies a grand position on the coast), Kingston SY9579, Langton Herring SY6182, Litton Cheyney SY5590, Puncknowle SY5388 (pronounced Punnel), Sutton Poyntz SY7083, Symondsbury SY4493, and West Knighton SY7387.

Walks

This area has the county's best walking. The Dorset Coast Path, part of the 500-mile, South-West Peninsula Path, follows the entire coastline where practicable; sheer, unfenced drops from the clifftops (particularly on Purbeck) are not to everyone's taste. The most remarkably varied short walk in the county is from **Studland** SZ0382 ⌂-1. In a couple of hours you can take in Ballard Down (huge views over Poole Harbour), Old Harry Rocks (tooth-like chalk pinnacles detached from the cliff) and the Agglestone (a rock standing solitary on Dorset's largest surviving heath). Nine Barrow Down SZ0081, the main Purbeck ridge, has far-ranging, two-way views and makes a good goal for walks from Corfe Castle SY9681.

Westwards from **Lyme Regis** SY3492 ⌂-2, a path snakes through an intriguing nature-reserve undercliff, still subject to landfalls, a celebrated area for fossils and flora. **Golden Cap** ⌂-3, the highest point on the county's coast, can be

reached from Seatown SY4291 (useful pub), a stiff but rewarding haul. Just E of Charmouth, a steep narrow road leads up to Stonebarrow Hill SY3893; nice easy walking, fine sea and inland views (disabled WC, NT shop in season).
Abbotsbury SY5785 ⌂-4 is the start for strolls around Chapel Hill SY5784 and on to the massive shingle bank of Chesil Beach (exhausting to walk any distance along). Paths leading N from the village get lovely views from the chalk downs.

The tiny ruined church at **East Fleet** SY6380 ⌂-5 is close to the great lagoon enclosed by Chesil Beach, which was used for trying out the dam-busting bouncing bomb; it is a peaceful spot with a diverse bird population.

At **Lulworth Cove** SY8280 ⌂-6 the classic mini-walk is westwards along the cliffs to Durdle Door, a natural arch eroded by the sea; inland is prairie-like monotony, and it is best to return the same way. East of Lulworth Cove is army training land, which means high-security fences and dire warning notices, but you are allowed in most wknds and daily in Aug and during Easter (keep to the paths). Information boards by road junctions off the A351 and the A352 nr Wareham give opening times; or ring (01929) 462721 ext 4824 and ask for the Guardroom. The excellent coastal walk between Lulworth Cove and Kimmeridge Bay SY9078 heads past the surreal 'fossil forest' (formed of petrified algae that once clung to tree-trunks) to Mupe Bay SY8479. Another path ascends Bindon Hill SY8380, looking down over the semi-circular cove.

At **Kingston** SY9579 ⌂-7 (where the Scott Arms, a pleasant family pub, has lovely views of Corfe Castle), an easy level path goes to Hounstout Cliff SY9577. Turn left at the end and you are into Dorset fossil country, presided over by the primitive hermitage chapel on St Aldhelm's Head SY9675; the path here is of the switchback sort, and the chalk mud can make it tough going. At Worth Matravers SY9777, the unpretentious Square & Compass (lovely views) is another good base for coastal walks in this area. Nr here, the rock pool at Dancing Ledge SY9976 is said to have been cut by a local schoolmaster.

Durlston Head Country Park SZ0377 ⌂-8, on the edge of Swanage SZ0278, has fine views from the headland and the Great Globe, a 40-ton global representation in Purbeck marble.

Above **Portesham** SY6085 ⌂-9, high heathland gives a view which covers the entire sweep of the West Dorset coast. A track along Bronkham Hill, SE from the summit, feels truly ancient, with prehistoric burial mounds flanking it. **Lamberts Castle** SY3799 ⌂-10 is an unspoiled hill fort, charming for strolls (especially in late summer when the heather is out).

Driving

Sandbanks Ferry (open Apr–Sept) makes a spectacular way of entering Dorset proper; from the leafy suburbs of Bournemouth you sail into a different world, with the unfenced toll road crossing naked heath before nearing the Purbeck Hills. The road W from Corfe Castle through Church Knowle is pretty. There are more toll gates in Purbeck on some of the lanes leading down to the prettiest coves, and the pleasant route from Church Knowle or Wareham over the West Creech Hills may sometimes be closed for army firing practice.

The B3157 coast road is very attractive, with fine views W of Abbotsbury. The B3159 between Weymouth and Winterbourne Abbas is a nice road, with good views; turning off at Martinstown up the Black Down road to Abbotsbury, you get tremendous views as you pass the hideous Hardy Monument (to the admiral). Most of the small back roads burrow into quietly interesting countryside, for the most part very unspoilt.

The A35 running right across this area gives a good feel of the changing scenery, with some excellent views particularly between Chideock and Lyme Regis; there can be queues of traffic in summer.

Where to eat

Chesil SY6973 COVE HOUSE (01305) 820895 Excellent sea views from a simple old pub virtually on the beach; separate seafood menu as well as bar food and à la carte. £17|£2.50/£7.80.

Upwey SY6684 SHIP 7 Ridgeway (01305) 812522 Pretty, white-washed cottagey pub with very good bar food, well kept beer, a fine range of wines, and friendly service. £17|£2.25/£6.50.

Lyme Regis SY3492 PILOT BOAT (012974) 43157 Welcoming old smugglers inn not far from the beaches; lots of seafood in both the bar and restaurant, children's menu, decent wines. £16.50|£2/£5.75.

Langton Herring SY6182 ELM TREE (01305) 871257 Busy pub in a pretty, thatched village with a good range of interesting, home-cooked bar food, children's menu; close to the coastal path. £2.50/£6.30.

NORTH AND CENTRAL DORSET

Interesting places to visit, charming country towns, good places to stay, and includes Hardy country.

This part of the county has more places to visit than the coastal area. Among them, Forde Abbey at Thorncombe is outstanding, and Athelhampton House is still very well worth visiting despite the 1992 fire. Dorchester, Sherborne, Beaminster, Shaftesbury and Blandford Forum are all interesting towns with much to explore, and have a good few craft and antique shops without being overtly touristy. In Dorchester, the National Trust have just opened Thomas Hardy's house Max Gate; not much to see inside, but an evocative garden. Of many charming villages here, Milton Abbas takes the crown. Though the area's main attractions are mostly of an adult nature, there's plenty to keep children amused, too: the butterflies at Over Compton and the rare farm breeds at Gillingham are particularly well displayed. New to this edition is an interesting re-creation of an Iron Age homestead at Bradford Peverell.

This is, of course, Thomas Hardy country, and many people get extra pleasure from the many direct memories of his books which particular villages and tracts of countryside conjure up. It has a fine mix of scenery from the chalk uplands and intricate valleys of the central area to the quiet seclusion of the more intimate farming country in the west. There is pleasant walking, though sometimes the longer paths can be difficult to follow. There is also a good choice of places to stay in and to eat at, and the area is much quieter in summer than the coast.

Where to stay

Gillingham ST8026 STOCK HILL Wyke, Gillingham SP8 5NR (01747) 823626 £200 inc dinner; 9 lovely, very comfortable rms. Marvellously relaxing, carefully run, Victorian manor house in 10 acres of parkland, with antiques and paintings in the opulent day rooms; particularly welcoming service, and excellent food in the no-smoking restaurant using home-grown herbs and veg, local meat and fish; all-weather tennis court, croquet; children over 7 only.

Evershot ST5704 SUMMER LODGE Evershot, Dorchester DT2 0JR (01935) 83424 *£135; 17 big, individually decorated rms. The Earl of Ilchester's former dower house is a beautifully kept, peaceful hotel with really lovely flower displays in the comfortable and elegantly furnished day rooms; very attractive restaurant with fine views of the pretty garden, excellent food using the best local produce, fine breakfasts, and personal, caring service; outdoor swimming pool, tennis and croquet; dogs allowed; disabled access.

Chedington ST4805 CHEDINGTON COURT Chedington, Beaminster DT8 3HY (01935) 891265 *£95; 10 attractive and spacious rms. Handsome, Jacobean-style hotel in a fine hillside setting with lovely views; an elegant lounge, pretty conservatory, library, billiard room, log fires, and a tranquil atmosphere; very good food in the civilised restaurant, and a fine wine list; 10 acres of gardens with croquet and a par 74 nine-hole golf course; cl 2 Jan–2 Feb.

Sherborne ST6316 EASTBURY Long St, Sherborne DT9 3BY (01935) 813131 £75; 14 pretty rms. Elegant Georgian townhouse with a comfortable lounge, library, good food, relaxing atmosphere, and garden; close to the abbey and castles.

Evershot ST5704 ACORN Evershot, Dorchester DT2 0JW (01935) 83228 £74; 8 comfortable rms. Comfortable, L-shaped lounge bar, pretty furnishings and fine old fireplaces; good food, decent wines and real ales, very good breakfasts, friendly service, and a no-smoking restaurant; surrounded by attractive Hardy walking country.

Dorchester SY6890 KINGS ARMS High East St, Dorchester DT1 1HF (01305) 265353 £65.90w; 33 rms – the Lawrence of Arabia and the Tutenkhamun suites are extraordinary. Smart, thriving coaching inn made famous by Hardy's *Mayor of Casterbridge*; different menus in the restaurant, coffee shop and bar, and old-fashioned public bar with real ales, live music twice a week; disabled access.

Evershot ST5704 RECTORY HOUSE Fore St, Evershot, Dorchester DT2 0JW (01935) 83273 £60; 6 rms in main house and converted stables. Neatly kept, 18th-c listed building with two comfortable lounges, log fire, and good home cooking using local produce in the pretty dining room; cl Dec; children over 10; disabled access.

Dorchester SY6890 WESTWOOD HOUSE 29 High West St, Dorchester DT1 1UP (01305) 268018 £52.50; 8 rms, most with own bthrm. Welcoming Georgian house built as a coaching house for Lord Ilchester, with a restful lounge and good breakfasts in the conservatory; no evening meals (lots of nearby restaurants).

Dorchester SU5794 CASTERBRIDGE 49 High East St, Dorchester DT1 1HU (01305) 264043 £50; 15 rms. Small Georgian hotel in the town centre with a modern annexe across a small courtyard; elegant drawing room, cosy library, and an attractive dining room and conservatory; no evening meals (lots of nearby restaurants); cl 25–26 Dec; disabled access.

Halstock ST5407 HALSTOCK MILL Halstock, Yeovil BA22 9SJ (01935) 891278 *£50; 4 rms. Attractive 17th-c house quietly set in 10 acres, with lots of surrounding walks; log fire in the cosy beamed lounge, pleasant little dining room, and good food using home-grown fruit and veg, local fish and cheese; stabling; cl Christmas; children over 5 only.

Milton Abbas ST8001 HAMBRO ARMS Milton Abbas, Blandford Forum DT11 0BP (01258) 880233 £50; 2 rms. Pretty and popular old inn in a beautiful, 1770s landscaped village, with a beamed front lounge, log fire, popular food, and prompt, friendly service; children over 10.

Powerstock SY5196 THREE HORSESHOES Powerstock, Bridport DT6 3TF (01308) 85328 £50; 4 rms, most with own bthrm. Busy, stone and thatch pub in a lovely setting, ideal for fishing nearby – and much of the imaginative food is based around fish; comfortable bar, open fires, and neat lawn with fine sea views. Mellow church bells every 15 minutes

Yetminster ST5910 MANOR FARMHOUSE High St, Yetminster, Sherborne DT9 6LF (01935) 872247 £47.50; 4 rms. Fine, carefully modernised 17th-c building with beams and oak panelling, inglenook fireplaces, helpful owners, and good traditional cooking; children over 10; partial disabled access.

Lydlinch ST7413 HOLEBROOK FARM Lydlinch, Sturminster Newton DT10 2JB (01258) 817348 £42; 2 rms in farmhouse, with 3 in comfortably converted stables. 18th-c house on a family-run, grassland farm in a very peaceful setting; good home cooking, small swimming pool, games room and clay-pigeon shooting; lots to do nearby; also self-catering cottages in a converted byre; disabled access.

Dorchester SY6789 MAIDEN CASTLE FARM, Dorchester DT2 9PR (01305) 262356 £40; 3 rms. Victorian farmhouse on a big working farm and set beneath the prehistoric earthworks from which the farm takes its name; views of the castle and countryside, and comfortable, traditionally furnished sitting room which overlooks the garden.

Cerne Abbas ST6601 NEW Long St, Cerne Abbas, Dorchester DT2 7JF (0130 03) 41274 £30; 5 comfortable rms, some with four-posters. Pretty 15th-c inn with a beamed, L-shaped lounge bar, warm atmosphere, carefully cooked food inc marvellous breakfasts, good, interesting wine list (around a dozen by the glass too), and considerate service; also, a sheltered back lawn.

To see and do

Dorchester SY6890 Thriving country town, with busy shopping streets (and several worthwhile antique and print shops). Though most of the more attractive Georgian buildings are just out of the bustle, there are a few distinguished buildings on the main streets, including the timbered building of JUDGE JEFFREYS' LODGINGS in High West St – this was where he stayed during his notorious Bloody Assizes. There are one or two traces of the Romans' occupation, including the fragmentary remains of a town house behind the County Hall, and of an amphitheatre on Weymouth Ave. Not far from here is ELDRIDGE POPE'S VICTORIAN BREWERY, which can be visited by arrangement, tel (01305) 251251.

🏠 ❧ Thomas Hardy lived here for most of his life, using the town as the centre of events in *The Mayor of Casterbridge*. Among the places still associated with the author is MAX GATE (Alington Ave), the house he designed and lived in from 1885 to his death in 1928, recently opened up by the National Trust. You can see only the drawing room (the study has been moved to the County Museum, see below), but the gardens are fascinating, not least because they inspired so much of Hardy's poetry. Open pm Sun, Mon and Weds Apr–Sept; *£2; NT. Just outside town at Higher Bockhampton (3m E, just off the A35), on the edge of Puddletown Heath ('Egdon Heath'), is HARDY'S COTTAGE, the writer's birthplace in 1840. The thatched house hasn't changed much since, though the heath's now largely forested (there is a stretch of open heathland much as he knew it just SE). House open mainly by appointment; gardens open without appointment (though not much to see), with disabled access, or you can peer in from the public path; shop; cl 1–2, Thurs, Nov–Mar; (01305) 262366; £2.50; NT.

👁 COUNTY MUSEUM (High St West) The study from Max Gate has been reconstructed here, but the author isn't the only Thomas Hardy commemorated; there's also a display on his less celebrated namesake, Nelson's flag-captain at the Battle of Trafalgar. Quite a traditional museum, though very comprehensive. Shop, disabled access to ground floor only; cl Sun (exc July and Aug), 25–26 Dec, Good Fri; (01305) 262735; £1.95. In High East St, the King's Arms Hotel, full of Hardy associations, is a good place for lunch (other places to consider include the Cornwall in Alexandra Rd, Stationmaster's House by South station and Trumpet Major, Alington Ave).

👁 ❗ The lively DINOSAUR MUSEUM (Icen Way) is the largest such single-minded display in the country, with skeletons, fossils, reconstructions and interactive displays. Children are encouraged to touch and feel things.

Shop, disabled access; cl 24–26 Dec; (01305) 269880; £3.50.

🛇 A similar approach is found at the TUTANKHAMUN EXHIBITION (High West St), recreating the discovery of ancient treasures using a mix of sights, sounds and smells; details as Dinosaur Museum above.

🏠🛇❀ The KEEP MILITARY MUSEUM (Bridport Rd) Recently extensively refurbished, this splendid building has been a local landmark ever since it was built as the Victorian gatehouse of the Dorset regimental barracks. It now houses exhibits from all the county's regiments, and this year for the first time you can climb the battlements and enjoy the view. Shop; reopens Easter, then cl 1–2pm Sat and all Sun; (01305) 264066; £1.50.

🏚 MAIDEN CASTLE a mile or so SW is one of best examples of an Iron Age fort, covering 47 acres.

Other things to see and do

🏠❀▣ **Athelhampton** SY7794 ATHELHAMPTON HOUSE Magnificent 15th-c house, now fully restored after the 1992 fire. The damage to the east wing was pretty grim, but miraculously most of the beautiful furnishings and contents (even much of the panelling) were saved, and are back in their original positions. It really is a handsome old place, and has the added bonus of acres of wonderful, formal and landscaped gardens with rare plants, topiary and fountain pools. Also antique and occasional craft fairs. Meals, snacks, shop, disabled access; open pm Weds, Thurs, Sun and bank hols Easter–Oct, plus Tues May–Sept and Mon and Fri in July and Aug; (01305) 848363; £4.20 house and gardens, £2.10 garden only. Also worth a look is ILSINGTON HOUSE at nearby Puddletown SY7594, with pleasant grounds, an eclectic art collection (especially good on modern art) and an early 19th-c royal scandal to boot. Disabled access to ground floor only; open pm Weds and Thurs May–Sept, or by appointment; (01305) 848454; *£3. The Martyrs at Tolpuddle is useful for something to eat.

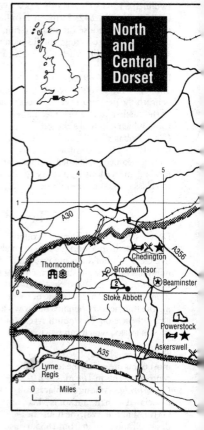

North and Central Dorset

🏠🐦❀❀ **Beaminster** ST4701 PARNHAM (A3066 towards Bridport) Surrounded by 14 acres of lovely gardens, this fine Tudor mansion is now famous as the home of John Makepeace the furniture-maker. His workshop is open, with completed pieces shown around the house, along with exhibitions by other designers and craftsmen. Meals, snacks, shop, mostly disabled access; open Sun, Weds and bank hols, Apr–Oct; (01308) 862204; *£4. The nearby woods of Hooke Park are a pleasant place for a stroll; you can get a combined ticket with the house. MAPPERTON GARDENS (off the B3163, E) Several acres of terraced hillside gardens in the grounds of a 16th-c manor house; specimen trees and shrubs, fountains, grottoes, fishponds, orangery, good walks and views. Shop, some disabled access; cl am, all

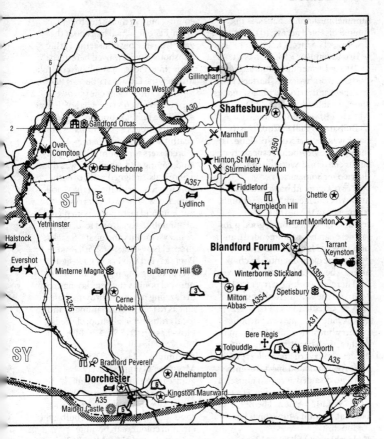

Nov–Feb; (01308) 863014; *£2.50. HORN PARK (A3066, N) Unusual plants in a series of gardens with bluebell woods, ponds, wild flowers and good views. Open pm Tues, Thurs and 1st and 3rd Sun of each month; *£2. Pickwicks is good for lunch, and the Greyhound is a useful alternative.

† **Bere Regis** SY8494 The CHURCH here has the finest timbered roof in Dorset, with extraordinary carved figures; 20p in a slot lights these up to remarkable effect. The Royal Oak is good value for lunch.

★ ☺ ☙ **Blandford Forum** ST8806 Georgian market town, rebuilt in 1731 by the curiously named Bastard brothers after the older buildings were destroyed by fire. Very interesting to walk round. ROYAL SIGNALS MUSEUM (Blandford Camp) The history of army communications from the Crimean War, with World War II spy radios, lots of uniforms, paintings and badges, and various military vehicles. Shop, disabled access; cl wknds exc Jun–Sept, 25 Dec; free. RINGROSE POTTERY Stoneware jugs, mugs, teapots, plates and bowls made and sold on premises; there should always be at least one potter you can watch in action. Shop, disabled access; cl some Suns, 25 Dec–2 Jan; free. The town also has a useful local history MUSEUM; disabled access to ground floor only; cl Sun, Nov–Mar; *30p. The Greyhound and Nelson's are decent pubs.

🏛 ☙ **Bradford Peverell** SY6593 NEW BARN FIELD CENTRE Authentic recreation of an Iron Age homestead, complete with animals and so on; also a working potter, bygones exhibition, wildflower reserve and nature trails.

Summer meals and snacks, shop, limited disabled access; (01305) 267463; cl 25 Dec; *£2.50.

🏵 **Broadwindsor** ST4302 has a CRAFT CENTRE in former farm buildings, with potters, woodworkers, hatters, gem-polishers and so forth. Meals, snacks, shop, disabled access; cl 23 Dec–Mar; (01308) 868362; free.

❋ **Bulbarrow Hill** ST7605, on the narrow lanes just S of Woolland, is a memorable viewpoint, especially on a summer evening with the sun going down over Somerset.

★ ✝ 🏛 🏵 **Cerne Abbas** ST6601 is an attractive village with a fine church, fragments of the old abbey, a remarkable collection of good pubs (all here can be recommended), and, of course, its famous, indelicate, prehistoric giant cut into the chalk above – best seen from the main road N. There's a working POTTERY (cl Mon) on the way up to the giant.

🏛 ❀ 🐄 **Chettle** ST9413 CHETTLE HOUSE Fine example of a baroque country house designed by Thomas Archer, with beautifully laid-out gardens, vineyard and gallery; various craft weekends and special events. Teas, no disabled access to house; cl Tues, Sat, 2nd Sun Oct–Easter; (01258) 830209; *£2. The Bugle Horn at Tarrant Monkton is handy for lunch.

🏛 **Hambledon Hill** ST8412 is a very imposing Neolithic hill fort in a commanding position just above Child Okeford – where the Saxon Inn is a good lunch stop.

★ **Fiddleford** ST8013 is an attractive village, and the Fiddleford Inn is a handy lunch stop.

🔌 🐄 ❀ **Kingston Maurward** SY7290 KINGSTON MAURWARD PARK Very close to Dorchester, but like being deep in the heart of the countryside, with lots of peaceful woodland and lakeside walks, a farm park, and plenty of gardens inc Edwardian gardens, formal gardens, the national collections of penstemon and salvia, and an Elizabethan walled garden. Snacks, shop, some disabled access; cl am, all Oct–Easter; (01305) 264738; £2.

★ ❀ ✝ 🐄 **Milton Abbas** ST8001 The prettiest thatched village in the county, built in the 18th c to replace an earlier one which had spoilt the view from the big house; the 17th-c almshouses were moved here at the same time. Pleasant stroll past the lake through the CAPABILITY BROWN PARK to the fine 15th-c ABBEY church of a former Benedictine monastery (it now serves the public school in the nearby house). Inside is a rather quaint, in-death-as-in-life effigy of the Dorchesters for whom all this landscaping and rebuilding was done. There's also a signed walk over the lane to a former chapel in the wood. PARK FARM MUSEUM Countryside museum and farm park, with plenty of animals to touch and feed, inc pigs, donkeys, rabbits and goats. Snacks, shop; cl Nov–Mar; *£2.50. RARE POULTRY, PIG AND PLANT CENTRE 10 breeds of pig and piglets, all sorts of unusual poultry inc hens laying eggs in dazzling blues and browns, baby chicks to touch, other animals, and local crafts. Snacks, shop; cl Weds, Nov–Easter; (01258) 880447; *£1.75. The village inn is good.

❀ **Minterne Magna** ST6504 MINTERNE GARDENS Lovely landscaped gardens, with lakes, cascades, streams, rare trees and impressive spring shows of azaleas, rhododendrons and spring bulbs; the autumn colours can be quite spectacular. Cl Nov–Mar; *£2.

🦋 **Over Compton** ST5817 WORLDWIDE BUTTERFLIES AND LULLINGSTONE SILK FARM Superb collection of butterflies from all over the world, flying free in reconstructions of their natural habitat inside Elizabethan Compton Hall. The silk farm demonstrates production of English silk used for coronations and royal weddings, and they have a new exhibition on conservation. Snacks, shop, some disabled access; cl Nov–Mar; (01935) 29937; £3.50. The Rose & Crown at Trent is good for lunch.

🏛 ❀ **Sandford Orcas** ST6220 MANOR HOUSE Interesting little Tudor manor house, largely unaltered since the 16th c, with fine furnishings and family portraits, and pleasant gardens, at their best in May and Jun. Open Easter Mon, then pm Sun and all Mon

May–Sept; (01963) 220206; £2. The Mitre tucked away nearby has decent food.

★ ❀ ⛰ ♿ **Shaftesbury** ST8622 Hilltop town with good views from Castle Hill and Park Walk; its most famous street is Gold Hill – thatched cottages stepped down a steep cobbled street, familiar from those Hovis TV advertisements. St James below is attractive. ABBEY RUINS AND MUSEUM Part of a nunnery founded by Alfred the Great, the abbey was destroyed in the Reformation, but the foundations still exist, and the museum has plenty of remains found during excavations, along with an Anglo-Saxon herb garden. Shop, disabled access; cl Nov–Easter; 90p. At the top of Gold Hill is a good LOCAL HISTORY MUSEUM, with a mummified cat found during the rethatching of a local cottage. Disabled access to ground floor only; cl Oct–Easter, may open some winter wknds; (01747) 852157; 80p. The Grosvenor Hotel, the Mitre (with wonderful Blackmore Vale views) and, down Gold Hill, the Two Brewers are all good for lunch, and the Ship is a quaint old tavern. There are several craft shops and workshops.

★ ✝ 🏠 ❀ ⛰ ♿ **Sherborne** ST6316 is an attractive town to wander through, given a feeling of unchanging solidity by the handsome, stone, medieval abbey buildings that mix in with later ones of the public school here, and by many other fine old buildings in and near the main street. The ABBEY itself is a glorious, golden stone building with a beautifully vaulted nave; at the Dissolution the townspeople raised the money to buy it, and it's remained the local parish church ever since. SHERBORNE CASTLE Built by Sir Walter Raleigh in 1594 and home of the Digby family since 1617, this striking old house stands out particularly for its fantastic period furnishings, though there are also interesting paintings and porcelain. Outside are gardens designed by Capability Brown, and beautiful parklands with an enormous lake. Snacks, shop; open pm Thurs, Sat, Sun, and bank hols Easter–Oct; (01935) 813182; £3.60 house and gardens, £1.50 grounds

only. Directly across the water, SHERBORNE OLD CASTLE is the original 12th-c castle, destroyed by Cromwell in the Civil War, but still with plenty of interesting and evocative ruins. Shop, disabled access (but no facilities); cl winter Mon and Tues; (01935) 812730; £1.25. It's reconstructed at the SHERBORNE MUSEUM, which also has some Victorian dolls' houses and ecclesiastical Roman remains. Shop; cl am Sun, Mon, Nov–wk before Easter; 50p. The Digby Tap and Cross Keys (both handy for the abbey) and Skippers (Horsecastles) are useful for lunch. Several craft shops include a working saddlery in the main street.

❀ **Spetisbury** ST9102 OLD MILL Pretty, medium-sized, riverside watergarden, with lots of plants for sale. Snacks; open pm Weds Apr–Aug, poss some wknds; (01258) 453939; £2. The Charlton Inn at Charlton Marshall is good for lunch.

🐄 🍎 **Tarrant Keynston** ST9204 KEYNSTON MILL FRUIT FARM Interesting vineyard and farm shop, with 21 different kinds of pick-your-own. Meals, snacks, shop; restaurant cl winter Mon and Nov–Easter, shop and vineyard cl Christmas–New Year; (01258) 452596.

❀ 🏠 **Thorncombe** ST3504 FORDE ABBEY The extensive gardens here really are special, with glorious trees and shrubs, a fine collection of Asiatic primulas, many interesting plants, and sweeping lawns. The striking abbey buildings still retain some of the features of the original 12th-c Cistercian monastery, but it was modernised in 1500 by Abbot Chard, and it's his great hall and tower that remain. Cromwell's Attorney-General later turned the abbey into a house, and the interior has changed little since, with magnificently furnished rooms, unusual plaster ceilings and a set of Raphael tapestries. Meals and snacks (in the 12th-c undercroft), shop, disabled access to gardens only; house open pm Weds, Sun and bank hols Apr–Oct, garden and nursery all year; (01460) 20231; £4.50, £3.25 garden only. The George over at Chardstock is the closest good place for lunch.

⏻ **Tolpuddle** SY7994 Famous for the agricultural workers who united to improve their working conditions and terms of employment. The MARTYRS' TREE under which they supposedly met still remains, and six cottages contain the TOLPUDDLE MUSEUM telling their story. Shop, disabled access by arrangement; cl Sun, Christmas wk; (01305) 848237; free. The Martyrs pub is useful for lunch.

★ **Other attractive villages** with decent pubs include Buckhorn Weston ST7524, Chedington ST4805, Evershot ST5704, Hinton St Mary ST7816 (superb manor house, medieval tithe barn), Powerstock SY5196, Tarrant Monkton ST9408, Whitchurch Canonicorum (fine church) and Winterborne Stickland ST8304. You might also like to explore the bridleway from Stubhampton ST9114 along Ashmore Bottom to Ashmore ST9217 (can be muddy in a wet spring).

Walks

Despite the ultra-English charm of much of inland Dorset – chalk downs, sleepy thatched villages, clumps of beechwoods and fine views – the area is surprisingly little walked, and careful map-reading is necessary as field routes are often not obvious. The best areas include those where agricultural improvement has been limited: the vicinities of **Powerstock** SY5196 ◠-1 and **Stoke Abbott** ST4500 ◠-2, for example, have delectable downland and valley landscapes, with a reasonably good path network (and both have decent pubs); another fine pub base for a country walk is the distinctive Fox at Corscombe ST5105. In the attractive downland W of **Bingham's Melcombe** ST7602 ◠-3, the dry ground of the Dorsetshire Gap ST7403 comes as a pleasant surprise on those days when you begin to think that all Dorset is turning to chalky mud.

The picturesque village of **Milton Abbas** ST8001 ◠-4 has attractive paths through the abbey estate and into Green Hill Down Nature Reserve; a longer walk continues NW to Bulbarrow Hill ST7605, which looks far into Somerset and Wilts. **Maiden Castle** SY6890 ◠-5, nr Dorchester, is so vast that the tour of its grassy ramparts almost qualifies as a fully fledged walk.

From the birthplace of Thomas Hardy at **Higher Bockhampton** SY7292 ◠-6, you can walk into nearby forest plantations and on to Black Heath and Duddle Heath, the 'untamed and untameable' Egdon Heath of Hardy's novels: further Hardyesque features abound locally, inc the church at Stinsford ('Mellstock') SY7191, where Hardy's heart is buried beside his first wife – a path from the river at Lower Bockhampton SY7290 leads to the village.

Cranborne Chase ST9217 ◠-7, shared with Wilts, offers good walking with some fine views, especially around Ashmore ST9217.

There's a pretty bluebell wood at **Bere Wood** SY8794 ◠-8 at the W end of Bloxworth; the track can be followed right through to Bere Regis SY8494. (There are even more bluebells at Delcombe Wood ST7805, but the only public track just skirts the W edge of the wood.)

Driving

The central downland has some interesting drives through largely unspoilt countryside. The valley road N from Winterborne Whitechurch, through the Winterbornes up to Okeford Fitzpaine, gives good changing views of the downland on either side, wooded and steeply chiselled as you approach Okeford. The high road E from Holywell, on the A37 nr Evershot, over Batcombe Hill and Gore Hill to Minterne Magna, offers memorable views. A pleasant circular drive is from Piddletrenthide through Plush (where the Brace of Pheasants is a very enjoyable lunchtime stop) and Mappowder to Hazelbury

Bryan, then S along the ancient ridge road over Bulbarrow Hill, through Ansty and Bingham's Melcombe, to turn right at Cheselbourne for Piddletrenthide again. There are some bracing views from the ridge road which forks off the A352 at Middlemarsh and runs along above Cerne all the way down to Dorchester. The zigzag road down to Shaftesbury from Ashmore has an almost alpine quality.

In the W of the county, there are tremendously atmospheric moments along the steep little lanes that track around Eggardon Hill, above Askerswell, Uploders and Nettlecombe; the hill is surmounted by a tremendous Iron Age hill fort, with wonderful views and impressive ramparts. The B3165 through Marshwood and then along the B3164 to Broadwindsor takes you through a little-known and quite unspoilt valley.

The E–W main roads across the county tend to be slow, with traffic queues building up quite readily.

Where to eat

Sturminster Newton ST7813 Plumber Manor Hazelbury Bryan Rd (01258) 72507 Fine 17th-c manor that has always belonged to the same family; at its heart are three stylish, evening dining rooms (though they also do Sun lunch); imaginative cooking, good wine list and friendly service; bedrooms; cl Feb; children over 10; disabled access. **£26**.

Blandford Forum ST8806 La Belle Alliance Whitecliff Mill St (01258) 452842 Attractive, little country-style restaurant in a Victorian house, with pleasant, friendly staff, excellent food, carefully chosen wine list, and an open fire in the cosy lounge; bedrooms; cl Sun, Mon (exc bank hols), first 3 wks Jan; children by arrangement, disabled access. **£20.45**.

Tarrant Monkton ST9408 Langton Arms (0125 889) 225 Thatched 17th-c pub in a pretty village, with a wide choice of good, fresh, home-made food, a bistro restaurant, well kept beers, decent wines, and a comfortable bar; also, an open fire, and skittle alley; disabled access. **£15|£1.95/£4.50**.

Chedington ST4805 Winyards Gap (01935) 891244 Comfortable pub with spectacular views and nearby walks; a wide choice of good bar food inc lots of fresh fish dishes, vegetarian choices, home-made puddings, daily specials, and children's menus; self-catering flats in a converted barn; cl pm 25 Dec. **£14|£1.20/£4.95**.

Marnhull ST7718 Blackmore Vale (01258) 820701 Relaxed and friendly atmosphere in this pleasant old pub, with good home-made bar food inc several vegetarian dishes, decent beer and wine, interesting furnishings in the comfortably modernised bar, and a log fire; can eat in the garden where one of the tables is thatched. **£14|£1.50/£4.75**.

Askerswell SY5292 Spyway (01308) 85250 Former smugglers' look-out with exceptional value, very popular bar food, lots of salads and cheesecakes; plenty of views and walks nearby; no children. **£11.50|£3.10/£3.95**.

Help this year from: Barbara Hatfield, B Widdowson, Mrs J A Powell, David Eberlin, M V and J Melling, Huw and Carolyn Lewis, Neil Hardwick, Gwyneth and Salvo Spadaro-Dutturi, Richard R Dolphin, Richard Burton, C J Pratt, Chris Warne, Brian Chambers, Marjorie and David Lamb, Mr and Mrs M P Aston, Douglas Adam, Trevor Scott, Charles Bardswell, WHBM, Bronwen and Steve Wrigley, John and Joan Nash, D G Clarke, David Sweeney, E G Parish, W H and E Thomas, Stephen and Anna Oxley, Alice Valdes-Scott, Bernard and Kathleen Hypher.

DORSET CALENDAR

Some of these dates were provisional as we went to press.

FEBRUARY

6 **Bournemouth** International Festival of Food and Wine – *till Thurs 9* (01202) 789789

11 **Dorchester** Wildlife Photographer of the Year Exhibition at the Dorset County Museum – *till 18 Mar* (01305) 262735

26 **Stinsford** Dorchester Book Fair at Kingston Maurward College of Agriculture and Horticulture (01258) 473561

28 **Corfe Castle** Marblers' and Stonecutters' Day to enforce rules laid down in 1651. *At noon*, the church's pancake bell summons the company from the Fox Inn to the town hall. New members are admitted for a fee, part of which is a quart of beer carried to the town hall while other members try to upset it. After the meeting, a football is kicked along the old road to Ower Quay by the participants (each carrying a pint of beer and loaf of bread) to preserve an ancient right of way used in the shipping of marbles. A tremendously amusing event (01929) 422885

MARCH

13 **Weymouth** Dorset Arts Conference – *till Sun 19* (01305) 772444

APRIL

7 **Weymouth** Easter Festival at Brewers Quay (01305) 772444

29 **Weymouth** International Beach Kite Festival at Weymouth Beach – *till Sun 30* (01305) 772444

MAY

1 **Dorchester** Annual Sheep Fair (venue to be confirmed) – *till Tues 2* (01305) 262126

5 **Weymouth** VE Day Celebrations and Commemorations – *till Mon 8* (01305) 772444

6 **nr Wareham** Corfe Castle Medieval Weekend – *till 8 May* (01929) 481294

8 **Cerne Abbas** Wessex Morris Men dance on Giant Hill at 7am (01305) 251481

12 **Bournemouth** Garden and Flower Show – *till Sun 14* (01202) 789789

13 **Abbotsbury** Garland Day (01305) 251481; **Bournemouth** International Festival – *till Sun 28* (01202) 297327; **Dorchester** National Maritime Museum Wrecks Exhibition – *till 23 Jun* (01305) 262735

14 **Weymouth** Vintage Motorcycle Rally with static display at Weymouth Pavilion (01305) 772444

20 **Dorchester** VE Parade (01305) 267992

27 **Weymouth** Oyster Festival – *till Sun 28* (01305) 772444

28 **Puddletown** Flower Festival at Athelhampton House and Gardens – *till Wed 31* (01305) 848363; **Weymouth** Dorset Tour – Vintage and Classic Car Rally at the Pavilion and Lodmoor Country Park (01305) 772444

29 **Blandford** Town Crier Competition and Fair (01258) 454500; **Weymouth** Trawler Race and Water Carnival (01305) 772458

DORSET CALENDAR

JUNE

2 **Cerne Abbas** Music Festival at St Mary's Church – *till Sun 4* (01300) 341456

12 **Dorchester** Carnival – *till procession on Sat 17*

24 **Bournemouth** Music Makers Festival – *till 8 July* (01202) 789789

25 **Beaminster** Gardens Open Day (01308) 862675; **Cattistock** Gardens Walkabout and Vintage Cars and Aeroplanes at Chalmington Manor (01300) 320226

JULY

1 **Weymouth** All-England Theatre Finals at the Pavilion (01305) 772444

8 **Puddletown** Carnival (01305) 848625; **Yetminster** Village Fair (01935) 872940

9 **Puddletown** MG Owners Club Car Rally at Athelhampton House and Gardens (01305) 848363

14 **Swanage** Jazz Festival – *till Sun 16* (01929) 422885

15 **Poole** Fisherman's Regatta – *till Sun 16* (01202) 675745

16 **Tolpuddle** Martyrs Rally: annual trade union rally with parade of banners (01202) 294333

22 **Lyme Regis** Lifeboat Week inc the Red Arrows – *till Sat 30* (01297) 443724

27 **Weymouth** Olympic Sailing Trials – *till 9 Sept* (01305) 772444

28 **Bournemouth** Firework Extravaganza *every Fri* – *till 1 Sept* (01202) 789789; **Weymouth** National Beach Volleyball Grand Prix Final – *till Sun 30* (01305) 772444

29 **Swanage** Regatta and Carnival – *till 6 Aug* (01929) 422885; **Dorchester** Dorset Cycling Weekend: 2 one-day cycle rides – *till Sun 30. Book in advance*: Bike 1 Bicycle Tours (01252) 624022

30 **Bournemouth** Kids Free Fun Festival – *till 28 Aug* (01202) 789789; **Poole** Hospital Gala; **Wareham** Military Day; **Weymouth** Family Beach Kite Festival and Fun Day

AUGUST

Weymouth Major Firework Display *every Mon night throughout Aug*

3 **Portesham** Possum Fez Wik (Fair Week) – *till Sun 6* (01305) 871316

6 **Bridport** West Bay Trawler Race Day (01308) 421808; **Dorchester** South Dorset Fayre at Came Park (01300) 348465; **Puddletown** Dorset County Arts and Crafts Association Annual Exhibition – *till Thurs 10* (01202) 553113

11 **Weymouth** VJ Day Celebrations and Commemorations – *till Wed 16* (01305) 772444

13 **Bridport** Carnival Week with procession *on Sat 19* (01308) 421808

14 **Weymouth** Kestrel National Sailing Championships – *till Thurs 17* (01305) 772444

16 **Weymouth** Carnival and Firework Festival (01305) 772444

18 **nr Wimborne Minster** Beating the Retreat at Kingston Lacy (01202) 880413

20 **Poole** Camden Trophy Powerboat Race with boats on view the day before (01202) 707227

DORSET CALENDAR

AUGUST cont

23 **Motcombe** Gillingham and Shaftesbury Show at Motcombe Turnpike Showground (01747) 823955

27 **Stinsford** Dorchester Book Fair at Kingston Maurward College of Agriculture and Horticulture (01258) 473561

30 **Tarrant Hinton** Great Dorset Steam Fair at the Showground – *till Sept 3* (01258) 860361

31 **Bridport** Melplash Agricultural Show (01308) 423337

SEPTEMBER

2 **Dorchester** Agricultural Show at Came Park (01305) 264249; **nr Wareham** Corfe Castle Medieval Weekend – *till 8 May* (01929) 481294

7 **Weymouth** Waterfest '95 at Weymouth Old Harbour (01305) 772444

17 **Weymouth** Beaulieu to Weymouth Vintage Classic Car Rally with static display at Weymouth Pavilion (*pm*) (01305) 772444

30 **Weymouth** Speed Sailing Championships – *till 7 Oct* (01305) 772444

OCTOBER

16 **Sherborne** Pack Monday Fair

21 **Corfe Castle** Civil War Garrison Weekend – *till Sun 22* (01929) 481294

22 **Weymouth** Beach Motocross Championships

NOVEMBER

5 **Weymouth** Guy Fawkes Night

19 **Stinsford** Dorchester Book Fair at Kingston Maurward College of Agriculture and Horticulture (01258) 473561

We welcome reports from readers . . .

This *Guide* depends on readers' reports. Do help us if you can – in return, we offer a discount on the next edition to people who've helped us with reports for it. Tell us what you think about places already in it, and anything extra you think we should say about them. And send us your ideas for inclusion in the next edition: places to visit, eat at or stay in, attractive drives or walks, maybe even unusual interesting shops you know of. Use the card in the middle, the report forms at the end, or just write – no stamp needed: *The Good Weekend Guide*, FREEPOST TN1569, Wadhurst, E Sussex TN5 7BR.

ESSEX

There is a quiet charm here which can bring visitors back again and again, though the countryside is far from spectacular and the coast is not the sort to fascinate most walkers. North Essex has a real East Anglian flavour, with some outstanding villages around the Stour Valley – Constable country, shared with Suffolk. South Essex is more of a mixed bag: some tranquil coast, but Southend and westwards is densely urbanised. The coastal areas have a wider choice of places to visit, particularly for families, but the inland villages and small towns tend to be more picturesque.

INLAND ESSEX

Saffron Walden is attractive, and there are several other pleasant places, particularly in the north.

Saffron Walden, the county's most attractive small town, scores doubly by having magnificent Audley End nearby – and is only a short drive from Cambridge, just over the county border. Castle Hedingham, Coggeshall, the toy museum at Stansted and the wildlife park at Widdington are all particularly enjoyable. The hotel we recommend at Broxted would make for a relaxing stay. Villages in this area often have handsome houses with distinctive colourwashed plasterwork – the intricate patterning on some is known as pargeting; many of the churches are well worth a look.

Where to stay

Broxted TL5726 WHITEHALL Church End, Broxted CM6 2BZ (01279) 850603 £105; 25 pretty rms. Fine old manor house set in lovely walled gardens, with a restful lounge, pleasant bar, ancient beams, big fireplaces, good food in the pretty timbered restaurant, and friendly service; outdoor swimming pool and tennis court; cl 25–30 Dec; disabled access.

Coggeshall TL8522 WHITE HART Coggeshall, Colchester CO6 1NH (01376) 561654 £65.60; 18 attractive rms. 15th-c hotel with a beamed lounge bar, log fires, friendly staff, and good food in both the bar and restaurant.

Thaxted TL6130 SWAN Thaxted, Dunmow CM6 2PL (01371) 830321 £65; 21 comfortably modernised rms. Four-gabled, late 15th-c inn with a pleasantly pubby, refurbished circular bar, soft lighting, traditional furnishings, and good food.

Saffron Walden TL5438 SAFFRON High St, Saffron Walden CB10 1AY (01799) 522676 £55; 17 rms. Friendly 16th-c hotel with a panelled bar, beams, comfortable lounge, and good food in the conservatory restaurant.

Rickling Green TL5029 CRICKETERS ARMS Rickling Green, Saffron Walden CB11 3YG (01799) 543210 £50; 7 rms in modern block behind. Cheerful, family-run pub by the village green, with cricketing mementos; beamed saloon bar with open fires, and decent food both in the bar and attractive restaurant.

Newney Green TL6507 MOOR HALL Newney Green, Chelmsford CM1 3SE (01245) 420814 £37; 2 rms, shared bthrm. Medieval house on a working farm with a 2-acre moated garden; friendly, family atmosphere, heavy timbers, log fires and big breakfasts; cl 13–31 Dec.

Duddenhoe End TL4636 DUDDENHOE END FARM Duddenhoe End, Saffron Walden CB11 4UU (0176 383) 8258 **£36**; 3 rms. 17th-c farmhouse with inglenook fireplaces and beams; no smoking; cl Christmas; children over 10.

To see and do

🏠 ❀ Ꮤ **Audley End House** TL5438 Spectacular Jacobean mansion and former royal palace remodelled by Robert Adam, serenely surrounded by splendid gardens landscaped by Capability Brown. It used to be much bigger, described by James I as 'too large for a king': two-thirds were demolished during 19th-c changes. Nothing inside can compete with the quite breathtaking façade but it's not for want of trying – there are around 30 rooms to see, crammed with fine furnishings and art, inc notable portraits by Lely and a Canaletto. Highlights are the beautiful great hall, drawing room and Strawberry Hill 'gothic' chapel. Suitably grand concerts and other events in the grounds. Snacks, shop, disabled access to gardens and ground floor; cl am, Mon (exc bank hols), Tues, Oct–Easter; (01799) 522842; £5.20, £2.85 grounds only. A miniature railway is nearby. The Queen's Head at Littlebury and Eight Bells in Saffron Walden have good food, and the Bell at Wendens Ambo is very pleasant.

↓T **Braintree** TL7622 WORKING SILK MUSEUM Fascinating look at silk production from start to finish, in a well restored old mill building; the hand-looms they use are over 150 years old. Also displays of fine silks and industrial machinery. Shop, disabled access; cl 12.30–1.30, all Sun and bank hols; (01376) 553393; *£2.75. The Green Dragon, just outside at Young's End, has good food.

★ † ᛗ ᕰ Ꮤ ℘ **Castle Hedingham** TL7835 has a good CHURCH with grand Norman masonry and interestingly carved choir seats, and some other attractive buildings. It's named for the Norman CASTLE which dominates it, its magnificent keep – one of the tallest in Europe – towering above the trees around the castle mound. The castle is exceptionally well preserved; the keep has four floors and a roof, and you can still see the banqueting hall and minstrels'

gallery. The wooded grounds are pleasant. Teas, shop; cl Nov–Easter; (01787) 460261; *£2.50. COLNE VALLEY RAILWAY & MUSEUM Lovingly restored Victorian railway buildings with a collection of vintage engines and carriages, plus short steamtrain trips pm every summer Sun, and pm Tues–Thurs in hols. Meals on Pullman coaches, snacks, shop, some disabled access; cl 23 Dec–Feb; (01787) 461174; £4, £2 when trains not running. There's a good working pottery in St James St, and the Bell is handy for lunch.

Ꮤ **Chappel** TL8927 EAST ANGLIAN RAILWAY MUSEUM Comprehensive collection of railway memorabilia, in restored old station buildings, with a new miniature railway and steamdays throughout the year. Snacks (not winter wkdys), shop, disabled access; cl 25 Dec, steamdays first Sun monthly as well as Weds in Aug and bank hols; (01206) 242524; £2, £4 steamdays. The prettily sited Swan is good for lunch, and the Chappel Viaduct is reputed to be the biggest brick structure in Europe.

† **Chelmsford** TL7006 is a big, busy city with little for visitors, but its 15th-c CATHEDRAL, consecrated as such only in 1914, has particularly harmonious Perpendicular architecture; they've just added a new organ.

★ 🏠 ❀ ℘ **Coggeshall** TL8522 This attractive small town has a good few antique shops, and PAYCOCKE'S (NT), a fine, timber-framed, medieval merchant's home with unusual panelling and carvings, and a pretty garden behind. Open pm Tues, Thurs, Sun and bank hols Easter–Mar-Sept; £1.40; NT. The ancient Fleece next door is useful for lunch, and there's a working POTTERY further along the st. Another inn, the Woolpack out by the church, is a magnificent timbered building. GRANGE BARN The oldest surviving timber-framed barn in Europe (now NT), dating from around 1140; it was originally part of

the Cistercian monastery here.
Disabled access; opening times as
Paycocke's (see above); £1.10, or joint
ticket with Paycocke's £2.

🐏 ♿ ✤ **Cressing** TL7920 CRESSING
TEMPLE A working farm for over 800
years, its present appearance owes
much to the Knights Templar in the
12th c – they commissioned the two
splendid timber barns here. Also
buildings from the 16th c and later, a
walled garden, and very varied events.
Snacks, shop, disabled access; cl am
Sun, Sat, Oct–Apr; (01376) 584903;
£1 wkdys, £2 Sun. The Three Ashes
has good-value food.

✤ nr **Feering** TL8621 FEERINGBURY
MANOR has a fine, big riverside garden
with ponds, streams, a little
waterwheel, old-fashioned plants and
bog gardens. Disabled access; open
8am–1pm wkdys May–July; (01376)
561946; £1.50.

★ 🏚 ✕ **Finchingfield** TL6832 is by
general agreement the county's
prettiest village, with charming
houses spread generously around a
sloping green that dips to a stream and
pond; just off it stands a pristine-
looking, small windmill. The Fox (one
of the most attractive buildings) and
Red Lion, and the Green Man just
outside, are useful for lunch.

✤ **Great Saling** TL7025 SALING HALL
Big garden with a late 17th-c walled
garden, watergardens and a growing
collection of unusual trees in
parkland. Disabled access; open pm
Weds mid-May–July; £1.50. The
White Hart is good, a handsome old
timbered inn.

✝ **Greensted** TL5303 ST ANDREWS The
country's oldest wooden church,
dating from the 9th c, with a later
Tudor chancel. The nearby Green
Man at Toot Hill is good for lunch.

👶 ✤ ✄ **Harlow** TL4510 is a new
town and not perhaps top of most
itineraries, but there are a couple of
surprisingly good museums. MARK
HALL CYCLE MUSEUM AND GARDENS
(Muskham Rd) Bewildering
assortment of bicycles from 1819 to
the present day – inc one that folds up,
another made from plastic – even one
where the seat tips forward and
throws its rider over the handlebars if
the brakes are applied too hard. Also a

Tudor herb garden and three walled
gardens. Shop, disabled access; cl Fri
(exc gardens), Sat and bank hols;
(01279) 439680; £1. The town
MUSEUM (Third Ave) has an important
Roman collection, and a butterfly
garden around the Georgian house.
Snacks, shop, disabled access to
ground floor only; cl Sun, Mon, 25–
26 Dec; £1.

🐏 ✤ **Lamarsh** TM8835 PARADISE
CENTRE Fun for children, with
miniature goats, bantams and play
area, and fascinating for gardeners,
with a very wide variety of unusual
plants beautifully laid out and for
sale, particularly woodland ones.
Snacks; open wknds and bank hols
Easter–Oct; (01787) 269449; *£1.50.
The Red Lion is good for lunch.

✤ **Langham** TM0233 THE FENS
Friendly little cottage garden with a
pond, woodland and ditch,
specialising in primulas. Garden open
mainly by arrangement, nursery Thurs
and Sat, or again by arrangement;
(01206) 272259; *£1. The Shepherd
& Dog is good for lunch.

🐏 **Little Dunmow** TL6521 PRIORY
VINEYARDS 10-acre working vineyard
in the grounds of a former
Augustinian priory. Shop, disabled
access; usually open all year, (01371)
820577 to check; £1. The Swan in
Felsted has good food.

✝ **Little Maplestead** TL8233 has an
unusual round CHURCH modelled on
the Holy Sepulchre in Jerusalem, and
used as a stopping-point for pilgrims
on their way there.

✝ **Nayland** TL9734 well rewards a
stroll – its fine church has an altar
painting by Constable; the White
Hart is a decent old inn, and the Angel
over at Stoke-by-Nayland is
exceptional.

★ ✝ 🏰 👶 ✤ ! 🏚 🏛 🏺 **Saffron Walden**
TL5438 is the finest small town in the
region. Throughout there are fine
examples of warmly colourwashed
pargeting. Walking around to look at
the buildings, you'll find it difficult to
avoid being tempted into one of the
many antique shops (or David Prue,
the fine cabinet-maker in Radwinter
Rd; cl wknds). From the town you can
walk straight into the park of Audley
End (see entry above). The grand airy

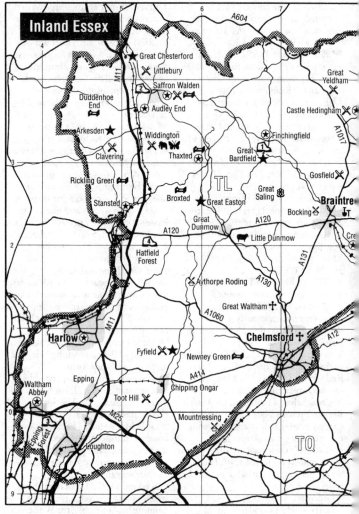

Inland Essex

Great Chesterford
Littlebury
Saffron Walden
Duddenhoe End
Audley End
Great Yeldham
Castle Hedingham
Arkesden
Widdington
Finchingfield
Clavering
Thaxted
Great Bardfield
Rickling Green
Gosfield
TL
Stansted
Broxted
Great Easton
Great Saling
Braintre
Bocking
Great Dunmow
Little Dunmow
Hatfield Forest
Aythorpe Roding
Great Waltham
Harlow
Chelmsford
Fyfield
Newney Green
Waltham Abbey
Epping
Chipping Ongar
Toot Hill
Mountnessing
Epping Forest
Loughton
TQ

CHURCH has a magnificent spire, and the very ruined CASTLE up on a grassy mound is worth prowling around. The local history MUSEUM nearby is small but unusually interesting, with the ruins of a 12th-c castle in the grounds. Shop, disabled access; cl am Sun and bank hols, 24–25 Dec; £1. BRIDGE END GARDENS Very pleasant, early Victorian gardens spread over 3½ acres, with rose garden, formal Dutch garden, kitchen garden and an atmospheric wilderness leading to a little grotto. Also Renaissance-style yew hedge maze, though until this is fully grown you'll probably need the key from the tourist information centre in the Market Place. Disabled access; cl 25 Dec; free. The Eight Bells does good food and welcomes families. About 4m S of town on the B184 at Wimbish, Grace's FARM SHOP is good, with PICK-YOUR-OWN fruit in summer.

☼ ↕T ✕ **Stansted** TL5222 HOUSE ON THE HILL TOY MUSEUM One of the biggest toy museums you're likely to come across; many displays are animated, and it's great fun watching the soldiers, trains and Meccano in

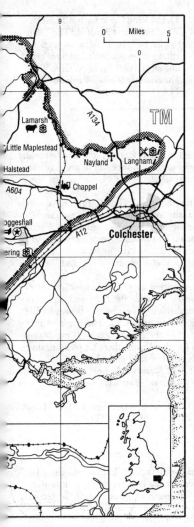

month, also bank hol Sun and Mon; cl Nov–Mar; 50p. Stansted Airport is well worth a look – quick to get in and out of – and the Cricketer's Arms at nearby Rickling Green is good for a lunch break.

★ ✝ 🏠 ⛄ ✗ ⚑ **Thaxted** TL6130 has a graceful, airy CHURCH with a tremendous spire, several handsome buildings inc nearby almshouses, a fine GUILDHALL (with a small local museum), and a restored WINDMILL. THE RAVEN ARMOURY (B184 towards Dunmow) does hand-forged steel and weaponry. The Star is good for lunch.

✝ 🏠 ⛄ ⚑ **Waltham Abbey** TL3800 Despite the surrounding housing developments, the centre has some handsome buildings – especially the ABBEY CHURCH with its famous peal of 13 bells (and a museum in the crypt). There are some associated ruins inc part of a Norman cloister, and the bridge dates back to the abbey's time. The EPPING FOREST DISTRICT MUSEUM (Sun St) is a good, local history museum in two timber-framed old houses, with lively holiday activities for children. Open pm Fri–Tues, cl Christmas wk; free. HAYES HILL FARM Traditional farmyard with plenty of animals, tools and equipment, an exhibition in the medieval barn, and Sun craft demonstrations; also includes Holyfield Hall working farm and dairy, with 150 cows milked every afternoon at 2.45, and seasonal events such as sheep-shearing and harvesting. Snacks, shop, disabled access; (0199 289) 2291; £2.20.

🐾 🦋 **Widdington** TL5331 MOLE HALL WILDLIFE PARK Family-run place with a wide variety of animals around a moated manor house. Otters a speciality, but also free-roaming wildfowl, deer paddock, butterfly house and insect pavilion. Summer snacks, shop, some disabled access; cl 25 Dec; (01799) 540400; £3.50 in summer, less in winter when butterfly house closed. The Fleur de Lys is a good dining pub.

✗ **Windmills** are quite a feature of this part of the county – given the relatively unhilly landscape, and they serve as attractive landmarks for miles around. As well as those we mention

action. Also a very good collector's shop. Cl most winter wkdys exc school hols; (01279) 813237; *£2.80. Next door (and run by the same enterprising people) is the intriguing MOUNTFICHET CASTLE AND 1066 VILLAGE, a fully reconstructed Norman castle and village, complete with animals, houses and gruesome examples of torture and punishment. Snacks, shop; cl mid-Nov–mid-Mar; *£3.75. Nearby, a well preserved 18th-c WINDMILL is unusual in having much of its equipment original rather than rebuilt. Shop; open pm 1st Sun of elsewhere, good examples can be seen at Aythorpe Roding TL5815, Bocking TL7524 and Mountnessing TQ6297.

★ **Other attractive villages** with decent pubs are Arkesden TL4834, Fyfield TL5606, Great Chesterford TL5143 and Great Easton TL6025. We'd add Great Bardfield TL6730 to this list for its fine old houses and village-edge windmill, but have heard nothing recently of its pub, the Vine. The church at Great Waltham TL6913 is beautiful.

Walks

For walkers, inland Essex lacks defined physical features and has too many vast arable fields. In places, a shortage of paths confines you to the road. That said, the prettiness of the villages, particularly in the N, encourages walks wherever there are connecting paths.

Finchingfield TL6832 ↻-1 and Great Bardfield TL6730 both have windmills and charming cottages, with an easily followed path along the Finchingfield Brook leading from one to the other. A goodish network of tracks serves the area around **Saffron Walden** TL5438 ↻-2, into the parkland of nearby Audley End House. Longer rambles can take in Newport TL5234, where the houses display characteristic pargeted plaster walls, and Wendens Ambo TL5136.

Epping Forest TQ4197 ↻-3 is a magnificent survival, an expansive tract of ancient hornbeam coppice, mainly tucked between the M25 and outer London. There are miles of leafy walks (and rides – you can hire horses locally), with some rough grazing and occasional distant views. There are so many woodland paths that getting lost is part of the experience; the long-distance Forest Way is, however, well marked. On the W side, there's a pleasant diversion to High Beach TQ4097, from where a few field paths lead SW.

Hatfield Forest TL5320 ↻-4, just S of Stansted Airport, is more of the same, not on quite the same scale but still extensive enough, with a nature trail and boating lake.

There are pleasant walks nr the White Hart at Margaretting Tye TL6800 and (in oak and chestnut woods) the Viper at Mill Green TL6401.

Driving

The B184 from Chipping Ongar right up to Saffron Walden and the B1053 between there and Braintree are admirable for country drives – little traffic, pleasant scenery, quietly attractive villages and quite a few distinctively colourwashed, often timbered houses that are surprisingly close to the road. The B1058 through Castle Hedingham, then left on the minor road through Gestingthorpe (where the Pheasant's a good stop) and the Belchamps up to Clare (just over the Suffolk border) is another very pleasant run, as is the back road down the Stour Valley from Sudbury through Henny Street, Lamarsh and Bures.

The area's trunk roads tend to be rather traffic-heavy, though the A12 is not usually clogged.

Where to eat

Clavering TL4731 Cricketers CB11 4QT (01799) 550442 Attractive and cosy, L-shaped dining pub with low beams, two open fires, and a wide choice of imaginative, well presented food in both the bar and restaurant; disabled access. £21|£2|£7.95.

Saffron Walden TL5438 Eight Bells Bridge St (01799) 522790 Handsome Tudor inn in a good walking area, nr Audley End; plenty of fresh fish, children's menu, splendidly timbered weekend restaurant; disabled access. £20|£2/£6.25.

Great Yeldham TL7638 WHITE HART Poole St (01787) 237250 Striking Tudor inn with an attractive garden, beams and oak-panelling, bar food and restaurant; cl pm Sun, Mon; disabled access. £20|£1.95/£5.

Toot Hill TL5103 GREEN MAN (01992) 522255 Simple pub in attractive countryside, close to Greensted with the country's oldest wooden church; good, interesting food in both the bar and restaurant, plenty of fish and game, over 100 wines; children over 10; cl 25 Dec. £17|£3/£3.

Littlebury TL5139 QUEENS HEAD (on the B1383, NW of Saffron Walden) (01799) 522251 Friendly, connected beamed areas, with real ale and good bar food inc some inventive dishes; no food pm Sun (except for residents), cl 25–26 Dec; disabled access. £16.25|£1.80/£6.20.

Gosfield TL7829 GREEN MAN (01787) 472746 Warm and friendly pub with a splendid cold table and really excellent, proper English cooking; fresh veg and home-made chips, decent wines, well kept beers, first-class staff and a fine atmosphere in the two bars. £14|£1.90/£6.50.

Langham TM0233 SHEPHERD & DOG (01206) 272711 Good-natured, warm, friendly local with hearty helpings of very good, often interesting, food, and popular theme nights. £12.50|£1.60/£4.75.

Castle Hedingham TL7835 BELL St James St (01787) 60350 Interesting old coaching inn with a log fire in the beamed lounge bar, traditionally furnished public bar, quickly served, decent food, and a lovely big walled garden behind; cl pm 25 Dec. £12|£2.50/£4.

Fyfield TL5606 BLACK BULL (01277) 899225 Enjoyable 15th-c pub with a wide choice of very good food inc Thurs evening fish specialities, and a relaxed atmosphere in the communicating rooms with beams and standing timbers. £1.60/£6.10.

Widdington TL5331 FLEUR DE LYS High St (01799) 40659 Wide choice of generous, reasonably priced bar food inc local game, and decent house wines in a well kept, unpretentious village pub; good real ales, log fire, and beams. £2.50/ £5.50.

COLCHESTER AND THE COAST

Interesting quiet corners, especially on the coast and in the north; a fair number of places to visit, with lots to see in Colchester.

This part of Essex has all sorts of peaceful corners, and out of season some of the smaller places on the coast have a secluded charm. Constable country – around Dedham along the border with Suffolk – is the county's prettiest area, though it has endured more than its fair share of visitors. There is plenty to see in Colchester, and many of the area's main family attractions are around it – more a place to visit by the day than a base for a short stay, as it's very much a busy working town.

Elsewhere, among the most appealing places are St Osyth Priory, Burnham-on-Crouch, Layer Marney Tower, Beth Chatto's garden at Elmstead Market, the developing garden at Rettendon, and the Heybridge barge basin at Maldon.

Southend is very much as you'd expect of this favourite seaside escape from London – lots to do in summer, a bit desolate in winter.

Where to stay

Dedham TM0533 MAISON TALBOOTH Dedham, Colchester CO7 6HN (01206) 322367 ***£120**; 10 carefully furnished rms. Tranquil Victorian country house in fine Constable country, with deeply comfortable seating in the elegant lounge, fresh flowers, and very good, imaginative food in the lovely timber-framed restaurant (a stroll away) which overlooks the river and gardens; disabled access.

Maldon TL8506 BLUE BOAR Silver St, Maldon CM9 7QE (01621) 852681 **£92 inc dinner**; 29 comfortable rms. 14th-c coaching inn with cosy, little, beamed and oak panelled rooms, open fires, good food inc interesting breakfasts, and friendly staff.

Burnham-on-Crouch TQ9596 WHITE HART, Burnham-on-Crouch CM0 8AS (01621) 782106 **£50.60**; 19 rms, 8 with shared bthrm. Old-fashioned, 17th-c yachting inn overlooking anchorage, with high ceilings, oak tables, polished parquet, sea pictures, panelling, decent bar food, and restaurant; cl 25–26 Dec.

Dedham TM0533 MARLBOROUGH HEAD Dedham, Colchester CO7 6DH (01206) 323250 ***£50**; 3 rms. Old-fashioned, comfortable, early 18th-c inn in the heart of Constable's home town; interesting carved woodwork in the central lounge, and a wide choice of interesting food; cl 25 Dec; disabled access.

West Mersea TM0112 BLACKWATER West Mersea, Colchester CO5 8QH (01206) 383338 **£50**; 7 pretty rms, most with own bthrm. Creeper-covered inn with a neat little sitting room, fresh flowers, good French food in the bistro-type restaurant, and big breakfasts; cl first 2 wks Jan.

West Mersea TM0112 VICTORY West Mersea, Colchester CO5 8LS (01206) 382907 **£35.50**; 3 rms. Decent pub in a fine spot overlooking the entrance to Strood Channel; good fresh fish; disabled access.

Tillingham TL9903 CAP & FEATHERS Tillingham, Southminster CM0 7TH (01621) 779212 ***£30**; 3 rms, shared bthrm. Quaint old pub nr the village green; extremely friendly and welcoming, and with good bar food inc meats from their own smokery.

To see and do

★ † **Bradwell-on-Sea** TM0006 is worth the long drive for the sense of being right out on the edge of things – the timeless emptiness if anything exaggerated by distant views of vast industrial installations. The walk eastwards down the old Roman road across the marshes takes you to a little, restored Saxon chapel right on the sea wall – the scene of an annual pilgrimage in July. The Cap & Feathers, on the way at Tillingham, is a lovely little pub.

★ � ☎ ☂ ✿ **Burnham-on-Crouch** TR9595 is an attractively old-fashioned yachting station, lively in summer, packed around the Aug bank hol for its regatta, nice in winter too – with rigging clacking forlornly against the masts of those yachts left to ride at anchor offshore. There's a little railway museum in a restored station, and the White Harte on the quay is good for lunch. The Limes (Southminster Rd) is

a decent FARM SHOP, with nature trails and PICK-YOUR-OWN fruit; cl Mon, and pm Sun and Tues.

☺ ✿ **Clacton** TM1715 and the quieter nearby **Frinton** TM2319 are roomy, family seaside resorts, with long stretches of gently shelving sandy beach and all the usual amusements. Beyond, the blowy open space of The Naze is pleasant for strolling, especially out of season when you're likely to have its 150 acres virtually to yourself, with good views out over the water.

🏛 ⛪ ⚓ ☂ 🏰 † ♠ ! ✗ **Colchester** TM0025 is Britain's oldest recorded town, the capital of Roman Britain. You can trace the Roman wall (the Hole in the Wall, Balkerne Gdns, is a decent pub built into the one surviving fragmentary gatehouse) – best armed first with a map-leaflet from the exemplary museum in COLCHESTER CASTLE. Ideal for families, this lets you try on Roman togas and helmets and touch some of the 2000-year-old pottery excavated nearby. Excellent collections of Roman relics, inc tombstones covered with detailed carvings, and a Civil War exhibition. Boasting the biggest Norman keep in Europe, the castle was built for William the Conqueror on the site of the Temple of Claudius, once the biggest Roman temple in the country; you can still see the remains, deep down in the building along with the prisons, used right up to the 19th c. Snacks, shop, good disabled access; cl am Sun in summer, all day Dec–Feb, and 24–26 Dec; (01206) 712931; *£2.50. The well established public park around the castle is very pleasant.

An interesting collection of museums include the NATURAL HISTORY MUSEUM and HOLLYTREES MUSEUM on the High St, the latter featuring lots of toys, costumes and curios from the last two centuries, and round the corner in Trinity St the SOCIAL HISTORY MUSEUM and TYMPERLEYS CLOCK MUSEUM, a particularly unusual selection in a lovely 15th-c house; there's something very special about coming here and hearing all the ticking. All four cl 1–2, Sun, Mon and 24–26 Dec, social history and clock museums also cl Nov–Mar; (01206) 712931; free. The High St has handsome buildings, some extravagantly timbered, and plenty more historical buildings inc ST BOTOLPH'S, the oldest Augustinian priory in the country. Town tours leave the Tourist Information Centre (Queen St) at 2pm in summer (11am Sun).

Two miles out of town in 40 acres of parkland is COLCHESTER ZOO, with thoughtfully designed enclosures for elephants, parrots, tigers, and sealions among others. Demonstrations such as feeding or snake-handling spread throughout the day, and fun underwater viewing area to watch the penguins. Meals, snacks, shop, some disabled access; cl 25 Dec; (01206) 331292; £5.70. Children should like ROLLERWORLD (Eastgates), the only international-standard, roller-skating rink in Britain. Cl Mon eve; £3. BOURNE MILL (just off the B1025, S) is a delightfully quaint, restored watermill by a pretty millpond; always worth looking at from the outside. Open Sun and Mon of bank hol wknds, also pm Sun and Tues in July–Aug only; £1.50. The Forrester's Arms (Castle St) and Rose & Crown (East St) are good for lunch.

† Copford TL9222 CHURCH is a fine Norman building with well restored, 12th-century wall paintings. The Swan at Stanway is quite handy for lunch.

★ † ▉ ▇ ☗ ⚘ Dedham TM0533 has several fine old buildings, especially the 15th-c flint CHURCH, its pinnacled tower familiar from so many Constable paintings; there's also the school Constable went to; good walks through the protected riverside meadows to his father's mill at Flatford (across the river lock, so in Suffolk). DEDHAM RARE BREEDS FARM Nicely undeveloped 16-acre farm, with two paddocks for children to walk through and stroke the animals. Snacks, shop, disabled access; open 4 Mar–16 Sept; (01206) 322176; *£2.75. There's a little TOY MUSEUM AND CRAFT CENTRE on the High St; cl Mon and Fri; museum 40p. The handsome Marlborough Head, a wool merchant's house dating from 1475, has good food, and the partly medieval Sun here is useful too.

❀ Elmstead Market TM0624 BETH CHATTO GARDENS A riot of colour in summer, these attractive gardens have been transformed from 4 acres of wasteland; lots of gardening ideas, plant sales inc unusual varieties. Cl Sun, bank hols and winter Sats; (01206) 822007; £2.

▉ ▉ ❀ ▟ ✕ Harwich TM2632 THE REDOUBT Circular fort built in 1808 in case of invasion by Napoleon, with three small museums. Shop; open Sat, some Suns, all Aug; (01255) 503429; *£1. Harwich also has an interesting little MARITIME MUSEUM in a lighthouse by the harbour. Shop; open Sun Easter–Sept; 50p. There are cruises around the harbour in summer. From the A120 W, there's an unusual sight for this part of Essex – a tall, narrow WINDMILL (actually an interloper, as it was brought from Suffolk).

❀ ⚘ Hockley TQ8293 VOLPAIA (54 Woodlands Rd) Lily specialist's small but beautiful woodside garden, with rare collected plants, species and own-bred hybrid lilies, as well as shade-loving shrubs; interesting plant sales. Teas; open pm Thurs and Sun mid-Apr–early July; (01702) 203761; £1. The Bull has decent food, and is handy for walks in Hockley Woods – and the following entry.

🐖 **Hullbridge** TQ8194 JAKAPENI FARM Small rare breeds park, specialising in pigs and sheep, with other pets and wildlife. Snacks, shop, disabled access; open Easter, then all Suns and bank hols till Nov; (01702) 232394; *£1.50.

🏠 ❀ **Ingatestone** TQ6499 INGATESTONE HALL is an interesting old house, nothing too remarkable but has enthusiastic tours by the family that live here, and lovely grounds. Teas; cl am, Mon (exc bank hols), Tues and all Oct–Easter; (01277) 353010; £3. The Hoop over at Stock is handy for lunch.

🏠 ❀ 🐖 **Layer Marney** TL9317 LAYER MARNEY TOWER The mansion here was never completed; its eight-storey Tudor gatehouse, the tallest of its kind in the country, is however very impressive – perhaps one of the most striking examples of 16th-c architecture in the country. Also formal gardens, rare breeds farm, medieval barn, farm shop and deer park. Snacks, shop, disabled access to grounds; cl am (exc Sun), all Sat, Oct–Mar; (01206) 330784; *£3.

❀ 🏠 ❀ ✝ ♨ **Maldon** TL8506 has a lively BOAT AND BARGE QUAY at Heybridge Basin just outside – the best chance to see one of the classic Thames barges with its ox-blood sails in action. The Old Ship here has decent food and lovely views. You can tour the old MOOT HALL, where they have been displaying an ambitious tapestry commemorating the 1000th anniversary of the Battle of Maldon, a crucial moment in English history. This may move to another site down the road this year, (01261) 857373 to check; cl Sun; £1. The MILLENNIUM GARDENS are named for the same event, and recreate what a garden would have looked like at the time of the battle. Also a CHURCH with an unusual triangular tower, some decent shops, a couple of small museums, and a riverside stroll past the golf course to the pretty weir by Beeleigh Abbey.

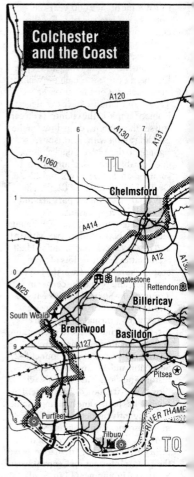

Colchester and the Coast

🐦 **Mersea Island** TM0413, much of it a National Nature Reserve for its shore life, is linked to the mainland by a little causeway, which can get covered by the tide. It does feel very much an island, and away from the extended village of West Mersea, popular for retirement homes, there are few people about out of season (in summer, the caravan parks bring in lots of families). In addition to the places mentioned in the **Where to stay** section, the Fox does good-value food.

✿ **Mistley** TM1231 has an interesting CRAFT CENTRE by the old barge quay, with musical-instrument makers as well as potters and so forth; vegetarian restaurant.

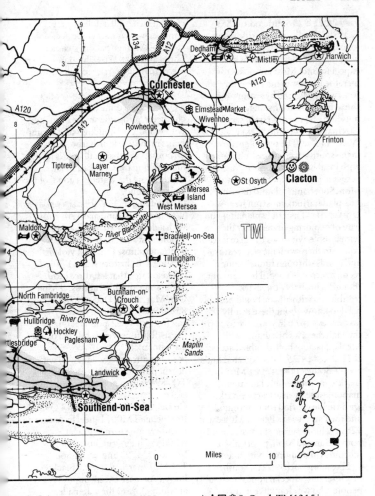

❀ ⚘ ❀ **Pitsea** TQ7488 PITSEA HALL COUNTRY PARK (formerly the Wat Tyler Country park) 120 acres with nature trails, craft workshops, rural life exhibition; free. There's also a MOTORBOAT MUSEUM, with a varied collection of vessels, and good guided tours (cl Tues and Weds; free).

❀ **Rettendon** TQ7698 RHS GARDEN (Hyde Hall) 8 acres of year-round hillside colour, with a woodland garden, big rose garden, ornamental ponds, shrubs, trees, and national collections of malus and viburnum. Teas, disabled access; cl Mon (exc bank hols), Tues, Fri and all Nov–Mar; (01245) 400256; £2.50. The Barge at Battlesbridge is quite handy for lunch.

★ † ▣ ❀ **St Osyth** TM1215 is a pretty little village distinguished by the remarkable, crenelled flint gateway leading to ST OSYTH PRIORY. Few people seem to find their way past the ancient gatehouse, perhaps surprisingly – the lovely towers and buildings on the other side cover a varied range of styles and periods, and the atmosphere is utterly peaceful and relaxed, with peacocks strutting across the wide shaded lawns. Notable paintings include works by Stubbs and Van Dyck, and there are 20 acres of gardens. Some disabled access; open May–Sept (and Easter wknd), grounds daily, art collection cl 12.30–2.30 and all Sat; (01255) 820492; £3.50.

! ♪ ⚓ 🍽 🏕 ☸ ⛴ Southend-on-Sea
TQ8885 Traditional seaside resort
long favoured by East Londoners,
with many of the attractions you'd
expect to find. Most famous is the
pier, the longest in the world if
somewhat battered by storms and
ships, excellent for fishing, with a
museum and restored train service.
CENTRAL MUSEUM AND PLANETARIUM
(Victoria Ave) The only planetarium
in the south-east outside London,
with local history too. Shop, disabled
access to ground floor only; cl am
Mon, Sun, bank hols and day after;
*£2 planetarium, museum free. SEA
LIFE CENTRE (Eastern Esplanade) Fun
way of exploring underwater life,
with bubble-windows to make it seem
you're in there with the sea creatures,
and a walk-through tunnel along a
reconstructed sea bed. The highlight
though is probably the shark
exhibition, with all you could possibly
need to know about these deadly
favourites – to go in you have to step
through the jaws of a giant shark.
Meals, snacks, shop, disabled access;
cl 25 Dec; *£4.25. Less expected finds
are the SOUTHCHURCH HALL MUSEUM
(Park Lane), a medieval moated
manor house in an attractive park,
with various period room settings,
and the PRITTLEWELL PRIORY MUSEUM, a
12th-c Cluniac priory in nice grounds;
both cl Sun and Mon, priory also cl
mornings in termtime; both free.

Like many such resorts, Southend
in winter has a special appeal for
people who wouldn't like it in
summer – seafront shops by the
endless promenade looking closed for
ever, the sea itself a doleful grey.
Summer BOAT TRIPS include occasional
runs on a vintage paddle-steamer:
phone (0634) 827648 for dates. There
are year-round ferries to Felixstowe;
£3 return.

Though attached, LEIGH-ON-SEA
TQ8385 has a quite distinct
character, altogether more intimate,
with wood-clad buildings and shrimp
boats in the working harbour; Ivy
Osborne's shellfish stall here is justly
famous, and the Crooked Billet
overlooking the water is a good, old-
fashioned pub.

🏰 ☸ Tilbury TQ6476 TILBURY FORT
Well preserved, unusual 17th-c fort
with a double moat; good views of the
Thames estuary, its boats and
container ships. The most violent
episode in its history was a 1776
cricket match that left three dead.
Shop, some disabled access; cl Mon
Oct–Mar, 24–26 Dec; (01375)
858489; £1.80. For an extra £1 you
can fire a 1943 12-pounder gun –
irresistible for several children of our
acquaintance.

★ **Other attractive villages,** all with
decent pubs, include Battlesbridge
TQ7894 (also a popular antique and
crafts centre, walks to the head of
Crouch estuary), Paglesham TQ9293,
Rowhedge TM0021 (nearby nature
reserve among former gravel
workings at Fingringhoe), South
Weald TQ5793 and Wivenhoe
TM0321 (particularly the Black
Buoy). All these except South Weald
are quite close to the waterside.
☸ Down at **Purfleet** TQ5578, the
Royal Hotel has good Thames views.

Walks

The county's low-lying, much indented coast does have opportunities for
walking, though the immediate hinterland is generally too dull to make circular walks worthwhile. The **Blackwater estuary** ⌂-1 has vast skies, with boats
and birdlife punctuating the flat sea and landscapes; the pick of local walks
include paths along the dykes from Tollesbury TL9510 and towards isolated
St Peter's Chapel from Bradwell-on-Sea TM0006. More boats are on view at
Burnham-on-Crouch TQ9596 ⌂-2, along the Crouch itself. The Ferryboat
down by the River Crouch, at the end of the lane through North Fambridge
TQ8597, is a good base for lonely waterside walks.

Mersea Island TM0413 ⌂-3 has a bracing coastal walk from East Mersea
along the sea-dyke overlooking the Colne estuary.

Despite the surrounding urbanisation, there are decent walks from the Shepherd & Dog at Crays Hill TQ7192 between Billericay and Basildon.

Driving

On the whole this is not an area for rewarding country drives, as it's mostly too flat to give worthwhile views. Also, the back roads are generally slow, and in the flatter parts many have unexpected turns. The A12 is now a good road, and the A120 between Colchester and Harwich is usually fairly quick. The A127 and A13 always seem a little nerve-wracking, perhaps because of the way their regular users jostle for quick getaway positions at the traffic lights.

Don't be tempted by the map into the long drive to Foulness Island; it is indeed an island, and wonderfully remote-feeling considering how close it is to London. But with a big atomic weapons establishment, it's almost entirely owned by the Ministry of Defence, and their checkpoint at Landwick TQ9687 will turn you back unless you've arranged a pass.

Where to eat

Burnham-on-Crouch TQ9596 CONTENTED SOLE 80 High St (01621) 782139 Though there's an obvious emphasis on fine seafood, meat dishes feature as well in this consistently good restaurant; disabled access; cl pm Sun, Mon, also last fortnight July and 4 wks around Christmas. £27|£3.50|£9.50.

West Mersea TM0112 WILLOW LODGE 108 Coast Rd (01206) 383568 Large, busy restaurant with a wide range of very good food, inc lots of fresh fish as well as vegetarian dishes; disabled access; cl pm Sun, Mon. £18|£1.80|£5.50

Dedham TM0533 MALLARD Riverside Cottage Mill Lane (01206) 322066 Unlicensed little riverside restaurant with a homely, relaxed atmosphere, and good, straightforward food; cl Mon, Tues, Thurs and Fri lunchtime, pm Sun, Jan. £15|£1.50|£3.90.

Colchester TM002S CLOWNS 61–62 High St (01206) 578631 Huge helpings of good, straightforward food in this clean and spacious restaurant; disabled access; cl 25–26 Dec. £11|£3.35.

North Fambridge TQ5136 FERRYBOAT (01621) 740208 Unspoilt and relaxed waterside pub, traditionally decorated, with very good-value, popular bar food, decent wines, well kept beer, and friendly service. £1/£3.

Help this year from: David Cardy, Jenny and Michael Back, George Atkinson, Quentin Williamson, Gwen and Peter Andrews, John Fahy, Adrian M Kelly, Penny and Martin Fletcher, Basil Minson, Trevor Scott, Mr and Mrs W R R Bruce, Judith Mayne, Bernard Phillips, Nigel Norman, Mike Beiley, Tony Beaulah

Essex Calendar

Some of these dates were provisional as we went to press.

MARCH

3 **Clacton** Real Ale and Jazz Festival – *till Sun 5* (01255) 474000

APRIL

16 **Chipping Ongar** Easter Show with vintage vehicles and arena events – *till Mon 17* (01277) 821143

25 **Thundersley** European Beer Festival at Runnymede Hall – *till Sat 29* (01268) 792711

MAY

8 **South Woodham Ferrers** May Day Carnival and Fête at Saltcoats Park (01245) 323228

13 **Chelmsford** Cathedral Festival – *till Sat 20* (01245) 359890; **Epping** Fighter Meet at North Weald Air Field – *till Sun 14* (01992) 524510

21 **Great Leighs** Essex Young Farmers Country Show at the Showground (01245) 362411

27 **Great Braxted** Braxted Park Show at Braxted Park – *till Sun 28* (01206) 251790; **Wormingford** Flower Festival at St Andrew's Church – *till Mon 29* (01787) 227292

28 **Great Leighs** Essex Motor Show at the Showground – *till Mon 29*; **Southend-on-Sea** Air Show at Western Esplanade – *till Mon 29* (01702) 215166

31 **Burnham-on-Sea** South-East Boat Show – *till Sun 4* (01359) 271311

JUNE

2 **Thaxted** National Morris Dancing – *till Sun 4* (01371) 831024

4 **nr Chelmsford** Annual Open Day at Writtle College (01245) 420705

11 **Cressing Temple** Essex History Fair

16 **Great Leighs** Essex County Show at the Showground – *till Sun 18* (01733) 234451

18 **Aldham** Gardens Open Day (01206) 240425; **Southend-on-Sea** Eastend to Southend Classic Car Run (01702) 215166

23 **Thaxted** Festival – *till July 16* (01371) 870296

24 **Leigh-on-Sea** Midsummer Folk Festival – *till Sun 25* (01702) 215166; **Southend-on-Sea** Midsummer Folk Festival – *till Sun 25* (01702) 215166

25 **East Tilbury** Historic Artillery Display at Coalhouse Fort; **Canvey Island** Castle Point Show at Waterside Farm (01268) 792711

JULY

1 **Colchester** Open-Air Concert 'Space and Time' at Castle Park; **Harwich** Festival – *till Sun 9* (01255) 506139; **Southend-on-Sea** Punch and Judy Festival, on and around the pier – *till Sun 2* (01702) 215166

2 **Burnham-on-Crouch** Transport Gala Weekend (01621) 784898

8 **nr Epping** Wings and Wheels Model Spectacular at North Weald Air Field – *till Sun 9* (01684) 594505; **Manningtree** Tendring Show at Lawford House Park (01206) 571517

ESSEX CALENDAR

JULY cont

9 **Southend-on-Sea** Triathlon (01702) 215564

15 **Southend-on-Sea** '999' Emergency Services Seafront Spectacular on Western Esplanade – *till Sun 16* (01702) 215166

20 **Cressing Temple** Festival – *till Sun 30*

29 **West Bergholt** Historic Vehicle Show – *till Sun 30 July* (01206) 271253

30 **East Tilbury** Classic Car Show at Coalhouse Fort; **Maldon** Carnival Week – *till Sat 5* (01621) 891105

AUGUST

4 **Southend-on-Sea** Jazz Festival – *till Sun 6* (01702) 215166

11 **Southend-on-Sea** Carnival Week – *till Sat 19* (01702) 713849

25 **Chelmsford** Spectacular – *till Tues 29* (01245) 283400

26 **Clacton-on-Sea** Jazz Festival – *till Mon 28* (01245) 436825; **Colchester** Open-Air Concert 'Space and Time' at Castle Park; **Saffron Walden** Festival of Gardening at Audley End House – *till Mon 28* (01525) 405771; **Southend-on-Sea** Thames Sailing Barge Race (0171) 5827070

27 **Purleigh** English Wine Festival at New Hall Vineyards – *till Mon 28* (01621) 828343

SEPTEMBER

2 **Orsett** Show; **Brentwood** Festival – *till Sun 17*; **Leigh-on-Sea** Regatta – *till Sun 3* (01702) 75183

9 **Billericay** Essex Steam Rally and Craft Fair at Barleylands Farm – *till Sun 10* (01268) 532253

30 **Burnham-on-Crouch** Carnival

NOVEMBER

4 **Harwich** Guy Carnival

6 **Southend-on-Sea** Music Festival – *till Sat 25*

DECEMBER

7 **Maldon** Victorian Christmas – *till Thurs 14* (01621) 860478

GLOUCESTERSHIRE

The Cotswolds area has a succession of delightful villages and small towns with handsome buildings largely unchanged since the heyday of the wool trade several centuries ago, many interesting places to visit, and charming countryside. Add to that civilised and individual places to stay in, and plenty of fine food, and it adds up to perfection for a short break.

The north Cotswolds area is the best known, with more famously beautiful villages and towns than the south, rather more in the way of tourist attractions, and the widest choice of really good places to stay at. But the south has a richer variety of relatively undiscovered villages and, in summer, is less swamped by visitors. Its countryside, although perhaps less classically Cotswoldy, has a great diversity of scenery, including the very up-and-down area around Stroud. Though there's no real division between north and south, we treat them separately – to provide areas of a manageable size to enjoy in a shortish break.

The Forest of Dean – very different indeed – has possibilities for a quiet weekend break, especially at those times of year when the Cotswolds are at their most popular. And it's within easy reach of Gloucester – a busy modern city, but with several things well worth seeing.

Though the county does have places that are a lot of fun for families, on the whole this wouldn't be first choice as an area to take young children to. But the Cotswolds country is classic for cycling – quiet, village-to-village lanes with ever-changing views.

NORTH COTSWOLDS

Idyllic villages and traditional small towns, lots of interesting places to visit, excellent places to stay.

Beautiful stone-built villages and small towns bulging with antique shops punctuate classic rolling countryside, traditional dry stone-walled fields with occasional beechwoods and meandering streams. A good many lovely places to visit include among their special highlights two glorious gardens near Mickleton, Stanway Manor, Snowshill Manor (the NT has just improved visitor facilities here), the farm park at Guiting Power, Sudeley Castle near Winchcombe, and the Batsford Arboretum at Moreton-in-Marsh. It's worth noting that several of the finest gardens and parks are clustered around Moreton-in-Marsh and Chipping Campden. There are good walks.

In the summer, the area does attract a lot of visitors, though even then you can find picturesque villages that have escaped the crowds. Springtime can be especially charming here.

An excellent choice of places to stay runs from small village inns and civilised B & Bs to some delightfully individual country hotels in former manor houses.

Where to stay

Buckland SP0836 BUCKLAND MANOR Buckland, Broadway, Worcs WR12 7LY (01386) 852626 **£155**; 14 sumptuous rms. Really lovely 13th-c building in 10 acres of beautifully kept gardens; comfortable lounges with magnificent oak panelling, flowers and antiques, and an elegant restaurant; outdoor swimming pool, riding, tennis, croquet, putting; children over 12.

Lower Slaughter SP1622 LOWER SLAUGHTER MANOR Lower Slaughter, Cheltenham GL54 2HP (01451) 820456 *****£120**; 14 luxurious rms with thoughtful extras. Grand 17th-c manor house on the edge of a particularly pretty village; with a lovely, wood-panelled drawing room, antiques and paintings, log fires, nice flower arrangements, fine plaster ceilings, excellent food in the elegant restaurant, and a very good wine list; 15th-c dovecot, croquet lawn and all-weather tennis court in the gardens and indoor heated swimming pool; cl 2 wks Jan; children over 10.

Charingworth SP2039 CHARINGWORTH MANOR Charingworth, Chipping Campden GL55 6NS (01386) 78555 **£110**; 24 lovely rms with thoughtful extras. Early 14th-c manor with Jacobean additions, set in fine grounds; mullioned windows, antiques, log fires and heavy oak beams in the relaxing sitting room, good, modern cooking in the charming restaurant, excellent breakfasts, and friendly staff; billiards, leisure spa with indoor swimming pool, and all-weather tennis court; children over 10 in evening restaurant; dogs by arrangement.

Stow-on-the-Wold SP1925 GRAPEVINE Stow-on-the-Wold, Cheltenham GL54 1AU (01451) 830344 *****£108**; 23 well furnished rms. Warm, friendly and very well run hotel, newly refurbished, with antiques, comfortable chairs and a relaxed atmosphere in the lounge, beamed bar, and good food in the attractive, sunny restaurant; cl 24 Dec–11 Jan.

Upper Slaughter SP1523 LORDS OF THE MANOR Upper Slaughter, Cheltenham GL54 2JD (01451) 820243 **£97.50**; 29 rms carefully furnished with antiques, Victorian sketches and paintings. Warm and friendly hotel with a mid-17th-c core (though it's been carefully extended many times); delightful views over 8 acres of grounds from the very comfortable library and drawing room, log fires, fresh flowers, fine, modern English cooking in the attractive candlelit restaurant (overlooking the original rectory gardens), good breakfasts, and kind service; the original cellars are lovely; cl 1–15 Jan; disabled access.

Chipping Campden SP1539 COTSWOLD HOUSE The Square, Chipping Campden GL55 6AN (01386) 840330 **£95**; 15 charming rms (the ones at the back overlook the pretty garden). Fine Regency building with antiques, open fires and beautiful flowers in the elegant rooms, an impressive spiral staircase, attractive and airy all-day eaterie, good food in the formal restaurant (pianist 3 evenings a week), and helpful professional staff; cl 24–28 Dec; children over 8.

Chipping Campden SP1539 NOEL ARMS High St, Chipping Campden GL55 6AT (01386) 840317 **£82**; 26 comfortable rms. Bustling 14th-c inn with old agricultural implements and an open fire in the bar, comfortable, traditionally furnished, small lounge areas, armour and antiques, conservatory, restaurant, and decent wines; disabled access.

Moreton-in-Marsh SP2032 WHITE HART ROYAL Moreton-in-Marsh GL56 0BA (01608) 650731 **£80**; 17 good rms. Comfortable, partly 15th-c inn with a blazing inglenook fire in the bar, and an attractive courtyard.

Willersey SP1039 OLD RECTORY Church St, Willersey, Broadway, Worcs WR12 7PN (01386) 853729 **£79**; 8 rms. Friendly and homely 17th-c house set opposite the little village church (the village itself is attractive); with good breakfasts and walled gardens; no evening meals – though several places nearby; cl Christmas; children over 8.

Stow-on-the-Wold SP1925 OLD STOCKS The Square, Stow-on-the-Wold, Cheltenham GL54 1AF (01451) 830666 **£70**; 18 good-value rms. Well run, 16th/17th-c, Cotswold stone hotel with a cosy, clean and welcoming small bar, beams and open fire, good food, friendly staff, and a sheltered garden; cl 19–29 Dec; disabled access.

Chipping Campden SP1539 SEYMOUR HOUSE High St, Chipping Campden GL55 6AH (01386) 840429 **£69.30**; 16 lovely rms. Comfortable, Georgian, Cotswold stone hotel with good food in the airy restaurant (which also has an ancient vine), beams, exposed stonework, open fires and antiques, and a terrace overlooking the quiet garden with its 500-year-old yew tree.

Nailsworth ST8499 EGYPT MILL, Nailsworth GL6 0AE (01453) 833449 **£65**; 16 comfortable airy rms. Carefully converted, 16th-century watermill with the original millstones and lifting equipment in the spacious lounge, a split-level restaurant, ground-floor bar where two waterwheels can be seen, good, freshly made food, friendly service, and seats in the waterside gardens.

Laverton Meadows SP0937 LEASOW HOUSE Laverton Meadows, Broadway WR12 7NA (01386) 584526 *£60.48; 7 spacious rms. Informal, 17th-c stone house with lovely views, friendly owners, and a comfortable library with drinks tray; good disabled access.

Chipping Campden SP1539 KINGS ARMS, Chipping Campden GL55 4AW (01386) 840256 **£60**; 14 rms. Civilised small hotel with a comfortably old-fashioned bar, log fires, excellent service, generously served good food, intimate candlelit restaurant, and lots of wines; they're kind to children.

Lower Swell SP1725 OLD FARMHOUSE Lower Swell, Cheltenham GL54 1LF (01451) 830232 **£60**; 14 rms, some in main building but most in various barns, stables and outbuildings, and most with own bthrm. Peaceful and unpretentious 16th-c manor farm with a log fire in the lounge bar, good, interesting food using fresh local produce, friendly staff, and a walled rose garden; cl 2 wks Feb.

Great Rissington SP1917 LAMB Great Rissington, Cheltenham GL54 2LP (01451) 820388 **£52**; 13 rms – one has a four-poster carved by the landlord. Civilised 17th-c inn in pretty countryside, with a sheltered hillside garden; cosy two-roomed bar, residents' lounge with a log fire, indoor swimming pool, and good nearby walks; cl 25–26 Dec; dogs allowed in bedrooms only.

Bledington SP2422 KINGS HEAD The Green, Bledington, Chipping Norton, Oxon OX7 6HD (01608) 658365 **£50**; 12 rms. Very nicely placed, 15th-c Cotswold inn by a duck-filled stream; cheery log fire in the atmospheric bar, lounge overlooking the garden, excellent food in both the bar and attractive restaurant (partly no smoking), and friendly service; cl 25 Dec; disabled access.

Oddington SP2225 HORSE & GROOM Oddington, Moreton-in-Marsh GL56 0XH (01451) 830584 **£50**; 7 quaint and comfortable rms. Attractive, well run inn in this pretty Cotswold village, with handsome old furnishings, a big log fire, candlelit dining room, and a good garden with aviary and large play area.

Winchcombe SP0228 WESLEY HOUSE High St, Winchcombe, Cheltenham GL54 5LJ (01242) 602366 **£45**; 6 cosy rms with showers. Pretty, half-timbered, 15th-c house with a quiet, friendly atmosphere, log fire in the comfortable lounge, and good food in the attractive, beamed restaurant; cl 17 Jan–10 Feb.

Greet SP0230 MANOR FARM Greet, Cheltenham GL54 5BJ (01242) 602423 **£40**; 3 rms. Mixed farm with a carefully restored, 16th-c manor house, fine views, big garden and croquet; also, self-catering cottages.

Winchcombe SP0228 SUDELEY HILL FARM Winchcombe, Cheltenham GL54 5JB (01242) 602344 *£40; 3 no-smoking rms. Friendly, 15th-c farmhouse on a working mixed farm, with log fires, guest sitting room, and dining room overlooking the large garden; barbecues too; no dogs; cl Christmas.

Moreton-in-Marsh SP2032 REDESDALE ARMS High St, Moreton-in-Marsh GL56 0AW (01608) 50308 **£36.40**; 16 individually decorated rms, some in an annexe. Lively, early 18th-c inn with a well renovated and comfortable pub bar and buttery, restaurant, and good food served by helpful staff; disabled access.

Bourton-on-the-Hill SP1732 HORSE & GROOM Bourton-on-the-Hill, Moreton-in-Marsh GL56 9AQ (01386) 700413 **£35**; 3 rms with showers. Quiet roadside pub with an attractive, high-beamed, little lounge bar, big log fire, a locals' bar, decent food, restaurant, and pretty hanging baskets.

Long Hanborough SP4214 OLD FARMHOUSE Station Hill, Long Hanborough, Witney, Oxon OX8 8JZ (01993) 882097 £35; 2 rms, one with own bthrm. 300-year-old farmhouse – not a working farm – with beams, flagstones and an inglenook fireplace, friendly owners, and good home cooking; no smoking; cl Christmas; children over 12.

To see and do

★ **Cotswold villages** The greatest attraction of the Cotswolds is the host of delightful, stone-built villages, usually with handsome medieval churches. The cottages and houses don't hide away behind gardens and high walls, but tend to be right by the road. Up in this part, they are usually built in a warm, golden-tinted stone, and roofed in picturesque slabs of heavy stone. Often, there's a strip of daffodil-planted grass between pavement and road, and sometimes a little stream. Lower Slaughter SP1622, with its sister village Upper Slaughter SP1523, is perhaps the prettiest village in Britain – a perfect harmony of stone, water, grass and trees. It's not nearly as overwhelmed by summer visitors as its nearby rival Bourton-on-the-Water SP1620 (see entry below), though it certainly gets its fair share.

Many lesser-known villages are almost as beautiful. We have picked out a short list which have the added attraction of a decent village pub: Bledington SP2422, Blockley SP1634 (where there's also the Sleepy Hollow Farm Park), Broad Campden SP1637 (the Baker's Arms), Broadwell SP2027, Ebrington SP1840, Great Barrington SP2013 (good, cheap bedrooms at the Fox), Lower Swell SP1725, Naunton SP1123, Oddington SP2225 (pleasant walks; the Fox at Lower Oddington has very good food), Stanton SP0734 (an absolute charmer) and Willersey SP1039. Though there's no pub to recommend there, Saintbury SP1139 is a winner when the daffodils are out.

CYCLING is a good way to see some of these places at their best, and the Cotswold Cycling Company not only hire bikes but can arrange your route and accommodation too; tel (01242) 250642.

Other things to see and do

❀ ♞ **Bourton-on-the-Hill** SP1732 BOURTON HOUSE Unusual plants, inc tender ones, in an attractive garden around a fine old house (not open). Teas in 16th-c tithe barn, shop; open pm Thurs and Fri late May–Sept; £2. The Horse & Groom is a civilised place for lunch. SEZINCOTE SP1730 (about a mile S, off the A44) Exotic, onion-domed forerunner of Brighton Pavilion, stunning from the outside, less interesting inside; also a classic, early 19th-c watergarden, and more recent Indian-style garden to match the building. Garden open pm Thurs, Fri and bank hols (cl Dec), house pm Thurs and Fri May–July and Sept; £3.50, £2.50 garden only. Children are not allowed in the house.

★ ☂ ⌂ ✗ ♩ ! **Bourton-on-the-Water** SP1620 One of the best-known Cotswold villages, disfigured by sprawly crowds in summer unless you get there very early in the morning – when it's enchanting. There is a wealth of attractions aimed at visitors. BIRDLAND Rare and exotic birds on the banks of the meandering River Windrush, inc the biggest colony of penguins outside America. Also a tropical house and play area for children. Snacks, shop, disabled access; cl 25 Dec; (01451) 820480; £3. COTSWOLD MOTOR MUSEUM In an old watermill, cars and motorcycles from the vintage years to the 1950s, along with 800 advertising signs, 8,000 pieces of automobilia, and toy collection. It's the home of Brum the children's TV character. Shop, disabled access; cl Dec–Jan, occasional winter wkdys; (01451) 821255; *£1.40. The price includes entry to the adjacent VILLAGE LIFE EXHIBITION, with recreated Edwardian rooms, village shop, and blacksmith's

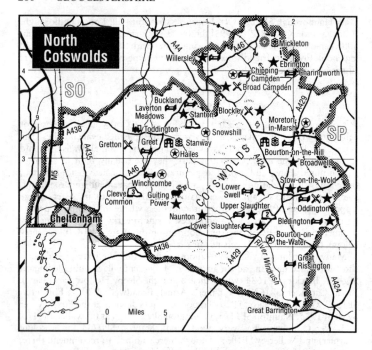

North Cotswolds

forge. Cl Dec–Feb, occasional winter wkdys; 70p for just here. MODEL VILLAGE A replica of the village modelled from Cotswold stone in the 1930s to a scale of one-ninth, complete with working waterwheel and music in the church. Snacks (in the adjacent, welcoming Old New Inn), shop; cl 25 Dec; £1.30. PERFUMERY EXHIBITION Aromatic displays and demonstrations of perfume-making and scent extraction, with scented garden, and audio-visual show in a specially designed theatre. Shop, disabled access; cl 25–26 Dec; (01451) 821717; £1.50. FOLLY FARM WATERFOWL (Just W on the A436) Lakes and pools with over 160 species of waterfowl, as well as friendly ducks, geese and poultry, and hand-reared animals. Good for children, and a nice spot for a picnic. Snacks, shop, disabled access; cl 25 Dec; (01451) 820285; *£3. The Old Manse has decent food and garden tables overlooking the Windrush.

★ ♠ † ☺ **Chipping Campden** SP1539
An extremely attractive town, with interesting old buildings inc an ancient, covered, open-sided market hall, a handsome Perpendicular church typical of the area's rich 'wool churches', enjoyable shops, and fine old inns. Many of our contributors would put it among the country's most delightful small towns, though until they get the cars out of the centre not all would agree. WOOLSTAPLERS HALL MUSEUM The 11 rooms of this 14th-c wool hall are packed with anything from phonographs to jelly moulds, and candlesticks to man-traps. Shop; cl Nov–Mar; (01386) 840289; *£2. In addition to places mentioned in the **Where to stay** section (above), the ancient Eight Bells by the church is good for lunch.

♠ ★ **Guiting Power** SP0924
COTSWOLD FARM PARK Ideal for children, a comprehensive collection of rare breeds in a typical Cotswold farm setting; at various stages of the year it is filled with lambs, foals, piglets and fluffy chicks. Also adventure playground, nature trails, seasonal events such as lambing and shearing, and temporary exhibitions. Meals, snacks, shop, disabled access; cl Oct–Mar; (01451) 850307; £3. The village itself is lovely, and the Olde Inne has good food.

🐚👑🍎 **Hailes** SP0228 HAILES ABBEY Graceful ruins of a 13th-c Cistercian abbey, once a centre for pilgrims who flocked to see a phial containing what they believed to be Christ's blood. Good museum, and Walkman tour. Shop, some disabled access; cl Mon and Tues Oct–Mar; £1.90; NT. Hailes Fruit Farm down the road is good for snacks, and has PICK YOUR OWN.

❀❀ **Mickleton** SP1643 HIDCOTE MANOR GARDEN Looking particularly trim these days, a delightful series of small gardens separated by walls and hedges of different species, with rare shrubs, trees and roses. Very popular, even mid-week. Meals, snacks, shop, some disabled access; cl Tues, Fri and Nov–Mar; £4.80; NT. The adjacent KIFTSGATE COURT GARDEN is renowned for its old-fashioned roses, inc the largest rose in England; also other rare plants, shrubs and trees. Good views across the Vale of Evesham – one of our correspondents is sure she caught a glimpse of Broadway Tower. Teas (between spring and Aug bank hols only – other days you could pop next door), rare plant sales; open pm Weds, Thurs, Sun and bank hols, Apr–Sept, as well as Sat Jun and July; (01386) 438777; £3. The King's Arms is good value for lunch.

★ 🐴❀❀🌿🦅📖 **Moreton-in-Marsh** SP2032 Attractively bustling old place, once an important linen weaving centre and coaching town, now with a popular Tues market. The White Hart Royal, Black Bear and Redesdale Arms are all useful for lunch. Just NW at Batsford Park, BATSFORD ARBORETUM is a private collection of over 1,000 rare and beautiful species of tree spread over 50 acres; hundreds of maples, 90 magnolias, flowering cherries, super views. Best in May and autumn, but ideal for a relaxing stroll at any time. Snacks, shop; cl mid-Nov–Feb; (01608) 50722; *£2.50. Also in Batsford Park, the COTSWOLD FALCONRY CENTRE has lots of eagles, hawks, falcons and owls, with daily flying demonstrations. In the breeding season, close-circuit TVs give a real bird's-eye view of life in the nest. Snacks, shop, disabled access; cl Nov–Feb; (01386) 701043; £2.50.

WELLINGTON AVIATION ART (Broadway Rd) Paintings, tie pins, prints and propellers, a unique collection of WWII aircraft pictures, sculpture and related material. Shop, disabled access; cl 12.30–2pm, all Mon; (01608) 650323; *£1.

🏠👑❀ **Snowshill** SP0933 SNOWSHILL MANOR Far more unusual than the ordinary Cotswold manor house it appears to be from the outside, with one of those extraordinary collections of ephemera great eccentrics manage to amass. There's real method to the madness – each room is carefully themed, full of maybe toys, musical instruments, bikes hanging from the ceiling, or even suits of Japanese Samurai armour, spookily arranged to look like a group of warriors meeting in the gloom. There's a charming cottage garden outside. Meals, snacks, shop; cl am, Tues and wkdys in Apr and Oct, and all Nov–Mar; £4.20; NT. This is one of the Trust's busier properties, and this year they're introducing a timed ticket system; you might find it best to come mid-week or out of season. They've also just bought an adjoining farm, with three cottages for holiday hire. The nearby Snowshill Arms is popular for lunch.

🏠❀ **Stanway** SP0632 STANWAY MANOR By any standards, one of the most beautiful 16th-c manor houses in the country – a cluster of gabled buildings popping up unexpectedly from the countryside, with charming and clearly lived-in rooms. Classic great hall and long passage, typical squire's family portraits and unusual furnishings. The early 18th-c grounds have fine trees and interesting buildings, inc a folly pyramid on a steeply wooded hill. Open pm Tues and Thurs Jun–Sept; (01386) 73469; £3, garden only £1.50.

★ **Stow-on-the-Wold** SP1925 is a handsome, stone-built market town with fine buildings around its square and in the narrow lanes off, and a good few antique shops, book shops and so forth. It's something of an antidote to the more sweetly pretty Cotswold villages, on quite a high plateau and altogether more austere in style – not for nothing was it known as 'Stow on the Wold, where the wind blows cold'. The Fosse Manor Hotel, Queen's Head and Old Stocks Hotel are all good for lunch here.

🚂 **Toddington** SP0333 GLOUCESTERSHIRE–WARWICKSHIRE RAILWAY Steam and diesel train trips through 4½ miles of quiet countryside, departing from restored GWR stations either here or at Winchcombe; trains run every wknd Mar–Oct and every day in summer and some school holidays. Snacks, shop, good disabled access (though watch out for the potholes in the car park); £5. It stops near the Harvest Home at Greet and Royal Oak at Gretton, both doing decent food.

★ ✝ 🏰 🖼 🕸 🎋 🚂 🍽 **Winchcombe** SP0228 Very peaceful and photogenic – once the capital of Mercia, now worth a stop for a look at the CHURCH with its grotesque gargoyles, or just to soak up the tranquil atmosphere. SUDELEY CASTLE AND GARDENS Delightful old house, once lived in by Catherine Parr, the luckiest of Henry VIII's wives. The original medieval castle was largely destroyed in the

Civil War, but the remains were skilfully blended into the 19th-c reconstruction. Rich furnishings, porcelain and tapestries, and notable paintings by Turner, van Dyck and Rubens. The 8 splendid gardens are unmissable. Various special events and regular craft workshops. Meals, snacks, shop and specialist plant centre, disabled access to garden; cl Nov–Mar; (01242) 602308; *£4.95. RAILWAY MUSEUM AND GARDEN Behind an ordinary-looking door is a rather more unusual Victorian garden full of lovingly rescued railway memorabilia inc a booking office, working signals and signal box. Snacks, shop, disabled access; usually open wknds Easter–Sept and daily in Aug, best to check, (01242) 620641; *£1.95. The FOLK AND POLICE MUSEUM has a collection of British and international police uniforms and equipment. Shop; cl Sun, Nov–Mar; 50p. Good High St eating places are the Plaisterer's Arms and the prettily set Corner Cupboard up at the top, and there are interesting craft and other shops here.

Walks

The **Cotswold Way**, a 100-mile path from Chipping Campden SP1539 to Bath ST7464, carefully picks out some of the most choice bits of landscape – a worthwhile aid for those planning a shorter stroll, for instance between the timeless villages of **Stanton** SP0734 ⌂-1, Stanway SP0632, and Buckland SP0836 (field paths and farm track let you detour to Snowshill SP0933, and from there it's a pleasant 3-mile walk to Broadway SP0937 just over the Heref & Worcs border).

Another attractive village-to-village stroll is the leisurely mile or so following the river between **Lower Slaughter** SP1622 ⌂-2 and Upper Slaughter SP1523. To make a longer walk for a circuit of a couple of hours, you can follow the signposted Warden's Way. The best way back out of Bourton-on-the-Water SP1620 is the exit by the church, heading out W past the school and over the old railway line, then following the lanes and tracks S of Upper Slaughter to rejoin the River Windrush to Bourton.

For views here, the steep grassy slopes of the W escarpment of the Cotswolds can't be bettered, and make for fine walking. **Cleeve Common** SO9925 ⌂-3, the highest point of the Cotswolds, has breezy, unkempt grassland on its open expanses and can either be reached from the nearby village of Cleeve Hill SO9826 on the A46, or integrated into a circular walk to include Belas Knap long barrow SP0125 and Winchcombe SP0228. There's also a pleasant walk up to Belas Knap from the Craven Arms (a decent pub, with a nice garden in a lovely setting) in Brockhampton SP0322.

Driving

The back roads through the villages we suggest visiting make for pleasant drives. The road along the sparkling River Windrush through Snowshill, Ford, Kineton and Naunton is a particular delight.

You can quickly get from this area to the south Cotswolds – from Chipping Campden down to Cirencester in under an hour, for instance.

Where to eat

Blockley SP1634 CROWN (01386) 700245 Smart and civilised, Elizabethan stone inn with very good food in the bar or one of two restaurants (seafood specialities, with up to 25 fresh fish main courses), lots of fine wines; children allowed if well behaved. Comfortable bedrooms. £28|£2.50/£4.95.
Lower Oddington SP2225 FOX (01451) 870888 Carefully restored, rather elegant place with a warm, friendly atmosphere, interesting food in the bar and lovely dining room, well kept beers, exceptionally good wines and other drinks like jugs of Pimm's, elderflower *pressé* and sloe gin. £17|£2.25/£7.50.
Gretton SP0131 ROYAL OAK (01242) 602477 Enterprising and original food in a long series of flagstoned or bare-boarded rooms; beams, dim lighting from candles in bottles, an entertaining medley of furnishings, and friendly, young service; cl 25–26 Dec. £15|£2.95/£4.95.
Broad Campden SP1637 BAKERS ARMS (01386) 840515 Atmospheric ex-granary in a tranquil village, with very good-value bar food (inc a children's menu), fine range of real ales, cosy, beamed bar, log fires, friendly cats, pleasant service, and a nice garden; cl 25 Dec, pm 26 Dec. £1.50/£3.50.

SOUTH COTSWOLDS

Excellent for a short break – even more variety of scenery and places to visit than in the north Cotswolds.

Besides the classic Cotswold scenery, this area also includes the quiet watermeadows of the upper Thames, the Severn estuary, and the tortuous steep hills around Stroud. It has a splendid choice of picturesque villages, many of them little-visited by tourists. Cirencester, Northleach and Painswick are all handsome Cotswold towns with interesting sightseeing possibilities. Cheltenham still has a considerable degree of Regency elegance, and makes a nice contrast to the older and more intimate style of the rest of the area. Among other places, the wildfowl reserve at Slimbridge is particularly rewarding these days, and Westonbirt Arboretum, the Chedworth Roman villa and the never-finished Gothic mansion at Nympsfield are all outstanding in their different ways.

Like the north Cotswolds, this part's main appeal is to adults – though there are attractions here which children enjoy.

There's no shortage of good places to stay in.

Where to stay

Bibury SP1106 SWAN Bibury, Cirencester GL7 5NW (01285) 740695 £150; 18 individually decorated rms. Handsome, creeper-covered hotel on the banks of the River Coln (the hotel has private fishing), with pretty, formal gardens;

cosy no-smoking parlour, carefully furnished, comfortable lounges, lovely fresh flowers, log fires, good food in the opulent dining room, nice breakfasts, and attentive staff; disabled access.

Shurdington SO9218 GREENWAY Shurdington, Cheltenham GL51 5UG (01242) 862352 **£110**; 19 well equipped, spacious and pretty rms. Very well run, lovely 16th-c manor house with antiques, fresh flowers and comfortable seats in the attractive drawing room, cosy cocktail bar, very good, modern British cooking, excellent wine list, pleasant service, and neatly kept gardens; no lunch Sat, cl 5 dys after 1 Jan; children over 7 only; disabled access.

Cheltenham SO9422 HOTEL ON THE PARK Evesham Rd, Cheltenham GL52 2AH (01242) 518898 ***£94**; 12 lovely rms. Warmly welcoming and handsome Regency house with an elegantly furnished drawing room and dining room, pretty flowers and antiques, and imaginative food inc good breakfasts; cl one wk Jan; children over 8.

Tetbury ST8893 CLOSE 8 Long St, Tetbury GL8 8AQ (01666) 502272 **£88**; 15 individually furnished rms, some with garden views. Civilised 16th-c hotel with a cosy little bar and relaxing, dome-ceilinged lounge, log fires, very good food, excellent service, and a walled garden – floodlit at night.

Painswick SO8609 PAINSWICK HOTEL Kemps Lane, Painswick, Stroud GL6 6YB (01452) 812160 **£87**; 20 well equipped, comfortable rms. 18th-c Palladian mansion – once a grand rectory – with fine views, antiques and paintings in the elegant rooms, open fires, good food (especially fish and shellfish) and a relaxed, friendly atmosphere; garden with croquet lawn.

Tetbury ST8893 CALCOT MANOR, Tetbury GL8 8YJ (01666) 890391 ***£87**; 20 individually decorated rms – as well as converted granary barn with child listening service, bunk beds, safe garden and play area for families. Charming manor house with a civilised lounge and smaller drawing room, log fires, friendly, relaxed atmosphere, and careful modern cooking in the airy restaurant, as well as lighter meals in the bar; outdoor swimming pool with re-laid terrace, croquet, clay-pigeon shooting, and tennis courts (planned); disabled access.

Tetbury ST8893 SNOOTY FOX, Tetbury GL8 8DD (01666) 502436 **£80**; 12 individually furnished rms. Charming 16th-c coaching inn with antiques and paintings in the comfortable lounges (one is no smoking), open fire in the bar, and good food in the oak-panelled restaurant.

Westonbirt ST8589 HARE & HOUNDS Westonbirt, Tetbury GL8 8QL (01666) 880233 **£80**; 30 comfortable rms. Cotswold stone hotel with a pleasant, old-fashioned bar, relaxed, spacious and comfortable lounges, open fires, good food, and friendly service; garden, tennis, squash, croquet, snooker; disabled access.

Withington SP0315 HALEWELL Withington, Cheltenham GL54 4BN (01242) 890238 ***£77**; 6 beamed and comfortable rms. Lovely, old Cotswold stone house, dating back to the 15th-c, with a relaxed house-party atmosphere, marvellously characterful beamed sitting rooms (one is a library), late breakfasts, and good English food in the panelled dining room; high tea is provided for children; 50 acres of private ground inc a big garden with stone terraces, heated outdoor swimming pool, and trout in the lake and River Coln; riding can be arranged; dogs allowed; good provision for the disabled.

Bibury SP1106 BIBURY COURT Bibury, Cirencester GL7 5NT (01285) 740337 ***£76**; 20 individual rms. Lovely, peaceful mansion house, dating from Tudor times, on the edge of a charming village; an informal, friendly atmosphere, panelled rooms, antiques, huge log fires, conservatory, and good imaginative food; beautiful gardens; cl 1 wk over Christmas.

Stratton SO0103 STRATTON HOUSE Gloucester Rd, Stratton, Cirencester GL7 2LE (01285) 651761 **£73.90**; 41 rms. Carefully extended, former wool merchant's house with lovely walled gardens; peaceful drawing room with an open fire, an oak parquet-floored bar, and an elegant restaurant; croquet.

Cheltenham SO9422 LYPIATT HOUSE Lypiatt Rd, Cheltenham GL50 2QW (01242) 224994 **£65**; 10 attractive rms. Carefully restored Victorian house in its own grounds; with friendly service, a light, comfortable drawing room, and a little conservatory bar; children over 5.

Ewen SU0097 WILD DUCK Ewen, Cirencester GL7 6BY (01285) 770310 £65; 9 rms. Attractive, old-fashioned, 16th-c inn with a handsome Elizabethan fireplace in the comfortable beamed bar, imaginative bar food (lots of fresh fish), and a prize-winning garden.

Cirencester SP0201 FLEECE Market Pl, Cirencester GL7 2NZ (01285) 658507 £60; 30 well equipped rms. Tudor coaching inn with oak beams and log fires in the comfortable lounge, good lunchtime food in the relaxing restaurant, and a pretty courtyard.

Fossebridge SP0811 FOSSEBRIDGE Fossebridge, Cheltenham GL54 3JS (01285) 720721 £55; 9 attractive rms. Ivy-covered, partly Tudor inn by the River Coln, with two attractively furnished, beamed bars, fine log fires, a good restaurant, and helpful service; pretty lawns and terraces.

Hampnett SP0915 HAMPNETT MANOR Hampnett, Cheltenham GL54 3NW (01451) 860806 £50; 3 rms. Victorian manor house in a pretty garden and set in a peaceful hamlet; with comfortable drawing room, big dining room, and a study; cl Christmas/New Year.

Painswick SO8609 PAINSWICK MILL Kingsmill Lane, Painswick, Stroud GL6 6SA (01452) 812245 £45; 2 beamed rms. Handsome, 17th-c, Cotswold stone house and a working mill until the 1920s, with oak panelled and beamed rooms and some fine old fireplaces; hard tennis court in the 3½ acres of gardens with two streams and a watergarden; children over 10.

Brookthorpe SO8312 GILBERTS Gilberts Lane, Gloucester GL4 0UH (01452) 812364 £44; 4 rms. 400-year-old house with woodburning stove and games in the sitting room, organic produce from the surrounding smallholding used for breakfast, and a relaxed atmosphere; very helpful advice about places to visit.

Northleach SP1114 MARKET HOUSE The Square, Northleach, Cheltenham GL54 3EJ (01451) 860557 £40; 3 rms, 2 with shared bthrm. Pretty, 400-year-old stone house, with flagstones, beams and an inglenook fireplace, and good breakfasts; children over 12.

North Nibley ST7496 NEW INN Waterley Bottom, North Nibley, Dursley GL11 6EF (01453) 543659 £35; 2 rms, shared bthrm. Simple country inn with a characterful landlady, wholesome home-made food, plentiful breakfasts, and several interesting ales; a neatly kept garden, small orchard, and good nearby walks; cl Christmas/New Year; no children.

To see and do

★ **Cotswold villages** One of the most popular villages of all here is Bibury SP1106 on the River Coln. In summer it is so busy as to blunt its appeal, but nearby on the same trout-stream you'll find other villages off the main road that are just as appealing though bypassed by most visitors, particularly Coln St Aldwyns SP1405 (the New Inn is excellent) and Quenington SP1404 (a decent village pub). On the far side of Bibury, the back road tracking along the river passes through a string of pleasant little villages such as Coln Rogers, Coln St Dennis and (lovely at daffodil time) Yanworth SP0713, and eventually reaches the pretty village of Withington SP0315 (delightful pub right on the stream).

Other villages well worth tracking down, all with decent pubs and many well off the usual tourist routes, include Amberley SO8401, Bisley SO9005, Chedworth SP0511, the Duntisbournes SO9709 (the Five Mile House is a real step back in time), Eastleach SP1905 (a lovely, ancient clapper bridge links the two Norman churches, very photogenic at daffodil time), Ewen SU0097, Frampton Mansell SO9102, North Cerney SP0208, Sapperton SO9403, Selsley SO8304 (William Morris, Maddox-Brown, Burne-Jones and Rossetti all worked on the church's windows), Sheepscombe SO8910, Slad SO8707 (the setting for Laurie Lee's *Cider With Rosie*), Woodchester (particularly for the views from the south) SO8302, Southrop SP1903 (another village that really

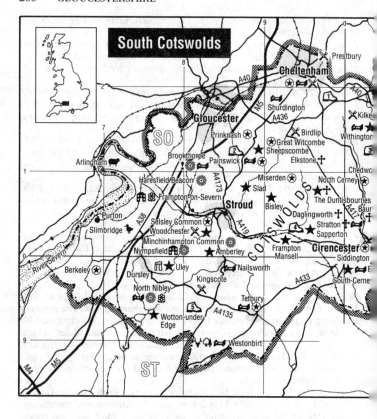

comes into its own when the daffodils are out, with a charming riverside church) and (more small town than village) Wotton-under-Edge ST7593, with a fine Schreider organ in its church, a new little heritage centre, and some handsome old buildings.

Other things to do and see

Arlingham SO7010 ST AUGUSTINE'S WORKING FARM Friendly dairy farm with cows, pigs, goats, hens, sheep and rabbits, all of which you can go right up to. Snacks, shop, disabled access; cl Oct–Mar; (01452) 740277; *£2.50. The Ship at Upper Framilode nearby has decent food in an attractive setting.

Barnsley SP0705 BARNSLEY HOUSE GARDEN Lovely little herb, vegetable and knot gardens, fruit trees and decorative plants, laburnum and lime walks and 18th-c summerhouses; especially attractive spring blossom and autumn colours. Plant sales; cl

Tues, Fri, Sun; (01285) 740281; £2. The Village Pub is good.

Berkeley ST6899 BERKELEY CASTLE Excellently preserved castle, very much a family home (24 generations of the Berkeleys have lived here over the last 850 years), but still keeping a flavour of its days as a Norman fortress. Impressive paintings, furnishings and silver, fine old keep and great hall, terraced gardens, park, extensive butterfly farm and the dungeon where Edward II was murdered in 1327. Snacks, shop, limited disabled access; cl am Sun and every day in Apr, Mon exc

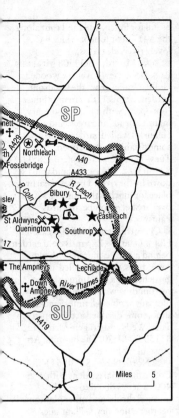

★ 🏠👹🏛 Cheltenham SO9422
Beautiful spa town useful for
exploring the Cotswolds, shopping or
admiring the elegant Regency
architecture of its tree-lined avenues.
PITTVILLE PUMP ROOM AND MUSEUM
(Pitville Park) Generally regarded as
the town's finest building – 19th-c
Greek Revival with a colonnaded
façade and balconied hall; spa water
available, super park and gardens.
The museum has a history of
Cheltenham, with well displayed,
original costumes from the city's
Regency heyday to the Swinging
Sixties. Shop; cl Mon (exc bank hols),
and Oct–May; (01242) 512740;
£1.50. ART GALLERY AND MUSEUM
(Clarence St) Excellent Arts and
Crafts collection inspired by William
Morris, fine paintings inc 17th-c
Dutch works, and rare porcelain and
ceramics. Meals, snacks, shop,
disabled access; cl Sun and bank hols;
free. HOLST BIRTHPLACE MUSEUM
(Clarence Rd, Pitville) Interesting
Regency house where the composer
was born in 1874; furnished in period
style, with his original piano. Shop; cl
Sun, Mon, bank hols, 25–26 Dec;
£1.50. Taylors in Cambray Pl is a
good wine bar, the Cotswold in
Portland St is useful for lunch, and the
well run café in the beautiful Imperial
Gardens is suitable for families.
★ ✝👹🗡🏠🏛👹 Cirencester SP0201 is
a busy country town, particularly on
its Mon and Fri market days, with a
succession of fine Cotswold stone
streets off the long market place. It has
many attractive buildings, and
interesting antique and other shops
inc traditional country saddlers etc.
Though one of the most handsome of
all the Cotswold towns, it is not too
touristy. The ST JOHN THE BAPTIST
CHURCH (Market Place) is very grand,
and has a striking late Gothic tower.
CORINIUM MUSEUM (Park St)
Cirencester was one of the most
important cities in Roman Britain,
and this spacious museum has one of
the finest collections of antiquities
from the period (all clearly displayed
and labelled). Also full-scale
reconstructions of a dining room and
kitchen (complete with menus), and
Saxon and medieval galleries. Snacks,

bank holidays, Oct exc Sun, all
Nov–Mar; (01453) 810332; £3.80,
£1 gardens only, £1 butterfly farm.
JENNER MUSEUM Largely unchanged
Georgian home of Edward Jenner,
who, as the museum here shows, not
only discovered the vaccine against
smallpox but also dabbled in
hydrogen balloons and hibernating
hedgehogs. He vaccinated the poor
free of charge from the thatched hut in
the attractive grounds. Shop, disabled
access; cl am, Mon exc bank hols, Oct
exc Sun, Nov–Mar; (01453) 810631;
£1.20. The Salmon at Wanswell
Green is a good nearby pub for lunch.
♪ ★ Bibury SP1106 TROUT FARM
Well placed by the oft-photographed
village, a working farm breeding
rainbow trout in 20 ponds. You can
feed the fish. Snacks, shop, disabled
access; cl 25 Dec; (01285) 740215;
£1.90. The Catherine Wheel is the
best place here for lunch.

shop, excellent disabled access; cl am Sun, Mon Nov–Mar, Christmas; (01285) 655611; £1.25. BREWERY COURT 20 independent craft businesses and shops in a former brewery building (cl Sun); plus theatre, gallery, café. Also worth a look are the 12th-c remains of ST JOHN'S HOSPITAL, the NORMAN ARCH, and the various well preserved wool merchants' houses. Cecily Hill, one of the town's most attractive streets, gives on to the pleasant strolling-ground of Cirencester Park. Decent places for lunch include the Slug & Lettuce, Fleece Hotel, Tatyans (Chinese) and (very local but good-value) Golden Cross.

🏛 ❀ **Frampton-on-Severn** SO7407 FRAMPTON COURT Elegant, lived-in Georgian house, with original furniture, porcelain and paintings, and fascinating gardens. The 18th-c orangery has been well converted into self-catering holiday flats. Disabled access to garden only; open all year by appointment; (01452) 740267; *£3.50. The village green is said to be the largest in the country, with the orangery on one side, and a civilised Georgian pub on another. Just outside the village, the Gloucester & Sharpness Canal passes grand, colonnaded, lock-keepers' houses by pretty swing bridges.

🏛 ❀ 🐀 ❀ **Great Witcombe** SO9114 WITCOMBE ROMAN VILLA Remains of a big villa built around a courtyard, with several mosaics and evidence of an underfloor heating system. Open only a few days each year – dates from English Heritage, 0171-973 3396. CRICKLEY HILL COUNTRY PARK (just N) has a few ancient sites, as well as nature trails, lovely woodland walks, and fine views. Some disabled access; visitor centre cl winter; (01452) 425674. The Royal George Hotel at Birdlip has decent food, and the Golden Heart at Brimpsfield is good.

★ **Lechlade** SU2199 is a graceful village with one or two worthwhile antique shops, a good, traditional toy shop, pleasant walks, and access to the quiet, reed-fringed Thames for footpath walks. The Red Lion and (with good arrangements for wheelchairs) Crown here are both

useful for lunch, and the Trout along the A417 at St John's Bridge has lovely riverside tables.

❀ ❀ 🐀 **Miserden** SO9308 MISERDEN PARK Good views over the wooded Golden Valley from the handsome gardens of this 17th-c manor house (not open), with a Lutyens topiary, mature shrubs and trees, and a colourful walled garden. Nursery, some disabled access; open Tues–Thurs Easter–Sept; (01285) 821303; £2. Also woodland trail down by the river. The best nearby place for lunch is the Butcher's Arms over at Sheepscombe, towards Painswick.

❀ 🐀 **North Cerney** SP0208 CERNEY HOUSE GARDENS Expansive old garden behind a 13th-c church, with old roses, trees, shrubs, walled and herb gardens, and a few animals. The surrounding woods are especially pleasant at bluebell time. Snacks, shop, some disabled access; open pm Tues, Weds and Fri Feb–Oct; (01285) 831300; *£1.50. The Bathurst Arms is useful for lunch.

❀ ❀ **North Nibley** ST7495 HUNT'S COURT Informal gardens with over 400 varieties of old roses, plus unusual shrubs and other plants inc heathers; fine views. Plant sales, mostly disabled access; cl Sun and Mon (exc spring bank hols) and some mid-summer Suns, all Aug; (01453) 547440; £1. The nearby Black Horse is useful for lunch, and the walk up to the Tyndale Monument above the wooded slope gives even better views.

★ † ! 🎵 **Northleach** SP1114 is a fine example of an unspoilt, small wool town, with a particularly interesting CHURCH. KEITH HARDING'S WORLD OF MECHANICAL MUSIC Unusual and quite captivating collection of clocks, musical boxes and instruments in an old, wool merchant's house, displayed and played in period settings. It's quite spooky watching the instruments work themselves. Shop, good disabled and blind access; cl 25–26 Dec; (01451) 860181; £3.50. COTSWOLD COUNTRYSIDE COLLECTION Museum of rural Cotswold life, with reconstructed rooms and quite an emphasis on horse-drawn equipment and wagons. Snacks, shop, disabled access to ground floor only; cl am Sun, all Nov–Mar; (01451) 860715; £1.25. The Red Lion (see **Where to eat** section) and Wheatsheaf Hotel are both pleasant for lunch.

🏠 ❀ **Nympsfield** SO8000 WOODCHESTER MANSION Construction of this splendid, unfinished Gothic mansion was inexplicably abandoned virtually overnight in 1870. It's being repaired but not finished, and you can usually see traditional building techniques like stonemasonry. Five species of bat add to the atmosphere. No children inside for safety reasons. Snacks, shop, disabled access to ground floor only; open first wknd of every month Apr–Oct, and bank hol wknds; (01453) 860531; *£3. The Rose & Crown in the village is good value for lunch, and the walk up Coaley Peak gives tremendous views over the Severn Valley.

★ ❀ 🏠 ✝ ☂ ❀ 🐦 **Painswick** SO8609 is a delightful little town often referred to as the 'Queen of the Cotswolds'. There's been a settlement here since Celtic times, and if you climb up PAINSWICK BEACON to look at the remains of the earliest structures, there are fine views towards the Malvern Hills. Plenty of old buildings to look at, such as the 15th-c POST OFFICE and the CHURCH OF ST MARY, with its fine tombs and fascinating churchyard – 99 immaculately clipped yews forming gateways and canopies, interesting tombstones, drifts of wild cyclamen in Sept. Also antique shops and craft workshops, notably that of Dennis French who has a showroom of woodware (cl Mon and wknds exc some summer Suns). PAINSWICK ROCOCO GARDEN (The Stables, Painswick House) Careful restoration of a sizeable 18th-c garden to match the 1748 painting showing its rococo mix of precisely trimmed hedging, paths and shrubs, with unrestrained trees and slightly zany garden buildings; pleasant vistas, woodland walks. Meals, snacks, shop, plant sales; cl Mon and Tues exc bank hols, all Dec–mid-Jan; (01452) 813204; £2.50. The Royal Oak is good for lunch.

✝ ☂ ❀ 🐦 **Prinknash** SO8614 PRINKNASH ABBEY AND POTTERY

Unusual 20th-c Benedictine monastery and earlier house, now home to the world-famous pottery. You can watch the crafts being made from the viewing gallery. Meals, snacks, shop, disabled access; cl 25–26 Dec, Good Fri; 75p for pottery viewing gallery. Good views over the Severn Vale from the attractive grounds, which also house the exotic pheasants, peacocks and other birds belonging to the PRINKNASH BIRD PARK. Lots of the birds are very friendly. Also deer, goats and waterfowl, monks' haunted fishpool, and pets' corner. Shop; cl 25–26; (01452) 812727; £2.80. The Black Horse at Cranham is handy for lunch.

❀ ❀ **Selsley Common** SO8304 The grassland common itself is quite high and has good views. SELSLEY HERB FARM Sizeable herb gardens, as well as old-fashioned roses and butterfly plants, and goats to feed. Shop, plant sales, cream teas summer Suns and bank hols, some disabled access; cl am Sun, and Oct–Mar; (01453) 766682; *£1 for garden. They also have a herb shop just down the A46 in Nailsworth ST8499 (which has plenty of trails around its old mills). The Ram at Woodchester is handy for lunch.

🎣 ♣ ❀ 🐦 ❦ **South Cerney** SU0497 COTSWOLD WATER PARK 2,000 acres of lakes with facilities for angling, windsurfing, sailing and other watersports, country park and walks, birdwatching, and nature reserves. Snacks, disabled access; (01285) 861459; £2 (£3 wkdys) car parking charge, poss not in winter. The Eliot Arms has decent food.

🐦 **Slimbridge** SO7703 WILDFOWL AND WETLANDS TRUST This enormous wildfowl reserve is the Trust's headquarters, and is filled with probably the world's most comprehensive collection of geese, swans and ducks, as well as six flocks of flamingos, rare and wild birds, and a tropical house. Some of the birds can be fed by hand. Excellent viewing facilities, varied events and talks, especially in school hols. Meals, snacks, shop, some disabled access; cl 24–25 Dec; (01453) 890065; £4.50. The Tudor Arms by the swing bridge across the canal is a useful food stop, and the village post office has details of a number of decent little walks around the area.

🏠 ⚲ 🏆 **Tetbury** ST8993 has a splendid raised MARKET HOUSE and some interesting little lanes, with quite a few antique shops and craft workshops. CHAVENAGE Friendly, unspoilt, 16th-c manor house with entertaining tours by the owner. Tapestries, furniture, Cromwellian relics, Edwardian wing, and big gardens. It's a popular location for TV programmes, providing a backdrop for characters from Monsieur Poirot to Mister Blobby. Disabled access to ground floor only; open pm Easter Sun and Mon, then pm Thurs and Sun May–Sept; (01666) 502329; £2.50. The Crown has decent food, and Hunter's Hall (A4135 towards Dursley) is even better.

★ 🏛 **Uley** ST7898 is an attractive, former weaving village with some 18th-c or older stone houses; the King's Head is very good for lunch. ULEY TUMULUS Quite daunting, 180ft-long burial mound known as Hetty Pegler's Tump (off the B4066, N), with a stone central passage and three burial chambers; key from nearby house.

🐜 ✝ **Westonbirt** ST8589 WESTONBIRT ARBORETUM Over 18,000 numbered trees and shrubs fill the 17 miles of pathways at this magnificent collection, begun in 1829 and run as a family hobby for years until it was bought by the Forestry Commission. Outstanding in spring and autumn, but worth a stop at any time, with lots of wildlife hidden away amongst the trees. Various events throughout the year. Meals, snacks, shop, disabled access; (01666) 880220; £2.50. The Hare & Hounds is handy for food.

🏛 🐜 🐚 **Yanworth** SP0513 CHEDWORTH ROMAN VILLA The best example of a 2nd-c Roman house in Britain, excavated in 1864 and nicely set in secluded woodland. Well preserved rooms, bath-houses and 4th-c mosaics, with smaller remains in the museum. Shop, some disabled access; cl Mon (exc bank hols), Tues in Nov, and all Dec–Feb (exc first 2 wknds in Dec); £2.60; NT. The Mill at

Withington, Seven Tuns in Upper Chedworth and Fossebridge Inn at Fossebridge are all quite handy for lunch – and the walk from each is very picturesque and unspoilt.

✝ Many villages have most **attractive churches**, few of them as yet locked. Cirencester is a good base for planning circuits of neighbouring villages – all with churches worth seeing. One such group, E of the town, consists of Ampney Crucis SP0602, Ampney St Peter SP0801, Ampney St Mary SP0802, Down Ampney SP1097 (Vaughan Williams was the vicar's son), Hampnett SP0915 and Northleach SP1114. Another group, NW of Cirencester, has Elkstone SO9612, Duntisbourne Abbots SO9707, Duntisbourne Rouse SO9806, Daglingworth SO9905 (with its finely preserved Saxon carving of Christ on the cross), Stratton SP0103, Baunton SP0204 and North Cerney SP0208.

🌼 🐜 ✝ The National Trust own quite a bit of **attractive countryside** around here, notably HARESFIELD BEACON SO8209 (3m NW of Stroud), nearly 450 acres of woodland and grassland on the Cotswold escarpment, with spectacular views, and nearby MINCHINHAMPTON AND RODBOROUGH COMMONS SO8600, 900 acres of open land with fine views, decent pubs, and a wide range of wildlife; both free.

❗ This part of the **River Severn** is well known for the Severn Bore, a tidal wave that occurs during high tide. Tides here are the second-highest in the world and, depending on conditions, can reach up to 6 ft in height. The National Rivers Authority produce a calendar listing the best times and places to catch the phenomena, with a rating of how spectacular it's likely to be in each; (01684) 850951. A good quiet spot to get down to the river is from Purton SO6904, where the Berkeley Arms has a wonderful estuary view.

🌼 ❗ Ongers Farm at Brookthorpe SO8312 organise GUIDED HORSERIDES, (01452) 813344; for more spectacular Cotswold views, BALLOON TRIPS can be booked on (01453) 885187.

Walks

The **Cotswold Way** (see north Cotswolds section) continues here, again with a good many worthwhile stretches from which to select walks. It takes in a series of excellent viewpoints: among them the **Devil's Chimney** SO9418 ⌂-1, a rock pinnacle amid old quarries on Leckhampton Hill, perched above Cheltenham SO9422; and **Painswick Beacon** SO8612 ⌂-2 and Haresfield Beacon SO8208, reached by short ascents from the road.

The **Chedworth Woods** SP0513 ⌂-3 provide scope for short walks if you want the satisfaction of reaching Chedworth Villa (see entry above) on foot. A field path from Chedworth SP0511 heading N through the woods is a little tricky to find; much easier is the level track along the N edge of the woods, which approaches the site from the E.

The rich, steeply sheltered valleys around Stroud make up a complicated landscape, seen to best advantage for example between Chalford SO8903 and Sapperton SO9403, where the derelict **Thames & Severn Canal** ⌂-4 is atmospherically overgrown, although its towpath survives as a walkway; the Daneway at Sapperton is an excellent jumping-off point. There are also pleasant walks nr the interesting Tunnel House at Coates SO9600, at the other end of the long former canal tunnel.

Not far from Wotton-under-Edge ST7593, the valley of **Ozleworth Bottom** ST7992 ⌂-5 has a nostalgically forgotten quality about it, providing a walk between Lasborough Manor and Ozleworth Park, with its unusual Norman church endowed with a hexagonal tower.

The **River Coln** ⌂-6 gives an appropriately quiet approach to Bibury SP1106, along the path from the toll-house just S of Coln St Aldwyns SP1405. This route takes you in by the mill and bridge over the Coln itself.

Extended walks over the Cotswold plateau are not always rewarding, with unchanging views of arable fields often the rule. Pubs that are good jumping-off points for walks here include the Black Horse at Cranham SO8912 for Cranham Woods, the Crown at Frampton Mansell SO9102 or the Daneway at Sapperton for the derelict canal mentioned above, the Edgemoor at Edge SO8509 (panoramic views), the Amberley Inn or Black Horse at Amberley SO8401, the Bell at Selsley SO8304, the Fleece at Hillesley ST7689, and the Berkeley Arms by the Severn estuary at Purton SO6904.

Driving

An area much less visited than most, yet with outstanding scenery is that between Wotton-under-Edge and Stroud, with the roads around there (B4066, B4058, the steep lanes up on to Minchinhampton Common nr Amberley, for example) all worthwhile. The main A46, which goes through this area, is not overly busy and gives some fine views.

The Cotswold plateau is intersected by Roman roads with far Cotswold views: of the modern roads following their course, the A429-A433 doesn't carry too much traffic and is a pleasant drive; the A435 is also quite enjoyable, but the A417 has too much traffic for leisurely driving. There are good views from the road off the A419 W of Cirencester, through Frampton Mansell and Sapperton.

Meandering along the back roads through and between any of the villages we've recommended is the best way of all of seeing the area; one of the nicest of these drives is along the Coln Valley – see Cotswold villages entry, above.

Where to eat

Birdlip SO9214 KINGSHEAD HOUSE (01452) 862299 17th-century former coaching inn, with lovely English cooking using the best fresh produce, helpful service, good wines; disabled access; cl am Sat, pm Sun, Mon, 26 Dec, 1 Jan. £27.90|£4/£4.50.

Northleach SP1114 WICKENS Market Place (01451) 860421 Cosy, low-ceilinged restaurant with good, modern English cooking, lovely puddings, pleasant service, and fine New World wines; cl Sun and Mon. **£22.50/£6.50**.

Kingscote ST8196 HUNTERS HALL (01453) 860393 Civilised, creeper-covered old inn with an elegant series of high-beamed connecting rooms, some fine old furniture, big log fires; good bar and restaurant food, a children's menu, excellent breakfasts, quite a few wines by the glass; big garden with a children's play area; bedrooms; disabled access. **£20l£1.95/£5.45**.

Southrop SP1903 SWAN (0136 785) 205 Civilised, creeper-covered, old stone-tiled pub in a pretty, daffodil-filled village; good, interesting food inc lovely ice-creams, respectable wine list, and log fires. **£18.50l£1.10/£4.50**.

Kilkenny SP0018 KILKENEY (01242) 820341 Spacious and smartly modernised, Cotswold country dining pub with attractive views, very good imaginative food, decent little wine list, and real ales; disabled access; cl pm Sun, Jan–Mar. **£17.75l£3/£5**.

Cheltenham SO9422 LE CHAMPIGNON SAUVAGE 24–26 Suffolk Rd (01242) 573449 Classic French cooking in this quietly and simply decorated restaurant, with helpful service and a good, thoughtful wine list; cl am Sat, Sun, 23 Dec–2 Jan, bank hols; disabled access. **£16.50 lunch, £22.50 dinner**.

Coln St Aldwyns SP1405 NEW INN (01285) 750651 Prettily placed, rather civilised country inn with a nicely old-fashioned atmosphere; attractively decorated bars, particularly good, imaginative food, well kept beer, half-a-dozen decent wines by the glass, and friendly, helpful service. **£15l£2.95/£7**.

Cheltenham SO9422 MORANS (01242) 581411 Bustling restaurant with good, varied food, lovely alcoholic ice-creams, and lots of cocktails; disabled access; cl Sun, bank hols. **£15l£2.95/£3.50**.

Northleach SP1114 RED LION Market Pl (01451) 860251 Good-value, well presented, simple food in a comfortable and friendly pub, popular Sun roast, open fire; disabled access. **£14.75l£2.30/£5.50**.

Siddington SU0399 GREYHOUND Characterful, friendly pub with two big log fires in the lounge, a happy mix of seats, interesting bric-a-brac, good, popular food, and well kept beers. **£13l£1.95/£5.50**.

Woodchester SO8302 RAM (01453) 873329 Bustling, cheerful pub with spectacular views of the valley from the terrace; an attractive beamed bar, good bar food, prompt, friendly service, and lots of real ales. **£11.25l£1.85/£4.95**.

GLOUCESTER AND THE FOREST OF DEAN

Gloucester is rewarding for day visits; the Forest of Dean has interesting walking especially if you're prepared to delve into its past.

Gloucester has a glorious cathedral and thriving dockland enjoyably revitalised for visitors, with fascinating waterways and advertising museums. It's a big city and, though it has other attractions too, it is perhaps best seen as a place to visit by the day (preferably on a weekend, when it's quieter), rather than as a place to stay in. It's quickly reached from Cheltenham, incidentally, as well as from other towns and villages within this area. It would be a tiring city to inflict on a family with children.

The Forest of Dean has a unique landscape: hilly woodland, much of it ancient, that shows many traces of the way it has provided a livelihood for the people living around it. And it's flanked by a spectacular stretch of the Wye Valley. Some people find the scenery of the forest itself a bit disappointing; it has most impact on those prepared to delve into its past a bit, perhaps at the heritage centre at Soudley. Given that, it's as attractive an area for walking as the Cotswolds. Its woodland colours are at their best in late May and autumn.

The quiet orchard and farming countryside around the Severn Valley and north of the Forest of Dean is well worth discovering. As the Severn itself is still a formidable barrier to travel here, with very few river crossings, there aren't that many people passing through, which has kept it very unspoilt. The little villages down by the west bank of the Severn have a timeless, unchanging feel.

There are not nearly so many places to visit in this part of the county. Newent has a reasonable number of worthwhile attractions, including plenty of interest for families; elsewhere, the most notable are Littledean Hall, the steam railway at Lydney, the caverns at Clearwell and, particularly in late May, the gardens of Lydney Park.

Prices over on this side of the Severn are rather lower than in the Cotswolds.

Where to stay

Upton St Leonards SO8614 HATTON COURT Upton Hill, Upton St Leonards, Gloucester GL4 8DE (01452) 617412 £95; 45 individually furnished rms. Carefully extended, ivy-covered manor house in 7 acres of neatly kept gardens and 30 acres of pastures (lovely views, too); with good modern cooking in the attractive restaurant, a comfortable lounge, and warmly helpful staff; outdoor heated swimming pool

Puckrup SO8836 PUCKRUP HALL Puckrup, Tewkesbury GL20 6EL (01684) 296200 *£92; 84 comfortably spacious rms. Handsome Regency mansion in over 140 acres of parkland with its own par 71, 18-hole golf course, and new leisure club inc indoor swimming pool, crèche, gym and so forth; an elegant lounge with fine plasterwork, relaxed bar overlooking the croquet lawn, and good food in four different dining areas; disabled access.

Clearwell SO5708 CLEARWELL CASTLE Clearwell, Coleford GL16 8LG (01594) 832320 *£90; 17 spacious rms mostly with four-posters or half-testers. Early 18th-c castle with huge, beautifully decorated halls, a comfortable lounge, antiques, fresh flowers and big fires, cosy bar, and a panelled restaurant with a fine fireplace; there's a chapel in the basement.

Corse Lawn SO8330 CORSE LAWN HOUSE Corse Lawn, Gloucester GL19 4LZ (01452) 780479 *£90; 19 individually furnished rms. Magnificent Queen Anne building with an attractive bar, comfortable lounge and three drawing rooms; a distinguished restaurant, excellent wines, and a relaxed atmosphere; dogs welcome; disabled access.

Clearwell SO5708 WYNDHAM ARMS Clearwell, Coleford GL16 8JT (01594) 833666 *£60; 17 well equipped rms. Smart old country inn nr the Wye Valley and Forest of Dean; with a comfortable, beamed bar, an open fire, big helpings of often unusual food, good service, neat gardens, and friendly dogs; disabled access.

Clearwell SO5708 TUDOR FARMHOUSE Clearwell, Coleford GL16 8JS (01594) 833046 £49; 9 cottagey rms. Carefully restored, Tudor farmhouse with lots of beams, sloping floors, and oak doors, delicious food in the candlelit restaurant, a small conservatory lounge, and friendly staff.

St Briavels SO5605 GEORGE St Briavels, Lydney GL15 6TA (01594) 530228 £40; 4 rms. Pleasant old pub in a particularly interesting village, overlooking the 12th-c castle; with three rambling rooms, a big stone fireplace, and a Celtic coffin lid dating from 1070 (found in a fireplace here) which is mounted next to the bar counter; and a cosy dining room with good food during all opening hours (and also served in a no-smoking area); outdoor chessboard.

Viney Hill SO6506 LOWER VINEY COUNTRY GUEST HOUSE Viney Hill, Lydney GL15 4LT (01594) 516000 £40; 6 well furnished, comfortable rms. Delightful, old, no-smoking farmhouse with half-acre garden, in lovely countryside; two cosy lounges (one with TV), lots of books and local information, a decent evening meal and good breakfast, friendly, efficient service; very pleasant walking all around.

To see and do

Gloucester SO8318 Despite its long history this is a busy modern city, and you have to search out the old buildings among today's big shops (for instance, the splendid timber-framed house tucked down a passageway off 26 Westgate St). The efficient tourist office at St Michael's Tower (itself a fine, ancient building at the central Cross) is particularly good at sending you off well equipped for the hunt. The Linden Tree (Bristol Rd out past docks), Tailor's House (Westgate St) and York House (London Rd) are all useful for a quick lunch.

✝ 🏛 The CATHEDRAL towers majestically over the city's more recent buildings. In 1330 the Abbot astutely purchased the remains of murdered Edward II, and the resulting stream of pilgrims paid for elaborate rebuilding, an early example of the Perpendicular style. Lovely fan-vaulted cloisters, the second-largest, medieval stained-glass window in the country, and a fine collection of church plate in the Treasury. Meals, snacks, shop, disabled access. Not far from here are the remains of 9th-c ST OSWALD'S PRIORY, the city's oldest structure. Other ecclesiastical remains nearby include GREYFRIARS and BLACKFRIARS, the latter pretty much unchanged since the 13th-c, with a rare scissor-braced roof. The revitalised GLOUCESTER DOCKS are worth exploring, with museums, smart shops, cafés and the like. The lively development deserves much of the credit for the city's current success as a tourist centre, with the docks now attracting over a million people each year. The next four attractions are all located here, and there are also guided walks and summer boat trips. The Waterfront in Llanthony Rd, at the S end of The Docks, has decent food.

✱ ⚓ NATIONAL WATERWAYS MUSEUM (Llanthony Warehouse, The Docks) The story of Britain's inland waterways, and the first heyday of these docks after the opening of the Gloucester & Berkeley Canal. Recently judged one of the top seven museums in Europe, this is a very good, lively place, with plenty to amuse children, who can even try their hand at steering a narrow boat. Also demonstrations, craft displays, and short cruises down the canal (£2 extra). Snacks, shop, disabled access; cl 25 Dec; (01452) 307009; £3.95.

♿ ROBERT OPIE COLLECTION MUSEUM OF ADVERTISING AND PACKAGING (Albert Warehouse, The Docks) Great for nostalgia-lovers – an enormous and quite fascinating assembly of packets, tins, bottles, posters, street signs and more from Victorian days onwards. Also continuous showing of vintage TV commercials. Snacks, shop, disabled access; cl Mon Nov–Jan, 25–26 Dec; (01452) 302309; £2.95.

♿ REGIMENTS OF GLOUCESTERSHIRE MUSEUM (The Docks) Unusually lively regimental museum with reconstructions and sound effects. Shop, disabled access; cl Mon (exc bank hols and during July and Aug), Christmas; (01452) 522682; £2.50.

🏛 GLOUCESTER ANTIQUES CENTRE (The Docks) Restored riverside warehouse with 68 varied antique shops, nicely arranged in Dickensian arcades. Meals, snacks, disabled access; cl am Sun, 25–26 Dec; (01452) 307161; free.

🏛 CITY EAST GATE (Eastgate St) Some Roman and medieval gate towers and the remains of a moat in an

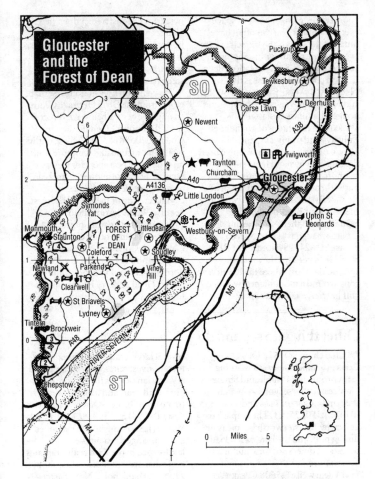

Gloucester and the Forest of Dean

0 Miles 5

underground exhibition chamber below the shopping centre; the adjacent walls may be open at times. Usually open Sat (not 12–2.15), May–Sept; (01452) 524131; 40p.

🖐🏛 FOLK MUSEUM (Westgate St) Social history museum in a group of Tudor and Jacobean timber-framed houses. Shop, some disabled access; cl Sun exc July–Sept, 25–26 Dec, 1 Jan, Good Fri; (01452) 526467; free.

🖐🏛 CITY MUSEUM AND ART GALLERY (Brunswick Rd) Local history (inc the oldest backgammon set known to exist), and paintings inc works by Gainsborough, Turner and others. Shop, disabled access; cl Sun (exc July–Sept), 24–26 Dec, Good Fri; free.

🖐 HOUSE OF THE TAILOR OF GLOUCESTER (College Ct) Inspiration for Beatrix Potter's story, now with an exhibition and shop. Disabled access downstairs; cl Sun and bank hols; free.

🌸❀ ROBINSWOOD HILL COUNTRY PARK (2m S) is a little outcrop of the Cotswolds, with 250 acres of walks and trails and wonderful views of the city from the summit. Snacks, disabled access; (01452) 413029; free. The GLOUCESTERSHIRE WILDLIFE TRUST VISITOR CENTRE here has displays and information on their 70 nature reserves in the area, as well as fun talks and events; (01452) 383333.

🐾✔🏛❀⛵ **The Forest of Dean** Still largely ancient oak woodland despite encroaching pine plantations, the forest rolls over many miles of hilly countryside, giving plenty of space – even in summer you can often have much of the woods to yourself. There are ponds, streams with stepping stones, cattle and maybe fallow deer (a good place to see these is the NAGSHEAD NATURE RESERVE SO6008), sudden distant views, the humps and gouges that mark ANCIENT IRON WORKINGS, the tracks of abandoned railways and tramways, and still one or two of the freeminers, who've been digging coal by hand from surface seams for hundreds of years. Good paths throughout. The paving of a ROMAN ROAD can be tracked just off the B4431 at Blackpool Bridge SO6508, and there's a pleasant CONIFER ARBORETUM near Speech House SO6212. SYMONDS YAT ROCK SO5616 is perhaps the most spectacular part, where the River Wye rolls around a monumental wooded cliff barrier, a favourite spot with peregrine falcons; tremendous views in all directions from the top, and at the bottom a ferry runs between two inns.

Around the edges of the forest the scenery changes to a patchwork of steep pastures – also very attractive.

It's well worth getting a forest map, either from the Dean Heritage Centre (see Soudley entry below) or direct from the Forestry Commission in Coleford (0594) 833057; these outline walks (inc an unusual sculpture trail), and mark the best spots for views or picnics. The information centres can also provide details of canoeing, caving, cycling or fishing in the forest. See also **Walks** section, below.

In addition to eating-places mentioned under other entries (eg Clearwell, Coleford, Newland, Parkend and St Briavels), the Royal Spring at Lower Lydbrook and King's Head at Berry Hill are useful food stops.

Other things to see and do

☛ **Churcham** SO7618 OLD LEY COURT (Chapel Lane) is a working farm producing Double and Single Gloucester cheese; you can watch them making it on Tues and Thurs; (01452) 750225; £1. The Apple Tree at nearby Minsterworth is a pleasant dining pub, and the lane past it leads to a good, quiet spot for watching the Severn Bore.

⦿ ♣ **Clearwell** SO5608 CLEARWELL CAVES Tours of huge caverns, a source of ore from the Iron Age right up to 1945; you can see all the caves tunnelled by miners, with deeper trips for the more adventurous. Stout shoes recommended. It's quite a labyrinth, with many miles of passageways. They create lively themed displays down here at Christmas. Meals, snacks, shop; cl all Nov, Jan and Feb, and am Dec wkdys; (01594) 832535; £2.80. The Wyndham Arms is good for lunch, and though the village is not in itself particularly pretty it's a very good centre for the lovely surrounding countryside.

🐾 ♨ ! ᠓ **Coleford** SO5710 GREAT WESTERN RAILWAY MUSEUM Converted Coleford GWR goods station with several large-scale, model steam locomotives, relics, photographs and a Victorian ticket office. Shop; open pm Sat all year, and usually Tues–Fri (from 3pm) Easter–Oct, best to check first, (01594) 833569; *£1.50. PUZZLE WOOD (Just off the B4228) Wooded paths arranged in a puzzle, landscaped in the 19th c; also remains of Roman iron mines. Snacks, shop; cl Mon (exc bank hols), Nov–Easter; (01594) 833187; £1.50. The Dog & Muffler at Joyford is useful for lunch.

✝ **Deerhurst** SO8729 has ancient remains including ODDA'S CHAPEL, a restored 11th-c chapel discovered as part of a farmhouse, and ST MARY'S PRIORY, an important, mainly Saxon church with a lovely atmosphere and some intriguing, original carvings and features. The riverside Coalhouse at Apperley has a wide choice of food.

☛ ⚘ **Little London** SO7019 ANGORA GOAT AND MOHAIR CENTRE (Blakemore Farm, Little London) Unusual farm with lots of angora goats and a shop selling clothes made from their fleeces. Also other animals and craft demonstrations. Snacks, disabled access; cl 25 Dec, Mon (exc bank hols) and Tues; (01452) 830630; free. The Red Hart at Blaisdon has good-value food.

🐴❋🏠👤 **Lydney** SO6303 DEAN FOREST RAILWAY Lots of locomotives, wagons and equipment, expanding steamtrips through the forest and other events. Snacks, shop, disabled access; cl Jan–2 wks before Easter; (01594) 843423 for train times; *£3. LYDNEY PARK Extensive, sheltered, spring garden rich with flowering shrubs, rhododendrons, azaleas and magnolias; also lakes and a deer park. Tucked away among the trees are the remains of a Roman temple, and a Roman museum has finds from the site, inc the astonishingly intricate Lydney dog. Snacks, shop, plant sales; usually open Sun, Weds and bank hols early Apr–early Jun, and every day late May, but best to check first; (01594) 42844; £2.

🐦👤🍴 **Newent** SO7226 is a small country town with some timbered buildings which have a bit of a Worcestershire or Herefordshire look. NATIONAL BIRDS OF PREY CENTRE Exceptional collection of birds of prey, with displays of falcons and other trained birds, breeding aviaries, and new Owl Courtyard to study them at close hand; birds flown four times each day. Meals, snacks, shop, some disabled access; cl Dec–Jan; (01531) 820286; £4. The Yew Tree out at Cliffords Mesne past here is handy for lunch. SHAMBLES MUSEUM OF VICTORIAN LIFE Enthusiastic re-creation of a Victorian cobbled square, shops and a furnished tradesman's house. Summer snacks, shop; cl Mon (exc bank hols), poss Christmas–Mar; (01531) 822144; £2.65. The George opposite is handy for lunch. THREE CHOIRS VINEYARD (off the B4215 towards Dymock) Tours of a rapidly expanding vineyard, now one of the six largest in the country, with tastings. Meals, snacks, shop, disabled access; cl Christmas wk; (01531) 890223; free. ST ANNE'S VINEYARD (Oxenhall, off the B4221) grow 150 varieties of vine. Many are for sale, as of course are the wines, with tastings. Cl am, all Mon (exc bank hols) Tues, Christmas; (01989) 720313, free.

👤 **Parkend** SO6208 has a good co-operative CRAFT CENTRE (cl Christmas). The Woodman is good for lunch, and the Fountain here is useful too.

★🏰❋👤 **St Briavels** SO5605 is an attractive and unusual small village focused on the ruins of its 13th-c castle (the inhabited part is a youth hostel), with a steeply grassy, former moat and views from the ramparts of the curtain wall. Kathy Boy organises weekend WATERCOLOUR WORKSHOPS in one of its medieval rooms; (01594) 530026. The George is handy for lunch, and there are a number of circular walks around the parish, devised by Mr McGubbin in the CRAFT SHOP (cl Tues, Weds and all winter wkdys).

🍴👤 **Soudley** SO6513 DEAN HERITAGE CENTRE Useful introduction to the Forest of Dean, set around an old watermill in a pretty wooded valley; reconstructed cottage and coal mine, nature trails, craft displays, and adventure playground. On certain dates they have traditional charcoal burning. Meals, snacks, shop, disabled access; cl wkdys Nov–Jan exc for pre-booked groups and during Christmas wk, also cl 24–26 Dec; (01594) 822170; £2.60.

★🍴 **Taynton** SO7321 is an attractive village, particularly when the daffodils are out, and the TAYNTON FARM CENTRE is a friendly little working farm (cl Nov–Mar exc shop).

★🏠👤✝ **Tewkesbury** SO8932 Important medieval town and site of the last battle in the Wars of the Roses in 1471, still full of attractive, half-timbered medieval buildings in a maze of little alleyways. Two of these old houses now house MUSEUMS. Most impressive is the ABBEY, its massively confident Norman tower one of the finest in existence; there are regular concerts in the abbey; snacks, disabled access. The historic Bell Hotel is useful for lunch.

🖼🏠 **Twigworth** SO8422 NATURE IN ART Growing collection of paintings, sculpture, and mosaics inspired by nature, in an imposing Georgian mansion. Regular events and talks. Meals, snacks, shop, disabled access; cl Mon (exc bank hols), 24–26 Dec; (01452) 731422; £2.80.

❀ † **Westbury-on-Severn** SO7114
WESTBURY COURT Formal Dutch garden
with canals, yew topiary, etc, restored
to its 1700s layout using pre-1700
cultivars inc old fruit varieties. Disabled
access; cl Mon (exc bank hols), Tues,
Good Fri, and all Nov–Mar; £2.20;
NT. The Red Lion has nice, generous
food, and the CHURCH has an unusual
detached tower. This is a good spot for
catching the Severn Bore at the spring
and autumn equinox.

Other good places to get down to
the river, with riverside pubs, are
Apperley SO8628, Norton via
Wainlode Hill SO8523 and
Twyning SO8936, though best of all
is Ashleworth Quay SO8125,
where there's a tithe barn of some
note and the very traditional pub has
been in the same family for centuries.
There's a handsome 15th-c TITHE
BARN in the village; cl Good Fri,
Nov–Mar; 60p.

Walks

The **Forest of Dean** ◮-1 rises and rolls, and is well equipped with car parks, picnic sites and forest trails. A good start is at the Soudley Heritage Centre SO6513 (see Soudley entry above). The Sculpture Trail takes a 4-mile route passing nearly 20 specially commissioned sculptures hidden deep in the forest (from the picnic site nr Speech House Hotel SO6611). The Kidnalls Forest Trail is a good way of tracking down some early industrial sites.

The Foundry Wood Trail passes Soudley fish ponds SO6212 and gains some fine views. The Wench Ford Forest Walk leads past a series of quite interesting rock outcrops. Signposted paths ensure easy route-finding up to the open summit of May Hill SO6921, where on a clear day you can see the Cotswolds, Malvern Hills, Welsh Marches and Severn Estuary.

The lower Wye Valley on the W side of the Forest of Dean cuts through a gorge giving some very picturesque views. As there are few crossing points, and the scenery away from the gorge is relatively unspectacular, walks along it are generally of the there-and-back sort. On this Gloucs side, the valley is tracked by the Offa's Dyke Path (the Wye Valley Walk takes in the western bank). Southern highlights include **Wintour's Leap** ST5496 ◮-2, a sheer cliff N of Chepstow, with dizzy views downwards, and the **Devil's Pulpit** ST5499 ◮-3, where trees frame a perfect vista of Tintern Abbey, far below on the opposite bank.

The Kymin SO5212 ◮-4 can be climbed from May Hill, just across the river border opposite Monmouth; at the summit is the Naval Temple, a quaint rustic conceit put up in 1800 to commemorate admirals of the Napoleonic Wars.

Useful pubs to start walks from include the Rising Sun at Moseley Green SO6308, Woodman at Parkend SO6208, Dog & Muffler at Joyford SO5813 and the White Horse at Staunton SO5412 (all Forest of Dean); the Yew Tree at Cliffords Mesne SO6922 (for May Hill), Glasshouse Inn by Newent Woods SO7122, the stunningly placed Boat, reached by a footbridge over the Wye from Redbrook SO5309, Brockweir Inn in Brockweir SO5401 and the Ostrich in the charming village of Newland SO5509 (both Wye Valley, too), and the Wyndham Arms at Clearwell SO5708. There's a pleasant short stroll down to the Severn from the Red Hart at Awre SO7108.

The countryside around Gloucester is pancake-flat, unrewarding for walkers.

Driving

On the whole this is not a very good area for country drives. Though there are decent roads through the heart of the Forest of Dean, the trees tend to cut off the views. The B4432 to Symonds Yat does give some reasonable views, and the B4228 down past St Briavels is a pleasant country road. Don't try to navigate the confusing little lanes around the edges of the Forest of Dean without a large-scale map – but if you can find your way around them, they are very rewarding.

Where to eat

Newland SO5509 OSTRICH (01594) 833260 Particularly attractive 13th-c inn in a pretty village; with a big log fire, comfortable seating, attentive service, and freshly prepared, good food; no children. £3.95/£7.50.

Help this year from: Joan Olivier, Martyn Kearey, Andrew and Catherine Brian, Audrey and Peter Dowsett, Neil and Anita Christopher, Andrew Shore, Pat and John Millward, B M Eldridge, Peter and Jenny Quine, Dave Irving, Tom McLean, Ewan McCall, Roger Huggins, Ted George, Mike and Jo, Michael and Derek Slade, Andrew and Liz Roberts, Andrew and Ruth Triggs, Pam Adsley, R A Baker, Martin Jones, Mr and Mrs W A Poeton, Michael Marlow, Graham Reeve, GA, PA, Mr and Mrs P R Bevins, Malcolm Davies, C W Channon, John and Shirley Dyson, Dr John A Evans, Paul Weedon, Jan and Dave Booth, Frank W Gadbois, Roger Entwistle, Jeff Davies, Simon and Amanda Southwell, Mike and Jill Steer, Jenny and Brian Seller, Mike Davies, John and Joan Calvert, E G Parish, June and Tony Baldwin, Ted George, David Hanley, Chris and Annie Clipson, Sue Cubitt, Tony and Lynne Starke, P and M Rudlin, Margaret Drazin, Robert Huddleston, Sheila Cooper, Mrs N. McCarthy, JCT; also special thanks to many clerks of parish councils here, who gave us particular guidance.

GLOUCESTERSHIRE CALENDAR

Some of these dates were provisional as we went to press.

MARCH

14 **Cheltenham** Gold Cup Meeting at the Racecourse nr Prestbury – *till Fri 17* (01242) 513014

18 **Toddington** Steam and Diesel Gala at Gloucestershire & Warwickshire Steam Railway (01242) 233845

APRIL

14 **Gloucester** Blues Festival – *till Sun 16*

22 **Nailsworth** Festival – *till 1 May* (01453) 835631

23 **Gloucester** St George's Day Celebrations with mummers and morris dancers

MAY

7 **Gloucester** Engine Rally at National Waterways Museum (01452) 318054; **Randwick** Cheese Rolling – after church service *at 10.30*, three cheeses are blessed and rolled anticlockwise round the church three times. One cheese is cut up and distributed to those present, the other two are kept until the following Sat when they are rolled down a slope to open the Randwick Rap

13 **Randwick** Rap – medieval fayre with carnival, maypole dancing and morris dancing

20 **Gloucester** Horses and Tugs at National Waterways Museum (01452) 318054

25 **Bisley** Well Blessings (01452) 770056

29 **Brockworth** Coopers Hill Cheese Rolling (old custom) *from 6pm*; **Tetbury** Medieval Fayre and Woolsack Races

JUNE

2 **Chipping Campden** Robert Dover's Games inc greasy pole, Scottish dancing, torchlight procession and fireworks

3 **Chipping Campden** Scuttlebrook Wake – fancy-dress parade with floats, morris dancing and competitions

GLOUCESTERSHIRE CALENDAR

JUNE cont

10 **Toddington** Bristol Bus Gathering at Gloucestershire & Warwickshire Steam Railway – *till Sun 11* (01242) 233845

24 **Cirencester** Festival of Music and the Arts – *till 8 July* (01285) 720150; **Toddington** Thomas the Tank Engine at Gloucestershire & Warwickshire Steam Railway (01242) 233845

JULY

1 **Cheltenham** International Festival of Music – *till Sun 16* (01242) 227979; **Stroud** Show at Stratford Park (01453) 765381; **Tewkesbury** Carnival

8 **Tewkesbury** Medieval Fayre – *till Sun 9*

16 **Toddington** Cotswold Transport Gala at Gloucestershire & Warwickshire Steam Railway (01242) 233845

22 **Cheltenham** Cricket Festival – *till Sun 30*; **Gloucester** Festival and Carnival – *till 5 Aug* (01452) 396620; also Museums Week and Cricket Festival – *till Sun 30*; **Guiting Power** Silver Jubilee Festival of Music and the Arts (01242) 603590; **Tewkesbury** Festival – *till Sun 30*

30 **Cirencester** Carnival

AUGUST

11 **Minchinhampton** British Open Horse Trials Championship at Gatcombe Park – *till Sun 13* (01454) 218272

19 **Fairford** Steam Rally and Show at Fairford Park – *till Sun 20* (01285) 655011; **Gloucestershire** Arts Week; **Gloucester** Three Choirs Festival at the Cathedral – *till Sat 26* (01542) 529819; **Painswick** Guild of Craftsmen Exhibition; **Tibberton** Horticultural Society Show (01452) 790424

20 **Temple Guiting** Open Day at David Nicholson's Racing Stables (01386) 584209

21 **Frampton** Deer Roast on the Village Green (01452) 740357

28 **Berkeley** Hunt Agricultural Show (01453) 860352; **Bourton-on-the-Water** Football in the River Windrush; **Frocester** Beer Festival

SEPTEMBER

2 **Moreton-in-Marsh** Traditional Agricultural and Horse Show (01608) 651908

9 **Stow-on-the-Wold** Day of Dance: morris dancing around the town *from 11am* (01451) 831082

17 **Painswick** Clypping of the Church Ceremony – *at 3pm*, St Mary's church is circled by parishioners and flower-bearing children singing the 'Clypping Hymn' (01452) 812334

23 **Cirencester** Cotswold Country Fair – *till Sun 24* (01285) 652007

OCTOBER

6 **Cheltenham** Festival of Literature – *till Sat 14* (01242) 521621

7 **Stroud** Arts Festival – *till Sat 21* (01453) 764502

9 **Cirencester** Mop Fair (funfair); **Tewkesbury** Mop Fair (01684) 296010

14 **Toddington** Steam and Vintage Gala at Gloucestershire & Warwickshire Steam Railway (01242) 233845

16 **Cirencester** Mop Fair (funfair)

DECEMBER

26 **Gloucester** Mummers and Morris Dancers in the Cathedral Precincts and New Inn Courtyard *at midday*

HAMPSHIRE

This county has an excellent choice of places to visit, yet in the main is far from touristy – its largely built-up coastline has saved it from being overrun by holiday-makers.

Away from the coast, a broad belt of gentle countryside stretches right across Hampshire from Andover, Stockbridge and Romsey along the Test Valley in the west, through Winchester and Alresford, to Alton and Petersfield in the east. Here is a quietly charming mix of rolling chalk downland, a patchwork of hedged fields and clumps of beechwood, the rich valleys of the clear chalk streams, and attractive, small villages often of brick and flint. Up in the north-east, the chalk downs give way to poorer heathy soils and fat fingers of urbanisation poking down the M3 and the trunk roads.

The New Forest feels quite different: some woodland, wide expanses of empty heathland, and a sheltered coast with yachting harbours.

CENTRAL HAMPSHIRE

A great many places for sightseeing, quiet countryside.

This area's strongest appeal is perhaps for those who like to spend much of their time out and about visiting things. It is outstanding for military and naval history, and museums dealing with this here, besides being among the country's most interesting for specialists, have a surprisingly broad and general appeal too. For most people, though, the rich choice of things to do and see here is topped by the exemplary Marwell Zoo at Colden Common, the lovely Watercress Railway Line from Alresford, and Mottisfont Abbey and its exceptional rose garden. Of the area's many great houses, Broadlands near Romsey, The Vyne near Sherborne St John, Hinton Ampner, Breamore and Stratfield Saye are all rewarding. The Hillier Gardens at Ampfield, the Sandham Memorial Chapel at Burghclere, the Hollycombe Steam Collection at Liphook and the Hawk Conservancy at Weyhill are much enjoyed even by people whose thoughts wouldn't normally turn in those directions. The practical reconstruction of an Iron Age farm at Chalton (new to the Guide) is unique.

Though the country areas don't have the obvious picturesque appeal of say the West Country, they do have their own rather retiring charm, with secluded valleys, quiet riverside villages, steep beechwoods and blowy downs. A good choice of places to stay runs from comfortable cottages and simple inns to stylish country-house hotels. There are plenty of attractive country pubs that serve good food, and that are well placed for after-lunch strolls.

The two main towns to consider as candidates for a weekend break are Winchester and Portsmouth. Winchester has a charming old quarter around its cathedral and plenty of opportunities for strolls nearby. Portsmouth, larger and busier, has the very specific appeal of its well preserved and displayed naval heritage – with a lot to amuse children.

Where to stay

Sparsholt SU4331 LAINSTON HOUSE Sparsholt, Winchester SO21 2LJ (01962) 863588 £145; 38 spacious rms. Close to Winchester, this elegant William and Mary hotel has 63 acres of fine parkland, a relaxing, elegant lounge, panelled bar and restaurant, flowers and paintings, a fine wine list, and good British cooking; disabled access.

Rotherwick SU7156 TYLNEY HALL Rotherwick, Basingstoke RG27 9AJ (01256) 764881 £118; 91 comfortable, well equipped rms. Grand Victorian mansion in 66 acres of gardens and parkland; with gracious day rooms, ornate plasterwork, oak panelling, oil paintings, log fires in big ornate fireplaces, interesting food in the candlelit restaurant, and good, attentive service; tennis, golf, indoor and outdoor swimming pools, gym and sauna.

Hurstbourne Tarrant SU3853 ESSEBORNE MANOR Hurstbourne Tarrant, Andover SP11 0ER (01264) 76444 £95; 12 individually decorated rms. Small Victorian manor with a calm, relaxed atmosphere, comfortable lounge, snug little bar, and good modern cooking; neat gardens with tennis, croquet and golf; children over 12; disabled access.

Winchester SU4829 ROYAL St Peter St, Winchester SO22 8BS (01962) 840840 £87.50; 75 comfortable rms in original building or annexe. Well kept, surprisingly peaceful hotel with pretty flowers, neat garden and terrace, a comfortable lounge, and conservatory restaurant; disabled access.

Middle Wallop SU2838 FIFEHEAD MANOR Middle Wallop, Stockbridge SO20 8EG (01264) 781565 £80; 16 spacious rms. Friendly and comfortable, old brick manor house in several acres of lovely gardens; with a restful atmosphere, pleasant, small lounge and bar, and good food in the candlelit restaurant; croquet; cl 2 wks at Christmas; disabled access.

Winchester SU4829 WYKEHAM ARMS 75 Kingsgate St, Winchester SO23 9PE (01962) 853834 £75; 7 well equipped, attractive rms. Very well run, smart old town inn, close to the cathedral, with bars interestingly furnished with old school desks from the college, military and historical memorabilia, royalty pictures, mugs and so forth; two small dining rooms serving an excellent daily changing menu (very good breakfasts, too), fine wines (lots by the glass), and prompt, friendly service; several no-smoking areas; no children.

Hayling Island SU7201 COCKLE WARREN COTTAGE 36 Seafront, Hayling Island PO11 9HL (01705) 464961 £64; 5 pretty, well equipped rms. Carefully run and attractive, traditional-style house on the seafront, with friendly, courteous owners, a log fire in the cosy lounge, very good food in the conservatory dining room, and heated swimming pool; children over 12 (or under 12 months).

Crawley SU4234 FOX & HOUNDS Crawley, Winchester SO21 2PR (01962) 776285 £55; 3 well equipped rms. Striking almost Tyrolean pub with elegant timbering and oak parquet, a lounge with log fire, good, interesting bar and restaurant food, and prompt, unobtrusive service.

Droxford SU6018 WHITE HORSE Droxford, Southampton SO32 3PB (01489) 877490 £50; 3 rms, 1 with own bthrm. Rambling 16th-c coaching inn with attractively furnished and low-beamed, cosy rooms, log fires, friendly staff (and ghost), and particularly good food; seats in the flower-filled courtyard; pleasant walks nearby.

Portsmouth SU6501 SALLY PORT High St, Old Town, Portsmouth PO1 2LU (01705) 821293 £49; 10 rms, some with own bthrm. Beautifully kept, 16th-c inn in a quiet position; good food, and very friendly, efficient service; said to have been a favourite of Nelson.

Lee-on-the-Solent SU5600 BELLE VUE, Lee-on-the-Solent PO13 9BW (01705)

550258 £47; 27 rms, some with sea view. Pleasant, quiet hotel on the seafront with fine views across to the Isle of Wight; decent bar and restaurant food, helpful and friendly staff, and nightly entertainment; cl 25–26 Dec; disabled access.

Cheriton SU5828 FLOWER POTS Cheriton, Alresford SO24 0QQ (01962) 771318 £42; 5 rms. Unspoilt and quietly comfortable village local, run by a very friendly family with their own-brew beers; pleasant, little bars, and decent bar food; disabled access.

Portsmouth SZ6498 FORTITUDE COTTAGE 51 Broad St, Old Portsmouth PO1 2JD (01705) 823748 £40; 3 neat and attractive rms, shared bthrm. Comfortable B & B in a cottage named after an old ship, with a pretty, beamed breakfast room looking over the fishing boats; no evening meals but places nearby; cl 25–26 Dec; no children.

Eastleigh SU4518 PARK FARM Stoneham Lane, Eastleigh SO5 3HS (01703) 612960 £32; 3 rms, 2 with shared bthrm. Lots of country walks around these converted coaching stables, coarse fishing in own lake; evening meals by arrangement.

To see and do

Portsmouth SZ6399 and its residential/resort part Southsea is an island town, with just two roads and the motorway bridging it to the mainland – traffic can be very slow indeed on the main approaches. Its great claim on the imagination is its place at the heart of English naval history, and the two parts that are interesting to visitors are the Old Town and the Historic Dockyard, on either side of the ferry berths and well away from the traffic. Overlooking the narrow harbour neck, Georgian buildings on an old-fashioned, cobbled hard give a good feel of the old days, and the little inner Camber Harbour still has fishing boats. By the harbour, the Bridge, Spice Island and Still & West are beautifully placed and useful for lunch, as is the Dolphin in the Old Town High St. The cathedral, dating from the 13th c to the present, is a delightful departure from the traditional layout.

✿ ⛵ HM NAVAL BASE is the main stop for most visitors – expensive, but with lots to see. It houses HMS VICTORY, the MARY ROSE, HMS WARRIOR, and the ROYAL NAVAL MUSEUM. The flagship (in more ways than one) is of course HMS *Victory*, still in commission, and manned by regular serving officers. Good guided tours bring those Trafalgar days very close, and include the spot where Nelson died. The raising of the *Mary Rose* from the Solent silt where it had sat for 437 years provided a wealth of material and information about the Tudor period. The discoveries are well shown in an airy hall, with an audio-visual display on the ship's rescue and conservation. The great oak hull itself is in a separate shed, sprayed almost constantly to prevent the timbers from drying out. HMS *Warrior*, when launched 140 years ago, the most fearsome battleship in the world: the first iron-clad dreadnought, with inches of armour-plating over her extraordinarily thick teak hull. She's been immaculately restored, and is manned by tars in period uniform. Again, tours are very vivid. The ROYAL NAVAL MUSEUM, in handsome 18th-c dockside buildings, has lively and varied displays on the development and history of the Navy up to and beyond the Falklands War (or as it's called here – the South Atlantic Campaign). Lots of Nelson memorabilia, inc his death mask, and quite a jolly gallery looking at popular images of the sailor. Each ship costs £4.50 to visit individually (though the HMS *Victory* ticket also includes entry to the Royal Naval Museum); there's a slight saving in a combined ticket – £8.50 for two ships, or £12.50 for everything. The site has snacks and a shop, and generally good disabled access to all the ships; ships cl 25 Dec, museum 24 Dec–1 Jan; (01705) 839766.

⛵ Several other places focus on the town's fighting history, notably the D-

DAY MUSEUM (Clarence Esplanade, Southsea), which vividly recalls and explains the Normandy landings from the point of view of both sides. Very realistic in places – you almost panic when the sirens sound. It also houses the remarkable 272 ft Overlord embroidery, telling the story of D-Day over 34 panels. Shop, disabled access; cl 24–26 Dec; (01705) 827261; *£3.50. ROYAL MARINES MUSEUM (Royal Marines Eastney Southsea) Vigorous museum rated by those in the know as one of the best of its type. It couldn't be more different from the usual military exhibitions, with lively recreations of major amphibious actions, a junior commando assault course, multi-media cinema and a jungle room with real snakes and scorpions. Meals, snacks, shop; cl few days over Christmas; (01705) 819385; £3.

The fortifications in defence of Portsmouth Harbour, here, around Gosport (see entry below) and up on Portsdown, give a remarkably complete picture of the development of defensive strategy from Tudor times to the fears of French invasion in the 1860s, though they have more appeal to people interested in warfare than to those who like the romantic idea of a regular 'castle'. SOUTHSEA CASTLE AND MUSEUM is the best place to start, built in 1545 as part of Henry VIII's coastal defences. Good displays on the development of Portsmouth as a military fortress (with some splendid fish-bone model ships made by Napoleonic prisoners-of-war here), and a dramatic new section on the castle itself. Snacks, shop; cl 24–26 Dec; (01705) 875261; *£1.50. Another formidable fortress is the 19th-c FORT WIDLEY up on Portsdown Hill. On the seaward side of Southsea there are sturdy Tudor and later towers, bastions and batteries, alongside the resort's gardens and entertainments, giving interesting sea views. Good guided walks around the Tudor fortifications and the best parts of the Old Town leave the Square Fort at 2.30 on Sun (not late Sept–mid-Apr).

A good way to wind up an exploration of Portsmouth's naval past is the boat trip out from the Naval Base to SPITBANK FORT, a mile out to sea. A granite, iron and brick fortress built on the seabed as part of the coastal defences against Napoleon

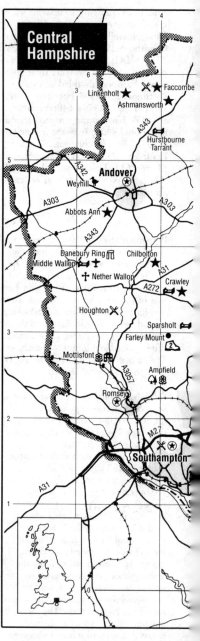

Central Hampshire

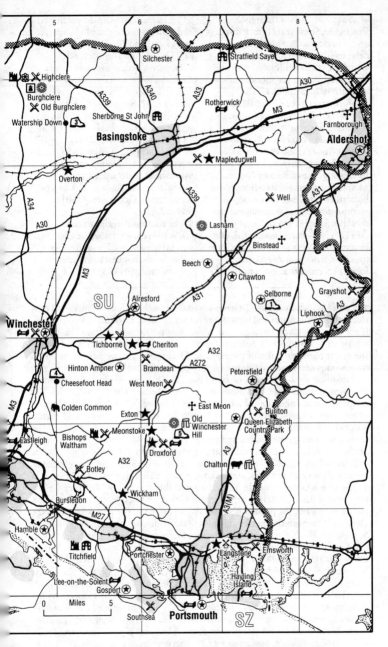

III, its two floors are linked by a maze of passages, and there's a 420-ft-deep well which still draws fresh water. The inner courtyard is now a sheltered terrace for summer refreshments from the café. Cl Mon (exc bank hols), Oct–Easter; (01329) 664286; £5.75 inc boat trip. You can stay out here if you really do want to get away from it all.

♪ ♣ SEA LIFE CENTRE (Clarence Esplanade, Southsea) Hi-tech displays and observation bubbles bring you close to all kinds of underwater creatures, with the illusion you're on the seabed. Also a very good shark exhibition. Meals, snacks, shop, disabled access; cl 25 Dec; (01705) 734461; £4.25. There are BOAT TRIPS round the harbour from nearby.

♻ 🦋 CUMBERLAND HOUSE NATURAL SCIENCE MUSEUM AND BUTTERFLY HOUSE (Eastern Parade, Southsea) Interesting natural history and geology museum, inc free-flying butterflies, a full-size dinosaur reconstruction, and seasonal ecology displays. Shop; cl 24–26 Dec; *£1.

♻ 🏚 CITY MUSEUM (Museum Rd, Old Portsmouth) Very good displays on the city's history, in an amazing former barracks that looks rather like a French château. Also decorative art and crafts. Snacks, disabled access; cl am wkdys, and 24–26 Dec; *£1.

🏚♻ DICKENS' BIRTHPLACE (Old Commercial Rd, in the main town) Restored to the modest, middle-class style it had when the author was born here in 1812. Still various Dickens-related objects such as the couch on which he died. Shop; cl am wkdys, all Oct–Mar; (01705) 827261; £1.

🏚 The GUILDHALL (Guildhall Sq) is an interesting old building, with free tours showing off what's said to be the world's biggest glass mural; tours by arrangement Oct–Mar; (01705) 834092.

✝ The roofless Royal Garrison CHURCH (French St) is where Charles II was married in 1662; usually open Mon–Weds, but best to make an appointment; (01705) 527667.

★ ✝ 🏰 🏚 **Winchester** SU4829 has a compact though fascinating medieval centre, with two city gates still intact; it was the capital of England in Saxon times. It's a nice old place, with guided walks around the sights from the tourist information centre every Sat, and some summer weekdays. There's a multi-storey car park at the top of the High St. The most attractive part of the city is the glorious and peaceful CATHEDRAL CLOSE, surrounded by a very harmonious and distinguished collection of buildings. The handsome old Eclipse Inn, nr the north-eastern edge, is a useful refreshment break. The CATHEDRAL itself is an awesome building, full of interest – one of Europe's finest, with the longest of all Gothic naves. The cathedral library has many rare books and manuscripts inc a wonderful, 12th-c illuminated Bible, and the sculpture gallery has some outstanding late Gothic sculpture. William of Wykeham paid for much of the rebuilding, and his tomb is appropriately the finest. Good guided tours (not bank hols; £2.00). The Queen recently opened a smart new visitor centre here, with very good meals and snacks, and there's a distinguished shop in a 16th-c coach house. Close by are the appreciable remains of Wolvesey Castle, the original Bishop's Palace begun in the 12th c, and beside it (not open, but a handsome sight), the present Bishop's Palace of 1684. The best way out of the cloisters is through the medieval King's Gate, which has above it the church of St Swithin. This takes you into Kingsgate St, calm and old-fashioned, with an excellent pub, the Wykeham Arms. Down on the left, a lovely riverside path takes you along to the City Mill and a mighty statue of King Alfred. All along Kingsgate St are buildings connected with WINCHESTER COLLEGE, the oldest school in the country. Most of the college's original buildings remain intact, especially around the grand 14th-c chapel and its calm, tilting cloisters with a delightful, two-storey chantry in their centre, and a glimpse of the Warden's garden through one gate. The modern War Cloisters are quiet and beautiful. Shop, some disabled access; guided tours Apr–Sept; cl 1–2, am Sun, 25–26 Dec; (01962) 868778; guided tours £2, otherwise free.

🏰 ❀ The 13th-c CASTLE now survives only in its huge great hall; hanging off one wall is a round table they call King Arthur's (actually much the same date as the castle, and painted with its Arthurian scenes later). A small but very interesting garden is laid out on the lines of what might have been there in the 13th c. Shop, disabled access; cl 25–26 Dec, Good Fri; free.

🕭 🏥 ❀ There's another clutch of MILITARY MUSEUMS; the GURKHA MUSEUM (Romsey Rd) probably has the broadest appeal, with dioramas and interactive displays taking you from Nepal to the North-West Frontier. Shop, disabled access; cl Sun, Mon (exc bank hols when cl following Tues), Christmas; *£1.50. More traditional regimental exhibitions are the ROYAL HUSSARS (PWO) MUSEUM (also Romsey Rd, cl wkdy lunchtimes, all Mon, Christmas; *£1.50), and the ROYAL HAMPSHIRE REGIMENT MUSEUM in a fine Georgian house down Southgate St, which also has the pleasant MEMORIAL GARDENS. Disabled access; cl 12.30–2, Christmas and wknds Nov–Mar; free.

🕭 🏥 ❀ WESTGATE MUSEUM (High St) More militaria and some local history above a formidable, medieval city gate – the panorama of the city and surrounding countryside is rewarding. Shop; cl 1–2 Sat, am Sun, Mon in Oct, Feb and Mar, all Nov–Jan; 30p.

🖼 GUILDHALL GALLERY (Broadway) Refurbished 19th-c building with changing exhibitions of fine art, crafts and photography. Snacks, shop, disabled access; cl am Sun, pm Mon Oct–Mar, Good Fri, 25–26 Dec, 1 Jan; free.

🕭 CITY MUSEUM (The Square) Well organised local history and archaeology, inc a telling Roman mosaic. Shop, disabled access to ground floor only; cl 1–2 Sat, am Sun, Mon Oct–Mar, 25–26 Dec; free.

🏥 ST CROSS is a short stroll along the watermeadows by the River Itchen. Very attractively set around two quadrangles, the quaint 15th-c almshouses still provide bread and ale to travellers who ask at the massive gate (you have to ask for 'Wayfarer's Dole'). Handsome 12th/13th-c chapel, medieval kitchen, walled Master's garden and Brethren's Hall. Shop, disabled access; cl 12.30–2pm, Sun, 25 Dec, Good Fri; *£1.50. The Bell out here is useful for lunch.

🏛 There are pleasant walks up rounded ST CATHERINE'S HILL, which has a small, medieval turf maze and traces of a hill fort.

Other things to see and do

✚ 🕭 ❀ ♤ Aldershot SU8650 AIRBORNE FORCES MUSEUM (Browning Barracks) The best of Aldershot's profusion of military museums (most of which are of rather specialist appeal), covering the creation and operation of the parachute forces from 1940. There's almost too much to take in. This year they're celebrating the 50th anniversary of Operation Varsity, the Crossing of the Rhine. Shop, disabled access; cl over Christmas; (01252) 349619; *£2. MILITARY MUSEUM (Queens Ave) Well done despite its specialist appeal, following the development of the military camps at Aldershot and Farnham and their impact on civilian and military life. Snacks, shop, disabled access; cl 2 wks over Christmas, bank hols; (01252) 314598; £1.50. The Aldershot/Farnborough area has quite a lot of parks, and open spaces

out in the surrounding pinewoods for children to let off steam, with boating lakes and so forth.

🐎 🏬 ★ Alresford SU5931 WATERCRESS LINE One of the nicest steam railways in the country, with 10-mile trips between Alresford and Alton through wonderful countryside and its watercress beds. They really try to create a pre-war feel, with stations en route decked out accordingly; you can get connections to Waterloo. Meals, snacks, shop, disabled access; phone for timetable (01962) 734866; £6.50. You may be able to combine it with a visit to the BASS BREWERY at the Alton end. Alresford is a charming little town, from the Roman ponds in Old Alresford to the so-called New Alresford founded around 1200; good antiquarian bookshop here. The Horse & Groom is the best simple place for lunch; the Old School House is a smart restaurant, and the Globe looks out over one of the ponds.

✿ ♘ **Ampfield** SU4023 SIR HAROLD HILLIER GARDENS AND ARBORETUM Impressive collection of trees and shrubs, the biggest of its kind in Britain, covering 160 beautifully landscaped acres. Full of colour and surprises all year, lots of good talks and events. Summer meals, snacks, shop, disabled access; cl Sat Dec–Feb, 25–28 Dec, 1 Jan; (01794) 68787; £3. The White Horse nearby is a comfortable lunch break.

♿ ▣ ☛ ♪ **Andover** SU3645 Nr the church at the top of the impressive High St of this very extended country town, the MUSEUM OF THE IRON AGE looks particularly at finds from Danebury Ring (see entry below), giving a vivid impression of life for the pre-Roman Celts. There's an adjacent, more general MUSEUM. Shop, limited disabled access; cl Sun (exc summer pm), Mon, Christmas; (01264) 366283; £1.20. The conference room of the borough council office (Weyhill Rd) houses the remarkable TEST VALLEY TAPESTRY, each of its many panels embroidered by a different village to show a scene relating to that community. Disabled access; generally open Mon lunchtimes and one pm Thurs each month – best to phone (01264) 364144 to check; free. FINKLEY DOWN FARM PARK (just NE of town) Well laid out working farm with a wide range of animals and poultry inc rare breeds; they positively encourage you to touch the tamer animals. Also, a countryside museum with Romany caravans, adventure playground and picnic site. Readers like this place a lot, especially as it has so much for children (and space for them to run around). Snacks, shop, disabled access; cl Oct–Apr; (01264) 352195; £3.30. Three or four miles down the Roman road, the Coronation Arms at St Mary Bourne is useful for lunch. There are well stocked trout-fishing lakes around Andover, for example at Rooksbury Mill.

♰ ♘ ✿ **Beech** SU6938 ALTON ABBEY The home of a community of Benedictine monks and set amid peaceful woodland – this is a relaxing place for a stroll. The grounds have a number of mature specimen trees and shrubs, especially rhododendrons and azaleas. The Sun at Bentworth is an appropriate sort of place for a meal.

♰ **Binsted** SU7740 CHURCH where Field Marshal Montgomery is buried; after the war he lived a mile away at Islington Mill SU7742 – a pretty spot. The Jolly Farmer at Blacknest is handy for lunch.

🏰 **Bishop's Waltham** SU5517 PALACE Impressive ruins of the Bishop of Winchester's majestic 12th-c palace, with the remains of the state apartments round a cloister court, and William of Wykeham's great hall and tower. Shop, disabled access to the ground floor; cl 1–2, Mon in winter, 24–26 Dec, 1 Jan; (01489) 892460; £1.80. The Bunch of Grapes and White Swan are quite useful for lunch.

▣ ✿ **Burghclere** SU4761 SANDHAM MEMORIAL CHAPEL Stanley Spencer's moving masterpiece, built in memory of H W Sandham who was killed in the First World War. The final resurrection scene is especially dramatic, best on a bright day as the room is quite dark. Cl Mon, Tues, wkdays Nov and Mar and all Dec–Feb; £1.30; NT. The Carpenter's Arms opposite is useful for lunch, with superb views.

✿ ♘ ♞ ☛ ♣ ✕ **Bursledon** SU4809 MANOR FARM COUNTRY PARK (Highlands Lane) Woodland and riverside walks based around a traditional working farm, with lots of animals, crafts and activities. Meals, snacks, shop, disabled access; park open all yr, farm cl winter exc Sun; (01489) 787055; *£2.80. There may be summer BOAT TRIPS from here along the Hamble. Bursledon also has a WINDMILL; open Sun and summer Sats. The Fox & Hounds (Hungerford Bottom) is an interesting place for lunch.

🏚 ☛ **Chalton** SU7315 BUTSER ANCIENT FARM (Bascombe Copse) Reconstructed Iron Age farm, with crops, animals, crafts and demonstrations. It's really a huge experiment, the aim being to find out more about life in ancient times. You can try your hand at grinding corn on a stone, and there's even a Celtic maze (planted with period herbs). Shop, disabled access; cl am Sat, all winter wknds – winter opening is mainly by arrangement; (01705) 598838; £1.50. The ancient Red Lion is good for lunch.

🏠♨❀ **Chawton** SU7037 JANE AUSTEN'S HOUSE Unpretentious 17th-c house where the author lived, worked and died, still with some of her letters and possessions (inc a table she's supposed to have used for writing). Rooms are furnished in period style, and the pleasant garden is good for picnics. Shop, disabled access to ground floor and garden; cl Mon and Tues in Nov, Dec and Mar and all wkdys Jan and Feb; (01420) 83262; *£2. The Rose & Crown at Upper Farringdon does good-value food.

🐾 **Colden Common** SU5021 (off the A333 towards Bishop's Waltham) MARWELL ZOO is a good one, in a spacious park, with plenty of room for its 1,000 animals, many of which no longer exist in the wild. Some can be approached and stroked. A glass wall at one end of the tiger cage lets you enjoy the terrifying, though completely safe, experience of one of the beasts jumping up at you. Meals, snacks, shop, disabled access; cl 25 Dec; (01962) 777406; £6. On the downs above, the Ship at Owslebury is useful for lunch, and the Queen's Head at Fisher's Pond is handy too.

🏛 **Danebury Ring** SU3237 is an Iron Age hill fort rich in (excavated) remains, interestingly waymarked. The Peat Spade at Longstock, to the E, does good food.

✝ **Farnborough** SU8753 Though the town itself is scarcely a place for visitors, ST MICHAEL'S ABBEY is an interesting old church with the tombs of Emperor Napoleon III of France, and his wife and son in the Imperial Crypt; it's still maintained by resident Benedictine monks. Best to ring for guided tour times, though usually 3.30pm Sat, and the same time Weds and Sun in July–Sept; (01252) 372822; crypt £2. The Prince of Wales (Rectory Rd) has decent lunchtime food.

❀🏛❀ **Gosport** SZ6199 ROYAL NAVY SUBMARINE MUSEUM The highlight here is the beached WWII submarine HMS *Alliance*, still in full working order, fascinating inside to small boys of any age. The more conventional part of the museum includes an audio-visual show giving the flavour of diving into the depths. Snacks, shop, disabled access to ground floor only; cl 24 Dec–1 Jan; (01705) 529217; £3.50. FORT BROCKHURST has a good overview exhibition of how the various series of forts protected Portsmouth; the view of the harbour and Portsdown Hill from the useful Hogshead & Halibut (Hardway), open all day, lets you work it out from a different perspective.

★ ♨❀🏛 **Hamble** SU4806 in HOWARD'S WAY country has interesting views of the yachts, and you can walk a long way up river or towards the Solent; there's a friendly little ferry from Warsash – about 10 people at a time (30p). The simple Olde Whyte Harte and smarter Bugle are both useful. Nearby Netley SU4508 has a coastal COUNTRY PARK and the extensive ruins of a 13th-c abbey.

🏛❀ **Highclere** SU4360 HIGHCLERE CASTLE (best approached from the A34 rather than Highclere itself) Magnificent pastiche of a medieval castle, as impressively grand inside as it is outside. Elaborate saloon and main staircase, and a number of paintings and other treasures worth studying, notably Napoleon's desk and a van Dyck of Charles I. Unusually, the main bedrooms are open to visitors. Exhibitions of Egyptian relics (the 5th earl discovered Tutankhamun's tomb with Howard Carter), and horseracing (the current earl is the Queen's racing manager), and lovely gardens and grounds, inc a Victorian tropical conservatory and walled garden. Good events and concerts. Snacks, shop and plant centre; open pm Weds, Thurs, and wknds July, Aug and Sept, plus Sun and Mon of bank hol wknds; (01635) 253210; £5. The closest pub for lunch is the Caernarvon Arms, but if you go a bit further the Yew Tree does excellent meals.

🏠❀❀ **Hinton Ampner** SU5927 HINTON AMPNER Good views from this Georgian house, sensitively restored after a terrible fire in 1960.

Fine Regency furniture, pictures and porcelain, and impressive grounds, with tranquil 20th-c shrub gardens. Teas, disabled access; open pm Tues, Weds and wknds (not house exc in Aug) Apr–Sept; *£3.70 house and garden, £2.40 garden only; NT. The Fox at Bramdean nearby is good for lunch.

★ ✕ **Langstone** SU7105 has thatched cottages, an old tidal mill, and a couple of decent pubs looking out over the thousands of acres of silted harbour – the winter sunsets are memorable. Swans float up at high tide, with oystercatchers and droves of darting dunlins on the low-tide mud flats. Interesting walks along the old sea wall.

✸ **Lasham** SU6742 is a pleasant place to watch gliders over the Downs. The Royal Oak does decent home cooking.

✸ ♤ ₪ **Liphook** SU8431 BOHUNT MANOR Lovely woodland gardens owned by the Worldwide Fund for Nature, with watergarden, roses and herbaceous borders, a lakeside walk, and unusual trees and shrubs. Disabled access; (01428) 722208; *£1.50 (usually free in winter). HOLLYCOMBE STEAM COLLECTION Huge collection of steam-driven equipment, from paddle-steamers to fairground equipment, with demonstrations, traction engine rides, and woodland steamtrain trips. Snacks, shop; open pm Sun and bank hols, plus some other days in July and Aug – best to tel (01428) 724900 to check; £4.50. The nearest place for a good lunch is the Red Lion over at Fernhurst.

✝ **Middle Wallop** SU2938 MUSEUM OF ARMY FLYING One of the country's best military museums, exploring man's efforts to fly. Kites, balloons, vintage aircraft, WWII gliders, and interactive displays. Some exhibits still fly occasional weekends, and there are quite a few interesting events – this year, on 10 Sept, a helicopter flying display. Meals, snacks, shop, disabled access; cl wk before Christmas–New Year; (01980) 674421; *£3.75. The Five Bells tucked away in nearby Nether Wallop is a pleasantly modest place for lunch.

⚙ ✸ **Mottisfont** SU3226 MOTTISFONT ABBEY 12th-c priory salvaged from the

Reformation as a splendid family house, in wonderful, peaceful surroundings. The gardens are an absolute delight, housing the National Collection of old roses (largely scented). A couple of rooms inc one decorated richly by Rex Whistler can be visited some days. Shop, good disabled access; open pm Sat–Weds Apr–Oct (till 8.30pm in Jun), rooms usually open pm Tues, Weds and Sun; £2.50, tour of rooms 50p extra; NT. The Mill Arms at Dunbridge has good home cooking.

⚙ ✸ **Old Winchester Hill** SU6420 The HILL FORT here gives wide views of Hampshire, the Solent and Isle of Wight, with nature trails through natural downland that's never been ploughed and resown; fairly busy on fine weekends, wonderfully remote on a blustery spring or autumn weekday. The George & Falcon at Warnford is popular for food.

♨ ▣ ✝ **Petersfield** SU7423 BEAR MUSEUM (Dragon St) Teddies, dolls and toys in a nursery setting. Children (or anyone else for that matter) can cuddle the exhibits. Shop, limited disabled access; cl most Suns exc Christmas; (01730) 265108; free. Petersfield also has a GALLERY commemorating the work of local artist Flora Twort in her old cottage (cl Sun and Mon), a collection of dolls in the Chapel St bookshop, and an interesting CHURCH (Market Sq). The Good Intent is useful for lunch.

⛪ ✝ ⚙ **Portchester** SU6105 PORTCHESTER CASTLE The imposing high walls and towers stretching right down to the waterfront were originally part of a 3rd-c Roman fort – they're the best example of their type in Europe. Other aged remains include a 12th-c church and 14th-c great tower. Richard II converted the buildings in the inner courtyard into a palace, and the remains of the kitchen, hall and great chamber can still be seen; there's a good exhibition. Snacks, shop, disabled access; cl 25–26 Dec; (01705) 378291; £2. The nearby Cormorant does good-value food.

♤ ✸ ! **Queen Elizabeth Country Park** SU7219 Lots going on all year, with woodland walks and rides (stables at the park), open downland, and events from hang-gliding through to sheep-shearing demonstrations and conker championships. Shop and café (cl wkdys Nov–Feb and Sat Jan–Feb); (01705) 595040; parking £1.50, 80p winter. The excellent Five Bells at Buriton is nearby.

🏠❀✝ **Romsey** SU3521 BROADLANDS (just S) Elegant Palladian mansion on the banks of the River Test, surrounded by beautiful, landscaped grounds. Fine furnishings and paintings, and a good exhibition on former resident Earl Mountbatten. Snacks, shop, disabled access; open pm July and Aug only; (01794) 516878; £5. Mountbatten is buried in the interesting 13th-c ROMSEY ABBEY, bought by the townspeople for their parish church at the Dissolution. There are some notable Saxon crosses and a 16th-c panel painting. The Dolphin (Cornmarket) is good for lunch.

🏠❀♨ **Selborne** SU7433 GILBERT WHITE'S HOUSE Impressive 18th-c former home of naturalist Gilbert White, furnished in period style. The extensive gardens are being restored to their original form, and separate galleries commemorate Captain Oates and Frank Oates. Shop, disabled access to ground floor and garden; cl wkdys Nov–Mar, Christmas; (01420) 511275; *£2.50. There are interesting walks tracing White's steps, and the Queen's Hotel is useful for lunch.

🏠 **Sherborne St John** SU6255 THE VYNE Magnificent Tudor mansion with splendid 17th- and 18th-c embellishments, inc the earliest classical portico on an English country house. Plenty of panelling in the long gallery, exquisite stained glass in the chapel, and a striking Palladian staircase. Snacks, shop, disabled access; cl am, Mon (exc bank hols when cl following Tues instead), Fri, Oct–Apr; £4, £2 grounds only; NT.

♨🏠✝ **Silchester** SU6262 CALLEVA MUSEUM Small collection of finds from the site of Calleva Atrebatum, a Roman town excavated nearby; free. The site itself has recently been restored, and has 1½ miles of city wall to walk along, as well as a 9,000-seat amphitheatre, and a 12th-c church on the site of the Roman

temples. The nearby Calleva Arms does cheap lunches, and also sells good guides to the site.

🏠♨❀✳✝🖼 **Southampton** SU4211 Once known as the 'Gateway to the World', this huge, bustling town rather unexpectedly has one of the three best-preserved, medieval town walls in the country. The best stretch is along the western side of the old core, around from the magnificent, partly Norman BARGATE (which includes a small local museum); there are usually guided walks along here on Sun mornings. There are lots of other old buildings dotted around the less appetising modern townscape, though if you're short of time it's probably best to concentrate your efforts on the area around St Michael's Sq, Bugle St and perhaps the old High St. Parking around the centre is metered. The quayside nearest here has been cleaned up, with modern café-bars overlooking yachting berths. In Bugle St is the pretty, 15th-c, timber-framed TUDOR HOUSE, with an excellent re-created Tudor knot garden behind, and a collection of mainly Victorian artefacts exhibited within the suitably creaky rooms. Shop, disabled access to ground floor only; cl 12–1, am Sun, Mon, Christmas; (01703) 332513; £1.50. Just down the road, the MARITIME MUSEUM is a fine 14th-c warehouse with an impressive timber ceiling, and useful displays on the history of the port – especially strong on the great liners. Shop, disabled access to ground floor only; cl 1–2, am Sun, Mon, Christmas; (01703) 223941; £1.50. GOD'S HOUSE TOWER (Winkle St) is an early 15th-c, prototype gun battery, now housing a Museum of Archaeology, with good displays on the city's Saxon forebear, Hamwic. Shop; cl 1–2, am Sun, Mon; *£1.50. The nearby bowling green is said to be the oldest in the world. HALL OF AVIATION (Albert Rd, S) Good exhibition of various aircraft of local interest – inc prototype helicopters and the Spitfire. Shop, disabled access; cl Mon (exc bank and school hols), Christmas; (01703) 635830; *£3. CITY ART GALLERY (Civic Centre, Commercial Rd) Very extensive and distinguished collection of British and European paintings and sculptures from the last 600 years, with particular emphasis on the 20th c. Meals, snacks, shop, disabled access; cl am Sun, all Mon, 25–27 and 31 Dec; free. The Red Lion in the High St does food all day, and is chiefly notable for its genuine, great medieval hall.

🏠 **Stratfield Saye** SU6861 STRATFIELD SAYE HOUSE A grateful nation granted the Duke of Wellington the money to buy this 17th-c house after Waterloo. Perhaps surprisingly, the Duke had a taste for French furniture, lots of which is still here, and there are a number of leather-bound books that belonged to Napoleon. Also the Duke's splendid funeral carriage, and his hearing aid – prolonged exposure to cannons having proved problematic for his hearing. Meals, snacks, shop, disabled access; cl am, all Fri, Oct–Apr; (01256) 882882; £4.50. The New Inn is pleasant for lunch. There are pleasant walks E of the park, on Heckfield Heath.

🏠🏠 **Titchfield** SU5305 TITCHFIELD ABBEY Ruined 13th-c abbey, almost overshadowed by the grand Tudor gatehouse built when it was converted into a mansion after the Dissolution. Some of Shakespeare's plays were reputedly first performed here. Disabled access; free. The riverside Fisherman's Rest opposite is a decent pub/restaurant.

🦅 **Weyhill** SU3146 HAWK CONSERVANCY One of the best birds of prey centres we've come across, really well thought out; you can handle some of the birds, and there are regular flying displays. The very keen can book a day's hawking under instruction. Meals, snacks, shop, disabled access; cl Nov–Feb; (01264) 772252; £4. The Star and Weyhill Fair are handy for lunch.

★ 🍴 🌼 Among the county's many **attractive villages**, ones with decent pubs include Abbots Ann SU3243, Cheriton SU5828, Chilbolton SU3939 (the Common is being carefully preserved), Crawley SU4234, East Meon SU6822 (splendid Norman church), Faccombe SU3858, Hamble SU4806 (the Olde Whyte Harte, nr the water), Mapledurwell SU6851, Meonstoke SU6119, Nether Wallop SU3036 (the Saxon church is well worth seeing), Overton SU5149 and Tichborne SU5630. Other good villages are Exton SU6121 (beautifully set by the river under the chalk hills), and Wickham SU5711, with its huge village square (and a good farm shop with pick your own at nearby Droxford SU6018), while in the N, Ashmansworth SU4157 and Linkenholt SU3658 are high enough to give fine views from many of their lanes (best explored by car).

Walks

In the E of the county, there are some good scenic pockets around **Selborne** SU7433 🚶-1, the countryside recorded in such detail by naturalist Gilbert White; the zigzag path he created with his brother in 1753 still climbs Selborne Hanger. The hangers hereabouts are beechwoods which cling to the abrupt escarpments; Noar Hill, close by, has been designated a nature reserve for its chalkland flora.

Farley Mount SU4029 🚶-2 is an attractive area for walking, with plenty of space in downland and woodland, and fine views.

Watership Down SU4957 🚶-3, just S of Kingsclere, was the home of the rabbits in the novel by Richard Adams – their final adventure was down at Freefolk SU4848, where the local pub fittingly has a batch of bunnies. Pleasant wooded walks through this area.

Cheesefoot Head SU5327 🚶-4 (locally pronounced Chesford) is nice for walks; a natural amphitheatre where Eisenhower and Montgomery addressed the troops before the Normandy invasion.

Old Winchester Hill SU6420 🚶-5 is a good place for breezy strolls.

Many of the woodlands in this part of Hampshire fill with snowdrops in Feb (Warnford SU6223 is a good example); in May there are bluebells, for example at Froxfield SU7025, East Tisted SU7032 and Ropley SU6431.

Decent pubs on which to base walks include the Milburys at Beauworth SU5726, Bat & Ball on Broadhalfpenny Down SU6716, Five Bells at Buriton SU7420, Red Lion at Chalton SU7315, Queen's Head at Dogmersfield SU7853, Mill Arms at Barley Hill, Dunbridge SU3126, the George at East Meon SU6822, Star at East Tytherley SU2929, Vine at Hannington SU5355, Hawkley Inn on Pococks Lane, Hawkley SU7429, John o' Gaunt at Horsebridge SU3430, Old House At Home at Newnham SU7054, Bush at Ovington SU5531, White Horse, nr Priors Dean above Petersfield SU7129 (our favourite country pub), Selborne Arms in Selborne SU7433, Coronation Arms at St Mary Bourne SU4250 (Test Way), Harrow at Steep SU7425 (the beechwood hangers), Elm Tree at Swanwick SU5109 (handy for the new Hants Wildlife Reserve) and the George at Vernham Dean SU3456 (Fosbury hill fort).

Driving

Some of the nicest drives are through the valleys of the rivers and tributaries of the Test (B3048, B3400, back road through Longstock and Houghton to Mottisfont), Itchen (back road from Ovington to Easton) and Meon (the back road through Soberton is preferable to the A32 N of Wickham). The B3046 N of Alresford gives a good impression of Downs farming country, and the A272 Winchester–Petersfield is another long-winded, downland road. Even better than the A272 is the old high road it replaced, running from Winchester through Alresford, Ropley, Hedge Corner and Stoner Hill to Steep.

There's an attractive circular drive from Bishop's Waltham N over Stephen's Castle Down, past the Owslebury crossroads and over Lane End Down to the Milburys pub S of Beauworth, and on to Warnford, getting back to Bishop's Waltham along the A32 to Corhampton and then the B3035. On this drive, the diversion to the viewpoint of Beacon Hill is well worthwhile – either from the Kilmeston crossroads between the Milburys and Warnford, or from Exton, just off the A32.

In the N of the county, relatively empty highlands overlapping with Wilts and Berks offer some fine views, though some of the lanes are narrow with sharp bends and steep hills. Hurstbourne Tarrant is a good centre for this largely unspoilt area, and attractive lanes include Hurstbourne Tarrant to Faccombe and Walbury or to Inkpen via the Netherton Valley, Faccombe to Walbury Hill, Walbury Hill to Inkpen Beacon, Faccombe to Linkenholt, and Vernham Dean to Oxenwood (via the Weyhill road up Conholt Hill, turning right on its summit).

Where to eat

Botley SU5112 COBBETTS 15 The Square (01489) 782068 Nicely presented, mainly French food in a 16th-c cottage, with a relaxed atmosphere and friendly staff; cl Mon and Sat lunchtimes, Sun; disabled access. £36/£13.10 (2-course lunch).
Emsworth SU7406 36 ON THE QUAY South St (01243) 375592 Very good French cooking in a charming quayside restaurant, with helpful service and a sound wine list; cl Tues, 2 wks Oct; children over 11. £35 for 4 courses.
Old Burghclere SU4758 DEW POND (01635) 278408. Beautiful 16th-c country house with log fires and a friendly atmosphere; lovely food using fresh local produce on a frequently changing small menu; no smoking; cl Sun, Mon, first 2 wks Jan, 2 wks Aug; children over 12; disabled access. £27.50.
Mapledurwell SU6851 GAMEKEEPERS (01256) 22038 Interesting old inn in a lovely thatched village, with a wide choice of enterprising food, good-value wines, and friendly service; cl pm Sun, 25–26 Dec; disabled access. £21|£1.40/£3.95.
Highclere SU4360 YEW TREE Hollington Cross, Andover Rd (on the A343, S) (01635) 253360 Cheerfully decorated, L-shaped bar with a big log fire, enterprising food such as lamb en croûte, river trout or crispy duck, and good, unobtrusive waitress service; disabled access. £20|£2.75/£6.80.

Buriton SU7420 FIVE BELLS (01730) 263584 Popular, unpretentious country local with a genuine welcome, simple and relaxing furniture, a log fire, very good bar food, and a good choice of well kept beers. £20l£2.50/£6.25.

Southampton SU4212 BROWNS Frobisher House, Nelson Gate, Commercial Rd (01703) 332615 Friendly, simply decorated restaurant nr the Mayflower Theatre, with good, innovative cooking and a short, sound wine list; cl am Sat, Sun, 14–30 Aug; children over 12. £18.75/£7.50.

Houghton SU3432 BOOT (01794) 388310 Flourishing dining pub with pleasant service and good restaurant food; cl Mon; disabled access. £18.50l£2.50/£5.95.

Well SU7646 CHEQUERS (01256) 862605 Neatly kept and rather smart country pub – quite handy for the Watercress Line; with a relaxed atmosphere, snug rooms, beams, lots of 18th-c country-life prints, and very good, unusual bar food; disabled access. £18.50l£3.50/£5.25.

Grayshott SU8735 WOODS PLACE Headley Rd (01428) 605555 Pretty restaurant in a former butcher's shop with panelling and wall tiles; most enjoyable modern cooking, and friendly service; cl Sun, Mon, Christmas, 2 wks Aug; disabled access. £17/£7.

Bishop's Waltham SU5517 TONY'S BRASSERIE The Old Granary, corner of Brook St and Bank St (01489) 896352 Cosy restaurant with friendly service, simple French and other international dishes, and decent wines; cl pm Sun, Mon. £16/£7.50 (2 courses).

Southsea SZ6498 A FISTFUL OF TACOS Albert Rd (01705) 293474 Evening restaurant with good Californian/Mexican food; partial disabled access. £15/£5.

Droxford SU6018 HURDLES (01489) 877451 Pretty, creeper-covered building, simple home cooking, and friendly staff; cl 25–26 Dec; no children; disabled access. £14l£2.30/£4.

West Meon SU6424 THOMAS LORD (01730) 829244 Attractive village local with a strong cricketing influence; welcoming atmosphere, generous helpings of good-value food, and helpful service. £12l£1.80/£4.

Winchester SU4829 PAPPAGALLOS City Rd (01962) 841107 Bustling, friendly restaurant with decent Italian food; cl Sun, bank hols; £12.

Faccombe SU3858 JACK RUSSELL (01264) 87315 Pleasant little place with an attractive dining conservatory, courteous service, and very good food; bedrooms; disabled access. £11l£2/£4.75.

Tichborne SU5630 TICHBORNE ARMS (01962) 733760 Attractive, thatched country pub in rolling countryside, with very good, imaginative bar food, and delicious puddings; big garden; cl pm 25 and 26 Dec; no children; disabled access. £11l£1.30/£3.50.

Bramdean SU6128 FOX (01962) 771363 Welcoming, 17th-c dining pub with famous fox masks on the wall, very appetising bar food (lots of fish), and obliging service. £2.60/£6.25.

NEW FOREST

Beaulieu and Exbury Gardens have strong appeal; the forest itself is remarkable for unrestricted walking.

The forest, which includes large tracts of heath as well as woodland, has the particular appeal for walkers that you can head off in virtually any direction you want without worrying about trespassing. Once away from the roads, it does give a great feeling of untrammelled space. Children like it: apart from the ponies and deer, there's plenty of scope for generally running riot without coming to grief.

Down on the coast there are sheltered yachting harbours, and the pleasant waterside town of Lymington with warm Georgian buildings. Beaulieu is immensely successful at pleasing visitors, with a wide range of attractions carefully organised to suit different tastes. The much less visited Exbury Gardens have a wonderfully rich, waterside garden landscape, irresistible in late spring. There are not that many other paid-entry attractions in this area; foremost among them are perhaps the maritime museum in the pretty village of Bucklers Hard, the imaginative Spinners garden at Boldre and the butterfly farm at Ashurst; children enjoy Paultons Park at Ower.

Where to stay

New Milton SZ2495 CHEWTON GLEN, New Milton BH25 6QS (01425) 275341 *£199; 58 really beautiful rms. Luxurious hotel in lovely grounds, with sumptuous day rooms, antiques, excellent modern French cooking, and very good service; nine-hole golf course, swimming pool, tennis (two indoor courts as well) and croquet; also a health club with an indoor swimming pool, gym, saunas, treatment rooms; children over 7 only; disabled access.

Lymington SZ3295 PASSFORD HOUSE Mount Pleasant Lane, Lymington SO41 8LS (01590) 682398 *£101; 55 neatly kept, airy rms. Attractive hotel on the edge of the New Forest, with a comfortable panelled lounge (three others, too), cocktail bar, open fires, excellent service; gardens and parkland with indoor and outdoor swimming pools, tennis, croquet, putting; disabled access.

Brockenhurst SU2902 CAREYS MANOR, Brockenhurst SO4 7RH (01590) 23551 *£99; 78 rms, some opening directly onto the garden. Attractive country house with landscaped gardens, a comfortable, airy lounge, and good food; fine sports complex with a big indoor pool, sauna, solarium, steam room and gym; disabled access.

Lyndhurst SU2908 PARKHILL Beaulieu Rd, Lyndhurst SO43 7FZ (01703) 282944 £98; 20 carefully furnished rms, some overlooking the lawns. 13th-c hunting lodge rebuilt by the Duke of Clarence in the mid-18th c and set in parkland with fine views; comfortable lounges, antiques, flowers, and a civilised atmosphere; good food in the attractive dining room, and friendly, professional staff; disabled access.

Beaulieu SU3802 MONTAGU ARMS Palace Lane, Beaulieu SO42 7ZL (01590) 612324 *£95.90; 24 individually decorated rms. Attractive, creeper-clad hotel in a beautiful setting, lovely terraced garden, comfortable sitting room, conservatory lounge, very good food in the beamed restaurant, and attentive staff; their health club is in the village; they also run the village shop, post office and bakery.

Bucklers Hard SU4000 MASTER BUILDERS HOUSE Bucklers Hard, Beaulieu, Brockenhurst SO42 7XB (01590) 616253 £85; 23 rms (the ones in the original building have most character). Extended 18th-century house on the banks of the River Beaulieu built for master builder Henry Adams who, among other fine ships, built Nelson's favourite, *Agamemnon*; homely residents' lounge with a log fire, heavy-beamed, bustling bar, an airy restaurant, and a relaxed atmosphere; disabled access.

Lymington SZ3295 STANWELL HOUSE High St, Lymington SO41 9AA (01590) 677123 *£85; 35 pretty rms. Handsome townhouse with a comfortable, attractively furnished lounge, cosy little bar, good, imaginative food, and a pretty, walled back garden; disabled access.

New Milton SZ2495 YEW TREE FARM Bashley Common Rd, New Milton BH25 5SH (01425) 611041 £50; 2 lovely, spacious rms. Marvellously comfortable and well run, traditional thatched smallholding on the edge of the New Forest; with a small, cosy hall, friendly welcome, extensive breakfasts (taken in bedroom), and good, home-made dinners (if required) using top quality produce; riding nearby; no children.

Rockbourne SU1118 SHEARINGS Rockbourne, Fordingbridge SP6 3NA (01725) 519256 *£46; 3 rms. Beside a winter stream in a charming village, this warmly welcoming and pretty, 16th-c thatched cottage has inglenook fireplaces, ancient beams (some nearly 1,000 years old), a comfortable sitting room, and home-cooked food; candlelit dinner if requested; cl mid-Dec–mid-Feb; children over 12; no dogs.

Copythorne SU3114 OLD WELL Copythorne, Southampton SO4 2PE (01703) 812321 *£45; 6 rms. Well kept, family-run restaurant with bedrooms, decent food, a pleasant bar, and friendly service; evening meals Fri and Sat.

Sway SZ2798 NURSES COTTAGE Station Rd, Sway, Lymington SO41 6BA (01590) 683402 *45; 3 rms. Small, immaculately kept house (formerly a district nurse's home) with very helpful owners, a neat garden, and good breakfasts; evening meal by arrangement; children over 5.

Lymington SZ3295 KINGS ARMS, St Thomas St, Lymington SO41 9NB (01590) 672594 £36; 2 rms, shared bthrm. Small inn with two bars (one for eating), very friendly licensees, real ales, and decent food; busy Sat lunchtimes when local market is on; no accommodation 25–26 Dec; children over 5 only.

Picket Hill SU1805 PICKET HILL HOUSE Picket Hill, Ringwood BH24 3HH (01425) 476173 £34; 3 rms (2 with own bthrm). Country house on the edge of the New Forest, with a large lounge, friendly and helpful owners, a pretty garden, and good breakfasts; lots to do nearby; cl Christmas; children over 10.

To see and do

The **New Forest** itself is an unchanging blend of woodland and heath, covering nearly 150 square miles, designated a royal hunting preserve by William the Conqueror not long after the Battle of Hastings. Still with quite a medieval feel, the ancient woodlands are very atmospheric to stroll through, especially when you come across an unexpected, sunlit leafy glade. It's most fun just to potter around (you can go pretty much wherever you please), but you'll get much more out of a guided tour with people who've lived or worked in the forest all their lives; tel (01703) 282269 for details. CYCLING is fun too; you can hire bikes at Brockenhurst SU2902, tel (01590) 24204. The Museum and Visitor Centre at Lyndhurst (see entry below) is a good place to start, and has details of watersports and riding. See **Walks** section below for ideas for exploring the area on foot.

🦋 **Ashurst** SU3310 NEW FOREST BUTTERFLY FARM Indoor tropical jungle with free-flying butterflies and moths from all over the world. Also an insectarium, woodland walk, dragonfly ponds, adventure playground and wagon rides. Meals, snacks, shop, disabled access; cl Nov–Mar; (01703) 292166; £3.50. The White Horse at Netley Marsh has decent food.

🏨🏠🏕️❄️🐴✝️🎣☺ **Beaulieu** SU3802 The attractions at this hugely popular place would each make rewarding visits on their own, so their combined appeal makes Beaulieu a very worthwhile choice for a family day out. For many the main draw is the NATIONAL MOTOR MUSEUM, a collection that from humble beginnings has grown to become one of the most comprehensive in the

world, with over 250 vehicles and displays, some in period reconstructions. Children should enjoy WHEELS, an automated trip through 100 years of motoring, and there's an exciting simulator ride that does pretty much the same in more robust style. Before the cars came along it was the PALACE HOUSE that visitors came to see, a fine old mansion based around the gatehouse of the huge Cistercian Abbey that stood here until the Reformation. It has some interesting paintings and furnishings, and what are thought to be the original, monastic, fan-vaulted ceilings. The beautiful lakeside parkland and gardens have graceful ruins of other abbey buildings, inc a lovely row of arches, and the monks' refectory (now the parish church) has an exhibition on their daily life. Other features include miniature car rides, a model railway, and a high-level monorail around the grounds; in summer, they have a daily parade of vehicles from the museum. All very slickly done – at times it's almost like a miniature Disneyland. Meals, snacks, shops, disabled access; cl 25 Dec; (01590) 612123; £7.50. In the village facing the Palace House gates, the Wine Press is popular for lunch, and a marked trail leads from it down to Bucklers Hard – see entry below.

❀ **Boldre** SZ3198 SPINNERS Wonderful gardens created since the 1960s. The nursery is famed for its rare trees (especially maples and magnolias), shrubs and plants, and attracts visitors from all over the world. Some disabled access; gardens open Weds–Sat from mid-Apr–mid-Sept (plus Sun Apr and May), or by appointment, nursery open all year exc Mon and Tues July–Apr; (01590) 673347; *£1.50. The Red Lion (no children) is good for lunch.

🏠👃 **Breamore** SU1517 BREAMORE HOUSE Good example of a late Elizabethan manor house, with fine furnishings, tapestries and paintings (mainly 17th- and 18th-c Dutch school), and countryside museum. Horse-drawn carriages and fire-fighting equipment in the stables, and there are some animals and a maze. Snacks, shop, disabled access; open pm Tues, Weds and Sun Apr–Sept, plus Thurs and Sat May–Sept, and every day in Aug and school hols; (01725) 512468; *£4.50. The home cooking at the Horse & Groom at Woodgreen is good.

★ ❀ ♪ ⚓ **Bucklers Hard** The little waterside village is very pretty, with long, red-roofed cottage rows flanking a wide, grassed waterside street. It was once an important centre for shipbuilding, and the MARITIME MUSEUM tells the story of the industry, right up to the voyages of Sir Francis Chichester. You have to pay to come into the village, though admission includes entry to the museum and the various other exhibitions and reconstructions dotted around, inc the carefully restored 18th-c homes of a shipwright and labourer, and a typical inn scene complete with costumed

figures, smells and conversation. Meals, snacks, shop; cl 25 Dec; *£2.60. There are summer boat trips, and the Master Builder's House is useful for lunch. A pleasant 2½-mile riverside walk takes you to Beaulieu (see entry above), run by the same people.

🏰 ❀ **Calshot Castle** SU4802, down past the oil refineries and power stations, is a Tudor fort at the end of the spit of land out over the tidal mudflats at the end of Southampton Water; splendid views of the shipping and the Isle of Wight. The Jolly Sailor at Ashlett Creek, nr Fawley, has a pleasant waterside setting for lunch.

★ **Damersham** ST1015 In spring, it's worth visiting the churchyard here to see the carpet of snowdrops.

❀ ♫ ❀ **Exbury** SU4200 EXBURY GARDENS Wonderful, 200-acre, landscaped woodland gardens on the E bank of the River Beaulieu, with a splendid rock garden, heather garden and river walk, and, above all, the Rothschild collection of rhododendrons, azaleas, magnolias and camellias – one of the world's finest, and at its best in May and early Jun. Meals, snacks, shop, disabled access; cl 25 Oct–26 Feb; (01703) 891203; price varies with the season, from £2 in summer when less is open to £4.50 on spring wknds. Nearby LEPE COUNTRY PARK is a nice place for a coastal stroll, with good views and lots of natural habitats. The Jolly Sailor (see Calshot, above) is quite handy.

🏰 **Hurst Castle** SZ3189 On a little spit commanding the Solent, and best reached on foot or by boat from Keyhaven (there's a pleasant walk from the characterful Gun pub), this was one of the most sophisticated fortresses around when built by Henry VIII. Fortified again in the 19th c, it still has two huge, 38-ton guns. Summer snacks, shop; cl wkdys Nov–Mar, 24–26 Dec, 1 Jan; (01590) 642344; £1.80.

★ **Lymington** SZ3295 is a handsome and relaxed waterside town, very popular in summer with yachting people; it has quite a number of attractive Georgian buildings and some good shops. The Chequers down Ridgeway Lane, S of Pennington, is the best place here for lunch, and the Ship is well worth knowing for its waterside position.

⛴ **Lyndhurst** SU2907 is the tourist centre of the New Forest, as well as the main shopping town for people living here – so has craft shops, antique shops etc. NEW FOREST MUSEUM Good themed displays and an audio-visual exploration of the forest's history and wildlife, and a 25-ft embroidery. It looks like a modern supermarket from outside. Shop, disabled access; cl 25 Dec; (01703) 283914; *£2.50. The Crown and Swan hotels are useful for lunch.

★ † ❀ ▣ **Minstead** SU2711 is pretty, with a fine old church at the top of the hill; the Trusty Servant by the green (where there may be summer cricket) does decent food. FURZEY GARDENS Eight, peaceful, heather-filled acres surrounding a 16th-c thatched cottage with a local craft gallery. Disabled access; cl 25–26 Dec; (01703) 812464; £2.50 Mar–Oct, £1.50 Nov–Feb.

🏍 **New Milton** SZ2495 SAMMY MILLER MUSEUM Some people consider this changing collection of fully restored motorbikes to be the best in Europe, and many of the 200 or so bikes are the only surviving examples in the world. Snacks, shop, disabled access; cl 25 Dec; (01425) 619696; *£3.

☺ ❦ ! ⛴ 🐄 **Ower** SU3216 PAULTONS PARK Agreeable family theme park with 140 acres of rides, gardens, animals, birds and wildfowl, as well as moving dinosaurs, a 10-acre lake with working waterwheel, Romany museum and miniature Rio Grande railway. Meals, snacks, shop, disabled access; cl Nov–Feb; (01703) 814442; £6.50. The White Hart at Cadnam is good.

♟ ❦ **Ringwood** SU1505 MOORS VALLEY COUNTRY PARK Nearly 400 hectares of forest, plenty of animals and nature trails. An unusual treetop walkway gives a rather different view of the forest. Snacks, shop, disabled access; (01425) 470721; car parking charge. The riverside Fish is nice for lunch.

🏛⛴ **Rockbourne** SU1118 ROMAN VILLA Remains of the largest known Roman villa in the area, found by chance 50 years ago by a farmer digging out a ferret. Interesting

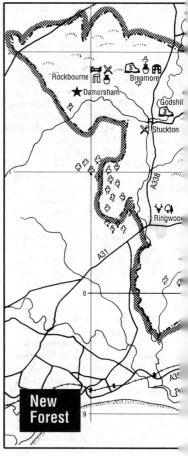

museum with mosaics, part of the hypocaust heating system, and a wide range of other items found on the site. Shop, disabled access; cl am wkdys exc July and Aug, all Oct–Mar; (017253) 541; *£1.30. The Rose & Thistle is useful for lunch.

✕ **Totton** SU3513 ELING TIDE MILL There's been a mill on this causeway for over 900 years, and the present one still works, making it the only mill still using tidal energy to produce flour. Snacks, shop, disabled access to ground floor only; cl Mon, Tues, and 25 Dec – ring for demonstration times, which of course depend on the tide; (01703) 869575; £1.15. In unpromising surroundings, the Anchor on Eling Quay is a good, cheap place for lunch.

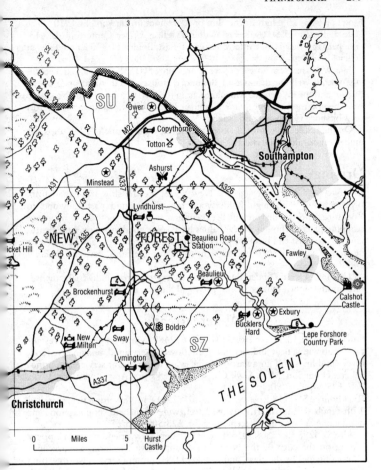

Walks

The path network in the New Forest is remarkably comprehensive, and anyone who just wants to walk at will in woodland and over open heaths will be well satisfied; moreover, in most places there's no obligation to stick to rights of way. The lack of major objectives can be a problem for purists: there are no obviously defined hills, and long walks in the eastern woodlands, many of which are coniferous, can become monotonous. Further W, the scenery is more intricate and a touch more varied. It is often a good idea to use routes which have plenty of landmarks to guide the way; the heath and forest can be fiendishly disorienting.

Besides the ponies, you see fallow deer, especially at the Bolderwood Deer Sanctuary SU2308 (and in the woods, very occasionally, the smaller, shyer roe deer; even in some places red deer).

The best walks alternate mixed forest with heathland; isolated ponds and country pubs provide focal points. Good starting places include **Beaulieu Road** railway station SU3406 △-1, for its surrounding remote-feeling heaths, **Burley Street** SU2004 △-2, **Godshill** SU1714 △-3 and **Brockenhurst** SU2902 △-4.

Pubs handy for New Forest walks are the Queen's Head or smarter White Buck at Burley SU2003, Royal Oak at Fritham SU2314, Forester's Arms at

Frogham SU1713, High Corner Inn or Red Shoot nr Linwood SU1910, Alice Lisle at Rockford SU1608, Sir Walter Tyrell at Upper Canterton SU2613, and perhaps the Turf Cutter's Arms at East Boldre SU3700 and Filly at Setley SU3000.

Just W of the New Forest proper is **Breamore** SU1518 ⌂-5, a thatched village within walking distance of Breamore House (Elizabethan, open to the public) and the mysterious Mizmaze, cut in the turf. Close by to the N, a steep walk behind the Cartwheel at Whitsbury SU1219 takes you up to the hill fort of Whitsbury Camp, for good views.

On the E side of the area is **Lepe Foreshore Country Park** SZ4598 ⌂-6, for mild saunters along the coast.

Driving

The two best drives through the New Forest are the slow back road from Brockenhurst N through Bolderwood and then round past Linwood to Rockford, and the drive from Brockenhurst to Burley. Both have plenty of stopping places. Though the A31 does have some good views over the heathland, it's too fast and busy for you really to appreciate them – and beware that heading W down it there are no right turns into the forest between Cadnam and Ringwood.

The B3054 from Dibden Purlieu is a quick retreat from industrial expanses into another much quieter world; pretty all the way to Lymington.

Where to eat

Stuckton SU1613 THREE LIONS (01425) 652489 Warmly welcoming, restauranty pub with a neat and airy bar, fresh flowers, very good, imaginative food, lovely puddings and an award-winning wine list; pleasant service and atmosphere; cl pm Sun, Mon, 1 wk Christmas, 2 wks July/Aug, 2 wks Oct, 2 wks Feb. £25|£4.80/£7.90.

Rockbourne SU1118 ROSE & THISTLE (017253) 236 Very attractive, thatched 17th-c pub with a smartly civilised feel, wide menu with popular food inc good game dishes, and a decent wine list. £23.50|£2.25/£5.

Boldre SZ3298 RED LION (01590) 673177 Very busy, friendly pub in a pretty setting on the edge of the New Forest; impressive bar food, a marvellous choice of wines by the glass, and well kept beer; prompt service; worth getting there early; no children; disabled access. £16.60|£2.80/£5.90.

Help this year from: G Hundleby, Sheila Cooper, D Horwood, Maurice Southon, Andrew Claiden, Sheena Anderson, D Horwood, Mrs Oliver, B M Eldridge, KCW, Peter and Audrey Dowsett, Ann and Colin Hunt, Ted Burden, Julie Mundy, Martin Robinson, Alan Bunt, D Grzelka, John and Joy Winterbottom, Colin Barnett, Ruth Trott, David Martin, Peter Churchill, E G Parish, Jenny and Brian Seller, John and Christine Simpson, John and Joan Calvert, Terry and Eileen Stott, Jo Goldsmith, A E Green, Mrs J Styles, J Watson, the Bailey family, Bill Capper, K Flack, Jim Penman, Christof Niklaus, Wendy Arnold, David Dimock, Dono and Carol Leaman, WHBM, Nick Twining, Keith Widdowson.

HAMPSHIRE CALENDAR

Some of these dates were provisional as we went to press.

FEBRUARY

22 **Southampton** English National Ballet, ROMEO AND JULIET at the
Mayflower Theatre – *till Sat 25* (01703) 229771

MARCH

3 **Southampton** International Women's Week – *till Sun 19*
(01703) 832525

27 **Southampton** Welsh National Opera at the Mayflower Theatre –
till 1 Apr (01703) 229771

APRIL

14 **Gosport** Easter Folk Festival at Thorngate Halls – *till Mon 17*
(01705) 522944

17 **Middle Wallop** Spring Vehicle Meet at the Museum of Army Flying
(01264) 384461

22 **Fordingbridge** Spring Festival Fair Day – festival will run for about two
more wks (01425) 653876

28 **Winchester** Folk Festival – *till Sun 30* (01962) 840500

29 **Butts** Spring Fair

MAY

7 **Southsea** Heavy Horse Parade at Castle Field Arena – *till Mon 8*
(01705) 834146; **Winchester** VE Service in Winchester Cathedral
(01962) 840500

8 **Winchester** VE Day Street Party (01962) 840500

27 **Havant** Country Show at Stansted Park – *till Sun 28* (01705) 412265

29 **Romsey** Spring Fair

JUNE

3 **Eastleigh** Southern Motor Fair at Itchen Valley Country Park – *till Sun 4*
(01703) 622205

8 **Southampton** Film Festival – *till Wed 22* (01703) 832457

17 **Exton** Bishop's Waltham Agricultural Show (01489) 891800;
Sarisbury Country Fair (01489) 573114

JULY

1 **Gosport** Carnival (01705) 584116; **Hedge End** Carnival and Gala Show
(01489) 785041; **Southampton** Balloon and Flower Festival – *till Sun 2*
(01703) 223855

7 **Winchester** Hat Fair: festival of street theatre – *till Sun 9*
(01962) 840500

8 **Fleet** Carnival Week – *till Sat 15* (01252) 617936; **Horndean** Hampshire
Country Fair and Sheepdog Trial at Queen Elizabeth Country Park
(01705) 595040; **Southampton** Carnival (01703) 398828

12 **Breamore** Hampshire celebrates VE Day at Breamore House –
till Thurs 13

15 **Eastleigh** Town and Country Show at Itchen Valley Country Park –
till Sun 16 (01703) 622205; **Fordingbridge** Show (01425) 652223

HAMPSHIRE CALENDAR

JULY cont

16 **Alton** Agricultural Show at Froyle Park (01420) 563492

21 **Gosport** Summer Festival – *till Sun 30* (01705) 522944

23 **Andover** Shetland Show at at Finkley Down Farm Park (01264) 352195; **Bucklers Hard** Village Festival (01590) 616203

25 **Brockenhurst** New Forest and Hampshire County Show at New Park Farm – *till Thurs 27* (01590) 22400

AUGUST

4 **Portsmouth** and **Southsea** Show at Southsea Common – *till Sun 6* (01705) 834146

5 **Havant** Grand Vintage Gathering and Country Craft Fair at Stansted Park – *till Sun 6* (01705) 412265

6 **Riseley** Heckfield Horticultural Show at Wellington Country Park (01734) 326444

12 **Breamore** Hampshire celebrates Victory at Breamore House – *till Sun 13* (01725) 22233; **Somerley** Ellingham and Ringwood Show at Upper Park (01425) 476601

26 **Middle Wallop** International Model Aircraft Competition – *till Mon 28*; **Portsmouth** International Kite Festival at Southsea Common – *till Sun 27* (01705) 824355

28 **Alton** Horticultural Society Autumn Show; **Emsworth** Show

SEPTEMBER

2 **Alresford** Agricultural Show at Titchborne Park (01962) 733887; **Riseley** Shetland Pony Show at Wellington Country Park (01734) 326444

9 **Romsey** Show at Broadlands Park (01794) 517521

15 **Winchester** Celebration of the Arts – *till Sun 24* (01962) 840500

16 **Southampton** International Boat Show – *till Sun 24* (01784) 473377

OCTOBER

23 **Titchfield** Carnival (01329) 846166

NOVEMBER

1 **Portsmouth** Fireworks Display (01705) 824355

4 **Aldershot** Firework Spectacular; **Winchester** Guy Fawkes Carnival and Fireworks Display at the Arbour (01962) 714288

DECEMBER

26 **Crookham Village** Mummers Play *at midday* (01252) 20968

HEREFORD AND WORCESTER

This area has attractive scenery, surprisingly good food (home-grown produce is more common here than usual), and plenty of interesting places to visit including an exceptional number of fine gardens. Worcestershire and the east of the area is more obviously geared to visitors. Over in the west, the countryside becomes quieter and progressively more unspoilt, with increasingly attractive prices: Herefordshire has most to recommend it for a really peaceful break.

The orchards in Herefordshire and the Vale of Evesham make blossom time (usually April through early May) and harvest time (September) attractive: local tourist board trails make it easy to see the best of this. Asparagus fanatics have a bonus in May, when there is an abundance of fresh local asparagus. In winter, big log fires and generous central heating are the rule – people here really seem to appreciate their warmth.

For a first-time visit there's a lot to be said for basing yourself somewhere around Ledbury, which puts virtually any part of the three areas that we've divided this county into within reach.

THE VALE OF EVESHAM, MALVERN HILLS AND LEDBURY

Mainly for quiet, adult holidays – Ledbury is a good base, with stirring scenery in the Malvern Hills.

This area has some lovely villages, often little-changed over the ages, with an interesting variety of building – from warmly handsome stonework around Broadway to the classic, black and white timbering of places like Bretforton. The Malvern Hills are scenically most alluring; the richer farmland and orchard country around the River Avon in the Vale of Evesham is less striking (except at blossom time), but still pleasant to drive around – and as well as the villages, the many farm shops punctuate it with points of passing interest.

Ledbury, Broadway, Great Malvern and Evesham are all attractive, with several appealing places to visit – generally quiet and for adults, though many children enjoy the Domestic Wildfowl Trust at Evesham; there's also a teddy bear museum and good country park at Broadway. Eastnor Castle is well worth a visit.

There are fine hotels and inns to choose from. Ledbury has a lot going for it as a base for exploration of this area – a charming town in its own right, and with good roads out. Broadway, of course, puts you on the doorstep of the Cotswolds, too.

Where to stay

Broadway SP0937 LYGON ARMS High St, Broadway WR12 7DU (01386) 852255 £155.10; 65 lovely period rms (some more modern, too). Strikingly handsome hotel with interesting, old beamed rooms, oak panelling, antiques and log fires; fine, traditional food in the great hall with a minstrels' gallery and heraldic frieze, excellent service, and a charming garden; Oliver Cromwell and King Charles I are said to have stayed here; health spa; disabled access.

Ledbury SO7138 HOPE END COUNTRY HOUSE Hope End, Ledbury HR8 1JQ (01531) 3613 £97; 9 rms. Once the home of Elizabeth Barrett Browning and a wonderfully peaceful place to stay, with a huge, organic walled garden where most of the veg, fruit and herbs are grown for the very good English cooking (roaming chickens provide the eggs); a fine, Georgian landscaped garden, lots of books, woodburning stoves, and comfortable seating in cosy sitting rooms, lovely breakfasts, and unobtrusive service; cl mid-Dec–early Feb; children over 12 only.

Malvern Wells SO7845 COTTAGE IN THE WOOD Holywell Rd, Malvern Wells WR14 4LG (01684) 573487 *£97; 20 compact but pretty rms. Georgian dower house with splendid views across the Severn Valley, antiques, lots of pot plants, and good food in the attractive restaurant; neat lawns in the 7 acres of grounds.

Great Malvern SO7846 FOLEY ARMS 14 Worcester Rd, Great Malvern WR14 4QS (01684) 573397 *£88; 26 rms. Surrounded by lovely countryside with lots of walks nearby, this comfortably modernised, balconied Regency hotel has open fires and fresh flowers in the lounges, a pubby bar, cosy restaurant, and marvellous views; lots to do nearby.

Broadway SP0937 COLLIN HOUSE Collin Lane, Broadway WR12 7PB (01386) 858354 *£86; 7 warm, comfortable and quiet rms. Golden stone, 16th-century Cotswold house in 3 acres of gardens, orchards and meadowland; restful public rooms, oak beams, log fires, very good English food in the candlelit, beamed restaurant (views through mullioned windows onto garden), and friendly service; outside swimming pool; cl 24 Dec for 4 nights; children over 7; partial disabled access.

Evesham SP0344 EVESHAM Coopers Lane, off Waterside WR11 6DA (01386) 765566 *£86; 40 spacious rms. Comfortably modernised and cheerfully run hotel with a friendly, relaxed atmosphere, lots of facilities for children, very good food (especially the lunchtime buffet) from a jokey menu, indoor swimming pool, and croquet; cl 25–26 Dec; partial disabled access; pets welcome (not in public rooms).

Harvington SP0548 MILL Anchor Lane, Harvington, Evesham WR11 5NR (0386) 870688 *£85; 15 comfortable rms overlooking grounds. Handsome Georgian hotel in 8 acres of wooded parkland, with 600 ft of river, mooring for guests' boats, fishing, hard tennis court and heated outdoor swimming pool; carefully refurbished, airy lounges with open fires, courteous, helpful staff, fine, imaginative food using fresh local produce, thoughtful wine list with helpful notes, and good breakfasts; cl 24–28 Dec; limited disabled access; children over 10.

Ledbury SO7138 FEATHERS High St, Ledbury HR8 1DS (01531) 635266 *£85; 11 carefully decorated rms making the most of the old beams and timbers. Very striking, mainly 16th-century, black and white hotel with a relaxed and attractively decorated, beamed and timbered bar, smart, comfortable lounge, country antiques and open fires; good food in both the bar and restaurant, and a decent wine list.

Upton-upon-Severn SO8540 WHITE LION High St, Upton-upon-Severn WR8 0HJ (01684) 592551 *£74.50; 10 rms. Handsome, former coaching inn with an open fire in the comfortable, cosy lounge bar, very good food in the restful, oak-beamed restaurant, and pleasant service; cl 25–26 Dec.

Broadway SP0937 BROADWAY The Green, Broadway WR12 7AA (01386) 852401 £70; 20 well kept rms. Lovely building dating back to 1575 and once a monastic guesthouse; attractively presented food served by attentive staff in the airy, comfortable restaurant or bar, a galleried and timbered lounge, and seats outside on the terrace.

Great Malvern SO7845 COTFORD 51 Graham Rd, Great Malvern WR14 2HU (01684) 572427 *£58; 16 rms. Family-run hotel with a really friendly atmosphere, generous helpings of decent food, and personal service; disabled access (single rm only).

Ledbury SO7138 OLDE TALBOT New St, Ledbury HR8 2DX (01531) 632963 £45; 7 rms, most with own bthrm. An inn since 1595, with a cosy, friendly bar, pleasant residents' lounge, good, imaginative food in the fine, oak-timbered dining room, and well kept beers.

Malvern SO7647 COWLEIGH PARK FARM Cowleigh Rd, Malvern WR13 5HJ (01684) 566750 £40; 3 rms. Carefully restored and furnished black and white timbered, 13th-century farmhouse in its own grounds and surrounded by lovely countryside; self-catering also; cl Christmas; children over 5.

To see and do

❧ **Beckford** SO9735 SILK SHOP prints, scarves and ties; processes demonstrated, shop with good-value seconds, café. The Gardener's Arms at Alderton has good food.

★ ✝ 🏠 **Bretforton** SP0943 is one of the prettiest, black and white thatched villages, with an interesting church and a splendid medieval pub, the Fleece – left to the National Trust after being in the same family for several centuries; a proper pub, it's kept just as it was, with a magnificent collection of Jacobean oak furniture and pewter.

★ 🏠🌺🐄‼ **Broadway** SP0937 is an exceptionally harmonious, stone-built Cotswold village, with the golden stone and uneven stone-tiled roofs perfectly blending the grand houses and the humbler cottages together, in a long, grass-lined main street. It's decidedly on the coach-tour trail, getting very busy indeed in summer. There are fine things for sale in extraordinarily expensive antique shops, and a very grand old inn, the Lygon Arms, with a useful side wine bar. A good escape from the tourists is the Crown & Trumpet in Church St, an archetypal Cotswold pub. The COTSWOLD TEDDY BEAR MUSEUM (High St) has a big collection of old bears, dolls and toys. Shop, some disabled access; cl 25 Dec; (01386) 858323; *£1.50. Above the village, the late 18th-c folly BROADWAY TOWER AND COUNTRY PARK There are marvellous views from the tower on a clear day – with the help of the telescope – said to stretch over 12 counties. Exhibitions on the tower's history, sheep and wool farming and regular visitor William Morris. Outside, the well laid-out and cared for country park has farm animals and rare breeds, nature trails, an adventure playground and giant chess and draughts boards. Good-value meals and snacks, shops, some disabled access; cl Nov–Mar; (01386) 852498; £2.75.

🏠❀♿❤ **Eastnor Castle** SO7336 (just E of Ledbury) Splendid neo-Gothic castle, especially dramatic in autumn, when the Virginia Creeper that all but envelops the stirring battlements turns a fierce red. Designed by Pugin, the richly decorated rooms are breathtaking, with fine collections of armour, tapestries, furniture and paintings; the attractive grounds have an arboretum and 300-acre deer park. The family that live here have really spruced it up in recent years. Meals, snacks, shop; open pm every Sun from Easter–Oct, plus bank hols and wkdys in Aug; (01531) 633160; £3.50. Eastnor village's thatched post office is lovely.

🏠✝🏛❀♿🐑🐄❧🏠 **Evesham** SP0344 has a pedestrianised market square with some fine buildings inc a 12th-c ABBEY GATEWAY. The church's striking, 16th-c bell tower is well preserved, and some altogether more ruined remnants in the town park beyond lead to riverside meadows. The tourist information centre is in another attractive abbey building, the Almonry, a Tudor timbered house with craft shows, a small museum,

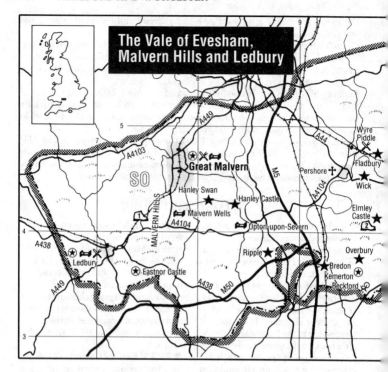

The Vale of Evesham, Malvern Hills and Ledbury

and nice gardens. The Royal Oak is useful for lunch, and around May the Round of Gras at Badsey (on the B4035, E) majors on fresh local asparagus. DOMESTIC FOWL TRUST (Honeybourne) Rare examples of hens, ducks, geese and turkeys, some of them quite extraordinary, over 10 acres of well labelled breeding paddocks. Also young chicks for children to handle (all year), children's farm and adventure playground. Snacks, shop, limited disabled access; cl Fri, Dec 25–26; (01386) 833083; £2.90. TWYFORD COUNTRY CENTRE (just N, on the A435) Busy little complex, with a farm and craft shops, adventure playground, conservatory, and wildlife and falconry centre – maybe weekend miniature train rides. They plan to add fishing lakes and woodland. Meals, snacks, shop, disabled access; cl Dec 25–26; (01386) 443348; free exc falconry and wildlife, £2.50.

★ † ☕ ✿ ❀ 🏛 **Great Malvern** SO7846 Elegant, hillside spa town with easy access to inspiring hill scenery. The beautifully symmetrical PRIORY has a notable collection of medieval wall tiles. Just along the road, the former gateway of a Benedictine monastery now houses a MUSEUM with displays on subjects as diverse as cars, radar, Malvern spring water, and the life of Sir Edward Elgar. Shop; cl Weds in termtime, all Nov–Easter; *50p. A good few craft workshops include musical instrument-makers such as Hibernian Violins, Players Ave; cl lunch and wknds. On the east side of the hills, BARNARDS GREEN HOUSE SO7945 has an attractive garden with a wide range of gardening ideas around a gracious, half-timbered, 17th-c house (not open). The owner is an authority on dried flowers. Teas, plant sales, disabled access; open pm Thurs Apr–Sept, a couple of Suns in May and Aug, and other times by appointment; (01684) 574446; *£1.50. The nearby Bluebell is useful for lunch. On the west side (Walwyn Rd, Colwall), PICTON GARDEN at Old Court Nurseries has a nicely laid out

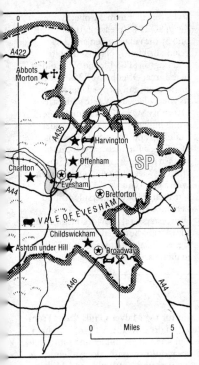

famous for their well balanced 15th- and 16th-c timbering, and there are plenty of similar structures. From the Market House an exceptional alley of ancient, jettied buildings leads to the partly Norman church of St Michael and All Angels, with an unusual spire tower detached from the main building, and its carillon ringing out a well known hymn every third hour. The Old Grammar School has been restored as a heritage centre (cl Oct–Whitsun exc Easter), and the council offices must be the only ones in the country decorated with medieval wall paintings; you can see these free any weekday between 11am and 2pm if there's someone available to show you them, or better still arrange a proper guided tour in advance on (01531) 635457; £1. There are craft workshops, antique shops and a decent bookshop, and in addition to the Feathers itself, the Olde Talbot is worth going to for food.

✝ **Pershore** SO9445 is very much a working town, the 'capital' of the fruit- and vegetable-growing area around it. It's a pleasant place, largely Georgian, with an impressive ABBEY and walks by the River Avon. The Miller's Arms has good-value home cooking. Heading out along the A4104 SW, when you've passed the Oak in Defford, keep your eyes skinned for a group of cottages on your right; the last, surrounded by farm animals and without an inn sign, is the MONKEY HOUSE SO9143, a uniquely old-fashioned cider tavern (cl pm Mon, Tues).

☞ **Farm shops** in the VALE OF EVESHAM, especially along the A44 W of Broadway, are good for all manner of local produce inc eggs, jams, pickles and trout as well as fruit and veg, but the highlights of the year are asparagus in May and apples and particularly plums in Sept. The Chapel Hill nursery about half a mile W of Broadway has good-value plants for sale.

★ A tremendous wealth of **attractive villages** include black and white Abbots Morton SP0353 (with a lovely church); Ashton under Hill SO9938 below Bredon Hill, with many charming, black and white timbered

cottagey collection of hardy plants and shrubs, best in summer, with a national collection of asters (late summer/autumn) and rock garden. Plant sales, disabled access; cl 1–2.15, Mon, Tues, and all Nov–Mar; £1.50. The Chase Inn at Upper Colwall is quite handy for lunch, and the Mount Pleasant Hotel (Belle Vue Terrace) has good views and decent food.

★ ✝ ❀ **Kemerton** SO9437, below Bredon Hill, is an attractively leafy village with pretty, stone-built houses among the trees. One of the most attractive is THE PRIORY, its big garden richly planted with colourful borders; also cool streamside plantings, handsome trees and shrubs. Plant sales; open pm Thurs May–Sept, plus several Suns under the National Garden Scheme; £1.50. The Crown is useful for lunch.

★ ⌂ ✝ ♫ ✿ **Ledbury** SO7138 has a spaciously leisured High St with some fine buildings, and feels very much a real town not just a tourist centre. The old MARKET HOUSE, the FEATHERS HOTEL and LEDBURY PARK HOUSE are houses, and a fine Norman church; Bredon SO9236, with a magnificent, medieval tithe barn (and a good pub, the Fox & Hounds); Charlton SP0145 (the Gardener's Arms is useful); Childswickham SP0738 (streamside, timbered stone cottages); largely black and white Elmley Castle SO9841 under Bredon Hill (a lovely church, and an unusual rustic tavern – the Queen Elizabeth); Fladbury SO9946 by the Avon, with riverside walks, a 9th-c Saxon cross, and a handsome Georgian village green (the Chequers, partly 14th-c, is good value for lunch and has bedrooms); Hanley Castle SO8442, a rustic little place around a great cedar tree, with both its church and its unusually unspoilt pub looking like an attempt to glue two half-buildings in entirely different styles together to make one; Hanley Swan SO8142 (pleasant, traditional pub by the village green and duck pond); brilliantly black and white Harvington SP0548, one of the oldest in the area; Offenham SP0546, with an original, gaily striped maypole in its wide, black and white main street; Overbury SO9537, an immaculate, stone-built estate village with older buildings and a nice church; Ripple SO8737, with finely carved choir seats in its imposing, largely 13th-c church; Wick SO9645, on the Avon, with a good church.

Much of the countryside around here (and running into Worcestershire) provided inspiration for Elgar as he cycled around; a signed ELGAR TRAIL leads you to all the main sites.

Walks

It is easy to understand Elgar's enthusiasm for the **Malvern Hills** ⌂-1. From the distance (and they form a splendid backdrop to the Vale of Evesham) they look a formidable mountain range, but seem to get milder and more welcoming as you approach. The gentle up-and-down path along their spine makes one of England's great ridge walks, with the Cotswolds and Midland plain on one side and wilder Wales on the other. The Herefordshire Beacon SO7640, capped by ramparts of an Iron Age hill fort, is easily reached from the car park on the A449 nr Little Malvern. For long circular walks based on the Malverns, Great Malvern is well placed for the Worcestershire Beacon SO7645, the highest point of the range (1,395 ft). The Chase Hotel at Upper Wyche SO7643 and Malvern Hills Hotel by the British Camp car park on Wynds Point SO7641 are also starting or finishing points for walkers. Ledbury SO7138 and Eastnor SO7337 are good bases for rambles into the attractive western slopes.

Bredon Hill ⌂-2 is the Vale of Evesham's one notable feature for walkers. It's an outlier of the Cotswolds, distinctively rounded and on cloudy days rather ominous. It can be easily reached from Overbury SO9537, but the best walk over it is from Bredons Norton SO9339 to Elmley Castle SO9841.

Driving

In and around the Malvern Hills, the B4232 from Upper Colwall to Wynds Point has some of the best high views, while the B4218 on the E side gives several good views of the hills themselves. There's nothing finer than to have Elgar playing on your car audio system as you drive.

N of Ledbury, there's quite a dramatic drive on the rather narrow road heading N through Wellington Heath, to bear right along the wooded hillside for views out over the farmland.

The classic circular tour of the Vale of Evesham orchards is the A435 N of Evesham to Harvington, left through Atch Lench and Church Lench, left opposite Church Lench church, then right at Handgate Farm to Badgers Hill, left at the Hill Furze T-junction to Fladbury Cross, then left on to the B4084 through Wood Norton and Chadbury, and back to Evesham. The Vale is at its best in Apr or early May when the orchards are full of blossom – first plum and then apple.

There's a fine panorama of the vale from the A44 dropping down out of Oxon towards Broadway.

Other drives based on the villages we recommend will take you through quiet lanes and past individual black and white farmhouses and cottages.

Where to eat

Malvern SO7742 CROQUE-EN-BOUCHE 221 Wells Rd (01684) 565612 Boldly decorated Victorian house with delicious, carefully cooked food from a short-ish menu with marvellous puddings and cheeses, and an exceptional wine list; cl am Sun, Mon, Tues, New Year, 2 wks Sept; disabled access. **£36.50 for 6 courses.**

Broadway SP9037 HUNTERS LODGE High St (01386) 853247 Pretty Cotswold house with lovely food cooked by the Swiss owner, and friendly, helpful service; open pm Weds, Thurs, Fri, Sat, open am Sat and Sun only; cl first 3 wks Feb; children welcome at lunch, but over 8 only at dinner; disabled access. **£18.40 lunch, £21.90 dinner**|£4/£6.

Wyre Piddle SO9647 ANCHOR (01386) 552799 Relaxing 17th-century pub with lovely views over the lawn and River Avon and on over the Vale of Evesham, ideal in summer; friendly little lounge with a log fire, comfortable bar, and good, popular food; restaurant cl pm Sun; disabled access. **£15**|£2.15/£6.

Ledbury SO7138 MARKET PLACE (01531) 634250 Pleasant, bustling restaurant open all day for morning coffee, lunch and afternoon tea with home-made cakes, flans and puddings; cl pm. **£10**|£1.70/£3.50.

HEREFORDSHIRE

Excellent for a quiet break in classic, unspoilt English countryside; exceptional gardens.

Virtually the whole of this quintessentially English county preserves the landscape at its unspoilt best. Its chief appeal is as an escape into the sort of peaceful world that elsewhere tends to survive only in people's memories. Where old villages have been extended, their appearance has rarely suffered. There's very little real urbanisation, and the county is outside the main motorway area: there aren't that many tourists or country-cottagers about, even at the height of summer. Remote yes, but also very civilised, with an unexpected abundance of art galleries and bookshops (Hay-on-Wye, that town-sized bookshop, is just over the border in Wales), and excellent natural cooking using local produce.

Of the towns, Hereford itself is engaging and relaxing, with plenty of varied attractions – well worth a day out. Kington, Leominster and Ross-on-Wye are also agreeable to wander around. Elsewhere, the black and white villages are a particular delight, and Berrington Hall at Ashton, Goodrich Castle and the nearby farm park, Lower Brockhampton House at Brockhampton, Croft Castle and Dinmore Manor all make pleasant outings. There are several fine gardens to look at, and no stay here would be complete without a visit to a cider farm. The area's not strong on conventional visitor attractions, and it might be difficult to keep young children amused here.

Where to stay

Eyton SO4861 Marsh Eyton, Leominster HR6 0AG (01568) 613952 £75; 5 individually decorated, comfortable rms with garden views. Carefully restored, 14th-c, timbered country hotel with a quietly relaxing atmosphere in prettily furnished beamed rooms (fine medieval hall), good food using lots of home-grown herbs, decent wines, and a colourful big garden.

Ullingswick SO5950 The Steppes Ullingswick, Hereford HR1 3JG (01432) 820424 *£75; 6 large, well furnished rms in a recently restored, timber-framed barn and stable set around a central courtyard. 17th-c, beautifully restored building with low beams, inglenook fireplaces and lots of antiques; cellar bar, cosy, atmospheric dining room, good food using local produce and home-grown herbs; decent wine list, attentive, friendly service, and big breakfasts; pleasant garden; cl 2 wks before Christmas, re-open 24 Dec, cl 3 Jan for 2 wks; children over 12.

Kington SO3256 Penrhos Court, Kington HR5 3LH (01544) 230720 £70; 19 elegant rms. Beautifully restored, 13th-c hall in 6 acres of grounds, with fine beams and flagstones and very good, carefully cooked food using home-grown herbs and veg; medieval banquests, too; disabled access.

Brimfield SO5368 Roebuck Brimfield, Ludlow S18 4NE (01584) 711230 £65; 3 rms. Very civilised dining pub with excellent food in an elegant, modern, no-smoking restaurant and panelled bar; open fires, caring pleasant staff, fine wine list; cl pm Sun, Mon, 1 wk Oct, 2 wks Feb; children by arrangement.

Ross-on-Wye SO6024 Kings Head 8 High St, Ross-on-Wye HR9 5HL (01989) 763174 *£60; 25 rms. Comfortable, 14th-c coaching inn with a good atmosphere, beamed and panelled bar, and decent food in both the bar and small restaurant; disabled access.

Trumpet SO6539 Verzons Country House Trumpet, Ledbury HR8 2PZ (01531) 670381 £60; 9 rms. Georgian country house, carefully restored to preserve many original features; a relaxed bar/restaurant and a more formal Garden restaurant overlooking the 4 acres of gardens and paddocks; families are most welcome; cl 24–25 Dec; partial disabled access.

Symonds Yat SO5616 Woodlea Symonds Yat, Ross–on–Wye HR9 6BL (01600) 890206 *£55; 9 rms, most with own bthrm. Family-run guesthouse in a fine position overlooking the Wye Rapids; with comfortable lounges and good food; cl part of Jan/Feb.

Weobley SO4052 Olde Salutation Hereford HR4 8SJ (01544) 318443 *£55; 4 rms. Friendly, 500-year-old inn looking down on an attractive, half-timbered village, with a good bar and elaborate restaurant food; also, a quiet lounge with standing timbers and log fires, and a small public bar; cl 25 Dec; no children except babies.

Fownhope SO5834 Green Man Fownhope, Hereford HR1 4PE (01432) 860243 £50; 19 rms. Attractive and atmospheric Tudor inn close to the River Wye, with an impressive oak-beamed lounge (the residents' lounges are no–smoking), log fire, and generously served popular bar food.

Symonds Yat SO5616 Saracens Head Symonds Yat, Ross-on-Wye HR9 6JL (01600) 890435 £50; 10 rms, 3 with shared bthrm. Small, comfortable hotel in a former cider mill and set on the banks of the River Wye; excellent restaurant food, a decent wine list, and friendly staff; good base for fishing and canoeing; cl Jan.

Carey SO5631 Cottage of Content Carey, Hereford HR2 6NG (01432) 840242 £48; 4 rms. Very pretty, 500-year-old country pub with attractive bars, lots of wines and decent breakfast; quiet village setting.

Ruckhall Common SO4539 ANCIENT CAMP Ruckhall Common, Hereford HR2 9QX (01981) 250449 £48; 5 rms, some with river views. Smart country inn in a delightfully remote spot, with fine views of the River Wye and beyond from the terrace; beamed and flagstoned bar, well stocked library, good bar and restaurant food (not pm Sun or Mon); children over 8.

Edde Cross SO6024 EDDE CROSS HOUSE Edde Cross, Ross-on-Wye HR9 7BZ (01989) 565088 £44; 4 rms. Carefully restored, no-smoking, Georgian town house with a relaxed, homely atmosphere, attractive dining room (no evening meals), and helpful owners; cl Dec–Jan; children over 10.

Leysters SO5663 HILLS FARM Leysters, Leominster HR6 9HP (01568) 750205 *£40; 5 rms. Traditional, stone and brick, 15th-c farmhouse in 120 arable acres, with rambling beamed rooms, a pretty sitting room, good fresh food, and fine views; no smoking; cl Nov–Feb; no children.

Woolhope SO6136 BUTCHERS ARMS Woolhope, Hereford HR1 4RF (01432) 860281 £39; 3 neat, attractive rms (shared bthrm), with fruit and chocolates. An exceptionally nice, family-run place with very friendly staff, lots of flowers, and decent food (good breakfasts); lovely surrounding walks.

Kinnersley SO3449 UPPER NEWTON FARMHOUSE Kinnersley, Hereford HR3 6QB (01544) 327727 *£30; 2 prettily decorated rms with hand-crafted items. 17th-c farmhouse in the middle of a working farm; open fires, beams, sloping floors, and good food (inc vegetarian) using fresh farm veg; no smoking or pets; self-catering cottage.

Woonton SO3552 ROSE COTTAGE Woonton, Almeley, Hereford HR3 6QW (01544) 340436 £30; 3 charming rms. Very pretty and rather romantic, ambling half-timbered house in quiet rural countryside, with an old-style English garden; lots of cottagey charm, panelled and sympathetically furnished sitting room with collections of teacups around a cosy breakfast area; and a welcoming owner.

To see and do

Hereford SO5140 grew as a regional market centre, and still has its busy livestock and general market every Weds. For the rest of the week it feels very quiet-paced and old-fashioned, its streets (some pedestrianised now) lined with handsome Georgian and other buildings (Church St is almost wholly medieval). The many antique shops are by no means over-priced. Guided walks leave the tourist information centre every day at 10.30am (2.30 Sun). Wye-side walks give a pleasing view of the city, its spires and towers. Saxtys, the Green Dragon Hotel and the Bunch of Carrots are all useful for lunch.

✝ The Norman CATHEDRAL, nicely placed on the banks of the Wye, is perhaps most famous as the home of the Mappa Mundi, the largest complete example of a 13th-c world map. Other notable features include the lovely 13th- and 15th-c chapel, and the country's biggest chained library (the second biggest is at All Saints church, at the opposite end of the main st). Restaurant, shop, and Mappa Mundi exhibition cl Sun; £2.60 exhibition.

🐾♿🏫 CIDER MUSEUM (Pomana Pl) Cider-making through the ages, with an enormous 17th-c French press, original cellars, 1920s bottling line and a working cider-brandy distillery – the first licensed for over 250 years. Also various craft demonstrations. Shop, disabled access to ground floor only; cl am and all Sun in winter, 25–26 Dec and 1 Jan; (01432) 354207; £1.95. The enormous modern BULMER'S CIDER MILL (Plough Lane) has tours and tastings; cl Jan, Feb, tours by appointment; (01432) 352000; £2.95.

🏫 THE OLD HOUSE (High Town) Glorious Jacobean house with period furnishings and paintings. Shop, some disabled access; cl 1–2 pm, Mon, Sun (exc bank hol wknds), pm Sat in winter, Christmas; £1.

♿ CHURCHILL GARDENS MUSEUM (Venns Lane, northern outskirts) Regency house in fine grounds, with good local history, room settings, and displays of 18th- and 19th-c furniture, costumes and paintings. Shop, some disabled access; cl am, Sun exc summer, Mon exc bank hols, Christmas; £1. You can get a joint ticket with the Old House (see above) for £1.40.

♿ WATERWORKS MUSEUM (Broomy Hill) Restored Victorian pumping station, with giant steam pumping engines, smaller handpumps (you can try working some), and interesting displays on the history of drinking water in the Marches. Snacks, shop, disabled access; open mainly pm summer Suns only, best to check on (01432) 268430; *£1.50.

♿ CITY MUSEUM AND ART GALLERY (Broad St) Natural history and archaeology, interesting beekeeping display, and changing exhibitions of paintings. Shop, disabled access; cl Mon and Sun (exc bank hols), 25–26 Dec, Good Fri; free.

♿ The ST JOHN AND CONINGSBY MUSEUM, in a 13th-c hospice in Widemarsh St, has provided an interesting look at the Ancient Order of St John and its role in the Crusades; it was closed as we went to press so best to check with the tourist information centre on (01432) 268430.

Other things to see and do

🏛 ❀ ✿ **Abbey Dore** SO3830 is primarily the impressive surviving part of a once-huge 12th/13th-c Cistercian abbey church, with Early English features and an awesome stone altar. ABBEY DORE COURT GARDEN Attractive riverside lawns and gardens, getting bigger all the time, with good views across to the ruins. Meals and snacks (in 17th-c stables), unusual plant sales and gift shop, teddy bear collection, disabled access; cl Weds, Nov–Feb (though shop open up to Christmas); £1.50. The Neville Arms uses local produce for its home cooking.

🏠 ✿ **Ashton** SO5164 BERRINGTON HALL Elegant, late 18th-c, neo-

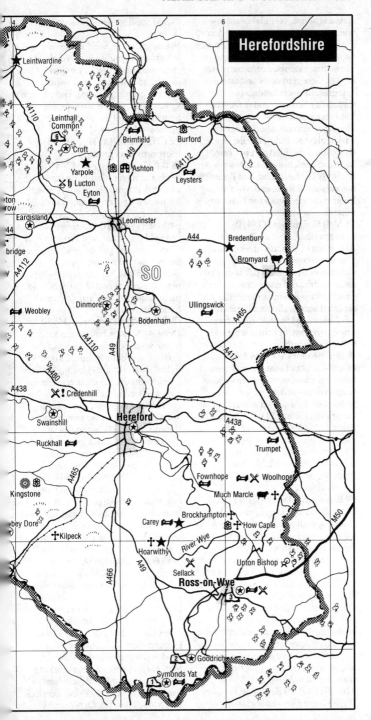

Herefordshire

Leintwardine

A4110

Leinthall
Common

Croft

Yarpole

Lucton

Eyton

Brimfield

Burford

A49

Ashton

A4112

Leysters

Eardisland

Leominster

A44

Bredenbury

Bromyard

A4112

bridge

SO

Weobley

Dinmore

Ullingswick

A465

A4110

Bodenham

A49

A480

A438

Credenhill

Swainshill

Hereford

A438

Ruckhall

A465

Trumpet

Fownhope

Woolhope

Kingstone

Much Marcle

bey Dore

Kilpeck

Carey

Brockhampton

How Caple

Hoarwithy

River Wye

Upton Bishop

M50

Sellack

Ross-on-Wye

A466

A49

Goodrich

Symonds Yat

classical house, very elaborate inside, with beautiful furnishings and decor, the Digby collection of mostly French furnishings, charming nursery, and interesting examples of 'downstairs' life in a Georgian dairy and laundry. The grounds were landscaped by Capability Brown – and in fact the house was built by his son-in-law. Pleasant circular walk through the park (July–Oct only). Meals, snacks, shop, some disabled access; cl am, Mon exc bank hols, Tues, Nov–Mar; £3.50; NT. The Roebuck at Brimfield has very good food, and towards Leominster, the Stockton Cross Inn is reliable.

🐾 ♈ ❀ **Bodenham** SO5450 QUEENSWOOD COUNTRY PARK AND ARBORETUM 170 acres of woodland and arboretum with over 500 varieties of tree; also wildlife displays, nature trails, and good views. Meals, snacks, shop and information centre, disabled access; shop and café cl 25–26 Dec; (0156884) 7052; free. The Crozen Inn at Felton is a good-value dining pub.

❀ ❀ 🖼 **Brobury** SO3444 BROBURY HOUSE GALLERY Eight acres of semi-formal gardens with fine views; also watercolours and prints for sale. Snacks, shop, disabled access (but no facilities); cl Sun, 25 Dec, 1 Jan; (01981) 500595; gardens £1.50 – the gallery is free. They now do B & B in the smart Victorian house, with fishing permits available. The Portway, nr Monnington-on-Wye, has good food.

🐖 **Bromyard** SD6554 SHORTWOOD DAIRY FARM Working farm ideal for children, with afternoon activities like milking Daisy or feeding the pigs and calves. Snacks, shop, disabled access; cl Sat, Oct–Easter exc for last wk Oct when open for cider-making; (01885) 400205; £2.50. The Crown & Sceptre does generous family lunches.

❀ **Burford** SO5868 BURFORD HOUSE GARDENS Charmingly designed landscaped gardens around an 18th-c house (not open). The nursery has hundreds of clematis cultivars for sale. Meals, snacks, shop, disabled access; cl am Sun, 25–26 Dec; (01584) 810777; £1.95. The Ship in Tenbury Wells is very pleasant for lunch.

! **Credenhill** SO4544 L'ESCARGOT ANGLAIS Part of the National Snail Farming Centre, with all the information you'll ever need about these misunderstood little slow-coaches. Snail trails show various species (even hairy ones), and you can sample dishes made with them. Snacks, shop; cl wkdys Apr and Oct, all Nov–Mar; (01432) 760218; *£1.70. The Bell at Tillington does more orthodox food.

🏰 ❀ 🏛 CROFT CASTLE SO4764 The walls and turrets date from the 14th and 15th c, while the inside is mostly 18th c, with an interesting staircase and plastered ceilings. Attractive parklands with an avenue of 350-year-old chestnuts, and a footpath to CROFT AMBREY, an Iron Age fort. Shop, disabled access; open pm Weds–Sun and bank hols May–Sept, plus wknds Apr and Oct; £3; NT. The picturesque Bell at Yarpole is quite handy for lunch.

🏠 ❀ 🐑 ✝ 🖼 **Dinmore** SO4950 DINMORE MANOR Hilltop manor house with spectacular views of the surrounding countryside. Closely linked to the Knights Hospitaller of St John, the house has cloisters, a grand hall, and a good stained-glass collection; the grounds have farm animals. Perhaps most interesting is the ancient chapel, incongruously placed between a rock garden and 1,200-year-old yew tree. Summer snacks, shop, plant centre, disabled access; cl 25 Dec; (01432) 830322; *£2.50. Nearby Green Acres has organically grown pick-your-own fruit and veg; DINMORE FRUIT FARM has a very wide choice of apple varieties, as well as more conventional pick-your-own.

★ 🏠 🖼 **Eardisland** SO4258 is a gorgeous riverside, black and white village; the spectacularly wonky weather-vane on one ivy-clad dovecot has been at that angle for years. BURTON COURT, just outside, is an interesting old house with a 14th-c great hall, and collections of ship models, costumes and natural history specimens. Also, a working model fairground, and pick-your-own berries. Teas, disabled access; cl am, Mon, Tues, Fri, Oct–Apr; *£2.

The nearby White Swan is charming for lunch.

Goodrich SO5719 GOODRICH CASTLE Proper-looking, 12th-c castle built using the same red sandstone rock it stands on, so that it seems almost to grow out of the ground. Still plenty to see, with towers, passageways, dungeon and marvellous views of the surrounding countryside. Interesting events from demonstrations of medieval life to Shakespeare. Snacks, shop; cl 24–26 Dec, 1 Jan; (01600) 890538; £1.80. WYE VALLEY FARM PARK Plenty of animals nicely set in old stone buildings; children are encouraged to touch most of them. The same family have run the farm since 1650. Also riverside walks and a cider press. Shop, disabled access; cl Nov–Easter; (01600) 890296; £3.50. The Crown, off the B4228 at Howle Hill, is the nearest recommended place for lunch.

How Caple SO6030 HOW CAPLE COURT 11 acres of peaceful, formal and woodland Edwardian gardens overlooking the river, with old roses and unusual herbaceous plants for sale. Open May–Sept; (01989) 86626; £2.50. Also an interesting medieval church and fabrics shop. The Green Man at Fownhope is quite handy for a meal.

Kingstone SO4235 KINGSTONE COTTAGES Charming, exuberant cottage garden, not to be missed at midsummer for its profusion of old-fashioned pinks and border carnations. Also fine views, and a tucked-away, little grotto – looking out it seems as though you're waist-high in water. Unusual plants for sale; open wkdys early May–late Jun, or by appointment; (01989) 565267. The prettily placed Three Horseshoes over at Allensmore is reasonably close.

★ **Kington** SO2956 Attractive border town by the River Arrow, well placed for walks (for example, up the Hergest Ridge). The Swan Hotel is useful for lunch. HERGEST CROFT GARDENS are the splendid result of inspired work by several generations of keen gardeners; some of the centenarian rhododendrons in the woods are of almost incredible size. Famous kitchen garden with colourful flowerbeds, and the national collections of birches and maples. Snacks, shop, disabled access; cl am, Nov–Easter; (01544) 230160; £2.30. OAKLANDS SMALL BREEDS FARM (off the A4111, S) Rare and unusual miniature horses, pigs and goats, poultry, pheasants and waterfowl, as well as a new owl garden and rabbit enclosure; the views are a bonus, and children love Dorrie, a miniature Dexter cow who even on tiptoe is only 32 inches high. Snacks, shop, disabled access; cl am Sat and Weds exc school hols, Nov–Easter; (01544) 231109; £2.50.

Lucton SO4464 MORTIMER'S CROSS MILL AND BATTLE CENTRE Charming watermill on the banks of the River Ludd, still in working order, with an exhibition on the decisive Wars of the Roses battle fought here in 1461. Open pm Thurs, Sun and bank hols Apr–Sept; (01568) 708820; £1.20. The Bateman Arms at Shobdon is useful for lunch.

Much Marcle SO6633 Weston's CIDER FARM, still alongside the family house, has an engaging combination of modern equipment and old-fashioned atmosphere. Enthusiastic guided tours, liberal tastings, interesting ciders and perries. The nearby Slip is good for lunch and has outstanding gardens; the memorial monuments in the village church are unrivalled in the area.

★ **Ross-on-Wye** SO5923 Picturesquely perched on a sandstone cliff by the river, with twice-weekly markets at the striking 17th-c MARKET HALL. The lower riverside part has attractive waterside walks, and a useful pub (the Hope & Anchor; the Hereford Bull very prettily set by the river in nearby Wilton is also worth knowing). LOST STREET MUSEUM Edwardian street with fully stocked period shops, and excellent collections of musical boxes, toys, gramophones, costume and advertising items. Snacks; cl wkdys Jan and Feb, all Dec; (01989) 562752; *£2. C & J HUGHES CANDLEMAKERS Workshop open to the public; cl 25–26 Dec. BUTTON MUSEUM Unique private collection of over 10,000 buttons from the last 200 years. Surprisingly interesting, and run by a real enthusiast. Shop, disabled access; cl Nov–Mar; (01989) 566089; *£1.50.

❋ ◑ **Staunton on Arrow** SO3660 STAUNTON PARK Big lakeside garden with a woodland walk, fine trees, attractive herb garden, new knot garden and old-fashioned herbaceous gardens. Nice teas with home-made jams and chutneys, shop, disabled access; open pm Weds and Sun Apr–Sept; *£1.50. HORSEWAY HERBS Friendly little place with lots of herb plants, other plants and gardens; the shop sells herbs as both plants and crafts, as well as pickles and jams. Teas, disabled access; cl Weds, all Nov–Mar; (01544) 388212; free.

❋ ◑ ❋ **Swainshill** SO4541 WEIR GARDENS Delightful riverside gardens at their best in spring, with displays of bulbs set in woodland walks, and fine views from clifftop walks. Cl Mon exc bank hols, Tues, Nov–mid-Feb; *£1.50; NT.

↑ ❋ ❋ ! ☺ ❦ **Symonds Yat** SO5616 (shared with Gloucs on the other side of the river) is a spectacular bend of the River Wye through a steep, wooded rock gorge, where peregrine falcons nest (the RSPB have a demonstration area); splendid Wye views, nature trails; two inns on either side of the river are linked by a hand-pulled ferry, and there's ample (walkers would say over-generous) parking. Among other things to amuse visitors here (it is a popular tourist destination) is the JUBILEE PARK, with unusual shops, the Jubilee Maze built for the Queen's Silver Jubilee, and a lively MUSEUM OF MAZES telling the history of similar labyrinthine creations. Meals, snacks, shop, disabled access; cl wkdys Oct–Easter exc school hols, all Dec–Jan; (01600) 890360; £2.50. On the same site, the WORLD OF BUTTERFLIES has hundreds of butterflies and humming birds in a big tropical indoor garden; cl Nov–Mar; £2.25.

❧ **Upton Bishop** SO6527 WOBAGE FARM CRAFT WORKSHOPS have several potters, a furniture-maker, wood-carver and jeweller; cl wkdys exc by appointment; (01989) 780233; free.

★ The many **black and white villages**

are a particular characteristic of the county. Besides Eardisland (see entry above), best of all is probably Pembridge SO3958, full of fine, timbered buildings inc a medieval market hall and the ancient New Inn. Dunkerton's small CIDER FARM (nearby at Luntley SO3956) uses ancient, traditional, local cider-apple and pear cultivars, for distinctive ciders and perries; free tastings; cl Sun. Another of the prettiest villages is Weobley SO4052, with its long sloping green; stroll out past the bowling green to the church; the Olde Salutation is good for lunch. Other favourite villages in the county, all with decent pubs, include Carey SO5631, Bredenbury SO6156 (despite the main road), Dorstone SO3141 (with an impressive, prehistoric burial mound nearby), Hoarwithy SO5429, the riverside Leintwardine SO4174 (its church is much bigger than usual for this county), and streamside Yarpole SO4765 (with a free-standing, medieval bell tower). Lingen SO3767 is prettily set among hills, with the Royal George a decent pub beside Kim Davis's renowned alpine nursery and garden.

✝ The area has many **charming churches**. The best-known is the small Norman one at Kilpeck SO4530 (a delightful little hamlet): amazing sandstone carving inside and out, beautifully preserved (except for the more uncomfortably pagan bits which prudish Victorians tried to remove). There are too many good churches in the county to list, but some wonderful curiosities include ALMELEY SO3351 (early 18th-c, half-timbered Quaker Meeting House – contemplative feel; key in porch), BROCKHAMPTON SO6032 (extraordinary, turn-of-the-century Arts and Crafts church designed by Lethaby; note that this is in the little village between Hereford and Ross-on-Wye), EARDISLEY SO3149 (12th-c font with wonderfully vivid carvings of a sinner being wrested from the clutches of evil), HOARWITHY SO5429 (Italianate, full of mosaics etc) and PEMBRIDGE SO3938 (unusual detached belfry where you can watch the clock mechanism).

Walks

Herefordshire's most satisfying walks are around its edges – in the Wye Valley on the southern fringes, around Woolhope SO6135 and the western part of the Malverns on its eastern margins, and up the Golden Valley and the hills of the Welsh Marches to the W and NW. The centre is for the most part an undulating plain, with a dozy agricultural charm and some very pretty villages.

The Herefordshire part of the Wye Valley includes **Symonds Yat** SO5616 ◠-1, something of a motorist's viewpoint over a tight meander of the Wye (there's a prominent car park), but with potential for more ambitious walks into the gorge, where an old railway line follows the river; SW, an entertainingly rickety, wire-mesh suspension bridge gives access to the W bank. To the N, the formidable ruins of **Goodrich Castle** SO5719 ◠-2 are a feasible objective or starting point for gorge walks.

Ross-on-Wye SO5923 ◠-3 in the more open stretches of the valley has pleasant woodland walks in Penyard Park, SE of the town. The elevated country around Woolhope has good variety, with the views from Ridge Hill, E of the village, and the more densely wooded hills nr Mordiford SO5737 among the highlights.

Merbach Hill SO3044 ◠-4 in western Herefordshire can be reached by driving up from Bredwardine SO3344, where Rev Francis Kilvert's grave can be seen in the churchyard, and then walking from the top of the lane; there's a view right over the Black Mountains, Herefordshire and Radnorshire, and a short stroll along the lane SE brings you to Arthur's Stone, a prehistoric burial chamber.

Hergest Ridge SO2556 ◠-5, reached via a cul-de-sac from Kington, is NW Herefordshire's answer to the Malvern Hills – and like them inspired Elgar, in this case to write his *Introduction and Allegro for Strings*. It's another of those ridges for those who can't decide whether they prefer the gentle lowland textures of England or the more rugged offerings of Wales. The walk gets better with every step, as the wide ridge tapers into horseback width at the far end, above Gladestry in Powys.

Leinthall Common SO4467 ◠-6, a brackeny expanse scattered with cottages, is a quiet corner of Herefordshire where you can walk around the estate of Croft Castle and scale the modest heights of Croft Ambrey, an Iron Age hill fort with a view into Shrops.

Other walks can start or finish at country pubs, such as the Penny Farthing at Aston Crews SO6723, Tally Ho! at Broad Heath SO6665, the Crown at Howle Hill SO6020, Three Horseshoes at Ullingswick SO5949 or the Carpenters at Walterstone SO3425.

Driving

For driving on relatively quiet roads in countryside studded by black and white farmsteads and villages, the best area is between Kingsland, Pembridge and Weobley, where there is a Black and White Villages Trail.

The B4347 and B4348 up the Golden Valley is a very pretty drive. If you keep on to Hay and loop back by the B4350, you can cross the old toll bridge over the Wye for the short stretch past Whitney-on-Wye, with distant lush views; the road becomes much less interesting as you approach Hereford, though. An alternative is to backtrack from Hay along the remote hill road through Michaelchurch Escley and Clodock: lovely scenery, decent food at the Bridge in Michaelchurch, a ruined riverside fort in Longtown, and a pretty church in Clodock. The lane off at Longtown takes you up into the pretty Olchon Valley (good walks) and back again to Hay.

A short stretch of back country road that gives an excellent taste of the quieter parts of the county is the one off the B4224 S of Fownhope at Crossway, through How Caple and Penalt to Hoarwithy; but many other country roads give a fine sense of time slowing right down.

Another approach to tracing your way through the area's lovely villages and country lanes is to take a group fairly close together, each of which has an attractive church – such as Bredwardine, Moccas, Tyberton and Eaton Bishop, strung along the upper Wye Valley; or rather more tortuously – Fownhope, Brockhampton, Hoarwithy, Kings Caple and Foy, again nr the Wye.

Where to eat

Ross-on-Wye SO6024 Pheasants 52 Edde Cross St (01989) 65751 Homely little restaurant with a cosy lounge, good, interesting food, nice cheeses, and a relaxed atmosphere; cl Sun and Mon, bookings only for lunch Oct–Apr; disabled access. **£25/£6.**

Sellack SO5627 Lough Pool (01989) 730236 Attractive, black and white timbered cottage in lovely countryside; with a log fire in the cosy, beamed room and excellent, tasty bar food; cl 25 Dec. **£15/£4.50.**

Credenhill SO4544 Jasmine House (01432) 760945 Very good Chinese food, decent wine; also take-aways; disabled access. **£14.50/£6.30.**

Woolhope SO6135 Crown (01432) 860468 Warmly welcoming and neatly kept old pub with popular, imaginative food, well kept beers, good wines, and helpful service; cl pm 25 Dec for food. **£12/£5.20.**

Dorstone SO3141 Pandy (01981) 550273 Cosy, half-timbered, ancient pub – very relaxed and friendly – with delicious, imaginative food, beamed and flag-stoned rooms, well kept beers, and wood-burning stove; cl am Mon, Tues from 1 Nov–Easter. **£12|£1.50/£3.95.**

Winforton SO2947 Sun (01544) 327677 Very friendly and neatly kept little pub with beamed rooms, wood-burning stoves, particularly good, interesting food, and a sheltered garden; cl am Tues (all day in winter). **£2.75/£8.**

WORCESTERSHIRE

Some attractive places; perhaps best for people who already know and like other parts of this twin county and want to explore more of it.

Worcester is a busy city: not a place for quiet relaxation, but with a good deal of interest at least for adults to track down. For younger people, a better bet would be Bewdley: the terminus for Britain's most lively steam railway, as well as other things to do. Elsewhere, highlights include Great Witley with its extraordinary ruin and splendid church, Britain's best garden centre at Wychbold, Hanbury Hall (with several other places to visit nearby), and the buildings' museum at Bromsgrove.

There are quite a few attractive villages, and some interesting patches of countryside for walkers – though on the whole those parts of the county already discussed are more beautiful, and, being further from Birmingham, less busy.

There's a reasonable choice of places to stay.

The Vale of Evesham is described separately, in the first section of this chapter.

Where to stay

Bromsgrove SO9570 Grafton Manor Grafton Lane, Bromsgrove B61 7HA (01527) 579007 **£105;** 9 individually decorated rms. Impressive, early 18th-c mansion with an Elizabethan core and lovely grounds; splendid restaurant with very good, modern British cooking using home-grown herbs, a comfortable lounge, decent service; croquet and riding.

Abberley SO7667 Elms Stockton Rd, Abberley WR6 6AT (01299) 896666 **£97**; 25 comfortable rms. Lovely Queen Anne mansion with fine views from the well kept grounds; an elegant, restful drawing room with antiques, log fires and flowers, very good food, and friendly, efficient staff.

Chaddesley Corbett SO8973 Brockencote Hall Chaddesley Corbett, Kidderminster DY10 4PY (01562) 777876 ***£95**; 17 individually decorated rms. Grand country-house hotel in 70 acres of grounds, with a half-timbered dovecot and lake; large, airy and attractively furnished rooms, a conservatory lounge with garden views, an elegant restaurant with fine, modern French and English cooking, and very good service; children under 12 free if sharing parents' room; no dogs; disabled access.

Knightwick SO7355 Talbot Knightsford Bridge, Knightwick, Worcester WR6 5PH (01886) 21235 **£56.50**; 10 comfortable rms, most with own bthrm. Rambling 14th-c inn of considerable character, with heavy beams, individual furnishings and nice prints in the bar, good, interesting food (tasty puddings), decent wines; glorious setting with pleasant walks and own fishing on the Teme.

Ombersley SO8463 Crown & Sandys Arms Ombersley, Droitwich WR9 0EW (01905) 620252 ***£35**; 7 no-smoking rms, most with own bthrm. Pretty Dutch-gabled inn with good views from the garden, a cosy, beamed bar area, open fire, and decent food; no dogs in bedrooms; cl 20–30 Dec.

Frith Common SO6969 Hunt House Farm Frith Common, Tenbury Wells WR15 8JY (01299) 832277 ***£32**; 3 rms. 16th-c timbered farmhouse on a 180-acre, arable and sheep farm in lovely surrounding countryside; friendly atmosphere, oak beams and open fires; cl Christmas; children over 8.

To see and do

Worcester SO8555 Though it's a busy commercial centre, this has some splendid medieval buildings dotted about, with lots of half-timbered houses, particularly around Friar St and New St. It's long been a place that interestingly combines industry (china and gloves, for instance) with the area's more established agriculture. Plenty of shops, inc some nice specialist ones, and cafés in Hopmarket Yard, a former coaching inn.

The Commandery (Sidbury) The only museum in the country wholly devoted to the English Civil War, in a striking, timber-framed, 15th-c building – used as the headquarters of Charles II's army at the end of the conflict. Lots of weaponry, spectacular audio-visual shows and life-size talking figures recreating events throughout the war. Unusual special events and military displays. Meals, snacks, shop; cl 25–26 Dec; (01905) 355071; £3.10.

Royal Worcester and the Museum of Worcester Porcelain (Severn St) Factory tours of the country's oldest continuous producer of porcelain (no children under 11), and an excellent museum – totally refurbished this year. Meals, snacks, shop, disabled access to museum only; cl Sun, 25–26

Dec, tours wkdys only; (01905) 23221; tours £3, museum £1.50.

✝ Cathedral Founded on the site of a Saxon monastery, in a calm and peaceful setting overlooking the river. It took from 1084 to 1375 to build, and has an attractive 14th-c tower, Norman crypt, and the tombs of Prince Arthur and King John, the latter topped by the oldest royal effigy in the country. Also lots of Victorian stained glass and some monastic buildings. Meals, snacks, shop, disabled access; £1.50 donation suggested.

Greyfriars (Friar St) Carefully restored, medieval, timber-framed town house with a delightful walled garden. Open Weds, Thurs and bank hols, Apr–Oct; £1.60. Down the same street, the 15th-c Tudor House has social history displays. Shop,

disabled access; cl Thurs, Sun, Christmas; £1.50.

◉▣ CITY MUSEUM AND ART GALLERY (Foregate St) Local and natural history, new River Severn gallery, and changing art exhibitions. Meals, snacks, shop, disabled access; cl Thurs, Sun, Christmas; free.

🏛 GUILDHALL (High St) Handsome, early Georgian building with one of the best Queen Anne rooms in the country. Meals, snacks, shop; cl Sun, Feb, Christmas; free.

♧ WORCESTER WOODS COUNTRYSIDE CENTRE 140 acres of ancient woodland on the edge of the city, popular orienteering course or nature trails; not as interesting as woodlands elsewhere, but useful for strolling in if you don't want to leave the city. Snacks, shop, disabled access; free.

🏛 JOLLY ROGER BREWERY (Lowesmoor) Tours of cheerful, traditional micro-brewery, inc the history of the brewing process and samples. Open normal licensing hours, preferably by arrangement; (01905) 22222; free.

🐄🐖♪ BENNETTS FARM PARK (Lower Wick) Working dairy farm with animals, weekend milking parlour and a vintage machinery museum in pretty, 16th-c farm buildings; walks and fishing in season. Snacks (inc their own ice-cream), shop, disabled access; cl Sept–Easter; (01905) 748150; £1.

and industries. Shop, disabled access; cl am wknds, Mon, Tues, and Oct–Easter; (01299) 403573; £1.
WEST MIDLANDS SAFARI AND LEISURE PARK Wildlife park with exotic animals, sea lions, reptile house, parrot show, deer park and drive-through reserves with lions and now rhinos. Lots of rides in the leisure area. Meals, snacks, shop, disabled access; cl Nov–Mar; (01299) 404604; £3.99.

🐖 ❀ **Bishop's Frome** SO6648 HOP POCKET HOP FARM Traditional hop farm, its 100 acres a hive of activity in the harvest season. Big craft shop and gardens, and tours of the kilns by arrangement. You can buy the hops by mail. Snacks, disabled access; cl Mon (exc bank hols) and Mon-Thurs Jan and Feb; (01531) 640323; tours £2. The Green Dragon is a good pub.

❀ 🐎 **Blakeshall** SO8381 KINGSFORD COUNTRY PARK 200-acre park with pine forests, birch groves and plenty of walks and trails (inc one for the disabled). Very nice, unspoilt feel – even the signposts and picnic tables are made at the saw mill here. (01562) 851129; free. The canalside Lock Inn at Wolverley is quite handy.

🏚🎋❀🐎❀ **Brockhampton** SO6955 LOWER BROCKHAMPTON Idyllic, timber-framed and moated, 14th-c manor house in attractive, secluded countryside. Particularly interesting and unusual 15th-c gatehouse, and the ruins of a 12th-c chapel. Shop, some disabled access; cl Mon exc bank hols, Tues, and Nov–Mar; £1.50; NT. The Trust also own the adjacent 1,700-acre BROCKHAMPTON ESTATE, with splendid views from its park and woodlands. The Live & Let Live, down a track off the A44 at Bringsty Common, is an interestingly basic, rustic tavern; the Talbot at Knightwick has good food.

🎋🐎🏚👤🎋 **Bromsgrove** SO9570 AVONCROFT MUSEUM OF BUILDINGS (Stoke Prior; on the B4091, S) Threatened buildings of historical interest are carefully re-erected and restored here – anything from a 14th-c monastic roof through an 18th-c dovecot and icehouse to a 1946 prefab. Demonstrations of traditional building techniques, varied events,

Other things to see and do

★ 🎋🐎 🐖 **Bewdley** SO7875 Attractive small town, with riverside walks and interesting side streets (and a very unusual pub, the Little Pack Horse, up towards the end of the old High St). SEVERN VALLEY RAILWAY Splendid steamtrain trips through the Wyre Forest and the Severn Valley between Kidderminster and Bridgnorth in Shrops, with lots going on – this railway is run with great verve. The Bewdley station has a fine model railway called Wribbenhall Junction. Various special events and weekends. Meals, snacks, shop; best to check (01299) 403816 for timetable; from £4.20, £9.50 full return trip. An 18th-c row of butchers' shops has a MUSEUM concentrating on local crafts maybe weekend miniature train rides. Snacks, shop, disabled access; cl Mon exc Jun–Aug, Fri in Mar and Nov, all Dec–Feb; (01527) 831363; *£3, slightly less out of season. The Country Girl here is useful for lunch. The town also has a decent MUSEUM (cl am Sun and all Dec; £1) and DAUB AND WATTLE'S POTTERY, a largely unchanged pottery building with displays and a shop; cl Sun; free.

✿ **Burcot** SO9771 BURCOT FORGE has potters, stained-glass firing, wrought ironwork etc; usually at least something open exc am Sun; free.

★ 🏠 † ♫ **Droitwich** SO9063 is famous as a spa town; you don't drink the water here, you float in it. The BRINE BATHS on St Andrews Rd are reckoned by correspondents to be just the thing after an exhausting day's sightseeing; (01905) 794894 to book; £5.50. Interesting buildings include the timbered houses around the High St and the Sacred Heart CHURCH with its fine stained-glass mosaics. The HERITAGE CENTRE (Victoria Sq) has an unusual radio exhibition. Cl Sun; free. Trotter Hall (Copcut Elm) is an extraordinary pub with decent food.

🏠 🏞 † ♫ **Great Witley** SO7664 WITLEY COURT Astonishing ruined shell of a Jacobean house transformed into an Italianate palace by the Earl of Dudley, and partly destroyed by fire in 1937. It's an elaborate place, with ceiling paintings, an enormous Perseus fountain, and a balustraded garden – very atmospheric to wander through. The splendidly baroque CHURCH by the house, overlooking the lake, is no less dramatic, and one of the county's great finds; almost certainly designed by James Gibbs, it has splendid paintings and stained glass around the largely papier-mâché interior, much of which came second-hand from a house in London. Snacks, shop; cl 1–2 pm, winter Mons and Tues, 25–26 Dec, 1 Jan; (01299) 896636; £1.25. EASTGROVE COTTAGE GARDEN (on the B4196 towards Shrawley) Interesting and unusual, hardy and tender perennial plants in a cottage-garden setting by an ancient, timbered house (not open). Good plants for sale, disabled access; cl Tues and Weds Apr–July, every day in Aug,

Sun–Weds Sept–mid-Oct, then up to Easter; *£1.50. The Bell on the B4202, nr Pensax, is the best nearby place we know of for lunch.

🏠 ❀ † ♫ ✿ **Hanbury** SO9664 HANBURY HALL 18th-c country house with outstanding painted ceilings and staircase, fine porcelain, and contemporary icehouse and orangery in the grounds. The formal gardens are being restored to their 18th-c form, and you can hire rooms in the lodge on the edge of the estate. Snacks, shop, some disabled access; open pm Sat, Sun and Mon Apr–Oct, maybe Tues and Weds in Aug; *£3.70 house and gardens; NT. The CHURCH, high on a hill, has superb views over the countryside. THE JINNEY RING CRAFT CENTRE (B4091, Droitwich Rd) has varied craft workshops in beautiful timbered barns, from pottery to violin-making. Meals, snacks, shop, some disabled access; cl Mon exc bank hols, Christmas; free. They also organise regular craft courses. Nearby at Stock Green SO9858 WHITE COTTAGE has a profusion of interesting plants in colourful borders, and a pretty streamside, springtime wild garden; plant sales inc rare-species geraniums. Disabled access; cl Thurs, alternate Suns, all Oct–Easter; (01386) 792414; *£1. The Gate Hangs High (Woodgate) has a good carvery.

🏞 ♖ **Hartlebury** SO8371 HARTLEBURY CASTLE STATE ROOMS Elegant rooms recounting the history of the castle and the Bishops of Worcester, who've used it as their official residence since 850. Shop, disabled access; open pm wknds and Weds, Easter–Sept; (01299) 250410; 75p. A wing of the castle is used for the COUNTY MUSEUM. Snacks, shop; cl am Fri and Sun, all Sat, and Dec–Feb; (01299) 250416 £1.50.

🚂 **Kidderminster** SO8376 is not an alluring place to visit, but is one terminus of the excellent Severn Valley steam railway (see Bewdley entry above), with a beautiful replica of the Edwardian station's refreshment rooms.

♖ **Lower Broadheath** SO8157 ELGAR'S BIRTHPLACE MUSEUM Modest cottage where the composer was born in

1857, now, as he wanted, a museum of his life and work, with displays of musical scores and letters, and the desk where he did his writing. Shop; cl Weds, am Oct–Apr, 25–26 Dec, mid-Jan–mid-Feb; £3. You can pick up routes and information here about the Elgar Trail around the area.

† **Martley** SO7559 has an interesting old CHURCH with some 13th-c wall paintings.

⬥† ❀ **Redditch** SP0467 FORGE MILL NEEDLE MUSEUM AND BORDESLEY ABBEY VISITOR CENTRE The only remaining water-driven, needle-scouring mill, with demonstrations of 18th-c machinery and needle-making, and finds from the nearby 12th-c Cistercian abbey. Very attractive grounds. Shop, disabled access with prior notice; cl am wknds, all Fri, and Dec–Feb; (01527) 62509; *£1.75.

❀ ❦ **Spetchley** SO8953 SPETCHLEY PARK GARDENS 140 acres of lovely gardens and park with both red and fallow deer, sweeping lawns and herbaceous borders, rose lawn, interesting trees and shrubs. Snacks, disabled access (but no facilities); cl am Sun, Sat, Mon (exc bank hols), Oct–Mar; (01453) 810332; £2.10. The Berkeley Knot is handy for lunch.

❀ **Stone** SO8574 STONE HOUSE Unusual walled garden with colourful plants, especially climbers and tender flowering shrubs; interesting plant sales. Disabled access; open Weds–Sat (plus some Suns May–Jun), Mar–Oct; (01562) 69902; £1.50. The Fox at Chaddesley Corbett has a good-value carvery.

❦ **West Hagley** SO9080 FALCONRY CENTRE Frequent flying displays of hawks, owls and other birds of prey; they organise falconry courses, some lasting just a day. Snacks, shop, some

disabled access; cl 25–26 Dec; (01562) 700014; *£2.50. The Holly Bush (on the A491 towards Bromsgrove) has popular, fresh food.

🏠 **Wichenford** SO7860 DOVECOT (NT) Unusually constructed, timber-framed, wattle and daub, 17th-c dovecot with nearly 600 nesting boxes. Open daily Apr–Oct, winter by appointment; (01684) 850051; 60p.

❀ **Wychbold** SO9265 WEBBS GARDEN CENTRE (on the A38 towards Bromsgrove) is probably the best in the country, attractively laid out and recently extended, with a massive choice of things to buy, fine amusements for children and good disabled access. The thatched café is exemplary; cl 25–26 Dec; (01527) 861777.

★ Other **attractive villages** include Belbroughton SO9277 (the Queen's is nice for lunch); Chaddesley Corbett SO8973 (there's a fine, partly Norman church, and the Fox has a good carvery); Clifton-upon-Teme SO7162 (lots of quiet strolls above the orchards; the Red Lion's useful here); Feckenham SP0061, with an attractive green and some fine Georgian red brick; Ombersley SO8463 – an attractive mix of handsome, black and white timbered houses with elegant, Georgian brick – both the Crown & Sandys Arms and the King's Arms are decent for lunch; Upper Arley SO7680 on the Severn (the Severn Valley Railway, see Bewdley entry above, stops at a station over the footbridge; the Harbour is useful for lunch); and Wolverley SO8279, with steeply gabled cottages below a brick-built, hilltop church, and the decent, cliffside Lock Inn by the quaint Staffs & Worcs Canal.

Walks

Paradoxically, it's over towards Birmingham that the topography is most interesting, with much of the land rising to over 1,000 ft. The **Lickey Hills Country Park** SO9975 ⌂-1 is densely wooded, a fragment of primeval forest, with the views suddenly opening out over the sprawling city; waymarking makes the maze of paths and tracks less confusing. **Clent Hills Country Park** SO9379 ⌂-2 is a fine hillscape, open and exhilarating; waymarked routes are provided. The Fountain at Clent SO9379 is useful for lunch.

The **Wyre Forest** SO7575 ⌂-3, on the Shrops border, is a major broadleaved woodland, with numerous, ready-made Forestry Commission trails (leaflets available from the Visitor Centre; the Royal Forester nearby, if open, is useful for lunch). The **Abberley Hills** SO7567 ⌂-4, nr Stourport, are far less trodden but rewarding – partly wooded, with good views and close to the extraordinary ruins of Witley Court SO7664 (see entry above).

Useful pubs for **waterside walks** are the Camp House at Grimley SO8359 on the River Severn; the Fox & Hounds at Lulsley SO7455, for quiet Teme-side orchards (and on up through Ravenshill Wood to Crews Hill, or instead along to the attractive Talbot at Knightwick SO7355); and on the Worcs & Birmingham Canal, the Firs at Dunhampstead SO9160, Navigation at Stoke Prior SO9468, Bowling Green at Stoke Works SO9468 (yes, it does have its own bowling green), and the Queen's Head at Stoke Pound SO9667.

Driving

This is not nearly such a rewarding area for leisurely country drives as either the Vale of Evesham and the Malvern Hills, or Herefordshire to the W. However, W of Worcester the B4197 through Martley has some quietly attractive views, and the B4204 crossing it is a pleasant country road. The B4194/B4196 S of Bewdley is quite a good road, though the Severn is not at its most engaging along here. The A456 has some worthwhile views, but can carry quite a bit of traffic.

Where to eat

Worcester SO8555 Browns 24 Quay St (01905) 26263 Most attractive and spacious warehouse conversion with big windows overlooking the river, excellent modern cooking inc fish and vegetarian dishes, and good wines; cl am Sat, pm Sun, 1 wk Christmas; children over 10. £20 lunch, £30 dinner.

Bransford SO7852 Bear & Ragged Staff (01886) 833399 Busy dining pub with interconnecting rooms, open fires, a wide choice of interesting food, decent wines, and friendly service. £16/£6.

Wychbold SO9265 Thatch (01527) 861412 Not a pub but part of Webbs Garden Centre (see entry above); open 9–7.30pm (till 5 Sat, Sun and in winter), with a wine licence, good-value snacks and meals in pleasant surroundings; cl 25–26 Dec; disabled access. £12.50/£2/£5.

Pensax SO7269 Bell (01299) 896677 Unspoilt and friendly 19th-c pub with good food, several changing real ales and open fires; dining room extension has a fine view over the hills to Wyre Forest; fair disabled access (one step). £12/£1.75/£3.75.

Help this year from: Pam Adsley, Michael Butler, Andrew and Ruth Triggs, A Y Drummond, K R Wood, Neil and Anita Christopher, Steve Goodchild, Derek Allpass, Jill White, DRS, Huw and Carolyn Lewis, Patrick and Mary McDermott, Rebecca Mortimer, A K Thorlby, Graham Reeve, Rebecca Mortimer, Sarah Edwards, Patrick Freeman, Mrs M M Westwood, Martin Richards, Dave Braisted, P Brown, J Penford, Bill Sykes, Paul and Karen Mason, Alan Skull, Jenny and Brian Seller, Mrs B Sugarman, Bronwen and Steve Wrigley, Mrs S le Bert-Francis, Derek and Sylvia Stephenson, C J Parsons.

Please let us know what you think of places in the *Guide*. Use the report forms at the back of the book or simply send a letter.

HEREFORD AND WORCESTER CALENDAR

Some of these dates were provisional as we went to press.

JANUARY

1 **Bewdley Bridge** Duck Race

21 **Worcester** Frost Fair at the Commandery – *till Sun 22* (01905) 355071

MARCH

18 **Stoke Heath** Hands on Science Weekend at Avoncroft Museum of Buildings – *till Sun 19* (01527) 831363

APRIL

14 **Worcester** Civil War Festival and Encampment at the Commandery – *till Sun 23* (01905) 355071

15 **Stoke Heath** Avoncroft in Steam at Avoncroft Museum of Buildings – *till Mon 17* (01527) 831363

27 **Malvern** Wales Championship Dog Show at the Three Counties Showground – *till Sun 30* (01684) 892751

MAY

2 **Hereford** May Fair – *till Thurs 4* (01432) 268430

5 **Malvern** Spring Gardening Show at the Three Counties Showground – *till Sun 7* (01684) 892751

6 **Worcester** VE Day Anniversary Celebrations at the Tudor House Museum – *till Mon 8* (01905) 355071

8 **Leominster** May Fair (01568) 616460

11 **Malvern** UK Quilt Show at the Three Counties Showground – *till Sun 14* (01684) 892751

20 **Malvern** Festival – *till 4 June* (01684) 892277

21 **Worcester** National Trust Centenary Service at the Cathedral (01684) 850051

27 **Stoke Heath** Activity Weekend at Avoncroft Museum of Buildings – *till Mon 29* (01527) 831363; **Worcester** Oak Apple Festival at the Commandery – *till Mon 29* (01905) 355071; **Worcester** Regatta (01905) 451831

24 **Bromsgrove** Court Leet and Court Baron – procession through town from *10.30am*, carnival *from 2pm*

JUNE

3 **Leominster** Festival – *till Sun 11* (01568) 612874

4 **Hartlebury** Vintage Transport Event at the Castle County Museum (01299) 250416

13 **Malvern** Three Counties Show at the Three Counties Showground – *till Thurs 15* (01684) 892751

17 **Kidderminster** Carnival (01562) 751634

23 **Upton-upon-Severn** Oliver Cromwell Jazz Festival – *till Sun 25* (01922) 30779

HEREFORD AND WORCESTER CALENDAR

JUNE cont

29 **Stoke Heath** Open-Air Theatre at Avoncroft Museum of Buildings *Much Ado About Nothing – till 1 July* (01527) 831363

JULY

1 **Worcester** Carnival (01905) 722320

4 **Leominster** Ludlow Festival Concert at Berrington Hall (01568) 615721

7 **Hereford** Summer Festival – *till Sun 16*

9 **Stoke Heath** Austin Sideley Vintage Car Rally at Avoncroft Museum of Buildings (01527) 831363

11 **Leominster** Tapestry of Music – music workshop for children and evening concert at Berrington Hall (01568) 615721

18 **Leominster** Classical Concert at Berrington Hall (01568) 615721

22 **Bromyard** Countryside Open Day at Brockhampton Estate (01684) 850051

25 **Leominster** Classical Concert at Berrington Hall (01568) 615721

29 **Upton-upon-Severn** Steam Rally at Ryalls Court Farm

AUGUST

5 **Ross-on-Wye** Carnival (01989) 562768; **Stoke Heath** Children's Activity Weekend at Avoncroft Museum of Buildings – *till Sun 6* (01527) 831363

6 **Hartlebury** Country Fair at the Castle County Museum (01299) 250416

12 **Worcester** Elizabethan Festival at the Commandery – *till Sun 20* (01905) 355071

20 **Harvington** Annual Pilgrimage at Harvington Hall

28 **Ledbury** Street Carnival (01531) 633034; **Leominster** Agricultural Show (01432) 830735; **Madresfield** Agricultural Show at Madresfield Court; **Ross-on-Wye** Regatta (01989) 562768

SEPTEMBER

2 **Stourport-on-Severn** Carnival (01562) 60020; **Worcester** Re-enactment of part of the Battle of Worcester: 'The Escape of Charles II' – *till Sun 3* (01905) 355071

22 **Stoke Heath** Apple and Cheese Day at Avoncroft Museum of Buildings (01527) 831363

29 **Malvern** Jazz Festival at the Winter Gardens Complex – *till 1 Oct* (01922) 30779

OCTOBER

9 **Ledbury** Hop Fair – *till Tues 10* (01531) 633034

NOVEMBER

4 **Worcester** Fireworks (01905) 722320

DECEMBER

7 **Worcester** Victorian Christmas Street Fair – *till Sat 9* (01905) 722320

HERTFORDSHIRE

Some rewarding days out – and St Albans could justify a short break.

St Albans has the well preserved remains of the Roman city behind its undeniably modern face, besides some other interesting old streets and historic corners. The best time to visit is summer, preferably late June, when the Royal National Rose Society's great garden there is most rewarding. Elsewhere, highlights include Hatfield House, the unusual zoological museum at Tring, Knebworth, and the gardens of Benington Lordship. Children particularly enjoy the wildlife park at Broxbourne.

Despite intensive urbanisation in the south, there are quite a few attractive villages and plenty of opportunities for decent walks almost throughout the county.

Where to stay

Chipperfield TL0401 TWO BREWERS Chipperfield, Kings Langley WD4 9BS (01923) 265266 *£85; 20 rms. Comfortable and very neatly kept, pubby Forte hotel with relaxing views of the pretty village green; dark, beamed, main bar with cushioned antique settles, a bow-windowed lounge with comfortable sofas and easy chairs, open fires, and good bar and restaurant food; pleasant nearby walks.

St Albans TL1407 WHITE HART Holywell Hill, St Albans AL1 1EZ (01727) 853624 £50; 11 rms, most with own bthrm. Comfortable and civilised former coaching inn with two bar areas, antique panelling, handsome fireplaces and furnishings, and a residents' lounge reached by a barleytwist staircase; courteous, friendly service, and a good restaurant.

To see and do

St Albans TL1407 is the sort of town that repays a keen-eyed stroll, with interesting corners of considerable antiquity tucked between the modern shops which, on first impressions, seem to dominate it. It was one of the most important Roman towns in Northern Europe, and has some fine, well excavated remains in peaceful surroundings.

🏛☕ The visible remains of VERULAMIUM, as it was known in Roman times, are down in the SW corner of town past the cathedral and park (coming from outside, most easily reached by the A4147, off the Hemel Hempstead exit from the M1, junction 7). The place to start is the excellent MUSEUM with its lively interpretation of everyday Roman life, as well as jewellery, wall paintings and other domestic items found on the site. Shop, disabled access; cl am Sun, Christmas; (01727) 819339; £2.50.

Follow signs from here into the adjacent playing-fields: an unassuming brick building – looking like a garage or changing rooms – houses the carefully restored mosaic floor and hypocaust underfloor heating system of an excavated Roman villa; free. Further on is a well preserved section of the Roman town wall. The ROMAN THEATRE is not large by the standards of some others in England (room for 1,600), but taking into account its good state of preservation it is unique. Shop, disabled

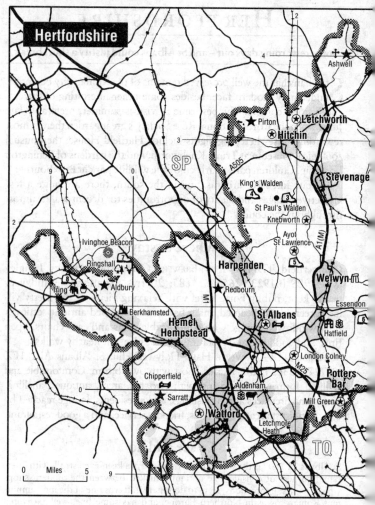

Hertfordshire

access; cl 25–26 Dec, 1 Jan; *£1.
✝ ❁ 🏠 ❀ There are other quiet
quarters too, most notably in and
around the CATHEDRAL. Up on a
mound with good views, the 11th-c
reddish exterior is made of flint,
handily procured from the Roman
remains. Once the country's premier
abbey, it suffered a little after the
Reformation, and its fortunes didn't
revive until Victorian times. It was
touched up a lot then, but the majestic
interior does have some earlier
features, inc 13th- and 14th-c
paintings in the nave, and some Saxon
transept pillars. Meals, snacks, shop,

disabled access; free. The great 14th-c
ABBEY GATEHOUSE beyond leads down
to a neat park, its lake and willow-
edged stream packed with ducks.
🏠 ❁ The most striking of the town's
non-ecclesiastical buildings is the
unusual, medieval, stone CLOCK
TOWER; its bell, striking on the hour, is
even older than the tower itself. Fine
views over the city and surrounding
country from the top. Open wknds
and bank hols Easter–mid-Sept; 25p.
Nearby, French Row is a narrow alley
of striking timbered buildings jettied
out over the street, right by a modern
shopping centre.

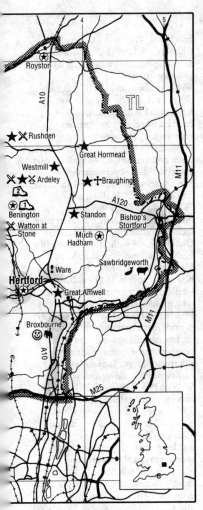

Rose & Crown is very civilised. Other pubs well worth visiting if you pass them include the Goat in Sopwell St, Garibaldi in Albert St and Six Bells in St Michael's (on the site of a Roman bath-house, though not visibly so). The Cock (Hatfield Rd) is worth looking out for because of its bizarre history; its floors were found to rest on thick foundations of human bones. ☉ ⚘ The MUSEUM OF ST ALBANS (Hatfield Rd) covers the area's history since the Romans left, and its development from medieval market town to commuter city. Shop, disabled access to ground floor only; cl am Sun; free. ORGAN MUSEUM (Camp Rd) Collection of automatically operated organs and other musical instruments, inc Wurlitzer and Rutt theatre organs. Recitals every Sun 2.15–4.30pm, and concerts all year. Teas, shop, disabled access (but no facilities); open pm Sun only; (01727) 869693; *£2. GREBE HOUSE WILDLIFE INFORMATION CENTRE (St Michael's St) Home of the regional nature conservation trust, with displays and activities, and information on reserves nearby. Shop, disabled access; cl over Christmas; (01727) 858901; free.

🌼 A mile or two outside the town at Chiswellgreen TL1304, the GARDENS OF THE ROSE (B4630, S) are the showgrounds of the Royal National Rose Society, with over 1,600 cultivars, many in mass plantings. Lots of interesting cultivation trials going on, new roses from all over the world, plenty of clematis, and new plantings for year-round interest. Snacks, shop, disabled access; cl mid-Oct–early Jun; (01727) 850461; £4. ✗ ☉ ▣ ♨ KINGSBURY WATERMILL 16th-c watermill, half a mile from the city, on the banks of the River Ver, still with one working waterwheel, as well as a museum and an art gallery. Meals, snacks, shop; cl Mon, Christmas; *85p. GORHAMBURY Two miles out of town, but peaceful enough to make you think it's in the heart of the country – an interesting 18th-c house with an extensive assemblage of 17th-c family portraits and some 16th-c enamelled glass. Open only pm Thurs May–Sept; *£3.50.

♨ A stroll through the town in search of other notable buildings (the tourist information office in the Town Hall, Market Pl, has helpful guide/maps) is rewarded by the surprisingly large number of decent pubs here. In French Row, the Fleur de Lys (though undistinguished as a pub) is a remarkable medieval building. Down between the abbey gate and park, the Fighting Cocks is based on a building which had some connection with the abbey, and its interesting layout includes the clearly discernible shape of a cockpit. In the quietly attractive, largely Georgian St Michael's St, the

Other things to see and do

✤ 🐑 **Aldenham** TQ1398 COUNTRY PARK has plenty of space for children to run around in, with an adventure play area, nature trails and a herd of longhorn cattle. The prettily placed Three Horseshoes, at Letchmore Heath, has weekday lunches and Sat snacks.

★ ✗ **Ardeley** TL3027 Attractive thatched village where the partly 13th-c CROMER WINDMILL is the last remaining post mill in the county, now lovingly restored. Usually open second and fourth Weds May–Sept, plus bank hols, but best to check, (01892) 584322; 75p. The Jolly Waggoner has excellent steaks and other food.

★ ✝ ₳ **Ayot St Lawrence** TL1916 is a delightful little backwater, with a very picturesque, 12th-c, ivy-covered, RUINED CHURCH; the existing CHURCH is an incongruously grand neo-Grecian affair. SHAW'S CORNER is much as it was when GBS lived here, from 1906–1950; Shaw devotees will enjoy seeing his exercise machine, pen, spectacles, and even the soft homburg he wore for 60 years. Try and go on a weekday when more is open. Cl am Sun, all Mon (exc pm bank hols) and Tues, Nov–Mar; £2.80; NT. The Brocket Arms is a fine, old-fashioned inn.

★ ✝ ✤ ₳ **Benington** TL3023 is one of the county's prettiest villages, its church lovely when the snowdrops are out in late Feb. BENINGTON LORDSHIP Kept well up to date, 7 acres of Edwardian terraced gardens with many unusual plants, fine herbaceous borders, roses and rock garden, and a particularly lovely splash of snowdrops. The grounds include a very picturesque, early 19th-c, 'Norman' ruined gatehouse, actually put together from stones of the genuine, moated, Norman ruined keep. Plant sales; open pm Weds Apr–Sept, Sun Apr–Aug, and bank hols, plus some dates Feb for snowdrops – ring for details; (01438) 869668; *£2.50. The lovely old Bell here has generous food.

🏰 **Berkhamsted** SP9807 BERKHAMSTED CASTLE Extensive remains of a motte and bailey castle built by the half-brother of William the Conqueror. Chaucer was later clerk of works; free. The Boat down by the canal is good for lunch.

🐍 ☺ **Broxbourne** TL3707 PARADISE WILDLIFE PARK Friendly little zoo and leisure park with lions, monkeys, camels and zebras; events from meeting the python to feeding the lions, and an adventure playground, crazy golf and woodland walk. Meals (they do a three-course carvery on Sun), snacks, shop, disabled access; cl 25 Dec; (01992) 468001; £4.

₳ ✤ **Hatfield** TL2308 is a big, modern, built-up area, but on its edge includes a charming original core – Old Hatfield – with a fine old pub (the Eight Bells), and alongside the park of HATFIELD HOUSE. This great Jacobean house was built in 1611 by Robert Cecil on the site of an earlier palace which had been a childhood home of Elizabeth I. Plenty from this and later periods in the splendid State Rooms, inc fine furnishings and tapestries, portraits of the queen, and even her silk stockings, perhaps among the earliest worn in this country. Also, a William IV kitchen and the national collection of model soldiers, with over 3,000 exhibits. Extensive rolling parkland, and gardens recreated in 17th-c style, with a scented garden and knot garden containing plants that were typical between the 15th and 17th c. Meals, snacks, shop, disabled access; open Apr–Sept, park every day, gardens cl Sun, house cl am and all Mon exc bank hols. No guided tours Sun or bank hols; (01707) 262823; £4.70, £2.60 park and gardens only.

🐎 ✤ ⛲ 🏮 ₳ ★ **Hertford** TL3212 has some quiet older parts, with handsomely pargeted buildings in the old main Fore St (inc the relaxing old Salisbury Arms Hotel). There are several antique shops in St Andrew St (one in a fine 15th-c house). The so-called CASTLE is in fact the 15th-c gatehouse for Edward IV's original moated castle – carefully restored and now occupied by the council. Open pm first Sun in month (not Oct–Apr), with a brass band outside. The extensive riverside grounds (always open) include the massive Norman flint walls of Henry II's castle, and a stone commemorating the first general synod of the English Church on 24 Sept 673. Opposite the castle remains, the White Horse is useful for lunch. There's a cheery, local history MUSEUM in an elegant 17th-c building, with a graceful Jacobean knot garden. Shop, disabled access to ground floor and garden; cl Sun, Mon, Christmas; (01992) 582686; free. Some summer weekends they also open the 18th-c SEED WAREHOUSE, with a well preserved Roman oven. The MCMULLENS BREWERY is a striking Victorian building on the river. The Old Barge by the Lee Navigation Canal has a wide choice of vegetarian food among other dishes. Nearby Hertingfordbury TL3012 is an attractive village, between river and beechwoods.

✝ ⏚ 🏛 Hitchin TL1829 has a lot of Georgian and some older buildings rather lost among the new, especially along Tilehouse St and Bridge St. The 14th-c riverside CHURCH is very attractive, and there's a decent MUSEUM AND ART GALLERY.

🏠 ✿ ⚘ ✤ Knebworth TL2520 KNEBWORTH HOUSE, GARDENS AND COUNTRY PARK Victorian author Sir Edward Bulwer Lytton was responsible for the spectacular, high-Gothic decoration that radically altered the appearance of the original Tudor mansion here; he wanted it to be a castle fit for the romantic characters in his novels. Still a lived-in home, the grand rooms include a splendid Jacobean great hall, an elaborately decorated State Drawing Room, mementos of former guests inc Dickens and Churchill, and an exhibition on the British Raj. The gardens were redesigned by Lutyens, and include a herb garden laid out to the plans of Gertrude Jekyll; the 250-acre park has a miniature railway, extensive adventure playground and a deer park. Lots of events, inc various high-profile concerts. Meals, snacks, shop, disabled access; house cl am, Mon (exc bank hols), Oct–Mar, with limited opening Apr, May and Sept – best to check first; (01438) 812661; £4.50. Along the outer edge of the park is the pretty little hamlet of Old Knebworth; the Lytton Arms here is particularly popular for its wide range of real ales.

🏚 🏛 ⚞ Letchworth TL2232 was the country's first garden city, begun in 1903. The interesting FIRST GARDEN CITY HERITAGE MUSEUM, set in the architects' charming Arts and Crafts style thatched cottages, shows the thinking behind this uniquely 20th-c idea. Shop, disabled access; cl am exc Sat (when cl 1–2), all Sun, 25–26 Dec and maybe other dates due to building work – check first; (01462) 683149; free. STANDALONE FARM (Wilbury Rd) Working farm with plenty of traditional animals to stroke and feed, inc shire horses; also daily milking, a working blacksmith and natural history displays. Snacks, shop, disabled access; cl Oct–Feb (exc autumn half-term); (01462) 686775; £2.40.

✝ ✤ ⚞ London Colney TL1803 MOSQUITO AIRCRAFT MUSEUM The Mosquito bombers were developed here in secret from 1939, and now the site houses a collection of 20 different de Havilland aircraft, as well as aero engines, full workshop, and other memorabilia. Snacks, shop, disabled access; open pm Thurs, wknds and bank hols Mar–Oct; (01727) 822051; £3. There are pretty riverside gardens down by the bridge; the Green Dragon here is useful for lunch. AYLETT NURSERIES Good garden centre specialising in geraniums, fuchsias and especially their award-winning dahlias. It's their 40th anniversary in Apr so expect celebrations then. Meals, snacks, disabled access; cl 25–26 Dec. The trial grounds for the dahlias are at BOWMANS FARM, five minutes away by car, and you can walk round free from Aug to the first frost of autumn. The farm itself is rapidly becoming quite a draw, not least because of its huge FARM SHOP, practically a supermarket (though cheaper for most things), with an enormous range of produce and a separate butcher's department. You can watch milking and look at the animals, and there are tractor rides, lakeside walks and a play area. Meals, snacks, disabled access; cl 25 Dec; (01727) 821253; shop free, farm £2.75.

✗☘☙♞ **Mill Green** TL2409 MILL GREEN MUSEUM Producing corn for around 1,000 years, a well restored working watermill with a little local history museum. Craft demonstrations most Suns, from paper-quilling to lovespoon-carving. Shop, disabled access to ground floor only; cl am wknds, all Mon, milling pm Sun only; free.

☙♔❀★ **Much Hadham** TL4319 FORGE MUSEUM AND VICTORIAN COTTAGE GARDEN Based around a working blacksmith, the story of such craftsmen through the ages, with examples of old equipment and tools. The Victorian-style garden has an unusual bee shelter. Snacks, shop, disabled access; open Sat and pm Sun all year, Tues, Fri and bank hols Apr–Sept (but cl Good Fri); *70p. The village is attractive, with fine Tudor and Georgian houses, and the Jolly Waggoners and Bull are useful for lunch.

♘❤ **Ringshall** SP9814 Right on the county border and nr Whipsnade Zoo in Beds, the ASHRIDGE ESTATE has 4,000 acres of unspoilt woodlands and open spaces, with plenty of deer and other wildlife (inc the dormouse, though you won't see it in daylight), and a monument erected for the Duke of Bridgewater. Teas summer wknds, shop and information centre, some disabled access; open pm wknds Easter–Sept; parking £1, monument £1; NT. The Valiant Trooper at Aldbury is quite handy for something to eat.

☙✝♘ **Royston** TL3540 Though the town's largely modern there are some attractive Tudor buildings in Upper King St, and interesting ones to be tracked down among the modern shops. The local MUSEUM is housed in a former monastic chapel (cl Mon, Tues, Fri), and the partly 13th-c CHURCH was also a part of this pre-Dissolution large monastery. There are probably a lot of interesting remains under the buildings of the town, as it seems to have been a continuously occupied settlement on the crossing of the Roman Icknield Way and Ermine St. Right by this central crossing is an odd, bell-shaped underground cavern with rough relief carvings; open pm summer wknds and bank hols; 50p. The Coach & Horses is a useful food stop.

🐖♪ **Sawbridgeworth** TL4814 KECKSYS FARM Working farm with sheep, cattle, poultry, rabbits and rare breeds of pig; right by the river, where coarse fishing is available. They also have a campsite. Disabled access; open daily Easter–Sept; (01279) 600896; *£2. The Coach & Horses up at Thorley Street is a good-value, family food pub.

🐖☙ **Tring** SP9211 WALTER ROTHSCHILD ZOOLOGICAL MUSEUM Largely consisting of the remarkably eclectic collections of the second Lord Rothschild, started when he was a little boy: thousands of preserved or stuffed mammals, insects, birds, fish and reptiles inc domestic dogs, giant tortoises and even a display of dressed fleas. Part of the Natural History Museum, it probably has more species on display than anywhere else in the world, and it's quite odd seeing now-extinct creatures such as the zebra-like quagga or huge giant moa. Snacks, shop, limited disabled access; cl 1 Jan, Good Fri, 24–26 Dec; (01442) 824181; £2. There's good access to the Grand Union Canal here, for long towpath walks, and the Royal Hotel (Station Rd) is right on the Ridgeway (see **Walks** section below).

! **Ware** TL3514 SCOTT'S GROTTO Built in the 1760s by the poet John Scott, this is perhaps one of the finest bits of romantic 'gothickry' in the world, extending 67 ft into the hillside under a modern housing development, with underground passages and chambers decorated with flints, shells, stones and minerals. Wear flat shoes and bring a torch; open pm Sat and bank hols, Apr–Sept; £1 donation requested. Several of the private gardens running down to the quiet River Lee have gazebos over the water, neatly restored with crisp white paintwork. The Sow & Pigs (on the A10, N) has good-value food.

❀♘⚓☙ **Watford** TQ1196 CHESLYN GARDENS are an unexpected pleasure in this largely modern urban area, with 3½ acres of woodland and formal gardens, and an aviary. Disabled access; cl 25–26 Dec. From

Cassiobury Park there are CANAL BOAT
TRIPS along the Grand Union Canal on
pm Sun and bank hols Easter–Oct, as
well as Tues and Thurs in Aug;
(01438) 714528; £3. The local
MUSEUM has a wartime exhibition
featuring the Watford Home Guard,
the basis for the TV series *Dad's
Army*. Shop, disabled access; cl 1–2
Sat, all Sun, bank hols; free.

🏛 **Welwyn** TL2316 ROMAN BATHS
Excavated before the construction of
the A1 and since then rather
ingeniously preserved within the
motorway embankment, this Roman
bath-house is all that remains of a 3rd-
c villa. Very good condition, with
explanatory displays. Shop, disabled
access; cl am, all Mon–Weds; *80p.

★ **Attractive villages** include Aldbury
SP9612 (with a perfect village green,
stocks etc, teas; the Valiant Trooper's
a pleasant pub); Ashwell TL2639
(with an unusually tall church tower;

the Bushel & Strike just beside it and
the Rose & Crown are both useful for
lunch); and Westmill TL3627 (a
happy combination of neat green,
tiled cottages and fine old church; the
Sword in Hand here's good). Others,
all with decent pubs, include:
Braughing TL3925 (pronounced
Braffing; its 14th-c riverside church is
pretty), Great Amwell TL3712 (a nice
conjunction of church, pre-Norman
Emma's Well and pool with islets),
Letchmore Heath TQ1597, Pirton
TL1431 (the village green is actually
the remains of a Norman motte and
bailey), Redbourn TL1012 (despite
motorway noise, Church End with its
workhouse and Norman church is
pretty), Rushden TL3031 and
Sarratt TL0499. The thatch and
timbering of Great Hormead TL4030 is
attractive, and Standon TL3922 has
some good timbered buildings in its
curving High St.

Walks

Large areas of this county are taken up by London's northward-stretching
fingers through Rickmansworth, Chorleywood, Watford, Borehamwood,
Potters Bar and the continuous Enfield/Cheshunt/Hoddesdon development,
and also by the first early 20th-c new towns, the garden cities of Letchworth
and Welwyn, and their more modern successors Hatfield, Hemel Hempstead
and Stevenage. But between and beyond these there are good green windows
of carefully preserved farmland and some more wooded countryside. These
yield pockets of good walking terrain, though there is little that is really
outstanding.

In the E, the villages and rolling farmland have an East Anglian flavour,
quite rural in many places such as around **Benington** TL3023 △-1, **Ardeley**
TL3027 △-2, **St Paul's Walden** TL1922 △-3 (birthplace of the Queen
Mother) and **King's Walden** TL1523 △-4. **Ayot St Lawrence** TL1916 △-5 is
conveniently close to link to a walk along the River Lea, which has been
dammed at Brocket Hall to form a lake (in view from the public right of way).
Shorter walks can start from Ayot Green TL2214, where an abandoned railway line is open to walkers and forms a useful link. The mildly hilly country
around **Essendon** TL2708 △-6 is popular with weekend walkers for its pleasantly varied, village-to-village paths; the Candlestick is well placed for refreshment, and the Salisbury Crest in the village itself is good for lunch.

In the extreme W (a wiggle in the county boundary puts it in Bucks), **Ivinghoe Beacon** SP9617 △-7 is a protruding finger of the Chilterns, and the finish
of the long-distance Ridgeway Path which begins in Wilts. The slopes, too
steep for ploughing, comprise woodland, scrub and unspoilt downland; from
the beacon itself you look down over eight counties. Aldbury SP9612 provides
the nearest good pub, and those looking for a shorter stroll from here can
explore the great woodlands of the Ashridge Estate, superb for autumn
colours. The **Grand Union Canal,** nr Tring SP9211, △-8 has a part-aban-
doned offshoot, the Wendover Arm, and the still-operational Aylesbury Arm;
feeder reservoirs at Wilstone SP9014 and Marsworth SP9214 (again, just over

the Bucks border) lie adjacent, both with waterside pubs within reach of the canal towpaths.

There's also canal access from the Boat at Gravel Path, Berkhamsted SP9807, Fisheries at Boxmoor TL0306 and the pretty Three Horseshoes at Bourne End TL0206.

Other pubs handy for walks include the Waggoners at Ayot Green TL2214, Two Brewers on Chipperfield Common TL0401, Bricklayer's Arms at Flaunden TL0100, Alford Arms at Frithsden TL0110, Huntsman at Goose Green TL3509 (for Hertford Heath), Cross Keys at Gustard Wood, nr Wheathampstead TL1716, Two Brewers at Northaw TL2802 (the ancient Great Wood is very pretty), Cabinet at Reed TL3636, Harvest Moon at Thorley TL4718, Sword in Hand at Westmill TL3627 and the Greyhound at Wigginton SP9410 (where the landlord's very helpful with suggestions; the 18th-c summerhouse in the woods is an odd find).

Scales Wood, up nr Anstey TL4133, is also good for strolls, and in the woods above Hexton is an easily traced Iron Age hill fort, Ravensburgh Castle TL1029 (the Live & Let Live in nearby Pegsdon is handy for refreshment). There are pleasant, unspoilt walks from Sarratt TQ0499 into the Chess Valley (see Bucks).

Driving

The back road through Dane End, Great Munden and on round past Wood End through Ardeley gives a good idea of the quiet, cut-off seclusion of this part of Herts, despite Stevenage being so close. Sandwiched between the M1 and the A1(M) N of Wheathampstead, the B651 runs through pretty countryside, as does the nearly parallel B656. An interesting back road is the Roman road through Coleman Green (where a ruined, roadside chimney-stack is preserved for its associations with John Bunyan – the nearby pub named after him is a useful stop).

N of Ware, the A10, an old Roman road, doesn't carry that much traffic now and gives good views, with pleasant, short detours to some of the villages mentioned above – and at Wadesmill there are some quaint, creeper-covered, Norman ruins by the river, nr a showy 19th-c bridge.

There are quite a few roadside farm shops in the area, with massive glasshouse installations along the Lee Valley.

Where to eat

Ardeley TL3027 JOLLY WAGGONER (01438) 832175 Friendly and genuine country pub with a thriving restaurant, two unspoilt bars, and a wide range of very good, home-made bar food; cl am Mon; children over 5. £20|£2/£5.50.
Rushden TL3031 MOON & STARS (01763) 88330 Unspoilt and cottagey country pub; nice atmosphere in the heavy-beamed bar with a huge inglenook and enjoyable food served by friendly staff; pleasant garden. £14|£2/£5.50.
Watton-at-Stone TL3019 GEORGE & DRAGON (01920) 830285 Civilised pub first licensed in 1603, with antiques and daily newspapers, friendly, efficient service, imaginative bar food, and good house wines; cl pm Sun, Christmas; partial disabled access. £14|£2/£5.

Help this year from: Martyn Kearey, David Goldstone, Huw and Carolyn Lewis, Martin and Jane Bailey, Peter Churchill, Alan Stourton, David Wright, Brian Marsden, Mark Hearn, Dr Paul Kitchener, Ted George, Neil and Anita Christopher, Charles Bardswell.

HERTFORDSHIRE CALENDAR

Some of these dates were provisional as we went to press.

APRIL

16 **Knebworth** American Civil War Battle Re-enactment – *till Mon 17* at Knebworth Park (01438) 811908

MAY

1 **Hertford** Music Festival – *till Weds 31* (01992) 524533

7 **Knebworth** Country Show at Knebworth Park – *till Mon 8* (01438) 811908

11 **Hatfield** Living Crafts at Hatfield House – *till Sun 14* (01707) 262823

13 **Knebworth** Hertfordshire Garden Show at Knebworth Park – *till Sun 14* (01438) 811908; **Rickmansworth** Week – *till Sun 21* (01923) 772325

20 **Rickmansworth** Canal Festival – *till Sun 21* (01923) 778382

21 **Hertford** Dressage Show at Hartham Common (01920) 463430; **Hitchin** Family Fun Day at Walsworth Common (01462) 455260

26 **Knebworth** Caravan Club National Rally at Knebworth Park – *till Weds 31* (01438) 811908

27 **Redbourn** Hertfordshire County Show – *till Sun 28* (01582) 792626

28 **New Mill** Wendover Canal Festival – *till Mon 29* (0144 282) 3378

29 **Hertford** Hertfordshire County Day at Hartham Meadows

JUNE

10 **Great Amwell** Steam Rally at Hillside Farm – *till Sun 11* (01992) 443161

11 **Knebworth** MG Owners' Club Rally at Knebworth Park (01438) 811908

17 **Ayot St Lawrence** George Bernard Shaw Summer Play at Shaw's Corner (01494) 522234

18 **Knebworth** Morris Minor Owners' Club National Rally at Knebworth Park (01438) 811908

22 **Ayot St Lawrence** George Bernard Shaw's *Candida – till Sun 23* (01494) 522234

24 **Hatfield** Festival of Gardening at Hatfield House – *till Sun 25* (01707) 262823; **Kings Langley** Carnival (01923) 270953; **Knebworth** North Hertfordshire Motor Fair at Knebworth Park – *till Sun 25* (01438) 811908; **Tring** Carnival (01442) 827190

JULY

1 **Ringshall** Victorian Craft Fair and Estate Day – *till Sun 2* (01494) 522234; **Ware** Week Carnival – *till Sat 8* (01920) 460316

16 **Knebworth** Pre-1950 American Auto Club Rally at Knebworth Park (01438) 811908; **Redbourn** St Albans Horse and Dog Show at the County Showground (01727) 855080

30 **Knebworth** Fireworks and Laser Symphony Concert at Knebworth Park (01438) 811908

HERTFORDSHIRE CALENDAR

AUGUST

5 **Knebworth** Hot Rod Supernationals at Knebworth Park – *till Sun 6* (01438) 811908

11 **Hatfield** Great British Pottery and Ceramics Festival at Hatfield House – *till Sun 13* (01707) 262823

19 **Knebworth** Hertfordshire Craft Fair at Knebworth Park – *till Sun 20* (01438) 811908

26 **Hertford** Horse Show at Hartham Common (01920) 463430

27 **Knebworth** Classic Car Roadshow at Knebworth Park – *till Mon 28* (01438) 811908

29 **St Albans** National Miniature Rose Show at The Royal National Rose Society, Chiswellgreen – *till Weds 30* (01727) 850461

SEPTEMBER

3 **Knebworth** Classic American Auto Club Rally at Knebworth Park (01438) 811908

22 **Stevenage** Charter Fair – *till Sat 23*

23 **Knebworth** Festival of Flowers at Knebworth Park – *till Sun 24* (01438) 811908

NOVEMBER

4 **St Albans** Gala and Firework Celebration at Verulamium Park (01727) 860780

5 **Welwyn Garden City** Firework Display at Stanborough Park (01707) 331212

We welcome reports from readers ...

This *Guide* depends on readers' reports. Do help us if you can – in return, we offer a discount on the next edition to people who've helped us with reports for it. Tell us what you think about places already in it, and anything extra you think we should say about them. And send us your ideas for inclusion in the next edition: places to visit, eat at or stay in, attractive drives or walks, maybe even unusual interesting shops you know of. Use the card in the middle, the report forms at the end, or just write – no stamp needed: *The Good Weekend Guide*, FREEPOST TN1569, Wadhurst, E Sussex TN5 7BR.

HUMBERSIDE

Beverley and Hull are contrasting and relatively untouristy candidates for a short stay; there are several good places to visit outside, but the scenery is not outstanding.

North of the Humber, in what used to be East Yorkshire (and will soon be again if Boundaries Commission proposals are accepted), there are quite a few places worth visiting, including ones to amuse children: we'd particularly pick out the Penny Arcadia in Pocklington, and three stately homes in splendid grounds – Burton Agnes Hall, Sledmere House and, at Sproatley, Burton Constable Hall. Bridlington on the coast has a certain charm.

Beverley is an archetypal quiet country town with fine old buildings and a magnificent minster church. Hull is a big port that has worked hard to make itself attractive and interesting for visitors. Both have decided character. As they are close to each other, you could stay in one and see the other too – as well as making forays into the countryside.

The rolling Wolds in the north (sweeping landscapes of low chalk downs dissected by dry valleys) have quite an appeal, though can hardly compare with the grander North York Moors a little futher north.

The coastal plain south of Bridlington, and the areas around and to the south of the Humber, are really too flat to stand out for a satisfying countryside weekend. However, the fishing heritage centre down in Grimsby is well worth a visit.

Prices are generally low in the area – you get a lot for your money here.

Where to stay

Beverley TA0340 BEVERLEY ARMS North Bar Within, Beverley HU17 8DD (01482) 869241 **£75**; 57 rms. Georgian-fronted, former coaching inn with a spacious and traditional, oak-panelled bar, flagstones, antique copper, and good restaurant food; disabled access; pets welcome.
Hull TA0928 FORTE CREST Castle St, Hull HU1 2BX (01482) 225221 **£69.40**; 99 rms. Modern purpose-built hotel with fine views over the marina, a bar-lounge with nautical decorations, and good restaurant food; disabled access.
Willerby TA9028 WILLERBY MANOR Well Lane, Willerby, Hull HU10 6ER (01482) 652616 **£64.50**; 36 rms. Family-owned Victorian house in 3 acres of gardens, with an airy, conservatory dining bar and a more formal restaurant; good food and helpful service.

To see and do

◨ ★ † **Beverley** TA0339 is an attractive country town, in a way like a small-scale York, with much the same sort of appeal. Its MINSTER is a wonderful 12th–14th-c building, with elegant buttressing and elaborately pinnacled towers. The W front is richly carved yet extraordinarily harmonious. Inside are several delights, inc the intricately carved Percy Tomb Canopy, the unusual Saxon Fridstol (one of only two such seats in the country), and the biggest collection of misericords in Britain. Shop, disabled access; cl am Sun, guided tours in summer only; £1 suggested donation. The former wealth of the town can be guessed at from the magnificence of another subsidiary church not far away, St Mary's Church in Hengate; the weather-vane on the SW turret is said to have been the last design by Pugin, who sketched it on the back of an envelope. Opposite is the White Horse, a quaint old gaslit, bare-boarded tavern. A more orthodox place for lunch is the Queen's Head. There are many fine Georgian buildings in the partly pedestrianised city, and several antique shops and the like – though it's still very much an honest market town rather than a tourist place. Up to 1,000 animals, mainly pigs, are still sold at the Tues and Thurs market, and the race-course is something of a local landmark.

✝ 🏛 Museum of Army Transport (Flamingate) Huge hangar with all sorts of military vehicles inc planes, tanks and cars, many displayed in realistic settings – down to farm-building camouflage for the Second World War and scratchy sand for the Gulf War. Children like it a lot: being able to get into the jeeps and so on makes it much more fun for them than many museums. Things are added all the time – this year a huge collection of over 6,000 models. Meals, snacks, shop, disabled access; cl 24–26 Dec; (01482) 860445; £2.99. 🏛⌂🏛 Guildhall (Register Sq) Now

used as a county court and mayor's parlour, the building was first established in 1500 and then rebuilt in 1762; exhibits include civic regalia and ancient charters. Tourist information centre, disabled access on ground floor only; cl Sun in winter, 25–26 Dec; free. Best to go on bank hols or Weds between May–Sept when more rooms are open and guides are in attendance. Art Gallery and Museum (Champney St) Local antiquities and pictures, inc lots of works by Fred Elwell the woodcarver, most famous for his work in the minster. Cl 12.30–2pm, pm Thurs, all bank hols; free.

Hull TA0928 Kingston-upon-Hull is the full name of this big port, so individual that it had its own flourishing, independent telephone service long before British Telecom was privatised; it's surprisingly pleasant for visitors. On the waterfront, the former docks have been well tidied up. The landing stage for the former Humber ferry is now an attractive pedestrian enclave with some solid, well restored, Georgian buildings. There are pleasant Humber views from the waterfront Minerva, which brews its own beer. Nearby, the original dock has become a yacht marina, with quite cheerfully buoyant, modern buildings around it. Away from the water, some of the most ancient buildings in the narrow streets of the old town have survived, notably on the High St. One of the most delightful old buildings is the Olde Whyte Harte just off Silver St; it was in its heavily panelled upper room that the town's governor made the fateful decision to lock the town's gate against King Charles in 1642, depriving him of the arsenal that might otherwise have swung the Civil War in his favour. These two enclaves, the old town and former docks, are separated from each other by good main roads through to the modern container and ferry docks; the traffic just sweeps by, leaving them as self-contained islands – very quiet at weekends.

❀⌂🏛⚔🏛🖼 Most of the museums and so forth are concentrated in the old town, so it's easy to walk from one to another; several are currently developing quite enthusiastically. It's impossible to miss the Town Docks Museum (Queen Victoria Sq), a massive yet solidly stylish, three-domed Victorian building, well set up with good displays on Hull's maritime history. There's a long-established section on whales and whaling, and

the huge skeletons on display were mentioned in *Moby Dick*. Shop, disabled access; cl am Sun, 25–26 Dec, Good Fri; free. Old Grammar School (South Church Side) Rapidly expanding social history museum; shop, disabled access; cl am Sun, 25-26 Dec, Good Fri; free. Wilberforce House (High St) William Wilberforce was born in this 17th-c house, and its Jacobean and Georgian rooms have a good exploration of the horrors of the slave trade and the struggle for its abolition, as well as period costumes, a chemist shop and a notable collection of dolls. Shop; cl am Sun, 25-26 Dec, 1 Jan, Good Fri; free. The Olde Black Boy nearby was the site of slave auctions. WATER MUSEUM (Springhead Ave) Interesting displays showing that getting water was once far more complicated than just turning a tap. The main feature is a beam engine that in its day could raise about a million gallons of water in four hours from the well below. Shop, some disabled access; cl am, all Mon, Dec; free. FERENS ART GALLERY (Queen Victoria Sq) Enterprisingly run general collection, with lots of maritime paintings and Dutch Old Masters, and good visiting exhibitions; particularly strong on Frank Brangwyn. Snacks, shop, disabled access; cl am Sun, 25–26 Dec, Good Fri; free. HULL MUSEUM OF TRANSPORT (High St) Another expanding collection, so far devoted to local public transport and bicycles, some weird and wonderful. Meals and snacks, shop; cl am Sun, 25–26 Dec, Good Fri; free. SPURN LIGHTSHIP Operating from the 1920s to the 1970s, and now moored in Hull Marina – interesting to go below decks and imagine being confined to this for weeks at a time, not going anywhere, tossed about in storms or blanketed in fog. Shop; cl am Sun, Mon and Tues in winter, Christmas; free. MAISTER HOUSE (High St) Only the staircase and entrance hall are open in this mid-18th-c rebuilding, but the staircase is splendid – Palladian stonework and wrought iron. The doors are ornate and finely carved. Cl wknds and public hols; 80p. NT. The HULL AND EAST RIDING MUSEUM, which has been very good, is closed until late 1995 for refurbishment.

Other things to see and do

✽ ❤ 🗡 ✺ 🏰🐕 Barton-upon-Humber TA0322 BARTON CLAY PITS Informative country park based around several old clay pits, with nature reserves, walks, fishing (extensive reed beds), sailing and other activities. Good views of the Humber Bridge. Shop, disabled access; visitor centre cl Mon, Tues and Oct–Mar; free. BAYSGARTH HOUSE MUSEUM Well displayed local history in a handsome 18th-c house, especially strong on rural crafts. Shop, some disabled access; cl Mon(exc bank hols) – Weds, 25–26 Dec, 1 Jan; (01652) 632318; free.

★ ❦ ⚘ Blacktoft SE8424 is an attractive village, and its pub the Hope & Anchor, with tables out by the waterside, is great for birdwatchers, being right by the RSPB marsh reserve. The SOUTH FARM CRAFT GALLERY has a pottery, doll's-house shop and other crafts. Teas, good disabled access; cl Mon and Tues, Christmas; free.

✚🐕🗡🏰✽🏛❢!🏚🏰❦ Bridlington TA1766 had the image of being bracing in the heyday of the traditional seaside resort, and the way the country rolls down to the long sands of the shore still gives that feeling. The centre is a quay and small harbour, with the usual summer attractions, but the original core of the town is half a mile in from the sea, with some charming old houses among the more modern ones around the heavily restored PRIORY CHURCH. A 14th-c gateway gives some idea of how imposing the priory must have been before the Dissolution, and now houses a local history and regimental museum. Open pm Tues–Thurs, Jun–Sept; £1. The HARBOUR MUSEUM AND AQUARIUM (Harbour Rd) is the best place to find out about the town's seafaring heritage. Cl winter wkdys, Christmas; 40p. On the NE edge of the town SEWERBY HALL, in spacious parkland right on the coast, has a miniature zoo and aviary as well as a charming garden. The elegant house dates from 1714–1720 and houses an art gallery and museum, inc Amy Johnson memorabilia – the pioneer aviator lived nearby; lots of events. Snacks, shop, disabled access (but not to the hall); grounds open daily all year, house and museum just Easter–Oct; £2 in summer, grounds free winter. There's a good MODEL VILLAGE in Bondville. Disabled access; cl Oct–Apr; *£2.50. A walk along the low cliff from here towards Flamborough Head TA2670 soon brings you to a strip of woodland by a stream; if you follow the lane up from here past the car park and along the wood, you come to Iron Age earthworks which cut right across the head – making it a pretty impressive, defensive position. In the opposite direction, by the leisure park at Carnaby, the PARK ROSE POTTERY (Carnaby Covert Lane) has factory visits and a seconds shop, as well as 12 acres of parkland with play areas and an owl sanctuary. Meals, snacks, shop, disabled access; cl Christmas wk; (01262) 602823; site entry free, some individual attractions have charges. Also at this end of town is JOHN BULL'S WORLD OF ROCK, where you can tour a factory producing biscuits, chocolate and rock. Cl winter wknds, Christmas; factory free, £1 exhibition.

✿ **Broughton** SE9608 MAYFIELD COURT CRAFTS (High St) is a decent craft shop; cl Weds and Thurs.

🏠 ✲ ✝ **Burton Agnes** TA1063 BURTON AGNES HALL Marvellous, richly decorated Elizabethan house, with a fantastically carved great hall, 16th-c antiques, and some splendid Impressionist paintings. A fine woodland garden has colourful borders, pets corner and a topiary walk to an orangery. Meals, snacks, shop, disabled access on ground floor only; cl Nov–Mar; (01262) 490324; *£3, grounds only £1.50. The Norman manor house which preceded the present one, refaced in brick but still showing its original structure, stands between here and the church. At nearby Kilham, the CHURCH is attractive, with a memorable Norman door.

✝ ✲ 🏠 ✖ 🍴 **Cleethorpes** TA3008 is a big, traditional seaside resort with extensive, gently shelving, tidal sands, and all the entertainments you'd expect (as well as a surprisingly ancient CHURCH among some attractive CHURCH older houses at its original

core). The Smugglers and Willys (which brews its own beer) are useful for lunch. Varied attractions down by the lakeside include FUCHSIA FANTASY, selling over 700 varieties of fuchsias, and other plants according to season (limited winter opening, best to check on (01472) 883075), and JUNGLE WORLD AND MINI-BEAST ZOO (Kings Rd), with lots of butterflies and birds flying through an indoor rainforest.

Humberside

Bugthorpe
Stamford Bridge
Bishop Wilton
Fangfoss
A166
A1079
Pocklington
Sutton-upon-Derwent
Market Weighton
SE
A163
A614
North Cave
Howden
M62
M180
Sandtoft
M18
Epworth
SK

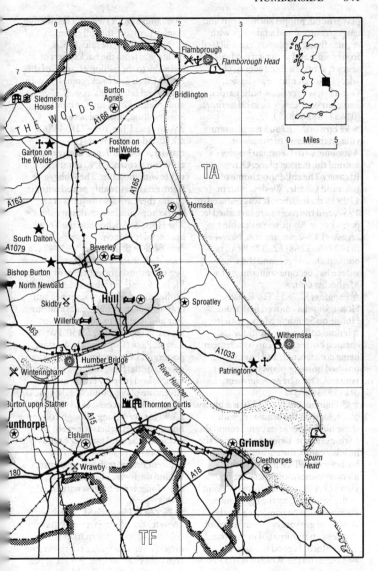

Shop, disabled access; cl 25 Dec; £1.75. The CLEETHORPES COAST LIGHT RAILWAY starts its trip around the local scenery from here.

🏠 ❀ nr **Driffield** SE9365 SLEDMERE HOUSE is a grand 18th-c mansion with a library bigger than most of the county's public ones, decorated and furnished in the style of the period, with one showpiece room done in Turkish tiling. The extensive park behind an immaculate stone wall was landscaped by Capability Brown. They play their pipe organ every afternoon. Cl am, all Mon (exc bank hols), Fri, and Oct–Easter; (01377) 236637; £3. The Triton nearby is useful for lunch.

🐑 🦆 ☺ ❀ ⚓ **Elsham** TA0312 ELSHAM HALL COUNTRY PARK Lots for families at this attractive place – farmyard animals, arboretum, adventure playground, puppet shows, craft and garden centres, and a falconry with regular flying displays. Carp will feed from your hand at the jetty. Meals, snacks, shop, disabled access; cl wkdys and Sat mid-Sept–Easter, Good Fri, winter bank hols; garden and craft centre may be cl other times; (01652) 688698; £3.95.

★ 🏰 **Epworth** SE7803 is a pleasant village, the centre of the isle of Axholme, with Georgian houses around the market place. OLD RECTORY The childhood home of John and Charles Wesley, built in 1709 by their father. It was restored in 1957, and the rooms are furnished in period style. Shop, some disabled access; cl 12–2pm, am Sun, Nov–Feb; (01427) 872268; £2. B & B can be booked ahead here, and the whole village has become something of a Methodist centre.

🎠 **Fangfoss** SE7653 THE ROCKING HORSE SHOP has moved here from Holme on Spalding Moor, with its splendid collection of antique rocking horses. You can watch them being constructed, and buy either a finished horse or plans for doing it yourself. Open by appointment; (01759) 368737.

✝ ❀ **Flamborough** TA2270 is a blowy place, high on the headland, with some old houses at its core around the 15th-c CHURCH. Down below, past the holiday camp, the natural rock harbour is well sheltered, with a lifeboat station, and there are fine views of coast and sea from the point of the headland, by the lighthouse. Flamborough Marine sell a local version of guernseys – weatherproof 'ganseys', hand-knitted in the round. The Seabirds is good for lunch.

🚩 **Foston on the Wolds** TA1055 CRUCKLEY FARM Friendly working farm, with lots of animals to fuss over – inc some very strange-looking rare breeds; daily milking displays. Snacks, shop, disabled access; cl Oct–Apr; (01262) 488337; *£2.30.

🛉 ❀ 🎠 **Grimsby** TA2710 is a declining fishing port which has not yet made itself entirely appealing to visitors, though it's making promising efforts in that direction. Outstanding is the NATIONAL FISHING HERITAGE CENTRE

(Alexandra Dock) where a fascinating display provides the full experience of a trawlerman of the mid-1950s, taking you from the backstreets of Grimsby to the fishing grounds of the Arctic Circle and back, complete with smells and sensations as well as sights and sounds. Great fun for families. Snacks, shop, disabled access; cl 25–26 Dec, 1 Jan; (01472) 344868; £3.10. Additional tours of a real trawler, the *Ross Tiger*, are available, £2.05 on its own, £3.90 combined ticket with museum. The Abbeygate Centre has reasonably priced antique shops; there are also upstairs craft workshops, inc lace-making; café. The Hope & Anchor and the Trawl are useful for lunch.

🛉 🎠 🦋 ☺ 🐦 🚂 **Hornsea** TA1947 is a sizeable E coast resort. MUSEUM (New-begin) Enthusiastic museum of village life in a former farmhouse and its outbuildings. Various activities and craft demonstrations. Snacks during July and Aug, shop, some disabled access; cl Oct–Easter; £1.50. POTTERY LEISURE PARK (Rolston Rd) Working potters and various family attractions such as butterflies, vintage cars, model village, birds of prey centre and an adventure playground. Meals, snacks, shop, disabled access; cl 24–26 Dec; £3.99 for everything, though you can buy individual tickets for each attraction. Several familiar brands and stores have sale shops in the adjacent Freeport shopping centre. Behind the town, Hornsea Mere, 2 miles long, is the biggest natural lake in this region.

★ 🏰 ✝ 🏛 ❀ **Howden** SE7528 is an unpretentiously attractive place, with cobbled alleys, a fine market hall, a majestic MINSTER with a tall tower, the ruins of a charming medieval chapter house, and a small, marshland country park down the lane opposite the minster, with ponds and raised walkways. The Plough is useful for lunch.

❀ 🛥 The **Humber Bridge** TA0224 is the longest single-span suspension bridge in the world – nearly a mile between the towers – and a very impressive sweep of engineering (there's a footway across, as well as the road). At the N end is the HUMBER

BRIDGE COUNTRY PARK, with plenty of woodland and clifftop walks and an old mill from the days when this area was the centre of the chalk industry. Meals, snacks, shop, good disabled access; free.

★ **Market Weighton** SE8742 is a neat and pleasant old market town with one or two useful antique shops; the Londesborough Arms is a civilised lunch stop.

☛ **North Newbald** SE9136 NORTHERN SHIRE HORSE CENTRE (Flower Hill Farm) Busy working farm with pedigree shire horse stud. Farming bygones, reconstructed rooms, decent walks and plenty of animals, inc rare sheep and cattle. Meals, snacks, shop, disabled access; cl Fri and Sat, all Oct–Easter; (01430) 827270; £2.25.

! ⚘ ❀ ♿ **Pocklington** SE8048 is an open-faced market town below the Wolds, with a good few handsome buildings; the Feathers is popular for lunch (and has decent bedrooms). PENNY ARCADIA Lively exploration of the varied world of slot-machines, with a comprehensive collection of antique and veteran, coin-operated amusements – great fun. Shop, disabled access; cl am exc Jun–Aug, all Oct–Apr; (01759) 303420; *£3. A mile or two outside the town, BURNBY HALL (Burnby Rd) is famous for its water lilies, with dozens of varieties in two large ponds; also a splendid rose garden, and an intriguing collection of all sorts of ethnic material and sporting trophies from across the world. Snacks, shop, disabled access; cl mid-Oct–first wk Apr; (01759) 302068; £2. From out here it's not far to the Plough at Allerthorpe – very good for lunch.

🏛 **Sandtoft** SE7408 TRANSPORT CENTRE Working trolley bus system and a collection of over 60 trolley and motor buses from Britain and the Continent, some working. Also models and other memorabilia. Snacks, shop; best to tel (01724) 3711391 for opening dates; £3.

❀ ✈ ⚘ ♿ 🖼 **Scunthorpe** SE8910 NORMANBY HALL COUNTRY PARK 350 acres of grounds with deer grazing in the park, lots of wildfowl, nature trails, riding, some interesting

sculptures, farm museum, and various special events. The Regency mansion itself has rooms decorated in period style. Meals, snacks, shop, disabled access to ground floor only; house cl am, and Oct–Mar, park open all year; (01724) 720588; free, though charge for car parking: 90p Mon–Fri, £1.60 Sat, £2.20 Sun. BOROUGH MUSEUM AND ART GALLERY (Oswald Rd) Local history and folklore, especially good on archaeology and geology. Shop, disabled access to ground floor only; cl am Sun, all Mon, Christmas; free.

⚘ ♿ ❀ ♪ **Sproatley** TA1934 BURTON CONSTABLE HALL The wonderful exterior gives away this delightful house's Elizabethan origins, but the inside was extravagantly and splendidly remodelled in the 18th c. Around 30 beautifully preserved rooms to see, inc a sweeping long gallery, as well as intriguing collections of fossils, 18th-c scientific instruments and assorted oddities from around the world. The 200 acres of parkland were landscaped by Capability Brown. Teas, disabled access to ground floor only; cl am, Fri, Sat (exc July and Aug), Oct–Easter; (01964) 562400; *£3. Camping, caravanning and seasonal fishing.

🏰 ⚘ nr **Thornton Curtis** TA1118 THORNTON ABBEY Ruins of a 12th-c Augustinian abbey, with a small exhibition in the magnificent 14th-c gatehouse. Disabled access (not into gatehouse); grounds open daily, gatehouse usually open only first and third Suns in month – best to check first; (01469) 540357; free.

❀ ♿ **Withernsea** TA3427 LIGHTHOUSE Towering above the houses of this little resort, with fantastic views for those keen enough to climb the 144 steps. Varied displays and exhibitions. Snacks, shop, disabled access to ground floor only; open pm wknds Mar–Oct, daily July and Aug; (01964) 614834; *£1.50.

✗ **Working windmills** at WRAWBY TA0209 (best to tel Mrs Day for opening dates on (01652) 653699; 60p) and SKIDBY TA0133 (cl am Sun, Mon, and Oct–Apr; 80p), which has gentle country walks nearby, and brilliant, filled Yorkshire puddings at the Half Moon.

★ **Attractive villages** include Bishop Wilton SE7955, Bugthorpe SE7758 (especially in spring; with a handsome church), Garton-on-the-Wolds SE9859 (another interesting church – 12th-c, and very High Church inside, with 19th-c mosaics and frescoes), North Cave SE8932 (for the view of the lake and park behind the church), Patrington TA3122 (a glorious church, with lovely carving inside – its graceful spire beckoning you from a long way off); and, all with decent pubs, Bishop Burton SE9939, Burton upon Stather SE8717 and South Dalton SE9645 (the picturesque Pipe & Glass has a fine position by Dalton Park).

Walks

Flamborough Head TA2670 ⌂-1 has some quite exciting walking, particularly around its N side, with the cacophony of thousands of kittiwakes sounding within the inlets; puffins can sometimes be seen on rock ledges. A level mile and a half from the lighthouse along clifftops leads to North Landing TA2273 (café and car park). A longer walk, making the Head the midway point, starts from Flamborough village TA2270 and heads around fields to join the coastal path; to avoid anti-climax, walk the southern cliffs first and keep the real drama for later on. To the N, the path follows the coast closely nearly all the way, and hilly country coming right to the coast makes for interest.

The area between the Wolds, Humber and coast, known as Holderness, is flat: rich farming country with huge fields and not many buildings, though the fine village churches – often with soaring towers or spires – reflect the wealth that this fertile land has put into them in the past. The long southern stretch of coast is flat country too, without a great deal of appeal for walkers – except for long, lonely, off-season walks by the edge of the North Sea.

A rough track open to cars makes it to the very end of **Spurn Head** TA4011 ⌂-2, the vulnerable-looking spit which protrudes like a claw at the mouth of the Humber estuary, a bleak place to some but a paradise for birdwatchers, who often wait here in spring and autumn for glimpses of rare migrant species. The estuary itself, looking a promising sight on the map, is actually not a beautiful piece of water, but grey, solemn and grim.

The southern part of the **Wolds Way** ⌂-3 has the best of inland walking, with the start of the 79-mile route passing along the N bank of the Humber for awesome views of the Humber Bridge. The Gate pub at Millington SE8352 is by quite a steep path up on to the Wolds Way, and other walks above it, with good views, take you up on to the track of an old Roman road, and around some of the county's rare woods.

Driving

Distances here are long, but the roads have little traffic and are generally good, so that you can cover ground quickly. People unfamiliar with the Wolds will enjoy any of the roads which sweep over these rolling stretches of farmland, with the views punctuated by distant clumps of trees and an occasional spire or tower proclaiming a village. The B1249 N of Driffield is one such (especially over the Yorkshire border, as it drops down over the Staxton Brow); on the way, it passes the Old Mill, a useful place to eat nr Langtoft. Also out from Driffield, the B1252 has some handsome views, and the B1248 N from Beverley is of similar character.

Towards the W, the countryside becomes more picturesquely hilly, with pastures replacing some of the big-field, arable farmland; the A163 passing Londesborough and the steeper B1246 between Driffield and Pocklington both take good account of this rather different scenery.

Further S, the B1230 from Howden to Beverley, relieved of traffic pressure by the M62, has reverted to the more relaxed character of an old coach road.

The B1242 up the coast certainly gives you plenty of sea views, but tends rather to emphasise the monotony of the North Sea. A more interesting coastal drive is the B1259 out to Flamborough Head, and then up the coast a bit on the B1229.

Where to eat

Winteringham SE9322 WINTERINGHAM FIELDS (01724) 733096 Restaurant with rooms in a 16th-c manor house; comfortable and very attractive Victorian furnishings, beams, open fires, excellent and inventive food in the no-smoking dining room, warm and friendly service; fine breakfasts, individual bedrooms with period furniture; cl Sun, am Mon and Sat, 2 wks Christmas, first wk Aug; partial disabled access. £40|£15.75 3-course lunch.

Stamford Bridge SE7155 THREE CUPS (01759) 71396 Spacious and friendly family pub with stripped brickwork, beams, panelling and a library theme; popular food (carvery Tues–Sun), and a good children's play area; restaurant cl Mon. £14.50|£1.90/£4.90.

Sutton-upon-Derwent SE7047 ST VINCENT ARMS (01904) 608349 Relaxed atmosphere in a traditional, panelled front parlour with an open fire, high-backed old settles, and good, solid, home-cooked food in the spacious dining room; friendly staff, well kept beers and a decent choice of wines; big garden. £14|£2/£5.

Flamborough TA2270 SEABIRDS (01262) 850242 Friendly old pub full of shipping memorabilia, with very good fish dishes amongst other home-made food, and lots of wines; cl pm Sun and Mon in winter; partial disabled access. £12|£1.75/£4.20.

Help this year from: Miranda Hutchinson, M and J Back, Lawrence Bacon, Jean Scott.

HUMBERSIDE CALENDAR

Some of these dates were provisional as we went to press.

JANUARY

6 **Haxey** Haxey Hood Ancient Game: created in the 13th-c by Lady de Mowbray whose hood was blown away and retrieved by labourers. Contest begins with a procession of players – colourfully dressed 'boggans', a king and a fool. The game resembles rugby played with leather hoods. The object is to get a hood away from the boggans by throwing, kicking or carrying. When a boggan touches the hood it is thrown again and the game continues *until dusk*

8 **Beverley** Epiphany Procession at Beverley Minster, *6.30pm* (01482) 868540

MARCH

16 nr **Market Weighton** Kiplingcotes Derby – starts at the Sandstone Post *at midday*, a mile N of the old railway station: possibly the oldest flat race in the country, and surely the only race where the winner gets less money than the runner-up (01482) 651207

HUMBERSIDE CALENDAR

APRIL

14 **Hull** Church Arts and Organ Festival (street and fairground organs, and exhibitions of all aspects of church arts) – *till Mon 17* (01482) 223559

29 **Bridlington** Festival – *till 13 May* (01262) 401392

MAY

1 **Bridlington** Open Golf Festival, also at Flamborough Head and the Links at Bridlington Bay – *till Sat 6* (01262) 606715

5 **Cleethorpes** Beer Festival at the Winter Gardens – *till Sun 7* (01472) 692925

7 **Sewerby** Spring Show at Sewerby Hall – *till Mon 8* (01262) 851052

8 **Cleethorpes** May Day Fair at the Showground (01472) 200220; **Normanby** Victorian Day with Victorian cavalry, school room and laundry at Normanby Hall (01724) 720588

11 **Beverley** Early Music Festival – *till Sun 14* (01904) 658338

13 **Bishop Burton** Gardens Open Day at Bishop Burton College (01964) 550481

20 **Cleethorpes** International Angling Festival at Boating Lake – *till Sun 21* (01472) 276760 (Steve Hallan)

26 **Cleethorpes** Folk Festival at the Winter Gardens – *till Mon 29* (01472) 692925

27 **Sewerby** Bridlington Horse Pageant at Sewerby Hall – *till Mon 29* (01262) 851052

28 **Elsham** Children's Festival Weekend at Elsham Hall Country and Wildlife Park – *till Mon 29* (01652) 688698; **Normanby** Horse Trials at Normanby Hall (01724) 720588

JUNE

3 **Hull** Lord Mayor's Parade and Gala from Walton Street Fairground to East Park (01482) 595080

4 **Hull** (East Park) to **Bridlington** (Limekiln Lane) East Coast Vintage Commercial Vehicle Rally (01482) 223559; **Messingham** Show at the Grange (01724) 763004

11 **Normanby** Motor Show at Normanby Hall Country Park (01724) 720588

16 **Beverley** Folk Festival – *till Sun 18* (01377) 217662

18 **Grimsby** Brass Band Festival at the Town Hall (01472) 242000; **Sewerby** Fur and Feather Show at Sewerby Hall (01262) 851052; **Walkington** Hayride in Victorian Costume *from 1pm*: dating from Victorian times when local folk had a day's holiday and hayride to the coast. Now the custom is celebrated by a 10-mile ride through Beverley and back to Walkington (01482) 864421

25 **Bishop Burton** Town and Country Day at Bishop Burton College (01964) 550481; **Normanby** Normanby Show at Normanby Hall (01724) 720588; **Sledmere** Vintage Car Rally at Sledmere House (01377) 236637

Humberside Calendar

JULY

1 **Driffield** Festival – *till Sun 9* (01262) 401392; **Hull** Festival inc buskers competition and powerboat racing – *till Mon 31* (01482) 223559

2 **Sewerby** Midsummer Show at Sewerby Hall (01262) 851052

7 **Grimsby** International Jazz Festival at King George V Stadium – *till Sun 9* (01472) 242000 ext 1473

15 **Barton-upon-Humber** Carnival at Baysgarth Park (01652) 635330; **Broughton** Show (01652) 656567

23 **Hull** Brass Band Competition and Concert (01964) 562400; **Normanby** Classic Car Rally at Normanby Hall Country Park (01724) 720588; **Sewerby** Sheep and Goat Show at Sewerby Hall (01262) 851052

AUGUST

1 **Sewerby** Summer Show at Sewerby Hall – *till Weds 2* (01262) 851052

5 **Bridlington** RYYC Annual Regatta in the bay – *till Sat 12* (01262) 672041

6 **Sledmere** Sheepdog Trials and Craft Fair at Sledmere House (01377) 236637; **Bridlington** Carnival (01262) 678255

8 **Hull** Jazz Festival on the waterfront – *till Sun 13* (01482) 223559

12 **Driffield** Steam and Vintage Rally at the Showground – *till Sun 13* (01377) 254384; **Howden** Show – *till Sun 13* (01757) 630247

13 **Normanby** Centenary Jaguar Day at Normanby Hall Country Park (01724) 720588

26 **Elsham** Folkdance Festival at Elsham Hall Country and Wildlife Park – *till Mon 28* (01652) 688698; **Sledmere** Flower Festival at Sledmere House (01377) 236637

28 **Epworth** Show

31 **Hull** International Sea Shanty Festival – *till 3 Sept* (01482) 223559

SEPTEMBER

9 **Normanby** Oil and Steam Engine Rally at Normanby Hall Country Park – *till Sun 10* (01724) 720588

OCTOBER

Hull Time-based Arts Festival – Root 95 (01482) 216446

6 **Hull** Comedy Festival – *till 2 Dec*, and Fair – *till Sat 14* (01482) 223559

8 **Cleethorpes** Brass Band Championships at the Beachcomber (01472) 200220

29 **Crowle** Scunthorpe Craft Fair and Agricultural Show

NOVEMBER

4 **Cleethorpes** Giant Bonfire and Fireworks (01472) 200220

5 **Hull** Bonfire and Fireworks (01482) 42331

9 **Hull** Literature Festival – *till Mon 20* (01482) 595625

19 **Cleethorpes** Victorian Christmas Fair (01472) 200220

24 **Hornsea** Lights On Night

26 **Beverley** Advent Procession at Beverley Minster, *6.30pm* (01482) 868540

ISLE OF WIGHT

Attractive countryside and coast, a great many places of interest; popular for summer family holidays, very good at other times for peaceful short breaks, with lovely walks.

The island has several traditional seaside resorts, and plenty to interest families, particularly in summer when it's a favourite for family beach holidays – many of the more child-oriented attractions close for six months over winter. Outside the main holiday season, it has a great deal of potential for short breaks – feeling fresh, uncrowded and leisurely. In May and June its south coast is generally the sunniest place in Britain, and even in winter really cold weather is rare here. There are plenty of good coastal walks in fine scenery, and among places to visit we'd particularly pick out Osborne House (with other interesting things close by), Ventnor, Arreton, Brading, Carisbrooke Castle, and the bird and animal attractions at St Lawrence (excellent rare breeds centre in a lovely setting), Shorwell (a really nice farm park), Seaview and Newchurch. In high summer, the main resorts and places to visit are very busy, with coach parties descending in droves on the prettiest villages (there are places, especially inland, where you can get away from them).

The crossing takes about 30 minutes – 15 for the Portsmouth–Ryde catamaran, 10 for the Southsea hovercraft. Foot fares start at £4.80, cars from around £29: tel (01705) 827744 for bookings from Portsmouth to Fishbourne or Ryde, and Lymington to Yarmouth; (01703) 33033 for Southampton to Cowes; (01983) 811000 for the hovercraft from Southsea to Ryde. The fare is to an extent offset by the fact that once you're there prices are rather on the low side compared with the mainland – even counting the car fare, hotels towards the top of the range are reasonable compared with ones of similar quality on the mainland. If you're planning to stay for two or three nights, it's always worth asking the hotel if they do a bargain package deal that includes the ferry fare; this can be good value.

The island has a bus service that would put most parts of the mainland to shame, especially between May and September; a week's bus pass is worth getting, as is a daily Rover road/rail ticket (£5.95).

Where to stay

Bonchurch SZ5778 PEACOCK VANE, Bonchurch PO38 1RJ (01983) 852019 £85; 12 very comfortable and very individually decorated rms. Country-house hotel with a relaxed atmosphere, a comfortable lounge with antiques and heavy drapes, and a Sat evening pianist; attractive breakfast room, conservatory, and a restaurant with good food and friendly service; pleasant garden; cl Mon and Tues in Jan and Feb.
Shanklin SZ5881 LUCCOMBE CHINE HOUSE, Shanklin PO37 6RH (01983) 862037 £72; 6 rms, all with four-posters. Very friendly small hotel at the end of a long drive and surrounded by large wooded grounds where you can watch

foxes and badgers at night taking food left for them on the lawn; a homely lounge, help-yourself drinks tray, beams and inglenook fireplaces, and very good food in the cosy dining room; nice walks; cl Dec–Jan; no children.

Seaview SZ6291 SEAVIEW High St, Seaview PO34 5EX (01983) 612711 **£65**; 16 attractively decorated rms. Small and friendly hotel with fine maritime photographs in the chatty and relaxed front bar, an old-fashioned, characterful back bar, good, freshly made bar food, and a highly regarded evening restaurant; children over 5 in evening restaurant; disabled access.

Yarmouth SZ3589 GEORGE Quay St, Yarmouth PO41 0PE (01983) 760331 **£65**; 11 comfortable rms. Pleasantly relaxing panelled bars, one with a nautical theme; log fires, good food, and prompt, courteous service; own gardens to a private beach, own fishing operation in Yarmouth and St Vaast.

Ventnor SZ5677 MADEIRA HALL, Ventnor PO38 1NS (01983) 852624 **£60**; 8 rms. Once the home of Miss Dick (Dickens based Miss Havisham in *Great Expectations* on her), this attractive, no-smoking, Victorian manor house stands in lovely quiet grounds with a swimming pool and putting green; a friendly, relaxed atmosphere, appealing day rooms, and good food in the elegant restaurant; children over 5; partial disabled access.

Ryde SZ5992 RYDE CASTLE Esplanade, Ryde PO33 1JA (01983) 563755 **£52.50**; 20 rms, most with four-posters. 16th-c castle with a comfortable lounge, tapestries, and good food in the restaurant designed to look like a galleon.

Yarmouth SZ3589 BUGLE The Square, Yarmouth PO41 0NS (01983) 760272 **£50**; 6 rms (best to have one not over the bar). Bustling inn with a bar decorated like a galleon stern, and other panelled rooms inc a peaceful lounge; friendly atmosphere, good bar and restaurant food, children's room, and a sizeable garden.

Bonchurch SZ5778 LAKE, Bonchurch PO38 1RF (01983) 852613 **£45**; 21 rms. Early 19th-c country house in 2 acres of pretty gardens; with three lounges (one is a conservatory), bar, restaurant and enjoyable food; cl Nov–Feb; children over 3.

St Lawrence SZ5376 LISLE COMBE Bank End Farm, Undercliffe Drive, St Lawrence, Ventnor PO38 1UW (01983) 852582 **£33**; 3 rms, shared bthrm. Elizabethan-style farmhouse in a 5-acre coastal garden, with lovely sea views, their own rare breeds and waterfowl park, and nearby coves and beaches; cl Christmas and New Year.

Carisbrooke SZ4888 GREAT PARK FARM Betty Haunt Lane, Carisbrooke, Newport PO30 4HR (01983) 522945 **£32**; 3 no-smoking rms. Lovely old farmhouse on arable farm, with panoramic views, good walks, a dining room and sitting room; no dogs; cl Oct-Mar; children over 8.

To see and do

! ☺ ❀ ₰ 🚐 🏚 Alum Bay SZ3484 The beach here is famous for its multicoloured sands from the different rock strata in the cliff that runs down to it; 20 different shades of pinks, greys and ochres, showing up brightest after rain. The NEEDLES PLEASURE PARK at the top of the cliffs sells little glass tubes with the sands inside carefully layered. It also has a fun-park and other entertainments, as well as a spectacular chairlift down to the beach, with wonderful views along the way. Meals, snacks, shop, disabled access; cl Oct–Mar; (01983) 752401; individual charge for all attractions (return trip on the chairlift is £1.75), or 'Supersaver' covering most activities £4.50. This includes entrance to ALUM BAY GLASS, with glass-blowing demonstrations (not wknds), and a factory shop. Disabled access; cl 15 Dec–4 Jan; *60p. From the park a minibus goes up to the NEEDLES OLD BATTERY (you can't go by car), where an extensive display in the powder house of the recently restored, 19th-c fort illustrates the history of this headland. On the parade-ground are two 12-ton gun barrels salvaged from the sea. A longish tunnel leads from the fort to a look-out spot that

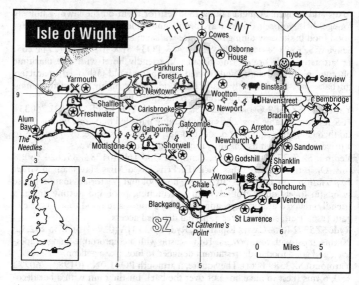

Isle of Wight

THE SOLENT

gives stunning views of the rock pinnacles of the Needles themselves, and their lighthouse. Meals, snacks, shop; cl Fri and Sat (exc July and Aug), Nov–Mar; £2.40; NT. The Freshwater nearby is handy for lunch.

✝ 🏠 🛏 🐖 🐑 🛶 🙂 **Arreton** SZ5386 is a pleasant place with a delightful 13th-c CHURCH (which has a brass-rubbing centre). The White Lion is good for lunch. Around is lots for families to enjoy. ARRETON MANOR Lovely, old, mellow stone house, dating from around 1600, with splendid period furnishings and panelling, and a variety of museums, inc collections of lace and dolls, and the NATIONAL WIRELESS MUSEUM – it was nearby that Marconi made his pioneering experiments. Meals, snacks, shop; cl am Sun, all Sat (exc bank hol wknds), and Nov–Feb; (01983) 528134; £3. The nearby Arreton Country CRAFT VILLAGE has craft workshops, pub, and a restaurant with home-baking. HASELEY MANOR The largest and oldest manor house open on the island – some parts dating from the original foundation of 1310 – with Tudor, Georgian and Victorian additions. The 20 or so rooms are decorated in period style, some with costumed figures. In the grounds is a reconstructed 18th-c farm with

animals, as well as herb gardens, and play area. Snacks, shop, disabled access; cl Nov–Easter; (01983) 865420; £3.50. An associated CRAFT CENTRE has the island's biggest pottery studio, as well as old-fashioned sweet-making (not wknds or Christmas), pets corner and teas; free. ROBIN HILL COUNTRY PARK is a nice place for a break or for children to let off steam, with woodland walks, toboggan rides, an assault course and other activities spread over 88 acres. Meals, snacks, shop, disabled access but rather hilly; cl Nov–Mar; (01983) 527352; £2.50.

❄ ✗ **Bembridge** SZ6488 even in summer is quiet for a coastal place, though with plenty going on in its yachting harbour, and a lifeboat station nearby. SHIPWRECK CENTRE AND MARITIME MUSEUM Six galleries of salvage and shipwreck items, models, early diving equipment and seafaring tales of pirates and mermen. Shop, disabled access to ground floor only; cl Nov–Feb; (01983) 872223; £2.10. WINDMILL The only surviving windmill on the island, built in 1700 and used until 1913. Shop; cl Sat (exc July–Aug) and Nov–Mar; £1.20; NT. The school has a big collection of books, letters, manuscripts and drawings by John Ruskin and his associates; by appointment only, tel

(01983) 872101. Out on the Foreland, the rock pools are magnificent and would keep any beachcomber happy for hours. The Row Barge nr the harbour is useful for lunch.

🐗 **Binstead** SZ5791 BRICKFIELDS HORSE COUNTRY (Newnham Rd) is a working farm with shire and miniature horses (inc the only shire horse twins in the country), tame farm animals, a carriage collection, agricultural bygones, and showjumping summer Weds evenings. Also a farrier, saddlery, cider-making and play area. Meals, snacks, shop, disabled access; cl 25–26 Dec; (01983) 566801; *£3.50. The old White Hart at Havenstreet is handy for lunch.

☺🐗👶❀❀ **Blackgang** SZ4971 BLACKGANG CHINE FANTASY PARK Attractive park with all sorts of different themed areas, inc Dinosaurland, Fantasyland and Jungleland, with a complete replica of a Victorian sawmill, and a display of woodland skills and traditional crafts. A museum on St Catherine's Quay has local and maritime history exhibits, and there are lots of lively events. Good views, and on a summer evening the gardens are well illuminated. Meals, snacks, shop, disabled access; cl Nov–Apr (exc Chine gardens open Christmas wk); (01983) 730330; *£4.99, sawmill and quay only £2.25.

★✝🏠👶🐗❀ 🐗 **Brading** SZ6087 is a busy, attractive place, with interesting monuments in its Norman CHURCH, and a pretty graveyard. The Bugle is useful for lunch. The remains of a ROMAN VILLA have good mosaics (cl Oct–Mar; £1.50) and there's a little local history museum in the town hall (cl Sat and Oct–Apr; *50p). LILLIPUT DOLL AND TOY MUSEUM (High St) Excellent private collection with over 2,000 exhibits dating from as far back as 2000 BC, and examples of almost every seriously collectable doll in Britain. Shop, disabled access (though there are two steps); cl 15 Jan–15 Mar; (01983) 407231; £1.25. MORTON MANOR (off A3055) 13th-c manor house, rebuilt in 1680 with further changes in the 18th c, set in lovely landscaped gardens with ornamental ponds and an Elizabethan turf maze. Also a little vineyard, with an exhibition of wine-making relics. Meals and snacks in thatched teashop, shop, disabled access; cl Sat, Nov–Mar; (01983) 406168; £2.90. NUNWELL HOUSE AND GARDENS (off A3055) Lovely, lived-in, 16th-c house with charming gardens; it has a Home Guard Museum as well as interesting furniture and family memorabilia. Charles I spent his last night of freedom here. Snacks, shop; cl Fri, Sat, Oct–Jun; (01983) 407240; £2.30. WAX MUSEUM (High St) You either like wax museums or you don't but this one, set in the partly 11th-c Ancient Rectory Mansion, is one of the best of its kind. Shop; cl 25 Dec; £3.99. The price also covers admission to the ANIMAL WORLD OF NATURAL HISTORY, which has a huge collection of animals, birds and reptiles displayed in their natural surroundings. Shop, disabled access; cl 25 Dec. The Bugle is a good, family pub.

★✝🏠🐗❀ **Calbourne** SZ4286 is an attractive village with photogenic, streamside thatched cottages, a 13th-c CHURCH, and working POTTERY (cl Sun Jan–Easter; 40p). It's worth getting here early to avoid the coach tours. WATERMILL AND RURAL MUSEUM A 20-ft waterwheel still powers this 17th-c mill, and the grounds have tame peacocks. Home-baked snacks, shop with stoneground flour etc, some disabled access; cl Nov–Easter; £2. The Sun is useful for lunch.

🏰👶❀ 🐗 **Carisbrooke** SZ4888 CARISBROOKE CASTLE An imposing entrance leads to the ruins of the only medieval castle on the island – between 1647 and 1648 home to the imprisoned Charles I (his daughter died here in 1650). The remains are mainly from the Norman castle, but there are also remnants of Elizabethan and Jacobean buildings. The site has two medieval wells – one in the 12th-c keep and the other in the 16th-c well-house in the courtyard, with entertaining demonstrations of the traditional method of driving the winding gear using a team of donkeys. Good museum; snacks, shop, disabled access to ground floor; cl 24–26 Dec, 1 Jan; (01983) 522107; £3.20. In summer they do costumed guided tours for an extra £1. The Eight Bells, with lakeside garden and good Solent views, is useful for lunch and quite handy for the nearby DONKEY SANCTUARY.

🐄 **Chale** SZ4877 CHALE FARM Small farm producing various flavours of ice-cream, inc Christmas pudding. You can see the ice-cream being made, and the cows being milked (around 4pm); cl am Sun; free. The Wight Mouse is an excellent family pub.

★ ❀ 👶 **Cowes** SZ4995 is stylish and lively, very much centred on its yachting connections, with interesting buildings and shops inc fascinating ships' chandlers in the long, narrow, High St, and the battery of over 20 brass cannons used to start the yacht races down by the harbour. The Globe (The Parade) does lots of seafood. The public library in Beckford Rd houses the COWES MARITIME MUSEUM, looking especially at local shipbuilders and naval architects. Mostly disabled access; cl Sun, Thurs and Sat before bank hols, Christmas; free. More maritime memorabilia at the pretty SIR MAX AITKEN MUSEUM. Open wkdys May–Sept; *£1. The TOY & MODEL MUSEUM (High St) is largely ship-oriented, too, with masses of warship models alongside working steamtrain models and so forth.

† 🏰 ❀ 👶 **Freshwater** SZ3484 is a very extended, rather sprawling village but has, tucked away, a charming quiet core. The picturesque, thatched CHURCH (built this century) includes quite a few Tennyson family memorials, and beyond it a causeway crosses the head of the Yar estuary. GOLDEN HILL FORT Former 19th-c, fortified barracks block with splendid views from the battlements; military museum and visitors centre. Meals, snacks, shop, disabled access; cl Christmas; £1.50 (free in winter). The bay's famous Arch Rock collapsed into the sea a couple of years ago. The Red Lion is good for lunch, and the Vine has a pleasant terrace for warm days. There are fine walks nearby, and Hill Farm has riding.

🏮 **Gatcombe** SZ4984 A TOUCH OF GLASS Traditional glassworks, with demonstrations and a shop selling particularly fine examples of the craft. Disabled access; cl 1–1.30pm, studio cl wknds, 25–26 Dec; free. They also have a shop in Shanklin (cl Tues). The Chequers at Rookley is good for lunch.

★ † 🏮 ❀ ! 👶 **Godshill** SZ5281 is best appreciated in winter, when the coach parties that descend on the teahouses and quaint little streets have gone home. Plenty of famously pretty, thatched cottages, and a good 15th-c CHURCH, with an interesting, 15th-c wall painting. OLD SMITHY TOURIST CENTRE Local crafts, gifts and fashions, an aviary of exotic birds, herb garden, and a garden in the shape of the island itself – all centred around a former blacksmith's forge. Snacks, shop, disabled access; cl Sun Jan–Feb, 25–26 Dec, gardens cl end Oct–Easter; 80p. MODEL VILLAGE Shanklin, its Chine Valley and Godshill painstakingly recreated in miniature, and nicely floodlit summer eves. Shop, disabled access; cl Nov–Mar; *£2. NOSTALGIA TOY MUSEUM Lots of pre-war toys with plenty of die-cast model cars. Shop, disabled access; cl Sat, and Nov–Easter; (01983) 840181; 95p. There's also a NATURAL HISTORY CENTRE with collections of minerals, fossils and precious stones. Cl Nov–Mar; £1.25. The Chequers at Rookley is the nearest recommended place for lunch.

🚂 **Havenstreet** SZ5690 STEAM RAILWAY Restored by volunteers, the railway now runs a very pleasant 10-mile trip from Wootton to Smallbrook Junction (where it's possible to change directly on to BR). Many of the engines and much of the rolling stock is vintage and there's a display of memorabilia at the old gas works at Havenstreet station. Snacks, shop, disabled access if accompanied; phone for timetable, (01983) 882204; £4.50. A good way of saving money is to buy the BR Island Line ticket, which for £6.50 gives you a day's unlimited, standard class travel on all BR trains and the Steam Railway. The White Hart does good, generous food.

★ ⚘ ⌂ ❀ **Mottistone** SZ4083 is a charming old village with a well in the centre of the green, and even the bus shelter is made out of stone. The Bluebell Wood, opposite the church, is lovely in spring. MOTTISTONE MANOR Medieval and Elizabethan manor house, with fine gardens. Open pm Weds and bank hols Apr–Sept, poss more in summer; (01983) 740552; £3.60 house and garden, £1.80 garden only; NT. The Sun at Hulverstone nearby is lovely in summer.

✙ **Newchurch** SZ5685 is a quiet village with a photogenic church; the Pointer beside it has decent food. ISLAND AMAZON ADVENTURE The exotic birds and animals you'd find in an Amazon rainforest, with monkeys, spiders, flamingos, crocodile and other extremely odd-looking creatures in lively jungle and village settings. Children can tunnel their way into the parrot enclosure, and there's also a playground and pets corner. Snacks, shop, disabled access; (01983) 867122; *£3.25.

★ ⌂ ☕ ❀ ✝ ❀ **Newport** SZ4989 has a good deal of character, with some fine old Georgian houses, and warm, red-brick, 18th-c buildings down by the quay. It's the main place on the island for antique shops. ROMAN VILLA Well preserved baths and reconstructed rooms on the site of a 3rd-c Roman villa, and a well laid-out and informative museum housing finds from the site; also a Roman garden. Shop; cl Nov–Mar; (01983) 529720; £1.50. The parish CHURCH OF ST THOMAS is worth a look – it has an interestingly carved Jacobean pulpit and a memorial to Charles I's daughter, constructed on the orders of Queen Victoria. The 17th-c Wheatsheaf nearby is useful for lunch. The Quay Arts Centre (Sea St) usually has weekend antique and craft fairs, and in the Quay itself, a restored PIRATES' SHIP (used in the filming of the *Onedin Line*) has summer activities (at various prices) and tours for children.

⌂ ✙ ☕ ❀ ❀ **Newtown** SZ4390 was for a while in the Middle Ages the island's capital, but began a slow decline after a disastrous fire in 1377, and eventually faded out altogether – what used to be rich merchants' streets are now just grassy tracks. The OLD TOWN HALL, rebuilt in 1699 but now left stranded and unusually isolated from any houses, is all that's left to mark the once thriving town. Open pm Mon, Weds and Sun Apr–Sept, plus Tues and Thurs in July and Aug; £1; NT. There are rewarding walks for birdwatchers at the nearby NATURE RESERVE. Just out of town, the CLAMERKIN FARM PARK is a 30-acre working farm with lots of friendly animals, fine views, craft demonstrations and a golf-driving range. Meals, snacks, shop, disabled access; cl Oct–Easter; (01983) 531396; *£1.60. The New Inn at Shalfleet, open all day in summer, is popular for seafood.

⌂ ❀ ☕ ✝ **Osborne House** SZ5285 Queen Victoria's favourite house, and where she died in 1901; the state and private apartments haven't changed much since. Designed by Prince Albert with professional help from Thomas Cubitt to resemble an Italian villa, it's a striking place. The grounds are filled with every conceivable English tree, and a horse-drawn carriage conveys you in style to the Swiss cottage, where the royal children learnt cooking and gardening. Snacks, shop, disabled access to ground floor only; cl Nov–Mar; (01983) 200022; £5.50. Next to the house's fine GARDENS, which were originally laid out by Queen Victoria and Prince Albert, BARTON MANOR GARDENS AND VINEYARD covers about 10 acres, and is one of England's finest vineyards, with lovely gardens and plants, and the biggest rose-hedge maze on the island. A restored old farm building has awards and memorabilia from the famous shows and films the current owner has been involved with. Meals, snacks, shop, disabled access; cl from second Sun in Oct–Mar; (01983) 292835; £3.50: includes two tastings and a souvenir glass. You can buy a combined ticket for the vineyards and Osborne House. Nearby WHIPPINGHAM CHURCH SZ5193 is said to have been another of Prince Albert's designs, and is a good deal more eccentric: a bizarre mix of different styles. Down on the River Medina, the beautifully placed Folly Inn has an appropriately nautical atmosphere. There is nothing in East Cowes itself to lure a holiday visitor. ☺ **Ryde** SZ5992 is now the biggest town here, with a long triple pier, good sandy beaches, and a full set of holiday-resort amusements – just right for a straightforward family holiday.

🐏 ✔ 🐦 ✿ ❀ **St Lawrence** SZ5376 RARE BREEDS AND WATERFOWL PARK (Lisle Combe, Undercliff Drive) Good rare breeds centre in a really lovely setting, covering 30 secluded coastal acres. A wide range of animals includes unusual examples of cattle, sheep, pigs, otters, miniature horses, donkeys, goats, waterfowl and poultry to name a few, and as we went to press they were planning to add a herd of buffalo. Meals, snacks, shop, disabled access (they prefer notice); cl winter wkdys, 25 Dec; (01983) 852582; *£2.70. They do B & B in the attractive old house. TROPICAL BIRD PARK Over 400 birds in the beautiful grounds of Old Park, in the almost subtropical Undercliff. Snacks, shop, disabled access; cl 25 Dec; (01983) 852583; £2.50. The park also houses ISLE OF WIGHT GLASS, with demonstrations and displays, and a shop; no glass-making at wknds or Christmas; (01983) 853526; 50p. The St Lawrence Inn is a popular dining pub with superb Channel views.

♨ ☺ 🐦 🐖 **Sandown** SZ5984 has all the usual things for a family beach holiday – pier, boat trips, canoeing lake, discos – and a fine beach. MUSEUM OF GEOLOGY Interesting displays of the island's fossils and rocks, with recently excavated dinosaur fossils. Shop, some disabled access; cl Sun, 25–26 Dec; (01983) 404344; free. The ZOO has rare and endangered animals like tigers, panthers and leopards, as well as birds, spiders and snakes. Cl Nov–Easter exc Sun; £3.99. Nearby ADGESTONE VINEYARD was one of the country's first commercial vineyards; walks round vineyard and part-underground winery (booking essential), tastings. Shop;

cl pm Sat, Sun, Christmas; (01983) 402503; free.

❀ 🐦 ❀ **Seaview** SZ6291 is a quiet retreat, with sedate streets of unassuming villas; the Old Fort inn has lovely sea views, and the Seaview Hotel does very good lunches. Just out of town, FLAMINGO PARK has hundreds of birds in award-winning, spacious, landscaped grounds; some can be fed by hand. They have a very successful breeding record. Snacks, shop, disabled access; cl Nov–Easter; (01983) 612153; £3.50.

🦢 ♪ ❀ 🐖 ❀ **Shanklin** SZ5881 SHANKLIN CHINE Glorious natural gorge with a magnificent, 45-ft waterfall. A heritage centre gives details of rare flora, nature trails and life in Shanklin during Victorian times. Snacks, shop; cl mid-Oct–Easter; *£1.50. The adjoining RYLSTONE GARDENS have a COUNTRYSIDE CENTRE with details and displays of the island's landscape and wildlife. Shop, disabled access to ground floor; cl Oct–Jun (exc Easter and spring half-term hols); *£1. They also organise guided walks. Right down on the beach, the thatched Fisherman's Cottage is useful for lunch (open all day in season, cl Nov–Feb). At the other end of the small resort town, the thatched Crab Inn makes a pretty picture, and on the Esplanade the Longshoreman has good sea views and interesting local photographs, inc one of the pier – finally demolished in 1993.

★ † 🐖 ✗ **Shorwell** SZ4582, one of the few really pretty villages on the island to have escaped a flood of tourist interest, has charming, streamside thatched cottages and a fine church; the attractive Crown is very good for lunch. YAFFORD MILL FARM PARK is fun: a seal lives in a special enclosure beside the millpond of the working 18th-c watermill, various species of waterfowl dwell in the pools of the stream, and rare breeds of sheep and cattle graze along its banks; there are nature trails along the sides. Also, old farm machinery, wagons and traction engines (sometimes in steam) and an adventure playground across the lane. Meals, snacks, shop, disabled access;

cl 25 Dec; (01983) 62117; £2.40.

❀☙♓✝❀ **Ventnor** SZ5677 is an interesting place, with a proper, relatively untouristy little town up on the cliff, a fairly restrained and decorous seafront down below linked to it by a tortuously steep loop of road, and between them, perched on ledges among the trees, quite a number of Victorian villas – many of them still private houses rather than guesthouses. Its great pride, developed over the last two decades or so, is the BOTANIC GARDEN, where an exceptional collection of subtropical plants make the most of the mild climate; the Garden Tavern here has decent food. In the grounds (in fact, more correctly, under them), the MUSEUM OF SMUGGLING HISTORY has displays and tableaux showing the tricks smugglers have used over the past 700 years, whether they were sneaking in wool, brandy, tobacco or drugs, as well as the more general story of a trade that could be described as an early form of duty-free. Meals, snacks, shop; cl Oct–Easter; *£1.80. HERITAGE MUSEUM (Spring Hill) History of the town and surrounding area; cl 1–2 pm, pm Weds and Sat, all Sun; *40p. The LONGSHOREMAN'S MUSEUM (Esplanade) has more local history, as well as model boats and fossils. Shop, disabled access; cl Jan and Feb; *50p. The Spyglass is an excellent pub with superb sea views.

Nearby **Bonchurch** SZ5778 is much quieter, with leafy lanes hugging the steep slopes and passing an unexpected tree-shaded pond; steep steps connect the different levels, and there's a quiet cove down below the cliff. The small 13th-c CHURCH has a lovely peaceful graveyard, and above the cliff, St Boniface Down has tremendous views. The Bonchurch Inn is rather unusual, with its Italian landlord and food. For several miles along this section of coast, the cliffs have been and to some extent still are subject to massive landslides. The UNDERCLIFF along here is formed from the irregular masses of earth which have come to rest below, with often rocky chasms between each other and the cliff itself. Sometimes planted and sometimes with profuse natural vegetation, the resulting scenery is unlike anything else on the island, with quite a subtropical aspect. Some of the attractions along it we've listed under St Lawrence (see entry).

❧✝❀❀ **Wootton** SZ5492 is a terminus for the STEAM RAILWAY – see Havenstreet entry above. It has an attractive CHURCH, part-Norman. BUTTERFLY WORLD, besides a 5-acre garden centre, has free-flying butterflies in a subtropical house, koi carp, Italianate garden, and an insectarium. Snacks, shop, disabled access; cl Nov–Easter; (01983) 883430; £2.65. The Woodman's Arms is pleasant for lunch, as is the Sloop down overlooking the creek.

❧❀ **Wroxall** SZ5480 APPULDURCOMBE HOUSE Intriguing Palladian ruin, on the site of a 12th-c one, nestling among grounds beautifully landscaped by Capability Brown. You can still catch something of the atmosphere of the days when this was one of the grandest houses on the island. Snacks, shop; cl 1–2pm, Oct–Mar; (01983) 852484; *£1.20.

★❧❀❧♓⚓ **Yarmouth** SZ3589 is a lively place, its old harbour busy with yachts in summer. The CASTLE was built as part of Henry VIII's coastal defences; it's in an excellent state, and you can see the Master Gunner's surprisingly homely parlour and kitchen. Also local watercolours and photographs. Outside, the open gun platform has good views of the harbour. Shop; cl 1–2pm, Oct–Mar; (01983) 760678; £1.70. FORT VICTORIA COUNTRY PARK Overlooking the Solent, this country park surrounds the ruined 19th-c fort which was built to provide defence for Portsmouth, and includes 50 acres of woodland and about one mile of pebbly beach. In the grounds are a maritime heritage centre, aquarium (£1.50) and planetarium (£2.00); snacks, shop, disabled access (though not yet in the planetarium). Maritime heritage centre cl Oct–Easter, café and aquarium open wknds in winter period; (01983) 760860; park free. The Wheatsheaf here is popular for lunch, and the Bugle and George are both worthy old inns.

Walks

The island's coastal walks equal and perhaps surpass anything else in the south-east: these alone would justify coming here for a break. **Tennyson Down** SZ3285 ⌂-1 on Wight's western tip is the best place of all for walkers here: a friendly grassy ridge and cliff walk rolled into one, with views over most of the island and across to the mainland. You pass the memorial to Alfred Lord Tennyson (who lived nearby) and the walk culminates in spectacular fashion above The Needles SZ2984, a group of wave-battered chalk pinnacles. There's a choice of start points, depending on how long you want to walk for. A close one is Alum Bay SZ3483; or you can walk the entire ridge from Freshwater Bay SZ3485 (summer bus service from Alum Bay to ferry you back), or walk the coast from Totland SZ3286 over Headon Warren.

Compton Down SZ3785 ⌂-2 is another good place for walks on this south coast, a hogback grassy hill E of Freshwater Bay; circular walks can take in the coast path along Compton Bay. **St Catherine's Hill** SZ4977 ⌂-3, capped by the ruins of a 14th-c lighthouse, is a short walk up from the coast path further E. The path skirts the undercliff of St Catherine's Point SZ4875, the isle's southern tip, which has a modern working lighthouse; there are several other paths through the undercliff here. **Bonchurch Down** ⌂-4 above Ventnor SZ5677 is somewhat dominated by unsightly radar installations but gives fine views. The unspoilt reed-fringed **Yar estuary** ⌂-5 is skirted by a footpath along the former railway line south from Yarmouth SZ3589.

On the N coast, the **Newtown Nature Reserve** SZ4191 ⌂-6 has walks around the creeks of the Newtown/Clamerkin estuaries, but there are few circular routes; Newtown village SZ4290 is a good starting point. The E coast is heavily developed; the coastal path sometimes follows roads and skirts large residential areas, but walk opportunities exist around **Bembridge** SZ6488 ⌂-7, particularly S to Culver Cliff SZ6385.

Inland, the island is characterised by long curving chalk ridges (tracks often follow the crests) and forestry plantations (with many signposted woodland trails). The hills north of **Brighstone** SZ4282 ⌂-8 represent some of the pick of the scenery. The Countryman on Limerstone Rd is a good refreshment break, with fine views down to the sea; not far away the pretty thatched Sun in Hulverstone is another useful break. **Parkhurst Forest** SZ4890 ⌂-9, just W of the prison, is a couple of miles across, with plenty of paths and a good chance of seeing red squirrels.

Driving

The A3055 along the SE coast can, out of season, give the quite pleasurable feeling of driving out into the back of beyond, and starts by dropping down from a splendid viewpoint below St Catherine's Hill (nervous drivers may or may not be reassured to know that this road has tiltmeters built into it, which are supposed to give automatic warning if there's a suddenly increased risk of a landslip dumping the road into the sea). The A3055 also has some fine sea and coast views best when driving from Ventnor to Shanklin. From Brading the road out over Bembridge Down to Culver Cliff has good views on the way, and ends at an isolated pub (the Culver Haven) which has terrific views in virtually all directions.

Inland, most of the roads give quietly attractive views, but particularly good are the back road between Brading and Newport – the one that tracks virtually the whole way down the island from Wootton Bridge through Downend to pass Bohemia Corner and track on down to Niton – and the one from Brighstone in to Calbourne.

Where to eat

Shorwell SZ4582 CROWN (01983) 740293 The big back garden with its trout-filled stream, ducks, doves and lilies is a really lovely place to eat in summer, and there's a small beamed two-roomed lounge with log fire, good food, and friendly staff; partial disabled access. £12.50/£1.60/£3.95.

Shalfleet NEW INN (01983) 78314 Engagingly traditional and partly flagstoned bar with roaring log fire, stripped stone dining lounge, no-smoking restaurant, good fresh fish dishes, and friendly staff; cl Sun. £1.95/£4.50.

Yarmouth SZ3589 WHEATSHEAF Bridge Rd (01983) 760456 Four comfortable and spacious eating areas with wide choice of good food (daily specials are the best choice), well kept beers and quick, friendly service. £1.95/£6.

Help this year from: B M Eldridge, Nigel Gibbs, HNJ, PEJ, Chris and Kim Elias, David Sweeney, Reg Nelson, Harry Hall, the Bailey family, Phil and Heidi Cook, Michael and Harriet Robinson, David White, Jack Barnwell.

ISLE OF WIGHT CALENDAR

Some of these dates were provisional as we went to press.

FEBRUARY

28 **Yarmouth** Pancake Races

APRIL

15 **Yarmouth** Easter Bonnet Parade (01983) 760108

MAY

1 **Arreton** Living History at Arreton Manor – *till Fri 19* (01983) 528134; **Newport** May Day Ceilidh and Morris men at Longstone, Mottistone Down (01983) 822300

4 **Newport** International Oboe Competition at Medina Theatre – *till Sun 7* (01983) 612451

6 **Shorwell** Military Vehicles and Traction Engines at Yafford Mill – *till Mon 8* (01983) 740610

8 **Niton** Island's Most Amazing Tea Party at Blackgang Chine (01983) 730330

13 **Sandown** Branstone Farm Open Day (01983) 865540

18 **Ventnor** Music for Fun Festival at the Winter Gardens – *till Sun 28* (01983) 852859

28 **Niton** Pirate Fiesta at Blackgang Chine (01983) 730330

29 **Ventnor** Crab Fayre at Ventnor Botanic Garden (01983) 853824

JUNE

3 **Ventnor** Smuggling Pageant – *till Wed 7* (01983) 853690

9 **Binstead** Isle of Wight Heavy Horse Festival at Brickfields Horsecountry and IOW Shire Horse Centre – *till Mon 12* (01983) 566801

10 **Cowes** Round the Island Yacht Race (01983) 296621

23 **Newport** Folk Festival at the Riverside Centre – *till Sun 25* (01983) 822300

ISLE OF WIGHT CALENDAR

JULY

21 **Northwood** Royal Isle of Wight Agricultural Society County Show at the Northwood Showground (01983) 524343

22 **Freshwater** Carnival (01983) 752904; **Newport** Randy (01983) 531396

26 **Sandown** Carnival (01983) 402024

28 **nr Brighstone** Jazz at Mottistone Manor Garden – *till Sat 29* (01983) 526445

29 **Cowes** Week – *till 6 Aug* (01983) 293303; **Shorwell** Traction Engine Rally at Yafford Mill – *till Sun 30* (01983) 740610

AUGUST

5 **Yarmouth** Carnival – *till procession on Sat 12* (01983) 760108

9 **Cowes** Festival – *till Mon 28* (01983) 295425

12 **Shorwell** Transport Through the Ages at Yafford Mill – *till Sun 13* (01983) 740610

13 **Arreton** Pageant at Arreton Manor (01983) 528134; **Sandown** Bay Regatta (01983) 406808

16 **Shanklin** Regatta at the Esplanade (01983) 862942

19 **Newchurch** Garlic Festival at the Fighting Cocks Cross Roads on A3056 – *till Sun 20* (01983) 865573

27 **Ryde** Carnival – *till 2 Sept* (01983) 566461

28 **St Helens** Carnival and Sports Day (01983) 522577

30 **Sandown** Illuminated Carnival (01983) 402024

SEPTEMBER

2 **Shorwell** Military Vehicle Rally at Yafford Mill – *till Sun 3* (01983) 740610

NOVEMBER

4 **St Helens** Bonfire (01983) 522577

5 **Niton** Giant Bonfire and Fireworks at Robin Hill Country Park (01983) 730330; **Yarmouth** Guy Fawkes Celebrations in the Square

DECEMBER

31 **Carisbrooke** New Year's Eve Ceilidh (01983) 822300

KENT

East Kent has many very rewarding places to visit, especially in Canterbury and Dover, including plenty to interest families. Its coast has several traditional resorts. The west of Kent is quite a good area for an adult break, with charming houses and gardens to visit, villages with attractive tile-hung and weatherboarded dwellings and old stone-built churches, a good smattering of antique shops, teashops and so forth, and the attractive Wealden countryside of little hills and valleys, oak woods and some peaceful far views.

There's a reasonable choice of places to stay in both halves of the county – rather wider, as is the choice of places to eat, in the west than the east.

CANTERBURY AND EAST KENT

Very good family attractions and some pleasant coastal resorts in this part of the county; Canterbury and Dover both well worth visiting.

Canterbury has many fine buildings besides the cathedral itself, and two interesting heritage centres. Elsewhere, there are many interesting places to visit, including plenty attractive to families: best among them are Dover Castle and the heritage centre there, enjoyable zoos at Bekesbourne and Lympne, the tropical bird park at Blean, and the famously quaint Romney Hythe & Dymchurch Railway. Two rewarding new entries this year are the extraordinary little-visited collections at Birchington, and the relatively unknown Godinton Park stately home at Ashford. The coast has some pleasant resorts dating from pre-railway Victorian days, when boats brought well-to-do Londoners down the coast. When the early coastbound railways took people further afield, these forerunners – most notably Broadstairs – settled into a tranquillity that at least to a degree they've kept till today.

The inland countryside is generally less picturesque than in the west of the county. In April and early May the remaining apple and cherry orchards still light up the scenery with their blossom (tall windbreak trees tend to interrupt the views later), and the many farm shops have local apples from September onwards – a fine time to visit the extraordinary collection of rare apple and other fruit varieties at the Brogdale Trust near Faversham. The flatlands of Romney Marsh in the south have a certain bypassed-by-time appeal.

Where to stay

Boughton Lees TR0247 EASTWELL MANOR Eastwell Park, Boughton Lees, Ashford TN25 4HR (01233) 635751 £120; 23 prettily decorated, spacious rms. Fine Jacobean-style manor (actually built in the 1920s) in 62 acres of private grounds; grand oak-panelled rooms, open fires, comfortable leather seating, fresh flowers, very good service and outstanding food in atmospheric restaurant; snooker, croquet, pitch-and-putt, riding, tennis and lots of walks; disabled access.

Chartham TR1054 THRUXTED OAST Mystole, Chartham, Canterbury CT4 7BX (01227) 730080 *£75; 3 charming rms. 4 miles from Canterbury, this carefully converted 18th-c oast house is surrounded by hop gardens and orchards, with pretty terrace and croquet; breakfast served in big farmhouse kitchen; picture-framing workshop and fine country walks; cl 24–26 Dec; children by arrangement.

Canterbury TR1557 FALSTAFF 8–12 St Dunstan's St, Canterbury CT2 8AF (01227) 462138 £65; 24 rms. Partly 16th-c coaching inn close to Westgate Tower with open fires and beams, polished oak furniture, comfortable lounge, and decent food.

Canterbury TR1557 THANINGTON 140 Wincheap, Canterbury CT1 3RY (01227) 453227 £58; 10 rms linked to main building by Georgian-style conservatory. Thoughtfully run and warmly welcoming hotel, with elegant little rooms, games room, walled garden, and indoor swimming pool; cl Christmas.

St Margaret's at Cliffe TR3644 CLIFFE TAVERN St Margaret's at Cliffe, Dover CT15 6AT (01304) 852749 £54.80; 12 rms, most in two little cottages across yard from main pub. Series of 17th-c buildings opposite the church, with pleasant lounge, good, popular food, large breakfasts, and quiet garden; very handy for ferries.

Canterbury TR1557 CATHEDRAL GATE 36 Burgate, Canterbury CT1 2HA (01227) 464381 £54; 24 rms, some with own bthrm and some overlooking cathedral. 15th-c hotel with bow windows, massive oak beams, sloping floors, antiques and fresh flowers, and a quiet, restful atmosphere.

St Margaret's at Cliffe TR3644 WALLETT'S COURT St Margaret's at Cliffe, Dover CT15 6EW (01304) 852424 *£50; 10 rms, 2 in recently converted stable block with gentle views. Fine old manor house with 13th-c cellars, beams, antiques and comfortable seating, helpful service, and marvellous food; cl 4 days over Christmas; very close to ferries.

Faversham TR0161 FRITH FARM HOUSE Otterden, Faversham ME13 0DD (01795) 890701 £45; 3 pretty rms. Fine restored Georgian house with comfortable sitting room, delicious food in lovely dining room, conservatory breakfast room, and friendly owners; garden with views over orchards and woods; children over 12; riding available.

Barham TR2050 DUKE OF CUMBERLAND Barham, Canterbury CT4 6NY (01227) 831396 £35; 3 rms. Pleasant and spacious 2-bar local with big helpings of good-value straightforward lunchtime food and more elaborate evening meals; caravan site.

To see and do

Canterbury TR1557 is one of the most satisfying places to visit in the country. Though redevelopment after WWII air-raid damage has been rather unsympathetic, there is still a wealth of historic buildings tucked away in surviving narrow medieval streets. Much of the centre is pedestrianised, with good car parks on the fringes of the old centre. Interesting guided walks leave from the Visitor Information Centre, 34 St Margaret's St; if you're making your own way, don't miss Palace St, Burgate with the Buttermarket Sq, and St Peter's St, all of which have fine buildings, and you can follow quite a lot of the ancient city wall on a walk passing the Norman castle (not open). The city's Roman and ecclesiastical heritage is well known, but there are other remains here too, notably a prehistoric tumulus in Dane John Garden. The Canterbury Tales (just off St Peter's St) is the best pub here for lunch; the smart Falstaff Hotel (St Dunstan's St), Cricketers (St Peter's St), Flying Horse (Upper Bridge St) and White Hart (Castle Row) are also good; the last has a garden.

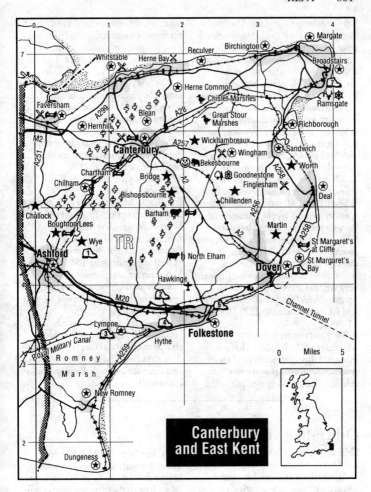

Canterbury and East Kent

✝ The famous CATHEDRAL
spectacularly lives up to expectations
– for the most overwhelming first
impression, it's best approached from
Queningate. The earliest parts are
Norman, with much added in the
15th c. Rewarding features are
everywhere – an airily impressive
nave, fascinating stained glass, the
Bell Harry Tower, lovely cloisters,
and the shrine of Thomas Becket,
murdered here in the 12th c. In the
crypt are some wonderfully grotesque
carvings, full of strange animals and
fantastic fighting monsters. The
church is dramatically floodlit in
summer, and has concerts throughout
the year. Shop, disabled access; may
be closed for services at certain times,
limited opening Sun; charges for
audio-visual show and guided or
Walkman tours. The ruins of the
former monastery can be seen in
Green Court in the cathedral
precincts, which include many fine
buildings related to the cathedral and
the impressive Norman Staircase. Not
far outside is the medieval King's
School (The Borough). More ruins
can be seen at ST AUGUSTINE'S ABBEY
(Longport) founded at the end of the
6th c and rebuilt in the 11th; it's
mostly the remains of the medieval
Benedictine abbey you can see today.
Shop, disabled access; cl 24–26 Dec, 1
Jan; £1.50.

Ͱᗲ CANTERBURY HERITAGE MUSEUM
(Stour St) Housed in the fine medieval
Poor Priests Hospital, a splendid
interpretation of the city's history, told
with deft use of lavish and up-to-date
display technology (inc holograms),
leaving many vivid visual impressions
– one of the most rewarding places in
the south-east. Shop, disabled access
to ground floor only; cl Sun (exc pm
Jun–Oct), Good Fri and Christmas
wk; (01227) 452747; £1.50. Hidden
away through an arch beside the
building is the charming Greyfriars,
above the River Stour.

ᗲ The ROMAN MUSEUM (Longmarket)
is underground, by the remains of a
Roman town house, and has good
lively reconstructions of a market and
aromatic kitchen, and hi-tech
displays. You can touch various
relics, and the house's mosaic floor is
very well displayed. Shop, disabled
access; cl Sun (exc Jun–Oct), Good Fri
and Christmas wk; (01227) 785575;
£1.50.

Ͱ THE CANTERBURY TALES (St
Margaret's St) Chaucer's characters
brought enthusiastically to life with
smells, sound effects and lively
celebrity voices. Very well put
together, though perhaps a little
pricey. Meals, snacks, good unusual
shop, disabled access (prior notice
preferred); cl 25 Dec; (01227)
454888; £4.50.

ᗲ WEST GATE MUSEUM (where St
Peter's St meets St Dunstan's St) The
city's last remaining fortified
gatehouse, built in the late 14th c,
with arms and armour, interesting
cells, and excellent views from the
battlements. Children can try on
replica armour. Shop; cl
12.30–1.30pm, Sun, Good Fri,
Christmas wk; 60p.

ᗲ▣ ROYAL MUSEUM, ART GALLERY AND
BUFFS REGIMENTAL MUSEUM (High St)
Fine porcelain, glass, clocks and
watches, and local archaeology inc
Roman and Anglo-Saxon jewellery,
as well as paintings by TS Cooper, the
Victorian animal painter; cl Sun,
Good Fri and Christmas wk; free. The
remains of the Norman castle are also
worth a look.

✝ ST MARTIN'S CHURCH (North
Holmes Rd) is the country's oldest
church in continual use; the Venerable
Bede says it was built by the Romans,
and there are certainly Roman bricks
in the walls.

Other things to see and do

🏚▣ ❀ **Ashford** TR0042 The town
itself is not a draw for visitors, but just
W GODINTON PARK (off A20) is a
rewarding old house, relatively
undiscovered by tourists, with
excellent guided tours. Highlights are
the Jacobean carving and panelling,
fine collections of 17th and 18th-c
porcelain, furnishings and paintings
(inc works by Lely and Reynolds),
14th-c hall with hammer-beamed
roof, and formal gardens with
topiary; open Easter wknd then Sun
and bank hols Jun–Sept; (01233)
620773; *£2.

🥕 **Barham** TR2050 ELHAM VALLEY
VINEYARDS Friendly little vineyard in
pretty sheltered valley; self-guided
tours of grounds and winery
producing award-winning still and
sparkling wines. Tastings and sales,
disabled access; cl Mon (exc bank
hols), Jan–Mar; (01227) 831266; £2.
The beautifully set Dolls House is
good value for lunch, and the village is
quite close to the farm heritage centre
at North Elham (see entry below).

🐾 ☺ **Bekesbourne** TR1955 HOWLETTS
WILD ANIMAL PARK Excellent animal
park, well spread out over lovely
grounds. They have the world's
largest colony of breeding gorillas, as
well as tigers, deer, antelope,
leopards, bison and the only herd of
breeding elephants in the country.
Readers rate it very highly, and
there's lots for children, who love it.
Meals, snacks, shop, limited
disabled access; cl 25 Dec; (01303)
264944; £6.50. The same people run
the Port Lympne Wild Animal Park at
Lympne (see entry below), and their
genuine devotion and dedication to
their animals is striking. Evenhill

House in nearby Littlebourne is good for lunch, and the Bow Window Hotel and King William IV there are both useful too.

🏠 ❀ ♿ **Birchington** TR3069 Quex House and Gardens and Powell-Cotton Museum One of Kent's most fascinating but least known museums, attached to a fine Regency house with furnished period rooms. Nine galleries display the collections of Victorian explorer and naturalist Major Powell-Cotton, with hundreds of well mounted animals, native artefacts, oriental art, firearms and cannons. They're restoring the walled gardens, and the grounds have an odd early 19th-c bell tower with bizarre wrought-iron spire (open last Sun of summer months only). Summer snacks, shop, disabled access; open pm Weds, Thurs, Sun and bank hols Apr–Oct, plus Tues July–Sept and Fri Aug, and Sun Mar, Dec and Jan; (01843) 842168; *£2.50. The Morton's Fork Hotel down at Minster does good lunches.

🐦 ♿ ✿ **Blean** TR1260 Blean Bird Park Friendly, family-run place with lots of exotic tropical birds flying free in natural settings. They have the biggest collection of breeding macaws, cockatoos and parakeets in England, as well as owls, peacocks, animals and woodland walks. Snacks, shops (they sell parrots), disabled access; cl 25–26 Dec; (01227) 471666; *£2.75. Nearby Blean Woods TR0860 are protected as a nature reserve, with well signed walks in the RSPB area. The Dove over at Dargate does decent food.

★ 🏠 ❀ ♿ **Broadstairs** TR3967 Appealingly unspoilt seaside resort, attractively meandering up among the trees on the low hill behind, with pleasant gardens, old-fashioned bathing-huts on its beach, and a good relaxed atmosphere. There are fishing boats and yachts in the lively little harbour, seven sandy bays, refreshing clifftop walks and lots of Dickens connections ('Our watering place', he called the town). Bleak House Dickens Maritime and Smuggling Museum (Fort Rd) The author's favourite seaside residence, where he wrote David Copperfield, and from

which he found the title for another novel. Lots of his belongings and related memorabilia, as well as displays on local wrecks and smuggling. Snacks, shop, some disabled access; cl Nov–Feb; (01843) 62224; £1.75. Dickens House Museum (Victoria Parade) Former home of Miss Mary Strong, the basis for Betsey Trotwood in David Copperfield – the parlour is furnished as in the book. Also some of Dickens' letters and possessions. Shop; cl am, 3rd wk in Oct–Mar; 80p.

★ ❀ 🍴 ♿ ✿ **Chilham** TR0653 This lovely village square is the prettiest in Kent, and several antique shops reflect its popularity with visitors – in summer, get there early to catch it at its most photogenic. Chilham Castle Gardens has been worth visiting, but the owners aren't sure whether they will be opening them this year; (01227) 766567 to check. The perfectly placed White Horse, and the Woolpack just down the hill, are useful for lunch. Nearby Badgers Hill Farm and Cidery is a cheerily unspoilt spot, with cider-making, local crafts, free-roaming pigs (you may find them in the shop) and other animals, unusual garden ideas, picnic and play areas, pick-your-own fruit, and anything else the friendly family in charge decide to try their hand at. Shop (with lots of home-made produce), disabled access; cl Jan; (01227) 730573; free.

🐦 **Chislet Marshes** TR2366 have thousands of geese and ducks; duck food by the bag from the nice little Gate Inn at Boyden Gate TR2265.

★ 🏰 ❀ ♿ **Deal** TR3752 Pleasantly understated seaside resort, full of nice little streets and alleys; once the busiest harbour town in the south-east, and Caesar's landing point in 55 BC. Deal Castle The biggest in Henry VIII's chain of coastal defences, shaped like a Tudor rose with every wall rounded to deflect shot. Good Walkman tour; snacks, shop; in winter cl 1–2pm and Mon and Tues; (01304) 372762; £2. Built at the same time and for the same reason, Walmer Castle later became the official residence of the Lords Warden of the Cinque Ports (inc the Duke of Wellington, who left behind his famous boot). It's more a stately home than a fortress, with rooms furnished in 18th-c style, and pretty gardens laid out mainly by a niece of William Pitt the Younger. Snacks, shop; cl winter Mon and Tues, all Jan and Feb; (01304) 364288; £3. TIME-BALL TOWER Museum of time, telegraphy and maritime communication, with working time-ball dropping on the hour every day. Shop; cl Mon, and usually Sept–May; £1.10. The Ship (Middle St) is useful for lunch, as is the Rising Sun nr the beach in Kingsdown.

🏰🏮✝🕯🕯♻⚓⚓✕🏛 **Dover** TR3141 The busiest ferry port in Europe, Dover is not in itself an attractive town but has several extremely interesting places to visit, reflecting the fascinating history it owes to its strategic importance. A useful way of exploring is with the Passport to Dover scheme, which gets you into the main attractions more cheaply. Top of anyone's list must be DOVER CASTLE, a magnificent and excellently preserved Norman fortress with its original keep, 242-ft well and massive walls and towers. There's a lot to see, with a lively collection of secret-agent gadgetry, regimental museum, and Hellfire Corner, the atmospheric complex of underground tunnels that played a vital role in WWII. Close by is the PHAROS TOWER, a Roman lighthouse using a 4-floor flaring brazier as a guide-light; there's a restored SAXON CHURCH right beside it. Meals, snacks, shop, disabled access; cl 24–26 Dec, 1 Jan; £5.25. From the castle there are interesting views of the comings and goings down in the harbour, and out to sea. The top and bottom of the famous cliffs are linked by the GRAND SHAFT, an unusual spiral stone staircase; open Weds–Sun Jun–Aug; £1. WHITE CLIFFS EXPERIENCE (Market Sq) Splendidly lively interactive museum telling the story of the port from the Romans to WWII. It's quite big, with a lot to do – you can row in a Roman galley, talk to soldiers or walk through a 1944 blitzed street. Snacks, shop, disabled access; cl 25

Dec; (01304) 214566; £4.99. The same site also has a MUSEUM with more conventional displays. OLD TOWN GAOL (High St) Experience life behind bars in a Victorian prison, with hi-tech effects recreating courtroom scenes and cell life. They'll even lock you (albeit briefly) in a tiny cell – just right for teasing children. Shop, disabled access; cl am Sun, Mon and Tues Oct–May, Christmas; (01304) 242766; £3.20. CRABBLE CORN MILL (Lower Rd) Beautifully restored working 19th-c watermill, still producing the flour that used to serve the troops. Snacks (made using their own flour), shop; open Weds–Sun May–Sept, plus wknds Oct and Apr and Sun Nov and Mar; (01304) 823292; £2. ROMAN PAINTED HOUSE (New St) Well preserved remains of Roman hotel with unique wall paintings and panels, and elaborate underfloor heating system. Shop, disabled access; cl Mon (exc bank hols), Nov–Mar; (01304) 203279; *£1.50. Blakes (Castle St) is useful for lunch.

⚓⚓✝♻🏮❀ **Dungeness** TR0916 is fascinatingly odd, a real curiosity and quite foreign-feeling, its acres of shingle colonised by fishing shacks and railway carriages converted into homes (Derek Jarman used to live here). It is a terminus for the little steam railway described under New Romney. DUNGENESS INFORMATION CENTRE AND POWER STATIONS Tours of either the A or the B power station, with hi-tech interactive displays, videos, models and nature trail. Snacks, shop, disabled access to visitor centre only; cl Sat Nov–Mar, 5 days over Christmas; no children under 5, as everyone has to wear a hard hat; (01679) 21815; free. The RSPB NATURE RESERVE on the shingle headland is interesting for its unusual plants and in late spring for the nesting terns; cl Tues; £1. The Pilot right on the beach is useful for lunch, and a stroll away from OLD DUNGENESS LIGHTHOUSE, which has fine views from the top (167 steps); cl wkdys Nov–Mar; £1.

★🏮♻✕🍺🏮❀ **Faversham** TR0161 Delightfully photogenic small town ideal for a stroll, plenty of colour-washed timbered old buildings such as the Elizabethan grammar school and the Guildhall (one of the few raised market halls still to shelter stallholders in the pillared market court beneath it – Tues, Fri and Sat). In another 16th-c building, the very good FLEUR DE LIS HERITAGE CENTRE, all the better for the impetus given it by enthusiastic volunteers, has an audio-visual show, colourful displays, reconstructions and a working vintage-telephone exchange. Shop (good for books on Kent), disabled access to ground floor only; cl Sun Nov–Mar; (01795) 534542; *£1 for museum. Walking tours of Faversham leave here at 10.30am every Sat Apr–Sept and cost £1. CHART GUNPOWDER MILLS (Westbrook Walk) Well restored old gunpowder mills, reputedly the last left in the country. Shop, limited disabled access; open pm wknds and bank hols Easter–Oct; £1. Reads is very good for lunch; the Elephant is also good. BROGDALE TRUST (Brogdale Rd) Mammoth fruit farm, beautiful but baffling to stroll through, its 30 acres of orchards producing hundreds of distinct varieties of every hardy fruit imaginable; there are 2,500 variants of apple alone. They also hold the National Fruit Collections, and are developing gardens to show how fruit farming has changed over the centuries. The shop sells trees, bushes, and plenty of examples of their crop – from pears, plums and cherries to cobnuts, quinces and medlars. Meals, snacks, shop, disabled access; cl Mon, Tues and Dec–Mar; (01795) 535286; *£2. Four miles W of town BELMONT is a pleasant 18th-c mansion in well placed parkland, with a walled garden, and collection of unusual clocks – one looks like a church steeple. Snacks, shop, disabled access; open pm wknds and bank hols Easter–Sept; (01795) 890202; £3.80. A track off the road to Oare leads to a remote waterside pub, the Shipwrights Arms: charming setting on summer evenings.

✝ 🏠 ✿ ❀ ⏰ ! ☺ ⬆️ 🏛 **Folkestone** TR2336 The second major cross-Channel port has developed a lot in the last 200 years. There is an intact pre-19th-c area called the Bayle around the interesting old CHURCH – very pretty and Kentish. Though the part around the harbour, previously a picturesque warren, was badly bombed in WWII, the fish stalls there contribute authentic local colour, and the Old High St has a certain Cornish-type quaintness. The remains known as CAESAR'S CAMP in fact long predate the Roman invasion. Particularly pleasant is a walk along the Leas, a clifftop expanse of lawns and flower gardens with good views. MUSEUM & ART GALLERY The town's history from fossils to WWII, with ceramics and glass, regular art exhibitions; cl Sun and bank hols; free. You can watch sweet and rock making at ROWLANDS CONFECTIONERY on the Old High St; cl Weds; free. The ROTUNDA AMUSEMENT PARK is a traditional fairground, with lots undercover, and a big market Sun and bank hols. The Lifeboat (North St) and old-fashioned British Lion (by the parish church) are good for lunch. EUROTUNNEL EXHIBITION CENTRE (out of town by M20, beyond Cheriton TR1936) By now the Channel Tunnel should be well and truly open, and the background and design of this remarkable achievement are well explained here, with lots of lively interactive displays. One simulates tunnel trips by car, bike or train. Meals and snacks (in French-style café), shop, disabled access; cl 25–26 Dec; (01303) 270111; £3.60. They also do coach trips from the centre around the Tunnel terminal itself; £2.50. Out here, the Master Brewer is handy for lunch. Also on the W edge of town, SANDGATE CASTLE is a well restored Tudor fortress right beside the sea; the grounds are a lovely place for a stroll. They do good Sunday lunches; open by appointment only, (01303) 221717; no charge, donations welcome. The nearby Clarendon (Brewers Lane, off the Hythe rd) does good cheap food.

✿ 🐌 **Goodnestone** TR2553 GOODNESTONE PARK Old-fashioned roses in traditional walled garden recalling Jane Austen's stays in the fine 18th-c house (not open); also woodland garden with good trees. Teas Weds and Sun May–Aug, nursery, disabled access; cl Tues and Sat, Sun in Oct, and Nov–Mar; (01304) 840107; £2. The Griffin's Head at Chillenden has decent food.

🐦 **Great Stour Marshes** TR2262 are interesting for their thousands of geese and ducks; access from the good Grove Ferry pub just off the A28 near Upstreet TR2263.

✈ **Hawkinge** TR2139 KENT BATTLE OF BRITAIN MUSEUM Plenty of aeroplanes, and extensive collection of relics and memorabilia of British and German aircraft involved in the fighting; also uniforms and full-sized reconstructions. They should have a new hangar ready by summer this year. Snacks, shop, some disabled access; cl Nov–Easter; (01303) 893140; £2.50.

✗ **Herne Bay** TR1768 is a decorous and spaciously laid out 19th-c resort. HERNE WINDMILL Early Kentish smock mill built at the end of the 17th c, much of the original machinery still working after an enthusiastic restoration. Shop; open pm Sun and bank hols April–Sept, plus pm Thurs and Sat summer hols; (01227) 361326; *75p. Other working windmills at Stelling Minnis TR1446, Willesborough TR0241 (open pm wknds and bank hols May–Oct; *£1), and Wittersham TQ8927 (open pm Sun and bank hols Jun–Sept, 50p).

🐐 🐘 🐑 ✾ **Herne Common** TR1865 BRAMBLES WILDLIFE PARK Cheery 20-acre woodland park with lots of animals inc deer, owls, foxes, wallabies and wildcats; also small rare-breed farm and indoor garden. Children should enjoy feeding the lop-eared rabbit. Snacks, shop, disabled access; cl Nov–Easter; (01227) 712379; *£2.40.

✾ 🐐 🐘 ✾ 🌿 ★ **Hernhill** TR0660 MOUNT EPHRAIM GARDENS Seven acres of pleasant gardens, with Japanese rock garden, topiary garden, water-garden, woodland walk and small vineyard; good views. Snacks, shop; cl Tues, Oct–mid-Apr; (01227) 751496; *£2. There's a craft centre on Sun (exc July). By the church and small green of this charming village, the ancient Red

Lion is good for lunch.

🐘 🏠 ✾ ✾ 🏛 **Lympne** TR1135 PORT LYMPNE WILD ANIMAL PARK, MANSION AND GARDENS 300-acre park spun off from Howletts (see Bekesbourne above) as the collection grew. Hundreds of rare animals inc the only pair of Sumatran rhinos in the western world, as well as elephants, wolves, leopards, monkeys, and gorillas. The handsome and well restored house includes the Hexagonal Library used to sign the Treaty of Paris after WWI and the incredible Tent Room by Rex Whistler, and the landscaped gardens are exemplary, with broad views over Romney Marsh, and beyond to the sea. Meals, snacks, shop; cl 25 Dec; (01303) 264646; *£6.50. LYMPNE CASTLE Fortified medieval manor house remodelled in Edwardian times, with various exhibitions and good views from Norman tower; cl occasional Sats and Oct–Easter; (01303) 267571; *£3. The Botolphs Bridge Inn just S has decent home cooking.

❗ ✾ 🍴 🏠 ☺ ✗ **Margate** TR3571 Often rather brash seaside resort, but plenty of fun for families, and excellent sandy beaches. An unexpected puzzle is the SHELL GROTTO (Grotto Hill), 2,000 sq ft of winding underground passages and exquisitely decorated tunnels leading to a mysterious ancient shell temple, thought to be the only one in the world. No one really knows its origins or what it was for. Shop; cl Nov–Mar; (01843) 220008; *£1. Similarly atmospheric are the MARGATE CAVES nearby, huge caverns with wall-paintings and spooky shapes and shadows; times and price as Grotto. The Old Town Hall has a good local history MUSEUM, and nearby is a very well preserved TUDOR HOUSE, closed to visitors at the moment, but still worth a look from outside. DREAMLAND THEME PARK is a good fairground, with the tallest big wheel in Britain. To the E of town on College Rd there's a working WINDMILL.

🚂 ☺ ★ ✈ **New Romney** TR0624 ROMNEY HYTHE & DYMCHURCH RAILWAY The world's smallest-scale public railway, with 13½ miles of 15in-gauge track between Hythe and

Dungeness. The station has a toy and model museum with two magnificent model railways. Snacks, shop, disabled access (they prefer notice); cl Oct–Mar; Santa Specials in Dec; (01797) 362353; fares start at around £2, £7.30 full fare. The hillside town of HYTHE TR1634 is itself well worth a look, with attractive old houses in its narrow High St and the pretty lanes around the church. Its beach stretches up to Sandgate, which is also pleasant to stroll through (with a couple of decent pubs, the Ship and, closer to Hythe itself, the Clarendon tucked up a steep cobbled track above the sea; the Lord Nelson in Hythe is also useful). Inland, ROMNEY MARSH is the most unspoilt corner of Kent, flat country laced with drainage ditches and isolated farmsteads: St Mary in the Marsh has a small but attractive church, and a good flagstoned pub – the Star. If you don't want to penetrate the Marsh quite so deeply, near Brookland TQ9825 (see West Kent map) on the main A259 (actually on Walland Marsh) the sign to the Woolpack leads you to a particularly good pub with the right sort of atmosphere for the area. Standing quite alone in the marshes FAIRFIELD CHURCH TQ9626 is a tent-roofed brick-and-timber building, remarkable for its utterly lonely surroundings – and attractive inside.

🐏 ♪ **North Elham** TR1844 PARSONAGE FARM Nicely unspoilt rural heritage centre dating from medieval times, with traditional and rare breeds, cereal production, nature trails, and old agricultural equipment. Snacks, shop, disabled access; cl Mon (exc bank hols), Oct–Easter; (01303) 840356; £2.50. The Kings Arms at Elham is useful for lunch.

★ ✿ **Ramsgate** TR3865 A quiet and civilised seaside resort, with some elegantly colonnaded Georgian buildings and other fine houses up on the cliffs (Pugin, the architect of the Houses of Parliament, designed the church – where he's buried – and the house next door), and a historic harbour (bustling now with its yacht marina and Hoverport). In a handsome early 19th-c clock-house in the harbour, the MARITIME MUSEUM looks at the seafaring heritage of East Kent, with a collection of historic ships and boats (some by prior arrangement only). Shop; cl wknds Oct–Mar; (01843) 587765; *£1.

🏰 ✝ ✿ **Reculver** TR2269 The 3rd-c ROMAN FORT was well preserved until the 18th c, when cliff erosion caused some of it to collapse into the sea; there are still some bits, though it's the proud pair of tall Saxon towers of the former church on the mound above the beach that stay in the memory. Surrounding these remains is a COUNTRY PARK, with a good visitor centre; (012273) 66444; free.

🏰 🏛 ⬛ **Richborough** TR3260 RICHBOROUGH CASTLE Ruined Roman castle, lots of walls and foundations and a museum about the site. Snacks, shop, disabled access; cl Nov–Mar; £1.80 (Walkman tours for a small extra charge).

✿ ⬛ 🏛 **St Margaret's Bay** TR3844 PINES GARDEN AND BAY MUSEUM Six acres of trees, shrubs, flowers and an ornamental lake, with a little local history museum. Disabled access; museum cl am, all Mon and Fri, bank hol wknds and Sept–May, garden cl 25 Dec; (01304) 852764; *£1. The SOUTH FORELAND LIGHTHOUSE on top of the cliffs has an exhibition on Marconi, who used it in his early radio experiments; open pm wknds and bank hols Apr–Oct; £1.50; NT. The spectacularly sited Coastguard is useful for refreshments.

★ ✝ ✗ ⬛ **Sandwich** TR3358 is a pleasant quiet town with a surprising number of medieval remains, including some sections of the old town wall and three handsome medieval CHURCHES, one part-Norman. In its day it was one of England's main commercial ports; the sea's now left it far behind. The best timbered buildings are in Strand St, with some by the attractive former quay on the River Stour (the old Bargate is very photogenic). As we went to press they were considering a festival for 1995, but had not decided (so no dates). A WINDMILL on the A258 just out of town has a little folk museum; open Sun (cl 12–2.30pm) and pm bank hols; (01304) 612076; *£1. The St Crispin not far from the sands S of the town is pleasant for lunch.

♪ ♫ ❀ ⚘ **Whitstable** TR1166 The OYSTER FISHERY EXHIBITION (East Quay) focuses on the traditional Kentish industry of oyster fishing, with live shellfish, and hands-on seashore exhibit for children. Shop; open wknds and school hols all yr, plus wkdys exc Weds May–Aug; (01227) 272003; *£1. They sell fresh oysters, which you can order by mail, along with a recipe book with some good ideas for cooking them. The town MUSEUM AND GALLERY (Oxford St) explores other maritime history and traditions. Shop, disabled access; cl 1–2 pm, Weds and Sun, Good Fri, Christmas wk; free. Small but friendly, the wonderfully named CHUFFA TRAINS RAILMANIA MUSEUM (High St) is ideal for children, with model trains to play on. Model-railway shop; cl Sun, Christmas–New

Year; *£1.50. Besides Pearsons (see **Where to eat**), the Old Neptune and Tankerton Arms, both overlooking the sea, have decent food inc vegetarian.

🐦 🐾 ★ **Wingham** TR2457 WINGHAM BIRD PARK Lots of endangered species of birds from all over the world, with the emphasis very much on breeding. Also racoons, wallabies and other animals. Snacks, shop, disabled access; cl 25–26 Dec; (01227) 720836; £2.75. The village is attractive, with a good restaurant (the Four Seasons); the Eight Bells over at Wingham Well is good for lunch.

★ **Other attractive villages**, all with decent pubs, include Bishopsbourne TR1852, Bodsham TR1045, Boughton Lees TR0247, Bridge TR1854, Challock TR0050, Chillenden TR2653, Martin TR3346, Wickhambreaux TR2158, Worth TR3356 and Wye TR0546.

Walks

Some of the most pleasant walks in this part of the county are on the North Downs – not that high, but steep enough along the escarpment to give some great views. The **Wye Downs** TR0745 ◔-1, designated a nature reserve for their chalkland flora that includes a variety of orchids, look across the orchards below to both the Thames Estuary and the Channel.

The long-distance Saxon Shore Way also yields some good views and interesting walks. From **Etchinghill** TR1639 ◔-2, it crosses under an old railway line, heads up an unspoilt dry valley, and leads along the top of the slope for sightings of Dungeness and the French coast (Cap Gris Nez in Picardy). Elsewhere it takes in the **Royal Military Canal** TQ9630 ◔-3, built along the north fringe of Romney Marsh as a defence against Napoleon; you can combine this section with a path along the escarpment at Lympne Castle. The towpath from **West Hythe** TR1234 ◔-4 takes you up into Hythe itself, where a path from the junction of Station Rd (B2065) and Mill Lane enters parkland and continues up to Saltwood Castle TR1634, which still has its impressive medieval curtain wall.

From the east cliff at Folkestone TR2336 you can walk out past the martello tower into **The Warren** TR2437 ◔-5, an intriguingly tumbledown undercliff; you can now climb from here up on to the clifftop, which makes for a good bracing walk from Folkestone all the way to Dover TR3141 for the train or bus back. At the Dover end, the famous **White Cliffs** ◔-6 provide an exhilarating walk (and interesting views of the harbour – you can even see France on a clear day) from Dover Castle to St Margaret's at Cliffe TR3644, passing the Roman lighthouse above Dover and a curious scaled-down windmill at St Margaret's at Cliffe. There's a bus back to Dover (no point making a circuit, as the inland scenery here is not worth while), or you can press on to Kingsdown TR3748 or to Deal TR3752.

On the Thanet coast, there's a pleasant walk from **Broadstairs** TR3967 ◔-7 to Ramsgate TR3865.

Driving

One of the most notable roads here is the B2068 and its unclassified link with Canterbury, an old Roman road running straight as a die down to the coast (the detour to the nice country pub outside Stowting, the Tiger, is well worth while). More twistily, the B2065 down the lovely Elham Valley is a pleasant drive, passing several good pubs such as the Dolls House near Barham and (both good for families) the New Inn and Rose & Crown in Elham itself. The lanes above Wye also give a good taste of the quieter parts of the East Kent countryside: the best route is the downs road to Hastingleigh, then round through Bodsham Green, Sole Street and on past the Crundale Downs.

The orchard country inland from Kent's N coast is pretty to drive through at blossom time (and there may be pick-your-own soft fruit here in summer): between Gillingham and Boughton Street it's worth following any of the little lanes off the A2 (which carries relatively little traffic these days). There's a decent pub in Boughton Street itself (the White Horse), and others well worth working into a drive through this area include the Dove at Dargate, White Lion at Selling, and Carpenters Arms at Eastling.

Where to eat

Faversham TR0161 Reads Painters Forstal (01795) 535344 Attractively decorated, comfortable restaurant with imaginative, carefully prepared food and an excellent wine list; cl Sun and Mon, 2 wks end Aug; disabled access. **£33.50 evening, £19.50 lunch.**

Wingham TR2457 Four Seasons (01227) 720286 Small restaurant, overlooking attractive garden, with a good choice of interesting food; cl 3–15 Jan. **£20|£4.85/£8.**

Canterbury TR1557 Sullys High St (01227) 766266 Very good modern cooking (inc vegetarian menu) in popular restaurant – part of the County Hotel – a civilised old place with timbers and panelling; bedrooms; disabled access. **£19|£2/£4.**

Whitstable TR1166 Pearsons (01227) 272005 Bustling, popular pub with consistently good very fresh seafood, traditional furnishings, and kind and quick service – even when very busy; upstairs restaurant; cl 25 Dec. **£18|£2.20/£9.**

Finglesham TR3353 Crown (01304) 612555 Pleasant 16th-c country pub, attractively refurbished, with wide choice of reasonably priced bar food, popular old-world restaurant with inglenook fireplace and flagstones, and good, friendly service; cl pm 25 Dec. **£15|£1.50/£3.95.**

WEST KENT

Lovely houses and gardens to visit, quietly attractive countryside.

This part of Kent is good for a quiet break, exploring villages (with their many antique shops) and countryside, taking in some of the sights at the same time. The main draw for visitors is the wealth of beautiful houses and gardens, especially Leeds Castle, the gardens of Scotney Castle near Lamberhurst, Sissinghurst Garden, Penshurst Place, Chartwell and Squerryes Court near Westerham, Ightham Mote, Hever Castle and the newly opened gardens at Groombridge. The Finchcocks collection of keyboard instruments at Goudhurst is fascinating to anyone interested in music. Other places here do have quite a lot for children to enjoy, most notably the Whitbread Hop Farm at Beltring, the farm park at Dartford, the little steam railway at Tenterden and, for older children, the Chatham dockyard.

North Kent is on the whole not pretty, though some bleak and lonely marshes on the Thames estuary appeal to some. Roughly south of the M25 it develops an intimate charm, with a wealth of detail in the village and country scenes, and some very pleasant walks. This is particularly true of the part known as the Weald, marked by the many villages whose names end in –den: to seem less of an outsider, you should know that the stress is always on the last syllable of these names, the reverse of how you'd guess they were pronounced. The local landmarks are oast houses, most now converted into homes but formerly used for drying hops, the white cowls topping their conical roofs turning with the wind. Any holiday in this part would almost certainly spill over, like the Weald itself, into neighbouring parts of East Sussex, which have a very similar appeal.

Tunbridge Wells is no longer the spa town that it once was, though the Pantiles there is still a pleasant spot, and the town usually has some interesting things going on – as well as comfortable places to stay. There's a good choice in other parts, too, though not cheap.

Where to stay

Tunbridge Wells TQ5639 Spa Mount Ephraim TN4 8JX (01892) 520331 *£84; 76 comfortable rms. Run by the same family for three generations, this Georgian hotel, set in 14 acres of landscaped gardens, has a comfortable and quietly decorated, partly no-smoking lounge, a popular and attractive bar, good food in the Regency-style restaurant, a nice old-fashioned atmosphere and friendly, long-serving staff; leisure centre with indoor heated swimming pool, gym, beauty salon, sauna, Jacuzzi, and solarium, and floodlit hard tennis court; disabled access.

Boughton Monchelsea TQ7751 Tanyard Wierton Hill, Boughton Monchelsea, Maidstone ME17 4JT (01622) 744705 *£80; 6 beamed rms. Appealing medieval yeoman's house with fine views, cosy day rooms with log fires and beams, newly opened restaurant in 13th-c part of building (open to non-residents, too), and garden; cl 1st 2 wks Jan; children over 6.

Tenterden TQ8833 White Lion High St TN30 6BD (01580) 765077 £70; 15 rms. 350-year-old coaching inn, comfortably refurbished, with very good food in bar and dining room, and friendly, efficient service.

Pluckley TQ9245 Elvey Farm Pluckley, Ashford TN27 0SU (01233) 840442 £55.50; 9 rms, some in oast house roundel, some in original barn and stable block. This 15th-c farmhouse is in a secluded spot on 75-acre working family farm with timbered rooms, inglenook fireplace, and French windows from lounge on to sun terrace; play areas for children; cl Christmas; disabled access.

Shipbourne TQ5952 Chaser Stumble Hill TN11 9PE (01732) 810360 *£55; 15 rms. Colonial-style building with porticoed front in a lovely position by the village church and green; comfortable and homely atmosphere in well kept bar, with a wide range of attractively presented good food in both the bar and the restaurant; disabled access.

Penshurst TQ5243 Swale Cottage Old Swaylands Lane, Penshurst, Tonbridge TN11 8AH (01892) 870738 *£52; 3 beamed rms. Careful conversion of 13th-c Grade II listed barn and hayloft, with good breakfasts and cottage garden; not far from Hever – Anne Boleyn's childhood home; children over 12.

Warren Street TQ9253 Harrow Warren Street, Maidstone ME17 2ED

(01622) 858727 **£49.50**; 15 rms. Immaculate country inn with quietly low-key atmosphere; flowers, candles and big woodburning stove, extensive comfortably modernised low-beamed bar, attentive service and generous helpings of well cooked food; cl 25 Dec.

Eastling TQ9656 CARPENTERS ARMS Eastling, Faversham ME13 0AZ (01795) 890234 *£48; 3 rms. Pretty pub with cottagey bric à brac and lace tablecloths, oak beams and big fireplaces; warm welcome, pleasant food in bar and restaurant, and decent wines; children over 12.

Goudhurst TQ7238 STAR & EAGLE High St TN17 1AL (01580) 21152 **£48**; 11 character rms, 9 with own bthrm. Striking medieval inn with comfortable, Jacobean-style furnishings in heavy-beamed day rooms, outstanding views, polite staff, good food, and well kept ales; disabled access.

Sissinghurst TQ7937 SISSINGHURST CASTLE FARM Sissinghurst, Cranbrook TN17 2AB (01580) 712885 **£46**; 3 rms, one with own bthrm. Victorian farmhouse in the grounds of Sissinghurst Castle, with spacious rooms and pretty garden; farm is mostly arable with cattle and sheep; children over 5.

Cranbrook TQ7835 HANCOCKS Tilsden Lane TN17 3PH (01580) 714645 *£45; 4 rms with home-made biscuits and fresh flowers. Lovely timbered 15th/16th-c farmhouse with particularly relaxed and friendly atmosphere, beamed rooms elegantly furnished with antiques, log fires, freshly prepared good food inc home-made rolls and cakes (tea and coffee at any time at no extra charge), and pretty garden.

Hawkhurst TQ7628 CONGHURST FARM Hawkhurst, Cranbrook TN18 4RU (01580) 753331 **£40**; 3 rms. Friendly Georgian farmhouse on 500-acre arable/sheep farm in lovely quiet countryside with comfortable drawing room, TV room, log fires, good breakfasts, and evening meals by arrangement; lots to do nearby; cl Dec–Jan; children over 12.

Headcorn TQ8344 BLETCHENDEN MANOR FARM Headcorn, Ashford TN27 0JB (01622) 890228 **£40**; 3 rms, most with own bthrm. 15th-c farmhouse surrounded by own farmland in Weald of Kent, with big beamed dining room, own sitting room; cl Christmas; children over 12; self-catering also.

Charing TQ9549 BARNFIELD Charing, Ashford TN27 0BN (01233) 712421 *£36; 4 beamed rms, shared big bthrm. Delightful early 15th-c farmhouse with fine beams, big open fires, comfortable sitting rooms, lots of books, antiques, big garden, good food and friendly owners.

Pluckley TQ9243 DERING ARMS Pluckley, Ashford TN27 0RR (01233) 840371 *£36; 3 rms, shared bthrm. Dutch gabled old inn with friendly and relaxed attractive bars, and wonderful food with emphasis on fish and gourmet evenings every six weeks; vintage-car rally once a month; cl 26 Dec.

Smarden TQ8842 CHEQUERS Smarden, Ashford TN27 8QA (01233) 770217 **£36**; 6 good-value rms, some with own bthrm. Comfortable old-world pub full of character, with beams, log fire, a varied choice of really good reasonably priced food inc vegetarian dishes and seasonal vegetables, and exceptionally good breakfasts; cl 25 Dec.

Teston TQ7053 COURT LODGE The Street, Teston, Maidstone ME18 5AQ (01622) 812570 *£36; 3 rms, 2 with own bthrm. 16th-c house with pretty garden overlooking orchards and hop gardens; inglenook fireplaces, oak beams, leaded windows, and good breakfasts; cl Christmas and New Year; children over 10.

Groombridge TQ5337 CROWN Groombridge, Tunbridge Wells TN3 9QH (01892) 864742 *£35; 4 rms, shared bthrm. Carefully preserved Elizabethan inn on village green, with snug atmospheric timbered bar rooms, log fire in big brick inglenook, traditional furnishings, good, popular food, well kept beers, good-value house wines, and quick service.

Marden TQ7444 TANNER Goudhurst Rd, Marden, Tonbridge TN12 9ND (01622) 831214 **£35**; 3 rms (showers). Quietly set Tudor farmhouse in 15-acre family mixed farm with residents' lounge, inglenook dining room, large garden, and walks and picnic areas around farm; they breed shire horses; children over 12; no pets.

To see and do

✝ ⚲ ❀ 🏚 **Aylesford** TQ7359
AYLESFORD PRIORY Often referred to as
the Friars, these carefully restored
13th/14th-c buildings are once again
the home of a group of Carmelite
monks. Fine cloisters and chapels,
sculptures and ceramics by modern
artists and potters, and beautiful
grounds. Snacks, shop, disabled
access; tearoom and shop cl
Christmas and Easter; (01622)
717272; free. KITS COTY HOUSE up the
road towards the A229 is a massive
Stone Age tomb chamber which
'mightily impressed' Pepys when he
saw it; free. The Little Gem is a very
quaint little pub.

🌳 **Bedgebury Pinetum** TQ7133 is a
lakeside landscaped valley full of
magnificent conifers, with walks up
through forest plots designed to try
out the commercial possibilities of all
sorts of little-known species; £1. The
Bull at Three Leg Cross, Ticehurst is
good for lunch.

🐄 🐗 🕊 **Beltring** TQ6747 WHITBREAD
HOP FARM The largest surviving group
of Victorian oast houses and galleried
barns, housing museums on hop-
farming through the ages, rural crafts
and farming machinery; also nature
trails, animals, birds of prey, shire
horses, pottery, and special events
most summer wknds – a very popular
family outing. Meals, snacks, shop,
some disabled access; cl 25, 26 and 31
Dec; (01622) 872068; £4.95. The
Walnut Tree at Yalding is quite handy
for lunch.

★ ✝ 🐖 **Biddenden** TQ8438 This
attractive village has several
interesting old houses on the south
side of the High St, and a handsome
13th-c CHURCH with a bold tower.
Towards Benenden, BIDDENDEN
VINEYARDS has pleasant strolls around
thriving wine- and cider-producing
vineyard. All-yr tastings, harvesting in
Oct and bottling in Mar. Summer
snacks, shop; cl Sun Jan and Feb, 24
Dec–2 Jan; (01580) 291726; free. The
Red Lion has decent food.

❀ **Borough Green** TQ6157 GREAT
COMP GARDEN (2 miles E) Interesting
collection of trees, shrubs, herbaceous
plants and heathers with fine lawns

and paths. Teas on Sun and bank hols,
plant shop; cl Nov–Mar; £2.50. The
Plough at Ivy Hatch a few miles S is
very good for lunch.

❀ ❀ **Brasted** TQ4755 EMMETT'S
GARDEN Charming hillside shrub
garden with magnificent views – it's
the highest garden in Kent; full of
bluebells in spring and a riot of colour
in autumn. Teas, shop, some disabled
access; cl am, Mon (exc bank hols),
Tues, Nov–Mar; £2.50; NT. The Bull
and White Hart Hotel are handy for
lunch.

❀ 🌳 **Brenchley** TQ6741 has some
attractive old houses, and the ancient
Rose & Crown has home-cooked
food. MARLE PLACE is a pretty garden
around a fine 17th-c house (not open),
with interesting scented plants in the
walled garden, woodland walk, and
showy bantams; herbs and other
plants for sale. Teas, disabled access;
cl Nov–Mar; (0189272) 2304; *£2.50.

❀ ⚲ ⛴ 🐖 ❀ **Chatham** TQ7567
HISTORIC DOCKYARD 80-acre working
museum set in the most complete
Georgian dockyard in the world. Lots
to see and do, one exhibition, Wooden
Walls, showing through sights, sounds
and smells how 18th-c warships such
as HMS *Victory* were built here. Also
restorations, craft workshops,
interesting Commissioner's House,
and lively events. A visit here can easily
last most of the day. Meals, snacks,
shop, disabled access; open Apr–Oct
plus wknds and Weds Nov, Feb and
Mar; (01634) 812551; £5.50. You can
get a ticket that includes BOAT TRIPS on
the paddle steamer *Kingswear Castle*.
FORT AMHERST The finest surviving
18th-c fort in the country, with
massive ditches, gun emplacements, a
warren of tunnels and a firing gun
battery. 18 acres of parkland and live
re-enactments most Sun. Snacks, shop;
cl 3 wks at Christmas; (01634)
847747; £3.50.

★ ✝ 🐖 📷 🎣 **Chiddingstone** TQ5045
A favourite Kentish village, an
unspoilt cluster of Tudor houses and
buildings owned by the NT, in lovely
countryside. The church and the
mysterious stone from which the
village takes its name are worth a

look. CHIDDINGSTONE CASTLE 17th-c house rebuilt in castle style at the start of the 19th c; renowned paintings and antiquities from England, Egypt and the Orient, inc fine collections of Japanese swords and Buddhist art. The pleasant landscaped grounds have just been restored, and you can fish in the lake (£8 a day). Various events and concerts. Snacks, shop, some disabled access; open pm Weds, Sun and bank hols Apr–Oct, plus Tues and Thurs–Sat Jun–Sept; (01892) 870347; £3.50. The Castle is good for lunch.

★ ✝ 🏠 ✿ **Cobham** TQ6768 Another attractive village, with a good mix of unspoilt buildings from various centuries – an excellent place to walk round (as Dickens liked to do). The partly 13th-c CHURCH is worth examining, with its magnificent brasses and tombs, as is the 14th-c NEW COLLEGE, like a miniature Oxford college but far less known to visitors. Disabled access; cl Thurs; free. The Earls of Darnley once lived in the impressive COBHAM HALL, now a girls' boarding and day school, but open to visitors in the school hols. The décor is quite splendid in parts (inc some notable marble fireplaces), and the lovely grounds are being restored. Snacks, shop; open pm selected Suns, Weds and Thurs in Mar, Jun and especially Apr, July and Aug; (01474) 824319; *£2.50. At the S end of the village, OWLETTS is a modest 17th-c yeoman's house with an interesting staircase and grand classical bird bath in the garden; open pm Weds and Thurs Apr–Sept; £1.50; NT. The Leather Bottle is OK for lunch, with lots of interesting Dickens memorabilia and a good garden.

✗ ★ ♨ **Cranbrook** TQ7735 has a very good working WINDMILL picturesquely set almost in its centre, and still grinding corn – it's a lovely sight; open pm Sat and bank hols Apr–Sept plus pm Sun mid-July–Aug; free. The attractive miniature town, with largely unspoilt lanes of tiled buildings, also has a friendly local history museum, and for picnics Perfect Partners (Stone St) is the best delicatessen for many miles.

🦢 🐘 **Crayford** TQ5174 DAVID EVANS CRAFT CENTRE OF SILK (actually just inside Gtr London, but handy for next entry) Demonstrations of traditional silk-making, with reconstructed Victorian shop, street and dockside, complete with sound effects. The only company still producing Madder silk. Snacks, good shop, disabled access; cl Sun and bank hols; (01322) 559401; *£2. Tours of factory too by arrangement.

🐃 ♥ **Dartford** TQ5474 STONE LODGE FARM PARK Well organised working farm, free from any modern trappings. Rare breeds, pets for children, daily milking, spinning and other events, birds of prey, aviaries and a collection of old farming equipment. Snacks, shop, disabled access; cl Nov–Feb; (01322) 292211; £2.75.

✿ 🦆 ❀ **Doddington** TQ9357 DODDINGTON PLACE Grand garden with formal plantings, old-fashioned rock garden, rhododendrons in woodland, and broad views. Plant sales, café, shop, disabled access; open Weds and pm Sun and bank hols Easter–Sept; (01795) 886101; *£2. The Carpenters Arms at Eastling is quite handy for lunch.

🏰 🏠 ✿ 🏯 **Eynsford** TQ5465 EYNSFORD CASTLE Ruins of Norman knight's castle, with impressive 30-ft walls, and remains of hall and ditch; cl winter Mon, 24–26 Dec, 1 Jan. LULLINGSTONE CASTLE Historic family mansion with fine state rooms, great hall, staircase and library, interesting collections and beautiful grounds. The 15th-c gate tower was one of the first buildings to be made entirely of brick. Snacks, shop, disabled access; open pm Sat, Sun and bank hols Apr–Oct; *£3.50. LULLINGSTONE ROMAN VILLA Remains of rather well-to-do 1st and 2nd-c family's villa, with exceptionally well preserved floor mosaics and an extensive bath complex. Also an early Christian chapel – the only one so far found in a private house. Snacks, shop, some disabled access; cl winter Mon, Christmas; (01322) 863467; £2. The Malt Shovel has good seafood.

♨ ✝ **Gillingham** TQ7768 ROYAL ENGINEERS MUSEUM Of more general appeal than you might at first think,

interesting displays with sound effects
about the soldier-engineers spanning
the years 1066 to 1945, with oddities
and arts brought back from various
countries. Snacks, shop, disabled
access; cl Fri, 25–26 Dec, 1 Jan;
(01634) 406397; *£2. The partly
Norman CHURCH is worth a look.

★ ❀ ✝ 🏠 🐾 👃 Goudhurst TQ7237
Charming Wealden village, with quite
a few antique shops and so forth, and
spectacular views from the graveyard
of the 14th-c hilltop church (but
during the day too much traffic for
comfort). The Spread Eagle up by the
church, one of the village's most
handsome old buildings, is useful for
lunch. FINCHCOCKS (off A262 W) The
early Georgian house and its lovely
gardens are attractive, but the main
draw here is the big collection of
working keyboard instruments from
the 17th c onwards. Some of these are
played whenever the house is open,
the well done recitals really adding to
the atmosphere. Snacks, shop, some
disabled access; open pm daily in Aug
exc Mon and Tues, as well as pm Sun
and bank hols Apr–Sept; (01580)
211702; £4.50. There are various
special events throughout the year,
notably the concerts in Sept. The
Green Cross Inn up by the main rd has
good home cooking.

🐝 🍸 Groombridge TQ5337
GROOMBRIDGE PLACE GARDENS
Beautiful walled gardens around
17th-c moated mansion, the
parkland and forest inspiring
generations of artists and writers.
Drunken topiary garden, oriental
garden, rose garden, sculpture garden,
and lots more, the paths patrolled by
peacocks, the moat guarded by black
swans. These are reckoned by many to
be among the country's most
spectacular gardens and have only
just been opened. Snacks, shop,
disabled access; cl am, wkdys Apr
and May, and Oct–Mar exc first 2
wknds of Oct; (01892) 863999; *£3.
The prettily placed Crown is handy
for lunch.

🐦 Headcorn TQ8344 HEADCORN
FLOWER CENTRE AND VINEYARD
Enormous all-weather flower centre
and vineyard, excellent
chrysanthemums and orchid lilies in

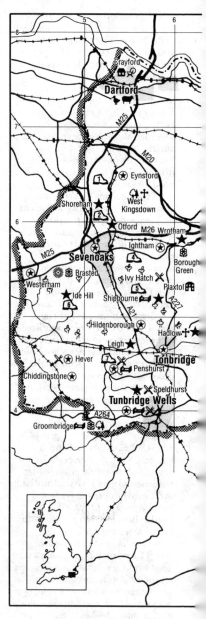

heated flower houses. Wknd snacks,
shop, disabled access; cl 25 Dec–1
Jan; (01622) 890250; £1.50 self-
guided tours, guided tours (wknds
Easter–Sept plus wkdys Jun–Aug)
£2.95, inc tastings. The simple George
& Dragon is useful for lunch.

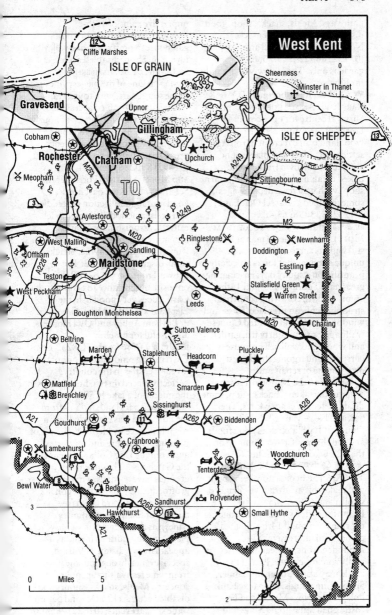

West Kent

Cliffe Marshes

ISLE OF GRAIN

Sheerness

Minster in Thanet

Gravesend

Upnor

Gillingham

ISLE OF SHEPPEY

Cobham

Rochester   Chatham

Upchurch

Sittingbourne

Meopham

TQ

A2

M2

Aylesford   A249

Ringlestone   Newnham

M20   Doddington

West Malling   Sandling   Eastling

Offham   Maidstone   Stalisfield Green

Teston   Warren Street

West Peckham   Leeds

Boughton Monchelsea   Charing

M20

Beltring   Sutton Valence

Marden   Staplehurst   Headcorn   Pluckley

Matfield   Smarden

Brenchley   A29

Goudhurst   Sissinghurst

A262   Biddenden

Cranbrook   Woodchurch

Lamberhurst

Tenterden

Bewl Water   Bedgebury

Sandhurst   Rolvenden

Hawkhurst   Small Hythe

0   Miles   5

Hever TQ4745 HEVER CASTLE AND GARDENS Double-moated 13th-c castle in 30 acres of beautiful gardens, little changed externally since Anne Boleyn lived here as a child. Inside it's a different story, as the rooms were magnificently restored by the Astor family at the start of this century, and filled with antiques, furnishings and art from all over Europe. The grounds are a draw in their own right, with lakes, Italianate garden with antique sculptures, walled rose garden and maze, and a quarter of a mile of pathways. Meals, snacks, shop, good disabled access to gardens; cl early Nov–mid-Mar, castle cl am; (01732) 865224; £5.20, £3.80 gardens only. The Henry VIII is handy for lunch.

🐄 🐤 ☺ 🐌 **Hildenborough** TQ5648 RARE FARM ANIMALS OF HOLLANDEN Survival centre for once common breeds of farm animals with woodland trails, recreated Iron Age settlement, adventure playground, and pick-your-own fruit. Home-baked meals and snacks, notable farm shop (with well regarded sausages), some disabled access; cl Oct–Easter; (01732) 833858; £3.40.

🏠 ❀ 🐤 **Ightham** TQ5956 IGHTHAM MOTE Lovely medieval manor house, still with its surrounding moat, a unique survival that looks especially beautiful on a sunny day. Fascinating great hall, Tudor chapel and 14th-c crypt, while the drawing room has a striking Jacobean fireplace, frieze and windows, and hand-painted Chinese wallpaper; pretty courtyard, garden and woodland walks. The house is currently undergoing the biggest programme of repair and conservation the National Trust has so far undertaken. Snacks, shop, some disabled access; cl am wkdys, Tues, Sat, and Nov–Mar; £4; NT. The Plough at Ivy Hatch does good food, and the cheaper Crown Point up on the A25 is good for families.

★ ❀ 🏠 🐤 🐄 🐌 **Lamberhurst** TQ6736 The bypass now being built will make this an attractive village to stroll around. SCOTNEY CASTLE Beautiful 19th-c gardens surrounding the ruins of a small 14th-c moated castle, with impressive rhododendrons, azaleas and roses – a really romantic place. Part of the castle may also be open in summer. Shop; cl am wknds, Mon (exc bank hols), Tues, Nov–Mar, Good Fri, castle open same hours May–mid-Sept; £3.20; NT. OWL HOUSE GARDENS 13 acres of sweeping lawns, flowers, shrubs and fruit trees around timber-framed 16th-c wool smugglers' house; sunken water-gardens and woodlands. Shop, disabled access; *£2.50. BAYHAM ABBEY Technically in Sussex but more handy from here,

impressive ruins of 13th-c Premonstratensian abbey and gatehouse in pretty wooded valley. A nice spot. Shop, disabled access; cl Oct–Mar; £1.80. LAMBERHURST VINEYARD One of the biggest vineyards in the south-east, with tours, trails and tastings. Disabled access; usually only cl 25–26 Dec, 1 Jan, with hourly guided tours Apr–Sept, but the vineyard was for sale as we went to press, so probably best to check first; (01892) 890286; tours £1.95. TOY AND MODEL MUSEUM (Forstal Farm) Set in a typical Kent oast house, a good nostalgic collection inc teddies and dolls in period settings, model railway, astonishingly detailed miniature fairground, and various Rupert Bear memorabilia. Snacks, shop, disabled access; £2. The Brown Trout, on the B2169 nearly opposite the entrance to Scotney Castle, does very good fish; the Elephant's Head at Hook Green out nr Bayham Abbey and Owl House is also useful for lunch.

🏰 ▣ 🐚 🍽 ! 🐄 🐾 **Leeds** TQ8253 LEEDS CASTLE Long renowned as one of the loveliest castles in the country, perfectly placed on two little islands in the middle of a lake in 500 acres of landscaped parkland. It dates from the 9th c, and was converted into a royal residence by Henry VIII. Lots of paintings, furniture and tapestries, and a unique Dog Collar Museum in the Gatehouse. The enormous grounds have gardens, a maze and grotto, duckery and aviary, golf course, and vineyard (with free tastings of English and country wines); as this suggests it's a busy place, and not quite as idyllic as it appears from a distance. Various special events throughout the year from wine festivals to open-air concerts. Meals, snacks, shop, good disabled access; cl 25 Dec and before some special events; (01622) 765400; £7, £5.50 park and gardens only. KENT GARDEN COSTUME DOLLS AND COUNTRY WINE A friendly little place specialising in two quite distinct crafts: the creation of reproduction antique porcelain dolls, and a vineyard producing traditional country wines. Demonstrations of each – with tastings of the latter. Shop, disabled access; cl Mon–Weds, 25–26 Dec; (01622) 861638; free. The Swan at Sutton Valence does decent food.

🏠🎵⌚✝🖼⛵ **Maidstone** TQ7555 is a busy modern town, but well worth penetrating on a Sunday (when it's quieter) for its good museums. ARCHBISHOP'S PALACE AND HERITAGE CENTRE Striking 14th-c palace used by the Archbishops of Canterbury as a stopping-place on their way from London. Recently very well restored, with a lively new heritage centre tracing the history of the building and the county. Meals, snacks, shop, disabled access to heritage centre, but not all rooms of palace; cl 25–26 Dec; £2.95. Admission covers entry to the TYRWHITT DRAKE MUSEUM OF CARRIAGES in the palace stables, a notable collection of horse-drawn carriages and vehicles. Shop, disabled access to ground floor only; cl as above; *£1.50 for this museum only. The site also includes the old parish CHURCH of All Saints. A handsome Elizabethan manor house in St Faith's St is now the MUSEUM AND ART GALLERY, with period furniture and fine pictures set out in original room settings. Snacks, shop; cl am Sun, 25–26 Dec; free. The Minstrel in Knightrider Rd is a useful wine bar, and the Pilot in Upper Stone St has decent bar food. You may be able to go on a BOAT TRIP along to Allington.

✝🌿 **Marden** TQ7444 has a 12th/14th-c ragstone CHURCH with a unique white weatherboarded tower, and other buildings going back to the 14th c; MARDEN MEADOW (Staplehurst Rd) is a lovely unimproved hay meadow, alive with wild flowers and butterflies in late spring and early summer. The Gun & Spitroast over at Horsmonden is popular for lunch.

🐄🦋🐖 **Matfield** TQ6541 BADSELL PARK FARM Rare breeds of cattle, pigs, goats and sheep, poultry and pets, butterfly house, pick-your-own soft fruits, good farm shop, and notable nature trail. Meals, snacks, shop, disabled access; (01892) 832549; £4. The Rose & Crown at Brenchley is quite handy for lunch.

✖ **Meopham** TQ6466 has an unusual 6-sided windmill, the base of which serves as a meeting place for the parish council. Shop, disabled access to ground floor only; open pm Sun and bank hols May–Sept; 60p. The Cricketers prettily set on the green does good-value food.

✝ **Minster in Thanet** TQ9573 MINSTER ABBEY Site of one of the earliest nunneries in the country, with ruins and cloisters of the 7th-c building. The current house is still run by Benedictine nuns. Shop, disabled access; open 11–12 am all yr exc Sun, plus 2–4.30 pm May–Sept; free.

★🏠🖼⌚🌸☺🚃 **Penshurst** TQ5243 is a pretty village, with antique shops, teas and so forth, and, above all, PENSHURST PLACE, a great medieval manor house, unchanged since the Sidney family first came here centuries ago. Interesting combination of architectural styles, huge chestnut-beamed baronial hall, state rooms with extensive collections of portraits and furnishings, toy museum, and marvellous formal gardens with nature trails and adventure playground. Meals, snacks, shop, improved disabled access (with a new garden for the blind); house cl am, wkdys Oct and Mar, all Nov–Feb; (01892) 870307; £4.95, £3.50 grounds only. The Leicester Arms in the village is good for lunch, and above it up on Smarts Hill the Spotted Dog has lovely views down over Penshurst Place. The Bottle House and the Rock out in this direction are also both well worth tracking down if you're walking in the area. Penshurst also has a VINEYARD (Grove Rd) with tours and tastings and various animals inc rare breeds of sheep; cl wkdys Jan and Feb; (01892) 870255; *£1.

🏠 **Plaxtol** TQ6053 OLD SOAR MANOR An ancient oak door at this 13th-c knight's dwelling has graffiti spanning the ages, and there's also a very well preserved solar block, chapel, lavatorium and barrel-vaulted undercroft; cl Oct–Mar; free. This general area is attractive orchard country, with good-value apples from the farm shops from Sept onwards; many here also have fresh cobnuts in

Sept. The Golding Hop is useful for lunch.

✝ ⛪ 🏠 ♿ **Rochester** TQ7468 is a busy town, but well worth walking round, with several attractive buildings besides those we mention; one of the quaintest is Kent's oldest pub, the Coopers Arms (St Margaret's St; cheap lunches). The Norman CATHEDRAL is the most spectacular, with its original richly carved door, vaulted crypt, St Gundolph's tower, tombs and effigies and huge 15th-c window. ROCHESTER CASTLE is one of the best examples of 11th-c military architecture, with an excellent storeyed keep and parts of the castle wall. Very dramatic, it looks a little like the Tower of London, only more forbidding. There's a good taped tour. Snacks, shop; cl 24–26 Dec, 1 Jan; (01634) 402276; £2. CHARLES DICKENS CENTRE (High St) Late Tudor house used in both *Pickwick Papers* and *Edwin Drood*, now with scenes and characters from the author's books brought vividly to life, especially in the new audio-visual show Dickens' Dream. Shop; cl 25–26 Dec; (01634) 844176; £2.60. Dickens fans should also try to visit GAD'S HILL SCHOOL at Higham just out of town, the only house the writer ever owned and where he wrote many of his novels. His first sight of the house, many years before he lived there, is described in *A Christmas Carol*. Shop; open out of school hours by arrangement; (01474) 822366; £2. Back in town the GUILDHALL MUSEUM has impressive decorated plaster ceilings, and some hands-on exhibits and audio-visual shows. Disabled access to ground floor only; free.

🏛 **Rolvenden** TQ8530 CM BOOTH COLLECTION OF HISTORIC VEHICLES The main feature is a unique collection of three-wheeled Morgan cars but there are also caravans, bikes, cars and toy and model-car displays. Shop; cl most Suns; (01580) 211234; £1.20. Another Hooden Horse nearby has decent food.

✝ 🌸 🐕 ⚘ **Sandhurst** TQ7928 has a fine 14th-c CHURCH with good views from the graveyard. SANDHURST VINEYARD (Hoads Farm, Crouch

Lane) has tours of vineyard and hop gardens, inc hop-picking in Sept. Tastings and shop; cl am wkdys, and Christmas–Easter exc by arrangement; (01580) 850296; free. They do B & B in a 16th-c farmhouse. Nearby at Standen Street, Iden Green TQ8031, TILE BARN NURSERY is the only one in the world to specialise in wild cyclamen, with four greenhouses filled with over two dozen miniature species, several of them hardy, in flower Sept–Apr; usually cl Mon, Tues and Sun, best to ring first to check they're open; (01580) 240221.

⛪ 🏚 🐾 ♥ **Sandling** TQ7558 MUSEUM OF KENT LIFE (Lock Lane) The story of the Kent countryside, told over 27 acres, taking in farming tools, gardens, a working oast house, machinery and animals, as well as various crafts and special events most wknds. Meals, snacks, shop, disabled access; cl Mon (exc bank hols), Oct–Easter; (01622) 763936; £3. TYLAND BARN Well restored 17th-c barn, now the headquarters of the Kent Trust for Nature Conservation, with displays and information of their many nature reserves in the area. Snacks, shop, disabled access; cl Mon (exc bank hols), Jan; (01622) 662012; free. The Chiltern Hundreds (Penenden Heath Rd, off M20 junction 7) is quite handy for lunch, as is the Little Gem in Aylesford.

🏚 🖼 ✾ 🍴 ✿ **Sevenoaks** TQ5255 This commuters' town has little to see apart from the handsome old buildings of Sevenoaks School. Just E is the great set piece of KNOLE. Originally a simple medieval manor house, this was gradually transformed into a palace by a 15th-c archbishop, followed by Henry VIII and then generations of the Sackville family. The largest – some would say the grandest – private house in the country still lived in, it's a calendar house, with 365 rooms, 52 staircases and 7 courtyards. The rooms are beautifully furnished and decorated, with magnificent tapestries and paintings by the likes of Reynolds and Gainsborough. Outside are 26 acres of attractive grounds and a 1,000-acre deer park. It really is a marvellous place to visit – but wrap up well, some of the rooms can get a little chilly. Meals, snacks, shop; cl am Thurs, Mon (exc bank hols), Tues, Nov–Mar; the garden is open only on the first Weds of each month May–Sept; £4, 50p garden only; NT. The Buck's Head at nearby Godden Green has interesting food. The WILDFOWL RESERVE (Bradbourne Vale Rd) has 135 acres of lakes, ponds, woodland and reedbeds, several viewing hides and a satisfying nature trail. Snacks, shop, disabled access; open Weds, Sat, Sun and bank hols, cl Christmas; (01732) 456407; *£2. RIVERHILL HOUSE GARDENS (A225 S) Hillside gardens with rose and shrub terraces, woodland walks among fine trees, rhododendrons, bluebells in spring, and fine views. Teas, plant sales; open pm Sun and bank hol wknds Apr–Jun; (01732) 458802; £2.

❀ **Sissinghurst** TQ7937 SISSINGHURST GARDEN Several charming gardens themed according to season or colour and cared for by obviously loving hands, all offset by the lovely tall-towered Elizabethan gatehouse (not open); rose garden, nuttery, moat walk and Tower Lawn. Get there early – a timed ticket sytem is in operation, and they may close once capacity has been reached. Meals, snacks, shop, disabled access; cl am wkdys, all Mon (exc bank hols), and mid-Oct–Mar; £5; NT. The Three Chimneys on the way to Biddenden is very good for lunch.

🏠 👶 🚗 ❀ **Small Hythe** TQ8930 SMALLHYTHE PLACE Originally a Tudor harbour-master's house, later the final home of Dame Ellen Terry and now a museum of her life, with mementos of her theatrical contemporaries; cl am, Thurs, Fri, Nov–Mar; £2.50; NT. TENTERDEN VINEYARD AND HERB GARDEN Acres of vines, attractive lakes ideal for picnics, winery, herb garden and agricultural museum. Snacks, shop, some disabled access; (01580) 763033; £1. Tenterden TQ8833 is nearby.

👶 🚗 ❀ **Staplehurst** TQ7843 BRATTLE FARM MUSEUM Country museum on a working farm, with tools and skills from the past few centuries, and a pair of working oxen called Stuff and Nonsense. Shop, disabled access; open Sun and bank hols Easter–Oct; (01580) 891222; *£1.50. IDEN CROFT HERBS (Frittenden Rd) Walled herb gardens, thyme rockery, trails and gardens designed for the blind or disabled; cl winter Sun; (01580) 891432; £1 suggested donation. The Lord Raglan (Chart Hill Rd) does interesting food.

★ 👶 🚗 **Tenterden** TQ8833 is a busy small town with lots of attractive old buildings, especially 17th and 18th-c character cottages on the N side of the High St. There's a small but interesting local history MUSEUM on Station Rd; cl am, Fri and all Nov–Mar; 75p. The striking 15th-c Woolpack has good-value home cooking. The KENT & EAST SUSSEX RAILWAY has steam trains running from here into Sussex, with lovely Wealden views, recalling those halcyon days when few places were more than 4 miles from a railway station. The regular Pullman dining-car runs are popular, as are the Christmas Santa Specials. Meals, snacks, shop, disabled access; (01580) 765155 for timetable; £5.80.

🏰 ❈ ❀ **Tonbridge** TQ5846 is a commuter town perked up a bit by the distinguished buildings of Tonbridge School. TONBRIDGE CASTLE 13th-c castle gatehouse with well constructed models and audio-visual displays depicting events from that period. Good views from the battlements and pleasant gardens. Shop; cl 25–26 Dec, 1 Jan; (01732) 770929; £2.50.

❗ 🏠 ✝ 👶 🏛 **Tunbridge Wells** TQ5839 Very much a busy commuters' shopping centre nowadays, but parts still show its former character as a genteel spa town. The allegedly health-restoring water still trickles through the Pantiles, the former centre of the town, full of elegant buildings now housing interesting shops. You can try the water at the Chalybeate Spring here, 25p a glass; cl Nov–Mar. A DAY AT THE WELLS Extravagant recreation of the town's Georgian heyday using very up-to-date display technology. Shop, disabled access (prior notice preferred); cl 25 Dec; (01892) 546545; £3.75. The CHURCH of King

Charles the Martyr is an interesting chapel built in the late 17th c for the gentry visiting the Pantiles; it has a remarkable plaster ceiling. The MUSEUM AND ART GALLERY has examples of Tunbridge ware, the area's speciality woodware. Shop, disabled access; cl Sun; free. Above the Pantiles the hillside Common is pleasant for strolls, with plenty of trees and rocks. The best place for a proper lunch is Sankeys fish restaurant (Mount Ephraim).

⛫ Upnor TQ7670 CASTLE Well preserved Elizabethan castle famous for failing to protect the Medway from the Dutch in 1667; attractive turrets, gatehouse and windows. Walkman tours. Shop, disabled access to grounds only; cl Oct–Mar; (01634) 718742; £2. Up towards the Thames marshes, the Black Bull at Cliffe is unusual for its authentic Malaysian food.

✝ ♤ West Kingsdown TQ5762 CHURCH is largely Saxon, with a rare Saxon tower; given great appeal by its unique tranquil setting, secluded in the middle of a wood. The yew tree by the west door looks very old indeed.

★ ✝ ⛫ West Malling TQ6757 Attractive little village, most of which is a conservation area thanks to its many old timbered houses and wells; lots of nice alleyways to explore. Particularly worth a look are the ABBEY, one of the country's oldest ecclesiastical buildings, and ST LEONARD'S TOWER, a fine Norman tower from an 11th-c castle. The Kings Arms at Offham has decent food.

★ 🏠 ❀ 🖼 ⛵ Westerham TQ4454 This pleasant country town is perhaps best known to visitors for its proximity to CHARTWELL, the home of Winston Churchill until his death. Still much as he left them, the interesting rooms are full of his possessions and reminders of his career. Very attractive gardens, and lakes with famous black swans. Meals, snacks, shop, disabled access; house cl Mon (exc bank hols), Fri, and Tues after bank hols, as well as Tues and Thurs in Nov and Mar, and all Dec–Feb – gardens cl Nov–Apr;

£4.50, £2 gardens only; 50p studio only; NT. Overshadowed by its more famous neighbour but to some people a good deal more satisfying is SQUERRYES COURT, a fine 17th-c manor house overlooking attractive grounds, with excellent collections of paintings, china and furniture. The garden was first laid out in 1689 and is now being painstakingly restored, and some of the magnificent lime trees are as old as the house. Snacks, shop; open pm Weds, wknds and bank hols Apr–Sept, and Sun in Mar; (01959) 62345; £3.50, £2 grounds only. QUEBEC HOUSE Gabled boyhood home of General Wolfe with exhibitions on his life and the battle that made his name; cl am, Thurs, Sat, and Nov–Mar; £2; NT. The Spinning Wheel (A233 towards Biggin Hill) is useful enough for lunch.

🚜 ✗ Woodchurch TQ9434 SOUTH OF ENGLAND RARE BREEDS CENTRE Acres of Kentish farmland with one of the largest collections of rare animals in Europe; lots of pigs, cattle, horses, goats and poultry, inc plenty to touch and fuss. Meals, snacks, shop, disabled access; cl 25 Dec; (01233) 861493; £3. Nearby is a well restored windmill, still grinding corn for demonstrations, and its sails turning whenever it's open. Shop; open pm Sun and bank hols Easter–Sept; *75p.

★ Other attractive villages, all with decent pubs, include Ide Hill TQ4851, Leigh TQ5446, Offham TQ6557, Otford TQ5359, Pluckley TQ9243, Shipbourne TQ5952, Shoreham TQ5161, Smarden TQ8842 (the Bell just outside is good, too – and very pretty), Speldhurst TQ5541, Stalisfield Green TQ9553, Sutton Valence TQ8149, Upchurch TQ8467 (where the 13th-c church has a unique 'candle snuffer' tower), West Peckham TQ6452 and Wrotham TQ6159. The church at Hadlow TQ6349 has the interesting Hop Pickers Memorial, dedicated to the 30 villagers who one wet day in 1853 drowned on their way back from the fields; the enormously tall folly of Hadlow Tower is worth a look.

Walks

The area surrounding Sevenoaks TQ5255 has more walk potential than a glance at the OS map might suggest. The terrain is complicated, the Wealden villages unspoilt to a remarkable degree, and the path network dense and very well kept. Orchards, hop gardens, pantile-clad timber-framed cottages and oast houses set the Kentish theme. Newcomers may be surprised to find such attractive and deeply rural countryside so close to London.

There are organised trails from the countryside centre at **Lullingstone** TQ5064 △-1, along the River Darent and into woods above the nearby golf course. **Shoreham** TQ5161 and **Otford** TQ5359 △-2 both have attractive village centres, linked by an easy track, with the downlands to the E giving scope for longer walks across Magpie Bottom and past Romney Street. Further E the farmland soon gets arable, and ploughed fields can be a tedious slog, but from **Trottiscliffe** (pronounced Trosley) TQ6460 △-3 the walk E to the Coldrum Stones TQ6560, a 4,000-year-old burial chamber, is recommended, with an extension on to the North Downs (Trosley Country Park), here densely wooded but open on the steep slope itself.

Knole Park TQ5454 △-4, just on the edge of Sevenoaks TQ5255, is criss-crossed with paths and tracks encompassing the deer park and the great house of Knole itself.

One Tree Hill △-5, reached from a National Trust car park TQ5553 south of Godden Green, has a grand view over the Weald. From here the Greensand Way (look for GW markers) follows the very edge of the lower Greensand escarpment which dips gently down to Ightham Mote TQ5853, two miles E; Ivy Hatch TQ5854 and Stone Street TQ5754 have handily placed pubs to make this into a circuit. **Ide Hill** TQ4851 △-6, with its pubs and picture-book green, is also on the scarp slope and on the Greensand Way: other targets for walks here include Toy's Hill TQ4751, French Street TQ4552, Chartwell TQ4551 and Westerham TQ4454.

The Weald's most luscious lowlands include the vicinity of **Penshurst** TQ5243 △-7, where the fields are predominantly pasture, the cottages characteristically pantile-hung and the paths just elevated enough to gain charming views. As with much of the rest of the area, route-finding is fiddly and patient map-reading is in order. One of the best circular routes is Penshurst–Chiddingstone Hoath TQ4942–Chiddingstone TQ4945, which passes several good pubs on the way.

Bewl Water TQ6732 △-8, dissected by the Kent/East Sussex boundary, is skirted by a 14-mile path on the banks of the reservoir (can be very busy on bank hols; sailing, fishing etc too).

A public footpath strides through pastures and woodlands of the **Scotney Castle** estate TQ6834 △-9, and can form a basis for circular walks from Kilndown TQ7035 to Lamberhurst TQ6736 and back.

There's an attractive round walk from Burnt House Farm on the Rye rd E of **Sandhurst** TQ7928 △-10, via Cledge Wood and Marsh Quarter Farm to the Kent Ditch and the River Rother, to take you round to Bodiam Castle (see Sussex chapter) and back via Northlands Farm and Silverden. The walk from **Cranbrook** TQ7735 △-11 to Sissinghurst TQ7937 and back is pleasant.

The Thames Estuary and North Kent coast are not really of mainstream appeal. However, **Cliffe Marshes** TQ7278 △-12, N of Rochester, are bounded by a long sea wall cum footpath which feels (and is) extraordinarily remote and not a little surreal. The **Isle of Sheppey** △-13 has a brief moment of interest at its eastern end, where you can walk the dyke S from Leysdown-on-Sea TR0370 to Shell Ness TR0567 at the mouth of the Swale.

Pubs useful for walkers include the Bald Faced Stag at Ashurst TQ5038, Wheatsheaf at Bough Beech TQ4846, Pepper Box at Fairbourne Heath above Ulcombe TQ8550, Woodman on Goathurst Common TQ4952, Buck's Head at Godden Green TQ5555, Ringlestone Inn TQ8755 N of Harrietsham, Cock at Ide Hill TQ4851, Golden Lion at Luddesdown TQ6766, Kentish Horse at Markbeech TQ4742, Horns & Bull at Otford TQ5359 (the ruined palace of the archbishops is well worth a look here), Rock at Hoath Corner TQ4943, Harrow at Warren Street TQ9253 and Rising Sun at Woodlands TQ5560.

Driving

All the B-roads in this area E of a line drawn up through Lamberhurst are worth taking, giving good views of the countryside without much traffic. W of this line, the B2188 through Groombridge and Fordcombe to Penshurst, and then left along the B2176 for a lovely view of Penshurst Place, is good. In the Weald particularly, almost any side road will take you past ancient tile-hung farmhouses, oast houses with their wind-vane cowl tops, and perhaps one of the declining number of hop yards with their twining hop bines climbing so high that men on stilts are needed to maintain the trellises.

Where to eat

Tunbridge Wells TQ5839 THACKERAY'S HOUSE 85 London Rd (01892) 511921 Civilised restaurant with excellent carefully cooked and presented food, an interesting wine list and quiet service; bistro downstairs; cl pm Sun, Mon, Christmas; limited disabled access. £27.50|£10 2-course lunch/£12.

Speldhurst TQ5541 GEORGE & DRAGON (01892) 863125 Distinguished old pub, based on a manorial great hall dating back to 1212, with good bar food, striking first-floor restaurant under the original massive roof timbers, and a splendid wine cellar; cl am Sat, pm Sun, Mon. £26|£4.25/£5.95.

Penshurst TQ5243 BOTTLE HOUSE (01892) 870306 Relaxed and friendly 15th-c pub with unpretentious beamed bar, popular food and efficient service. £23|£4.25/£5.95.

Penshurst TQ5243 SPOTTED DOG (01892) 870253 Quaint tiled house with lovely view, neatly kept timbered bar, and a wide choice of very good food that changes twice a day; lots of fresh fish. £22|£4.05/£6.95.

Tunbridge Wells TQ5839 SANKEYS 39 Mount Ephraim (01892) 511422 Excellent fresh fish and seafood cooked in all sorts of ways in several cosy and relaxed restaurant rooms; lively downstairs cellar wine bar too; cl 25 Dec. £22|£2.75/£10.

Tenterden TQ8833 KENT & E SUSSEX RAILWAY Tenterden Town Station TN30 6HE (01580) 765155 Steam-hauled and ornately decorated Pullman dining car with English food (Sun lunch/afternoon tea/5-course dinner) served by authentically dressed stewards; great fun; cl Jan and Feb £20|£2/£3.50.

Ivy Hatch TQ5854 PLOUGH (01732) 810268 Relaxed and friendly tile-hung house with imaginative and constantly changing food, well kept beers, good wines and efficient service; cosy bar areas, elegant conservatory restaurant, and nearby walks; disabled access. £19.50/£6.95.

Lamberhurst TQ6635 BROWN TROUT (01892) 890312 Very popular dining pub with friendly, prompt service and extremely good fish dishes – the daily specials are a bargain. £18|£3.15/£7.35.

Ringlestone TQ8755 RINGLESTONE (01622) 859900 Welcoming atmosphere in interestingly decorated, deservedly popular country pub, with very good food, especially the lunchtime buffet (no chips or fried food), and lots of real ales and country wines; no food 25 Dec; partial disabled access. £17.50|£3.95/£5.

Newnham TQ9557 GEORGE (01795) 890237 Distinctive 16th-c pub furnished with great character, atmospheric bar rooms, friendly staff, excellent imaginative food using fresh local produce, well kept beers and well chosen wines; no credit cards; no food pm Sun, Mon; children tolerated, dogs welcome; disabled access. £17|£2.50/£6.50.

Hever TQ4744 GREYHOUND (01732) 8622221 Pleasant place to eat before musical or theatrical performances in Hever Castle; English food as well as Belgian dishes (and beers); disabled access. £15|£2.50/£5.

Biddenden TQ8538 THREE CHIMNEYS (01580) 291472 Atmospheric country pub with small beamed rooms, log fires, and excellent, imaginative food from a large seasonal menu; cl 25–26 Dec; children in garden dining room only. **£14.50**|£3.25|£5.50.

Help this year from: Stephen Barney, Martyn G Hart, Michael and Jenny Back, Jenny and Brian Seller, Andy and Jill Kassube, Mrs S J Findlay, Dave Braisted, Thomas Nott, L G Milligan, George Atkinson, Chris and Anne Fluck, Geoff Lindley, Simon Small, M A and C R Starling, A B Dromey, P Walker, Ian Phillips, Louise Weekes, Mrs J A Trotter, Paul McKeerer, Nigel Gibbs, Tony Gayfer, Ralph A Raimi, Comus Elliott, S J Elliott, Colin Harnett, Simon Morton, Mark Thompson, K Flack, E G Parish, J R Biesmans.

KENT CALENDAR

Some of these dates were provisional as we went to press.

JANUARY

1 **Leeds** New Year's Day Treasure Trail at Leeds Castle (01622) 765400

MARCH

4 **Canterbury** National Trust Centenary Concert in the Cathedral (01892) 891001

6 **Dover** Film Festival – *till Fri 10* (01304) 208382

19 **Folkestone** European and All England Sea Angling Championship (01303) 276039

25 **Leeds** Spring Gardens Week at Leeds Castle – *till 2 April* (01622) 765400

APRIL

8 **Dover** Easter Fun Trail at the White Cliffs Experience – *till Sun 23* (01304) 210101

15 **Leeds** Celebration of Easter at Leeds Castle – *till Mon 17* (01622) 765400

16 **Chatham** Mad Hatter's Tea Party at the Historic Dockyard – *till Mon 17* (01634) 812551

18 **Folkestone** Children's Festival at the Metropole Arts Centre – *till Sat 22* (01303) 255070

22 **Canterbury** Medieval Fair, Costumed Cavalcade and Chaucer Commemoration Service (01227) 470379

28 **Folkestone** Dance Festival at the Leas Cliff Hall – *till Sun 30* (01303) 850388

MAY

1 **Rochester** Sweeps Festival Procession (01634) 843666

5 **Folkestone** VE Day Anniversary Celebrations at the Leas Cliff Hall – *till Mon 8* (01303) 253193

6 **Hever** Day of Dance at Hever Castle (01732) 865224; **Rochester** Sweeps Festival – *till Mon 8* (01634) 843666

7 **Dover** Festival – *till Sun 21* with VE Day celebrations on *Mon 8* (01304) 821199

8 **Chatham** VE Day Celebrations at the Historic Dockyard (01634) 812551

13 **Leeds** Festival of English Wines at Leeds Castle – *till Sun 14* (01622) 765400

KENT CALENDAR

MAY cont

21 **Ramsgate** Spring Festival of Arts and Architecture – *till 4 Jun*
(01843) 580994; **Sandling** Kent Day at the Museum of Kent Life
(01622) 763936

27 **Hever** Merry England Weekend at Hever Castle (01732) 865224;
Sandwich Great East Kent Garden Show at Windmill Farm
(01304) 201644; **Sellinge** Steam Festival – *till Mon 29* (01303) 813000

28 **Goudhurst** Spring Garden Fair at Finchcocks – *till Mon 29* (01580) 211702

30 **Detling** Smallholders Show at the Kent Showground (01306) 741302

JUNE

1 **Rochester** Dickens Festival – *till Sun 4* (01634) 843666

3 **Leeds** Balloon and Vintage Car Fiesta at Leeds Castle – *till Sun 4*
(01622) 765400

10 **Westerham** Music, Memories and Moonlight at Chartwell (01892)
891001; **Wrotham** Vintage and Veteran Steam and Transport Rally at the
Wings of the Morning Field, Wrotham Hill – *till Sun 11* (01732) 885568

17 **Sandling** Midsummer Folk Festival at the Museum of Kent Life –
till Sun 18 (01622) 763936

20 **Sevenoaks** Summer Festival – *till Thurs 29* (01732) 455133

24 **Brookland** Fhilippino Festival at the Philippine Village – *till Sun 25*
(01797) 344616; **Canterbury** Chaucer Festival – *till 22 July*
(01227) 470379; **Leeds** Open Air Concert at Leeds Castle (01622) 765400;
Sittingbourne Carnival

25 **Dover** Roman Festival at the White Cliffs Experience (01304) 210101;
Gravesend Riverside Fayre – *till Sun 26*

JULY

1 **Dover** Carnival (01304) 821498; **Hever** Summer Festival at Hever
Lakeside Theatre – *till end Aug* (01732) 866114; **Leeds** Open Air
Concert at Leeds Castle (01622) 765400; **Swale** Festival – *till Mon 31*
(01795) 580068

7 **Dymchurch** Kent Custom Bike Show at Angel Field – *till Sun 9*
(01634) 576991

9 **Chatham** River Day at the Historic Dockyard (01634) 812551

13 **Detling** Kent County Show at the Showground – *till Sat 15* (01622) 630975

14 **Ivy Hatch** National Trust Centenary Concert at Ightham Mote –
till Sat 15 with Family Concert *on Sun 16* (01892) 891001

15 **Cobham** Kent County and Countryman's Fair at Cobham Hall –
till Sun 16 (01243) 544181

20 **Lamberhurst** Open Air Opera at Scotney Castle – *till Sun 23* (01892) 891001

21 **Deal** Summer Music Festival – *till 5 Aug* (01304) 369576

22 **Rochester, Chatham, Strood** Medway Arts Festival – *till Sun 30*
(01634) 843666

23 **Chatham** Heavy Horse Day at the Historic Dockyard (01634) 812551

27 **Deal** Carnival (01304) 380556; **Lamberhurst** Open Air Opera at
Scotney Castle – *till Sat 29* (01892) 891001

KENT CALENDAR

JULY cont

28 **Chatham** South East Garden Festival at the Historic Dockyard (01634) 812551

29 **Tunbridge Wells** Georgian Festivities on the Pantiles – *till 6 Aug* (01892) 526121; **Whitstable** Regatta – *till Sat 30* (01227) 263595

AUGUST

7 **Sandwich** Open Amateur Golf Week at Prince's Golf Club – *till Fri 11* (01304) 611118

12 **Chatham** Victorian Fair at the Historic Dockyard – *till Sun 13* (01634) 812551

13 **Brookland** Festival of the Orient and Martial Arts at Philippine Village (01797) 344616

16 **Hythe** Venetian Fête – floating carnival viewed from Royal Military Canal (01303) 850388 ext 363

18 **Broadstairs** Folk Week – *till Fri 25* (01843) 865650

19 **Detling** Steam and Transport Rally at the Showground – *till Sun 20* (01622) 630975; **Ide Hill** Country Fair at Emmetts Garden – *till Sun 20* (01892) 891001; **Sheerness** Carnival

24 **Sandwich** Festival – *till Mon 28* (01304) 612392

26 **Ide Hill** Jazz Concert at Emmetts Garden (01892) 891001; **Rochester** Norman **Rochester** – *till Mon 28* (01634) 843666; **Shepway** Festival with airshow – *till Sept 3* (01303) 850388 ext 321

SEPTEMBER

2 **Canterbury** Hop Hoodening at the Cathedral – hop-picking festival with folk dancing groups from all over the country (01843) 591701; **Faversham** English Hop Festival – *till Sun 3* (01795) 424341; **Goudhurst** Finchcocks Festival, *every weekend till 1 Oct* (01580) 211702; **Ramsgate** Victorian Street Fair

9 **Strood** Steam Festival – *till Sun 10* (01634) 843666

15 **Leeds** Flower Festival at Leeds Castle (01622) 765400

16 **Chatham** Beat Retreat at the Historic Dockyard (01634) 812551

25 **Folkestone** Kent Literature Festival at the Metropole Arts Centre – *till 1 Oct* (01303) 255070

OCTOBER

7 **Canterbury** Festival – *till Sat 21* (01227) 472820; **Goudhurst** Autumn Fair at Finchcocks – *till Sun 8* (01580) 211702

14 **Faversham** Carnival

NOVEMBER

4 **Leeds** Grand Firework Spectacular at Leeds Castle (01622) 765400

17 **Tudeley** Henry Purcell Tercentenary Tudeley Festival at All Saints Church – *till Sat 25* (01732) 773322

DECEMBER

2 **Rochester** Dickensian Christmas – *till Sun 3* (01634) 843666

26 **Folkestone** Boxing Day Dip at East Cliff Sands (01303) 258083

LANCASHIRE
(INCLUDING GREATER MANCHESTER AND MERSEYSIDE)

Manchester and Liverpool both have lots of interesting things to do, making for excellent day visits. Elsewhere, in complete contrast, the little-known Forest of Bowland is good value for very quiet country breaks. The Silverdale area up towards Cumbria, even less well known, is also a possibility for country-lovers. Closer to Manchester, there is Pennine moorland of real beauty, with more places of interest to visit within easy reach. A newcomer to Lancashire will be surprised at its many beautifully timbered houses and halls (though not all live up to expectations inside).

The famous traditional seaside resorts are a tremendous draw to some – Blackpool gets more visitors each year than does the whole of Spain. Out of season, when those long stretches of beach and dune are empty, they have a certain lonely charm.

There's also an element of fascination about the tidal sands of Morecambe Bay stretching for miles into the distance, north of Lancaster, though the north Cumbrian side is much the most beautiful. Lancaster itself is a town of attractive streets and interesting buildings – some possibilities as a place to stay, even more as a place to visit for the day.

In general, prices in this area are appealing.

LANCASTER AND ITS COAST

Good quiet countryside in the north; Lancaster itself is civilised and attractive, Blackpool in summer is packed with lively fun.

The coast and its hinterland south of Lancaster is rather flat and featureless. This flatness is all part and parcel of the broad beaches which originally made Blackpool and its altogether more decorous neighbour Lytham St Annes popular beach resorts. Nowadays, with people more dubious about plunging into the Irish Sea, Blackpool has become more a place for young adults to have summer fun, with lots of discos, fun pubs and so forth as well as its vivid array of entertainments – an ideal place if that's the sort of thing you want, and a must for tram freaks.

North of Lancaster the countryside comes into its own. The Silverdale/Arnside area up by the Cumbrian border has a lot to recommend it for a quiet break: charming hilly countryside, by no means overrun with visitors even in summer, a coastline that's particularly interesting to bird-watchers and naturalists, and several places to visit.

Lancaster itself is an attractive town of considerable character, with a lot to do – and splendid countryside virtually on its doorstep.

There are quite a few things to see and do elsewhere here; highlights include Leighton Hall and the Carnforth steam railway centre.

Where to stay

Blackpool SD3035 IMPERIAL North Promenade FY1 2HB (01253) 23971 £98; 183 comfortable rms. Lots of Victorian features such as marble-pillared entrance hall and chesterfields, full health and fitness club with indoor swimming pool, gym. Jacuzzi, steak and sauna room and solarium free to residents.

Lancaster SD4862 POST HOUSE Waterside Park, Caton Rd LA1 3RA (01524) 65999 £71.90; 115 well equipped rms. Well run bustling modern hotel with waterside garden, buffet-style restaurant and lots of leisure facilities; disabled access.

Bilsborrow SD5139 GUY'S THATCHED HAMLET Bilsborrow, Preston PR3 0RS (01995) 640010 £42; 32 smartly modern rms. Bustling complex alongside canal, thatched old tavern, restaurant and pizzeria, outside terrace, children's play area and craft shops; good base for exploring the area; open all day; disabled access.

To see and do

☺ 🐾 ❅ 🗡 🖼 🏠 **Blackpool** SD3036 Britain's most loved and loathed seaside resort, in summer offering more bed spaces than the whole of Portugal. The atmosphere then is unashamedly boisterous (it's pretty dreary in winter), and though it's now more geared to young adults, most children love it, with plenty for them to do from donkey rides along the beaches (they have a day off on Fri) to days at the SANDCASTLE leisure complex. BLACKPOOL TOWER (until May proudly painted gold to celebrate its centenary) has several attractions geared towards families, inc a circus, laser shows, aquarium, insect exhibition, science gallery, and dark ride. Meals, snacks, shop, disabled access; cl winter wkdys; (01253) 292013; £5.95, more during the Illuminations. These famous autumn light displays are probably the best of their kind – if you don't mind travelling at a snail's pace along the Golden Five Hundred Yards (or Mile as they call it here). The town is now more than ever dominated by its redoubtable PLEASURE BEACH, where the new rollercoaster, quite reasonably called the Big One, stands 235 ft high; it travels at up to 85mph, and has not been entirely problem-free in its first few months – which perhaps adds to the thrill. Crowded and noisy, with a sprawling mass of 150 other breath-taking rides, the fairground might not be everyone's cup of tea, but this last year has again been Britain's most visited attraction.

There's more to Blackpool than ice-creams and eyesores: the ZOO (East Park Drive) has over 400 animals in 32 acres of spaciously landscaped gardens, as well as a miniature railway and play area. Meals, snacks, shop, disabled access; cl 25 Dec; (01253) 765027; £3.80, half price Dec–Mar. SEA LIFE CENTRE (Golden Mile Centre) Broadly similar to the other centres around the country, but this one has a bonus: the biggest display of tropical sharks in Europe. There's a walk-through tunnel underneath so you feel you're in there with them. Meals, snacks, shop, disabled access; cl 25 Dec; (01253) 22445; £4.45. GRUNDY ART GALLERY (Queen St) Works by 19th and 20th-c artists, various temporary exhibitions. Shop, disabled access to ground floor only; cl Sun and bank hols; free. No pilgrimage to this granddaddy of rollicking resorts would be complete without a visit to the factory where they make the famous BLACKPOOL ROCK: Coronation Rock Co, Cherry Tree Rd North. Shop, disabled access; cl 1–2 pm, wknds. They shut at 3.30pm, an hour earlier on Fri (01253) 21988; free. The tram to Fleetwood is a great survivor. The Ramsden Arms opposite Blackpool North station is the best of the town's pubs and has good-value bedrooms.

🐎 🏠 **Carnforth** SD4970 STEAMTOWN RAILWAY CENTRE Impressive collection of British and Continental locomotives, plus miniature engines. Snacks, shop; cl 25–26 Dec; *£3.50

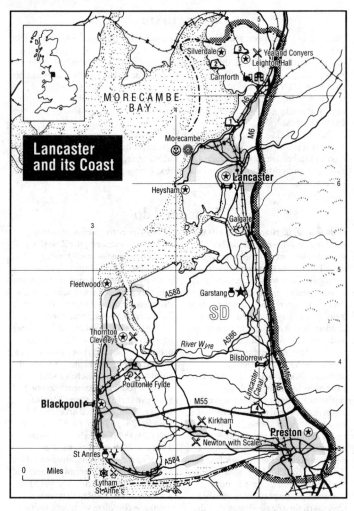

Lancaster and its Coast

MORECAMBE BAY

Silverdale · Yealand Conyers · Leighton Hall · Carnforth · Morecambe · Lancaster · Heysham · Galgate · Fleetwood · Garstang · Thornton Cleveleys · River Wyre · Bilsborrow · Poulton-le-Fylde · Lancaster Canal · Blackpool · Kirkham · Newton with Scales · Preston · St Annes · Lytham St Anne's

M6 · A6 · A588 · A586 · M55 · A584

SD

0 Miles 5

full steam days ((01524) 732100 for dates), £2.10 otherwise. The steam rides are unusual – especially with 125s belting past the ancient carriages. *Brief Encounter* was filmed partly at the adjacent station. A mile or so N, WARTON OLD RECTORY is the ruin of a 14th-c manor house – easy to trace the various living rooms among the attractively arched remains. Some disabled access; cl 1–2pm, winter Mon, 25–26 Dec, 1 Jan; free.

⚓✿♪ **Fleetwood** SD3348 Developed as a rather elegant 19th-c resort, with landscaping by Decimus Burton, plenty of smart buildings, lively harbour (boat trips in summer), trams from Blackpool right through the town, and two elegant if not entirely practical lighthouses, one in the middle of the street; excellent market. A MUSEUM concentrates on the town's fishing and shipping history. Shop; open pm Tues, Weds, Fri and Sat, Easter–Oct; *£1. The Marine Hall exhibition centre on the front has a decent bar (the Wyre – no food) with excellent views of the harbour and Morecambe Bay. STANAH SD3542 some way up the Wyre has a stretch of waterside country with reedbeds, birds and views, attractive despite the

ICI chemical works in the background, and on the opposite bank the Shard Bridge Inn at Hambleton SD3741 is nicely placed for lunch; SKIPPOOL SD3540 has lots of yachting activity in an attractive boating area, with a decent small café.

⚓ **Galgate** SD4855 CANALSIDE CRAFT CENTRE Converted farm buildings by canal with various crafts inc woodturner producing unusual clocks, barometers and bowls; cl Mon; (01524) 752223; free. The Plough is useful for lunch.

★ ♨ **Garstang** SD4845 is quite an attractive small market town, with a good deal of canal activity (and a fine aqueduct crossing the River Wyre). The entertaining waterside Owd Tithebarn (with a canal museum upstairs) is fun for lunch, and the more traditional Wheatsheaf and Kings Arms are useful too.

Glasson Dock SD4456, once an important port for Lancaster, still has the occasional coaster berthing, but is now a lively summer boating place, with attractive countryside around; good Sunday car-boot sales.

⚓ ✠ ✝ **Heysham** SD4160 HEYSHAM POWER STATIONS Hi-tech interactive exhibition on electricity generation, with tours of power station and nuclear reactor, and 25-acre nature reserve. Snacks, disabled access; cl am wknds, 25–26 Dec, 1 Jan, tours are in the afternoon, and in summer it may be worth booking; (01524) 855264; free. A tremendous contrast is the quaint squint-walled little village CHURCH, partly Saxon, with Norse-carved hogback tombstone inside. The unusual waterside Golden Ball at Heaton with Oxcliffe off the Lancaster road (should be signposted Overton, may be cut off by very high tides) is fun for lunch.

⚓ 🏰 ✠ 🏯 ✿ ♨ ⚓ ❀ 🦋 **Lancaster** SD4761 always manages to seem friendly and relaxed despite the grandeur of many of its stone buildings; ambling down the cobbled streets and alleyways (much is pedestrianised), you find it hard to believe that this was once one of the major West Indies shipping ports. These days the water traffic is more sedate, and you can hire punts or cruise along the canal in the summer months; the Water Witch on the canal is good for lunch, and other lunch spots worth knowing here include the Cross Keys, John of Gaunt, Mill Hotel and West Bank Hotel. The dramatic 12th-c Norman CASTLE, famous for hangings and witch trials, is owned by the Queen as Duke of Lancaster, and part of it is still used as a prison. The cells and the tower are open to the public, as is the 18th-c Gothic Revival Shire Hall. Shop; open wknds Apr–Oct and occasional wkdys if Court not in session; (01524) 64998; £2.50. PRIORY CHURCH Dates back to before the Conquest but the present hilltop building is mainly 14th and 15th c, with very interesting medieval choir-stalls, needlework and Anglo-Saxon cross fragments. Snacks, shop, some disabled access; cl winter lunchtimes. Nearby are the remains of a Roman bath house. MARITIME MUSEUM (St George's Quay) Lively and up-to-date look at the local maritime trade and fishing industry; the audio-visual show is good fun. Snacks, shop, disabled access; cl am Nov–Apr; £1.50 summer, free in winter. JUDGES LODGING (Church St) 17th-c house with well restored period rooms and plenty of Gillow furniture, inc the recently acquired very fine library table from Denton Hall. Also museum of childhood inc doll collection; cl am exc wkdys July–Sept (when cl 1–2 pm), Sun exc pm July–Sept, and all Nov–Easter; (01524) 32808; £1. The CITY MUSEUM (Market Sq) is firmly traditional, though still interesting, housed in a very grand Georgian former town hall. Shop; cl Sun; free. COTTAGE MUSEUM (Castle Hill) Old cottage opposite the castle furnished in the style of an early 19th-c artisan's house; cl am, Nov–Easter; 50p. WILLIAMSON PARK, ASHTON MEMORIAL AND BUTTERFLY PARK Magnificent folly clearly visible from the motorway, set in 38 acres of lovely landscaped parkland; displays on Edwardian life and unrivalled views from upper galleries. The butterfly house has a good collection of plants and lepidoptera, as well as free-flying birds and various creepy-crawlies.

Snacks, shop, disabled access; cl 25–26 Dec, 1 Jan; (01524) 33318; *£2.50.

🏠 🖼 ⛵ 🦋 Leighton Hall SD4974 LEIGHTON HALL Notably friendly neo-Gothic mansion (more restrained inside), still the home of the Gillow family and with early examples of their furniture, as well as clocks and paintings. The grounds have a collection of birds of prey (flying displays 3.30pm), nature trails, and beautifully kept gardens. The first glimpse of the house as you approach is lovely, with Lakeland hills rising up behind. Snacks, shop, disabled access; cl am, all Sat and Mon (exc bank hols), Oct–Apr; (01524) 734474; £3.20. The New Inn at Yealand Conyers is handy for lunch.

✗ ❀ Lytham St Annes SD3627 has a splendidly restored WINDMILL in the centre of the green, with an exhibition of its history. There's also a little LIFEBOAT MUSEUM in the adjacent old lifeboat house; both open Tues, Thurs and wknds Oct–Apr, cl 1–2pm; free. The Taps is a good real-ale pub here.

☺ ❀ Morecambe SD4364 Five miles of promenade and more of beaches to stroll along at this cheery resort, with pretty sunsets over the bay. FRONTIERLAND Wild West theme park with 30 family rides and attractions – spectacular views across the bay from the Sky Ride. Meals, snacks, shop, disabled access; cl Nov–Easter; £6.99. The town's new theme park, THE WORLD OF CRINKLEY BOTTOM, is at Happy Mount Park.

🏛 ✗ Poulton le Fylde SD3539 has quite an attractive pedestrianised market square, with a lovely church (as others in Lancashire, looking a good deal older than in fact it is), and several useful places to eat – the Old Town Hall is particularly good value. There's a good range of craft shops by the working WINDMILL at nearby Thornton SD3342; excellent teashop.

👶 🖼 ♒ ✝ 🏰 Preston SD5329 has a couple of decent museums, the impressive if rather dour Greek revival HARRIS MUSEUM AND ART GALLERY (Market Sq), with a good range of fine and decorative art (cl Sun and bank hols; free), and the COUNTY AND REGIMENTAL MUSEUM (Stanley St),

focusing on county history; cl Thurs, Sun and bank hols; £1. There's a good big market (the space is used for car-boot sales on Thurs), and the Olde Blue Bell (Church St) has a good choice of lunchtime food. MOOR PARK OBSERVATORY is usually open the last two Fri evenings of the month Sept–Mar (exc Dec); (01772) 201201 to check. Just out of town at Penwortham the CHURCH of St Mary has a 14th-c chancel, and the scant remains of a motte and bailey castle in the churchyard. The Fleece (Liverpool Rd, Penwortham Hill) is useful for lunch.

👶 ⛵ St Annes SD3228 TOY AND TEDDY BEAR MUSEUM Porritt-built Victorian building with big collection of old toys, dolls, trains, bears and other nostalgic children's items. Good shop, disabled access; open school hols, bank hol wknds and Sun all year, and daily exc Tues Whit–Oct; (01253) 713705; *£1.70. There's a sand dune NATURE RESERVE running alongside Clifton Drive North.

🛶 ⛵ ❀ 🐾 ☺ ❀ 🏨 Silverdale SD4674 looks out over the tidal sands to the Cumbrian hills, with streets of quiet houses and a church that looks 14th-c but was built barely a century ago. There are good woodland walks behind the town, and the Silverdale Hotel on Shore Rd is well worth knowing. LEIGHTON MOSS NATURE RESERVE (off Yealand Redmayne rd) RSPB reserve with several roomy hides looking out on to reedbeds where bitterns, bearded tits and marsh harriers breed; good walks and views, picnic areas, and guided talks (the otter-watching evenings in Jun and July are esp popular). Meals, snacks, shop, disabled access; cl 25 Dec; (01524) 701601; *£3. WOLF HOUSE GALLERY (Gibraltar) Georgian buildings selling paintings, knitwear, glass, rocking horses and other crafts; good views, and an adventure playground. Snacks; cl 1–2 pm, Mon, all wkdys 25 Dec–end Mar. Reginald Kaye's NURSERY has unusual alpine and other plants. Not far away, the FRIENDS' MEETING HOUSE in the pleasant village of Yealand Conyers SD5074 is unobtrusively charming; the New Inn here is a good dining pub.

✗ ✗ ⌁ **Thornton** SD3342 Marsh Mill Village Striking 18th-c flour and meal mill, now restored as the centrepiece of a bustling complex with various craft and gift shops, a dried flower specialist, and even a clog museum. Meals, snacks, shops, disabled access; cl 25 Dec; (01253) 860765; admission to the village is free, mill £1.20.

⌁ The **Lancaster Canal** which runs up the whole of this area from Preston to Carnforth is ideal for boating – 40 miles without a single lock; often through quiet countryside, with herons and even occasional kingfishers – best in spring or early summer, with ducklings and cygnets bobbing about, and lambs in the fields alongside. Boats can be hired by the day at Catforth SD4735 (01772) 690232, where there's a decent teashop.

Walks

The vast mudflats and sands of **Morecambe Bay** ⌂-1 are home to 200,000 waders, and are famous for their galloping tides. Walks over them are described in the Cumbria chapter – foot access is easier from that side, though guided walks are also available from Hest Bank (details from local tourist information centres; the tides and stretches of quicksand do make a guide essential). **Warton Crag** SD4973 ⌂-2 just N of Carnforth gives fine views over the bay and coast, and pleasant walking. **Leighton Moss Nature Reserve** ⌂-3 (see Silverdale above) is a short walk N, and is crossed by a public footpath.

The **Lancaster Canal** towpath ⌂-4 allows pleasant walks, largely through quiet countryside; Catforth SD4735 is a good departure point.

Driving

The Fylde is too low-lying to see much beyond the next bend. Once past Lancaster, there's a vivid change, with roads around Yealand Conyers and Silverdale looping through attractively wooded hilly countryside, and on the coastal side giving good views across Morecambe Bay.

Where to eat

Thornton Cleveleys SD3342 River House Skippool Creek (01253) 883497 Delightful restaurant with very good honest cooking using the freshest local ingredients; decent wine list, fresh flowers and log fires, and fine views (they also have bedrooms); cl Sun pm; children must be well behaved; partial disabled access. £45|£3/£10.
Kirkham SD4231 Cromwellian 16 Poulton St (01772) 685680 Tiny evening restaurant in 17th-c house with consistently good, interesting food from a fixed-price menu – thoughtful wine list, too; cl Sun and Mon, 1st wk Jan, 2 wks Aug. £25.
Yealand Conyers SD5074 New Inn (01524) 732938 Welcoming and atmospheric creeper-covered pub with good food in two communicating cottagey dining rooms, simply furnished little beamed bar, log fires, well kept beers, decent wines and a good choice of malt whiskies; a welcoming spot after a hard day on the fells. £15.55|£1.95/£4.95.
Newton with Scales SD4532 Prachee Preston New Rd (01772) 685896 A wide choice of classical Indian cooking in comfortable surroundings with consistently good standards over many years; disabled access. £12.75.

THE LANCASHIRE HEARTLAND

Manchester and Liverpool excellent for day visits; plenty of places to visit outside, grand walks on the moors.

Both Manchester and Liverpool are full of grand Victorian buildings, and interesting things to do and see – Manchester particularly so. To explore them, it might be best to stay outside and come in by day – particularly at the weekend, when traffic is very light and both are quite quick to get into by car, with easy parking. As they tend to be depressing in cold wet weather, a summer visit gives you most chance of seeing these two great cities at their best. Manchester's Museum of Science and Industry is a must for families; in Liverpool, the new Pleasure Island and Wester Approaches are already proving popular. Southport, too, has a good many attractions. Elsewhere, highlights include Bramhall Hall, Speke Hall, the Martin Mere wildfowl reserve, Rufford Old Hall, the warships in Birkenhead, the Camelot theme park at Charnock Richard, and the good re-creation of 1900s life at Wigan Pier. It's an easy area in which to find things to keep children amused.

There's magnificent countryside up on the moors here – plenty of exhilarating drives and some scope for walking.

Where to stay

Manchester SJ8284 VICTORIA & ALBERT Water St M60 9EA (0161) 832 1188 £80; 132 rms, individually styled and named after TV programmes. Carefully converted Victorian warehouse opposite Granada TV studios, with original iron pillars, oak beams and exposed brickwork, particularly good service, comfortable bar overlooking river, and good, imaginative food in restaurant and all-day brasserie; disabled access.

Bury SD8010 NORMANDIE Elbut Lane, Birtle, Bury BL9 6UT (0161) 764 3869 £69; 23 attractive rms. Unpretentious hotel high on the Pennines with fine views, homely lounge and snug bar, excellent French and English restaurant food, fine wine list, and friendly, professional service; cl Sun, last wk Dec, 1st wk Jan, 1st wk over Easter; disabled access.

Bromley Cross SD7213 DROP INN Hospital Rd, Last Drop, Bromley Cross BL7 9PZ (01204) 591131 £67w; 83 rms. Spacious, creeper-covered pub with lots of beamery and timbering, popular one-price hot and cold buffet, and heavy tables out on attractive flagstone terrace; village is an odd pastiche of old-world stone-and-cobbles street complete with gift and tea shops, bakery, etc – all part of a big well equipped Rank hotel complex; disabled access.

Darwen SD6922 OLD ROSINS Pickup Bank, Hoddlesden, Darwen BB3 3QD (01254) 771264 £49.50; 15 well equipped rms. Friendly old pub in centre of moors and ideal as base for exploring the area; good views from cosy open-plan bar, and interesting bar and restaurant food.

Ashworth Valley SD8913 LEACHES FARM Ashworth Valley, Rochdale OL11 5UN (01706) 41116 *£34; 3 rms, shared bthrm. 17th-c hill farm with really wonderful views; beams, and log fires; cl 22 Dec–2 Jan.

To see and do

Manchester SJ8498 On a fine weekend strolling around the city's very impressive buildings is a real pleasure. Albert Sq is one of the finest areas, with the great Albert Memorial (which predates London's), the main cultural centres, and some lively café-bars. The Town Hall is a massively impressive piece of Victoriana, facing colourful summer gardens. The CATHEDRAL is a very wide 15th-c church, with notable choir stalls; the small medieval centre around it, and Shambles Sq, deserve a look, as do Exchange St and St Ann's Sq. The Castlefield area by the basin where the Bridgewater and Rochdale canals meet is interesting – grimy warehouses, viaducts and the like, with some lively redevelopment inc the good Dukes 92 pub and maybe street theatre. The Rochdale canal towpath is a fascinating seamy-side walk. The council produces a good map detailing a walk round town. Chinatown here, incidentally, is the second largest Chinese community in England: lots of authentic restaurants and a Chinese Arts Centre.

! GRANADA STUDIOS TOUR (Water St) Downing Street, Baker Street and Coronation Street all in one go; if peering through the window of the Rovers Return doesn't excite you, there are also shows, sets, hi-tech 3-D rides, and exhibitions covering all aspects of television and cinema. Meals, snacks, shop, disabled access; cl Mon (exc bank hols), winter Tues, 24–26 Dec and wkdys; (0161) 833 0880; £10.99 – one of the most expensive visits in this book, but great fun, lively, and very slickly done – a visit can easily last all day.

↓⊺ ☺ MUSEUM OF SCIENCE AND INDUSTRY (Castlefield) Enormous museum on the site of the oldest passenger railway station in the world, hours of things to do, and plenty to touch and fiddle with. Highlights inc the power hall, air and space gallery (inc an exciting simulator), interactive science area, reconstructed sewer in the underground exhibition on sanitation, and the electricity gallery – which on its own covers four storeys. Enough to keep most families intrigued and entertained for most of the day. Meals, snacks, shop, disabled access; cl 23–25 Dec; (0161) 832 2244; £3.50, car parking may be extra.

☺ ♔ GALLERY OF ENGLISH COSTUME (Platt Hall, Rusholme) The best museum of its kind that we know of, a Georgian mansion with comprehensive examples of fashion styles over the last 400 years. The collection is so big that all the displays are changed frequently – though like the styles themselves you can guarantee they'll eventually come back. Shop, disabled access to ground floor only; the opening times do vary – best to tel first; (0161) 236 7369; free.

▣ CITY ART GALLERIES (Mosley St) Esp strong on Pre-Raphaelite paintings, as well as decorative and applied arts from early times; fascinating reconstruction of LS Lowry's studio, with soundtrack of the great man. Meals, snacks, shop; cl am Sun, Good Fri, 25–26 Dec; free.

♔ ♍ JOHN RYLANDS LIBRARY (Deansgate) Magnificent neo-Gothic building with lovely old-fashioned reading room and over five million books. Displays and tours of splendid old manuscripts and archival material; they may be closed for rewiring up to March – best to check first, (0161) 834 5343. Shop; cl pm Sat, Sun, bank hols, 24 Dec–1 Jan; free.

♔♍ MUSEUM OF TRANSPORT (Boyle St) Local transport through the ages inc over 80 buses and other vehicles, with photos, tickets and other items. Sun snacks, shop, disabled access; open Weds, Sat, Sun and bank hols; (0161) 205 2122; £1.60.

▣ WHITWORTH ART GALLERY (Oxford Rd) British watercolours from Sandby to Turner, as well as plenty of modern paintings and sculpture, and unusual collections of textiles and wallpaper. Meals, snacks, shop, disabled access; cl Sun, Good Fri, Christmas wk; free.

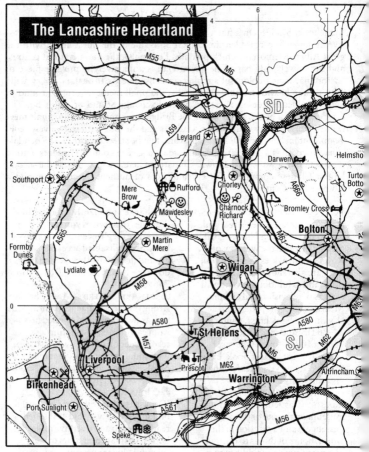

The Lancashire Heartland

⚕ ❀ ⚑ PANKHURST CENTRE (62 Nelson St) Emmeline Pankhurst launched the Suffragette movement from this Georgian semi. Displays on the fight for the vote, period-furnished parlour, interestingly planted garden and contemporary arts and crafts. Meals, snacks, shop, disabled access; cl wknds and bank hols; (0161) 274 3525; free.

⚕ MANCHESTER JEWISH MUSEUM (Cheetham Hill Rd, 1 mile N on A665) Housed in a former synagogue, the story of Manchester's Jewish community over the last 200 years, with interesting recorded recollections of life earlier this century. Shop, disabled access to ground floor only; cl Fri, Sat and Jewish holidays; (0161) 834 9879; £2.

⚕ ♪ MANCHESTER MUSEUM (Oxford Rd) Good Japanese collection, Egyptian relics, aquarium, beehive, and local history and crafts. Shop, disabled access; cl Sun, Good Fri, May Day, Christmas; free.

⚕ MANCHESTER UNITED MUSEUM AND TOUR CENTRE (Old Trafford) The country's first purpose-built football museum, covering the club's history from its foundation in 1878 to the more recent glory days; hundreds of changing exhibits and tours of the ground (not match days, limited pre-match days). Snacks, shop, disabled access; cl Mon, 25 Dec; (0161) 877 4002; £4.95 tour and museum, £2.95 museum only.

See also Salford and Prestwich, below.

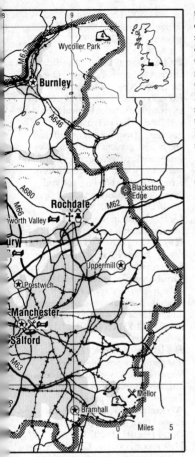

Liverpool SJ4395 The fine 19th-c buildings which mark Liverpool's past as one of the world's great ports have in the last few years taken on a cleaner and prouder look. At the same time a good few varied family attractions have opened, making it a rewarding place for a visit if you know what's going on. Several really good museums and art galleries are free. The Philharmonic (Hope St) is probably the country's grandest late Victorian pub; nearby the Everyman Bistro has good-value food. You can tour the Liver Building pm wkdys by arrangement – (0151) 236 2748 – though it's best viewed from one of the famous ferries across the Mersey, which leave regularly from Pier Head. Other well known buildings include

the two CATHEDRALS, both built this century though in wildly differing styles. Walk along Hope St (the heart of the city's 18th-c area, with many Georgian brick terraces) to the modern Metropolitan Roman Catholic cathedral, designed by Frederick Gibberd after a vast earlier scheme by Lutyens ran out of money; the crypt of the Lutyens design is beneath the present impressive structure, with the blue light from the 16-sided glass tower reflecting on its marble. The Anglican cathedral, designed by Giles Gilbert Scott when he was only 21, is undeniably powerful, though its soaring proportions and cavernous scale make it impersonal. Both churches have good concerts.

♨ The ALBERT DOCK is a spectacular restoration of previously redundant warehouse buildings by the river, now a lively complex of shops, cafés and exhibitions with regular entertainers, performers, events and boat trips. The Pump House, one of the renovated buildings on the dockside, is good for lunch, and the next three attractions are housed in the complex – you can easily base a whole day around a visit here.

▣ TATE GALLERY (Albert Dock) The National Collection of Modern Art, with plenty of sculptures, paintings and various special events. Not for the traditionalists, though there are only occasional blackspots – like the 1994 absurdity of that notorious empty room by some American non-artist. Exhibitions until spring on post-war European art, and Matisse, Maillol and Rodin. Meals, snacks, shop, disabled access; cl Mon (exc bank hols), Good Fri, 25–26 Dec; (0151) 709 3223; free, exc some major exhibitions.

! BEATLES STORY (Albert Dock) Bouncy tribute to the local boys made good and the sights and sounds of the 60s. Shop, disabled access; cl 25–26 Dec; (0151)709 1963; *£4.45. Beatles fans can also go on a 2-hour magical mystery tour around related city sites; (0151) 709 3631.

✿☉♫ MERSEYSIDE MARITIME MUSEUM (Albert Dock) Huge museum with varied displays on the port; boats, ships, craft demonstrations and a vivid interpretation of what it was like for the millions who travelled from here to the New World. It takes in the MUSEUM OF LIVERPOOL LIFE (the former Labour Museum), looking at social history over the last century or so, and the Customs and Excise museum, ANYTHING TO DECLARE – a lot more fun than it sounds, with bizarre confiscated and counterfeit goods, an intriguing look at concealment techniques, and even demonstrations by sniffer dogs. Meals, snacks, shop, disabled access; cl Good Fri, 24–26 Dec, 1 Jan; £3 – good value considering all there is to see.

🖼 WALKER ART GALLERY (William Brown St) Excellent collection of European paintings and sculpture with esp notable Italian, Dutch and Pre-Raphaelite pictures. Snacks, shop, disabled access; cl am Sun, 1 Jan, Good Fri, 24–26 Dec; free.

♿☺ LIVERPOOL MUSEUM (William Brown St) You could spend hours at this excellent museum and still not see everything. There's a particularly good planetarium (shows 3.15 pm wkdys, around 1, 2 and 4 pm wknds; cl Mon), and a lively natural history centre with lots to play with (cl Mon). From 12 Feb–4 Jun they'll have the touring Dinosaurs Alive exhibition, featuring roaring moving lifesize models; cl am Sun, Good Fri, 24–26 Dec, 1 Jan; free, planetarium £1.20.

♿🖼 LIVERPOOL LIBRARIES AND ARTS (William Brown St) Tours of one of Europe's biggest public libraries, taking in first editions, prints and fine bindings. Snacks, shop, disabled access; cl Sun, all bank hols and Tues after spring and summer bank hols; (0151) 225 5445 to book; free.

🏠 WESTERN APPROACHES (Rumford St) Restored underground command centre for the Battle of the Atlantic,

the only WWII bunker of its kind open to the public. Shop, disabled access; cl 25–26 Dec; (0151) 227 2008; *£3.99.

🌼♿☺ PLEASURE ISLAND (Riverside Drive, A5036 continuation S) One of the country's most successful new attractions, based around the site of the International Garden Festival a few years back. They still have the traditional Japanese, Chinese, Indian and English gardens from then, along with woodland walks and trails, a lively interactive science centre, and leisure activities such as bowling, golf and roller-skating. Meals, snacks, shop; cl 25–26 Dec, 1 Jan; (0151) 728 7766; £5.95. The Britannia in an excellent Merseyside setting is handy for lunch.

🏠🐄🌼 CROXTETH HALL AND COUNTRY PARK (5 miles NE) Period displays in Edwardian house, and working farm, Victorian walled garden, miniature railway, and country walks in the grounds. Meals, snacks, shop, some disabled access; house cl Oct–Easter; (0151) 228 5311; *£2.50, £1.10 hall or farm only.

🏠🌼🖼 SUDLEY (Mosley Hill) Interestingly unspoilt private Victorian house with good gardens, attractive furniture and paintings by Turner and Pre-Raphaelites. Weekend snacks, disabled access to ground floor only; cl Good Fri, 24–26 Dec, 1 Jan; (0151) 207 0001; free.

! LIVERPOOL FOOTBALL CLUB (Anfield Rd) A chance for fans to see behind the scenes at Anfield, with tours of the grounds, dressing room and pitch. The trophy room has cups, programmes and other treasured memorabilia, as well as a video of some of the club's greatest moments. Shop, some disabled access; tours pm wkdys and summer Sats (except match days), am May–Sept, booking recommended, (0151) 263 2361; *£3.

Other things to see and do

🏠🖼🌼✕ **Altrincham** SJ7687 DUNHAM MASSEY HALL 16th-c moated manor house extensively remodelled in the 18th c, with impressive collections of silverware, paintings and furnishings, and restored kitchen, pantry and

laundry. The largely unaltered grounds have plenty of deer wandering about, formal avenues of trees, and a working Elizabethan saw mill (usually Weds and Sun only). Various concerts and events – even in winter when the house is closed. Meals, snacks, shop, some disabled access; house cl am, Thurs, Fri and Nov–Mar, garden cl Nov–Mar except weekends from 25 Feb; £4.50 house and garden (inc lively new Walkman guide), £2 garden only; NT. In town the attractive Old Packet House (Navigation Rd, Broadheath) by the canal does good food.

✝ ❀ ! ▣ ☗ 🏚 Birkenhead SJ3288 Waterfront views over to Liverpool, of course, but a surprise in BIRKENHEAD PRIORY (Priory St), a ruined 12th-c Benedictine priory with notable visitor centre. Shop, some disabled access; cl 1.30–2 pm, Mon (exc bank hols), 25–26 Dec, 1 Jan; free. Good views from the tower of the neighbouring church. The docks have a couple of HISTORIC WARSHIPS, HMS *Plymouth* and the submarine *Onyx*, both of which played a part in the Falklands War. The *Onyx* is the only floating submarine open to the public in the country – you can peep up the periscope. Quite a few ladders to negotiate. Snacks, shop; cl 25 Dec, 1 Jan; (0151) 650 1573; £4 both ships. WILLIAMSON ART GALLERY AND MUSEUM (Slatey Rd) English watercolours and art by the Liverpool school, sculpture and ceramics, model ships, and a collection of cars and motorcycles in period garage setting. Shop, disabled access; cl am Sun, Mon; (0151) 652 4177; free. On summer Suns (mid-May–mid-Sept) there are generally free concerts at either the Museum or the Priory. The Shrewsbury Arms out in Claughton Firs is the best place for lunch, while at Shore Rd, Woodside, there's an unusual STEAM PUMPING STATION; cl 1.30–2 pm and all Mon; (0151) 650 1182; *£1. BIRKENHEAD PARK laid out in 1853 was the world's first public park.

❀ Blackstone Edge SD9716 PENNINE RIDING EXPERIENCE Guided rides through windswept moors and valleys along ancient packhorse routes. They have 15 horses, and do trips lasting from a day to full wk hols. The views are fantastic; (01706) 377061.

🏠 ⬆ ☗ ▣ ▣ 🎭 ➶ ♪ ☙ Bolton SD7108 SMITHILLS HALL (Smithills Dean Rd) Interesting (though much restored) old manor house with fine 14th-c

Great Hall and splendid panelled drawing room; lots of Stuart furniture. Shop, disabled access to ground floor only; cl am Sun, Mon (exc bank hols), all Oct–Mar; (01204) 841265; £1.55. The nearby 15th-c HALL I' TH' WOOD was the home of Samuel Crompton and where he developed his spinning mule in 1779; there's a museum of his life. It was restored and refurnished by Lord Leverhulme at the start of this century; details as above, a joint ticket is available. The MUSEUM AND ART GALLERY is quite good, with Egyptian mummies, lots of watercolours and 20th-c sculpture. Snacks, shop; cl Weds, Sun and bank hols; free. You can tour WARBURTONS BAKERY by arrangement; (01204) 23551; free. BUTTERFLY WORLD (Queen's Park) Free-flying butterflies and moths, as well as fish pools, tarantulas, scorpions and locusts. Snacks, shop, disabled access; cl Dec–Mar; £1.75. The King's Head (Junction Rd, Deane), with a bowling green behind, is useful for lunch, as is the restaurant of the Queen's Moat House – an interesting church conversion. LAST DROP VILLAGE Just outside Bolton, this former farm village has been transformed into a pastiche of an 18th-c village, very rustic and quaint, with cottages, shops, decent pub and craft centre.

🏠 ▣ ❀ Bramhall SJ8984 BRAMHALL HALL One of the finest houses in the area (particularly from the outside), a splendid timber-framed 14th-c hall with rare 16th-c wall paintings and furniture, and extensive parkland; there was a fair bit of prettifying restoration in the last century. Meals, snacks, shop, disabled access to ground floor; house cl am, Mon Oct–Dec, all wkdys Jan–Mar; (0161) 485 3708; £2.75.

☗ ▣ ♪ ⸙ ✝ 🐦 Burnley SD8432 TOWNELEY HALL ART GALLERY AND MUSEUMS 14th-c house with local crafts and industry, paintings, furniture and glassware, period rooms, and natural history centre with aquarium. Snacks, shop, disabled access; cl Sat, Christmas; free. The CANAL WHARF (Manchester Rd) has a small museum with weaver's cottage etc, and short towpath walks along the Leeds & Liverpool Canal here give you a vivid impression of the towering old weaving mills; the raised canal embankment across the valley is a remarkable sight. ROCKWATER BIRD CONSERVATION CENTRE (Cliviger – A646 N) Pheasants, bantams, foreign birds and owls as well as rabbits, chipmunks and miniature sheep. Snacks, disabled access (but no facilities); cl Mon (exc bank hols), Thurs and Nov–Easter; (01282) 415016; *£2. Nearby CLIVIGER GORGE has pleasant walks, with stream, woodland and farmland; moors above. The Kettledrum up at Mereclough to the S has good home cooking.

🐃 Bury SD8011 EAST LANCS RAILWAY Well regarded by enthusiasts, a scenic 17-mile steam journey along the pretty Irwell valley; you can get on or off along the way, so it's a good way of leisurely exploring the area. Snacks, shop, disabled access; open wknds and bank hols; (0161) 764 7790 for timetable; *£5 return for the full trip. The Tap & Spile (Manchester Old Rd) is useful for a bite to eat, and the Lord Raglan up at Nangreaves SD8115 is a popular nearby moorland dining pub.

☺ ⚘ Charnock Richard SD5515 CAMELOT ADVENTURE THEME PARK 130-acre theme park recreating the mythical Camelot, with jousting and falconry displays, a medieval village and dozens of rides and attractions – rather better than other such places. Crafts Sun. Meals, snacks, shop, disabled access; open wknds and school hols Apr, May, Sept and Oct, daily Jun–Aug; (01257) 453044; £9.99.

🎪 ✿ ♠ ▣ Chorley SD5817 ASTLEY HALL Unusual-looking timber-framed 16th-c house with extensive gardens and woodland. Elaborate carvings and plasterwork, interesting pottery and paintings. Meals, snacks, shop, disabled access to ground floor; cl 12–1 pm, Mon–Thurs Nov–Mar, 25 Dec–2 Jan; (01257) 262166; *£2. The Malt 'n' Hops behind the station in the town itself is useful for lunch.

↓T Helmshore SD7821 HELMSHORE TEXTILE MUSEUMS Two stone mills with comprehensive collection of textile machinery, much of it in its original environment and still in working order. Also waterwheel and good explanatory displays – this is undoubtedly one of the best textile museums in the country. Snacks July–Sept, shop, disabled access; cl am (exc Sun Easter–Oct), Sat (exc July–Sept), all Nov–Easter (exc pm Sun); (01706) 226459; £1.50. The Duke of Wellington on the B6232 W of Haslingden is a good family dining pub in fine surroundings.

🏠🛍️ ▣ ♪ ⚘ ❀ ✝ Leyland SD5422 BRITISH COMMERCIAL VEHICLE MUSEUM Biggest commercial-vehicle museum in Europe, with over 40 perfectly restored British wagons, buses, trucks, vans and fire engines – they shine so much you'd think they were new. Snacks, shop, disabled access; cl Mon (exc bank hols), wkdys in Oct and Nov, all Dec–Apr; (01772) 451011; £3. OLD GRAMMAR SCHOOL MUSEUM AND EXHIBITION CENTRE Sturdy 16th-c building with changing local art and history; open all Tues and Fri, am Sat and pm Thurs; free. WORDEN ARTS AND CRAFTS CENTRE (Worden Park) Art displays and nine varied craft workshops, surrounded by 157 acres of parkland. Meals, snacks, shop, disabled access; cl 25 Dec; free. Leyland also has a pleasant little town trail, and the 15th-c CHURCH has some fine stained glass. The friendly little Rose & Crown (A581 S) has decent basic food.

🌱☺🍲 Martin Mere SD4310 WILDFOWL AND WETLANDS TRUST Thousands of wild geese, swans, ducks and flamingoes regularly visit the recreated natural open water habitats at this important 376-acre centre; in the winter swans come from Iceland and Siberia. Lots of the birds will feed straight from your hand. Good displays in visitor centre, well organised walks, lively Wetlands Adventure for children, and plenty of instructive and entertaining events. Meals, snacks, shop, disabled access; cl 24–25 Dec; (01704) 895181; £3.95. About 400 yards down the road, in **Burscough**, the WINDMILL ANIMAL FARM is a friendly 40-acre site with various animals and their babies to feed (inc rare breeds), as well as tractor rides and adventure playground. Snacks, shop, disabled access; cl winter wkdys; (01704) 892282; £2.25. The canalside Ship at Lathom has good-value lunches.

🏵 ☺ **Mawdesley** SD4915 has a decent CRAFT CENTRE (Back Lane) in former farm buildings, with animals and play area for children; the tea room has a good range of teas and coffees; cl Mon exc bank hols. The Robin Hood in pretty country N of the village has good-value food.

🐾 ✔ **Mere Brow** SD4118 TARLETON LEISURE LAKES Attractive lake and woodland area with 90 acres of countryside; watersports, fishing, golf, walks, nearby farm shop. Meals, snacks, disabled access; (01772) 814502; £5 per car. The Cock & Bottle in Tarleton has a popular dining pub.

★ ✤ 🖻 ♄ **Port Sunlight** SJ3384 The most famous of the garden villages built by 19th-c philanthropists, contriving something better than the appalling squalor of northern England's factory towns. Historically important as the precursor of garden cities, garden suburbs and New Towns, it's perfectly preserved, with groups of mock-Tudor cottages, swathes of greenery and parkland: no two groups of houses are alike. Lord Leverhulme, who had built his Sunlight Soap factory here, donated the village its outstanding LADY LEVER ART GALLERY Interesting Victorian paintings inc Turners and Pre-Raphaelites – many adapted for use in soap ads, to the fury of the artists; noted Wedgwood ceramics. It will be closed for refurbishment until early summer, so best to ring first, (051) 207 0001 ext 613; free. PORT SUNLIGHT HERITAGE CENTRE sets the scene, with useful village trail leaflets; also period soap packaging (you can buy soap in similar style wrappings). Shop; cl winter wknds; *40p. THORNTON HOUGH SJ3081 was built by Lord Leverhulme as a mock-Tudor estate village – Port Sunlight on a much smaller scale; the Seven Stars there is useful for lunch. Other parts of the Wirral are described in the Cheshire chapter.

🐾 ↓↑ **Prescot** SJ4692 KNOWSLEY SAFARI PARK Five-mile drive through very natural-looking reserves of lions, tigers, rhinos, monkeys and other animals; they have the biggest herd of African elephants in Europe. Also pets corner and miniature railway. Meals, snacks, shop, disabled access; cl Nov–Mar; (0151) 430 9009; *£8 per car – load in all your friends and it's very good value indeed. MUSEUM OF CLOCK AND WATCH MAKING 18th-c town house with exhibits on former local clockmaking industry. Shop; cl am Sun, Mon (exc bank hols), Good Fri, 25–26 Dec, 1 Jan; (0151) 430 7787; free. The Clock Face is a pleasant old mansion-house pub here.

🏠 ✤ 🖻 **Prestwich** SD8104 HEATON HALL Splendidly decorated 18th-c neo-classical house in extensive well used public parkland; fine paintings, plasterwork and furniture, unusual circular Pompeiian room, and various recitals and temporary exhibitions. Snacks, shop, disabled access; cl 1–2 pm, am Sun, Mon–Weds, Oct–Apr; (0161) 236 5244; free.

♂ ✝ **Rochdale** SD8713 was the birthplace of the Co-operative movement, and a good MUSEUM in the original shop on Toad Lane has the full story; cl Mon; 50p. There's also a decent museum devoted to Gracie Fields and an 800-yr-old CHURCH with stained glass by Burne-Jones and William Morris.

🏠 ♂ **Rufford** SD4615 RUFFORD OLD HALL Lovely timber-framed Tudor house built by the Hesketh family in the 16th c, with an intricate hammer-beam roof and movable wooden screen in the Great Hall, and impressive collections of 17th-c Lancashire oak furniture, 16th-c arms, armour and tapestries. Some later rooms too. Snacks, shop; cl am, Thurs, Fri, Nov–Mar; £3. NT. The Black Horse at Croston has good-value home cooking.

↓↑ **St Helens** SJ5195 PILKINGTON GLASS MUSEUM The surprisingly interesting history of glass production, well told via interactive displays and exhibitions. Snacks, shop, limited disabled access; cl am wknds and bank hols, all Christmas–New Year; (01744) 692014; free.

↓↑ 🏠 ♂ 🖻 **Salford** SJ8197 MINING MUSEUM (Eccles Old Rd) Georgian building with two reconstructed mines, and displays showing the history and development of coal-mining. Shop; cl 12.30–1.30 pm, am Sun, Sat, Good Fri, 25–26 Dec; (0161) 736 1832; free. ORDSALL HALL MUSEUM (Taylorson St) Timbered Tudor manor house with local history and Victorian farmhouse kitchen. Shop, some disabled access; cl 12.30–1.30 pm, am Sun, Sat, Good Fri, 25–26 Dec; (0161) 872 0251; free. MUSEUM AND ART GALLERY Most notable for the unrivalled L S Lowry collection; also good collection of Victorian arts, and nostalgic reconstruction of industrial street scene, with some wonderfully over the top period advertisements. Snacks, shop, disabled access; cl am Sun, Sat, Good Fri, Easter, 25 Dec, 1 Jan; (0161) 736 2649; free. The waterside Mark Addy (Stanley St) has a great choice of cheeses and pâtés.

✿ 📠 🙂 😊 🏮 👃 ★ 🏠 ⚘ **Southport** SD3317 Smartish Victorian seaside resort, long famed as the most pleasant shopping town in the area, and as the place where the sea doesn't come in – in fact it comes in as often as anywhere else, but doesn't stay quite as long. Nice parks and gardens, and bracing trips down the PIER, either on foot or on the little train. Lord St is the elegant main shopping street; there's an excellent antiquarian bookshop down the Wayfarers Arcade just off it. In summer you can generally get pleasure flights over the area from the beach. SOUTHPORT RAILWAY CENTRE (Derby Rd) Biggest centre of its type in the area, with plenty of old locomotives, and other vehicles. Snacks, shop, disabled access; cl wkdys exc summer school hols; (01704) 530693; £2 steam days, £1.50 non-steam days. ATKINSON ART GALLERY Specialises in 19th and 20th-c watercolours, oil paintings, prints and sculpture; shop, disabled access; cl pm Thurs and Sat, all Sun, bank hols; free. PLEASURELAND Typical fairground, plenty of rides and attractions; the wooden rollercoaster is well regarded by connoisseurs. There's a little ZOO (Princes Park) next door; cl 25 Dec; (01704) 38102; *£2.50. BRITISH LAWNMOWER MUSEUM (Shakespeare St) Fully restored

machines from the 1830s to the present, taking in all the famous brands (these were the days when plenty of people could say they had a Rolls Royce). Also one of the first racing lawnmowers – the curator used to be a champion; cl Sun and bank hols; (01704) 535369; *£1. CHURCHTOWN VILLAGE SD3618, the oldest part of town, has a number of pretty thatched cottages and the lakeside BOTANIC GARDENS, which are very attractive as well as being interesting to plantsmen; boats to hire, fernery, pets corner, and local history MUSEUM (open 11–3 Tues–Fri and pm wknds and bank hols; free). Just opposite, MEOLS HALL is worth a look mainly for its paintings, inc works by Ramsey, Reynolds, Romney and Poussin. They hope to develop a craft area in the courtyard this year. Shop; usually open pm mid-Jul–Aug; (01704) 28171; price not fixed as we went to press. The Hesketh Arms is good for lunch out here.

🏮 ✿ **Speke** SJ4383 SPEKE HALL A remarkable manor house built around a square courtyard, this is one of the most beautiful and richly timbered black and white houses in the country; the inside is mainly Victorian, though there's a vast Tudor Great Hall, as well as interesting servants' quarters, intricate plasterwork and priest's hole. The garden is being restored in Victorian style. It's hard to believe the centre of Liverpool is just 6 miles away. Meals, snacks, shop, disabled access; cl am, all Mon, Jan–Mar; £3.40, 60p grounds only; NT. They now do occasional roof tours for those interested in finding out more about how the timbers were put together; best to tel (0151) 427 7231 for dates and times.

🏮 👃 ✿ **Turton Bottoms** SD7315 TURTON TOWER 15th-c Renaissance house with Elizabethan buildings and earlier peel tower; mostly a museum inside, but there are a couple of period rooms, as well as a major collection of carved wood furniture. Formal Victorian gardens. It was interestingly extended by followers of the Romantic and later Arts and Crafts movement. Snacks, shop; open daily May–Sept (cl am wknds, and 12-1 pm for lunch), pm Sat–Weds in Mar, Apr and Oct, and pm Sun only in Nov and Feb; (01204) 852203; *90p. The White Horse at Edgworth nearby is useful for lunch.

★ ☀️▣ **Uppermill** SD9905 This whole area of mill settlements in steep valleys cut through the moors is full of interest, and Uppermill itself is one of the most attractive places.

SADDLEWORTH MUSEUM AND ART GALLERY Based around an old mill, with regular days when the mill and weaver's cottage are brought to life by appropriately dressed volunteers. Shop, limited disabled access; cl am Nov–Feb, 25 Dec; £1. Up above the town is a lonely moorland church, with good walks around it; the ancient pub opposite, the Cross Keys, is good.

ᛁ ↓T ❁ ♠🐾 **Wigan** SD5805 WIGAN PIER Rather different from when Orwell knew it, this is now a dynamic and hugely enjoyable wharfside centre demonstrating local life in the early 1900s, with actors bringing the reconstructed coal mine, pub, school, music hall, houses and even seaside vividly to life. An ingenious mix of museum and theatre, it's great fun, and you really do get a tangible impression of what life at the turn of the century was like. Across the canal a textile mill has the world's largest working mill engine and other machines. Meals, snacks, shop, disabled access; cl Fri, maybe other days in winter; (01942) 44888; *£4.10. The Old Pear Tree on Frog Lane does decent lunches; the atmospheric Orwell on Wigan Pier has quick food. HAIGH HALL COUNTRY PARK 250-acre country park with guided walks, nature trails, mini zoo, golf course, craft centre, walled gardens and miniature railway. Meals, snacks, shop, some disabled access; (01942) 832985; park free, though charges for car parking and attractions.

🍎 **Pick-your-own** is popular, with lots of places on the flat ground in the W of the area – soft fruit the speciality, late June–Aug; LYDIATE FRUIT FARM SD3604 (Pilling Lane) has a good farm shop in attractive 18th-c former stable buildings.

★ The area has few conventionally pretty villages, but there are unexpected corners even quite close to urban areas – such as Ringley SD7605 with its village stocks and ancient bridge over the Irwell (and a decent pub).

Walks

Rivington SD6214 ⌂-1, just outside Horwich, lies close to attractive reservoirs. Lower Rivington Reservoir SD6213 has a waterside path along its eastern edge, and a curious mock-up of Liverpool castle built in 1912 as an adornment to the vast and atmospherically decayed gardens of Lever Park SD6313, which cover the hillside. A trail guides you around the undergrowth and up to the Pigeon Tower SD6314, within a few minutes of Rivington Pike – the summit. The Great House Barn SD6313 is the place to start, with a good information centre, maps, guides, etc.

From Marple SJ9588, the towpath along the **Peak Forest Canal** ⌂-2 soon leaves suburbia for green countryside; N is the famous set of Marple locks SJ9689 and aqueduct over the River Etherow. To the S, you can leave the canal at Strines SJ9868 and climb on to Mellor Moor SJ9987.

Down on the coast, **Formby Dunes** SD2809 ⌂-3 reached from the NW edge of Formby is a large tract of sweeping sandy dunes which are in some areas being stabilised by pine plantations; broad beaches, good walks through the adjacent pinewoods, made interesting by the chance of seeing and even feeding red squirrels (you can buy nuts for them here). Best in spring and autumn – can be busy in summer; parking in some places may cost £1.50, but keep looking – a number of other spots are free.

Wycoller Park SD9339 ⌂-4 is Lancashire Brontë country (the ruined hall at Wycoller features in *Jane Eyre*), and has walks along a beck to Clam Bridge, an Iron Age slab, and up to Foster's Leap SD9439, a finely placed crag.

This area is outstanding for the number of pubs which are well sited as good jumping-off points for walks – or places to look forward to getting back to. Up on the moors, many of these are closed during lunchtime Mon–Thurs. Good pubs for walkers include the Hare & Hounds at Abbey Village SD6422, Pack Horse at Affetside SD7513, Black Dog at Belmont SD6716, Dog at Belthorn SD7224, White House on Blackstone Edge SD9716, Owd Betts at Cheesden on Ashworth Moor SD8316, Rams Head near Denshaw SD9710, Diggle Hotel at Diglea Hamlet above Diggle itself SE0008, Strawbury Duck by Entwistle Station SD7217, Bull's Head on Grains Bar SD9608, Duke of Wellington on B6232 W of Haslingden SD7522, Egerton Arms off the narrow Ashworth rd above Heywood SD8513, Romper at Ridge End above Marple SJ9686, Kettledrum at Mereclough SD8632, Old Rosins at Pickup Bank, Old Hoddlesden SD6922, Roebuck on Roebuck Low SD9606, Royal Arms at Tockholes SD6623 (for Roddlesworth Valley woodlands, maybe on to the ruins of Hollinshead Hall and its restored curative well; the Victoria and Rock are also good, though slightly less well placed), Railway at White Coppice SD6118.

Driving

The best drives are over to the NE and E of the area. In the NE, the A635 out of Mossley quickly soars up on to Saddleworth Moor; the A670 takes you up over equally wild moorland countryside, over Standedge; the B6197 from Delph down to Grains Bar and then right along the A672 to Denshaw, where both the A672 and the A640 strike magnificently off into the moors. All these roads soon take you into Yorkshire.

The A675 N from Bolton is a fine drive, with attractive but narrow side roads branching off at Belmont; the back road forking off to the right through Tockholes is wider, and a pleasant drive. The A666 Bolton–Darwen, and the parallel loop of the B6391 out from Bromley Cross, are fine moorland roads; coming into Darwen you pass some very striking industrial relics such as the extraordinary campanile-style mill chimney and massive complex stationary steam engine. There are attractive views from the old Roman road heading N through Edgworth. The B6232 from Haslingden to Blackburn has fine views. The moorland roads S from Burnley are quite attractive, with the best views from the back road angling off SE from the A52 to the junction of the A671 and B6238.

Perhaps best of all in this area are the old packhorse roads between Burnley and Hebden Bridge through Mereclough and over Stansfield Moor, and between Nelson/Colne and Hebden Bridge over Widdop Moor.

In the SE, the hill roads climbing up from Marple above the Goyt Valley yield good views, taking you quickly over the border into the high country of that part of Cheshire and Derbyshire.

West of the M6 there's a patch of surprisingly pleasant countryside around the area sometimes known over-generously as the Wigan Alps, with several popular dining pubs dotted around such as the Robin Hood on the Mawdesley–Croston road, the Stocks in Alder Lane, Parbold, the Farmers Arms at Bispham Green, and the Brook House on Barmskin Lane, the road between Wrightington Bar (which has yet more eating houses such as the Rigbye Arms and High Moor Restaurant) and Mawdesley. Any of these will provide a decent meal, and the various roads looping between them make the most of this gently attractive and modestly hilly countryside – which also yields plenty of possibilities for quiet walks.

Where to eat

Manchester and Liverpool both have plenty of good ethnic restaurants – excellent for locals.

Manchester SJ8498 YANG SING 34 Princess St (0161) 236 2200 Exceptionally good Chinese food using the best fresh ingredients (tanks of live fish, too), wonderful dim-sum, unusual dishes like ducks' tongues and goose webs among traditional Cantonese specialities, good-value set meals, and bustling atmosphere; cl 25 Dec; limited disabled access. **£19.**

Birkenhead SJ3289 PASTIME RESTAURANT 42 Hamilton Sq (0151) 647 8095 Popular restaurant in handsome Victorian building with good food (the fixed price menu is good value), a relaxed atmosphere, and friendly, helpful service; cl Mon; partial disabled access. **£17.50.**

Manchester SJ8498 GAYLORD Amethyst House, Marriott's Court, Spring Gardens (0161) 832 6037 Outstandingly good, long-standing Indian restaurant, traditionally and smartly decorated, with very carefully cooked food and efficient service; cl 25 Dec, 1 Jan. **£16.60.**

Southport SD3317 SCARISBRICK HOTEL Lord St (01704) 543000 Busy Victorian hotel with popular, reasonably priced restaurant; also bar food in comfortable lounge; disabled access. **£14.40|£1.95/£3.25.**

Manchester SJ8498 ROYAL OAK 729 Wilmslow Rd, Didsbury (0161) 445 3152 Busy pub with exceptional choice of cheeses from around the world, huge helpings; bread, cheese and salad **£2.80.**

Manchester SJ8498 MARK ADDY Stanley St, Salford (0161) 832 4080 Smart pub in converted boat waiting rooms with a good range of food – though it's the choice of 50 different cheeses served in huge single chunks that is the main feature; doggy-bags provided; bread and cheese **£2.80.**

Mellor SJ9888 DEVONSHIRE ARMS Longhurst Lane (0161) 427 2563 Relaxed and distinctive pub on the edge of the Peak District with home-made, interesting bar food. **£2.75/£4.95.**

NORTH LANCASHIRE AND THE FOREST OF BOWLAND

Striking moorland, though with limited access; attractive countryside elsewhere, with pretty villages; a good area for a quiet break.

The Forest of Bowland is a striking area of Pennine moorland. It's less visited than most areas of comparable scenery, as much of the moorland, privately owned, is closed to walkers. Development in some of the villages (also in private hands) is controlled too strictly to allow for any significant expansion of holiday accommodation – let alone a proliferation of camp sites and so forth. Despite this, indeed in many ways because of this, the area does have a lot of appeal for people who want peace and quiet. There is at least some potential for walking here – for instance, along the pretty Rivers Hodder and Dunsop.

Elsewhere, Pendle Hill has always held the imagination, and other areas of fine countryside include the great whaleback of Longridge Fell, and the wooded Beacon Fell country park. Some of Lancashire's most attractive villages are to be found here, and there are plenty of places to visit.

Where to stay

Slaidburn SD7152 PARROCK HEAD FARM Slaidburn, Clitheroe BB7 3AH (01200) 446614 **£91 inc dinner**; 9 rms – 3 in main house, 6 in garden cottages. Lovely converted 17th-c farmhouse in wonderful spot between Lakes and Dales, with cosy, low-beamed bar, carefully converted hay-loft to create comfortable lounge and elegantly furnished timbered library, fresh flowers, very good food in spacious restaurant, well chosen wine list, generous breakfasts, and friendly staff; dogs allowed; disabled access.

Cowan Bridge SD6477 HIPPING HALL Cowan Bridge, Kirkby Lonsdale, Carnforth LA6 2JJ (015242) 71187 £74; 7 pretty rms. Relaxed country-house atmosphere and delicious food in handsome small hotel with help-yourself drinks in conservatory, open fire, lovely beamed Great Hall with minstrel gallery where guests dine together, and 4 acres of walled gardens; cl Jan-Feb; children over 12.

Gibbon Bridge SD6342 GIBBON BRIDGE Gibbon Bridge, Chipping, Preston PR3 2TQ (01995) 61456 £70; 30 rms. Family-owned country hotel with beautiful landscaped gardens and a quiet, relaxing atmosphere; good, straightforward English cooking, an excellent bakery, spacious, airy restaurant and adjoining conservatory, fine wines, and very good service; health and gym area; a good base for walking and short driving trips; disabled access.

Whitewell SD6546 INN AT WHITEWELL Whitewell, Clitheroe BB7 3AT (01200) 448222 *£67; 10 rms, some with open peat fires. Civilised stone inn in the Forest of Bowland, attractive setting and grounds with views down valley, interesting period furnishings, plenty of room, good food, fine wines, and unusual facilities such as art gallery and 6 miles of trout, salmon and sea-trout fishing; friendly dogs welcome.

Capernwray SD5371 NEW CAPERNWRAY FARMHOUSE Capernwray, Carnforth LA6 1AD (01524) 734284 £55; 3 comfortable rms. Pretty 300-year-old ex-farmhouse with helpful, friendly owners, cosy lounge, stone walls and beams, and candlelit dinner in what was the dairy; children over 10.

Hurst Green SD6838 SHIREBURN ARMS Hurst Green, Blackburn BB7 9QJ (01254) 826518 *£49; 16 rms. Lovely 17th-c country hotel with a refined but friendly atmosphere, airy and neatly modernised bar, comfortable lounge, open fires, good-value food in restaurant, and fine view of the Ribble Valley from the conservatory; disabled access.

Colne SD8839 HIGHER WANLESS FARM Red Lane BB8 7JP (01282) 865301 £38; 2 rms, one with own bthrm. Warmly welcoming farmhouse with beams, log fires and lovely surrounding farmland used mainly for breeding of shire horses, as well as sheep; cl Dec–Jan; children over 3.

Clitheroe SD7441 BROOKLYN GUEST HOUSE 32 Pimlico Rd BB7 2AH (01200) 28268 £36; 4 rms. Very friendly and spotlessly kept Victorian town house with comfortable, homely residents' lounge, and generous, well cooked breakfasts; close to town centre and Forest of Bowland; no pets.

Waddington SD7243 BACKFOLD COTTAGE The Square, Waddington, Clitheroe BB7 3JA (01200) 22367 £36; 3 rms. Tiny 17th-c cottage in cobbled street, beautifully furnished with antiques; very good service, candlelit evening meals, and log fires; self-catering cottage, too; cl Christmas; children at owner's discretion.

Lower Dolphinholme SD5153 OLD MILL HOUSE Lower Dolphinholme, Lancaster LA2 9AX (01524) 791855 £35; 3 rms. 17th-c no smoking house, originally a corn mill, in 3 acres of lovely gardens and woodland on the River Wyre; relaxed lounge with open log fire, good food in dining room, and gas lighting; no children.

Waddington SD7243 PETER BARN Cross Lane, Waddington Clitheroe BB7 3JH (01200) 28585 *£35; 3 lovely rms. Converted old stone tithe barn with beamed sitting room, antiques, lovely home cooking, warmly welcoming owners, a gentle atmosphere, and surrounded by a delightful garden; fine walking country; cl 23 Dec–1 Jan.

Chipping SD6243 CARR SIDE FARM Chipping, Preston PR3 2TS (01995) 61590 £34; 3 comfortable, warm rms with magnificent Pennine views – as there are from the dining room. Immaculately kept B & B in farmhouse on a working farm with land that runs right up on to the fells; huge breakfasts and very good service; pony trekking; children over 3.

To see and do

⬇T **Barnoldswick** SD8746 BANCROFT MILL ENGINE The last working steam mill in the area (not that long ago Barnoldswick had 13), with the engine and boilerhouse as they were in its glory days. Snacks, shop, disabled access; best to tel (01282) 813932 for dates of steam days; £1. The Fanny Grey (B651 towards Colne) has decent food.

⬇ ❀ ▬ 🏠 ✝ **Barrowford** SD8539 PENDLE HERITAGE CENTRE Local history, 18th-c walled gardens, farm and country trails, 14th-c barn with pot-bellied pig, and displays on the Pendle witches – the house itself certainly looks appropriately witchy. Snacks, shop, disabled access; cl 20 Dec–2 Jan; (01282) 695366; *£1.50. The CHURCH at nearby unspoilt Newchurch SD8239 has the witches' grave, and the Old Sparrow Hawk on Wheatley Lane towards Fence does good lunches.

⬇T 🜃 ▣ ✝ ❀ ✿ **Blackburn** SD6827 Put firmly on the map by the Industrial Revolution, this has bustling shops and market, some fine buildings and lots of beautiful unspoilt countryside around. LEWIS MUSEUM OF TEXTILE MACHINERY (Exchange St) Development of textile industry from the 18th c, displayed in period rooms with various changing exhibitions. Shop, limited disabled access; cl Sun, Mon, bank hols and Christmas; free. MUSEUM AND ART GALLERY (Museum St) Fine books and manuscripts, English watercolours, Japanese woodblock prints, Greek and Russian Orthodox icons, and a fantastic collection of beetles – some of them really big and pretty scary. Shop, disabled access to ground floor only; cl Sun, Mon, bank hols and Christmas; free. The parish CHURCH (actually now a cathedral) is very handsome – grand yet elegant. WITTON COUNTRY PARK 480 acres of attractive countryside with walks, nature trails, viewpoints, displays of carts and horse-drawn carriages, small mammal centre and other displays. Wknd snacks, shop, some disabled access; visitor centre cl am (exc Sun), and all Mon, Tues and

Weds Nov–Mar – the park is always open; admission to the park is free, though there is a small charge for the visitor centre.

🜃 🜚 ✿ **Clitheroe** SD7441 Bustling old market town, its High Street dominated by the CASTLE perched on its limestone rock. One of the oldest buildings in Lancashire, it has one of the smallest Norman keeps in the country. The CLITHEROE CASTLE MUSEUM nearby has an extensive geology exhibition, as well as cloggers' and printers' shops; good views of the Ribble Valley. Shop; cl Nov-Easter; *£1. The Starkie Arms below is handy for lunch. Every Weds evening hundreds of poultry and small livestock enthusiasts travel to the auctions here, some from as far away as Scotland.

🜚 **Colne** SD8839 BRITISH IN INDIA MUSEUM Interesting history of the British rule of India from the 17th c to 1947, with models, photographs, uniforms and other related objects. Shop; cl Sun and Tues, all bank hols, 4–13 July and 5–11 Sept, all Dec and Jan; (01282) 870215; *£1.50.

🏠 ▣ **Cow Ark** SD6745 BROWSHOLME HALL Unpretentious-looking Tudor house on the edge of the Forest of Bowland, with a surprisingly rich range of contents. Guided tours by members of the family show off the 17th-c furnishings and paintings by the likes of Turner, Romney, Batoni and Northcote. Shop, disabled access; open Easter and spring bank hol wknds, Sat in July, all wknd Aug; (01254) 826719; £2.80. The Inn at Whitewell in one direction and Red Pump at Bashall Eaves in the other offer a choice of good places to eat.

★ **Downham** SD7844 is an outstandingly pretty village below Pendle Hill; carefully preserved, on the side of a steep pasture valley with a stream winding along the bottom; the Assheton Arms is pleasant for lunch, and there are pretty walks nearby.

🏠 ❀ ✿ **Hoghton** SD6125 HOGHTON TOWER Splendid 16th-c fortified hilltop mansion, with grand state

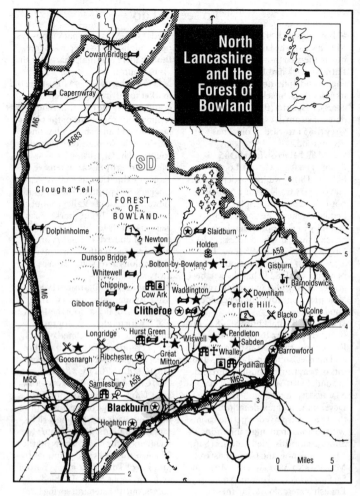

North
Lancashire
and the
Forest of
Bowland

rooms and royal bedchamber. The Tudor well house has a horse-drawn pump, and there are stone cells once used to jail cattle thieves; also a collection of dolls and dolls' houses. The gardens are lovely (particularly the Rose Garden) and walks through the surrounding grounds offer wonderful views of the sea, moors, Lakeland hills and Welsh mountains. Snacks, shop; open pm Sun Easter–Oct, plus Tues–Thurs July and Aug; (01254) 852986; £2.50, £1 garden only. The Royal Oak and (all day) canalside Boatyard at Riley Green have decent food.

🌺 **Holden** SD7749 HOLDEN CLOUGH NURSERY Old-fashioned nursery with thoroughly up-to-date approach to raising interesting plants in Victorian kitchen garden of Holden Clough Hall; beds of alpines, trough gardens, herbaceous perennials, shrubs and rhododendrons. Shop, disabled access; cl am (exc Sat), all Fri, Sun (exc pm Apr and May), and 25 Dec– 1 Jan; (01200) 447615; free. The Coach & Horses in the lovely village of Bolton by Bowland has good food.

🏠 **Hurst Green** SD6838 STONYHURST COLLEGE Magnificent 16th-c manor house, home to famous Catholic boarding school, and one of the biggest buildings in the area. The library, chapel, other historic rooms and the extensive grounds can be seen. Snacks, shop; open pm Aug exc Mon, gardens open July too; (01254) 826345; £3.50, £1 garden only. The Bayley Arms, Punch Bowl and Shireburn Arms Hotel here are all useful for lunch; it's good walking country.

🏠 🖼 **Padiham** SD7933 GAWTHORPE HALL Early 17th-c manor house with fine panelling and moulded ceilings, minstrel gallery and Jacobean long gallery. Important collections of costume, embroidery and lace, and paintings from the National Portrait Gallery. Snacks, shop, some disabled access; cl am (exc bank hols), Mon, Fri, Nov–Mar; £2.30; NT. The hilly cobbled alleyways in the town's centre are now a conservation area.

★ 👁🏚♣† **Ribchester** SD6335 is an attractive little town, many of its buildings incorporating masonry plundered from the former Roman town here: the White Bull pub, with decent food, has a couple of Tuscan pillars for its porch and an excavated Roman bath house behind. There are several small antique shops. MUSEUM OF CHILDHOOD Enormous collection of over 250,000 toys, models, and other items inc dolls' houses, teddies (one rescued from the *Titanic*), and working model fairground. Snacks, shop; cl Mon exc bank hols; (01254) 878520; £2.45. RIBCHESTER ROMAN MUSEUM Small museum on the site of a fort occupied by the Romans between the 1st and 4th c; lots of coins, pottery and the famous Ribchester helmet, as well as a new audio-visual display on the area's history. Shop, disabled access; cl am wknds; (01254) 878261; £1.25. There are also excavated granaries behind STYDD NURSERY, a specialist plant nursery with lots of old-fashioned roses and hardy perennials. Some disabled access; cl am (exc Sat), all Mon; free. The 15th-c CHURCH stands on the site of the Roman fort, and no doubt uses much salvaged material from it.

🏚 ⚘ **Samlesbury** SD6230 SAMLESBURY HALL Well restored half-timbered 14th-c manor house, with good changing exhibitions and sales of antiques, crafts and collector's items. Tours are good at bringing out how the building has changed and developed over the centuries. Meals, snacks, shop, disabled access; cl am, all Mon exc bank hols, mid-Dec–mid-Jan; (01254) 812010; *£2. The Myerscough Hotel (A59) is good for lunch.

★ 🏚† **Slaidburn** SD7152 in the Forest of Bowland is perfectly preserved: charming stone cottages, a green with the River Hodder running by, and at the opposite end an early 18th-c schoolhouse and a CHURCH with a very 18th-c feel inside. The Hark to Bounty is good for lunch and has comfortable bedrooms.

† 🏚 **Whalley** SD7336 WHALLEY ABBEY Striking remains of 14th-c Cistercian abbey – the monks' quarters, rather than the church which has virtually disappeared – in grounds of Blackburn Diocesan Retreat and Conference House, an interesting 16th-c manor house (where they do B & B). Two gatehouses are intact, and there's a new visitor centre. Snacks, shop, disabled access; cl Oct–Apr; (01254) 822268; *£1.50. The separate 13th-c parish CHURCH is very attractive, with interesting woodwork inside and three Celtic-Scandinavian crosses dating back a thousand years. The Freemasons Arms at Wiswell does good food.

★ **Other attractive villages** in or on the edges of the Forest of Bowland are Bolton by Bowland SD7849 (with a fine church), Gisburn SD8248, Newton SD6950 and Waddington SD7244. Elsewhere, we'd recommend Goosnargh SD5537, and, on the slopes of Pendle Hill, Pendleton SD7539, Sabden SD7737 and Wiswell SD7437. All these villages have decent pubs and good surrounding scenery. Great Mitton SD7139 has an attractive church with an outstanding range of memorial tombs. Dunsop Bridge SD6550 is the nearest village to the exact centre of Great Britain.

Walks

The major snag about the **Forest of Bowland** ⌂-1 is its lack of legal access, with only a few paths crossing the impressive massif that forms some of the county's most significant scenery; the Ramblers' Association has often organised mass trespasses as demonstrations against denial of access. There are, however, a few fine walks on rights of way – for instance, up Clougha Fell from Quernmore SD5259; above Tarnbrook Wyre SD5855; up Dunsop Fell from Slaidburn SD7152 or Dunsop Bridge SD6550; up Fairsnape and Wolf Fell from Chipping SD6143 or Bleasdale SD5745. Beacon Fell Country Park SD5642 is an atmospheric place to wander through. There are some pleasant walks around the Coronation Arms at Horton SD8550.

You can walk round and almost all over **Pendle Hill** SD7941 ⌂-2, so thorough is the path network, and although Pendle's witch-persecuting days are happily over the place still has a haunting elemental appeal. The view that enraptured George Fox, the founder of the Quakers, is as good as ever. The quickest way up is from Barley village SD8240.

Driving

Crossing the Forest of Bowland, the B6478 takes in some of its most appealing if not grandest scenery; from Slaidburn the narrow old road N past Stocks Reservoir gives a sense of adventure. One of the nicest roads in this part is up from Clitheroe through Bashall Eaves and then the Trough of Bowland, eventually taking the right fork up towards Quernmore.

The back roads up over Longridge Fell give some fine views over much of Lancashire, especially the old road from Longridge up past the New Drop Inn (lovely views over the Ribble Valley) to Waddington. Around Pendle Hill, the steep road up through Pendleton and down through Sabden also gives some splendid views, as does the road around the hill's eastern flank – passing through some very attractive scenery around Downham.

Where to eat

Longridge SD6037 PAUL HEATHCOTES 104 Higher Rd (01772) 784969 Pretty restaurant with flowers, beams and candlelit tables, exceptional modern British cooking, marvellous puddings, and exemplary service; cl Mon; children tolerated; disabled access. £80|£22.50 3-course lunch.

Downham SD7844 ASSHETON ARMS (01200) 441227 Popular pub among peaceful pastures in prettily preserved village, rambling beamed bar, reasonably priced and generously served bar food, and decent wines; disabled access. £16|£3.10|£5.50.

Goosnargh SD5537 BUSHELLS ARMS (01772) 865235 Friendly modernised pub close to Chingle Hall, with excellent range of imaginative food from a constantly changing menu, and good range of wines; may cl Mon; well behaved children only; partial disabled access. £14.40|£2.50|£6.

Blacko SD8541 MOORCOCK (01282) 614186 Spaciously comfortable lounge bar with wonderful views from the picture windows, very good and generously served food, and efficient friendly service; cl 25 Dec, disabled access. £13|£2|£4.95.

Help this year from: Alan and Margaret Griffiths, Mrs Ada Bradley, Keith Croxton, Dilys Unsworth, Bronwen and Steve Wrigley, LM, Andrew Hazeldine, M G Lavery, Michael Butler, Mike and Wendy Proctor, G L Tong, Paul McPherson, Jim and Maggie Cowell, Paul Wreglesworth, Lynn Sharpless, Bob Eardley, Sarah Elliott, Gary Goldson, Julie and Andie Hawkins, Fred Collier, S R and A I Ashcroft, A and M Dickinson, Graham Reeve, Brian Kneale, Ada Bradley, GA, PA, Brian Jones, Brian Wainwright, Andrew and Ruth Triggs, Nic Armitage, D Grzelka, Ian Phillips, M and J Back, Margaret and Allen Marsden, Caroline Wright, D Stokes, Steve and Karen Jennings, Tony and Lynne Stark, David Templar.

LANCASHIRE CALENDAR

Some of these dates were provisional as we went to press.

JANUARY

11 **Lancaster** Old Calendar Walk – New Year's Eve torchlit walk round the historic town, starts 7pm from the John o'Gaunt Gateway (01524) 32878

28 **Liverpool** Chinese New Year Celebrations – *till 5 Feb* (0151) 709 8151

FEBRUARY

25 **Lancaster** Old Calendar Walk – Valentine's Day torchlit walk round the historic town, starts 7pm from the John o'Gaunt Gateway (01524) 32878

MARCH

6 **Liverpool** Festival of Music – *till Fri 10* (0151) 225 6306

8 **Liverpool** Merseyside International Festival of Women at the Blackburn House Centre For Women – *till Mon 13* (0151) 709 4356

18 **Oldham** William Walton Festival at Queen Elizabeth Hall – *till Mon 20* (0161) 678 4072

20 **Liverpool** Festival of Speech and Drama – *till Fri 24* (0151) 225 6306

26 **Manchester** L S Lowry: The Man and His Art at Stockport Art Gallery – *till 21 May* (0161) 474 4453

APRIL

6 **Liverpool** Grand National meeting at Aintree Racecourse – *till Sat 8* (0151) 523 2600

14 **Lancaster** Maritime Festival – *till Mon 17* (01524) 32878

15 **Bacup** Britannia Coconut Dancers – colourful elaborately costumed black-faced clog dancers from 9am, thought to be pirate dances brought with miners moving N from Cornwall

17 **Preston** Egg and Orange Rolling in Avenham Park – in pagan times Easter is associated with the renewal of life, symbolised by the brightly painted eggs which since Christian times also represent the stone rolled away from the entrance to the Sepulchre

MAY

4 **Merseyside** VE Day Celebrations – *till Tues 9* (0151) 709 2444

13 **Lancaster** Old Calendar Walk – May Day torchlit walk round the historic town, starts 7pm from the John o'Gaunt Gateway (01524) 32878

14 **Fylde** Red Rose Carriage Driving Event

19 **Chorley** Canal Festival – *till Sun 21* (01257) 481778

26 **Blackpool** British Open Ballroom and Latin American Dance Championships at Winter Gardens – *till 2 Jun* (01253) 25252; **Morecambe** International Festival of Country Music – *till Mon 29* (01524) 582828

27 **Liverpool** Show at Wavertree (0151) 225 6351; **Morecambe** Chess Congress – *till Mon 29* (01524) 582828

28 **Churchtown** Children's Festival

LANCASHIRE CALENDAR

JUNE

2 **Cark-in-Cartmel** Great Garden and Countryside Festival – *till Sun 4*

3 **Bilsborrow** Gala; **Lancaster** Annual Punt Races (01524) 849484; **Liverpool** Lord Mayor's Parade (0151) 734 2851

4 **Morecambe** Carnival (01524) 414379; **Skippool** Gymkhana and Gala Horse Show with gala procession *on Sat 10*

9 **Liverpool** Festival of Comedy – *till Wed 21* (0151) 709 8151; **Liverpool** Africa Oye 95 (African, Latin and Caribbean festival) – *till Sat 17* with free festival at Birkenhead Park *on Sat 10* (0151) 708 6344

8 **Wirral** Show – *till Sun 9* (0151) 639 2718

10 **Calverdale** Children's Festival

17 **Liverpool** Mozart's Requiem at the Metropolitan Cathedral (0151) 724 6644

JULY

1 **Carnforth** Jazz and Fireworks at Leighton Hall; also Classical Concert *on Sun 2* (01865) 864466

4 **Lancaster** Old Calendar Walk – Midsummer Eve torchlit walk round the historic town, starts 7pm from the John o'Gaunt Gateway (01524) 32878

8 **Wigan** Jazz Festival – *till Sun 9*; **Winmarleigh** Gala; **Wirral** Show – *till Sun 9* (0151) 639 2718

16 **Morecambe** International One Man Band Shebang (01524) 582828

21 **Chorley** Royal Lancashire Show at Astley Park – *till Sun 23* (01254) 813769

22 **Liverpool** Trains, Boats and Planes at the Southport Railway Centre – *till Sun 23* (01704) 530693

28 **St Helens** Show at Sherdley Park – *till Sun 30* (01744) 456000

30 **Morecambe** Combined Services (military parade) – *till 6 Aug* (01524) 582828

AUGUST

5 **Garstang** Agricultural Show; **Morecambe** Peripatetic Promenaders (Street Theatre Weekend) – *till Sun 6* (01524) 582828; **Southport** Woodvale Rally, large display of model aircraft and classic cars at Woodvale Airfield – *till Sun 6* (01704) 578816

11 **Merseyside** VJ Celebrations – *till Wed 16* (0151) 709 2444; **Morecambe** World of Music and Dance – *till Sun 13* (01524) 582828

12 **Fleetwood** Firework Display and Birdman Competition at Fleetwood Pier; **Rochdale** Rushbearing Weekend; **Southport** Friends of Thomas the Tank Engine Gala Party – *till Sun 13* (01704) 530693

17 **Southport** Flower Show – *till Sat 19* (01704) 533133

20 **Morecambe and Lancaster** Folklore Fiesta – *till Weds 23* (01524) 582501

25 **Bolton** Festival at Central Library – *till 3 Sept* (01204) 22311 ext 2170; **Colne** R'n'B Festival with over 200 bands – *till Mon 28* (01282) 864721; **Lancaster** Georgian Legacy Festival – *till Mon 28* (01524) 32878; **Liverpool** Beatles festival – *till Tues 29* (0151) 236 9091

LANCASHIRE CALENDAR

AUGUST cont

28 **Liverpool** Woolton Show at Camp Hill (0151) 236 9091; **Liverpool** Matthew Street Festival – free festival with music, street performers and carnival atmosphere (0151) 236 9091

31 **Over Kellett** Burton, Milnthorpe and Carnforth Show at Mason's Field (01524) 701066

SEPTEMBER

1 **Blackpool** Illuminations on the Promenade – *till 5 Nov* (01253) 25212; **Fleetwood** Train and Transport Festival – *till Sun 3*

3 **Crumpsall** Trans Lancs Historic Vehicle Rally (0161) 205 2122; **Lancaster** Horticultural Society Summer Show

22 **Morecambe** Autumn Festival of Country Music – *till Sun 24* (01524) 582828

OCTOBER

8 **St Helens** North West Labrador Club Show (01744) 810910

10 **Lancaster** Old Calendar Walk – Michaelmas Day torchlit walk round the historic town, starts 7pm from the John o'Gaunt Gateway (01524) 32878

14 **Manchester** Complementary Medicine Festival at the Dominion Hotel – *till Sun 15* (01943) 609454

20 **Lancaster** Literature Festival – *till Sun 29* (01524) 62166

23 **Blackpool** Sequence dance festival at Winter Gardens – *till Thurs 26* (01253) 25252

NOVEMBER

4 **Lancaster** Fireworks Spectacular at Castle Hill (01524) 32878

5 **Fleetwood** Firework Display and Birdman Competition at Fleetwood Pier; **St Helens** Bonfire and Fireworks at Sherdley Park (01744) 24061

10 **Lancaster** Old Calendar Walk – Hallowe'en torchlit walk round the historic town, starts 7pm from the John o'Gaunt Gateway (01524) 32878

12 **Lancaster** Horticultural Society Late Show

DECEMBER

17 **Lancaster** Old Calendar Walk – St Nicholas Day torchlit walk round the historic town, starts 7pm from the John o'Gaunt Gateway (01524) 32878

We welcome reports from readers ...

This *Guide* depends on readers' reports. Please tell us what you think about places in it. And do recommend additions. Use the card in the middle, the report forms at the end, or just write – no stamp needed: *The Good Weekend Guide*, FREEPOST TN1569, Wadhurst, E Sussex TN5 7BR.

LEICESTERSHIRE, LINCOLNSHIRE AND NOTTINGHAMSHIRE

Leicestershire has the most varied and appealing countryside here, undulating and with interesting views. Parts of Lincolnshire have a somewhat similar rolling character, and, like Leicestershire, the county is studded with attractive villages and remarkably fine churches. Both these counties have plenty of grand houses and castles to look at, though rather less in the way of things to keep children entertained; that's where Nottinghamshire tends to score. This is not a part of Britain to come to if you want to spend the time looking around fine gardens.

All three counties treat visitors well, with exhaustive maps, trails and guide leaflets from information centres. A bonus in Leicestershire is unusually good public transport.

Of the three county towns, Lincoln is the best bet for most people: it's preserved a more universally appealing character, and has lots to see. If you enjoy sightseeing, Nottingham might well be a choice – again with lots to see, and a gentler place at weekends than you'd expect. Though Leicester has a good many attractions, most people will probably find it too busy a workaday city to enjoy a weekend stay.

LEICESTERSHIRE

Good for a civilised break, with interesting places to visit, and expansive varied scenery.

The eastern side of the county has quite a lot to offer for a short break. The rolling countryside has long views and is pleasantly varied, with patches of woodland, attractive stone-built villages, many delightful churches, and several fine houses in handsome parkland. Among places to look around and things to do, we'd pick out Belvoir Castle, Stamford Hall at Swinford, the steam railway running from Shackerstone past the battlefield of Bosworth Field, followed by the ruined castles at Ashby-de-la-Zouch and Kirby Muxloe. There are other attractions for railway enthusiasts at Loughborough and Cottesmore. Rutland Water is a reservoir, but now has the look of a huge natural lake, pleasant to walk around, with nature reserves at the western end, bicycle and boat hire, and even launch trips. A smattering of things for children to enjoy elsewhere includes particularly the working farm at Oadby, the zoo at Twycross and the discovery park in Coalville. There's a good deal to see and do in Leicester itself, but it's more a place for day visits than for a stay.

Where to stay

Packington SK3614 SPRINGS HYDRO Packington, Ashby-de-la-Zouch LE65 1TG (01530) 273873 **£150** inc lunch and dinner and one massage; 41 rms. Britain's first purpose-built health hydro with all the facilities, good healthy food, and friendly staff; cl 5 days over Christmas; no children.

Stapleford SK8018 STAPLEFORD PARK Stapleford, Melton Mowbray LE14 2EF (01572) 787522 ***£135**; 35 lavishly decorated rms, plus cottage. Luxurious country house, extravagantly restored, in lovely extensive grounds, with lots of mahogany, opulent furnishings, fine oil paintings, and impressive library, good restaurant food, enthusiastic American owner and warmly welcoming staff; riding, stabling, tennis, croquet, miniature golf, coarse fishing, clay-pigeon shooting, hunting; cots/babysitting; dogs welcome; disabled access.

Oakham SK8609 HAMBLETON HALL, LE15 8TH (01572) 756991 **£130**; 15 luxurious rms. Set in beautiful grounds on the edge of Rutland Water, this grandly restored Victorian manor house has elegant day rooms with fine views, antiques, open fires and exceptional flower arrangements; professional, friendly staff, wonderful food, a grandly stimulating wine list and a marvellously pampering atmosphere; disabled access.

Rothley SK5812 ROTHLEY COURT, Rothley LE7 7LG (0116) 237 4141 **£102**; 36 rms (the ones in the main house have more character). Mentioned in the Domesday Book, this carefully run manor house with its beautifully preserved 13th-c chapel has some fine oak panelling, open fires, a comfortable bar, conservatory, a terrace and garden, and courteous staff; disabled access.

Oakham SK8609 WHIPPER INN Market Pl, Oakham LE15 6DT (01572) 756971 **£80**; 24 rms. Attractive and well run 17th-c stone coaching inn with oak-beamed and panelled lounge opening into cosy eating area; good food and well kept ales; disabled access.

Stretton SK9416 RAM JAM INN Great North Rd, Stretton LE15 7QY (01780) 410776 ***£59**; 8 comfortable and well equipped rms. Actually on the A1, this is a civilised place with smart all-day continental-style snack bar from breakfast-time on, comfortable airy modern lounge bar, good choice of food quickly served from buffet counter, and useful small wine list; cl 25 Dec.

Lyddington SP8798 MARQUESS OF EXETER Lyddington, Oakham LE15 9LT (01572) 822477 **£55**; 17 rms. Rambling 16th-c family-run stone hotel in charming village, with beams, huge log fire surrounded by comfortable easy chairs – very tempting on a cold winter evening; excellent value bar food inc vegetarian dishes; disabled access. Fire damage repairs should be completed by early 1995 at the latest.

Market Harborough SP7387 THREE SWANS 21 High St, Market Harborough LE16 7NJ (01858) 466644 ***£55**; 36 rms. Fine old coaching inn with plush lounge bar, attractive conservatory and glorious courtyard, very friendly and helpful staff, and good food; disabled access.

Empingham SK9408 WHITE HORSE Main St, Empingham LE15 8PR (01780) 460221/460521 ***£52**; 14 pretty rms, some in a delightfully converted stable block, and most with own bthrm. Popular old refurbished pub on edge of Europe's largest man-made lake, relaxed and friendly atmosphere, big helpings of excellent food inc fine breakfasts even for non-residents, coffee and croissants from 8 am and cream teas all year round; log fire, attractive restaurant, and efficient, friendly service; cots/highchairs; disabled access.

Glooston SP7595 OLD BARN Main St, Glooston, Market Harborough LE16 7ST (0185 884) 215 ***£49.50**; 3 rms. Attractively restored 16th-c pub with civilised décor and open fire in beamed main bar, charming little restaurant, good meals and breakfasts, and decent real ales; cl 25 Dec.

Breedon on the Hill SK4022 HOLLY BUSH Breedon on the Hill, Derby DE7 1AN (01332) 862356 **£45**; 2 attractive pine-furnished rms. Pleasant and popular very low-beamed, partly Tudor pub with comfortable plush bar and dining room, good food, and friendly service.

Medbourne SP7993 NEVILL ARMS Medbourne, Market Harborough LE16 8EE (0185 883) 288 £39.50w; 3 rms. Old mullion-windowed inn just across footbridge over stream. Bright and busy with excellent food and friendly, prompt service; lots of bar games; cl 25 Dec; disabled access.

Sibson SK3500 MILLERS Main Rd, Sibson CV13 6LB (01827) 880223 £31.90w; 40 rms. Well placed, clean hotel converted from a mill and village bakery with working millwheel and stream in lounge bar; disabled access.

To see and do

🏰 ⛵ ⚓ ♀ ✝ Ashby-de-la-Zouch SK3516 ASHBY-DE-LA-ZOUCH CASTLE Impressive ruins of Norman manor house and 15th-c extension, destroyed in the Civil War. Notable features include the walls, solar and large kitchen, and especially the tower in which Mary Queen of Scots was imprisoned. The adjoining fields were the setting for Sir Walter Scott's *Ivanhoe*. Snacks, shop, some disabled access; cl winter Mon and Tues; £1.25. There's a little MUSEUM next to the tourist information centre on North St; cl 12–2 pm and am Sun, Oct–Easter; *25p. MOIRA FURNACE (Moira, B5003 W) 19th-c blast furnace and foundations of engine house and casting shed, along with a series of lime kilns. Snacks, shop, disabled access; cl am, Mon, and Nov–Mar; free. A few craft workshops in the grounds; the Rawdon Arms is useful for lunch. Off B587 N in pretty Staunton Harold the FERRERS CENTRE has good craft shops and exhibitions around a striking Georgian courtyard; cl Mon (exc bank hols); free. The CHURCH out here (owned by the National Trust) was one of the few built during the Commonwealth. A little further on the Holly Bush at Breedon on the Hill has popular food.

❀ Beacon Hill Country Park SK5114 The hill itself (above Woodhouse Eaves) is one of the best viewpoints in the area – an intriguing mix of the industrial and the very rural; it's popular locally as a beauty-spot, rising almost like a volcano above its lower woodland slopes. The Wheatsheaf is handy for lunch.

🏛 ❀ 🖼 ⛵ Belvoir SK8133 BELVOIR CASTLE Overlooking the Vale of Belvoir (pronounced Beaver), the house, rebuilt grandiosely in 1816, is a glorious fantasy of turrets and battlements, pinnacles and towers, surrounded by terraced gardens peopled with sculptures. The Dukes of Rutland have lived here since Henry VIII's reign, and the collections of furniture, tapestries and master paintings bear witness to their unerringly good taste. Also regimental museum and collection of arms and armour. Meals and snacks, shop, limited disabled access – it's quite a walk up the hill; cl Mon (exc bank hols), Fri and Nov–Apr; (01476) 870262; £4. The Peacock at Redmile not far off is excellent for lunch, and the Wheel at Branston SK8129 is handy too.

✝ Bottesford SK0838 has an interesting CHURCH full of elaborate tombs and monuments; they had to raise the roof to fit them all in.

❀ Bradgate Country Park SK5209, on the edge of Newtown Linford, is an extensive tract of former hunting park, little changed over the last 750 years. At its heart are the ruins of the 15th-c home of Lady Jane Grey, and a visitor centre tells her sad story; visitor centre cl am, Mon and winter wkdys; park free, car parking 30p, visitor centre £1.20. Fallow deer still roam these heathy slopes among the rock outcrops, and below the park Cropston Reservoir has waterfowl. The Bradgate Arms at Cropston and Pear Tree (particularly good food) in Woodhouse Eaves are handy for lunch.

🏛 ❀ Burrough Hill SK7611 is an imposing Iron Age hill fort, its high ramparts still largely intact; a splendid viewpoint. The determinedly simple Stag & Hounds in the village below is useful for refreshment, and the Old Brewery over at Somerby has good-value home cooking and brews its own good beers.

⛵ ☺ 🎵 Coalville SK4214 SNIBSTON DISCOVERY PARK Originally a colliery (the first shaft was sunk by George and Robert Stephenson), this is now a thriving 100-acre centre with fun exhibitions and interactive displays covering a huge range of topics: the environment, weather, human body, underground and overground engineering, transport, local history and fashion. Outside are reassembled wheelwright's and blacksmith's shops, a huge play area, nature trails, golf course and fishing lagoons. Enough here to keep most people busy (and entertained) for quite some time. Meals, snacks, shop, disabled access; cl 25–26 Dec; (01530) 510851; *£4. The Bull's Head above Whitwick has decent food and great views.

Cottesmore SK9013 RUTLAND RAILWAY MUSEUM A collection of 28 industrial steam and diesel locomotives and 70 other wagons and vehicles used in the ironstone quarries and industry. On steam days there are unlimited rides along part of the former Midland Railway mineral branch, and there's quite a nice lineside walk to the old Oakham Canal. Open wknds and bank hols Easter–Sept, and over Christmas – best to tel (01572) 813203 for dates of this year's steam days; £2.50. The Sun is good for lunch.

Donington Park SK4427 DONINGTON COLLECTION Largest private collection of single-seater racing cars in the world, with unique vehicles driven by all the greats and lots of related memorabilia; if you're a racing fan try to go on a day when some of the exhibits are being exercised. Meals and snacks, shop, disabled access; (01332) 810048; cl 25–26 Dec, 1 Jan; *£4. The Priest House by the Trent at Kings Mills is good for lunch.

East Midlands Airport SK4525 on the Derbys border has a lively AEROPARK AND VISITOR CENTRE, with plenty of aeroplanes inc a Canberra, Vulcan and Lightning, and displays on the history of flight and how a modern airport works. Viewpoints are just 180m away from the runways of the main airport. Snacks, shop, disabled access; visitor centre cl winter wkdys; (01332) 810621; £2 per car. The Cap & Stocking just over

the motorway in Kegworth SK4826 is a fine old tavern.

Egleton SK8707 RUTLAND WATER NATURE RESERVE is a strip of land stretching 9 miles around the lake, sensibly divided into two parts. Lyndon Reserve is for the general public (with a useful visitor centre), and Egleton Reserve is aimed at the more serious birdwatcher. Both have observation hides overlooking the water – and a varied procession of feathered visitors. Lots of talks, walks and events. Snacks, shop, disabled access; Lyndon Reserve open wknds all year, plus Tues, Weds and Thurs in summer (£1), Egleton daily exc Thurs (£2.50). On the other side of Rutland Water (Europe's biggest man-made lake) there are nature trails, places to hire bikes, and hourly BOAT TRIPS. The White Horse at Empingham is good for lunch, and other handy dining places are the Finches Arms at Upper Hambleton (the best views over the water), the Normanton Park Hotel, and the Noel Arms at Whitwell.

★ **Exton** SK9211 is a handsome village around a tree-studded green; the Fox & Hounds has good home cooking. BARNSDALE PLANTS (The Avenue) Well known gardens with five acres of interesting plants and useful ideas and techniques. All plants are organically grown using peat-free compost. Shop; cl 25 Dec, 1 Jan; (01572) 813200; free.

Eyebrook Reservoir SP8595 is rewarding for birdspotters and fishermen, though as it has no hides or facilities appeals mainly to true enthusiasts.

Houghton on the Hill SK6703 The lane N brings you after a mile to the site, on its right, of Ingarsby DESERTED VILLAGE, its inhabitants evicted in the 15th c by the Abbot of Leicester who wanted their land for grazing sheep – which may still be seen here, among the clearly discernible mounds and hollows that mark the long-gone settlement.

Kibworth Harcourt SP6894 has the county's only remaining post mill, a fine example from the early 18th c. The Three Horseshoes is a civilised place for lunch. Other well preserved windmills can be found at

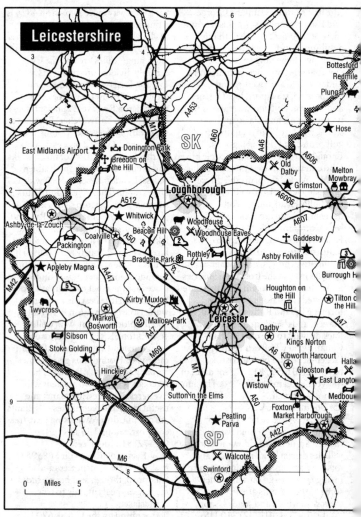

Leicestershire

Arnesby SP6192, Shepshed SK4719 and Wymondham SK8518, one of only four 6-sailed mills in the country, with a tea room and craft shops; cl Mon and winter wkdys (there are boat trips near here).

Kirby Muxloe SK5104 KIRBY MUXLOE CASTLE Peaceful 15th-c ruins, barely used by their original owner before he was executed. An imposing gatehouse, water-filled moat and one tower are still in good shape. Shop, disabled access; may be admission charge in summer. The Royal Oak is useful for lunch.

Leicester SK5904 In this busy city's mix of ancient and modern, it's the modern which makes the most immediate impression. But a bit of digging around among the shops, office blocks and traffic schemes does turn up quite a few interesting reminders of its long and varied past; most of the main exhibitions and museums are free. JEWRY WALL MUSEUM AND SITE (St Nicholas Circle) Former site of Roman baths, the courtyard now excavated to reveal porticos and shops sheltered by the remains of a

recreated scenes of domestic life and collections of clocks and musical instruments. There's a quiet period garden. Shop, some disabled access; cl am Sun, Good Fri, 25–26 Dec; free. More on the edge of the city, BELGRAVE HALL (Church Rd) is a fine example of 18th-c architecture, furnished with period pieces. Charming gardens. Shop, limited disabled access; cl am Sun, Good Fri, 25–26 Dec; free. Nearby, the MUSEUM OF TECHNOLOGY looks at the area's industrial heritage, with a power-generation gallery, transport displays, and a galaxy of knitting machinery that makes the home version look decidedly primitive. Shop, disabled access (except to engine house); it's been closed recently for restoration, so best to check for opening times, (0116) 251 0851. LEICESTERSHIRE MUSEUM AND ART GALLERY (New Walk) Interesting displays of 18th- to 20th-c art, and a collection of German Expressionist art that for this country must be unique. Shop, disabled access; cl am Sun, Good Fri, 25–26 Dec; free. The unusual GAS MUSEUM (Aylestone Rd) has a comprehensive study of the industry, and examples of its application, from cookers and washing machines to hairdryers and magic lanterns. Disabled access to ground floor only; open pm Tues (exc after a bank hol) to Fri; (0116) 253 5506; free. Other oddities worth a look if passing inc the ECO HOUSE (Hinckley Rd), an ordinary house converted to show over 100 ways to make the modern home more environment-friendly (cl am wkdys, all Mon and Tues), and the JAIN CENTRE (Oxford St), with some fantastic examples of traditional Indian architecture; open pm wkdys. GORSE HILL CITY FARM (Anstey Lane) Friendly little community farm with the usual animals and activities, and a developing organic garden. Meals, snacks, shop, disabled access; cl Weds; (0116) 253 7582; £1 donation requested. Towpath walks along both the Grand Union Canal and the River Soar give a relatively tranquil back view of the city's industrial life. The Welford Place (on Welford Pl) is good for lunch here, serving food all

massive stone wall. Useful archaeology displays, inc excellent collections of mosaic pavements and painted wallplaster, and models. Shop, disabled access; cl am Sun, Good Fri, 25–26 Dec; free. A short walk away WYGSTON'S HOUSE MUSEUM OF COSTUME has English costume from the 17th c to the present, with entertaining reconstructions of various specialist clothing shops from the 1920s. Meals and snacks, shop, disabled access; cl am Sun, 25–26 Dec, Good Fri; free. NEWARKE HOUSES (The Newarke) Local history and crafts, inc through the day; and the Melton on the A607 N is fascinating for its authentic on-view Bombay cooking (Thurs–Sun eve). Just S of town at Wigston, the FRAMEWORK KNITTERS MUSEUM is a restored 18th-c knitter's house and workshop, with original hand frames; open pm Sun and bank hols Apr–Sept plus first Sat of each month; £1.

⬆ ♿ **Loughborough** SK5354 BELL FOUNDRY MUSEUM Part of the largest working bell foundry in the world, a look at bells and their application – the array of bells in the tuning room is quite remarkable. Shop, disabled access; cl 12.30–1.30 pm, all Mon (exc bank hols) and Sun; (01509) 233414; *75p. GREAT CENTRAL RAILWAY Main-line steam railway to Leicester, with a museum this end. Meals, snacks, shop, disabled access; cl wkdys Oct–Apr; (01509) 230726; £5.60. The Swan in the Rushes (A6) has good home cooking, and the picturesque canalside Boat (Meadow Lane) is good value.

🏠 **Lyddington** SP8797 BEDE HOUSE Until the Reformation this fine 15th-c house was a residence of the Bishops of Lincoln; it was later converted into an almshouse. Notable carved ceilings in the bishop's quarters upstairs, which still have 15th-c glass; interesting smaller rooms, and tranquil garden. Shop; cl 1–2 pm, Oct–Mar; *£1.25. The Marquess of Exeter and Old White Hart are good for lunch.

☺ **Mallory Park** SK4500 provides a complete change of mood, with motorsport meetings held every wknd Mar–Oct. Meals, snacks, shop, disabled access; from £5.50. The Royal Arms at Sutton Cheney is the nearest good eating place.

★ ♿ **Market Bosworth** SK4003 is an attractive market town which used to specialise in the production of corsets; bizarre, florid and even agonising examples can be seen in the town MUSEUM. Softleys, the Black Horse and the comfortable Inn on the Park all have good value food. It's more famous however for hosting the deciding action in the War of the Roses, when Richard III's defeat led to the Tudors seizing the English throne.

The BOSWORTH BATTLEFIELD VISITOR CENTRE AND COUNTRY PARK to the south has explanatory exhibitions, models, a film theatre, and a detailed trail. Reconstructions and similarly lively events throughout the year. Meals and snacks, shop, disabled access; cl am wkdys exc bank hols and during July and Aug, all Nov–Mar (exc prebooked parties); (01455) 290429; £2. From Shackerstone SK3706 the BATTLEFIELD STEAM RAILWAY LINE runs through Market Bosworth to Shenton by the battlefield, a rather nice return trip of just over 9 miles; a museum at the Shackerstone station has enthusiastically mounted displays on the age of steam, and a Victorian tea room (open Tues–Sun). Open wknds only; tel for details of timetable, (01827) 880754; £4.50 return. The Rising Sun here is useful for lunch, as are the Royal Arms at Sutton Cheney SK4100 and canalside Dog & Hedgehog at Dadlington, at the battlefield end.

★ ✝ ♿ **Market Harborough** SP7387 The attractive town centre has some fine old Georgian buildings, and above them the gracefully soaring 14th-c spire of the church. There's a local history MUSEUM in the council offices, with plenty of local corsetry. Shop, disabled access; cl am Sun, Good Fri and 25–26 Dec; free. The Three Swans Hotel does good lunches.

♿ 🏛 **Melton Mowbray** SK7518 Stilton cheese, pork pies and the Quorn hunt all originate in this little town. The MELTON CARNEGIE MUSEUM celebrates its fashionable 19th-c days, with a look at contemporary life in the area. Shop, disabled access; cl Sun exc summer pm; free. Plans are well advanced for an adjacent Museum of Fox Hunting. Dickinson & Morris (Nottingham St) still make the pies to a traditional recipe (tours on Tues and Sat in season). Websters at nearby Saxelby SK7020 make Stilton in their 19th-c dairy, tel (01664) 812223; just beyond, the Black Horse at Grimston has decent food and a remarkable collection of cricket memorabilia.

🚌 ☺ ✿ ♿ **Oadby** SK6200 FARMWORLD Working farm in

charming countryside, with Children's Farmyard and rare breeds, milking parlour, and enchanting pastiche of an Edwardian alehouse. Also crafts and walks. Meals, snacks, shop, disabled access; cl 25–26 Dec and 1 Jan; (01530) 710355; *£4. The UNIVERSITY BOTANIC GARDENS (Stoughton Drive South) are set around student halls of residence: 16 acres filled with a wide variety of plants in different and delightful settings, inc a hardy fuchsia collection. Plant sales, disabled access; cl wknds and bank hols; (01530) 717725; free.

★ 🏠 ⛴ 🐄 ♣ **Oakham** SK8609, the capital of the former Rutland, is an attractive small town with a good sense of country bustle about it, and one or two interesting antique shops. OAKHAM CASTLE The magnificent Norman banqueting hall is all that remains of the late 12th-c manor house which once stood here, though earthworks and walls give a good idea of what it must have been like. The hall itself is decorated with a droll collection of extraordinary horseshoes, some grossly opulent, some simply enormously oversized. Shop, disabled access; cl 1–2 pm, Mon (exc bank hols). RUTLAND COUNTY MUSEUM Good local history museum with emphasis on rural life, as well as Roman and Saxon finds. Shop, disabled access; cl am Sun, 25–26 Dec and Good Fri; free. RUTLAND FARM PARK (Uppingham Rd) Lots of animals inc various breeds of cattle, pig, sheep and poultry, as well as old farming equipment, and pretty walks round the woodland and stream, with fine trees and Victorian rockeries. Snacks, shop, disabled access; cl am out of season, all Mon (exc bank hols) and mid-Sept–mid-Apr; (01572) 756789; £2.30. The Whipper Inn, Waycotts and Barnsdale Lodge are all good for lunch – see alsoEgleton, above.

🐄 ♣ **Plungar** SK7633 OUR LITTLE FARM A friendly little place, with traditional and rare breeds in the farmyard, an incubator and hatchery with tiny ducklings and the like, and 8-acre nature trail. Also wknd craft displays and events. Snacks, shop, disabled access; cl Mon (exc bank

hols), Nov–mid-Mar; (01949) 860349; £2.20. The Belvoir Inn is a handy stop.

🕊 **Sutton in the Elms** SP5194 FALCONRY CENTRE (Mill on the Soar, Coventry Rd) Flying demonstrations of owls, hawks, falcons and buzzards; they really try to get the audience involved. Thriving family dining pub on same site, disabled access; cl 25 Dec; £1.60.

🏠 🖼 🍴 ✝ ♣ **Swinford** SP5779 STANFORD HALL AND MOTORCYCLE MUSEUM 5,000 books line the library of this handsome 17th-c house, an elegant place that still keeps a cosy lived-in atmosphere. Particular highlights are the painted ceiling in the ballroom, the portraits that accompany the winding grand staircase, and a collection of well preserved old costume. The excellent motorcycle museum is in the grounds, which also have a lovely 14th-c church with splendid stained glass, an old forge, walled rose garden, Sunday craft centre, and a reconstruction of the first successful flying machine in the country. Regular car rallies out here too. Snacks, shop, some disabled access; open pm Sat, Sun, bank hols and Tues after bank hols from Easter Sat–end Sept; (01788) 860250; house and grounds £3.20, grounds only £1.80, motorcycle museum £1 extra. The Cherry Tree at Catthorpe and Bell at Lilbourne both have good-value food.

🐄 🌙 🐛 **Tilton on the Hill** SK7405 HALSTEAD HOUSE FARM Specialist poultry farm, with a display on poultry rearing, nature trail, fishing lake and gardens. Meals, snacks, shop, disabled access; cl Mon and all Nov–Easter; £2 for displays. The Rose & Crown is handy for lunch.

🐒 **Twycross** SK3305 TWYCROSS ZOO PARK Specialises in primates, with an enormous and varied range of apes, gibbons, orang-utans, and chimpanzees every shape, size and species. Plenty of other animals too, inc giraffes, sea-lions, elephants and penguins. Can be crowded in the afternoons. Meals, snacks, shop, disabled access; cl 25 Dec; (01827) 880250; £4. The Cock at Sibson is an attractive place for lunch.

! Welland Viaduct SP9197 nr Seaton is one of the county's most striking sights: nearly a mile long, swooping across the pastures of the valley, it is the country's longest viaduct.

★ **! Wing** SK8902 is a quietly attractive Rutland village, notable for its small medieval TURF MAZE. The Kings Arms is good for lunch.

🐾 **Woodhouse** SK5315 WHATOFF LODGE (E towards Quorn) A decent nature trail starts from this working farm, where there's an exhibition of rural bygones and some farm animals. Snacks, shop, disabled access; cl Mon (exc bank hols), mid-Oct–mid-Mar; (01509) 412127; *£2. The Pear Tree at Woodhouse Eaves is the best nearby place for lunch.

✝ Though not to quite such a degree as neighbouring Lincolnshire, this is church country, with many fine **churches** in both towns and villages. We'd particularly pick out those at Breedon on the Hill SK4022 (on an interesting partly quarried Iron Age hill fort), Exton SK9211 (beautifully placed in a park), Gaddesby SK6813 (elaborate 13th-c workmanship), King's Norton SK6800 (graceful Gothic Revival), Normanton SK9306 (with Rutland Water and a museum nearby), Stoke Dry SP8596, Tilton on the Hill SK7405 and Wistow SP6496.

★ **Other attractive villages** here, all with decent pubs, include Appleby Magna SK3109, Ashby Folville SK7011, Barrowden SK9400, Branston SK8129, Braunston SK8306, East Langton SP7292, Grimston SK6821, Hallaton SP7896, Hose SK7329, Knipton SK8231, Knossington SK8008, Lyddington SP8798, Medbourne SP7993, Peatling Parva SP5889, South Luffenham SK9402, Stoke Golding SP3997 and Whitwick SK4316.

Walks

The walk around **Rutland Water** ᗐ-1 totals 24 miles – information centres have details of shorter trails. The best walk, starting from Hambleton and touring the peninsula which protrudes into the reservoir, is little publicised.

The former great hunting park of **Charnwood Forest** ᗐ-2 has two good surviving chunks here: Bradgate Park SK5209 (see above, To see and do), and nearby Beacon Hill SK5114. Surprisingly for the E Midlands, both have miniature patches of moorland with suitably scaled-down crags. Both are part of country parks, with general access, plenty of waymarked paths, and lots of opportunities for picnics. From the 800-ft summit of Beacon Hill, the Jubilee Walk heads N and E through partly wooded country. A trail S makes a small circuit around Broombriggs Farm SK5114, with boards explaining farming methods by the path. The friendly Bull's Head (B587 Whitwick–Copt Oak), with a big garden and lots of animals, has fine views over the Forest.

Burrough Hill SK7611 ᗐ-3 S of Melton Mowbray SK7518 has an enjoyable path along its escarpment. The summit has an Iron Age hill fort, and a view indicator.

Foxton Locks SP7090 ᗐ-4 on the Grand Union Canal nr Market Harborough SP7387 are a famous example of canal engineering, and next to an interesting inclined plane, now abandoned – a failed attempt at preserving water over this section. A handy pub, Bridge 61 (SP7090), is right next to the towpath.

The **Ashby Canal** ᗐ-5 towpath has good countryside walking, with green fields and stone-arched bridges, as well as coots, moorhens, herons and maybe even the flash of a kingfisher. The best parts run from the tunnel under Snarestone SK3409 past Gopsall Park SK3605, and then on through Shackerstone SK3706 and Congerstone SK3505 to pass Shenton Park SK3800 on an embankment, before heading into Warwickshire and its junction with the Coventry Canal. It also makes an ideal link between Bosworth battlefield and the steam railway to the N.

Pubs useful for walkers here include the the Pear Tree and Bull's Head in

Woodhouse Eaves SK5214 and the Copt Oak SK4812 (for Charnwood Forest); the Priest House at Kings Mills near Castle Donington SK4427 (for the River Trent); and, all handy for canals, the Three Horseshoes at Stoke Golding SP3997, old-fashioned Navigation in Barrow upon Soar SK5717, Griffin at Congerstone SK3605, and Navigation at Kilby Bridge SP6097.

Driving

Driving is a pleasure in much of the county, with good views from long-striding old coach roads such as the one running below Belvoir Castle from Long Benington up in Lincolnshire through Bottesford, Harby and Hose. Another runs from just below the castle NW of Knipton down through Eastwell and past Grimston all the way to Barrow upon Soar. The road N from Oakham through Ashwell, Wymondham and Waltham on the Wolds to Harby is very fine. Further S, a similar road runs easily across the county from Uppingham through Hallaton, Tur Langton and Kibworth Harcourt, past Wistow to Kilby, Countesthorpe and Cosby.

There are fewer views and more traffic over in the W of the county, though the road through Peckleton, Kirkby Mallory, Sutton Cheney and Fenny Drayton is quite scenic.

Where to eat

Old Dalby SK6723 Crown (01664) 823134 Converted farmhouse, unspoilt and welcoming, serving a wide range of drinks (14 real ales and 20 malt whiskies), and big helpings of imaginative and completely fresh food (no freezers, microwaves or chips); no food pm Sun; disabled access. £25|£2.75/£10.
Hallaton SP7896 Bewicke Arms (0185 889) 217 Thatched cottage by village green with warm welcome and traditional feel in its two beamed bar rooms, generous helpings of good, popular food inc fine puddings, well kept real ales, and friendly service; no dogs. £18|£2.40/£8.90.
Redmile SK7935 Peacock (01949) 842554 Atmospheric little village house opposite Belvoir Castle with extremely popular, imaginative food in bar or pretty restaurant, well kept real ales, good wine, and courteous service; open fires, attractive conservatory, and several no smoking areas. £17|£2.50/£6.
Woodhouse Eaves SK5214 Pear Tree (01509) 890243 Full of Edwardian character, with a comfortably furnished and attractively decorated bar and dining area serving very good food; cl pm Sun. £16|£2/£5.50.
Walcote SP5683 Black Horse (01455) 552684 Authentic Thai food cooked by Thai landlady, unusual drinks, chatty atmosphere, large open fire and seats out behind in summer; cl Mon/Tues am (open bank hols); disabled access. £14.50 for 5-course meal, appointment only, 6 people minimum|£5.
Leicester SK5904 Altro Mondo 52 Chatham St (0116) 255 5563 Popular Italian restaurant with good food, nice wine, and helpful, quiet and attentive service; cl Sun. £6.95 wkdys.

LINCOLNSHIRE

Some lovely houses, castles and villages in this little-visited area, with plenty of scope for quiet breaks away from the crowds; Lincoln and Stamford are enjoyable towns.

Lincolnshire's main appeal is as a get-away-from-it-all break for adults, in a part of England decidedly different from any other. It's best in late spring, summer, or autumn; in winter it can be one of England's chilliest areas. There's quite a good choice of places to stay, and to eat out in.

The best of the countryside is north and east of Lincoln: rolling wolds, attractive villages and small towns, soaring church spires, rich farmland with huge fields of arable crops – a better area for country drives than for walks. Nearer the Wash, and up the coast towards Wainfleet and Coningsby, the land is very flat, reclaimed from the sea: pretty dull, except in springtime when the endless bulbfields around Spalding burst into spectacular bloom.

Stamford and Lincoln are interesting towns with a good deal of character. The county has some fine old mansions and castles to look at, most notably Burghley House (just outside Stamford), Belton House, Woolsthorpe Manor, and Tattershall and Grimsthorpe Castles. Though there are things to entertain children, and the coast is famous for its traditional family summer seaside resorts, it's not a very good area for a shorter family break. One of the best family outings is the butterfly park at Long Sutton.

Where to stay

Lincoln SK9872 WHITE HART Bailgate, Lincoln LB1 3AR (01522) 526222 £100; 48 restful rms. 15th-c hotel next to cathedral, with antique-filled lounges, small panelled bar, attractive restaurant, and welcoming service; partial disabled access.

Stamford TF0207 GEORGE 71 St Martins, Stamford PE9 2LB (01780) 55171 *£99; 47 rms. Historic ancient former coaching inn with quietly civilised atmosphere, sturdy timbers, broad flagstones, heavy beams and massive stonework, open log fires, wonderful food in Garden Lounge (tempting help-yourself buffet), restaurant and courtyard (in summer), excellent range of drinks – very good value Italian wines, and welcoming staff; well kept walled garden and sunken lawn where croquet is played.

Washingborough SK9872 WASHINGBOROUGH HALL Church Hill, Washingborough, Lincoln LN4 1BE (01522) 790340 £69; 12 rms. Georgian manor house in 3 acres of grounds, with comfortable homely lounge, attractive dining room, open fire, good food, swimming pool and croquet; cl 4 days over Christmas.

Sandilands TF5280 GRANGE & LINKS Sandilands, Mablethorpe LN12 2RA (01507) 441334 £65; 31 rms. Popular hotel, noted for good food and comfortable surroundings, with own golf course and good nearby beach; disabled access.

Lincoln SK9872 D'ISNEY PLACE Eastgate, Lincoln LN2 4AA (01522) 538881 *£63; 17 rms. Friendly 18th-c hotel with lovely gardens, fine furniture and relaxed atmosphere; disabled access.

Woodhall Spa TF1963 DOWER HOUSE Manor Estate, Woodhall Spa LN10 6PY (01526) 52588 £60; 7 rms, most with own bthrm. Edwardian hotel in its own grounds on a private road with friendly welcome, log fires, and comfortable lounge.

Skegness TF5660 VINE Vine Rd, Seacroft, Skegness PE25 3DB (01754) 763018 £52; 22 rms. 17th-c hotel with extensions built on in character, cosy lounges, oak-panelled bar, open fires, good food in dining room, attractive grounds; close to golf course.

Alford TF4575 WHITE HORSE 29 West St, Alford LN13 9DG (01507) 462218 £40; 9 prettily furnished and comfortable rms, most with own bthrm. Picturesque thatched 16th-c inn, carefully restored over the years, with plush beamed lounge, superb range of vodkas (the licensee is from Poland), good range of well prepared reasonably priced bar food, popular communicating restaurant; cl 24–26 Dec.

East Barkwith TF1781 GRANGE Torrington Lane, East Barkwith, Lincoln LN3 5RY (01673) 858249 £40; 3 pretty rms. Particularly enjoyable Georgian house with charmingly decorated rooms, warmly welcoming owners, very good food, open fires, conservatory, and conservation and wildlife award-winning farmland with trails; cl Christmas; children over 12.

Dyke TF1022 WISHING WELL Dyke, Bourne PE10 0AF (01778) 422970 *£39; 7 rms, most with own bthrm. The wishing well is at the dining end of the long rambling bar – heavy-beamed with dark stone, brasswork, candlelight and a big fireplace; excellent popular food, helpful service and a friendly atmosphere; disabled access.

Lincoln SK9872 CARLINE 1–3 Carline Rd, Lincoln LN1 1HL (01522) 530422 *£38; 12 well equipped rms, 10 with own bthrm. Spotlessly kept and comfortable double-fronted Edwardian guest house 5 mins from cathedral, with helpful, cheerful owners, quiet sitting rooms, and fine breakfasts; cl Christmas and New Year.

North Hykeham SK9465 LOUDOR 37 Newark St, North Hykeham LN6 8RB (01522) 680333 *£38; 10 rms. Family-run hotel with pleasant lounge, small bar, good, plentiful food, and quick, friendly service; disabled access.

Buslingthorpe TF0885 EAST FARM HOUSE Middle Rasen Rd, Buslingthorpe, Lincoln LN3 5AQ (01673) 842283 *£36; 2 rms. 18th-c farmhouse surrounded by family farm, with beams, stripped pine, log fires, relaxed atmosphere, and good breakfasts.

Barkston SP9241 BARKSTON HOUSE Barkston, Grantham NG32 2NH (01400) 50555 £35; 3 rms. Warm and comfortable restored 18th-c house with open fires and beams, relaxed atmosphere, accomplished English cooking, and 7 acres of grounds; cl 1 wk Christmas.

Lincoln SK9872 EDWARD KING HOUSE The Old Palace, Lincoln LN2 1PU (01522) 528778 £35; 17 rms, shared bthrm. B&B in what was once the Bishop's house and situated in the centre of the city with Lincoln Cathedral views; cl 24 Dec–1 Jan.

To see and do

Lincoln SK9872 The cathedral and castle, both very striking, share the hilltop in the centre of the town, with enough old buildings around them to keep a sense of unity. There's a lot to appeal up here, and in the steep streets (Steep Hill and Strait St) of ancient buildings running down from them to the 15th-c Stonebow Gate at the top of the High St below. This lower part of the town is much more of a normal bustling shopping and working centre, though even here there are a good few interesting old buildings – inc several Saxon churches and the Norman guildhall.

✝ The CATHEDRAL strikes many as England's finest. On the site of a former Roman fort, the original building was largely destroyed in an 1185 earthquake, but the magnificent west front survived, and after nearly a century of rebuilding (and a hiccough in 1239, when the new central tower collapsed) it was complete by 1280. The triple towers rise spectacularly above the nearby rooftops, looking especially good when lit up at night. Inside, the carvings and stained glass are stupendous, and the architecture gracefully harmonious. It's the home of the Lincoln Imp, a carving on one column in the choir. Snacks, shop, disabled access. From here you can visit the ruins of the once formidable Bishop's Palace.

🏰 CASTLE In beautiful surroundings on a formidable earthwork, the castle was originally built in 1068 for William the Conqueror, but only two towers and two impressive gateways date back to that time. Later additions include 19th-c prisoners' chapel, unusually designed so that none of the

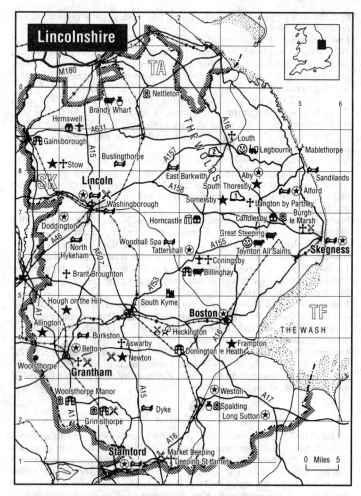

Lincolnshire

congregation could see each other. Super views from the ramparts. One of only four remaining originals of Magna Carta is on display, and an exhibition fills in the background. Lively events throughout the year. Snacks, shop, disabled access; cl 25–26 Dec; (01522) 511068; *£2.

🏛 Some Roman remains in the city include the high wall along Westgate, and the largely reconstructed Newport Arch N of the cathedral; the canal between Lincoln and the River Trent is Roman – you can walk out into the country along it from the city.

🏚 🕯 Museum of Lincolnshire Life (Burton Rd) Big former barracks interestingly illustrating county life over the past two centuries. Summer snacks, shop, disabled access; cl 24–27 Dec, Good Fri and am Sun in winter; (01522) 528448; *£1.20. A lawn in the courtyard makes a good picnic area.

🕯 🌀 ❀ National Cycle Museum The best collection of bicyclabilia in the country, made up of over 140 bicycles, and lots of photographs, trophies and medals. You couldn't pedal down to the shops on all of these – one bike, the Eiffel Tower, has its seat more than ten feet higher than the wheels. Shop, disabled access; cl 1 wk over Christmas; *£1. The Museum has recently moved

to the grounds of the site of THE LAWN, the county's first lunatic asylum in 1820. It now has hands-on history and archaeology displays, an exotic glasshouse, and an aquarium in its landscaped grounds, as well as a restaurant, coffee shop and bar; free.
🖼 USHER GALLERY (Lindum Rd) Attractive gallery with fine watches, porcelain and miniatures, Tennyson memorabilia, Peter de Wint watercolours, medals and coins. Shop, disabled access; cl 25–26 Dec, Good Fri and am Sun; *£1, free on Fri.
❗ INCREDIBLY FANTASTIC OLD TOY SHOW (Westgate) Old toys and end-of-pier amusements, close to both the cathedral and the castle, so a good treat for unwilling culture buffs.

There's something new every year. Shop, disabled access; cl am Sun, all Mon (exc pm bank hols), and winter wkdys (except school hols); (01522) 520534; £1.50.
The CITY AND COUNTY MUSEUM on Broadgate is closed this year for refurbishment.
The Wig & Mitre and Brown's Pie Shop, both in Steep St, are good for lunch, and behind the cathedral and castle the Victoria and the Adam & Eve each have a good lively atmosphere. The Green Dragon (Waterside North) by the canal is an extremely handsome old timbered building, and there are pleasant canal strolls near the Woodcocks, a popular family pub at Burton Lane End off A57 W.

Other things to see and do

✗ ❀ ✔ ♙ **Aby** TF4178 CLAYTHORPE WATER MILL AND WILDFOWL GARDENS Pretty spot around an 18th-c watermill, the grounds full of ornamental wildfowl and poultry, and animals such as rabbits and a miniature pony. Fun to wander through the woods too. Meals, snacks, shop, mostly disabled access; cl Nov–Feb; (01507) 450687; £2.35. The Vine at South Thoresby is a civilised place for lunch.
★ ☗ ⚸ ✗ **Alford** TF4575 is a pleasant town with some attractive brick and thatch buildings, including the 17th-c ALFORD MANOR HOUSE, now a folk museum. Snacks, shop; cl am Sun, Oct–Easter; 80p. In summer the town has a crafts market (Fri). There's a tall restored 5-sailed WINDMILL on the road towards Sutton on Sea (open Sat and bank hols, plus pm Tues, Fri and Sun in July and Aug; £1), and another a little further along at Bilsby. The White Horse Hotel is good for lunch.
✝ **Bardney** TF1468 Just off the B1190 SE of the village are the remains of a 12th-c abbey, TUPHOLME ABBEY; interesting to wander around, and normally quite deserted. The village has some handsome almshouses.
🏠 🖼 ❀ **Belton** SK9339 BELTON HOUSE Splendid Restoration-period mansion full of wonderful carvings (some of them possibly by Grinling Gibbons),

ornate plasterwork, sumptuous furnishings, tapestries, paintings and ceramics. Outside is a beautiful 1,000-acre deer park, with orangery and formal Italian garden, and adventure playground. Meals, snacks, shop, disabled access to gardens only; open pm Weds–Sun and bank hols Apr–Oct, grounds open 11; £4.30; NT. The Stag's Head at Barkston has decent food.
🐖 🏠 **Billinghay** TF1555 BILLINGHAY CHILDREN'S FARM Small but very friendly; they take time to show you the differences between various breeds. Snacks, shop, disabled access; cl Nov–Mar; (01526) 860305; *£1. There's an interesting old thatched cottage open nearby. The Penny Farthing over at Timberland is a popular dining pub.
★ ✝ ❀ ✗ ☗ **Boston** TF3244 Still the county's leading port, this little town has a number of pretty spots and handsome historic buildings. Most famous is the BOSTON STUMP, the graceful tower of magnificent 14th-c St Botolph's church. Climb to the top for far views over this flat landscape – it's the second tallest parish church in the country (the tallest is in Louth – see **Churches**, below); the inside is spectacular too. Another prominent feature of the skyline is the MAUD FOSTER MILL, the tallest working

windmill in the country, and surely one of the most photogenic. The Kings Arms opposite has lovely views of it, and decent food; Goodbarns Yard (Wormgate) is a more central pub/restaurant. GUILDHALL MUSEUM In 1607 this 15th-c building became the prison of the Pilgrim Fathers after their unsuccessful attempt to flee to Holland (they did, of course, eventually escape further afield, taking their former town's name to one of their first settlements). Displays cover this and the rest of the town's history. Shop, disabled access to ground floor only; cl am Sun (all day in winter); (01205) 365954; 95p.

ö ☛ **Brandy Wharf** TF0197 CIDER CENTRE 18th-c cider house with up to 60 different varieties, also a little museum and orchard – the enthusiastic owner is very knowledgeable about cider. Meals, snacks, shop, disabled access; open licensing hrs; free.

† ※ **Burgh Le Marsh** TF5065 has a notable CHURCH; a nearby WINDMILL has unusual left-handed sails; open pm 2nd and last Sun each month; 50p.

❀ 🐄 **Candlesby** TF4567 CANDLESBY HERBS Good range of herb plants for sale and on display in the garden, as well as hints and advice on all sorts of things you can do with them; cl Mon (exc bank hols); free.

† † **Coningsby** TF2258 BATTLE OF BRITAIN MEMORIAL FLIGHT VISITOR CENTRE Subject to operational commitments you can see the aircraft of the Battle of Britain Memorial Flight – inc the only flying Lancaster in Europe. The Visitor Centre has exhibitions. Summer snacks, shop, disabled access; cl wknds, bank hols, and 2 wks over Christmas; (01526) 44041 – it is worth checking first if you're hoping to see a particular aircraft; *£3. The CHURCH has what's said to be the biggest dial of any clock with just a single hand. Just out of town, the interesting old Leagate Inn is useful for lunch.

🏛 ❀ † **Doddington** SK9070 DODDINGTON HALL Striking lived-in Elizabethan mansion, the exterior unchanged since it was built, and still with its walled gardens, gatehouse and family church. The elegant rooms

are mostly Georgian, with porcelain, pictures and furniture acquired by the family over the last four centuries. Regular concerts in the Long Gallery. Meals, snacks, shop, disabled access; open Easter Mon, then Weds, Sun and bank hols May–Sept, and daily except Sat in Aug; (01522) 6943098; £3.50.

🏛 **Donington le Heath** SK4112 DONINGTON LE HEATH MANOR HOUSE Pretty much unaltered since it was built in 1280, so one of the very rare examples of an almost untouched medieval manor house. Snacks, shop; cl am, Mon, Tues, all Oct–Easter; (01530) 831259; free.

🏛 **Gainsborough** SK8189 OLD HALL Restored medieval manor house with interesting Great Hall and original kitchen. Good walkman tour. Snacks, shop; cl winter Sun; (01427) 612669; £1.50. The Trent Port is useful for lunch.

☛ **Great Steeping** TF4464 NORTHCOTE HEAVY HORSE CENTRE Besides the gentle giants themselves (showcased at 12 and 3pm), there's a collection of old vehicles, and other animals, from rare breeds of cattle and sheep to miniature ponies and working dogs. Meals, snacks, shop, disabled access; open Sun, Weds and Thurs Mar–Oct, plus Tues May and Jun, and every day exc Sat July and Aug; (01754) 830286; *£3.75. The Bell at Halton Holegate has good home cooking.

🏛 ❀ **Grimsthorpe** TF0422 GRIMSTHORPE CASTLE A patchwork of styles from its medieval tower and Tudor quadrangle to the baroque north front by Vanbrugh; the state rooms and galleries are full of fine furnishings. Outside are formal gardens and parkland with lake, and red deer tame enough for children to feed. Meals and snacks, shop, some disabled access. They're reorganising their opening times and prices – best to check first on (01778) 32205. The Five Bells at Edenham is a good dining pub.

※ ⚘ **Heckington** TF1444 is an understated but pleasant small town, with a well restored WINDMILL – the only one in Britain with eight sails; open pm Sun all yr, daily Easter–Sept, poss longer this year; (01529) 60765;

80p. Nearby the Pearoom is a decent CRAFT CENTRE, and the Nag's Head is good for lunch. Another fine restored mill, a splendid six-sailed model, is at Sibsey TF3550; £1.10.

✤ 🏛 **Hemswell** SK9391 BOMBER COUNTY AVIATION MUSEUM Small but enthusiastic collection in former RAF base, where you can watch restoration work being carried out on Hunter, Vampire and Mystère planes. Snacks, shop, disabled access; open Sun; free. Collectors should find something to interest them at the HEMSWELL ANTIQUES CENTRE close by – three buildings with around 270 shops selling books, period furniture, ceramics, rugs and jewellery.

🏛 🏚 **Horncastle** TF2669 A popular stop for antiques, with a number of shops, 30 of which are grouped together in the Bridge St Antiques Centre. You can still see parts of the town's ROMAN WALL. Old Nick's (North St) has a good value carvery.

🚂 ☺ **Legbourne** TF3684 RAILWAY MUSEUM Varied local railway memorabilia at the oldest preserved Great Northern Railway station. Also model railway and pets' corner. Snacks, shop, disabled access; cl Mon (exc bank hols), all Oct–Easter; (01507) 603116; £1.50. The Royal Oak at Little Cawthorpe is useful for lunch.

🦋 ✤ ☺ ✿ ✝ **Long Sutton** TF4222 BUTTERFLY AND FALCONRY PARK One of Britain's biggest walk-through tropical houses, with hundreds of butterflies flying freely. Also creepy-crawly little insectarium, wildflower meadows, nature trail, farm animals, adventure playground and pets' corner. The falconry centre has twice-daily displays and you can handle some of the birds. A well organised place. Meals and snacks, shop, disabled access; cl Nov–Mar; (01406) 363833; £3.40. The village CHURCH SPIRE is unusual for the hundreds of tons of lead sheathing it. The Crown & Woolpack has good simple food.

✤ **Mablethorpe** TF5185 ANIMAL GARDENS AND SEAL TRUST Rescued seals unable to return to the wild find a permanent home here, along with monkeys, parrots, porcupines, llamas, emus and all sorts of other creatures.

It's right by the beach. Snacks, shop, disabled access; cl Nov–Easter; (01507) 473346; £2.50.

❀ **Nettleton** TA1100 Potterton & Martin's NURSERY (Moortown Rd)has a lot of unusual and interesting plants – mainly alpines and small bulbs. The Nickerson Arms at Rothwell has decent food.

✤ 🐘 🎣 🦋 ⚓ **Skegness** TF5663 was built as a late 19th-c resort, and has been an archetypal one, with the first Butlin's Holiday Camp just up the coast. It has the regular amusements, though it lost its pier in a storm 15 years ago. The rewarding NATURELAND SEAL SANCTUARY (North Parade) is renowned for its seal rescuing activities. It's fascinating watching the seals performing tricks – none of them were trained in any way, they just seem to like showing off. Also other animals inc crocodiles, snakes and a tarantula, an aquarium, and free-flying tropical butterflies (May–Oct). Snacks, shop, disabled access; cl 25–26 Dec, 1 Jan; (01754) 764345; £2.95. CHURCH FARM MUSEUM (Church Rd South) Good recreation of daily farm life at the end of the 19th c, with changing exhibitions, craft demonstrations, and quite a lot of Lincoln longwool sheep. Snacks, shop, disabled access; cl Nov–Mar; (01754) 766658; *£1. The Vine Hotel on the southern edge of the town was here long before the resort, welcoming Tennyson among others; it's useful for lunch.

🏰 **South Kyme** TF1749 has a fine 14th-c battlemented tower standing in a meadow quite near the road.

👑 ❀ **Spalding** TF2422 MUSEUM OF ENTERTAINMENT (Millgate) Unusual and quirky collection tracing the development of entertainment from barrel and church organs to puppets and phonographs, taking in a history of the fairground along the way. Many of the exhibits are working, and the owners clearly love their subject. Snacks, shop, disabled access; open wknds Easter-Oct plus pm wkdys July-Sept; (01406) 540379; *£2. SPRINGFIELDS GARDENS 25-acre garden with glasshouses; there's a fantastic bedding plants display in summer, and in spring over a million bulbs in bloom. Meals and snacks, shop, disabled access; cl Oct–Mar; *£2.50. AYLSCOUGHFEE HALL MUSEUM (Church Gate) Spooky-looking medieval manor house with exhibitions on the local land and the people who've worked on it. Summer snacks, shop, disabled access; cl winter wknds, gardens open all yr; free. The Olde Dun Cow and riverside Lincolnshire Poacher are useful for lunch. All around this area, the flat fields by the roadside are a mass of colour in spring, first daffodils and then a multicoloured sea of tulips – very Dutch.

★ ✝ 🏠 🖼 🌸 ⚓ ☗ ! **Stamford** TF0307 John Betjeman considered this to be England's most attractive town, though it's now doomed to be mixed up with the town of Middlemarch it portrayed in the recent TV adaptation. Within the medieval walls are no fewer than 500 listed buildings, inc a good number of attractive medieval CHURCHES – particularly All Saints' in the centre, St George's with excellent 15th-c stained glass, and St Mary's near it. The lasting impression is of timeless stonework, in a particularly attractive creamy buff. On the edge of town is the splendid BURGHLEY HOUSE built by William Cecil and still the home of his family. Its exterior is Tudor at its most solidly showy. The inside was restyled between 1680 and 1700, and the state rooms are largely baroque with wonderful frescoes by Antonio Verrio – the Heaven Room is particularly impressive; notable paintings, furnishings, early Japanese ceramics and temporary exhibitions. The peaceful grounds, where the Burghley Horse Trials are held, were landscaped by Capability Brown. Meals, snacks, shop, limited disabled access; cl end of 1st wk Oct–Maundy Thurs; (01780) 52451; £5.10. STEAM BREWERY MUSEUM Vivid recreation of a Victorian brewery, which they hope to have working soon. Snacks, shop, disabled access; cl Mon (exc bank hols), Tues, mid Oct–Feb; (01780) 52186 £1.50. The local history MUSEUM includes life-size figures dressed in the clothes of Tom Thumb (only 3 ft 4 in) and Daniel Lambert, a portly fellow who weighed 50 stone

when he died on a racing outing here. Shop, disabled access to ground floor only; cl 12.30–1.30 pm winter, all Sun exc pm summer; *50p. The George, one of the town's grandest buildings with some parts going back to Saxon times, is excellent for lunch; the Bull & Swan and Lord Burghley are also good. Nearby Tolethorpe Hall has an open-air theatre in its grounds (covered auditorium), with a good Shakespeare season; (01780) 54381.

🏰 ✝ ! **Tattershall** TF2157 TATTERSHALL CASTLE The magnificent turreted keep of this 15th-c castle is 100 ft high and has fine heraldic chimneypieces on each of the four storeys; there's a double moat with peacocks and waterfowl. Snacks, shop (with food for the birds), some disabled access; open Sat–Weds Apr–Oct plus wknds Nov and Dec; £2.20; NT. The airy 15th-c CHURCH is also attractive, and just off the A153 towards Sleaford, on the left before you reach Tattershall Bridge, is a preserved steam engine which worked at keeping this area of fens drained for nearly a century. The Abbey Lodge Hotel (B1192 towards Woodhall) has good food.

🐐 ☺ **Toynton All Saints** TF3964 FENSIDE GOAT CENTRE Cheery dairy farm with various breeds of goat and demonstrations of milking around 4 pm; also sheep, rare cows, pigs and other animals, spinning displays and a play area. Children are encouraged to touch the animals. Shop, disabled access; cl am, all Tues and Sat, Oct–Mar; (01790) 752452; *£1.80.

🦉 🌸 ☗ **Weston** TF2924 BAYTREE OWL CENTRE Plenty of owls, many in a free-flying area; some can be handled. The entire centre is part of an expanding complex with ducks and rabbits in a landscaped glasshouse, a garden centre and a little museum. Meals, snacks, shop, disabled access; cl 25–26 Dec; (01406) 371907; £1.80.

🏠 🌸 **Woolsthorpe** SK9224 (this is the small village nr Colsterworth, not the bigger Woolsthorpe to the NW) WOOLSTHORPE MANOR The birthplace of Isaac Newton, where he later conducted some of his more important experiments, one of which, analysing the nature of white light, is recreated today. Geometry workings said to be in his handwriting are scratched into the plasterwork – and of course the garden has a venerable apple tree. Cl am, Mon and Tues, Nov–Mar; £2.30; NT.

✝ ❀ This county has a remarkable collection of great **churches**. Even villages which are tiny now and can never have been very large are graced by buildings of often impressive power. The remarkable height of the spires is a particular feature, with the tallest of any parish church in Britain being the very elegant 16th-c church in Louth TF3387 (the tower can be climbed on summer afternoons; hundreds of steps for a fabulous view). Other notable spires are those in Grantham SK9135 (the early 19th-c jingle about it, 'Grantham, now two rarities are thine, A lofty steeple and a living sign', refers to the hive with living bees still used as an inn sign by the Beehive pub there) and Brant Broughton SK9154. Other country churches worth seeing if you're near include those at Aswarby TF0639 (good food and bedrooms at the Tally Ho), Deeping St James TF1609, Langton by Partney TF3970 and Stow SK8882, while at Croyland you can see the remains of a once great abbey, part of which is still used as the parish church.

Many **village cottage gardens**, easily seen from the road, add a welcome splash of colour that seems a particular Lincolnshire characteristic. Tealby TF1590 is the best example: a great variety of neat and charmingly planted gardens adorn the stonebuilt cottages on its main street which runs down from the 12th-c church to a watersplash near a watermill, and there is more colour in the quaintly named side lanes.

Other **attractive villages**, all with decent pubs, include Newton TF0436, Frampton TF3239 (perhaps the prettiest Fenland village), Hough on the Hill SK9246, South Thoresby TF4077, Stow SK8882, Allington SK8540 (despite the proximity of the A1) and Woolsthorpe SK8435 (the one near Belvoir). Somersby TF3472 is also worth a visit.

Walks

The Lincolnshire Wolds, a tract of chalk hills in the E, rise gently: fields are mostly large (some like prairies), the scene interrupted by patches of woodland. The long-distance **Viking Way** ⌂-1 assists village-to-village walks, with 'Tennyson country' a popular focus (Tennyson was born at the rectory in Somersby TF3472, when his father was rector at Bag Enderby).

From Louth TF3387 a walk SW out of town enters **Hubbard's Hill** TF3186 ⌂-2, not in fact a hill but a surprisingly deep river valley for the Wolds.

Driving

The most interesting drive in the county is probably the Bluestone Heath hill road off the A16, just N of its junction with the A1104 W of Alford. This runs past South Ormsby and then swings round N to reach the A157 W of Louth; fine views most of the way. In similar vein, if not quite so rewarding, is the old road known as the High Street, which forks off the A158 about 3 miles N of Horncastle and runs almost due N up past Ranby, Market Stainton and Ludford all the way to Caistor. Both these roads follow Iron Age trackways. The A153 between Horncastle and Louth is a good road for getting a perspective on the rolling Wolds country, and doesn't usually carry heavy traffic. If you're prepared to take things gently, the B1398 northwards out of Lincoln has quite a few typically Lincolnshire views. Running S from Lincoln, the A607 through Leadenham (where the George is a pleasant stop) to Grantham follows the Lincoln Cliff, giving some good views.

Around Horncastle, an interesting day's drive includes Scrivelsby and its deer park, the pretty market town of Horncastle itself, Belchford (Blue Bell useful for lunch), Fulletby (perhaps a stroll on the footpaths here), Somersby (Tennyson's birthplace – his bust is in the church), Old Bolingbroke (castle ruins), Spilsby (good delicatessen in the quiet market place with its statue of Sir John Franklin), and, if you've made good time, Wainfleet and Boston.

In the N a lane hugging the embankment of the Trent between Gainsborough and the Humberside border gives a good impression of the flood plain of this powerful brooding river; there's a good lunch stop at the Jenny Wren at Susworth.

Over in the E and further S, driving is generally less interesting. The coast road has a lot of twists and turns, and even those side roads which look quite good on a map can turn out to be tryingly slow in practice, with agricultural vehicles too wide to pass trundling along at a snail's pace.

Where to eat

Market Deeping TF1310 CAUDLE HOUSE (01778) 347595 Georgian house with two small dining rooms and a little bar area, friendly, helpful staff (the wait-resses wear Victorian dress), a good choice of carefully cooked food, and a thoughtful wine list; bedrooms; cl 2 wks Aug. **£24.50 for 5 courses.**

Grimsthorpe TF0422 BLACK HORSE (0177 832) 247 Large open fire and rustic atmosphere in narrow bar, cosy Buttery Bar with another open fire, and inti-mate, candlelit dining room – all with excellent food; decent wine and pleas-ant, friendly staff; cl Sun, 1 wk over Christmas; children over 8; disabled access. **£23|£3.15/£5.75.**

Lincoln SK9772 JEWS HOUSE 15 The Strait (01522) 524851 Small, intimate and elegantly furnished restaurant in one of the oldest buildings in the city, with very good, imaginative food, professional, friendly service, and upstairs coffee lounge for those who want to smoke after the meal; cl Sun, am Mon. **£22.50|£3.50/£4.95.**

Newton TF0436 RED LION (0152 97) 256 Full of charm and character, this civilised pub specialises in imaginative choose-as-much-as-you-like salads – home-made soups and daily specials are good, too. **£20|£2.10/£9.45.**

Lincoln SK9772 WIG & MITRE Steep St (01522) 535190/523705 Attractively restored 14th-c building with imaginative food served all day (breakfast too), excellent puddings; more elaborate restaurant menu, interesting wine list, and consistently efficient, prompt service; cl 25 Dec; disabled access. **£18.55|£2.75/£5.**

Lincoln SK9772 BROWN'S PIE SHOP Steep St (01522) 527330 Spectacular pies (and lots of other food), helpful staff, comfortable seats and pleasant tradi-tional atmosphere; cl 1 Jan. **£15|£1.50/£3.50.**

Grantham SK9135 BLUE BULL 64 Westgate (01476) 70929 Popular food in bustling pub; cl Sun pm. **£9.50|£1.25/£3.**

NOTTINGHAMSHIRE

Nottingham has unexpected pleasures as a sightseeing break; some surprises out in the country too, with interesting smaller towns and villages, a few good places to visit, and some fine landscapes.

The county has some charming and interesting villages, one or two attractive old towns such as Newark and Southwell, and some pleas-ant countryside. In the north, the Dukeries, named for the noble fam-ilies and their great seats which used to occupy the area, still have extensive tracts of landscaped, largely forested parkland left after the grand houses and families have gone – even quite close to the indus-trial and mining centres around Mansfield.

Where to stay

Nottingham SK5639 ROYAL MOAT HOUSE Wollaton St, Nottingham NG1 5RH (0115) 941 4444 £90; 201 well equipped rms. Large and very popular modern hotel with glass-roofed arcade of tropical trees and plants, lots of bars (one with fine city views) and four restaurants; cl 25–26 Dec, 1 Jan, disabled access.

Langar SK7234 LANGAR HALL Langar, Nottingham NG13 9HG (01949) 860559 *£80; 12 lovely rms. Fine country house in spacious grounds with beautifully furnished, elegant rooms, pillared dining hall with paintings for sale, antiques and fresh flowers, a relaxed, informal atmosphere, a lively and friendly owner, and very good food; regular theatricals and murder weekends.

Southwell SK7053 SARACEN'S HEAD Market Pl, Southwell BG25 0HE (01636) 812701 £62w; 27 well kept rms. Interesting old hotel (Charles I spent his last free night here) with characterful main beamed bar, pleasant staff, straightforward bar lunches, and restaurant.

Barnby Moor SK6684 OLDE BELL Barnby Moor, Retford DN22 8QS (01777) 705121 £60w; 55 comfortable rms. Old coaching inn with open fires, beams, fine old furniture, and relaxed atmosphere.

Drakeholes SK7090 GRIFF INN Drakeholes, Doncaster, S Yorks DN10 5DF (01777) 817206 *£50; 3 rms. Handsome brick house with beautiful landscaped gardens and excellent views over River Idle valley and basin of Chesterfield Canal; wide range of bar food – carvery and salad bar open all week, substantial breakfasts and good vegetarian meals, friendly, helpful service; one bar is no smoking; disabled access.

Bestwood Country Park SK5646 BESTWOOD LODGE Bestwood Country Park, Nottingham NG5 8NE (0115) 920 3011 £40w; 40 rms. Attractive Victorian hotel set in lovely parkland, with minstrels' gallery, spacious bar, open fires, and good food in elegant restaurant; cl 25 Dec.

To see and do

Nottingham SK5739 on a weekend or a summer evening quickly loses its big city character, and is then easy to park in and stroll through, without the river of traffic that otherwise swarms so thickly along its inner ring road. It has an amazing number of decent pubs scattered through it – handy for the thirsty work of serious sightseeing. The parts around the parish church (which has some interesting carvings) and the Lace Market are particularly attractive. The rock on which the old town once stood is honeycombed with hundreds of galleries, cellars and passageways (one attractive old pub, the Olde Trip to Jerusalem, has a fascinating bar tunnelled right into the rock face). CAVE TOURS leave the Castle daily (exc Sun) at 2pm and 3pm (and 4pm in summer); £1. The tourist information centre on Wheeler Gate has a useful half hour audiovisual introduction to the town.

🏰👑⚙✿⚔✕🏛❀🔔🎶❦ Up on the summit the current CASTLE dates from the 17th c, but the gateway is from the earlier 13th-c fortress. It now houses a MUSEUM, with a good history of the site and the subterranean passageways. Meals, snacks, shop, disabled access; cl 25 Dec; (0115) 948 3504; free exc wknds and bank hols when £1. This also covers entry to the good BREWHOUSE YARD MUSEUM (Castle Boulevard), spread over five 17th-c houses, with interactive and thematic displays on local life in post-

medieval times. Quite a few of the activities – such as the feelie boxes – have been designed with children in mind. Also period toy shop and cottage garden with award-winning historic roses. Shop, some disabled access; cl 25 Dec; (0115) 948 3504. The LACE HALL (High Pavement) tells the story of the local lace industry, with demonstrations of the craft – you can have a go yourself; a lively place, with a lot of commitment and surprisingly interesting displays, touching on social conditions and

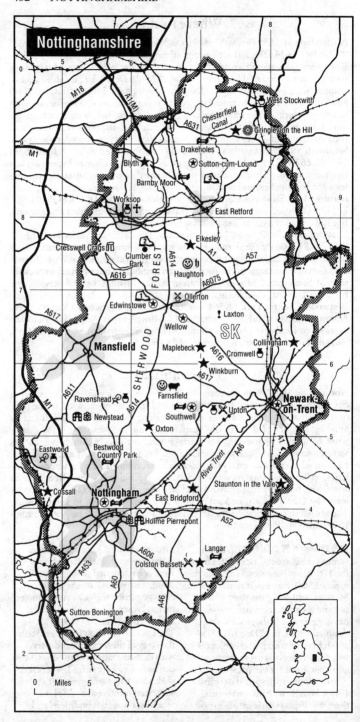

Nottinghamshire

West Stockwith
Chesterfield Canal
Gringley on the Hill
Drakeholes
Sutton-cum-Lound
Blyth
Barnby Moor
Worksop
East Retford
Cresswell Crags
Clumber Park
Elkesley
FOREST
A614
Haughton
A6075
A57
A616
A617
Edwinstowe
Ollerton
Laxton
Wellow
SK
Mansfield
Maplebeck
Collingham
A616
Cromwell
Winkburn
A617
SHERWOOD
Ravenshead
A614
Farnsfield
Newstead
Southwell
Upton
Newark-on-Trent
Oxton
Eastwood
Bestwood Country Park
M1
A611
Cossall
Nottingham
East Bridgford
Staunton in the Vale
River Trent
A46
Holme Pierrepont
A52
A606
Langar
Colston Bassett
A453
A60
A46
Sutton Bonington
0 Miles 5

child labour. Very good snacks and teas, shop, disabled access; cl 25–26 Dec; (0115) 948 4221; *£2.75. The INDUSTRIAL MUSEUM (Courtyard Buildings, Wollaton Park) also looks at lace making, as well as the pharmaceutical industry, engineering, printing and tobacco making. Shop, disabled access; cl am Sun, all Mon–Weds Oct–Mar; £1 joint with Wollaton Hall and Park (see below). CANAL MUSEUM (Canal Street) 19th-c warehouse recounting the history of the River Trent from the Ice Age, using interesting presentations. Shop, disabled access; cl 12–1 pm, Mon, Tues; free. GREEN'S MILL AND SCIENCE CENTRE (Windmill Lane, Sneinton) Flour is still produced and sold at this restored tower mill whenever conditions allow, and you can try grinding corn on part of an old millstone. The next door Science Centre has various hands-on exhibits, as well as a weather satellite receiver showing pictures live from space. Shop, disabled access; cl Mon (exc bank hols), Tues, and 25 Dec – best to tel (0115) 950 3635 to check the mill is working; free. MUSEUM OF COSTUME AND TEXTILES (43–51 Castle Gate) Embroidery from all over the world, map tapestries, dress accessories and costume from 1730 to 1960. Shops, some disabled access; cl 25 Dec; free.

WOLLATON HALL AND PARK Splendidly ornate Tudor building, now home to the city's natural history museum. The 500-acre grounds are a delight; cl am Sun; free, £1 joint with Industrial Museum (see above). The University ART GALLERY is worth a look; cl am Sun and bank hols. THE TALES OF ROBIN HOOD (Maid Marian Way) Nottingham wouldn't be complete without a reference to the county's legendary hero. Cars carry you through recreated medieval Nottingham and Sherwood Forest, ingeniously designed so that the experience seems to surround you. A film looks at the truth behind the stories and you can try your hand at shooting the sheriff using a real bow and arrow. Special events last wknd of every month. Meals, snacks, shop, disabled access; cl 24–26 Dec; (0115) 948 3284; £3.95. Useful lunch places are Fellows Morton & Clayton (Canal Rd; brews its own beer), Limelight (attached to the Playhouse), Lincolnshire Poacher (Mansfield Rd), Bell (Angel Row) and Sir John Borlase Warren (Canning Circus). There's an unusual NATURE RESERVE down by Beeston at the extensive partly wooded Attenborough lakes SK5234; on the far side a path takes you along the narrow spit of land dividing them from the mighty Trent.

Other things to see and do

🏚 Creswell SK5274 CRESWELL CRAGS VISITOR CENTRE Stone Age man lived in the caves and rock shelters of this limestone gorge right by the Derbyshire border (the village is actually over in Derbys). They don't have tours of the cave every day, but it's still a very interesting prehistoric site, with a good visitor centre explaining the period, reconstructions of family life in the Ice Age, and other displays and activities. They sometimes have children's stories in one of the caves (booking required). Snacks, shop, disabled access; cl Nov–Jan exc Sun best to check for cave tour dates (though you can usually count on them having them on

summer Suns); (01909) 720378; site free, cave tours £1. Take a torch. The Half Moon (Chesterfield Rd, Whitwell) has good-value food.
👹 Cromwell SK7961 VINA COOKE MUSEUM OF DOLLS AND BYGONE CHILDHOOD Thousands of interesting objects related to childhood – prams, costumes, toys and dolls from the last 250 years, all set in an imposing 17th-c rectory. It's especially lively on Easter Mon, with Morris dancers, crafts and the like. Snacks, shop; cl 12–2 pm, 25–26 Dec; (01636) 821364; *£2. The riverside Muskham Ferry at North Muskham is a decent family dining pub.

⚬ ⚘ **Eastwood** SK4646 D H
LAWRENCE BIRTHPLACE MUSEUM The
writer's early experiences played an
important formative role in his
writing, and here you can explore the
carefully restored Victorian working-
class setting of that childhood.
Various craft workshops next door.
Shop, limited disabled access; cl 25
Dec–1 Jan; *£1.75. Another home of
Lawrence's, furnished as he
described it in *Sons and Lovers*, is
open by appointment only on
(01773) 719786.

♪ ⚬ ⚘ ⚘ ⚘ **Edwinstowe** SK6266
SHERWOOD FOREST VISITOR CENTRE AND
COUNTRY PARK The visitor centre
includes a Robin Hood exhibition,
celebrating the legendary figure and
the many stories surrounding him.
Snacks, shop, disabled access; (0115)
982 3202. It's a good springboard for
the forest itself, only a fraction of
what it once was but still miles across
– and altogether more forested than
the heathland that Robin himself
would have known. It has good
waymarked paths and footpaths.
Near the village church (supposedly
where Robin Hood and Maid
Marian were married), the Church
Farm CRAFT WORKSHOPS have various
crafts in former farm buildings.
SHERWOOD FOREST FARM PARK Unusual
breeds of traditional farm animals,
foreign-bird aviaries, pets' corner and
colourful waterfowl on a sizeable
lake. Home-baked teas, shop,
disabled access; cl mid-Oct–Easter;
(01623) 823558; *£3. For lunch with
a good view over the forest, the
Bird in Hand at Blidworth SK5956
is useful.

⚘ ☺ **Farnsfield** SK6456 WHITE POST
MODERN FARM CENTRE Great for
children, a bustling modern working
farm with exhibits ranging from a
mousetown through 20 acres of
demonstration arable crop plots to
llamas, quails, snakes and fish. Lots of
amiable farm animals to fuss over,
and new pet learning centre with hints
on handling and health care. The pig-
breeding unit is fun, and you may be
able to watch eggs hatching in the
huge incubator. Snacks, shop,
disabled access; (01623) 882977;
£2.95. The Waggon & Horses at

Halam is a popular dining pub.

★ ❀ **Gringley on the Hill** SK7391, an
attractive village, gives magnificent
views in all directions from Beacon
Hill above the Chesterfield Canal;
you can make out the towers of
Lincoln cathedral on a clear day. The
Griff Inn at Drakeholes is a civilised
place for lunch.

♪ ☺ **Haughton** SK6872 WORLD OF
ROBIN HOOD Lively recreation of
medieval times and the background to
the tales of Robin Hood, with lots of
settings and costumed characters
giving the stories their historical
perspective. They've constructed an
entire medieval village, with moated
drawbridge, cobbled streets and
authentic shops and houses – a castle
is nearing completion. Children will
love it – they can even handle
weapons from the period. Meals,
snacks, shop, some disabled access;
probably only cl 25 Dec, but it may be
a good idea to check first in winter;
(01623) 860210; *£3.95. The
Robin Hood at Elkesley has good
value food.

⚑ ❀ **Holme Pierrepont** SK6239
HOLME PIERREPONT HALL Early Tudor
manor house with interesting early
15th-c timbers, and an elaborate
parterre in the formal courtyard
garden. Snacks, shop, disabled access
to gardens only; open pm Sun
Jun–Sept, plus Thurs July and Aug,
and Tues and Fri Aug; (0115) 933
2371; *£3.

❗ **Laxton** SK7268 is unique for having
kept the pattern of its MEDIEVAL
FARMING, with different villagers each
owning strips of the three great fields.
You can walk the grass paths or sykes
which divide groups of these strips.
The court of the manor, consisting of
local villagers, does its rounds
ceremoniously each year to check that
boundaries and paths are being
properly kept, and holds court in the
Dovecote, a good village pub. In the
pub's yard a small interpretation
centre explains the system.

★ ✝ ⚒ ⚒ ♪ ✝ ⚬ **Newark** SK7953 is an
attractive old market town with some
interesting buildings in its side streets,
a fine CHURCH, and walks by the River
Trent with summer BOAT TRIPS. The
Old Kings Arms, Mail Coach and

Malt Shovel are all useful for lunch. The CASTLE ruins date from the 11th c, and there's still a fair bit to see; it was destroyed during the Civil War then had periods as a cattle market and a bowling green – at one stage there were even plans to turn it into a quarry. The history of the site is well interpreted at the GILSTRAP HERITAGE CENTRE in the grounds. Shop, disabled access; cl 25–26 Dec, 1 Jan; free. AIR MUSEUM Good collection of over 40 assorted aircraft inc rare jet fighters and bombers; half the exhibits are under cover so fine all year round. On certain days you can sit inside some of the aircraft. Snacks, shop, disabled access; cl 24–26 Dec; (01636) 707170; *£3. MILLGATE MUSEUM OF SOCIAL AND FOLK LIFE Recreation of domestic and working life from Victorian times through to the 1950s. Teas, shop, some disabled access; cl am wknds and bank hols; free. The town also has a decent local history MUSEUM on Appletongate (cl 1–2 pm, all Thurs, and Sun exc pm summer).

🏠 ❀ **Newstead** SK5152 NEWSTEAD ABBEY Set in gorgeously romantic grounds, this splendid house was the home of Lord Byron, many of whose possessions can still be seen in his former bedroom. Other rooms are decorated in a variety of period styles ranging from medieval through to Victorian, and there are substantial remains of the original abbey. Meals and snacks, shop, disabled access; cl Oct–Mar; (01623) 793557; *£3.50, £1.50 gardens only. The Burnstump in the Country Park at Papplewick is a good value family dining pub.

✗ **Ollerton** SK6667 OLLERTON MILL The only working watermill in the county, still producing flour as it did in the early 18th c. There's a good video, and it's a pleasant setting, on the edge of Sherwood Forest. Meals, snacks, shop; mill working pm Sun and bank hols Apr–Sept; (01623) 824094; *£1.50.

🏊 ♨ **Ravenshead** SK5755 LONGDALE CRAFT CENTRE (Longdale Lane) Very good craft centre, now the most visited tourist attraction in the county. It's set out as a Victorian village street, with rows of period workshops – carving, toy-making, jewellery and so

forth, and a museum of craft tools. Decent restaurant; (01623) 794858; cl 25–26 Dec; £1.75 for museum. The Little John at Blidworth on the far side of the town is pleasant for lunch.

✝ ♨ ➡ **Southwell** SK7053 has a magnificent 12th-c MINSTER, a fine sight from miles around (especially at night when it's imaginatively floodlit), and glorious to walk through. Fine leaf carvings and lovely choir screen; it's well worth catching one of the regular concerts. As well as being attractive in its own right, this small quiet town is the home of the Bramley apple, developed by Henry Merryweather in the last century. The whole story is in an exhibition at his descendant's garden centre on Halam Rd, where one of the original trees still prospers. The aptly named Bramley Apple next door is useful for lunch. There's a FRUIT FARM in the grounds of nearby Norwood Park.

🐦 ♥ ➡ **Sutton-cum-Lound** SK7285 WETLANDS WATERFOWL RESERVE AND EXOTIC BIRD PARK Two lagoons full of birds ranging from ducks through swans to flamingos; many more wild birds inc parrots live in the surrounding countryside. Also new owl and fox sanctuary, llamas, wallabies and other animals, and children's farm. Meals, snacks, shop, disabled access; cl 25 Dec; (01777) 818099; £1.50. The canalside Boat at Haydon has decent food.

♨ **Upton** SK7354 UPTON HALL is the home of the British Horological Institute, and a museum of clocks and timepieces from marine chronometers to the first telephone speaking clock; as some of the exhibits are over 300 years old don't expect all the ones that work to be keeping perfect time. Snacks, disabled access; open pm Sun Apr–Sept; (01636) 813795; *£2.50. The French Horn is good for lunch, and the Cross Keys is also worth knowing.

★ ! ❀ ✝ **Wellow** SK6766 is an attractive village, unusual for being one of the only five in the country with a permanent MAYPOLE – which used to be the trunk of a Sherwood Forest tree, but is now metal. It stands on the only genuine village green in the county, kept that way since the village was founded in the 12th c (all the others were just open spaces used by the villagers and itinerant traders for buying and selling, which have been grassed over since all that stopped). The Olde Red Lion is good for lunch. There's a pleasant COUNTRY PARK nearby at Rufford SK6465, with the ruins of a 12th-c abbey.

♿ West Stockwith SK7995 WORLD IN MINIATURE Made from wood, wax or wool, all kinds of dolls from the 19th c onward, with a number of their houses and tiny shops, gardens and furniture. They restore dolls made before the 1960s. Meals, snacks, shop, disabled access; cl Mon (exc bank hols) and Tues, and all Jan; (01427) 890982; *£1.50.

♿ † Worksop SK5879 If you're passing this little market town it's worth popping into the Museum for the PILGRIM FATHERS STORY, following the New World colonists from their N Notts roots to the early days in New England; cl pm Thurs and Sat, all Sun, free. The PRIORY CHURCH is worth a look too; the elaborate scrollwork on its 12th-c yew door is said to be the oldest of its kind in the country. The Newcastle Arms (Carlton Rd) has good-value food.

The **River Trent** gives a tremendous sense of power even when it's on its best behaviour, sliding swiftly and massively along; its occasional floods are devastating, and most years it claims lives. Villages giving pleasant access to it include Laneham SK8076 and Thrumpton SK5031; decent pubs in good riverside spots include the Hazleford Ferry at Bleasby SK7149,

Lazy Otter in Wyke Lane, Farndon SK7651, Bromley Arms at Fiskerton SK7351 and Muskham Ferry at North Muskham SK7958. On the gentler Soar the Plough at Normanton on Soar SK5123 is in a pretty spot.

★ Other interesting and **attractive villages** in the county include the delightfully rustic Maplebeck SK7160 (the Beehive's an attractive country tavern; nearby Woodborough is also worth a look – and Lambley, partly for its unusual unspoilt miners' tavern the Woodlark), Blyth SK6287 now that the A1's left it aside (the White Swan's good for lunch, there are interesting wall paintings in the church, and Hodsock Priory Gardens are lovely at snowdrop time), Collingham SK8663, Cossall SK4842 (D H Lawrence country: he was once engaged to the girl who lived in Church Cottage), East Bridgford SK6943 (the Reindeer has good fresh fish), Elkesley SK6975 (working potter nr church; the Robin Hood is useful for lunch), Oxton SK6251 (the lane up hill northwards below the power lines takes you up to an Iron Age hill fort), Sutton Bonington SK5025 (interesting spinning/weaving workshop on Bucks Lane; cl pm Weds, Sun and summer hols), Winkburn SK7158 (unusual in that its simple 12th-c village church is a temple of the Knights Hospitaller), and, with their more 'Leicestershire-ish' character, Colston Bassett SK7033 (the Martins Arms is excellent for lunch), and Staunton in the Vale SK8043 (the Staunton Arms is useful) over in the Vale of Belvoir.

Walks

Though the county is far from being ideal for walkers, it does have some pleasant forest walks. **Sherwood Forest** ⌂-1 no longer covers a fifth of the county as in Robin Hood's day, and the heathland it once contained has been swallowed up into farmland. However, it is well endowed with trails, the most popular being to the Major Oak SK6267 (a huge tree in the heart of the forest).

Of the great Dukeries estates, **Clumber Park** SK6275 ⌂-2 is outstanding for its walks, with enough paths through its woodland and parkland for a full-day excursion.

There's scope for walks along the **Chesterfield Canal** ⌂-3; one quiet stretch is by the Boat at Hayton SK7384.

Driving

The best drives are in the N of the county: most notably, the B6034 from Edwinstowe through Sherwood Forest, left along the A616 for a mile or two, then right along the B6005, to turn right for Carburton and keep on through the fine landscapes of Clumber Park. A drive which runs with little traffic over the wolds in the S and along the Vale of Belvoir is the back road through West Leake, East Leake, Wysall, Widmerpool, Kinoulton, Colston Bassett, Granby and Orston. The B6386 coming into Southwell from the W, and connecting there with the A612 running E, is quite pleasant.

Where to eat

Colston Bassett SK7033 MARTINS ARMS (01949) 81361 Homely, comfortable pub with imaginative, often unusual food in bar and civilised restaurant, well kept real ales, a good choice of malt whiskies, quite a few wines by the glass, and an open fire; cl Sun and Mon pm; no children. **£17.50|£2.75/£6.95.**

Upton SU7354 CROSS KEYS (01636) 813269 Atmospheric and heavily beamed 17th-c pub with rambling bar, lots of interesting pictures, enterprising and generously served food inc very good daily specials, well kept beers, decent wines, and welcoming, efficient service. **£14|£2/£5.**

Help this year from: Michael and Jenny Back, Roy Bromell, Derek and Sylvia Stephenson, H Bramwell, Jim Farmer, Peter Burton, Stephen and Julie Brown, Norman and Gill Fox, R M Taylor, Chris Walling, Norma and Keith Bloomfield, George Atkinson, WHBM, A M McCarthy, K Walton, Ian and Val Titman, D W Gray, David and Ruth Hollands, Ruth and Alan Cooper, Gordon B Thornton, George and Sheila Edwards, Michael Swallow, Eric Locker, Elizabeth and Anthony Watts, J V Dadswell, Jane Kingsbury.

LEICESTERSHIRE, LINCOLNSHIRE AND NOTTINGHAMSHIRE CALENDAR

Some of these dates were provisional as we went to press.

JANUARY

22 **Brandy Wharf** Lincolnshire Wassailing Sunday at the Cider Centre (01652) 678364

FEBRUARY

2 **Spalding** Springfields Horticultural Exhibition at Springfields Gardens – *till Sun 5* (01775) 724843

26 **Newark** Dolls Fair at Kelham Hall (01480) 216372

APRIL

14 **Goulceby** Redhill Good Friday Service, cross-bearing parishioners lead procession up hill and re-enact erection of the crosses

17 **Hallaton** Bottle Kicking, Hare Pie Scrambling and general festivities

30 **Leicester** Dolls Fair at De Montfort Hall (01480) 216372

MAY

5 **Winthorpe** Nottinghamshire County Show at Newark Showground – *till Sat 6* (01636) 702627

LEICESTERSHIRE, LINCOLNSHIRE AND NOTTINGHAMSHIRE CALENDAR

MAY cont

6 **Spalding** Flower Parade – *till Mon 8* (01775) 724843

7 **Loughborough** Leicestershire County Show at Dishley Grange – *till Mon 8* (01509) 646786

8 **Castle Donington** Medieval Mayday Market

13 **Boston** Taverner Festival (450th anniversary) – *till Sun 21* (01205) 363108

14 **Belvoir** Jousting at Belvoir Castle (01476) 870262

20 **Tallington** Steam Fair – *till Sun 21* (01780) 63063

21 **Leicester** Historic Transport Pageant and Vehicle Parade at Abbey Park (0116) 251 2512

24 **Leicester** Early Music Festival at St Mary de Castro – *till 10 Jun* (0116) 267 3389

28 **Carlton** Country Fair at East Carlton Park – *till Mon 29* (01536) 402551

29 **Woodhall Spa** Agricultural Show at Jubilee Park

JUNE

2 **Little Casterton** Stamford Shakespeare Company Season at Rutland Open Air Theatre – *till 26 Aug* (01780) 54381

3 **Lincoln** Water Festival – *till Sun 4*; **Market Deeping** Agricultural Show – *till Sun 4*

4 **Melton Mowbray** Brooksby College Farm Open Day

10 **Cadeby** Steam and Brass Rubbing Day at The Old Rectory; **Market Harborough** Carnival (01858) 462626

17 **Grantham** Carnival at Wyndham Park – *till Sun 18* (01476) 74484; **Leicester** International Music Festival – *till Sun 25* (0116) 259 5693

21 **Grange de Lings** Lincolnshire Show at the Lincolnshire Showground – *till Thurs 22* (01522) 524240

24 **Boston** Carnival – *till Sun 25* (01205) 355570; **Grantham** Concert at Belton House (01476) 66116

25 **Belvoir** Jousting at Belvoir Castle (01476) 870262

JULY

1 **Castle Ashby** Country Fair at Castle Ashby House – *till Sun 2* (01604) 696521

8 **Wymeswold** Rempstone Steam and Country Show

15 **Tattershall** Gilbert and Sullivan Concert at Tattershall Castle (01526) 342543

16 **Bruntingthorpe** Big Thunder Airshow at the airfield (0116) 247 8030; **Measham** Ashby Show at Measham Lodge Farm (01530) 412125

17 **Kirkby Mallory** Pre-1960s Vehicles Race Meeting at Mallory Park Circuit (01635) 44411

21 **Peckleton** Festival in and around St Mary Magdalen's Church – *till Sun 23* (01455) 822604

23 **Grantham** Family Day at Belton House (01476) 66116; **Spalding** Vintage Vehicle and Classic Car Show at Springfields (01775) 724843; **Lutterworth** Vintage Motorcycle Club Founder's Day Rally at Stanford Hall and Motorcycle Museum (0116) 288 4619

Leicestershire, Lincolnshire and Nottinghamshire Calendar

JULY cont

24 **Loughborough** Festival of Dance at Charnwood Theatre – *till Fri 28* (01509) 263151

28 **Gunby** Evening Concert at Gunby Hall (01909) 486411

29 **Heckington** and District Agricultural Show at the Showground – *till Sun 30* (01529) 304145; **Stamford** Fireworks and Laser Symphony Concert at Burghley House (01625) 575681

30 **Belvoir** Jousting at Belvoir Castle (01476) 870262

31 **Edwinstowe** Robin Hood Festival at the Sherwood Forest Visitor Centre and Country Park – *till 6 Aug* (01623) 824490

AUGUST

5 **Leicester** Caribbean Carnival at Victoria Park (0116) 253 0491; **Uppingham** Summer Fair

6 **Skendleby** Lincolnshire Sheepdog Trials at Lodge Farm (01775) 713930

12 **Market Bosworth** Medieval Fayre – *till Sun 13* (0116) 239 4366; **Spalding** Springfields Summer Show at Springfields Gardens – *till Sun 13* (01775) 724843

18 **Oakham** International Bird Watching Fair – *till Sun 20* (01572) 770651

19 **Leicester** Castle Park Festival – *till Sat 26* (0116) 265 7088

20 **Sutton Cheney** Jousting at Bosworth Field (01455) 290429

27 **Belvoir** Jousting at Belvoir Castle (01476) 870262; **Leicester** International Air Display at the airport (0116) 259 3484; **Leicester** Show at Abbey Park – *till Mon 28* (0116) 252 7356

31 **Stamford** Burghley Horse Trials at Burghley Park – *till 3 Sept* (01780) 52131

SEPTEMBER

2 **Tattershall** Pageant at Tattershall Castle (01526) 342543

9 **Bourne** Thurlby and Northorpe Carnival at Lawrence Park – *till Sun 17* (01778) 425670

10 **Sutton Cheney** Re-enactment of the Battle of Bosworth at Bosworth Field (01455) 290429

17 **Loughborough** Raft Race and Family Fun Day at Charnwood Water

OCTOBER

5 **Nottingham** Goose Fair – *till Sat 7*

2 **Castle Donington** Wakes (small traditional street fair) – *till Mon 30 (not Sun)* (01332) 810432

NOVEMBER

4 **Cadeby** Steam Day and Bonfire at The Old Rectory

12 **Newark** Dolls Fair at Kelham Hall (01480) 216372

DECEMBER

26 **Swithland** Morris Dancing at the Griffin Inn (0116) 267 5654

30 **Leicester** Dolls Fair at De Montfort Hall (01480) 216372

The Midlands
(Warwickshire, West Midlands and Northamptonshire)

Aconsiderable number of most impressive old houses head the long list of interesting places to visit here, and there are some notable motor collections; it's not so strong on things to keep children happy.

North Warwickshire and the West Midlands are packed with things to see and do. As many of the most interesting are buried in relatively unappealing urban areas, they are best suited to day visits, preferably on a weekend. Warwick and its closely coupled neighbour Leamington Spa do have potential for short-break stays.

Stratford is great for Shakespeare lovers, though other people will find more to enjoy out in the south Warwickshire countryside. On the edge of the Cotswolds, this part of the county is given additional interest by the neighbouring parts of Gloucestershire and Oxfordshire.

Northamptonshire has a lot of appeal for a short break – relatively undiscovered countryside, with a good mix of places to visit (though little for children), plenty of places to stay, the most scenic driving in the area, and good-value prices.

This is not very good countryside for walkers, though there are some pleasant strolls.

Birmingham, Warwick and North Warwickshire

Some great day visits, particularly in and around Birmingham; Warwick is a possibility for a stay, and there are other comfortable places for a short break.

Birmingham has excellent art collections, lively museums, a surprisingly interesting factory visit at Bournville, good botanic gardens, many other things worth seeing, and a burgeoning cultural identity typified in Simon Rattle's conductorship of the City of Birmingham Symphony Orchestra. Though we have included one good-value hotel here for the determined sightseer, the city itself is not ideal for a weekend break: most people would find it better to go in by the day. Coventry also has quite a lot to see on day visits. Warwick, by contrast, has the character and atmosphere to provide short-stay appeal, coupled as it is with its neighbour Leamington Spa – which still has the gardens, parks and spacious terraces of its heyday as a spa resort. Outside these towns, the high points for most people are Kenilworth Castle, the open-air museum at Dudley, Arbury Hall, and Wightwick Manor in Wolverhampton.

Laced with canals, the area gives some of its better walking possibilities along their towpaths; otherwise, it has less to hold the attention of walkers. It has quite a good choice of comfortable places to stay in.

Where to stay

Wishaw SP1794 BELFRY Wishaw, Sutton Coldfield B76 9PR (01675) 470301 *£160 inc dinner; 219 rms in four wings named after famous golfers. Set in 500 acres of parkland and with two world-class 18-hole golf courses, this creeper-covered hotel has light, modern day rooms inc 8 bars and 4 restaurants, lots of plants, a floodlit driving range, putting green, golf centre, fine leisure complex, and nightclub; disabled access.

Leamington Spa SP3161 MALLORY COURT Harbury Lane, Bishops Tackbrook, Leamington Spa CV33 9QB (01926) 330214 *£150; 10 wonderfully comfortable and luxurious rms. Fine, ancient-looking house – actually built around 1910 – with elegant, antique and flower-filled day rooms, attentive staff, excellent food using home-grown produce in panelled restaurant, and 10 acres of lovely gardens with outdoor swimming pool, tennis, squash, croquet; cl 3–12 Jan; children over 9.

Barford SP2760 GLEBE HOUSE Church St, Barford, Warwick CV35 8BS (01926) 624218 £110; 41 pretty and comfortable rms. Carefully extended former rectory with spacious conservatory restaurant, restful lounge bar, leisure club with indoor swimming pool, sauna, steam room, and a trimnasium, and croquet in the landscaped gardens.

Ansty SP3983 ANSTY HALL Ansty, Coventry CV7 9HZ (01203) 612222 *£100; 31 luxurious rms. Handsome 17th-c hotel in 8 acres of grounds, with quiet, relaxing atmosphere, comfortable and elegantly furnished day rooms, helpful staff, and fine modern English cooking – much produce is grown in the walled garden.

Hockley Heath SP1573 NUTHURST GRANGE Nuthurst Grange Lane, Hockley Heath B94 5NL (01564) 783972 £99; 15 airy, pretty rms. At the end of a long drive through attractive parkland stands this handsome Edwardian house with warmly welcoming staff, excellent food, and comfortable day rooms with lots of flowers; disabled access.

Sutton Coldfield SP1296 NEW HALL Walmley Rd, Sutton Coldfield B76 8QX (0121) 378 2442 £94; 60 lovely rms (the ones in the manor house are the best). The oldest moated manor house in England; 26 acres of beautiful grounds, luxuriously furnished day rooms, a graceful panelled restaurant with carefully cooked imaginative food using very fresh (often home-grown) produce, excellent service; children over 8; disabled access.

West Bromwich SP0091 MOAT HOUSE Birmingham Rd, West Bromwich, Birmingham B70 6RS (0121) 553 6111 £85.40; 172 rms. Decent modern hotel, handy for the motorway, with good food (especially carvery), and attentive helpful service; playroom with nursery maid and childminder, disabled access.

Kenilworth SP2871 CLARENDON HOUSE Old High St, Kenilworth CV8 1LZ (01800) 616883 £65; 30 cosy rms. Carefully restored and friendly 15th-c hotel with Cromwellian armour in the beamed public rooms, and set in the oldest part of town.

Warwick SP2865 FORTH HOUSE 44 High St, Warwick CV34 4AX (01926) 401512 £46; 2 pretty and spacious suites (one almost a flat). Prettily decorated house with lovely surprisingly big garden, and good food; disabled access.

Sherbourne SP2661 OLD RECTORY Vicarage Lane, Sherbourne, Warwick CV35 8AB (01926) 624562 *£43; 14 rms, all with antique brass or brass and iron beds. Carefully furnished Georgian house not far from Warwick, with cosy sitting room, big log fire, beams, flagstones, honesty bar, hearty breakfasts, pretty walled gardens; converted coach house is popular with families; cl 23–27 Dec; dogs welcome; good disabled access.

Avon Dassett SP4049 CRANDON HOUSE Avon Dassett, Leamington Spa CV33 0AA (01295) 770652 £35; 3 rms. Welcoming farmhouse on a small working farm with a variety of livestock, fine views, big garden, comfortable sitting rooms (one with woodburning stove), and fine breakfasts; evening meals by arrangement; cl Christmas; children over 8.

Birmingham SP0787 Wharf 20 Bridge St, Birmingham B1 2JH (0121) 633 4820 £33.50; 54 comfortable, modern rms. Decent very good value hotel overlooking the Worcester & Birmingham Canal; disabled access.

To see and do

↓ᴛ ℩ Birmingham SP0786 There are masses of things to see and do here, but for most people it is disqualified as a place to stay by its lack of an attractive town centre – plans to replace the notorious Bull Ring with a centre more in tune with the city's growing cultural pride seem permanently on hold. However, the formidably efficient traffic system which ploughs through its heart means that, particularly at weekends, you can easily tap in on this rich reservoir of things to see, just coming in as it suits you. The centre today is mostly modern, but the city has a long heritage, dating back long before it was valued at £1 in the Domesday Book, and has a rich and varied industrial history taking in everything from buckles to chocolate buttons, and cloth to Crunchies. There's a surprising absence of that essential for big-city visits: good pubs. A few acceptable ones which do at least some lunchtime food include the Atkinson Bar (Midland Hotel), Bellefield (Winson St, Winson Green), Black Eagle (Factory Rd, Hockley), Brewer & Baker (Ravenhurst St, Camp Hill), Prince of Wales (Cambridge St) and Rope Walk (St Paul's Sq, Hockley).

▥ ▦ ᕒ ⱡ Aston Hall (Aston, 2m NE) Strikingly grand Jacobean mansion with panelled long gallery, balustraded staircase and magnificent plaster friezes and ceilings. Snacks, shop; cl am, Nov–Easter; (0121) 327 0062; free (and more satisfying than a good many houses you'd have to pay for). City Museum and Art Gallery (Chamberlain Sq) Perhaps the best collection of Pre-Raphaelite paintings anywhere. Also other French, Dutch, Italian and English works from the 14th c on; excellent coins and archaeology sections and displays on local and natural history. Meals, snacks, shop, disabled access; cl am Sun, 25 Dec; (0121) 235 2834; free. **▣ Barber Institute** (University) Excellent collection of paintings and sculptures, well housed in a very attractive gallery; just the right size to be enjoyable without being overwhelming. Shop, disabled access; cl Sun am; (0121) 472 0962; free. **ᕒ ⱡ Museum of Science and Industry** (Newhall St) Concentrating on the city's contribution to science and engineering, with displays of tools, equipment and working engines, and the oldest still-working steam engine in the world. Splendid Locomotive Hall and aircraft section with Spitfire and Hurricane steam days. Meals, snacks, shop, disabled access; cl

several days around Christmas and New Year; (0121) 236 1022; free. **ⱡ Birmingham Railway Museum** (Warwick Rd) Working railway museum with fully equipped workshop, many steam locomotives and several historic carriages, waggons and other vehicles. Meals, snacks, shop, disabled access; cl 25–26 Dec and 1 Jan; (0121) 707 4696 for details of steam days; £2.50. They organise full or half-day courses in steam train driving (adults only) – in winter you may be able to try driving the famous *Flying Scotsman*. **↓ᴛ ▨ Jewellery Quarter** Birmingham's importance in the jewellery trade is much smaller than it used to be, but the Quarter is still Britain's biggest producer of gold jewellery. There are around 100 jewellery shops lining the streets, useful for browsing or repairs. The Discovery Centre on Vyse St is built around the well restored workshops of the Smith & Pepper company, still much as they were at the start of the century. There's a good overview of the industry, as well as tours of the factory and demonstrations of jewellery-making techniques. It recently won the Museum of the Year Award for best industrial museum. Snacks, shop, disabled access; cl Sun; (0121) 554 3598; £2. The Rosevilla nearby has decent food.

☎ ! CADBURY WORLD (Bournville SP0481) Fascinating displays on the origin, production and marketing of the world-famous chocolate, with plenty of samples along the way to satisfy any cravings created by the sumptuous smells. Watch out for the bizarre little cars shaped like Creme Eggs. The new Fantasy Factory is good for children, with a more light-hearted look at chocolate-making. A very enjoyable place, but it gets busy, so book in advance to avoid queues. Meals, snacks, shop, disabled access; cl some Mons, Tues and Fris – best to check first: (0121) 451 4180; £4.75.

❀ BOTANICAL GARDENS (Edgbaston) 15 acres featuring Tropical House with lily pool, bananas and cocoa, Palm House, Orangery, the National Bonsai Collection, Cactus House and the gardens themselves, filled with rhododendrons and azaleas and a good collection of trees. Bands play on summer Sun afternoons. Meals, snacks, shop, disabled access; cl 25 Dec; (0121) 454 1860; £2.90 (£3.20 Sun).

🐾 BIRMINGHAM NATURE CENTRE (Edgbaston) British and European animals in indoor and outdoor enclosures designed to resemble natural habitats. Meals, snacks, shop, disabled access; open pm Tues–Fri Easter–early Oct; (0121) 472 7775; free.

🏰 WEOLEY CASTLE (Alwold Rd) Ruins of 13th-c castle with interesting little museum. Shop; cl am, Sat–Mon, Nov–Mar; (0121) 427 4270; free.

🏠 BLAKESLEY HALL (Yardley) Timber-framed 16th-c merchant's house, furnished according to an inventory of 1684. Displays on timber building, pottery and rural crafts. Shop; cl am, and Nov–Mar; (0121) 783 2193; free.

✗ ⬇ SAREHOLE MILL (Hall Green) Working 18th-c water mill, with several displays explaining the milling process. Tolkien often came here as a child. Shop; cl am, and Nov–Mar; (0121) 777 6612; free.

♿ SELLY MANOR MUSEUM (Selly Oak SP0382) Two timber-framed medieval manor houses re-erected on new site, with herb garden, crafts and exhibitions. Snacks, shop, some disabled access; cl wknds, Mon (exc bank hols), 15 Dec–15 Jan; (0121) 472 0199; *£1.

Warwick SP2865 This year is the 450th anniversary of Henry VIII's granting the town charter. Though many older buildings survive despite a major fire in 1694, today's centre is dominated by elegant Queen Anne rebuilding. Some of the old-est structures are to be found around Mill St, which is very attractive to stroll along; there are a good few antique shops. The Zetland Arms (Church St) and Tilted Wig (Market Pl) are useful for quick food, and the Saxon Mill (Guys Cliffe) is a straightforward family dining pub in attractive waterside surroundings.

🏰 ! ❀ WARWICK CASTLE One of the country's most splendid castles and certainly the most visited. Begun by William the Conqueror, it's a lively place, with lots of displays specially geared for families, such as the gruesome torture chambers in the dungeon or the Royal Weekend Party exhibition, both of which show the influence of Madame Tussaud's, which owns the site. A similar exhibition re-creating the medieval household's preparations for battle has recently opened in the 14th-c undercroft. Also excellently preserved rooms, magnificent Hall, fine furnishings and art, and marvellous grounds designed by Capability Brown; the views from its parklands are dramatic, stirring stuff. Very busy, but worth braving the crowds for. Meals, snacks, shop, disabled access to grounds only; cl 25 Dec; (01926) 495421; £7.75. The nearby MILL GARDEN is a delightful series of plantings in a super setting on the river beside the castle – a very nice place to stroll through, with plenty of old things to look at along the way. Shop, disabled access; open pm Sun and bank hol Mons, Easter–mid-Oct, more often than not at other times by appointment; (01926) 492877; £1 suggested donation.

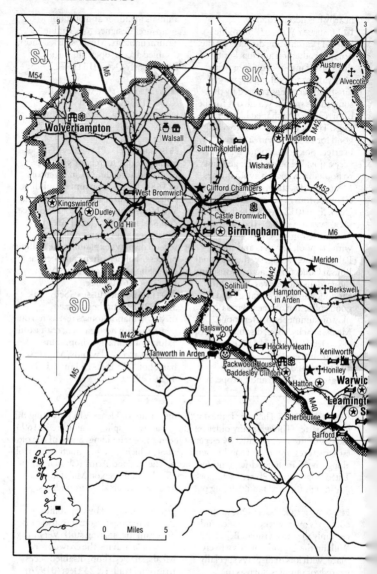

✝ ❋ St Mary's Church (Old Square)
Splendid medieval church on the
town's highest point, Norman crypt,
chapter house and magnificent 15th-c
Beauchamp chapel. In summer you can
go up the tower which has excellent
views – small admission charge.

🏠 Lord Leycester Hospital (High St)
Lovely half-timbered building built in
1383, still used as a home of rest for
retired servicemen (there's a

regimental museum). You can see the
fine old Guildhall, candlelit chapel,
gatehouse and courtyard, and they've
recently opened up the garden (pm Sat
only), with its Norman Arch and
2,000-yr-old vase from the Nile.
Snacks, shop; cl Mon, Good Fri, 25
Dec; (01926) 491422; *£2.25.

🏠 🍽 St John's House (St John's) Fine
17th-c house with exhibits from the
county museum, inc a reconstructed

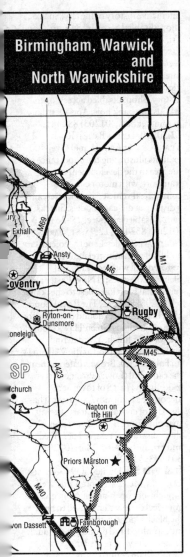

Birmingham, Warwick and North Warwickshire

to life. Shop; cl Sun am, Oct–Easter exc Sat and local school hols; *£1.
🖐 WARWICKSHIRE MUSEUM (Market Place) County museum in the 17th-c market hall, with local history and archaeology inc good fossils, habitat displays and Sheldon tapestry map of the county. Shop; cl Sun exc pm Apr–Sept; free.

The impressive flight of CANAL LOCKS on the Grand Union Canal west of the town can be reached most easily from Hatton SP2467, on the A4177 just past the hospital complex.

Other things to see and do

✝ **Alvecote** SK2404 14th-c PRIORY RUINS, including a doorway and dovecot, in countryside by Coventry Canal – useful towpath walks. There are fine views from the Wolferstan Arms at Shuttington, a good family pub.

🏠🖐🌳 **Arbury** SP3389 ARBURY HALL They like to call this the 'Gothic Gem of the Midlands' and it is a splendid-looking place, the original Elizabethan house elaborately spruced up in the 19th c with soaring fan vaulting and filigree tracery in most of the rooms, and the outside additions making it one of the best examples of the Gothic Revival style. The writer George Eliot was born on the estate, and in her *Mr Gilfil's Love Story* describes some of the rooms – not unreasonably comparing the dining room to a cathedral. There's also some work by Wren in the stables (which now house a collection of vintage cycles) and the gardens are a pleasure. Shop, limited disabled access; open pm Sun and bank hols Easter–Sept, gardens also open pm Mon; (01203) 382802; £3, garden only £1.60. A major display on the life of George Eliot can be seen at the Museum up the road in Nuneaton SP3592, nicely set in colourful Riversley Park (good craft centre nearby); cl Mon; free. From here there are occasional guided tours around local places with an Eliot connection (inc Arbury Hall); (01203) 384027 for dates.

🏠🌼✝ **Baddesley Clinton** SP2070 BADDESLEY CLINTON HOUSE Romantic

Victorian parlour, kitchen and schoolroom and regimental museum. Shop, disabled access to ground floor only. Cl 12.30–1.30 pm, Sun exc pm Apr–Sept, Mon; (01926) 410 410 for this and two museums below; free.
🖐 DOLL MUSEUM (Castle St) Carefully restored half-timbered Elizabethan house with comprehensive collection of antique and period dolls and toys. A fun video shows the exhibits come

13th-c moated manor house, mostly unchanged since the 17th c. Interesting portraits, priest's holes and garden with chapel and pretty walks. Meals, snacks, shop, disabled access; house cl am, Mon (exc bank hols), Tues, and Nov–Feb (though shop and restaurant stay open till Christmas); £4, grounds only £2; NT. A timed ticket system is in operation. The nearby CHURCH has a lovely east window. The prettily set Cockhorse at Rowington does good simple food.
❁ **Castle Bromwich** SP1489 CASTLE BROMWICH HALL GARDEN is an authentic collection of plants grown here in the 18th c, inc ancient vegetables as well as herbs and shrubs, in a classic 18th-c formal layout. Snacks, shop, plant sales, disabled access; cl am, Fri, Oct–Easter; (0121) 749 4100; £2.
✝ ☺ ▦ ▥ ♨ ✝ **Coventry** SP3378 Like Birmingham, more of a place to dip into than to fix as your full weekend-stay menu; its most interesting street is Spon St, with one or two ancient buildings that started their lives here and others that have been rescued from elsewhere and rebuilt here (the picturesque Old Windmill does cheap basic lunches). One of the town's most famous inhabitants was Lady Godiva, commemorated by a statue in Broadgate and the Coventry Clock where she pops out in the pink every hour. CATHEDRAL (Priory Row) Bombed during the war, the old cathedral ruins have been carefully preserved, and parts of it such as the 14th-c tower remain intact. These have been joined by the new cathedral designed by Sir Basil Spence, with windows by John Piper. It is in no way an orthodox church building, and is worth a look for unusual modern art (inc a tapestry by Graham Sutherland) and even holograms; the visitor centre has more, as well as a full history of its development. Meals, snacks, shop, disabled access; cl 4 days in July and Nov for degree ceremonies. TOY MUSEUM (Much Park St) Toys from 1740 to 1990, inc dolls, trains and games, housed in a 14th-c monastery gatehouse. Shop; cl am and 25 Dec; *£1.50. HERBERT ART GALLERY AND MUSEUM (Jordan Well) Fine silver and furniture, Chinese art, and a lively new interactive history of the city. Snacks, shop, disabled access; cl Sun am, Good Fri, 25 Dec; (01203) 832 381; free. LUNT ROMAN FORT (Coventry Rd) Fun reconstruction of a 1st-c Roman fort, interesting to see such a site in all its glory. Good interpretative displays and history. Shop, disabled access; open wknds and bank hols, Apr–Oct, daily in summer hols; (01203) 832381; £2.50. MUSEUM OF BRITISH ROAD TRANSPORT (St Agnes Lane) Over 400 exhibits illustrating the importance of the area in the development of transport, with motor cars, commercial vehicles and bicycles, and a display of die-cast models. Snacks, shop, disabled access; cl 25–26 Dec; (01203) 832425; £2.95. ST MARY'S GUILDHALL (Bayley Lane) Medieval city guildhall with minstrels' gallery, restored hall with portraits and Flemish tapestries; cl Nov–Easter and for official functions, best to check first tel (01203) 832272. The Royal Court Hotel and the Greyhound out at Sutton Stop (Aldermans Green/Hawkesbury) are good for lunch. You can find authentic Indian food at the William IV on Foleshill Rd. Browns café-bar near the cathedral (Lower Precinct) serves food all day. Just S of town at the airport, the MIDLAND AIR MUSEUM has displays of civil and military aircraft spanning more than 70 years. Snacks, shop, disabled access; cl Tues, Weds and Fri, and all Nov–Mar; (01203) 301 333; £2.50.
⬆ ⛟ 🎠 ⛲ ☺ ▣ **Dudley** SO9490 BLACK COUNTRY MUSEUM (Tipton Rd) Well thought-out open-air museum giving a good feel of how things used to be in the Black Country, the heavily industrialised and proudly individual areas on the west part of the Birmingham conurbation. Reconstruction of typical turn-of-the-century Black Country village, complete with cottages, chapel, chemist, school, baker and pub, and trips along the canal or even down a mine. All the staff are in period costume. Plenty of things to do here – it could be a whole day out. Meals, snacks, shop, some disabled access; cl Mon and Tues in Nov–Feb, and wk before and during Christmas; (0121) 557 9643; £4.95. The Dudley Canal

Trust do BOAT TRIPS along the Dudley Tunnel, part of a unique network of canal tunnels and limestone mines; there's an audio-visual show in the Singing cavern. Best to ring for dates, and they prefer prior notice for disabled visitors; (0121) 520 5321; £1.90. DUDLEY ZOO Popular traditional zoo in the wooded grounds of an impressive RUINED CASTLE, with animals from all over the world; there's a train up to the top of the hill good views. Meals, snacks, shop, disabled access; cl 25 Dec; (01384) 252401; £4.40. MUSEUM AND ART GALLERY (St James's Rd) Good collection of 17th-, 18th- and 19th-c European paintings, furniture, and ceramics, with other local history and fossils in the lively new geology gallery. Shop, disabled access; cl Sun; free.

✿ **Earlswood** SP1173 MANOR FARM CRAFT WORKSHOPS (Wood Lane) Ceramics, furniture restoration, stained glass, print-making, needlework etc, and farm shop with home-made ice cream; disabled access; cl Mon. The canalside Bluebell is a popular family dining pub.

🏠🖐 **Farnborough** SP4349 FARNBOROUGH HALL Wonderful Palladian villa filled with splendid sculptures, paintings and fine rococo plasterwork; the staircase, hall and two main rooms are on show, and the gardens have a temple and views from the terrace walk – less impressive than they were thanks to the arrival of the M40. Some disabled access; open pm Weds and Sat Apr–Sept, and terrace also open pm Thurs and Fri; £2.60, terrace walk only £1; NT. In the yard is the enthusiastic EDGEHILL BATTLE MUSEUM, commemorating the first major battle of the English Civil War, fought nearby in 1642. Weapons, uniforms, models and dioramas, with appropriate period music. The friendly staff really are dedicated to their subject. Snacks, shop; open pm Weds and Sat Apr–Sept; (01295) 690593; £1. The reopened Butchers Arms has good food.

✿🐏🍦 **Hatton** SP2367 COUNTRY WORLD (Dark Lane) Britain's biggest crafts village, made up of some three dozen workshops; the 100-acre site also includes a collection of rare breeds (some in walk-through paddocks), adventure playground, and summer pick-your-own soft fruits. Meals, snacks, shop, disabled access; (01926) 842436; craft village free, farm £2.70. Some of the craftsmen and women offer courses in their skills. A nature trail leads to the Stairway to Heaven – a flight of 21 canal locks over 2 miles. Good farm shop nearby at Windmill House Farm; the Durham Ox at Shrewley is handy for lunch.

🏰 **Kenilworth** SP2871 KENILWORTH CASTLE Dramatic castle begun in the 12th c and later transformed by John of Gaunt into a spectacular fortress. These are among the finest castle ruins in the country, with a still impressive keep and various other buildings within the sandstone walls. Also restored Tudor garden, and various re-enactments, plays and operas in the grounds. Snacks, shop, disabled access; cl 24–26 Dec, 1 Jan; (01926) 52708; £1.80. The town itself has some pleasant strolls, especially around the castle area, where the Clarendon House Hotel is a civilised place for lunch; the Clarendon Arms is also good value.

🖐! 🏰 **Kingswinsford** SO8888 BROADFIELD HOUSE GLASS MUSEUM (Barnett Lane) Excellent collection of glass from nearby Stourbridge, recently redisplayed to dazzling effect. Clever use of lighting shows off the exhibits quite spectacularly, and even the audio-visual shows create a sense of excitement. One of the area's least expected treasures. Shop; cl Sat lunch, am exc Sat, all day Mon; (01384) 273 011; free. Nearby Himley SO8791 has the CROOKED HOUSE, an extraordinary pub bent by mining subsidence into a three-dimensional optical illusion that'll have you imagining things roll uphill here, instead of down; perhaps surprisingly, it's a good pub too. Down by the canal, the Navigation (Greensforge) gives pleasant views of narrow boats working their way through the lock. Just down the A449 at Amblecote SO8985 you can tour the ROYAL DOULTON FACTORY or visit the factory shop (cl Sun); tours 10am and 11.15am wkdys only; (01384) 440

442; free. The Robin Hood here (Collis St) has good value food.

❦ ♨ 🏛 **Leamington Spa** SP3265 Elegant spa resort popularised by the rich who came to take the waters in the 18th c and 19th c. There are still many fine Regency buildings, though today the town is better seen as a civilised shopping centre, and perhaps as a base for sallies into the surrounding countryside – or into Warwick, across the River Avon. The JEPHSON GARDENS (The Parade) are beautifully laid out and worth a look, with wild ducks on the lake. Meals, snacks, shop, disabled access; free. WARWICK DISTRICT COUNCIL ART GALLERY AND MUSEUM (Avenue Rd) has collections of ceramics, pottery and glass, and British, Dutch and Flemish paintings from the 16th c to the present. Shop, disabled access; cl 1–2pm, Weds, Sun, Good Fri, 25–26 Dec, 1 Jan; free.

🐄 🏠 ⅋ 🐾 **Middleton** SP1798 ASH END HOUSE FARM Friendly farm specifically set up for children; animals from shire horses to baby chicks and fluffy ducklings, as well as various rare breeds of goats, pigs and sheep. A pony ride is included in the price. Snacks, shop, disabled access; cl 25–27 Dec; (0121) 329 3240; £2.60 children, £1.30 adults. MIDDLETON HALL Varied architecture in the house (still being restored), nature reserve, walled gardens, orchards and woodlands, and a craft centre in the stables; workshops inc lace bobbin makers, glassblowing, knitwear, jewellery, upholstery and ceramics. Snacks, shop, some disabled access; house open pm Sun and bank hols Apr–Oct, craft centre cl Mon and Tues; (01827) 283095; house £1.20. The Green Man is a decent family dining pub.

★ ❀ 🐄 **Napton on the Hill** SP4661 is an attractive village on a rounded hill above a curve in the Oxford Canal – perhaps the prettiest in this part of the world, with pleasant towpath walks. Great views of seven counties from the hill. CHURCH LEYES FARM is a friendly 40-acre family-run organic farm with animals, walks and wild-flower conservation headlands by the hedges – lovely views. Cl Sat and Jewish holy days; (0192681) 2143;

*£1. The Folly by the canal locks is good for lunch.

🏠 ❦ **Packwood House** SP1671 (off A34) Friendly old house with origins as a 16th-c farmhouse, now carefully restored and not at all commercialised; interesting panelling, furniture and needlework, and in the garden unusual yew trees clipped to represent the Sermon on the Mount. Shop, some disabled access; cl am, Mon (exc bank hols), Tues, Nov–Mar; £3, garden only £2. NT. The Navigation by the canal at Lapworth is the best nearby place for lunch.

♨ **Rugby** SP5075 RUGBY SCHOOL MUSEUM (Little Church St) The history of the famous school and the people it's educated. Shop, disabled access; cl am, Sun, Mon and two wks at Christmas; (01788) 574117; *£1. Guided tours of the school itself leave here at 2.30pm (not Sun or Mon), or other times by arrangement; *£1.75, or £2.50 combined ticket with museum. The game the school invented is commemorated at the JAMES GILBERT RUGBY FOOTBALL MUSEUM down the road. Gilberts have made their well known rugby balls in this shop since 1842, and there are demonstrations of their production, with displays and collections relating to the game. Shop; cl Sun and a few days over Christmas; (01788) 542426; free. The Three Horseshoes not far off in Sheep St is useful for lunch.

❦ **Ryton on Dunsmore** SP3874 RYTON GARDENS The home of the Henry Doubleday Research Association, the organic farming and gardening organisation, so the grounds are landscaped with thousands of organically grown plants and trees; herb garden, rose garden, garden for the blind, and shrub borders among the displays, as well as some free-range farm animals. Lots of events. Very good meals and snacks in wholefood café, shop, disabled access; cl 25 Dec, 1 Jan; (01203) 303517; *£2.50.

🏍 **Solihull** SP1679 NATIONAL MOTORCYCLE MUSEUM (Coventry Rd, Bickenhill) Five halls displaying over 650 gleamingly restored motorcycles, all British, from around 150 different factories. Also a permanent display on the Norton Racing team, Britain's first TT winners for nearly 40 years, and, more incongruously, the biggest theatre organ in Europe. Meals, snacks, shop, disabled access; cl 24–26 Dec; (01675) 443311; *£4.50.

🐑☺ **Tanworth in Arden** SP1479 UMBERSLADE CHILDREN'S FARM Friendly family-run farm with animals to stroke and feed, and play areas for letting off steam. Also nature trails and walks, and a new goat milking area. Snacks, shop, disabled access; cl Nov–mid Mar; (01564) 742251; *£2.75.

♿ 🏠 **Walsall** SP0198 JEROME K JEROME BIRTHPLACE MUSEUM (Bradford St) Dedicated to life and work of the author of *Three Men in a Boat*, with a reconstructed 1850s parlour. Cl 1–2pm, pm Sat, Sun; free. WALSALL LEATHER MUSEUM (Wisenmore) 19th-c leather goods factory with tours of aromatic workshops and displays and demonstrations of leather production and development. Meals, snacks, shop (with a variety of local leather goods), disabled access; cl Mon; (01922) 721153; free. The New Inn (John St), called Pretty Bricks locally, does decent cheap food.

🏠 ❀ **Wolverhampton** SO9198 WIGHTWICK MANOR (Wightwick, just off A454) Only a century old, but beautifully and unusually designed by followers of William Morris, this house is a fine testimonial to the enduring qualities of his design principles. Flamboyant tiles, fittings, furnishings and glass, and lots of Pre-Raphaelite art, cannily acquired while it was unfashionable. Also period garden with yew hedges and topiary. Shop, some disabled access; open pm Thurs, Sat and bank hol wknds, Mar–Dec, garden also wkdys by arrangement; (01902) 761108; *£4.20. In the town, the Great Western in Sun St and the Press wine bar in Queens St are useful for lunch. Around 4 miles N of town, MOSELEY OLD HALL is a Tudor house famed as a hiding place for Charles II after the Battle of Worcester. The façade has altered since, though the furnishings and atmosphere in its panelled rooms don't seem to have changed much, and there's a 17th-c knot garden. Teas, shop, limited disabled access; open pm Weds, wknds and bank hols Apr–Oct plus Tues in July and Aug; £3.20; NT.

★ **Other attractive villages** include Priors Marston SP4857 (attractive old houses around the village green, unusual blue brick paths; good pubs – the Falcon and ancient Holly Bush; there's a walk up Marston Hill behind, and quite a good network of paths around nearby Priors Hardwick taking you down to the Oxford Canal); Austrey SK2906 (timbered houses and cottages, some thatch); Barston SP2078; Berkswell SP2479 (pretty Norman church); Clifford Chambers SP1092 (timbered houses and a Tudor rectory which has some claim to being the true birthplace of Shakespeare); Exhall SP3385 (pretty black and white timbering and some pleasant gently hilly walks nearby despite the proximity of the M6); Hampton in Arden SP2081 (the White Lion is useful for lunch); Honiley SP2472 (well, not exactly – the village has gone now, and there are only vestiges of the big house, but the surviving 18th-c church still makes this feel like a village); Meriden SP2482 (a cross on the green marks what the village feels is the centre of England – it's true that of the streams rising in the village pond one ends up in the Severn and the other over in the Humber); and Stoneleigh SP3372 (sandstone Norman church, timber-framed houses – the one called Forsythia Cottage was a pub till 1890, when the local landlord closed it in disgust at the way the cyclists out from Coventry whistled at his daughter). Near Stoneleigh is the headquarters of the Royal Agricultural Society of England, and the showground for the Royal Show.

Walks

This is not notable walking country. The canal towpaths offer some possibilities. The **Ashby Canal** △-1 heading off into the Leics countryside from its junction with the Coventry Canal at Marston Junction SP3688 is perhaps the prettiest.

From the Stags Head in **Offchurch** SP3665 ⌂-2 a pleasant walk W winds through the riverside parkland of Offchurch Bury.

Hartshill Hayes Country Park SP3294 ⌂-3 is mixed woodland, opening out at the top for broad views towards the Peak District. The Coventry Canal below allows more extended rambles.

Besides the places already mentioned, there are several useful canalside pubs including the Navigation at Lapworth SP1670, Two Boats at Long Itchington SP4164 (the flight of Stockton Locks just E usually has plenty going on), George & Dragon at the Wharf nr Fenny Compton SP4152 (A423 – a popular family pub, with aviaries and so forth) and Dog & Doublet at Bodymoor Heath SP2096 (useful for the Kingsbury Water Park too).

There are some pleasant strolls near the Anchor at Leek Wootton SP2868 and Falcon at Priors Marston SP4857.

Driving

There are few pleasant country drives here, but the old drovers' road, the Welsh Road from Cubbington through Offchurch and Southam (a pleasant small town, where the ancient Old Mint is a good refreshment break) to Priors Marston and on into Northamptonshire gives a good taste of some of the quietest gently rolling farmland, getting hillier on the county boundary. A surprisingly quiet cross-country back road follows the straight line of the Roman Foss Way down from the Leics border through Brinklow (where the Raven is a useful stop), Stretton on Dunsmore and Princethorpe to Halford in the southern part of the county.

Where to eat

Leamington Spa SP3165 PHOENIX BAR Regent Hotel (01926) 427231 Extremely popular, elegant and comfortable hotel bar with lovely *trompe l'oeil* on the walls, open fire, relaxed atmosphere; very good food and helpful service; two other restaurants also; disabled access. £20|£1.50/£5.

Old Hill SO9685 WATERFALL 132 Waterfall Lane (0121) 561 3499 Small busy refurbished Black Country local with good value food, decent range of real ales from all over the country, and enthusiastic licensee; partial disabled access. £9.75|£1/£3.50.

SOUTH WARWICKSHIRE

Stratford is rewarding if you know and love your Shakespeare; elsewhere there is quietly appealing countryside.

Many of the things to see and do here are concentrated in Stratford, the tourist centre of the area which, while full of interest for people on the Shakespeare trail, can be disappointing to others. Around Stratford are quite a few pretty villages, with further Shakespeare connections for those who want to look for them: his wife's cottage at Shottery and mother's house at Wilmcote are both very attractive. There are three great houses in fine grounds worth visiting, at Alcester, Charlecote and Coughton. The countryside is not spectacular, but appealing in a quiet way, with some possibilities for leisurely drives and gentle strolls. There's very little to amuse children, though small boys may be riveted by the remarkable Heritage Motor Centre at

Gaydon. Nostalgia and music enthusiasts will also enjoy Ashorne.

The area has a reasonable choice of comfortable places to stay, though in Stratford prices are high. On the fringes of the Cotswolds, South Warwickshire has a lot to see and do. For good walks you'd be better to stray over into nearby parts of Gloucestershire and Oxfordshire.

Where to stay

Stratford-upon-Avon SP2055 WELCOMBE Warwick Rd, Stratford-upon-Avon CV37 0NR (01789) 295252 *£145; 76 rms with antiques and luxurious bthrms. Jacobean-style mansion in parkland estate with an 18-hole golf course and two all-weather floodlit tennis courts; deeply comfortable day rooms inc a fine panelled lounge, open fires and fresh flowers; elegant restaurant, immaculate service; cl 28 Dec–3 Jan; disabled access.

Stratford-upon-Avon SP2055 SHAKESPEARE Chapel St, Stratford-upon-Avon CV37 6ER (01789) 294771 £125.90; 63 comfortable, well equipped rms. Smart Forte hotel based on handsome, lavishly modernised Tudor merchants' houses, with comfortable bar, well kept real ales, good food, quick friendly service, tables in back courtyard, and civilised tea or coffee in peaceful chintzy armchairs by blazing log fires; 3 minutes' walk from theatre.

Stratford-upon-Avon SP2055 ARDEN THISTLE 44 Waterside, Stratford-upon-Avon CV37 6BA (01789) 294949 £98; 63 rms. Elegant Regency house opposite Royal Shakespeare and Swan Theatres and overlooking River Avon, with stylish bar and lounge, elegant restaurant, private gardens and a relaxed, friendly atmosphere.

Stratford-upon-Avon SP2055 STRATFORD HOUSE Sheep St, Stratford-upon-Avon CV37 6EF (01789) 268288 £85; 11 comfortable rms. Georgian house close to theatre with open fire and lots of flowers in the lounge, fine food in airy restaurant (pre-theatre dinner, too), and friendly, helpful service; cl Christmas; disabled access.

Stratford-upon-Avon SP2055 COACH HOUSE 16 Warwick Rd, Stratford-upon-Avon CV37 6YW (01789) 204109 £62; 23 comfortable rms, most with own bthrm. Not far from the Royal Shakespeare Theatre, this partly Georgian hotel has a cosy bar, pleasant cellar restaurant and good reasonably priced food (pre-theatre meals, too); partial disabled access.

Wilmcote SP1657 SWAN HOUSE The Green, Wilmcote, Stratford-upon-Avon CV37 9XJ (01789) 267030 *£60; 8 decent rms. Popular Georgian hotel overlooking the village green and Mary Arden's house; enjoyable home-cooked food and winter log fire.

Stratford-upon-Avon SP2055 PAYTON 6 John St, Stratford-upon-Avon CV37 6UB (01789) 266442 £52; 5 rms. Quietly set Georgian house, handy for theatre, with caring owners and tempting breakfasts; cl 24–26 Dec.

Ilmington SP2143 HOWARD ARMS Ilmington, Shipston-on-Stour CV36 4LN (01608) 682226 £50; 2 rms. Neatly kept golden stone inn opposite village green with pleasant sheltered garden, beamed and flagstoned dining bar, open fires, friendly service, rewarding food and decent wines; no accomm 25–26 Dec.

Stratford-upon-Avon SP2055 MELITA 37 Shipston Rd, Stratford-upon-Avon CV37 7LN (01789) 292432 *£49; 12 well equipped rms. Friendly family-run Victorian hotel with pretty, carefully laid-out garden, comfortable lounge with open fire, extensive breakfasts, and some provision for no-smokers; close to town centre and theatre; cl Christmas; pets by arrangement; disabled access.

Blackwell SP2443 BLACKWELL GRANGE Blackwell, Shipston-on-Stour CV36 4PF (01608) 682357 £48; 2 pretty rms. 17th-c Cotswold farmhouse with log fire in comfortable beamed sitting room, large inglenook fireplace in flagstoned dining room, good home cooking using own free-range eggs, pretty garden, and nice views of the surrounding fields; children over 12; disabled access.

Stratford-upon-Avon SP2055 CARLTON 22 Evesham Place, Stratford-upon-Avon CV37 6HT (01789) 293548 £40; 6 homely rms, most with own bthrm.

Neatly kept and very welcoming no smoking Victorian house, close to theatre and restaurants, with helpful owners, very good breakfasts, and little garden. **Wilmcote** SP1657 PEAR TREE COTTAGE 7 Church St, Wilmcote, Stratford-upon-Avon CV37 9UX (01789) 205889 £40; 7 rms. Charming half-timbered Elizabethan house owned by the same family for three generations, with beams, flagstones, cosy atmosphere, good breakfasts, and shady garden; self-catering also; cl Christmas–1 Jan; children over 2.

Little Compton SP2630 RED LION Little Compton, Moreton in Marsh GL56 0RT (01608) 674397 *£36; 3 rms, shared bthrm. Simple but civilised low-beamed Cotswold stone inn with log fires, separate dining area, big menu with speciality steaks, extensive wine list, and large, attractive garden; children over 8.

To see and do

Stratford-upon-Avon SP2055 Visitors who look at the town just as a town can be disappointed, but for those who have a grounding in Shakespeare's plays the genius of the man does somehow add a special gloss to everything, so that the interesting buildings seem that bit more interesting and not so outnumbered by the workaday ones, the overpriced antique shops and the gift shops. There are, indeed, buildings of undoubted appeal here, and the gardens by the River Avon make a memorable setting for the Memorial Theatre. If you're looking forward to a good production at the theatre, or, better still, able to run through much of the verse in your head, then you'll love Stratford. But if you've always thought Shakespeare overrated, then you'll think the same about Stratford, too. You can buy joint tickets for most of the Shakespearian properties. The pub with the most theatrical Shakespeare connections is the Mucky Duck, or more properly White Swan (Southern Way) – traditionally where the RSC actors and actresses drink. Other useful places for lunch here include the quaint old Garrick (High St), Vintner Wine Bar (Sheep St), Lamplighters (Rother St), Slug & Lettuce (Guild St/Union St) and smart Shakespeare Hotel (Chapel St).

🏠 SHAKESPEARE'S BIRTHPLACE (Henley St) The house where the writer is reputed to have been born in 1564; lots of exhibits from the period with good interpretative displays. Shop, disabled access to ground floor only; cl 24–26 Dec, am Good Fri and 1 Jan; (01789) 204016; £2.60.

🏠 NEW PLACE/NASH'S HOUSE (Chapel St) The place where Shakespeare died in 1616; the house was destroyed in the 18th c, but the Elizabethan knot garden remains, and the adjacent house, former home of the writer's granddaughter, has a good collection of furniture and local history. Shop, limited disabled access; cl am Sun in winter and 1 Jan, 24–26 Dec; (01789) 292325; £1.80.

🏠 KING EDWARD VI SCHOOL A half-timbered building where Shakespeare reputedly had his lessons; open by arrangement, tel (01789) 293351.

✝ HOLY TRINITY Church by the river where Shakespeare was baptised and buried – many fine 15th-c features. Cl am Sun (all day winter); 50p to

enter the chancel where the grave is.

🏠 HALLS CROFT (Old Town) Lovely gabled Tudor home of Dr John Hall, who married Shakespeare's daughter; good displays on the medicine of the time, and Elizabethan and Jacobean furniture. Snacks, some disabled access; cl am winter Suns and 1 Jan, 25 Dec; (01789) 292107; £1.70.

🏠 WORLD OF SHAKESPEARE (Waterside) Probably the best way of maintaining the interest of children less happy with real history; 25 life-size tableaux recreate Elizabethan life with the help of sound effects, music and dramatic lighting. Snacks, disabled access; cl 25 Dec; (01789) 269190; £3.

🏠 ROYAL SHAKESPEARE COMPANY COLLECTION (Waterside) Over 1,000 costumes, props, pictures and other items demonstrating the changes in staging from medieval times to the present; other exhibitions and displays. You can book full guided tours; shop; cl 24–25 Dec; (01789) 296655; £2.

The town has a few other attractions

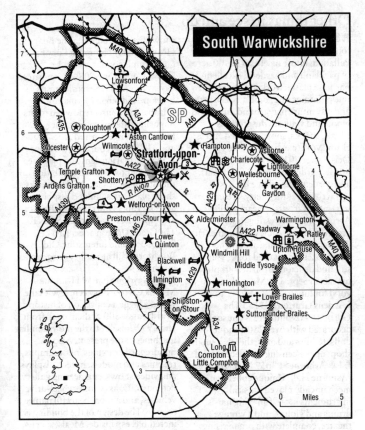

South Warwickshire

that have nothing to do with
Shakespeare at all, all useful for
children bored with the Bard:

🏠 HARVARD HOUSE (High St) has no
direct connection with Shakespeare,
but it's a fine late 16th-c town house, a
striking example of houses of his day.
Cl Sun, and all Oct–late May; (01789)
204 507; £1.

🧸 NATIONAL TEDDY BEAR MUSEUM
(Greenhill St) Furry friends of all
shapes and sizes – old ones, mechanical
and musical ones, ones that belonged
to famous people, and some that are
famous themselves. Shop; cl 25–26
Dec; (01789) 293160; *£1.95.

🦋 ! BUTTERFLY FARM AND JUNGLE
SAFARI (Tramway Walk) The
difference from over the river
couldn't be more striking – quaintly
gabled houses here give way to
cascading waterfalls and tropical
forests, with up to 1,500 exotic

butterflies flying free in a recreation of
their own jungle habitat. Good
explanations and knowledgeable
staff – as well as a number of less
friendly creatures in the Insect City,
safely behind glass. Snacks, shop,
disabled access; cl 25 Dec; (01789)
299288; £3.25.

🐎 SHIRE HORSE CENTRE AND FARM
PARK (Clifford Rd) Parades and
demonstrations of the huge horses, as
well as goats, pigs, rare breeds of
sheep and cattle, owl sanctuary with
falconry displays and an adventure
playground. Meals, snacks, shop,
disabled access (can be a bit bumpy);
cl 25 Dec; (01789) 266276; £4.

📺 RAGDOLL (Chapel St) makes
children's TV programmes like *Rosie
and Jim* and *Tots TV*; the ground
floor of their headquarters has a shop,
play areas and plenty to amuse young
children; cl am Sun.

Other things to see and do

Alcester SP0857 RAGLEY HALL (on A435) Perfectly symmetrical Palladian house nicely set in 400 acres of parkland and gardens; excellent baroque plasterwork in Great Hall, fine paintings (inc some modern art), and adventure playground, maze and woodland walks in the grounds. Meals, snacks, shop, disabled access; cl am, Mon (exc bank hols), Fri, Oct–Easter; (01789) 762090; £5 house, garden and park, £3.50 park and garden. The village itself is attractive, as is the pretty stream that separates it from the nearby village of Arrow – also interesting to stroll around (despite some development). Though fruit farming around here is much rarer than it used to be, you can still find delicious fresh dessert plums for sale in Sept. The Moat House is good for lunch.

! Ardens Grafton SP1153 The GOLDEN CROSS inn here is unusually decorated with over 250 antique dolls, teddies and toys; there's a small shop; open licensing hrs, decent food.

Ashorne SP3057 NICKELODEON (Ashorne Hall) Unique collection of mechanically played musical instruments inc self-playing harps, drums and violins, and a vintage theatre, complete with organ rising from the floor. They show silent comedies and 1950s Pathé newsreels; various teas and events. Meals, snacks, shop, disabled access; open pm Sun Mar–Nov, and some other days in summer; (01926) 651444; *£5.25. The Leopard at Bishops Tachbrook has good value food.

Charlecote SP2656 CHARLECOTE PARK 250 acres of parkland, full of deer (Shakespeare is said to have poached them from here), along with the descendants of reputedly the country's first flock of Jacob sheep. Well furnished rooms inc the Great Hall and Victorian kitchen, and there's an impressive Tudor gatehouse. Meals, snacks, shop, disabled access; cl Weds, Thurs, Good Fri, all Nov–Mar, and house also cl 1–2pm every day; £4; NT. By the park is a charming little 19th-c estate village of timbered cottages, and a show Victorian church. The Boars Head in pretty Hampton Lucy has good simple food.

† Coughton SP0860 COUGHTON COURT (on A435) Several priest's holes are hidden in this mainly Elizabethan house, renowned for its imposing gatehouse. Notable furniture, porcelain and relics inside, and a lake, two churches, pleasant walks, formal gardens and play area in the grounds. Also an exhibition on the Gunpowder Plot. Meals, snacks, shop, plant sales, limited disabled access; cl am, Thurs, Fri, wkdys Oct and Apr, all Nov–Mar; £4.50; NT. The Green Dragon at nearby Sambourne and interesting Old Washford Mill at Studley are good for lunch.

Gaydon SP3654 HERITAGE MOTOR CENTRE Busy centre with the world's biggest collection of historic British cars – 300 of them in all from an 1895 Wolseley to the more familiar machines of the present. Also hundreds of drawings, photographs, trophies and models, hi-tech displays and video shows, engineering gallery, demonstrations of four-wheel-drive vehicles, and a more peaceful nature reserve. The design of the building is incredible, esp inside. Meals, snacks, shop, disabled access; cl 25–26 Dec; (01926) 641188; £5.50. The Malt Shovel is useful for lunch.

Long Compton SP2832 is a pleasant Cotswoldy village of thatched stone houses inc some antique shops. Nearby, a mile or so to the S, are the ROLLRIGHT STONES, the King Stone on one side of the lane, and on the other two groups of stones known as the King's Men and the Whispering Knights. Legend has it that this well preserved stone circle is a king and his men, tricked by a witch into falling under her spell, and petrified. The stones straddle the Oxfordshire border, and just E, at Rollright, the Gate Hangs High is useful for lunch.

Shottery SP1854 ANNE HATHAWAY'S COTTAGE Substantial thatched Tudor farmhouse, the home of Anne Hathaway until her marriage to William Shakespeare; good displays of domestic life during the period, pleasant cottage garden. Snacks, shop; cl 25–26 Dec; (01789) 292100; £2.20. There's a craft centre next door, and the Bell is handy for something to eat away from the tourists.

🏠▣ **Upton House** SP3746 (A422 near Ratley) The exceptional art collection is the main draw at this late 17th-c house; the enormous range of paintings includes works by Bosch, El Greco, Brueghel and Hogarth, all sensibly arranged and displayed. Also Brussels tapestries, Sèvres porcelain and woodland and terrace walks. The house was remodelled earlier this century, and in the last year there have been a number of improvements. Snacks, shop, disabled access; cl am, wkdys in Apr and Oct, Thurs and Fri, all Nov–Mar; £4.30, garden only £2.15; NT. There's a timed ticket system at peak periods. The Bell at Shenington is the closest good place for lunch.

✗ ⬥⬦ ☗ **Wellesbourne** SP2855 WELLESBOURNE WATERMILL Historic watermill in secluded rural setting, the striking wooden wheel still producing flour. Helpful staff, and crafts and nature trails. Snacks, shop, some disabled access (though there are steep steps); open Thurs–Sun Easter–Sept, pm Sun only in Oct, Nov, Feb and Mar; (01789) 470237; £2. WARTIME MUSEUM Housed in the underground HQ of a former RAF base, a collection of aeronautical relics and wartime memorabilia. Also a few restored aircraft inc a Vampire, Provost and Sea Vixen. Shop, some disabled access; open Suns only; £1.

🏠☗✦ **Wilmcote** SP1658 MARY ARDEN'S HOUSE Picturesque home of Shakespeare's mother, with the barns given over to countryside memorabilia; daily falconry displays, rare breeds. Snacks, some disabled access; cl am winter Sun, 24–26 Dec; (01789) 293455; £3. The Swan House, overlooking it, is good for lunch, and the Masons Arms is useful too.

★ **Other attractive villages** include Aston Cantlow SP1460 (timbered houses, fine guildhall, lovely church where Shakespeare's parents married); Lower Brailes SP3039 (lovely slender-spired church, pretty stone houses, good views; the George is useful for lunch); Shakespeare's 'Hungry Grafton', now Temple Grafton SP1255 (the Blue Boar is good for lunch); Hampton Lucy SP2557 (the Boars Head is useful for lunch); Honington SP2642 (church on edge of lawn of late 17th-c Honington Hall); Ilmington SP2143 (path to partly Norman church, lovely inside; pleasant walks on hills above; Howard Arms is good for lunch); Lighthorne SP3355 (the Antelope is good for lunch); Lower Quinton SP1847 (College Arms useful for lunch); Middle Tysoe SP3344 (with a very traditional cottage bakery); Preston on Stour SP2049; Radway SP3748, Ratley SP3847 and Warmington SP4147 (where the ancient Plough is good); these last three are all below Edge Hill, where the castellated folly of the Castle Inn enjoys great views from its garden and has good-value food); Sutton under Brailes SP2937; and Welford on Avon SP1452 (the Bell is good for lunch). Shipston-on-Stour SP2450 is a small town with quite a busy shopping centre, but is rewarding to stroll through, with a good church and a good few handsome old stone buildings, antique shops among them; the Horseshoe currently seems best value for lunch here.

Walks

The S part of the county has some pleasing **Cotswold countryside** ⌂-1 around Sutton under Brailes SP2937, and we've mentioned some other walking possibilities in this general area above. From **Upper Tysoe** SP3343 ⌂-2 the walk S over Windmill Hill (which does have a windmill) takes you to the church on the edge of Compton Wynyates park, giving views of the attractive Tudor manor – a refreshing bit of brick building, in this Cotswold-edge stone country.

There's a short walk along the **River Avon** ⌂-3 from the Ferry, a good dining pub in Alveston SP2356. The Cottage of Content at **Barton** SP1051, which has day fishing tickets, also gives on to an Avon walk ⌂-4. The Fleur de Lys at **Lowsonford** SP1868 ⌂-5 is a pleasant start for canal walks.

Driving

Perhaps the nicest country drive here is the circular route around Alcester, through Walcote, Aston Cantlow, Wilmcote, Temple Grafton and Wixford, and then over the Gloucs border through Radford, Inkberrow, Holberrow Green, and back by New End and Kings Coughton. From its junction with the M40 (junction 13, nr Bishops Tachbrook), the B4087 to Wellesbourne and then either on to Alderminster or turning right for Charlecote and Hampton Lucy is also quite attractive.

The arrival of the M40 has turned the former A41, now the B4100, into a pleasantly empty road that gives a good general impression of the area, as does the Foss Way heading like a die up across country from Halford where it forks off the A429.

Where to eat

Stratford-upon-Avon SP2055 THE OPPOSITION 13 Sheep St (01789) 269980 Small restaurant with generous helpings of very good food; handy for theatres and open for after-show meals; cl Sun Dec–Mar; no children in evening. £19|£3.75/£6.80.
Stratford-upon-Avon SP2055 CELLARS 16-17 Warwick Rd (01789) 204109 Renovated and attractive cellar restaurant in hotel (separate entrance) with a smoking and a no-smoking room and daily-changing, interesting home-cooked food; friendly service, and reasonably priced wine list; best to book Sat evenings; cl 25 Dec. £18.50|£1.40/£4.50.
Alderminster SP2348 BELL (01789) 450414 Very popular and rather civilised dining pub close to Stratford, with excellent, imaginative food, daily-changing food relying on fresh local produce; cl pms 24 Dec–2 Jan; disabled access. £16.75|£2.95/£6.50.
Stratford-upon-Avon SP2055 SIR TOBY'S 8 Church St (01789) 268822 Cheerful and popular bistro in 17th-c malt house with very good, imaginative food and good value, simple wine list; pre-theatre meals, too; cl Sun–Tues; partial disabled access. £15/£7.30.
Lowsonford SP1868 FLEUR DE LYS (01564) 782431 Bustling canalside pub with comfortable, civilised atmosphere, smart spreading bar with lots of low black beams, open fires, unusually elegant family room, good, interesting food (inc extensive children's menu), well kept real ales, and lots of New World wines by the glass; cl Sun pm; disabled access. £15/£5.

NORTHAMPTONSHIRE

Delightful untouristy countryside, with pleasant drives and some fine houses to visit; good value for a peaceful break.

A great attraction of the countryside here is its untouristy feel – subtle landscapes of gentle hills, a fair amount of woodland, quietly attractive villages built in a warm stone that recalls the Cotswolds. Rockingham Castle, Castle Ashby House, Althorp Hall at Great Brington, Canons Ashby House, Sulgrave Manor, Deene Park, Cottesbrooke Hall, Lamport Hall and Boughton House make up a most impressive collection of grand houses to look at, most with interesting and handsome grounds. The gardens of Holdenby House and Coton Manor are delightful, the canal museum at Stoke Bruerne is interesting, and Oundle is a graceful small town. Along the wide valley of the River Nene, running across the county from Badby round Northampton and Wellingborough and then up past Oundle, some fine churches are to be found.

There are one or two things dotted around for children to do, though on the whole this county does not score as highly for family breaks as it does for older people going away for a relatively quiet weekend – in a part of the country that's not yet been discovered. The choice of places to stay at and to eat out in is good, and prices are attractive.

Where to stay

Oundle TL0388 TALBOT Oundle, Peterborough PE8 4EA (01832) 273621 £82; 39 most attractive big rms. Mary, Queen of Scots walked down one of the staircases in this carefully refurbished 17th-c hotel to her execution; attractive, cosy lounges, big log fires, good food in timbered restaurant, and garden; limited disabled access.

Towcester SP6948 SARACENS HEAD Watling St, Towcester NN12 7BX (01327) 350414 £65; 21 well appointed rms. Handsome Georgian coaching inn with parts dating back to the 17th c, and strong *Pickwick Papers* connections.

Ashby St Ledgers SP5768 OLDE COACH HOUSE Ashby St Ledgers, Rugby CV23 8UN (01788) 890349 £48; 6 rms. Busy old inn in attractive village full of thatched stone houses, with rambling atmospheric rooms, winter log fire, good food in bar and partly no smoking dining room, well kept beer, smiling service, and big gardens; cl 25 Dec.

Weedon SP6046 CROSSROADS Weedon, Northampton SP9 277 (01327) 340354 £46.40; 48 comfortable and attractive rms. Civilised modern main-road hotel with smartly refurbished extensive dining bar, light and airy separate coffee parlour, restaurant; disabled access.

Culworth SP5446 FULFORD HOUSE The Green, Culworth, Banbury, Oxon OX17 2BB (01295) 760355 £45; 3 pretty rms. Relaxing 400-year-old stone house with lovely views over pastures with horses, charming garden, beams, log fire in comfortable drawing room, and good food around circular Georgian table using fresh home-grown veg; cl mid-Dec–mid-Feb; children over 5.

Sudborough SP9682 VANE ARMS High St, Sudborough, Kettering NN14 3BX (01832) 733223 £45; 2 rms. Thatched inn on picturesque village street, attractive and welcoming, with comfortable main bar, open fires, friendly, helpful staff, a marvellous range of real ales, and good, freshly cooked food.

Badby SP5559 WINDMILL Badby, Daventry NN11 6AN (01327) 702363 £40w; 8 rms. Traditional, carefully modernised thatched stone inn with beams, flagstones and huge inglenook fireplace in front bar, cosy, comfortable lounge; good generously served bar and restaurant food, and decent wines; fine views of the pretty village from car park; disabled access.

East Haddon SP6668 RED LION East Haddon, Northampton NN6 8BU (01604) 770223 £39; 5 rms. Golden stone hotel with pretty gardens and lawns, a neatly kept and comfortable lounge with oak-panelled settles, soft modern dining chairs, wooden or cast-iron tables; a comprehensive choice of good bar and restaurant food, and friendly service.

Old SP7872 WOLD FARM Old, Northampton NN6 9RJ (01604) 781258 *£38; 6 rms, 3 with shared bthrm. 18th-c house at the heart of beef and arable farm, with spacious, characterful rooms, good food in beamed dining room, attentive, welcoming owners, and two pretty gardens; disabled access in one ground-floor room.

To see and do

♠ ❀ **Boughton** SP7565 BOUGHTON HOUSE (off A43) Impressively grand old place often compared to Versailles (some of its treasures were in fact made for there). Richly furnished and decorated, with gorgeous mythical scenes painted on the ceilings, and works by El Greco, Murillo and Caracci lining the walls. Everything is in mint condition – some of the tapestries and carpets look as good as new. Excellent armoury, beautiful parklands, and adventure playground and garden shop. Snacks, shop, disabled access; grounds open pm May–Sept (exc Fri), house pm Aug only; (01536) 515731; *£4, grounds only £1.50.

❀ † ♠ **Brigstock** SP9485 HILL FARM HERBS Popular herb nursery with plants displayed in old farmyard; also selection of dried flowers. Summer snacks, shop; cl 25–26 Dec; (01536) 373694; free. The CHURCH has a Saxon tower, and a bell that used to be rung three times a day to help anyone lost in the woods; the Olde Three Cocks does good-value food. BRIGSTOCK COUNTRY PARK here is a good place for a wander, esp around wildlife-filled Fermyn Forest on the edge. LYVEDEN NEW BIELD Unfinished 'new building' started in 1595 but abandoned after the owner Sir Thomas Tresham's son died in the Tower; intriguing and unusual, it was intended to celebrate the Passion of Christ, and is shaped like a Greek cross; *£1, NT. Another oddly designed building of Tresham's, the TRIANGULAR LODGE, can be seen at nearby Rushton SP8482. There are three walls, with three windows and three gables on three levels, and a three-sided chimney – logically, it represents the Holy Trinity. Cl Oct-Mar; 85p.

♠ ❀ † **Canons Ashby** SP5750 CANONS ASHBY HOUSE (on B4525) Exceptional little manor house, more northern-looking than Midlands, beautifully restored with Elizabethan wall paintings and glorious Jacobean plasterwork. The formal gardens have also been carefully restored over the last 20 years, and now closely reflect the layout of the early 18th c, with lovely stonework and plants that would have been used then rather than more recent introductions. A reasonably sized park has a hilltop 12th–14th-c PRIORY CHURCH. Brewhouse café, shop, disabled access; cl am, Mon (exc bank hols), Tues, Good Fri and all Nov–Mar; £3; NT – it's one of their busier properties. The Olde House at Home at Moreton Pinkney is handy for lunch.

♠ ❀ † 🌳 **Castle Ashby** SP8659 CASTLE ASHBY HOUSE itself is not open, but is well worth seeing from outside, as it's one of the finest mansions in the Midlands, a splendidly palatial Elizabethan building at the end of a magnificent miles-long avenue planted at William III's suggestion nearly 300 years ago. The gardens, which can be visited, include grand Victorian terraces, sweeping lawns, Italianate gardens with an orangery, and lakeside parkland that may well be the prolific Capability Brown's most enduring achievement; nature trail, disabled access; £2. The CHURCH, within the park, is very attractive; there's a public path to it. CRAFT CENTRE AND RURAL SHOPPING YARD Variety of goods in restored farm buildings, inc farm produce, furniture, knitwear, toys and ceramics. Snacks, shops, disabled access; cl Mon.

❀ 🕊 **Coton** SP6771 COTON MANOR (off A428) Attractive views over countryside and Ravensthorpe Reservoir from charming gardens around 17th-c stonebuilt manor house (not open); interesting plantings, water gardens with flamingos, cranes and ornamental waterfowl wandering freely. The neighbouring woods are lovely at bluebell time. Snacks, plant sales, disabled access; open pm Weds–Sun Apr–Sept; *£2.70. The Red Lion at East Haddon is good for lunch.

♠ ❀ **Cottesbrooke Hall** SP7173 COTTESBROOKE HALL Very attractive Queen Anne house reputed to be the model for Jane Austen's *Mansfield Park*, with a renowned collection of mainly sporting and equestrian paintings, and fine furnishings and porcelain. The lovely garden has formal borders, venerable cedars, greenhouses, extensive wild garden, and the separate cottage garden of Gamekeepers Cottage. Teas, shop (some unusual plants for sale), disabled access to gardens only; open pm Thurs and bank hols 20 Apr–28 Sept; (01604) 505808; *£3.50, garden only *£2.50. The George in nearby Brixworth (see **Churches**, below) has decent simple food.

🏠 ❀ **Deene** SP9492 DEENE PARK (off A43) Lord Cardigan who led the Charge of the Light Brigade used to live in this beautifully presented partly Tudor house; there's a high-spirited contemporary portrait of him in full attack gallop. Perfect hammer-beamed roof, attractive period furnishings, and extensive parklands with woodside and lakeside walks. The gardens have old-fashioned roses, rare trees and shrubs, and reflect continuing interest by the owners over the generations – there's a terrace designed by David Hicks. Meals, snacks, shop, some disabled access; open pm Sun Jun–Aug, plus Sun and Mon of bank hol wknds in Apr and May; (01780) 450223; £3.50, garden only £2. KIRBY HALL (off A43) Splendidly ruined Elizabethan mansion with a bizarre mixture of styles and design; from some angles it still looks intact – even close up. The 17th-c gardens are being restored to their original plan, with fruit and yew trees, and it's a tranquil spot for a picnic. Shop, disabled access; cl winter Mon and Tues, 24–26 Dec, 1 Jan; (01536) 203320; £1.25.

★ ✝ 🏰 **Fotheringhay** TL0593 is a lovely village with a charming if slightly out-of-proportion 14th-c CHURCH across a watermeadow from the River Nene. It was part of a small pre-Reformation college and doubles as a memorial to the House of York, with some interesting heraldry. There's only a fragment left of the CASTLE where Mary, Queen of Scots was imprisoned, beside the castle mound. The Falcon is excellent for lunch.

★ ✝ **Geddington** SP8963 has a very well preserved elaborate 13th-c cross erected by Edward I where Queen Eleanor's funeral cortege rested on its

way to Westminster. The photogenic packhorse bridge is even older, and there's a 12th-c church. The Star has good food.

🏠 🖾 🔲 ⌖ ✝ **Great Brington** SP6665 ALTHORP The home of the Spencer family since 1508, the house has been remodelled several times, esp in the 17th and 18th c, and is most notable for what's inside – esp the splendid collection of furnishings and porcelain, and paintings by Rubens, Van Dyck and Lely. They sometimes do longer tours on Weds to linger over these. Snacks, shop, some disabled access; 1995 opening times undecided as we went to press – it's usually open every day in Aug, but best to check on (01604) 770209; £4.50. On the edge of the estate there's public access to a sandy-floored area of pine woods and heathland known as Harlestone Firs SP7164, pleasant for walking. The village itself is charming, and the graveyard of the attractive CHURCH on the edge of the park has fine views. The Fox & Hounds here is a good pub, as is the Saracens Head in nearby Little Brington (which at least in summer does teas too).

❀ 🔲 ⌖ ↟ **Holdenby** SP6967 HOLDENBY HOUSE GARDENS In Elizabethan times this was one of the biggest houses in the country, and the extensive gardens and grounds have been restored in the original style. Also a museum, rare-breeds farm, and falconry centre with flying displays. Snacks, shop, disabled access; cl am and Oct–Mar; *£2.50, less on Sat when only the falconry centre is open. The Red Lion at East Haddon is good for lunch.

☺ 🙂 🔲 **Kettering** SP8678 WICKSTEED PARK Big amusement park created in the 1920s; as then it has swings and slides, but these have been joined by more modern sophisticated rides. There are still train and steamer rides, also canoeing etc. Meals, snacks, shop, disabled access; cl Oct–Easter; £4 parking charge (less wkdys out of high season), various charges for rides. ALFRED EAST GALLERY National, regional and local art, craft and photography; shop, disabled access; cl Sun and bank hols; free. Next door

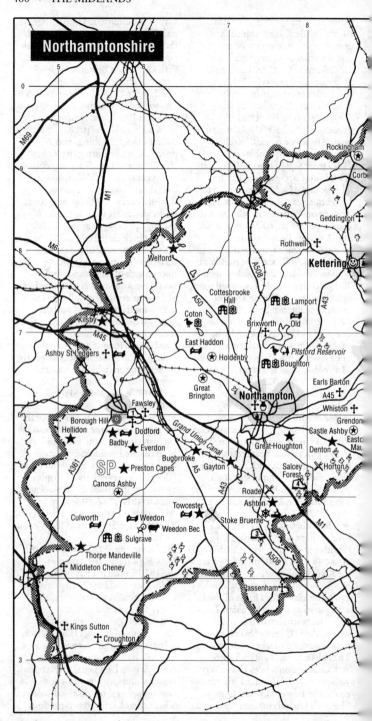

Northamptonshire

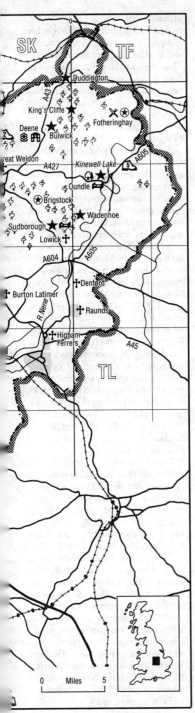

the MANOR HOUSE MUSEUM has several hands-on exhibits.

🏚 ✿ **Lamport** SP7574 LAMPORT HALL Mainly 17th- and 18th-c house in spacious park, with tranquil gardens containing a remarkable alpine rockery – the home of the first garden gnomes, only one of which now survives. Fine collections of art and furnishings, and frequent antique fairs, concerts and other events. Snacks, shop, disabled access to ground floor only; open pm Sun and bank hols Easter-Oct, and Thurs in July and Aug (guided tours then); (0160 128) 272; £3. In outbuildings local enthusiasts keep a collection of ancient tractors and agricultural bygones; similar opening hours, no extra charge. The Swan, with great views, has good-value food.

! Naseby SP6878 The owner of Purlieu Farm has set out a model of the BATTLE OF NASEBY battle lines, using many hundreds of model soldiers, with a 10-minute commentary, also some battlefield relics. The site also has re-created period rooms, vintage farm machinery and tools, village history, and a spacious picnic area; only open pm bank hol Sun and Mon Easter-Sept; £1. One BATTLE MONUMENT (Sibbertoft Rd) marks the position of Cromwell's New Model Army before his devastating counter-attack; there's another on the B4036 towards Clipston. The Fitzgerald Arms is useful for lunch.

✝ ♨ **Northampton** SP7560 Daniel Defoe would no longer describe this prosperous shoemaking town as one of the most handsome in the country, but it has a few interesting buildings. There are several fine CHURCHES, most notably the 12th-c Holy Sepulchre (one of only four remaining round churches in the country), the very grand central All Saints, and the ornate Norman St Peters in Marefair right by the dual carriageway. The Welsh House (now a china shop) and Hazelrigg House are also very handsome. The CENTRAL MUSEUM (Guildhall Rd) houses the famous Boot and Shoe collection, with features as diverse as an elephant's boot, Margot Fonteyn's ballet shoes,

Roman sandals and Queen Victoria's wedding slippers. Shop, disabled access; cl Sun am; free. The ABINGTON MUSEUM (Abington Park) is interesting, in the 15th-c former home of Shakespeare's granddaughter. Cl am, Sun; free. The Newt & Cucumber (College St) does quick good-value food, but has been shut on Sun.

★ 🐟 **Oundle** TL0388 is a charming and elegant stone-built town with a graceful church and several antique shops; the Ship is useful for lunch, as is the waterside Mill just outside town. Nr here BARNWELL COUNTRY PARK has meadows, woodland and reedy corners around former gravel workings that have now been landscaped as lake. A good spot for a walk, with a variety of birds; the Montagu Arms in Barnwell itself does good Sunday lunches.

🐦 🐟 **Pitsford Reservoir** SP7669 is a good spot for birdwatching, esp in winter when wildfowl flock to the northern part of the lake; the south part is useful for fishing. Nearby SYWELL COUNTRY PARK SP8265 has woodland and lakeside walks, and a little wildlife display in a former pumphouse.

🏰 🏠 ❀ **Rockingham** SP8691 ROCKINGHAM CASTLE (on A6003) Lovely old house still tucked away behind the curtain wall of the original Norman fortress – obviously quite an effective defence, as the castle was able to resist repeated assaults in the Civil War. The site of the original keep is now a rose garden, but the outline of the two baileys and the drum towers still remain, and the later Elizabethan building has a very good range of furnishings and art. Fine views from the hilltop setting. Snacks, shop, disabled access; open Sun, Thurs, and bank hols Easter–Sept, as well as Tues in Aug or after bank hols, or by appointment; (01536) 770240; £3.60, garden only £2.20. The Sondes Arms in the village, also pretty despite the main road, is good for lunch, with super views.

❀ ⚓ **Stoke Bruerne** SP7449 CANAL MUSEUM Close to a flight of locks on the Grand Union Canal, with fine old canal buildings (inc a popular pub, the Boat), and lots happening on the water, this is a handsome former corn warehouse housing a good collection of canal memorabilia, inc a reconstructed traditional narrow boat complete with immaculately packed-in colourful furniture and crockery. Also other working boats, interesting displays and boat trips through nearby tunnel. Shop, limited disabled access; cl winter Mon, 25–26 Dec; (01604) 862229; *£2.50. Good towpath walks from here.

🏠 ❀ **Sulgrave** SP5544 SULGRAVE MANOR George Washington's family lived in this modest manor house until his grandfather emigrated to America, and there are several relics of the first president, as well as interesting furnishings, elegant period rooms and well kept gardens. Lots of special events inc cavalry demonstrations and several jolly Living History exhibitions, when for nine days the Manor is run exactly as it was in a particular era. Snacks, shop; cl 1–2 pm, Weds, wkdys Nov–Mar (exc by appointment), all Jan; (01295) 760205; *£3. The Star is good for lunch.

🐄 🐾 **Weedon Bec** SP6456 OLD DAIRY FARM CRAFT CENTRE (Upper Stowe) has sheep, pigs, peacocks, ducks and donkeys, as well as craft workshops, antiques, farm shop, wool collection and Liberty materials. Meals, snacks, shop, disabled access; cl for two wks from 25 Dec; (01327) 40525; free, exc for special wknds. The Heart of England and Narrow Boat are pleasant for lunch.

✝ The county is notable for its lovely stone-built **churches**, many with elegant spires visible a long way off and a memorable feature of the county's landscape – particularly along the valley of the River Nene. A shortlist of these might include Ashby St Ledgers SP5768, Brixworth SP7470 (a particularly fine Anglo-Saxon church, one of England's oldest – mostly 7th c with much reused Roman material), Burton Latimer SP9075, Croughton SP5433 (14th/15th-c murals), Denford SP9976 (for its nature-reserve churchyard by the River Nene, waterside walks from here), Dodford SP6160 (striking memorials), Earls Barton SP8563 (fine Saxon tower), Easton Maudit SP8858, Fawsley SP5556 (above Capability Brown's lakes), Great Weldon SP9289, Higham Ferrers SP9669, Kings Sutton SP4936, Lowick SP9780, Middleton Cheney SP4941, Passenham SP7739 (17th-c murals), Raunds SP9972, Rothwell SP8181 and Whiston SP8460. With many of these, the village is well worth seeing, too.

★ Other attractive villages, all with decent pubs, include Ashton TL0588, Bugbrooke SP6757, Bulwick SP9694, Denton SP8358, Duddington SK9800, Gayton SP7054, Geddington SP8963, Great Houghton SP7958, Grendon SP8760, Hellidon SP5158 (pleasant walks nearby), Kilsby SP5671, Sudborough SP9682, Thorpe Mandeville SP5344, Wadenhoe TL0383 and Welford SP6480. Towcester SP6948 is a town not village (and pronounced Toaster not Towcester), but despite some light industry on the edge has regained something of a pleasantly villagey feel since its bypass, and has some attractive Georgian and Victorian buildings. We'd also recommend Kings Cliffe TL0097 (a large handsome stone village, rather Cotswoldy), and a trio of lovely mellow orange ironstone villages, Preston Capes SP5754, Everdon SP5957 and Badby SP5559 – the last has two good pubs.

✸ The best views in the region are from Borough Hill SP5862 above the golf course; an Iron Age hill fort shares the top with a formidable array of television and telecommunications masts, but on a clear day the views are tremendous.

☎ The county's Enterprise Agency runs a very full programme of guided factory visits, mostly free, covering all sorts of local manufacturing and service industries from the big shoe companies and places like Carlsberg or Barclaycard to helicopter makers, narrow-boat builders and blacksmiths; tel (01604) 671400 and ask for their 'Tours of the Unexpected' brochure; all tours must be pre-booked.

Walks

Gorgeous orange-coloured stone adds to the charm of buildings around Badby SP5658, where the well waymarked **Knightley Way** ⌂-1 takes a pleasant 12-mile course to Greens Norton SP6649. The finest part is between Badby Wood SP5658 and Fawsley Park SP5657, where the path drops to landscaped lakes by the hall and estate church. The bluebells in May in Badby Wood are lovely; no right of way, but public access.

Rockingham Forest SP9490 ⌂-2 has enough country houses scattered around it to spice interest, and grey-stone cottages are a local feature; on its NW edge the Exeter Arms at Wakerley, a former hunting lodge, gives access to both Wakerley Woods and the Welland Valley. For **Grand Union Canal** walks ⌂-3 Stoke Bruerne SP7450 is a popular start, with its waterside pub and waterways museum. Other pubs handy for the towpath are the Royal Oak at Blisworth SP7253, Admiral Nelson at Braunston SP5466 (very busy in summer), New Inn at Buckby Wharf SP6065, Navigation at Thrupp Wharf near Cosgrove SP7942, Narrow Boat at Weedon SP6046 (attractive Chinese restaurant) and Wharf in Welford SP6480. **Salcey Forest** SP8052 ⌂-4 is a couple of miles of ancient forest, largely oak, now managed for nature conservation, with well marked trails including one good for wheelchairs. **Kinewell Lake** SP9875 ⌂-5 is a well managed local nature reserve around former gravel-pit lakes by the River Nene.

Driving

Just E of Northampton, there's a pleasant drive around the northern edge of the Castle Ashby estates, through Cogenhoe, Whiston, Grendon and Easton Maudit. Further N, the B4036 from off the A5 near Watford Gap through West Haddon, Naseby and Clipston to Market Harborough just over the Leics border gives a good feel of the quieter parts of the county. Up in the NE corner of the county, pleasant back roads track through the Forest of Rockingham; though there are considerable stretches of woodland dotted about, this former hunting forest is now mostly farmland, with attractive stone villages.

The A5, relieved of much of its traffic by the M1, is a good road, swooping and gliding along the track of the old Roman Watling Street; the bit between the southern county boundary and Weedon is best.

Where to eat

Horton SP8254 FRENCH PARTRIDGE (01604) 870033 Lovely little evening restaurant run by the Partridges for 30 years with consistently excellent food, a relaxed atmosphere, and fine wines; cl Sun, Mon, 2 wks around Christmas, 2 wks Easter, 1st 3 wks Aug; disabled access. **£29 for 4 courses.**

Roade SP7551 ROADHOUSE 16 High St (01604) 863372 Very good food in attractive and comfortable popular restaurant; good wine list; cl am Sat, pm Sun, Mon; disabled access. **£15 lunch, £22 dinner.**

Fotheringhay TL0593 FALCON (018326) 254 Atmospheric and comfortable pub near interesting church and site of Fotheringhay Castle, with good, imaginative bar food, well kept real ales, comfortable lounge and more simple public bar, open fires, and neat garden; cl Mon; disabled access. **£15.50|£2.50|£8.**

Help this year from: Cdr Patrick Tailyour, Michael and Derek Slade, Sir Simon Tilden, Martyn Hart, L G Holmes, Joan Olivier, Michael and Jenny Back, B M Eldridge, Stephen and Julie Brown, Mr and Mrs C Roberts, Graham Richardson, Frank W Gadbois, L Harvard, George Atkinson, Thomas Nott, Keith Croxton, David and Mary Webb, John Baker, P J Hanson, Ted George, Mr and Mrs R C Allison, J H Peters, Martin Jones, Bob and Maggie Atherton, Norma and Keith Bloomfield, John and Marianne Cooper, Sheila and Terry Wells, John and Elizabeth Gwynne, C Driver, Margaret Dyke, WHBM, John Atherton, Paul Amos, Bill Sykes, Don Kellaway, Angie Coles, Mr and Mrs G Hart, CMW, JJW, Derek and Sylvia Stephenson, Brian and Anna Marsden, Ian Phillips, Susan and John Douglas, Hilary Aslett, Kate and Harry Taylor.

MIDLANDS CALENDAR

Some of these dates were provisional as we went to press.

JANUARY

17 **Kenilworth** Antique and Collectors Fair at the National Agricultural Centre (NAC), Stoneleigh Park (01636) 702326

18 **Birmingham** LAPADA Antiques and fine art fair at the National Exhibition Centre (NEC) – *till Sun 22* (0121) 780 4141

FEBRUARY

22 **Birmingham** Forties Festival – *till mid-April* (0121) 2354175

25 **Kenilworth** Vintage and Classic Event at NAC, Stoneleigh Park – *till Sun 26* (01203) 696969

28 **Atherstone** Shrovetide Football (01827) 716410

MARCH

5 **Kenilworth** Vintage and Classic Event at NAC, Stoneleigh Park (01203) 696969

7 **Birmingham** World Figure Skating Championships at the NEC – *till Sun 12* (01827) 872005; **Kenilworth** Antique and Collectors Fair at NAC, Stoneleigh Park (01636) 702326

9 **Birmingham** Great British Innovation and Inventions Fair and the International Inventions Fair at the NEC – *till Sun 12* (01202) 765009, also Individual Homes Exhibition

10 **Alveston** Minstrels and Melodies Weekend at the Youth Hostel – *till Sun 12* (01789) 297093

16 **Birmingham** Crufts Dog Show at the NEC – *till Sun 19* (0171) 493 6651

APRIL

1 **Sulgrave** Living History 1645 (English Civil War) at Sulgrave Manor – *till Sun 9* (01295) 760205

4 **Birmingham** British International Antiques Fair at the NEC – *till Sun 9* (0121) 780 4141

16 **Kenilworth** Classic Event at NAC, Stoneleigh Park – *till Mon 17* (01203) 696969

22 **Stratford-upon-Avon** Shakespeare Birthday Celebrations in the town centre (01789) 415536

23 **Warwick** St George's Day at Warwick Castle (01926) 495421

29 **Sulgrave** American Indian Encampment at Sulgrave Manor – *till 1 May* (01295) 760205

MAY

1 **Daventry** and District Arts Festival – *till Weds 31* (01327) 71100

5 **Warwick** and **Leamington** Weekend of Czech music – *till Tues 9* (01926) 410747

6 **Birmingham** BBC Top Gear Classic and Sportscar Show at the NEC – *till Mon 8* (0181) 943 5000

8 **Rushden** Historical Transport Society Cavalcade at Lancaster Farm (01933) 318983

10 **Rothwell** Festival – *till Weds 17* (01536) 710268

Midlands Calendar

MAY cont

12 **Birmingham** National Dog Show at Perry Park Showground – *till Sun 14* (01536) 791399; Readers and Writers Festival – *till Sat 20* (0121) 235 4244; **Solihull** Festival – *till Sat 20* (0121) 704 6979

14 **Moulton** College Spring Fair and Open Day (01604) 491131

27 **Braunston** Boat Show – *till Mon 29* (01788) 890666

28 **Lamport** Country Festival – *till Mon 29* (01604) 686272; **Northampton** British Falconry and Raptor Fair and Northamptonshire Game Fair at Althorp House – *till Mon 29* (01588) 672708

JUNE

1 **Warwick** Family Day at Charlecote Park (01789) 470277

3 **Wellingborough** Carnival – *till Sun 4*

14 **Birmingham** BBC Gardeners' World Live at the NEC – *till Sun 18* (0181) 943 5000

15 **Warwick** Midsummer Music Festival at Charlecote Park – *till Weds 21* (01789) 470277

17 **Corby** Carnival at the Boating Lake (01536) 402551; **Northampton** Battle of Naseby at Holdenby House – *till Sun 18*; **Stratford-upon-Avon** Regatta (01926) 400234

18 **Northampton** Carnival (01604) 784534

24 **Warwick** Carnival (01926) 491311

30 **Knowle** Outdoor Opera at Baddesley Clinton – *till 1 July* (01564) 783294

JULY

1 **Hollowell** Steam and Heavy Horse Show – *till Sun 2* (01604) 505422; **Kenilworth** Carnival (01926) 56299; **Sulgrave** Living History 1580 (Elizabethan England) at Sulgrave Manor – *till Sun 9* (01295) 760205; **Warwick** and **Leamington** Festival – *till Sun 16* (01926) 410747

3 **Kenilworth** Royal International Agricultural Show at NAC, Stoneleigh Park – *till Thurs 6* (01203) 696969

8 **Leamington Spa** Carnival (01926) 429062; **Stratford-upon-Avon** Festival – *till Sat 22* (01789) 267969

9 **Market Bosworth** Show at the Park (01530) 271169

14 **Northampton** Show at Abington Park – *till Sun 16* (01604) 233500; **Towcester** British Grand Prix at Silverstone Circuit – *till Sun 16* (01327) 857271

15 **Corby** Highland Gathering at West Glebe Park (01536) 402551; **Oundle** International Festival – *till Sun 23* (01832) 272227

29 **Canons Ashby** NT Centenary Concert at Canons Ashby House (01327) 860044

AUGUST

4 **Warwick** Folk Festival – *till Sat 5* (01203) 678738

5 **Alcester** Fireworks and Laser Symphony Concert at Ragley Hall (01625) 575681; **Chasetown** Chase Wakes with carnival and steam engines at Burntwood Recreation Centre (01543) 682911; **Dudley** Dudley Show at Himley Park – *till Sun 6* (01384) 453521

MIDLANDS CALENDAR

AUGUST cont

6 **Sulgrave** Outdoor Theatre at Sulgrave Manor – *till Mon 7* (01295) 760205

10 **Yardley Gobion** National Sheepdog Trials – *till Sat 12* (01234) 352672

13 **Northampton** Fireworks and Laser Concert at Althorp House (01625) 575681

18 **Northampton** Hot Air Balloon Festival at Northampton Racecourse – *till Sun 20* (01604) 233500

26 **Dudley** Canal Festival – *till Mon 28*; **Stoneleigh** Town and Country Festival at the NAC – *till Mon 28* (01676) 533536

27 **Corby** Family Fun Weekend at the Boating Lake – *till Mon 28* (01536) 402551; **Sulgrave** Living History 1780 (Georgian England) at Sulgrave Manor – *till Mon 30* (01295) 760205

SEPTEMBER

1 **Alcester** Last Night of the Proms at Ragley Hall (01625) 575681

2 **Stratford-upon-Avon** Shakespeare Run – *till Sun 3*

9 **nr Oundle** Son et Lumière at Lyveden New Bield (0183 25) 358; **Sulgrave** American Civil War Re-enactment at Sulgrave Manor – *till Sun 10* (01295) 760205

OCTOBER

12 **Birmingham** British Ski Show at the NEC – *till Sun 15* (01895) 677677

14 **Warwick** Hog Roast and Mop Fair (01926) 492212

20 **Birmingham** Ideal Homes Show at the NEC – *till Sun 29* (01895) 677677

21 **Sulgrave** Apple Day Festival at Sulgrave Manor – *till Sun 22* (01295) 760205; **Warwick** Runaway Mop Fair (01926) 492212

27 **Birmingham** International Motorcycle Show at the NEC – *till Sun 5* (01634) 711445

NOVEMBER

3 **Corby** Bonfire Night at Corby Boating Lake (01536) 402551

11 **Birmingham** National Classic Motor Show at the NEC – *till Sun 12* (0121) 780 4141; **Ryton-on-Dunsmore** Wroth Silver Ceremony at dawn – one of the oldest continuous ceremonies in the British Isles where payment of dues is made to the Earl of Buccleuch (01788) 576956

18 **Birmingham** Cat Show at the NEC (01278) 427575

23 **Birmingham** Good Food, Cooking and Kitchen Show at the NEC – *till Sun 26* (0181) 948 1666

DECEMBER

1 **Birmingham** Clothes Show Live at the NEC – *till Weds 6* (0171) 637 3313

2 **Sulgrave** Tudor Christmas at Sulgrave Manor – *till Sun 3*, *also every wknd in Dec and Weds 27–Fri 29 Dec* (01295) 760205

7 **Warwick** Victorian Street Fair and Christmas Lights Switch On (01926) 492212

26 **Moulton** Mummers Play and Morris Dancing in the village centre (01604) 646818

NORFOLK

The north part of the county includes a good deal of largely unspoilt coast, and the hinterland has the feel of being undiscovered territory for visitors. The area has a distinct character of its own. There are some interesting places to visit (and traditional seaside resorts which pull the summer crowds), but its great appeal is as a place for a quiet break, really getting away from it all. It's one of the best parts of England for birdwatchers.

There is a wider choice of attractions and things to do in the southern part of the county, though this has a rather less individual feel. The Norfolk Broads are a magnet for boating people, and for land-based people do add interest to the countryside – though there are not that many points of access for landlubbers, and the roads very rarely track alongside the water. The flat coast is largely given over to family beach resorts.

The county has some fine walks, but you have to choose your places carefully – much of the countryside is flat and repetitive. However, it's excellent for cycling – quiet lanes, attractive villages and country churches, fair views.

Norwich itself can well support a weekend visit; it never seems visibly a tourist city, which is a big plus.

There's a good choice of places to stay here, covering a wide range of styles and prices – and no shortage of decent places in which to eat out.

Early spring, when the snowdrops are out, is a pleasant time for driving through the county; they crowd under many of the roadside hedges – and of course the more touristy parts of the county are virtually unvisited then.

NORTH NORFOLK

Largely unspoilt, yet with plenty of interesting places to visit; expansive coastal scenery.

This corner of Norfolk has a quite distinct character, with a real sense of style about even the simplest buildings, a coast that's full of fascination for birdwatchers, and a splendidly broad canvas of sea, saltings and sky.

Sandringham itself is a big draw. Holkham Hall, Houghton Hall and Felbrigg Hall are actually grander, and other interesting places include the castle at Castle Rising, the lavender gardens at Heacham, the Anglo-Catholic pilgrimage centre of Little Walsingham, the longest really narrow-gauge railway in Britain at Wells-next-the-Sea, another steam railway at Sheringham (which has handsome parkland), and the splendid collection of steam organs and steam engines at Thursford Green. There are quite a few decent museums in King's

Lynn. The shire horse centre at West Runton and open farm at Snettisham are fun, and Hunstanton and Cromer are civilised seaside resorts with a fair amount of individuality.

We can recommend quite a good choice of reasonably priced hotels and inns to stay at here, and cooking in the area is above average.

The line we draw between here and the rest of Norfolk is the A148 to Cromer.

Where to stay

Grimston TF7222 CONGHAM HALL Grimston, King's Lynn PE32 1AH (01485) 600250 £110; 14 individually decorated rms. Warmly welcoming and handsome Georgian manor in 40 acres of grounds that include herb, vegetable and flower gardens (herbs for sale and garden open to the public), paddock, orchards, and cricket pitch; fine day rooms, and a pretty orangery restaurant with excellent modern cooking; children over 12.

Blakeney TG0243 BLAKENEY HOTEL Blakeney, Holt NR25 7NE (01263) 740797 £106; 60 very comfortable rms, many with views over the salt marshes and some with own little terrace. Overlooking the harbour with fine views, this friendly hotel has appealing public rooms, good food, very pleasant staff, an indoor swimming pool, saunas, spa bath, billiard room, and a garden; good disabled access.

Great Snoring TF9434 OLD RECTORY Great Snoring, Fakenham NR21 0HP (01328) 820597 *£87.50; 6 comfortable rms. Wonderfully tranquil country house dating back to the 16th c, with a church next door; lovely walled gardens, fresh flowers in the homely lounge, good food in the beamed dining room with stone-mullioned windows, fine breakfasts, and courteous service; cl 24–27 Dec; self-catering cottage suites also.

Titchwell TF7543 MANOR HOTEL Titchwell, King's Lynn PE31 8BB (01485) 210221 £78; 15 rms. Smart but relaxed hotel handy for the RSPB reserve, with pleasant views down to the beach; comfortable lounge with an open fire, pretty little bar, and an attractive family room; ornithologist chef does good bar and restaurant food (especially local seafood), and summer buffets; dogs welcome.

Burnham Market TF8342 HOSTE ARMS The Green, Burnham Market, King's Lynn PE31 8HD (01328) 738257 £72; 15 comfortable rms. Handsome inn sited on the green of a lovely Georgian village, with attractive bars, some interesting period features, good food in both the bar and restaurant, inc morning coffee and afternoon tea, and friendly staff; disabled access.

Thornham TF7343 LIFEBOAT Thornham, Hunstanton PE36 6LT (01485) 512236 *£65; 13 pretty rms, most with sea view. Well placed on the edge of the coastal flats, with a very cosy atmosphere – especially in winter, when there are five fires and antique paraffin lamps; good food in the bar and elegant restaurant; disabled access.

King's Lynn TF6220 TUDOR ROSE St Nicholas St, King's Lynn PE30 1LR (01553) 762824 £50; 14 rms. Attractive, half-timbered, 15th-c inn with an interesting medieval door; friendly and chatty atmosphere, decent food in both the bar and no-smoking, raftered restaurant, and good breakfasts; disabled access.

Dersingham TF6830 FEATHERS Manor Rd, Dersingham PE31 6LN (01485) 540207 £40; 5 well furnished, comfortable rms, shared bthrm. Solidly handsome, Jacobean sandstone inn with relaxed and comfortably modernised, dark-panelled bars opening on to an attractive garden with a play area (summer barbecues); reasonably priced bar food, restaurant (not pm Sun), and pleasant service.

Hillington TF7225 FFOLKES ARMS Hillington, King's Lynn PE31 6BJ (01485) 600210 £35; 20 good rms, many in new wing. Large, comfortable inn with a good choice of food, inc a carvery, wide range of real ales, and a country club; cl 25 Dec; good disabled access.

To see and do

🐦 ⚓ **Brancaster/Scolt Head** TF8045
Miles of these dunes, flat coastal
saltings, broad tidal beaches and Scolt
Head Island are owned by the
National Trust: a fine lonely place,
full of birds – the island is an important
breeding ground, and in good weather
a boat takes people across from
Brancaster Staithe. The Ship and Jolly
Sailors are useful for lunch.

🏠 ✝ **Burnham Thorpe** TF8441 has
strong Lord Nelson connections, inc
the pub named after him where he had
several celebration dinners, and which
is now richly decorated with really
interesting Nelson memorabilia. The
lectern in the village church uses wood
from HMS *Victory*, and the church
has other Nelson mementos.

🏰 **Castle Rising** TF6624 CASTLE
RISING CASTLE Massive earthworks
surround this fine Norman keep,
probably built by the Earl of Arundel.
It's a marvellous setting for the
summer jousting they stage here.
Snacks, shop; cl winter Mon and
Tues, 24–26 Dec, 1 Jan; (01553)
631330; £1.25. The Black Horse is a
popular dining pub.

☺ ✝ ☀ ♨ ❀ **Cromer** TG2242 Popular
seaside resort since Victorian times,
with lovely sandy beaches, more sun
than average, bustling markets, golf
courses, interesting shops and
galleries and lots of entertainments.
The pier is one of the last in the
country to present an end-of-pier
show – very popular, so worth
booking early. The tower of the
imposing CHURCH (Church St) gives
spectacular views of the surrounding
countryside. By the church, the
CROMER MUSEUM, has good local
history in five 19th-c, fishermen's
cottages. Shop; cl Mon 1–2pm, am
Sun, Good Fri, 23–27 Dec, 1 Jan; £1.
On the promenade the LIFEBOAT
MUSEUM (The Gangway) presents the
history of the RNLI in general, and
looks at the famous local lifeboatman
Henry Blogg, who over 53 years saved
873 lives. Shop, disabled access; cl
Nov–Easter; free. Nearby you may
find dressed crabs for sale; the crab
boats still work from here, and
Cromer crabs are the best on

England's E coast. The Bath House on
the promenade is useful for lunch.

🐦 ▣ **Fakenham** TF9229 PENSTHORPE
WATERFOWL TRUST (Pensthorpe) Lots
of wild and exotic waterfowl, many of
them rare. They've recently opened a
new visitor centre with displays of
wildlife art and photography. Also
woodland, meadow, lakeside and
riverside nature trails, and various fun
talks and events. Several readers have
recommended this over the last year.
Meals, snacks, shop, disabled access;
cl wkdys Jan–mid-Mar, 25 Dec;
(01328) 851465; £3.95. The Crown
in the town's market square is an
interesting old place for lunch.

🏠 ❀ ▣ **Felbrigg** TG2039 FELBRIGG
HALL Magnificent 17th-c house in
splendid grounds, inc an orangery
with a wonderful collection of
camellias and a colourfully restored
walled garden overlooked by a
dovecot that in its day held 2,000
birds. The house is decorated with
paintings and furnishings from the
18th c, and has a wonderful Gothic
library; they've recently opened up a
further 11 rooms. Lots of events, with
something going on at the stable block
most pm Sun. Meals, snacks, shop,
disabled access; cl Tues and Fri,
Nov–Mar, hall also cl am, grounds cl
25 Dec only; £4.60, garden only
£1.80; NT. There's public access to
the woods and lake.

♨ **Glandford** TG0441 SHELL MUSEUM
Curious little museum housing the
often very beautiful seashells and
other interesting objects collected by
Sir Alfred Jodrell, who lived in nearby
Bayfield Hall. Also has some
painstakingly constructed models
made of shells. Shop, disabled access;
cl 12.30–2pm, am Fri and Sat, all Sun,
and Nov–Feb exc am Mon–Thurs in
Nov and Feb; 50p. The King's Head at
Letheringsett is quite handy for lunch.

✗ ❀ **Great Bircham** TF7732
WINDMILL Not far from Houghton
Hall, this great mill, the most striking
in the county, is set atop a windy hill
ensuring glorious views of the
surrounding country. The milling
process is well explained, and they sell
bread baked at the mill's own bakery.

Snacks, shop, some disabled access; cl Oct–Easter, tearooms and bakery also cl Sat; (0148 523) 393; £2. You can hire bikes here and they provide good routes. The King's Head Hotel (a favourite with Sandringham shooting parties) is pleasant for lunch.

❀ ⌂ **Grimston** TF7222 The HERB GARDEN of Congham Hall Hotel (see **Where to stay** section above) has 200–300 different herbs, in traditional layouts, with many unusual varieties for sale. Open 2–4pm, cl Sat and Oct–Mar; free. In addition to the hotel itself, the Jolly Farmers is good for lunch.

❀ ⌂ **Heacham** TF6737 NORFOLK LAVENDER The largest lavender-growing and distilling operation in the country, as well as the National Collection of lavender species and cultivars. The guided tour (daily spring bank hol–Sept) really adds interest, and at harvest time they may drive visitors out to the fields. Also, rose and herb gardens. Snacks (inc their lavender and lemon scones), shop, disabled access; cl 23 Dec–13 Jan; (01485) 570384; free. The Rose & Crown at Snettisham is the closest decent place for lunch.

⌂ ❀ ▣ ♨ ⌖ **Holkham** TF8944 HOLKHAM HALL Splendid Palladian mansion in delightful and very extensive tree-filled grounds with an ornamental lake and an 18th-c walled garden. Sumptuously furnished state rooms, with fine paintings by Claude, Rubens, Van Dyck and Gainsborough. An ancestor of the present owner was Thomas Coke, whose revolutionary farming techniques are described in a new farming exhibition in the porter's lodge. Also Holkham pottery and a collection of agricultural tools. Meals, snacks, shop, some disabled access; cl am, all Fri and Sat, Oct–Easter; (01328) 710227; £5 for everything, £3 hall only. The Victoria Hotel is handy for lunch. The beach has a bird reserve, though spotters may get more twitchy than usual if they stray on to the adjacent nudist beach.

⌂ ❀ ♨ ⌂ **Houghton** TF9235 HOUGHTON HALL Built for Robert Walpole and obviously designed to impress, this is a spectacularly grand Palladian mansion set in charming parkland. The state rooms were decorated and furnished by William Kent, and house an important collection of 20,000 model soldiers and other militaria. Heavy horses, Shetland ponies and llamas in the stables. The house was closed for major repair work as we went to press and no details had been decided for 1995; (01485) 528569.

♨ ⌖ ☺ **Hunstanton** TF6740 is a clean, fresh and well kept resort with gently shelving tidal sands (donkey rides still), summer boat trips, pleasant dune walks past the golf course up to the BIRD RESERVE on Gore Point, and a hi-tech SEA LIFE CENTRE (Southern Promenade), with an ocean tunnel bringing you face to face with deep-water creatures as well as octopuses and toothy copper eels. Also a seal hospital with pools of sick or injured animals. Meals, snacks, shop, disabled access; cl 25–26 Dec; (01485) 533576; £4.25. There are also the more conventional resort entertainments, such as OASIS, a giant leisure park on The Promenade with tropically heated indoor and outdoor pools with both towering and toddler aquaslides. The low cliffs around the town are quite colourful, with different rock strata. The Ancient Mariner, part of the Le Strange Arms Hotel in Old Hunstanton, is good value for lunch.

★ ⌂ † ♨ ♭ ⌖ **King's Lynn** TF6220 was once the fourth largest town in England; it is quieter now, with pleasant corners, some attractive Georgian brick buildings and a few much older places such as the 17th-c Custom House on the quay by the River Purfleet, the 15th-c CHURCH of St Nicholas (Chapel Lane), the South Gates, Red Mount Chapel and the two medieval guildhalls. The first of these, the 15th-c ST GEORGE'S GUILDHALL (King St), is now the town's theatre, and home of the King's Lynn Festival; on the tour they like to say Shakespeare himself performed here. Meals, snacks, shop, disabled access to galleries; cl 12.30–2pm Sat, Sun (exc pm summer), and bank hols; £1. The handsome Trinity Guildhall

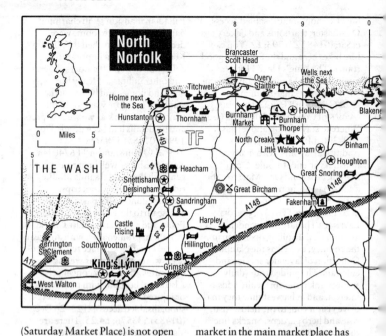

North Norfolk

(Saturday Market Place) is not open to the public, but the 14th-c King John Cup and other fabulous examples of civic paraphernalia housed in its undercroft are included in the tour of the OLD GAOL HOUSE (also in Saturday Market Place), a lively new journey through the town's rich history; spirited models, and spooky sights, sounds and smells, particularly good for children. Shop, disabled access; cl Weds and Thurs from Nov–spring bank hol; (01533) 763044; £2. TRUES YARD Restored old fishermen's cottages giving a good picture of what life was like here in the last century, when families of up to 11 were often squeezed in the two little rooms. Snacks, shop, disabled access; cl 25 Dec; (01553) 770479; £1.90. The TOWN HOUSE MUSEUM (Queen St) has further displays of social history, with room reconstructions, costumes and toys. Shop, disabled access to ground floor only; cl Mon and Sun (exc pm May–Sept), Christmas; £1. The LYNN MUSEUM (Old Market St) includes the skeleton of a Saxon warrior, as well as a surprisingly interesting collection of medieval pilgrim badges. Shop, disabled access; cl Sun, bank hols, 25–26 Dec, 1 Jan; 60p. The Tues

market in the main market place has some decent craft stalls. The Tudor Rose between there and St Nicholas is good for lunch, and in the market place, the Globe and Maydens Heade are useful for food, as is the Wildfowler on the Gayton rd.

† ✗ Letheringsett TG0538 has a CHURCH with an unusual round tower, and a restored waterpowered WATERMILL in a pretty setting, still milling flour from local wheat. Cl 1–2 pm, pm Sat, all Mon, and Sun exc pm Whit–Sept, Christmas, demonstrations are usually on pm Tues, Weds, Thurs and Sun; (01263) 713153; £2.25 when they're demonstrating, otherwise £1.25. The King's Head is an attractive place for lunch.

★ † ❀ ✪ ❧ Little Walsingham TF9336 WALSINGHAM ABBEY GROUNDS The original 12th-c priory was destroyed by Henry VIII in 1538, but parts of the building still remain, inc the abbey gates, great arch, part of the refectory and the Holy Wells. The ruins are overlooked by the new building, and there are pleasant gardens and woodland walks, with masses of snowdrops in early spring. Meals, snacks, shop, disabled access; gates of site open Apr–Sept Weds, Sat

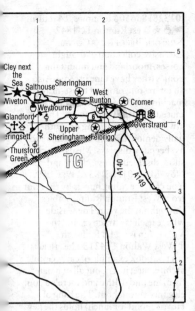

and Sun, plus Mon and Fri in Aug.
You can also gain entrance through
the estate office whenever it's open –
generally Mon–Fri, 9–5; (01328)
820259; *£1. THE SHIREHALL MUSEUM
has a particular emphasis on the
pilgrimage to Walsingham; displays
are in an almost perfect Georgian
courtroom complete with original
fittings. Shop, limited disabled access;
cl 1–2 pm Mon, am Sun, wkdys Oct,
and all Nov–Easter; 60p. The Bull is
useful for lunch.

★ **North Creake** TF8538 CREAKE
ABBEY All that remains of this early
13th-c Augustinian priory is the
crossing and E arm, but it's still worth
a passing look if you're here for the
good food at the very traditional Jolly
Farmers (see **Where to eat** section
below). The village itself is charming.

Overstrand TG2440 PLESAUNCE
Gardens laid out by Gertrude Jekyll,
currently being restored. You can also
see a couple of rooms in the house
designed by Lutyens, and admission
includes a cream tea. Open pm Mon,
Weds and Thurs May–Oct; (0126
378) 212; £2.50. Good beach walks
nearby.

† **Sandringham** TF6928
For many people an important reason

for coming to this part of Norfolk is
its connection with the royal family.
SANDRINGHAM HOUSE was bought by
Queen Victoria for her son Edward in
1862 and has become famous as the
Christmas royal residence; the 19th-c
building is filled with their portraits
and those of their European
counterparts, and has various gifts
presented to the family over the years.
The parish CHURCH OF ST MARY
MAGDALENE, as well as being full of
treasures of its own, has a cross set
into the chancel floor where the
coffins of George V and VI rested
before being transported to Windsor.
The house's grounds and surrounding
country park are lovely. Meals,
snacks, shop, disabled access; open
Easter–Sept, exc during summer royal
visit – best to check for dates; tel
(01553) 772675; £4.00, grounds and
museum only £3.00. In summer, pick-
your-own lets you sample fruit that
might otherwise have graced the royal
table. On the journey to the house, the
royal family often used the small
building at WOLFERTON STATION to
rest. Many of the original, late 19th-c
fittings survive, as well as period
posters and royal train furniture,
letters and photos. Shop, disabled
access but no special facilities; cl am
Sun, Sat (exc grounds and shop), all
Oct–Easter; (01485) 540674; *£1.95.
The Feathers on the Sandringham rd
out of Dersingham is useful for lunch.

† **Sheringham** TG1443 still has
a working fishing harbour, with some
old buildings around it, though there's
a lot more modern building up behind.
The seafront Two Lifeboats is useful
for lunch. NORTH NORFOLK RAILWAY
Full-size steam railway, chugging
through five miles of lovely coastal
scenery, with a museum of railway
memorabilia at the station, and a
collection of steam engines and vintage
rolling stock. Meals, snacks, shop,
disabled access; steamtrain operates
Mar–Dec – best to tel (01263) 822045
for dates and times; *£5 full return
journey. The extensive parkland of
SHERINGHAM PARK, gloriously
landscaped by Humphrey Repton (it
was his favourite work), gives excellent
coastal views from viewing towers.
Also mature trees and fine

rhododendrons (best late May/June), with nice walks to the coast. Disabled access; free, but parking £2.30; NT. The 14th-c church in the quiet village of Upper Sheringham nearby is very attractive, and the Red Lion there is good for lunch.

🐷 ⚘ ✕ **Snettisham** TF6834 PARK FARM Working farm offering a good insight into seasonal farming operations – lambing, shearing, and red deer calving. Lots of animals, as well as an adventure playground and indoor play area, craft centre and mini golf. Meals, snacks, shop, disabled access; cl Nov–20 Mar (exc shop and craft centre, open all year); (01485) 542425; *£3.50, plus £3 for a 45-minute guided ride around the deer park. Nearby is a restored working WATERMILL, with pretty walks in the vicinity. Open pm Thurs July–mid-Sept; £1. The Rose & Crown is good for lunch.

❀ **Terrington St Clement** TF5419 AFRICAN VIOLET CENTRE Good range of plants besides the African violets it's developed so successfully as house plants. The Woolpack at Walpole Cross Keys has decent food.

🐚 ᕬ ☺ **Thursford Green** TF9833 THURSFORD COLLECTION Rather jolly collection of organs – the musical kind, whether barrel, street or fairground. Most are demonstrated every day, as is the Wurlitzer cinema organ, which stars in Tues evening concerts in summer. Also showmen's steam engines, ploughing engines and a 2-ft-gauge steam railway, and, for those seeking greater thrills, an adventure playground and Venetian Gondola switchback ride. Meals, snacks, shop, disabled access; cl am exc in summer, all Nov–Mar and bank hols; (01328) 878477; £4.35. The Crawfish is useful for lunch.

★ ᕬ **Wells-next-the-Sea** TF9143 is a pleasant and rather gracious little village-sized town; the Crown is good for lunch. WELLS & WALSINGHAM LIGHT RAILWAY Passing through delightful countryside, this railway is remarkable for being the longest track in Britain to use a 10¼-in-gauge track, with a steam locomotive built specially for it a few years ago. Snacks, shop; cl Oct–Easter; tel

(01328) 856506 for times; £4 return.

🐷 ♘ ★ **West Runton** TG1842 NORFOLK SHIRE HORSE CENTRE Extensive collection of draught horses, moorland and mountain ponies (they have nine breeds). Also an interesting range of horse-drawn machinery, children's farm, and a museum of rural equipment. There's always something going on, with daily demonstrations and events such as sheepdog displays. Meals, snacks, shop, disabled access; cl Sat, and Nov–Mar; (01263) 837339; £3.50. You can hire riding horses by the hour from West Runton Riding Stables throughout the year. The seaside village itself is attractive, and the Village Inn is useful for lunch.

✝ **West Walton** TF4213 The CHURCH is a textbook example of early Gothic architecture; just about all of it dates from the mid-13th c and there's a cool elegance throughout. The King of Hearts (good for lunch) holds the key.

♘ **Weybourne** TG1042 MUCKLEBURGH COLLECTION World War II fighting vehicles and other materiel on the site of a former military camp, once the lynchpin of defences on this coast; tanks, trucks, guns, missiles and bombs from all over the world. They add new things every year, inc recently rare field guns, and the only guns to have fired atomic shells. Also other local history and model ships. Meals and snacks served in a NAAFI-style café; shop, disabled access; cl Nov–Easter; (01263) 588210; *£3.

🦅 ⚓ This stretch of coast is particularly worthwhile for **birdwatching**. We mention a few reserves elsewhere but other observation points that have been recommended to us include Holme-next-the-Sea TF7043, Thornham TF7343, Titchwell TF7543 (a good RSPB reserve; in addition to the Manor Hotel, the Three Horseshoes has good-value food and bedrooms), and Blakeney TG0243 (which besides having a decent pub, the King's Arms, has a windmill, and boat trips out to see seals).

★ **Other attractive villages** here, all with pleasant pubs, include Binham TF9839, Burnham Market TF8342 (also a gatehouse and the 13th-c remains of a priory), Cley-next-the-Sea TG0443 (handy for the bird-sanctuary marshes towards the Blakeney Point sandspit, and another windmill; the church is magnificent), Harpley TF7825, South Wootton TF6422 and Wiveton TG0342.

Decent pubs in other attractive coastal areas include the Red Lion at Stiffkey (pronounced Stukey) TF9743, Three Horseshoes at Warham TF9441, Sandpiper at Wighton TF9340 and the marshside Dun Cow at Salthouse TG0743.

Walks

Dutch-gabled buildings, flint walls, huge skies, saltmarshes and the odd wind-mill give the area a real sense of place and make it distinctive for walkers. The North Norfolk Coastal Path follows the length of this coast, although not always right next to the sea. The weather is often kinder on the coast, when conditions a few miles inland can be quite different. Going over sand can be tiring, despite the lack of contours. Between **Wells-next-the-Sea** TF9143 △-1 and Overy Staithe TF8444, the sandy beach never quite looks the same from one day to the next – this is the best stretch of coast for walks. At Holkham there is a car park quite close to the beach, where pine trees meet the sands, while westwards the crowds rapidly thin out. From Overy Staithe, the path follows a zigzagging dyke – saltmarsh on one side, neat farmland on the other – to the dunes and beach.

Another good stretch is **Blakeney Point** TG0046 △-2 which gets better as you walk along it, although the shingle bank needs patience and is hard on the ankles; pleasant dunes await at the far end. The dyke walk between **Blakeney** TG0243 △-3 and Cley-next-the-Sea TG0443 is less arduous, with the birds on the mudflats for company.

The coastal **Holkham Hall** estate TF8842 △-4 allows walkers throughout the year on its driveways; the parkland is a bit gloomy, but impressively land-scaped with a lake, a temple and an obelisk. Further W, **Holme-next-the-Sea** TF7043 △-5 gives access to a sandy beach for a 2-mile walk past a bird sanc-tuary and saltings to Thornham TF7343.

Only **Beacon Hill** TG1841 △-6, nr Cromer, rises to any height (a humble 300 ft); the coastal path here detours over the sandy heath and through wood-lands. **Salthouse** TF0743 △-7 and Kelling TG0942 back similar heathy hinterlands, where you can tie in a walk along the coast (here unvaryingly straight) as part of the same excursion.

Sandringham Country Park TF6727 △-8, with its majestic trees and glades, is the most notable parkland walking area. There are also some pleas-ant inland walks around Ringstead TF7040, where the Gin Trap has decent home cooking.

Driving

The A149 round the coast is not a quick road, except at quiet times of year, but does give the feel of the area very well indeed. The B roads are all quite good, with the roads N out of Fakenham (quite a pleasant, small market town) passing through attractive villages.

Where to eat

King's Lynn TF6220 ROCOCO 11 Saturday Market Pl (01533) 771483 Deli-cious and imaginative modern cooking using local produce, in a pretty dining room decorated with lots of fresh flowers and paintings; a cosy lounge area, relaxed atmosphere, good, informal service, and decent wines. £29/£6.75.
Wells-next-the-Sea TF9143 MOORINGS 6 Freeman St (01328) 710949 Pretty

restaurant close to the harbour, with lovely, locally caught seafood, good vegetarian dishes, and decent wines; cl Tues and Weds, am Thurs, mid-Dec, mid-Jun; disabled access. £22.50.

Burnham Market TF8342 Hoste Arms The Green (01328) 738257 Good bar food, inc interesting vegetarian dishes, in a handsome old inn, civilised, bustling bars, open fires, friendly staff and a restaurant; bedrooms; disabled access. £21|£2|£5.

Blakeney TG0243 White Horse (01263) 740574 Good food, inc fresh fish, in a popular bar with friendly, enthusiastic licensees; reasonably priced wines, and an attractive evening restaurant; bedrooms; disabled access (not bedrooms). £19|£1.50/£4.95.

North Creake TF8538 Jolly Farmers 1 Burnham Rd (01328) 738185 Cosy and friendly little pub with a chatty atmosphere, good, fresh, local fish, home-made puddings, and Thai food Weds and Fri evenings; children in dining room only. £13.50|£1.75/£4.95.

Upper Sheringham TG1441 Red Lion (01263) 825408 Simple, friendly little flint cottage with good, interesting bar food using fresh, local produce; 3-course special pm Weds, seafood specials pm Thurs, relaxed atmosphere, and an open fire. £2.95/£5.95.

SOUTH AND EAST NORFOLK

Norwich is good for a city break, and a fine choice of things to do and see elsewhere makes this area appealing for out-and-about weekends.

Norwich is an enjoyable, historic cathedral city with plenty to see – certainly one of Britain's dozen or so most rewarding places for a city break. Elsewhere, this part of the county has a lot to offer people who want to get out and about, visiting places of interest. Prime among these are Blickling Hall, the wildfowl centre at Welney, Bressingham Gardens and Steam Museum, Castle Acre, the extensive wooded watergardens at South Walsham, and the many animal and wildlife centres such as the South American zoo park near Thetford, the Asian one at Filby, the European one at Great Witchingham and the otter trust at Earsham.

In general the countryside isn't a major draw in this part of Norfolk. The famous Broads tend to hide away from land-based visitors unless you make a determined effort to get to them. They are, of course, obviously best seen from a boat. Broads cruising is usually a week-long affair, but could be worked into a short-stay holiday, by the day or even a whole weekend. Wroxham is a popular centre for this, though one of the quieter bases in the north might make a better choice for just a day on the water.

The coast is strung with beach resorts, some large and lively (most obviously, Great Yarmouth), some relaxed and more individual. But for most people a weekend break in this area is more likely to concentrate on the interesting interior.

We've found some very civilised places to stay here, including this year somewhere good in Norwich itself, and there's no problem finding decent food.

Where to stay

Sprowston TG2411 SPROWSTON MANOR Wroxham Rd, Sprowston, Norwich NR7 8RP (01603) 410871 £101.50; 97 individually decorated, spacious rms. Extended 16th-c manor house in 10 acres of parkland and surrounded by Sprowston Park golf course; comfortable day rooms, fine food in the elegant orangery and attractive restaurant, a leisure club with palms and stone balustrades, and poolside bar; disabled access.

Swaffham TF8109 STRATTON HOUSE Ash Close, Swaffham PE37 7NH (01760) 723845 *£80; 7 interesting, pretty rms. Warmly welcoming, elegant Queen Anne house, with delicious English food using home-grown herbs and vegetables from a family smallholding; a carefully chosen wine list illustrated with owner Mrs Scott's own watercolours; comfortable drawing rooms with open fires and lots of china cats, dried flowers, and books; big cupboard full of toys and games for children; cl 24–26 Dec; dogs welcome.

Hethersett TG1505 PARK FARM Hethersett, Norwich NR9 3DL (01603) 810264 *£70; 37 rms. Carefully extended Georgian house, with fine food in the pretty restaurant, friendly staff, a leisure complex with swimming pool, and landscaped gardens with tennis court; partial disabled access.

Scole TM1579 SCOLE INN Scole, Diss IP21 4DR (01379) 740481 £63; 23 rms. Stately 17th-c coaching inn with a colourful history and one of the few pubs with a Grade I preservation listing; handsome beams and fireplaces, antique settles and oak refectory tables, good bar and restaurant food, well kept real ales, and pleasant service.

Blickling TG1728 BUCKINGHAMSHIRE ARMS Blickling, Norwich NR11 6NF (01263) 732133 *£60; 3 rms, one with own bthrm. Handsome Jacobean inn in the grounds of Blickling Hall, with a civilised atmosphere, helpful staff, good food in both the bar and restaurant (best to book), nice breakfasts, and well kept real ales.

Erpingham TG1631 SARACENS HEAD Wolterton, Erpingham, Norwich NR11 7LX (01263) 768909 *£45; 3 rms. Remote and civilised, 19th-c brick inn with an atmospheric two-room bar, log fires and fresh flowers; extremely fine food, inc good-value, two-course lunches, a pretty little dining parlour, well kept beers and decent whiskies and wines; pleasant courtyard and a walled garden; cl 25 Dec.

Mundford TL8093 CROWN Crown St, Mundford, Thetford IP26 5HQ (01842) 878233 *£45; 10 good rms. Friendly, small village pub – originally a hunting inn – rebuilt in the 18th c, with an attractive choice of good-value, straightforward food, very welcoming staff, a happy atmosphere, and well kept real ales.

Winterton-on-Sea TG4919 FISHERMANS RETURN The Lane, Winterton-on-Sea, Great Yarmouth NR29 4BN (01493) 393305 *£45; 3 characterful rms, shared bthrm. Traditional, 300-year-old pub in a quiet village, close to the beach, with warmly welcoming owners, a relaxed lounge bar, open fire, good home-made food, fine breakfasts and a sheltered garden; low beams, steep stairs.

Northwold TL7596 GRANGE Northwold, Thetford IP26 5NF (01366) 728240 £44; 5 rms, two with own bthrm. Lovely 18th-c rectory in 12 acres of garden behind the church, with a log fire in the drawing room, views over lawns with peacocks and ducks, and a heated swimming pool; cl Christmas.

South Lopham TM0481 MALTING FARM Blo'Norton Rd, South Lopham, Diss IP22 2HT (01379) 88201 £38; 3 well furnished rms, some with own bthrm. Friendly, welcoming, Elizabethan farmhouse on a working dairy farm, with woodburning stoves in inglenook fireplaces in both the sitting and dining rooms, big breakfasts with home-baked bread and preserves around a large table, and a small play area with toys; non-smokers preferred; the owner's passion is embroidery, patchwork, spinning and quilting; cl Christmas and New Year.

Norwich TG2308 EARLHAM GUEST HOUSE 147 Earlham Rd, Norwich NR2 3RG (01603) 54169 £34; 7 rms, some with own bthrm. Friendly, terraced Victorian house with a small residents' lounge, good breakfasts with vegetarian choices, and helpful owners.

Stoke Holy Cross TG2301 SALAMANCA FARM Stoke Holy Cross, Norwich

NR14 8QJ (01508) 492322 £34; 4 rms. Mainly Victorian farmhouse, a short stroll from the River Tas, with a guest lounge, spacious dining room, big garden, and a farm shop; cl 15 Dec–15 Jan.

Shelfhanger TM1083 SHELFHANGER HALL Shelfhanger, Diss IP22 2DE (01379) 642094 £32; 3 rms, 2 with own showers. 16th-c moated farmhouse overlooking a big garden and farmland; snooker table and table tennis; cl Christmas; children over 10; self-catering also.

To see and do

Norwich TG2308 is busy but civilised, with quite a concentration of attractive streets and buildings in the old centre. All sorts of surprises pop up in the narrow streets and lanes that still follow its medieval layout; Elm St is especially handsome, and there are plenty of antique shops and so forth. Even in the more commercial/industrial centre N of the River Wensum there are fine patches (such as Colegate). Fortunately, the visually disappointing university is hidden away out on the western edge, though in termtime its students do bring a good bit of life into the centre. Norwich is the home of Colman's mustard, and the Mustard Shop (Bridewell Alley) has some varieties you may not have come across before. The ancient Adam & Eve (Bishopgate) is good for lunch, and other central pubs and wine bars useful for a bite to eat without being overrun by students include the Edith Cavell (Tombland), riverside Rib of Beef (Wensum St), Take Five (St Andrew's Hill) and Wild Man (St George St).

🏰 👹 🖼 CASTLE (Castle Meadow) Set on the city hill, this impressive, four-square Norman structure dominates the city. It houses the CASTLE MUSEUM, with guided tours of the dungeons, battlements and the 12th-c keep, and displays of art (with particular emphasis on the Norwich School), silverware (for which the town was famous) and ceramics, as well as archaeology and natural history. If you like stuffed birds, don't miss this part, which among countless other exhibits includes Norfolk's last pair of great bustards. Snacks, shop, disabled access; cl am Sun, Good Fri, 25–26 Dec, 1 Jan; (01603) 223624; £2.20. Linked to this museum via a secret passage is a former courtroom in the historic Shirehall, now the ROYAL NORFOLK REGIMENTAL MUSEUM – the passage was once used to transfer prisoners to the court. The displays are more lively than in many regimental museums, telling the story of the domestic and military life of a soldier in the county regiment from 1685. Small shop; cl am Sun, Good Fri, Christmas period, 1 Jan; entrance is included in the Castle Museum ticket, or you can buy a ticket for £1 which also covers several other museums in the city, as do the prices we quote for several below.

✝ 🏛 CATHEDRAL With the cloisters and the many well preserved buildings of its extensive precincts this makes an awe-inspiring impression behind the great medieval gateways that shut out the modern city. Basically medieval, the cathedral has some fine features from later periods – the flying buttresses for example, and the late 15th-c vaulted roof, spire and W window with Victorian glass. The NORMAN CLOISTERS are the largest in the country, rebuilt after a serious riot between city and cathedral in 1272, and remarkable for the 400 bosses which are carved with scenes of medieval life (there are hundreds more in the cathedral itself, though less easy to see). Snacks, shop, disabled access; free. The precincts are delightful, with several closes, medieval alleys and secluded gardens, and all sorts of varied buildings from the cottages of Hooks Walk through the finer houses in the Upper Close to the buildings of Norwich School. The best view of the cathedral is from the river by Pulls Ferry; it's not easy to see from other parts of the town.

🖼 SAINSBURY CENTRE FOR VISUAL ARTS (University of East Anglia) Striking Norman Foster building with notable 19th- and 20th-c European art, and a fascinating range of ethnographic art, inc African tribal sculpture, and Egyptian and Asian antiquities. Meals, snacks, shop, disabled access; cl am, Mon, 23 Dec–2 Jan; *£1.

🏠👶 BRIDEWELL MUSEUM (Bridewell Alley) 14th-c building used as a prison from 1583 to 1828, now with exhibits on the town's trade and industries over the past 200 years. Shop; cl Sun, Good Fri, 25–26 Dec, 1 Jan; £1.40.

🏠👶 STRANGERS HALL (Charing Cross) Interesting medieval house right in the city centre, with period rooms and temporary exhibitions of toys, costumes and textiles. Lots of stairs; shop; dates and price as Bridewell Museum (see above).

🏠 DRAGON HALL (King St) Well preserved, medieval merchant's hall, with a splendid, timber-framed roof,

intricate carvings, cellars, vaulted undercroft, and some finely painted roundels. Shop, disabled access; cl wknds exc summer Sats, 23 Dec–2 Jan, bank hols; *£1.

✝👶 MEDIEVAL CHURCHES – literally dozens of them, in great variety – are one of the city's joys. Perhaps the finest of all is St Peter Hungate (Princes St), an impressive, 15th-c church with a grand hammerbeam roof, museum of church art and brass rubbing centre. Small shop, disabled access; dates and price as Bridewell Museum (see above).

⚓ BOAT TRIPS on the river give an interesting light on the city. You can see how some of its older buildings were designed for water-borne traffic, rather than road transport.

The Broads

Norfolk's network of linking waterways is not easy to visit on foot or by car; the best way to see the Broads is undoubtedly by boat. Wroxham with its neighbour Hoveton is a main centre for boat hire, but, like the other principal centre Horning, is probably better thought of as a base for longer spells afloat than for short breaks or day trips. If you want a boat for just the day, the quieter reaches of the more northern Broads would probably suit you better – say, from Barton Turf TG3522, Hickling TG4123, Stalham TG3725 or Wayford Bridge TG3424.

Good places to get down to the Broads but remain on land include Hickling itself (with a pleasant path along the N shore) and Ormesby St Michael TG4614, where the Eels Foot pub has attractive waterside lawns, and the Norfolk Rare Breeds Centre has an interesting range of animals; cl Sat and Oct–Mar exc Sun; £2.

Other waterside pubs handy for watching boating activity include the Woods End at Bramerton TG2904; the Rising Sun at Coltishall TG2719 (on a pretty bend of the River Bure); the Crown at Dilham TG3325; the Swan, or the Ferry – a busy Chef & Brewers – at Horning TG3417; the quaint Walpole Arms at Itteringham TG1430; the Old Bridge at Potter Heigham TG4119 (good riverside garden); the Ferry at Reedham TG4101 (the little car ferry here is fun); the Ferry House at Stokesby TG4310; the Ferry House at Surlingham TG3206 (there's still a rowing-boat ferry here), or nearby Coldham Hall (lovely riverside garden); the Sutton Staithe Hotel at Sutton Staithe TG3823 (a pretty, quiet spot); or the Lock, a remote candlelit pub down by the River Waveney at Geldeston TM3991.

For a sense of adventure you can take the long walk across the marshes from Wickhampton TG4205 or Halvergate TG4206 past former windpumps to the Berney Arms on Breydon Water.

The Maltsters at Ranworth TG3514 is just across the lane from one of the few Broads the boats can't get to – the conservation centre of Ranworth Broad (though you can take a different kind of boat across it). The Broadland Conservation Centre here has nature trails and displays of local and natural history; disabled access; cl Nov–Mar; free. There are guided tours of the wildlife here on Suns, and the local CHURCH has the best painted rood screen in the county.

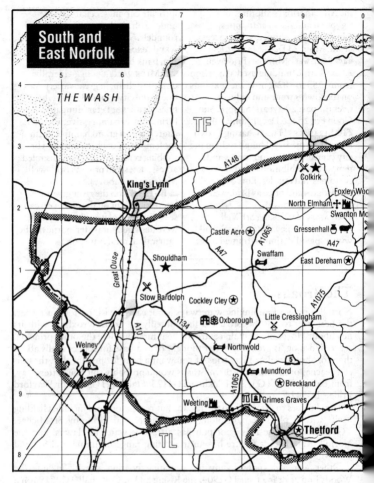

South and East Norfolk

THE WASH

TF

A148

Colkirk

Foxley Wood

North Elmham

Swanton Mc

King's Lynn

Castle Acre

Gressenhall

A47

A1065

Swaffam

East Dereham

Shouldham

A47

Great Ouse

A1075

Stow Bardolph

Cockley Cley

Little Cressingham

Oxborough

A134

A10

Welney

Northwold

Mundford

A1065

Breckland

Weeting

Grimes Graves

TL

Thetford

Other things to see and do

❀ ✝ **Attleborough** TM0495 has PETER BEALES ROSE NURSERY, a specialist in old-fashioned roses that you won't find for sale elsewhere. The 15th-c CHURCH is interesting, with an unusual round tower and a screen decorated with the arms of the 24 bishoprics in England when it was built. The nearby Crown at Great Ellingham TM0196 is attractively located and useful for lunch.

Baconsthorpe TG1237 BACONSTHORPE CASTLE The gatehouses, curtain walls and towers are all that's left of this moated and semi-fortified 15th-c house, but the displays on the site give a good idea of what it must have looked like in its glory. It's a very pretty, peaceful spot, with swans on the lake adding to its charm; free. You can find information booklets at the nearby post office. The Hare & Hounds on the way to Hempstead is good for lunch.

🐒 ☺ ❀ **Banham** TM0688 BANHAM ZOO and APPLEYARD CRAFT COURT Over 20 acres of parkland and garden with rare and endangered species, particularly monkeys and apes – though alas the bulk of their parrot collection was stolen not so long ago. Also indoor activity centre, ice-cream

parlour, play area, putting green and craft courtyard. Readers rate this very highly. Meals, snacks, shop, disabled access; cl 25–26 Dec; (01953) 887771; £5.50. The George or King's Head in New Buckenham would do for lunch.
🏠 ❀ **Blickling** TG1728 BLICKLING HALL Magnificent house dating mainly from the early 17th c, though the hedges that flank it may be older. Dramatic, carved oak staircase, splendid paintings inc a famous Canaletto, and intricate decor and furnishings. Best of all are the 125-ft long gallery with its ornate Jacobean plaster ceiling, and the Chinese bedroom, still lined with 18th-c hand-painted wallpaper. The gardens and

grounds are lovely. Meals, snacks, shop, good disabled access with a lift in the house; cl Mon (exc bank hols), Thurs, all Nov–Mar; £4.90, £5.50 Sun and bank hols; NT. There's free public access to the park on the W side of the pike-filled lake, with a pleasant walk from the Buckinghamshire Arms (which is good for lunch).
🛶 ✿ 🐾 **Breckland** around Thetford is a region of poor, flat, sandy heathland with scattered shallow meres and originally scrubby mixed woodland, extensively planted now with pines instead; there are forest walks, for example from car parks on the A134 NW of Thetford, where you may disturb roe deer. A good place to see it

as it was is the East Wretham Heath NATURE RESERVE TL9188, off the A1075 NE of Thetford: plenty of wild flowers, nature trails, and hides for watching the birds and deer; free.

❀ ▦ ⬥ **Bressingham** TM0780 BRESSINGHAM STEAM MUSEUM AND GARDENS The founder, Alan Bloom, has successfully combined his two interests to great effect at this rewarding site. The 6 acres of informal gardens are planted with 5,000 species and cultivars of alpines and perennials in island beds, with lots of the dwarf conifers Bloom has done so much to popularise. Then there's the excellent steam collection, inc 50 road and rail engines, mostly restored to working order, a steam roundabout and Norfolk fire museum. Four steam-hauled trains run through the charming countryside – one running through 5 miles of the Waveney valley – and parts of the garden. Meals, snacks, shop, disabled access; cl Nov–Mar, and gardens only Mon; (0137) 988382; £3.70. The Garden House is handy for lunch.

▦ ✕ **Burgh Castle** TG4805 CASTLE You can still see sections of the massive walls of this coastal Roman fortress, built in the 3rd c to protect the coast from Saxon marauders. The bastions topping some parts of the walls were probably for ballistae, giant catapults which could sink or set fire to boats; free. Across the water from here, and accessible only by foot, by boat, or by rail from Great Yarmouth, the seven-storey BERNEY ARMS WINDMILL dates from the 19th c when it was used to grind clinker and to drain the water from the marshes. Disabled access; cl 1–2pm, and Oct–Mar; (01493) 700605; 85p.

▥ ⓘ ▦ **Caister-on-Sea** TG5212, like all the other settlements down this coast, plays host to a good many summer visitors, with all the usual attractions, inc long sandy beaches. It's also got a lifeboat station, right by the beach. The ruined, moated CASTLE is set back from the town, a little way inland. Falstaff (the original behind Shakespeare's creation) built it on returning from Agincourt; its walls surround a 98-ft tower. The grounds contain a MOTOR MUSEUM with a good collection of vehicles from 1893 onwards. Snacks, shop, some disabled access; cl Sat, and Oct–mid-May; £4. The town contains various remains of an excavated ROMAN FORT, inc the S gateway and a town wall.

★ ✝ ▥ **Castle Acre** TF8115 is a delightful village, with an 18th-c feel along the tree-shaded walk of Stocks Green (the Ostrich here is nice for lunch). CASTLE ACRE PRIORY Ruins of a gorgeous Cluniac priory built by William the Conqueror's son-in-law. The remains are extensive, inc the fine, arcaded W front of the 11th–12th-c church, and a chapel and 15th-c gatehouse; there's a good Walkman tour. Well laid out, and very picturesque. Snacks, shop, some disabled access; cl winter Mon and Tues; (01760) 755394; £2.10. Beside these relics are the sparser yet still awe-inspiring ruins of a great CASTLE built at the same time. The site is on the Peddar's Way, a Roman rd following the track of an earlier herding way – which is now a path extending the Norfolk Coastal Path (see North Norfolk Walks section). West Acre, 2 or 3 miles to the W, has a few further priory remains, and (like Castle Acre itself) picturesque fords over the River Nar.

▧ ♨ ✝ ▦ ! **Cockley Cley** TF7904 Lots of interesting historical things to see around this village (pronounced to rhyme with 'fry'). There's a MUSEUM of agricultural equipment, vintage engines and carriages, a 15th-c COTTAGE FORGE housing models and exhibits following local life from prehistoric times, and a 7th-c SAXON CHURCH. Most unusual is the ICENI VILLAGE, built as and where it was believed to exist 2,000 years ago. Snacks, shop, disabled access; cl Nov–Mar; (01760) 721339; £2.80 for all attractions. The unusually named village pub, the Twenty Churchwardens, is useful for lunch.

⋎ **Earsham** TM3289 OTTER TRUST This charitable trust works towards reintroducing otters to rivers from which they've disappeared, but which now seem likely to support the animals again. You can see the little creatures here in a natural environment. They're obviously cheerful and intelligent, but don't perform on demand and you may have to wait a while to see anything. Snacks, shop; cl Nov–Mar; (01986) 893470; £3.50.

⚱✝✗ **East Dereham** TF9913 BISHOP BONNERS COTTAGE MUSEUM is interesting if you're passing through, with various changing local history. Shop, disabled access to ground floor only; open pm May–Sept, not Sun; free. The CHURCH has a medieval well, and there's a working windmill on the Norwich rd, with useful displays. Cl am, all Mon–Weds, Oct–Mar. The George has decent food.

🕷⚱🐦 **Erpingham** TG1631 ALBY GARDENS Four acres of interesting shrubs, plants and bulbs, with a museum devoted to lace, another concentrating on bottles (over 2,000 of them, mainly from regional brewers), a bee observation hive, and various crafts inc woodturning, stained glass, photography, furniture and ceramics. Very good roses and lilies in July. Meals, snacks, shop, mostly disabled access; cl Mon (exc bank hols), all wkdys Jan–mid-Mar (lace museum also cl Sat); (01263) 761226; crafts free, gardens £1, bottle museum 30p. The Ark, and the Saracen's Head out at Wolterton, are both very good for lunch.

🕷✔🐦♪⚱ **Filby** TG4613 THRIGBY HALL WILDLIFE GARDENS 18th-c park filled with animals and birds from Asia, with tropical and bird houses, a tree walk, willow-pattern garden, and ornamental wildfowl on the lake. Also a huge, jungly, swamp hall where you can watch somnolent crocodiles dozing under water. Summer snacks, shop, disabled access; (01493) 369477; *£4.50. Not far away at Burgh St Margaret TG4414, the BYGONE HERITAGE VILLAGE is a recreated 19th-c village, with animals, classic cars, steam-driven sawmill, crafts and various other attractions. Meals, snacks, shops, disabled access; cl Nov–Easter; (01493) 369770; £4.80.

↓T **Forncett St Mary** TM1694 INDUSTRIAL STEAM MUSEUM Unusual collection of stationary steam engines rescued from all over the country, inc the one that used to open Tower Bridge. Snacks, shop, disabled access; open usually first Sun of month, May–Dec, when the engines are in steam; (01508) 488277; £2.50. The Bird in Hand over at Wreningham does good-value food.

🍂 **Foxley Wood** TG0321 is a big block of ancient woodland, mainly deciduous and grown naturally for many centuries; lovely woodland spring flowers. Cl Thurs.

🐎 **Frettenham** TG2417 HORSE SANCTUARY (Hill Top Farm, Hall Lane) Very dedicated and friendly place caring for hundreds of rescued horses and donkeys. Snacks, shop, disabled access; open pm Sun and bank hols from Easter to mid-Dec, plus pm Mon in July and Aug; (01603) 737432; £2.

✔🐾☺ **Great Witchingham** TG1021 NORFOLK WILDLIFE PARK 40 acres of gorgeous parkland with a huge collection of British and European wildlife; tame animals include a team of trained reindeer who take children for rides on a wheeled sledge. Also a narrow-gauge steam railway, trout pool and commando play areas. Snacks, shop; cl Nov–Mar; (01603) 872274; £3.80. The Ratcatchers at Cawston is the nearest good place for lunch.

☺♪🦋❗⚱🌸 **Great Yarmouth** TG5207 still has a fishing harbour, and most of the Broads cruising boats seem to end up passing through the town at one time or another. It's a cross between working town and resort, with lots of holiday entertainments – more a place for lively family holidays than for a weekend break. The first three attractions we list here are all good for families and holiday-makers, but the others might well tempt older visitors into the town if they were nearby. SEA LIFE CENTRE (Marine Parade) Displays of the kinds of marine life found on the Norfolk coast, as well as underwater tunnels through shark-infested oceans and tropical fish. Meals, snacks, shop, disabled access; cl 25 Dec; £4.25. LIVING JUNGLE AND BUTTERFLY FARM (sea front) Indoor tropical paradise, with butterflies, birds and fish in a recreated jungle environment – along with terrapins, tarantulas and scorpions. Snacks, shop, disabled access; cl Nov–Feb; (01493) 842202; *£3. MERRIVALE MODEL VILLAGE (Wellington Pier Gardens) Attractive landscaped gardens with children's rides and remote-controlled cars, and the exceptionally detailed village – it covers an acre and features a railway, radio-controlled boats and over 200 models. Meals, snacks, shop, disabled access; cl Oct–Easter; £2.50.

ELIZABETHAN HOUSE MUSEUM (South Quay) A patchwork of historical detail – built in 1596, it has a Georgian façade, 16th-c panelled rooms and, among features from later periods, some rooms decorated and furnished in 19th-c style. Interesting carved chimney and, as well as toys, a collection of Lowestoft porcelain and 18th–19th-c drinking glasses. Shop, disabled access to ground floor only; open 9–24 Apr, then 28 May–Sept, cl 1–2pm and all Sat; £1. The MARITIME MUSEUM OF EAST ANGLIA (Marine Parade) looks at the local fishing industry, with some more incongruous features, inc a mummified hand and an Indian scalp. Shop; cl Sat and much of Oct–May, tel (01493) 842267 for details; 80p. TOLHOUSE MUSEUM (Tolhouse St) This 13th-c building used to be the town's gaol and courthouse (you can still see the dungeons), and now has various local history and archaeology displays, as well as a brass rubbing centre. Shop; open 28 May–1 Sept, not Sat;*50p. OLD MERCHANT'S HOUSE 17th-c house standing among the narrow lanes or Rows nr the waterfront, with some well restored rooms. Cl 1–2pm and all Oct–Mar; £1.20. The 144-ft NELSON'S MONUMENT has fine views of the town at the top of the 217 steps. Open pm July and Aug and 21 Oct, Trafalgar Day; 60p. The White Swan (Caister Rd) is useful for lunch.

🐄🐖Gressenhall TF9615 NORFOLK RURAL LIFE MUSEUM AND UNION FARM Recreation of a typical 1920s farm, with rare breeds of sheep, pigs, cattle and poultry, and working reconstructions of rural and agricultural life. Snacks, shop, disabled access; cl am Sun, all Mon (exc bank hols), and Nov–Mar; (01362) 860563; £3.50.

🎟🐗 Grimes Graves TL8189 GRIMES GRAVES Bring a torch to this site in Breckland (see entry above), as you can climb into one of the 300 pits and vertical shafts which lead down into the galleries – some around 30ft deep

– where the Neolithic people mined their flint. The rough stone, not yet knapped into shape, would have travelled from this site to provide raw material for tool- and weapon-makers around the country. No lavatories at the site, but there are some within a mile. Shop, disabled access; cl Apr–Oct 1–2pm, cl Mon and Tues Nov–Mar, 25 Dec, 1 Jan; (01842) 810656; £1.25.

★ Heydon TG1127 is rather cut off from the surrounding countryside – a big green with an entirely unspoilt village around it; even the pub the Earle Arms, still with horses stabled in its yard, is the very basic sort of country tavern that died out years ago elsewhere.

✗ 🌿 Horsey TG4522 is in a quiet corner of the coast, below sea level – among the places most at risk of flooding if the sea defences are breached. There's a good path to the dunes and the sea from the lane past the Nelson's Head (pleasant for lunch). On the other side of the main road, HORSEY WINDPUMP is a restored drainage windmill, now in full working order. Teas, small shop, some disabled access; cl Sept–Mar; *£1.20; NT. A path from here goes round the N side of quiet Horsey Mere, and on up the New Cut to another former drainage windmill, from where you can walk back to the village; the marshes on the far side of the Cut have a lot of birds.

✝ Horsham St Faith TG2114 NORWICH AVIATION MUSEUM Enthusiastic displays of local aeronautical history, with aircraft (there's a Vulcan bomber), engines, and other paraphernalia; as it's on the edge of Norwich Airport you get a good view of the live article too. Snacks, shop; open Sun and bank hols, and some other summer pms and evenings; (01603) 625309; *£1.50. The thatched Chequers at Hainford has decent food.

🐝 🌿 Hoveton TG3018 HOVETON HALL GARDEN Large and attractive, spring woodland garden with daffodils and rhododendrons, a lakeside walk, a walled, old-fashioned, herbaceous garden and a kitchen garden. Teas, shop, disabled access; open pm Weds, Fri, Sun and

bank hols Easter–mid-Sept; £1.75.
Wroxham Barns CRAFT CENTRE
(Tunstead Rd) has several craft
workshops in 18th-c restored farm
buildings, inc pottery, boatbuilding,
and folk art as well as a children's
farm and traditional fair; nice walks
in parkland. Meals, snacks, shop, play
area, disabled access; cl 25–26 Dec;
(01603) 783762; £1.50 for farm,
otherwise free. The waterside King's
Head Hotel is useful for lunch.

❁ **Loddon** TM3698 READS NURSERY
(Hales Hall) has specialised for a
century in unusual conservatory
plants, inc a good range of lemon,
orange and other citrus fruits, also nut
trees etc. Cl 1–2pm, am Sun, and Mon
(exc bank hols) 25 Dec; (01508)
548395. The White Horse at
Chedgrave does good simple food.

✝ ⛪ **North Elmham** TF9820 The
CHURCH here is an attractive 13th-c
building, odd in that there's a step
down into it. A little further N are the
interesting ruins of a SAXON
CATHEDRAL. The King's Head here is
useful for lunch.

🏠 ❁ **Oxborough** TF7401 OXBURGH
HALL Henry VII stayed in this moated
manor in 1487, and the room is now
decorated with wall hangings worked
by Mary Queen of Scots.
Unfortunately, most of the house was
thoroughly refurbished during
Victorian times, but the 80-ft-high
gatehouse remains as an awe-inspiring
example of 15th-c building work. The
garden has a colourful French parterre.
Meals, snacks, shop, disabled access; cl
am, Thurs, Fri, and Oct–Mar; £3.80;
NT. The Twenty Churchwardens at
Cockley Cley is quite handy for lunch.

❁ 🌼 **Raveningham** TM3996
RAVENINGHAM HALL GARDENS Victorian
conservatory with an interesting
collection of rare shrubs and shrub
roses; also, a traditional kitchen garden
and arboretum. Open pm Weds, Sun
and bank hols mid-Mar–mid-Sept,
nursery and arboretum open daily exc
wknds in Nov–Feb; (01508) 548222;
£2. RAVENINGHAM CRAFT WORKSHOPS
(Beccles Rd) Victorian farm buildings
with furniture-making and other
workshops. Shop, antiques, teas; cl
Christmas.

☺ 🌼 ♥ 🏰 **Reedham** TG4101 PETTITTS

FEATHERCRAFT AND ANIMAL ADVENTURE
PARK You can still watch the
demonstrations of feathercraft,
though they've become a little
swamped by the other attractions
here, inc aviaries, a gnome village, an
American-style locomotive ride
around the grounds, a half-mile
miniature railway, big adventure
playground, miniature horse stud,
deer-petting park and crazy golf.
Meals, snacks, shop; cl Sat, and
Nov–Easter; (01493) 701403;
*£5.50. The Ferry is useful for lunch.

🏰 **St Olaves** TM4599 ST OLAVES
PRIORY Ruins of a 13th-c Augustinian
priory; it's still possible to see the fine
brick undercroft in the cloister – a
remarkable early use of this material;
free. The riverside Bell, very old
indeed though much modernised, is
useful for lunch.

❁ 🌿 ♥ **Saxthorpe** TG1130
MANNINGTON GARDENS AND
COUNTRYSIDE The most beautiful
feature of these gardens is the summer
rose display, but they also have 20
miles of footpaths around the hall and
woodland which are open all year.
Snacks, shop, disabled access; open
pm Sun Apr–Oct, plus Weds–Fri
May–Aug; (01263) 874175; *£2.50.
The paths lead to the grounds of
Wolterton Park, where the NATIONAL
OWL CONSERVATION CENTRE has
exhibitions and displays. Open Weds,
Fri and Sun, Easter–Oct; (01263)
761718; admission charge.

❁ 🌿 ♥ **South Walsham** TG3613
FAIRHAVEN GARDEN TRUST Charming
wooded watergardens set beside the
private South Walsham Inner Broad,
the waterways linked by little bridges.
Rare plants, masses of rhododendrons
among the flowers and a tree – the
King Oak – which is said to be 900
years old. It's an extensive place,
running to some 230 acres, inc a big
BIRD SANCTUARY – to visit this part you
need permission from the warden Mr
Debbage. Boat trips every half-hour.
Snacks, shop, disabled access – but
paths are quite uneven; open Easter
wk, then Weds–Sun plus bank hols
May–Sept, cl am Sat; (01603) 270449;
*£3. The Ship has good home cooking.

♥ **Strumpshaw Marsh** TG3306 (off
Low Rd, Brundall) Partly drained

watermeadows and fen between woodland and the River Yare; RSPB hides for watching marsh birds, inc harriers and bearded tits, winter geese, and maybe swallowtail butterflies in Jun; £2.50. The Yare Inn in Brundall is popular for food. ✿ ⚘ **Taverham** TG1513 has a very large GARDEN CENTRE, with an adjoining CRAFT WORKSHOP COURTYARD; teas.

♦ ⚱ † **Thetford** TL8783 ANCIENT HOUSE MUSEUM Early Tudor house with fine oak ceilings, now a local history museum with a small, period herb garden in the back courtyard. Shop; cl Sun (exc pm Jun–Sept), 25–26 Dec and 1 Jan; free exc in Aug, when 60p. THETFORD PRIORY Ruins of a 12th-c Cluniac monastery; you can easily make out the full ground plan of the cloisters, and the 14th-c gatehouse still stands. Disabled access; free. WARREN LODGE was a 15th-c flint hunting lodge, worth a look. The Bell and Thomas Paine are both civilised places for lunch.

▥ **Weeting** TL7788 WEETING CASTLE Remains of a three-storeyed cross-wing among the ruins of an 11th-c, fortified manor house. The New Inn over at Hockwold has good-value food.

✦ **Welney** TL5294 WILDFOWL AND WETLANDS TRUST Wonderful 1,000 acre nature reserve, with numerous hides and a spacious observatory. In winter the sights include up to 4,000 migratory swans and numerous species of duck (wrap up well then), while in spring the emphasis switches to waders and other birds. There's a nature trail in summer. Snacks, shop, disabled access; cl 24–25 Dec; (01353) 860711; £2.95. The riverside Jenyns Arms at Denver Sluice TF5900 is fairly handy for lunch.

♤ ! ☺ ♖ **Weston Longville** TG1115 DINOSAUR PARK 300 acres of unspoilt woodland with life-sized reconstructions of dinosaurs lying in wait around every corner – good for children to appreciate properly how big some of these beasts were. Also a maze, an adventure playground and a rural bygones museum. Snacks, shop, disabled access; cl Nov–Mar; £3.50. The Parson Woodforde is useful for lunch.

★ **Winterton-on-Sea** TG4919 is one of the quieter seaside resorts scattered all along this coast, with a pleasantly villagey feel, and a particularly good beach over the dunes – a nice place for a wander by the sea; the 17th-c Fisherman's Return is worth a stop for lunch.

⚓ **Wroxham** TG3017 is the main centre for BROADS BOAT CRUISING, and has several boat hire firms. So it's a good place to watch the boating activities from dry land, or to use as the start of a longer cruising holiday. The Bell here has kept more character than many places around.

✗ We've already mentioned several **windmills** around the area; other fine examples are at Acle TG3910, Little Cressingham TF8700, Paston TG3134 and, best of all, Sutton TG3823 (the tallest mill in the country, nine floors high – cl Oct–Mar; £1).

★ **Other attractive villages**, all with decent pubs, include Aldborough TG1834, Colkirk TF9126, Coltishall TG2719, Hainford TG2218, Mundford TL8093, Neatishead TG3420, the interesting, medieval New Buckenham TM0890, Reepham TG1022 (the station has an interesting nostalgia collection), Shouldham TF6708, Swanton Morley TG0116, Woodbastwick TG3315 (a picturesque, thatched estate village) and Worstead TG3025.

Walks

The Peddars Way – the first half of the long-distance path that makes a strikingly straight beeline across the county, and later metamorphoses into the more significant North Norfolk Coastal Path – starts at Knettishall Heath TL9480 nr Thetford, and follows ancient-feeling green ways and quiet lanes to reach the coast up in N Norfolk at Holme-next-the-Sea TF7043, passing through Castle Acre TF8115 on the way. Some may find there is a little too much road-walking to sustain interest.

Few paths get close enough to the Broads themselves, often tantalisingly out of sight, and once away from the waterside and fenny woodlands you are immediately into the flat, humdrum agricultural landscapes found in much of the rest of the area. There is some scope for strolling along rivers, such as the reedy estuarine River Yare nr Great Yarmouth, and the canalised parts of the Bure ⌂-1, Yare ⌂-2, Thurne ⌂-3 and others; pumping-mills, birdlife and the boating scene are the principal features. Horsey TG4522 ⌂-4 does have the ingredients for a varied round walk: a path along reed-fringed Horsey Mere (NT – owned for its wildfowl and otter population) and the New Cut, then for a total contrast joining the beach for sea views near Horsey Corner.

Elsewhere, the chief distinguishing marks are woodland plantations and parkland. Of the forests, the largest is Thetford Forest TL8783. This is mainly conifers and more conifers, though you may see the flash of a roe deer between the trees. For most people there's more interest in the unforested part of the adjacent Breckland grasslands, largely an army training area, which can be appreciated from the 8-mile **Pingo Trail** ⌂-5 starting from Stow Bedon TL9596. This passes through three Sites of Special Scientific Interest (inc Cranberry Rough, an alder swampland), taking you along a disused railway line before joining the Peddar's Way at Hockham Heath TL9292. The Chequers at Thompson TL9296 (comfortable bedrooms) makes an attractive base for woodland and field walks.

For bird-lovers the Wildfowl Trust Refuge at **Welney** TL5294 ⌂-6 has a floodlit lagoon and observatory from which you can watch the thousands of wintering Bewick swans and varied waterfowl, and there are conducted summer evening walks; tel (01353) 860711 for details.

Driving

The territory here is on the whole too flat to make driving interesting, as views tend to be rather repetitive and not very far-ranging. Some worthwhile roads N of Norwich include the B1149 from Norwich to Holt, the B1145 from King's Lynn right across to North Walsham and beyond, and the B1110 from East Dereham to Holt.

In the E of the county it's quite difficult to travel from S to N without going through Norwich – or at least round its ring road.

Where to eat

Norwich TG2308 ADLARDS 79 Upper St Giles St (01603) 633522 Warm and friendly, quietly decorated restaurant serving delicious, carefully thought-out food from a menu that changes daily; lovely puddings, fine service, and a good wine list; cl Sun and Mon. **£20 lunch, £35 dinner**.
Erpingham TG1631 ARK (01263) 761535 Lovely individual food inc home-made bread and home-grown vegetables in a simple, relaxed cottage with a log fire and courteous service; bedrooms; cl Mon, cl am Tues–Sat (unless by arrangement); disabled access. **£24**.
Stow Bardolph TF6205 HARE ARMS (01366) 382229 Good-value, quickly served, interesting lunchtime bar food in a pleasantly refurbished country pub with cheerful licensees; prompt, courteous service even when busy, fresh flowers, a separate, elegant evening restaurant, and a big conservatory for children (not allowed in main bar); cl 25–26 Dec. **£20|£1.50/£5.25.**
Cawston TG1323 GREY GABLES (01603) 871259 Very good English cooking using fresh local produce in a little Georgian restaurant; pleasant service and a fine wine list; bedrooms; cl 24–26 Dec. **£17.50.**
Briston TG0532 JOHN H STRACEY (01263) 860891 Wide choice of notable but reasonably priced bar food in an attractive, spotless pub with nicely set-out tables, friendly licensee, and good real ales; also, a popular restaurant; pleasant countryside; cl pm 25 Dec; disabled access. **£17|£1.85/£5.50.**

Swanton Morley TG0117 DARBYS (01362) 637647 Cosy, beamed country pub decorated with lots of farm tools and so forth; very well kept real ales, good, generously served and often interesting bar food, a log fire, and friendly staff; children's room and adventure playground; also bedrooms, self-catering, camping, caravan site, horse facilities, country trails; disabled access. £15|£2.75|£5.

Colkirk TF9126 CROWN (01328) 862171 Unpretentious but comfortable and welcoming pub with good, honest, well presented food, well kept real ales, decent wines, a restaurant, and a friendly landlord; own bowling green behind; disabled access. £15|£2|£4.

Cawston TG1323 RATCATCHERS (01603) 871430 Cheery pub serving big helpings of very good food from a huge menu; local meat, fresh fish and home-grown herbs, daily specials and vegetarian dishes; cosy, candlelit dining room too; cl 25–26 Dec. £14.50|£2.75|£5.95.

Reedham TG4101 FERRY (01493) 700429 Perfectly placed pub beside the River Yare, with plenty of tables to watch boats or swans, and very popular, good bar food. £13.95|£1.25|£3.80.

St Olaves TM4599 PRIORY FARM (01493) 488432 Good, interesting food, inc fresh fish and a children's menu; right by St Olaves Priory; open all day Jun–Sept; disabled access. £13|£1.50|£4.

Help this year from: Miss C Gammon, R C Vincent, Charles Bardswell, Jenny and Michael Back, Sheila and Brian Wilson, Mrs E Stratton, Alastair Campbell, Mrs R Cotgreave, Geoff Lee, John Wooll, John and Elizabeth Gwynne, Sue Demont, Tim Barrow, Bryan Hay, S G MacSwiney, Frank Cummins, John Beeken, Sue and Dominic Dunlop, David and Mary Webb, Eric Locker, Bronwen and Steve Wrigley, Peter and Pat Frogley, Margaret Drazin, G E Stait, AHNR, Sheila and Brian Wilson, A H Denman, Ian Phillips, Mrs M A Kilner, Thomas Nott, R P Berry.

NORFOLK CALENDAR

Some of these dates were provisional as we went to press.

JANUARY

1 **Norwich** Sculpture Park Winter Show – *till Sat 14* (01603) 611549

26 **Norwich** London Mime Exhibition – *till Fri 27* at the Arts Centre (01603) 662661

MARCH

2 **Norwich** Blues Festival at the Arts Centre – *till Sat 4* (01603) 662661

25 **Norwich** Complimentary Medicine Festival at St Andrew's Hall – *till Sun 26* (01943) 609454

APRIL

1 **Norwich** Sculpture Park Summer Show – *till end Oct* (01603) 611549

15 **Blickling** Country Skills and Working Craft Fair at Blickling Hall – *till Mon 17* (01263) 734711

17 **Cromer** Drama and Speech Festival (01263) 513811

28 **Norwich** Women in Music Festival at the Arts Centre – *till 1 May* (01603) 662661

MAY

9 **Cromer** Dialect Festival (01263) 513811

27 **Felbrigg** Coast and Countryside Fair at Felbrigg Hall – *till Mon 29* (01263) 734711

NORFOLK CALENDAR

MAYcont

28 **Felbrigg** Folk Music Festival at Felbrigg Hall (01263) 734711

JUNE

10 **Hunstanton** and District Festival of Arts – *till Sun 18* (01485) 532722

24 **Blickling** Open-Air Concert at Blickling Hall – *till Sun 25* (01263) 734711

28 **Norwich** Royal Norfolk Show at the Showground – *till Thurs 29* (01603) 748931

30 **Sandringham** Country Weekend and Horse Driving Trials – *till 2 July* (01733) 234451

JULY

7 **Felbrigg** Music Weekend at Felbrigg Hall – *till Sun 9* (01263) 734711; **North Walsham** Carnival (01263) 513811

8 **Norwich** Lord Mayor's Street Procession (01603) 662661

15 **King's Lynn** Festival – *till Sat 29* (01553) 773578

16 **Holt** Carnival – *till Sun 23* (01263) 513811

22 **Wells-next-the-Sea** Holkham Country Fair at Holkham Park – *till Sun 23* (01328) 830367

28 **Worstead** Festival – *till Sun 30* (01603) 662661

29 **Cromer** Cricket Week – *till 6 Aug* (01263) 513811; **Wells-next-the Sea** Carnival Week – *till 6 Aug* (01263) 513811

AUGUST

2 **Sheringham** Carnival Day (01263) 513811

3 **Blickling** Family Garden Party at Blickling Hall (01263) 734711

5 **Felbrigg** Vintage Transport and Classic Car Rally at Felbrigg Hall – *till Sun 6* (01263) 734711

6 **Mundesley** Festival – *till Sat 12* (01263) 513811

10 **Oxborough** Children's Fun Festival at Oxburgh Hall – *till Fri 11* (01263) 734711

12 **Cromer** Carnival Week – *till Fri 18* (01263) 513811

18 **Blickling** Fireworks and Laser Concert at Blickling Hall – *till Sat 19* (01625) 575681; **Felbrigg** Woodland Open Day at Felbrigg Hall (01263) 734711

28 **Aylsham** Show (01263) 732432; **Sandringham** Craft Fair

SEPTEMBER

9 **Aldborough** Village Show – *till Sun 10* (01263) 513811

10 **Norwich** Town and Country at the Showground (01603) 748931

OCTOBER

5 **Norwich** Norfolk and Norwich Festival – *till Sun 15* (01603) 764764

18 **Thursford** Christmas Show (01263) 513811

23 **Norwich** CAMRA Beer Festival at St Andrew's Hall (01603) 662661

25 **Felbrigg** Woodland Open Day at Felbrigg Hall (01263) 734711

DECEMBER

6 **North Holt** Christmas Festival (01263) 513811

25 **Hunstanton** Christmas Day Fun

NORTHUMBRIA
(DURHAM, NORTHUMBERLAND, CLEVELAND, TYNE & WEAR)

Durham is one of England's best four or five cities for a short stay. The countryside includes, in the Northumberland National Park, a tremendous spread of largely unspoilt scenery, quiet and uncrowded even in summer, embracing the rolling grassy uplands of the Cheviot Hills, miles of monotonous conifers in Kielder Forest, and Hadrian's Wall, Britain's largest Roman monument – but few other sights or facilities for visitors. People up here are among Britain's friendliest, prices are low, and the area is very good both for walking and for driving (there is less traffic than elsewhere in England).

Teesdale in County Durham and North Tynedale in Northumberland have the best of the countryside, but other areas here share the same basic qualities of interesting scenery enlivened by streams, high moorland, solid stone buildings, unhurried small market towns, and peaceful unspoilt landscapes. There is a long, mainly low-lying coastline (outside the National Park); away from industrial Tyneside it has some fine solitary places and ruined castles.

There are fewer sights to visit here than in many other areas, but they are well worth tracking down. The Beamish open-air museum is outstanding.

May and June are the most attractive months, with long days of generally dry weather. September can be delightful, but autumn tends to set in quite fiercely in October, and winter is bleak.

NORTH AND EAST NORTHUMBERLAND

Very good value for a quiet break: grand, lonely countryside and coast, lots of interesting castles, some other places well worth visiting; Newcastle well worth a short visit.

This section includes Tyneside; Hadrian's Wall and Kielder Water are discussed separately in the next. The country areas here are rich in fine landscapes and seascapes, with many classic castles, ruined or inhabited – Bamburgh, Warkworth, Lindisfarne on Holy Island, Chillingham (with its ancient white cattle) and Alnwick prime among them. The magnificent Cragside at Rothbury, the villages of Ford and Etal linked by their little narrow-gauge railway, and Bede's World at Jarrow (developing well as an interpretation of Anglo-Saxon life here), are also worth a visit.

The local authority museums, especially in Newcastle, are very go-ahead, with lots of appeal for families; the new children's gallery at the Laing Art Gallery in Newcastle, and Newcastle Discovery, are fine examples of this family approach. Hartlepool is currently making great strides towards being an interesting place to visit. The best of the countryside is up in the empty Cheviots, though plenty of other parts are rewarding; the rocky sandy coast has many lovely stretches, but its hinterland is less interesting. Newcastle has lots of things to see and a great deal of character – good for day visits (preferably on a weekend so as to avoid the traffic).

Where to stay

Cornhill-on-Tweed NT8639 TILLMOUTH PARK, Cornhill-on-Tweed TD12 4UU (01890) 882255 £95; 13 spacious, pretty rms with period furniture. Solid, stone-built country house in 15 acres of parkland (fishing on the River Till); with comfortable, relaxing lounges, open fires, a galleried hall, and good food in the bistro or restaurant; dogs welcome.

Belford NU1033 BLUE BELL, Belford NE70 7NE (01668) 213543 £80; 17 comfortable rms. Pleasantly old-fashioned dining room overlooking an attractive garden, a comfortable and relaxing lounge, family bar in former stables, plentiful bar food, and polite, friendly service; disabled access.

Warkworth NU2506 WARKWORTH COUNTRY HOUSE Warkworth, Morpeth NE65 0XB (01665) 711276 £72.50; 14 comfortably furnished rms. Warmly welcoming 16th-c hotel with a comfortable lounge, a bar with real ales, and interesting *objets d'art* and paintings; very good food inc excellent breakfasts, and quick, efficient service; disabled access.

Longframlington NU1301 EMBLETON HALL Longframlington, Morpeth NE65 8DT (01665) 570249 £69.95; 10 comfortable, pretty and individually decorated rms. Charming hotel in lovely grounds and surrounded by fine countryside, with a particularly friendly, relaxed atmosphere, and courteous staff; neat little bar, an elegant lounge, log fires, excellent-value bar meals, and very good food in the attractive dining room.

Bamburgh NU1835 LORD CREWE ARMS, Bamburgh NE69 7BL (0166 84) 243 £62; 25 comfortable rms, most with own bthrm. Relaxing and comfortable old inn, beautifully placed in a charming coastal village below the magnificent Norman castle; with entertaining bric-a-brac and a log fire in the back bar, and good food under the new French chef; cl 4 Jan–15 Mar; children over 5.

Seahouses NU2232 OLDE SHIP Main St, Seahouses NE68 7RD (01665) 720200 £62; 12 rms. Thriving harbourside inn, full of nautical items and fishing memorabilia, popular bar food and good service; ideal for coastal walks; looks out towards the Farne Islands (boat trips bookable in harbour); cl Dec–Jan; no children.

Wylam NZ1265 LABURNAM HOUSE, Wylam NE41 8AJ (01661) 852185 £50; 4 comfortable rms. Attractive 18th-c house-cum-restaurant with pretty furnishings, generous helpings of unfailingly good, modern French cooking (the fish is recommended), and unobtrusive service.

Chatton NU0628 PERCY ARMS Chatton, Alnwick NE66 5PS (0166 85) 244 £40; 7 rms. Partly creeper-covered stone inn with a neatly kept, comfortable and spacious bar, an open fire, and good-value food inc very tasty fresh fish; 12 miles of private fishing for residents; sauna, solarium, keep-fit facilities.

Edlingham NU1109 LUMBYLAW FARM Edlingham, Alnwick NE66 2BW (01665) 574277 £33; 3 rms, one with shower. Peacefully set working farm on 350 acres with sheep and South Devon cattle, and marvellous views; warm welcome and good breakfasts; no smoking or pets; self-catering also available; cl Oct–Apr.

Newton-by-the-Sea NU2426 JOINERS ARMS Newton-by-the-Sea, Alnwick NE66 3EA (01665) 576645 £30; 5 rms, shared bthrm. In easy walking distance of the best two beaches in Northumberland, and very much the village focal point, this popular inn offers good food inc fresh fish in both the bar and lounge/restaurant, and has welcoming staff; cl wkdy lunchtimes Nov–Mar.

To see and do

★ 🏛 🔲 🛎 🏠 **Alnwick** NU1813 Busy town at the heart of prosperous farming country, with some attractive old streets nr its market square. ALNWICK CASTLE The 'Windsor of the North' dates back to the 11th c, and is the second largest inhabited castle in the country. Stone soldiers perched on the battlements seem to stand guard, but once inside all is Italian Rennaissance grandeur, with a magnificent art collection taking in works by Titian, Van Dyck and Canaletto, and an outstanding Claude. Some of the rooms are quite breathtaking. Also has a famous collection of Meissen china, regimental museum, and Roman remains. Shop; cl Nov–Easter; (01665) 510777; *£4. The hillside CHURCH of St Michael and All Angels, above the river, is a perfect example of a complete, late Gothic building. The Market Tavern has bargain food.

🏛 ★ 🛎 † **Bamburgh** NU1835 BAMBURGH CASTLE Huge, square, Norman castle on a mighty cliff, its clock serving as timekeeper for the cricket green in the attractive village below. Despite the forbidding exterior, the inside is very much a lived-in stately home, with armour from the Tower of London. Snacks, shop; cl am, Nov–Apr; (016684) 208; £2.50. GRACE DARLING MUSEUM Pictures, documents and other reminders of the local heroine, inc the boat in which Grace and her father rescued nine survivors from the wrecked SS *Forfarshire*. Shop, disabled access; cl Oct–Easter; free (donations to RNLI). There's a neo-Gothic shrine to Grace in the yard of the interesting 13th-c CHURCH. The Lord Crewe Arms is well placed for lunch.

🏛 🏛 ❀ **Belsay** NZ1079 BELSAY HALL, CASTLE AND GARDENS The same family have lived here for nearly 600 years, first in a medieval castle, then a Jacobean manor house and finally a grand mansion designed to look like a Greek classical temple – all can still be seen. The 30 acres of landscaped parkland are especially pleasant, with a rhododendron garden, formal terraces, and woodland walks. Snacks, shop, disabled access; cl winter Mon, 25–26 Dec, 1 Jan; (01661) 881043; £2.40. The Highlander has reasonably priced food.

★ 🏛 † 🛎 🕸 **Berwick-upon-Tweed** NT9953 is largely unspoilt, with some handsome 18th-c buildings and a fine 17th-c church; most people who come here seem to while away at least a bit of time watching the swans on the River Tweed. Alternatively, look out over the sea from the Rob Roy (Spittal Rd), which has good local fish. The town walls, partly grassed over and easy to walk round, were a masterpiece of 16th-c military planning. BERWICK BARRACKS (The Parade) Britain's oldest surviving, purpose-built barracks, built in the early 18th c (the design attributed to Vanbrugh), now a local history museum and gallery, with an interesting exhibition on the British soldier. Snacks, shop, disabled access; cl winter Mon and Tues, 24–26 Dec, 1 Jan; (01289) 330044; £2.20. WINE AND SPIRIT MUSEUM (Palace Green) The mainland base of Lindisfarne mead-makers (see St Aidan's Winery listed under Lindisfarne entry below), with a collection of objects from the wine and spirit industries, traditional working potter, home-made pot-pourri, and a Victorian chemist' shop. Snacks, shop, disabled access; cl Sun and 24 Dec–5 Jan; free.

🏛 ❀ 🔩 **Cambo** NZ0285 WALLINGTON HOUSE Built in 1688 and altered in the 1740s, with fine plasterwork and porcelain, and works by the pre-Raphaelite circle often found here in the house's 19th-c cultural glory days. Outside are 100 acres of lawns, terraces, lakes and woodland, with showpiece fuchsias in the conservatory. Meals and snacks, shop and plant centre, disabled facilities; house cl am, all Tues, and Nov–May, grounds and garden open all year; house, walled garden and grounds £4.40, grounds only £2.20; NT.

🏛 ❀ ✔ 🏠 ❀ **Chillingham** NU0525 CHILLINGHAM CASTLE Striking old castle dating back to the 12th c, full of antiques, tapestries, arms and armour. Formal gardens, woodland walks, lake, and splendid views of the surrounding countryside; occasional concerts and special events. Brave souls can rent one of their haunted rooms. Snacks, shop, some disabled access; cl am, Tues, and Oct–Apr; (016685) 359; £3.30. CHILLINGHAM WILD CATTLE PARK The famous, large-horned white cattle have been here for the last 700 years, the only animals of their kind still pure and uncrossed with domestic breeds. As they're potentially aggressive, tours are conducted by a warden, and binoculars are recommended for a closer view. Shop; cl 12–2pm, am Sun, all Tues, and Nov–Mar; (01668) 5250; *£2.50. Above the park is Ross Castle HILL FORT NU0825, with great views. The Percy Arms at Chatton is good for lunch.

Embleton NU2322 DUNSTANBURGH CASTLE A favourite spot with artists (Turner painted it three times), these huge ruins stand imposingly on the cliff above the North Sea, with screeching seagulls adding much to the atmosphere. Cl 24–26 Dec, 1 Jan and Mon Oct–Mar; £1.20; NT. The NT also owns much of this stretch of coastline, inc the pleasantly bracing walk to the Jolly Fisherman pub at Craster.

★ ☆ ☜ ✗ ☷ ☳ **Ford** NT9437 was built as a model estate-workers' village, for Ford Castle; very attractive, with one or two craft workshops. HEATHERSLAW LIGHT RAILWAY Steam or diesel journeys on a narrow-gauge railway along the pretty valley of the River Till up to Etal. Snacks, shop, disabled access; cl wkdys Nov–Christmas, all Jan–Easter, (01890) 820244 for times; *£2.95. HEATHERSLAW CORN MILL Well restored, 19th-c, water-driven double corn mill, with displays and demonstrations. Snacks, shop, some disabled access; open daily Easter–Oct, then wknds in Nov, Feb and Mar; (01890) 820338; £1.50. Flour from here is used at the HEATHERSLAW BAKERY where on some days there may be free samples of the resulting cakes and biscuits; (01890) 820208. **Etal** NT9339, close by, is a

pretty row of white cottages running down to a ford across the river, with a working forge, and an attractive, thatched pub – the Black Bull. ETAL CASTLE Evocative ruins of a 14th-c fortress, with very good walkman tours and a new exhibition on Border history. Shop, disabled access to exhibition area; cl Nov–Mar; £2. You can hire bikes: tel (01890) 820527.

✝ ☷ ☛ **Jarrow** NZ3065 ST PAUL'S CHURCH AND MONASTERY The Venerable Bede lived here for most of his life, producing the 37 books that encompass much of what is now known of life in early Christian England. Along with the other half of the monastery, St Peter's, at nearby Monkwearmouth (see entry below), the site is still a major Christian shrine; in medieval times pilgrims took bits off Bede's chair and put them in water, which they then drank to cure their ills. Very little remains of the original monastery, but there's Saxon stained glass in the church, and the chancel incorporates one of the earlier chapels. A good museum in the adjacent Georgian Jarrow Hall has a collection of finely carved Anglo-Saxon stones, more stained glass, and various excavated relics. The whole site is now known as BEDE'S WORLD, and is developing rather rapidly – several lively new displays are due to open this year, and the creation of an authentic, 11-acre, period farm is well under way. Meals, snacks, shop, some disabled access; cl am Sun, all Mon (exc bank hols), Christmas wk; (0191) 489 2106; *£3.

❋ ✝ ☷ ❀ ☛ ☳ **Lindisfarne** NU1413 is another important centre for Christian pilgrims. Otherwise known as Holy Island, it's linked to the mainland by a causeway which you can drive over at low tide; tide tables are posted at each end – or tel (01289) 89200. There are nature-reserve dunes, a restored tide-mill, fishermen's huts made of upturned former boats, old limekilns, a small extended village with tourist cafés and pubs, and good views from the close-grazed, grassy crags. The main draw is LINDISFARNE PRIORY, from where in the 7th c St Aidan and monks from Iona replanted the seeds of Christianity in

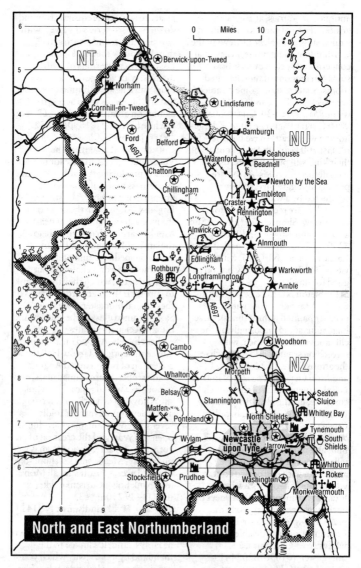

North and East Northumberland

Dark Age England. These early monks were driven out by Vikings but the priory was re-established in the 12th c, and it's the extensive remains of this foundation you can see today – a very peaceful and romantic spot, with graceful, red sandstone arches bordered by perhaps incongruously neat lawns. The visitor centre has vivid displays. Shop, disabled access to visitor centre; cl 24–26 Dec, 1 Jan; (01289) 89200; £2.20. LINDISFARNE CASTLE The rather lonely and austere exterior belies what's within; the 16th-c fortress was restored by Lutyens for the editor of *Country Life* in a suitably monolithic, quasi-medieval style. Sumptuous furnishings include a fine collection of antique oak furniture, and there's a walled garden designed by Gertrude Jekyll to protect against the North Sea winds. Cl am, Fri (exc Good Fri), and Nov–Mar; £3.40; NT. St Aidan's Winery Home of Lindisfarne Mead, a fortified wine made from grapes, honey, herbs and water from an island well. They make honey too, and the craft shop has a range of local pottery and jewellery. You can sample the mead, apparently a traditional aphrodisiac. Cl winter wknds, 23 Dec–1 Jan, and occasional wknds; (01289) 89230; free. The Lindisfarne Hotel is good for more conventional refreshment.

✝ **Longframlington** NU1201 Brinkburn Priory Well preserved 12th-c church (thanks to some Victorian restoration), still with medieval grave slabs, font and double piscina. Occasional services and concerts. Shop; cl 1–2 pm, and Oct–Mar; (01665) 570628; £1.25. The Granby is useful for lunch.

✝ 🐾 **Monkwearmouth** NZ4058 St Peter's church Sister church of St Paul's at Jarrow, its early years equally well documented by the Venerable Bede. Much of the original Saxon church still remains, inc the W wall and tower, and there's a little exhibition. Just outside is a striking sculpture by Colin Wilbourn commemorating the church's 7th-c founder, Benedict Biscop. Monkwearmouth Station has a railway museum, with as well as trains the chance to learn to drive a bus. Cl Mon, am Sun, Christmas; free. N of here (on the A183 towards South Shields) the Grotto at Marsden is unique: a lift down to a pub cut into the seaside cliffs.

♂ **Morpeth** NZ2086 Morpeth Chantry Bagpipe Museum Harmonious collection of small pipes and bagpipes from around the world. Headphoned sound displays explain the difference between a rant and a reel. Shop; cl lunchtime, all Sun and bank hols; (01670) 519466; £1. The Tap & Spile, open all day, has good-value food.

✝ 🏰 ☼ ♂ ! 🔲 🎠 ☺ **Newcastle upon Tyne** NZ2464 This big industrial conurbation is far from being conventionally pretty, but has a strong, vibrant atmosphere. An hour or two is ample for exploring its best parts, as they are grouped very compactly high above the River Tyne with its three great bridges – particularly what has become almost the city's trademark, the two-decker High Level Bridge for road and rail designed by Robert Stephenson in the 1840s. The famous metro system makes it quick and straightforward to get around here, or for example to the attractions noted under North and South Shields, Tynemouth and Whitley Bay; a one-day Rover ticket (available from the tourist information centre) costs £3. The 14th/15th-c Anglican cathedral is worth a look. A lot still remains of the Norman castle that gives the city its name, though it's a little spoiled by the main railway line which cuts the gatehouse off from the keep. Cl Mon, Christmas; *£1. You can trace some stretches of the medieval city wall (especially from St Andrew's Church along the cobbled lane W of Stowell St – Chinese restaurants around here – and past the Heber Tower along Bath Lane). You can get a good bird's-eye view of the centre's lofty Victorian terraces from the top of Grey's Monument; a steep climb, Sat only. It's at the head of Grey St, which like Eldon Sq is a fine, early 19th-c contribution to the townscape. Fitzgeralds down the street is useful for a bite to eat. Steep alleys and steps lead from the centre down to The Quay, the oldest part of the town, with several unexpected and quaintly attractive, timber-framed medieval buildings; one of the oldest, the Cooperage, is a good pub. Downstream, E of the 1920s Tyne Bridge, an area of recently refurbished, 19th-c wharf buildings is also enjoyable to walk through, with crafts and a bric-a-brac market on Sun, and a useful pub for food – the Baltic Tavern. Newcastle Discovery (Blandford Sq), formerly the Museum of Science and Engineering, is a wonderfully quirky and enjoyable, interactive museum, with a very good section on the history of the city. The Science Factory goes down well with children. As we went to press they were adding new galleries on fashion, photography, and life in the armed forces, and some displays from the John George Joicey Museum (curently closed) are likely to move here. Snacks, shop, disabled access; cl Sun, Good Fri, 25–26 Dec, 1 Jan; (0191) 222 1222; free.

HANCOCK MUSEUM (Barras Bridge) Very good natural history museum, with magnificent collections of stuffed birds and mammals. Exhibitions planned for 1995 include the Creepy Crawly Roadshow looking at insects and spiders (Feb–Jun), and Megabugs, showing off the biggest moving insects in the world (July–Oct); an exhibition on cats finishes at the end of Feb. Lively events and activities for children – best to check first what's going on. Meals, snacks, shop, disabled access; cl am Sun, 25–26 Dec, 1 Jan, Good Fri; (0191) 222 7418; £1.80. LAING ART GALLERY (Higham Pl) is a good one, with an unusual new children's gallery, where play areas and activities are specially designed to encourage children up to 8 to think about shapes, texture and patterns. Cl 25–26 Dec, 1 Jan, Good Fri; (0191) 232 7734; free. MUSEUM OF ANTIQUITIES (the University) Major collection of ancient relics from NE England, particularly strong on Roman remains. Shop, disabled access by arrangement; cl Sun, Good Fri, 24–26 Dec, 1 Jan; (0191) 222 7844; free. Besides the pubs mentioned above, the Bridge Hotel (Castle Sq), Crown Posada (The Side, off Dean St), Duke of Wellington (High Bridge) and the recently converted Off Shore (Quayside) are all pleasantly civilised.

On the S side of the Tyne, Gateshead's METRO CENTRE (A1, just W) is a useful family place for a rainy day. It's a massive modern shopping and leisure complex with several different, themed undercover areas, inc all sorts of fairground attractions, and the Spitting Image hall of fame; do remember exactly where you put your car – there are 12,000 parking spaces. If you're in this area the SHIPLEY ART GALLERY (Prince Consort Rd) is worth a look (cl Mon and Christmas).

🏰 **Norham** NT9048 CASTLE Formidable remains of a 12th-c border fortress on a steep, sheep-terraced grassy mound. It was the locale for Scott's *Marmion*; some disabled access; free.

🚌🚂✿ **North Shields** NZ3468 has steamtrain trips at the STEPHENSON RAILWAY MUSEUM (Middle Engine Lane) (open wknds and bank hols), and the FISHING EXPERIENCE CENTRE (Fish Quay) exploring the underwater world of the North Sea, from the point of view of both fishermen and fish – good fun. Snacks, shop, disabled access; cl Mon and Tues and Nov–Mar; £2.10. The Wooden Doll (Hudson St) is a decent pub with memorable Tyne views.

✤🏡🍎 **Ponteland** NZ1773 KIRKLEY HALL GARDENS Attractive and thoughtfully maintained, with a big collection of herbaceous perennials, Victorian walled garden, pretty sunken garden, woodland garden and lots of unusual trees and shrubs. Snacks, FARM SHOP with PICK-YOUR-OWN; £1.50. The Blackbird is useful for lunch.

🏰 **Prudhoe** NZ0962 PRUDHOE CASTLE 12th–14th-c ruined castle on an impressive mound (the name means 'proud hill') overlooking the Tyne, once the stronghold of the powerful Percy family. Remarkable restored gatehouse, and an exhibition in a nearby 19th-c manor house. Snacks, shop, disabled access; (01661) 833459; cl 1–2pm, Nov–Easter; £1.80. The Feathers at Hedley on the Hill does good weekend food; on weekdays the Crown & Anchor at Horsley is useful.

✝ **Roker** NZ4159 has an interesting CHURCH designed by leading members of the Arts and Crafts movement at the turn of the century.

🏘✤ **Rothbury** NU0602 CRAGSIDE Opulent Victorian mansion of Lord Armstrong, the armaments king, with some spectacularly grand rooms. Best of all are the miles of landscaped, well wooded grounds, with lakes, glorious rhododendrons, showy formal garden, and a walk illustrating the various elements of the hydroelectric scheme he devised to light the house. Meals, snacks, shop, disabled access (inc fishing pier on a trout lake); cl Mon exc bank hols, and Nov–Mar (though garden, grounds and visitor centre open Tues, Sat and Sun Nov and Dec); £5.50, £3.40 grounds only; NT. The splendidly placed Angler's Arms has good food.

⚓ Seahouses NU2232 has a busy fishing harbour, overlooked by a good interesting pub, the Olde Ship. From here there are boat trips around the FARNE ISLANDS so you can see their eider ducks, thousands of other seabirds, and grey seals – breeding from the end of summer into autumn, with the plaintive-voiced pups staying on shore for only a few weeks. In fine weather, landing may be possible on the Inner Farne, which has a lighthouse and 14th-c chapel, with a small exhibition about the islands in a former chapel beside it.

🏠 † Seaton Sluice NZ3477 SEATON DELAVAL Vanbrugh's Palladian masterpiece, a splendid design of central porticoed main block and massive outer wings. Not all the interior has survived unscathed, and much of the original park and grounds has been submerged by surrounding developments. Open pm Weds, Sun and bank hols, May–Sept; (0191) 237 3040; *£2. The buildings around the Norman CHURCH are attractive. Down near the front, the Waterford Arms has excellent fresh fish.

🏠 🥄 South Shields NZ3567 In the 2nd c ARBEIA ROMAN FORT played a crucial role in the campaign against the Scots. Huge variety of remains, recreated scenes of camp life, and a museum with excellently displayed finds. Snacks, shop, disabled access; cl, Christmas, Mon (exc bank hols), and Sun exc summer pm; (0191) 456 1369; free. Just round the corner the MUSEUM AND ART GALLERY has some good hands-on exhibitions, especially in the new land, river and sea gallery. Cl Mon and am Sun, Christmas; free. The Harbour Lights (Beacon St), nr the river mouth, has good-value food, and the Marsden Rattler (South Foreshore) is an enjoyable seafront bar complete with two original railway carriages.

🏠 � 🌸 Stocksfield NZ0661 CHERRYBURN (Mickley) Well preserved 18th-c farm, the birthplace of artist, engraver and naturalist Thomas Bewick, with an exhibition on his life and work. A nice spot, with farm animals running about the yard (they have various rare breeds), craft demonstrations, and good valley views. Shop, some disabled access; cl am, all Tues and Weds, and Nov–Mar; *£2.50; NT.

🏰 🥄 Tynemouth NZ3669 CASTLE AND PRIORY Evocative clifftop ruins, high above the Tyne estuary. The 11th-c Benedictine priory was once one of the richest in England but little now remains beyond its stirring nave and chancel, and the spooky gravestones outside. Even less is left of the 11th- and 14th-c castle. It's unusual to find two such ruins next to each other, and it's a great spot for picnics. Shop, disabled access; cl winter Mon and Tues, 24–26 Dec, 1 Jan; (0191) 257 1090; £1.25. SEA LIFE CENTRE The same reliable mixture as at their other centres, with a spectacular underwater tunnel surrounded by gallons of water populated by sharks and other creatures. Snacks, shop, disabled access; cl 25 Dec; £4.25. Fitzpatricks (Front St) is comfortable for lunch.

★ 🏰 † Warkworth NU2403 is a quietly picturesque small town. The main street rises attractively from the Norman church by the river to the striking CASTLE on its hill above the River Coquet. It's virtually complete, so it is wonderfully atmospheric wandering round the crooked passageways and dark staircases. Very much the sort of place where you imagine dark deeds afoot, and, sure enough, sneaky plots were once hatched here by Harry Hotspur – events immortalised in Shakespeare's *Henry IV*. Shop; cl 24–26 Dec, 1 Jan; (01665) 711423; £1.80. There's a pleasant riverside path upstream to the WARKWORTH HERMITAGE, a cell of retreat cut into the sandstone cliff in the 14th c, with some crude wall carvings and a tiny vaulted chapel. A rowing boat can take you across to it on summer wknds (Apr–Sept); 80p. In the town, the Warkworth Country House Hotel, Hermitage and Mason's Arms are all useful for lunch, and there are one or two antique shops.

The 12th-c CHURCH has a finely vaulted chancel. In the other direction, this stretch of sea coast has some lovely beaches.

🏠⚓🏴 **Washington** NZ3156 is an unspoilt old village that comes as a real surprise when you've penetrated the surrounding new town. WASHINGTON OLD HALL Well restored, stone-built, 13th-c manor, for several hundred years the home of George Washington's family, though his ancestors had been established elsewhere (notably Sulgrave Manor in Northants) for quite a while by the time he was born. Rooms are laid out in 17th- and 18th-c style, and they're in the process of recreating a Jacobean formal garden. Snacks, shop; cl Fri and Sat, all Oct–Apr; (0191) 416 6879; £2.20; NT. The nearby Washington Arms is good value for lunch, and there's a MINING MUSEUM down Albany Way. Just E of Washington at District 15, the 100-acre WILDFOWL AND WETLANDS CENTRE has hides, walks and a good visitor centre. Lots of the birds will feed from your hand. Snacks, shop, disabled access; cl 24–25 Dec; (0191) 416 5454; £3.40.

🏠 **Whitburn** NZ4262 SOUTER LIGHTHOUSE When built in 1870 this was the most advanced lighthouse of the day, and the first to be powered by electricity. You can still see the period rooms and equipment. Meals, snacks, shop, disabled access (but not to tower); cl Mon (exc bank hols), Nov–Mar; £2.30; NT. The Trust also own the Leas, the spectacular stretch of coastline around here, leading to Marsden Rock with its colony of kittiwakes, cormorants and fulmars. The Jolly Sailor has decent food.

🏠 **Whitley Bay** NZ3572 ST MARY'S LIGHTHOUSE is actually out on St Mary's Island, reached by a causeway at low tide. It's said that every exiled Geordie has a picture of it. Shop; adjacent café; cl wkdys Nov–May, and possibly other times depending on the tide; (0191) 252 0853; £1.50. When the lighthouse is closed the island is worth a visit for the rockpools alone, and is visited all through the year by a wide range of birds. Back in Whitley Bay, the Delaval Arms has good home cooking.

⚓🏠⚓✝🏴 **Woodhorn** NZ3088 WOODHORN COLLIERY MUSEUM Former colliery buildings recreating life in the pit and the communities around it, with the help of life-size models, working machinery and sound effects. Display of art by local miners, craft workshops and woodland walks. Meals, snacks, shop; cl Mon, Tues, Christmas; (01670) 856968; free. The partly Saxon and Norman WOODHORN CHURCH close by is said to be the oldest on this coast; it has a local history museum and weekend craft demonstrations. Shop, disabled access; cl 12.30–1pm, Mon, Tues, Christmas; free.

★ A number of attractive **coastal villages** and towns dotted along this underpopulated coast include Amble NU2704 (solid old fishing harbour, new yacht marina; RSPB boat trips around nearby Coquet Island with its colourful eider ducks and puffins); Alnmouth NU2511 (attractive beaches, pleasant coastal walks, a lot for summer visitors); Beadnell NU2329 (boats on the beach, and an interestingly restored waterside limekiln) and nearby Benthall, Boulmer NU2714 (active fishing boats), Craster NU2620 (tidal fishing harbour, good kippering factory, excellent pub) and Newton-by-the-Sea NU2426 (little more than a circle of houses above the sea, and a useful little inn, with a bird reserve nearby). Inland, Matfen NZ0372 is pretty, with a riverside village green.

Walks

Rothbury Terraces NU0501 ◁-1, nr Rothbury itself, and **Hulme Park** NU1414 ◁-2, just out of Alnwick's centre, are both excellent for parkland walks; in the latter, don't miss the whimsical Brizles Tower and hermit's cave.

The Northumberland coast has much of interest along its sandy and rocky shores, but the hinterland is rather dull, so it's better for pottering and for there-and-back walks than for round ones. A coastal path covers the finest sections, which include Craster NU2620 to **Dunstanburgh Castle** NU2521 ⌂-3, and the windswept solitude of **Ross Back Sands** NU1437 ⌂-4. These overlook **Holy Island** NU1413 ⌂-5, which itself has an easy but fascinating 3-mile walk around its shores.

The Cheviots, part of the Northumberland National Park, are strikingly empty and solitary, with only the characteristic local breed of hardy sheep for company in most places. The Pennine Way's penultimate stages take a long, lonely plod over the grassy moors, inc a fine, high ridge section along the English/Scottish border past the 2,036-ft summit of **Windy Gyle** NT8515 ⌂-6. You have to walk some way from the road to attain this main ridge: start from Coquetdale NT8511 and walk along the Street, an ancient drovers' track. Gradients are mild but the peaty ground can get boggy after rain; not all routes are defined on the ground, but stone boundary walls and forest plantations are useful guides. **Clennel Street** ⌂-7, another drove road leading from Coquetdale, can be followed from nr Alwinton NT9206, and offers much the same sort of scenery; there's a pretty way back, along a track by the River Alwin.

A stiff walk up the Pennine Way through the **Redesdale Forest** ⌂-8 above Byrness NT7602 takes you to the spectacular earthworks of the little-visited Chew Green Roman camps NT7808, surrounded by wild country. The Pennines up here contain a great many more unspoilt prehistoric and other archaeological remains, many of them reached only by quite a long walk. This does set goals for walkers in these magnificent hills, which often reward with remarkable views. Ordnance Survey large-scale maps show their position; Sheets 74 and 75 of the *Landranger* series are the most useful. Some areas N of the A68 and W of the B6341 may temporarily be put out of bounds by Army training, and in early 1995 the Army is expected to propose an increase in its use of this area.

Berwick-upon-Tweed NT9953 ⌂-9 has an extraordinary trio of bridges, and deserves to be approached along the Tweed: there are paths on both banks, starting from the East Ord picnic site by the A1 road bridge. The town ramparts, impressively intact, give good views. Industrial Tyneside provides a few reasonable coastal walks, inc **Marsden Bay** nature reserve NZ4065 ⌂-10 near South Shields.

Driving

Once clear of Tyneside, the traffic generally thins out a lot, so that getting to any of the places we've mentioned as worth visiting will normally be part of the pleasure.

The most attractive drive in the whole area is along Coquetdale, on the B6344 through Rothbury, the B6341 to Swindon, and then on through Holystone, Harbottle and Alwinton. If you want you can keep right on to the end, along the increasingly desolate road to Blindburn.

In the Cheviots, scenic roads tend to be dead ends – there is no road going up over the Cheviot ridge.

Where to eat

Whalton NZ1382 BERESFORD ARMS (01670) 75225 A wide choice of good, waitress-served food in a pleasant bar or dining room; attractive village; cl winter pm Sun. £21.50|£3.95|£4.95.

Matfen NZ0372 BLACK BULL (01661) 886330 Striking, creeper-covered, stone building by the green, with a wide choice of generously served, interesting food in an extended, Turkey-carpeted and pleasant restaurant; efficient service; disabled access. £19|£2.50|£4.50.

Stannington NZ2279 RIDLEY ARMS (01670) 789216 Spacious, open-plan bars with cosy furnishings, a quiet lounge, and particularly good food in the sepa-rate restaurant and pleasant bar; excellent A1 stop-off. **£17|£2.20/£4.75**.

Rennington NU2118 MASONS ARMS (01665) 577275 Friendly pub with a wide choice of generously served bar food (fine puddings); also, a comfortable lounge bar, cheery licensees, and decent breakfasts; bedrooms. **£15|£1.95/£5.95**.

Warenford NU1429 WARENFORD LODGE (01668) 213453 Old, very individual, though rather modern feeling pub with stripped stonework and a big stone fire-place; serves really good, attractively presented, imaginative food and decent wines; children only in the evening dining room; disabled access. **£14|£3/£7**.

Seaton Sluice NZ3477 WATERFORD ARMS (0191) 237 0450 Comfortably mod-ernised pub with generous helpings of excellent food – their fish comes fresh from the harbour just down the road. **£13.75|£2.25/£8.50**.

HADRIAN'S WALL, TYNEDALE AND KIELDER WATER

Hadrian's Wall is a must-see; lovely, unspoilt countryside, especially in the North Tyne valley.

The chief charm of this area is its countryside, with the great Roman wall as an interesting bonus – indeed a fascinating one, if you've not seen it before. In high summer, the wall, a favourite walk, does get swarms of visitors, but even then its sheer length means that away from the excavated fortresses it's never crowded. At other times of year you can often look along great stretches without seeing anyone else.

The North Tyne valley has some extremely relaxing and fulfilling scenery (and good fishing), and would be ideal for a quiet weekend. But all the places to stay that we recommend in this area put you within easy reach of open spaces and high moors. There is a scattering of places with decent food.

There are very few places to visit here apart from the Roman wall and things associated with it, and the attractive recreational area around Kielder Water behind the Kielder Forest's leagues of conifer plantations. In summer, the evenings here are long; one tip is to stay away from water then, unless you're midge-proof.

Where to stay

Chollerford NY9372 GEORGE Chollerford, Hexham NE46 4EW (01434) 681611 **£105**; 48 well equipped rms. Quiet hotel with fine gardens sloping down to the river, and a 17th-c bridge over the North Tyne visible from the can-dlelit restaurant; thoughtful, attentive service; swimming pool; disabled access.

Tarset NY7985 EARLS LODGE Tarset, Hexham NE48 1LF (01434) 240269 **£50**; 4 rms. Licensed guesthouse (used to be a pub) with health-conscious food, and set in attractive surrounding scenery – three mountain bikes for res-idents' use (free of charge); cl 25 Dec; no children.

Slaley NY9858 ROSE & CROWN Slaley, Hexham NE47 0AA (01434) 673263 ***£39**; 3 attractively modernised rms. Traditional village inn with mugs hang-ing from the beamed ceiling in the bar, popular food in both the bar and restaurant, and friendly service; lots to do nearby.

Haltwhistle NY7164 BROOMSHAW HILL FARM Willia Rd, Haltwhistle NE49 9NP (01434) 320866 **£32**; 2 rms, shared bthrm. Partly 18th-c farmhouse on a

5-acre livestock farm and close to Hadrian's Wall; with an attractive lounge and robust breakfasts eaten round a communal table; cl Nov–Feb.

West Woodburn NY8987 BAY HORSE West Woodburn, Hexham NE48 2RX (01434) 270218 *£32; 5 rms, shared bthrm. Pretty, welcoming, 18th-c coaching inn with a curious Roman stone in the garden which runs down to the River Rede (trout and salmon fishing); comfortable, open-plan bar with open fire, and good standard food.

The Pheasant at Stannersburn NY7286, a new main entry in our companion *Good Pub Guide*, has bedrooms and is very well placed for Kielder Water: (01434) 240382.

To see and do

Hadrian's Wall The wall amazes people first seeing it. It's extraordinary to imagine those Roman military engineers, so far from their warm homeland, building this remarkable construction in such inhospitable surroundings. Much of it runs along the natural crag of the great Whin Sills, making it that much more formidable.

With its associated forts, the wall has a lot to hold the interest, and an overall sense of grandeur that is a definite part of its appeal. The stone wall itself, with its turret watchtowers, milecastles and more sporadic forts, defines the northern side of a narrow frontier zone, bounded on its S side by a ditch between turf ramparts, with a military road running between wall and ditch. It was this whole installation rather than just the wall itself which the Romans used to control trade and cross-border travel.

We mention below some of the more striking and accessible features connected with the wall, inc the bigger behind-the-lines forts and camps. The section at Cuddys Crag NY7868 is perhaps the most beautiful of all, very photogenic and giving glorious views. In the six weeks of the school summer hols, a tourist bus can take you from Hexham to several of the main sites; check with the information centre on (01434) 605225 for times.

The best place to eat nr the wall and its main sites is the Milecastle Inn on the B6318 NE of Haltwhistle.

Bardon Mill NY7868 VINDOLANDA Started well before the wall itself, this Roman fort and frontier town soon became a base for 500 soldiers. Lots of well preserved remains, and a full-scale reconstruction of Hadrian's turf and stone wall, complete with turret and gate tower. The adjacent museum has a fascinating selection of handwritten letters and documents found on the site, inc party invitations, shopping lists and a note that could have been written by many a modern mother: 'I have sent you socks and two pairs of underpants'. Another 400 2nd-c letters have recently been discovered, adding much to historians' understanding of the period. Shop, disabled access to museum but not site; museum cl late Nov–mid-Feb; (01434) 344277; £3, less when museum cl in winter.

Carrawbrough NY8971 MITHRAIC TEMPLE Three 3rd-c altars to Mithras were found here, on the line of the Roman wall near the fort of Brocolitia. They're now in Newcastle's Museum of Antiquities, but you can see replicas in their original setting.

Chollerford NY9365 CHESTERS ROMAN FORT The best-preserved example of a Roman cavalry fort in Britain; in the bath-house you can see exactly how the underfloor heating system worked. Also a museum with sculptures and inscriptions from sites all along the wall; attractive riverside setting. Snacks, shop, disabled access; cl 24–26 Dec, 1 Jan; (01434) 681379; £2.

★ **Corbridge** NY9964 is an attractive village (or very small town) above the Tyne; the Wheatsheaf here is good for lunch. CORBRIDGE ROMAN FORT Granaries, portico columns and what may be the legionary

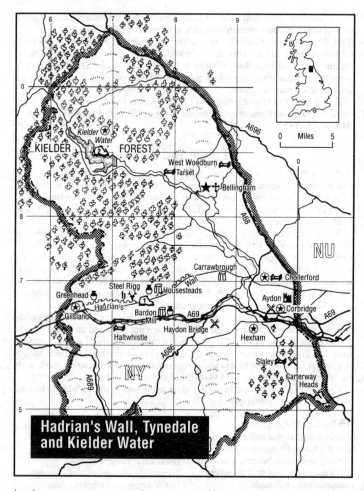

Hadrian's Wall, Tynedale and Kielder Water

headquarters survive among these 3rd-c remains. The adjacent museum has the magnificent Corbridge Lion. Shop, disabled access; cl winter Mon and Tues, 25–26 Dec, 1 Jan; £2.

🏛 ♄ ❀ **Gilsland** NY6366 Birdoswald Roman Fort Overlooking the Irthing Gorge (and in fact just over the Cumbrian border), this is one of the most impressive sites, partly because it has so many features in such a small area and partly for its grand views. Good visitor centre. Snacks, shop, some disabled access; cl Nov–Easter; £1.75.

♿ **Greenhead** NY6666 Roman Army Museum (Carvoran) Entertaining and informative intrepretation of what it

was like to be a Roman soldier, with everything you could possibly want to know about his training, pay, and off-duty hobbies. Snacks, shop, disabled access; cl mid-Nov–early Feb; (016977) 47485; £2.50.

🏛 ♿ **Housesteads** NY7969 Housesteads Roman Fort and Museum The best known and most visited section of the wall, pretty much slap bang in the middle. It owes its fine state of preservation partly to the fact that while other stretches were being used as a handy source of free, recycled, quality masonry, this fort was base camp for a powerful group of border bandits; woe betide anyone who tried to use their

fortifications as material for cowsheds or churches. You can still see the remains of all the fort's main buildings, and a museum has altars, inscriptions and models. Good walks from here, in either direction. Snacks, shop; cl 24–26 Dec, 1 Jan; (01434) 344363; £2.20.
ƕ ∀ **Steel Rigg** NY7667 ONCE BREWED

Very useful Northumberland National Park Information Centre, handy for Housesteads and Vindolanda, with exhibitions and audio-visual presentations about the wall and the park. Guided walks leave from here. Snacks, shop, disabled access; cl wkdys Nov, then all Dec–Feb; (01434) 344396; free.

Other things to see and do

🏰 **Aydon** NZ0166 has a remarkably well preserved 13th-c CASTLE in a lovely setting. Snacks, shop, some disabled access; cl Oct–Easter; (01434) 632450; *£1.80.
Blanchland NY9750 is the archetypal border village, every house looking a stronghold, alone in a great bowl of magnificent scenery. The Lord Crewe Arms here is an interesting hotel, in parts very ancient indeed.
❀ **Chollerford** SY9372 HEXHAM HERBS (nr Chesters Fort – see entry above) Over 800 varieties of herbs beautifully laid out in attractive walled gardens, inc national collections of thyme and marjoram; also old-fashioned roses, many other plants, and a woodland walk. Shop, some disabled access, plant sales; cl Nov–Feb exc by appointment; (01434) 681483; £1.
★ ☉ † **Hexham** NY9364 is the main town in the area, a pleasant market town, not too big, with some attractive stone buildings. One, the country's first purpose-built prison, now houses the BORDER HISTORY MUSEUM, colourfully charting the chequered contacts between the English and Scots over the centuries. Cl Dec and Jan; £1.30. HEXHAM ABBEY Founded around 674 by St Wilfrid, this was once the largest church N of the Alps. The bulk of what is seen today dates from the 12th c, though there are two splendid Saxon survivals – the superbly atmospheric crypt, and the throne of the bishop (St Wilfrid's Chair or Frith Stool). It's unique for the Night Stairs, down which the choir still descend for services. Summer snacks, shop, disabled access; free, but donations

welcome. The County Hotel is reliable for lunch. A little way N, WARDEN CHURCH NY6265, down a lane by the Tyne, is a fine example of the sturdy northern churches that had to do double duty as holy places and watchtowers to warn of Border raiders.
♣ ∀ 🏠 ♤ ! 🛥 **Kielder Water** NY6688 is an extremely large reservoir which has done quite a lot to open up a remote part of the Borders. It's an interesting shape, modelled by the steep folds of the land, and is already beginning to look as if it's always been tucked away in these pine-blanketed hills. A sensible first stop is the Tower Knowe VISITOR CENTRE down at the foot of the lake, with an exhibition and useful information about the area and its wildlife. They can organise what they call safaris around rarely seen parts of the area; tel (01434) 240398. CRUISES start from here too, and call all around the lake (takes about an hour and a half). LEAPLISH WATERSIDE PARK, slightly round to the W, is another good starting point, and has lots to do in summer, inc plenty of watersports, trails, and canoe and other BOAT HIRE. You can rent LOG CABINS by the week; tel (01502) 500500. Up at the top of the lake, the BAKETHIN CONSERVATION AREA is particularly rewarding for wildlife. CYCLING is fun round here – the very friendly Kielder Bikes company hire bikes from Hawkhope car park, tel (01434) 250392; a good mountain bike costs around £9 for three hours. Their main shop is in the village of **Kielder** NY6293 itself, opposite KIELDER CASTLE, an 18th-c hunting

lodge built for the Duke of Northumberland. It's now a very good Forestry Authority visitor centre with exhibitions (inc closed-circuit TV birdwatching). Shop, meals and a play area; (01434) 250209; cl Nov–Easter. Guided walks set off from here into the surrounding Kielder Forest – miles of pine trees with a good chance of seeing red squirrels, as well as deer; some nice spots for picnics. The Kielder Heavy Horse Co may do HORSE-DRAWN WAGON TRIPS: tel (01434) 250319. HIGH YARROW FARM nearby is a working farm with spring lambing, tame animals, ornamental pheasants – even free-ranging, hand-feeding reindeer. If wet the animals can be seen under cover. Some disabled access; cl Oct–Mar; (01434) 240264;

*£2. The Pheasant at Stannersburn is handy for lunch.
★ † North Tynedale is one of the least known and most unspoilt parts of Northumberland. Between the Pennines and the Cheviots, it's a peaceful river valley surrounded by wild moorland, with fine scenery and a particularly unrushed atmosphere – very relaxing. The main town of the upper North Tyne is **Bellingham** (pronounced Bellingjum) NY8383, a small country town with an attractive 13th-c church, stone-roofed to protect it against arson-minded Border raiders. There's a pretty walk just N of the town, to the 30-ft cascade of Hareshaw Linn. Summer PONY-TREKKING from Brown Rigg Farm, (01434) 220210. The Cheviot Hotel does decent food.

Walks

Hadrian's Wall ⌂-1 has easy access from the parallel B6318 and numerous car parks on the way. The best-preserved sections include those around Walltown Crags NY6666, Cawfield Crags NY7167 and Housesteads Fort NY7969. There's not a lot of point trying to make walks into circuits: all the interest is along the wall itself, although in places you may prefer to drop down beneath the switchback Whin Sill (the ridge of hard rock on which the wall stands), which itself can be quite tiring. The views are bleak and exhilarating. Even in fine summer weather the wind can be chilly on the wall, so go well wrapped up.

The great tract of **Kielder Forest** ⌂-2 has been set up as a recreational area, with self-guided forest walks (easy to follow).

Driving

In Kielder Forest, there is a 12-mile forest drive with some open views among the millions of conifers, starting from the Forestry Authority's visitor centre at 18th-c Kielder Castle. The approach roads to Kielder Water from Bellingham also make an attractive drive, passing several isolated villages, and the B6320 from Wall through Wark to Bellingham traces through a lovely part of the North Tyne valley.

The B6318 from Humshaugh to Gilsland follows the old Roman military road along the line of Hadrian's Wall, and gives some good views of it, while the B6295 down Allendale has some fine scenery.

The A68 runs through increasingly grand scenery in Redesdale as it approaches the Scottish border; up in this lonely area the Gun at Ridsdale is a useful stop.

Where to eat

Carterway Heads NZ0552 MANOR HOUSE (01207) 55268 Simple, slate-roofed, stone house with a pleasant view over moorland pastures; plentiful and imaginative food with a menu that changes daily; cl 25 Dec. £18.50|£1.70/£6.
Slaley NY9858 ROSE & CROWN (01434) 673263 Friendly, family-run inn with decent bar food and interesting restaurant food, inc several vegetarian dishes

and a good-value Sunday lunch; bedrooms; disabled access (not bedrooms). £15.75|£1.30/£4.75.

Corbridge NY9964 VALLEY Old Station House, Station Rd (01434) 633434 Extremely friendly Indian restaurant in an attractively converted, sandstone station house, with a wide choice of very good Indian food and kind service; also, a special train service for parties, with a uniformed escort and free travel: your order is phoned ahead to be ready on arrival – good fun; cl Sun; limited disabled access. £15.

Haydon Bridge NY8464 GENERAL HAVELOCK (01434) 684283 Old, very civilised, stone terraced house without machines or piped music; the stripped-stone, back dining room overlooks the Tyne; good, popular food. £14.

DURHAM

Grand, unspoilt scenery, especially in Teesdale; Durham City is good for a weekend stay; Beamish has an exceptionally enjoyable open-air museum.

The county's prime attractions are its scenic beauty and the fact that it's not touristy. Among a great deal of other fine countryside, Teesdale, above Barnard Castle, stands out for its beautiful peaceful scenery, and gives good access to the high moors (with splendid fishing, too). The city of Durham has much character, a lively atmosphere and plenty to see besides its cathedral, which is one of the three most impressive in Britain; it's an enjoyable place for a short stay.

The magnificent open-air museum at Beamish stands out as Britain's most appealing and rewarding attraction, excellent for keeping children interested, though fun whatever your age. The Bowes Museum at Barnard Castle is also tremendously worth while – a surprisingly under-visited storehouse of treasures. There is an expanding range of other interesting places to visit here, from Raby Castle at Staindrop to the lead-mining relics in Weardale and the mining museum at Skinningrove.

We also include the predominantly industrial area of Cleveland in this chapter; Hartlepool has several sights worth visiting.

Where to stay

Durham NZ2743 ROYAL COUNTY Old Elvet, Durham DH1 3JN (0191) 386 6821 £120; 150 rms. Close to the centre of the city with views of the castle and cathedral, this extended hotel has attractively furnished rooms, several restaurants, and lots of leisure facilities; disabled access.

Easington NZ4143 GRINKLE PARK Easington, Belford TS13 4UB (01287) 610515 £80; 20 individually decorated rms. Charming country house in 35 acres of parkland between moors and coast, with croquet and all-weather tennis court; comfortable lounges, an open fire, friendly and efficient service and enjoyable food using local produce when possible; full-sized snooker table.

Romaldkirk NY9922 ROSE & CROWN Romaldkirk, Barnard Castle DL12 9EB (01833) 50213 *£75; 12 rms, the ones in the main house have lots of character. Interesting old coaching inn by the green of this delightful Teesdale village; with a beamed traditional bar, Jacobean oak settle, log fire, old black and white photographs, and lots of brass; excellent, unusual food inc wonderful home-made puddings in the fine, oak-panelled restaurant; cl 25–26 Dec; disabled access.

Headlam NZ1819 HEADLAM HALL Headlam, Darlington DL2 3HA (01325) 730238 *£70; 26 pretty rms, 17 in the main house and 9 in an adjacent coach house. Jacobean mansion in 4 acres of carefully kept gardens, with a little trout lake, tennis court, small golf practice area, and croquet lawn; elegant rooms, a fine, carved oak fireplace in the main hall, and good food in the four individually decorated rooms of the restaurant; indoor swimming pool, snooker and sauna; cl 24–25 Dec; disabled access.

Greta Bridge NZ0813 MORRITT ARMS Greta Bridge, Barnard Castle DL12 9SE (01833) 627232 £68; 16 rms. Smartly old-fashioned coaching inn where Dickens stayed in 1838 to research *Nicholas Nickleby* – one of the characterful bars has a colourful Dickensian mural; comfortable lounges, fresh flowers, good open fires, and a pleasant garden; coarse fishing; no children in evening dining room.

Middleton-in-Teesdale NY9526 TEESDALE Middleton-in-Teesdale, Barnard Castle DL12 0QG (01833) 40264 £60.50; 14 rms. In summer, this warm, pleasant and comfortable place is a riot of colour with lovely hanging baskets, window boxes and borders; well presented, good, fresh food in the attractive dining room (wonderful, wild Scottish salmon), decent bar food, and fine service; also, self-catering cottages.

Cotherstone NZ0119 FOX & HOUNDS Cotherstone, Barnard Castle DL12 9PF (01833) 650241 *£55; 3 no-smoking rms. Attractive building in a lovely setting overlooking the green of this Teesdale village; comfortably furnished, cosy beamed bar with alcoves and recesses, local photographs, and an open fire; good food in the no-smoking dining room and courteous, friendly service; handy for walks; cl 25 Dec; children over 9.

Durham NZ2743 GEORGIAN TOWN HOUSE 11 Crossgate DH1 4PS (0191) 386 8070 £45; 6 pretty rms. Attractive building with an extravagantly comfortable sitting room, a handsome, airy, conservatory dining room, and a friendly atmosphere; cl mid-Dec–mid-Jan; children over cot age.

Shincliffe NZ2941 SEVEN STARS Shincliffe, Durham DH1 2NU (0191) 384 8454 £42.39; 8 rms. Small but comfortably smart inn in an attractive village; traditionally furnished in one half, remarkable fireplace in the other; friendly staff and a quiet atmosphere; decent bar and restaurant food and big breakfasts.

High Force NY8728 HIGH FORCE HOTEL High Force, Barnard Castle DL12 0XH (01833) 22222 £42; 6 rms. Close to England's highest waterfall (for which it's named), this is a cheerful and friendly place under new owners, with decent food and lots of malt whiskies; it includes a mountain rescue post.

Wolsingham NZ0737 GREENWELL FARM Wolsingham, Tow Low, Bishop Auckland DL13 4PH (01388) 527248 £32.50; 3 rms. 300-year-old farmhouse with fine views, sitting and dining rooms, and good food using naturally reared meats and locally grown produce; there are also spring lambs, calves and chicks, nature trail and conservation areas; you can bring your own horse or mountain bike; self-catering too.

Bowes NY9112 ANCIENT UNICORN Bowes, Barnard Castle DL12 9HA (01833) 28321 £30; 4 comfortable rms. Coaching inn with *Nicholas Nickleby* connections and a welcoming, open-plan, plush bar with good, honest bar food; also, self-catering in well converted stables block.

To see and do

Durham NZ2743 The ancient core of the town stands on a crag defended by an almost complete loop of the River Wear, with a rewarding riverside path going from Prebends Bridge up to South St (with some of the best views of the cathedral's magnificent pinnacled towers), recrossing the river by Silver St Bridge. The old part of town is largely pedestrianised, with attractive cobbled alleys and narrow medieval lanes, and fine medieval buildings among the Georgian and later ones, particularly around the 12th-c, pedestrians-only

Elvet Bridge. There are several medieval churches, and interesting little shops. You can hire rowing boats nr Elvet Bridge, which is also the departure point for launches; and paths track along the riverside. The City Hotel (New Elvet) and Swan & Three Cygnets (Elvet Bridge) are useful for lunch.

✝ � 🏛 The huge CATHEDRAL is one of England's finest, and among the places which our contributors say they prize above all in Britain. It's a fiercely beautiful and unusually well preserved Norman building, breathtaking and very masculine inside; the first in Britain to use pointed arches. St Cuthbert's shrine is here, and they say that the Lady Chapel owes its odd position at the W end to his hatred of women; every time they tried to build it in the right place his spirit apparently caused the foundations to collapse. Try to spot the unique bronze knocker that seems to have a cheery grin. The TREASURY contains many valuable and beautiful objects from the church's 900 years, and there's a collection of rare books and manuscripts in the 15th-c monks' dormitory. Meals, snacks, shop, disabled facilities; monks' dormitory open 11am–3pm Mon–Sat, 2–4pm Sun (20p), Treasury cl am Sun (£1). There are handsome old houses around The Close behind the cathedral, which with its precincts is the best example in the country of what was once a Benedictine monastery.

🏰 The CASTLE nearby started as an early Norman motte and bailey. Still a proud building, the chapel dates from about 1080 and the great hall from 1284. It's now used for university accommodation, and you can stay here. Shop; guided tours Mon, Weds and Sat 2–4.30pm, maybe every day in university vacations – best to check first; (0191) 374 3863; £1.50.

� UNIVERSITY MUSEUM OF ARCHAEOLOGY On the river bank below the cathedral's SW corner, a former fulling mill with finds from the city and surrounding area. Shop; cl am Nov–Mar; 80p. Also along these banks is a sculpture of the Last Supper carved by Colin Wilbourn from 13 trees that died of Dutch elm disease.

� ORIENTAL MUSEUM (Elvet Hill) Unrivalled collections of oriental artefacts, with remarkable displays of everything from plates, carvings, and paintings to costumes and mummies.

Shop; cl 1–2pm, am wknds, Christmas–New Year; (0191) 374 2911; *£1.

🌺 🌱 UNIVERSITY BOTANIC GARDENS (Hollingside Lane) Hugely enjoyable 18-acre garden in mature woodland, with exotic trees from America and the Himalayas, a tropical house, cactus house and visitor centre, and an unusual garden with Colin Wilbourn sculptures. Snacks, shop, disabled access; open daily Apr–Nov, and pm the rest of year, weather permitting; (0191) 374 2671; free.

✝ 🕈 St Mary le Bow CHURCH (The Bailey) has a HERITAGE CENTRE with exhibitions and an audio-visual show on the city's history. Shop, disabled access; cl am (exc July and Aug), wkdys in Apr and May and all Oct–Mar; *70p.

🌺 HOUGHALL COLLEGE GARDENS (Shincliffe Rd) The county's main horticultural training centre, with 10 acres of hardy plants, a watergarden, woodland garden, alpine rock garden, parterre and arboretum. This area records some of the lowest temperatures in the country so they like to say that if something grows here, it'll grow anywhere; disabled access; cl am, Christmas; free.

🌺 🌼 ST AIDAN'S COLLEGE GROUNDS (Windmill Hill) are currently being redeveloped and probably won't be finished until next year, though if you're nearby there should still be something to see, inc good views of the cathedral. Cl Christmas, New Year and Easter wk; free.

� 🖼 DURHAM LIGHT INFANTRY MUSEUM AND DURHAM ART GALLERY (Aykley Heads) Regimental history and good art gallery with unusual temporary exhibitions. Snacks, shop, disabled access; cl am Sun, Mon (exc bank hols), Christmas hols; (0191) 384 2214; *80p.

🏰 FINCHALE PRIORY (3m NE, on a minor road off the A167) St Godric chose this site as a place to meditate in 1110, and it's still a pleasant spot for contemplation, beside the graceful ruins of the 13th-c church; 80p.

Other things to see and do

✿ ✔ **Acklam** NZ4917 BOTANIC CENTRE Thriving environmental demonstration centre, with organic gardens, wildlife areas and sound exhibitions. Growing and developing all the time, with a number of natural habitats (moorland, wetlands etc) under construction. Meals, snacks, shop, disabled access; cl Mon, Tues, Oct–Mar; (01642) 594895; £1.50.

★ 🏠 🚌 🖼 ✿ ⛏ † **Barnard Castle** NZ0516 is a pleasant market town, still coming to life on Weds market day, with several attractive buildings. Most notable is the BOWES MUSEUM – not so much a museum as a beautiful, French-style château in 20 acres of meticulously kept and appropriately formal grounds. The 40 rooms are filled with sumptuous fine arts and an outstanding display of paintings by Canaletto, Goya, El Greco and others (the biggest collection of Spanish paintings in Britain); also a children's room and local history section. Because of its location, relatively very few people visit this treasure-house, though it's one of the most worthwhile places to see in the entire country; on a cold winter's day you'll have it and its frost-sparkling grounds virtually to yourself. Note that this year they will be closed until Apr for rewiring. Meals, snacks, shop, disabled access; reopens Apr, then only cl am Sun and 20–25 Dec; (01833) 690606; £2.50. CASTLE Dramatically set 12th-c ruins; the original keep and the 14th-c hall survive. Snacks, shop, disabled facilities; cl winter Mon and Tues, 24–26 Dec, 1 Jan; £1.80. Nr it the White Swan is an ancient pub, perched in a similarly striking position over the river. In the centre, the Golden Lion is good value for lunch, and nearby there are decent places like the Morritt Arms Hotel at Greta Bridge and the Fox & Hounds at Cotherstone. The riverside walk a couple of miles downstream to ruined EGGLESTONE ABBEY is well worthwhile (it can also be reached by car). Substantial remains include gracefully arched windows, and some remnants of the monastic buildings. Disabled access;

free. Just SE of town ROKEBY PARK is an elegant 18th-c villa in a fine setting, most famous for its Rokeby Venus by Velasquez (though the original is now in the National Gallery). The best of the other pictures is probably Pellegrini's *Venus Disarming Cupid*. Shop, disabled access to ground floor only; open May bank hols then pm Mon and Tues Jun–2ndTues in Sept; (01833) 37334; *£3.

♪ ⛏ **Beamish** NZ2253 THE NORTH OF ENGLAND OPEN-AIR MUSEUM Amazingly ambitious, 300-acre museum exhaustively recreating life in the North of England at the turn of the century. Shops, workshops, dentist, houses, trams, omnibus, colliery, drift mine, vintage fairground, Victorian bandstand, shire horses – something for everyone, though best on a dry day. They're constantly adding things – new this year are a period garage and sweet factory with demonstrations. It's by far the best open-air museum we've seen, and more of our contributors rate it among Britain's top attractions than

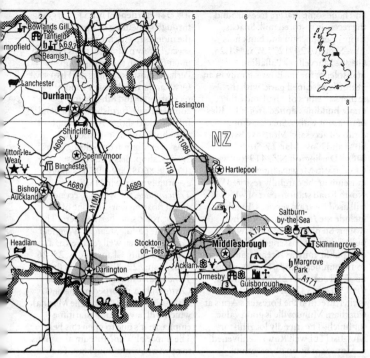

any other place to visit. Meals, snacks, good shop, disabled access; cl Mon and Fri Nov–Mar, phone for details of Christmas opening, (01207) 231811; summer £6.99, less in winter when less is going on – though of course the plus side is there are fewer people too, so guides can take more time to explain things. The Shepherd & Shepherdess not far from the gate is useful for lunch.

Binchester NZ2332 ROMAN FORT Quite a lot left of this 1st-c, 10-acre fort, inc the best preserved military baths in the country, with an exceptional hypocaust system. Interesting events include days when you can sample Roman food. Shop; open Easter wknd, then daily May–Sept; (01388) 663089; 80p. A 3rd-c fort can be seen a few miles S at **Piercebridge** NZ2116 (where the riverside George, with its famous grandfather clock which stopped when the old man died, is good for lunch), and finds from both sites are shown at the Bowes Museum in Barnard Castle (see entry above).

Bishop Auckland NZ2130 AUCKLAND CASTLE Since Norman times the main country residence of the Bishops of Durham, a grand series of buildings entered through a splendid Gothic gatehouse in the town's market place. Some rooms are relatively stark, but a highlight is the chapel, splendidly transformed from a 12th-c banqueting hall by John Cosin from 1660. The grounds are attractive, with an unusual 18th-c deercote. Shop; open May–mid-Sept, all Tues, pm only Sun, Weds, Thurs, bank hols and Sat in Aug; (01388) 601627; £2.

Bowes NY9913 BOWES CASTLE was built inside the earthworks of a Roman fort, and remains include the great Norman keep, three storeys high; free. A few miles W the Bowes Moor Hotel, one of England's highest, is a welcoming moorland oasis.

Burnopfield NZ1757 LEAP MILL FARM Working farm and watermill, hardly changed since the 18th-c – even the pigsty is a listed building. Rare breeds of cattle, old-fashioned roosters, ganders and goats, and handsome mature trees around the recently restored mill. Snacks, shop; open pm Sun and bank hols Apr–Sept; (01207) 271375; *£1.25. GIBSIDE Marvellous Palladian mausoleum for the Bowes family in an 18th-c landscaped park, with the rather sad ruins of a hall and other estate buildings dotted around. Miles of pleasant walks. Snacks, shop, disabled access; cl Mon (exc bank hols) and Nov–Mar; £2.50; NT.

ⓌⒺ✝ Darlington NZ2419 RAILWAY CENTRE AND MUSEUM Interesting museum in the carefully restored North Road station, part of which is still used for train services. Exhibits include the *Locomotion* built by Robert Stephenson in 1825, which pulled the first passenger steamtrain on a public railway. Steamtrain rides some summer wknds. Snacks, shop, disabled access; cl 25-26 Dec, 1 Jan; (01325) 460532; £1.70. Further out in this direction the Forester's Arms at Coatham Mundeville is good value for lunch. The friendly local history MUSEUM (Tubwell Row) is enlivened in May–Sept by an observation beehive. Shop, disabled access to ground floor only; cl 1–2, pm Thurs, Sun, some bank hols; (01325) 463795; free. St Cuthbert's (Church Row) is an interesting early English CHURCH.

★ ❀ Eggleston NY9924 is an attractive, moorside, Teesdale village. EGGLESTON HALL GARDENS Good example of an updated, 19th-c, country-house garden, with rare and unusual trees, shrubs, perennials, other plants and seven greenhouses. They sell plants, organically grown herbs, and fruit and vegetables from the walled kitchen garden. Snacks, disabled access; (01833) 50378; 50p (or £1 for a good-value season ticket). The Three Tuns is useful for lunch.

✝ ⓜ Guisborough NZ6115 GISBOROUGH PRIORY 14th-c ruined church, one huge window rising dramatically from the rest of the more or less foundation-level ruins. The gatehouse is fairly well preserved, and it's an atmospheric spot for a picnic. Disabled access; cl winter Mon and Tues, 24–26 Dec, 1 Jan; 80p. The Tap & Spile is handy for a bite to eat.

ⓗ❀Ⓔ✝ Hartlepool NZ5133 is going through something of a renaissance at the moment, with the development of several lively new attractions likely to put it firmly on the tourist map. Perhaps most exciting is the HISTORIC QUAY at the old docks, a vivid recreation of an 18th-c seaport complete with furnished houses and fully stocked shops. Also a couple of film shows and a dramatic (and noisy!) exhibition on fighting ships. Snacks, shop, disabled access; (01429) 860888; £4.95. It's likely eventually to take in HMS *Trincomalee*, the world's second-oldest floating warship, one of the two HISTORIC SHIPS berthed here. The other, the paddle steamer *Wingfield Castle*, has been well restored as a living museum. Cl am wkdys, 25–26 Dec, 1 Jan; £2 for both. When the *Trincomalee* moves, the *Wingfield Castle* will be absorbed by the new MUSEUM OF HARTLEPOOL(The Marina), which will have quite a maritime emphasis; it's due to open this Feb. The Imperial War Museum also plans to open a new museum here. The old part of town has some remains of the medieval wall. 3m S of town the ENERGY INFO CENTRE at Hartlepool Power Station has lively displays and tours (best to book for these). Shop, disabled access; cl wknds exc pm Apr–Oct; (01429) 869201; free. The Causeway at Stranton, right by Camerons brewery, is a decent pub.

☛ Lanchester NZ1647 HALL HILL FARM Friendly working farm with lots of animals, nature trails, a riverside walk and trailer rides. Snacks, shop; cl am, all Sat, and all Sept–Mar exc Sun in Sept and Dec; (01388) 730300; *£2.75. The Queen's Head does good food.

ⓗ Margrove Park NZ6516 Right on the edge of the moors, the SOUTH CLEVELAND HERITAGE CENTRE has exhibitions on the area's natural history and wildlife. They organise walks and nature trails. Snacks (from summer this year), shop, disabled access; cl am Sun, all Fri and Sat, every am in winter 25–26 Dec, 1 Jan; (01287) 610368; free.

Ⓔ❀ ☙ ☛ Middlesbrough NZ4920 Though the town itself is not a

particular attraction for visitors, it does contain a clutch of decent museums and galleries. The DORMAN MUSEUM (Linthorpe Rd) has lively summer activities for children; (01642) 813781; cl Sun, Mon, 25–26 Dec, 1 Jan; free. CAPTAIN COOK BIRTHPLACE MUSEUM (Stewart Park, Marton, 3m S) Good account of the life of James Cook and his discoveries, some displays accompanied by the sound of creaking ship's timbers; they celebrate his birthday on 25 Oct. The impressive grounds also have a conservatory with various tropical plants, animals and birds. Snacks, shop, disabled access; cl Mon exc bank hols, 25–26 Dec, 1 Jan; (01642) 311211; £1.20. NEWHAM GRANGE LEISURE FARM (Coulby Newham) Rare breeds, agricultural museum, reconstructed vet's surgery and merchant's shop, and plenty of other animals and poultry. Snacks, shop, disabled access; cl wkdys Nov–Mar; (01642) 300202; £1.20. The Transporter Bridge across the Tees is unique, with the central section serving as a ferry shuttling cars and pedestrians across the river. Cl Sun am; car 57p, pedestrian 18p.

🏠 ❀ **Ormesby** NZ5416 ORMESBY HALL Elegant 18th-c house with elaborate plasterwork, a newly renovated Victorian laundry and kitchen, pleasant gardens and grounds. The first Sun of each month is a Family Fun Day. Snacks, shop, disabled access; cl am, Mon, Tues, Fri, Nov–Mar; £2; NT.

⛏ **Rowlands Gill** NZ1759 DERWENTCOTE STEEL FURNACE (on the A694 between Rowlands Gill and Hamsterley, where the Cross Keys does good-value food) The earliest and most complete steel-making furnace to have survived, with an exhibition on steel production. Shop, disabled access; cl Oct–Mar; (01207) 562573; 80p.

❀ ⛴ **Saltburn-by-the-Sea** NZ6722 Originally a superior Victorian seaside resort, with traces of those days still in the Italianate valley garden and the water-operated, sloping tramway by the pier. The SHIP INN, a good pub right by the boats pulled up on the beach, is probably

the most ancient building. The old cottages alongside it house a vivid exhibition on the town's smuggling heritage. Cl wkdys Oct–Easter; £1.50. The beach is sheltered by the great headland of Warsett Hill to the S.

⛏ **Skinningrove** NZ7119 is an industrial village with a steel-rolling mill – far from picturesque, but it has strong local colour. TOM LEONARD MINING MUSEUM Good mining museum demonstrating well the reality of work underground. You can see how the stone is drilled, charged with explosives and fired. Snacks, shop; cl am, Nov–Easter; (01287) 642877; *£2. The monumental Boulby Cliff is fairly nr (see **Walks** section below), and a bit further on, just over the Yorks border, the very pretty seaside village of Staithes has several decent pubs.

🏠 ☕ 🍴 ❀ **Spennymoor** NZ2634 WHITWORTH HALL AND GARDENS Bobbie Shafto went to sea from this neat old house, now with period furnished rooms, a miniature village, clock museum, vineyard and brewery. The handsome grounds have been restored to their original state, and they've recently added a waterwheel. Teas, shop, some disabled access; open wknds and bank hols Easter–Aug, plus Mon, Tues and Weds spring bank hol wk and July and Aug, and Sun in Sept, hall cl am; (01388) 817419; £4. Bonnie Bobbie is buried in the parish church.

🏰 ❀ ✟ **Staindrop** NZ1220 RABY CASTLE Imposing old fortress with Saxon origins, since the 17th c the home of Lord Barnard's family. Vast medieval hall, 14th-c kitchen, and a Victorian octagonal drawing room – this year fully restored to its original dazzling splendour. Also interesting furniture, paintings and china, walled gardens and deer park. As you approach it looks just like a castle ought to. Snacks, shop (selling oven-ready game from the estate), disabled access (prior notice appreciated); open bank hol wknds from Easter, then Weds and Sun in May and Jun, and daily except Sat July–Sept, castle pm only; (01833) 60202; £3.30. The village is pretty. Over at

Summerhouse the Raby Hunt has decent food.

🜨⚲♀♐ ⚶ **Stockton-on-Tees** NZ4419 GREEN DRAGON MUSEUM (Theatre Yard) Local history inc a lively audio-visual presentation on the birth of the railways here in 1825. Shop, some disabled access (prior notice preferred); cl Sun and bank hols; (01642) 781184; free. There's also a railway heritage trail around town. PRESTON HALL MUSEUM (Yarm Rd, 2m, S) Very well constructed, Victorian high st and other period rooms, plus working craftsmen, aviary, and woodland and riverside walks. Snacks, shop, disabled access; cl 1 Jan, Good Fri, 25–26 Dec; (01642) 781184; free, though there is a £1 charge for parking. On the same site BUTTERFLY WORLD has a recreated jungle environment with hundreds of exotic butterflies flitting between the trees, rocks and waterfalls. Shop, disabled access; cl Dec, Jan; £2.50.

🚂🏛 **Tanfield** NZ1855 TANFIELD RAILWAY Built in 1725 to carry coal to the Tyne, the world's oldest surviving railway, set in a picturesque wooded valley. Steamtrains still chuff along the route, and you can get off by a wooden gorge spanned by CAUSEY ARCH, the world's first railway bridge. They often have a blacksmith forging new parts for restoration work. Summer snacks, shop, disabled access; trains usually run every Sun plus Thurs and Sat in summer hols, tel (0191) 274 2002 to check times; from £3 for trains.

♈★🗡 **Teesdale** has the best of the county's scenery, and Upper Teesdale is famous for its limestone flora, inc rare, arctic, alpine species and the unique Teesdale violet; Widdybank Fell is a National Nature Reserve. England's most powerful WATERFALL at High Force NY8728 drops into a craggy cauldron at the end of a striking wooded gorge (the nearby High Force Hotel is useful). The **attractive villages** of Middleton-in-Teesdale NY9526, Romaldkirk NY9922 (there's an especially distinguished church here) and Eggleston NN9924 all have decent pubs and inns. Side tracks with rewards at their end include the cosy Strathmore Arms in Holwick NY9027 and the Cow Green Reservoir (a short drive or walk above the pleasant Langdon Beck Inn NY8631, with the 200-ft cascade of Cauldon Snout below it); good fishing on the river or the reservoirs above it, and fine landscapes all the way along.

♨⛏★ **Weardale** runs through the heart of the county, and was the source of much of its wealth, with lead and iron mining along its length and in the moors above. There's little reminder of those days now, but high at the top of the dale nr the Cumbrian border at Cowshill is the KILLHOPE LEAD MINING CENTRE NY8243, probably the best-preserved lead mining site in Britain, and unmissable if you're at all interested in industrial history. Snacks, shop, some disabled access; cl Nov–Mar; (01388) 537505; £2. At Ireshopeburn NY8639, nr the source of the river, the WEARDALE MUSEUM recreates life in the mining days, with period rooms and furnishings, and an exhibition on John Wesley, who often preached in the adjacent chapel. Shop; cl am, all Mon, Tues and Fri (exc in Aug and bank hols), and Oct–Easter; 80p. Along the dale is a string of **attractive villages** like Cotherstone NZ0119 (where the Fox & Hounds has the best food in the valley), Stanhope NY9939 (the 'capital' of Weardale, with an odd fossil tree stump in the churchyard) and Wolsingham NZ0737 (good-value food at the Black Bull), as well as pleasant waterside and moorland walks. The Golden Lion at St John's Chapel NY8838 also has good-value food.

♈★ **Witton-le-Wear** NZ1730 LOW BARNS NATURE RESERVE 100-acre reserve with nature trails, woodland, grassland, a lake and lots of interesting wildlife. More observation hides are planned. Snacks, shop, good disabled access (by this summer the nature trail should be completely suitable for wheelchairs); (01388) 488728; free. The village is attractive, with a tree-lined sloping green; the Victoria is useful for lunch.

Walks

Though this county can't quite compete with Northumberland for serious walking, it does have a good many very enjoyable walks in fine scenery. **Upper Teesdale** ⌂-1 has much of the best walking in the Durham Pennines. Most popular of all is the short path from the main road to the High Force waterfall NY8728. From Bowlees Visitor Centre NY9028 you can make more of a walk of it, first detouring N to Gibson's Cave NY9028, a pretty waterfall at the top of a gorge, and then heading S to cross the Tees for an easy two miles upriver, passing Low Force NY9028 on the way. Beyond High Force, the Pennine Way encounters some truly wild landscape as the Tees rushes along a gorge beneath Cronkley Scar NY8329 and tumbles down Cauldron Snout NY8229 – a cascade which can be reached from the dam at Cow Green Reservoir NY7930 (where there is also a nature trail).

There is more gorge scenery around **Barnard Castle** NZ0516 ⌂-2, here wooded, romantic and unmistakably lowland in character; the valley path W eventually climbs above the river and follows field routes as it leads towards Cotherstone NZ0119. Similar pockets of scenery are found along the River Greta, S of town, and the Deepdale Beck, to the W; both have attractive paths along them.

The Cross Keys at Hamsterley NZ1231 is a useful base for good walks in the nearby fellside Hamsterley Forest.

Cleveland, though solidly built up and much industrialised, has rural fringes, inc the northern flanks of the North York Moors, where **Roseberry Topping** NZ5712 ⌂-3 is a memorable viewpoint reached by a walk over moors from Gribdale Gate car park E of Great Ayton NZ5611; a popular circuit goes by way of Airy Home Farm, the childhood home of Captain Cook. **Eston Nab** NZ5618 ⌂-4, outside the National Park, has a massive view over industrial Teesside. The **Cleveland Way** ⌂-5, most of which is actually in North Yorks, begins its grand coastal finale at Saltburn-by-the-Sea NZ6722, passing Skinningrove NZ7119 (an odd shantytown of pigeon-fanciers' sheds spreads over the cliff) and ascending Boulby Cliff NZ7619, the highest point on the E coast, before re-entering North Yorks and the National Park.

The county council's environment department runs a busy programme of guided walks throughout the county, with some emphasis on country pursuits, local history and geology; tel (0191) 386 4411 ext 2354 for programme.

Driving

One of the finest drives in the N is the B6277 through Teesdale right over to Alston in Cumbria. Others include the B6278 from Barnard Castle through Egglestone to Stanhope, and then on to Edmondbyers where a left turn on to the B6306 takes you down through Blanchland and over the border into Northumberland; and the A689 up Weardale.

If you are passing through on the way to or from Scotland, a splendid route is to turn off the A1 just N of Scotch Corner down in Yorks, then take the B6275 through Piercebridge to join the A68 and plunge on over the hills into and through Northumberland.

Where to eat

Romaldkirk NY9922 ROSE & CROWN (01833) 50213 Civilised old coaching inn by the village green, with a friendly atmosphere, warming log fire, interesting decorations, and very good bar and restaurant food using local produce. £15|£2.50/£5.

Eggleston NY9924 THREE TUNS (01833) 50289 Peacefully atmospheric pub by the village green, with a warm welcome, nice beamed bar, log fire, and reliable food. £2.50/£5.

Good food is also to be found in the places we recommend in the **Where to stay** section above.

Help this year from: Jonathan Mann, Abagail Regan, GSB, JJW, CMW, Peter Race, Ian Phillips, Stephen Brown, D Irving, P D and J Bickley, John Allsopp, Leonard Dixon, Graham and Karen Oddey, Brian Webster, Dr A and Dr A C Jackson, J S Poulter, Ken Smith, Mrs M Kilner, John Oddey, Noel Jackson, Louise Campbell, Mr and Mrs R J Foreman, John Fazakerley, Pat Woodward, M and J Back.

NORTHUMBRIA CALENDAR

Some of these dates were provisional as we went to press.

This year is the 1,000th anniversary of Durham Cathedral which was founded in 995.

JANUARY

28 **Durham** Wildlife Photographer of the Year at Durham Light Infantry Museum and Durham Art Gallery – *till 26 Feb* (0191) 384 2214

FEBRUARY

5 **Newcastle upon Tyne** Chinese New Year in Chinatown with lion dance, procession, fireworks, unicorn dance and Chinese market (0191) 384 6905

12 **Newbiggin-by-the-Sea** Wansbeck Brass Band Contest at the Sports and Community Centre (01670) 81444

22 **Washington Village** National Trust Centenary Concert at Washington Old Hall (0191) 416 6879

MARCH

17 **Cambo** Early Music Demonstration and Talk at Wallington (01669) 20333

APRIL

1 nr **Rowlands Gill** Walk, Balloon Event and Fireworks at Gibside (01207) 542255

21 **Morpeth** Northumbrian Gathering: festival of traditional Northumbrian music, song, dance and crafts – *till Sun 23* (01670) 513308

22 **North Pennines** Spring Festival – *till 8 May* (01434) 381806

MAY

1 **Berwick-upon-Tweed** Riding the Bounds: ancient and colourful custom where about 100 horses and a procession ride out of the town for races and games (01289) 307384

18 **Whitburn** Living History Day at Souter Lighthouse (0191) 529 3161

21 **Berwick-upon-Tweed** Border Marches Festival: circular walks through River Tweed valley with refreshment points and entertainments along the way (01289) 330044

26 **Berwick-upon-Tweed** May Fair – *till Mon 29* (01289) 330044

27 **Eastgate** Spring Sheep Show (01388) 517381

28 **North Shields** Fishquay Festival – *till Mon 29* 0191-266 7421

29 **Corbridge** Northumberland County Show at Tynedale Park (01434) 344443

JUNE

3 **Allendale** Fair (01434) 683269

NORTHUMBRIA CALENDAR

JUNE cont

4 **Ormesby** June Jaunts at Ormesby Hall: family fun day (01642) 300937

10 **Corbridge** South Tyne Traction Engine Society Steam and Vintage Rally at Tyndale Park – *till Sun 11* (01434) 321029; **Durham** Regatta – *till Sun 11* (0191) 386 8752

16 **Cambo** Outdoor Concert with Lasers and Fireworks at Wallington (01669) 20333; **Newcastle upon Tyne** Newcastle Hoppings at Town Moor – *till Sat 24* (0191) 261 0691

17 **Cambo** Open-Air Shakespeare at Wallington – *till 1 July* (01669) 20333; **Ovingham** Goose Fair: traditional event with Morris men and Northumbrian pipes (01661) 832711; nr **Rowlands Gill** Young Musicians Festival in the walled garden at Gibside (01207) 542255

18 **Bywell** Country Fair inc gun dog trials (01669) 20607

24 nr **Rowlands Gill** Midsummer Music Concert at Gibside (01207) 542255

25 **Alnwick** Fair: costumed re-enactments with courts, duckings and processions – *till 1 July* (01665) 605004

JULY

1 **Lanchester** Show (off the A691) – *till Sun 2* (0191) 373 4565; **South Shields** South Tyneside Show at Bents Park – *till Sun 2* (0191) 427 1717; **Washington** Northern International Kite Festival at Northern Playing Fields – *till Sun 2* (0191) 512 0444

2 **Belford** Carnival – *till Sun 9*

7 **Tynemouth** Whitley Bay Traditional Jazz Festival at the Park Hotel – *till Sun 9* (0191) 279 2382; **Whitley Bay** North of England Motor Show at the Links – *till Sun 9* (0191) 516 0085

8 **Durham** Miners Gala: colourful march culminating in trade union rally (0191) 384 3515; **South Shields** Cookston Country Festival – *till 13 Aug* (0191) 427 1717

14 **Redcar** International Folk Music, Dance and Song Festival at the Redcar Bowl – *till Sun 16* (01947) 840928; nr **Rowlands Gill** Flower Festival and Country Fair at Gibside – *till Sun 16* (01207) 542255

15 **Bishop Auckland** Early Music Festival at Auckland Castle – *till Sun 16* (01388) 765555; **Chester-le-Street** Durham County Show at Clondyke Garden Centre – *till Sun 16* (0191) 388 5459

16 **Middlesbrough** Mela at Central Gardens: Asian day with music, dancing, food and children's entertainment (01642) 264130

22 **Middlesbrough** Cleveland County Show at Stewart Park (01642) 327583

28 **Middlesbrough** Cleveland International Eisteddfod – *till 3 Aug* (01642) 327088

AUGUST

3 **Stockton-on-Tees** Stockton Riverside International Festival – *till Sun 6* (01642) 670067

4 **Kielder** Folk Festival – *till Sun 6* (01434) 220643

5 **Alnwick** International Music Festival – *till Sat 12* (01665) 602398; **Sunderland** International Air Show – *till Sun 6* (0191) 510 9317

6 **Saltburn** Victorian Festival – *till Sun 13* (01642) 231212

NORTHUMBRIA CALENDAR

AUGUST cont

12 **Billingham** International Folklore Festival – *till Sat 19* (01642) 558212; **Cambo** Open-Air Classics with fireworks at Wallington (01669) 20333; **Slaley** Show at Townhead Field (01434) 682569

13 nr **Rowlands Gill** Teddy Bears Picnic at Gibside – *till Sun 16* (01207) 542255

19 **Whittingham** Show at the Showground (01669) 21121

20 **Cambo** Wallington Fun Day (01669) 20333

26 **St John's Chapel** Agricultural Show (01388) 537298

27 **Ormesby** Teesside Festival of Transport at Ormesby Hall – *till Mon 28* (01642) 300937

28 **Blanchland** and Hunstanworth Show at the Showfield (01434) 675385; **Newcastle upon Tyne** Free Festival (0191) 273 0311; **Wooler** Glendale Agricultural Show at the Showfield (01665) 578380

SEPTEMBER

2 **Wolsingham** and Wear Valley Agricultural Show at Scotch Isle Farm – *till Mon 4* (01388) 527862

8 **Sunderland** Illuminations – *till 3 Nov* 0191-416 6440

9 **Berwick-upon-Tweed** Military Tattoo at Berwick Barracks – *till Sun 10* (0129) 304493; **Bowes** Agricultural Show (01833) 628208; **Stanhope** Agricultural Show and Country Fair at Unthank Park – *till Mon 11* (01388) 528347; **Seaham** East Durham Show at the Showground – *till Sun 10* (0191) 581 7016

10 **Cambo** Gardeners Open Day at Wallington (01669) 20333; **Newcastle upon Tyne** Science Festival at Newcastle University – *till Fri 15* (0191) 261 0691

16 **High Shipley** Eggleston Agricultural Show (01833) 38749

30 **Belford** Show (01668) 213501

OCTOBER

1 **Ashington** Festival – *till Tues 31* (01670) 814444

7 **Houghton-le-Spring** Houghton Feast: traditional festival – *till Sun 15* (0191) 416 6440; **Middlesbrough** Write-around Literary Festival – *till Sat 21* (01642) 243425

13 **Tyneside** Irish Festival – *till Sun 22* 0191-261 5677

14 **Alwinton** Border Shepherds Show at the Haugh (01669) 30246

28 nr **Rowlands Gill** Halloween BBQ and Final Fling at Gibside (01207) 542255

NOVEMBER

5 **Stockton-on-Tees** Fireworks Party (01642) 670067

DECEMBER

16 nr **Rowlands Gill** Christmas Carols at Gibside – *till Sun 17* (01207) 542255

26 **Sunderland** Boxing Day Dip: over 1,000 dippers in fancy dress are hosed by the fire brigade before braving the sea (0191) 548 6118

31 **Allendale** Baal Festival: villagers parade in costume with tar barrels on their heads which are later thrown on to a huge bonfire

OXFORDSHIRE

Oxford itself is a treasure-house of great museums and one of the best half-dozen or so English cities for a short break – though much more frenetic than its rival Cambridge. Just north of the city are Blenheim and its small town of Woodstock, where you could easily spend a day.

Away from these two places, the county's appeal is primarily rural. The very varied countryside includes the fringes of the Cotswolds in the north of the county and, in the south, part of the Chilterns, the lush Thames Valley, and the much emptier northern crest of the downs. Many of the county's villages and small towns have considerable charm, ideal to potter around. We have added several new places to visit this year, most notably Kelmscott Manor in South Oxfordshire. The county has quite a few great houses and some fine gardens to visit, though not many of the more organised types of visitor attractions. This is a particularly good county for eating out.

OXFORD

A vibrant, bustling city, Oxford is packed with memorable medieval university buildings and magnificent collections.

Oxford is not a restful city: the ancient university buildings in their medieval lanes are surrounded by a bustling, largely industrialised town, and a formidable amount of traffic. Yet there are many quiet corners, if you know where to look for them.

Most of the oldest or most interesting colleges are grouped near the centre of town, particularly around the Bodleian Library, the Sheldonian Theatre and the splendid, domed Radcliffe Camera (also a library). The cluster of ancient buildings around this partly cobbled area makes it one of the most attractive parts of the city, and easily the most photographed. Throughout, the honey-coloured stone of most university buildings makes for a uniformity that bridges different styles and different centuries.

Besides the colleges themselves, the art collections of the Ashmolean Museum, the extraordinary Pitt Rivers Museum and the Bodleian Library are all extremely rewarding; the university's botanic garden is the oldest in the world.

The one-way system and difficulties in parking away from the NCPs combine to make it a driver's nightmare; if you can, it may be best to leave your car at the Park and Ride on the ring road. Walking is anyway the only way you can see more than tantalising glimpses of college quads through the tiny doorways.

As so many readers enjoy staying here, we have this year added more recommended places to stay in the city; several of those listed in North and South Oxfordshire are also within easy reach.

Where to stay

RANDOLPH Beaumont St OX1 2LN (01865) 247481 £150; 109 rms. Fine Victorian hotel, facing the Ashmolean Museum, with elegant, comfortable day rooms, grand foyer, a graceful restaurant with a lovely plasterwork ceiling, and a cellar wine bar; disabled access.

OLD PARSONAGE 1 Banbury Rd OX2 6NN (01865) 310210 £145; 30 lovely rms. Handsome and civilised 17th-c parsonage with very courteous staff, good breakfasts and excellent light meals in the cosy bar (Browns Restaurant – under the same ownership – is over the rd), a small lounge, and a pretty, little garden; they have their own punt; cl 23–28 Dec; disabled access.

COTSWOLD HOUSE 363 Banbury Rd OX2 7PL (01865) 310558 £52; 7 comfortable rms. Beautifully kept, Cotswold stone house with particularly helpful owners; residents' lounge, very good breakfasts, pretty flowers throughout, and a neat back garden; cl 10 days over Christmas; children over 5.

PINE CASTLE 290 Iffley Rd OX4 4AE (01865) 241497 £50; 7 rms, most with own bthrm. Small, family-run, Edwardian hotel with a comfortable, cosy lounge, and good breakfasts in the small restaurant; cl Christmas wk.

DIAL HOUSE 25 London Rd, Headington OX3 7RE (01865) 60743 £45; 8 no-smoking rms. Attractive, half-timbered house in a pretty garden, with a comfortable and restful lounge, and helpful, attentive owners; cl Christmas–New Year; children over 6; dogs welcome.

To see and do

The various COLLEGES are generally the main attraction for visitors. Newcomers to the town are often surprised to discover that these are all separate bodies with little in common, each firmly maintaining their own dons, rules and traditions; the university itself is little more than an administrative umbrella. Most colleges allow visitors into at least some of the quads, although this may be more limited in term-time, and some are starting to charge. A good way of making sure you see a reasonable cross-section is to join one of the walking tours that leave the tourist information centre (now located in the old school building in Gloucester Green) every day at 11am and 2pm, and other times too in summer; afternoon tours are the best. Ideally, though, it's worth trying to explore at your own pace away from the crowds – again, afternoons are the best time for this, with more colleges open then.

🏠 ✌ 🐾 MAGDALEN (High St) is the most beautiful college, its tower a dramatic sight for visitors entering the city from the S. The quads and cloisters are very pleasant to stroll through, but the chief attraction is the DEER PARK, an unexpected haven in the heart of the bustling city. There's a circular path around this called Addison's Walk – in spring a mass of snowdrops and daffodils, and full of wildlife. Over a small bridge is the Fellows' Garden with a small ornamental lake – a very peaceful, sheltered spot.

🏠 ✝ 🖼 CHRIST CHURCH (St Aldates) is better known: a magnificently stately place begun by Cardinal Wolsey in the 16th c, but soon taken over by Henry VIII. The main entrance into the front quad is through Tom Tower, designed by Christopher Wren and named after its famous bell that rings out 101 times at nine o'clock every night – in less liberal times, the hour when students were due back in their rooms. The Hall is worth a look, with its remarkable hammerbeam roof, paintings of alumni and benefactors by all the most expensive portrait-painters of the period, and the long tables laid out with silver for meals. The elaborate little CATHEDRAL is England's smallest, and doubles as the college chapel. It has some excellent stained glass by Burne-Jones, fantastic pendant vaulting in the choir, and some of the original Norman priory work. The college's PICTURE GALLERY

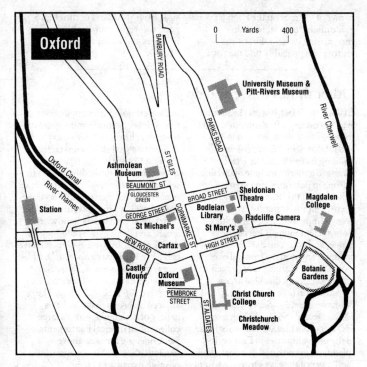

Oxford

0   Yards   400

BANBURY ROAD

University Museum & Pitt-Rivers Museum

PARKS ROAD

River Cherwell

Oxford Canal

ST GILES

Ashmolean Museum

River Thames

BEAUMONT ST

GLOUCESTER GREEN

BROAD STREET

Sheldonian Theatre

Magdalen College

Station

GEORGE STREET

CORNMARKET ST

Bodleian Library

St Michael's

St Mary's

Radcliffe Camera

NEW ROAD

Carfax

HIGH STREET

Botanic Gardens

Castle Mound

Oxford Museum

PEMBROKE STREET

ST ALDATES

Christ Church College

Christchurch Meadow

(Canterbury Quad) is a hidden treasure unnoticed by most visitors, with an important collection of Old Master paintings and drawings. Works by Tintoretto, Carracci and Van Dyck, and various temporary exhibitions, this year inc a look at military drawings (28 Feb–10 May) and a study of mannerism (5 Oct–18 Dec). Shop; cl 1–2pm, am Sun, 10–16 Apr, 23 Dec–1 Jan 1996, guided tours Thurs at 2.15pm; *£1.

🏛✝✳❀ Other interesting colleges are NEW (Holywell St), with its impressive chapel, atmospheric, wisteria-covered cloisters, and remains of the city wall; MERTON (Merton St), the most ancient buildings with the first quad and the country's oldest library (tours available); UNIVERSITY (High St), which has an interesting monument to Shelley despite having thrown him out; the brightly Victorian, very red-brick KEBLE (Parks Rd) (with perhaps the most famous Pre-Raphaelite painting of all, Holman Hunt's *Light of the World*, in its chapel); and ST

EDMUND HALL (Queens Lane), the only surviving medieval college, complete with Norman crypt. Amble down some of the town's prettiest streets and there are more, such as charming EXETER, JESUS and LINCOLN down Turl St, and CORPUS CHRISTI and ORIEL around Merton Lane and Oriel Sq. This latter college has a very attractive and unusual entrance to its dining hall. TRINITY on Broad St is very grand. Around Radcliffe Sq, BRASENOSE is quaint (and has fine views of the surrounding skyline from its quads), and Hertford has its BRIDGE OF SIGHS over New College St – in itself worth exploring for some more unusual and less busy views and a good look at the gargoyles on the backs of some of the buildings. Colleges with particularly nice GARDENS include Worcester and the more modern St Hughs, though many of the private fellows' gardens not usually open to visitors can be seen under the National Gardens Scheme.

More GUIDED WALKS leave from the

corner of Catte St on the High St; your guide might turn out to be an enterprising student. First-time visitors will probably find the TOUR BUSES from St Aldates or the High St good value; the routes take in all the best sites and last about 1½ hours; *£6.50.

Other things to see and do

ð▣ ASHMOLEAN MUSEUM (Beaumont St) The country's first museum, and still one of its finest, opened in 1683 and rehoused in this imposing building from 1845. The well arranged galleries include marvellous European paintings, an extensive collection of Pre-Raphaelite pictures, a representative range of work by French Impressionists, antiquities from ancient Egypt, Greece and Rome, and coins, medals, porcelain, ceramics and pottery from all over the world. A fascinating place to spend an afternoon. Shop, disabled access; cl am Sun, Mon (exc bank hols), Good Fri–Easter Sun, 3–5 Sept (St Giles Fair), 23–26 Dec; (01865) 278000; free.

🏠ð BODLEIAN LIBRARY (Broad St) One of the oldest libraries in Europe, its splendidly grand quad dominated by the Tower of the Five Orders. Most of it isn't open to the public, but guided tours take in the beautifully vaulted 15th-c Divinity School, which shows some of the library's treasures, and Duke Humfry's Library, the oldest reading room. There are usually various changing exhibitions in the Schola Naturalis Philosophiae. Guided tours usually take place at 10.30am, 11.30am, 2pm and 3pm (cl pm Sat and Sun), but probably best to check first on (01865) 277165. No children under 14, excellent shop, limited disabled access; *£3. Altogether the library houses over 5,500,000 books, going down six storeys under the centre of the city.

🏠 SHELDONIAN THEATRE (Broad St) A grand classical building, with a lovely painted ceiling. In its time it's been used for parliaments, and nowadays university ceremonies are held here; you may see students heading for these on some weekends, though the theatre is closed to the public then.

ð PITT RIVERS MUSEUM (Banbury Rd) Shrunken heads, totem poles and fertility rites – a fascinating, close-packed ethnological museum off the tourist track, with art and ingenuity from all cultures and periods. The million or so exhibits range from Captain Cook's Pacific Islands collection and 18th-c ship models to severed fingertips and an Eskimo coat made from seal intestines. Everything is displayed in firmly traditional cases or drawers, with neatly handwritten labels, and there's still something of the Victorian atmosphere it must have had when it originally opened. Disabled access by arrangement, shop; cl am, Sun, a few days over Christmas and Easter; (01865) 270927; free. The adjacent BALFOUR BUILDING has a gallery of archaeology and a large collection of musical instruments. Same opening times as above.

✽ CHRISTCHURCH MEADOW is an unspoilt expanse of green astonishingly close to the busy city streets. You can gaze across the fields of grazing Christchurch cattle to the spires in the distance, or walk under overhanging trees along the banks of the river to the boathouses. From here you can usually see college eights rowing down the water.

✽ ♧ OXFORD BOTANIC GARDEN (High St) Britain's oldest botanic garden, founded in 1621, with 8,000 species of plant from all over the world. The London plane tree was born here. It's a lovely, relaxing place to sit for a while, or to wander through on the way to the river. Disabled access; cl Good Fri and 25 Dec; (01865) 276920; £1 part of Jun, July and Aug, free at other times. The 55-acre UNIVERSITY ARBORETUM (SU5599 5m SE of the town) is also worth visiting. Some disabled access; cl am Sun, all Nov–Apr; free.

♭☺ THE OXFORD STORY (Broad St) Europe's longest dark ride, with cars designed as desks whisking you through a lively recreation of university history, complete with sights, sounds and smells. A useful introduction to the city (especially for families). Shop, disabled access; cl 25 Dec; (01865) 790055; £4.50.

! The COVERED MARKET (High St) is a maze of stalls with something different at every turn: chic boutiques, speciality shops, cafés, old-fashioned butchers and poultry merchants with whole birds and animals hanging gruesomely outside the stalls. The Oxford Sandwich Co do excellent take-away sandwiches here, and Ben's Cookies are a firm favourite with students.

 GLOUCESTER GREEN by the bus station has been interestingly rejuvenated, with trendy shops and cafés; you'd hardly believe this was once one of the less desirable parts of town. On Weds there's a bustling market here. The Old Fire Station complex now houses a theatre and CURIOXITY, a lively, interactive science gallery where visitors can experiment with the exhibits. Meals, snacks, shop; cl 25–26 Dec, some bank hols; (01865) 794494; £1.75. They've just started a science trail around the city. Not too far from here in Little Clarendon St, George & Davies is a wonderful ice-cream parlour; our favourite flavours are the Baileys or Double Chocolate Fudge Brownie.

 BATE COLLECTION OF MUSICAL INSTRUMENTS (St Aldates) Outstanding – and constantly developing – collection of early keyboards, woodwind, brass, percussion and other instruments, inc a complete Japanese gamelan. Cl am, wknds, 25 Dec, Good Fri; free.

 UNIVERSITY MUSEUM (Parks Rd) Victorian Gothic building specialising in natural history – fossils and dinosaurs, a popular, working beehive (May–Nov) and even bits of Alice's dodo. Shop; cl am, Sun, some days over Easter and Christmas; free.

 HISTORY OF SCIENCE MUSEUM (Broad St) Scientific and medical equipment, clocks, cameras and other exhibits, housed in one of the city's nicest old buildings. Cl 1–2.30pm, wknds, bank hols, and a wk at Christmas and Easter; free.

 MUSEUM OF MODERN ART (Pembroke St) Modern art museum with the sort of exhibitions and displays of paintings and sculpture not often found in galleries outside London. Meals, snacks, good bookshop, disabled access; cl am Sun, Mon; (01865) 722733; cl Christmas; *£2.50.

 MUSEUM OF OXFORD (St Aldates) Interesting little museum about the archaeology and history of the city, with recreated rooms, models, maps, period music and sound effects. Shop; cl Sun, Mon; cl 25–26 Dec, 1 Jan; free.

 CASTLE MOUND Not much left of Oxford's Norman castle other than the tower and crypt of the castle church, and an underground, medieval well chamber, but the mound gives quite good views over the city and its surroundings. Tours pm Weds twice a month July–Sept – tel Mrs O'Neill on (01865) 815559 for dates; £2.

 There are particularly fine VIEWS from the tower of the interesting university church of ST MARY on the High St (shop, snacks; cl am Sun, 24–26 Dec; £1.40), or from Oxford's oldest building ST MICHAEL AT THE NORTH GATE on Cornmarket St, a Saxon church with interesting displays of silver, clocks and bells. Cl during services; £1. Right at the traditional centre of the city CARFAX TOWER, all that remains of a 14th-c church, also has good views, and the bells in the tower are interestingly designed. Shop; cl Nov–Mar; £1.20.

 PUNTING is good fun in sunny weather; once you've got the knack it's a very nice way of spending a lazy afternoon. You can hire boats from Magdalen Bridge or Folly Bridge; usually about £6 an hour, but you'll probably have to put down a big deposit. From Folly Bridge, Salters also run steamer trips to Abingdon.

 TELECOM MUSEUM (Speedwell St) Unusual collection of telephone and telegraph equipment, well illustrating the development of telecommunications. Disabled access; open by appointment only; (01865) 246601; free.

 ROTUNDA MUSEUM OF ANTIQUE DOLLS' HOUSES (SP5203 Grove House, Iffley Turn) 2 m S of the city centre, a private collection of over 40 historic houses, dating from 1700–1900, with period furniture, carpets, dinner services, books and inhabitants. No under-16s; open pm Sun May–mid-Sept, or by written appointment; *£2. Iffley's Norman CHURCH is one of the county's finest. There are a few worthwhile shops dotted about; Blackwells is the main bookseller, with several branches around the Broad St area (their music shop on Holywell St is good). Nr the station, the OXFORD ANTIQUE TRADING Co is one of the largest, permanent antique centres in the country, with 80 dealers under one roof.

Walks

Most of the walking you do here will be from college to college and building to building, but there are more countrified walks almost from the city centre.

The university parks are the closest place to the centre for a good stroll – and in summer you can watch first-class cricket matches for free.

The best outlying area is **Port Meadow**, an expanse of waterside common land with grazing horses and flocks of geese, which extends N from Jericho and can be reached on the far side of the Oxford Canal via Walton Well Rd, crossing the Thames and turning right along the W bank. Just beyond the far end of Port Meadow is the ruin of 12th-c Godstow Nunnery, where 'Fair Rosamund', the mistress of Henry II is buried; nearby, the riverside, medieval Trout pub is attractive, with peacocks wandering around. A second, well sited riverside pub, the thatched Perch at Binsey, is another popular objective in this direction.

Iffley Meadows on the other side of the centre are conserved for wildlife, and in late spring are a sea of purple snakes-head fritillaries.

The rivers **Thames** and **Cherwell** make strikingly rural corridors through the city, though walks along the Cherwell may be impeded by closed college gates. They are most likely to be open in mid-afternoon.

From the big garden of the Fishes at South Hinksey SP5004, a footpath towards the town partly follows a causeway built originally by John Ruskin to give students experience of healthy outdoor labour.

Where to eat

15 NORTH PARADE (01865) 513773 Smart, French-style restaurant, run by women, with comfortably cushioned chairs, changing paintings on the walls and a calm, informal atmosphere; very good food inc delicious home-baked bread and a vegetarian dish, decent wines; the service is efficient, friendly and unobtrusive; cl pm Sun, 25 Dec, 1 Jan, disabled access. £23/£12.

GEES 61a Banbury Rd (01865) 53540 Relaxed, airy atmosphere in a genuine old conservatory, fresh herbs and spices to enliven interesting vegetarian pastas, wild mushrooms and so forth as well as good meat and fish dishes, unusual wines; partial disabled access (spiral stair to lavatories). £19/£3.95.

TIBERIO 260 Banbury Rd, Summertown (01865) 54117/67210 Welcoming Italian restaurant with good food and pleasant, efficient and friendly service; cl Sun; disabled access. £18/£7.50.

CAFÉ MOMA Museum of Modern Art Pembroke St (01865) 722733 Clean, light and very popular self-service café in the museum basement; simple modern furnishings, exhibitions, largely vegetarian food, excellent cakes, and efficient, friendly service; cl Mon, Good Fri, Christmas; disabled access. £10/£3.80.

The ancient Turf Tavern in Bath Pl between Holywell St and New College Lane is the most interesting pub, and other decent pubs include the Bear (Alfred St), Kings Arms (Holywell St), Rose & Crown (North Parade) and the White Horse (Broad St). The Victoria Arms at Old Marston, with a big garden on the Cherwell, is a popular punters' destination, and the Isis by Iffley Lock is another pleasant riverside pub.

Other useful places include, for full meals, Bath Place Hotel (Bath Pl), Blue

Coyote (Cowley Rd), L'Escargot, Georginas and Hi-Lo (Covered Market), Hot Pot (St Clements), Michaels and Nosebag (St Michaels), Whites (Turl St); for pizzas etc, Coco's (Cowley Rd), Mama Mia (South Parade) and Pizza Express (Golden Cross – interesting medieval building); for snacks etc, Beatons and Browns (Covered Market), a different Browns (Woodstock Rd), Heroes (Ship St), Mortons (Broad St), Queens Lane Café (High St), Rosie Lee teashop (High St) and St Giles Café (St Giles); for Chinese, Liaison (Castle St) and Opium Den (George St); for Indian, Jamals (Walton St); for Indonesian, Munchy-Munchy (Park End St); for cocktails and jazz, Freuds (Walton St).

NORTH OXFORDSHIRE

Attractive Cotswolds countryside in the west, civilised places to stay, good eating out; Blenheim is the great attraction, other interesting places too.

Blenheim is the county's great showpiece; it's genuinely a palace, with memorable lakeside grounds, as well as lots of things to do if you (or your children) want to be amused. Nearby Woodstock is an attractive small town. Elsewhere, the gardens at Waterperry (and those of Cornwell Manor, if you can time your visit right), Broughton Castle and Rousham House are all particularly appealing.

The villages and countryside have a distinctly Cotswolds flavour over in the west, and up in the north-west corner of the county many of the buildings use a particularly beautiful golden stone. There are some really lovely villages, and a special pleasure here is tracking down ones that are far less well known than the famous visitor honeypots such as Burford: Great Tew, heavily protected by listed building orders, is remarkably unspoilt for such a pretty village. Most of the small towns and even the larger villages have antique shops and craft shops that are at least worth a look.

There are a few attractions to take children out to, but on the whole this area is not well served in this respect.

A good choice of places to stay includes quite a few charming, old small inns and a couple of friendly family farmhouses that seem particularly to suit the character of the area. In addition to the restaurants we list, a great many of the local pubs have decent food.

Where to stay

Horton-cum-Studley SP5912 STUDLEY PRIORY Horton-cum-Studley, Oxford OX9 1AZ (0186 735) 616 **£125**; 19 rms. Once a Benedictine nunnery, this lovely 12th-c building (which has little changed since Elizabethan times) stands in 13 acres of wooded grounds; fine panelling, 16th- and 17th-c stained-glass windows, antiques and open fires in the elegant drawing room and cosy bar, seasonally changing menus, and an attractive restaurant.

Woodstock SP4416 BEAR Park St, Woodstock OX20 1SZ (01993) 811511 **£121**; 45 comfortable, traditionally furnished rms. Originally a coaching inn and owned by Blenheim Palace, this 16th-c hotel has massive oak beams, a fine staircase, first-rate service, a cosy bar with paintings and cushioned Windsor chairs, and very good English cooking; disabled access.

Burford SP2512 BAY TREE 12–14 Sheep St, Burford OX18 4LW (01993 82) 2791 £110; 23 individually furnished rms. Attractive Tudor inn with a low-ceilinged bar, beams and flagstones, log fires, an airy conservatory, a pretty, terraced garden, and good, imaginative food.

Woodstock SP4416 FEATHERS Market St, Woodstock OX20 15X (01993) 812291 £99; 17 individually decorated rms. Lovely old building with a relaxing drawing room and study, open fires, first-class, friendly staff, a gentle atmosphere, and daily-changing imaginative food, inc lovely puddings; also, a sunny courtyard with attractive tables and chairs.

Chadlington SP3222 MANOR Chadlington, Chipping Norton OX7 3LX (01608) 676711 *£95; 7 attractive rms. In a pretty village, this small, Cotswold-stone manor house is set in 18 acres of grounds, with comfortable, graceful lounges, a relaxed atmosphere, open fire, very good, seasonally changing food, and an excellent wine list.

Weston-on-the-Green SP5318 WESTON MANOR Weston-on-the-Green, Bicester OX6 8QL (01869) 50621 £95; 36 rms with garden views. Imposing manor house in 13 acres of informal gardens, with a fine, oak-panelled, baronial hall dining room complete with minstrel gallery, carefully furnished lounges, and an outdoor swimming pool, squash and croquet; 10 mins to north Oxford; disabled access.

Kingham SP2523 MILL HOUSE Kingham, Chipping Norton OX7 6UH (01608) 658188 £90; 23 good rms. Carefully renovated, 17th-c flour mill with a comfortable, spacious lounge, an open log fire in the lounge bar, and original features such as two bread ovens; cosy, popular restaurant, and very good, interesting food; children over 5; disabled access.

Minster Lovell SP3111 OLD SWAN Minster Lovell, Witney OX8 5RN (01993) 774441 £90; 60 rms. Ancient and charming, Cotswold inn, with restful and attractive, low-beamed rooms opening off a small central bar, antiques, good china in corner cupboards, log fires in huge fireplaces, fine food in the restaurant (housed in what used to be the brewhouse), and extensive, pretty gardens with a medieval well; tennis, croquet; a sister hotel, the Minster Lovell Mill, is just opposite.

Burford SP2512 LAMB Sheep St, Burford OX18 4LR (01993) 823155 £80; 13 rms, 12 with own bthrm. 500-year-old Cotswold inn with a lovely, restful atmosphere, a spacious, beamed, flagstoned and elegantly furnished lounge, civilised public bar, bunches of flowers on oak and elm tables, three winter log fires, antiques, and good food in the airy restaurant; also, a pretty little garden; cl 25–26 Dec.

Charlbury SP3519 BELL Charlbury, Chipping Norton OX7 3AP (01608) 810278 *£75; 14 spotless, attractive rms. Small, neatly kept, 17th-c hotel with a warm and friendly atmosphere, quiet and civilised, flagstoned bar, a huge open fire, notable bar lunches, decent restaurant, and good breakfasts.

Chipping Norton SP3127 CROWN & CUSHION High St, Chipping Norton OX7 5AD (01608) 642533 £69; 40 splendid rms. 500-year-old coaching inn with a civilised and attractive, flagstoned bar, log fires, a flower-filled conservatory, good food in both the bar and restaurant; a sheltered garden and sun-trap terrace, and an indoor swimming pool/leisure centre.

Shipton-under-Wychwood SP2717 LAMB Shipton-under-Wychwood, Chipping Norton OX7 6AQ (01993) 830465 *£65; 5 comfortable rms. Ancient, Cotswold-stone pub with friendly and helpful licensees; a relaxed and civilised atmosphere, bar with an open log fire, highly polished furniture, and newspapers to read; extremely good food, especially breakfasts; no children.

Burford SP2512 ANGEL Witney St, Burford OX18 4SN (01993) 822438 £50; 2 rms. Pleasantly unassuming old inn with one attractive, flagstoned bar and another charmingly cosy one, generous, home-made bar food, inventive evening meals in the restaurant, inc lots of fish and seasonal theme menus, and a pretty, secluded garden and dining terrace.

Chipping Norton SP3127 FOX Market Place, Chipping Norton OX7 5DD

(01608) 642658 **£50**; 6 comfortable rms. Ancient old inn with an open fire and some antique oak settles in the rambling lounge, and friendly service from the Italian landlord; a wide choice of good food in both the bar and upstairs restaurant, and fine views from the back garden; cl 25 Dec.

Asthall SP2811 Maytime Asthall, Burford OX18 4HW (01993) 822068 **£48**; 6 quiet, cottage-style rms. Attractive, 16th-c, Cotswold-stone inn with a warmly welcoming landlord; a popular, plush dining bar, good food and decent wines, and huge breakfasts; worth an early spring-morning walk through the pretty village, across the fields to Swinbrook and back along the river.

Duns Tew SP4528 White Horse Duns Tew, Bicester OX6 4JS (01869) 340272 **£45**; 13 rms. In a picturesque village, this inn has lovely flagstones, old oak panelling on stripped masonry, ancient beams and enormous inglenook fireplaces; friendly staff, real ales, and good food in both the bar and restaurant; own golf course; disabled access.

Church Enstone SP3724 Crown Church Enstone, Chipping Norton OX7 4NN (01608) 677262 **£42**; 4 well appointed rms, most with own bthrm. Cotswold-stone inn in a pretty village, with an attractive horseshoe bar, friendly atmosphere and staff, good food in both the bar and restaurant, and decent breakfasts; no children.

Minster Lovell SP3111 Hill Grove Farm Minster Lovell, Witney OX8 5NA (01993) 703120 ***£41**; 2 rms. Friendly B & B on a mixed, family-run, 300-acre working farm, with good breakfasts; no smoking; cl Christmas.

Charlbury SP3519 Danbury Mill Farm Charlbury, Chipping Norton OX7 3JH (01608) 810314 **£40**; 3 rms. Cotswold-stone farmhouse with lovely views to Wychwood Forest; friendly atmosphere, decent food, and good service; can watch animals.

Stratton Audley SP6026 Old School Stratton Audley, Bicester OX6 9BJ (01869) 277371 **£40**; 4 rms, shared bthrm. Lovely, 400-year-old house with a quiet, restful atmosphere, peaceful drawing room, tea, coffee and home-made cake on arrival, and good breakfasts; all-weather hard tennis court, and an attractive garden; nearby thatched pub for evening meals.

Clifton SP4831 Duke of Cumberland's Head Clifton, Banbury OX15 0PE (01869) 38534 ***£35**; 3 rms with own showers in new, sympathetically built extension. Simply but stylishly refurbished, thatched, 17th-c stone inn with a friendly atmosphere; very good food in both the bar and restaurant, log fire, well kept beers and wines, and helpful service.

North Leigh SP3813 Woodman North Leigh, Witney OX8 6TT (01993) 881790 ***£32**; 2 comfortable rms, shared bthrm. Friendly little village pub with attentive licensees, good-value, freshly prepared food, well kept real ales, daily papers, and a big garden; no food Mon.

To see and do

🕊 🍎 **Banbury** SP4540, a busy shopping town, was actually without its famous cross for 250 years, between the Puritans destroying it in 1602 and the construction of its replacement in 1859. Also interesting is the tomb in St Mary's Church graveyard (on Horsefair) from which Jonathan Swift borrowed the name Gulliver for his traveller. Nearby there's a good local history museum. Snacks, shop, disabled access; cl Sun, winter Mon, Christmas; free. The splendid old Reindeer and the Wine Vaults, both in Parsons St, are useful for lunch. Out on the B4035 towards Broughton, there's good, summer pick-your-own.

🏛 🍎 **Broughton** SP4138 Broughton Castle Striking, early 14th- and 16th-c house with a proper moat and gatehouse, originally owned by William of Wykeham. Exceptional oak panelling, period furniture, paintings, and Civil War relics (in the Civil War an ancestor of the present Lord Saye and Sele was known as Old Subtlety, for his political skills). Some rooms have stone walls under elaborately plastered ceilings, an unusual combination that works rather well. Snacks, shop, disabled access to ground floor only; open Easter, then 18 May–14 Sept pm Weds, Sun and bank hol Mons, plus Thurs in July and Aug; (01295) 262624; £3.20. The Elephant & Castle at Bloxham is useful for lunch, and there's a decent little village MUSEUM here too.

★ † ☺ 🐾 ↕ ♪ 🏞 **Burford** SP2512 Lovely little Cotswold town with interesting shops and tearooms along its pretty main street. The CHURCH is particularly intriguing, with a super graveyard (some of the rich wool merchants who lived here had stone woolpacks as gravestones), and 17th-c graffiti by some of the 400 Leveller mutineers imprisoned here by Cromwell. The town also has an interesting little MUSEUM (open pm Apr–Oct, 40p), and is full of attractive pubs: the best for food and atmosphere are the Lamb and the Angel. Just outside town, the COTSWOLD WILDLIFE PARK has animals, birds and reptiles from all over the world in re-creations of their natural environment, with an aquarium, tropical and insect houses, brass-rubbing centre, adventure playground and summer train rides, all set in acres of attractive parkland. Meals, snacks, shop, disabled access; cl 25 Dec; (01993) 823006; *£4.60. In an area not especially rich in family attractions, this should prove popular with children. Burford does get very busy indeed with visitors, and it's worth noting that several smaller and altogether quieter nearby villages are, in their way, as pretty: TAYNTON SP2313, the BARRINGTONS SP2013 (just over the Gloucs border), FULBROOK SP2513, SWINBROOK SP2712 and ASTHALL SP2811. All except the first have the additional attraction of a decent pub. You can walk between these, along the River Windrush for much of the way.

★ ☺ † **Charlbury** SP3519 is a nice little town on the edge of the Cotswolds, with some fine old buildings, a small museum looking at the town's now-vanished, glove-making industry (open pm Sun and bank hols; free), and decent riverside and woodland walks. A mile or so W, the CHURCH at Shorthampton has some ancient wall paintings.

★ † 🏠 ☺ **Chipping Norton** SP3127 Very pleasant, old, stone-built wool town with an unusually wide market place, and a good few antique shops. The pretty ST MARY'S CHURCH (Church St) is one of the longest in the country, and has some interesting brasses. Among other attractive buildings, there are also some fine, 17th-c ALMSHOUSES. The interesting local history MUSEUM is scheduled to reopen on a new site this year. There are some unusual, old carved heads under a shop called the Playpen (High St), usually on view pm Thurs by appointment – check with the tourist information centre on (01608) 644379. The ancient Fox and the Blue Boar are civilised for lunch.

🏞🏠 **Deddington** SP4631 DEDDINGTON CASTLE Not much left of this 12th-c castle, but the huge earthworks of the outer and inner baileys can still be seen; free. There are some attractive stone buildings around the village square, and the Holcombe Hotel and King's Arms are good for lunch.

★ **Great Tew** SP3929 is the most charming village in the area (some would say in all England). It's an outstanding series of golden stone, 17th- and 18th-c cottages, some thatched and others with stone-slabbed roofs, around an attractive sloping green and among ancient trees, with wooded slopes above; the Falkland Arms here is a classic country tavern.

🏛 **Little Rollright** SP2930 ROLLRIGHT STONES Dramatic and mysterious Bronze Age stones, chiefly in a circle about 100ft across, dating from around 1800–550 BC; as they straddle the border with Warwicks, we've mentioned them in the Midlands chapter too. The Gate Hangs High nr here is useful for lunch.

🚗 **Long Hanborough** SP4214 OXFORD BUS MUSEUM Around 40 vehicles, from Oxford horse-trams to more modern machines up to the 1960s, some roadworthy, others in the course of restoration. Disabled access; open Sun only; (01993)

North Oxfordshire

Cropredy
Wardington
Shenington
Epwell
Wroxton
Banbury
Swalcliffe
Broughton
Adderbury
Clifton
Little Rollright
Deddington
Souldern
Chipping Norton
Great Tew
Duns Tew
Stratton Audley
Kingham
Church Enstone
Bicester
Chadlington
Rousham
Milton-under-Wychwood
Charlbury
Weston-on-the-Green
Shipton-under-Wychwood
Woodstock
Otmoor
North Leigh
Horton-cum-Studley
Burford
Widford
Long Hanborough
Asthall
Witney
Barnard Gate
Waterperry
Minster Lovell
Oxford

0   Miles   5

883617; £1. The Bell has good-value food.

★ † 🏠 **Minster Lovell** SP3111 is one of the prettiest and most unspoilt old villages in the area. There's an attractive, 15th-c CHURCH and village green, and a 15th-c bridge over the River Windrush narrow enough for the Welsh drovers to use for counting the sheep in the flocks they brought this way each year. MINSTER LOVELL HALL Imposing and attractively set, the 15th-c house was being used as ramshackle farm buildings until its 'restoration' as neat ruins in the 1930s. Enough survives to make it easy to believe the story about Richard III's favourite, Lord Lovell, being hidden in a secret room here after the king's downfall at Bosworth, and then dying of starvation with his dog when a trusted servant stopped feeding him; or even the Mistletoe Bough tale, about the girl playing party games on her wedding night, and hiding herself

in a chest which unfortunately locked on her, leaving her hidden till the discovery of her skeleton decades later. The medieval DOVECOT has been well restored. Snacks, shop; open Thurs–Sun (and bank hols) Apr–Sept; (01993) 775315; £1.05. The Old Swan Hotel does good light lunches, the White Hart up on the main rd does cheaper food.

🏠 🦆 † **North Leigh** SP3813 ROMAN VILLA Occupied between the 2nd and 4th c, when it was a very grand place with several dozen rooms. Ruins include an almost complete mosaic tile floor (though this may be not open in 1995), and the wooded setting is very pleasant; free. The medieval village CHURCH, with a Saxon tower, is lovely inside. The Woodman is handy for lunch.

♈ 🏠 🌼 ❅ **Otmoor** SP5615 is several square miles of flatland, so poorly drained that in very wet weather its river actually flows backwards.

Because serious farming is virtually out of the question, it does have more natural wildlife than most places in the county; there are several paths through it. The Abingdon Arms at Beckley, with excellent food, is one good starting point (and there's a decent farm shop there on the B4027 from Stanton St John); the Nut Tree at Murcott also has reasonable food, and the Plough at Noke is a good-value, country local. On one edge, the PICK-YOUR-OWN fruit farm at Elsfield SP5410 has nice views over the wilderness, as well as an unusually wide range of varieties.

🏠🖼🌼🐾 ⚘ † **Rousham** SP4724 ROUSHAM HOUSE Nicely unspoilt, 17th-c house embellished by court artist and architects, and remodelled in the 18th c by William Kent to give the external appearance of a Gothic Tudor mansion. It still has Civil War shooting holes in the door, as well as 150 paintings and fine, period furnishings. Excellent, 18th-c, classically landscaped garden with buildings, cascades, statues and vistas in 30 acres of hanging woods above the River Cherwell, and walled flower and vegetable gardens. No children under 15; some disabled access to grounds; house open pm Weds, Sun and bank hols Apr–Sept, gardens all year; £2.50 house, £2.50 garden. There's also a 12th-c church. The Red Lion at Steeple Aston is good for lunch (no children here, either), and the Gardiners Arms at Tackley is handy too.

† **South Newington** SP4033 The CHURCH here has some fine, medieval wall paintings; if it's locked you can get the key from the College Farmhouse next door.

🏠👁 **Swalcliffe** SP3737 SWALCLIFFE BARN One of the best-preserved barns in the country, with much of its medieval-timber, half-cruck roof intact. There's a display of agricultural and trade vehicles. Shop, disabled access; open pm Sun Apr–Oct, bank hols and Sat Jun–Aug; free. The village is pretty, and the Stag's Head is useful for lunch.

🌼🖼† **Waterperry** SP6206 WATERPERRY GARDENS Peaceful gardens and nurseries, between 1932 and 1971 the home of a celebrated

horticultural school; fine herbaceous borders, a rock garden, riverside walk, shrub borders, lawns, trees and useful nurseries. The grounds include a new arts and craft gallery, and a wonderfully tranquil little CHURCH, mainly Norman, but incorporating some Saxon work, with fine, ancient glass and brasses. Meals, snacks, excellent garden shop, good disabled access; cl Christmas and New Year and several days in July; (01844) 339254; *£2.20. The Clifden Arms in Worminghall just over the Bucks border is nice for lunch.

★🏠†🐾⚘⚘ **Witney** SP3510 Saxon kings used to hold their meetings, or witans, here, which is where the name comes from. It was a prosperous town in the Middle Ages, and is well known for its blankets, made here since medieval times. Quiet and relaxed, with picturesque stone buildings, a market square still with its ancient butter cross and 17th-c clock, and quite a few interesting old buildings such as the 13th-c church and 18th-c blanket hall. The Three Horseshoes in Corn St is attractive for lunch. COGGES FARM MUSEUM SP3609 Great fun – an entertaining and informative, Victorian, living farm museum, with period farmhouse kitchens and dairy, walled gardens, and local breeds of farm animals. Daily feeding, agricultural and craft demonstrations. Meals, snacks, shop, disabled access; cl am wknds, Mon (exc bank hols), Nov–Mar (exc Advent wknd when there are various seasonal events); (01993) 772602; £2.75.

🏠🌼🖼🦌⚘🗡⚘†❋ **Woodstock** SP4416 Civilised and prosperous small town, with good antique shops and fine stone buildings. In addition to the excellent if pricey Feathers Hotel, and cheaper Woodstock Arms are all good for lunch. BLENHEIM PALACE One of the most impressive stately homes in the country, Blenheim was given to the Duke of Marlborough by Queen Anne as a reward for his military achievements against the French. Fantastically grand, the house itself covers 14 acres, and the grounds stretch for well over 2,000. There's a lot to see: sumptuous State Rooms and 183-ft Long Library, an exhibition about Churchill (born here in 1874), and tapestries, sculpture and fine furnishings. The grounds, landscaped by Capability Brown, have an enormous maze and lots of other children's play areas, a walled garden and butterfly house. Rowing boats can be hired for the lake, and they can arrange fishing and shooting. Very much geared to visitors, and all carried out with great efficiency, yet it hasn't moved too far downmarket; this really is a splendid place for a day out. Meals, snacks, several shops and plant centre; disabled access in house, but limited in garden; house cl Nov–mid-Mar; (01993) 811091; £6.90, grounds only £4. OXFORDSHIRE COUNTY MUSEUM (Fletcher's House) Elegant town house with pleasant gardens and good displays of the county and its people. Snacks, shop, some disabled access; cl am Sun, Good Fri, winter Mon, 25–25 Dec; free. The graveyard of BLADON CHURCH, where Churchill is buried, has views over Blenheim Park.

✝ Among the county's many **fine churches**, one of the most interesting is at Widford SP2612, just outside Burford: very simple, but notable for three things – its medieval wall paintings, the remains of a Roman pavement at the W end of the chancel, and its surroundings, a former village that's now virtually disappeared. The one house that's left was in the past, in turn, a fulling mill, paper mill and flour mill.

★ **Other attractive villages** here, all with decent pubs, include Adderbury SP4635, Chadlington SP3222, Church Enstone SP3724, Cropredy SP4646, Duns Tew SP4528, Epwell SP3540, Milton-under-Wychwood SP2618, Shenington SP3742, Shipton-under-Wychwood SP2717 (interesting bookshop, lovely green, two good inns – one very ancient), Souldern SP5131, Wardington SP4945 and Wroxton SP4142.

Walks

Opportunities for walking are more limited here than over in the Gloucs Cotswolds, and there's rather more for walkers in the S of the county. However, there are quite a few attractive, shorter walks in the area.

Blenheim SP4416 ⌂-1 has plentiful paths and tracks through its huge estate, inc a public right of way. **Otmoor** wilderness SP5615 ⌂-2 is interesting to walk through: see entry in the **To see and do** section above.

The **Oxford Canal** ⌂-3 towpath closely parallels the railway as well as the River Cherwell, so you can walk from one village to another, for example from Lower Heyford SP4824 to Nethercott SP4820, and return by train. There's also access from the Boat and (with a new conservatory) Jolly Boatman at Thrupp SP4815.

Over in the W, the Cotswolds offer a handful of decent walks, such as along the **River Windrush** ⌂-4 from Burford SP2512 or Swinbrook SP2712, and around **Sibford Gower** SP3537 ⌂-5 (the thatched Wykham Arms is good for lunch here). There's also a nice, 8-mile, circular walk from the Plough at Finstock SP3616.

Closer to Oxford, there are several pleasant walks from the White Horse at **Forest Hill** SP5807 ⌂-6.

Driving

Some of the nicest country drives in this part of Oxfordshire are along the back roads around the valley of the River Windrush just N of the A40, W of Witney. These are all worth exploring, with a succession of attractive views.

The A44 (formerly the A34), N out of Oxford through Woodstock and on to Stratford (changing to the A3400 as it passes Chipping Norton), is probably the best road of all for giving an overview of the rolling North Oxfordshire scenery with its Cotswold overtones, but does carry quite a bit of traffic.

The B4035 from Banbury to Sibford Ferris, or the more northerly unclassified road looping off it through North Newington, Shutford and Epwell, takes you through attractively hilly farming country – very quiet; you can then track down through Hook Norton to Chipping Norton for a Cotswoldy drive, and on down to Charlbury and Witney on the B4026/B4022.

Since the opening of the M40 extension, the A4260 Oxford–Banbury road carries much less traffic and is a reasonably quick way of getting an overall picture of much of the area, with worthwhile detours into Tackley, Steeple Aston, Duns Tew, Deddington and Adderbury (all of which have decent pubs).

Where to eat

Chinnor SP7500 SIR CHARLES NAPIER Spriggs Alley 10 mins from exit 6, M40 (01494) 483011 Though most of the emphasis in this civilised pub is on the very good, stylish back restaurant, decorated with works by local artists, you can enjoy fine food from the short bar menu as well; a really good wine list, homely furnishings, winter log fire, and relaxed, friendly service; you can eat on the terrace in summer; it gets busy at weekends; cl pm Sun, Mon; children over 8 in evening; partial disabled access. £25|£4.75/£8.50.

Adderbury SP4635 RED LION (01295) 810269 Pleasantly civilised, 16th-c coaching inn with comfortable and attractive bar rooms, a lovely big inglenook, good, home-made bar food, decent wines, well kept beers, and friendly licensees; also bedrooms. £20/£9.

Barnard Gate SP4010 BOOT (01865) 881231 Thriving and well decorated, extended dining pub with an impressive choice of good, generous food, prompt and friendly service, well kept beers, decent wines, a big log fire, and a restaurant; £16.50|£2.50/£6.20.

SOUTH OXFORDSHIRE

Prosperous and civilised, with some fine hotels and restaurants – but not cheap.

This area has rather more varied countryside than in the north of the county, including as it does long reaches of the Thames, the edge of the Chilterns, and the altogether more open, sweeping downland south of the B4507/A417; it offers a wider range of possibilities for walkers. Like the rest of the county, it has attractive small towns and villages, and a fair number of places to visit, prime among them Stonor House, Buscot Park, Mapledurham House, the railway collection at Didcot, Greys Court near Henley, Dorchester Abbey, and – a new addition to the guide - Kelmscott Manor. Children enjoy the bird and animal collection at Ipsden, the model landscape at Long Wittenham, and trips on the river. It's one of the more expensive places for a short stay, though there's a fine choice of hotels and good food.

Where to stay

Great Milton SP6202 LE MANOIR AUX QUAT' SAISONS Great Milton, Oxford OX44 7PD (01844) 278881 £194; 19 opulent rms. Luxurious Jacobean manor in 27 acres of parkland and lovely gardens, with heated pool, and a kitchen garden (providing many of the cooking ingredients); sumptuous lounges with fine furniture, beautiful flowers and open fires, exemplary service, and exquisitely presented, superb food (at a price); residential cookery courses; disabled access.

Henley-on-Thames SU7882 RED LION Hart St, Henley-on-Thames RG9 2AR (01491) 572161 £112; 26 rms, most with own bthrm, some with river views. Handsome family-run and neatly kept, 16th-c riverside hotel with comfortable public rooms, very good, interesting food in the elegant, Regency-style restaurant, and particularly helpful, warm and friendly staff.

North Stoke SY6086 SPRINGS Wallingford OX10 6BE (01491) 836687 £110; 36 well furnished, spacious rms. Grand, mock-Tudor hotel with a restful atmosphere in the old-fashioned, panelled lounge and snug bar, fresh flowers, good restaurant food, friendly, helpful staff, and 30 acres of grounds with tennis, outdoor swimming pool, and a spring-fed lake; children by arrangement only; disabled access.

Moulsford SU5983 BEETLE & WEDGE Moulsford, Wallingford OX10 9JR (01491) 651381 £95; 10 pretty rms, most with a lovely river view. Civilised riverside hotel where Jerome K Jerome wrote *Three Men in a Boat* and where H G Wells lived for a time (it was The Potwell in *The History of Mr Polly*); informal, old, beamed Boathouse bar, lovely conservatory dining room, very good food, a carefully chosen wine list, open fires, fresh flowers, riverside terrace and waterside lawn with moorings, and a warmly welcoming atmosphere; no food 25 Dec; disabled access.

Stonor SU7388 STONOR ARMS Stonor, Oxford RG9 6HE (01491) 638345 *£92.50; 9 rms. Carefully restored, 18th-c hotel with an elegant restaurant and a pretty conservatory, relaxed, flagstoned bar, friendly staff, and good, imaginative food; disabled access.

Clanfield SP2801 PLOUGH Clanfield, Bampton OX8 2RB (0136 781) 222 £85; 6 rms. Rose-clad, 16th-c, Cotswold-stone manor house with a relaxed, beamed lounge bar, an open fire, friendly, helpful staff and very good food in the pleasant restaurant.

Wallingford SU6089 SHILLINGFORD BRIDGE Ferry Rd, Shillingford, Wallingford OX10 8LX (01865) 858567 £74; 42 rms. Riverside hotel with own river frontage, fishing and moorings; comfortable, bustling bars and an attractive restaurant (all with fine views), squash, swimming pool, and dinner-dance every Sat evening; disabled access.

Kingston Bagpuize SU4098 FALLOWFIELDS Southmoor, Kingston Bagpuize, Abingdon OX13 5BH (01865) 820416 £73; 5 rms. Delightful, Gothic-style, old manor house with elegant, relaxing sitting rooms, open fires, good food in the attractive dining room, and 2 acres of pretty gardens, with outdoor heated swimming pool and tennis court; children over 10.

Dorchester SU5794 GEORGE Dorchester, Wallingford OX10 7HH (01865) 340404 £70; 18 rms. Lovely, 500-year-old building with a comfortably old-fashioned and civilised bar, old beams, big fireplace, exceptionally fine wines, good food, and pleasant service; first used as a brewhouse for the Norman abbey opposite.

Clifton Hampden SU5495 PLOUGH Clifton Hampden, Abingdon OX14 3EG (01865) 407811 £55; 2 rms with thoughtful extras. Quaint little village pub close to the Thames and run by an extraordinarily obliging Turkish couple; a relaxed and friendly atmosphere, cosy bar with beams and panelling, two civilised lounge areas, a no-smoking restaurant, and good, fresh food (no chips).

Exlade Street SU6582 HIGHWAYMAN Exlade Street, Reading RG8 0UA (01491) 682020 £55; 4 rms. 17th-c pub in magnificent rolling countryside with fine views; an interesting variety of furniture in unusual, rambling, low-beamed rooms, and friendly, courteous service.

Uffington SU3089 CRAVEN Fernham Rd, Uffington, Faringdon SN7 7RD (01367) 820449 *£54; 7 pretty rms, most with own bthrm. Most attractive, 17th-c thatched house with a beamed sitting room, log fire in the inglenook fireplace, antiques, and a friendly, relaxed atmosphere; good food in the beamed, farmhouse kitchen, and lots of nearby walks; disabled access.

Faringdon SU2895 Crown Market Place, Faringdon SN7 7HU (01367) 242744 £39.50w; 11 rms, most with own bthrm. Interesting 16th-c inn with an old-fashioned, atmospheric bar, a fine inglenook fireplace, flagstones and panelling, good bar and restaurant food, friendly staff, and a lovely courtyard; cl 25–26 Dec.

Little Wittenham SU5693 Rooks Orchard Little Wittenham, Abingdon OX14 4QY (01865) 407765 £38; 3 rms. Comfortable 17th-c house in lovely gardens, with beams, inglenook fireplaces, and good breakfasts; dogs by arrangement; next to the Little Wittenham Nature Reserve and Clumps.

Weald SP3002 Morar Weald, Bampton OX18 2HL (01993) 850162 £38; 3 rms. Warm, friendly and neatly kept, modern stone house (no smoking) with helpful and knowledgeable owners; separate lounge and dining room, lovely English cooking in winter using home-grown produce (home-made bread and preserves, too); a pretty, flower-filled, big garden, and cats, a dog and goats (no visiting dogs allowed); cl 20–28 Dec; children over 6.

To see and do

★ 🏠✝👁 **Abingdon** SU4997
Attractive, Thames-side town, until 1974 the county town of Berkshire. Much expanded around its old, partly pedestrianised core, which was originally the easternmost centre for the area's wool industry. There's a fine old gatehouse, several handsome old buildings and almshouses around the impressive, 15th–16th-c, Wren-style CHURCH OF ST HELEN off Thames St, and the 17th-c former county hall (on High St) which has now become a good MUSEUM (cl Mon; free). The remains of the partly Norman, Benedictine ABBEY, once the second most powerful in England, have been restored, with part now housing a local theatre. The prettily placed, riverside Old Anchor is useful for lunch.

👁 **Benson** SU6191 Benson Veteran Cycle Museum Private collection of over 500 bicycles from between 1818 and 1930. Open Easter–Sept by appointment with Mr Passey, on (01491) 838414; free. The Queen's Head at Crowmarsh has good-value food.

✌ 🦋👁 **Bix Bottom** SU7288
Warburg Reserve is an extensive area of wildflower-rich, rough grassland and ancient beechwood, good for wild orchids and butterflies, besides birds and maybe deer. The Fox is handy for lunch.

🏠▣👁 **Buscot** SU2298 Buscot Park What makes this 18th-c house really special is the amazing collection of art and furnishings amassed by its owners; paintings by Reynolds, Gainsborough, Rembrandt, Murillo and several of the Pre-Raphaelites (inc a splendid series by Burne-Jones), with some more recent pictures too. The attractive grounds have formal water-gardens and a mouth-watering kitchen garden. Teas; open Apr–Sept pm Weds–Fri, also open every 2nd and 4th wknd in each month; *£4; NT. The Trout at St John's Bridge on the Lechlade rd is useful for lunch.

🚂 **Didcot** SO5290 Didcot Railway Centre The biggest collection anywhere of Great Western Railway stock, housed under cover, inc 20 steam locomotives, a diesel railcar and lots of passenger and freight rolling stock. Snacks, shop, disabled access; open wknds all year and wkdys Easter–Sept, best to ring for dates of steamdays, though they usually have them every Sun and Weds in the summer hols; (01235) 817200; £3–£5 depending on event. The town itself has nothing to detain a visitor.

✝👁★ **Dorchester** SU5794
Dorchester Abbey Very impressive and well preserved old abbey, with a 12th-c nave and rare lead font, and other parts from the next few centuries. The tower was rebuilt in 1605 and has a 14th-c spiral staircase, as well as a very rare Jesse window from the same period, and some mosaic-like, 12th-c glass in other windows. The adjacent former guesthouse now houses a little MUSEUM about the abbey and the area. In summer they do very English teas (pm Weds–Sun). Shop, disabled access;

museum cl 12.30–2pm, am Sun, Mon, Oct–Easter (exc first 2 wknds in Oct); free. The whole Thames-side village is a lovely place to explore, with interesting antique shops. The handsome old George is good for lunch, and there's home cooking in the Fleur de Lys and Plough.

⬥ 🐾 🏚 **Filkins** SP2304 COTSWOLD WOOLLEN WEAVERS Friendly, working woollen mill demonstrating traditional production methods in 18th-c buildings. Snacks, very good, well stocked shop, disabled access; (01367) 860491; cl am Sun, 25–31 Dec; free. The Lamb is useful for lunch. Craft workshops in the village include natural dyers (Filkins Farmhouse, appointment only (01367) 860253), traditional chair-makers (Calf Pens, Cross Tree) and saddlers (Oxleaze Farm).

🍎 🐷 🏚 **Frilford** SU4497 MILLETS FARM CENTRE has pick-your-own-fruit, animals, walks, and an unusually extensive farm shop, which takes in a bakery, delicatessen, garden centre, and wine merchant. Cl a few days over Christmas; (01865) 391555.

🏚 **Great Coxwell** SU2693 GREAT COXWELL BARN As noble as a cathedral according to William Morris, a 13th-c, stone-built, tithe barn 152ft long and 44ft wide, with beautifully crafted timbers supporting the roof; free. The Woodman at Fernham, on the other side of the A420, is an interesting old country tavern, nice for lunch.

★ ♨ 🏚 ❀ **Henley-on-Thames** SO7682 Pleasant, well heeled, Thames-side town famed for its summer regatta; you can usually see other rowing races or practices on the river throughout the year, and hire river boats: tel (01491) 572035. The Three Tuns has good food, and the riverside Little White Hart and Anchor are useful too. Nearby GREYS COURT (Rotherfield Greys) SO7283 is an attractive, gabled, Jacobean house with the interesting ruins of its medieval predecessor, but the gardens are the best feature, with white and rose gardens, ancient wisterias, a kitchen garden, wheelhouse and brick maze. They've recently added a new ornamental garden, brick ice-house, and 1830s carousel. Teas; open

Apr–Sept, house pm Mon, Weds and Fri, garden pm daily exc Thurs and Sun; £3.80 house and gardens, £2.80 gardens only; NT. The Maltsters Arms is handy for it.

🐦 ⬥ ❗ **Ipsden** SU6385 WELLPLACE BIRD FARM Hundreds of different kinds of birds and animals inc lambs, goats, otters, donkeys and monkeys. You can feed lots of the animals, so it's great for children. Meals, snacks, shop, disabled access; cl wkdys Oct–Easter; (01491) 680473; *£2. They have car-boot sales on bank hols. The King William IV, at Hailey nearby, is an excellent country pub with sweeping views and lots of old farm equipment which the landlord really knows about; he also has a shire horse which pulls a brewer's dray. A friend of his, Ian Smith, tel (01491) 641364, can arrange HORSE-DRAWN WAGGON RIDES through these pretty Chilterns fringes. Most fine summer days, he runs two-horse waggons from the old brick kiln by the main road through Nettlebed SU7086.

🏚 ❀ 🅱 **Kelmscot** SU2499 is a peaceful little village by the Thames; the Plough here is very good. KELMSCOTT MANOR The summer home of William Morris until his death in 1896, now filled with a sumptuous collection of his furnishings and fabrics, and a good number of his possessions. It's easily one of the best assemblages of Morris memorabilia, standing out all the more for its domestic setting. Also works by other Pre-Raphaelite artists, inc splendid paintings by Rossetti, who initially shared the lease. Snacks, shop, disabled access to ground floor only; open Weds Apr–Sept, cl 1–2pm; (01367) 252486; *£5. We follow the Ordnance Survey spelling for the village, though many people now give it two ts.

🏚 ❀ **Kingston Bagpuize** SU4098 KINGSTON HOUSE Charming 17th-c manor house with lovely panelling, a fine staircase, attractive furnishings and a friendly, unstuffy feel; peaceful garden with mature flowering shrubs, woodland walks, and Georgian gazebo over a former Elizabethan cockpit. Snacks, shop; open pm Sun and bank hols Apr–Sept; (01865) 820259; *£3.50, garden only *£1. The Hind's Head is good value for lunch.

⊙ **Long Wittenham** SU5493 PENDON MUSEUM OF MINIATURE LANDSCAPE AND TRANSPORT Charming exhibition showing a highly detailed model railway and meticulously researched, 1930s, model village scenes; you can often see modellers working on the exhibits, and they're always happy to chat. Snacks, shop, disabled access by arrangement; open pm wknds and bank hols, cl mid-Dec–early Jan; (01865) 407365; £2. The Machine Man and riverside Plough are handy for lunch.

★ ⚘ 🏠 🕸 ✕ **Mapledurham** SU6776 Very attractive little community with lovely beechwoods full of birds. The best way to reach it is by boat from the Caversham Promenade at Reading, operating whenever MAPLEDURHAM HOUSE is open. This is an impressive Elizabethan mansion in pretty parkland running down to the Thames, with lots of paintings and family portraits, great oak staircases and moulded Elizabethan ceilings. In the grounds is the MAPLEDURHAM WATERMILL, the last mill on the Thames to use wooden machinery, still fully operational and producing flour, bran, semolina and grain. Also riverside walks and an island with picnic area. Teas, shop, disabled access to ground floor only; open pm Sat, Sun and bank hols Easter–Sept; (01734) 723350; £4 house and watermill, £3 house only, £2.50 watermill only.

🏠 🕸 **Milton** SU4892 MILTON MANOR Elegant, 17th-c manor house with a splendid, Strawberry Hill 'gothick' library and interesting wings, chapel, stables, walled garden and grounds; unusual collections of teapots and fine china. Snacks; grounds open pm Easter wknd, then Weds and Sun May–Aug, plus bank hols, and Tues and Thurs in Aug, tours of house 2.30 and 3.30pm; (01235) 831287; £3, grounds only £1.50. Caltons nearby has good food.

🍒 **Milton Hill** SU4790 is surrounded by CHERRY ORCHARDS, a fine sight when the white blossom is out in spring, and with plump, red-black, fresh cherries from roadside stalls around July.

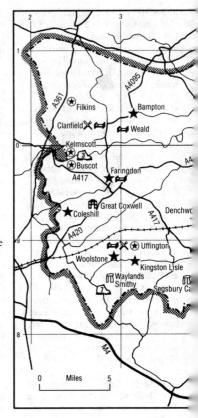

🏠 🕸 **Nuffield** SU6687 NUFFIELD PLACE The home of Lord and Lady Nuffield from 1933–1963, with the original 30s furnishings; very good gardens with mature trees and shrubs, inc rhododendrons, lawns, pond and rockery, as well as Lady Nuffield's own Wolseley. Teas, shop, limited disabled access; open pm 2nd and 4th Sun each month May–Sept; (01491) 641224; £2.50. The Crown pub here has good food.

✝ **Rycote** SP6604 RYCOTE CHAPEL Peaceful, little private chapel founded in the 15th c and visited by both Elizabeth I and Charles I; still has the original font and fine 17th-c interior. Shop, disabled access; open 11 Apr, 2 May, 13 Jun, 18 July, 29 Aug, 19 Sept; 95p. The Bell at Great Milton has good, home-cooking.

🏛 🌼 **Segsbury Camp** SU3884, reached by the dead-end lane up past the

South Oxfordshire

Sparrow in Letcombe Regis, is a big Iron Age hill fort, also used by the Romans, with good views.

❀ **Sonning Common** SU7080 HERB FARM Extensive range of herb plants and products, with over 3,200 different species in the display garden. A restored 19th-c granary has an exhibition of agricultural implements and there's a maze. Snacks, disabled access; cl Mon (exc bank hols and in Dec), 25–26 Dec; (01734) 724220; free, 50p for maze. The Butcher's Arms is an enjoyable dining pub with weekend family entertainment.

★ ⌂ ❀ **Stanton Harcourt** SP4105 is an attractive village, with the medieval MANOR HOUSE really rather unusual and well worth a look. The conical great kitchen has no chimney – the smoke from ovens and fireplaces collected in the cone of the roof and drifted out through wooden louvres;

the gardens too are appealing. Disabled access; open roughly pm Thurs and Sun fortnightly from Easter–Sept, plus bank hols – best to check first; (01865) 881928; *£3, garden only *£1.50. The Harcourt Arms nearby does good meals.

⌂ ▣ ❀ ♿ **Stonor** SU7388 STONOR HOUSE AND PARK Despite the stately Tudor façade this ancient house actually dates back to 1180, and there are beautiful furnishings, paintings, sculptures and tapestries from all over the world. The lovely gardens have an unusual exhibition of sculpture from Zimbabwe, and there's a wooded deer park. Snacks, shop, disabled access; open Apr–Sept pm Sun, plus May–Sept pm Weds, July/Aug pm Thurs and Aug pm Sat; (01491) 638587; *£4, garden only £2. The Stonor family still use the chapel to celebrate Roman Catholic mass, as they have for 800 years; St Edmund Campion used it in 1581. The smart Stonor Arms is useful for lunch.

★ † **Thame** SP7005 is worth a look for its splendid range of unspoilt architecture. The main street is very wide and has escaped any significant development this century, so there are a number of medieval, timber-framed buildings next to stately Georgian houses; the 13th-c CHURCH is attractive. The 15th-c Birdcage Inn used to be the town lock-up; the Abingdon Arms is useful for a bite to eat, and at Easington, out past Long Crendon, the Mole & Chicken does very good food.

★ ☗ 🏛 ❈ ! **Uffington** SU3089 is a charming village, and the Fox & Hounds opposite John Betjeman's former house has decent food. TOM BROWN'S SCHOOL MUSEUM Young Mr Brown's schooldays must have been based on those the author Thomas Hughes passed here; the building now has a very interesting exhibition on his life and work. Shop, disabled access; open pm wknds and bank hols Easter–Oct; *30p. UFFINGTON CASTLE Iron Age fort that covered 8 acres but had only one gateway, now offering great views over the vale below; free. On the hillside is a 375-ft WHITE HORSE carved into the chalk, very Celtic in style, and now thought to be at least 2,000 years old. If you stand in the centre of the eye and turn around three times with your eyes closed, any reasonable wish will be granted. This is one good setting-off point for the Ridgeway – see **Walks** section, below. Off the B4507 below the White Horse, a bit over a mile E, the turning off up towards the downs opposite the Kingston Lisle rd almost immediately passes a cottage on the left which has outside a huge, pitted, flint rock, locally known as the blowing stone: if you blow in the right hole and in the right way you can produce a splendid, deep blast of sound.

🏰 ☗ **Wallingford** SU6089 Ruins of a 13th-c CASTLE on a hill, the history of which can be found at the nearby MUSEUM, along with other local history, and a reconstructed Victorian street. Cl am, all Mon (exc bank hols), winter Suns, and Dec–Feb; £1. The Little House Around the Corner By the Brook is a civilised family pub in a lovely, streamside spot by the church.

† 🏛 ☗ ✕ **Wantage** SU4087 Historic town where King Alfred was reputedly born; recently much expanded, though there's an attractive, quiet corner by the 13th–15th-c CHURCH with its raised graveyard, and in Newbury St, 17th-c almshouses have a courtyard cobbled with bones, nr the King Alfred tearooms (which John Betjeman's wife used to run). The Lamb down in Mill St is the best pub here. VALE AND DOWNLAND MUSEUM CENTRE (Church St) Lively local history and geology museum. Meals, snacks, shop, disabled access; cl am Sun, Mon, Good Fri, Christmas; free. A few miles N on the A338 at Venn, the WATERMILL is the regularly used working corn mill in the area; open 2nd Sun in month Apr–Oct; £1.

🏛 **Waylands Smithy** SU2885, midway along the Ridgeway between White Horse Hill (see Uffington entry, above) and the B4000 above Ashbury (where the Rose & Crown is ideally placed for walkers), was even in Saxon times reputed to be the forge of a magic blacksmith, who would invisibly shoe your horse overnight if you left it there with a silver coin – and exact horrid penalties if you tried to slip by without paying. It's an impressive place, alone on the downs, an excavated NEOLITHIC BURIAL CHAMBER over 5,000 years old, made with massive sarsen stones each weighing several tons; free.

✕ 🏚 🐾 **Wheatley** SP5905 has an unusual octagonal WINDMILL, open by appointment, (01865) 874610; free. Just S at Garsington SP5702, JENNINGS FARM SHOP has a wide range of produce as well as craft workshops and a working blacksmith's forge.

★ 🚂 🏚 **Whitchurch** SU6377 is an attractive little village, with nice walks nearby; the Greyhound does good-value food. The BOZE DOWN VINEYARD has won several awards in recent years, and they have free tastings at weekends (cl am Sun, Christmas); (01734) 844031. Nearby Path Hill Farm has a shop selling various organic products.

★ **Other attractive small towns and villages** here, all with decent pubs, include Ardington SU4388 (several craft workshops in the Home Farm buildings), Bampton SP3103, Blewbury SU5385, Brightwell Baldwin SU6595, Chalgrove SU6396, Clifton Hampden SU5495, Coleshill SU2393 (lots of good walks nearby), Denchworth SU3791, East Hendred SU4588, Ewelme SU6491, Faringdon SU2895, Kingston Lisle SU3287, Lewknor SU7198, Marsh Baldon SU5699, Stoke Row SU6784 (with its unusual Maharajah's Well), Sutton Courtenay SU5093 (the food at Notcutts Garden Centre here is praised by readers), Sydenham SP7201 (lovely church), Woolstone SU2987 and Wytham SP4708.

Walks

SE of Oxford the **River Thames** passes Dorchester SU5794 △-1, a fine old town with timber-framed houses and a venerable old coaching inn (the George). Paths lead from here to the river, which can be crossed at Day's Lock SU5693; a short walk brings you to Sinodun Hills SU5692 (alternative access from the adjacent car park), a pair of hillocks which look across the Chilterns and Berks Downs. The **Thames Valley** proper △-2, shared with Berks and Bucks, has a classic, very English sort of beauty, with boating scenes, superb trees and riverside architecture. Riverside walks on the Oxon side are possible only in places, notably between Henley SU7682 and Sonning SU7575; you can also get down to the Thames from the attractive Perch & Pike at South Stoke SU5983.

The **Upper Thames,** △-3, W of Oxford, flows through low-lying country, not outstanding for walking along – although the towpath itself is pleasant enough, with Cotswold villages making good focal points: from William Morris's house at Kelmscot SU2899, for example, it is a straightforward mile and a half E to the Swan at Radcot Bridge SU2899. Other useful pubs for enjoyable if undramatic riverside strolls are: the Trout on the unclassified rd between Bampton and Buckland at Tadpole Bridge SP3300; the Maybush, on the A415 at Newbridge SP4001 (the Rose Revived here is worth knowing for its big Thames-side lawn); the Ferry, off the B4449 S of Stanton Harcourt at Bablock Hythe SP4304 and the Talbot, on the B4044 nr Swinford Bridge SP4408.

The Chilterns have numerous possibilities for exploring the beechwoods and farmlands, though the chalk hills' more memorable viewpoints and landscapes mostly lie outside the county (see Bucks chapter). **Stonor Deer Park** △-4 is skirted by an attractive right of way from Stonor village SU7388, and you can link this with the famous Maharajah's Well at Stoke Row SU6784; or you can continue E to Turville SU7690 (see Bucks chapter). At **Cowleaze Wood** SU7295 △-5, between Christmas Common SU7193 and the M40, forest art exhibits are scattered around as part of a sculpture trail. On the **Oxfordshire Way** △-6, a short walk with a palpable sense of peace is the one from the lane out of Bix, past Bix Hall to Valley End Farm SU7286. Useful pubs for walkers in and around the Oxon Chilterns include the Fox at Bix SU7285, Black Horse or Four Horseshoes at Checkendon SU6683, Fox & Hounds on Christmas Common SU7193, Highwayman at Exlade Street SU6582, King Charles Head on Goring Heath SU6678, Five Horseshoes at Maidensgrove SU7288, Olde Leathern Bottle at Lewknor SU7198, Crown at Pishill SU7389, Beehive at Russells Water SU7089, Maltsters Arms at Rotherfield Greys SU7282 (lovely church) and Crooked Billet at Stoke Row SU6784.

Nr the northern crest of the downs, the Ridgeway tracks right across the county from Wilts to Berks. This broad, grassy trackway was used as a herding highway for some 2,000 years before the Romans came, and after the break-up of the Roman Empire came back into use for the same purpose, well into medieval times. It's now part of the long-distance path network, and gives good walking with fine views. Nr Compton Beauchamp SU2787 △-7 is a particularly atmospheric short stretch, taking in the ancient sites of Waylands Smithy, the White Horse and Uffington Castle.

Driving

On the whole this area is not very good for country drives: there is least traffic in the W of the area, and the downland roads from here S into Berks have some long views. The B4507, below the downs W of Wantage, has some attractive views of the downs above it. Another decent downland road is the A417 through Blewbury, but it does carry rather a lot of traffic.

Over towards the Chilterns, the B480 Henley–Watlington through attractive rolling countryside – some wooded – is fairly quiet. Side roads in this same part are rewarding – for instance, the loop largely through woodland from off the B481 S of Nettlebed at Highmoor Cross, through Stoke Row and back up to Nuffield. The road steeply uphill from Watlington through Christmas Common and over the Bucks border to Northend is pleasant; going back down, there are fine views out over Oxon. The car park beside it gives access to Watlington Woods SU7093, with good views and a mass of bluebells in spring. Below the Chilterns escarpment, the B4009 running along on the edge of the plain from Watlington to Chinnor and beyond gives nice views of the hills above. Though the A423 Henley–Wallingford goes through attractive scenery, it does carry quite a bit of traffic.

Where to eat

Goring SU6080 LEATHERNE BOTTEL (01491) 872667 Smart restaurant overlooking a quiet stretch of the Thames, with excellent food using home-grown herbs, local game and vegetables, and fresh fish delivered daily; cl 25 Dec. £30/£12.50.

Stoke Row SU6784 CROOKED BILLET (01491) 681048 Country dining pub with pubby furnishings and a wide choice of interesting, often inventive, waitress-served food; decent wines, well kept beers, log fires, and a big garden by Chiltern beechwoods. £26.50/£8.50.

Sutton Courtenay SU5093 FISH 4 Appleford Rd (01235) 848242 Outstanding, imaginative food in this popular dining pub, with daily fresh fish and local produce (vegetarian dishes, too); good wines, well kept real ale, lovely nibbles, and friendly staff; cl 3/4 days between Christmas and New Year; disabled access. £25|£4.95/£11.95.

Brightwell Baldwin SU6595 LORD NELSON (01491) 612497 Busy, 17th-c inn with a very good, daily-changing menu featuring some imaginative dishes in both the bar and restaurant, friendly waitress service, a good wine list, and popular Sunday lunches; cl pm Sun; children over 7; disabled access. £21.50|£4.95/£8.50.

Maidensgrove SU7288 FIVE HORSESHOES (01491) 641282 17th-c, little brick house with a log fire in the rambling bar; very good, often imaginative bar food, well kept real ales, decent wine list, and a walkers' bar – the surrounding Chiltern beechwoods are popular; summer barbecues in the nice garden; children allowed away from bars; disabled access. £18.50|£3.50/£7.50.

Watlington SU6894 CHEQUERS (01491) 612874 Rambling, candlelit pub with a wide choice of very good food in the bar, and a pretty garden; no children. £18|£2.50/£6.

Nuffield SU6687 CROWN (01491) 641335 Attractive, brick-and-flint pub in fine countryside; with roaring winter log fires, a wide choice of good, home-made food, a comfortable and relaxed atmosphere, well kept beers, decent wines and prompt, friendly service; cl 25–26 Dec, pm 1 Jan; children in own room lunchtimes only. £17.75|£2/£6.50.

Clanfield 2802 CLANFIELD TAVERN Pretty pub with welcoming staff, heavy-beamed, stone-walled, small rooms leading off the main bar and very good, interesting food from a daily-changing menu, inc lovely puddings. £15|£1.75|£2.25.

Uffington SU3087 BRITCHCOMBE FARM (01367) 820667 Working farm, in a lovely spot right underneath White Horse Hill, offering afternoon teas on Sat, Sun and bank hol Mons, with home-made scones, cream teas, cakes and so forth; very friendly service, a log fire in winter, tables outside amongst the geese and sheep in summer; some fruit and vegetables, home-made mohair knitwear and crafts, mobile home for hire, and certified camping/caravan site; disabled access. £2.50.

Help this year from: Rolf Schneider, Roger Giffard, Jack Gerber, Richard Morley, David Domeracki, Dr P J Hoozman, Lizzie Broadbent, Joan Olivier, Simon Briston, Tim Brierly, Lorraine Webster, Pete Baker, Lynn Sharpless, Bob Eardley, Peter and Audrey Dowsett, Jim and Maggie Cowell, P and J Shapley, Elizabeth Chalmers, Jon Carpenter, Christopher and Sharon Hayle, Mrs J Burton, George Atkinson, John Sanders, Mr and Mrs N Hazzard, Heather Couper, Nigel Herbert, A P Seymour, Jamie and Sarah Allan, Chris Warne, Roderic Plinston, Ian Phillips, Walter Reid, Sue Demont, Tim Barrow, Brian and Anna Marsden, Peter and Anne Hollindale, Geoff Lee, Paul Randall, Mr and Mrs G D Amos, Tony Walker, Marjorie and David Lamb, Dick Brown, Nick Cox, David Heath, Graham Reeve; we are also grateful for particular help from the clerks of a number of parish councils here.

OXFORDSHIRE CALENDAR

Some of these dates were provisional as we went to press.

MAY

6 **Woodstock** Craft Fair at Blenheim Palace – *till Mon 8* (01993) 811091

7 **Tackley** Horse Show and Sheepdog Trials at Tackley Showground (01235) 520858

25 **Oxford** Beating the Bounds at St Michael's Church (01865) 240940

28 **Woodstock** Grand Charity Cricket Match at Blenheim Palace (01865) 247427

29 **Oxford** Lord Mayor's Parade and Show at South Park (01865) 252826

JUNE

3 **Great Milton** Oxfordshire Federation of Young Farmers Club Country Show and Rally at Views Farm Barns (01865) 872334

4 **Coleshill** Children's Day at Buscot and Coleshill Estate (01494) 528051; **Henley-on-Thames** VW Rally at Stonor Park (01491) 638587

17 **Abingdon** Election of the Mayor of Ock St: tradition since 1700 with a fight over an ox, votes counted *at 4pm*, new mayor invested with the regalia of office, drinks from a 200-year-old mace, and is chaired down Ock St; Morris dancing into the evening

28 **Henley-on-Thames** Henley Royal Regatta – *till 2 July* (01491) 572153

OXFORDSHIRE CALENDAR

JULY

1 **Hook Norton** Rural Fayre – *till Sun 2* (01608) 737861

5 **Henley-on-Thames** Arts Festival – *till Sat 8* (01491) 410414

8 **Oxford** Horse Races and Craft Fair on Wolvercote Common (01865) 58845

13 **Waterperry** Art in Action at Waterperry Gardens – *till Sun 16* (0171) 381 3192

14 **Radley** Fireworks Concert at Radley College – *till Sun 16, also Fri 21– Sun 23* (01865) 864056

15 **Sonning Common** Country Fayre at the Herb Farm and Saxon Maze – *till Sun 16*; **Woodcote** Rally and Country Fair at Crays Pond (01491) 680240

29 **Woodstock** Fireworks Concert at Blenheim Palace – *till Sun 30* (01865) 864056

AUGUST

5 **Claydon** Vintage Fayre at the Granary Museum, Butlins Farm – *till Sun 6* (01295) 690258; **Woodstock** Flower Show at Blenheim Palace – *till Sun 6* (01525) 405771

11 **Cropredy** Folk and Rock Festival with Fairport Convention – *till Sat 12* Fax (01869) 337142

12 **Henley-on-Thames** Traditional Boat Rally at Fawley Meadow – *till Sun 13* (01753) 852413

25 **Henley-on-Thames** Chilterns Craft Show at Stonor Park – *till Mon 28* (01491) 638587; **Towersey** Village Festival – *till Mon 28* (01296) 394411

26 **Woodstock** Craft Fair at Blenheim Palace – *till Mon 28* (01993) 811091

27 **Abingdon** Horse Show at Rye Farm Meadow (01235) 520858; **Uffington** White Horse Show – *till Mon 28* (01235) 760176

28 **Heathfield** Show

SEPTEMBER

4 **Oxford** St Giles Fair – *till Tues 5* (01865) 726871

9 **Beckley** Otmoor Country Show and Fair at Lower Woods Farm – *till Sun 10* (01865) 351741; **Hambleden** Henley Show (01491) 410948

10 **Abingdon** MG Vintage Rally starting at the works (01235) 522711

14 **Woodstock** Blenheim International Horse Trials at Blenheim Palace – *till Sun 17* (01993) 813255

21 **Thame** Agricultural Show (0184 421) 2737

OCTOBER

18 **Banbury** Michaelmas Fair (01295) 259 855

SHROPSHIRE

This county is extremely rewarding, with lovely, quiet countryside, some unusually well preserved old houses and ruins, and attractive old towns and villages. Shrewsbury is one of England's dozen or so most interesting towns, with plenty to fill a weekend stay, and Ludlow is a classic, picturesque small town. Readers have particularly enjoyed Attingham Park and the farm at Atcham, and Hawkstone Park. The aerospace museum at Cosford, the working farm at Acton Scott, the gardens of Hodnet Hall, and Stokesay Castle are also well liked. On the whole the county has more to offer adults than children, but for people of any age the Ironbridge museums, especially the lively open-air one, are among Britain's most enjoyable places to visit, and the Severn Valley Railway running out of Bridgnorth is perhaps the liveliest and most fun of all the country's steam railways.

The unspoilt countryside is the county's most appealing feature, with remarkable views from its set of distinctive hills. The partly heather-covered Long Mynd, the country's southernmost grouse moor, has great character, with the much smaller but very striking Caer Caradoc facing it across the valley; the rather eery Stiperstones, west of the Long Mynd, are outcrops of harder, quartzy rock leaving strange-shaped boulders, tors and crests on the skyline – and strange tales among the people living nearby; Wenlock Edge, to the east, is long and smoother, wooded along its flanks. Other notable hills are the rather volcanic-looking Titterstone Clee north-east of Ludlow, the aptly named Brown Clee north of that, and the bold Wrekin towering over Telford. Though there is some quarrying, it's not too obtrusive.

Down in the valleys of farmland, woods and streams, buildings are often of stone, with a lot of picturesque, black and white timbering.

The county scores for value, with low prices: there's a splendid range of comfortable and charming places to stay.

Where to stay

Ludlow SO5175 FEATHERS Bull Ring, Ludlow SY8 1AA (01584) 875261 **£98**; 40 comfortable rms. Hotel with an exquisitely proportioned and intricately carved, timbered frontage; Jacobean panelling and carving within, period furnishings, decent food in the bar, artistically presented restaurant dishes, and efficient, pleasant service; limited disabled access.

Shifnal SJ7508 PARK HOUSE Silvermere Park, Park St, Shifnal TF11 9BA (01952) 460128 **£97**; 54 individually decorated rms. Two 17th-c houses, quite different in style, make up this comfortable hotel; welcoming, helpful staff, fresh flowers, relaxing lounges, fine food in the restaurant and grill room, and a health club and leisure complex; good disabled access.

Ludlow SO5175 DINHAM HALL Dinham, Ludlow SY8 1EJ (01584) 876464 **£89.50**; 12 well equipped rms. Graceful Georgian hotel, opposite the castle, with a comfortable lounge, courteous service, very good food in the restaurant, lighter meals in the terrace bar, and secluded gardens.

Shrewsbury SJ4912 ALBRIGHT HUSSEY Ellesmere Rd, Shrewsbury SY4 3AF (01939) 290571 ***£85**; 5 lovely rms. Fine, moated, medieval manor house, partly timber-framed and partly stone and brick, in 4 acres of gardens; particularly good food in the timbered and panelled restaurant, and excellent service; children over 3.

Worfield SO7595 OLD VICARAGE Worfield, Bridgnorth WV15 5JZ (01746) 716497 £85; 14 pretty rms. Restful and carefully restored, Edwardian rectory standing in 2 acres of grounds, with 2 airy, conservatory-style lounges, very good, interesting food (lots of British cheeses, lovely puddings), a fine wine list, and warm, friendly, helpful service; cl 1 wk from 26 Dec; disabled access.

Albrighton SJ4918 ALBRIGHTON HALL Ellesmere Rd, Albrighton SY4 3AG (01939) 201000 £79.50w; 39 rms. Carefully restored country house with an attractive cocktail bar, good food and wine in the oak-panelled restaurant, and a relaxed atmosphere; also, a leisure complex with an indoor-heated swimming pool.

Cleobury Mortimer SO6775 REDFERN Cleobury Mortimer, Kidderminster DY14 8AA (01299) 270395 £70; 11 rms. Small Georgian hotel run by a friendly couple; with a cosy bar, farmhouse-style dining room, good, home-cooked food, and a log fire; disabled access, children £10 if sharing parents' rm.

Shrewsbury SJ4912 LION Wyle Cop, Shrewsbury SY1 1UY (01743) 353107 £70; 59 comfortable and attractive rms. Imposing old coaching inn with a cosy, oak-panelled bar and a sedate series of high-ceilinged rooms opening off, lots of beams, open fires, and comfortable sofas and seats; obliging staff and good food in both the bar and restaurant.

Norton SJ7200 HUNDRED HOUSE Bridgnorth Rd, Norton, Shifnal TF11 9EE (0195 271) 353 £69; 10 cottagey rms. Carefully refurbished, mainly Georgian inn with quite a sophisticated feel; neatly kept bar with old, quarry-tiled floors, beamed ceilings and oak panelling, handsome fireplaces, consistently good, popular bar food, excellent breakfast and afternoon tea, and elaborate evening meals using the inn's own herbs; delightful garden, no dogs.

Hopton Wafers SO6476 CROWN Hopton Wafers, Kidderminster DY14 0NB (01299) 270372 *£60; 8 rms. Attractive, creeper-covered stone inn in pleasant countryside, with an interestingly furnished bar, inglenook fireplace, good food, decent house wines, beers and malt whiskies, and friendly, efficient service; also, a streamside garden.

Much Wenlock SO6299 TALBOT High St, Much Wenlock TF13 6AA (01952) 727077 £60; 6 rms. Dating from 1360 and once part of Wenlock Abbey, this converted, 18th-c malthouse is very civilised, with lovely flower arrangements, prints, very quiet music from 30s' and 40s' dance bands, warm, friendly and helpful staff, and justifiably popular food in the bar and no-smoking restaurant; cl Christmas; children must be well behaved.

Church Stretton SO4593 MYND HOUSE Little Stretton, Church Stretton SY6 6RB (01694) 722212 *£58; 8 rms, most with extensive views and period furnishings. Friendly Edwardian hotel at the foot of the Long Mynd, with comfortable lounges, a cosy bar, log fire, caring staff and good food and fine wines in the candlelit restaurant; lots of walks; cl Christmas, Jan, 2 wks summer; dogs accepted in some bedrooms.

Hopesay SO3883 OLD RECTORY Hopesay, Craven Arms SY7 8HD (0158 87) 245 £56; 4 comfortable rms, one with own sitting room. 17th-c rectory with a lovely, 2-acre garden overlooking Hopesay Hill (National Trust); comfortable drawing room with a log fire and baby grand piano, an attractive dining room, and excellent home cooking; no smoking; cl Christmas; children over 12.

Hodnet SJ6128 BEAR Hodnet, Market Drayton TF9 3NH (01630) 685214 *£55; 6 rms. Clean, comfortable, 16th-c hotel, serving a good range of reasonably priced and imaginative food in the big main bar and restaurant (small no-smoking area); also, a cocktail bar with an unusual sunken garden in the former bear pit, and a Baronial-style room for popular medieval banquets; ample parking.

Wenlock Edge SO5796 WENLOCK EDGE INN Wenlock Edge, Much Wenlock TF13 6DJ (0174 636) 403 £55; 3 rms, showers only. Family-run and wonderfully welcoming inn by the Ippikins Rock viewpoint, with lots of walks through NT land that runs along the Edge; lovely, chatty and relaxed atmosphere, very good, fresh, home-made bar food (not Mon), fine breakfasts, good, old-fashioned puddings, and a wide range of drinks; 2nd Mon evening of month is story-telling night; cl 24–26 Dec; no children.

Wrockwardine SJ6212 Church Farm Wrockwardine, Telford TF6 5DG (01952) 244917 £48; 6 rms, most with own bthrm. Friendly, Georgian farmhouse, built on a very ancient site overlooking the attractive garden and church; with a relaxed atmosphere, beams and a log fire in the lounge, and good, home-cooked food in the traditionally furnished dining room; disabled access.

Bishop's Castle SO3289 Castle The Square, Bishop's Castle SY9 5BN £45; 7 rms with fine views. Standing on the site of the old castle keep, this 18th-c hotel has good fires, a relaxed and friendly atmosphere, lovely, home-made food, well kept beers, and welcoming owners.

Cleobury Mortimer SO6775 Talbot High St, Cleobury Mortimer DY14 8DQ (01299) 270036 £45; 8 comfortable rms. Tastefully refurbished and very welcoming, 16th-c inn, serving well cooked and nicely presented food, inc good breakfasts.

Llanfair Waterdine SO2476 Red Lion Llanfair Waterdine, Knighton LD7 1TU (01547) 528214 *£45; 3 rms, 1 with own bthrm. In an area of outstanding beauty and overlooking the River Teme, this pub has a heavily beamed, rambling lounge bar with a big open fire, a small, black-beamed tap room, a little dining room, friendly service and a determinedly traditional atmosphere – no noisy machines, music or children.

Gretton SO5295 Court Farm Gretton, Cardington, Church Stretton SY6 7HU (01694) 771219 £42; 4 rms. Large, comfortable, stone-built farmhouse on a 325-acre arable stock farm; with a warm welcome, big, woodburning stove in the inglenook fireplace and good food using home-grown and local produce; no smoking; cl Dec–Jan; children over 14; no pets.

Ludlow SO5174 Church Inn Church St, Ludlow SY8 1AW (01584) 872174 *£40; 9 rms. Georgian stuccoed building opening behind on to a quiet walk by the parish church; with a comfortable, airy bar, well served, popular food in both the bar and no-smoking restaurant, and well kept real ales.

Ludlow SO5174 Unicorn Lower Corve St, Ludlow SY8 1DU (01584) 873555 *£40; 5 rms, most with own bthrm. Pleasantly refurbished, family-run inn with good, popular food in both the bar and restaurant (inc vegetarian and vegan dishes), real ales, winter log fires, and riverside terrace; cl 25 Dec.

Shrewsbury SJ4315 Mytton Hall Montford Bridge, Shrewsbury SY4 1EU £40; 3 rms. Rather grand, white Georgian house in lovely gardens by the River Perry, with an elegant sitting room, log fire, good food in the lovely dining room where breakfasts are served around a communal table, welcoming owners; private fishing and tennis court; children over 12.

Woolstaston SO4599 Rectory Farm Woolstaston, Church Stretton SY6 6NN (01694) 751306 *£38; 3 comfortable rms. Lovely, half-timbered, 17th-c farmhouse on the lower slopes of the Long Mynd, with fine views, a friendly welcome, big, beamed lounge, cosy TV room, and hearty breakfasts; no evening meals; cl Christmas–Jan; children over 12; no dogs.

Clun SO3081 New House Farm Clun, Craven Arms SY7 8NJ (01588) 638314 *£36; 3 big rms. Up in the hills, friendly and very comfortable, 18th-c farmhouse of a stock-rearing farm, with its own Iron Age hill fort; breakfasts include own honey, and evening meal (by arrangement) using home-grown produce; excellent nearby walks, riding and fishing (lake and fly-fishing); cl Nov–Jan.

Strefford SO4485 Strefford Hall Farm Strefford, Craven Arms SY6 6NN (01588) 6722383 *£36; 3 rms. Stone-built, Victorian farmhouse surrounded by 360 acres of working farmland; woodburning stove in the sitting room, no smoking, lots of walks; cl Christmas and New Year.

Ludlow SO5175 Wheatsheaf Lower Broad St, Ludlow SY8 1PQ (01584) 872980 £35; 5 oak-beamed rms with showers. Attractively furnished, small

17th-c pub spectacularly built into the medieval town gate; traditional atmosphere, a wide range of good bar food, real ales and farm ciders, and friendly owners. **Hampton Loade** SO7586 OLD FORGE HOUSE Hampton Loade, Bridgnorth WV15 6HD (01746) 780338 £32; 3 rms, 1 with own bthrm. Family-run, homely Georgian house close to the River Severn, with fine breakfasts, friendly owners, and a lovely, quiet garden; cl 25 Dec.

To see and do

🏛 **Acton Burnell** SJ5302 ACTON BURNELL CASTLE Ruined, red sandstone manor house built in the 13th c, but almost abandoned by 1420. Disabled access; free. The Plume of Feathers at Harley is fairly handy for lunch.

🐖 🐾 **Acton Scott** SO4589 ACTON SCOTT WORKING FARM Vivid introduction to traditional rural life, with lots of rare breeds, and the kinds of crop they used to grow around the turn of the century, cultivated using old rotation methods. All the work is done by hand or horsepower, with period farm machinery. Lots of different craft demonstrations, and daily butter-making. Perhaps unusually, this is a farm aimed just as much at adults (perhaps more) as at children. Meals, snacks, shop, disabled access; cl Mon (exc bank hols), Nov–Mar; (01694) 781306; £2.75. The best nearby places for decent lunches are the Plough at Wistanstow (which brews its own beer) and up on Wenlock Edge, the Wenlock Edge Inn.

🏚 🏞 🐖 🐾 **Atcham** SJ5409 ATTINGHAM PARK Splendidly grand, late 18th-c house on the site of an old Roman town, with an imposing, three-storey, colonnaded portico and elaborate, intricate decor. The extensive picture gallery was designed by Nash, who made imaginative use of early curved cast iron and glass for the ceiling; attractive mature gardens and deer park outside. Snacks, shop, disabled access by prior arrangement; house cl am, all Thurs and Fri, and Nov–Easter; house and grounds £3.30, grounds only £1.30; NT. The nearby HOME FARM has rare breeds of farm animal and traditional farm machinery; you can watch the milking of the Jersey cows, and play with the pets. Farmhouse teas, shop, limited disabled access; cl am, Thurs and Fri

(exc school hols), Nov–Mar; (01743) 709243; £2. The Corbet Arms over at Upton Magna does good-value food.

🐖 🐾 **Billingsley** SO7185 RAYS FARM COUNTRY MATTERS Traditional farm in pleasant countryside, with pigs, sheep, cattle, miniature ponies, a llama, and a good collection of owls and other animals. Also, pleasant woodland walks, and bicycles can be hired for exploring the surrounding scenery (£3 an hour). Meals, snacks, shop, disabled access; cl 25 Dec; (01299) 841255; *£2.50. Both pubs in nearby Chelmarsh have decent food and lovely reservoir views.

★ 🏚 🍺 **Bishop's Castle** SO3289 is a historic, little market town, well liked by readers, with some fine Elizabethan and Georgian buildings, railway and local history museums, good shops, and the odd House on Crutches. It's handy for exploring Offa's Dyke. The Three Tuns has a unique Victorian, tower brewhouse, still in use.

★ 🏚 🏛 ❀ ❄ † 🏍 🏞 🍺 🍽 **Bridgnorth** SO7193 is an old market town on the River Severn, picturesque without being touristy. It's divided into the High Town and Low Town and connected by the hair-raising CLIFF RAILWAY which passes some small caves that people lived in till 1856 (they're not open, but labelled). As well as some handsome red brick, High Town has lots of fine, timbered buildings, such as the odd town hall built on a sandstone-arched base that straddles the road in the high st. The old CASTLE was mostly destroyed in the Civil War, but part of the keep remains, left at a scary tilt by the constant bombardment; the grounds are now a park with good views – the best views are from Castle Esplanade. The unusual CHURCH nearby (East Castle St) was designed by Thomas Telford. SEVERN VALLEY RAILWAY The leading standard-gauge steam railway, with a great collection of locomotives, a splendidly lively atmosphere, and trips through beautiful scenery; for full details see entry under Bewdley, in Hereford and Worcester chapter. It's worth taking the excellent return dining trip, or the Railwayman's Arms in the station is an atmospheric place for a snack. Other useful pubs for food here are the Falcon (St John's St), King's Head (Whitburn St) and especially the Bear (Northgate); or for attractive views with your meal, head out on the B4364 to the Punch Bowl or Down.

MIDLAND MOTOR MUSEUM (Stourbridge Rd) Over 100 well restored sports cars, racing cars and motorcycles in converted stables in the beautiful grounds of Stanmore Hall. Also steam traction engines. Snacks, shop, disabled access; open wknds and bank hols, daily July–Sept; (01746) 762992; £3.50. The grounds also have a caravan site. COSTUME AND CHILDHOOD MUSEUM (Newmarket Building) Lots of old costumes, dolls, and a Victorian nursery; also, collections of art and minerals, and a play house for children. Meals, snacks, shop; cl Tues, Christmas wk; *£1.25. DANIELS MILL The biggest waterwheel powering a working corn mill in the country; a picturesque old place, run by the same family for 200 years. Also, a good collection of country tools, old maps and documents. Snacks, shop; open pm wknds, Weds and bank hols Easter–Sept; (01746) 762753; £1.50.

🏠 ❀ ✝ **Broseley** SJ6602 BENTHALL HALL Elizabethan sandstone house with fine oak woodwork and panelling, decorative plasterwork, an interesting garden, and a 17th-c church (services 3.15pm most Suns). Shop, some disabled access; open pm Weds, Sun and bank hols Apr–Sept; £3, garden only £2; NT. The Forester's Arms and Cumberland Hotel are both useful for lunch.

✝ **Buildwas** SJ6204 BUILDWAS ABBEY Beautiful remains of a 12th-c Cistercian abbey – apart from the roof it's practically all still here. Shop, disabled access; cl Oct–Mar and maybe 1–2pm; £1.25. It's right next

to the gigantic cooling towers of a power station, which oddly have a space-age, geometrical beauty of their own, seen this close. The best places for lunch are in nearby Much Wenlock.

🏠 ❀ **Bury Ditches** SO3384 is an Iron Age ring fort, high up on a hill, with superb views of S Shropshire and N Herefordshire.

★ ♤ 🏠 ❀ **Clun** SO3081 Attractive, stone-built village on the edge of CLUN FOREST, a peaceful, pastoral area of rolling, partly wooded hills. The ruined Norman CASTLE gives fine views from the castle mound; free. Down by the River Clun, the 16th-c stone bridge is very picturesque. The Sun and White Horse are useful for lunch.

✝ 🏠 ✕ **Cleobury Mortimer** SO6775 is a civilised small town, most notable perhaps for its church's CROOKED SPIRE, though timbered Tudor buildings among its more elegant Georgian ones are picturesque. A restored WATERMILL produces its own stoneground flour. The Bell is pleasant for lunch.

✝ 🏠 **Cosford** SJ7904 AEROSPACE MUSEUM Spectacular collection of aircraft inc Victor and Vulcan bombers, Hastings, York and British Airways airliners, the last airworthy Britannia and plenty more, as well as lots of missiles and a new display of engines. Snacks, shop, disabled access; cl Christmas; (01902) 374872; *£4.20. There's a decent farm shop on Holyhead Rd, and the Bell at Tong is a good, family dining pub.

❀ **Dudleston Heath** SJ3736 ERWAY FARM HOUSE Small woodland garden with an interesting profusion of snowdrops, hellebores, daphnes and shade-loving plants; unusual plant and seed sales. Open only once a month – pm last Sun of month Feb–Sept; £1. The nearby Ellesmere Inn is useful for lunch.

🐖 **Harmer Hill** SJ4921 PIM HILL FARM (Lea Hall) Rare breeds, picnic site, friendly donkey, and an organic produce shop. Snacks; cl Mon, Tues and winter Suns; (01939) 290342; free. The Bridgewater Arms is handy for lunch.

✝ 🏠 **Haughmond Abbey** SJ4414 (off the B5062, E of Shrewsbury) HAUGHMOND ABBEY Extensive ruins of an Augustinian abbey, partly converted into a house after the Dissolution. Fine Norman doorway in the chapter house, some interesting sculpture, and well preserved lodgings and kitchens. Disabled access; cl Mon and Tues, Nov–Mar; £1.25.

✿ ⚘ ❄ ♨ ⊖ ! **Hawkstone Park** SJ5830 Created in the 18th c, this remarkable wooded parkland with its magnificent series of follies was for a while one of the most visited attractions in the country, though this century it became neglected and mostly forgotten. It's now been restored to its original grandeur, and has spectacular views from the monuments dotted around its 100 acres. Highlights include the ruins of a medieval red castle, intricate arches and pathways, a hermit in his hermitage and a fantastic underground grotto; it's a rewarding place to stroll around – the full circuit can easily take over three hours, and sensible shoes are recommended. The BBC filmed their *Chronicles of Narnia* here. Meals, snacks, shop, limited disabled access; cl Nov–Mar (exc wknds in Dec); (01939) 200611; *£4. The Caspian Bar of the Hawkstone Park Hotel has good-value food, and Hodnet – see entry below – is not far.

✿ **Hodnet** SJ6128 HODNET HALL GARDENS 60 acres of landscaped gardens with spacious lawns, lush pools, plants and trees; also, a 17th-c dovecot and an astonishingly decorated tearoom, full of big-game trophies. A very pleasant place to spend an afternoon. Snacks, shop, disabled access (prior notice preferred); cl am, Mon, and Oct–Mar; (01630) 685202; £2.60. The Bear Hotel opposite is good for lunch.

★ ⚘ ⬆ � ⌂ ♪ ❄ **Ironbridge** SJ6703 This steep town, with intriguing hillside paths and narrow lanes to explore, was the birthplace of the Industrial Revolution: it was Abraham Darby's use here of coke instead of charcoal for smelting which made mass-production of iron possible. As with other early industrial areas using both minerals and water, the surroundings are lovely – in this case, the Severn Gorge, with woods and steep, grassy slopes running down to the river. It was

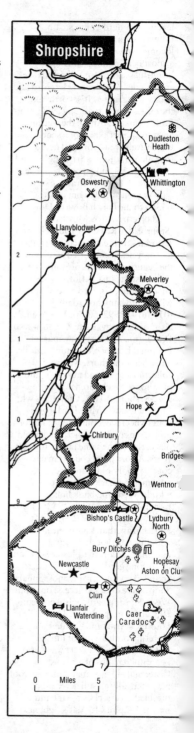

Shropshire

Dudleston Heath

Oswestry

Whittington

Llanyblodwel

Melverley

Hope

Chirbury

Bridges

Wentnor

Bishop's Castle

Lydbury North

Bury Ditches

Hopesay

Newcastle

Aston on Clun

Clun

Caer Caradoc

Llanfair Waterdine

0   Miles   5

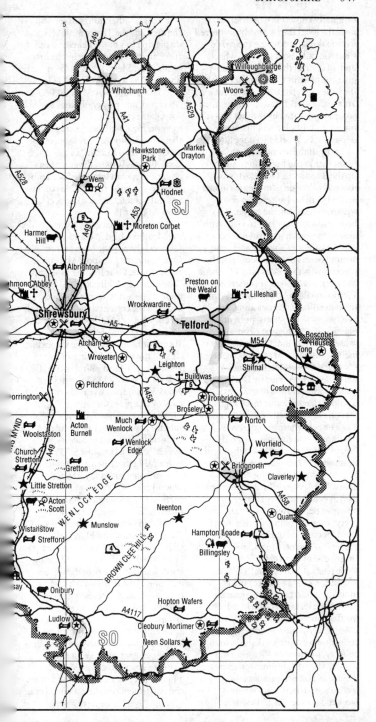

originally known as Coalbrookdale, until the local Darby family pioneered iron-making, producing the world's first iron rails, boats, trains, wheels and, of course, the bridge that now gives the place its name. For some while the valley was the biggest iron-making area in the world, and its importance is commemorated by the fact that it's one of only 14 places in Britain designated a World Heritage Site.

Many of the former industrial monuments and buildings now make up the IRONBRIDGE GORGE MUSEUM, more a collection of museums in fact, several of them scattered over 6 square miles along the gorge. It's a hugely rewarding place to visit, with almost too much to see in one go – you could easily base a whole weekend around here. For most people the best place of all is the BLISTS HILL OPEN-AIR MUSEUM, a complete, reconstructed Victorian village, showing everything from the offices, houses and machinery to the shops, pubs and pigsties; it's the biggest open-air museum of its kind. Other highlights include the MUSEUM OF IRON, where it's well worth seeing the original working furnace used by Darby; the outstanding ceramic displays at Coalport (remarkable brick kilns there have wonderful echoes); and the Tar Tunnel, where bitumen was produced. You can also visit old houses belonging to the Darby family. In summer, a bus service runs between the sites, which are some distance apart. Don't worry if you haven't time to visit everything – special-offer passport tickets (which include everything at a reduced price) remain valid indefinitely until you've seen all the bits you want. Meals, snacks, shops, disabled access; cl 24–25 Dec, some parts cl Nov–Mar; (01952) 433522; £8 for a passport ticket, individual tickets to each museum available. Across a footbridge from the Coalport Museum, the MAWS CRAFT CENTRE is one of the biggest collections of craft workshops in the country, in a former Victorian tile works. They display and sell things as diverse as pottery, puzzles and pictures, and there are various weekend courses; cl 25 Dec; free.

Plenty of other things to see around the area, inc the TEDDY BEAR MUSEUM, displaying lots of the bears and other furry animals made here by the long-established Merrythought Company. Shop; cl 25 Dec; (01952) 433116; free. IRONBRIDGE TOY MUSEUM Lots of Meccano, and plenty of other British toys, games and childhood memorabilia, with interesting, themed exhibitions. Toyshop; cl 25 Dec; (01952) 433926; *£1. UNDERWATER WORLD River Severn aquatic life, with lots of fish and other creatures in good re-creations of their natural habitat. Snacks, shop; cl Nov–Mar; *£1.

Attractively placed by the riverside, the Meadow, Bird in Hand, Boat at Jackfield (handy for Maws Craft Centre and the Coalport Museum), Malt House, Olde Robin Hood and Woodbridge are all useful for lunch; there's a pleasant, terraced walk between the river and the Golden Ball (Wesley Rd, off Madelet Hill). Just W of Ironbridge and Telford is the abrupt hill, wooded on the slopes but clear at the top, with magnificent views, known as the Wrekin SJ6208.

† ⛪ **Lilleshall** SJ7315 LILLESHALL ABBEY Very impressive ruins of a 12th-c abbey in a pleasant setting surrounded by yew trees – it's a nice spot for a picnic, very peaceful and undisturbed. Disabled access; free.

★ 🏠 ⛪ † ☉ ⚲ 🏛 **Ludlow** SO5175 A beautiful 12th-c town, its original grid plan still obvious today. Dotted around are 500 listed buildings, with particularly good examples down Broad St, a charming mixture of Tudor and Georgian architecture. The most famous building is the lavishly carved and timbered FEATHERS HOTEL on the Bullring, worth seeing inside and out. The Broadgate, the only one of the town's 13th-c gates to have survived, is interesting. The splendid old CASTLE, dating from around 1086, was for a while a seat of government when the Council for Wales and the Marches met here. Lots of original parts survive, inc the Norman keep and chapel with its unusual circular nave, and the towers and battlements on their wooded crag over the River Teme have a very properly 'castle-ish' feel; Shakespearean plays are performed here during the festival. There's a lovely view of it from over at Whitcliffe. Shop, disabled access; cl Dec and Jan; (01584) 873355; £2. Dominating the town almost as much is the PARISH CHURCH (off King St) with its magnificent pinnacled tower; it's in an attractive, tranquil enclave behind the old buttermarket, and has a wonderful sense of timeless peace inside, with sumptuous, intricate carving, especially on the ceiling and the choir stalls. Shop, disabled access. There are quite a few antique shops in the town, as well as a good local history MUSEUM in Castle St (cl 1–2pm, Sun exc July and Aug, all Oct–Apr; 50p), and DINHAM HOUSE, (Dinham) a craft centre with art exhibitions and various workshops, as well as regular outdoor music and drama in summer. Snacks, shop; cl 25–26 Dec; (01584) 874240; crafts free, £2 for exhibitions. The Church Inn, Unicorn, Olde Bull Ring and Wheatsheaf are all good for lunch.

🏠 ❀ ♪ **Lydbury North** SO3483 WALCOT HALL Fine Georgian house built for Clive of India; free-standing ballroom, stable yard with matching clock towers, a big walled garden, a dovecot, and an arboretum with good rhododendrons, azaleas and specimen trees. Open pm bank hols, Weds May, Jun and Sept, Sun May, July and Aug, and Fri May and Jun; (0171) 581 2782; £2.50. You can stay in various wings of the house, and they can arrange fishing and riding.

Market Drayton SJ6734 is the traditional home of gingerbread; the unique local recipe is locked in a bank.

✝ 🐾 ⊕ **Melverley** SJ3316 ST PETER'S CHURCH is a beautiful, black and white building; it was rebuilt in 1406 after Owen Glendower burned the previous structure, and has a fine Jacobean pulpit and chain bible. The stables of the Old Rectory have a CRAFT CENTRE. The Old Three Pigeons over at Nesscliffe has decent food, with Kynaston Cave and good cliff walks nr it.

🏰 ✝ **Moreton Corbet** SJ5623 The CASTLE was destroyed by Parliament in 1644, but you can still see a small, 13th-c keep and the substantial ruins of the once grand Elizabethan house; free. There are some elaborate tombs in the adjacent CHURCH.

★ 🏠 ✝ 🏰 ⊖ **Much Wenlock** SO6299 Lovely, little, medieval market town, with lots of timbered and jettied buildings. The famous PRIORY has its origins in the 7th c, but it's the magnificent remains of the 11th-c building and later additions you can see today. The chapter house has remarkably patterned, interlaced arches. Good Walkman guide. Shop, disabled access; sometimes cl 1–2pm, and cl Mon and Tues Nov–Mar, 24–26 Dec, 1 Jan; £1.80. There's a good local history MUSEUM. Shop, disabled access; cl 1-2 pm, Sun (exc Jun–Aug), Oct–Mar; *50p. The Talbot is useful for lunch.

🦃 **Onibury** SO4579 WERNLAS COLLECTION OF RARE POULTRY Mostly large fowl, also rare breeds of pheasant, unusual European species, and several breeds of animal. About 6,000 chicks are hatched each year, so there are usually plenty for children to handle or feed; attractive surroundings. Snacks, shop; cl Mon (exc mid-July–mid-Sept), 25 Dec; (01584) 77318; £2.75. The Hollybush is handy for lunch.

🚂 ⊖ 🏚 ❀ **Oswestry** SJ2929 CAMBRIAN RAILWAY MUSEUM and OSWESTRY CYCLE MUSEUM (Oswald Rd) Joint museum with lots of old bicycles and a history of cycling through the ages (especially good on Dunlop), as well as steam engines and railway memorabilia; some locomotives may be in steam on bank hols and selected wknds. Shop, disabled access; cl Christmas; (01691) 671749; £1.50. OLD OSWESTRY (just N) Impressive, Iron Age hill fort covering 68 acres. The elaborate, western defensive entrance and five ramparts remain; free. The ancient, black and white, timbered Fox is good for lunch, the Wynnstay Hotel a comfortable refuge. The OLD RACECOURSE (2 or 3m W, on the B4580) is a high stretch of common with splendid views into Wales.

❀ ❀ ⊖ **Pitchford** SJ5404 GOLDING GARDEN Steeply terraced, 16th-c gardens with tender plants in sheltered corners, good views, and pick-your-own asparagus – best to check first at either end of the season. Open mid-Apr–mid-Jun, or by appointment; (01694) 731204; £1. The Fox at Cross Houses does good-value food.

☛ **Preston upon the Weald** SJ6815 HOO FARM ANIMAL KINGDOM All the ingredients you'd expect on a traditional working farm – animals, pets, nature trails and sheep shearing, but they race the sheep too, and there are other unusual features such as ostriches, pheasant-rearing and beekeeping. Children can bottle-feed the lambs, and there's also a maze. Snacks, shop, disabled access; cl Mon (exc bank hols), mid-Sept–Easter exc month up to Christmas for trees; (01952) 677917; £2.50. The Tayleur Arms over at Longdon upon Tern is a decent, family dining pub.

🏠 ❀ ♤ 🖼 **Quatt** SO7488 DUDMASTON 17th-c house in extensive parklands with lakeside and woodland walks; fine furnishings and paintings, inc the old flower-painting collection of Francis Darby of Coalbrookdale, and a collection of modern art and sculpture. Snacks, shop, disabled access to house, parts of garden and woods; open pm Weds and Sun Apr–Sept; £3.50 house and garden, £2 garden only; NT. There's usually free pedestrian access to the woods all year. The Lion of Morfe over at Upper Farmcote is fairly handy for lunch.

★ 🏠 ❀ ⚒ † ! 👹 ♖ **Shrewsbury** SJ4912 still has a largely medieval, central street layout, with oddly named streets (such as Shoplatch, Murivance, Wyle Cop), and plenty of quiet corners up narrow alleys and courtyards among its more modern shops and offices. It has a wealth of striking architecture, both Tudor timbering and Georgian brick. Around The Square, numerous buildings reflect the medieval wool fortunes, inc the old market hall; in the adjacent High St, Owens Mansion and Irelands Mansion (not open) are fine, half-timbered houses well worth looking at from outside. The original town is almost entirely ringed by a loop of the Severn (quiet waterside paths and parks); only a narrow neck of land needed guarding by the 12th-c CASTLE. It was refurbished by Thomas

Telford in 1790, but parts of the earlier building remain, such as the Norman gateway and the great hall. It's being restored at the moment, so may not be open, but much can be seen from the pleasant grounds; free. The walk up Castle St is well worthwhile, passing the original Grammar School building and the half-timbered Council House Court. The 14th-c ABBEY with its statue of Edward III is impressive, and has a memorial to Wilfred Owen.

SHREWSBURY QUEST (Abbey Foregate) is a lively, new reconstruction of medieval monastic life; you can create your own decorated manuscript or try your hand at ancient games and crafts. Also, Brother Cadfael's workshop and herb garden, and puzzles and activities for children. Meals, snacks (inspired by medieval recipes), shop, disabled access; cl 25 Dec, 1 Jan; (01743) 243324; £3.50. Nearby the church of ST MARY has one of the tallest spires in England. CLIVE HOUSE MUSEUM (College Hill) Old town house associated with Clive of India, with excellent displays of Coalport and Caughley porcelain, fine paintings in period rooms, a walled garden and various other exhibitions. Shop, disabled access to ground floor only; cl Mon and winter Suns; £1. ROWLEY'S HOUSE MUSEUM (Barker St) Impressive, timber-framed building with social and natural history, as well as interesting Roman remains and a new medieval gallery. Shop, disabled access to ground floor only; cl Mon and winter Suns, Christmas; £1.20.

It's a rewarding town to walk around, with several attractive riverside parks. Among other interesting shops is a good CRAFT CENTRE in 12th-c St Julian's church (top of the High St), with several cheery workshops, a bustling craft fair every Sat and a good restaurant (especially useful for vegetarians). Some disabled access; cl Thurs (exc school hols), Sun and Christmas; free. The Castle Vaults, a black and white, timbered building nr the station, surprises by having a decent Mexican restaurant, the building now occupied by McDonalds is one of the last secular, medieval stone buildings in town, and other places to mention for food include the riverside Boat House (New St/Quarry Park), Coach & Horses (Swan Hill/Cross Hill), Pig & Truffle (Mardol) and Three Fishes (Fish St).

🏛 ❀ **Stokesay** SO4381 STOKESAY CASTLE Perhaps the finest example of a medieval manor house in existence – 13th c – in a charming setting; timbered Tudor gatehouse, solar, and hall with cruck-framed roof and Early English windows – just as it was 700 years ago. It really is a pretty spot, and there are good views from the top of the tower. Snacks, shop; cl Mon and Tues Oct–Mar; (01588) 672544; £2.30. The Plough at Wistanstow is the nearest good place for lunch.

🏛 ❀ 🏰 **Nr Tong** SJ8308 BOSCOBEL HOUSE Renowned for hiding Charles II after the Battle of Worcester, this is an interesting old place with an unusually well preserved 17th-c garden and cobbled courtyard, and 19th-c decor giving a romanticised view of the king's drama. Meals, snacks, shop, disabled access to gardens only; cl winter Mon and Tues, 25 Dec, all Jan; (01902) 850244; £3.15. The ROYAL OAK here is said by some to have been the hiding place of the king, by others to be a descendant, and by others still to be just a fine old tree. WHITELADIES PRIORY Ruins of an Augustinian nunnery destroyed in the Civil War; free. The Bell is good for lunch.

🏚 🏛 **Wem** SJ5128 ROCKING HORSE WORKSHOP An interesting opportunity to watch the production of traditionally styled rocking horses; the workshop also has horses at various stages of renovation, and a display of period toys. Shop; cl 25 Dec, check first at wknds, tel (01939) 232335; free.

🐄 🏰 **Whittington** SJ3331 PARK HALL WORKING FARM MUSEUM The powerful shire horses here still work the land as they have for decades. The Victorian stables also have lots of livestock from that period inc cattle, sheep and several breeds of pig, and there are examples of vintage farm machinery and equipment. Snacks, shop, disabled access; cl Fri exc July–mid-

Sept, all Nov–Easter; (01691) 652175; *£2.50. Nearby are the handsome remains of a CASTLE, with good-value food at the Olde Boot alongside.

❀ ❀ **Willoughbridge** SJ7540 DOROTHY CLIVE GARDEN 7-acre, hillside, woodland garden created from an old gravel quarry; rock and watergardens, rare trees and shrubs, splendid rhododendrons, fine views. Snacks, disabled access; cl Nov–Mar; £2. The Falcon at Woore does good food. Actually just over the Staffs border, but usually listed under nearby Market Drayton – so we've included it in this chapter instead.

🏛 ⚱ 🍷 **Wroxeter** SJ5608 ROMAN CITY The name is slightly misleading – most of the remains of the excavated Roman town of Virconium (once the fourth biggest town in the country) are buried under fields, but there's a well preserved colonnade and municipal bath, with very useful explanatory boards, and the MUSEUM has a good range of finds from the town and the earlier fortress. Snacks, shop, disabled access; cl 1–2pm, Mon and Tues Nov–Mar; (01743) 761330; £1.80. There's also a Roman wall on the neighbouring ROMAN VINEYARD, a friendly little place producing several wines – it's the most northerly producer of red wine in the world. Also, a lavender farm (Romans used lavender to keep insects off their vines), rare breeds, and some interesting glacial stones. Teas, shop (with various lavender-based products), disabled access; cl Mon and Oct–Mar, shop open all year; (01743) 761888; £1.50–£2 tour, depending on time of year.

❗ The local tourist information centres have details of a number of imaginative trails round the region, centring on the work of Thomas Telford, haunted villages, the novels of Ellis Peters, and sites connected with King Arthur (recent theories suggest the mythical king was a 5th-c warlord ruling from a post-Roman city – possibly Wroxeter – in the heart of Shrops). They can also give details of BALLOON TRIPS over the largely unspoilt countryside.

★ **Other attractive villages**, almost all of them with decent pubs, include

Aston on Clun SO3982, Bridges SO3996 (handy for the Stiperstones and Long Mynd), Chirbury SO2698 (with its famously haunted graveyard), Claverley SO7993 (the church here has impressive, medieval wall paintings), Leighton SJ6105, Little Stretton SO4392, Llanyblodwel SJ2423 (with an exuberantly decorated church and a charming, old, black and white, riverside pub), Lydbury North SO3586, Munslow SO5287, Neen Sollars SO6672, Neenton SO6488, Newcastle SO2582, Shifnal SJ7508 (another interesting church); Weston Park at Weston under Lizard is nearby – see Staffs section of Derbys/Staffs chapter, Tong SJ7907, Wentnor SO3893 and Worfield SO7696.

Walks

S Shropshire's hills rise to nearly 1,800 ft, and have a real Welsh Marches feel. The ridge of the **Stiperstones** SJ3600 △-1 is crowned by dramatic rocks and has a splendid view; reached from a nearby car park (you can make an interesting 8½-mile circuit with a stop at the More Arms at Hope SO3298), or you can take the longish walk up from spoil-heap-dominated Snailbeach SJ3702. The **Long Mynd** SO4092 △-2 is best reached from Church Stretton SO4593; this bracken-and-bilberry-clad massif has a flat, plateau-like top, crossed by the Port Way, an ancient track dating from Neolithic times. Its sides are cut into by a series of narrow, remote-feeling valleys, of which Cardingmill Valley is best known because of its relative accessibility. **Caer Caradoc** SO3075 △-3, E of Church Stretton, has a pleasingly compact summit, and the pick of the local views. The best start is at Hope Bowdler SO4792, not far from the county's oldest pub, the Royal Oak at Cardington SO4792. **Brown Clee Hill** SO5985 △-4, Shropshire's highest point, has a disappointingly flat top but a certain solitary grandeur.

The **Severn Gorge** △-5 has such charming scenery that its industrial monuments are ideal for a tour on foot. Steep lanes and paths connect Ironbridge SJ6703 and Coalbrookdale SJ6604, and an old railway track and a path along the base of Benthall Edge Wood SJ6603 assist routes along the gorge. A fine linear walk can be taken from Broseley SJ6701, descending NW into the gorge via Corbett's Dingle to Coalport SJ6902. From Coalport, you can follow the river all the way S to Bridgnorth SO7193.

The **Wrekin** SJ6208 △-6, just W of Telford SJ6810, is no Everest (an easily attained 1,334 ft), but because it's so isolated on the edge of the Shropshire uplands it commands a huge panorama spanning places over 100 miles apart. Further S, the Lion at Hampton Loade SO7586 is a good base for walks by the **River Severn** △-7 – and quiet, except when the Severn Valley Railway has one of its weekend steam spectaculars.

N Shropshire is in general less interesting for walkers, but does have some places that are worth seeking out. Around **Ellesmere** SJ3934 △-8 are a number of meres or lakes – the mere by Ellesmere itself, Blake Mere SJ4133, and Cole Mere SJ4333, which has a country park around it. This is close enough to the Shropshire Union Canal to include a walk along the towpath, with Colemere village SJ4332 a suitable starting place. **Grinshill Hill** SJ5223 △-9, between Grinshill SJ5223 and Clive SJ5124, has much wider views than you'd expect from its modest height, and quite an atmospheric summit, where woods open out by sheer, quarried rock-faces.

Driving

Driving in Shropshire is made pleasurable by the relative lack of traffic – and by the fact that a good many roads take you through lovely scenery and past picturesque houses and villages. There are pleasant views from the old coaching road SW from Shrewsbury, through Longden, Pulverbatch and beyond, with increasingly attractive scenery the further you go. Other enjoyable roads include the B4371 from Much Wenlock to Church Stretton, along Wenlock Edge, with bracing views except in places where woods line it; and the back road from Wigmore through Leinthall Starkes to Ludlow, giving lovely views as you approach the town. The back roads up over the top of the Long Mynd from Church Stretton are scenic but steep.

S of Bridgnorth, the back road through Chelmarsh to Highley has very pleasant views of the Severn Valley and Chelmarsh Reservoir.

The main roads tend to be quite civilised here; there are good views from the A4117 Cleobury Mortimer–Ludlow at Cleehill. In towns like Ludlow and Shrewsbury the traffic does tend to pile up, but even the busiest road, the A49, is tolerable.

Where to eat

Dorrington SJ4703 COUNTRY FRIENDS (01743) 718707 Cosy, half-timbered restaurant with good, interesting food, inc lovely puddings and British cheeses served with home-made bread; cl Sun, Mon, 12–28 July; partial disabled access. **£29.50**|£2.10/£7.

Woore SJ7342 FALCON (01630) 647230 Small, simple pub with a wide choice of generous, well presented, good food, friendly service, and well kept beer; nr Bridgemere garden centre; cl 25 Dec, children over 12 in restaurant. **£18.50**|£1.60/£8.50.

Bridgnorth SO7293 MAGPIE HOUSE (01746) 763977 Little, timbered, evening restaurant backing on to the River Severn, with excellent food from a smallish menu, and very attentive staff; resident ghost. **£17**/£9.45.

Hope SJ3401 STABLES (01743) 891344 Warmly welcoming, charming inn with promptly served, particularly good food (fine, home-made ice-creams); a blazing log fire in the beamed, L-shaped bar, well kept real ales, decent wines and spirits, cottagey dining room, and a good view to Long Mountain from the front, and over Hope Valley to the Stiperstones at the back; cl Mon; children lunchtimes only. **£16**|£1.50/£5.50.

Shrewsbury SJ4912 CASTLE VAULTS Castle Gates (01743) 358807 Mexican restaurant attached to a black and white pub, with generous helpings of good-value food; cl pm Sun, 25–26 Dec, 1 Jan; disabled access. **£16**|£2.50/£8.50.

Oswestry SJ2929 FOX Cross St (01691) 653311 Ancient, black and white façade and little local entrance bar; attractive, low-beamed and panelled main room, a good choice of decent food, an open fire, and speedy, friendly service; cl pm 25 Dec. **£14**|£1.50/£5.75.

Wistanstow SO4385 PLOUGH (01588) 673251 Simply furnished pub with lots of chairs and tables; fine, own-brewed beers (Woods), very good choice of wines by the glass, and popular, home-made food, with a fuller evening menu; cl am Mon; children lunchtimes only. **£13.90**|£1.50/£4.95.

Help this year from: Michael and Jenny Back, Martyn G Hart, Basil Minson, Rita Horridge, Ann Griffiths, Nigel Woolliscroft, G E Stait, Dave Braisted, Margaret Horner, Mr and Mrs H S Hill, George Atkinson, Mike and Wendy Proctor, Paul McPherson, Jenny and Brian Seller, Susan Holmes, Brenda and Derrick Swift.

Shropshire Calendar

Some of these dates were provisional as we went to press.

MARCH

18 **Minsterley** and District Eisteddfod – *till Sun 19* (01743) 791508

APRIL

14 **Ironbridge** 'An Ironmaster's Home' – opening of Dale House at Blists Hill Open-Air Museum (01952) 583003

16 **Newport** Driving Society Rally (01952) 291370

MAY

8 **Ironbridge** Glory Days: VE Day commemoration with street party, fireworks and music at Blists Hill Open-Air Museum (01952) 583003

19 **Shrewsbury** Shropshire and West Midland Agricultural Show at the Showground – *till Sat 20* (01743) 362824

27 **Ludlow** Craft Fair – *till Mon 29* (01983) 552554

29 **Aston on Clun** Arbor Tree Dressing: ancient ritual when a 250-year-old poplar is decorated on Royal Oak Day; **Ludlow** Carnival (01584) 875053

JUNE

2 **Bridgnorth** English Haydn Festival – *till Sat 10* (01952) 825235

5 **Quatt** Open-Air Theatre performing *The Merry Wives of Windsor* at Dudmaston Hall; *also on Sat 29* (01746) 780866

10 **Lydbury North** Shropshire Game Fair at Walcot Hall – *till Sun 11* (01588) 672708

11 **Bridgnorth** Open-Air Opera Gala with fireworks at Dudmaston Hall (01746) 780866

18 **Shifnal** Cosford Air Show (01902) 374872; **Shrewsbury** Open Day at Attingham Park (01743) 709203

23 **Jackfield** and Ironbridge Bluegrass and Roots Festival at the Maws Craft Centre – *till Sun 25* (01743) 235257; **Shrewsbury** International Music Festival – *till 3 July* (01743) 350763

24 **Bridgnorth to Kidderminster** Wartime Weekend at the Severn Valley Railway – *till Sun 25* (01299) 403816; **Ludlow** Festival – *till Sun 9* (01584) 875070

24 **Shrewsbury** Shrewsbury Abbey Fair (01743) 232723

29 **Ludlow** Jazz and Fringe Festival at the Bull Hotel – *till 9 July* (01584) 873611

JULY

2 **Bishop's Castle** Carnival (01588) 638371

9 **Shrewsbury** World Music and Cajun Day at the Castle (01743) 231142

21 **Wenlock Edge** Festival at the Edge: international storytelling festival at the Wenlock Edge Inn – *till Sun 23* (01952) 883936

22 **Church Stretton** and South Shropshire Arts Festival – *till 5 Aug* (01694) 722836

AUGUST

11 **Shrewsbury** Flower Show at Quarry Park – *till Sat 12* (01743) 364051

27 **Bicton** Shropshire Steam Rally at Onslow Park – *till Mon 28* (01694) 723799; **Lydbury North** Traction Engine Rally at Walcot Hall – *till Mon 28* (0158 88) 640

28 **Ironbridge** Coracle Regatta (01952) 813667

SEPTEMBER

22 **Shrewsbury** International Ballooning Fiesta at Attingham Park – *till Sun 24* (01743) 709203

SOMERSET AND AVON

This varied and interesting area has plenty of places to visit (including quite a few new additions to this year's *Guide*). Bath, sophisticated and elegant, is one of Britain's three or four most rewarding cities – excellent for a weekend break. Bristol is lively and vigorous, with lots of things to see and do: great for day visits, though not necessarily for a stay. The countryside is dotted with attractive villages and small towns, and a profusion of church towers, pinnacled, turreted and gargoyled, landmarks both in the flatlands and among the trees of the hills and valleys. In east Somerset, Wells is a charming, largely unspoilt small cathedral city, and Glastonbury has the pull of its Arthurian legends; the Mendip Hills have some spectacular scenery. West Somerset is quieter and more secluded, with the Quantock Hills having the most attractive countryside.

In the hillier parts, buildings are generally of stone, varying in colour and character from the Cotswold style of Avon, through the pale limestone of the Mendips and the golden warmth of south Somerset's Ham stone, to the rugged and stolid greys of the hamlets tucked into the folds of the Quantocks.

Over in the west, Somerset includes a large part of Exmoor. We have covered this in a separate Exmoor section, included at the end of the Devon chapter.

BATH

A lovely city, excellent for a short stay, with lots to see.

Graceful and elegant, Bath's mellow squares, crescents and terraces of fine 18th-c buildings gain added appeal and even a touch of drama from the steepness of the hills they cling to. They were built for people planning to enjoy themselves, and a strong sense of this still runs through the atmosphere here: you feel it's somewhere to be entertained and pampered, that there's a lot going on that is fun.

Many places here recall the days of Beau Nash and the building of Bath as a fashionable resort. Other attractions go back to the Roman Baths, and come right up to date with the city's interesting and unusual shops.

In the Walks section we note the greatest of the Regency buildings to look at; just strolling around the city is a special pleasure, but among many places to visit we'd pick out particularly the Roman Baths, Pump Room, Museum of Costume at the Assembly Rooms, Building of Bath Museum, Industrial Heritage Centre, No 1 Royal Crescent, and Bath Abbey. The American Museum on the edge of the city at Claverton is very special.

This is not a cheap city to stay in, but the places we recommend, all stylish and comfortable, give you the feeling that you're getting value for money.

In midsummer, during the week the centre floods with school parties, sometimes from other countries. Weekends are better; but for a weekday summer visit it might be best to wait until the school holidays.

If you want to go during the early summer Festival, book accommodation well ahead.

Where to stay

PRIORY Weston Rd BA1 2XT (01225) 331922 £164; 21 charming rms. Gothic-style Georgian country house hotel in 2 acres of gardens, with elegant and civilised day rooms, friendly, helpful service, reliably good food in 3 dining rooms, fine wines, and croquet and outdoor heated swimming pool.

ROYAL CRESCENT 16 Royal Crescent BA1 2LS (01225) 319090 £160; 42 luxurious rms. Elegant Georgian hotel with comfortable, antique-filled lounges, very attractive garden room (with its own menu), open fires and lovely flowers; excellently presented, very well prepared fine food in the Dower House Restaurant with its own relaxed spacious drawing room and well balanced, extensive wine list; impeccable service; children over 7 in restaurant in the evening; disabled access.

QUEENSBERRY Russel St BA1 2QF (01225) 447928 *£98; 22 lovely rms. Three beautifully decorated Georgian town houses in quiet residential street, with comfortable, restful drawing room, open fire, attractive modern restaurant, good robust cooking, and professional service; may cl 1 wk Christmas.

PARADISE HOUSE 86–88 Holloway BA2 4PX (01225) 317723 £65; 9 rooms, most with own bthrm. Classically elegant early 18th-c hotel, lovingly restored, with pretty breakfast room, restful drawing room, log fire, spacious walled gardens, and marvellous views over the city; cl 23–27 Dec; disabled access.

Bathford ST7964 OLD SCHOOL HOUSE Church St BA1 7RR (01225) 859593 £64; 4 rms. Quietly relaxed hotel in early Victorian village school house 3 miles from Bath, with winter log fires, a friendly atmosphere and candlelit dinner (24 hrs' notice); no smoking; good nearby walks; disabled access.

Bathford ST7964 EAGLE HOUSE Church St BA1 7RS (01225) 859946 £59; 8 comfortable big rms, 2 in cottage. Lovely Georgian house with an informal, friendly atmosphere, particularly helpful owners, open fires, spacious drawing room and smaller sitting room, good breakfasts, and big garden with fine views; very good for families; cl 20 Dec–4 Jan.

DORIAN HOUSE 1 Upper Oldfield Park BA2 3JX (01225) 426336 £55; 8 individually decorated rms. Gracious and neatly kept Victorian house with fine views of the city (only 10 mins' stroll away); charming, friendly owners, small bar, comfortable sitting room and elegant little dining room.

HAYDON HOUSE 9 Bloomfield Park BA2 2BY (01225) 427351 £55; 5 good rms with thoughtful extras. Deceptively unassuming-looking Edwardian house with comfortable, elegant and restful rooms, antiques, excellent breakfasts (no evening meals), warmly welcoming owners, and pretty garden; no smoking; children by arrangement.

BROCKS 32 Brock St BA1 2LN (01225) 338374 £48; 8 rms, most with own bthrm. Georgian house with fine breakfasts in big dining room, lounge area, helpful staff, and close to some shops, restaurants, secondhand bookshops and theatre; cl 24–26 Dec, 2 wks Jan.

BADMINTON VILLA 10 Upper Oldfield Park BA2 3JZ (01225) 426347 £48; 4 rms. Big Victorian house with marvellous city views, comfortable lounge, good breakfasts, and helpful, friendly owners; cl 24 Dec–2 Jan; children over 8.

To see and do

✝ BATH ABBEY Particularly renowned for its fan vaulting, the current building (begun in 1499) is the third great church to be built on this site. The Elizabethans called it the Lantern of the West because of its profusion of stained glass. Most impressive is the great east window, depicting 56 scenes from the life of Christ. On one side of this is the finely carved memorial to Bartholomew Barnes (1608), and on the other the beautiful medieval carving of the Prior Birde Chantry. Shop, disabled access; cl Good Fri, 25 Dec; £1 suggested donation. They've recently opened a good exhibition on the Abbey's history in carefully restored 18th-c cellars. Disabled access; cl Sun; £2.

🏛👌 The ROMAN BATHS were founded by AD 75, and are undoubtedly one of the most remarkable Roman sites in Britain. N of the spring the Romans laid out a colonnaded precinct containing the temple of Sulis Minerva, while to the S a range of cleansing and curative baths was built. The Sacred Spring was both a focus for worship – receiving the required offerings – and also a reservoir supplying the baths with spa water. They were all but forgotten until the 18th c, when workmen chanced upon a bust of Minerva, and it was not until 1878 that the great baths you can view today were uncovered. The main baths are pretty much intact, and there's lots to see; in August they're open at night and quite beautifully floodlit. The MUSEUM shows finds made during excavations of the spring, inc the bust of Minerva and a remarkable Gorgon's Head pediment, as well as altars, tombstones, and fascinating curse tablets, and a model of the site as it would have appeared in the 4th c. Meals, snacks, shop, disabled access; cl 25–26 Dec; (01225) 461111; £5 (combined ticket with Museum of Costume and Assembly Rooms available £6.60).

🏠 PUMP ROOM The stylish 18th-c mecca for the fashionable, built directly above the Roman temple courtyard, with a restaurant serving morning coffee, lunches and teas to the gay strains of the Pump Room trio. You can sample the spa water. Meals and snacks, shop, disabled access (but not to the baths themselves); cl 25–26 Dec; free.

📷👌 BRITISH FOLK ART COLLECTION (The Vineyard, Paragon) Formerly known as the Museum of English Naive Art, a wonderful collection of 18th- and 19th-c paintings depicting ordinary people, pursuits and incidents. This is the first museum devoted to the journeyman painters who would knock up any picture from an inn sign to a snapshot portrait of your favourite cow. Also a display of shop signs, weathervanes and country furniture. Shop; cl am Sun, Mon, 22 Dec–1 Jan, Easter; (01225) 446926; £2.

👌 On the same site the BUILDING OF BATH MUSEUM looks at how the city was transformed in the 18th c, with scale models, original tools, and a fabulous city model. It's housed in a chapel, and those who have difficulty walking might find the floor slightly uneven. Shop, disabled access but no facilities; cl Mon, and 16 Dec-1 Mar; (01225) 333895; £2.50.

🏠 NO 1 ROYAL CRESCENT in 1768 was the first house built in Bath's most regal terrace, and now has two floors restored and furnished in the style of that time. Also an interesting kitchen. Shop; cl Mon, mid-Dec–Feb; (01225) 428126; £3.

🌸 GEORGIAN GARDEN (Gravel Walk, between Royal Crescent and Queen Sq) Typical small town garden of 1760, with the original layout and the plants that would have been used then – the emphasis clearly on strolling and chatting rather than horticulture itself, given the high ratio of walking-space to plants; cl wknds (exc pm Sun in Aug), and Nov–Apr; free.

🏠👌 HERSCHEL HOUSE AND MUSEUM (New King St) Interesting Georgian home and workplace of William Herschel, the composer and astronomer, with models of his telescopes and other scientific equipment. Also period drawing and music rooms, historical instruments, kitchen, and the workshop where he cast the specular metal mirrors that were to be so important to

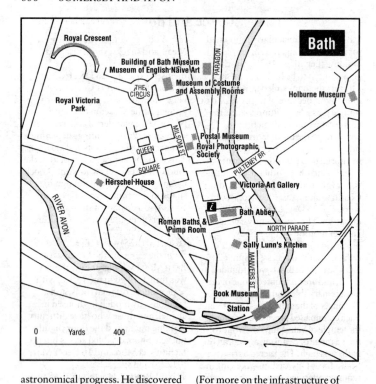

Bath

Royal Crescent

Building of Bath Museum
Museum of English Naïve Art

PARAGON

THE CIRCUS

Museum of Costume
and Assembly Rooms

Holburne Museum

Royal Victoria Park

MILSOM ST

QUEEN

Postal Museum
Royal Photographic Society

SQUARE

PULTENEY BR

Herschel House

Victoria Art Gallery

i

Bath Abbey

Roman Baths &
Pump Room

NORTH PARADE

Sally Lunn's Kitchen

MANVERS ST

Book Museum

Station

RIVER AVON

0   Yards   400

---

astronomical progress. He discovered
the planet Uranus from the back
garden. Shop; cl am and wkdys
Nov–Mar; (01225) 311342; *£2.50.
🅰 ⚭ HOLBURNE MUSEUM (Gt Pulteney
St) Fine old building displaying the
decorative and fine-art collection of
Sir Thomas William Holburne
(1793–1874), as well as lots of 20th-c
art and crafts. Interesting temporary
exhibitions. Meals, snacks, shop,
disabled access; cl am Sun, Mon Nov–
Easter; (01225) 466669; *£3.50.
🜲 INDUSTRIAL HERITAGE CENTRE (Julian
Rd) The highlight is the engaging MR
BOWLER'S BUSINESS, a well restored
factory first established in 1872,
providing various plumbing,
engineering, gas-fitting, bell-hanging
and other services. Everything is just
as it was then, inc the antique soda
fountain that turned out such
charmingly named drinks as Cherry
Ciderette. Also the story of Bath stone,
with a replica of a mine face before
mechanisation. Snacks, shop, disabled
access by arrangement; cl wkdys
Nov–Easter; (01225) 318348; *£3.

(For more on the infrastructure of
Bath's 18th-c revolution, see also the
Underground Quarry, included under
Corsham in our Wiltshire chapter.)
🜲 🏛 MUSEUM OF COSTUME AND
ASSEMBLY ROOMS (Bennett St)
Dazzling – over 200 figures dressed in
original costumes from the late 16th c
to the present, one of the most
impressive displays of fashions in the
world. Also fashion accessories.
Guided tours of the museum and the
Assembly Rooms built in 1771 by
John Wood the Younger. Shop,
disabled access; cl 25–26 Dec,
Assembly Rooms may cl for
functions; (01225) 461111; £3.20
(combined ticket with Roman Baths
available £6.60).
🜲 POSTAL MUSEUM (Broad St)
Development of the postal system
since the days of Henry VIII, inc a
full-scale replica Victorian post
office (it was from Bath's Central
Post Office that the first postage-
stamp, the Penny Black, was posted).
Snacks, shop, disabled access to
ground floor only; cl Sun Jan and

Feb, 25 Dec, bank hols; (01225) 460333; £2.

🕭 📖 BOOK MUSEUM (Manvers St) Bath's elegant atmosphere has long proved popular with book buyers and writers, and part of this museum has displays and first editions relating to authors who lived or worked here, esp Jane Austen and Charles Dickens. There's a reconstruction of Dickens' study at Gadshill Place. The other half of the exhibition is devoted to the history and art of bookbinding, and adjoining this is the shop of GEORGE BAYNTUN, who has been binding and selling antiquarian books for 50 years; cl 1–2 pm, pm Sat, all Sun and bank hols; (01225) 466000; *£2.

🔳 ROYAL PHOTOGRAPHIC SOCIETY (The Octagon, Milsom St) Five galleries with major international exhibitions and useful displays on the development of photography, inc the first picture ever taken. Meals, snacks, shop, disabled access; cl 25–26 Dec, bank hols; (01225) 462841; £3 (free to members).

🏠🕭 SALLY LUNN'S KITCHEN (North Parade Passage), reputedly the oldest house in Bath, is a charming partly timbered medieval structure, still preserving in its cellars the original kitchen of the legendary Sally Lunn, who in the 17th c created her famous brioche bread buns here. Extensive excavations have revealed Roman and Saxon remains below the present house. Meals and snacks (inc of course the buns, made to a secret recipe), shop; cl am Sun; 30p.

🔳🕭 VICTORIA ART GALLERY (Bridge St) European Old Masters and 18th- to 20th-c British paintings and drawings, as well as decorative arts, inc porcelain, glass and watches. They've recently purchased Turner's painting of the west front of Bath Abbey. Shop, disabled access to ground floor only; cl Sun, 25-26 Dec and bank hols; free.

❀🕭 BECKFORD'S TOWER (Lansdown Rd) Italianate tower with fine views from the top, and a little museum commemorating the well travelled collector William Beckford; open pm wknds and bank hols Apr–Oct; (01225) 338727; £1.50.

⚓ BOAT CRUISES leave on the hour from the landing stage by Pulteney Bridge (not Oct–Easter), and boats and punts can be hired in summer from the Boating Station on the River Avon, Forester Rd, Bathwick: (01225) 466407.

! To see the city as it's shown in the great architectural drawings, and go as much further afield as the wind will allow, you can book hot-air BALLOON TRIPS, subject to weather, perhaps taking off from the Royal Victoria Park; (01225) 466888; from £99.

Bath is famous for **shopping** – yet it's all too easy for strangers here for the day to end up near the Roman Baths paying high prices for things they could get in any other High Street. Here are some suggestions for things you won't so easily find elsewhere.

BARTLETT ST MARKETS (both sides of street) Every day: from junk to top-drawer antiques, often buzzing with dealers from elsewhere.

CHINA DOLL (Walcot St) Excellent collection of doll's-house accessories, not cheap – probably best to keep children's noses glued to the window rather than letting them loose inside.

FINE CHEESE CO (Walcot St) Huge range of interesting cheeses, mouthwatering olive bread, helpful staff.

GUINEA LANE MARKET Very early am Weds, antiques changing hands quickly.

HITCHCOCKS (Chapel Row) Specialised craft gallery on four floors.

ROOKSMOOR GALLERY (Brock St) Modern limited-edition prints, sculpture, light and well presented.

ST JAMES GALLERY (Margaret Buildings) Fine British crafts, wide range; small – don't try to squeeze a pushchair in.

SHEPHERDS PURSE (John St) Long-established knitting wool/patterns shop.

THE GREEN SHOP (Green St) Vetted environmentally sound products, from unbleached cotton bedclothes to long-life light bulbs – lots of gift ideas for 'green' friends.

WALCOT ST FLEA MARKET is best of all for bargains; Sat, occasional Sun.

Other things to see and do near Bath

⏱ 🏠 ❀ **Claverton** ST7862 AMERICAN MUSEUM IN BRITAIN (Claverton Manor) Quite a contrast to the rest of Bath's attractions, a fascinating illustration of American history and life in lovely gracious surroundings. Eighteen rooms are fully furnished and decorated to re-create the style of American homes from the 17th to the 19th c, while the grounds include a replica of part of George Washington's garden at Mount Vernon, as well as an American arboretum. Collections of pewter, glass, folk art, patchwork quilts and maps, with special sections on the Indians and the Shakers, various special events, and changing exhibitions. Well liked by readers, it's the only museum in the country completely devoted to our colonial cousins. Snacks, shop, some disabled access; cl am, Mon, and Nov–Mar; (01225) 480726; £5.

📷 **Farleigh Hungerford** ST8057 Extensive ruins of 14th-c CASTLE, with monuments in the chapel to the Hungerford family, who once owned the land from here to Salisbury. Shop; cl 1–2pm, winter Mon and Tues; £1.25.

✗ ☺ **Priston** ST6961 PRISTON MILL Set in charming countryside, this working watermill has produced flour for the citizens of Bath for centuries, and was once run by the monks of Bath Abbey. Good explanations of how it works, as well as play areas, pets' corner, trailer rides and nature trails. A relaxing place, ideal for families. Meals, snacks, shop; cl am wkdys, Oct–Mar; (01225) 423894; £2.50.

Walks

Walking around Bath is a delight; there are flat parts, though to make the most of it you have to be prepared to climb some of the steeper streets. Places not to be missed include the great showpieces of 18th-c town planning, Queen Sq, The Circus and the Royal Crescent; the quieter Abbey Green and cobbled Abbey St and Queen St; and the great Pulteney Bridge (there's a fine view of it from the bridge at the end of North Parade, or the riverside Parade Gardens, where brass bands play in summer). The revivified Kennet & Avon Canal is one of Bath's pleasures, with quiet towpath walks along to Bathampton (where the George is popular for lunch); it has quite a few colourful narrowboats in summer.

Driving

Not recommended. Bath's streets were laid out for travel by sedan chair, not car, and a tortuous one-way system seems designed to deter drivers rather than to make traffic flow more easily.

Where to eat

DOWER HOUSE Royal Crescent Hotel, 16 Royal Crescent (01225) 319090 Luxuriously decorated restaurant with delicious, innovative food, attractively presented, a well chosen wine list, and good service; children over 7 only for dinner; disabled access. £40|£4.50/£10.

WOODS 9–13 Alfred St (01225) 314812 Bustling bright restaurant with horse-racing pictures, excellent set menus as well as interesting daily specials (good fish), and cheery staff; cl pm Sun, 24–26 Dec; disabled access. **£10.95 midweek, £18.95 Sat**|£3.75/£6.30.

Bathford ST7966 CROWN Bathford Hill (01225) 852297 Four or five attractively decorated rooms lead off main bar; good food with nice puddings, wide choice of drinks inc good cafetière coffee with fresh cream; no smoking garden room; cl am Mon, 25–26 Dec; disabled access. £16|£2.50/£6.50.

There's no shortage of entertaining snack places, and good pubs providing at least some decent food include the Old Green Tree (Green St), Crystal Palace (Abbey Green) and Hare & Hounds (Lansdown Hill – great views).

AVON

Bristol is lively and interesting for day visits, and elsewhere there are one or two other worthwhile attractions; some very comfortable places to stay.

Bristol is the real focus of attention in the county, with masses of things to do (the wine museum is an interesting addition). It is well worth a day visit, though probably too busy an industrial city to use as a base for an enjoyable stay. Better to cosset yourself in one of the two splendid country-house hotels we list – excellent bases too for excursions into Bath or down into Somerset.

Dyrham Park is attractive, and there's some pleasant countryside down towards the Mendips. On the coast, Weston-super-Mare has possibilities as an undemanding family resort, and Clevedon is also quite attractive.

Where to stay

Hunstrete ST6462 HUNSTRETE HOUSE Hunstrete, Pensford, Bristol BS18 4NS (01761) 490490 £120; 24 individually decorated rms. Classically handsome mainly 18th-c country-house hotel on the edge of the Mendips in 92 acres of grounds including a walled garden and deer park; comfortable and elegantly furnished day rooms with antiques, paintings, log fires, and fresh flowers from the garden. Tranquil atmosphere, excellent service, and very good enjoyable food using produce from the garden when possible; lovely gardens, croquet lawn, heated swimming pool, all-weather tennis court, and nearby riding; children by arrangement; disabled access.

Thornbury ST6390 THORNBURY CASTLE Thornbury, Bristol BS12 1HH (01454) 281182 £105; 18 opulent rms, some with big Tudor fireplaces or fine oriel windows. Impressive and luxuriously renovated early 16th-c castle with deeply comfortable seats, antiques, tapestries, huge fireplaces and mullioned windows in the baronial public rooms; 2 restaurants (1 in the base of a tower), fine cooking, extensive wine list (including their own wine from their expanding vineyard), thoughtful, friendly service, and vast grounds; cl 2 days Jan; children over 12.

Stanton Wick ST6162 CARPENTERS ARMS Stanton Wick, Pensford, Bristol BS18 4BX (01761) 490202 £59.50; 12 no smoking rms. Warm and attractively furnished tile-roofed inn converted from a row of miners' cottages with big log fire, woodburning stove, a wide choice of good food inc generous breakfasts, good wines, well kept beers, and friendly, efficient staff.

Stanton Drew ST5663 VALLEY FARM Sandy Lane, Stanton Drew, Bristol BS18 4EL (01275) 332723 £36; 3 rms, 1 with own bthrm. Quietly set modern farmhouse on working beef farm with homely big lounge, hearty breakfasts and a genuinely warm welcome; walks from the door.

To see and do

Bristol ST5872 is much more down-to-earth and radical than elegant and conservative Bath. The city's prosperity still stems from its port, where facilities have been kept up to date so as to accommodate increasingly sophisticated vessels, and it is a major industrial centre, with aerospace predominating among many other manufacturing interests. It's more a place to dip into for small doses by the day than to choose for a stay; the best part for leisurely strolls is its elegant suburb of Clifton, with handsome Georgian terraces and its famous suspension bridge. Day visits are made easy by the motorway that plunges right into the city's heart. Useful central pubs for a lunchtime bite to eat are the Bridge (Passage St), Le Château (Park St), waterside Cottage (Baltic Wharf) and Shakespeare (Victoria St); a little further out, the Highbury Vaults (St Michaels Hill, Cotham) is the best in the city. In the evening Millwards (see Where to eat) is good.

🏚 🏚 † The city is full of splendid architecture. Two of the finest buildings are the CORN EXCHANGE (Corn Street), built in 1743, and the OLD COUNCIL HOUSE (Corn Street), built in 1827 – one in a series standing on that spot since 1552; in Broad Street, there is the Grand Hotel (1869), the Guild Hall (1843) and the art-nouveau façade of the former Edward Everard printing house built in 1900. Also in this area are the famous CHRISTMAS STEPS dating from 1669, quaintly lined by steep buildings: this is a good area for shops selling antiques, stamps and old books. At the top of these steps is the CHAPEL OF THE THREE KINGS OF COLOGNE dating from the 1480s (the 'three kings' are the three wise men whose shrines are in Cologne cathedral). The warden of the nearby almshouses will provide access to this tiny chapel. At the bottom of the steps is the lodge of ST BARTHOLOMEWS – all that remains of the 13th-c hospital and almshouse which once stood on this site.

🏚 ❋ Houses that can be viewed inside include the RED LODGE (Park St), built in the 16th c and then altered in the 18th, with interior features and furnishings from both periods. On the first floor is the last surviving suite of 16th-c rooms in Bristol, as well as a wonderful carved stone chimney-piece, plasterwork ceilings and fine oak panelling; other rooms contain walnut and gilt furniture and early 18th-c portraits. There's a reconstructed Tudor-style garden open Sat Jun and July; cl 1–2 pm, Sun, Mon and over Christmas; £1. You can buy a combined ticket that takes in the nearby GEORGIAN HOUSE (Great George St), one of several examples in this street of 18th- and early 19th-c architecture. Built in 1790 for a wealthy sugar merchant, it's a fine illustration of a typical town house of the day. Three floors are still

decorated in period style, inc the below-stairs area with kitchen, laundry and housekeeper's room; times and price as for Red Lodge.

⚓ 🏚 ♨ ❋ The DOCKS are being restored in a way that's making them increasingly attractive to visitors. Distinctive blue and yellow FERRIES (Apr–Sept) link several points around the harbour – the complexity of the docks is better understood when viewed from the water. The old part around King Street, between the waterfront and the Bristol Old Vic, has quiet cobbled streets of Georgian buildings, pleasant to wander through, and elsewhere some of the bigger warehouses are being pressed into service as museums, café-bars and the like. One bar is in a converted lightship, another steamer has become a restaurant/bar, and a former coaster has become the Old Profanity, an entertainment showboat popular with students. The ARNOLFINI, a big former tea warehouse, is now a contemporary arts complex with bar, restaurant, exhibitions, cinema, theatre and so

forth. BRISTOL INDUSTRIAL MUSEUM (Floating Harbour off Wapping) Housed in a converted dockside transit shed, comprehensive coverage of the city's role in trade and industry, esp good on transport, with locally built steam locomotives and aircraft (inc a mock-up of Concorde's flight deck), and a good look at the development of the port. Also reconstructions, lots of special events and (usually one Sun a month only) a hands-on printing workshop. Shop, disabled access; cl Mon, 25–26 Dec, 1 Jan, Good Fri; (0117) 925 1470; *£1. Bristol's long heritage of ship-building is well shown at the MARITIME HERITAGE CENTRE (Floating Harbour), with original machinery, full-sized reconstructions, models and videos. Snacks, shop, disabled access; cl 24–25 Dec; free.

On the dockside outside, usually running summer wknds, is a small steam railway, the BRISTOL HARBOUR RAILWAY, which for 80p has a return trip down along the old cargo route to the SS *Great Britain*. This ship was the first iron, screw-propelled, ocean-going vessel, designed by Isambard Kingdom Brunel, and really was a departure from what had gone before. It's being restored, after a half century or so lying neglected in the Falkland Islands. Snacks, shop; cl 24–25 Dec; (0117) 926 0680; £2.90 (good walkman tours for 80p extra). Also

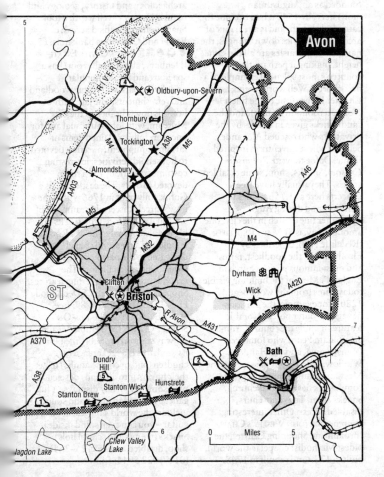

moored here is the 1860s steam-tug *Mayflower*, which has interesting trips round the docks every hour most wknds in summer. It's only small so best to book with the Industrial Museum (see above); £2. The nearby diesel-powered firefloat *Pyronaut* (1934) and Fairbain steam-crane (1876) also operate occasional summer wknds. From Apr to Oct the PLEASURE STEAMERS *Waverley* and *Balmoral* run fairly frequent day cruises from here, along the Avon and Severn or to Devon, Wales or Lundy; (0117) 926 0767 for programme.

† Supposedly on the very spot where St Augustine met the Celtic Christians in the early 7th c is the imposing edifice of the CATHEDRAL. Originally founded as an Augustinian monastery, by 1542 it had become the cathedral church, and is a real mix of architectural styles down the ages; the nave, choir and aisles are all the same height, making it perhaps the country's most splendid example of a hall-church. Well worth seeing are the Chapter House (one of the finest Norman rooms in Britain), and the candlesticks given in thanks by the privateers who rescued Alexander Selkirk (whose adventures inspired Daniel Defoe to write *Robinson Crusoe*). Snacks, shop, some disabled access. They usually have free concerts here at 1.15pm Tues in termtime and during Aug.

† Another fine church in the city, one among many, is ST MARY REDCLIFFE (Redcliffe Hill), described by Elizabeth I as 'the goodliest, fairest and most famous parish church in England'. Most of the building visible today dates from the work begun in 1280 – for example, the glorious hexagonal outer porch. Notable features include the tomb of Admiral Sir William Penn, who founded Pennsylvania, and the Handel Window, where eight passages of the Messiah commemorate the great composer's ties with this church. Snacks Mon, Tues and Thurs, disabled access. Other interesting churches inc JOHN WESLEY'S CHAPEL (Broadmead Shopping Centre), the oldest Methodist chapel in the world, built in 1739 and rebuilt in 1748.

Both chapel and living rooms are preserved in their original state and include the famous double-decked pulpit from which John Wesley preached. Shop, disabled access to ground floor only; cl 1–2pm, Sun, and Weds Oct–Mar; (0117) 926 4740; £1.50. The LORD MAYOR'S CHAPEL (Park Street) is all that remains of the medieval Hospital of the Gaunts founded in 1220. Since 1722 this has been the Corporation's official place of worship – the only civic church in the country. The 16th-c stained-glass windows, floor tiles and fan-vaulted ceiling are glorious.

CITY MUSEUM AND ART GALLERY (Queens Rd) Good collections of applied art, fine art, Oriental art, archaeology and history, geology and natural history – well worth a look. Snacks, shop, disabled access; cl Easter and Christmas bank hols; £2.

BLAISE CASTLE ESTATE (Henbury, about 4 miles out) has a spacious and locally popular undulating park with some woodland and refreshments. The late 18th-c house is now a branch of the City Museum, with lots of unusual and for once carefully explained items of farming equipment, a section devoted to household activities, interesting costume collection, and a room devoted to dolls. The castle itself is a Gothic folly built in 1766 within the now scarcely discernible ramparts of an Iron Age hill fort, which in its busy life has also been the site of a Roman temple and a medieval chapel dedicated to the patron saint of woolcombers – St Blasius. The grounds are full of interesting features. Shop; cl 1–2pm, Mon, 25 Dec, Good Fri, 1 Jan; (0117) 950 6789; free.

EXPLORATORY HANDS-ON SCIENCE CENTRE (by Temple Meads railway station) Probably the best of its kind, this is a great place for children (and of course adults) to get their fingers into all kinds of science, with some very lively displays. A fun gallery devoted to music and sound includes the world's biggest acoustic guitar – you can even stand inside it. Snacks (wknds and school hols), shop, disabled access; cl 25–26 Dec; (0117) 922 5944; £4.

🍷 Harveys Wine Museum (Denmark St) Unique collection of antique corkscrews, decanters, glasses, bottles, furniture and other items associated with the production and serving of wine, housed in the medieval cellars of the company perhaps best known for their Bristol Cream. There's a very good shop, and you may be able to join one of the guided tours with tutored tastings – best to check first. Meals, snacks; cl 1–2pm, Sun (exc pm summer); (0117) 927 7661; £2.50 (inc a glass of sherry).

❀ ❀ The Cabot Tower, in attractive gardens at the top of Brandon Hill, gives good views of the city, but there are hundreds of steps. Snacks, cl 25–26 Dec; free. Nearby St George's has good Thurs lunchtime concerts, rarely booked up completely in advance.

★ 🏠 ❀ 🍴 ! Clifton is the quiet side of Bristol. It's well worth a visit, with some fine late 18th- and 19th-c terraces, an antiques market (Mall, cl Sun, Mon), a big park right on the spectacular Avon gorge facing the NT woodlands on the crags opposite, and the remarkably modern-looking Suspension Bridge, based on an 1836 design by Brunel and finished in 1864; a Victorian girl leapt off here after a tiff with her boyfriend, but was saved when her huge skirts acted as a parachute. The Somerset House (Princess Victoria St) is useful for something to eat.

🐾 ❀ 🍴 Bristol Zoo Gardens out here is the fourth most visited zoo in the country, nicely set in 12 acres of pleasant gardens. There's a lot going on, with hundreds of mammals and birds, and an aquarium with walk-through tank containing fantastic species of tropical, freshwater and saltwater fish. Also Insect House, and hands-on exhibition centre. Meals, snacks, shop, disabled access; cl 25 Dec; (0117) 973 8951; £5.50.

Other things to see and do

⚓ 🍴 ❀ 🏠 ❀ Clevedon ST4071 The Victorian Pier is being lovingly restored (it partly collapsed in 1970) and is pleasant for a stroll. Upstairs, above the tollhouse, is a gallery selling paintings, and there are sailings and fishing from the pier itself. Shop, disabled access; cl Weds Nov–Feb, 25 Dec; *50p. The pleasure steamers call in summer; (01275) 878846. Good views from Church Hill, and in Moor Lane the Clevedon Craft Centre has 15 varied workshops and a tea room; some parts cl Mon. The Little Harp (Promenade) has decent food and views to Exmoor and Wales.

Clevedon Court (just E, ST4271) Most of the original structure of this manor house, built in 1320, is still intact, though there are interesting additions from other periods inc a charming 18th-c garden. Snacks, limited disabled access; open pm Sun, Weds, Thurs and bank hols Apr–Sept; (01275) 872257; £3.30.

🏠 ❀ Dyrham ST7475 Dyrham Park Set in an ancient park grazed by fallow deer, this fine William and Mary house has hardly changed since the late 17th c. The interiors have Dutch-style furnishings, Delft ware, Dutch bird paintings and a remarkable *trompe l'oeil* by Hoogstraten. Shop; house cl am, all Thurs and Fri, all Nov–Mar, park open all yr; *£5, £1.50 deer park only; NT. The Crown at Tolldown on the A46 is quite useful for lunch.

♿ Oldbury-on-Severn ST6292 Oldbury Power Station (just N) Tours of nuclear power station, with good hands-on displays, new multi-media show, and nature trail. Shop, disabled access; cl winter Sat, 24 Dec–1 Jan; (01454) 419899; free. The Anchor has good food.

✚ ❀ ⚓ Steep Holm ST2260 This island a few miles off shore is a nature reserve, 50 acres teeming with rare plants, wildlife and historic remains, owned by the Kenneth Allsop Memorial Trust. Terrific views from the rugged cliffs; snacks, shop in former Victorian barracks; not suitable for the disabled. Boat trips to the island run from Knightstone Causeway, Weston, and occasionally from Clevedon, Apr–end Oct; contact Mrs Joan Rendell (01934) 632307; all-day trip £12.

✝ ☗ ♿ 🏚 **Weston-super-Mare**
ST3261 Friendly family seaside
resort, its Latin epithet added in the
19th c in an attempt to be one up on
the fashionable French resorts. An
unexpected find is the INTERNATIONAL
HELICOPTER MUSEUM, with over 50
helicopters and autogyros on display,
as well as photographs, models and
explanations of how the various parts
of the machines work. On the second
Sun each month (exc Jan and Feb)
they have an Open Cockpit Day,
when some of the helicopters are
opened up for visitors to inspect.
Snacks, shop, disabled access; cl
25–26 Dec, 1 Jan; (01934) 635227;
£3. The WOODSPRING MUSEUM
(Burlington St) looks mainly at
Victorian domestic life, with
elaborately reconstructed shops and
lots of seaside displays. Adjacent
Clara's Cottage is a Westonian home
of the 1900s with period kitchen,
parlour, bedroom, toys and dolls, and
back yard. Also displays on mining
and local archaeology, and an audio-
visual display of night-time animals.
Snacks, shop, disabled access on
ground floor only; cl Mon; £1.60
(which entitles you to as many return
visits as you like over the next year).
The Claremont Vaults on the
seafront is useful for lunch, and there
are pleasant walks through the
woods around the Iron Age fort above
the town.

🎣 The **lakes** in the Chew Valley – the
Chew Valley Lake ST5656 itself and
Blagdon Lake ST5159 – are more
popular as breathing places for people
living nearby than as places for
visitors from afar; both are pleasant
large stretches of water, with
managed fishing. The Live & Let
Live at Blagdon ST5059 is nicely set
for lunch.

★ **Attractive villages,** all with decent
pubs, include Almondsbury ST6084,
Oldbury-on-Severn ST6292 (the
church on the nearby knoll is
unusual), Tockington ST6186 and
Wick ST7072; the last three all have
pleasant nearby walks.

Walks

The N edge of the **Mendips** ◠-1 offers good walks, and useful starting points
include the Crown at Churchill ST4459, Swan at Rowberrow ST4558 (just
over the Somerset border) and Ring o' Bells at Compton Martin ST5457. The
great limestone gorge of Burrington Combe ST4858, an easy walk by the
B3134, can be combined with walks up on to Black Down ST4757 for memorable views in all directions, and over the heather and cranberry moors to Dole-
bury Warren ST4558, also in E Somerset, where the site of an Iron Age hill
fort marks a splendid Mendip viewpoint.

The attractively restored **Kennet & Avon Canal** ◠-2 has a good footpath
alongside. The canal runs across the county from Bristol through Hanham
ST6472 (where the Chequers is a welcome stop), Saltford ST6867 and Bath to
the spectacular aqueduct at Avoncliff ST8059 (and beyond, across Wiltshire
and into Berkshire).

The Iron Age hill fort of **Cadbury Camp** ST4572 ◠-3 can be reached from
the Black Horse in Clapton-in-Gordano ST4773, by a lane past the church,
which leads to a footbridge high over the M5.

The sea wall of the **Severn estuary** ◠-4 makes for some lonely walks, with
power station cooling towers emphasising the emptiness of the tidal flats. The
White Hart in Littleton-on-Severn ST5990, Anchor in Oldbury-on-Severn and
right on the embankment the Windbound at Shepperdine ST6295 are useful
starting points.

Dundry Hill ST5566 ◠-5 just beyond Bristol's southern suburbs has views
over the city, Chew Valley and Blagdon Lakes and the Mendips.

There are some pleasant walks around the Dog at Old Sodbury ST7581.

Driving

The steep wooded hills and valleys around Bath, particularly towards the S, are very picturesque. The A36 from Bath towards Warminster has some fine views of the richly wooded Avon valley, but except at very quiet times is too busy for pleasure. Better is the B3110 to Norton St Philip, but best of all, to view this steep and intricate scenery, are the narrow side roads such as the one through South Stoke (where the Pack Horse is an interesting ancient pub) or the one between Monkton Combe and Combe Hay (the Wheatsheaf here is good).

In the Chew Valley, the B3130 and B3114 are quite pleasant drives. The B3134 up into the Mendips is one of the prettiest roads in the area.

Where to eat

Bristol ST5872 HOWARDS 1a Avon Crescent, Hotwells (0117) 926 2921 Relaxed, friendly and charming restaurant with a wide choice of very good, honest cooking, and good value wines; cl Sun, 25–26 Dec. £18 dinner, £13 lunch.
Bristol ST5872 MILLWARDS 40 Alfred Place Kingsdown (0117) 924 5026 Small candlelit no smoking vegetarian evening restaurant with simple, clean furnishings, very good imaginative food, decent wine list inc many organic choices, and smiling service; cl Sun, Mon, 1 wk Christmas/Easter, 2 wks Oct. £17.
Oldbury-on-Severn ST6292 ANCHOR Church St (01454) 413331 Attractively modernised village pub with good daily-changing bar food, enterprising puddings, friendly service, no smoking dining room; cl 25 Dec; children in dining room only; disabled access. £13.50l£2.10/£4.95.

EAST SOMERSET

Some interesting countryside and places to visit; Wells and Glastonbury are very popular.

Wells cathedral is glorious; it, Glastonbury, the Wookey Hole Caves and Cheddar Gorge do attract a good many summer visitors, and are best explored out of season. Other less visited highlights include the Fleet Air Arm museum at Yeovilton, Castle Cary (with Hadspen Gardens), and Lytes Cary Manor at Kingsdon; Ebbor Gorge is a quieter alternative to the Cheddar one, and throughout the region there are pretty villages and interesting small towns. The edge of the Mendips has the best of the area's scenery (and offers the county's best walking). The dead-flat marshy pastures of the Somerset Levels provide an interesting contrast, and the richer more rolling farmland with small secluded valleys and wooded hillsides towards the east offer some gentle country drives.

There's enough to keep children entertained (and Longleat's just over the Wiltshire border), though on the whole it's adults who will enjoy this area most. And of course Bath itself is within easy reach.

Where to stay

Ston Easton ST6253 STON EASTON PARK Ston Easton, Bath BA3 4DF (01761) 241631 £145; 21 really lovely rms. Majestic Palladian mansion of Bath stone with beautifully landscaped 18th-c gardens in 26 acres of parkland;

elegant day rooms with antiques and flowers, attractive restaurant with good food (much grown in the kitchen garden), and extremely helpful, friendly and unstuffy service; babies and children over 7 welcome by prior arrangement.

Freshford ST7859 HOMEWOOD PARK Freshford, Bath BA3 6BB (01225) 723731 *£99; 15 lovely rms. On the edge of the ruins of Hinton Priory stands this charming Victorian hotel, with flowers and fine furniture in graceful day rooms, elegant restaurant with very good, imaginative food, and 10 acres of gardens and woodlands; tennis, croquet; disabled access.

Glastonbury ST5039 NUMBER 3 3 Magdalene St, Glastonbury BA6 9EW (0458) 832129 *£65; 6 rms. Attractive creeper-clad Georgian house next to the ruins of Glastonbury Abbey, with antiques and paintings, comfortable residents' lounge, little bar, particularly good imaginative food in restful dining room, and fine wine list; cl Dec and Jan; children over 8.

Ansford ST6333 BONDS HOTEL Ansford, Castle Cary BA7 7JP (01963) 50464 £60; 7 rms. Small listed Georgian house, once an inn, with antiques, open fires, personal caring service, and lots of charm; interesting weekly-changing food (many local cheeses on the cheeseboard) and good wine list in cosy restaurant; cl 1 wk Christmas; children over 8.

Glastonbury ST5039 WHO'D A THOUGHT IT 17 Northload St, Glastonbury BA6 9JJ (01458) 834460 *£55; 6 cosy rms. Friendly inn with lots of interesting original features and fittings, well kept real ales, and popular food inc good breakfasts.

Wells ST5545 TOR Tor St, Wells BA5 2US (01749) 672084 £45; 8 rms, most with own bthrm. 17th-c family house close to the cathedral, with comfortable lounge, good breakfasts in pretty dining room, and helpful owners; no smoking; children over 5.

Croscombe ST5844 BULL TERRIER Croscombe, Wells BA5 3QJ (01749) 343658 £44; 3 rms. One of the oldest pubs in Somerset, with neat, civilised decor, warm, courteous service, decent choice of wines, and consistently good food inc enterprising daily specials and particularly good imaginative puddings; cl Mon Oct–Mar; no children or pets.

Axbridge ST4255 LAMB The Square, Axbridge BF26 2AP (01934) 732253 £40; 3 spacious old-world rms. Interesting rambling old place in attractive, partly medieval square; log fires, welcoming service, good-value bar food, real ales, and pretty little garden with cockatiels; quite handy for M5; cl 25 Dec.

Bleadon ST3357 PURN HOUSE FARM Bleadon, Weston-super-Mare BS24 0QE (01934) 812324 £40; 6 spacious rms, most with own bthrm. Working family farm with 700 acres, dairy and stock animals, sheep and family pets, good food using home-produced meat and vegetables, comfortable sitting room, attractive, partly panelled dining room, games room with table tennis and so forth; riding, golf and fishing nearby; cl Dec and Jan; disabled access.

Milborne Port ST6718 QUEEN'S HEAD Milborne Port, Sherborne DT9 5DQ (01963) 250314 £35; 3 cosy rms, 1 with own shower. Old coaching inn with beamed lounge, good food, friendly service, quiet restaurant, 7 well kept beers and 4 ciders, and tables in sheltered courtyard and garden.

Horsington ST7023 HALF MOON Horsington, Templecombe BA8 0ED (01963) 370140 £32; 4 rms, in chalets with showers. Nicely refurbished inn, with stripped stone, oak floors, beams and inglenook fires, home-made food in bar and restaurant, decent wines and real ales, and garden with play area.

Polsham ST5142 SOUTHWAY FARM Polsham, Wells BA5 1RW (01749) 673396 £32; 3 rms, shared bthrm. Friendly Georgian farmhouse with open fire in comfortable lounge, attractive dining room, good breakfasts and pretty garden; cl Dec–Feb.

Emborough ST6151 REDHILL FARM Emborough, Bath BA3 4SH (01761) 241294 £30; 3 rms, shared bthrm. Friendly old farmhouse high on the Mendips, with animals and poultry to amuse the children and good fresh food; riding, sailing, fishing nearby; no dogs.

To see and do

★🏠♨ **Axbridge** ST4254 This pleasant small town has an attractive largely medieval square and narrow winding high street, unusual in this part of the world for its jettied timber-framed buildings. One of them is KING JOHN'S HUNTING LODGE, actually built around 1500 so having no connection with King John (nor in fact with hunting) – but no less attractive for that. It houses a local history museum. Disabled access to grounds; cl am, all Oct–Easter; £1; NT. The little market square is a tranquil place, and the rambling old Lamb on the corner is good for lunch.

★ ✝ 🏚 🏛 **Bruton** ST6834 Fascinating little town; worth looking out for are the Bartons, narrow alleys leading down from the High Street to the river (which you can cross either by footbridge or by using stepping stones); also ST MARY'S CHURCH, which stands on the site of a medieval Augustinian priory and abbey – the old abbey wall with its buttresses still stands in Silver Street. The church has a spectacular altar-piece, and in the chancel is a fine effigy of Sir Maurice Berkely, a great survivor who was standard-bearer to Henry VIII, Edward VI and Queen Elizabeth. Interesting and individual shops – antiques, books and prints. The Castle Inn is good for lunch.

✝ 🐄 ☺ **Burnham-on-Sea** ST3050 is in summer a bustling low-cost family seaside resort with its wide beaches, sandy dunes, and the usual holiday facilities. Its plain-looking CHURCH surprises with its collection of Grinling Gibbons carvings from the long-demolished Palace of Whitehall in London. Children enjoy ANIMAL FARM COUNTRY PARK AND THE LAND OF LEGENDS at nearby Berrow ST2952, where there are animals and conservation trails, and displays of folk tales and other myths and stories; cl Nov–Mar; (01278) 751628; £2.80. The Red Cow at Brent Knoll has good food.

🐟 ❄ **Burrington Combe** ST4758 is a steeply wooded roadside combe on the north flank of the Mendips, with good viewpoints above it.

❄ 🏠 ★ ♨ 🐄 **Castle Cary** ST6332 HADSPEN GARDENS Covering about 8 acres, these beautiful gardens surround a fine 18th-c house. A delightful 17th-c walled garden has all sorts of herbaceous plants and old-fashioned roses. Also lily pond and ancient flower meadow. Many old favourite plants, but also many exotics. Sun snacks, nursery, some disabled access; open Thurs–Sun Mar–Sept; (01749) 813707; £2. The village itself is also very attractive, basically a medieval market town, now offering a useful range of traditional family-run shops, hotels and inns; the George Hotel is recommended. The Castle Cary VINEYARD produces decent wine (cl am Sun and Nov–Apr), and the ROUNDHOUSE, Britain's smallest prison, built in 1779, and the local museum are worth a look if you've time.

✗ ❄ **Chapel Allerton** ST4050 The 18th-c ASHTON WINDMILL here is the only complete mill left in the county, and has splendid views over the Cheddar Gorge and Somerset Levels; open pm Sun and bank hols Easter–Sept, plus pm Weds July and Aug; (01934) 712694; free. The New Inn down in Wedmore has wholesome home cooking.

✝ 🍴 ❄ 🎠 🏚 ☺ ♨ 🏛 🍴 **Cheddar** ST4754 has a very fine market cross, with some interesting shops and a 14th/15th-c CHURCH with a fine tall tower in the older part of the extended village; the Galleries is quite useful for lunch, and outside there are roadside strawberry stalls and pick-your-own in summer. CHEDDAR GORGE is the attraction here, a magnificent limestone gorge with picturesque cliffs, formed when a cavern roof collapsed; a road goes along the bottom, and Jacob's Ladder climbs to an excellent viewpoint. CHEDDAR SHOWCAVES Two beautiful caves beneath the Gorge; quite cathedral-like with spectacular stalagmites and stalactites joining to form columns. Also an exhibition devoted to 'Cheddar Man', Britain's oldest complete skeleton, with a re-creation of his world of 9,000 years ago. Good clifftop walks, and plenty of activities for children inc the lively Crystal Quest. Meals, snacks, shop; cl 24–25 Dec; (01934) 742343; £5. CHEDDAR GORGE CHEESE CO RURAL VILLAGE Shops and traditional crafts based around a factory that thanks to its location claims to make the only genuine cheddar cheese in the world. You can watch each stage of the seven-hour process, and of course taste the matured product. Also fudge-making, scrumpy sampling, and reconstructed 1920s sweet factory, as well as less flavoursome crafts inc cooperage, and lace- and candle-making. Meals, snacks, shops, disabled access; cl Nov–mid-Mar; (01934) 742810; *£3. There's an AQUARIUM near here too.

🐄 ✿ † **Chewton Mendip** ST5953 CHEWTON CHEESE DAIRY Another traditional cheese dairy, one of the few to mature their cheeses properly, so producing not just the characteristic rind but also the true depth of flavour. They start at 7am and go on till 3pm, with the best time to watch between 11.30am and 2.30pm. A video shows the stages you may have missed, and there are various animals and a few other craft shops. Meals, snacks, shop, disabled access; no cheese-making Thurs or Sun, cl 25–26 Dec, 1 Jan; (01761) 241666; £2 guided tour. The 15th-c CHURCH TOWER is perhaps the most magnificent in any village in the area, and the Decoy Duck Gallery is interesting; cl Sun and Mon, and all Jan and Feb. The Waldegrave Arms has good value home cooking.

🚂 🖼 ✿ **Cranmore** ST6843 EAST SOMERSET RAILWAY Engine shed and workshops, with nine steam locomotives and rolling stock, art gallery with wildlife paintings by David Shepherd, and steam trips along part of what's known as the Strawberry Line. Meals and snacks, shop, disabled access; open wknds (exc Jan and Feb) plus Weds–Fri May–Sept, though trains don't run all these days; (01749) 880417; £3.50, £1.50 when no trains running. The Strode Arms in this quiet and pleasant village is very good for lunch, and there are good views from the top of

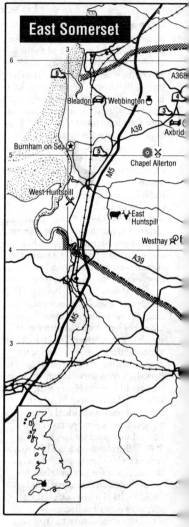

CRANMORE FOLLY; cl Oct–Mar; £1.

† **Cucklington** ST7527 CHURCH of St Lawrence is 13th c with small side chapel dedicated to St Barbara, whose well lies further down in the village.

🐄 ✟ **East Huntspill** ST3444 NEW ROAD FARM Family-run working farm, with quite an emphasis on wildlife rescue. The best feature is the unique observation badger sett in the Nocturnal House, with glass viewing panels to watch the creatures' life underground. Also farm trail, barn owl release scheme, demonstrations

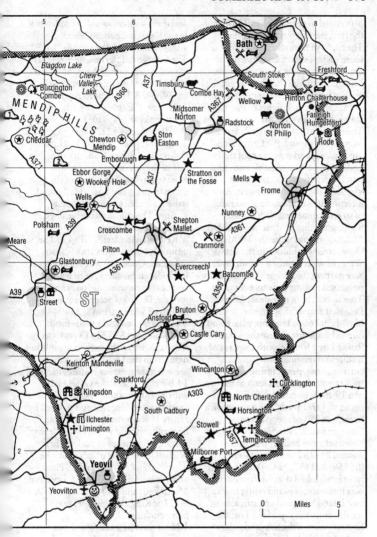

of various farming methods, and special events. Meals, snacks, shop, disabled access; cl wkdys Oct–Mar; (01278) 783250; £3.75. The Crossways Inn over at West Huntspill is good for lunch.

Ebbor Gorge ST5248 If you like Cheddar Gorge but don't like the souvenir stall, coach parties and all, then Ebbor Gorge is for you. It's the same sort of thing, above Wookey Hole, but altogether more unspoilt. The New Inn or Queen Victoria up at Priddy have sensibly priced food.

★ † ⚘ 🐄 🚂 ❄ 🏰 🎪 🏤 **Glastonbury** ST4938 and its immediate surrounding area are rich in myth and legend. Tales of King Arthur can be found all over the country, but are especially prominent here; they like to say that bones reinterred in the abbey in 1191 were those of Arthur and Guinevere. The noble ruins of GLASTONBURY ABBEY are said to mark the location of the birth of Christianity in this country. The story goes that Joseph of Arimathea struck his staff into Wearyall Hill, where it proceeded to take root. (Offshoots of the tree, the famous Glastonbury Thorn, have flourished to this day and there's a fine specimen in the parish churchyard.) He is also said to have brought with him the Holy Grail, the chalice from the Last Supper, which Arthur's table of knights heroically sought through so many famous tales. The remains of the church date mainly from 1524, though the Lady Chapel is much older, and massive roof timbers and richly decorated gable ends and porches testify to the enormous wealth of the order who ran it. An interpretation area has a good range of stories connected with the site. Shop, some disabled access; cl 25 Dec; *£2. Legend has it the chalice of the Holy Grail was hidden in the CHALICE WELL, now set amidst a colourful 2½-acre garden; the spring has apparently possessed healing powers ever since. True or not, it's a nice peaceful spot. Disabled access, shop; cl am Nov–Feb; *60p. The abbey barn and outbuildings now house the SOMERSET RURAL LIFE MUSEUM, with displays of traditional regional skills such as cider-making, peat-cutting and basket-weaving, and a look at the life of a 19th-c Somerset labourer. Also orchard, rare breeds, bee garden with hives, and lots of special events. Summer snacks, shop, some disabled access; cl am wknds and all Sun in winter, 25–26 Dec, 1 Jan, Good Fri; (01458) 831197; *£1.50. Historians have established that Glastonbury was formerly an island rising from a vast inland lake, and you can almost see this from the top of the Tor, the highest point of the hills and ridges among which the little town nestles. Excavations here have revealed a prehistoric LAKE VILLAGE covering three or four acres below it, consisting of nearly a hundred mounds surrounded by a wooden palisade. Lots of items and timbers from the village have been unusually well preserved thanks to the waterlogged state of the site, and some of the finds, providing a fascinating insight into the life of the settlement, are displayed in the GLASTONBURY TRIBUNAL, a fine 15th-c town house on the High St. The tourist information centre is here too,

and there's some notable plasterwork in the lower back room. Shop; cl winter Sun; (01458) 832954; *£1.50. The George & Pilgrims, its medieval carved façade one of the sights of the town, is quite useful for lunch, as is the Who'd A Thought It. ADAMS & JONES near the abbey car park will hand-make shoes to measure.

★ ⌂ **Ilchester** ST5222 Charming, with a useful range of well stocked little shops. Used to be a Roman town, and one of the houses has a piece of Roman paving. The whole of the green fronting the Town Hall is said to be the burial ground of Plague victims. The comfortable Ivelchester Hotel has good food.

⚘ **Keinton Mandeville** ST5430 The unique ICELANDIC TAPESTRY SCHOOL (The Firs, Queen St) teaches medieval Icelandic embroidery, with wknd courses (some going abroad) and kits for sale. Disabled access; cl Sun and 25 July–25 Aug; (01458) 224044. The Quarry has good-value food.

⌂ ❁ **Kingsdon** ST5326 LYTES CARY MANOR Most of the surviving building dates from the 16th c, though there are interesting earlier features inc the 14th-c chapel, and the Great Hall with its 15th-c stained glass. The gardens were designed and stocked by Henry Lyte, a notable Elizabethan horticulturist and writer on gardening, and are being brought back to their original state, using plants which he described and recommended. Plant sales, limited disabled access; open pm Mon, Weds and Sat Apr–Oct; £3.50; NT. The Kingsdon Inn does good home cooking.

† **Limington** ST5422 Worth seeing is the fine CHURCH with effigies of the Giverney family dating back to the 1300s.

⌂ **North Cheriton** ST6825 Close by the church are the remains of a court with five walls where Napoleonic officers imprisoned in 'The Dogs' (manor house at Wincanton) used to play Fives.

🐄 ❁ **Norton St Philip** ST7755 NORWOOD RARE BREEDS FARM Friendly farm on high open land with plenty of traditional and rare breeds of cattle, sheep, pigs, goats and poultry, and good views. You can go right up to the animals, and watch the pigs being fed at 4.15 pm. Meals, snacks, good farm shop, disabled access; cl Oct–Easter; (01373) 834356; £3. The George is useful for lunch – and one of the most interesting ancient inn buildings in Britain.

★ 🏠 † **Nunney** ST7345 has a small market place just above a quiet river, and 18th-c weavers' cottages. NUNNEY CASTLE Reduced to ruins by the Parliamentarians during the Civil War, this 14th-c crenellated manor house has one of the deepest moats in the country; it and its feeder stream running through the green of this quaint and quiet village are very popular with ducks. The castle's layout and round towers were supposedly modelled on France's Bastille; free. The church, as usual in so many Somerset villages, is well worth a look, and the George is a useful food stop (does teas, too).

🐚 **Radstock** ST6854 MUSEUM (Haydon) Once a dairy and cheese-making farm set in the old North Somerset coalfield, now an unusually interesting local history museum, inc reconstructed coalface, miner's cottage, workshop and schoolroom, model railway, agricultural implements, blacksmith's forge and 1930s Co-op shop. Snacks, shop, disabled access; cl wkdys (exc bank hols), am Sun and bank hols, all Dec; £1.50.

🐦 ❀ **Rode** ST8053 TROPICAL BIRD GARDENS Huge collection of around 200 species of colourful and exotic birds flying through 17 acres of grounds, with ornamental lakes, ponds and masses of trees and shrubs. Also pets' corner and (Easter–mid-Sept) woodland miniature railway. Summer meals, snacks, shop (inc sales of clematis, of which they have a notable collection), disabled access; cl 25 Dec; (01373) 830326; £3.90. The Red Lion nearby at Woolverton is useful for lunch.

★ † 🏚 **South Cadbury** ST6225 has an attractive scatter of golden cottages huddled around the church with its strikingy gargoyled tower; Waterloo Crescent is a row of farmworkers' cottages built in 1815. CADBURY CASTLE Arthurian connections crowd this area; the legendary king and his knights are still said to sleep in the castle, waking on Christmas Eve to ride down the hill, along what is still called King Arthur's Hunting Causeway, and through the village on their pilgrimage to Glastonbury. The castle, covering about 18 acres, is in fact a massive Iron Age camp: many relics have been found there – especially Roman artefacts. It's quite a steep climb (and can be muddy). The Queens Arms at Corton Denham has decent food, and in the opposite direction nearby COMPTON PAUNCEFOOT ST6425 is pretty.

🚗 **Sparkford** ST6026 HAYNES SPARKFORD MOTOR MUSEUM Lots of vintage and classic cars and motorcycles restored to working condition, where possible using original parts; you should be able to see some being test-driven outside, and there's a video theatre. Meals, snacks, shop, disabled access; cl 25–26 Dec, 1 Jan; (01963) 40804; £3.85.

🐚 🚃 **Street** ST4836 SHOE MUSEUM In the oldest part of Clarks shoe factory, footwear from Roman times to the present day, as well as machinery, tools and advertising material. The adjacent CLARKS VILLAGE has over 20 factory outlets, with some good bargains. Meals, snacks, shop, disabled access; museum cl am Sun; free. The Mullions opposite is useful for lunch.

★ † **Templecombe** ST7022 Ancient village with stocks still standing in place; the name comes from the medieval order of Knights Templar, who were dedicated to the protection of pilgrims and religious treasures. The church, founded by King Alfred's daughter, houses a 13th-c painting of Christ, found by accident 30 years ago in an outhouse which had once formed part of the priest's house; possibly an early copy of the Turin Shroud, which the Knights Templar may have had in their possession for a while. The Half Moon at nearby Horsington has good value food.

🐎 **Timsbury** ST6658 RADFORD FARM Friendly little farm with shire horse stables, the huge creatures still doing most of the work. Lots of animals for children to fuss, milking and other activities, nature trail. Meals, snacks, shop; cl Nov–Mar (exc some wknds before Christmas); (01761) 470106; £3.

♨ Webbington ST3855
WHEELWRIGHTS WORKING MUSEUM AND GYPSY FOLKLORE COLLECTION Wheels, carriages and caravans next to working old workshop, as well as Edwardian fairground and Romany museum. Snacks, shop, disabled access; cl Mon (exc bank hols) and Tues (exc July and Aug), usually all Jan and Feb; (01934) 750841; £2.50. The New Moon at Biddisham is a good value family dining pub.

★ † 🏛 🌲 ♨ 🏛 Wells ST5445 With a population of only 9,500 this delightful place wouldn't normally even qualify as a big town, but in fact it's England's smallest city. The CATHEDRAL that grants it this honour is a stunning structure right in the centre, its three towers stretching up against the Mendip foothills. This is the way cathedral cities were meant to be, their skylines dwarfed by the grandeur of the cathedral itself. The spectacular west front is the first sight to greet you as you come through one of the several surviving medieval gateways, and is reckoned by many to be the finest cathedral façade in the country; dating from the 13th c, it carries 293 pieces of medieval sculpture. Inside be sure to see the wonderful inverted arches – scissor-shaped and designed to take the additional weight of the tower which was heightened in 1338. In the nave the austere lines of the Perpendicular minstrels' gallery help make up one of the earliest completely Gothic designs. The clock in the north transept dates from 1390, and horsemen still joust on it every quarter of an hour. Plenty of fine carvings in the south transept, inc various victims of toothache, and four graphic scenes of an old man stealing fruit and getting what for. The embroidered stallbacks in the choir (1937–1948) are a riot of colour – a labour of love for needleworkers across the country. The chapter house is a gem of the Decorated style; the library (with documents dating back to the 10th c) at 168 ft long is possibly the largest medieval library building in England. Meals, snacks, shop, disabled access; £1.50 suggested donation. The 15th-c Chain Gate links the cathedral with the Vicars' Close, where the Vicars Choral still live, in the original medieval houses. It's said to be one of the oldest complete medieval streets in Europe. The moated and fortified BISHOP'S PALACE nearby can be approached only through the 14th-c gatehouse, and it's quite dramatic going across the drawbridge. The beautiful series of buildings still has some original 13th-c parts, notably the banqueting hall and undercroft, as well as several other interesting state rooms and a long gallery hung with portraits of former bishops. The grounds are the site of the famous wells that give the town its name, bubbling up from the pool below the cathedral and producing on average 40 gallons of water a second. Also decent arboretum and a rather clever flock of swans, trained to ring a little bell under the gatehouse window when they want feeding. Meals, snacks, shop, disabled access; open Tues, Thurs, bank hols and pm Sun Apr–Oct, daily in Aug; (01749) 678691; £2, maybe more for special exhibitions. A Tudor building in Cathedral Green houses a good local history MUSEUM, with mementoes of the Witch of Wookey Hole who lived in the caves, and notable embroidery samplers. Disabled access to ground floor only; cl winter Mon and Tues; £1. There are a good few other attractive old buildings, many now used as offices and shops (inc several antique shops), and several grouped around the Market Place; the Fountain and City Arms near here are good for lunch, and there's a big cheese shop not far away.

🏛 ✿ Westhay ST4341 PEAT MOORS VISITOR CENTRE (Shapwick Rd) In the heart of the peat-cutting area of the Somerset Levels, a fascinating insight into the area's archaeology, history and natural history, with an excellent exhibition on peat-cutting and a reconstructed Iron Age village. Craft demonstrations most summer wknds. Meals and snacks, shop, disabled access; cl 25–26 Dec; (01458) 860257; *£1.50. You can get a joint ticket with the museums in Glastonbury. The

King William down at Catcott is a nice friendly place for lunch.

★ ✝ 🏠 **Wincanton** ST7128 Fine Georgian houses and many of the multitude of inns and hotels survive from the coaching era; many still have old coach-entry gates (for a meal we'd recommend the Smithy just outside at Charlton Musgrove). The CHURCH PORCH has a medieval relief of St Eligius. ROSIE'S CIDER (Rose Farm, Lattiford) sell a good range of local ciders (inc their own), as well as country wines and local preserves; open Thurs–Sat, but give them a ring on other days and if they're in they'll open then too; (01963) 33680.

🍺 ↧ ☺ ✗ ♣ **Wookey Hole** ST5347 WOOKEY HOLE CAVES AND PAPERMILL Guided tours of half a mile of dramatic subterranean tunnels and caverns, using remote-controlled lighting to spotlight the geological features and illustrate the history and myths associated with the caves. Just along the river the papermill demonstrates paper production, and also houses an authentic Edwardian fairground, Victorian portrait studio, Magical Mirror Maze and an Old Penny Arcade. A bustling place, and all under cover, so ideal for a day when the sun's not shining. Meals, snacks, shop, disabled access exc to caves; cl 17–25 Dec; (01749) 672243; £5.60. The Burcott Inn nearby is useful for lunch, and in Burcott itself there's a working WATERMILL with several craft shops and animals; cl Mon and Tues, no milling wkdys; £1.80.

🗝 **Yeovil** ST5516 has little to interest visitors, but the MUSEUM OF SOUTH SOMERSET (Hendford) is worth a look if passing, with a good range of local history and reconstructed Roman and Georgian rooms. Disabled access to ground floor only; cl Sun and Mon; free.

✝ ☺ **Yeovilton** ST5422 FLEET AIR ARM MUSEUM Big, bustling place concentrating on the story of aviation at sea from 1908, and the history of the Royal Naval Air Service. Lively displays on the WRNS, the Falklands and Gulf Wars, jets and helicopters, as well as nearly 50 historic aircraft, and lots of models, paintings, weapons and photographs. There's a very good new exhibition on aircraft carriers, and viewing galleries look out over the aircraft using this busy base. Also children's adventure playground and hi-tech flight simulator. You can spend a good few hours here. Meals, snacks, shop, disabled access; cl 24–26 Dec; (01935) 840565; *£5.50. The Carpenters Arms at Chilthorne Domer has good home cooking.

★ **Other attractive villages** in this area are Batcombe ST6838, Brent Knoll ST3350 (remarkable carved bench-ends in the church), Combe Hay ST7359, Croscombe ST5844 (great 17th-c woodwork in its 15th-c church), Evercreech ST6438, Mells ST7249 (marvellous church), Pilton ST5940, South Stoke ST7641, Stowell ST6822, Wellow ST7458 and Winscombe ST4157. Stratton on the Fosse ST6550 is notable for the spectacular modern (though not modern-looking) Downside Abbey.

Walks

Excluding Exmoor (discussed separately, in the Devon chapter), the Mendips have the county's most interesting walks – not on the top, which is mostly unremarkable farmland, but along its edges, particularly in the two great limestone gorges. The **Cheddar Gorge** ST4553 ⌂-1 is a straightforward walk along the road. It rapidly loses its commercialised trappings, and when you reach the far end two worthwhile paths leave the road. On the E side is a quiet dale with two nature reserves, Black Rock ST4854 and Velvet Bottom ST4955. On the W side, the West Mendip Way climbs through woods and gives access to another path which skirts the top of the gorge (the views into it are hair-raising). **Ebbor Gorge** ST5248 ⌂-2, altogether quieter than Cheddar Gorge, has an attractive nature trail. A good walk runs from Wookey Hole ST5347 through the Gorge to Pen Hill ST5548 for panoramic views. Burrington Combe on the north side has been mentioned above, under Avon. The

West Mendip Way △-3 (Wells to Weston-super-Mare) crosses the Mendip plateau and ascends some medium-sized hills: there are stunning views from the walk from Compton Bishop ST3955 over Crook Peak ST3855, Compton Hill ST3856 and Wavering Down ST4055 to Kings Wood ST4155. The **Strawberry Line** △-4 below the Mendips at Winscombe ST4257 is an abandoned railway, now mainly a footpath, with steam trips along part of it from Cranmore.

Brent Knoll ST3450 △-5, a detached Mendip outlier, has a path to its summit from Brent Knoll village (the Red Cow here is useful). **Brean Down** ST2958 △-6, sandwiched between Weston-super-Mare and acres of holiday camps, protrudes into the Bristol Channel and provides the finest coastal walk in E Somerset. The pleasant walk to **Wells** ST5445 △-7 from Croscombe ST5844 gives unforgettable views of the cathedral.

Driving

The best road into the Mendips is the B3135 up through the Cheddar Gorge, passing the dramatic limestone cliffs, and then coming out on the plateau of the Mendips.

Many of the back roads in the E part of the area, towards the borders with Wiltshire and Dorset, take you through countryside with a very secluded feel. A good part for exploration, more open, is east of Bruton and up towards Alfred's Tower.

The B3139 through Wells and Wedmore is an old coach road running along land which rises very slightly above the flood-prone Somerset Levels. The B3151 down to Glastonbury gives a good view of the town below the Tor as you approach.

Where to eat

Shepton Mallet ST6143 Blostins 29 Waterloo Rd (01749) 343648 Friendly candlelit evening bistro with consistently good interesting food inc lovely puddings; cl Sun, Mon, 2 wks Jan, 2 wks Jun, 1 wk Nov. **£18.95.**
Blagdon Hill ST2217 White Lion (01823) 142296 Gently refurbished village pub with good china ornaments, log fire, very pleasant service, and a wide choice of good home-made food; cl 25 Dec; children in dining room. **£18|£1.75/£4.**
West Huntspill ST3044 Crossways (01278) 783756 Popular, spacious dining pub with lovely atmosphere and very good food (esp puddings). **£18|£3/£5.50.**
Combe Hay ST7359 Wheatsheaf (01225) 833504 Pleasantly old-fashioned rooms, sloping lawn looking down to church and ancient manor stables, wide choice of good food (lots of game and fish), and friendly staff; summer barbecues. **£16|£3/£5.25.**
Cranmore ST6643 Strode Arms (01749) 880450 Carefully run former farmhouse with charming country furnishings and generous helpings of good home-made dishes; also excellent puddings; cl winter pm Sun; children in restaurant only; disabled access. **£14.50|£1.75/£5.50.**
Freshford ST7859 Freshford Inn (01225) 722250 Picturesque three-storey building in lovely setting, comfortable interestingly decorated bar, good generous restaurant and bar food, well kept ales and helpful staff. **£1.70/£5.50.**

WEST SOMERSET

Many interesting places to visit, good value places to stay, some very unspoilt if undramatic countryside.

What strikes visitors most about much of the countryside in this part of Somerset is its secluded and self-contained nature: without the splendid church towers peeking up out of the trees, you'd often not know a village was there at all. The Quantock Hills, above all, exemplify the private feel of Somerset, with their small valleys each seeming to be a little individual world. In the south-east the Blackdown Hills are classic English countryside, surprisingly little visited, with some charming untouristy villages. The vivid green fenny pastures of the Levels, including Sedgemoor, are an important habitat for wildlife and on slightly misty days have haunting views across to Glastonbury Tor and the Mendips.

A good many interesting places to visit here include particularly Montacute House, Dunster and its castle, Barrington Court with its lovely gardens, the fine old gardens of Clapton Court at Crewkerne, the Cricket St Thomas wildlife park, the garden of Lambrook Manor at East Lambrook, the unusual indoor jungle at Washford, and one of the enjoyable cider mills at Dowlish Wake or Bradford-on-Tone.

Minehead is a pleasant traditional resort, most notable perhaps for the steam railway which runs up below the Quantocks, a much longer route than usual for private railways.

A wide choice of places to stay runs from a good many little country inns and civilised farm or country-house B & Bs, which seem particularly to suit the area's character, to very comfortable small hotels; prices in this part of the county represent good value for money.

The Somerset parts of Exmoor have been described in the section devoted to Exmoor, in the Devon chapter; places like Dunster, off the moor though within the National Park, are included here.

Where to stay

Dunster SS9943 LUTTRELL ARMS Dunster, Minehead TA24 6SG (01643) 821555 £112; 27 rms. Comfortably modernised THF hotel in ancient building of great character with individual atmosphere, good popular food and interesting evening meals; cannon emplacements in the garden date from the Civil War; close to Exmoor National Park.

Middlecombe SS9645 PERITON PARK Middlecombe, Minehead TA24 8SW (01643) 706885 £90; 8 rms with views of surrounding countryside. Fine Victorian country house on the edge of Exmoor with comfortable lounge, books, log fire, a relaxed atmosphere, friendly service, and good food in panelled dining room; excellent walks and very good riding centre next to hotel; children over 12; disabled access.

Langley Marsh ST0729 LANGLEY HOUSE Wiveliscombe, Taunton TA4 2UF (01984) 623318 £83; 8 individually decorated, pretty rms. Spotlessly kept Georgian house with 16th-c heart, charming lounge and dining room, antiques, fresh flowers, log fires, friendly service, very good carefully cooked food using home-grown herbs and vegetables, and neatly kept landscaped gardens.

Barwick ST5613 LITTLE BARWICK HOUSE Barwick, Yeovil BA22 9TD (01935) 23902 *£76; 6 rms. Listed Georgian dower house in pretty garden, 2 miles south of Yeovil. Excellent food, lovely relaxed atmosphere, open fire in lounge, and good service; cl 3 wks Jan; dogs by arrangement.

Kilve ST1442 MEADOW HOUSE Sea Lane, Kilve, Bridgwater TA5 1EG (01278) 741546 £75; 10 rms, 5 of them in cottage in courtyard. Beautifully kept Georgian house with relaxed atmosphere, fresh flowers, antiques and comfortable seats, traditional English food using their own fruit and vegetables, a fine wine list, landscaped gardens, croquet, streamside walks, and sea fishing (5 mins); a smugglers' passage runs from the hotel to the church.

Hatch Beauchamp ST3220 FARTHINGS Hatch Beauchamp, Taunton TA3 6SG (01823) 480664 £65; 8 rms with thoughtful extras. Charming little Georgian house in three acres of gardens, with caring, friendly owners, open fires in quiet lounges, and good food using fresh local produce; children under 8 must eat by 7pm.

Kilve ST1422 HOOD ARMS Kilve, Bridgwater TA5 1EA (01278) 741210 £62; 5 rms. Popular village inn with straightforwardly comfortable main bar, wood-burning stove decorated with horse brasses, cosy little lounge, attentive service and very good food in bar and no smoking restaurant; cl 25 Dec.

Holford ST1541 COMBE HOUSE Holford, Bridgwater TA5 1RZ (01278) 741382 *£58; 19 rms. Warmly friendly hotel in pretty spot, with comfortable rooms, good home-made food, and relaxed atmosphere; cl Nov–Mar.

Lower Vellow ST0938 CURDON MILL Lower Vellow, Williton, Taunton TA4 4LS (01984) 56522 £50; 6 smallish but pretty and individually furnished rms. Charming and beautifully furnished hotel on the edge of Exmoor National Park; very good evening meal in antique-filled dining room, substantial breakfasts, friendly staff (and other guests), and lovely garden – as well as 200 acres of working farm to wander over; the waterwheel and mill shaft have been carefully preserved and still work; outdoor heated swimming pool; children over 8.

Somerton ST4828 LYNCH COUNTRY HOUSE 4 Behind Berry TA11 7PD (01458) 272316 £45; 5 prettily decorated rms. Carefully restored, homely Georgian house with comfortable lounge, books, and good breakfasts (no evening meals) in airy room overlooking grounds and lake, where there are black swans and exotic ducks; cl Christmas.

North Perrott ST4709 MANOR ARMS North Perrott, Crewkerne TA18 7SG (01460) 72901 £44; 5 rms. Comfortable and attractive little 16th-c inn with friendly, helpful licensees, beams, exposed stone and inglenook fireplace, good home-made food in bar and restaurant, and garden with play area; free coarse fishing and free entry into classic gardens of S Somerset; disabled access.

Waterrow ST0425 ROCK Waterrow, Taunton TA4 2AX (01984) 23293 £44; 7 rms. Welcoming pub prettily placed in small valley village; log fire, smallish bar, civilised lunchtime dining room that doubles as smart evening restaurant, wide choice of good food, decent coffee, real ales; no accomm Christmas.

Wiveliscombe ST0827 DEEPLEIGH Wiveliscombe, Taunton TA4 2UU (01984) 623379 £40; 5 cottagey rms with lovely views. Pink-washed 16th-c house in 3 acres; beams, panelling, log fire in inglenook fireplace, comfortable drawing room, cosy bar and attractive dining room with good food; lots of walks; riding or clay-pigeon shoots can be arranged.

Pinksmoor ST1320 PINKSMOOR MILLHOUSE Pinksmoor, Wellington TQ21 0HD (01823) 672361 £37; 3 comfortable rms. Though the old mill is no longer in use, you can walk along the millstream (conservation area with lots of wildlife) or around family-run dairy farm; log fire, 2 lounges, friendly welcome, and farmhouse cooking; no smoking; cl Christmas and New Year; no dogs.

Roadwater ST0338 WOOD ADVENT FARM Roadwater, Watchett TA23 0RR (01984) 40920 £37; 5 rms. Relaxed, spacious farmhouse on 340 acres of working farm; log fire in comfortable lounge, good country cooking using their own produce in dining room with woodburning stove; grass tennis court, outdoor heated swimming pool, and clay-pigeon- and pheasant-shooting.

Stogumber ST0937 HALL FARM Stogumber, Taunton TA4 3TQ (01984) 56321 £37; 6 rms, 5 with own bthrm. Old-fashioned B & B with evening meals (bring your own wine) – wonderfully unpretentious, and warmly friendly staff; cl 23 Dec–21 Jan; well behaved dogs welcome.

Bradley Green ST2438 MALT SHOVEL Blackmoor Lane, Bradley Green, Cannington, Bridgwater TA5 2NE (01278) 653432 *£36; 4 comfortable rms. Friendly, family-run pub with woodburning stove in homely, no-frills main bar, a little beamed snug, family room, dining room, good-value and popular food and real ales; cl 25 Dec.

Cannington ST2438 BLACKMORE FARM Cannington, Bridgwater TA5 2NE

(01278) 653442 £36; 3 rms. Grade I listed manor house dating back to 14th c with garderobes, beams and stone archways, good breakfasts around a huge table in the Great Hall, and log fire in comfortable sitting room.

Holford ST1541 QUANTOCK HOUSE Holford, Bridgwater TA5 1RY (01278) 741439 £36; 3 rms. Thatched 17th-c house with large cottagey garden, big inglenook in residents' lounge, delicious English cooking (evening meals by arrangement) and a friendly welcome; pets welcome; cl 25 Dec.

Stoke St Gregory ST3527 ROSE & CROWN Stoke St Gregory, Taunton TA3 7EW (01823) 490296 £35; 5 rms, 2 in cottage annexe, mostly shared bthrm. Warmly friendly 17th-c cottagey inn with a cosy and pleasantly romanticised stable theme, generous helpings of particularly good-value food in no smoking dining room, excellent breakfasts, decent wine list, and popular skittle alley; children over 12.

West Bagborough ST1633 RISING SUN West Bagborough, Taunton TA4 3EF (01823) 432575 £35; 4 rms, with showers. Pleasant quiet little place in tiny Quantocks village, with friendly family service, short choice of fresh generously served food inc big breakfasts, well kept real ale, and big log fires.

Isle Brewers ST2224 BUSHFURLONG FARM Isle Brewers, Taunton TA3 6QT (01460) 281219 *£34; 4 rms, 2 with own bthrm. Ham stone farmhouse, dating from early 1700s, on family-run arable farm with fine country views, breakfast room with access to garden, and guest lounge; no smoking, no evening meals (pubs nearby), bikes for hire, fishing; cl Christmas.

To see and do

🏠 ❀ **Barrington** ST3918 BARRINGTON COURT In the grounds of a splendid 16th-c house, a magnificent series of gardens influenced by Gertrude Jekyll, inc a rose garden, and traditional walled kitchen garden, the produce from which is on sale in the shop. Snacks, shop, disabled access; garden open pm Apr–Sept exc Fri and Sat, house Weds only; £3.10, house extra £1; NT. The village itself is attractive, and the Royal Oak does good lunches.

🐄 ⅃┬ 🏠 **Bradford-on-Tone** ST1722 SHEPPY'S CIDER (Three Bridges) The Sheppys have been making cider here since the early 19th c, and you can follow the entire process over the 370-acre farm. Tastings in the shop, and a little museum. Snacks, shop, disabled access; cl Sun exc 12–2 pm Easter–Christmas; (01823) 461233; £1.50. The Anchor at Hillfarrance has good bar food (and a nice family room).

👞 **Bridgwater** ST3037 has industrial outskirts, but some central bits worth seeing if you're passing: Castle St is the finest early 18th-c street in the county. ADMIRAL BLAKE MUSEUM Now the town museum, this picturesque house was the birthplace of the admiral in 1598, and shows his personal possessions (inc his sea chest) and a diorama of his great victory over the Spaniards at Santa Cruz. Also displays on the Battle of Sedgemoor in 1685, and other local history. Shop; cl am Sun, 25–26 Dec; free. The adjacent waterwheel is being restored.

🎣 **Burrow Bridge** ST3630 SOMERSET LEVELS BASKET CENTRE have been making baskets from local materials cut on the surrounding Levels for nearly 150 years; also other crafts. Shop, disabled access; cl Sun, 25–26 Dec; free. The George at Middlezoy is a pleasant old-fashioned Levels country pub.

⅃┬ ✕ ❀ 🎣 ✝ **Chard** ST3208 has a good local history MUSEUM looking at regional industries from cloth- and lace-making to agricultural engineering. Also a bizarre collection of artificial limbs. Shop, disabled access; cl Sun (exc July and Aug), mid-Oct–early May; £1.50. There are a couple of places to hire bikes; the local tourist board do good cycle routes. Just N of town HORNSBURY MILL ST3310 is a 200-year-old watermill, with landscaped water garden, trout lake, play area and craft shops. You can stay here too. Meals, snacks, shop, disabled access; (01460) 63317; free, museum £1.50. Another handy place to eat in this direction is the

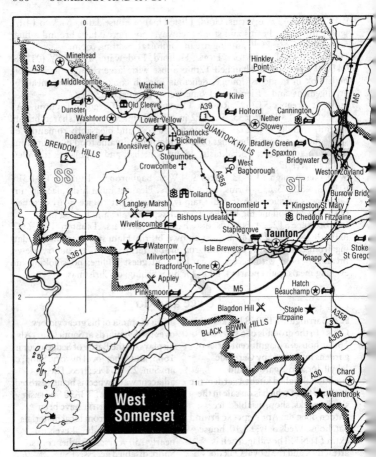

West Somerset

Haymaker at Wadeford. FORDE ABBEY nearby is listed under Dorset – particularly worth visiting, just over the border.

❀ **Cannington** ST2539 CANNINGTON COLLEGE HERITAGE GARDENS Extensive gardens inc over 10,000 different types of plant, with eight National Collections, display and ornamental beds, tropical and sub-tropical glasshouses, and gardens of bees and butterflies. Snacks, shop; cl am, and Nov–Easter; (01278) 652226; *£1.50. The King's Head is useful for lunch.

❀ **Cheddon Fitzpaine** ST2428 HESTERCOMBE GARDENS Raised walks, sunken lawns and a water garden are all part of the grand design which Lutyens and Gertrude Jekyll created for this garden (now beautifully restored) set around the headquarters

of the Somerset Fire Brigade; cl wknds exc pm May–Sept; *£2. If you don't want to go into Taunton, the Bathpool Inn at Bathpool on the A38 is a handy family dining pub.

✚ ☺ **Cricket St Thomas** ST3708 The WILDLIFE PARK here has seen a few changes over the last year; they've still got a wide variety of animals in well designed enclosures, but have added a series of attractions based around the TV series *Noel's House Party*. No stranger to TV shows (*To the Manor Born* was filmed here), the park is reckoned by some to be not what it was, but it's not too difficult to ignore the brashness of Mr Blobby and enjoy the rest of the surroundings. They've had some success in breeding (esp with black swans) and there's also a woodland railway. Meals and snacks,

shop, disabled access; cl 25–26 Dec, tel to check open in winter; (01460) 30755; £6.80.

🐄 ♨ 🏠 **Dowlish Wake** ST3713 PERRY'S CIDER MILLS They've been making cider here for centuries, and between Oct and Christmas you can watch it being produced. The cider mill is in a group of thatched 16th-c buildings around a yard with brightly painted old farm waggons and so forth, with more agricultural bygones under cover. Enthusiastically run, with liberal tastings and half a dozen different ciders for sale, in old-fashioned earthenware flagons if you want. Shop, disabled access; cl 1–1.30pm, 25–26 Dec, 1 Jan; free. The nearby New Inn is very good for lunch.

★ ✝ 👃 ✗ 🏰 ♨ ❄ ! **Dunster** SS9943 has fine medieval houses along the wide main street below the wooded castle hill, with a handsome former yarn market and market cross, a lovely 15th-c priory CHURCH with particularly tuneful bells, and a doll museum. An 18th-c WATERMILL still produces stoneground flour for sale (teas; cl Sat exc July and Aug, all Nov–Mar; *£1.50). The handsome old Luttrell Arms Hotel is good for lunch. DUNSTER CASTLE Dramatically placed, set in a 28-acre park teeming with exotic flora and even subtropical plants. The castle's current appearance is largely 19th c, but there are older features inside such as the 17th-c oak staircase and gallery with its brightly painted wall hangings. Excellent views. Shop in 17th-c stables, limited disabled access; cl Thurs, Fri, Nov–Mar (exc garden, only cl Dec and Jan); £4.70, £2.70 garden and park only; NT. You can also see from a distance the 12th-c OLD DOVECOT, special for still having its potence or revolving ladder, used for harvesting the plump squabs from the nesting boxes.

♨ **East Lambrook** ST4319 EAST LAMBROOK MANOR GARDEN This well loved cottagey garden around a 15th-c house (not open) is now Grade I listed; it was started by Walter and Margery Fish in 1937, and Margery Fish described the process in her book *We Made A Garden*, which became immensely popular. They keep the National Collection of geraniums. Plant sales, shop; cl Sun, and all Nov–Feb; (01460) 40328; *£2. The Rose & Crown opposite is useful for lunch.

🏠 ♨ 👃 **Hatch Beauchamp** ST3220 HATCH COURT Fine Palladian mansion with impressive hall, walled kitchen garden, deer park, plenty of china and a small military museum. It's one of those places where the family really take care showing you round, enlivening the tour with plenty of anecdotes. Teas; open pm Thurs mid-Jun–mid-Sept, and garden only the two Thurs before and after; (01823) 480058; £3, £2 garden only. The Hatch Inn is useful for lunch.

♨ HINKLEY POINT ST2646 POWER STATION Quite a contrast to most of the other places we recommend in this region, with hi-tech displays and interactive videos explaining how electricity is generated, and information on local ecology and wildlife (there are nature trails from here); cl winter Sat, 25–26 Dec, 1 Jan; free. Tours (also free) of the station too, which must be booked in advance: (01278) 652461.

★ † Huish Episcopi ST4226 Attractive village with a fine CHURCH, and a quaint old pub, the Rose & Crown.

↓T ⚐ Kingsbury Episcopi ST4321 SOMERSET CIDER BRANDY CO England's first fully licensed cider distillery, with huge copper stills, oak vats and wooden presses, and traditional cider orchards to stroll through. Shop; cl Sun; (01460) 240782; free. The village green has an ancient lock-up, and the Wyndham Arms is useful for lunch.

† 🏚 Martock ST4619 Magnificent CHURCH with splendid roof; look out for the old court house turned into a grammar school by William Strode in 1661, with the inscription above the door 'Martock neglect not your opportunities' in English, Latin, Hebrew and Greek. The Fleur de Lis in Stoke sub Hamdon is useful for lunch.

❀ ⚘ Merriott ST4412 SCOTTS OF MERRIOTT Perhaps the last of the big general retail nurseries to raise and grow most of their own trees and shrubs, on 90 acres – a sea of colour when the 500 varieties of roses are in flower in July. Snacks, shop, disabled access; (01460) 72306; free. In the village D B POTTERY (Highway Cottage, Church St) make attractive teapots and other stoneware. Shop, disabled access; cl 12–2pm wkdys; (01460) 75655; free. The Poulett Arms on the attractive main street of nearby Hinton St George is good for lunch.

🚃 🏍 ⚐ Minehead SS9746 has a sweet easily missed area of sloping streets and thatched cottages around its church, with Church Steps a quaint steep back lane. Around this original fishing village is a spacious resort, its beach and promenade sheltered by the wooded hills to the NE. It has the usual attractions, a lively harbour, a sizeable holiday camp, and a modern shopping area. The Old Ship Aground has good-value food and pleasant harbour views. There's an unusual

POTTERY SHOP (cl Sun) on Park St, and a little SHOE FACTORY you can visit on North Rd (cl 1–2pm and wknds exc am Sat). Minehead is the terminus for the WEST SOMERSET RAILWAY, whose steam trains run along the coast to Watchet and then inland to Bishops Lydeard – a splendid long run stopping at several little stations (the one at Washford – see below – has a museum devoted to the old Somerset & Dorset Railway). Meals and snacks, shop, very good disabled access, with a specially adapted coach; cl wkdys Mar, Nov and Dec, and all Jan and Feb, best to check on (01643) 707650 for dates and times; *£2-£8 depending on the length of the journey. From the harbour you may be able to catch the *Waverley* (paddle steamer) or *Balmoral*, along the Bristol Channel or to Lundy Island.

❀ ♤ ♨ ✕ 🏚 Monksilver ST0736 COMBE SYDENHAM COUNTRY PARK Halfway through a 40-yr restoration plan, 580 acres of Exmoor-edge woodland, with Elizabethan-style garden, National Museum of Baking (inc working corn mill), children's play area and woodland walks; 16th-c house. Meals and snacks, good shop with meat and fish from the estate; cl Sat (exc shop open am), Nov–Mar; (01984) 56284; £4. The Notley Arms is excellent for lunch.

🏚 ★ 🖼 ❀ Montacute ST4917 MONTACUTE HOUSE Magnificent 16th-c honeyed stone house in beautiful little village, with a wealth of interesting tapestries, furniture, paintings and ceramics, set in rooms with decorated ceilings, ornate fireplaces and fine wood panelling. The highlight is the collection of Tudor and Jacobean paintings from the National Portrait Gallery in the Long Gallery. The main body of the house is original but the heraldic beasts and fluted columns were added in the 18th c; impressive formal gardens. Meals and snacks, shop, limited disabled access; cl am, Tues, Good Fri, Nov–Mar; £4.70; NT. In the village, features worth seeing include the Borough – a square of two-storey houses – which is quite charming, while Abbey Farm and the Monk's House are all that remain from the Cluniac Priory founded in Norman times and destroyed by Henry VIII during the Dissolution. The Kings Arms and Phelips Arms are good for lunch.

✝ 🏠 ⚲ **Muchelney** ST4224 MUCHELNEY ABBEY The abbey was founded in the 9th c (perhaps earlier), but the well preserved ruins date from the 15th, inc part of the cloister, and the abbot's lodging with its splendidly carved fireplace. Shop, limited disabled access; cl 1–2 pm, Oct–Mar; £1.25. The tiny 14th-c priest's house opposite is worth a quick look; open pm Sun and Mon Apr–Sept; £1.30; NT. The Wyndham Arms at Kingsbury Episcopi is pleasant for lunch. The other way, the JOHN LEACH POTTERY (Langport) is famous for its striking signed designs by Bernard Leach's grandson; cl lunchtime, pm Sat, Sun.

★ ❀ 🏠 ⚲ **Nether Stowey** ST1939 is an appealing large village with winding streets, handy for both Exmoor and the Quantocks, with good views over the Levels from the mound of the former Norman castle; the QUANTOCK HILLS INFORMATION CENTRE in Castle St is a valuable source of information. COLERIDGE COTTAGE (off the A39) Little has changed since Coleridge moved here in 1796; he lived here with a pig or two, and his friends the Wordsworths resided in considerably more style not far away – the two families were regarded with suspicion by the local population. It was here that Coleridge was inspired to write *The Ancient Mariner*; open pm Tues–Thurs and Sun Apr–Sept; £1.50; NT. The Cottage Inn at Keenthorne just E of the village is good for lunch. Up at Over Stowey ST1838, QUANTOCK WEAVERS (Old Forge, Plainsfield) carry out hand spinning, knitting and weaving using natural dyes, in former 17th-c forge; cl am wknds.

🏠 **Old Cleeve** ST0342 John Wood (Old Cleeve Tannery) is a SHEEPSKIN FACTORY with wkdy guided tours (not Nov–Mar; 50p), café, and a shop selling rugs, coats, slippers etc inc cheap seconds; cl Sun, 25–26 Dec, 1 Jan; (01984) 40291. The White Horse at Washford has good-value food.

★ ✝ **Somerton** ST4828 is a market town built in light grey stone, with a 17th-c market cross and fine old Georgian buildings in the quiet main square. ST MICHAEL'S CHURCH is stupendous, its roof supposedly created by monks of Muchelney from 7,000 fetter pieces, among which is a beer barrel – apparently a reference to Abbot Bere. The Globe, Red Lion and White Hart are useful for lunch.

🏠 ✝ 🏠 **South Petherton** ST4316 This houses the HQ and two shops of Global Village, a company importing ethnic art and lo-tech products from over 30 countries, including many of the Third World. The CHURCH has the second-highest octagonal tower in the country. Opposite Nat West in the High Street is Market House, where three local men were hanged in the courtyard after the Monmouth Rebellion of 1685.

🍴 **Staplegrove** ST2126 STAPLECOMBE VINEYARDS Friendly little vineyard, with self-guided tours of the fields, then back at the house a cheery couple happy to chat; open pm exc Sun Apr–Oct, or by appointment; (01823) 451217; free. Avoiding Taunton, the Kingfisher's Catch at Bishops Lydeard does decent lunches.

★ ✝ 🍴 ☺ **Stogumber** ST0937 is a charming village with cottage gardens, an unblemished main street, and an interesting CHURCH; the White Horse is good for lunch. BEE WORLD AND ANIMAL CENTRE Rather jolly bee farm with observation hives, and demonstrations of the uses to which the honey can be put, from candles to face cream. Also rare breeds and other animals, pony rides for children at 12 pm and 2.30pm, nature trails, and adventure playground. Meals, snacks, shop, disabled access; cl Nov–Easter; (01984) 56545; £2.75.

🏠 ! ❀ ♘ ✟ 🏠 ❀ **Stoke sub Hamdon** ST4419 This village is overlooked by Ham Hill, which has provided the stone for many of the villages in the area, producing that distinctive warm honey-coloured look. The former 14th- and 15th-c STOKE SUB HAMDON PRIORY manor house has long since vanished, but its fine thatched barn and the screens, passage and Great Hall of the chantry can still be seen; free. Though the Fleur de Lis is a useful pub, Montacute is probably the best nearby place for lunch, and on the way is a striking folly, St Michael's Tower; it's one of three, all built by neighbouring friends in the 18th c – whenever one had a flag up it was an invitation for the others to go round for a hearty evening. Just S, HAM HILL COUNTRY PARK has 140 acres of grassland and woodland. Once an Iron Age fort, it's full of wildlife and plants, and the views from the top of the hill are really quite splendid.

✔ ♄ ✿ **Stoke St Gregory** ST3426 The WILLOW AND WETLANDS VISITOR CENTRE shows how this area – the most important area of wetland in the country – developed from marsh and swamp, and looks at its wildlife and industries, esp willow-growing and basket-making. Shop, some disabled access; cl wknds (exc shop Sat), Easter Mon; (01823) 490249; £1.95. Nearby, the ENGLISH BASKET CENTRE produces baskets from its own willow plantations, as well as art charcoal. Also working blacksmith and display of willow sculptures. Shop, disabled access; cl Sun; (01823) 698418; free. The Rose & Crown at Woodhill on the edge of the village is good for lunch.

† ♣ ☗ ✿ **Taunton** ST2324 is a busy and prosperous shopping country town with a lively Saturday cattle market. It's not of great visual distinction; the best bit is Hammett St, a short street of 18th-c red brick terraces leading to the county's biggest CHURCH, which has an exceptionally ornate roof, lovely pinnacled tower and lofty Perpendicular chancel. The Tudor House on Fore St is attractive. The 13th-c portcullised gatetower of the town's former castle is now absorbed into the County Hotel. Another part houses the fine SOMERSET COUNTY MUSEUM, with local history and archaeology, ceramics, glass, and dolls, and a regimental museum. Judge Jeffries conducted some of his Bloody Assizes after the Monmouth rebellion of 1685 in the castle's Great Hall. Shop, disabled access to ground floor only; cl Sun, Good Fri, 25–26 Dec; £1.20. SOMERSET CRICKET MUSEUM (Priory Ave) Balls, bats and blazers, cards, cuttings and caps, with a cricketing reference library too. The building is one of the town's oldest, thought to have been the gatehouse for the priory that once stood on the cricket ground. Shop, some disabled access; open wkdys, poss wknds when there's a match on – best to check first in winter; (01823) 275893; *60p. Just behind Riverside Pl the SHAKESPEARE GLASSWORKS have demonstrations of glassblowing (not Sun or Mon), and in Bath Pl MAKERS is a decent craft shop selling local hand-made crafts; cl Sun. There's a good collection of antique shops on East Reach. The Masons Arms in Magdalene St is good for lunch, as is the Vivary Arms across the park from the centre.

❀ **Tintinhull** ST5019 TINTINHULL HOUSE GARDEN Colourful and attractive 1930s formal garden sheltered by walls and hedges, around 17th-c house (not open) with Queen Anne façade. Teas, disabled access; cl am, Mon, Fri, Oct–Mar; £3.30; NT.

♟ ❀ **Tolland** ST1032 GAULDEN MANOR Nicely tucked-away medieval manor house distinguished for its early plasterwork. The gardens are pleasant too, with a rose garden and bog garden. Snacks, shop, plant sales, disabled access; open pm Sun and Thurs May–Aug, plus bank hols; (0198 47) 213; *£3. The excellent Three Horseshoes at Langley Marsh is quite handy for lunch.

🐾 ♪ ❀ † ♖ **Washford** ST0441 TROPIQUARIA Amazing transformation of 1930s BBC transmitting station into an indoor jungle with 15-ft waterfall, tropical plants, free-flying birds and all sorts of weird and wonderful-looking animals – the more dangerous ones caged. Outside are aviaries, landscaped gardens and an adventure playground. Also radio exhibition and puppet shows. Meals and snacks, shop, disabled access (exc to aquarium); cl winter wkdys exc school hols; (01984) 40688; £3.40. CLEEVE ABBEY Remarkably well preserved 12th-c Cistercian abbey, the gatehouse, dormitory and refectory all in good condition. Fine timbered roof, detailed wall paintings and traceried windows, and an exhibition on monastic life. Snacks, shop, some disabled access; cl 1–2pm, winter Mon; (01984) 40377; £1.80. The nearby station has a little RAILWAY MUSEUM; cl Nov–Feb (01984) 40869; free. The Notley Arms at Monksilver not far off is excellent for lunch. **Watchet** ST0743 is a small working port, with fishing boats and coasters using its tidal harbour, and enough industry to keep it from being too touristy – though it's by no means unattractive. The West Somerset Hotel has good cheap food.

✿ **West Bagborough** ST1633 is a tiny village well placed below the Quantocks. QUANTOCK POTTERY Traditional working pottery with demonstrations and shop. Meals and snacks. The Rising Sun has fresh generous food.

✝ Some of the **churches** in this area have very finely carved 15th- and 16th-c bench ends, with fascinating figures, beasts, fertility symbols and grotesques. The most interesting are at Bishops Lydeard ST1629 (attractive village), Combe Florey (Evelyn Waugh buried outside), Hatch Beauchamp ST3220, Kingston St Mary ST2229 (pretty village), Milverton ST1225 (where there's also a little pottery on the charming High St) and Stogumber ST0937; in the Quantocks Bicknoller ST1139, Broomfield ST2231, Crowcombe ST1336 and Spaxton ST2237 are all good. Many of these churches have fine oak waggon roofs, brass candelabras and carved screens. The church at Ilminster ST3514 has a magnificent 15th-c tower, all turrets, pinnacles and gargoyles; Stogursey ST2042 has an exceptional Norman church.

Other attractive villages in the area, all with decent pubs, include East Coker ST5412 (T S Eliot's ashes are buried here), Hinton St George ST4212, North Perrott ST4709, Staple Fitzpaine ST2618, Wambrook ST2907 and Waterrow ST0425. High Ham ST4230 and Weston Zoyland ST3534 are also pretty. East Quantoxhead ST1343 with its archetypal duckpond, tiny church with fine oak carvings, and walks to the coast, is delightful; the Hood Arms over at Kilve is good for lunch.

Walks

In this region, only the **Quantocks** ⌂-1 have anything substantial to offer the walker. The hills' secretive quality is illustrated by the dense broad-leafed woodlands on the northern side, where shady combes display splendid spring and autumn colours. The village of Holford ST1541 is a good starting point: the paths begin with helpful signposts, although you may soon get bemused by the complexity of the path junctions; Holford Combe ST1540 is reasonably easy to find, and a map will get you to the ancient hill-fort site capping Dowsborough ST1639, from where a moorland track leads gently N to Holford.

The less wooded western slopes have some attractive valleys enclosed by plunging slopes, with tracks along the bottom: Bicknoller ST1139 is a pleasant start; the Blue Ball at Triscombe ST1535 is another useful port of call. The moorland tops are quite a different world, where ancient trackways lead past prehistoric cairns and burial mounds; Exmoor, the Bristol Channel, South Wales and the Mendips are in sight. The tiny road from Nether Stowey ST1939 to Crowcombe ST1336 crosses the ridge and gives easy access on to the moor.

The Royal Oak at Luxborough SS9837 is a good place for walkers in the **Brendon Hills** ⌂-2.

Down towards the Blackdown Hills south of Taunton, the well marked woodland walks around **Castle Neroche** ST2715 ⌂-3, an isolated ruined Norman fortification with more the aspect now of a hill fort than a castle, are well worth it for the fine views at the top. Further towards Chard, the Cotley Inn at Wambrook (bedrooms) is in quiet countryside suiting both walkers and cyclists.

Driving

This area is full of little lanes winding quietly around without getting you anywhere very significant. The road up wooded Cockercombe from Nether Stowey seems to be taking you right into the unknown. In this same general area, there's a nice road running from Cannington on the A39 west of Bridgwater to Combwich, then round to Stogursey (worth a stop to look at the charming carved pew ends in the church), and then on to rejoin the A39 either at Nether Stowey or further on near Kilve.

Inland, a quiet road with good views is the one forking off the B3170 past the Holman Clavel Inn (a useful stop), over Culmhead and the Blackdown Hills, to pass the Wellington Monument above Wellington itself.

Where to eat

Appley ST0621 Globe (01823) 672327 Cheerfully run and unspoilt 15th-c pub with a relaxed, chatty atmosphere, generous helpings of good, interesting food inc adventurous daily specials and vegetarian meals, and gorgeous puddings; no smoking dining room; cl Mon lunch exc bank hols; limited disabled access. £20|£1.30/£5.50.

Knapp ST2925 Rising Sun (01823) 490436 Fine 15th-c longhouse with friendly atmosphere, stripped beams and stonework, inglenook fireplaces and good food with a strong emphasis on fish dishes; cl 25 Dec. £20|£3.75/£8.

Dowlish Wake ST3713 New Inn (01460) 52413 Neatly kept 17th-c stone pub with spotlessly kept dark beamed bar, woodburning stove in inglenook fireplace, good-value basic snacks as well as a fuller à la carte menu inc Swiss specialities, well kept real ales and Perry's ciders – it's possible to visit the nearby 16th-c stone cider mill – and pleasant back garden; no food winter pm Sun; children in family room; disabled access. £18|£1.25/£4.

Haselbury Plucknett ST4711 Haselbury Inn (01460) 72488 Popular and inviting pub with very wide choice of food inc lots of daily specials, a fine choice of real ales, good wines, and friendly service. £16|£3.15/£5.75.

Langley Marsh ST0729 Three Horseshoes (01984) 623763 Popular red sandstone pub with imaginative, daily-changing food, vegetables from their own garden, no chips or fried food, a wide choice of often unusual real ales, no fruit machines or pool tables, skittle alley, and sloping back garden with farmland views; good nearby walks; children must be well behaved; disabled access. £12|£1.85/£4.50.

Monksilver ST0737 Notley Arms (01984) 56217 Relaxed and friendly pub, with characterful beamed L-shaped bar, woodburning stoves, particularly good, popular food, well kept beers, and neatly kept cottagey garden that runs down to a swift clear stream; cl 25 Dec, 1st 2 wks Feb; limited disabled access. £12|£2.25/£5.

Help this year from: Ian Jagoe, John Oddey, Peter Churchill, Dr and Mrs A K Clarke, Dilys Unsworth, John and Joan Wyatt, B M Eldridge, Steve Goodchild, A E and P McCully, Mike and Sue Moss, J Morrell, JCW, Simon and Amanda Southwell, P M Lane, Mark and Diana Bradshaw, Brian and Jill Bond, K R Harris, S G Brown, Frank and Daphne Hodgson, Peter and Audrey Dowsett, Jed and Virginia Brown, Peter Neate, David Eberlin, Barry and Anne, Mr and Mrs Bird, Hilary Aslett, Mark Undrill, Rex Miller.

SOMERSET AND AVON CALENDAR

Some of these dates were provisional as we went to press.

JANUARY

Bath Exhibition: Top International Fashion 1963–1993 at the Museum of Costume – *till Dec* (01225) 461111

14 **Bath** 'Pictures at an Exhibition' works inspired by Mussorgsky at Victoria Art Gallery – *till 30 Sept* (01225) 461111

17 (the old Twelfth Night) **Carhampton** Wassailing the Apple Trees: ancient ritual (01643) 702624

MARCH

4 **Bath** Mid-Somerset Competitive Festival – *till Sat 18* (01225) 466558

26 **Monkton Heathfield** Orchid Festival at the Jubilee Hall (01823) 442063

APRIL

14 **Bristol** Harveys Wine Museum (Denmark St) 30th Anniversary and 200th Anniversary of Harveys in Bristol – *till 24 Dec* (0117) 925 3253

22 **Rode** Railway Weekend at the Bird Garden – *till Sun 23* (01373) 830326

28 **Bath** Spring Flower Show at Royal Victoria Park – *till Sun 30* (01225) 448433

29 **Hatch Beauchamp** Plant Hunters Fair at Hatch Court – sale of less common plants by nurserymen in the south-west (01275) 462700; **Shepton Mallet** South-West Custom and Classic Bike Show at the Royal Bath & West Showground – *till Sun 30* (0117) 940 5809

30 **Minehead** Hobby Horse Parade: horse (maybe originally to scare away Danish invaders) made of painted canvas with ribbons and a long tail goes through the streets accompanied by musicians – *till 3 May* (01643) 703607

MAY

4 **Badminton** Horse trials – *till Sun 7* (01454) 218375

13 **Cannington** College Open Day (01278) 652226

19 **Bath** International Festival – *till 4 June* (01225) 463362; **Cheddar** Fair and Folk Festival – *till Sun 14* (01934) 742320

24 **Bristol** Charles Wesley Festival – *till Nov* (0117) 926 4740

26 **Bath** Balloon Fiesta at Royal Victoria Park – *till Sun 28* (01225) 448433

27 **Shepton Mallet** Welsh Motorcycle Extravaganza at the Royal Bath & West Showground – *till Sun 28* (0117) 940 5809; **Thornbury** Plant Hunters Fair at Armstrong Hall – sale of less common plants by nurserymen in the south-west (01275) 462700

28 **Watchet** Spring Festival (01984) 631781

29 **Bishops Lydeard** Sandhill Park Country Fair (01823) 432237; **Long Ashton** North Somerset Show at Ashton Court Estate (0117) 964 3498

31 **Shepton Mallet** Royal Bath and West of England Show at the Royal Bath & West Showground – *till 3 June* (01749) 823211

JUNE

2 **Ellicombe** West Somerset Folk Festival and Craft Fayre at the Rugby Ground – *till Sun 4* (01643) 702994

3 **Bath** Kite Festival at Royal Victoria Park – *till Sun 4* (01225) 448433; **Bridgwater** Somerset Waterways Festival at the Bridgwater & Taunton Canal, Albert Street – *till Sun 4* (01278) 787852; **Dunster** Civil War Garrison at Dunster Castle – *till Sun 4* (01460) 241938

SOMERSET AND AVON CALENDAR

JUNE cont

10 **Bristol** Leisure and Motor Show at Durdham Downs – *till Sun 11*
(0117) 926 0080; **Saltford** Plant Hunters Fair at the Community Centre
– sale of less common plants by nurserymen in the south-west
(01275) 462700; **Shepton Mallet** Collett Day Festival

11 **Long Ashton** Bristol to Bournemouth Vintage Vehicle Run starting at
Ashton Court Estate (01272) 260767

14 **Dunster** Open Air Theatre: A MIDSUMMER'S NIGHT'S DREAM at Dunster
Castle – *till Thurs 15* (01460) 241938

16 **Great Elm** Music Festival – *till Sun 18, also weekends of 23 and 30 June,
Fri–Sun* (01373) 812383

23 **Barrington** Open Air Theatre: THE LION IN WINTER at Barrington Court –
till Sat 24 **Pilton** Glastonbury Music Festival at Worthy Farm – *till Sun 25*
(01749) 890254

24 **Bath** Steam and Vintage Festival – *till Sun 25* (01225) 840915; **Bristol**
Elizabethan Midsummer Eve Musical Evening at Harveys Wine
Museum (Denmark St) (0117) 927 5027; **Glastonbury** Pilgrimage to the
Abbey (Anglican) (01458) 832267

25 **Glastonbury** Pilgrimage to the Abbey (Roman Catholic)
(01458) 832267; **Long Ashton** Festival of Retirement at Ashton Court
Estate (0117) 920 7704

JULY

2 **Watchet** Carnival

8 **Dunster** Victorian Weekend at Dunster Castle – *till Sun 9* (01460) 241938;
Montacute Horse Trials at Montacute House Park – *till Sun 9* (01963) 32750;
Somerton Summer Arts Festival – *till Sat 15* (01458) 272041

15 **Ilchester** International Air Day at RNAS Yeovilton (01935) 841008;
Rode Clematis Weekend at the Bird Garden – *till Sun 16* (01373) 830326

22 **Long Ashton** Ashton Court Festival – *till Sun 23* (0117) 942 0140

29 **Bradford-on-Tone** Craft and Cider Country Fayre at Sheppy's Cider
Farm – *till Sun 30* (01823) 433933; **Somerton** Horse Show at Home
Farm (01935) 840735; **Weston-super-Mare** Holidays: helicopter fly-ins,
static displays and pleasure flights – *till Sun 30* (01934) 822524

AUGUST

5 **Bristol** Harbour Regatta at Bristol City Docks – *till Sun 6* (0117) 929 7704

8 **Thurlbear** Taunton Agricultural Show at Netherclay Farm (01823) 421267

12 **Long Ashton** International Bristol Balloon Fiesta at Ashton Court Estate
– *till Mon 14* (0117) 953 5884; **Montacute** Victorian Longbow Display
at Montacute House (01935) 823289; **Yeovil** Festival of Transport at
Barwick Park – *till Sun 13* (01935) 22319

18 **Dunster** Show at Dunster Lawns (0139 84) 490

19 **Bath** Society of Artists Annual Exhibition at Victoria Art Gallery –
till 30 Sept (01225) 461111; **Bristol** Festival of Transport – *till Sun 20*
(0117) 942 2851; **Brompton Regis** Show and Gymkhana (01398) 7438;
Frome St Catherine's Medieval Street Fair; **Shepton Mallet** County and
Agricultural Show at the Royal Bath & West Showground – *till Sun 20*
(01306) 741302; **Whitchurch** Bristol Festival of Transport at Hengrove
Park – *till Sun 20* (0117) 942 2851

SOMERSET AND AVON CALENDAR

AUGUST cont

23 **Priddy** Sheep Fair, colourful mixture of travellers and commercial stock (01749) 677667

25 **Glastonbury** Children's Festival – *till Mon 28* (01458) 832925

27 **Bristol** Avon Rowing Regatta at Bristol Historic Harbour (0117) 930 3810

SEPTEMBER

2 **Long Ashton** International Kite Festival at Ashton Court Estate – *till Sun 3* (0117) 946 6852; **Montacute** Band of the Royal Marines, Joust, Laser Show and Ox Roast at Montacute House – *till Sun 3* (01935) 823289

9 **Shepton Mallet** Countryside Cavalcade at the Royal Bath & West Showground – *till Sun 10* (01458) 46645

16 **Bristol** Plant Hunters Fair at the Botanic Garden – sale of less common plants by nurserymen in the south-west (01275) 462700; **Rode** Steam Attractions at the Bird Garden – *till Sun 17* (01373) 830326

20 **Frome** Cheese Show at the Showfield (01373) 463600

23 **Frome** Illuminated Carnival; **Shepton Mallet** Great West Classic Motorcycle Show at the Royal Bath & West Showground – *till Sun 24* (0117) 940 5809

27 **Bridgwater** Fair at St Matthew's Field – *till Sat 30* (01454) 323974

30 **Wellington** Carnival (01823) 662339

OCTOBER

7 **Chard** Carnival Procession (01460) 64185; **Ilminster** Carnival; **Weston-super-Mare** Speed Trials and Vintage Sprint (01934) 626838

21 **Taunton** Illuminated Carnival and Cider Barrel Rolling Race (01823) 286137; **Wincanton** Carnival (01963) 34037

26 **Hinton St George** Punkie Night: children carry elaborately carved hollowed candlelit mangel-wurzels from house to house singing the 'Punkie Night Song'

31 **Dunster** Ghost Tour of Dunster Castle at 7pm and 10pm (01460) 241938

NOVEMBER

2 **Bridgwater** Guy Fawkes Carnival, one of Europe's most spectacular illuminated parades (01278) 786206

4 **North Petherton** Guy Fawkes Carnival (as Bridgwater above)

5 **Cricket St Thomas** Fireworks Party at the Wildlife and Leisure Park (01460) 30755

6 **Burnham-on-Sea** Guy Fawkes Carnival (as Bridgwater above)

8 **Shepton Mallet** Guy Fawkes Carnival (as Bridgwater above)

10 **Wells** Guy Fawkes Carnival (as Bridgwater above)

11 **Glastonbury** Guy Fawkes Carnival (as Bridgwater above)

13 **Weston-super-Mare** Guy Fawkes Carnival (as Bridgwater above)

26 **Bristol** Advent Sunday at the Lord Mayor's Chapel, College Green: Lord Mayor, Council and the city's two trumpeters all in traditional dress proceed in state to the only civic chapel in the kingdom

SUFFOLK

Suffolk has many good opportunities for short breaks, with delightful villages, charming if unspectacular countryside, and largely unspoilt seaside scenery. There are quite a lot of interesting things to see and do, a good few of them small enough to be friendly and personal. The area's Anglo-Saxon past is attractively explored in a number of places, and wool made the area wealthy in medieval times: there's a rich legacy of Perpendicular church architecture to show for those heady days. First-time visitors will be struck by the large number of antique shops.

There's no shortage of civilised places to stay in. This is not a particularly cheap county, but many of the area's pubs do decent food in pleasant surroundings, and at sensible prices.

This is poorish country for walkers, but like the Stour Valley in northern Essex, which it borders, is excellent for cycling – quiet back roads, lots of villages, gentle gradients without being dead flat.

Whichever area you are in, the Museum of East Anglian Life at Stowmarket, described in the West Suffolk section but centrally placed for all three areas, is well worth a visit.

SOUTH SUFFOLK

Gentle appeal, with charming old villages, some attractive houses and gardens.

This area's quiet attraction is summed up in the four classic English villages, fairly close to one another, which draw visitors from all over the world for their harmoniously colour-washed, timbered buildings. Long Melford, Lavenham, Cavendish and Clare are all pleasant to potter about in. The first two in particular have plenty of places to visit. Constable country, around East Bergholt by the border with Essex, has perhaps had more than a comfortable share of summer visitors, but it is very pretty, and people interested in traditional British painting can easily combine visits to Flatford Mill, Christchurch Mansion in Ipswich and Gainsborough's House in Sudbury. Elsewhere, Ickworth at Horringer is the most interesting place to visit, and there are also several attractive gardens. It's not a good area for determined walkers.

Where to stay

Lavenham TL9149 SWAN High St, Lavenham CO10 9QA (01787) 247477) £122; 47 rms. Handsome and comfortable, Elizabethan hotel with a pubby little bar, lots of cosy seating areas and alcoves with beams, timbers, armchairs and settees; good food in both the bar and lavishly timbered restaurant, afternoon teas, and friendly, helpful staff.

Hintlesham TM0843 HINTLESHAM HALL Hintlesham, Ipswich IP8 3NS (01473) 652334 £97; 33 lovely rms. Magnificent mansion, mainly Georgian but dating back to Elizabethan times, in 175 acres with big walled gardens, 18-hole golf course, outdoor-heated swimming pool, tennis, trout fishing, snooker, croquet, sauna and steam room; restful and comfortable day rooms with books, antiques, and open fires, fine modern cooking in several restaurants, a marvellous wine list, and exemplary service; children over 10 in evening restaurant; well behaved dogs welcome (not in bedrooms or public rooms).

Long Melford TL8645 Bull Hall St, Long Melford CO10 9JG (01787) 378494 £90; 25 rms, ancient or comfortably modern. An inn since 1580, this fine, black and white building was originally a medieval manorial hall; handsome and interesting stripped woodwork and timbering, a large log fire, old-fashioned and antique furnishings, decent food, and pleasant, friendly service; beautiful village.

Lavenham TL9149 Angel Market Pl Lavenham, Sudbury CO10 9QZ (01787) 247388 £60; 8 well equipped rms. 15th-c inn in the heart of an excellently preserved medieval town, with the original cellar and a pargeted ceiling, several Tudor features such as a rare, shuttered shop window front, a civilised atmosphere, very good food, well kept real ales, lots of decent wines, several malt whiskies; live classical piano pm Fri, and quiz pm Sun; cl 25 Dec; disabled access.

Stoke-by-Nayland TL9836 Angel Stoke-by-Nayland, Colchester CO6 4SA (01206) 263245 £57.50; 6 rms. Elegant dining pub in the Stour Valley, busy but relaxed, with Tudor beams in the cosy bar, stripped brickwork and timbers, fine furniture, a huge log fire and woodburning stove, decent wines, and imaginative and reasonably priced bar food; cl 25–26 Dec; children over 10.

Bildeston TL9949 Crown Bildeston, Ipswich IP7 7EB (01449) 740510 £49; 15 rms, most with own bthrm. Lovely, timber-framed, Tudor inn with welcoming, courteous service, comfortable, well furnished, beamed lounge, open fires, good food in the popular restaurant, an attractive, 2-acre garden – and a resident ghost; no food pm 25 Dec; disabled access.

Hadleigh TM0242 Edgehill 2 High St, Hadleigh, Ipswich IP7 5AP (01473) 822458 £47.50; 9 pretty rms. Friendly, family-run, Tudor house with a Georgian façade; comfortable, carefully restored rooms, personal service, very good English food using home-grown produce, and an attractive walled garden; croquet; cl Christmas.

Chelsworth TL9848 Peacock The Street, Chelsworth IP7 7HU (01449) 740758 £45; 3 rms, shared bthrm. Elegantly restored, 14th-c inn with plenty of exposed Tudor brickwork and timbers, a fine inglenook fireplace, generous helpings of good bar food, well kept real ales, decent wines; craft shop behind, and just over the bridge is the rich parkland of Chelsworth Hall.

Needham Market TM0855 Pipps Ford Norwich Rd, Needham Market, Ipswich IP6 8LJ (01449) 760208 £45; 6 pretty rms with antiques and fine old beds; 4 rms in converted Stables Cottage. Lovely, 16th-c farmhouse in a quiet garden; log fires in the big inglenook fireplaces and good, imaginative food served in the conservatory with subtropical plants; home-baked bread, home-produced ham and pork, and own honey, eggs, and preserves, with organically home-grown veg and herbs; surrounded by farmland and set on a beautiful stretch of the River Gipping; cl mid-Dec–mid-Jan; babies and children over 5 welcome.

Hintlesham TM0843 College Farm Hintlesham, Ipswich IP8 3NT (01473) 652253 *£36; 3 rms, 1 with own bthrm. Late 15th-c house on a farm and with a neat garden; comfortably furnished rooms, lots of beams, log fire in the inglenook fireplace, and friendly owners; no pets; walks around the farm (beef and arable), and riding and golf nearby; cl Christmas and New Year; children over 5.

Lawshall TL8654 Brighthouse Farm Melford Rd, Lawshall, Bury St Edmunds IP29 4PX (01284) 830385 £36; 3 rms. Homely B & B in a timbered, Georgian farmhouse with log fires, lounge and games room; self-catering and camping also.

To see and do

★ † ☛ ♫ 🖻 **Cavendish** TL8046 is a lovely sight, its green framed by colourfully plastered, timbered houses with behind them the tower of the attractive, medieval Church.

Cavendish Manor Vineyards and Nether Hall 15th-c manor house nicely surrounded by vineyards; the house has paintings and interesting old exhibits, and there are tours and tastings in the vineyard. Shop; cl 25 Dec; (01787) 280221; *£2.50. Nearby PENTLOW FARM is a children's farm with lots of baby animals – unusually, it's free. Open Sun and pm wkdys in school hols, Mar–Sept; (01787) 280748. The old Bull has good-value food.

★ † ☎ **Clare** TL7645 is another of the area's charming, timber and plaster villages, with a huge church, the sketchy ruins of a castle on a former Iron Age earthwork above the River Stour, and some remains of a 13th-c Augustinian priory; nature trails around the castle. There's a three-storey antiques warehouse, and the Bell is good for lunch.

☎ ☛ † **East Bergholt** TM0733 BRIDGE COTTAGE, FLATFORD A 17th-c cottage nr the mill immortalised by Constable. Inside is a good interpretative centre for his paintings. Teas; cl Mon and Tues (exc Jun–Sept), most of Dec, all Jan–mid-Mar; free; NT. Guided walks through areas that inspired his work leave here three times every afternoon Jun–Sept (£1.50). You can hire rowing boats for trips along the River Stour – very relaxing if you can persuade someone else to man the oars. The mill itself and its famous partner WILLY LOTTS HOUSE are both owned by the National Trust and leased by them to the Field Studies Council, which runs arts courses here; (01206) 298283. The King's Head nearby is attractive for lunch, and the church with its uncompleted tower has a unique, 16th-c, timber-framed bell cage.

† **Great Bricett** TM0450 WATTISHAM AIRFIELD MUSEUM Small exhibition related to the airfield. Open pm Sun Mar–Oct, or wkdys by appointment; (01449) 728940; free.

🐑 ❀ **Hartest** TL8352 has an attractive village green; at the end, the Crown is pleasant for lunch. GIFFORDS HALL 33 acres with vineyard and winery, wild flower meadows, rare breeds of sheep and domestic fowls, and a rose garden. It's perhaps best known among gardeners for its sweet peas, and they have a Rose and Sweet Pea Festival the last wknd in Jun. Meals, snacks, shop, disabled access; cl am, and Nov–Easter; (01284) 830464; £1.25–£2.75, depending on season.

☎ ❀ **Hintlesham** TM0843 HILLSIDE NURSERIES Farm shop with organically

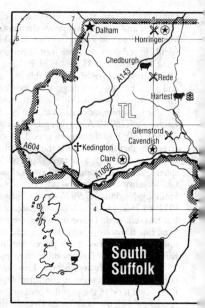

South Suffolk

grown veg, pick-your-own, and plant sales. Usually cl pm, and most Suns – best to check first; (01473) 652682; free. Hintlesham Hall does marvellous lunches (see **Where to stay** section above); on a humbler level, the George here is good.

★ 🏠 🖼 ❀ ✟ ꙮ **Horringer** TL8261 is attractive, with well spaced, colour-washed buildings; the Beehive is pleasant for lunch. ICKWORTH Very untypical stately home, a 100-ft-high oval rotunda, with two curved corridors filled with a fascinating art collection and other treasures: good furniture, porcelain, pictures by Gainsborough amongst others, and an exceptional collection of Georgian silver. The gardens have fine trees and a deer enclosure. Meals, snacks, shop; house cl am, all Mon (exc bank hols) and Thurs, and Nov–Mar (though shop and restaurant open wknds to Christmas), park open all year; £4.30, park and gardens only £1.50; NT. From Mar–Dec you'll usually find various crafts in the Community Centre.

🏠 🖼 ❀ ☎ 🏠 🖈 † **Ipswich** TM1644 A regional centre since the Stone Age, Ipswich flourished as a port sending cloth to the continent after King John granted it a charter in the 13th c. It's too busy to compete with other places

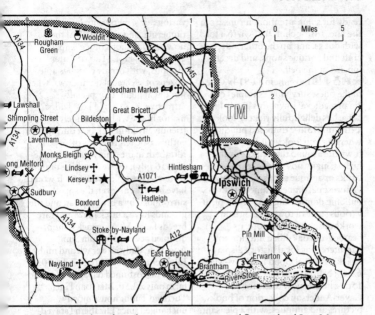

in this area as a base for a short holiday, but has quite a few things to look at on briefer visits (traffic schemes make getting in and out rather slow). Cardinal Wolsey set up a college here, but all that remains is the 16th-c gatehouse in College St. The Ancient House in the Butter Market (now a bookshop) has some 15th-c carvings and exceptionally neat pargeting. CHRISTCHURCH MANSION (Soane St) The original 16th-c house was altered in the following century after a fire, but since then it's escaped any further redevelopment. The rooms are furnished in period style, with a Victorian wing inc servants' quarters, and the Suffolk Artists' Gallery has the best collection of works by Constable and Gainsborough outside London. There's a pleasant park. Shop, disabled access to ground floor only; cl am Sun, Mon (exc bank hols), 24–26 Dec, 1 Jan, Good Fri; (01473) 253246; free. Attached is the Wolsey Art Gallery, with various changing exhibitions. IPSWICH MUSEUM (High St) is a good one, its natural history section (painstakingly restored to how it was in its Victorian heyday) inc the first gorillas brought to Europe in the mid-19th c. Quite an emphasis on Roman Suffolk. Shop, disabled access to ground floor only; cl Sun, Mon, 24–26 Dec, 1 Jan, Good Fri; free.

TOLLY COBBOLD BREWERY (Cliff Rd) Striking, waterside Victorian brewery, with tours taking in the whole brewing process. They've got some particularly interesting old equipment, inc a Victorian steam engine, and there are beer tastings in the Brewery Tap (which functions as a separate pub, with decent meals and snacks). Shop; tours at noon, daily Jun–Sept, otherwise Fri–Sun only, cl Christmas; (01473) 231723; £3.25 (inc drink). The old trolleybus depot on Cobham Rd is now home to the TRANSPORT MUSEUM, with over 70 ancient, commercial vehicles built or used in the area. Snacks, shop, disabled access; open Sun and bank hols Easter–Oct; (01473) 832260; £1.50. Dotted about the town are several attractive MEDIEVAL CHURCHES, especially the 15th-c St Margaret's (Constable Rd); St Mary at the Elms (Belstead Rd) has the town's oldest cottages behind it. If you're there on a winter's night, five medieval churches are nicely floodlit. The port is quite busy. ★ † Kersey TL9944 is a very pretty, one-street village, full of timbering and attractive, colourful plasterwork – though one or two buildings look ready for some attention. It runs from the fine, 14th-c church down to a ford with ducks, and up the other side; craft and antique shops, and decent lunches at the Bell.

★ 🏠🍽🌼🔲 **Lavenham** TL9149 One of the finest surviving examples of a small medieval town, this lovely little place has delightfully rickety-looking, 14th- and 15th-c timbered buildings wherever you look, still centres of town life around the market sq and high st; many now house tearooms, banks or antique shops. GUILDHALL Picturesque, timber-framed, 16th-c building dominating the market pl, at various stages a town hall, prison, workhouse and wool store; its beamed and oak-filled interior now has interesting local history displays. Snacks, shop; cl Good Fri, Nov–Mar; £2.40; NT. LITTLE HALL Delightful, 15th-c house, now featuring the Gayer-Anderson collection of books, pictures and antiques, with a pleasant, enclosed garden. Cl am, Mon (exc bank hols), Tues, Fri, all Nov–Easter; (01787) 247179; *£1. THE PRIORY Very well restored Benedictine house with interesting drawings and Elizabethan wall paintings, fascinating stained glass by Ervin Bossanyi, and a uniquely designed herb garden. Meals, snacks, shop; cl Nov–Easter; (01787) 247417; *£2.50. The old wool hall has been incorporated into the Swan Hotel, itself well worth seeing. Both it (at a price) and the Angel are good for lunch.

✝ **Lindsey** TL9745 ST JAMES'S CHAPEL Charming little thatched, flint and stone chapel, built some time during the 13th c, but inc some earlier work too; free. The Red Rose in nearby Lindsey Tye is useful for lunch.

🌼 🐦 **Little Blakenham** TM1048 BLAKENHAM WOODLAND GARDEN Woodland garden richly planted with camellias, rhododendrons, magnolias and the like; lovely in May when the bluebells are out. Lots of rare trees and shrubs. Open pm exc Sat Mar–Jun; *£1. The Sorrel Horse over at Barham has decent food.

★✝🏠🍽🐄🌊☗ **Long Melford** TL8645 A very nice old place to stroll around: the fine green and long main st (Hall St) are lined with buildings from various eras, many with lovely timbering, and around 20 of them now antique shops (not cheap, but interesting). HOLY TRINITY CHURCH is glorious, with ornate carvings and dozens of spectacular windows; when floodlit at night it's especially attractive. KENTWELL HALL Tudor manor house with a genuinely friendly, lived-in feel, best during their enthusiastic re-creations of Elizabethan life (this year, wknds 18 Jun–16 July), with everything done as closely as possible to the way it would have been then – even the speech. It's surrounded by a broad moat, and the grounds have a brick maze and rare breeds farm. Meals, snacks, shop, disabled access; open pm Sun Apr–Sept, daily Easter wk and mid-July–Sept; (01787) 310207; £4.50, (more on costumed days), garden and farm only £2.50. MELFORD HALL Turreted Tudor house mostly unchanged since Elizabeth I stayed here in 1578 (with a retinue of 500, and 1,500 servants); it still has the original panelled banqueting hall. Displays include a collection of Chinese porcelain, and an exhibition on Beatrix Potter, who was related to the owners and often stayed here; the gardens have a Tudor pavilion. Some disabled access; open pm wknds and bank hols Apr–Oct, plus pm Weds and Thurs May–Sept; £2.70; NT. The Bull Hotel, one of the finer old buildings here, does good light lunches; the George & Dragon and, at the end of the truly long village, the Hare are also useful for food.

🌾 **Monks Eleigh** TL9647 CORN CRAFT Traditional corn dollies and their production; in Aug and Sept you can walk through the fields and pick the flowers. Snacks, big shop, disabled access; cl Christmas; (01449) 740456; free. The Swan Hotel has good home-cooking.

★ **Pin Mill** TM2037, below the wooded slopes by the River Orwell, has Thames barges on tidal moorings, and is a nice spot; the Butt & Oyster here is attractively placed for a bite to eat.

🌼 **Rougham Green** TL9061 NETHERFIELD COTTAGE (towards Hessett) shows that you don't have to have a massive garden to make it very special indeed: hundreds of different herbs, beautifully yet sensibly grouped by how you'd use them, with two small knot gardens. Best May–Oct, but a peaceful haven at any time. The cheery owner is happy to chat. Plant sales; cl 25 Dec; (01359) 270452; free, guided tours by appointment. The Rushbrooke Arms at Sicklesmere has decent food.

✝ 🏠 **Stoke-by-Nayland** TL9836 has a lovely 15th-c CHURCH with a tower familiar from several Constable paintings, and some handsome Tudor buildings; the Angel is excellent for lunch, but get there early.

★ 🏠 🅰 **Sudbury** TL8741 is a pleasant market town (good Sat market stalls); the Waggon & Horses is good-value for lunch, as is the Mill, which has a lovely view over the water meadows. GAINSBOROUGH'S HOUSE The famous painter was born here in 1727, and the house now has an excellent collection of his work; unexpected finds include his efforts at sculpture. Plenty of period furniture and china

too, and contemporary arts and crafts. Shop; cl am Sun, Mon (exc pm bank hols), Good Fri, Christmas; (01787) 372958; *£2.50.

✝ Apart from the places already mentioned, lots of villages have **Constable and Gainsborough connections,** as both were raised in the area. Constable painted altarpieces for the churches at Brantham TM1034 and Nayland TL9734, and often painted the church at Stoke-by-Nayland TL9836, while Gainsborough painted the church at Hadleigh TM0242 (an old market town with some other striking buildings and a nearby woodland RSPB reserve). There are also **nice churches** at Kedington TL7046 (Saxon crucifix) and Needham Market TM0855, where the marvellous hammer beam roof has been described as 'a whole church seemingly in the air'.

★ **Other attractive villages** in the area, all with decent pubs, include Boxford TL9640, Chelsworth TL9848, Dalham TL7261 and Shimpling Street TL8752.

Walks

The views immortalised by Constable make the walk from **East Bergholt** TM0734 ⌂-1 along the water meadows by the Stour East Anglia's most famous walk – picturesque and well worthwhile, though there is no real point in leaving the path to make a circular route. Elsewhere, unfortunately, the Stour Valley's attractive villages don't quite compensate for the humdrum scenery in between, and although it is possible to find field paths, it's difficult to work these into circular walks.

   Shotley Gate TM2433 ⌂-2, at the meeting of the Stour and Orwell estuaries, is at the hub of a rewarding walk that follows the two rivers, with pleasant views across to Harwich and its shipping; the Bristol Arms is a good stop. Start inland at Shotley TM2335 and cross the fields either N to the Orwell or S to the Stour, then follow the waterside.

   Just S of **Stutton** TM1534 ⌂-3, where the King's Head is useful, is another fine stretch of the broad Stour estuary; on its N side, Alton Water is a reservoir recreation area.

Driving

The classic drive is the back road between Long Melford and Lavenham, and then the A1092 along to Cavendish and Clare, linking these four lovely villages. The back roads in the triangle between these and the A143 and A134 up to Bury St Edmunds all give plenty of pleasing views of colour-washed, old houses, generally set close enough to the road to enjoy.

   In the opposite direction, the A1141 E of Lavenham through Monks Eleigh, and then the B1115 through Chelsworth and Bildeston to Hitcham, are attractive, as is the back road through Buxhall and Rattlesden to Woolpit.

Where to eat

Long Melford TL8645 CHIMNEYS Hall St (01787) 379806 Lovely, beamed 16th-c building, with very good, carefully prepared food and a thoughtful wine list; the paintings are for sale; cl pm Sun; disabled access. **£27.50 dinner, £14.50 lunch/£10.50.**

Sudbury TL8741 MABEYS BRASSERIE 47 Gainsborough St (01787) 74298 Simply but attractively furnished restaurant, with very good cooking using first-class ingredients, a relaxed atmosphere, friendly service and a fine wine list; cl Sun, Mon (inc bank hols), 25–26 Dec, 1 Jan; disabled access. **£18/£4.95.**

Horringer TL8261 BEEHIVE (01284) 735260 Pretty, ivy-covered pub with a friendly atmosphere, particularly good, often imaginative food, prompt and helpful service, attractively furnished, little rambling rooms, woodburning stove, well kept real ales and decent wines; disabled access. **£17|£2/£4.95.**

Rede TL8055 PLOUGH (0128 489) 208 Welcoming, partly thatched cottage in a lovely spot, with particularly helpful owners, lots of well presented, fresh fish and game in season, imaginative daily specials, a good evening restaurant, and decent wine. **£14.50/£5.50.**

Erwarton TM2134 QUEENS HEAD (01473) 787550 Remote and unspoilt little pub with a homely atmosphere, lovely views, cosy coal fire in the beamed bar, good, well priced bar food inc fresh fish and game in season, well kept real ales and friendly service; cl 25 Dec; children in restaurant only; disabled access. **£13.15|£1.90/£4.95.**

Glemsford TL8247 BLACK LION (01787) 280684 Wide choice of very good fresh food in both the pleasant bar and little restaurant, with obliging service and decent real ales; cl pm Sun, pm 25 Dec. **£10|£1.50/£3.**

EAST SUFFOLK

Good for quiet breaks, with an unspoilt, interesting coast, pleasant small towns and villages, attractive places to visit.

This area has a lot of appeal for quiet breaks, with a largely unspoilt coast giving wide sea- and skyscapes that most would say constitute Suffolk's loveliest scenery. Even in summer you can walk for miles along fairly empty beaches and coast. Southwold, Walberswick, Aldeburgh and Orford are all relatively unspoilt, very pleasant for anyone wanting to be by the sea without being too seasidey. There is a lot of interest for nature-lovers.

Inland there are attractive villages and small towns, with prettily timbered and plastered buildings (though not so many as you'll find in the southern part of the county). Interesting places to visit include the farm park at Easton, Helmingham Hall, Framlingham Castle and the wildlife park at Kessingland; there are several things in the area that children like. Lowestoft, England's busiest fishing port, doubles as a summer beach and boating resort, and has plenty to do.

Where to stay

Woodbridge TM2749 SECKFORD HALL, Woodbridge IP13 6NU (01394) 385678 **£99**; 32 rms. Handsome Tudor mansion with beams, flagstones, big fireplaces, a comfortable, panelled lounge with antiques, a cosy bar, good food and service; 32 acres of gardens and parkland with a trout-filled lake; indoor heated pool, gym, 18-hole pay-and-play golf; cl 25 Dec; disabled access.

Southwold TM5076 SWAN Market Pl, Southwold IP18 6EG (01502) 722186 **£89**; 45 rms, most with own bthrm. 17th-c inn with a comfortable and restful drawing room, upstairs reading room, convivial bar, good food in the elegant dining room, well kept real ales, decent wines and helpful staff; disabled access.

Brome TM1376 OAKSMERE Brome, Eye IP23 8AJ (01379) 870326 ***£87.50**; 11 lovely rms. Warm, friendly, partly 16th-c hotel with a bustling bar in what was the original Tudor hall; good food in the elegant restaurant, conservatory, neatly kept gardens with a fine collection of box and yew topiary, and its own cricket pitch; limited disabled access.

Framlingham TM2863 CROWN Framlingham, Woodbridge IP13 9AN (01728) 723521 **£85**; 14 comfortable rms. Bustling and friendly, little, black and white, Tudor coaching inn with a comfortable lounge and open fire, a cosy bar with heavy beams and log fire, an attractive small courtyard with a winter-flowering cherry, good food in both the bar and restaurant, and friendly, helpful staff. A Forte hotel, though pleasantly individual and old-fashioned.

Aldeburgh TM4656 WHITE LION Market Cross, Aldeburgh IP15 5BJ (01728) 452720 **£80**; 38 rms, some with sea view. Popular, rather smart, 16th-c, family-run seafront hotel with comfortable lounges, two bars, log fires, good food in the panelled and beamed restaurant and cheerful, friendly staff.

Westleton TM4469 CROWN Westleton, Saxmundham IP17 3AD (01728) 648777 **£69.50**; 19 rms, some with Jacuzzis. Very relaxing inn in excellent walking country nr Minsmere bird reserve; pretty, landscaped garden and floodlit terrace, comfortably furnished bar with an open fire, a smart, no-smoking dining conservatory, good food inc lovely puddings, a helpful wine list with a wide choice, lots of malt whiskies, well kept real ales and courteous service; cl 25–26 Dec; disabled access.

Southwold TM5076 CROWN High St, Southwold IP18 6DP (01502) 722275 **£58**; 12 rms. Outstanding old pub in the centre of town, with a smart but relaxed, elegant main bar, excellent imaginative food in the bar and no-smoking restaurant, lots of wines, properly kept, by the glass, and friendly, helpful staff; cl 1 wk Jan.

Halesworth TM3877 ANGEL Thoroughfare, Halesworth IP19 8AH (01986) 873365 **£57.50**; 7 rms. 16th-c hotel carefully refurbished in keeping with the building; friendly bars, good restaurant food, well kept beers and wines; disabled access.

Campsea Ashe TM3255 OLD RECTORY Campsea Ashe, Woodbridge IP3 0PU (01728) 746524 **£50**; 9 comfortable and pretty rms. Very relaxed and genuinely welcoming Georgian house next to the church, with a log fire in the comfortable, restful drawing room, lovely food from a set menu in the summer conservatory or the more formal dining rooms with more log fires, a good wine list, peaceful gardens; dogs allowed (but not in dining room); cl Christmas.

Lowestoft TM5492 BAYFIELDS 159 High St, Lowestoft NR32 1HU (01502) 568617 **£50**; 10 rms. Pleasant hotel within walking distance of both town and beach, with good-value, fresh fish straight from the market.

Great Glemham TM3361 CROWN Great Glemham, Saxmundham IP17 2DA (01728) 663693 **£35**; 3 old-fashioned rms. Welcoming and pleasantly placed, old brick house with a beamed, open-plan lounge, a huge double fireplace with woodburning stove on one side and logs blazing on the other, good, promptly served bar food, decent wines, well kept real ales, and a neat garden.

To see and do

★ ❀ ☗ ❄ **Aldeburgh** TM4656 Fishing village with quaint little streets running down to the shingle beach where the fishermen still haul in and sell their catch; quite touristy, especially at festival time, but not at all garishly so. MOOT HALL MUSEUM Good local history displays in a 16th-c, brick and timber Moot Hall (reached by an outside staircase). There's a special emphasis on maritime history and coastal erosion, plus finds from the Anglo-Saxon ship burial at Snape (see entry below). Cl am exc July and Aug, wkdys Apr and May, all Oct–Easter; 35p. The attractively placed Cross

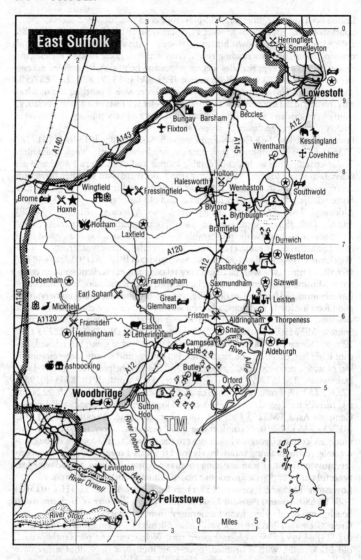

East Suffolk

Herringfleet
Somerleyton
Lowestoft
Bungay Barsham
Flixton
Beccles
Wrentham
Kessingland
Covehithe
Halesworth Holton
Wingfield
Fressingfield
Wenhaston
Southwold
Brome
Hoxne
Blyford
Blythburgh
Horham
Bramfield
Laxfield
Dunwich
Debenham
A120
A12
Westleton
Framlingham
Eastbridge
Sizewell
Earl Soham
Saxmundham
Mickfield
Great
Glemham
Leiston
A1120
Framsden
Friston
Aldringham
Thorpeness
Helmingham
Easton
Letheringham
Snape
Campsea
Ashe
Aldeburgh
Ashbocking
River Alde
Butley
Orford
Woodbridge
Sutton
Hoo
TM
River Deben
Levington
River Orwell
Felixstowe
River Stour

0 Miles 5

Keys is nice for lunch, and the rather old-fashioned Brudenell Hotel on the beach has great sea views; there's an RSPB reserve just N at North Warren. ℘ **Aldringham** TM4461 CRAFT MARKET Three extensively stocked galleries of local crafts and fine art. Teas, disabled access; cl 12–2pm Sun (maybe all day in winter), 25–28 Dec, 1 Jan; (01728) 830397; free. The Parrot & Punchbowl has good wines and decent food.

Ashbocking TM1654 JAMES WHITE CIDER BREWERY Cider- and apple-juice-making and tasting, with pick-your-own in season. Snacks, shop, some disabled access; open daily but tel first at wknds; (01473) 890111; free. The Barley Mow at Witnesham has home-cooking. **Beccles** TM4289 WILLIAM CLOWES PRINT MUSEUM (Newgate) Interesting look at the development of printing from 1800 onwards, with a wide range of machinery, woodcuts and books. Open 2–4.30pm wkdys Jun, July and Aug, or by appointment; (01502) 712884; free. Down the same road there's a good local history MUSEUM. Open pm Sun, plus Weds and Sat Apr–Oct. The King's Head Hotel is useful for lunch.

🏰 **Bungay** TM3389 Ruins of a Norman CASTLE right in the centre of this little market town, with twin towers and massive flint walls. Bungay straddles the border with Norfolk, and we've described the nearby Otter Trust in our Norfolk chapter, under the Earsham entry. The Green Dragon is useful for lunch.

🎨🏰 **Butley** TM3650 BUTLEY POTTERY Working pottery, with shop, tearoom and restaurant. Cl Mon and Tues in winter; free. The Oyster Bar is good for lunch – and does have local oysters. S of here, by the quiet back road to Capel St Andrew, are the remains of a medieval abbey gatehouse.

★ ✝ 🎨 **Debenham** TM1763 is an attractive village with a fine, partly Saxon church, and another POTTERY (Carters Ceramics, Low Rd). Cl Sun (exc pm summer) – best to tel first (01728) 860475.

🗿 **Dunwich** TM4770 is slipping slowly under the sea; most of what was once quite a sizeable town is now submerged, and they do say as how on quiet nights, when there's a swell running after a storm, you can hear the bells of a submerged church tolling. There are some fragmentary ruins of a friary, but more interesting is the little MUSEUM on the subject of the village's gradual erosion (cl Nov–Easter; free). Excellent coastal walks along the cliffs, beaches and heathland of Dunwich Heath, which has a NT tearoom. The Ship is pleasant for lunch, and the Flora Tearooms have superb, freshly caught fish and chips.

🐄 **Easton** TM2858 EASTON FARM PARK Friendly farm with plenty to see; demonstrations of milking and other operations at the Victorian dairy set up by the Duke of Hamilton – and in the more modern version alongside – as well as animals and rare breeds, a display on food production, working blacksmith, adventure playground, and nature trails. Meals, snacks, shop,

disabled access; cl Oct–mid-Mar; (01728) 746475; £3.85. The White Horse is good for lunch.

🏰🗿🐄 **Felixstowe** TM2831 LANDGUARD FORT AND MUSEUM Guided tours of an early 18th-c, coastal defence fort, with displays of its history. Also, materials from the RAF and HMS *Beehive*, and, from this year, a big collection of elaborate, model paddlesteamers. Shop, disabled access; open pm Weds and Sun end of May–Sept, plus Thurs in summer hols; (01394) 286403; *£1.50 fort, 50p museum. The town itself is quite a busy port, with a ferry (passengers, not cars) across to Harwich, and thanks to its beaches and relatively dry climate has developed into a popular, low-price, family resort. Along the coast N of the town, past another Martello Tower, golf course and sand dunes, is the gently attractive and altogether quieter little settlement of Felixstowe Ferry, with another foot-ferry across the estuary of the River Deben.

✝ **Flixton** TM3186 NORFOLK AND SUFFOLK AVIATION MUSEUM Aircraft and related items from the Wright Brothers to the present day, with aeroplanes displayed outside and in the Blister Hangar. Shop, disabled access; open Sun and bank hols Easter–Oct, plus Tues–Thurs in summer hols; (01502) 562944; free.

🏰❀🗿✝ **Framlingham** TM2863 CASTLE This 12th-c castle was the place where Mary I heard that she had become Queen. Unusually, the entire curtain wall has survived (you can walk all the way along it), and there are also 13 towers, some 17th-c almshouses, and an array of Tudor chimneys. Good views, and an interesting museum. Shop, disabled access to ground floor only; cl 25–26 Dec, 1 Jan; (01728) 724189; £1.80, museum 30p extra. The CHURCH has an excellent hammerbeamed roof. The town's sloping market sq is quite attractive, and the Crown at its head is useful for lunch, as is the Castle Inn.

❀🏚❦♠ **Helmingham** TM1857 HELMINGHAM HALL GARDENS Beautiful gardens still much as they were in Tudor times. The grand battlemented house they stand around is ringed by a moat, over which the drawbridge is still raised each night. Extensive deer park with hundreds of red and fallow deer, as well as Highland cattle and Soay sheep, and magnificent old oak trees. Constable painted a number of views of the woodlands – it is a pretty spot. Cream teas, shop (inc Helmingham produce), disabled access; open (gardens only) pm Sun 30 Apr–10 Sept; (01473) 890363; *£2.50.

🦋 **Horham** TM2072 The churchyard here has been conserved as natural grassland around its older graves for generations, just scythed for hay in the first wk of July; so from spring onwards it's a mass of wild flowers, with plenty of butterflies (and beehives). The Ivy House in the quiet village of Stradbroke has good-value food.

🐾 ⵎ **Kessingland** TM5286 SUFFOLK WILDLIFE PARK Over 100 acres of very attractive grounds filled with rare animals and birds – they like to call it the African Wildlife Experience. Birds of prey demonstrations pm Weds, and good road-train journeys round the park. Meals, snacks, shop, disabled access; cl 25–26 Dec; (01502) 740291; £5.

† ♨ ⵎ **Laxfield** TM2972 has an interesting CHURCH, and the old Guildhall has a MUSEUM with a cottage kitchen, village shop and an observation beehive. Shop; open pm wknds and bank hols late May–Sept. The King's Head is a charmingly preserved old pub. The EAST OF ENGLAND BIRDS OF PREY AND CONSERVATION CENTRE Aviaries with hawks, falcons, eagles and owls, three flying displays a day, and closed-circuit TVs to watch young birds in their nests. Meals, snacks, shop, disabled access; cl Nov and Dec; (01986) 798844; *£3.50.

🏭 ⵎ **Leiston** TM4462 is a sizeable shopping town with the fragmentary remains of a 14th-c abbey, off the B1122 just N. LONG SHOP MUSEUM Big industrial museum in the preserved buildings of Garrett Engineering Co, with steam engines, steam rollers, traction engines, memorabilia from the nearby WWII air base and other local history. Shop, disabled access; cl Nov–Mar; (01728) 832189; *£2.00. The Engineer's Arms opposite has so much memorabilia it seems almost an extension.

† ♨ ! ✿ ⵎ ☺ **Lowestoft** TM5493 is the most easterly town in the country, and the main fishing port in the area, so there's always lots to see in the harbour. It's developed as a resort thanks to its beaches and proximity to the Broads. Cobbled streets of old buildings survive in the part known as The Scores, and the early medieval church is imposing and attractive. In the High St, the Bayfields Hotel and Volunteer are useful for lunch. There are regular summer harbour tours and sea BOAT TRIPS; details from the Tourist Information Office, Esplanade (01502) 523000. This is housed in a rather grand old pavilion, along with the multi-sensory LOWESTOFT STORY, and a play area themed as a North Sea rig. Also in the harbour is the *Lydia Eva* STEAM DRIFTER, the last surviving herring drifter, with an exhibition on life aboard and the herring industry in general. Open Apr–Oct, but may be in Great Yarmouth for some of the time – best to check first with the information centre (see above); free. At BOATWORLD (Oulton Broad) you can watch boats being made in the traditional manner. Open wkdys Whit–Sept; £1.95. EAST ANGLIA TRANSPORT MUSEUM (Carlton Colville) The best part is the reconstructed 1930s street scene – used as a setting for working vehicles such as trams, trains and trolley-buses, but there are lots of other vehicles displayed on the 3-acre woodland site, all lovingly restored. Snacks, shop; open Sun May–Sept, pm Sat Jun–Sept and pm wkdys in summer hols; (01986) 798398; £2.50. MARITIME MUSEUM (Whapload Rd) Ancient and modern fishing and commercial boats, as well as fishing gear, tools, art gallery and a lifeboat display. Shop, disabled access, cl Oct–Apr; *50p. There's a small ROYAL NAVAL MUSEUM in Sparrow's Nest. Cl 12–2pm, all Sat, mid-Oct–mid-May; free. PLEASUREWOOD HILLS AMERICAN THEME PARK (Corton Rd) Lots of rides and family attractions, with special features for younger visitors, and parrot and sealion shows. Trains and chairlifts speed up travel round the grounds, and there's an unusual 100-ft revolving tower. One of Suffolk's most popular attractions. Meals, snacks, shop, disabled access;

open daily May–Sept, some wknds in Apr and Oct; (01502) 508200; £9.

✿ ➜ **Mickfield** TM1361 Fish and Watergarden Centre 2 acres of ornamental watergardens and working nursery, with displays of tropical, marine and freshwater fish. Wknd teas, garden centre, disabled access; cl 25 Dec, 1 Jan; (01449) 711336; free.

🏰 ❀ † ♿ **Orford** TM4250 Orford Castle When Henry II commissioned this castle it was right on the shore, but since then the river has silted so much that it's now slightly inland. It has an amazing 18-sided keep rising up to 90ft, supported by three extra towers. Good views from the top (as usual, at the end of a spiral staircase). Shop; cl 1–2pm, 24–26 Dec, 1 Jan; £1.80. The church has the ruined chancel arches of a Norman predecessor in the graveyard. The process of coastal erosion is well illustrated by the Dunwich Underwater Exploration Exhibition at the Craft Shop in Front St, and there are displays on other aspects of marine life. Cl 25–26 Dec; 40p. The Oysterage is nice for lunch. There's a long lane down to the shore, looking across to the desolate Orford Ness, where avocets breed.

★ 🍖 ✿ † ♿ **Saxmundham** TM3863 is an attractive village with yet another fine church. The Queen's Head has reasonable food. Just NE at Bruisyard TM3266, Bruisyard Vineyard (signed off the B1119 Framlingham rd) Picturesque, 10-acre vineyard producing decent English wine, with herb garden, watergardens and woodland picnic area. Meals, snacks, shop, some disabled access; cl Christmas wk; (01728) 75281; free, Walkman tours £3. Nearby Yoxford TM3968 has a couple of good craft workshops.

✗ **Saxtead Green** TM2564 Saxtead Green Post Mill Traditional Suffolk post mill dating from 1854, although there's been a similar mill on the site for much longer. It's a steep climb up the staircase, but once inside you'll see that all the equipment has been meticulously brought back into perfect working order. Cl 1–2pm, Sun, Oct–Mar; (01728) 685789; £1.25. Attractive surroundings.

↓† 🏠 ✗ **Sizewell** TM4762 Sizewell Visitor Centre Interactive displays and exhibitions of energy, nuclear power and the environment, with tours of Sizewell B power station (booking essential). Cl 25–26 Dec, 1 Jan; (01728) 642139; free. Nearby, the long Sizewell Beach is generally virtually deserted out of season, with agate and other semi-precious stones common among the pebbles, even sometimes amber after stormy E winds. At its S end is the curious village of Thorpeness, built as a holiday village in a deliberately fanciful, olde-worlde style, with quite a few attractive, mock-Tudor houses (one even masking a water tower); it has a sizeable, artificial but now thoroughly natural-looking, picturesque lake, and the windmill here was brought over from Aldringham.

🏠 🖼 ♿ **Snape** TM3959 Maltings Converted 19th-c maltings, home of the Aldeburgh Music Festival begun by Benjamin Britten, as well as other concerts throughout the year. The centre is pleasant to wander around, with unusual shops and galleries, and in summer there are one-hour boat trips down the River Alde. The Plough & Sail, just outside, is recommended for lunch. Up in Snape village, the Golden Key is also good.

🏠 ✿ 🦃 🐄 ➜ **Somerleyton** TM4997 Somerleyton Hall Interesting Jacobean house rebuilt in the Anglo-Italian style in 1840, still very much lived-in, with period furnishings and paintings. The lovely gardens have a maze and miniature railway. Snacks, shop, disabled access; open pm Thurs and Sun Apr, May, Jun and Sept, plus Tues and Weds in July and Aug; (01502) 730244; £3.50. Nearby, with access from the Hall, is Fritton Lake, which attracts numerous wildfowl, particularly in the autumn and winter. Country World here has woodland walks, fishing, heavy horse stables, birds of prey (displays 11.30am and 3pm, not Fri), rowing (£2 per hour), children's rides, and plenty of space for pottering. Snacks, shop, disabled access; cl Oct–Mar; (01493) 488208; £3. The Plough at Blundeston, home of Barkis the carrier in *David Copperfield*, is useful for lunch.

★ † ♿ ✿ **Southwold** TM5076 Once an important fishing port, now a quite

enchanting and civilised little resort with a distinctive lighthouse as its main landmark, an attractive, unspoilt green by the sea, and no end of good pubs and inns supplied by the local Adnams brewery (their wholesale wine shop has interesting stock). For food, the Crown is outstanding, and though more straightforward the King's Head is good, as is the smart Swan Hotel; the Sole Bay and Lord Nelson have the most atmosphere. Southwold Jack on the tower of the interesting CHURCH is worth a look; he's an automaton that rings the bell for services. MUSEUM 17th-c, Dutch gabled cottage, with displays on the Southwold light railway and a local battle against the Dutch in 1672. Open pm Easter–Sept; free. LIFEBOAT MUSEUM Small museum with RNLI related material and models. Open pm daily spring bank hol–Sept; free. Across the golf course or along the breezy sea wall you come to the harbour, a tidal inlet, with its cheerful mix of beached fishing boats, multitudes of sailing boats, and fishing shacks; the Harbour Inn here is full of character. There's a footbridge over to Walberswick on the other side of the water – a pleasantly decorous, seaside village, popular with artists ever since Wilson Steer's days there in the 1890s. The Bell here is an attractive if very informal old inn, and the 15th-c church, parts now destroyed and other bits looking shaky, is picturesque. (The drive round by car between Southwold and Walberswick is several miles.)
🏛 **Sutton Hoo** TM2849 One of the most famous archaeological sites in the country, where in 1939 the discovery of an Anglo-Saxon ship burial caused historians to reinterpret the period completely. Knowledge of the Dark Ages is still patchy in parts, and you can't help wondering if there's another hoard of treasure waiting to be discovered that will have a similarly dramatic effect on current theories. Most of the treasure from here is in the British Museum, but you can go round the site and see the burial mounds, and there's an exhibition centre explaining its importance. Shop; tours at 2 and 3pm wknds and bank hols, Apr–early Sept; *£1.50. Further down the B1083,

the Plough at Sutton itself is good for lunch; or you can turn off down to Ramsholt for the Ramsholt Arms among the waterside pine woods, with quiet walks along the Deben estuary.
★ ♥ ⚘ 🏨 **Westleton** TM4469 is a pleasant village with an attractive green. MINSMERE RESERVE Big RSPB reserve with lots of different species among the heath, woods, marshes and lagoons, and good observation hides to see them from. Snacks, shop, disabled access; cl Tues; (01728) 873281; £3 for non-RSPB members. Nearby there are public walks over similar country, heath and pinewoods; Dunwich itself is within quite an easy walk. The Eel's Foot at Eastbridge is the pub favoured by birdwatchers; the Crown on Westleton Green by those who like to fortify themselves with more stylish food. Fisks Clematis Nursery has many varieties of clematis on show and for sale; cl winter wknds.
🏨 ❀ **Wingfield** TM2277 WINGFIELD COLLEGE Quite a surprise to find a splendid, medieval, timber-framed building behind the Georgian façade. Founded in 1362, the college flourished in the 15th c, but after the Reformation declined and became a private house. One of its 18th-c owners constructed the Palladian exterior to make his home more fashionable, using false ceilings, floors and windows so skilfully that for 200 years the house's earlier parts were forgotten. Striking great hall, topiary and kitchen gardens. Snacks; open pm wknds and bank hols Easter–Sept; *£2.50. They also organise Wingfield Arts, a varied programme of events in churches, halls and other everyday buildings all over the region; tel (01379) 384505 for details and programme. The Ivy House at Stradbroke is quite handy for lunch.
★ † ♨ ✕ **Woodbridge** TM2649 Quietly attractive and rather dignified market town, with many fine buildings and interesting book and antique shops, and a CHURCH of great style and interest. The local history MUSEUM looks at the ship burial at nearby Sutton Hoo, as well as the recent Anglo-Saxon finds at Burrow Hill. Cl am Sun, Mon (exc bank hols and summer hols), Tues (exc summer

hols), Weds, all Nov–Easter; *50p.
TIDE MILL Restored 18th-c mill on the
busy quayside. Shop, disabled access
to ground floor only; open Easter,
then daily May–Sept and wknds in
Oct; *80p. On Burkitt Rd, BUTTRUMS
MILL is a six-storey tower mill, now
fully restored, with displays of its
history. Open pm wknds and bank
hols May–Sept; 50p. The Melton
Grange Hotel is good for lunch, and
the Cherry Tree opposite Notcutts
Nursery (off the A12) is good value.
ₒ Woolpit TL9762 BYGONES MUSEUM
Small museum showing life in a
Suffolk village, with annually
changing displays and an exhibition
on brick-making. Shop, disabled
access; open pm wknds and bank hols
Oct–Easter; donations. They also look
at the village tale that in the 12th c,
two slightly strange-looking, green-
skinned children were found by a pit
that was suddenly blasted in the earth
one night; the boy soon died, but the
girl lived, was taken in by the priest
and learned English. She never said
more about her origins than that she'd
come from a land far far away, and
grew up to marry a local lad and have
children. The Brewer's Arms at nearby
Rattlesden does very good food.
๕ Wrentham TM4982 WRENTHAM
BASKETWARE (London Rd) make and
sell traditional willow baskets and
hampers, with up to 320 styles. Cl
Sun, Christmas; (01502) 75628; free.
✂ Lots of Suffolk's famous windmills
are found in this coastal region, and
although many fell into disrepair
earlier this century a large number
have been painstakingly restored. As
well as those already mentioned
there's a good example at
Letheringham TM2757, which also
has nice gardens (open pm Sun and
bank hols Apr–May, July–Aug,
£1.50); and others at Herringfleet
TM4797 and Holton TM4077,
though you can't often get into these.
✝ Interesting old churches can be
found at Blythburgh TM4475 (a
magnificent building in a lovely setting
above the marshes; there's a little
working pottery nearby), Bramfield
TM3973 (unusual, detached round
tower), Covehithe TM5282, Eye
TM1473 (beautiful stonework and
rood screen) and Wenhaston TM4276
(15th-c wall painting in excellent
condition full of lovely devils).
★ Other attractive villages here, all
with decent pubs, include Blyford
TM4277, Eastbridge TM4566,
Fressingfield TM2677, Hoxne
TM1777 and Huntingfield TM3374.
Levington TM2339 is a pleasant spot,
with ancient almshouses, a marina
below, and the Ship, a good pub (no
children) with estuary views.

Walks

Large areas of the flat, formerly heathy land nr the coast have been covered with
pine plantations, which are also pleasant for undisturbed walks, with the chance
of seeing red squirrels, and, in summer, with that lovely, fresh, foreign pinewood
smell. In some places the heath and marshy ground below it has been left undisturbed, and these reserves are interesting for birdwatchers. **Minsmere** bird reserve
TM4369 ◠-1 is the best-known: the lake, surrounding heathlands and woods,
and the coast supply walks for all seasons. The reserve is skirted by public paths,
and a hide is available for public use, but you need a permit to enter the rest of the
reserve. Approach points are Dunwich TM4770 and Eastbridge TM4566.

The **River Blyth** ◠-2 nr Southwold TM5076 and the **River Deben** ◠-3 nr
Shottisham TM3144 are broad rivers close to the coast, with delightful water-
side paths. **Coast walks** ◠-4 around Thorpeness TM4759 and S to Aldeburgh
TM4656 are pleasurable despite the rather graceless Sizewell nuclear power
plant, and diverse heathland, an old railway track walk and The Meare
(Thorpeness's lake) justify detours inland.

The short **Tangham Nature Trail** TM3450 ◠-5, among the plantations off
the B1084 towards Woodbridge, is specially designed for disabled people;
there are also longer walks through the pinewoods here, where red squirrels
often show themselves.

Driving

From this part of Suffolk, the A1120 – quite a pleasant drive passing some attractive villages with little traffic – would get you down to Lavenham in about 1¼–1½ hours: so the delightful villages around there are well within reach.

Within this northern area, the B1077, an old coach road up through Debenham and Eye, is considerably more interesting than the A140 for N–S trips. The B1116 through Framlingham and Fressingfield is another pleasant N–S coach road. An attractive back road is the one NE of Wickham Market, through Easton, Brandeston and Cretingham to Debenham. Nearer the coast, the B1084 from Woodbridge to Orford is a nice drive, as is the little-travelled, good road from Orford past the pinewoods of Iken Heath to Snape. The farming country up past Halesworth has plenty of quiet back roads through it, though the scenery is not that striking.

Most of the A12 is now a decent road, getting you quickly across this area and offering a good impression of the countryside as you go: it gives perhaps the finest view in the area, approaching Blythburgh from the S.

Cycling is one of the best ways to get around, as this area is so relatively flat, without too much traffic on the back roads; bicycles of all kinds can be hired from Byways Bicycles in Saxmundham – tel (01728) 77459.

Where to eat

Fressingfield TM2677 Fox & Goose (0137 986) 688 Early 16th-c, timbered inn with a cosmopolitan range of exceptionally good food, prettily presented, inc lovely puddings, generous helpings and fine wines; cl Mon and Tues, 2 wks Nov, Christmas. £25/£5.95.

Framsden TM1959 Dobermann (01473) 890461 Charmingly restored thatched pub with a twin-facing fireplace separating the friendly, spotlessly kept bars; good, popular food and a decent choice of beers and spirits; no children. £17.50|£1.75/£5.50.

Orford TM4250 Butley Orford Oysterage (01394) 450277 Simple restaurant with its own oyster beds, fishing boat and smoke house; very popular locally and with the yachting fraternity for its wonderfully fresh fish, decent wines and brisk, friendly service; disabled access. £15/£4.50.

Earl Soham TM2363 Victoria (01728) 685758 Unassuming pub with a particularly friendly landlord, welcoming atmosphere, very interesting, own-brewed beers, and good, reasonably priced, home-made food. £15|£1.25/£4.

Friston TM4160 Old Chequers (01728) 688270 Friendly pub in an interesting village, with a wide choice of lovely food, woodburning stoves, fresh flowers, well kept real ales and decent wines. £14|£3.25/£6.50.

Hoxne TM1777 Swan (01397) 975275 Carefully restored, late 15th-c house with heavy oak floors, fine fireplaces, and lots of atmosphere; promptly served, interesting bar food, well kept beer, decent wines, and a tranquil back garden; cl 25 Dec; disabled access. £1.30/£5.

WEST SUFFOLK

Several good places to visit; Newmarket is very enjoyable indeed for anyone interested in horse-racing, but other people find other parts of the county better to stay in.

This is not in general the most appealing part of the county, though anyone at all interested in racehorses could spend a very enjoyable weekend based at Newmarket. For others, the most interesting place in the area is the lively Museum of East Anglian Life in Stowmarket.

The reconstructed Anglo-Saxon village at West Stow country park, and Euston Hall are also well worth visiting, and the collection of music machines at Cotton is fun. Bury St Edmunds itself has quite a lot to see, and though busy during the week quietens down at weekends when it's very pleasant to stroll through.

Where to stay

Rougham TL9061 RAVENWOOD HALL Rougham, Bury St Edmunds IP30 9JA (0359) 270345 **£77**; 14 comfortable rms with antiques, some rms in mews. In 7 acres of carefully tended gardens and woodland, this tranquil, Tudor country house has a comfortable lounge with a log fire, a cosy bar, good food using home-preserved fruits and veg, home-smoked meats and fish served in the timbered restaurant with its big inglenook fireplace, a decent wine list, and helpful service; croquet, heated swimming pool, and hard tennis court.

Mildenhall TL7174 RIVERSIDE Mill St, Mildenhall, Bury St Edmunds IP28 7DP (01638) 717274 **£76**; 20 rms. 18th-c country house on the banks of the River Lark, with a relaxed restaurant overlooking the lawns, a comfortable bar, welcoming staff, decent food and real ales; croquet, and boats to hire.

Bury St Edmunds TL8564 ANGEL Angel Hill, Bury IP33 1LT (01284) 753926 *__£64__; 42 individually decorated rms. Thriving, creeper-clad, 15th-c, country-town hotel with particularly friendly staff, a comfortable lounge and relaxed bar, log fires and fresh flowers, and good food in both the elegant restaurant and downstairs medieval vaulted room.

Newmarket TL6463 RUTLAND ARMS High St, Newmarket CB8 8NB (01638) 664251 **£62.50**; 43 rms. Imposing, Georgian coaching inn built around a lovely cobbled courtyard, with an elegant, two-room bar, open fires, good restaurant, friendly, efficient service and a happy mix of customers; no accommodation Christmas.

Worlington TL6973 WORLINGTON HALL Worlington, Bury St Edmunds IP28 8RX (01638) 712237 **£55**; 9 comfortable rms. 16th-c, former manor house in 5 acres of grounds with a 9-hole pitch and putt course; comfortable, wood-panelled lounge bar with a log fire, good food in the relaxed, candlelit bistro, and friendly staff.

Newmarket TL6463 WHITE HART High St, Newmarket CB8 8JP (01638) 663051 **£49.95**; 23 rms. Comfortable hotel with racing pictures and an open fire in the spacious lounge, traditional restaurant, reliable bar food, and friendly staff; a front bar where the trainers meet, and a solid, back cocktail bar where they take their more important owners.

To see and do

ⓗ ⓠ **Brandon** TL7886 BRANDON HERITAGE CENTRE Brandon used to be the centre of the flint industry, and among the local history of the area here is a reconstructed flint-knappers' workshop; also displays on the fur industry and Thetford Forest. Shop, disabled access; open Thurs, Sat, pm Sun, and bank hols, Easter–mid-Dec; (01842) 813707; 50p. BRANDON COUNTRY PARK, largely pinewoods, is pleasant to stroll around.

★ † ☋ ♔ Ⓔ **Bury St Edmunds** TL8564 is a busy shopping town, but has a good deal of character, with quite a few attractive Georgian and earlier houses. The town has several antique shops, and the Linden Tree (Out Northgate St), Mason's Arms (Whiting St) and Queen's Head (Churchgate St) all do decent food. The tranquil precincts of the former medieval abbey include little of its remains beyond the 12th- and 14th-c gatehouses, and, of course, the old church building that in 1913 was given the status of CATHEDRAL. Parts are 15th c, but the hammerbeamed ceiling is 19th c, and work still goes on. SAMSONS TOWER MUSEUM has the history of the site, with

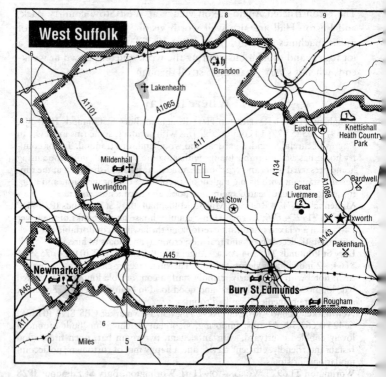

West Suffolk

remains of the earlier building. Cl am Sun, 25–26 Dec, Good Fri, and winter wkdys exc Weds; free, though good Walkman tour £2.50. An oddity near the abbey is the pretty little Nutshell (Traverse), probably the country's smallest pub, with long church connections – it closes on Sun and Holy Days. MANOR HOUSE MUSEUM (Honey Hill) Georgian mansion with a marvellous collection of watches, clocks and other timepieces, as well as prints, ceramics, paintings, furniture and costume. Quite a few fun, hands-on displays. Snacks, shop, disabled access; cl am Sun, 25–26 Dec, Good Fri; (01284) 757072; *£2.50. MOYSES HOUSE MUSEUM (Cornhill) Unusual, 12th-c, flint and stone house with a good range of Suffolk history, inc gruesome relics of the 'murder in the Red Barn' – the murderer's account of his trial is bound in his own skin. Displays are firmly traditional, but there's lots to grab the attention. Trips up the clock tower by arrangement. Shop, disabled access; cl am Sun, Good Fri, 25–26

Dec; (01284) 757072; free. A handsome Robert Adam building is now the ART GALLERY (Market Cross), with good, changing exhibitions. Shop, disabled access; cl Sun, Mon and Christmas; *50p. The handsome THEATRE ROYAL on Westgate St is Britain's third oldest working theatre, built in 1819 by William Wilkins, the designer of London's National Gallery. It's now owned by the National Trust, and you can look round when productions or rehearsals are not in progress.

☞ **Chedburgh** TL7957 REDE HALL FARM PARK Working farm based around agricultural life in the 1930–50s, with rare breeds, huge working horses and seasonal activities. Cl Oct–Easter (01284) 850695; £3. The Plough at Rede has good food.

☺**Cotton** TM0666 MECHANICAL MUSIC MUSEUM Big collection of instruments and musical items taking in not just the expected organs, street pianos, polyphons and gramophones, but dolls, fruit bowls and even a musical chair. A reconstructed cinema has an

!👑 **Newmarket** TL6463 Newmarket has been the centre of racing since James I used to slope off here from 1605, and in the early morning people driving through are quite likely to have to give way to a string of racehorses. NATIONAL HORSERACING MUSEUM (High St) Constantly expanding museum telling the stories and scandals of the sport's development through the centuries. Art, trophies, videos of classic races, a display on the history of betting, and racing relics from saddles to skeletons. You don't have to be interested in racing to get something out of this. Meals, snacks, shop, disabled access; cl am Sun, Mon (exc July and Aug), Dec–Mar; (01638) 667333; *£3.30. They also organise informative tours of the local breeding and racing scene, with a look at horses at work on the gallops, and visits to a training yard, stud and to the handsome, Georgian Jockey Club itself; booking is essential, prices start at £12. You can tour the NATIONAL STUD (A1304, W) by arrangement, (01638) 663464; guided tours are at 11.15am and 2.30pm wkdys, 11.15am Sat and 2.30pm Sun; £3.50, not bank hols or all Oct–Mar. The Rutland Arms across the road from the Jockey Club is useful for lunch and another place you'll see racing people; the King's Head out past the paddocks at Dullingham is also good.

✿ 🍴 🛍 **Stanton** TL9673 WYKEN HALL GARDENS Formal herb, knot and woodland gardens, walled, old-fashioned rose garden, copper beech maze, and a woodland walk to a 7-acre vineyard. A very nice, unspoilt estate, just right for exploring. Meals and snacks in medieval barn, unusual country shop, disabled access; open Thurs, Fri, Sun and bank hols, cl 25 Dec–31 Jan; (01359) 250240; *£2. The Six Bells at Bardwell has good, fresh food.

🏠 🎨 **Stonham Aspal** ST1359 The garden centre at Stonham Barns has an orchid centre, as well as various other small businesses, such as picture-framing and glass-engraving.

⬆🍴✝🎨☺ **Stowmarket** TM0458 MUSEUM OF EAST ANGLIAN LIFE (Iliffe Way) Very good and growing open-air museum, now covering 70 acres,

unusual Wurlitzer theatre pipe organ. Teas, shop, disabled access; open pm Sun Jun–Sept, plus the first Sun in Oct, a fair organ enthusiasts' day; (01449) 781988; *£2.50. The Greek-run, Trowel & Hammer is good for lunch.

🏠 🖼 🎨 ✝ **Euston** TL9079 EUSTON HALL Elegant old house built by Charles II's Secretary of State, Lord Arlington. The highlight is probably the excellent art collection, with several portraits of the Merry Monarch and his family and court, inc works by Lely and Van Dyck. The grounds were laid out by John Evelyn, William Kent and Capability Brown – so reflect centuries of development – with stately terraced lawns, fine trees, a lake, lovely rose garden and classical temple; there's also a 17th-c church in the style of Christopher Wren. Teas in former kitchen, shop, disabled access to grounds and tearoom; open pm Thurs Jun–Sept, plus pm Sun from late Jun–first wk Sept; (01842) 766366; *£2.50. The Thomas Paine in Thetford has good-value food.

with reconstructed buildings inc a watermill, chapel, smithy and wind-pump, and demonstrations of traditional crafts and skills such as woodturning and basket-making. Also, displays on Victorian domestic life, gypsies, farming and industry, with working steam engines and horses; always lots going on. Snacks, shop, disabled access; cl Mon (exc Jun–Sept), Nov–Easter; (01449) 612229; £3.70. The Victoria at Earl Soham is quite handy for lunch.

✿ ♨ ☂ ✔ ▣ ⌧ ! ☛ **West Stow** TL8071 West Stow country park is attractive, with 125 acres of heath and woodlands bordered by the River Lark. Over 120 different species of bird have been sighted here, and 25 species of animal; the visitor centre often has art and craft exhibitions. The most interesting feature is the Anglo-Saxon Village, an expanding reconstruction of an Anglo-Saxon settlement from around the 5th c, with the buildings constructed by the same methods and tools as originally used. Crops, crafts and costumed characters, with interesting special

events such as their Easter Sun market. Snacks, shop, disabled access; cl 25–26 Dec; (01284) 728718; park free, village *£2.50, inc very good Walkman guide. Cow Wise Working dairy farm with cows, goats, lambs and hens. Plenty to touch and feel, and milking and feeding every afternoon. Shop, disabled access; open pm Sun and bank hols 5 Mar–29 May, plus every day 25–28 Aug; (01284) 728862; *£1.80. The Red Lion at Icklingham has good food.

✗ Notable **windmills** include those at Bardwell TL9473 (cl am Sun, Sat and Mon; free), Pakenham TL9267 (open pm wknds and Weds Apr–Sept; £1.25 guided tour), and Thelnetham TM0178 (open every Sat, Easter wknd and then Sun and bank hols from July–Sept; 60p).

† ★ **Attractive, old churches** around here can be found at Mildenhall TL7174 and Lakenheath TL7182; **pleasant villages** include Risby TL8066 (with a decent antique centre), Haughley TM0262 (its Jacobean manor house in lovely grounds) and Ixworth TL9370.

Walks

Apart from the one or two places mentioned above, there's little interesting walking here. **Knettishall Heath Country Park** TL9480 △-1 has some pleasant strolls. There's a nice, shortish walk from **Great Livermere** church TL8871 △-2 past the Ampton Water lake to Ampton church TL8671. A longer path leads up through farmland to Great Livermere from Ixworth TL9370.

Driving

A decent road across Thetford Heath is the B1106 from Bury St Edmunds to Brandon, carrying much less traffic than the busy A11. The A1101, though not a quick road, and the B1112 forking off it, also give a good impression of these relatively unyielding flatlands. E of the A1088, the countryside's more rolling, with a few pleasant patches of woodland, richer farming country, and lots of small villages.

Where to eat

Ixworth TL9370 Theobolds 68 High St (01359) 231707 Consistently good, imaginative food in cosy rooms with log fires and beams, a very good wine list, and kind service; cl pm Sun, Mon, am Sat, bank hols, 25–26 Dec, 1 Jan, children in evening over 8 only. £25/£8.50.

Help this year from: John C Baker, Basil Minson, George Atkinson, Mrs P J Pearce, Dave Braisted, Simon Morton, Basil Minson, Jeff Davies, J D Burbidge, Hugh Stewart, Rita Horridge, Mrs Hilarie Taylor, GA, PA, Mr and Mrs Albert, John McGee, G E Rich, Mrs P M Goodwyn, M G and S M Keegan, Mrs B Sugarman, Susan Kerner, Nigel Woolliscroft, Ian Phillips, Richard Goss, D Edwards.

Suffolk Calendar

Some of these dates were provisional as we went to press.

FEBRUARY

18 **Santon Downham** Breckland Forestry Rally at Thetford Forest Park: competitive driving (01842) 810271

APRIL

14 **Long Melford** Historical Re-creation at Kentwell Hall – *till Mon 17* (01787) 310207; **Needham Market** East Anglian Art and Craft Exhibition and Sale at the Community Centre (01449) 722202

16 **West Stow** Saxon Market at West Stow Country Park and Anglo-Saxon Village – *till Mon 17* (01284) 728718

29 **Long Melford** Historical Re-creation at Kentwell Hall – *till Weds 30* (01787) 310207; **Otley** Open Weekend at Otley College of Agriculture and Horticulture – *till Sun 30* (01473) 785543

MAY

6 **Long Melford** Historical Re-creation at Kentwell Hall – *till Sun 7* (01787) 310207

7 **Felixstowe** Historic Vehicle Run (01394) 276770

8 **Mendlesham** Street Fayre (01449) 766483

11 **Bury St Edmunds** Festival – *till Sat 27* (01284) 757080

13 **Felixstowe** Folk Festival – *till Tues 16* (01394) 276770

14 **Ingham** South Suffolk Show at Ampton Park (01638) 750879

26 **Long Melford** Historical Re-creation at Kentwell Hall – *till Mon 29* (01787) 310207

27 **Mildenhall** Air Fête at RAF Mildenhall – *till Sun 28* (01638) 542995

29 **Felixstowe** Drama Festival: national amateur dramatics competition at the Spa Pavilion Theatre – *till 5 Jun* (01394) 282126

31 **Ipswich** Suffolk Show at Suffolk Showground – *till Thurs 1* (01473) 726847

JUNE

9 **Snape** Aldeburgh Festival of Music and Arts – *till Sun 25* (01728) 453543

10 **Long Melford** Country Fair at Melford Hall – *till Sun 11* 01787) 379783

11 **Long Melford** Red Rose Rent at Hadleigh Guildhall: a rose is placed on the tomb of Sir William de Clopton (who gave the Guildhall to the town for the rent of one red rose) with Mayor and Council in attendance

18 **Bury St Edmunds** Country Fair at Nowton Park (01284) 757088; **Long Melford** Historical Re-creation at Kentwell Hall – *every wknd till 16 July* (01787) 310207

25 **Bury St Edmunds** Hidden Gardens: over 20 private gardens open in the historic town centre (01284) 764667

26 **Ickworth** Craft Festival at Ickworth House – *till Mon 28* (01263) 735134

SUFFOLK CALENDAR

JULY

1 **Ipswich** Vintage Fair at Christchurch Park – *till Sun 2* (01473) 251477

12 **Bury St Edmunds** Viennese Evening with Fireworks – *till Fri 14* (01625) 575681

14 **Horringer** Open-Air Concert at Ickworth House Park and Gardens (01284) 735270

15 **Framlingham** Horse Show at Castle Meadow (01473) 822790; **Hadleigh** East Anglian Summer Music Festival – *till 6 Aug* (01473) 822596

20 **Snape** East Anglia Antiques Fair at the Maltings – *till Sun 23* (01986) 872368

28 **Horringer** Centenary Spectacular Open-Air Concert at Ickworth House – *till Sat 29* (01284) 735270

AUGUST

1 **Snape** Proms at Snape Maltings – *till Thurs 31* (01728) 452935

4 **Beccles** Carnival and Regatta Week – *till Mon 7* (01502) 712109

5 **Saxmundham** Carnival (01728) 602009

12 **Horringer** Mozart and Salieri in the Open-Air at Ickworth House (01284) 735270

20 **Thornham Magna** Open Sheepdog Trials at Thornham Field Centre (01379) 788153

21 **Aldeburgh** Olde Marine Regatta and Carnival (01394) 444333

25 **Long Melford** Historical Re-creation at Kentwell Hall – *till Mon 28* (01787) 310207

27 **Eye** Show at the Showground with military and civilian entertainment – *till Mon 28* (01379) 870224; **West Stow** Saxon Summer Market at West Stow Country Park and Anglo-Saxon Village – *till Mon 28* (01284) 728718

SEPTEMBER

16 **Ipswich** County and Agricultural Show at the Suffolk Showground – *till Sun 17* (01306) 741302

17 **Hadleigh** British Horse Society Horse Trials at Chelsworth Park, on the A1141 (01206) 262224

23 **Long Melford** Historical Re-creation at Kentwell Hall – *till Sun 24* (01787) 310207

We welcome reports from readers . . .

This *Guide* depends on readers' reports. Please tell us what you think about places in it. And do recommend additions. Use the card in the middle, the report forms at the end, or just write – no stamp needed: *The Good Weekend Guide*, FREEPOST TN1569, Wadhurst, E Sussex TN5 7BR.

SURREY

Some really quiet, attractive countryside, with plenty of places to visit.

Surrey's main surprise is its large proportion of beautifully preserved scenery, with relatively free access for walkers, and good, quiet back roads through some of the best of it. Unexpectedly for somewhere so close to London, it's the most heavily wooded county in England, and the National Trust owns several thousand acres in the finest parts. We have found a number of good places to stay close to some of the best countryside – some of these represent exceptional value.

Among the most enjoyable outings in the county are Polesden Lacey at Great Bookham, Wisley Garden, Loseley House near Guildford, Hatchlands at East Clandon, the arboretum at Winkworth, Clandon Park at West Clandon and, among many pretty villages, Shere, Outwood and Chiddingfold. The local history museum in Farnham is exceptionally good. Some popular family attractions are headed by the zoo and theme park at Chessington, the zoo at Charlwood, Thorpe Park at Chertsey, the rural life centre at Tilford and the Horton Park Rare Breeds Farm near Epsom. Epsom has a lively new attraction – the Derby Day Experience.

Where to stay

Bagshot SU9163 Pennyhill Park, Bagshot GU19 5ET (01276) 471774 £150; 76 spacious rms. Impressive country house in over 100 acres of well kept gardens and parkland, with friendly, courteous staff, a comfortable, two-level lounge with panelling and beams, a little bar, and very good, imaginative cooking; outdoor swimming pool, tennis, 9-hole golf course, riding, stabling, game fishing, and clay-pigeon shooting; indoor pool and gym planned; disabled access.

Nutfield TQ3050 Nutfield Priory Nutfield, Redhill RH1 4EN (01737) 822066 *£122; 52 rms. Impressive, Victorian, Gothic-style hotel with lovely, elaborate carvings, stained-glass windows, a fine panelled library, cloistered restaurant, and even an organ in the galleried grand hall; also, an extensive leisure club with indoor heated swimming pool; cl 25–31 Dec.

Haslemere SU9032 Lythe Hill Petworth Rd, Haslemere GU27 3BQ (01428) 651251 £111; 40 individually decorated rms, 5 in the house, the rest in carefully converted farm buildings. Lovely, 14th-c timbered house with more modern additions, in spacious grounds with a bluebell wood, lakes (coarse fishing), tennis and croquet; comfortable lounges, cocktail bar, and good food in the two restaurants; limited disabled access.

Dorking TQ1649 Burford Bridge Box Hill, Dorking RH5 6BX (01306) 884561 £102.90; 48 well equipped rms. At the foot of Box Hill, this mainly 18th-c hotel has flowers and antiques in the day rooms, a relaxed atmosphere, friendly staff, and lovely gardens with an outdoor swimming pool.

Chertsey TQ0466 Crown 7 London St, Chertsey KT16 8AP (01932) 564657 £58w; 30 comfortable, modern rms. Bustling, friendly place with some original features and an open fire in the large bar; conservatory extension, good food in the attractive restaurant, and a lovely, big garden; disabled access.

Farnham SU8446 Farnham House Alton Rd, Farnham GU10 5ER (01252) 716908 £43.90; 20 comfortable rms. Attractive, Victorian, Gothic-style manor house, newly named and refurbished, with oak panelling and open fires in the comfortable public rooms, a newly styled, split-level restaurant, and a tennis court and outdoor heated swimming pool in 5 acres of gardens.

Albury TQ0547 DRUMMOND ARMS The Street, Albury GU5 9AG (01483) 202039 *£40; 7 rms. Attractively furnished, well run pub with a wide choice of good, quickly served food, and a pretty garden; children over 10.

Ewhurst TQ0940 HIGH EDSER Shere Rd, Ewhurst, Cranleigh GU6 7PQ (01483) 278214 £40; 3 rms, shared bthrm. 16th-c, timber-framed, old farm-house in lovely countryside, with a comfortable residents' lounge, friendly owners, and a tennis court in the grounds.

Holmbury St Mary TQ1144 BULMER FARM Holmbury St Mary, Dorking RH5 6LG (01306) 730210 *£38; 8 big, comfortable rms, 5 in outbuildings with own showers. Attractive and welcoming, 17th-c farmhouse on a 30-acre beef farm in lovely countryside; with oak beams and an inglenook fireplace in the attractive sitting room, breakfasts with home-made preserves in the neatly kept dining room, and a large garden; self-catering also; children over 12; disabled access.

Godstone TQ3551 GODSTONE The Green, Godstone RG9 8DT (01833) 742461 £35; 8 rms. Well run, late 16th-c hotel with an open fire in the com-fortable residents' lounge, good, popular food in the attractive, beamed restaurant, summer cream teas, and helpful service; disabled access.

Abinger Hammer TQ0947 CROSSWAYS FARM Raikes Lane, Abinger Hammer, Dorking RH5 6PZ (01306) 730173 £32; 3 spacious rms, 2 with own bthrm. Interesting Jacobean farmhouse in lovely countryside, with a huge chimney, fine oak staircase, a log fire in the comfortable sitting room, good home-cook-ing using own-grown vegetables, croquet, and a small garden.

To see and do

❋ 🏠 † **Bletchingley** TQ3250 TILGATES (Little Common Lane) Sizeable garden enthusiastically planted with a very wide variety of well labelled rare trees and shrubs, with the National Collection of magnolias and an exceptional display of daffodils in spring. Disabled access, teas, plant sales; cl 25 Dec, all Jan and Feb; £1.50. The village itself has a good few attractive old houses and cottages, tile-hung or timber-framed, especially on the rd up to the Norman CHURCH. The Plough, Whyte Harte and William IV are all useful for lunch.

🖑 **Camberley** SU8860 SURREY HEATH MUSEUM (Knoll Rd) Good local history museum, with plenty of geology, archaeology and crafts from the area. Shop, disabled access; cl Sun and Mon, 25 Dec, 1 Jan; (01276) 686252; free.

🐎 🐓 🦋 **Charlwood** TQ2340 GATWICK ZOO AND AVIARIES Hundreds of mammals and birds, many in big naturalistic settings – some of which visitors can walk through, inc the two large tropical houses with plants and butterflies from around the world. Meals, snacks, shop, disabled access; cl wkdys Nov–Feb, 25–26 Dec;

(01293) 862312; *£3.50. The Fox Revived at Norwood Hill is a useful nearby dining pub.

🏠 🐄 🐚 🦰 ☺ 🐎 ✏ **Chertsey** TQ0466 has a good few Georgian buildings in its main streets, the remains of a medieval ABBEY, and pleasant walks by the Thames. The Crown and Golden Grove are useful for lunch. The late Georgian MUSEUM (Windsor St) has displays on the abbey, as well as an exhibition on Victorian fashion, and a pleasant little garden. Shop; cl am wkdys, Sun, Mon, 25 Dec and bank hols; free. Slightly NW at Lyne, the GREAT COCKROW RAILWAY (Hardwick Lane) is a notable miniature steam railway, with a unique signalling system. They've recently extended the track and added a new locomotive, the *Jubilee Bell*. Snacks; open pm Sun May–Oct; (01932) 565474; from £1.20. THORPE PARK TQ0368 Enormous, 500-acre amusement park built around former gravel pits, with lots of rides and attractions, many of them water-based – inc the Loggers' Leap, the highest log flume in the country. Also, a working farm with rare breeds, and various craftsmen and women. Done with flair and thought, and ideal for families. Meals, snacks, shop, good disabled access (they recently won an award for it); cl Nov–Easter; (01932) 562633; £11.25.

☺ 🐾 **Chessington** TQ1762
CHESSINGTON WORLD OF ADVENTURES Another superior theme park, one of the country's most-visited attractions, with over 100 rides and amusements, circus, and the famous zoo; latest addition is the spooky Terrortomb; there really is lots to do. Meals, snacks, shop, disabled access; cl Nov–Mar; (01372) 729560; £13. Special events on summer evenings, when the park is open late. It's actually in Greater London, but as everyone thinks of it as being in Surrey we include it here.

★ † ❀ **Chiddingfold** SU9635 is a lovely village in fine surroundings, with one window of its church made up from locally excavated fragments of 13th-c glass made here. The handsome old Crown is useful for lunch. RAMSTER (A283, S) has a splendid, Edwardian, woodland spring garden. Wknd teas, plant sales, disabled access; open pm wknds and bank hols Apr–July, every day in May; (01428) 644422; *£2.

🏠 ❀ 👶 ╳ **Cobham** TQ0960 is quite a busy shopping town, with some attractive older buildings around the church and in Church St; just outside Downside Common there is a classic cricket green, with cottages scattered around it, and a good pub – the Cricketers. PAINSHILL PARK These beautifully restored, 18th-c landscape gardens are a continual surprise, with Gothic temples, Chinese bridges and other follies at every turn, and a lake with seemingly endless bays and inlets. Lots of unusual trees and shrubs. Snacks, shop, limited disabled access; usually open Sun only Apr–Oct, but this year they hope to be open other days too; (01932) 864674; £3. Almost opposite the gates, the Little White Lion is handy for lunch. BUS MUSEUM (Redhill Rd) Private collection of London buses from the 1930s to the present. Open wknds and bank hols; free. The WATERMILL (Mill Rd) has been authentically restored by enthusiastic locals and is working for the first time in 60 years. Open pm 2nd Sun of month Apr–Oct; free.

🔲 † **Compton** SU9546 (nr Guildford)
WATTS PICTURE GALLERY Memorial gallery to Victorian painter and sculptor G F Watts, filled with his work; few people today seem to know his work but in his time he was one of the most celebrated artists in the world. Shop, disabled access; cl am, Thurs, Christmas; (01483) 810235; free. Just down the rd, the art nouveau tomb built by his widow is worth a look, and the village church is attractive. The Withies is good for lunch.

🐂 ! ❀ ★ 👶 **Dorking** TQ1450 DENBIES (London Rd) Britain's biggest vineyard – at 250 acres it's larger than many of the famous French ones it resembles. The tour is quite unlike any you'd find elsewhere, almost like a theme park in places, with an audio-visual show and 3-D theatre, where four months of vine growth is condensed into four minutes, and grapes being loaded on to a lorry look as if they're flying out of the screen. There are tastings at the end. Good fun, and you don't have to be a wine buff to enjoy it. Meals, snacks (in unusually designed restaurant), big shop, good disabled access; cl am Sun, 25–26 Dec; (01306) 876616; £4. Fine views and walks nearby. CHAPEL FARM TRAIL (Westhumble, TQ1651) Working farm with lots of animals in lovely countryside. Also trailer rides (£1 extra) and pleasant walks. Shop, disabled access; cl Nov–mid-Feb; (01306) 882865; £1.60. Dorking itself is a pleasant market town, with a lot of antique shops, and a local museum, in West St. The Cricketers (South St – A2003 towards Horsham) has good-value food.

🏠 👶 ❀ **East Clandon** TQ0652
HATCHLANDS Handsome, 18th-c brick house with more floors than are visible from the outside, thanks to an ingenious use of false windows. The grand rooms are especially notable for their fine ceilings and fireplaces, early examples of the work of Robert Adam. Also good paintings and furnishings, and the Cobbe Collection of keyboard instruments, inc a piano once played by Mozart; some instruments are usually played on Weds. The garden has a parterre by Gertrude Jekyll. Meals, snacks, shop,

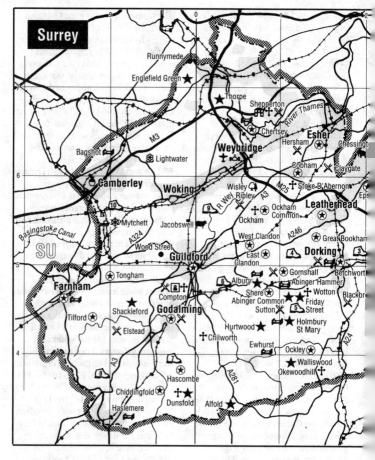

Surrey

disabled access (with notice); cl am, Sat (exc in Aug), Mon, Fri, Nov–Mar; (01483) 222482; £4; NT. The Queen's Head is useful for lunch.

! ☛ ✗ Epsom TQ2259 is best known for its racecourse, where the Derby (first run in 1780) is still the most prestigious race for three-year-old thoroughbreds. The DERBY DAY EXPERIENCE (Queen's Stand) re-creates the excitement of the event, with the help of audio-visual shows, archive film, interactive displays and various relics and mementos. A Hall of Fame recalls past winners, and there's an interesting look at the changing style of grandstands. Very good on the social side of things, so worth a look even if you're not a racegoer. Meals, snacks, shop, disabled access; cl first wk of Jun (Derby wk), 29 Jun, 27 July, 29–30 Aug, Christmas; (01372) 726311; £5.50. Other famous racecourses in this area include Sandown Park TQ1364, (01372) 463072; Kempton Park TQ1168, (01932) 782292; and Lingfield TQ3843, (01342) 834800; all have good facilities. On the B280 W of Epsom, HORTON PARK FARM has rare breeds, an adventure playground and craft shops. Snacks, shop, disabled access; cl 25–26 Dec; (01372) 743984; £1.95.

❀ ☎ ☞ Esher TQ1263 CLAREMONT LANDSCAPE GARDEN The oldest surviving landscaped garden in the country, laid out by Vanburgh and Bridgeman before 1720 and extended and naturalised by Kent; 50 colourful acres to lose yourself in. Meals (not

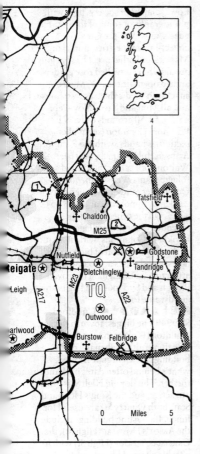

Tatsfield

Chaldon

M25

Nutfield

Reigate

Leigh

A217

M23

Godstone

Bletchingley

Tandridge

TQ

A22

Outwood

arlwood

Burstow Felbridge

0   Miles   5

last year voted the best museum in Britain in the European Museum Awards – quite an achievement for somewhere so traditional. It has some William Cobbett memorabilia and a pleasant walled garden. Shop, disabled access; cl Sun, Mon, Christmas; free. Cobbett's picturesque birthplace in Bridge Sq is now a pub named after him. The CASTLE was for 800 years a residence of the Bishops of Winchester, and Charles I stayed here on the way to his trial. Most of the buildings have been adapted to suit the briefing organisation based here, but the major rooms, inc the great hall, can be visited pm Weds; (01252) 721194; £1.20. The Norman keep, administered separately, includes the massive foundations of a Norman tower; it's open daily Apr–Sept; £1.80, inc Walkman tour. The JOHNSON WAX KILN GALLERY in Bridge Sq has diverse arts and crafts, with workshops and demonstrations. Cl Sun and bank hols; free. BIRDWORLD (off the A325, SW) Wide variety of birds in 18 acres of garden and parkland – all shapes and sizes from the tiny tanagers to the huge ostrich, with many rare species. Woodland walks and trails, and an adjacent UNDERWATER WORLD, with tropical, freshwater and marine fish. Meals, snacks, shop, disabled access; cl 25 Dec; (01420) 22140; £3.85. This is actually just over the Hants border at Holt Pound SU8143, but as this is rarely shown on maps we've included it under Farnham, the nearest big place.

★ 🏠 ⛪ 🌳 🐦 **Godalming** SU9643 is an attractive town with quite a few interesting buildings and, because of its narrow streets, a more old-fashioned feel than most in Surrey. Opposite the town hall, known affectionately by the locals as the Pepper Pot, is a 15th-c house with an absorbing local history MUSEUM, and a Gertrude Jekyll-style walled garden. Shop; cl Mon, Sun, bank hols exc Good Fri; free. The town is the terminus for the River Wey & Godalming Navigation, a 17th-c CANAL extended here in 1763. Its original locks and towpath have been

Mon), snacks, shop, disabled access; cl Christmas, Jan–Mar; *£1.80, going up to *£2.60 on Sun and bank hols; NT. There's a farm shop with PICK-YOUR-OWN fruit on Winterdown Rd.
★ 🏠 ⛪ 🏛 🖼 ✕ 🐦 🌳 🎵 **Farnham** SU8446 The Romans and Saxons both had settlements here, but it was in Georgian times that this handsome town had its heyday, thanks to the importance of local corn and hops. Many elegant buildings from this period remain, and there are some even older ones such as the early 17th-c Spinning Wheel (on Castle St, now a shoe shop). The area in the vicinity of Castle St is especially nice to stroll round. The Spotted Cow (Tilford Rd, Lower Bourne) is good for lunch. The local history MUSEUM (West St) was

restored for the National Trust; the wharf has some fine Georgian buildings (you can walk all the way to Weybridge, some 20 miles). BUSBRIDGE LAKES SU9742 (Hambledon Rd, off the B2130) A very pretty spot set on three lakes in fine parkland, with exotic waterfowl, peacocks, ornamental pheasants and 100 other kinds of bird, as well as follies and grottoes throughout the grounds. In spring, there are lambs and newly hatched ducklings and chicks. Wknd snacks, shop; open (1995) 9–17 Apr, 30 Apr–1 May, 28–29 May, 20–28 Aug; (01483) 421955; £3. The Inn on the Lake (A3100, S) is good for lunch, and in the High St the interesting old King's Arms & Royal Hotel is also useful.

★ † ⚘ ⌂ 🍴 **Godstone** TQ3551, despite its main roads, is attractive, spread around a broad green with a duck pond, and a pretty group of houses around the imposing CHURCH – 14th/15th c with a Norman tower. The Bell and the Hare & Hounds are useful for lunch. PILGRIM HARPS (Stansted House, Tilburstow Hill Rd) make and restore harps of all sorts; by appointment only, (01342) 893242. GODSTONE FARM (Tilburstow Hill) Friendly, 40-acre working farm; children are encouraged to touch the animals. Snacks, shop, disabled access; cl Nov–Mar; (01883) 742546; £2.80. FLOWER FARM (Quarry Rd, just off the A22 towards Oxted), looking up to the downs, has organically grown pick-your-own produce and a vineyard. Snacks, shop, disabled access; cl Nov–May (exc vineyard, open all year); (01883) 744590; free.

✗ ❀ ⚘ 🏠 **Gomshall** TQ0848 GOMSHALL MILL is a restored and working, two-wheeled watermill dating back to 1086, with the mill pond converted to riverside gardens and the buildings housing various craft shops. Meals and snacks (not Sun pm), disabled access; cl Christmas; free. The GOMSHALL GALLERY in Station Rd has contemporary arts and crafts; cl Sun, Christmas; free. The Compasses is useful for lunch.

🏠 ▣ ❀ ✤ ⚘ nr **Great Bookham** TQ1352 POLESDEN LACEY Attractive Regency house once at the centre of Edwardian high society, now with photographs of some of the notable guests, as well as the Greville collection of tapestries, porcelain, Old Masters and other art. The spacious grounds have a walled rose garden and an open-air theatre. Meals, snacks, shop, disabled access; house cl am, all Mon and Tues, Nov–Feb; £5.50, £2.50 grounds only; NT. Ranmore Common (see **Walks** section) is handy, with the Ranmore Arms useful for lunch; nearby, Walton Poor sell herb, scented and foliage plants Weds–Sun, not Oct–Easter, and open their pretty garden by appointment (0148 65) 2273. On the other side of the extended commuter village, the Bookham Commons, with a mixture of thorny scrub (full of birds), small lakes, marshy bits and oakwoods, are attractive. In Effingham nearby, the Plough and Sir Douglas Haig both do good-value food.

🏠 ▣ † ⛰ 🏰 ❀ ⌂ 🍴 **Guildford** SU9949 The biggest town in the area, Guildford is older than you might at first think; although many of the buildings are Georgian-fronted, what's behind often dates back much further. The sloping High St is most attractive, and the King's Head and Star (both Quarry St) are useful for lunch. Interesting buildings include the ABBOT'S HOSPITAL (High St), the GRAMMAR SCHOOL (High St) with its notable chained library, and GUILDFORD BOAT HOUSE (Millmead), now an art gallery. Best of all is the mainly Tudor GUILDHALL (High St), which has one of the few existing sets of Elizabethan standard measures. Open Tues and Thurs, guided tours at 2, 3 and 4pm; free. More recent is the CATHEDRAL, begun in 1936 and one of the only two entirely 20th-c cathedrals in the country; it's quite austere, but has a cool elegance inside. Shop; disabled access. Good shopping facilities are usually briskly modern; for a change of pace, you can hire a boat on the river. The riverside Jolly Farmer, nr the Yvonne Arnaud Theatre, has decent food. The hill of the ruined, 12th-c CASTLE has fine views of the town, and a garden in the former castle ditch. A 600-year-old, royal wine cellar was recently discovered in the grounds. Shop; open wk after Easter–end of Sept; 70p. Nearby is a good local history MUSEUM (Quarry St), with archaeology and needlework exhibits, and a display on Lewis Carroll, who died here in 1898. Shop, limited disabled access; cl Sun, Good Fri, 24–26 Dec; free.

LOSELEY HOUSE (3 miles SW off B3000) Most people are familiar with the name from the wonderful ice-cream and yoghurts produced here (the white chocolate and butterscotch flavours are delicious), and you can tour the dairy farm that makes them; afternoon tours usually feature milking. The stately Elizabethan country house was built in 1562 from stone taken from the older Waverley Abbey, and has fine panelling, ceilings, paintings and tapestries. Meals, snacks, shop, limited disabled access; open Weds–Sun May–Sept, though house cl am and all Sun; (01483) 304440; £3.50 house and grounds, £2.50 farm tours.

★ † ⚘ ❀ **Hascombe** SU9941 is a pretty village with an interesting church; the White Horse is good for lunch. WINKWORTH ARBORETUM Nearly 100 acres of lovely hillside woodland, with fine views over the North Downs – especially nice in spring, and with unusual flaring colours in the autumn. Meals, snacks, shop, disabled access; £2; NT.

🐄 **Jacobswell** TQ0053 BURPHAM COURT FARM PARK (Clay Lane) Over 75 acres of countryside with rare breeds of cattle, sheep, goats, pigs and poultry; good explanations and interpretative displays. Also, more familiar breeds, a pets' corner, play area and pretty riverside walks. Snacks, shop; cl wkdys Nov–Feb; (01483) 576089; £2.50.

🎦 👟 ❀ 🐄 🎨 **Leatherhead** TQ1656 FIRE AND IRON GALLERY (Oxshott Rd) Unusual exhibitions of ornamental metalwork. Shop, disabled access; cl 1–2pm, pm Sat, all Sun; free. A local history MUSEUM (Church St) is in a pretty, 17th-c, timber-framed cottage with garden. Open Sat, pm Thurs, am Fri Apr–Christmas; free. The Duke's Head in the pedestrianised High St is

pleasant for lunch, and there are riverside walks nearby. BOCKETTS FARM PARK, at nearby Fetcham TQ1456, is a working farm in a pretty, historic setting, with traditional and rare breeds, cart rides, and craft demonstrations. Meals and snacks (not 9–26 Jan), shop, disabled access; cl 25 Dec; (01372) 363764; £2.40.

❀ **Lightwater** SU9362 LIGHTWATER COUNTRY PARK AND HEATHLAND VISITOR CENTRE has good interpretative displays of the county's rich natural history, and, in particular, the sandy heathlands; nature trails. Snacks, shop, disabled access; park open all year, but visitor centre usually only open pm Sun and wkdys in summer hols; (01276) 479582; free.

✿ ⛴ **Mytchett** SU8855 BASINGSTOKE CANAL VISITOR CENTRE Displays on the canal, with boat trips along the water; you can hire rowing boats and there are pleasant towpath walks. Snacks, shop, disabled access; cl Mon (exc bank hols), winter wknds, Christmas; (01252) 370073; *£1.50.

🏠 ❀ ⚘ nr **Ockham Common** TQ0859 Chatley Heath Semaphore Tower (entrance on Old Lane, off the A3 to Effingham) Unique tower rather like a lighthouse, the only surviving member of a chain of 13 stations that once sent messages between the Admiralty in London and Portsmouth; excellent views from the top of the 88 steps. Surrounding it are 700 acres of heath and woodland, with a nature trail and good walks (inc the 20-minute trek from the car park to the tower). Shop; open pm wknds and bank hols wk before Easter–Sept, and Weds in school hols; (01932) 862762; £1.60. The Black Swan at Martyrs Green is useful.

🏠 ❀ 🖼 🎪 🎨 **Ockley** TQ1439 Some attractive old houses along the Roman rd here, with the King's Arms and Old School House doing decent food; the Scarlett Arms out at Walliswood is a delightful old place. HANNAH PESCHAR GALLERY AND GARDEN (Black and White Cottage, Standon Lane) Lush garden filled with contemporary sculpture: the watergarden is now more like a tropical rainforest than the cottage garden it started off as, and the atmospheric sculptures and ceramics blend in perfectly with its unusual design. Also, a small indoor gallery. Disabled access (but no lavatory); open Fri, Sat and pm Sun and bank hols 9 May–31 Oct, other times (exc Mon) by arrangement; (01306) 627269; *£4. There's a good, big farm shop with PICK-YOUR-OWN fruit nearby.

★ ♤ ✕ 🐄 🐂 Outwood TQ3246, spread around the common, is attractive, with an antique shop, and the adjacent National Trust woodlands are ideal for a picnic. The Dog & Duck out towards Coopers Hill is good for lunch. POST MILL The oldest working windmill in England, built in 1665, and one of the best preserved. It's a very nice spot, 400ft above sea level, with ducks, goats and horses all wandering freely about its grounds. Also, a small museum and collection of coaches. Shop, disabled access; open pm Sun and bank hols Easter–Oct; (01342) 843458; *£1.50.

🐂 ✕ † Reigate TQ2550 Few of the town's original buildings survive, but there are a couple of timber-framed houses around the high st. Below the peaceful castle grounds is a network of old tunnels, notably the intriguingly elaborate BARON'S CAVE – a splendidly atmospheric passageway with a wealth of myths and stories attached; the tours are enthusiastic and entertaining. Open one day a month or by appointment – check with Matthew Clarke (01737) 241179; 75p. OLD WINDMILL AND CHURCH On the heath just outside town, this 220-year-old, former windmill was converted into a church in 1882. They still have services the 3rd Sun each month in summer. Disabled access; open all year – if closed, key at golf club clubhouse. Nr it, the Skimmington Castle, an archetypal country tavern, is good for light lunches, and there are pleasant walks here.

Runnymede SU9972 is a field by a main road; not worth visiting unless you are quite fascinated by Magna Carta, though up the hill beyond the trees, the nearby memorials to John F Kennedy and, with their names, to the aircrew who died during World War II, are dignified and touching.

🏠 † Shepperton TQ0867 is one of the best places to watch the comings and goings on the RIVER THAMES, with the Wey Navigation joining the river here; the waterside Red Lion (Russell Rd) is useful for lunch, and away from the water there's a quiet and attractive, 18th-c, village square with a pleasant church.

★ † 🐂 Shere TQ0747 Very picturesque village, with 17th-c, timber-framed cottages, a grassy-banked stream with ducks and a ford, and lots of interesting corners. In the partly Norman CHURCH, a quatrefoil blocked hole in the chancel wall marks the spot where a 14th-c anchorite had herself walled in, being fed through another hole outside. The ancient White Horse nearby is useful for lunch (as is the Prince of Wales), and the Malt House is a decent local history museum. The village is within reach of both the North Downs around Ranworth Common and the greensand hills to the S (see **Walks** section below).

🐂 ♤ 🏛 Tilford SU8743 RURAL LIFE CENTRE Carefully displayed, private collection of farm implements and machinery, and examples of related crafts and industry. It's spread over 10 acres of field and woodland, with an arboretum. Snacks, shop, disabled access; cl Mon (exc bank hols), Tues, all Oct–Easter; (01252) 795571; £2.50. The village has a massive oak tree, thought to be 800 years old; the Barley Mow between the river and the goose-cropped cricket green is good for lunch, and it's not far from here to the remains of Waverley Abbey.

🍺 🐂 ✎ Tongham SU8848 HOGS BACK BREWERY Tours of a friendly, little brewery, still using traditional full mash and top fermentation methods to produce its six distinctive ales. The shop sells not only their own beer but over 500 different English, Belgian and German varieties, alongside English wines and farm ciders. Tours Weds evening at 6.30pm, other times by arrangement, shop open daily exc Sun, cl 25 Dec; (01252) 782328; tour *£4.50 (inc tastings). Manor Farm has PICK-YOUR-OWN fruit in Tongham Jun–Sept, and a CRAFT CENTRE in adjacent **Seale** SU8947, with dried flowers, furnishings, jewellery and general crafts. Meals, snacks, shop, disabled access; cl am Sun, Mon (exc bank hols), Christmas; free. The Jolly Farmer at Runfold is useful for lunch.

🏠👁📷🌸 **West Clandon** TQ0351 CLANDON PARK Grand, 18th-c house with an unusual collection of porcelain birds, fine furnishings and paintings. Also, a regimental museum and regular concerts in the two-storeyed Marble Hall. The gardens have a Maori house brought over from New Zealand in 1892. Meals, snacks, shop, disabled access to ground floor; cl am, Thurs and Fri (exc Good Fri), and Nov–Apr (though restaurant and shop open wknds till Christmas); £3.60. NT. The smart Onslow Arms is good for lunch.

🏛✝ nr **Weybridge** TQ0662 BROOKLANDS MUSEUM Motoring records were being set here even before the first race was held in 1907, and it later became the place where man first travelled at 100 mph, where the first British-made plane was flown, and the site of the first British Grand Prix. The exhaustive museum re-creates the racing circuit's 1920s and 30s heyday, with plenty of racing cars, motorbikes and bicycles displayed in the restored clubhouse. Also a look at aircraft production at the site, with a comprehensive collection of vintage Vickers and Hawker planes; demonstrations and events most weekends. Snacks, shop, good disabled access; cl Mon (exc bank hols), 25 Dec; (01932) 857381; £4.50. In the town, the Prince of Wales (Cross Rd/Anderson Rd) is nice for lunch.

🌸🌿 **Wisley** TQ0659 WISLEY GARDEN These 300-acre gardens have come a long way since they were set up in 1904 as experimental gardens for the Royal Horticultural Society; half the area is devoted to garden, some to vegetables, and the rest to farm, orchard and woodland, with lots of unusual plants, shrubs and trees. The gardens get very busy (especially at weekends) but are quite big enough to cope. Meals, snacks, shop (lots of hard-to-get gardening/plant books), garden centre (good plants from a wide range of nurseries, but expensive), disabled access; cl Sun (exc to RHS members), 25 Dec; (01483) 224234; £4.50. The canalside Anchor at Pyrford Lock (turn left down the exit road) is useful for lunch if the queues at the good café here daunt you; and the pub is well placed for walks along the prettiest section of the Wey Navigation Canal.

⚓ **Boat hire** is possible on the **Wey Navigation**, from Farncombe Boat House, Godalming, (01483) 421306, or Guildford Boat House, Millbrook, (01483) 504494; the canal passes through some fine scenery.

★ **Other attractive villages,** all with decent pubs, include Abinger Common TQ1145 (pretty church and duckpond, woods around), Albury TQ0547 (where the Victorian mansion Albury Park is famed for its chimneys), Alfold TQ0334, Betchworth TQ2049, Dunsfold TQ0036, Englefield Green SU9970 (handy for Savill Garden – see Berks chapter), Friday Street TQ1245, Holmbury St Mary TQ1144, Hurtwood TQ0845, Leigh TQ2246, Shackleford SU9345, Thorpe TQ0268, Walliswood TQ1138 and Wood Street SU9550.

✝ Though Surrey's village **churches** are not as notable as those in, say, Somerset, Lincs or Suffolk, and though you'll usually have to get the key from a local keyholder, most are at least worth a look. A shortlist, for the intrinsic appeal of the churches themselves or for their surroundings, would include Burstow TQ3140, Chaldon TQ3155 (with its unique wall painting of the Ladder of Salvation), Chilworth TQ0247, Dunsfold TQ0036, Okewoodhill TQ1337, Ockham TQ0756, Tandridge TQ3750, Tatsfield TQ4156 and Wotton TQ1247. The one at Stoke d'Abernon TQ1259 has the earliest surviving brass in Britain, dating from the 13th c; set in the floor of the chancel, it's very well preserved.

! You can book BALLOON TRIPS over the county on (01483) 232662.

Besides places already mentioned for the River Thames, the Swan at Staines TQ0471 (The Hythe) and the Swan at Walton-on-Thames TQ1066 (Manor Rd) have good views and access to the river and towpath.

Walks

In this well wooded and surprisingly hilly county, it's easy to escape from the suburbia that covers much of its northern part. Even quite close to the M25, the traffic is out of earshot at popular strolling-grounds such as **Banstead Wood** TQ2657 ◿-1 and **Marden Park** TQ3655 ◿-2.

Further W, the North Downs have a more untouched, rural character. **Box Hill** TQ1850 ◿-3 is the most popular viewpoint, with a summit car park and walks on its steep juniper and boxwood slopes: great views, wild orchids and butterflies in early summer, and field mushrooms in early autumn; the attractively placed King William IV at Mickleham is excellent for lunch. On the other side of the Mole Gap, the North Downs Way continues along **Ranmore Common** TQ1451 ◿-4, chalk downland with sheep, wild orchids and dense woodlands, within close range of Polesden Lacey.

The upper greensand country ◿-5 to the S, though much wooded, displays some satisfying variety and is arguably Surrey's best walking territory. Leith Hill TQ1342 has heather, sandy walks, a steep pinewood, and tremendous views. An 18th-c tower on top of the hill, the highest point in SE England, is the best viewpoint of all, with a surprising view of S London – which feels 100 miles away. It's open with teas on pm Weds and Sat, Sun and bank hols, but cl Oct–Mar exc fine wknds; 50p. Friday Street TQ1245, with a pleasant pub and a lake, is one starting point for switchback routes S through a series of brackeny summits to the tower; the Abinger Hatch at Abinger Common TQ1145 is another attractive start from this side. Leith Hill can also be approached from the S, from Ockley TQ1440 or the useful Parrot at Forest Green TQ1241 – this approach through attractive farmland may be preferable for people who like open country. There's a similarly open approach from Ewhurst TQ0940 to Pitch Hill TQ0842, where the Windmill has decent food. Around Hurt Wood TQ0943 large areas of private forest are open to walkers; relatively unfrequented, so it's a good place to spot birds and wild animals. The Royal Oak and King's Head at Holmbury St Mary TQ1144 are handy for walkers.

St Martha's Hill TQ0248 ◿-6, E of Guildford, has a church on its summit that can be reached only on foot, and by starting from Chilworth TQ0247, where the Villagers at Blackheath is useful for walkers, you can see the long-abandoned gunpowder mills by the Tilling Bourne (even if you don't find the tawny balsam J S Mills found there in 1822, when retreating from a tiresome house party at Albury Park). Further SW the terrain is lower but unspoilt around **Winkworth Arboretum** SU9941 ◿-7, nr Godalming. The **Devil's Punchbowl** SU8936 ◿-8, nr Hindhead, is a spectacular fold of the downs, with nature trails through a landscape characterised by mixed woodlands, quiet valleys, scattered ponds and sandy heaths. The area is quite developed but the woods and intricacy of the landscape give it a wholesome rurality, and the footpath network is dense. Gibbet Hill SU9035, above the A3, gets a view over most of it.

As we've said, the **Wey Navigation towpath** ◿-9 in the W of the county has the best waterside walks. The **Basingstoke Canal** ◿-10, formerly derelict, has been undergoing a tremendous programme of rehabilitation over the last 15 years or so. In its Surrey section it does not pass through such fine scenery as the Wey Navigation, but its towpath has been well restored. A visitor centre at Mytchett SU8855 explains the restoration.

Other country areas attractive for strolling include parts of wooded Netley Heath above Gomshall TQ0848; Frensham Common SU8540 (heather and woodland around a lake formed in the 13th c for fish breeding); Headley Heath TQ2053 (sandy walks and rides through heather, birchwoods and rather too much bracken; the Cock at Headley is good for lunch); Holmwood Common TQ1745 (undulating oak and birchwoods, lots of pleasant paths; the Plough at Blackbrook is handy for lunch); Horsell Common SU9959 (the sandpits which inspired and saw the start of H G Wells's *War of the Worlds*; the Bleak House at the Anthonys and the Red Lion in Horsell have decent food); and Thursley Common SU9040 (more heather, unusual birds, and boggy patches with shallow ponds where dragonflies breed; the Three Horse-shoes at Thursley is useful for lunch). The William IV at Albury Heath TQ0646, Sportsman at Mogador TQ2452 and Botley Hill Farmhouse at War-lingham (Limpsfield Rd) TQ3558 are popular starts or finishes for weekend walks, and the Thurlow Arms at Baynards Station Yard, nr Cox Green TQ0734, is handy for the disused railway Downs Link Path.

The Environment Unit of the County Council's Planning Department co-ordinates an ambitious programme of guided walks throughout the year, gen-erally exploring some historical or – more usually – natural history theme; on a typical Sunday there might be eight or more different walks to choose from. For the current programme, tel 081-541 9454 and ask for the Environment Unit.

Driving

The county's best drives are over on the W side of the A24, with all the side roads that lead S off the A25 between Dorking and Albury giving enjoyable views and little other traffic. The road from Shere, dropping steeply down over Pitch Hill, towards Ewhurst is particularly memorable. Further W, there's a pretty drive from Godalming down through Hascombe on the B2130, turning off on the side road to Dunsfold and on to Chiddingfold.

The A3 coming into Hindhead gives a good passing view of the Devil's Punchbowl, and the A31 between Guildford and Farnham has nice views from the Hog's Back ridge; both, however, are scarcely roads you'd seek out for a quiet country drive.

The roads around and steeply over Box Hill are attractive, and nearby is a pleasant route off the A25, through Betchworth and Brockham, then S through Newdigate and on to Rusper over the Sussex border.

Where to eat

Claygate TQ1563 Les Alouettes High St (01372) 464882 Particularly fine French cooking in an attractive, civilised restaurant, lovely puddings, and courteous service; cl am Sat, pm Sun, last wk Aug–1st wk Sept, 24–30 Dec, 1 Jan; limited disabled access. £35/£10.

Ripley TQ0556 Michels 13 High St (01483) 224777 Fine modern cooking in an attractive restaurant with good wines and professional service; cl pm Sun, Mon, am Sat, 1 wk Jan; partial disabled access. £33.

South Godstone TQ3749 La Bonne Auberge (01342) 892318 Comfortable, quietly set Victorian house, with very good French food and helpful staff; cl pm Sun, Mon; disabled access. £30.

Dorking TQ1649 Partners West Street 2, 3 and 4 West St (01306) 882826 Cosy, popular restaurant in a 16th-c building, with very good food inc good-value set meals and a well thought-out wine list; cl pm Sun, am Sat; children over 5. £25.50/£7.95.

Godalming SU9743 Inn on the Lake Ockford Rd (01483) 415575 Comfort-able and attractive restaurant surrounded by lawns, gardens and a lake, with very good and popular, modern British cooking; cl pm 25 Dec. £23|£2.20/£5.

Shepperton TQ0867 Edwinns Restaurant Church St (01932) 223543 Very good, popular food from an interesting menu, and friendly service; cl am Sat, pm Sun. £20.95.

Compton SU9546 Harrow (01483) 810379 Smart dining pub in interesting village close to the North Downs Way, with particularly good fish and seafood – though other dishes, too; little, beamed rooms, nice furnishings, and well kept real ales. £20|£3/£8.

Sutton TQ1046 Partners Brasserie 23 Stonecot Hill (01816) 447743 Cosy and pretty restaurant with really good, modern cooking and carefully chosen wines; cl Sun and Mon, am Sat, 25 Dec–1 Jan; disabled access. £20/£8.

Hersham TQ1164 THE DINING ROOM The Village Green (01932) 231686 Five little rooms with log fires, very good English food inc huge puddings, a relaxed atmosphere, and cheerful, friendly staff; cl am Sat, pm Sun, 10 days over Christmas, bank hols; limited disabled access. £19/£8.95.

Elstead SU9143 WOOLPACK (01252) 703106 Cheerfully old-fashioned pub, bustling and friendly, with huge helpings of good, interesting bar food, real ale tapped from the cask, a fair amount of wool industry memorabilia, open fires, and a children's play area in the garden; cl pm 25 Dec, 26 Dec; children in family room or dining room only; disabled access (though one step to lavatory). £18.75|£3.75/£4.25.

Felbridge TQ3639 WOODCOCK (01342) 325859 Spacious pub with lots to look at and some unusual touches in the various, differently styled areas; good, imaginative home-made food using fresh hand-picked produce from the markets, and hardworking, helpful staff; disabled access. £18.25|£3.25/£5.50.

Gomshall TQ0847 MULLIGANS Station Rd (A25) (01483) 202242 Friendly staff in an attractively decorated and relaxed fish restaurant, with live French café music on Thurs; cl 25–26 Dec; disabled access. £18|£3/£8.

Blackbrook TQ1846 PLOUGH (01306) 88603 Popular pub with colourful hanging baskets and window boxes and set in attractive walking country; generous helpings of good, imaginative food, particularly well kept real ales, very friendly service, a marvellous choice of wines by the glass, and a pretty, cottagey garden with a Swiss playhouse for children; no food pm Mon; no children; disabled access. £16|£2.95/£5.50.

Help this year from: Michael and Jenny Back, E G Parish, Mrs Hilarie Taylor, Susan and John Douglas, W J Wonham, Clem Stephens, Shirley Pielou, Alex and Beryl Williams, Dick Brown, Ian Phillips, D J and P M Taylor, Joy Heatherley, Tim Galligan, P Gillbe, Jenny and Brian Seller, Mr and Mrs Williams, R B Crail, Andy and Jackie Mallpress, D and J Tapper, A J Blackler, John Pettit, LM, Nic Armitage, Maurice Southon.

SURREY CALENDAR

Some of these dates were provisional as we went to press.

JANUARY

6 **Guildford** Wassailing: Twelfth Night pub tour by Morris men who act out the old tiptearers' or mummers' play and drink spiced beer from the wassail bowl

26 **Guildford** Dicing for the Maid's Money at the Guildhall: a will made in 1674 instructed two maids of long service to throw dice competing for a year's income

MARCH

3 **Guildford** International Music Festival – *till Sun 26* (01483) 259167

MAY

5 **Banstead** Arts Festival – *till Sun 21* (01737) 353738

6 **Guildford** May Day Ceremony: *at about 5.30* the Pilgrim Morris Men dance to greet the sunrise on the Downs, the procession then carries the summer pole up the High St to castle green; folk dancing around the pole and elsewhere throughout the day (01483) 444751

25 **Tilford** Bach Festival at All Saints Church – *till Sat 27* (01252) 782167

26 **Virginia Water** PGA Golf Championship at Wentworth – *till Mon 29* (01344) 842881

29 **Guildford** Surrey County Show at Stoke Park (01483) 425697; **West Ewell** Festival of Fun

SURREY CALENDAR

JUNE

10 **Abinger Common** Old Fair of Abinger with maypole and Morris dancing (01306) 731083; **Caterham** Carnival

16 **Great Bookham** Son et Lumière: the history of Polesden Lacey at Polesden Lacey – *till Sun 18* (01372) 459950

17 **Lightwater** Country and Craft Fair – *till Sun 18* (01276) 472791

21 **Great Bookham** DIE FLEDERMAUS at Polesden Lacey – *till Sat 24* (01372) 459950

24 **East Molesey** Metropolitan Police Horse Show and Tournament at the Metropolitan Police Mounted Branch at Imber Court – *till Sun 25* 0181-247 5480; **Farnham** Carnival (01252) 715538

28 **Great Bookham** A COMEDY OF ERRORS at Polesden Lacey – *till 1 July* (01372) 459950

JULY

1 **Guildford** Festival inc boat gathering – *till Sun 16* (01483) 444995

2 **Great Bookham** Promenade Concert and Fireworks at Polesden Lacey (01372) 459950

8 **Chertsey** Black Cherry Fair

9 **Great Bookham** Concert with the Glen Miller Band at Polesden Lacey (01372) 459950

12 **Esher** Fête Champêtre at Claremont Landscape Garden – *till Sat 15* (01372) 459950

15 **Reigate** Music Festival in Reigate Park – *till Sun 30* (01737) 823231

16 **Esher** Big Jazz Night at Claremont Landscape Garden (01372) 459950

30 **Tilford** Rustic Sunday at Old Kiln Rural Life Centre (01252) 792300

AUGUST

5 **Cranleigh** Show at the Showground (01306) 621505; **Crawley** International Festival of Arts at the Hawth – *till Sun 6* (01293) 552941; **Guildford** Classic Car Show and Country Fayre at Loseley Park – *till Sun 6* (01403) 891620

11 **Frimley Green** Berkshire Country Music Festival at Lakeside Country Club – *till Sun 13* (01734) 884422; **Guildford** Viennese Evening with fireworks at Loseley Park (01625) 575681

12 **Crawley** Juggling Convention at the Hawth – *till Sun 13* (01293) 552941; **Sunbury on Thames** Regatta; **Wisley** Flower Show at Wisley Gardens – *till Sun 13* 0171-630 7422

19 **Sunbury on Thames** Regatta at Rivermead Island (01932) 780067

26 **Egham** Royal Show at Runnymede – *till Sun 27* (01784) 434833

27 **Lingfield** Edenbridge and Oxted Agricultural Show at Ardenrun Showground – *till Mon 28* (01737) 645843

28 **Guildford** Family Festival of Folk and Blues at Stoke Park (01483) 36270

SEPTEMBER

9 **Chertsey** Agricultural Show – *till Sun 10* (01932) 872272

23 **nr Guildford** Surrey County Ploughing Match in a field off the A246 (01483) 414651

OCTOBER

20 **Farnham** Southern Counties Craft and Design Show at the Maltings – *till Sun 22* (01597) 851875; **Guildford** Book Festival – *till Sun 29* (01483) 259167

SUSSEX

This county has a good, interesting spread of different types of places particularly worth visiting, and attractively varied scenery.

West Sussex has one of Britain's most fascinating open-air museums, and the pick of the county's rich collection of impressive houses and fine gardens, including Uppark, to be reopened this year after a five-year closure. It also has a wider choice of really splendid country-house hotels than East Sussex. However, East Sussex has some outstanding attractions, too, including rather more for families, with quite a few newcomers this year. It has plenty of nice places to stay, and Rye is a particularly attractive town for a short visit.

There is plenty of good walking in both halves of the county. The South Downs with their expansive views run right across. East Sussex also has the sparsely wooded, high heathland of the Ashdown Forest, and the more intricate countryside of the Weald. Though most of the coast is densely built up, there are grand cliffs near Eastbourne and Hastings in the east.

EAST SUSSEX

Lots to see and do, attractive scenery and plenty of variety – ideal for a short stay.

The excellent choice of places to visit and things to do here is topped by Bodiam Castle, Sheffield Park garden, the wonderful Bluebell steam line nearby, Drusillas zoo (a children's favourite) and nearby Alfriston. Among new places, we'd particularly pick out the Bird Park at Flimwell, the English Wine Centre at Alfriston, Wilderness Wood at Hadlow Down and Pashley Manor Gardens at Ticehurst. Families really like the sheep centre at East Dean and Bentley at Halland; culture-minded people thrill to the Bloomsbury trail around Firle and Rodmell. On the coast, Eastbourne stands out as an unusually civilised, old-fashioned, seaside resort, well placed for a lot of the places to see out in the countryside.

The most picturesque countryside here is in the Weald towards the Kent boundary: steep slopes and valleys, ancient woods, pretty villages, tile-hung or weatherboarded oast houses and wood and tile Sussex barns with their long 'cats'-slide' roofs. Walkers find more scope, though, in the open downland culminating on Beachy Head that towers above the sea, or in the open, sandy heaths and woodland of the Ashdown Forest.

Brighton combines elegant Regency architecture, including the remarkable Royal Pavilion, with a more brassy side; it's a great place for antiques. Hastings has interesting parts. Rye, also by the sea, is a really interesting old town of considerable character; very good for a short stay or day visit.

Where to stay

Uckfield TQ4721 Horsted Place Little Horsted, Uckfield TN22 5TS (01825) 750581 £130; 17 individually decorated, spacious rms. Imposing, Victorian country house in 23 acres of grounds, with antiques, flowers and log fires in the luxurious lounges, delicious food and a good wine list in the no-smoking dining room; croquet, tennis, indoor heated swimming pool, and reduced green fees at East Sussex National; babies or children over 8 in restaurant; disabled access.

Eastbourne TV6199 Grand King Edward's Parade, Eastbourne BN21 4EQ (01323) 412345 £120 (minimum stay is 2 nights); 164 rms, many with sea views. Very well run, gracious, Victorian seaside hotel with a lovely, tranquil atmosphere; opulent drapes, chandeliers and marble pillars, spacious lounges, lovely flowers, excellent, imaginative food in the elegant restaurant, particularly good service, and fine leisure facilities; disabled access.

Brighton TQ3105 Grand Kings Rd, Brighton BN1 2FW (01273) 321188 £110; 200 handsome rms, many with sea views. Famous Victorian hotel with luxurious and elegant day rooms, fine moulded plasterwork and marble columns and floors, very good food and decent wines; popular afternoon tea in the sunny conservatory, a bustling nightclub, and health spa; disabled access.

Alfriston TQ5103 Star High St, Alfriston, Polegate BN26 5TA (01323) 870495 £102; 34 rms. Fascinating and atmospheric Forte hotel, built in the 15th c as a guesthouse for pilgrims; lots of medieval carvings, sanctuary post in the bar, decent food and drinks, and excellent service; disabled access.

Battle TQ7416 Netherfield Place Netherfield, Battle TN33 7PP (01424) 774455 £100; 14 lovely rms. Handsome, Georgian-style hotel in 30 acres of gardens and parkland; light, attractive day rooms, a log fire, really lovely flowers, and imaginative food using home-grown produce from the garden; two hard tennis courts, croquet, and putting green; cl last wk Dec, first 2 wks Jan.

Alfriston TQ5103 Deans Place Alfriston, Polegate BN26 5TW (01323) 870248 £85; 36 rms. 13th-c hotel with a pleasant lounge, cosy bar, log fires and fresh flowers, good food, landscaped gardens, swimming pool, croquet lawn, and pitch and putt; nice walks in every direction; disabled access.

Rye TQ9220 George High St, Rye TN31 7JP (01797) 222114 £85; 22 rms. 16th-c, former coaching inn with fine old beams said to have come from a Spanish Galleon; open fires, cosy bar, good food in the charming, timbered restaurant, and friendly staff.

Brighton TQ3105 Topps 17 Regency Sq, Brighton BN1 2EG (01273) 729334 £79; 15 lovely comfortable rms, 11 with gas-effect coal fires. Carefully furnished and well kept Regency town house nr the seafront; friendly, helpful service, good breakfasts and unpretentious dinners in the attractive basement restaurant, and a library/reception room; cl 25–26 Dec.

Telham TQ7614 Little Hemingfold Farmhouse Telham, Battle TN33 0TT (01424) 774338 *£65; 13 rms, most with own bthrm. Partly 17th-c, partly early Victorian farmhouse in 40 acres of woodland, with a trout-filled lake, gardens, and lots of walks; comfortable sitting rooms, open fires, restful atmosphere and very good food using home-grown produce – served either in the style of a dinner party or at own candlelit table; children can feed farm animals; tennis court.

Rye TQ9220 Jeakes House Mermaid St, Rye TN31 7ET (01797) 222828 *£57; 12 rms overlooking the rooftops of this medieval town or across the marsh to the sea, 10 with own bthrm. Fine, 16th-c building, well run and friendly, with good breakfasts, lots of well worn books, comfortable furnishings, linen and lace, and a lovely, peaceful atmosphere.

Sedlescombe TQ7718 Brickwall Sedlescombe, Battle TN33 0QA (01424) 870253 *£56; 23 attractive rms. Well run hotel with some Tudor originals, a happy atmosphere, comfortable residents' lounge, lively bar and oak-panelled lounge bar, fine food in the beamed restaurant, and an outdoor heated swimming pool; good base for exploring the area.

Brighton TQ3105 Dove 18 Regency Sq, Brighton BN1 2FG (01273) 779222 £55; 10 rms, 4 with sea views. Lovely, neatly kept bow-windowed Regency house with warmly welcoming, helpful owners, good breakfasts in the light and airy dining room (evening meals by prior arrangement); they are kind to families, with toys and baby-sitting available; disabled access.

Mayfield TQ5827 Middle House, Mayfield TN20 6AB (01435) 872146 £55; 8 rms. Old-world, Elizabethan hotel with a lovely panelled restaurant, leather chesterfields and armchairs in the morning coffee/afternoon tea area, chatty locals' bar with an open fire (maybe spit roasts), an attractive back garden, and pleasant views.

Rye TQ9220 Old Vicarage 66 Church St, Rye TN31 7HF (01797) 222119 £55; 6 pretty rms, with complimentary newspaper and glass of sherry. Quietly situated and charming, mainly 18th-c house with helpful, friendly owners, comfortable sitting room or small library, a log fire in the elegant dining room, and marvellous breakfasts with free-range eggs, fresh pork sausages, freshly made scones with home-made marmalade, specially selected tea and freshly ground coffee and local mushrooms; cl Christmas; children over 10.

Hartfield TQ4735 Bolebroke Mill Perry Hill, Edenbridge Rd, Hartfield TN7 4JP (01892) 770425 *£53; 4 charming, rural rms. Attractively and interestingly converted, family-run watermill and barn, very comfortable and spotlessly clean, with grindstones and internal machinery, low ceilings and beams, particularly good breakfasts, and excellent, personal service; cl Jan, Feb, Dec; children over 7; no pets.

Frant TQ5835 Old Parsonage Frant, Tunbridge Wells, Kent TN3 9DX (01892) 750773 £52; 3 very pretty rms, 2 with four-posters. Just 2 miles from Tunbridge Wells is this carefully restored, imposing, former Georgian rectory with antiques, watercolours and plants in the elegant sitting rooms, a spacious Victorian conservatory, good food in the candlelit dining room, and a balustraded terrace overlooking the quiet, 3-acre garden; several nearby walks.

Rye TQ9220 Holloway House High St, Rye TN31 7JF (01797) 224748 £50; 6 charming, beamed and timbered rms. Interesting Tudor house built on a medieval vaulted cellar, with warmly welcoming owners, a residents' parlour with fine, original, Elizabethan oak panelling, and generous breakfasts and summer evening meals in the spacious dining room.

Mayfield TQ5827 Rose & Crown Fletching St, Mayfield TN20 6TE (01435) 872200 £48; 5 charming, beamed rms. Pretty, weatherboarded, 16th-c inn with unspoilt, oak-beamed bars, two log fires, lots of real ales, very good food, a cosy little restaurant; decorated with flowering tubs and baskets in summer; children over 7.

Fletching TQ4223 Griffin Fletching, Uckfield TN22 3SS (01825) 722890 £45; 4 rms, 3 with four-posters. Extremely civilised and genuinely old country inn in a pretty village on the edge of Sheffield Park; enthusiastic and friendly service, attractive, beamed rooms with a relaxed 1930s feel, very good, imaginative food, and lots of wines; cl 24–25 Dec.

Offham TQ4012 Ousedale House Offham, Lewes BN7 3QF (01273) 478680 *£44; 3 pretty rms. Victorian country house with good views, and 3½ acres of garden and woodland; friendly owners, a spacious lounge, and traditional cooking using home-grown, seasonal produce; children over 10.

Wadhurst TQ6431 Newbarn Wards Lane, Wadhurst TN5 6HP (01892) 782042 £44; 3 pretty rms. Tile-hung and carefully renovated, 18th-c farmhouse in a marvellous position by Bewl Water reservoir (15-mile circular walk, bikes for hire, watersports, picnic areas and so forth); very friendly, helpful owners, an inglenook fireplace in the attractive and comfortable sitting room, good breakfasts with home-made preserves, lakeside gardens; self-catering cottages also.

Ditchling TQ3215 Bull Ditchling, Hassocks BN6 8SY (01273) 843147 £42.50; 3 well equipped rms. Attractive 14th-c inn in a charming old village, with a relaxed atmosphere in the beamed main bar, three inglenook fireplaces, decent bar food, well kept real ales, and a nice garden; many nearby walks and views.

Arlington TQ5407 BATES GREEN HOUSE Bates Green, Arlington, Polegate BN26 6SH (01323) 482039 *£42; 3 rms. Originally an 18th-c gamekeeper's cottage, now a no-smoking farmhouse on a 130-acre, turkey and sheep farm; with beams and a log fire, home-made cake and tea on arrival, big breakfasts, good, Aga-cooked evening meals, and a neatly kept garden; close to the South Downs and Arlington Reservoir; cl Christmas; children over 10; no pets.

Eastbourne TV6199 SEACROFT 9 St Aubyns Rd, Eastbourne BN22 7AS (01323) 735433 £38; 6 rms, with showers. Small, comfortable and popular hotel close to the pier, theatres and shopping centre; with a comfortable lounge and homely, friendly owners; may close much of the winter – phone to check; children over 10.

Lewes TQ4110 DORSET ARMS 22 Malling St, Lewes BN7 2RD (01273) 477110 £37; 2 comfortable rms, showers. Popular, 17th-c pub with friendly service, good bar food (especially fresh fish Fri lunch), restaurant, a well equipped family room, and terraces.

Winchelsea TQ9017 NEW INN German St, Winchelsea TN36 4EN (01797) 226252 £36; 6 rms, 2 with own showers. Rambling but well organised, 18th-c pub in an interesting and historic village, with comfortable furnishings, hearty, popular food inc local, fresh fish specialities and home-made pies; good views of the interesting church from the bars.

Burwash TQ6724 ASHLANDS COTTAGE Burwash, Etchingham TN19 7HS (01435) 882207 £34; 2 rms, shared bthrm. In a lovely spot nr Batemans, this pretty cottage has marvellous views, a homely sitting room, an attractive dining room (no full suppers but pubs nearby), and a pretty garden; children over 12.

Gun Hill TQ5614 GUN Gun Hill, Horam, Heathfield TN21 0JU (01825) 872361 £34; 3 rms, 1 with own bthrm. Run by the same people for 22 years, this charmingly furnished pub in good walking country has a very nice country feel, lots of flowers, generous helpings of proper, home-made bar food, several wines by the glass, and real ales; very attractive surroundings and a big garden with swings for children; cl 25–26 Dec.

To see and do

★ † 🏠 👶 🐾 🏢 ⚲ **Alfriston** TQ5103 has thatched, tiled and timbered houses in a sheltered spot below the Downs – it strikes some as the prettiest village they've ever seen. Its fine CHURCH is built on a Saxon funeral barrow, by a large green just off the single main street. Nr the church, CLERGY HOUSE, a 14th-c priest's hall house, was the first building to be taken over by the National Trust. Carefully restored, it now gives a faithful impression of medieval life. Shop; house cl Nov–Mar, shop cl Jan–Mar; *£2; NT. One of the most engaging buildings in the village is the Star Inn, with its Old Bill, a bright-red, figurehead lion on one corner taken as a trophy from a 17th-c Dutch ship, and some intricate, painted, 15th-c carvings among its handsome timbering. In high summer the ice-cream eaters, teashops and curio shops somewhat blunt the village's appeal, but at quieter times it's very

special. In addition to the Star, the Market Cross and George are good for lunch. Nearby DRUSILLAS (up towards the A27) is an excellent little zoo, very popular with children, with well organised specialist areas inc an otter valley, the world of owls, meerkat mound and flamingo lagoon. They pack a lot into a small area, and it's all very well done. Good meals and snacks, shops, disabled access; cl 24–26 Dec; (01323) 870234; £4.95. Next door, the ENGLISH WINE CENTRE has long been a supporter of wines made in this country; the shop sells a good cross-section (limited hours Sun). Also a museum, and regional foods and crafts, with a regional food fair the first wknd of Sept. Snacks, shop, disabled access; cl am Sun, 23 Dec–2 Jan; (01323) 870164; free, £4.25 tours and tastings. On the other side of the Cuckmere Valley, the small village of Litlington TQ5201 is notable for its CHURCH, down a footpath – so small there can scarcely be room in it for a congregation of more than about 15. The Plough & Harrow here is good.

✝ ☗ 🏠 ! **Battle** TQ7415 takes its name from certainly the most celebrated and perhaps the most disorganised skirmish in English history, thrashed out here in 1066. It took just one chaotic day for William of Normandy to secure the Crown (which he did have a claim on), the Battle of Hastings ending with King Harold's death from an arrow in the eye. The BATTLEFIELD has a mile-long walk around it, with models demonstrating what happened. Four years after the bloodshed, William built BATTLE ABBEY on the site as penance, the altar supposedly on the very spot where Harold fell. Not too much is left of the original building, but later remains include the monks' dormitory and common room, and the great 14th-c gatehouse which looms over the small market square. There's an exhibition about the site, with an interactive video on daily monastic life. Snacks, shop, disabled access; cl 24–26 Dec, 1 Jan; (01424) 773792; £3. The main streets (carrying a fair bit of traffic, so not exactly peaceful) have a lot of attractive old buildings, some now antique shops and cafés; beyond them the town extends into spreading new estates. The local history MUSEUM (High St) has a diorama of the Battle of Hastings and a reproduction of the Bayeux Tapestry. Shop; cl am Sun, Oct–Easter; *80p. A similar exhibition can be seen at the old ALMONRY (High St), which also has teas and a pretty little garden. Shop, some disabled access; cl am Sun, 25–26 Dec; *£1. A few doors along, BUCKLEYS YESTERDAY WORLD is a lively exploration of the shopping and social habits of the past, with reconstructed shops, railway station and the like; lots of hands-on activities, and a nostalgic film show. Snacks, shop; may cl wkdys in Jan; (01424) 775378; £3.65. The George has decent food, and the CHURCH of St Mary has some 13th-c wall paintings.

🏠 ☗ **Bexhill** TQ7407 is a low-key, seaside town, an unlikely setting for a gem of Bauhaus architecture – the shoreside De La Rue Pavilion designed by Mendelsohn and Chermayeff. The Italian-run café opposite is very good value. BEXHILL MUSEUM OF COSTUME AND SOCIAL HISTORY Set in the delightful grounds of the Old Manor House up in the tiny 'Old Town', a good look at the period 1740–1960, augmenting the collection of costumes with many other domestic items and clothing accessories. Shop, disabled access; cl am wknds, Mon (exc bank hols and Jun–Aug), Nov–Easter; (01424) 210045; £1.

🏰 ☀ ☗ 🍴 🐟 🏠 ☗ **Bodiam** TQ7825 BODIAM CASTLE This dramatic old place is the perfect picture-book castle, and a classic example of 14th-c fortification at its peak. Virtually complete from the outside, the massive walls still rise sheer from the romantic moat, with round drum towers at each corner. Thanks to conservation-minded landowners a fair bit of the interior structure survives too, inc over 30 fireplaces and 28 garderobes; there are a couple of audio-visual shows in the towers. The view from the battlements is splendid; the best view of the castle itself is from up on the Ewhurst rd. Meals, snacks, shop, limited disabled access; cl Mon in Oct–Mar, 25–29 Dec; £2.50; NT. Nearby QUARRY FARM has a collection of steam engines and associated antique machinery in an attractive country setting, as well as animals, nature trails and play area. Meals, snacks, shop, disabled access; open wknds and school hols Easter–Sept; (01580) 830670; £3. Up the hill in Ewhurst, BODIAM BONSAI grow, show and sell these miniature trees. Subject to weather, 45-minute BOAT TRIPS run to the castle through peaceful countryside from Newenden (where the White Hart is a useful pub); not Oct–Mar; tel (01797) 280363 for times. *£6.50 return. This can link with a STEAMTRAIN on the Kent & East Sussex Railway (see Tenterden entry, in the West Kent section of the Kent chapter). The White Horse in Ewhurst Green above the castle has decent food.

★ 🏚 ✿ 🛏 🖾 ♪ ! † ⛪ ⬆ ❁ ✗ **Brighton** TQ3105 Despite its many modern blocks, huge shopping centre and vast, modern sports halls, Brighton still has plenty of glistening, white, Regency buildings dating from its fashionable days in the early 18th c. Its atmosphere gets a real kick from its vigorous young university and from its several language schools for foreign students. The most lively part is the Lanes – 17th-c fishermen's cottages squeezed together in narrow twisting byways, now crammed with jewellery and antique shops, restaurants and bars; English's here is entertaining for lunch. Top of anyone's itinerary should be Nash's flamboyant, Indianesque ROYAL PAVILION, the most eccentric of all royal palaces – a riot of chinoiserie inside. The apartments of Queen Victoria (the last monarch to own the Pavilion) have been restored to their full overblown glory, and the gardens to the original Regency plan. They've recently opened a previously unseen suite of rooms, and the whole building is now beautifully floodlit at night. Snacks, shop, disabled access to ground floor only; cl 25–26 Dec; (01273) 603005; £3.75. Around the corner, the Prince Regent's stables and riding school now house the town's excellent MUSEUM AND ART GALLERY (Church St), quite sumptuous in parts, with outstanding Art Nouveau and Art Deco objects ranging from vases, tapestries and sculpture to shoe heels and Salvador Dali's Mae West lips sofa. Also a good exhibition of non-Western art and culture. Snacks, disabled access to ground floor only; cl am Sun, Weds, 25–26 Dec, 1 Jan, Good Fri; free. BOOTH MUSEUM OF NATURAL HISTORY (Dyke Rd) Magnificent, well presented collection of animal skeletons (inc some dinosaur bones), as well as the Victorian collection of birds the museum was first built to house. Shop, disabled access; cl am Sun, Thurs, bank hols, 25–26 Dec, 1 Jan; free. PRESTON MANOR (Preston Rd) Entertaining and vivid illustration of life in Edwardian times, with fully furnished period rooms, and pleasant walled gardens. Shop; may be cl 1–2pm, am Sun and Mon, 25–26 Dec, Good Fri; (01273) 603005; £2.60. The SEA LIFE CENTRE (Marine Parade) has excellent, lively displays of creatures found off the British coast, with a walk-through underwater tunnel and pools where you can touch the creatures. Meals, snacks, shop, disabled access; cl 25 Dec; £4.50.

The modern MARINA, E of the centre, is lively in summer, with lots of boutiques, bars, tables out by the water and so forth. On Sun mornings there's a good MARKET by the station approach; you do have to get there well before breakfast for the bargains, as it's become a major source of supply for the countless Brighton antique dealers. There's no shortage of simple places to eat here, inc the Cricketers (Black Lion St), Greys (Southover St, Kemp Town), Mary Packs Cliftonville (good local fish; Hove Pl), and the Royal Standard (Queen's Rd). ST BARTHOLOMEW'S CHURCH is an odd building, like a huge brick barn.

Just W of Brighton proper is Hove TQ2905, the quieter half of the resort. The BRITISH ENGINEERIUM (Nevill Rd) out here has all sorts of road, locomotive and marine steam engines, as well as tools, models, and a restored Victorian water-pumping station; good, instructive displays. Snacks, shop, limited disabled access; cl wk before and over Christmas, 1 Jan, engines in steam first Sun in month and bank hols; (01273) 559583; £3. Nearby, the FOREDOWN TOWER COUNTRYSIDE CENTRE (Foredown Rd, Portslade) has a CAMERA OBSCURA (best on bright days) and nice, related displays, as well as a weather station with satellite images, walks, and splendid views. They can arrange visits to Portslade Old Manor, a ruined medieval house a short stroll away. Snacks, shop; cl Mon–Weds in winter (exc by arrangement), Christmas; (01273) 422540; £1.80. There's a WINDMILL with local history displays on Holmes Ave (open pm Sun and bank hols May–Sept; 50p), and on Waterloo Rd ST ANDREW'S CHURCH was designed by Sir Charles Barry; quite dull from the outside, but inside rather elaborate in places. The BARLOW COLLECTION at the university, just out of town at Falmer (off the A27 towards Lewes), is reckoned to be Europe's finest collection of Chinese ceramics. It's usually open Tues and Thurs (not Aug), but best to check first on (01273) 606755; free.

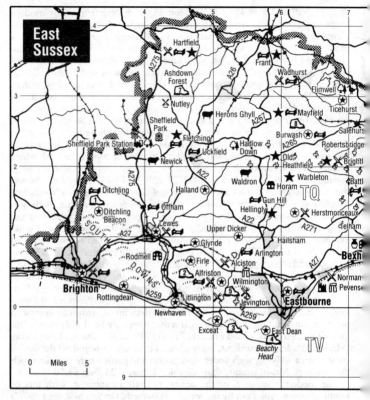

★ † ✿ 🏛 ❀ ✕ **Burwash** TQ6724 The single main street of this ridge village has many attractively restored, tile-hung cottages, inc a good antique centre and teashop, with lime trees along its brick pavement. The graveyard of the Norman-towered church gives fine views over the Dudwell Valley, and the Bell opposite is useful for lunch. Just below the village, BATEMANS was home to Rudyard Kipling from 1902 to 1936. His study is preserved much as it was then, as is the hefty pipework he installed for a hydroelectric plant to light the handsome, stone-built house. Lots of his possessions around the estate, inc his 1928 Rolls-Royce, and the attractive gardens have a quaint operating watermill (grinding flour every Sat at 2pm). A couple of friendly donkeys are paddocked opposite. Meals, snacks, shop, disabled access to ground floor only; cl Thurs, Fri (exc Good Fri), Nov–Mar; £3.50, Sun and

bank hols £4; NT. Their popular annual concert and firework display should be a bit special this year, as it's the Trust's centenary; it should be around the first wknd in Aug, tel (01435) 882302 to check. There are good, little-used walks along the wholly unspoilt valley from here, where you can look for Kipling landmarks such as Pooks Hill.

✿ ✕ ♿ **Ditchling Beacon** TQ3313 right by the road gives superb views all around, especially out over the villages and towns to the N; a nice area of preserved, sheep-cropped, unimproved downland, with chalk hill blue butterflies in summer. The village below is pleasant, with a decent MUSEUM; the Bull is recommended.

★ † ♿ 🏛 🚶 ♪ ✕ ✿ **Eastbourne** TV6199 Built largely in the second half of the 19th c, this civilised and restrained resort has a splendid line of imposing, white-faced edifices along its long seafront. The Duke of Devonshire

Services Museum (more interesting than the average military exhibition), as well as an aquarium grotto with marine and freshwater fish; open-air concerts every Weds and Fri Jun–Aug. Meals, snacks, shop; cl 6 Nov–Easter; (01323) 410300; *£1.70. Just along the front is a BUTTERFLY CENTRE; cl Nov–Easter; *£2.25. There's an enthusiastic little LIFEBOAT MUSEUM (cl Dec–Mar; free) on Grand Parade, and the Town Museum (High St, Old Town) has good, temporary exhibitions. Cl Mon, Tues, 24–26 Dec; 1 Jan; £2.

★ 🐑 🏛 ❀ **East Dean** TV5596 SEVEN SISTERS SHEEP CENTRE (Birling Manor Farm) Family-run, downland sheep farm with a compact visitor centre, and paved paths between pens of many breeds of sheep, some rare. Lambing (mid-Mar–early May), ancient flint barn with demonstrations of shearing (Jun–mid-July), spinning, milking and cheese-making, as well as plenty of young animals to cuddle, and baby lambs to bottle-feed. The farm shop sells sheep cheeses and yoghurts. Snacks, disabled access; cl am wkdys, all mid-Sept–mid-Mar, and some days in May – best to check first; (01323) 423302; £2. The village itself is prettily set around a sloping green, much improved by the recent closing of the roads around it, with an attractive pub, the Tiger. A lane past the farm continues to the BIRLING GAP TV5595, a cleft in the coastal cliffs famous since smuggling days, with a lighthouse and coastguard station (the Birling Gap Hotel is nicely set just above the shore); and on to BEACHY HEAD TV5995, the towering, cliffy edge of the Downs which is such a landmark for miles around: an unspoilt spot with terrific views, inc the lighthouse dwarfed far below. The BEACHY HEAD Countryside Centre has exhibitions and nature trails, and wild flower walks every summer Weds at 11.30am and 2.30pm. Cl winter wkdys, Christmas, poss all Jan and Feb; (01323) 430198; free.

🐘 🥄 ❀ **Exceat** TV5298 LIVING WORLD Set in two 18th-c barns in lovely countryside above Cuckmere Haven, a remarkable collection of small creatures and exotic insects, from snails through scorpions to

still owns much of the town, and as he prohibits seaside tat the place has a more dignified and solid feel than most seaside resorts. ST MARY'S CHURCH in the Old Town is lavish; next to it the Lamb is a nice old pub. MUSEUM OF SHOPS AND SOCIAL HISTORY (20 Cornfield Terrace) One of the most comprehensive collections of its type – 20 reconstructed and very well filled shops and rooms (inc an old seafarers tavern), and other nostalgic displays. Shop, disabled access on ground floor only; cl 25–26 Dec, Jan; (01323) 737143; £2. The WISH TOWER (King Edward's Parade) is one of the 103 Martello Towers built in case of French invasion; an exhibition looks at the history of this and similar towers, and there's a fascinating collection of model soldiers, some centuries old. Shop; cl late Sept–Easter; (01323) 410440; *£1.50. Another splendid tower, the REDOUBT FORTRESS (Royal Parade), houses the Sussex Combined marine life. Meals, snacks, shop, disabled access; cl Nov–mid-Mar exc wknds and school hols; (01323) 870100; £2.30. It's surrounded by the SEVEN SISTERS COUNTRY PARK, running down to the sea by the River Cuckmere – protected meadow, saltings, shingle and the flanking chalk headlands; you can hire bikes. The roomy Golden Galleon does good food and brews its own beer (besides selling other fine beers such as the award-winning Brewery on Sea Riptide which comes from Lancing and is not, as our sister publication *The Good Pub Guide* wrongly stated, brewed here).

★ ⊞▣❀✝ Firle TQ4707 is an attractive, quiet village, with a good pub, the Ram. FIRLE PLACE Beautiful house, essentially Tudor but remodelled in the 18th c, with some real treasures of European and English painting, and wonderful furnishings. Also, interesting mementos of General Gage, commander of the British forces at the start of the American War of Independence. Meals, snacks, shop; open pm Weds, Thurs and Sun May–Sept, as well as Easter, spring and summer bank hols; (01273) 858335; £3.50. Try and go on the first Weds in the month, their Connoisseur Days, when there are longer, unguided tours, and more rooms open. The delightful, 17th/18th-c CHARLESTON FARMHOUSE TQ4906 (over towards Alciston, where the Rose Cottage has good home-cooking) was the home of Duncan Grant and Clive and Vanessa Bell; decorated by them, it and its magical garden still evoke the atmosphere of those Bloomsbury days. Teas Sat, shop; open pm Weds–Sun and bank hols Apr–Oct, poss am too 19 July–10 Sept; (01323) 811265; *£4.50. Fri (exc 19 July–10 Sept) is Connoisseur Day, when tours are longer and children under 8 aren't admitted; these cost £6. Off the A27, a couple of miles E, BERWICK CHURCH TQ5105 has murals by the Bloomsbury Group; the Cricketers has nice home-cooking. See also Rodmell entry, below.

🍃 ♔ Flimwell TQ7131 BIRD PARK (Hawkhurst Rd) Enthusiastic wildfowl centre with over 110 species from all over the world. Also, a woodland walk (good at bluebell time). Snacks, shop; cl Mon (exc bank and school hols), Oct–Mar; (01580) 879202; *£2.95.

⊞❀✝ Glynde TQ4509 GLYNDE PLACE Elizabethan manor house in a beautiful setting, extensively remodelled inside in the 18th c. Portraits and mementos give a good grounding in the family history, while outside are pleasantly wild parklands and lawns. Snacks; open pm Weds, Thurs, Sun and bank hols May–Sept; (01273) 858224; £3, less for garden only. There's a neat, neo-Palladian CHURCH nearby, the Trevor Arms has decent food, and there are nice walks.

♔ Hadlow Down TQ5323 WILDERNESS WOOD Acres of working woodland, good for learning about forests and their wildlife, or just for a pleasant stroll. Lots of trails, displays on timber and its uses, and picnic and play areas. Snacks, shop (they make chestnut furniture and other goods), disabled access; (01825) 830977; *£1.60.

⊞▣👶🦆🐑🚐 Halland TQ4815 BENTLEY WILDFOWL AND MOTOR MUSEUM Tudor farmhouse converted into a Palladian mansion, filled with fine furnishings and paintings, inc 150 watercolours by local artist Philip Rickman. The motor museum has gleaming veteran, Edwardian and vintage vehicles, while the lakes and ponds that surround it are home to a countless variety of exotic wildfowl. Also, a small, children's farm, and a recently extended, narrow-gauge railway. Snacks, shop, disabled access; cl all Dec and Jan, and wkdys Nov–late Mar, house cl am and winter; (01825) 840573; £3.60. The Forge is useful for lunch.

★✝⊞🏚▣👶❀✒!♔ Hastings TQ8205 The Old Town up on the cliff at the E end is very attractive – two medieval churches, a couple of streets with raised pavements, lots of medieval buildings, and relatively unobtrusive, more recent infilling. Down below, the fishermen still haul their boats up on to the beach and sell excellent fresh fish by the unusual, tall, black, wooden net huts. The rest of the town is a typical, busy shopping town, with 19th-c resort buildings nearer the seafront, seaside hotels and B & Bs, a good promenade, pier and shingle beach.

HASTINGS CASTLE AND 1066 Bracingly set above crumbling cliffs, the evocative ruins of the Norman castle are close to the site of William the Conqueror's first motte and bailey castle in England. In the grounds is a lively audio-visual exhibition on the battle and its aftermath. Shop; cl 3 Jan–4 Feb; (01424) 422964; *£2.50. The town MUSEUM AND ART GALLERY (John's Pl, Cambridge Rd) is a little out of the centre, but worth a look for its new American-Indian gallery, with interesting weapons, clothing and art. Children may prefer the dinosaur gallery. Shop; cl am Sun, Christmas; free. Other useful museums include the MUSEUM OF LOCAL HISTORY (Old Town Hall, High St), with quite a maritime emphasis (cl Mon, Oct–Mar exc pm Sun; free), the FISHERMEN'S MUSEUM (Rock-a-Nore, Harbour), interestingly housed in a former fishermen's chapel (cl am wknds, and Nov–mid-May; free), and, a few doors along, the SHIPWRECK HERITAGE CENTRE, with an audio-visual display of 500 years of dramatic wrecks, and plenty of rescued treasures (cl am Apr–Jun, all Oct–Easter; £2). Down the same road, the SEA LIFE CENTRE is another in the lively chain – the usual, reliable formula joined here by a high-tech 3-D film. Snacks, shop, disabled access; cl 25 Dec; £4.25. HASTINGS EMBROIDERY (in the Town Hall, Queen's Rd) Ambitious, 80-yard tapestry depicting great events in British history, created by the Royal School of Needlework: also dolls and a scale model of the famous battle itself. Shop, disabled access; cl wknds and Christmas wk; *£1.25.

SMUGGLERS ADVENTURE A labyrinth of caverns and passages deep below West Hill, with models, a museum and life-size tableaux illustrating life for an 18th-c smuggler. Very good for children. Shop, disabled access; cl 25 Dec; (01424) 422964; £3.60. At each end of the cliffs is an unusual, sloping, tracked lift down to sea level (55p). The First In Last Out in the Old Town has interesting food.

✿ 🏠 ! ☉ 🞄 Herstmonceux TQ6312 Extensive gardens around a very handsome, 15th-c, brick-built CASTLE (SE of the village), with nature trails, a hands-on science centre, and astronomy displays in the former buildings of Greenwich Royal Observatory. Snacks, shop, disabled access; cl Nov–Mar; (01323) 834444; £2.50. Nearby on Hailsham Rd, Thomas Smith demonstrates the local art of trug BASKET-MAKING. Cl 1–2 pm, wknds, Christmas; (01323) 832137; 35p. The Ash Tree over at Brownbread Street has good home-cooking.

🏠 Horam TQ5818 is the home of MERRYDOWN VINTAGE CIDER; you can tour the factory, with tastings and an audio-visual show. Tours at 10am, 11.15am, 2pm, and 3.15pm Mon–Fri; cl Christmas; best to book, (01435) 812254; £2. The Gun is useful for food.

★ 🏠 🞄 ⚘ ☉ 🏠 Lewes TQ4110 The administrative capital of East Sussex, this is a pleasantly unrushed country town below the quarried white edge of the South Downs. It has some attractive old buildings, mainly Georgian though with a few older, stone-built or timber-framed specimens, particularly along its steep main street and in the little narrow alleys and other streets alongside. This is where you'll see Sussex tile-hanging at its best; there's also quite a lot of 'mathematical tiling' – sham bricks over timbered buildings to make them look more progressive. There are several decent antique shops, and a pleasing complex of CRAFT SHOPS in a former candlemaker's factory in Market Lane. Café (cl Sun). The Norman CASTLE is unusual for being built on not one but two artificial mounds (Lincoln is the only other such place we know of). Much of the surviving walling still stands, and the best view of the town is obtained from the roof of the keep. On the same site, a MUSEUM has displays on prehistoric, Roman, Saxon and medieval Sussex, with an audio-visual show on the town's history. Shop; cl Christmas; (01273) 486290; *£2.80. ANNE OF CLEVES HOUSE (Southover High St) Not all Henry VIII's wives came away from the marriage with anything to show for it, but Anne of Cleves was certainly ahead of the others, receiving this fine 16th-c house as part of her divorce settlement. She may never even have come here, but its rooms give a good idea of regional life over the following two centuries. Shop; cl am Sun, Dec; (01273) 474610; *£1.60. You can get a combined ticket for here and the castle complex for £3.50. The Dorset Arms, Pelham Arms and Snowdrop are useful for lunch. Local brewers Harveys have a good shop attached to the brewery on Cliffe High St. From Bell Lane, on the SW edge, you can follow the old Juggs Road track – used by the Brighton fishwives – up past Kingston and the downland nature reserve by Newmarket Hill to the outskirts of Brighton itself.

Newhaven TQ4401 NEWHAVEN FORT Built 120 years ago in case of French attack, this is a big place to explore, with underground installations and tunnels burrowing into the cliffs, and super views from its ramparts. Comprehensive museum, and an assault course for children. Snacks, shop; cl Oct–Mar; (01273) 517622; £2.95. GARDEN PARADISE AND PLANET EARTH (Avis Rd) Garden centre with a lively exhibition on the last few million years of evolution, complete with an earthquake experience and life-size dinosaurs. Also desert, tropical and subtropical plant houses, and a miniature railway. Meals, snacks, shops, disabled access, cl 25–26 Dec; (01273) 512123; £2.99 for exhibition. You can take the four-hour FERRY TRIP to Dieppe in France from here. The harbourside Hope has decent food.

Northiam TQ8125 GREAT DIXTER Timbered 15th-c house, carefully restored and added to by Lutyens in the early part of this century. The great 15th-c hall is particularly worth a look, its hammerbeams carved with armorial bearings. The gardens, also designed by Lutyens, are attractive; originally arranged as a series of distinct areas, they were later stocked more informally with interesting plants by the gardening writer Christopher Lloyd who lives here. Plant sales; house and gardens open pm Apr–10 Oct (open earlier Sun in July and Aug), cl Mon exc bank hols;

(01797) 253160; £3.50, £2.50 gardens only. Another fine old building here is the partly 15th-c BRICKWALL HOUSE, with splendid 17th-c plastered ceilings and very pleasant formal gardens. Shop, disabled access; open pm Sat and bank hols Easter–Sept; (01797) 223329; *£2.

Nutley TQ4427 The 300-year-old WINDMILL here is the only working, open trestle post mill in the country, saved from decline by enthusiastic locals before such action became more common (until then it was precariously propped up by telegraph poles). Open last Sun of month Apr–Sept; 60p. The Griffin at Fletching is the nearest place for a good lunch.

Pevensey TQ6404 PEVENSEY CASTLE Formidable castle based around a huge 4th-c Roman fort, with massive bastions and walls of Roman masonry still up to 30ft high in places. The Norman keep was built by William the Conqueror, and you can see interesting interior details inc fireplaces, dungeons and an oubliette. Shop, some disabled access; cl 1–2pm, winter Mon and Tues 24–26 Dec, 1 Jan; (01323) 762604; £1.80. The Royal Oak & Castle, right by the gate, is useful for a bite to eat, and the nearby Smugglers is an appropriate-feeling sort of place.

Rodmell TQ4106 MONKS HOUSE Just a quiet, lived-in village house, in a pleasant village, but a beautifully kept place of pilgrimage for followers of the Bloomsbury Group, as Leonard and Virginia Woolf lived here from 1919 until their deaths. Her writing hut is in the garden. Open pm Weds and Sat Apr–Oct; £2; NT. The Juggs at Kingston on the way from Lewes is good for lunch.

★ **Rottingdean** TQ3702 is a pretty place worth a stop. Enthusiastic locals are reponsible for preserving both the handsome Georgian grange, now a MUSEUM (cl am Sun, Christmas; free), and the pleasant, 2-acre KIPLING GARDENS – well restored, Victorian gardens (free) named after the author who lived here for five years from 1897. Burne-Jones was a resident for a while too, designing the windows built by William Morris for the Early English CHURCH.

★ ✝ 🏠 ☀ ♪ ♬ ♪ ✔ 🐑 📷 Rye TQ9220 is an enchanting town, easily worth spending a day or longer wandering through. Before the wind and sea currents did their work, it was virtually surrounded by sea, and as one of the Cinque Ports played an important part in providing men and ships for coastal defence – most notably in the 13th and 14th c. The town is built on a hill crowned by a partly Norman CHURCH (with a very early turret-clock, two quarter-jacks by it striking the quarter-hours); up here the largely cobbled streets still follow a 12th/13th-c narrow layout, with most of the houses lining them dating from the 16th c. The views from up here are lovely, and steep Mermaid St, in particular, is famously photogenic (the Mermaid itself is a grand old inn). The town is still almost encircled by three rivers, and its unique, peaceful atmosphere has inspired artists in all media. Readers love coming here, mainly because despite its many charms it remains relatively unspoilt. The HERITAGE CENTRE on Strand Quay is a useful introduction, with a sound and light show based around an intricate town model (not winter wkdys). Shop, disabled access; cl 25 Dec; free, sound and light show £2. RYE MUSEUM (Gun Gdn) Striking 13th-c Ypres Tower (as in Wipers), originally built to defend the town, but later used as a courthouse and prison. It's now a local history museum, with good views from the roof terrace. Shop; cl wkdys Nov–Mar, Christmas; *£1.50. The nearby Ypres Castle pub has decent food in a nice setting. LAMB HOUSE (West St) was built in 1723 for James Lamb, who, like his son, was mayor of the town. It's chiefly devoted now to mementos of the author Henry James, who lived here from 1898 to 1916; after his death E F Benson, who also became mayor, moved here. Open pm Weds and Sat Apr–Oct; *£2; NT.

The town is full of antique shops, book shops and craft shops – mostly good stuff, not tat. The Hope & Anchor is useful for food. The HARBOUR, because of the build-up of shingle along this coast, is now a mile or two from the town, though yachts and fishing boats do still come right up the river to the pretty quay. The Inkerman Arms has good fresh fish. Tony Easton will take you SEA FISHING for the day; (01797) 252104; from £20. The expanse of shingle stretching around the river mouth is now preserved as a NATURE RESERVE, with hides to watch the sea birds. CAMBER CASTLE is a massive Tudor fort, originally built right on the coast, but now stranded a mile or so inshore by the encroaching shingle. Guided tours usually leave the Heritage Centre at 10am and 2pm Sun, Weds and Fri in summer; best to check first on (01797) 226696. Beyond it, the Ship on Winchelsea Beach is a welcoming refuge.

❀ **Sheffield Park** TQ4124 Wonderful 200-acre garden landscaped by Capability Brown, since then imaginatively planted with many varieties of tree unknown to him, especially chosen for their autumn colours; each of the several hundred black gums, for instance, seems to flare into a different colour in Sept and Oct, despite their all being a single species (*Nyssa sylvatica*). Also marvellous rhododendrons, azaleas and waterlilies on the lakes. Snacks, shop, disabled access; cl Mon (exc bank hols) all year, Tues Nov–Dec, all mid-Dec–Feb, and wkdys in Mar; £4 May and Oct, otherwise £3.50; NT. The Griffin at Fletching nearby is good for lunch.

🚂 🚃 **Sheffield Park Station** TQ4023 BLUEBELL LINE The earliest preserved steam railway in Britain, and one of the best, with splendid stations decked out with period advertisements and wonderful, genuine period carriages; 9-mile trips through Horsted Keynes to Kingscote (where there are period bus connections to BR East Grinstead). The journey goes past woodlands that are a mass of bluebells in late spring, usually at their best in mid-May – hence the name of the line. Part of the station is a museum housing the region's largest railway collection, inc some 30 locomotives. Pullman dining specials, Santa specials, shop, café; some trains all year, daily Jun–Sept – best to tel (01825) 723777 for dates and times; £7. The Sloop, at Scaynes Hill not far off, is good for lunch.

❃ 🏛 ❃ ★ 🍎 **Ticehurst** TQ6930 PASHLEY MANOR 8 acres of beautifully restored, mainly Victorian, formal gardens around the handsome house once owned by the Boleyn family. Ancient trees, fine shrubs, ponds, moat and good views; very relaxed, charming and peaceful. This year they plan a Festival of Tulips to celebrate the 400th anniversary of their first bloom in England (11–16 May), and an old-fashioned Rose Festival in Jun. Snacks in fine weather (served outside), plant sales, limited disabled access; open Tues–Thurs and Sat Easter–mid-Oct; (01580) 200692; *£3. The village is attractive; up a side road at Three Legged Cross, Maynards has good pick-your-own and the Bull is a fine old place for lunch.

🏛 ✝ ✿ ✗ ♁ **Upper Dicker** TQ5509 MICHELHAM PRIORY Charming, 16th-c house based around a 13th-c Augustinian priory, with a 500-year-old gatehouse by the moat (which has plenty of waterfowl). Interesting furniture, tapestries and local ironwork, as well as crafts, a working watermill, and rope-making museum. Meals, snacks, shop, disabled access to ground floor only; cl Nov–Mar exc Sun in Mar and Nov; (01323) 844224; *£3.50. The Plough is good for lunch.

🏛 **Wilmington** TQ5403 Famous for its LONG MAN, a gigantic chalk-cut figure so far impossible to date – guesses hover anywhere between the early 18th c and the Bronze Age. The Giant's Rest has good home-cooking, and the Sussex Ox at Milton Street is a pleasant family pub.

★ ♪ ✝ **Winchelsea** TQ9017 Storms and French raids pretty much put paid to this once flourishing port's importance; today it's a quiet and pleasant little place, dwarfed by the distances between the three surviving town gates around it. The ROYAL MILITARY CANAL runs from here to Hythe in Kent, a never-used Napoleonic defence that was meant as a sort of glorified coastal moat – now a peaceful spot for coarse fishermen. The New Inn is good for lunch, and the tranquil CHURCH has some fine, old stained glass and medieval tombs.

🐑 Among several flourishing **vineyards** here, notable ones that do tours or vineyard trails and tastings include ST GEORGE'S at Waldron TQ5419, well laid out for visitors, with changing art and craft exhibitions in a 15th-c tithe barn, craft shop, adopt-a-vine scheme, and a charming village amid fine scenery. Cl wkdys Nov–Easter, Christmas; (01435) 812156; free, tours £1.50. BARNSGATE MANOR, at Herons Ghyll TQ4828, which also has llamas, donkeys, and an attractive restaurant with great views from the terrace. Shop, good disabled facilities; cl Christmas; (01825) 713366; £1.50 self-guided trails. BARKHAM MANOR, nr Newick TQ4321, appealingly set around a striking manor house with an 18th-c thatched barn. Shop, disabled access; cl Mon, and Dec-Mar; (01825) 722103; £1.50; and CARR TAYLOR at Westfield TQ8115, one of England's most successful commercial vineyards, producing sparkling wine as well as still. Disabled access; cl wknds Jan and Feb, Christmas; (01424) 752501; £1.25. See also the English Wine Centre, in Alfriston entry above.

★ **Attractive villages**, all with decent pubs, include Brightling TQ6921 (though Jack Fullers on Oxley's Green is now more restaurant than pub), Fletching TQ4223, Frant TQ5835, Hartfield TQ4735, Hellingly TQ5812, Mayfield TQ5827, Old Heathfield TQ5920 (not Heathfield itself, a mile or two W), Robertsbridge TQ7323, Salehurst TQ7424, Sedlescombe TQ7718 (where there's an unusual organic vineyard), and Warbleton TQ6018 (more pre-1750 Sussex barns here than anywhere else in the county).

Walks

The South Downs Way has the area's best or, at least, most expansive walks. There are fine stretches with distant views up over **Ditchling Beacon** TQ8813 ⛰-1 (easy access from the road) and **Firle Beacon** TQ4805 ⛰-2, a lovely walk above Firle, E of Lewes. At Alfriston TQ5103, the Way splits into two. The coastal route joins the sea at Cuckmere Haven TV5196 for a march along the **Seven Sisters** TV5396 ◠-3, a series of chalk cliffs which, together with Beachy Head, are the spectacular finale of the South Downs; for an interesting circular route you can head inland by Friston Forest TV5499, Westdean TV5299 and East Dean TV5597. **Beachy Head** TV5995 ◠-4, the giant of these cliffs, has a lighthouse far below, and is within close reach of Eastbourne TV6199.

The inland South Downs Way route from Alfriston, bound for Jevington TQ5601 and Eastbourne, passes **Lullington Heath** TQ5401 ◠-5, a rare survival of downland untampered with by modern farming practices, and managed as a National Nature Reserve for its chalkland and heathland flora; a diversion to Wilmington TQ5403 gives a view of the enigmatic chalk figure, the Long Man of Wilmington.

From the Old Town in the E of Hastings TQ8205, a path climbs on to the sandstone cliffs for a rugged couple of miles towards **Fairlight Cove** TQ8711 ◠-6. The coast here has a tumbled appearance and cliff-falls occur occasionally.

The **Ashdown Forest** ◠-7 is a major inland attraction, part forest, part heathland. Don't be put off by the OS map: there are far more walking routes than it suggests. Sandy tracks, clumps of Scots pines, secretive glades and exhilarating views comprise the key factors. It looks just like the E H Sheppard drawings for A A Milne's *Winnie the Pooh* stories, which were set here. Five Hundred Acre Wood TQ4832 is the Hundred Acre Wood of Pooh's world, and with a little searching you can find, SE of Hartfield TQ4735, the Pooh-sticks Bridge and, by the B2026, Gills Lap TQ4631 (the 'enchanted place' at the top of the forest, nr Piglet's house), where a memorial to Milne has been placed nr the triangulation point. Camp Hill TQ0311, nr Nutley Windmill, is one of the best walking areas in the Ashdown Forest. Handy pubs for Ashdown Forest walks include the Forester's Arms at Fairwarp TQ4646 and Hatch at Coleman's Hatch TQ4533.

There is very pleasant, hilly terrain around **Mayfield** TQ5827 ◠-8, with a reasonable network of paths. East Sussex shares Bewl Water with Kent – see West Kent section of Kent chapter.

Driving

Attractive downland routes include: the clifftop road E from Fairlight to Winchelsea; the busy A27 between Polegate and Brighton along the N slope of the South Downs, for the views of the Downs themselves; the B2116 from Offham to Ditchling, for quieter Downs views; the back road S of Ditchling up over the Downs towards Brighton, for terrific views over both the Weald and then Brighton itself and the coast.

In the Weald, the back road from Northiam through Ewhurst Green and Bodiam towards Hurst Green, but taking the southwards loop through Salehurst, is good. The B2096, from just W of Battle towards Heathfield, gives views S to Beachy Head from its highest points, nr Netherfield and just before Dallington. Off this road, any of the narrow side roads N into the countryside between Burwash and Dallington take you into what is probably the most unspoilt expanse of hilly, Wealden woods and pasture anywhere.

In the Ashdown Forest, the B2026 right across its heart is pleasant.

Where to eat

Herstmonceux TQ6312 SUNDIAL (01323) 832217 Pretty, 17th-c cottage with invariably excellent food inc lovely vegetables and delicious puddings, a praiseworthy wine list, a relaxed atmosphere, warm and friendly service, and a terrace and garden for summer eating; cl pm Sun, Mon, last 3 wks Aug, 25 Dec–mid-Jan. **£33 dinner, £23.50 lunch.**
Hastings TQ8109 ROSERS 64 Eversfield Pl, St Leonards (01424) 712218

Extremely rewarding, imaginative food (lots of fish and game in season) in a cosy little restaurant opposite the pier; fine wines, too; cl Sun and Mon, am Sat, 1st wk Jan, 1st wk Aug; disabled access. £30.

Wadhurst TQ6630 SPINDLEWOOD COUNTRY HOUSE Wallcrouch (01580) 200430 Good, interesting, country cooking from a varied menu in this Victorian hotel with friendly service, a thoughtful wine list, chatty bar and comfortable restaurant; 5 acres of gardens; cl bank hols, Christmas. £28.50.

Jevington TQ5601 HUNGRY MONK The Street (01323) 482178 Under the same ownership (and many of the same staff) for 26 years, this popular, candlelit evening restaurant (they do Sun lunch) has 3 sitting rooms, a bar and a little dining room, open fires, beams, a friendly, dinner-partyish atmosphere, and good, interesting food; cl bank hols, exc Good Fri. £25.

Alfriston TQ5103 MOONRAKERS (01323) 870472 Reliably enjoyable food in this cosy little cottage, with a log fire, good wine list, and friendly staff; cl pm Sun, 14–31 Jan; children over 6. £23.60/£3.45.

Hartfield TQ4735 ANCHOR (01892) 770424 Relaxed and friendly pub on the edge of Ashdown Forest, with impressive seafood as well as other satisfying dishes, well kept real ales, friendly, quick service, a chatty, heavily beamed bar, and popular front verandah. £20|£2.50/£4.75.

Brighton TQ3105 IL TEATRO 7 New Rd (01273) 202158 Friendly and enjoyable, Italian restaurant next to the Theatre Royal; cl Sun; disabled access. £18/£5.25.

Alciston TQ5005 ROSE COTTAGE (01323) 870377 In the same family for over 30 years, this charming, wisteria-covered cottage is popular for its home-made, traditional food with daily specials that change twice a day, fine, fresh local fish, real ales and good house wines; small no-smoking evening restaurant; cl 25–26 Dec. £17|£3.50/£5.25.

Brighton TQ3105 IL BISTRO 6 Market St, The Lanes (01273) 324584 Friendly place with a wide choice of popular food, decent wine list, and efficient, friendly service; cl 25–26 Dec; children over 4. £16/£4.50 for 2-course lunch.

Litlington TQ5201 LITLINGTON TEAROOMS (01323) 870222 Established 150 years ago, these tearooms still keep their quaint, Victorian elegance, with seating on an attractive sheltered lawn under a copper beach or ginko, in renovated beach huts with open fronts, or tearoom/restaurant; colourful hanging baskets and flowering tubs, quick, efficient service, and snacks, proper English teas, and weekend French lunches; handy for Alfriston; cl Oct–Apr; disabled access. £16|£1.40/£4.75.

Lewes TQ4110 LA CUCINA Station Rd (01273) 476707 Attractive Italian restaurant with good, popular food; cl Sun, am Mon–Weds, 2 wks over Christmas. £14.95/£8.50.

Brightling TQ6821 JACK FULLERS Oxley's Green (0142 482) 212 Smart dining pub with interesting pies, fine steamed puddings, unusual side dishes, some vegetarian choices, excellent wines (English ones, too), and pleasant service; cl Mon, Tues, winter Weds, pm Sun. /£8.50.

Norman's Bay TQ6805 STAR (01323) 762648 Friendly, ex-smugglers pub with a spaciously modernised bar, friendly atmosphere and huge helpings of popular food inc lots of puddings; paths inland to the marshy nature reserve. £3/£5.50.

WEST SUSSEX

Magnificent gardens, impressive houses, many other places of interest; some luxurious hotels.

West Sussex has some of England's most gorgeous gardens, the larger ones beautifully laid out in settings of great natural beauty, with many of the finest specimen trees and shrubs to be found anywhere, and many species which are either too tender or simply too rare to turn up elsewhere. The best are Wakehurst Place at Ardingly, Leonardslee at Lower Beeding, Nymans at Handcross and Borde Hill near Haywards Heath. The open-air museum at Singleton and the chalk-pits museum at Amberley are both excellent. Arundel Castle, Goodwood House, Parham House at Pulborough, Petworth House and Uppark are all marvellous places to visit, and the Roman villas at Bignor and Fishbourne are very splendid in their way. A refreshing change is Rejectamenta at East Wittering. Chichester and Arundel are both rewarding places to spend time strolling around, and the area has many attractive villages.

There's a good range of countryside, from the rich woodlands up in the north towards Haslemere, to the downlands north of Chichester, while the great sea inlet of Chichester Harbour has some very quiet places by its shore.

There are some lovely hotels, at a price, as well as a decent selection of less expensive places to stay.

Where to stay

East Grinstead TQ3938 GRAVETYE MANOR , East Grinstead RH19 4LJ (01342) 810567 *£208; 18 lovely rms. Elizabethan manor house in beautiful grounds, with antiques and fine paintings in the spacious, panelled public rooms, an excellent restaurant using home-grown produce (inc spring water and free-range eggs) and their own home-smoked fish and meats, an exceptional wine list, and a relaxed, almost old-fashioned atmosphere; children over 7.

Turners Hill TQ3435 ALEXANDER HOUSE East St, Turners Hill, Crawley RG10 4QD (01342) 714914 £150; 15 luxurious rms. Standing in 135 acres, this magnificent country mansion has grand day rooms with hand-painted, silk wall panels, crystal chandeliers, fine antiques and paintings, courteous, friendly service, lovely flowers, and good, modern cooking; no facilities for children under 7; no pets.

Lower Beeding TQ2227 SOUTH LODGE Brighton Rd, Lower Beeding, Horsham RG13 6PS (01403) 891711 £110; 39 individually decorated, spacious rms. Fine, creeper-clad, Victorian house in 90-acre grounds with marvellous views; open fires, antiques, chandeliers and panelling in the elegant public rooms, helpful staff, good modern cooking in the restful restaurant, and carefully chosen wines; tennis, croquet and clay-pigeon shooting; disabled access.

Chichester SU8605 DOLPHIN & ANCHOR West St, Chichester PO19 1QE (01243) 785121 £102; 49 rms. Handsome hotel, originally two medieval inns, opposite the cathedral; comfortable lounge, friendly service, and good food in the all-day coffee house and elegant restaurant.

Rusper TQ2037 GHYLL MANOR High St, Rusper, Horsham RH12 4XX (01293) 871571 £97.90; 25 rms in the main house, converted stable block or extension. Fine old manor house in 40 acres of grounds, with a log fire in the oak-panelled library-cum-lounge, and an attractive, candlelit restaurant; tennis and croquet; disabled access.

Amberley TQ0211 AMBERLEY CASTLE Amberley, Arundel BN18 9ND (01798) 831992 £95; 14 well equipped, charming rms. Magnificent, 900-year-old castle with day rooms filled with suits of armour and weapons as well as antiques, roaring fires and panelling; friendly service, imaginative cooking and well kept gardens; disabled access.

Climping TQ0002 BAILIFFSCOURT Climping, Littlehampton BN17 5RW (01903) 723511 £95; 24 rms, many with four-poster beds and open log fires in winter. Mock 13th-c manor built only 60 years ago, but with tremendous character – fine old iron-studded doors, huge fireplaces, heavy beams and so forth, and set in 22 acres of pastureland and walled gardens; outdoor swimming pool, tennis and croquet.

Cuckfield TQ3025 OCKENDEN MANOR Ockenden Lane, Cuckfield RH17 5LD (01444) 416111 *£95; 22 rms. Dating from 1520, this carefully extended manor house has antiques, fresh flowers and an open fire in the comfortable sitting room, a cosy bar, good, modern cooking in the fine, panelled restaurant, and lovely views from the neatly kept garden.

Bosham SU8003 MILLSTREAM Bosham Lane, Bosham, Chichester PO18 8HL (01243) 573234 *£89; 29 rms, some refurbished this year. Warm and friendly, small hotel in a picturesque fishing village, with an attractive bar and lounge, very good food using fresh local produce, a decent wine list, and a garden through which the stream runs; close to the 1,000-year-old church; disabled access.

Midhurst SU8821 SPREAD EAGLE, Midhurst GU29 9NH (01730) 816911 £86.50; 41 rms. Historic old inn dating back in part to 1430, with an impressive, beamed and timbered lounge, a dramatic fireplace and imposing leaded-light windows, handsome furnishings, a neatly modernised, airy, barrel-vaulted cellar bar, very good food, and friendly service; disabled access.

Storrington TQ0814 ABINGWORTH HALL Storrington, Pulborough RH20 3EF (01798) 813636 *£80; 20 rms. Country hotel with a warm, family atmosphere, good food using the freshest local produce and breakfasts with home-baked bread and croissants, decent wines, excellent service, an oak-panelled sitting room, open fire in the cocktail lounge, and a conservatory; the grounds have a small, outdoor heated swimming pool, hard tennis court, 9-hole pitch and putt course, croquet, boules, and coarse fishing; disabled access.

Arundel TQ0107 NORFOLK ARMS High St, Arundel BN18 9AD (01903) 882101 £73; 34 rms. Comfortable Georgian coaching inn with log fires in the pleasant bars, good food and service, and a nice, old-fashioned atmosphere.

Chichester SU8605 BEDFORD Southgate, Chichester PO19 1DP (01243) 785766 £65; 22 attractive rms. Family-run, Georgian hotel in the centre of the city, with a friendly atmosphere, and a comfortable, no-smoking lounge and restaurant opening out on to a quiet terrace.

Bramber TQ1710 OLD TOLLGATE The Street, Bramber, Steyning BN44 3WE (01903) 879494 £60; 31 good rms. On the site of the old tollhouse, this neatly kept hotel has a popular, carvery-style restaurant, a small lounge, and friendly staff; disabled access.

Chichester SU8605 SUFFOLK HOUSE 3 East Row, Chichester PO19 1PD (01243) 778924 £59; 10 comfortable, spacious rms. Warm and friendly, 18th-c town house in a quiet back street; with a relaxed atmosphere, extremely helpful, thoughtful service, very good food inc lovely breakfasts, and a little walled garden; close to the cathedral, theatre and station; they are kind to children; disabled access.

Sutton SU9715 WHITE HORSE The Street, Sutton, Pulborough RH20 1PS (017987) 221 *£58; 6 comfortable rms. Attractive, creeper-covered inn in a pretty village nr Bignor Roman villa, with log fires, a pleasant garden, and good South Downs walks; children welcome but limited facilities for them.

Fittleworth TQ0118 SWAN Fittleworth, Pulborough RG20 1EN (01798) 865479 £55; 10 rms. Handsome 15th-c inn with a big inglenook log fire in the comfortable lounge, friendly service, decent food, an attractive, panelled side room, and a sheltered back lawn; good nearby walks.

Bognor Regis TQ2623 ROYAL NORFOLK, Bognor Regis PO21 2LH (01243) 826222 *£50; 51 rms. Comfortable Regency hotel on the seafront, with good food and pleasant service.

Rogate SU8023 MIZZARDS Rogate, Petersfield GU31 5HS (01730) 821656 *£46; 3 rms. 16th-c house in a quiet country setting, with a comfortable and elegant sitting room, a vaulted dining room, outside swimming pool, landscaped gardens and a lake, and fine farmland views; no evening meals and no smoking; cl Christmas; children over 8.

West Hoathly TQ3532 Coneybury Hook Lane, West Hoathly, East Grinstead RH19 4PX (01342) 810200 £45; 2 rms, shared bthrm. Comfortable house in 6 acres of grounds with lovely country views; decent breakfasts, and pleasant owners; cl Christmas; children over 8.

Bosham SU8003 Kenwood Bosham, Chichester PO18 8PH (01243) 572727 £40; 3 large rms. Comfortable and well kept Victorian house with harbour views, a plushly furnished lounge, pleasant dining room, heated swimming pool, croquet, and free-range poultry; disabled access.

Chidham SU7903 Old Rectory Chidham Lane, Chidham, Chichester PO18 8TF (01243) 572088 £40; 3 rms. Handsome country house with an elegant sitting room, friendly owners, good breakfasts (pleasant pub nearby for evening meals), and a summer swimming pool in the big garden.

Wisborough Green TQ0526 Old Wharf Wharf Farm, Wisborough Green, Billingshurst RG14 0JG (01403) 784096 £40; 4 rms with views over farmland and canal. Carefully restored canal warehouse with a fine, old hoist wheel, comfortable sitting room with a log fire, breakfasts using free-range eggs from the farm, walled canalside garden, and a friendly atmosphere; no smoking, no pets; cl Christmas/New Year; children over 12.

Poynings TQ2612 Manor Farm Poynings, Brighton BN45 7AG (01273) 857371 *£37; 3 rms, shared bthrm. Quietly set, old manor house on a 260-acre, family-run, arable/sheep farm; evening meals by arrangement; lovely walks; cl Jan and Feb.

West Chiltington TQ0918 New House Farm Broadford Bridge Rd, West Chiltington, Pulborough RH20 2LA (01798) 812215 £36; 3 rms. 15th-c, oak-beamed farmhouse on a 50-acre mixed farm, with log fires in inglenook fireplaces; children over 10; two pubs close by – as is golf course, open to non-members.

Coolham TQ1222 Blue Idol Old House Lane, Coolham, Horsham RH13 8QP (01403) 741241 £32; 5 rms, shared bthrm. Timbered, Tudor farmhouse with a peaceful garden, comfortable lounge, good breakfasts (other food by arrangement), and croquet; dogs welcome.

Shipley TQ1422 Goffsland Farm Shipley, Horsham RH13 7BQ (01403) 730434 *£30; 1 family rm. Friendly, 17th-c farmhouse in the Sussex Weald on a 260-acre, family farm; good walks.

To see and do

★ ❀ ⅃ᴛ ℘ **Amberley** TQ0313 is a delightful, thatched village; from the churchyard you can peer into the castle (see **Where to stay** section above), and there is public access to the Wild Brooks (see **Walks** section below). The unspoilt Black Horse has good food, there are lovely views from the Sportsman's conservatory and garden, and the riverside Bridge at Houghton Bridge is great in summer. Amberley Chalk Pits Museum Carefully thought-out, open-air museum covering 36 acres of former chalk quarry and limeworks, with plenty of traditional crafts and re-created workshops. There really is lots going on, from pottery and cobbling to the village telephone exchange; also, exhibitions on concrete, engineering, and road-building, lime kilns, grinding mill, miniature railway and a collection of vintage buses. It's handily placed right by the station. Meals, snacks, shop, disabled access; cl Mon and Tues (exc school or bank hols), Nov–Mar; (01798) 831370; £4.50.

❀ ♤ **Ardingly** TQ3331 Wakehurst Place Garden The 'Southern Kew', administered by the Royal Botanic Gardens, with a tremendous variety of interesting trees and shrubs inc many tender rarities; lakes and watergardens, steep Himalayan glade, woodland walks and fine rhododendron species. Plenty to see throughout the year, and all very peaceful – there's even a nature reserve. Meals, snacks, plant and book sales, disabled access; cl 25 Dec, 1 Jan; £4; NT. Weekend guided walks usually leave from in front of the mansion at 11.30am and 2.30pm (Sun only in winter); tel 0181-332

5585 to check. The appropriately named Gardener's Arms does good lunches (children in garden only), and the White Hart at Selfield is also handy.
★ 🏠 ⛴ 🎵 🏭 🖼 ♿ ✝ ⚘ ♣ ✕ **Arundel** TQ0107 dates back to pre-Roman days, and is dominated by the magnificent walls and towers of the castle on a mound high over the River Arun. Attractive buildings, inc antique shops and so forth, cluster along the sides of the steep main st climbing up from the bridge to the castle itself. The MUSEUM AND HERITAGE CENTRE along here has a good potted history of the area. Shop; cl 1–2pm, am Sun, wkdys in Apr, May and Sept and all Oct–Easter; £1. The CASTLE was built at the end of the 11th c, and has been the seat of the Dukes of Norfolk for over 700 years (a plaque in the main sq says 'Since William Rose and Harold Fell, There have been Earls at Arundel'). It's a magnificent sight, a great spread of well kept towers and battlements soaring above the village and the trees around it. The keep is the oldest part; the rest dates mainly from the 19th c. Excellent art collection, inc portraits by Van Dyck, Reynolds, Lely and Gainsborough, as well as 16th-c furniture, and personal possessions of Mary Queen of Scots. Meals, snacks, shop; cl Sat, Nov–Mar; (01903) 883136; £4.50. The 19th-c Roman Catholic CATHEDRAL complements the castle well, giving rather a French feel to the whole small town. TOY AND MILITARY MUSEUM (High St) Good private collection housed in an attractive, little Georgian cottage. Shop, disabled access to ground floor only; open wknds all year, daily Jun–Sept and school hols; (01903) 883101; £1.25. ENGLISH COUNTRY CRAFTS, in a converted chapel in Tarrant St, has a nice range of local crafts – they have another branch in Worthing. WILDFOWL AND WETLANDS TRUST (Mill Rd) 55 acres of well landscaped pens, lakes, and paddocks, home to over 1,000 ducks, geese and swans from all over the world; the site also acts as a sanctuary for wild birds. Hides overlooking the different habitats make observing the birds easier. Meals, snacks, shop,

disabled access; cl 25 Dec; (01903) 883355; £3.95. The lane past the Trust ends at a little cluster of houses by an isolated church and a former watermill. On the way to the Trust, the Black Rabbit has a superb location and does food; in the town, the Bridge House, Red Lion and White Hart have decent food.
❀ **Ashington** TQ1315 HOLLY GATE CACTUS GARDEN Over 30,000 succulents and cactus plants from both tropical and arid habitats all over the world – a cactus enthusiast's prickly paradise. Summer snacks, plant sales, disabled access; cl 25–26 Dec; (01903) 892930; *£1.50. The Franklands Arms at Washington is a useful lunch stop.

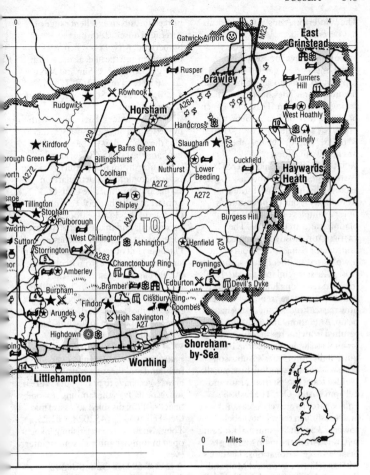

Bignor SU9814 ROMAN VILLA AND MUSEUM One of the largest villas yet discovered, with marvellous mosaics inc the longest in Britain – 82ft long, and still in its original position. The hypocaust is also very well preserved. Snacks, shop, disabled access, and largely under cover; cl Mon (exc bank hols and Jun–Sept), Nov–Feb; (017987) 259; £2.50. The Black Dog & Duck at Bury and Cricketer's Arms at Duncton have decent food.

Bognor Regis SZ9399 is an old-fashioned, seaside family resort, popular above all for its sandy beaches; the usual attractions. The Lamb (Steyne St) is a refuge for those who don't like traditional seaside food and cafés.

Bosham SU8003 The Saxon CHURCH here figures in the Bayeux Tapestry, and the village is a lovely cluster of old cottages around it, the green, and a broad, almost landlocked inlet of Chichester harbour – busy with boating in the summer. A very pleasant place to stroll around, with good antique shops and craft galleries. The Anchor Bleu, right by the water, is popular for lunch.

Boxgrove SU9007 BOXGROVE PRIORY Now the parish church, this 12th-c priory is one of the most outstanding Early English churches in the region, with a surprising, 16th-c, painted ceiling, free-standing chantry chapel, and the atmospheric remains of various monastic buildings outside.

The Winterton Arms at Crockerhill has decent food.

🏠 ✤ **Bramber** TQ1710 St Mary's Striking medieval house, with fine panelling, a pretty garden with topiary, and an unusual, Elizabethan painted room. They have concerts in spring and autumn. Teas, shop; open pm Sun and Mon Easter–Sept, plus pm Weds and Thurs in Aug; (01903) 816205; *£3.50. The Bramber Castle has good-value food.

★ ✤ ✤ 🐛 🏠 ▣ 🦊 ⚓ **Chichester** SU8604 Partly pedestrianised and easy to get around, this handsome, former Roman city is one of the country's finest examples of Georgian town planning and architecture. The CATHEDRAL is mostly Norman, and is unusual for rising straight out of the town's streets rather than a secluded close. The spire collapsed in the 1860s (the latest in a long line of structural problems), and was rebuilt, but even now the scaffolding always seems to be up. Alterations and additions have resulted in an interesting variety of styles, with highlights in the 14th-c quire stalls, John Piper's Aubusson tapestry, and the window by Chagall. Guided tours (not Sun) at 11am and 2.15pm Easter–Oct. The Bishop's Palace gardens are very pleasant. Snacks, shop in the medieval bell tower (23 South St – unusual for being separated from the main building), disabled access; donations. The city's MUSEUM (Little London, cl Mon and Sun, free) houses its archaeological displays in the interesting former GUILDHALL (Priory Park), which began life as a Grey Friars church in medieval times. It's usually open pm Tues–Sat Jun–Sept; free. MECHANICAL MUSIC AND DOLL COLLECTION (Church Rd, Portfield) Lots of interesting curiosities in this former Victorian church, but the main feature is the multitude of barrel, fair and Dutch street organs, musical boxes and phonographs – all restored and ready to play. Shop, disabled access; open pm exc Sat Easter–Oct, then just pm Sun (not Dec); (01243) 785421; £2. PALLANT HOUSE (North Pallant) Queen Anne town house with Edwardian kitchen and fine furnishings. The gallery has a fine collection of Bow

porcelain, and an excellent range of carefully chosen, 20th-c art – Sutherland, Klee, Leger, Ben Nicholson and the like; also, an 18th-c style garden. Shop; cl Sun and Mon 25–26 Dec, 1 Jan; (01243) 774557; £2.50. In St Paul's St, the White Horse is useful for lunch.

S of Chichester is flat country with nurseries and huge glasshouses; there's also the peaceful NATURE RESERVE of Pagham Harbour SZ8796, largely silted, marshy tidal flats, full of wading birds and wildfowl, particularly in spring and autumn. The Crab & Lobster at Sidlesham, on the edge of the reserve, has local seafood and other meals and snacks. Peter Adams runs BOAT TRIPS around Chichester Harbour, full of yachts and dinghies in summer. They leave from Itchenor SU8001 and are best at high tide; (01243) 786418; £3.50. There's also an hourly passenger ferry between here and the landing at the end of the lane S from Bosham (daily Jun–Aug, wknds only Apr, May and Sept).

🐄 🥄 **Coombes** TQ1908 CHURCH FARM organise trailer rides over farmland and through conservation areas – you have to book, but it's great fun, especially in the lambing season. Snacks, shop, disabled access; cl mid-Oct–Feb; (01273) 452028; *£2.25. They also have a coarse fishing lake, open in summer and also some winter eves.

★ 🏚 ✤ ✤ 🏠 **Dell Quay** SU8302 Attractive waterside hamlet with remains of a Roman quay, and good harbour views from the Crown & Anchor. APULDRAM ROSES Over 300 kinds of old-fashioned and new roses in a harbourside field and gardens made from former orchards; the shop sells various types, and everything needed to look after them; they have a sale at the end of the season in Sept. Shop open all year, field from Jun; (01243) 785769; free.

🏠 ✤ **East Grinstead** TQ3938 The town itself is really to be avoided, with long weekend traffic queues, but its main attractions are actually on the outskirts, off the B2110, just W. STANDEN Designed by Philip Webb, a friend of William Morris, and little-changed since, this house is a fine example of the many talents of the 19th-c Arts and Crafts Movement. The interior is decorated with several different William Morris wallpapers, and many of the furnishings are of the period, even down to the unusual light fittings designed by Webb. Snacks, shop, limited disabled access; open pm wknds in Mar, then Weds–Sat Apr–Oct; £4 (£4.80 wknds and bank hols), £2.50 garden only (£3 wknds); NT. INGWERSENS NURSERY (Birch Farm, Gravetye) is a very long-established, alpine plants specialist. Disabled access; cl 1–1.30pm, wknds Oct–Feb; (01342) 810236. Out this way, the Cat in the pretty village of West Hoathly TQ3632 (see entry below) has good food, and the White Hart at Selsfield and the Crown at Turners Hill are also useful.

♂ ✝ **East Wittering** SZ7997 REJECTAMENTA NOSTALGIA MUSEUM (Church Rd) Over 25,000 everyday objects from this century, collected over 22 years by a cheery, ex-art student who says she just can't stop; everything from gasmasks through knickers to pre-war lavatory paper, with period music and TV programmes like *Andy Pandy* and Bill and Ben, *The Flower Pot Men*. Refreshingly informal, the museum is unusually located in an old CHURCH, parts of which date back to the 12th c. Shop, disabled access; open Sun all year (pm only in winter), plus wkdys Easter–Oct; (01243) 868725; *£1.80. The Lamb between West Wittering and Birdham has interesting food.

🏛 ♂ ❀ **Fishbourne** SU8304 ROMAN PALACE This magnificent villa with its 100 or so rooms was occupied from the 1st to the 3rd c, and is the largest known residence from the period in Britain. A good museum details its history, while on the site itself you can see 25 of the superb mosaic floors (a bigger collection than anywhere else in Europe). A garden has been laid out according to its 1st-c plan. Meals, snacks, shop, disabled access; cl mid-Dec–mid-Feb; (01622) 871344; £3.40. The Black Boy has a wide choice of food.

❀ **Fontwell** SU9507 DENMANS GARDEN Colourful series of vistas over 3½ acres, inc exuberantly Oriental-

feeling areas with a gravel stream, ornamental grasses, bamboos, and flowering cherries, as well as a beautiful, richly planted, walled garden. Meals, snacks, plant sales, disabled access; cl Christmas, Jan and Feb; (01243) 542808; £2.25. The George at Eartham is a good nearby place to eat.

☺ **Gatwick Airport** TQ3041 right at the top of the area is quite exciting for children and should be even more so soon – they're developing part of it as a theme park.

🏰 ▣ ❀ **Goodwood** SU8808 GOODWOOD HOUSE Unusual looking house in beautiful downland countryside, notable for its furniture, tapestries and Sèvres porcelain, but renowned especially for its paintings, inc works by Canaletto and Stubbs. There's quite an equestrian feel – the house was acquired by the first Duke of Richmond in 1697 so that he could ride with the local hunt, and the stables added during 18th-c alterations are grander even than the house. Snacks, shop, some disabled access; open pm Sun and Mon Easter–Sept, plus Tues–Thurs in Aug, cl occasional event days, so best to check first; (01243) 774107; £3.40. The adjacent RACECOURSE is the setting for Glorious Goodwood, and as well as around 19 race days a year has monthly antique markets. The Fox Goes Free at Charlton is the best nearby place for a meal.

❀ **Handcross** TQ2629 NYMANS Some very impressive rare trees here, inc magnificent southern beeches and eucryphias, as well as fine camellias, rhododendrons and magnolias, countless other interesting flowering shrubs, a secluded sunken garden, and an extensive, artfully composed wilderness. Meals, snacks, plant sales, shop, disabled access; cl Mon, Fri, and Nov–Feb; *£3.50; NT. The Fountain, Red Lion and Royal Oak are all reliable for lunch.

❀ ♧ ♪ **Haywards Heath** TQ3226 BORDE HILL (Balcombe Rd, N) Lovely, 40-acre gardens with woodland walks through rare maples, oaks, conifers and many other fine trees, as well as a lake, herbaceous borders and magnificent rhododendrons. You can fish on the lake. Meals, snacks, plant sales, disabled access; cl mid-Oct–Mar; (01444) 450236; £3. The Cowdray Arms at Balcombe is handy for somewhere to eat.

🐗 ✗ ✌ **Henfield** TQ2116 WOODS MILL COUNTRYSIDE CENTRE 18th-c watermill with wildlife exhibitions, and nature trails over 15 acres of the surrounding countryside. Snacks, shop; open Sun, bank hols and pm Sat Apr–Sept, plus pm Tues, Weds and Thurs in school hols; (01273) 429630; £2.

❋ ❋ **Highdown** TQ0904 HIGHDOWN HILL Excellent views from this famous garden, which differs from most of the other famous Sussex gardens in that it's on very uncompromising chalk – laid out in and around a chalk pit high on the Downs above Angmering; many rarities, inc unusual Chinese plants. Some disabled access; cl wknds Oct–Mar, Christmas; (01903) 501054; free. The Spotted Cow, at the foot of Highdown Hill, is a useful place for lunch.

✗ **High Salvington** TQ1206 WINDMILL Early, 18th-c black post mill, currently being restored. Teas, shop; open pm 1st and 3rd Sun Apr–Sept; 50p.

🏠👢❋ **Horsham** TQ1730 has seen considerable development, but a particularly attractive, quiet corner is The Causeway, by the church. A timber-framed, Tudor house here is now a well organised local history MUSEUM, with dinosaur bones, an extraordinary collection of early bicycles, Shelley gallery, and an exhibition of shops and shopping. The small but pretty garden has some unusual wild cyclamen. Shop, limited disabled access but full facilities; cl Mon and Sun; free. The Black Jug (North St) and Boar's Head (Tower Hill, S towards Worthing) do decent food.

👢 **Littlehampton** TQ0202 Considering that the town was a port of some importance for several centuries up to the 1500s, it shows little sign of real age, but its long sandy beaches make it a popular, simple, family resort. There's a decent MUSEUM in an early 19th-c manor house; cl Sun and Mon; free. Towards the W, beyond the River Arun, there's quite an extensive area of unspoilt dunes between the beach and golf course. The Arun View right on the river does decent lunches.

❋ ✌ 🦜 **Lower Beeding** TQ2225 LEONARDSLEE GARDENS Enormous, Grade 1-listed garden, landscaped by Sir Edmund Loder of rhododendron fame, set in a 240-acre valley with six beautiful lakes; marvellous rhododendrons, magnolias, oaks and unusual conifers, a delightful rock garden, an extensive greenhouse and Japanese garden, bonsai exhibition, and wallaby and deer. The gardens are on the edge of the ancient St Leonard's Forest, and there's a new, summer, wild flower walk. Meals, snacks, plant sales, limited disabled access; cl Nov–Mar; (01403) 891212; May £4, other times £3. The Crabtree does excellent food.

★ 🐗 **Lurgashall** SU9327 Attractive small village, with an unusual loggia outside the church where parishioners walking in from a distance could eat their sandwiches. The unusual LURGASHALL WINERY produces a wide range of traditional country wines, meads and cordials. Tastings, cl am Sun, Christmas; (01428) 707292; self-guided tours £1. The Noah's Ark here is good for lunch.

🏠▣❋✌★ **Petworth** SU9721 PETWORTH HOUSE The magnificent rooms of this splendid old house, rebuilt in the 17th c, are filled with one of the most impressive art collections in the country, inc Dutch Old Masters and 20 pictures by Turner, a frequent visitor. Other highlights include the 13th-c chapel, grand staircase with frescoes, and the carved room, elegantly decorated by Grinling Gibbons. They usually open more rooms on wkdys, and this year you can visit the carefully preserved kitchens. Meals, snacks, shop, disabled access; cl am, Mon (exc bank hols when cl following Tues), Fri, Nov–Mar; £4; NT. The deer park, with stately trees and prospects still recognisable as those glorified by Turner, is free. The village, clustered by the great stone wall of the park, has narrow streets of attractive old houses, inc a good few antique shops. The New Star is handy for lunch, though the short trip out to the Black

Horse at Byworth or Horseguards at Tillington might be more memorable.
🐾 🏠 ✿ ✚ ⚔ ✗ Pulborough TQ0614 The town has some attractive buildings down towards the river; the Water's Edge, with lake views, has a good choice of food. There's an RSPB Reserve nearby. PARHAM HOUSE Charming Elizabethan house, still a family home, its panelled rooms full of notable portraits, furniture, Oriental carpets and lots of rare needlework. The surrounding grounds are really very special – popular with birds, they include a rose garden and a vegetable garden, the produce from which is sold in the shop. Also, a deer park, and a maze designed with children in mind. Snacks, shop; open pm Weds, Thurs and Sun Easter–Oct; (01903) 742021; £4, gardens only £2.50. NUTBOURNE VINEYARDS 18-acre vineyard with tours and tastings and a new visitor centre in a former windmill. Shop; cl Nov–Easter; (01798) 815196; free.

🐖 Selsey SZ8593 By this busy holiday village, NORTHCOMMON FARM CENTRE has a wide range of friendly animals, and HORSE RIDING from full-day treks over the Downs to half-hour rides for beginners. Snacks, shop; open pm wknds and school hols Easter–Sept; (01243) 602725; farm £1.65, riding £10 per hour.

✗ Shipley TQ1422 Striking, working WINDMILL, a smock mill built in 1879 and once owned by Hilaire Belloc. Teas, shop; tel (01243) 775888 for opening dates; £1.

🏠 ☉ ✚ † Shoreham-by-Sea TQ2105 Though not one of England's more famous ports, this is quite a busy one; several attractive old buildings around the harbour show this has long been the case. One such is MARLIPINS MUSEUM (High St) – a Norman building which may once have been a customs house, now a local history museum. Shop; cl 1–2pm, am Sun, Mon, Oct–Apr; £1. The airport (England's oldest, with an appealing Art Deco terminal) has a MUSEUM OF D-DAY AVIATION, with uniforms, engines, artefacts and a replica Spitfire. Cl Dec–Easter; £2.50. Inland, in Old Shoreham, the early Norman CHURCH is surrounded by some

handsome old houses, and the Red Lion here is a nice old place for lunch.
⬆ 🏠 ✗ ☛ Singleton SU8713 WEALD AND DOWNLAND OPEN-AIR MUSEUM Fascinating and unusual collection of rescued, historic buildings from all over the SE, dismantled and re-erected here. They're arranged to form a village, with an outlying farm and agricultural buildings, a Tudor market hall, blacksmith's forge, tollhouse and Victorian schoolroom. Some are furnished, and you can even buy flour from the medieval farmstead's working watermill. Also displays of rural industries and traditional local crafts. Snacks, shop; cl Nov–Feb exc wknds and Weds; (01243) 811348; £4.20. CHILSDOWN VINEYARD A 13-acre vineyard and winery based around an unusual Victorian station. Shop; cl am Sun, Oct–Apr; (01243) 63398; £1.50. The Fox Goes Free at Charlton is handy for lunch.

★ 🏠 ✿ ⚘ ❀ South Harting SU7819 is a pretty village, with good-value food in the nicely set Ship. UPPARK (B2146, S) This splendid, 17th-c house has been closed since a fire in 1989, but after a remarkable restoration programme (the biggest in the NT's history) will reopen again this Jun. Incredibly, most of the houses's treasures were rescued, even the wallpaper, so everything should look as it did the day before the blaze; only one carpet and a grand piano were totally destroyed. An exhibition will have the full story. The grounds, designed by Humphrey Repton, have a woodland walk and fine views towards the Solent. Snacks, shop, disabled access; open from Jun, pm Sun–Thurs till Oct; £5; NT. As it's likely to be busy, entrance will be by timed ticket, though a few tickets should be available in advance on (01730) 825317.

† Tangmere SU9006 MILITARY AVIATION MUSEUM Good collection of photographs, models, uniforms, aircraft and aircraft parts based around the former RAF base where H E Bates finished writing *Fair Stood the Wind for France*. Meals, snacks, shop, disabled access; cl Dec–Jan; (01243) 775223; £2.50. The Anglesey Arms at Halnaker and the quaint Gribble at

Oving are both quite handy.

🐄 ★ **Tillington** SU9421 NOAH'S
FARMYARD (Grittenham Farm) Lambs,
calves, goats, rabbits etc for children
to pet and feed, along with barn owls,
a short nature trail, and riverside
picnic area. Snacks, shop; cl mid-
Sept–Mar; (017985) 264; *£2.25.
The Horseguards is quite a stylish
dining pub, and the village is pretty.

🌼 🍴 **West Dean** SU8512 WEST DEAN
GARDENS Old roses, 100-yard pergola,
wild garden, walled kitchen garden
and an interesting collection of
stately, mature conifers in the park
and arboretum; a splendid downland
setting, notably peaceful and relaxed.
A new visitor centre is planned for this
year. Snacks, shop, some disabled
access, plant sales; cl Nov–Feb;
(01243) 811303; £2.50. The Fox
Goes Free at Charlton is quite useful
for a good meal.

★ 🌼 ✝ 🏠 🍴 🌼 **West Hoathly** TQ3632
Attractive village tucked quietly away
from the road, with tremendous views
from the lane downhill past the Cat (a
good pub with authentic Italian food).
On a clear day you can see the whole
sweep of the South Downs between
Chanctonbury Ring and the Long
Man of Wilmington. Nr the 13th-c
church is the 15th-c, timbered PRIEST
HOUSE, now a folk museum with a
little cottage garden. An exhibition on
herbs in medicine and folklore is

called A Brief History of Thyme.
Shop; cl am Sun, Tues, Nov–late Mar;
(01342) 810479; £1.75.

🍴 🏠 🍴 🌼 **Worthing** TQ1402
Restrained but rather charming town,
with a pleasant seafront; in the same
mould as Brighton but altogether
quieter and less gaudy. The MUSEUM
AND ART GALLERY (Chapel Rd) has an
extremely rich archaeological
collection, and a new sculpture
garden. Shop, disabled access; cl Sun,
Christmas; free. In the formerly
separate village of West Tarring are
some attractive old cottages, a 250-
year-old fig garden by the 14th-c
parish hall, a folklore museum in a
row of 15th-c cottages, and a
welcoming old pub, the Vine.

! The BRITISH SCHOOL OF BALLOONING
at Ebernoe, just N of Petworth
SU9721, organises champagne
balloon trips over the countryside – tel
(01428) 707307; £120; cheaper if
more people.

★ **Attractive villages** in the area, all
with decent pubs, include Barns
Green TQ1227, Burpham TQ0308,
Easebourne SU8922, East Dean
SU9013, Elsted SU8119, Findon
TQ1208, Fittleworth TQ0118,
Funtington SU7908, Henley SU8925,
Kirdford TQ0126, Rudgwick
TQ0833, Slaugham TQ2528, South
Harting SU7819, Stopham TQ0218
and Sutton SU9715.

Walks

The chalk South Downs dominate much of this part of the county, and have
the best of its walks. The South Downs Way makes for quick progress along
their crest. **Harting Downs** SU9718 △-1 involve no more than a level stroll
from the road nr South Harting SU7819. **Kingley Vale** SU8210 △-2 needs
much more stamina, whether you approach via the nature trail on the S side or
from Stoughton SU8011 to the N (the Hare & Hounds will fuel you well).
This nature reserve is Europe's largest yew forest, a magical place where the
trees create some eerie pools of darkness on the S slopes of the Downs; above,
you can look over Chichester Harbour from a prehistoric burial mound. At
Bignor Hill SU9813 △-3, the trees that obscure views for much of the way
hereabouts give way to open ground; Stane St, a Roman road here relegated to
a path, takes a strikingly straight course SW over a woodland and pasture
landscape.

At **Arundel** TQ0107 △-4 you can walk along the canalised River Arun and
into Arundel Park, with its lakes and woodlands beneath the slopes of the
Downs. From Amberley TQ0313, you can climb on to the Downs or take a
path across **Amberley Wild Brooks** TQ0314 △-5, a large expanse of watermeadows which form an important habitat for wetland plants and birdlife.

N of Worthing TQ1402 are two of the great landmarks of the Downs, both of them ancient hill forts. **Chanctonbury Ring** TQ1312 ⌂-6, now a prominent hilltop clump of trees, is reached from Steyning TQ1711 or Washington TQ1212. The huge ramparted site of **Cissbury Ring** TQ1308 ⌂-7 is quite close to Findon TQ1208 (where the Village House and Gun are both good lunch places). The **Downs above Brighton** ⌂-8 are open; arable farming and the presence of pylons rather distract from the pleasure of walking, but the steep northern slopes are still impressive, as at Devil's Dyke TQ2611 (with its tremendous view over Brighton, even more startling at night than by day), Wolstonbury Hill TQ2813 and the Jack and Jill windmills nr Clayton TQ3014.

Fernhurst SU8928 ⌂-9 up in the NW of the county has nicely varied countryside nearby; much is densely wooded, but there are some chances to get out on to the open hillsides as on Woolbeding Common SU8625 and the southern tip of Black Down SU9129. Further E, you can stroll by the shore of **Ardingly Reservoir** TQ3229 ⌂-10, or plan a longer walk around the elevated farmland and woodlands surrounding Wakehurst Place TQ3331 and Balcombe TQ3130. Another reservoir walk can be had along the N side of **Weir Wood Reservoir** TQ3934 ⌂-11, with paths leading up to Standen House TQ3835.

The coast is densely developed, but Chichester Harbour still has unspoilt waterside. A shoreside path skirts the quiet peninsulas of **Thorney Island** SU7503 ⌂-12 and Chidham SU7903. **East Head** SZ7694 ⌂-13, a NT-owned promontory on the eastern entrance of the harbour, is a sandy spit with dunes overlooking the marshes and mudflats of the estuary. The only other appreciable stretch of undeveloped coast is between Littlehampton TQ0202 and Middleton-on-Sea SU9700, which includes an attractive few miles along **Climping Beach** SU9902 ⌂-14.

The Bridge pub at Copsale TQ1725 is a popular base for local walks.

Driving

Good Downs roads include the B2141 from Chichester to South Harting, the B2146 S from South Harting past Uppark (a splendid NT property, still being restored after a fire) to Walderton, and the back road up the valley from there through Stoughton and East Marden, where you can either go on to meet the B2141 again, or keep round to the left behind Telegraph Hill and rejoin the B2146 nr Compton. From South Harting, taking the back road through East Harting and then a right turn in Elsted to take you slowly through the little villages of Treyford, Didling and Bepton, joining the A286 at Cocking, gives good views of the steep, wooded N slope of the Downs, on your right. All the back roads around Goodwood are pleasant, mainly open country drives, and to the E of that area, the B2139 has lovely views of a fine stretch of downland between Storrington and Houghton (where the George & Dragon is an a nice stop).

The A272, though not a quick road, gives a good cross-section of West Sussex, and goes through Midhurst, Petworth and Pulborough, all of them attractive, small towns. The A286 N and S through Midhurst carries relatively little traffic for a trunk road, and passes through some splendid countryside.

Where to eat

Chilgrove SU8214 WHITE HORSE (01243) 59219 18th-c pub/restaurant in a charming South Downs setting; very good, generously served, wholesome food and a superb wine list; cl pm Sun, Mon, last wk Oct, Feb, pm 25 Dec, 26 Dec; children in restaurant only. **£31 dinner, £25 lunch**|£2/£6.

Storrington TQ0814 OLD FORGE (01903) 743402 Good, imaginative food in a converted, beamed forge and an excellent choice of sweet wines to go with the rich puddings and home-made ice-creams; cl am Sat, pm Sun, Mon, am Tues,

2 wks late spring, 3 wks autumn; children must be well behaved; **£25**.

Chichester SU8605 COMME CA 67 Broyle Rd (01243) 788724 Busy little restaurant close to the Festival Theatre, with good, classic French cooking, popular Sun lunches and a children's menu; cl pm Sun, Mon, bank hols (exc Good Fri); disabled access. **£23.50|£4.25/£7.95**.

Elsted SU8119 THREE HORSESHOES (01730) 825746 Cosy Tudor pub in a lovely setting, with fine views of the South Downs from garden (and nice walks); snug, rustic rooms with huge log fires, ancient beams and antique furnishings, very good English cooking inc delicious puddings, well kept real ales, decent wines by the glass; disabled access. **£20|£4.50/£7**.

Burpham TQ0308 GEORGE & DRAGON (01903) 883131 Smartly comfortable, old pub with splendid views down to Arundel Castle and the river, popular with walkers; good, promptly served bar food with unusual specials, inc tasty vegetarian dishes, and an elegant restaurant; cl 25 Dec. **£18|£2.25/£5.50**.

Edburton TQ2311 TOTTINGTON MANOR (01903) 815757 Cosy, country house, with particularly good food using fresh seasonal produce in both the bar and restaurant; winter log fire, friendly service and a relaxed atmosphere; bedrooms; children over 5; disabled access. **£17.50|£3.50/£5.50**.

Nuthurst TQ1926 BLACK HORSE (01403) 891272 Warmly welcoming, black-beamed pub in lovely walking country, with a log fire in the inglenook fireplace, good, promptly served bar food, well kept real ales and country wines, friendly service. **£17.50|£2.50/£4**.

Elsted SU8119 ELSTED INN (01730) 813662 Simple but very friendly country inn, with very good, daily-changing bar food, well kept real ales, and log fires in the two small bars. **£16.50/£6.50**.

Lodsworth SU9223 HALFWAY BRIDGE (01798) 861281 Stylish and civilised, but warm and friendly, family-run pub; big helpings of inventive home-cooking in the no-smoking restaurant or attractively decorated, comfortable bar rooms, log fires, well kept real ales, ciders and wines. **£16|£3.10/£6.25**.

Easebourne SU8922 OLDE WHITE HORSE (01730) 813521 Neatly kept, old stone local, with good food in the comfortable bars and restaurant, a small log fire, and friendly service. **£15|£2.85/£6**.

Rowhook TQ1234 CHEQUERS (01403) 790480 Pleasantly rustic and old-fashioned pub, with well presented meals in the low-ceilinged, carpeted lounge or unpretentious, beamed front bar, well kept real ales, a fine choice of wines by the glass, and friendly service. **£3.10/£5.80**.

Help this year from: Michael and Jenny Back, Amanda Hodges, S V Bishop, John Beeken, David Dimmock, Colin Laffan, Mr and Mrs D E Powell, Jenny and Brian Seller, Carol Riddick, LMM, J H Bell, Brian Jones, Jack Taylor, Mrs M Rice, A and A Dale, J and P Maloney, Mrs M Rice, Ann and Colin Hunt, Alen and Marie Lewery, John and Joy Winterbottom, A J Blackler, Mr and Mrs J Stern, A E and P McCully, Martin and Catherine Horner, A Preston, Joan and John Calvert, A C Morrison, Klaus and Elizabeth Leist, Dr T E Hothersall, Peter and Lynn Brueton, Derek and Sylvia Stephenson, T M Fenning, H R Taylor, Peter Churchill, A G Drake, Penny and Martin Fletcher, A M Pickup, J F Rogers, E G Parish, L G Holmes.

We welcome reports from readers . . .

This *Guide* depends on readers' reports. Please tell us what you think about places in it. And do recommend additions. Use the card in the middle, the report forms at the end, or just write – no stamp needed: *The Good Weekend Guide*, FREEPOST TN1569, Wadhurst, E Sussex TN5 7BR.

SUSSEX CALENDAR

Some of these dates were provisional as we went to press.

The largest antiques shows in the county are at the Ardingly South of England Showground and take place on Jan 10–11, Feb 28–1 Mar, Apr 25–26, July 18–19, Sept 19–20, Oct 31–1 Nov (01636) 702326

JANUARY

1 **Hastings** Foreign and Colonial Chess Congress at Cinque Ports Hotel and Pier Ballroom – *till Fri 6* (01424) 439222

MARCH

13 **Haywards Heath and Mid-Sussex** Arts Festival – *till 30 Apr* (01444) 458166

27 **Hastings** Musical Festival at the White Rock Theatre – *till 25 Mar* (01424) 443116

APRIL

13 **West Sussex** International Music Festival – *till Tues 18* 0171-401 9941

16 **Singleton** Traditional Food Fair at the Weald and Downland Open-Air Museum – *till Mon 17* (01243) 811348

28 **Hastings** Jack in the Green Morris Dancing Festival – *till 1 May* (01424) 433830

MAY

5 **Brighton** Festival – *till Sun 28* (01273) 713875; **Brighton** Horse Driving Trials at Stanmer Park – *till Sun 7* (01323) 841641; **Eastbourne** International Folk Festival (01435) 830092

7 **Ardingly** Greenfingers Garden Fair at the South of England Showground (01342) 842345; **Bexhill** Festival of Motoring – *till Mon 8* (01424) 730564; **Bodiam** Medieval Fair at Bodiam Castle – *till Mon 8* (01892) 890651

13 **Battle** Festival – *till Sat 27* (01580) 880684

22 **Glyndebourne** Opera Season – *till 27 Aug* (01273) 812321

25 **Firle** Charleston Festival at Charleston Farmhouse – *till Mon 29* (01323) 811626

26 **Brighton** Old Ship Royal Escape Race at the beach in front of the Old Ship, King's Rd (01273) 329001; **Pevensey** Cuckoo Vintage Transport Fayre at Mill Farm – *till Mon 29* (01323) 845866

27 **Broad Oak** Heathfield and District Agricultural Show (01825) 790977

28 **Hastings** Rogationtide Blessing the Sea Ceremony on the Harbour Arm, nr the Lifeboat House *at 2pm* (01424) 422023

29 **Selsey** Donkey Derby

JUNE

1 **Hickstead** British Nations Showjumping Cup and Grand Prix – *till Sun 4* (01273) 834315

3 **Hadlow Down** Tinkers Park Traction Engine Rally – *till Sun 4*

7 **Boxgrove** Music of Boxgrove at Boxgrove Priory – *till Sat 10* (01734) 813190

8 **Ardingly** South of England Agricultural Show at the Showground – *till Sat 10* (01444) 892700

Sussex Calendar

JUNE cont

10 **East Preston** Festival Week – *till Sun 18* (01903) 771161

11 **Singleton** Heavy Horses at the Weald and Downland Open-Air Museum (01243) 811348

14 **Arundel** Corpus Christi Carpet of Flowers and Floral Festival at Cathedral of Our Lady & St Philip Howard – *till Thurs 15* (01903) 882297

17 **Danehill** Sheffield Park Garden Musical Evening (01892) 890651; **Pulborough** Steam Rally at Parham Park – *till Sun 18* (01903) 743939

18 **London to Brighton** Bike Ride (01225) 480130; **Lamberhurst** Austin Seven Owners Club Rally at Bewl Water (01892) 890661

19 **Eastbourne** International Ladies Lawn Tennis Championship at Devonshire Park (01323) 415442; **Singleton** Midsummer Marvels at the Weald and Downland Open-Air Museum – *till Fri 23* (01243) 811348

23 **Petworth** Open-Air Concerts at Petworth Park – *till Sun 25* (01372) 453401

24 **Bodiam** Jazz at the Castle (01892) 890651; **Crawley** Festival – *till 8 July* (01293) 535235

28 **Eastbourne** 1812 Night Military Band Concert with fireworks at the Redoubt Fortress *every Weds and Fri night – till 1 Sept* (01323) 410300

JULY

1 **Petworth** Festival at Petworth Park – *till Sun 9* (01798) 42207

2 **Chichester** Festivities – *till Tues 18* (01243) 785718

8 **Ardingly** Self-Sufficiency County Show at the South of England Showground – *till Sun 9* (01306) 741302; **Horsham** Festival and Carnival – *till Sun 9* (01403) 217799

13 **Hickstead** Royal International Horse Show – *till Sun 16* (01273) 834315

15 **Lamberhurst** Fireworks and Laser Concert at Bewl Water (01892) 890661

20 **Chichester** Southern Cathedrals Festival at Chichester Cathedral – *till Sun 23*

21 **Burwash** Bateman's Play at Bateman's – *till Sat 22* (01892) 890651

23 **Singleton** Rare and Traditional Breeds Show at the Weald and Downland Open-Air Museum (01243) 811348

25 **Goodwood** Glorious Goodwood at the Racecourse – *till Sat 29* (01243) 774107

28 **Petworth** National Trust Craft Festival at Petworth House and Park – *till Sat 2* (01798) 42207

29 **Bognor Regis** Carnival; **Lamberhurst** Have-a-go Weekend at Bewl Water: outdoor sports inc windsurfing, sailing, rowing, sub-aqua diving and archery – *till Sun 30* (01892) 890661

AUGUST

5 **Burwash** Fireworks Concert at Bateman's (01892) 890651; **Hastings** Old Town Week: inc open days at private houses and a carnival *on Weds – till Sun 13* (01424) 431213

SUSSEX CALENDAR

AUGUST cont

12 **Rye** Medieval Week – *till Sun 13* (01797) 223404

20 **Alfriston** Festival – *till Mon 28* (01323) 870650; **Eastbourne** Airbourne 95 on the seafront – *till* the Birdman competition (won last year by Patsy Quick, friend of the editor of this calendar) *on Sun 20* (01323) 410044

25 **Arundel** Festival – *till 3 Sept* (01903) 883690; **Worthing** British and Irish Country Music Festival at the Pavilion Theatre – *till Sun 27* (01903) 239999

26 **Hellingly** Festival of Transport at Broad Farm – *till Mon 28* (01323) 484926; **Rotherfield** Torchlight Procession and Fireworks (01273) 515451

31 **Rye** Carnival, also *on Sat 2 Sept*

SEPTEMBER

2 **Alfriston** English Wine and Regional Food Festival at the English Wine Centre – *till Sun 3* (01323) 870164; **Uckfield** Torchlight Procession and Fireworks (01273) 515451

9 **Crowborough** Torchlight Procession and Fireworks (01273) 515451; **Findon** Sheep Fair at Nepcote Farm (01435) 866688

16 **Mayfield** Torchlight Procession and Fireworks (01273) 515451

23 **Burgess Hill** Torchlight Procession and Fireworks (01273) 515451

29 **Chiddingly** Festival – *till 8 Oct* (01825) 872338

OCTOBER

14 **Newhaven** Torchlight Procession and Fireworks (01273) 515451

20 **Chichester** Sloe Fair at Oaklands Park

21 **Singleton** Steam Threshing and Ploughing at the Weald and Downland Open-Air Museum – *till Sun 22* (01243) 811348

28 **Littlehampton** Torchlight Procession and Fireworks (01273) 515451

NOVEMBER

4 **Battle** Fireworks with effigy (01424) 773721, a quieter alternative to **Lewes** Torchlight Procession and Fireworks: the best of Britain's bonfire celebrations; town closed to traffic *at 5.30pm*; spectacular celebrations include 'no popery' banner, bands, effigies and burning tar barrel race (01273) 515451

5 **Brighton** end of London to Brighton Veteran Car Run at Madeira Drive (01753) 681736

11 **East Hoathly** Torchlight Procession and Fireworks (01273) 515451

20 **Petworth** Fair at Petworth Park (01798) 42207

WILTSHIRE

For people who enjoy wandering around pleasant small towns and villages, and looking at beautiful houses and gardens and the like, Wiltshire can hardly be bettered. It's not too touristy even in summer, and has a good choice of places to stay, with plenty of individual character.

The south of the county includes the elegant and civilised old city of Salisbury, with one of England's most beautiful cathedrals; Longleat, with plenty to keep a family on the go all day; Wilton House, another place with very wide appeal; the wonderful grounds of Stourhead; and Stonehenge, Britain's most famous ancient monument.

The countryside in the north of the county is on the whole more attractive; up here, Corsham Court is magnificent, inside and out, and can be combined with a visit to the interesting nearby underground quarry centre. Most people would say that Castle Combe is England's prettiest village, and Lacock is also outstanding; Avebury, less flooded with visitors than Stonehenge and easier to see at close quarters, is well worth a visit.

SOUTH WILTSHIRE

Salisbury with its glorious cathedral is a good civilised base for a short break; lots to see and do outside.

Besides its elegant cathedral, Salisbury has a lot of appeal for a civilised quiet break, and makes a good base for exploring the surrounding countryside. The pick of the area's places to visit includes Stourhead at Stourton, Longleat near Warminster, Stonehenge and Wilton House. You can escape the crowds among the imposing yet very peaceful ruins of Old Wardour Castle near Tisbury.

The Salisbury Plain is better for driving over than walking – an almost unbroken expanse of rolling high ground, a mixture of pasture and broad, unhedged arable fields intersected by military training tracks. The most attractive countryside is along the valleys of the chalk streams – intimate scenery with stone or flint houses and sparkling rivers. There are a good many attractive villages.

Where to stay

Salisbury SU1429 ROSE & CROWN Harnham Rd, Salisbury SP2 8JQ (01722) 327908 £137.50; 29 rms in the original building or smart, modern extension. It's almost worth a visit just for the view – nearly identical to that in the most famous Constable painting of Salisbury cathedral; elegantly restored inn with friendly beamed and timbered bar, good restaurant and bar food, and charming Avonside garden; disabled access.
Warminster ST8744 BISHOPSTROW HOUSE Boreham Rd, Warminster BA12 9HH (01985) 212312 £123; 32 sumptuous rms. Charming ivy-clad Georgian

house in 27 acres with heated indoor and outdoor swimming pools, indoor and outdoor tennis courts, and fishing on own stretch of River Wylye; homely informal atmosphere, log fires, lovely fresh flowers, antiques and fine paintings in elegant day rooms, very good food.

Teffont Evias ST9831 HOWARDS HOUSE Teffont Evias, Salisbury SP3 5RJ (01722) 716392 £107.50; 9 rms. Very well run, welcoming and comfortable little hotel in 2 acres of gardens and surrounded by quiet countryside; log fire and lots of fresh flowers from the garden in restful sitting room, delicious food, fine breakfasts, particularly good wines, extremely good service.

Salisbury SU1429 RED LION Milford St, Salisbury SP1 2AN (01722) 323334 *£90; 56 individually decorated rms. Handsome family-run 700-year-old hotel with a mix of antique settles, leather chairs and modern banquettes in small 2-roomed panelled bar, spacious old-fashioned lounge with interesting furnishings inc clock with skeleton bellringers, and medieval restaurant; disabled access.

Salisbury SU1429 OLD MILL Town Path, W Harnham, Salisbury SP2 8EU (01722) 327517 *£65; 11 comfortably converted rms. Based on a former mill and warehouse – there's been a mill here since 1135 – with terrace out by mill pool and meadow walks with classic views of Salisbury cathedral; good honest English cooking in evening restaurant and beamed bar.

Stourton ST7734 SPREAD EAGLE Church Lawn, Stourton BA12 6QE (01747) 840587 £59; 5 comfortable and spacious rms. Fine position at the head of Stourhead Lake, popular with older people; old-fashioned furnishings, straightforward waitress-served food in bar and restaurant, good residents' lounge; cl 25 Dec.

Warminster ST8744 OLD BELL Market Pl, Warminster BA12 9AN (01985) 216611 *£58; 20 rms, most with own bthrm. Old-world country-town hotel with traditional bar food, bistro and restaurant, good choice of wines, friendly service; lots to do nearby; cl 25–26 Dec.

Hindon ST9132 LAMB High St, Hindon, Salisbury SP3 6DP (01747) 820573 £55; 13 rms. Solidly built, welcoming and civilised old inn with log fires in fine old bar, attractive lounges, imaginative food, friendly helpful service, and no smoking restaurant.

Beckington ST8051 WOOLPACK Beckington, Bath BA3 6SP (01373) 831244 £54.50; 10 comfortable rms. Genuinely welcoming old coaching inn, carefully refurbished, with log fire in bar and good food using fresh produce inc fish from Brixham; lots to do nearby.

Horningsham ST8141 BATH ARMS Horningsham, Warminster BA12 2LY (01985) 844308 £52; 7 well equipped and clean rms. By the entrance to Longleat House, this comfortable old inn has been modernised without being spoilt; good interesting food, pleasant service, well kept real ales; restaurant cl 25 Dec.

Heytesbury ST9242 ANGEL High St, Heytesbury BA12 OED (01985) 40330 *£49; 4 comfortable rms. Beautiful little coaching inn with superb service from very friendly staff, well kept real ales, good home-made food in charming bistro-style restaurant that opens on to secluded garden; cl 25 Dec.

Semley ST8926 BENETT ARMS Semley, Shaftesbury, Dorset SP7 9AS (01747) 830221 *£46; 5 rms. Friendly little Gothic village inn by large common, with cheery service, traditional home-made bar food using local produce, and extensive range of drinks; cl 25–26 Dec.

Salisbury SU1429 FARTHINGS 9 Swaynes Close, Salisbury SP1 3AE (01722) 330749 *£40; 4 rms, shared bthrm. Spotlessly kept no smoking house with friendly owners, good breakfasts, and pretty garden; close to cathedral; cl Christmas.

Ebbesbourne Wake ST9824 HORSESHOE Ebbesbourne Wake, Salisbury SP5 5JG (01722) 780474 £35; 2 rms. Consistently friendly inn with beautifully kept little bar, open fire, fresh flowers and interesting bric-a-brac on beams, popular home-made food in bar or no smoking restaurant, good breakfasts, well kept real ales, pretty little garden and pets' corner in paddock with goats and a Vietnamese pot-bellied pig; cl pm 25 Dec; disabled access.

West Grafton SU2460 ROSEGARTH West Grafton, Marlborough SN8 3BY (01672) 810288 *£33; 2 rms. Charming 16th-c thatched and half-timbered cottage in 3-acre garden, with comfortable lounge, good breakfasts, and friendly owners; no evening meals but free taxi service for guests taking supper at any of 4 local pubs.

Corsley ST8246 Lane End Cottage 72 Lane End, Corsley, Warminster BA12 7PG (01373) 832392 *£32; 3 rms, 1 with own shower. Quiet and secluded 17th-c cottage, very well kept, with delightful atmosphere, pleasant furnishings, excellent breakfasts, caring service, and neat garden; children over 11. The nearby White Hart has good food.

To see and do

Salisbury SU1429 A beautiful and gently relaxed city, with a good many fine old buildings, particularly around the lovely cathedral close. The most extensive close in the country, it's always been a distinct area of town, and the gates to it are still locked every night. The buildings cover a variety of architectural styles from the 13th c to the present, and while of course its great glory is the elegant cathedral itself, you can't help being struck by how impeccably mown the lawns are. Outside the close, there are some interesting antique and other shops, and the Market Square still has a traditional market each Tues and Sat; parking in town can be tricky then. The Haunch of Venison (Minster St) is a delightful old town tavern, while the Red Lion (Milford St), New Inn (New St) and Avon Brewery (Castle St) are all good for lunch, as is the waterside Old Mill out at West Harnham.

✝ CATHEDRAL Begun in 1220, this took just 38 years to build, making it uniform in style. The magnificent spire (added in 1334 along with the tower) is at 404 ft the tallest in the country, and some would say the finest in the world. Christopher Wren discovered it was leaning, but successfully corrected it, a feat now commemorated by a brass plaque. Also notable are the 14th-c clock, now the oldest working mechanical clock in the world, and the tomb of the first Earl of Salisbury, who gave the church one of only four surviving copies of the Magna Carta; it's still on display. The cloisters are some of the best in the country. Snacks, shop, disabled access; cl during services.
🏠 ❋ There's a good view of the cathedral from outside the 13th-c BISHOP'S PALACE (Cathedral Close), though the one immortalised by Constable, and still much as then, is from across the meadows by the River Avon over by West Harnham.
🏠 Mompesson House (Cathedral Close) Exquisite Queen Anne building, probably the most interesting in the close, with period furnishings, china and paintings, remarkable collection of 18th-c

drinking glasses, and interestingly carved oak staircase. Teas; cl am, all Thurs and Fri, Nov–Mar; £3; NT.
♿ 🖼 SALISBURY AND SOUTH WILTSHIRE MUSEUM (Cathedral Close) Good local history and archaeology in lovely building, with excellent Stonehenge gallery, collections of Wedgwood, costume, lace and embroidery, and some beautiful local watercolours by Turner. Snacks (Apr-Oct), shop, disabled access; cl Sun exc pm July, Aug and during the Salisbury Festival; (01722) 332151; *£2.50 – the ticket gives unlimited visits all year.
🏠 ♿ ❋ ✝ Also worth a look in the close are ST ANNE'S GATE, MALMESBURY HOUSE, the regimental museum, and NORTH CANONRY GARDENS, a peaceful place for a stroll near the river (open certain dates in summer, best to check with the notably friendly tourist information centre on 01722 334956). Nearby, the CHURCH of St Thomas was built for the cathedral workers, so in part is slightly older than the cathedral itself; it's notable for the unusually expansive medieval Painting of Doom.
🏛 ❋ OLD SARUM SU1332 (A345 on northern outskirts) This substantial and easily defended Iron Age hill fort

held a township right through the Roman occupation and Dark Ages into Norman times, when a castle and cathedral were built. In the early 13th c, through lack of either space or water, there was a general move to the much more fertile site of the present city, and the fort gradually fell into decline, becoming a quarry for the new centre; consequently there's not much left of the old cathedral and castle, but the views are splendid, and the foundations give interesting clues to ancient architecture and styles. Snacks, shop; cl 24–6 Dec, 1 Jan; (01722) 335398; £1.35.

Other things to see and do

⌂ There are around 4,500 **ancient sites and monuments** in Wiltshire – more than anywhere else in the country. Not all these places have much for the non-archaeologist to notice beyond a few mysterious humps in the ground. The major sites are described in the alphabetical listing below, but others worth a look if passing can be found near Enford SU1351, Norton Bavant ST9043 and White Sheet Hill ST8034 (its traditionally maintained downland now a nature reserve), with a white horse near Pewsey SU1560.

ⱷ⌖ **Brokerswood** ST8352 WOODLAND HERITAGE MUSEUM AND WOODLAND PARK 80 acres of woodland, with lakes, wildfowl, campsites, wildlife and conservation displays, adventure playground, walks, and little railway. Snacks, shop, some disabled access; park open daily, museum cl Sat (exc pm in summer), and am Sun in winter; (01373) 823800; £2. The Woolpack at Beckington has good food.

🐖 ✹ ❀ **Cholderton** SU2242 CHOLDERTON RARE BREEDS FARM Living museum of farm animals and poultry through the ages, with pigs, goats, sheep and cattle to feed. Also 50 breeds of rabbit, water gardens and some lovely views. Lots going on at wknds, from trailer rides and talks to pig-racing. Meals, snacks, shop, disabled access; cl Nov–Mar; (01980) 64438; £3.20. The Crown is useful for lunch.

✹ ✝ **East Knoyle** ST8731 WATERDALE HOUSE (Milton) Woodland garden at its best in late spring/early summer, with long-established camellias, rhododendrons and magnolias; also other plants inc water garden. Teas if fine; open Sun Apr–May; £1.50. The plasterwork in the chancel of the church was designed by Wren's father; he was the parish priest. The Seymour Arms is useful for lunch.

✿ **Hindon** ST9132 has a good CRAFT SHOP in a converted chapel, while up the hill a bit and round the corner the Lamb is good for lunch.

🏰 ✝ **Ludgershall** SU2650 CASTLE Former royal castle and hunting palace, ruined since the 16th c. You can still see some of the original large Norman earthworks, as well as the later flint walling; free. The CHURCH is also Norman. The nearby area is very pretty and unspoilt, the little villages of the Chutes, Tangley and Vernham Dean straddling the Hampshire border all worth a look (with the pubs over that way worth exploring too).

✿ **Middle Woodford** SU1236 HEALE GARDENS Eight acres of lovely formal gardens beside the River Avon, with lots of varied plants; the water garden is especially nice in spring and autumn. Snacks, specialist plant sales with many rare types propagated from the main gardens, shop, disabled access; (01722) 782504; £2.50. The Wheatsheaf in nearby Lower Woodford is good for lunch.

✿ ⌂ **Pepperbox Hill** SU2124, 5 miles SE of Salisbury, is named after the strangely shaped 17th-c tower on its summit. You can't get into the tower, but the site commands fine views over Salisbury itself, and southwards as far as Southampton. Another viewpoint over Salisbury is the Iron Age hill fort of FIGSBURY RING SU1833.

✿ **Stockton** ST9738 LONG HALL Series of meticulous mainly formal gardens laid out along Gertrude Jekyll lines, set against lovely partly medieval hall (not open); also fine trees with profusion of spring bulbs, and hellebores. Plant sales; open Weds

Apr–Sept; £2. The Bell at Wylye is good for lunch.

🏚🐾🍽 **Stonehenge** SU1142 One of the most famous prehistoric monuments in the world; everyone knows what it looks like, and the mechanics of getting the stones here have been pretty much sorted out (the larger ones local, the smaller ones all the way from Wales), but no one's really sure exactly what Stonehenge with its careful astronomical alignments was for. All very mysterious, and that's part of the attraction, though if you've made a long journey to see it you may end up slightly disappointed; in the interests of conservation, you'll have to stand and look from a distance. The best views are very early in the morning from the track from Larkhill, on the other side of the A344, or on a cold clear winter evening looking W past the monument towards the sunset; the ancient stones look very impressive silhouetted against the sky. In broad daylight when the crowds are there (not to mention the busy traffic – there's still argument rather than action about the nearby trunk road), the place loses much of its power to inspire awe, and at the best of times is not somewhere to impress young children. Plans for a new visitor centre rumble on, with nothing sorted as we went to press. Museum, snacks, shop, disabled access; (01980) 624715; cl 24–26 Dec, 1–2 Jan; £2.85; NT. WOODHENGE SU1543 nearby has the scant traces of another prehistoric monument which consisted of six rings of timber posts in a ditch; the positions are now marked by concrete posts, and a cairn marks the central spot where the tomb of a little girl ceremoniously axed to death was found. There's good PICK-YOUR-OWN fruit from late Jun to late July at Rolleston Manor Farm on the B3086 NW of Stonehenge.

✿❃🏚✝ **Stourton** ST7734 STOURHEAD Marvellous 18th-c gardens, gradually laid out in Italian style by the banker Henry Hoare II following his return from an Italian tour; a beautifully harmonious landscape of temples, lakes, bridges and splendid trees and other plants. Fine views from the very tall 18th-c folly at the far end of the

South Wiltshire

estate, though there are 221 steps (cl Mon and Fri). The early Georgian house has some good Chippendale furniture, and the church in the grounds is in a lovely hillside setting. Snacks, shop, disabled access; garden open all year, house pm daily exc Thurs and Fri, Apr–Oct; £4.10 for the gardens (less Nov–Feb), then another £4.10 for the house – if you can only do one, make it the gardens; NT. STOURTON HOUSE GARDEN An informal garden nearby, profusely planted with interesting and colourful shrubs, trees and other plants, inc unusual daffodils and over 250 species of hydrangea. Plant and dried-flower sales, teas, disabled access; open

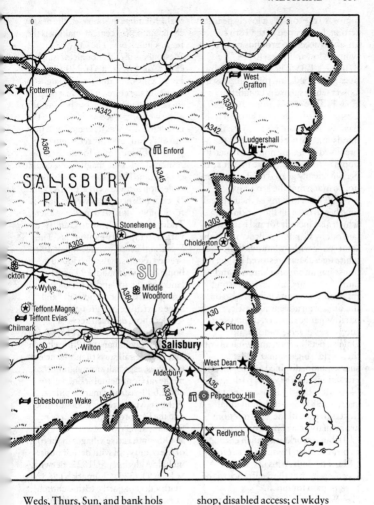

Weds, Thurs, Sun, and bank hols Apr–Nov; (01747) 840417; *£2. The Spread Eagle at the entrance to Stourhead is useful for lunch.

★ 🐂 ☺ **Teffont Magna** ST9832 is very attractive, full of charming stone-built cottages with neatly banked stone-walled gardens. The Black Horse is good for lunch. FARMER GILES FARMSTEAD Working dairy farm with 150 cows milked every afternoon, as well as calves, cattle, shire horses, donkeys, pigs, goats, rabbits and poultry; children can fuss the animals, feed the lambs in late spring, and play on the tractors. Also historical exhibitions, adventure playground, and a little vineyard. Meals, snacks,

shop, disabled access; cl wkdys Nov–Mar; (01722) 716338; £3.

★ † 🏠 🏚 ❀ **Tisbury** ST9429 Charming small town, left behind by the main roads so largely unspoilt, with some fine old buildings, riverside church, and just outside to the E an immensely long medieval tithe barn. OLD WARDOUR CASTLE, a couple of miles S, is the remains of a substantial 14th-c lakeside castle, badly damaged in the Civil War when a formidable elderly chatelaine with a handful of servants and estate workers held off a thousand Roundheads for quite a time before surrendering. The walls still stand to their original 60 ft, and you can walk almost to the top. It's a lovely peaceful setting, landscaped in the 18th c. Disabled access to grounds only; cl winter Mon and Tues; (01747) 870487; £1.35. The lovely old Crown does good food, and the Compasses at Lower Chicksgrove is delightful.

🏠 ✿ 🏃 🏦 ! ☺ Nr **Warminster** ST8043 LONGLEAT (off A362 W) Easily a full day's activities on this lively estate, its handsome 16th-c house one of the first lived-in stately homes to open its doors to the public. Since then it's all become firmly geared to visitors, but not so much that the attractive grounds have lost any of their appeal. Fine beech trees fill the parklands, which also include formal gardens laid out by Capability Brown, and the safari park with its famous lions and white tiger. Much restored inside, the house has impressive libraries and family portraits, and an interestingly restored Victorian kitchen. Also on the site are an adventure castle, narrow-gauge railway, displays on subjects as diverse as dolls and Daleks, pets' corner, and what may be the world's biggest maze. Meals, snacks, shop, disabled access; most attractions, inc the safari park, are cl Nov–Mar, but the house is open all year; (01985) 844400; individual tickets to each of the 17 attractions are available (the house on its own is *£4), but it works out much cheaper to buy the all-in Passport ticket for *£11. The Bath Arms at Horningsham at the S entrance to the park is good for lunch.

🏛 ✿ **Westbury** ST8751 To the E you can see the huge Westbury WHITE HORSE cut into the chalk of the downs; late 18th-c, it was an 'improvement' on an altogether older one which may have been Saxon, and which faced in the opposite direction. Above the white horse is an extensive Iron Age hill fort, with good views right down to the Mendips in Somerset; the nearby chalk quarry for cement-making is the biggest in Europe. The Crown in Westbury is useful enough for lunch.

🏠 🏦 ✿ 🍺 † **Wilton** ST0930 WILTON HOUSE One of the most satisfying houses in the country, not just because there's so much to see, but because it's all so well organised and friendly. The original house was damaged by a fire in 1647, and superbly redesigned by John Webb and Inigo Jones, the latter responsible for the magnificent double cube room. There's an outstanding art collection inc works by Rubens, Van Dyck and Brueghel, as well as fine furnishings, dolls and model soldiers, Tudor kitchen, Victorian laundry, and various temporary exhibitions. The Wareham Bears, a collection of 200 dressed teddies, have also found a home here. Outside are 21 acres of landscaped parkland, with water and rose gardens, woodland walk, and huge adventure playground. Meals, snacks, shop, disabled access; cl Nov–Easter; (01722) 743115; £5.50. The ornately Italianate 19th-c church incorporates all sorts of more ancient treasures, especially its magnificent medieval Continental stained glass and 2,000-year-old marble pillars. Wiltons (Market Pl) is good for lunch, and the Pembroke Arms has a good Sunday carvery.

★ **Other attractive villages** in this part of the county, all with decent pubs, include Alderbury SU1827, Berwick St John ST9323, Chilmark ST9632 (with a decent partly 13th-c church), Great Hinton ST9059, Kilmington ST7736, Mere ST8132 (dominated by its 100-ft church tower and with good views from Castle Hill), Pitton SU2131, Potterne ST9938, The Green ST8731 (nr East Knoyle), West Dean SU2527 and Wylye SU0037. Ansty ST9526 has England's tallest maypole.

Walks

Walking is not this area's strong point. The most attractive possibilities are to be found on the Cranborne Chase ST9317, on the Dorset borders, where the county's abundant chalk downland shows at its best. **Ashcombe Bottom** ST9319 ⌂-1, N of Tollard Royal, is a deep, remote valley which plunges into the heart of the Chase. The Harepath on **White Sheet Hill** ST9523 ⌂-2 near

Old Wardour Castle, is a high track giving sweeping views; you can branch off into a forest plantation.

Haydown Hill SU3156 ⌂-3, reached from the E by a walk up from Vernham Dean SU3456 (itself in Hampshire), has the ramparts of a hill fort bounded by steep gradients on its southern side; the three counties of Berkshire, Hampshire and Wiltshire meet close by at SU3559. In this same general area there are some pleasant walks around the Cross Keys at Upper Chute SU2954.

For **Salisbury Plain** ⌂-4, the County Council has a leaflet mapping out clearly way-marked walks around the edges of the Army's Imber firing range, totalling some 30 miles for the complete circuit.

Driving

The area's prettiest drives are those through the valleys of its chalk streams: the back road along the E side of the Avon valley from Upavon through East Chisenbury to Amesbury, then switching to the W bank for the run down to Salisbury through Wilsford and the Woodfords; the back road along the S side of the Wylye Valley, through Great Wishford, Wylye itself, Stockton and Corton; and the delightful road winding narrowly along the Ebble Valley, through euphoniously named villages such as Odstock, Stratford Tony, Stoke Farthing and Ebbesbourne Wake.

Where to eat

Redlynch SU2020 LANGLEY WOOD (01794) 390348 Very good innovative food and decent wines in homely creeper-covered restaurant set in its own grounds; bedrooms; cl pm Sun, Mon and Tues; children welcome Sun lunch but must be over 11 for dinner; disabled access. £25.

Pitton SU2131 SILVER PLOUGH (01722) 712266 Stylish village inn with lots to look at in beamed and comfortable front bar, good bar snacks and more elaborate meals with emphasis on imaginatively done fresh fish and seafood, well kept real ales, country wines, efficient service. £22|£3.95/£8.95.

Berwick St John ST9323 TALBOT (01747) 828222 Well run and friendly village pub with simply furnished heavily beamed bar, huge inglenook fireplace and decent food in bar and restaurant. £16.50/£6.50.

Potterne ST9958 GEORGE & DRAGON (01380) 722139 Much restored 15th-c thatched cottage with welcoming atmosphere, good food, pleasant service, and unique antique indoor rifle range; bedrooms; cl am Mon. £16|£1.50/£3.95.

NORTH WILTSHIRE

Beautiful villages, attractive small towns, very rewarding places to visit – deserves to be better known than it is.

This part of the county has many charming quiet villages – including Castle Combe and Lacock, two of the country's prettiest. As well as its little streets of attractive buildings, Lacock has other things well worth seeing. Elsewhere the most rewarding places to visit are Bowood House at Calne, Littlecote Manor at Chilton Foliat, Corsham Court and the nearby underground quarry centre, Sheldon Manor at Chippenham and the intriguing gardens of Hazelbury Manor at Box. Bradford-on-Avon has a lot to see. Other attractive small towns with a good deal of character are Devizes, Marlborough and Malmesbury. The Avebury stone circle is in its way as impressive as Stonehenge, and gives you altogether more scope for pottering around; other remarkable prehistoric sites are within easy reach of it.

The countryside, though undramatic, is quite attractive and offers a fair range of pleasant walks. There's a good choice of excellent places to stay .

Where to stay

Colerne ST8171 LUCKNAM PARK Colerne, Chippenham SN14 8AZ (01225) 742777 **£161**; 42 rms. Noble Georgian house reached by a long beech-lined driveway, with extensive grounds and carefully furnished elegant day rooms and panelled library; lovely flowers, antiques and paintings, excellent food and extremely good service in charming restaurant; leisure spa with indoor swimming pool, gym, beauty salon, hairdresser, snooker and floodlit tennis courts; croquet; children over 12 in evening restaurant; disabled access.

Castle Combe ST8477 MANOR HOUSE Castle Combe, Chippenham SN14 7HR (01249) 782206 **£145**; 36 lovely rms. 26 acres of garden and parkland, including an Italian garden, are the setting for this 14th-c manor house with its gracious day rooms, panelling, antiques, log fires and fresh flowers; very good innovative food; disabled access.

Malmesbury ST9387 WHATLEY MANOR Easton Grey, Malmesbury SN16 0RB (01666) 822888 **£112**; 29 rms with antique furniture, 18 in manor house, 11 in Court House across courtyard. Lovely Cotswold manor house in quiet gardens with paddocks by the River Avon; spacious and rather fine oak-panelled drawing room, pine-panelled lounge, log fires, relaxed atmosphere, lots of books in the library-bar, and attractive dining room overlooking garden; tennis court, swimming pool, croquet lawn, putting green, billiards, sauna, solarium and Jacuzzi; disabled access.

Nettleton ST8277 FOSSE FARMHOUSE Nettleton Shrub, Nettleton, Chippenham SN14 7NJ (01249) 782286 *** £98**; 6 rms. 18th-c Cotswold-stone house extensively restored with French decorative antique furniture and pretty English chintzes; morning coffee, lunch and afternoon cream teas served on the lawns or in very attractive dining room; antique shop with dried flowers and decorative items in former dairy behind the house.

Bradford-on-Avon ST8261 WOOLLEY GRANGE Woolley Green, Bradford-on-Avon BA15 1TX (01225) 864705 **£90**; 20 rms. Civilised Jacobean manor house with a relaxed, informal atmosphere, lovely flowers, log fires, antiques and comfortable seating in the beautifully decorated day rooms, and a pretty conservatory; delicious food using local (or home-grown) produce, often organic, inc home-baked breads and muffins and home-made jams and marmalades for breakfast, marvellous staff; very good for children – nursery with full-time nanny, games room, their own sort of food, and outdoor toys; swimming pool, tennis and croquet; disabled access.

Purton SU0887 PEAR TREE Church End, Purton, Swindon SN5 9ED (01793) 772100 *** £90**; 18 very comfortable, pretty rms. Impeccably run former rectory with elegant comfortable day rooms, fresh flowers, fine conservatory restaurant with good food using home-grown herbs, and 7½ acres of grounds inc a traditional Victorian garden; disabled access.

Crudwell ST9592 CRUDWELL COURT Crudwell, Malmesbury SN16 9EP (01666) 577194 **£88**; 15 pretty rms. Delightful warmly welcoming 17th-c rectory with comfortable restful day rooms, log fires, good food in airy and attractive dining room, friendly staff, and neatly kept walled gardens; swimming pool; disabled access.

Beanacre ST9066 BEECHFIELD HOUSE Beanacre, Melksham SN12 7PU (01225) 703700 **£75**; 20 rms. Victorian mansion of Bath stone with very comfortable lounges, antiques and ornate moulded ceilings, and 7 acres of well kept gardens; disabled access.

Lacock ST9168 AT THE SIGN OF THE ANGEL Church St, Lacock, Chippenham SN15 2LA (01249) 730230 £75; 9 lovely rms. This fine 15th-c house in a lovely NT village is full of character, with heavy oak furniture, beams and big fireplaces, an oak-panelled restful lounge, and good English cooking in two candlelit restaurants; cl 1 wk Christmas; disabled access.

Malmesbury ST9287 OLD BELL Abbey Row, Malmesbury SN16 0BW (01666) 822344 £75; 34 rms. With some claim to being one of England's oldest hotels and standing in the shadow of the Norman abbey, this fine wisteria-clad building has traditionally furnished rooms with Edwardian pictures, an early 13th-c hooded stone fireplace, 2 good fires, cheerful and helpful service, and attractively old-fashioned garden.

Devizes SU0061 BEAR Market Pl, Devizes SN10 1HS (01380) 722444 £70; 24 rms. An old-fashioned feel to this inn which dates from the 16th c and is very much at the town's heart; wide choice of food from snacks to more elaborate meals served in the oak-panelled Lawrence room, two more formal restaurants, beams and fresh flowers and prompt service.

Bradford-on-Avon ST8261 WIDBROOK GRANGE Trowbridge Rd, Bradford-on-Avon BA15 1UH (01225) 864750 *£69; 19 rms, 17 with own bthrm, and many in carefully converted courtyard cottages. Handsome stone ex-farmhouse in 11 acres, with comfortable drawing rooms, good food in elegant dining room, sunny conservatory, and indoor swimming pool and exercise machines; disabled access.

Box ST8268 BOX HOUSE Box, Corsham SN14 9NR (01225) 744447 £65; 9 individually decorated, spacious rms with antiques. Handsome Georgian mansion with restful and elegant sitting room, attractively presented fine food in airy dining rooms, a decent wine list, smart helpful staff, and lovely gardens.

Corsham ST8670 METHUEN ARMS High St, Corsham SN13 0HB (01249) 714867 £65; 25 rms. Georgian inn (a former nunnery) with mullioned windows, heavy oak beams, comfortable seats, good food, and friendly staff; pretty walled garden and fine skittle alley; cl 24–25 Dec; disabled access.

Burbage SU2361 OLD VICARAGE Burbage, Marlborough SN8 3AG (01672) 810495 *£60; 3 rms. Carefully run Victorian house in 2 acres of lovely grounds, with log fires, books and magazines in very attractive solidly comfortable drawing room, and good breakfasts (pubs and restaurants nearby for evening meals); no smoking; croquet and nearby riding; cl Christmas and New Year; no children.

Bradford-on-Avon ST8261 BRADFORD OLD WINDMILL 4 Masons Lane, Bradford-on-Avon BA15 1QN (01225) 866842 £59; 4 rms, 1 with giant waterbed, another with round bed. Interesting and carefully converted windmill with log fire in attractive circular lounge (formerly the grain store), good evening meals inc vegetarian dishes from Thailand, Nepal, Mexico and so forth, and fine breakfasts eaten around communal refectory table, lots of books, a friendly atmosphere, and pretty cottagey garden; no smoking; children over 6.

Ford ST8374 WHITE HART Chippenham SN14 8RP (01249) 782213 £59; 11 rms. Attractive ivy-covered inn in lovely spot by trout stream, with old-fashioned atmosphere, unusual and popular food, day rooms of real character, good service, and secluded small swimming pool; disabled access.

Willesley ST8488 TAVERN HOUSE Willesley, Tetbury Glos GL8 8QU (01666) 880444 £59; 4 pretty rms. Carefully restored and neatly kept 17th-c Cotswold-stone house, once an inn and staging post, with antiques and flowers in elegantly furnished rooms, and charming walled garden; children over 10.

Marlborough SU1869 IVY HOUSE High St, Marlborough SN8 1HJ (01672) 515333 £50; 26 rms. Handsome Georgian hotel with flowers and open fires in attractive lounge and reception area, very good food and wines in elegant restaurant, and helpful friendly staff.

Alderton ST8382 MANOR FARM Alderton, Chippenham SN14 6NL (01666

840271) £45; 3 rms, 2 with own bthrm. Warmly friendly 17th-c house on busy working farm, with homely lounge and good breakfasts; children over 12.

Wilcot SU1360 GOLDEN SWAN Wilcot, Pewsey SN9 5NN (01672) 62289 £35; 4 rms, shared bthrm. Ancient and very picturesque steeply thatched village inn in the quiet Vale of Pewsey, with lots of china jugs and mugs hanging from beams in 2 small rooms, a friendly atmosphere, bar food and dining room, and pretty front lawn; cl Christmas.

Rowde ST9762 LOWER FOXHANGERS FARM Rowde, Devizes SN10 1SS (01380) 828254 £32; 3 rms, 1 with own bthrm. 18th-c farmhouse on a 90-acre work-ing beef farm, with dining room and lounge; boating, fishing and walking on Kennet & Avon Canal; mobile homes also; cl Oct–Apr.

Gastard ST8868 BOYDS FARM Gastard, Corsham SN13 9PT (01249) 713146 £30; 3 rms. Friendly and handsome 16th-c house on family-run working farm with pedigree herd of Herefords; homely lounge, woodburning stove, tradi-tional breakfasts; no evening meals.

To see and do

★ ⌂ ☺ ⚲ ⌘ ✿ **Avebury** SU1069 This spectacular stone circle shares its site with a village. The big difference from Stonehenge is that as there haven't been the same hordes of tourists there's free and open access to the site with its 200 stones enclosed in a massive earthen rampart nearly a mile in circumference. It's the largest stone circle in Europe, and probably older than Stonehenge. Leading away from the circle is a 1½-mile avenue of stones known as WEST KENNET AVENUE – a good stretch has been restored. An interesting MUSEUM has an important collection of archaeological finds from the area, inc from WINDMILL HILL ST9623, a Neolithic enclosure a little over a mile away, but still on the same property. Shop, disabled access; £1.35. Management of the site was changing from English Heritage to National Trust as we went to press, so opening times weren't decided – it has been open daily exc winter Mon and Tues, but best to check on (01672) 539250. GREAT BARN MUSEUM OF WILTSHIRE LIFE Close by, in the pretty village, this magnificent 17th-c thatched barn has interesting rural life displays, and craft demonstrations every Sun; also occasional craft and food fairs. Snacks, shop, disabled access; cl wkdys mid-Nov–mid-Mar; (01672) 539555; *95p. AVEBURY MANOR dates from before the Conquest, but is mainly 16th-c; it was closed for restoration as we went to press, but you can usually see the intriguing gardens; best to check

what's open on (01672) 539388; NT. Stones does good vegetarian food.
⌂ Many more **prehistoric remains** around Avebury include towering SILBURY HILL SU1068, purpose unknown, the largest man-made mound in Europe – it would have taken a thousand men about ten years to build. Also close by is the 5,000-year-old chambered tomb and barrow at WEST KENNET SU1067, where several dozen people were buried – take a torch if you want to venture in behind the massive entrance stone: the chamber with two side chapels runs some 30 ft or more into the barrow. The Waggon & Horses at Beckhampton (of *Pickwick Papers* fame) is quite handy.
★ ✿ ✝ **Box** ST8268 is an attractive up-and-down village, its interesting parts hidden down the steep valley below the A4, with cottages and houses using the same stone that's been quarried near here since Roman times. There's a story that on 9 April, Brunel's birthday, the rising sun shines right through the great railway tunnel he quarried through the hill above here, in its day the longest in the world (you can see the restored grand entrance from the A4). HAZELBURY MANOR (off B3109 just E of centre) Richly varied landscaped gardens, with a medieval archery alley, stone and yew circles, fountain, waterfall, pond, large rockery, formal areas, and laburnum walk, all laid out as a sort of giant maze. Some disabled access, plant sales; open Thurs, Sun and bank

hols May–Sept, or by appointment; (01225) 812952; *£2.80. In Chapel Plaister ST8367 on the way, look out for the 15th-c CHAPEL for Glastonbury pilgrims on the little hilltop green. The Quarrymans Arms tucked away on Box Hill is good for lunch.

★ 🏰 † 🏠 ❀ ✤ **Bradford-on-Avon** ST8261 is an attractive hillside town given a distinguished air by the same sort of golden stone as was used in Bath; it's very steep, and has some handsome buildings reflecting its past wealth as a wool town. There are quite a few serious antique shops. Near the Norman parish church is a tall narrow late SAXON CHURCH, unusual for having virtually no later additions. The Bunch of Grapes (Silver St), Dandy Lion (Masons Hill) and Barge down by the canal are useful for lunch. A medieval TITHE BARN can be seen at nearby Barton Farm down by the river and canal, its massive stone-slab roof supported by an impressive network of great beams and rafters. A short walk along the canal from here is AVONCLIFF, quite a steep gorge shared by canal, river and railway, the canal stepping over the river by way of an aqueduct. The Cross Guns has remarkable views over all of this, and is a good place for lunch. Up the hill from here, just SE of Bradford itself, is WESTWOOD MANOR, a fully furnished 15th-c stone manor house with its original Gothic and Jacobean windows, fine 17th-c plasterwork, and a modern topiary garden; open pm Sun, Tues and Weds Apr–Sept; (01225) 863374; £3.20. The New Inn in Westwood village has good value food, and the CHURCH has some interesting late medieval stained glass. Just past here is IFORD MANOR ST8058, notable for its stylish Edwardian Italianate riverside terraced garden, with romantic cloisters, colonnade and statues; house not open. Teas Sun and bank hols; open pm exc Mon and Fri May–Sept, plus bank hols, and Sun Apr and Oct; (01225) 863146; £2. Out to the NE of town, past Bradford Leigh, is GREAT CHALFIELD MANOR ST8663, a beautiful moated manor house, restored in 1920 and still with its original Great Hall; open

Tues–Thurs Apr–Oct, guided tours only, at 12.15, 2.15, 3, 3.45 and 4.30 pm; £3.50; NT. Next door is a small 13th-c church.

🐖 🍴 🏰 **Bromham** ST9464 SANDRIDGE FARM Farm curing bacon and Wiltshire ham using traditional recipes – not pumping them full of slimy water; a viewing window shows the curing process. Also exhibition, nature trail through woodland and pig paddocks (wellies recommended), and baby farm animals. Shop (with good bacon and sausages), disabled access; cl Sun Oct–Apr; (01380) 850304; free. The Greyhound in the village is good for lunch.

✤ 🍴 🏰 🖼 🖿 **Calne** ST9769 BOWOOD The extensive parkland (laid out by Capability Brown) and colourful pleasure gardens are the glory of Bowood, with their temples, cascades and hermit's cave shielded from the outside world by further miles of partly wooded grounds; in May and Jun a separate woodland garden is open for rhododendron walks. Much of the main building was demolished in 1955, but there's plenty left; the impressive library was designed by Robert Adam, who also created the Orangery now used to house most of the fine displays of art and sculpture. Notable collection of English watercolours, as well as the laboratory where Joseph Priestley discovered oxygen in 1772, and an outstanding adventure playground. Meals, snacks, shop, limited disabled access; cl Nov–Mar; (01249) 812102; £4.50. The Lansdowne Arms at Derry Hill, near the house, is popular for lunch, and Calne also has a MOTOR MUSEUM.

★ † **Castle Combe** ST8477 For many the prettiest village in Britain, this has a classic group of stone-tiled Cotswoldy cottages by the turreted CHURCH at the bottom of the tree-clad hill that descends to the trout stream and its ancient stone bridge. Preservation of the village is taken so seriously that you won't even see television aerials on the houses. Some of the villagers open their beautifully kept gardens for charity the last wknd of Jun. Best of all during the week out of season; at other times it does get a great many visitors, even though the car park is sited some way up the hill. The Castle and White Hart are charming old places for something to eat.

🏠✳😊🍽️🎡🎭 **Chilton Foliat** SU3070
LITTLECOTE MANOR Handsome red-brick gabled Tudor house in lush Kennet Valley parkland, where Henry VIII courted his wife Jane Seymour. Civil War armour in the oak-panelled great hall, unique Cromwellian chapel, fine collections of period furniture, china and glass, and some intricately hand-painted Chinese wallpaper. The grounds may seem a touch commercialised to some, but it's a good mix for families, with as well as the medieval and Tudor gardens a collection of classic cars, pets' corner, rare breeds, and adventure playground. There's also a little Roman museum around the remains of a villa containing a beautiful 4th-c mosaic. Jousting every day in summer. Meals, snacks, craft shops, garden centre, some disabled access; cl Oct–Easter; (01488) 684000; £5.50. The Wheatsheaf has good value food.

🏠▣✳✝❗ **Corsham** ST8770
CORSHAM COURT Fine house and park begun in 1582 but subsequently added to and developed by those busy masters Capability Brown, John Nash, Robert Adam and Humphrey Repton. The collection of beautiful paintings is among the best of any stately home in the country, inc works by Caravaggio, Reynolds, Rubens and Van Dyck, and there are some fine statues and furnishings. In the gardens, the peaceful lake and a Georgian bath house are patrolled by a number of peacocks – if they haven't decided to wander off into the village. Shop, disabled access; cl am, Mon (exc bank hols), Fri (exc Easter–Sept), and all Dec; (01249) 712214; £3.50. Nearby there are some attractive former weavers' cottages; the CHURCH, on the edge of the park, is largely 12th-c, partly Saxon. UNDERGROUND QUARRY (Park Lane) The only shaft stone mine open to the public anywhere in the world. Don a miner's helmet and descend the 159 steps into a fascinating labyrinth of surprisingly spacious tunnels and galleries, from where the gorgeous Bath stone was

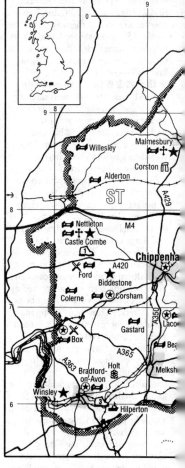

quarried. Privately owned, this is a refreshingly unspoilt place, well off the tourist routes, and as it's rarely busy you can really get a lot out of it. Wrap up well though – it always stays chilly. Snacks, shop; open daily exc Fri May–Sept, only open Sun Apr and Oct, guided tours roughly every hour and a half from 10.15 am (11.45 am Sat) to 3.30 pm; (01249) 716288; *£3.50. The town has a surprising number of antique shops, some very fine, and the Methuen Arms, which includes parts of a former priory, is good for lunch; anyone who likes real ale will enjoy the Two Pigs.

🏠✝✳🍽️ **Chippenham** ST8874
SHELDON MANOR Charming lived-in

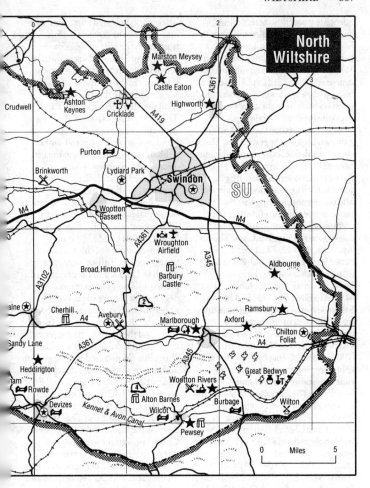

North
Wiltshire

Marston Meysey

Castle Eaton

Highworth

A361

Crudwell

Ashton
Keynes

Cricklade

A419

Purton

Brinkworth

Lydiard Park

Swindon

SU

M4

Wootton
Bassett

M4

A3102

Wroughton
Airfield

A345

Broad Hinton

Aldbourne

Barbury
Castle

alne

Cherhill

A4

Avebury

Marlborough

Ramsbury

Axford

Chilton
Foliat

Sandy Lane

A361

A4

Heddington

Kennet & Avon Canal

Rowde

Devizes

Wootton Rivers

Great Bedwyn

Alton Barnes

Wilcot

Burbage

Wilton

Pewsey

0   Miles   5

13th-c manor house, still with original (and highly unusual) porch, and a 15th-c CHAPEL. The panelled rooms have oak furnishings and collections of glass and porcelain, while the lovely terraced gardens include a mass of old-fashioned roses, yew trees as old as the house, and other interesting trees. Good meals and snacks, shop with plant sales, disabled access; open pm Sun, Thurs and bank hols, Apr–Oct; (01249) 653120; £3. Chippenham itself has a decent local history MUSEUM in the 16th-c Guildhall; cl Sun, Nov–Mar; free.
† ⅄ **Cricklade** SU1093 Small town quietly separated from the busy A419, with some attractive buildings and a

glorious tower crowning the fine parish CHURCH. At the end of the High St, just N of the Thames, a path on the left off the slip road heading back towards the A419 leads to a broad RIVERSIDE MEADOW kept unimproved for decades, and mown only in July after the numerous wild flowers have seeded.
★ ♨ ▣ ❁ **Devizes** SU0061 Lots of grand old buildings in this interesting and friendly town, and a good town trail takes most of them in. The 29 locks of the Kennet & Avon Canal coming up Caen Hill from the W form one of the longest flights of locks in the country; recent droughts have made it difficult to maintain an

adequate water flow here, and an appeal has been launched for funds to build a new pumping station. The headquarters of the Canal Trust on the Wharf has a museum and information centre; (01380) 721279; £1. The local history MUSEUM (Long St) is particularly good on finds from the area's ancient sites (the Bronze Age gallery is especially interesting), and has an art gallery with John Piper window. Shop, some disabled access; cl Sun and bank hols; (01380) 727369; £1.75. BROADLEAS (Potterne Rd) Rare plants in secluded dell among rhododendrons and other fine flowering shrubs, unusual trees, spring and autumn colour too. Teas Sun, unusual plant sales; open pm Sun, Weds and Thurs, Apr–Oct; (01380) 722035; *£2. The Bear Hotel, Elm Tree and White Bear, all tied to Wadworths, the local brewery, are all good for lunch.

↓t ☘ **Great Bedwyn** SO2764 BEDWYN STONE MUSEUM Fascinating little open-air museum demonstrating the ancient art of stonemasonry. Meals, snacks, shop, disabled access; (01672) 870234; free. CROFTON BEAM ENGINES Old pumping station housing the oldest working beam engines in the world, the 1812 Boulton & Watt, and an 1845 Harveys of Hayle, again pumping water into the Kennet & Avon Canal. Snacks, shop; open Sun, bank hols and pm Sat Easter–Oct, engines static most wknds but in steam in 1995 on 16–17 Apr, 29 Apr–1 May, 27–29 May, 29–30 July, 26–28 Aug, 30 Sept–1 Oct; (01672) 851639; static *£1.50, steam wknds *£3. The Harrow nearby at Little Bedwyn is good for lunch.

✿ **Holt** ST8661 THE COURTS Weavers used to come here to settle their disputes; the 15th-c house isn't open, but there are lovely and extensive formal gardens full of yew hedges, pools and borders, with the other half of the grounds given over to wild flowers among interesting trees. Disabled access; cl am, Sat, Nov–Mar; £2.50; NT. The Old Bear at Staverton has a wide food choice.

★✝ film ☘ ☕ ♉ ☕ film ☀ **Lacock** ST9168 A favourite village, this has a grid of quiet and narrow streets which are a delightful harmony of mellow

brickwork, lichened stone and timber-and-plaster; the CHURCH is 15th-c, and nothing in the village looks more recent than 18th-c. It's remained so remarkably unspoilt because most buildings in the village were owned for centuries by the Talbot family, until they left them to the NT in 1944. The showpiece is LACOCK ABBEY, a tranquil spread of mellow stone buildings, around a central timber-gabled courtyard, based on the little-altered 13th-c abbey. Cloisters, impressive Great Hall, medieval nunnery buildings and so forth, with some Tudor additions inc a romantic octagonal tower, and a successful 18th-c Gothicisation – even an old brewery. Surrounded by quiet meadows and trees, this was the setting for Fox Talbot's experiments which in 1835 led to the creation of the world's first photographic negative – a picture of part of the abbey itself. There's a museum (£2.30 entrance) devoted to this in a 16th-c barn, and the gardens are evidence of Fox Talbot's skills in other fields. Shop, limited disabled access; grounds and cloisters open every day, house and museum cl am, Tues, Good Fri, Nov–Mar; *£4.20, grounds and cloisters £2.10; NT. LACKHAM COUNTRY ATTRACTIONS This 500-acre estate is the home of the Lackham College of Agriculture, and attractions include a farm museum, walled garden and glasshouses, rare-breeds farm, pleasant woodland and riverside walks and a children's playground; the old roses are worth catching from May to July. They have ambitious plans for extending the garden. Snacks, shop, plant sales, disabled access; cl Nov–Mar; (01249) 443111; *£3. The NT, which owns the village, has preserved it against a surfeit of antique shops, but you'll find all you want in the nearby old market town of Melksham ST9063. The village does on the other hand have a splendid collection of pubs and inns – all good in their way; the Rising Sun out on Bewley Common up Bowden Hill has tremendous views.

film ☘ ✝ **Lydiard Park** SU1085 Grand Georgian house painstakingly restored after a long period of neglect up to WWII, with interesting early wallpaper and rare painted glass window, and elegant furnishings much as they would have been when first installed. Outside are extensive lawns, lakes and well wooded parkland, with nature walks and adventure playgrounds. The adjacent parish CHURCH has interesting monuments to the St John family, who lived in the house for 500 years. Snacks, shop, disabled access; cl 1–2 pm, am Sun, Good Fri, 25-26 Dec; (01793) 770401; car parking *£1, house *50p – quite a bargain.

★ † **Malmesbury** ST9287 Yet another charming old town, especially around the green facing its serene Norman ABBEY, from the tower of which a medieval monk called Elmer made one of the earliest semi-successful attempts at flight – he covered a couple of hundred yards, but did break both legs when he crash-landed. The Suffolk Arms up the Tetbury road is the best place here for lunch, and the Smoking Dog (High St) and Whole Hog (Market Cross) can also be recommended; the picturesque Old Bell is almost as old as the abbey beside it.

★ ⚘ **Marlborough** SU1868 One of the area's most attractive towns, this has a very pleasing wide High St, scene of the annual autumn Mop Fair which used to be held in most market towns for the hiring of servants, but which has been revived here as a general celebration – there's also a regular market each Weds and Sat. Even the more modern additions don't look obtrusively out of place among the harmonious mix of Georgian and Tudor buildings. The side streets are well worth exploring, too. To the N, the downs give great open spaces, not all turned over to monotonous arable farming (see Walks, below); to the E there are woody walks through the surviving miles of SAVERNAKE FOREST. The Bear, Sun and Green Dragon are useful for lunch.

🚩👹🅱 **Swindon** SU1484 This bustling hill-top market town and business centre is much older than you might think, and is mentioned in the Domesday Book. Later it was caught up with a vengeance in the railway

age, and in the Railway Village had one of the earliest examples of a planned workers' estate. In the heart of this, the excellent GREAT WESTERN RAILWAY MUSEUM (Faringdon Rd) is excellent, with lots of locomotives and related train memorabilia celebrating this most highly regarded railway, inc the historic Dean Goods and Lode Star. Also an exhibition on the GWR village itself, with recreated workshop displays. They're looking into moving premises so it may be worth checking first. Shop; cl am Sun; (01793) 493189; £1.80. Next door, the RAILWAY VILLAGE HOUSE AND MUSEUM (34 Faringdon Rd) is a restored foreman's house furnished in typical turn-of-the-century working-class style. Shop; cl 1–2 pm, am Sun; 85p. SWINDON & CRICKLADE RAILWAY One of the only live steam projects in the area, gradually being restored, with occasional trips through the countryside, and a museum. Meals, snacks, shop, disabled access; open wknds; (01793) 721252 for train times, wknds only; around £2. The Glue Pot (Emlyn Sq, in the Railway Village) is an entertaining local. MUSEUM AND ART GALLERY (Bath Rd) Small local history collection; also pictures by important 20th-c artists such as Moore and Sutherland. Shop, limited disabled access; cl am Sun, bank hols; free.

✠ **Wilton** SU2661 (not to be confused with the larger town in the south of the county) WILTON WINDMILL The only working windmill in the county, built in 1821 after the construction of the Kennet & Avon Canal had taken away all the water previously used to power mills. It's been restored, and on its prominent chalk ridge is beautifully floodlit every evening. Shop; open pm Sun Easter–Sept, plus Mon and Sat bank hol wknds; (01672) 870427; 80p. The Tipsy Miller at Marten has decent food.

† 🏛 **Wroughton Airfield** SU1378 has a branch of London's SCIENCE MUSEUM, housing growing national collections of aircraft, rockets, hovercraft, and road transport vehicles. Not really aimed at entertaining the general public, it's usually open around five times a year,

with lively special events or air displays; (01793) 814466 for 1995 dates; charges vary.

⌂ As well as the places we've mentioned, there are **ancient sites** at BARBURY CASTLE SU1677 (a splendidly remote and atmospheric place) and several near Marlborough, with good WHITE HORSES at Alton Barnes SU0962, Broad Hinton SU1076, Cherhill SU0370 and Corston ST9284.

⌂ The recently restored **Kennet & Avon Canal** runs right across this part of the county (see also Devizes above), and there are pleasant boat trips from several places along its route. Several correspondents have particularly enjoyed boats hired at Hilperton ST8759 and Bradford-on-Avon ST8261, and you can also embark from Devizes SU0061 or Wootton

Rivers SU1963, though we've had no reports on these. In the canal's restoration, a great deal of attention has been paid to the natural environment, and it's attractive for walks alongside; in winter you may even see a kingfisher flashing along it. For a more sedentary view, try the Barge Inn at Seend Cleeve ST9361.

★ **Other attractive villages** in this part of the county, all with decent pubs, include Aldbourne ST2675, waterside Ashton Keynes SU0494, Axford SU2370, Biddestone ST8773, Castle Eaton SU1495 (by a quiet stretch of the upper Thames, pleasant for strolling), Heddington ST9966, Highworth SU2092, Marston Meysey SU1297, Pewsey SU1560, Ramsbury ST2771, Sandy Lane ST9668, Winsley ST7961 and Wootton Rivers SU1963.

Walks

Castle Combe ST8477 ⌂-1 has surroundings that are as appealing as the village, and attractive paths along deep peaceful valleys.

Much of the Wiltshire chalklands are unvarying green mono-agricultural expanses, but the **Marlborough Downs** ⌂-2 harbour archaeological bounties which you can use to punctuate walks around Avebury SU1069 – for example, to the major prehistoric sites of Silbury Hill SU1068, West Kennet Long Barrow SU1067 and the neolithic camp on Windmill Hill SU0871. Fyfield Down SU1470 is primeval-feeling and unkempt, scattered with outcrops known as Sarsen stones, the raw material of Avebury stone circle and of part of Stonehenge. At the northernmost point of the Marlborough Downs, Barbury Castle SU1476 is an ancient hill-fort site with formidable ramparts, on the long-distance Ridgeway Path. There is a car park nearby, but you can also walk up to it from Ogbourne St George SU1974 along Smeathe's Ridge SU1775, a preserved stretch of downland (gorse and all).

The **Kennet & Avon Canal** ⌂-3 has a long flight of locks on the W side of Devizes SU0061, and can form part of a river and canal walk around Barton Farm Country Park at Bradford-on-Avon ST8261. At **Alton Barnes** SU1062 ⌂-4, the canal lies close enough to Pewsey Down nature reserve for an afternoon's walk to incorporate both features; the spine of the downs here is followed by the Wansdyke, an ancient earthwork which runs across the downs for miles from Morgans Hill SU0267 nr Calne nearly as far as the Savernake Forest.

Driving

The back road from Marlborough over the downs to Broad Hinton gives a good view of the open downland farming country – and covering the ground at car speed rather than walking speed, the scenery seems altogether more varied. Another quiet downland road, giving a view of one of the area's several white horses cut into the chalk of the downs, is from Marlborough to Alton Priors, where a right turn takes you along a pleasant valley road through Allington and Horton to Devizes. In the opposite direction from Marlborough, the quiet road through Mildenhall, Axford and Ramsbury has some charming Kennet Valley views, with good stops at the Red Lion in Axford and Bell in Ramsbury, and pleasant walks.

Relatively quiet main road through attractive countryside is the A342 out of Devizes; a left turn at Sandy Lane takes you on a very pretty back road to Lacock.

The countryside is not bad for cycling, with some quite quiet and not too hilly roads – good routes and maps are available from the County Council, and you can hire bikes in most of the towns in the area (though you need a permit to ride on the canal towpath).

Where to eat

Ford ST8374 WHITE HART (01249) 782213 In a lovely spot by a trout stream, this charming inn serves imaginative meals, a fine range of real ales, farm cider and country wines; bedrooms; £25|£2.25/£4.50.

Brinkworth SU0184 THREE CROWNS (01666) 510366 Friendly atmosphere in villagey pub with generous helpings of unusual and elaborate dishes, well kept real ales, wide choice of wines and spirits, and garden that looks out towards church and over rolling country. **£19 for 2 courses**|£3/£12.

Wootton Rivers SU1963 ROYAL OAK (01672) 810322 Prettily thatched 16th-c pub with relaxed friendly atmosphere, huge choice of well prepared food, well kept beer, decent wines, friendly service; bedrooms with help-yourself breakfasts; cl Christmas. **£16**|£1.75/£6.50.

Box ST8268 QUARRYMANS ARMS (01225) 743569 Tucked-away unspoilt hillside pub with fine views, 2 small knocked-together rooms with quarrying memorabilia, wide choice of good home-cooked food, well kept real ales, and very friendly staff; children welcome; bedrooms. **£13.95**|£1.50/£3.95.

Avebury SU0969 STONES RESTAURANT (01672) 3514 Relaxed but civilised restaurant with very good generously served vegetarian food and friendly service; open all day (not eve), wknds only Nov, Dec, Feb, Mar, cl all Jan; disabled access. £13/£4.95.

Help this year from: G Hart, Ian Jagoe, Bill Capper, Joy Heatherley, S J Penford, Audrey and Peter Dowsett, Buck and Gillian Shinkman, Jan and Dave Booth, Chris Cook, P Neate, R T and J C Moggridge, S G N Bennett, D B McAlpin, Colin and Ann Hunt, A R and B E Sayer, N K Kimber, John Rumney, Lawrence Bacon, M V Ward, Susan and John Douglas, Alan and Heather Jacques, Andrew Shore, W K Struthers, C H and P Stride, Tim Barrow, Sue Demont, GA, PA, Brian Bannatyne-Scott, S H Godsell, Tim and Felicity Dyer, Georgina Cole, JE, Don Mather.

We welcome reports from readers . . .

This *Guide* depends on readers' reports. Do help us if you can – in return, we offer a discount on the next edition to people who've helped us with reports for it. Tell us what you think about places already in it, and anything extra you think we should say about them. And send us your ideas for inclusion in the next edition: places to visit, eat at or stay in, attractive drives or walks, maybe even unusual interesting shops you know of. Use the card in the middle, the report forms at the end, or just write – no stamp needed: *The Good Weekend Guide*, FREEPOST TN1569, Wadhurst, E Sussex TN5 7BR.

WILTSHIRE CALENDAR

Some of these dates were provisional as we went to press.

APRIL

8 **Salisbury** Concert: War Requiem at Salisbury Cathedral (01722) 328726

14 **Devizes** Start of the Westminster International Canoe Race from Wharf Car Park (01491) 872042

15 **Warminster** Balloon Fiesta and Easter Egg Hunt at Longleat House – *till Mon 17* (01985) 844400

16 **Salisbury** St George's Spring Festival – *till Sun 23* (01722) 334956

29 **Malmesbury** Choral Concert at Malmesbury Abbey (01666) 824924

MAY

7 **Amesbury** Sarsen Trail Walk and Marathon which starts at Avebury, crosses Salisbury Plain (normally closed to the public) and ends at Stonehenge (01380) 725670

13 **Castle Combe** Steam Rally at the Race Circuit – *till Sun 14* (01249) 782417; **Salisbury** Festival – *till Sat 27* (01722) 323883

20 **Warminster** Family Cycling Festival at Longleat House – *till Sun 21* (01985) 844400

21 **Lacock** Lackham Country Day at Lackham College Country Attractions (01249) 443111

26 **Chippenham** Folk Festival – *till Mon 29* (01249) 657733

28 **Castle Combe** Classic Run at the Race Circuit (01249) 782417

29 **Chippenham** Celebrity Pro-am at Bowood Golf & Country Club (01249) 822228

30 **Chippenham** Western Golf Open at Bowood Golf & Country Club – *till 1 Jun* (01249) 822228

JUNE

3 **Amesbury** Carnival (01980) 622173

13 **Lacock** Open Air Theatre: A MIDSUMMER NIGHT'S DREAM at Lacock Abbey (01249) 730227

17 **Lacock** Open Air Theatre: THE LION IN WINTER at Lacock Abbey (01249) 730227; **Stourton** Viennese Symphony Concert with Fireworks and Lasers at Stourhead House and Gardens (01747) 840348

18 **Whiteparish** Salisbury and South Wiltshire Agricultural Show (01794) 884355

21 **Stonehenge** Druid Summer Solstice Ceremony *from midnight Tues 20*, vigil till dawn when service celebrates first rays of sun on altar, Presider crowned at noon

24 **Chippenham** Carnival (01249) 660149

25 **Warminster** Amateur Radio Rally at Longleat House (01272) 860422

JULY

1 **Malmesbury** Choral Concert by the Bath Camerata at Malmesbury Abbey (01666) 824924

3 **Bradford-on-Avon** Festival – *till Sun 9* (01225) 867444

8 **nr Marlborough** Open Air Theatre: THE LION IN WINTER at Avebury Manor Garden – *till Sun 9* (01672) 539388; **Warminster** Outdoor Concert with Fireworks at Longleat House (01985) 844400

WILTSHIRE CALENDAR

JULY cont

9 **Marlborough** Festival – *till Sun 23* (01672) 512656

10 **Box** Open Air Theatre: Shakespeare Production at Hazelbury Manor Gardens – *till Sat 15* (01249) 714317

14 **Marlborough** Jazz Weekend – *till Sun 16* (01672) 512656

15 **Devizes** Canal Festival and Boat Week – *till Sun 16* (01225) 700198

19 **Stourton** Centenary Fête Champêtre at Stourhead House and Gardens – *till Sat 22* (01747) 840348

21 **Trowbridge** Village Pump Festival – *till Sun 23* (01373) 830110; **Warminster** Wiltshire Balloon Festival at Longleat House – *till Sun 23* (01985) 844400

29 **Newbury** National Working Boat Gathering at Newbury Wharf – *till Sun 30* (01380) 721279

AUGUST

4 **Stourton** A MIDSUMMER NIGHT'S DREAM at Stourhead House and Gardens – *till Sat 5* (01747) 840348

11 **Marlborough** Wiltshire Artists Annual Exhibition at St Peter's Church: about 275 works by 60 artists for sale – *till Sat 19* (01672) 512771

12 **Calne** Open Air Fireworks and Laser Symphony Concert at Bowood House and Gardens (01625) 572839

19 **Castle Combe** Classic Action Day at the Race Circuit (01249) 782417; **Warminster** Outdoor Jazz Festival at Longleat House (01985) 844400

26 **Devizes** Carnival – *till 2 Sept* (01380) 723775

27 **Neston** Vintage Car Rally at Neston Park – *till Mon 28* (01225) 810211

28 **Corsham** Annual Flower Show; **Lacock** Village Fair (01249) 730320

SEPTEMBER

2 **Bradford-on-Avon** Wharfside Show – *till Sun 3* (01225) 864378; **Chippenham** Garden Allotment Society Annual Flower Show at Neeld Hall (01249) 653051; **Devizes** Carnival Festival – *till Sun 16* (01225) 700198; **Malmesbury** Carnival

9 **Castle Combe** Mini Action Day at the Race Circuit (01249) 782417; **Trowbridge** Carnival (01225) 777054; **Westbury** Medieval Fayre (01373) 827158

17 **Salisbury** Kite and Juggling Festival at Hudson's Field (01722) 410588

20 **Malmesbury** Organ Recital at Malmesbury Abbey (01666) 824924

23 **Castle Combe** Kit Car Action Day at the Race Circuit (01249) 782417; **Pewsey** Illuminated Carnival Procession (01672) 63378

29 **Cricklade** Music Festival at St Sampson's Church – *till 7 Oct* (01793) 750338

OCTOBER

16 **Salisbury** Charter Fair – *till Weds 18* (01722) 434526

28 **Warminster** Carnival – *till Sun 29*

NOVEMBER

18 **Stourton** NT Centenary Concert at Stourhead House – *till 5 Dec* (01747) 840348

DECEMBER

23 **Salisbury** Cathedral, Christmas Carol Concert

YORKSHIRE

Yorkshire has a great deal to offer for short or longer holidays. It has a tremendous variety of interesting places to visit, and glorious scenery for both walkers and drivers – especially in the Yorkshire Dales and North York Moors. It's one of the friendliest areas in Britain, and has dozens of most enjoyable places to stay. York itself is an excellent holiday city, appealing to older children as well as to adults.

The area around the very civilised spa town of Harrogate is particularly rich in beautiful places to visit. What we've called East Yorkshire, less well known to visitors than the dales and the moors, has a quietly untouristy appeal. South and west Yorkshire are the parts where you'll find the most places to visit, including some outstanding museums – many of them free; Calderdale and the south Pennines have a real Yorkshire mix of steep stone cottage terraces, remarkable mill buildings and some dramatic countryside. There are some notable centres of 20th-century art.

YORK

Outstanding for a short stay: largely pedestrianised medieval walled centre, with lots to interest visitors – including older children.

The magnificent minster is one of Britain's great sights, and the Jorvik Centre among the country's best heritage centres. The National Railway Museum and the Castle Museum are also impressive, and there are many other things well worth visiting here. Particularly in the summer, York does flood with visitors, which means queues and crowds at the main attractions; but most people find that all the other visitors actually seem to add to the atmosphere, rather than detracting from it. The centre, enclosed in 13th-c city walls, has lovely medieval buildings, fascinating twisting alleys, interesting shops and lots of lively cafés, pubs and bars; much is pedestrianised.

Where to stay

MIDDLETHORPE HALL Bishopthorpe Rd YO2 1QB (01904) 641241 **£134.90**; 30 fine rms, most in the converted stables. Lovely, immaculately restored William III country house just S of the city, with fine gardens and parkland, antiques and fresh flowers in comfortable, quiet day rooms, and excellent food and service; children over 8.

VIKING North St YO1 1JF (01904) 659822 **£125**; 188 rms. Smart and comfortable modern hotel on the banks of the River Ouse with fine city views, spacious public rooms, and good English cooking in two restaurants; leisure club.

GRANGE Clifton, York YO3 6AA (01904) 644744 **£108**; 30 individually decorated rms with antiques and English chintz. Close to the minster, this Regency town house has elegant public rooms, open fire, newspapers, good breakfasts, excellent restaurant food (there's also a brasserie), and warmly friendly staff; car park; disabled access.

4 SOUTH PARADE YO2 2BA (01904) 628229 £70; 3 lovely rms with Edwardian-style furnishings, original fireplaces and fresh flowers. Beautifully decorated house in small elegant Georgian terrace on private cobbled street 15 mins from minster and 5 mins from station; pretty drawing room, very helpful owners, good breakfasts and candlelit suppers by arrangement in delightful dining room; no smoking; cl Christmas; children over 12.

Shipton by Beningbrough SE5559 SIDINGS Shipton by Beningbrough, York YO6 1BS (01904) 470221 *£65; 8 rms in 2 converted coaches. A railway enthusiast's paradise, based on restored former railway carriages with excellent food served at Pullman-style tables, decent wine list, railway viewing platform, models, videos, and paintings and artefacts; disabled access.

CURZON LODGE 23 Tadcaster Rd, Dringhouses YO2 2QG (01904) 703157 *£56; 10 rms, some in former old coach house and stables. Charming early 17th-c house in marvellous spot overlooking Knavesmire Racecourse, with attractive, comfortable drawing room, sunny farmhouse dining room (good breakfasts), and secluded walled garden; cl Christmas and New Year; children over 7.

HOLMWOOD HOUSE 114 Holgate Rd YO2 4BB (01904) 626183 *£55; 12 pretty rms, most no smoking. Carefully restored mid-19th-c hotel 5 mins from city walls with open fire and books in homely lounge and very good breakfasts; you are given keys and can come and go as you please; own car park; cl first 2 wks Jan; children over 8.

HAZLEWOOD 24–25 Portland St, Gillygate YO3 3EH (01904) 628032 £47; 16 rms, most with own bthrm. Just 4 mins from the minster, this no smoking, neatly kept Victorian house has a lounge, attractive dining room, helpful owners, and a pretty little garden; disabled access.

ARNOT HOUSE 17 Grosvenor Terrace YO3 7AG (01904) 641966 £32; 6 rms. Comfortable house in Victorian terrace with original features, good breakfasts in neat dining room (evening meals on request), a pleasant atmosphere, and helpful owners; cl Dec and Jan; children over 5.

To see and do

✝ ✮ 🏠 MINSTER Britain's largest medieval building, started in 1220 and taking a staggering 250 years to build – a glorious example of Gothic architecture, in soft-coloured York stone. The west front is particularly impressive. It's very richly detailed inside, and contains more original medieval glass than any other church in England; look out for the beautiful ceilings of the central tower and the chapter house, the splendid five sisters window in the north transept, and the great east window which shows Genesis and Revelation in 27 panels. The choir stalls are 19th-c copies, but still worth finding, and the choir screen has 15 niches containing statues of the kings of England from William the Conqueror to Henry VI. The south transept vault has now been restored after the disastrous 1984 fire. There's a good display on the church's often turbulent history in the Foundations Museum and Treasury (inc the 1967–72 work to prevent collapse of the tower). Shop, disabled access; cl am Sun, and occasionally for major services. Largely traffic-free, the close outside is fairly quiet, but not enclosed, and without the tranquil serenity of say Exeter, Salisbury or Winchester. ST WILLIAM'S COLLEGE here has an exhibition on the minster, as well as a restaurant and three finely timbered rooms.

✝ The city has a good few other fine medieval CHURCHES, though many are no longer used for services. Most were built during the prosperous 15th and 16th c, and among the finest are Holy Trinity (Goodramgate) and St Helen's (St Helen's Sq). All Saints (North St) has some fascinating windows illustrating the last 15 days of the world.

♄ JORVIK VIKING CENTRE (below Coppergate Shopping Centre) Probably the first place in the country to utilise the sights-sounds-and-smells technology that's gradually revolutionised the heritage industry,

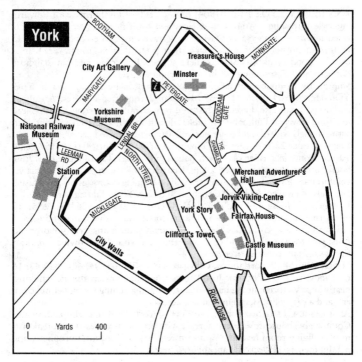

York

BOOTHAM

MONKGATE

Treasurer's House

City Art Gallery

MARYGATE

Minster

PETERGATE

THE GOODRAMGATE

Yorkshire Museum

National Railway Museum

LENDAL BR.

NORTH STREET

LEEMAN RD

THE SHAMBLES

Station

Merchant Adventurer's Hall

Jorvik Viking Centre

MICKLEGATE

York Story

Fairfax House

Clifford's Tower

City Walls

Castle Museum

River Ouse

0   Yards   400

and still easily one of the best. On the excavated site of a Viking street, time-cars whisk you through an exact reconstruction of the street, market and quayside, with quite astonishing detail: some of the faces were painstakingly constructed from actual Viking skulls. At the end are thousands of excavated finds from the site, with an interesting reconstruction of the dig itself. Queues here can be horrifically long, but almost everyone finds the wait well worth while; for the shortest wait, get there early or late. Snacks, shop, disabled access; cl 25 Dec; (01904) 627097; £3.95.

⚒🏠✝⚘🏚 The ARC (St Saviourgate) Refreshingly interesting and accessible archaeology centre; with the help of hands-on interactive displays you can decipher Viking-age writing, learn to make a Roman shoe, and sift through the remains of the past – all with professional archaeologists there to give information and advice. During the summer months you may even be able to watch a dig on Walmgate. Very much on the school-trips circuit, so

best out of termtime. The building itself is also well worth a look – the medieval CHURCH OF ST SAVIOUR, which has been beautifully restored, with an interesting old-fashioned garden. Shop, disabled access; cl am wknds, 18–31 Dec; (01904) 640029; *£3.50. The Archaeological Trust that run the ARC (and the Jorvik Centre, see above) also have a Georgian coffee-house THOMAS GENT's (off Stonegate), serving appropriate snacks on three candlelit floors furnished in period style; cl Sun. It joins on to BARLEY HALL, a medieval family home currently being restored. The full process will take some time, but several completed rooms are already open, and glass panels let you see restoration work in progress. There's a fascinating Walkman tour. Shop (the Trust have a couple more good shops nearby), disabled access to ground floor only; cl Sun, Good Fri, 20 Dec–1 Jan; (01904) 663046; £3.

⚒✖ CASTLE MUSEUM (Tower St) Housed in 18th-c prison buildings on the site of the former castle (part of the outer wall still stands), this is for many one of the best museums in the country, with a huge range of everyday objects from the past four centuries, shown in convincingly reconstructed real-life settings, from individual rooms and craft workshops to whole cobbled streets of shops. There's even a watermill, by the river outside. The collection of militaria is especially impressive, inc one of only three Anglo-Saxon helmets in the world, found here in York in the 1980s. Again, a favourite for school trips, so best out of termtime. Snacks, shop, disabled access to ground floor only; cl 25–26 Dec, 1 Jan; (01904) 653611; £3.95; joint ticket with York Story (see below) available. A REGIMENTAL MUSEUM is nearby; cl Sun and bank hols; 50p.

National Railway Museum (Leeman Rd) The great railway age is celebrated here with lots of panache and flair. The centrepiece is the great hall in which two sets of tracks and platforms radiate from central turntables, one with a changing display of two dozen great locomotives from the museum's huge collection, the other with all sorts of carriages and waggons, from the humblest and most utilitarian to Queen Victoria's sumptuous royal coach; you can go inside most of them. In the background is a well reproduced soundtrack of recorded station noises from the steam era, while alongside a mass of material vividly illustrates the history of rail and how it changed the world, from a lock of Robert Stephenson's hair to Channel Tunnel trains. Timetabled working demonstrations and rides – one place where the trains are always on time. Meals and snacks, shop, disabled access; cl 24–26 Dec; (01904) 621261; £4.20. The nearby Maltings (Wellington Row) has generous food.

City Art Gallery (Exhibition Sq) Well displayed collections running from Old Masters to the lusciously romantic nudes of William Etty, with some very handsome stoneware pottery – a veritable treasure house of paintings from over seven centuries. Shop, disabled access; cl am Sun, 25 Dec, 1 Jan, Good Fri; free. They usually have guided tours on Weds Jun–Sept at 12.30pm.

Clifford's Tower (near the Castle Museum in the castle precincts) After the minster, perhaps York's most interesting building, originally the 14th-c castle keep. You can walk around the top of the walls, which enclose a garden, and there are good views of the city. It gets its name from Roger de Clifford, who was hanged from it by chains. There's an unusual Lowry painting of the tower in the City Art Gallery. Shop; cl winter 1–2pm, 24–26 Dec, 1 Jan; £1.50.

Fairfax House (Castlegate) Magnificently restored mid-18th-c townhouse now probably one of the finest in England, its richly decorated rooms fully furnished in period style. Much of the impressive collection of paintings, pottery, clocks and Georgian furniture was donated by the great-grandson of the confectionery baron Joseph Terry. Among some very interesting displays is a re-created meal of 1763. Shop, some disabled access by arrangement; cl am Sun, Fri (exc Aug), Jan and Feb; (01904) 655543; *£3.20.

Friargate Museum (Lower Friargate) Rather jolly wax museum, with over 60 lifesize models, all posed, often wittily, in realistic sets to illustrate moments in history, from Alfred the Great through Drake to the Yeti. Also unusual and infectious display of laughter machines. Shop; cl Jan; (01904) 658775; £2.75.

Guildhall (St Helen's Sq) Exact replica of the original building of 1446, destroyed in a 1940 air raid. The stone walls of the earlier building survived and form the framework of the new one. There's an interesting arch-braced roof supported by solid oak pillars and decorated with colourful bosses, and some 17th-c glass in the west window. Disabled access; cl wknds exc pm Sun in summer, and most bank hols; (01904) 613161; free.

Merchant Adventurers Hall (Piccadilly) The largest timber-framed building in the city, and one of the finest in Europe. Built for the powerful Merchant Adventurers' Company in the 1350s and hung with banners of medieval guilds, it has a chapel and undercroft as well as the Great Hall itself. Shop, disabled access; cl winter

Sun, 10 days over Christmas and New Year; (01904) 654818; *£1.80.

🔔 MUSEUM OF AUTOMATA (Tower Street) Unusual collection of ingenious machines from the last 2,000 years, from simple moving figures to more hi-tech modern robots. Highlights include the Contemporary Gallery where you can start up the exhibits yourself, and the French Gallery, with video, sound and light bringing the famous figures of Parisian café society to life. Shop, disabled access; cl 25 Dec; (01904) 655550; £3.20.

🏠 TREASURER'S HOUSE (Chapter House St) There's been a house here since Roman times – this one dates from the 17th c, although the staircase dates from the 18th, and the basement has an exhibition of the site's history. The timbered hall is very fine, as is the period furniture, useful as an indication of how the officials of the nearby minster used to live. Snacks, shop; cl Nov–Mar; £3; NT.

🔔🏛☘ YORKSHIRE MUSEUM (Museum Gardens) A real treasure-trove, crammed with myriad archaeological finds and riches from Roman, Anglo-Saxon, Viking and medieval times, inc the fabulous and recently discovered medieval Middleham Jewel. All set out very sensibly, with the displays effectively put into context; they do notable temporary exhibitions. One esp good display is the reconstruction, complete with sound effects, of part of the abbey which stood here. Summer snacks, shop, disabled access; cl 25–26 Dec, 1 Jan, and am Sun in winter; (01904) 629745; £3, less in winter. Outside are 10 acres of botanical gardens by the wall: peaceful and attractive, around a shapely group of ruins inc the Benedictine St Mary's Abbey and the Multangular Tower (medieval, on a Roman base), as well as a working observatory.

❗ YORK DUNGEON (Clifford Street) Carefully researched exploration of superstition, torture and various forms of death, full of grue and gore; these were the days when justice really did need reforming. There's a quite extensive new Guy Fawkes Experience. Shop, disabled access; cl 25 Dec; (01904) 632599; £3.

🚂 YORK MODEL RAILWAY (York BR Station, Tearoom Sq) Extensive model railway in painstakingly recreated miniature town and country landscape, running as many as 20 trains at the same time; a second much smaller model shows a typical German town at night. Shop, disabled access; cl 25–26 Dec; (01904) 630169; £2.50.

🔔✝ YORK STORY (Castlegate) Elaborate exhibition tracing York's last thousand years, with a big 3-D model of the city and comprehensive audio-visual display. It's based in the partly 15th-c church of St Mary, whose spire at 152ft is the tallest in the city; shop, disabled access ground floor only; cl am Sun, 25–26 Dec, 1 Jan; £1.50, joint ticket with castle available.

🍖🔔🚂 MURTON PARK (just E of town, at Murton SE6552) is a busy 8-acre park best known for its MUSEUM OF FARMING, with exhibitions of agricultural equipment, some animals and a Land Army display, but there's also the DERWENT VALLEY LIGHT RAILWAY, which on summer Suns has trips along what was once known as the Blackberry Line, and a reconstructed Dark Age settlement (aimed mostly at children). Snacks, shop, disabled access; cl 25-26 Dec; (01904) 489966; *£2.80.

Walks

Inside the city walls, York is largely pedestrianised: it's the most rewarding of all English cities to walk around. You can do the circuit of the 13th-c city walls and their many towers in a couple of hours or so, mostly on top. One of the best stretches, with good views of the minster, is between the Monk Bar, the most striking of the turreted medieval gateways, and Bootham Bar. If you plan on doing the whole circuit it's well worth using one of the Walkman guides rented by the helpful Tourist Office (Exhibition Sq).

Around The Shambles, jettied medieval buildings leaning towards each other across the alleys are enlivened by witty architectural details such as the red figure of the printer's devil almost opposite the courtyard entry to the Olde Starre (a touristy pub, but genuinely old, with a view of the minster from seats in its yard). This area has some of the city's most interesting shops, inc good bookshops, all sorts of unusual specialist shops, and, especially in Stonegate, nearer the minster, and in elegant Micklegate, some serious silver and antique shops.

The River Ouse flows right through the centre: the staithe below Clifford St is one quiet place beside it (with a decent pub, the Kings Arms).

Driving

This can be summed up in one word – don't. It's best not to drive into the centre, within the walls, there's a dreadful morning and evening rush hour, and during the day car parks are often full. However, once the evening rush hour is over you can find parking even in the centre fairly easily. There's a good park-and-ride from the Tesco superstore (A64 SW). All the hotels we list have parking.

Where to eat

MELTONS 7 Scarcroft Rd (01904) 634341 Smart little restaurant with very good modern and more straightforward dishes, seafood specialities Tues eve, and a relaxed, friendly atmosphere; cl pm Sun, am Mon, 3 wks over Christmas, last wk Aug. £25|£4|£9.

19 GRAPE ST (01904) 636366 Close to the minster, this neat timbered restaurant serves a good mix of traditional and imaginative dishes (lovely nursery puddings) in a warmly friendly atmosphere; cl Sun and Mon, 1st 2 wks Feb, last 2 wks Sept, 25–26 Dec. £24.45|£2.50|£7.95.

ST WILLIAM'S COLLEGE RESTAURANT College St (01904) 634830 Enjoyable, varied food (inc vegetarian dishes) in pleasant self-service restaurant in fine building with enclosed courtyard for eating outside in summer; open 10–5; cl 25–26 Dec, Good Fri. £1.50|£3.10.

Useful bars, cafés and food pubs include Bettys (St Helen's Sq), the 15th-c Black Swan (Peaseholme Green), Brigadier Gerard (Monkgate), Hansom Cab (Market St), Red Lion (Merchantgate), Royal Oak (Goodramgate – a very handy break from wall-walking), Spread Eagle (Walmgate) and Tap & Spile (Monkgate).

THE NORTHERN DALES

Magnificent unspoilt scenery the main draw; some good castles and ruined abbeys, attractive prices.

Wensleydale has very beautiful and varied scenery including some magnificent waterfalls, a succession of attractive villages and small towns, and a good few pleasant places to stay – generally not grand, but comfortable, warm, very friendly and invitingly priced.

The upper reaches of Swaledale up in the north are largely unspoilt and with a remote feeling, more dramatic if more austere than Wensleydale, with a quieter road running through; we've found a couple of attractive places to stay up here, and it's in easy reach of the pleasant and interesting town of Richmond downriver.

Apart from the scenery itself, which is unquestionably the area's main draw, places to visit in these dales and in the flatter country to their east tend to be relatively low-key. Among the most rewarding, we'd include the ruined abbeys of Jervaulx and Easby, the castle remains at Richmond, Middleham and Castle Bolton, and Aysgarth for its waterfalls and carriage museum; a newcomer to this edition, the Wensleydale cheese creamery in Hawes, is interesting.

The Yorkshire Dales National Park extends over the border into areas such as Dentdale which we describe in the Cumbrian chapter.

Where to stay

Simonstone SD8791 SIMONSTONE HALL Simonstone, Hawes DL8 3LY (01969) 667255 £80; 10 pretty rms. Carefully restored, warmly welcoming country house in beautiful countryside with spacious panelled drawing rooms, antiques, paintings and old maps of the area; fine views, good, carefully cooked food, and interesting wines; cl 2 wks Jan; dogs always welcome; limited disabled access.

Askrigg SD9591 KINGS ARMS Askrigg, Leyburn DL8 3HQ (01969) 50258 *£75; 11 rms. Smart Georgian manor house with a homely, friendly atmosphere in several bars – one used in the television series *All Creatures Great and Small*; attractive furnishings, low beams and oak panelling, open fires (one in a fine green marble fireplace), imaginative restaurant dishes, excellent bar food, and very good wines.

Newby Wiske SE3688 SOLBERGE HALL Newby Wiske, Northallerton DL7 9ER (01609) 779191 £75; 25 rms. Victorian country house in 16 acres of gardens and woodland with open log fires, elegant lounge, attractive wood-panelled reception rooms, and good food (and lovely views) in Garden Room restaurant; croquet; disabled access.

Thornton Watlass SE2486 OLD RECTORY Thornton Watlass, Ripon HG4 4AH (01677) 423456 £65; 3 character rms. Wisteria-clad Georgian-faced ancient house nr green, well polished antiques and bookcases, fresh flowers, fire in guests' sitting room, lots of attention to detail; no evening meals, no daytime access to rooms; children over 8.

Reeth SE0499 ARKLESIDE Village Green, Reeth, Richmond DL11 6SG (01748) 84200 £60; 8 pretty rms. Charming small Swaledale hotel with friendly, caring owners, an attractively furnished lounge, airy conservatory bar overlooking the gardens, relaxing atmosphere, and good Yorkshire cooking in candlelit restaurant; cl Dec and Jan; children over 10.

Sedbusk SD8891 STONE HOUSE Sedbusk, Hawes DL8 3PT (01969) 667571 *£60; 18 rms, 17 with own bthrm. Small, warmly friendly Edwardian hotel with country-house feel and appropriate furnishings, stunning setting with magnificent views, attractive oak-panelled drawing room, billiard room, log fires, exemplary service, good local information; pleasant dining room with excellent wholesome food (special needs catered for) inc super breakfasts, reasonable choice of wines; part of the coach house will be converted into a fitness room; tennis lawn in the grounds, wonderful walks; P G Wodehouse stayed here as a guest of the original owner who employed a butler called Jeeves – it was on him that Wodehouse based his famous character; cl wkdys mid-Nov–Christmas (open then and New Year), cl midweek Nov and Dec, all Jan; good disabled access. Dogs may be allowed.

Middleham SE1288 GREYSTONES Market Pl, Middleham DL8 4NR (01969) 22016 *£56; 4 rms. Friendly, family-run Georgian house with log fire, books and magazines in restful lounge, generous helpings of good, wholesome food using home-grown vegetables and home-made bread, cakes and sweet and savoury biscuits; cl mid-Nov–mid-Feb; babysitters available.

Bainbridge SD9390 ROSE & CROWN Bainbridge, Leyburn DL8 3EE (01969) 650225 *£54; 12 comfortable rms. 15th-c coaching inn overlooking lovely village green, with antique settles and other old furniture in beamed and panelled front bar, open log fires, cosy residents' lounge, big wine list, and home-made traditional food in bar and restaurant; cl 25 Dec, 1 Jan.

Hawes SD8789 COCKETTS Market Pl, Hawes DL8 3RD (01969) 667312 £54; 8 warm rms, 6 with own bthrm. Friendly, hardworking owners make this a most attractive and enjoyable place to stay with woodburning stove in small bar, candlelit restaurant, and residents' lounge with books; cl 1–27 Dec; children over 10.

Leyburn SE1191 GOLDEN LION Market Pl, Leyburn DL8 5AS *£52; 15 good-value rms, most with own bthrm. Homely inn with comfortable and quietly friendly bay-windowed 2-room bar with light squared panelling, good, home-cooked traditional food in bar and evening restaurant, well kept real ales (inc one brewed to their own recipe), and helpful service; cl 25–26 Dec; no children; disabled access. Also has comfortable s/c in nearby Hawnby.

Thornton Watlass SE2486 BUCK Thornton Watlass, Ripon HG4 4AH (01677) 422461 *£48; 5 rms. Warmly friendly country pub overlooking cricket green in very attractive village, interesting beamed and panelled rooms, open fire, live music wknds in function room, excellent food inc summer barbecues, and lots of nearby walks (the Arboretum is very popular). The inn offers guided walking hols.

West Burton SE0186 FOX & HOUNDS West Burton, Leyburn DL8 4JY (01969) 663279 £48; 8 rms in cobbled courtyard. Unspoilt simple local in idyllic Dales village around long green, with homely welcoming atmosphere; small bar with extension, generous wholesome home-cooked food in residents' dining room and in bar, good service from friendly staff; children over 12; disabled access.

Pickhill SE3584 NAG'S HEAD Pickhill, Thirsk YO7 4JH (01845) 567391 £45; 15 rms. Cheerful and popular old inn with lots of ties, ale-yards, jugs and such around bar, stylish no smoking restaurant, good bar food, huge breakfasts, well kept beer, lots of malt whiskies, and fine wine list; disabled access.

East Witton SE1586 HOLLY TREE East Witton, Leyburn DL8 4LS (01969) 22383 *£42; 4 good rms. Very attractively decorated, partly 12th-c house in peaceful village with carefully cooked, good food, a homely, welcoming atmosphere, open fire in sitting room, TV lounge, and small garden; cl Jan and Feb; children over 10.

Middleham SE1288 BLACK SWAN Market Pl, Middleham DL8 4NP (01969) 22221 £42; 7 recently refurbished rms. Handsome 17th-c inn in charming village, with heavy-beamed bar, stripped stonework, very sturdy furniture inc high-backed settles built in by big stone fireplace, separate dining room, cheerful local atmosphere and wide choice of filling food; dogs welcome away from public rooms; no accomm 24–26 Dec.

Gunnerside SD9598 OXNOP HALL Low Oxnop, Gunnerside, Richmond DL11 6JJ (01748) 86253 £40; 6 rms. Extended 17th-c farmhouse on working beef cattle and sheep farm; old part has open fire in sitting room and beams, and good homely cooking; children over 8.

Richmond NZ1801 WHASHTON SPRINGS FARM, Richmond DL11 7JS (01748) 822884 *£40; 8 comfortable rms. Attractive Georgian stone-built farmhouse several miles N towards Ravensworth, on 600-acre mixed farm with comfort-able sitting room, log fire, country home-cooking using home-produced meat, fruit and veg, and lovely surrounding countryside; cl 12 Dec–1 Feb; children over 5.

Carperby SE0189 OLD STABLES Carperby, Leyburn DL8 4DB (01969) 663590 £38; 3 rms. Carefully converted stables with warmly welcoming, helpful own-ers, pleasantly furnished and neatly kept lounge and dining room, log fire, marvellous breakfasts with home-made marmalade, and lovely Swaledale views from the terrace; no smoking; no children or pets.

Richmond NZ1801 BLACK LION Finkle St, Richmond DL10 4QB (01748) 823121 £36; 14 rms, shared bthrms. Old coaching inn with cosy fires and beams, comfortable residents' lounge, well kept real ales in the bars, and very good, generously served food.

Danby Wiske SE3499 WHITE SWAN Danby Wiske, Northallerton DL7 0NQ (01609) 770122 *£31; 3 comfortable rms, shared bthrm. Cosy little pub in the middle of nowhere, handy for walkers on coast-to-coast footpath; very friendly licensees, and decent choice of good-value food inc free-range eggs from their chickens.

To see and do

🐃 🐄 🐾 **Aysgarth** SE0088 is most famous for its romantic series of WATERFALLS. The Lower Fall is the most spectacular, seen from the path on the opposite side of the road. The waterfalls do get crowded, particularly through August (when even parking can be a problem here). They're better in late spring or early autumn, when there tends to be more water in the river and therefore a better show. In severely cold weather they can be stunning, with wonderful ice sculptures building up. There's generally a small charge to view the Upper Fall (it's on private land), but you can see it just as well without paying from the bridge on the road. The main car park (60p for three hours) has a NATIONAL PARK CENTRE, with displays on the history and natural history of the Yorkshire Dales, and lots of useful walks, maps, and guides. Café, shop, disabled facilities; best to check winter opening, usually just wknds; (01969) 663424; free. YORKSHIRE CARRIAGE MUSEUM Some magnificent coaches and carriages among this collection of horse-drawn vehicles, with a decent craft and pottery shop; cl Nov–Good Fri; (01748) 823275; *£2. The George & Dragon Hotel and Palmer Flatt both have decent food.

★ ✗ 🏨 **Bainbridge** SD9390 is delightful, its broad sloping green still with the village stocks, and still ringing with the blowing of a buffalo-horn to guide shepherds down through the mists each night at 9 from the end of Sept till late Feb, as it has done for centuries. The Rose & Crown is good, and there's a restored 18th-c CORN MILL, with a collection of fully furnished hand-made doll's houses, all produced on the premises. The shop sells assembled houses or plans to make your own; open pm bank hol wknds and Weds and Fri July–mid-Sept, or by appointment; (01969) 50416; *75p.

🏨 🐄 🌸 🐃 **Bedale** SE2687 Partly Palladian BEDALE HALL is now mainly a community centre, but has a small folk museum with various domestic items, and an unusual fire engine dating from 1742. Shop, disabled access; cl Sun, and Nov–Easter (exc Tues); free. A little way south is THORPE PERROW, a well laid out 60-acre landscaped lakeside collection of rare trees and shrubs among some splendid mature specimens that have been growing here for over 400 years; particularly strong on oaks, ornamental cherries, willows and hazels, and lovely in spring when the bulbs are out. Snacks, shop, disabled access; (01677) 425323; *£2.75. The bustling Olde Black Swan does good-value food. The BIG SHEEP AND LITTLE COW at Aiskew SE2889 is a small-scale dairy farm, with friendly sheep and Dexter cows (Britain's smallest), and pigs and chicks – the family in charge love talking to visitors. Shop; cl Oct–Easter; (01677) 422125; *£2.50.

🏰 **Castle Bolton** SE0392 14th-c BOLTON CASTLE is a massive structure towering over the tiny single-street village built for it. Considering it was partly dismantled in 1645 and has been empty ever since, it's still in fine shape, its 100ft towers giving a great view. They'll show you Mary Queen of Scots' bedroom – she was locked up here in 1568. Snacks, shop; cl Nov–Mar; (01969) 23981; *£2.50. The Kings Arms at Redmire has good food.

✗ 🐄 **Crakehall** SE2490 The 17th-c CRAKEHALL WATERMILL stands on the site of a still earlier one; restored in 1980, it's now busily producing flour. Even when they're not milling, the wheel should still be turning. Snacks, shop; cl Mon, Fri, Oct–Easter; (01677) 423240; *£1. Nearby is a little MUSEUM OF BADGES AND BATTLEDRESS. Shop; cl am wknds, Mon (exc bank hols), Oct–Easter; (01677) 424444; *£1. The Bay Horse in a nice spot on Little Crakehall green has good-value food.

✝ ※ **Croft** NZ2909 Right on the border with Co Durham is a pleasant CHURCH, where Lewis Carroll's father was parson; there's a plaque in memory of the writer, complete with an enamelled White Rabbit, and an unusual family pew, reached by a staircase. If the church is closed, the key is kept at the hotel across the road, and there are nice river views.

★ ➍ 👶 🏰 **Hawes** SD8789 Busy in summer with hikers and coach-parties, but pretty, and a proper market town, its Tues mart alive with cattle and sheep in late summer. The WENSLEYDALE CREAMERY (Gayle Lane) seemed to be headed for closure when Dairy Crest decided to transfer the cheese's production to Lancashire a couple of years back, but after a timely management buy-out is thriving once again. From the unexpectedly interesting new visitor centre, with a well set out dairying/cheese museum, you can watch the cheese being made by the traditional method, all by hand, and there's a video and other displays. The price includes a sample, and the shop sells a good range of other cheeses. Meals and snacks in very good café, disabled facilities; (01969) 667644; £1.95. DALES COUNTRYSIDE MUSEUM AND NATIONAL PARK CENTRE (Station Yard) Developing centre exploring how man has changed and developed the area over the last 10,000 years, with interesting displays of local crafts and domestic and industrial life. Shop, disabled access; cl Nov–Mar exc some wknds; (01969) 667450; *£1.50. Outhwaites ROPEMAKERS (Town Foot) have been making rope for 200 years – see how it's done. Shop (not just great hawsers, useful things too like dog-leads), disabled access; cl wknds (exc Sat July–Oct and Easter), 10 days over Christmas; (01969) 667487; free. The White Hart, Board and Crown are useful for lunch. Just N is HARDRAW FORCE SD8691 England's tallest waterfall cascading over a 100ft lip – best after rain, though the paths can be muddy then; the Green Dragon pub charges visitors a fee (around 50p). The valley above the falls is attractive, and this can be a start for the long day's walk to Great Shunner Fell.

✝ **Jervaulx Abbey** SE1785 is less imposing than Fountains, Rievaulx and Bolton, but in some ways even more appealing – perhaps because the rough-cropped grass and wild flowers around the shattered walls emphasise the slightly melancholy atmosphere of a place of great worldly wealth and power that's come to nothing. Teas, shop, disabled access; always open; (01677) 460391; £1. The Blue Lion at East Witton nearby has excellent food.

★ 🏰 ※ **Middleham** SE1288 Attractive and civilised basically Georgian stone-built village, still with the style that came from its days as the country's top racehorse-training centre in the 18th and early 19th c. Even now there are times when it seems to have more horses than people: pick up breeding and gallops gossip in the bar of the good Black Swan. The village is dwarfed by 12th-c MIDDLEHAM CASTLE, for a time the home of young King Richard III which but for Bosworth Field might have become one of England's most powerful fortresses. Only the huge keep and some later buildings remain, but there are marvellous views from the top. Snacks, shop, disabled access; cl 1–2pm, winter Mon and Tues; *£1.25. This is a good area for self-catering accommodation – and fine walking country.

★ 🏰 ※ 🏠 👶 **Richmond** NZ1701 is a most attractive riverside country town, with steep and pretty streets of old stone buildings, and a splendid broad sloping market square (still cobbled, and perhaps the biggest in the country; market day is Sat). It's dominated by the austere and intricate ruins of RICHMOND CASTLE, which overlook the River Swale from a high rocky outcrop. The castle was begun in 1071 and the 100ft triangular keep still stands, as do two of the towers on the curtain walls, with great views from the top. Shop, some disabled access; cl 1–2pm in winter; (01748) 822493; £1.80.

Scollards Hall, which was built in 1080, is possibly the oldest domestic building in Britain. GEORGIAN THEATRE ROYAL The country's oldest and most authentic working theatre still in its original form, complete with gallery, boxes and pit. Built in 1788, the theatre closed in 1848 but was immaculately restored and reopened in 1962. Shop; guided tours and museum, Easter–Oct (not am Sun); (01748) 823021; *£1. The GREEN HOWARDS MUSEUM in a converted 12th-c church includes amongst other regimental history the blood-stained pistol holsters of the Grand Old Duke of York; cl Sun (exc pm Apr–Oct), Sat in Feb, all Dec and Jan; £1. The army connection with the town is still strong; nearby Catterick Camp is the biggest in the north. The Black Lion in Finkle St is good value for lunch.

★ Particularly **attractive villages** here include Askrigg SD9591 – a delightful collection of elegant stone houses around neat streamside greens, walks to nearby waterfalls, fine 15th-c church, and good pub, the Kings Arms; and Reeth SE0499, with another high, wide, sloping green (the Kings Arms is best for lunch here). Other pretty villages, all with decent pubs, include East Witton SE1586 (ancient houses, long wide green), Gilling West NZ1804, riverside Grinton SE0598 (charming church, pleasant walks), Hudswell NZ1400, Langthwaite NZ0003 (good circular walks from the pub), Low Row DD9897 (popular with potholers), Muker SD9198 (woollens shop),

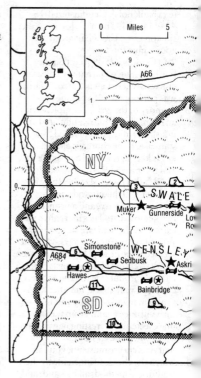

Redmire SE0591, Snape SE2784, Thornton Watlass SE2486 and West Burton SE0186. Leyburn SE1191 is a bustling little agricultural town rather than a village, but a good stop, with a proper country atmosphere and lively Fri market: the Sandpiper's the nicest pub, and the town is now home to Tennants, Europe's largest auction room for house clearances and antiques.

Walks

Swaledale is the northernmost of all the dales, and one of the least visited – giving more chance of getting away from it all at even peak times. Its bold hills, abundant stone barns and extreme tranquillity make it a walkers' favourite. It's grandly austere for the most part, though quite heavily wooded as it drops down towards Richmond NZ1801. In the steeper parts there are some fine waterfalls. The upper slopes, especially towards the Durham and Cumbrian borders, are wild and empty, except for the huge scattered flocks of hardy clean-limbed Swaledale sheep with their dark faces, grey muzzles, thick fleeces, and curly-horned rams. The meadowland down in the valleys of this dale and its broad tributary **Arkengarthdale** NZ0003 ⌂-1 is largely unimproved, with slow-growing natural grasses and lots of wild flowers. Many of

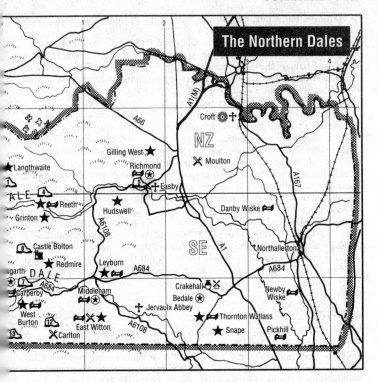

The Northern Dales

the area's 1,200 traditional stone hay barns which are such a distinctive feature here have been rehabilitated in the last four years, with generous National Parks grant aid. Until Victorian times the area was an important lead-mining centre, and still shows signs of the working methods: ruined mill buildings, tunnel entrances, spoil heaps and the so-called 'rushes', particularly around **Gunnerside** SD9598 ⌂-2, where streams were dammed to form torrents that could break up the lead-bearing rock strata below.

Between **Muker** SD9097 and **Keld** NY8901 ⌂-3, the Swale enters a deeply cut valley and tumbles over waterfalls; there are paths on both sides of the river, or you can take a more upland route over neighbouring Kisdon SD8999. **Reeth** SE0499 ⌂-4 is a centre for rambles ranging from pottering along the meadows by the Swale to walks over moors into adjacent Arkengarthdale (where the ascent on to Fremington Edge NZ0400 is recommended). **Richmond** NZ1701 ⌂-5 is well placed for walks, along the riverside beneath the towering bulk of its castle – E to Easby Abbey NZ1800, or W through Hudswell Woods NZ1400, with an extension to Whitcliffe Scar NZ1302, a cliff above the Swale with an exciting path along its top.

Wensleydale is more expansive in character and not quite as dramatic as Swaledale, but its scenery is richly picturesque, and its unspoilt villages and numerous waterfalls make for pleasurable walking. It was in the past one of the richest dales, its broad pastures and countless sheep supporting the wealthy abbeys and castles whose ruins now add so much interest to its scenery. Wensleydale sheep are very distinctive, with long fleecy dreadlock curls. **Upper Wensleydale** ⌂-6 around and W of Hawes SD8789 is steep and wild; E of here the valley starts broadening out, with richer lower pastures, and more regular farmland below Middleham SE1288. Hardraw Force SD8691, a 96ft waterfall, is, as we've said, reached through the Green Dragon at Hardraw, but a longer excursion follows the Pennine Way from Hawes SD8789 and over the River Ure.

Aysgarth Falls SE0888 △-7, the National Park's chief visitor honeypot, involve a short amble from the car park; or you can contrive longer routes along the S bank of the Ure from the delightful village of West Burton SE0196.
Apedale Head SE0095 △-8 is reached by a 3-mile plod up tracks NW of Castle Bolton SE0392; on fine days it feels like the top of the world, with views encompassing both Wensleydale and Swaledale.

Raydale SD8288 △-9 nr Bainbridge SD9390 is the most interesting of Wensleydale's subsidiary valleys for walkers. Its lower neck is quite narrow, but it broadens out into quite a broad sheltered bowl of valley, with Semer Water SD9187, a sizeable glacial lake which legend has it was conjured up by a wandering beggar to drown a village which had spurned him. It's Yorkshire's third largest natural lake, and has a path along its half-mile-long S side, but the local path network requires some road-walking for circular routes. The walled track (a Roman road) just N has wide-ranging views as it descends to Bainbridge.

Widdale SD8288 △-10, with extensive conifer plantations above it, **Sleddale** SD8586 △-11 above Hawes SD8789, and the broader **Bishopdale** △-12 SD9885 are steep-sided and dramatic. **Coverdale** SD0582 △-13, Wensleydale's major tributary valley, is relatively very quiet; fairly gentle in its lower reaches, climbing high into a wild and untamed-feeling world of lonely high sheep farms.

Driving

All the side roads off the A684 W of Leyburn are well worth exploring, particularly the Coverdale road over to Kettlewell (see next section); the B6160 up Bishopdale and into the top of Upper Wharfedale – after you pass Cray there's a pretty turning off on the right which brings you back to Hawes via Hubberholme; the B6255 up over Newby Head; the B6259 N into the headwaters of the Eden Valley in Cumbria; the steep and spectacular Buttertubs Pass road up to Swaledale (stop to look at the Buttertubs themselves, deep ferny holes near the summit where carriers used to cool their butter in hot weather); and the hill road through Carperby and Castle Bolton up to Reeth.

The B6270 along Swaledale is less travelled yet a very fine drive, with a splendid lonely loop off it up through Arkengarthdale to the Tan Hill Inn NY8906 (Britain's highest pub), where a left turn brings you back down to rejoin the B6270 near Keld.

Where to eat

East Witton SE1586 Blue Lion (01969) 24273 Stylish and civilised dining pub with distinctive old rooms, enterprising food, decent wines, and good restaurant (not pm Sun); bedrooms; disabled access. £20|£2/£5.
Moulton NZ2404 Black Bull (01325) 377289 Decidedly civilised, well run pub with old-fashioned style and standards of service, memorable bar snacks (excellent smoked salmon), conservatory restaurant or one in the Brighton Belle, and good wines. £18|£2.50/£7.50
Carlton SE0684 Foresters Arms (01969) 40272 Friendly, carefully restored inn with well kept real ales, a good choice of whiskies, reasonably priced good food in bar and restaurant, pleasant atmosphere and very friendly staff. £2.95/£6.95.

CENTRAL DALES

Outstanding countryside for walkers and for drivers, with plenty of beautifully located places to stay.

Wharfedale has the most varied scenery and is the most visited. Ribblesdale above Settle climbs into austerely impressive countryside with challenging walks, and does have some fine scenery, though is relatively tame in its lower reaches. Malhamdale, quite small, has some of Yorkshire's most striking landscape features and is a magnet for day visitors. Nidderdale has fewer paths than the other dales, but plenty of walking to fill a short stay, and though like the others it has lovely scenery it has the advantage of being rather off the tourist track.

Skipton Castle, the show cave at Ingleton and Bolton Abbey are all memorable, and the railway over the Pennines from Settle to Carlisle is a wonderful ride on a clear day.

Most of the places we recommend to stay in here let you walk straight from their door into fine scenery, and are very quietly placed – perfect for a relaxing quiet break. Though you have to get your boots on to make the most of the area, you can take in a great deal without leaving your car. On the whole, food here is robust and heartening rather than specially imaginative, though there are one or two outstanding exceptions; there's good value throughout.

Where to stay

Bolton Abbey SE0754 DEVONSHIRE ARMS COUNTRY HOUSE Bolton Abbey, Skipton BD23 6AJ (01756) 710441 £135; 40 individually furnished rms with thoughtful extras. Close to the priory itself and in lovely countryside, this country house is owned by the Duke of Devonshire and has been carefully furnished with fine antiques and paintings from Chatsworth; log fires, impeccable service, and beautifully presented, imaginative food in elegant restaurant, and fine breakfasts; disabled access.

Settle SD8264 FALCON MANOR Skipton Rd, Settle BD24 9BD (01729) 823814 £74; 20 rms. Quietly set, imposing hotel in its own grounds with spacious public rooms, log fires, fine food and lovely views in elegant restaurant, fine service; a well placed touring base; disabled access.

Ramsgill SE1271 YORKE ARMS Ramsgill, Harrogate HG3 5RL (01423) 755243 £69; 13 attractive rms. Carefully refurbished and civilised old inn with interesting antique furnishings, log fires, and good English cooking in bar and no smoking restaurant; short walk from bird sanctuary; cl 1st wk Feb; children over 10.

Burnsall SE0361 RED LION Burnsall, Skipton BD23 6BU (01756) 720204 *£67; 11 recently refurbished rms. Pretty 16th-c family-run ferryman's inn overlooking river and village green with tall maypole, attractively panelled bar, log fires and beams, decent bar and restaurant food (emphasis on fish), a good wine list, and big gardens and terrace on river banks; 75 yds of private fishing and permits for further 7 miles; disabled access.

Buckden SD9478 BUCK Buckden, Skipton BD23 5JA (01756) 760228 £62; 14 comfortable rms, most with own showers. Busy pub surrounded by moorland views (lots of walkers) with snug original area and bustling extended open-plan bar, well kept real ales, decent wines, and popular food which is served by smartly uniformed staff in attractive restaurant.

Wath in Nidderdale SE1467 SPORTSMANS ARMS Wath in Nidderdale, Harrogate HG3 5PP (01423) 711306 £55; 7 recently upgraded rms, some with own bthrm. Friendly 17th-c hotel with elegant bar, good range of wines, excellent lunchtime bar food (esp fish) and no smoking evening restaurant; lots of fine cheeses. A smashing place to stay if you're after good-value rooms and really enjoy fine food; cl 25 Dec.

Grassington SE0064 BLACK HORSE Garrs Lane, Grassington BD23 5AT (01756) 752770 £54; 15 rms. On the edge of the cobbled square, this is a bustling place with open fires and beams in comfortable bar, friendly service, and enjoyable food in small but attractive restaurant; sheltered terrace.

Elslack SD9249 TEMPEST ARMS Elslack, Skipton BD23 3AY (01282) 842450 £52; 10 rms. Warmly friendly 18th-c inn with comfortable bar and other quietly decorated areas, a log fire in the dividing fireplace, lots of wines, and excellent bar and restaurant food; disabled access.

Malham SD8963 BUCK Malham, Skipton BD23 4DA (01729) 830317 *£50; 10 rms. Comfortable and homely country hotel overlooking Malham Beck in small village with oak-panelled lounge, relaxed atmosphere, open fires, spacious bar for hikers/ramblers, decent food; wonderful walking country; self-catering also.

Wigglesworth SD8157 PLOUGH Wigglesworth, Skipton BD23 4RJ (01729) 840243 £46.40; 12 well equipped rms. Pleasant and well run country inn with highly regarded barn/conservatory restaurant (popular bar food, too), and lots of little rooms surrounding bar area, some smart and plush, others spartan yet cosy; friendly service, big breakfasts, and views of the Three Peaks disabled access.

Arncliffe SD9473 FALCON Arncliffe, Skipton BD23 5QE (01756) 770205 £45; 6 rms, some with own bthrm. Friendly delightfully basic Georgian inn ideal for walkers, functional little rooms and a fire, homely front lounge, airy conservatory, no smoking dining room, generous plain lunchtime snacks; cl end Nov–mid-Mar for accomm.

Darley Head SE1959 WELLINGTON Darley Head, Harrogate HG3 2QQ (01423) 780362 *£45; 12 well furnished rms. Carefully extended old pub with big open fire in spacious beamed bar, other smaller day rooms, too, decent food in attractive restaurant, and colourful gardens; disabled access.

Cray SD9379 WHITE LION Cray, Skipton BD23 5JB (01756) 760262 *£44; 5 rms. Friendly little pub 1,100ft up with super views of countryside, lots of walks, traditional feel with flagstones, beams, and log fires, and decent bar food; pleasant to sit by stream; disabled access.

Starbotton SD9574 FOX & HOUNDS Starbotton, Skipton BD23 5HY (01756) 760269 £44; 2 rms. Prettily placed and rather smart little Upper Wharfedale village inn with warmly welcoming atmosphere, flagstones, beams, big log fire, imaginative food, and well kept real ales; cl mid-Dec–mid-Feb.

Austwick SD7668 GAME COCK Austwick, Lancaster LA2 8BB (01524) 251226 £40; 4 rms, shared bthrms. Prettily placed inn with views over Dales National Park, notably friendly welcome, simple furnishings and a heartening fire in beamed back bar, good food in bar and no smoking restaurant; disabled access.

Kilnsey SD9767 TENNANT ARMS Kilnsey, Skipton BD23 5PS (01756) 752301 £40; 10 rms. In a nice spot by the River Wharfe, this spacious beamed and flagstoned inn has open fires (one fireplace made from an ornate carved four-poster), weapons collection, maps and stuffed or skeleton animals and fish; up for sale as we go to press, but has had friendly service and good-value food; views over spectacular overhanging Kilnsey Crag from restaurant.

Malham SD8963 MIRESFIELD FARM Malham, Skipton BD23 4DA (01729) 830414 £40; 14 rms, 12 with own bthrm. Spacious old farmhouse with good freshly prepared food, big conservatory, 2 lounges and lovely garden by stream and village green; disabled access.

Chapel le Dale SD7477 OLD HILL Chapel le Dale, Carnforth, Lancs LA6 3AR (01524) 241256 £35; 5 warm, basic but well furnished rms; shared bthrms. Popular with walkers and potholers, this inn has stripped stone walls, flagstone floors, old woodwork and partitions with waggon wheels in the bar, roaring log fire in cosy back parlour, and popular food inc big breakfasts; also, 2 bunk rms with 8 beds in each and camping.

Feizor SD7867 SCAR CLOSE FARM Feizor, Austwick, Lancaster LA2 8DF (01729) 823496 *£35; 4 clean, well appointed rms. Friendly converted barn on working farm with big guest lounge, books, magazines and TV, and big breakfasts and homely evening meals; lovely quiet surrounding countryside; cl 25–26 Dec, disabled access.

Stainforth SD8267 CRAVEN HEIFER Stainforth, Settle BD24 9PB (01729) 822599 £33; 4 good-value rms, shared bthrm. Small cosy village pub with friendly licensees, log fire, and reasonably priced bar food; well placed for walking in this Upper Ribblesdale area.

To see and do

✝ ❀ **Bolton Abbey** SE0754 Beautiful spot in lovely rolling wooded parkland on a knoll above the River Wharfe. Most of the priory buildings, dating from the 12th to the 16th c, are in ruins, but the central core of the main church is still used for Sunday services. 19th-c additions such as stained glass (some by Pugin) and murals oddly don't strike a false note. It's a popular place, and the car park does get full in summer. Attractive walks lead off in most directions, and the Devonshire Arms is very fine for lunch.

❄ **Brimham Rocks** SE2164 Spectacular and extraordinarily weathered gritstone pinnacles, tors and boulders facing the winds at a height of 950ft, conjuring up people, animal heads and other strange figures. A Victorian guidebook declared they were 'wrecked with grim and hideous forms defying all description and definition'. Children like them a lot – Henry Moore said that when he was a boy they sculpted quite a few ideas in his imagination. Information centre, shop and tea room open wknds Easter–Oct, and daily in school hols; parking £1.30; NT. The Half Moon on the B6265 does good quick food.

★ ❄ ☛ **Clapham** SD7569 is an attractive village that has turned walking and caving into something of an industry. The outdoors centre of Ingleborough Hall was formerly the family home of the great plantsman Reginald Farrer, who in his short life introduced and wrote about a great many notable plants from the Himalayas and China. A NATURE TRAIL leads past his own woods and small

lake to the entrance to INGLEBOROUGH CAVE, one of the most easily visited of the vast network of caverns plunging into the limestone hills around here – and probably the only one that wheelchairs can go all the way through. Snacks, shop, disabled access; cl wkdys Nov–Feb; (015242) 61249; *£3.50. There's a good NATIONAL PARK CENTRE with audio-visual show and useful local information; cl Nov–Mar; (015242) 251419; parking 50p. The New Inn is useful for lunch (and a good place for walkers to stay).

🚂 **Embsay** SE0053 EMBSAY STEAM RAILWAY Steam trips along a couple of miles of railway, prettily set below the limestone crags. It's being extended, with the eventual aim of running as far as Bolton Abbey. Back at the Embsay end is a ticket office originally at Ilkley, and a collection of old locomotives and carriages. Snacks, shop (remarkable range of books), disabled access; usually open Sun all yr, plus Tues and Sat July and daily Aug – best to tel (01756) 795189 for timetable; *£3. The Elm Tree is good for lunch.

★ **Grassington** SE0064 is a pleasant small town or large village around a sloping cobbled square, depending a lot on walkers and other visitors, with some attractive shops and a few interesting old buildings. The Black Horse and Devonshire Hotel both have decent food.

✝ **Hubberholme** SD9178 has a good 13th-c CHURCH, built on an ancient burial site, with Norman tower, unusual rood loft and pews by Thompson of Kilburn (see East Yorkshire section below) – with their little carved mouse trademark. The charmingly set George is useful here.

✠ **Ingleton** SD7174 WHITE SCAR CAVERN (B6255 towards Hawes) The country's biggest show cave and easily one of the most spectacular, with underground waterfalls and streams and an Ice Age cavern. Some amazing sights and atmospheric formations, and stunning stalactites and stalagmites that have been here for 100,000 years. Wrap up well – the guided tour takes about 80 minutes so it gets chilly. They provide hard hats. Snacks, shop; cl 25 Dec (and sometimes after heavy rain); (015242) 41244; £5.75. The Wheatsheaf and Bridge both do generous food.

🏠 ✿ ❋ **Parcevall Hall Gardens** SE0661 Surrounding an Elizabethan house, woodland gardens charmingly set on a hillside E of the main Wharfedale Valley; good views. Plant sales, some disabled access; cl Nov–Easter exc by appointment; (01756) 720311; £2. The Craven Arms at nearby Appletreewick is good for lunch, with lovely views.

🚃 🏛 🏠 ♦ **Settle** SD8264 The SETTLE–CARLISLE RAILWAY has a magnificent 70-mile route carved up through Ribblesdale across the wild moors between here and Cumbria, and then dropping down through the lovely Eden Valley; (01228) 44711 for times and fares. On Sat and most Suns throughout the year there's a programme of walks connecting with the moorland stops; they start quite early (8.45am Sat), with dates and times listed on the timetable. Aside from the setting, it's an ordinary BR line: steam trains do run most Sats in summer, but only from cities in the south – (01543) 419472 for routes and times – resulting in the bizarre situation that you can travel by steam if you're coming from Norwich or London, but not if you're in the immediate vicinity. Back in Settle Mary Milnthorpe & Daughter is a good antique jewellery and silver shop, and market day (Tues) around the Shambles is particularly attractive; look out to the right of here for the Folly, an extraordinary 17th-c townhouse. Just across the Ribble, Giggleswick SD8164 is a peaceful

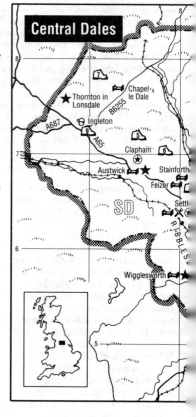

contrast to the hectic little town. Just N of the A65 Settle bypass at the top of Crows Nest, the YORKSHIRE DALES FALCONRY AND CONSERVATION CENTRE is a well organised newish centre with lots of vultures, eagles, hawks, falcons and owls. Birds fly at regular intervals (from 12), and they can organise full days with a falconer. Meals, snacks, shop, disabled access; cl 25 Dec; (01729) 825164; £3.95.

🏰 ✝ **Skipton** SD9851 On Sat the main street has a colourful market (at least some stalls here on most other days too, exc Sun and Tues). A canal runs through the town, and the Royal Shepherd in an attractive spot beside it is good for lunch; the Greenbank Hotel also does good lunches. CASTLE Properly romantic 12th-c castle, with sturdy round towers, broad stone steps, and a lovely central flagstoned and cobbled courtyard with a seat

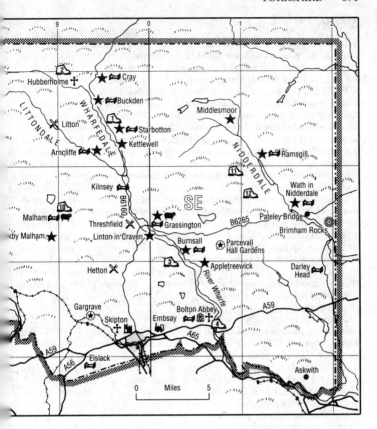

around its venerable central yew tree. One of the best-preserved medieval castles in Europe, it really is remarkable how much is left, interior and all – very few other castles have kept their roofs and stayed habitable. The original Norman arched gateway still stands – the word 'Desormais' carved above it is the family motto of the Cliffords, who lived here from 1310 to 1676. Shop; cl am Sun, 25 Dec; (01756) 792442; £2.90. The 14th-c CHURCH nearby has a 16th-c rood screen and interesting stained glass.

★ Numerous **attractive villages** or tiny hamlets in the area, all with decent pubs and most in delightful surroundings, include Appletreewick SE0560, Arncliffe SD9473 (the inspiration for Kingsley's *Water Babies*), Austwick SD7768 (the pub still shows a poster advertising a 1927 total eclipse), Buckden SD9477,

Burnsall SE0361, Cray SD9379, Gargrave SD9354 (on the Pennine Way), Kettlewell SD9772 (the Racehorses seems currently the best place here), Kirkby Malham SD8961, Linton in Craven SD9962 (a gem), Middlesmoor SE0874, Ramsgill SE1271, Stainforth SD8267, Starbotton SD9574, Thornton in Lonsdale SD6873, Wath SE1467 and Wigglesworth SD8157. A quaint spot for lunch in Nidderdale is the Watermill just north of Pateley Bridge SE1466; a converted flax mill with one of the largest waterwheels in Britain.

🐗 As well as at Clapham (see above), there are National Park Centres in Malham SD9062 and Grassington SE0064. Besides local information, maps, leaflets with suggested walks etc, the centres have displays on the natural history of the area, the life of the local community, and conservation work.

Walks

Wharfedale, with its tributary valley Littondale and its headwaters up in the steep conifer plantations at the top of Langstrothdale, is one of England's most popular areas for walkers, and very beautiful indeed in parts. The Dales Way follows the River Wharfe for the length of the dale, except between Kettlewell SD9772 and Grassington SE0064. Upper Wharfedale above Grassington has a level floor of sheltered well drained pastures with the river winding through, a few grey stone barns, and steep sides laced with dry stone walls, gnarled woodland and occasional austere crags, climbing up to high fairly level tops some 1,200ft above the valley floor. Kettlewell and particularly Grassington are sizeable villages, major bases for walkers; the smaller villages are delight-fully private and unspoilt, their grey or whitewashed stonework blending per-fectly with the long scars of the limestone terraces above them. Away from the valley floor, stone-walled grassy tracks are the easiest ways of gaining height: you can return over the high land, after a walk along the river, from **Starbot-ton** SD9574 △-1 to Kettlewell, or follow less obvious paths W to Arncliffe SD9473 in Littondale – which is very similar to the parent valley, though with a flatter damper valley floor. From **Hubberholme** SD9178 △-2 a walk not to be missed is up to Scar House SD8998 and along a level turfy terrace, which commands magnificent views down the dale, to Cray SD9379. Both hamlets have inns, and the walk can be expanded to include Buckden SD9477 – in fact there are good walks between all the Wharfedale/Littondale places marked on our map above and including Kilnsey SD9767, with good pub food available in each of them.

Below Grassington there's an extremely pretty stretch where the valley winds more sinuously past **Burnsall** SE0361 △-3, Appletreewick SE0560 and Bolton Abbey SE0754. There's a pleasant walk from Hebden SE0263 down to the Burnsall-Appletreewick stretch. Around **Bolton Abbey** △-4 the landscape has a lowland beauty: the ruined abbey, the turf banks of the Wharfe and the oaks of the Strid Wood SE0656, where a leaflet detailing nature trails is avail-able. A steep ascent from Howgill SE0659 is rewarded by views from Simon's Seat SE0759, an unmistakably upland perch on the edge of moors.

Ribblesdale, although partly marred by quarrying in its lower southern por-tions, climbs above Settle into severe and grand mountain scenery, craggy and remote: this is a major magnet for walkers on the Three Peaks Walk, 24 miles taking in the summits of Ingleborough SD7474, Pen-y-ghent SD8473 and Whernside SD9975. This is a tough undertaking in its entirety, but each of the peaks on its own is a manageable half-day excursion: choose a clear day – not just for the magnificent views but for your own safety.

Ingleborough (2,376ft) △-5 is best approached from Clapham SD7569, along the Reginald Farrer Trail (a tree collection adjoining an artificial lake, see To see and do above), past Ingleborough Cave SD7571 (guided visits) and Gaping Gill SD7572 (a vast pot-hole); the panorama extends far across Lan-cashire and into Cumbria. **Pen-y-ghent** (2,277ft) △-6, reached from Horton in Ribblesdale SD8072, has a satisfyingly compact summit, the craggiest fea-ture on the Pennine Way, which near here passes close to some pot-holes including Hull Pot. **Whernside** (2,415ft) △-7, sometimes criticised as the bor-ing one of the three, is Yorkshire's highest point, and has an exhilarating ridge section; start from the magnificent Ribblehead Viaduct SD7779 carrying the Settle–Carlisle railway over the head of the dale. Upper Ribblesdale is riddled with impressive pot-holes, some of them gaping chasms of sensational size that can be admired from the surface, as well as the intricate underground passages that make the area so popular with cavers. Up in the loneliest parts, useful refuges are the cheerful cavers' inn in the Old Hill at Chapel le Dale SD7477, and the isolated Station Inn at Ribblehead SD7779. At **Stainforth** SD8267 △-8 there is a pleasant gentle riverside walk from Stainforth Force SD8167 to Langcliffe SD8971. **Ingleton** SD6973 △-9 on the other side of Ingleborough

Hill has a lovely wooded walk up the River Twiss, over the moor and back down the River Doe, past a series of picturesque waterfalls; not too strenuous, very varied scenery, two or three hours – the admission fee for this Ingleton Glen is amply justified by the delightful gorge and waterfalls.

Malhamdale ◁-10 is much smaller, its upper stretches cut tortuously and deeply out of the limestone by the River Aire and its steep tributaries, leaving spectacular cliffs, extensive bare upland limestone 'pavements', craggy bowls carved out of the overhanging hillsides, and sparkling waterfalls. This area is understandably very popular indeed with walkers, and a magnet for day visitors. Walk along the beck from Malham SD8963 (where the Lister Arms is best for food) to Janet's Foss waterfall SD9163 and to the romantic severity of dramatic Gordale Scar SD9164, the dale's most memorable natural feature, where a beck makes a spectacular leap from the rocks. The Pennine Way N of Malham waterfall ascends the side of Malham Cove SD9864, a great cliff, then crosses a natural rock pavement and heads over a landscape of limestone scars, disappearing streams and green turf to Malham Tarn SD8966, a lovely mountain lake skirted on its E side by a nature trail.

Nidderdale ◁-11 is a quiet yet beautiful valley with an impressive solitary grandeur. Just outside the National Park, it and the hills above are less liberally laced with footpaths and open-access moorland than the other two dales here, and attract far fewer visitors – yet certainly have a sufficiency of relatively unfrequented walks, often on good paved but untarred tracks. The Nidderdale Way allows a fine fairly gentle walk of a couple of hours or so, up on to the high pastures (see lambs being born in spring) and moorland at Glasshouses SE1764 and back, with spectacular views almost all the way. It's well signposted with yellow arrows or Nidderdale Way signs; start from Dacre Banks SE1962 and take the lane a couple of hundred yards past the church. The stretch between the attractive small town of Pateley Bridge SE1566 and the little village of Lofthouse SE1073 is dominated by the sheltered two-mile waters of Gouthwaite reservoir SE1269, serenely set below the hills with some tall trees alongside. From Lofthouse SE1073 a path runs along beside the River Nidd, with picturesque tracks among small woods and ruined farmhouses, to Scar House Reservoir SE0576, quite exposed at the valley head (there's also a toll road up to it); high, exposed routes line the N side of the dale up here. To the W of Lofthouse, How Stean Gorge SE0673 ◁-12 is a spectacular ravine pocked with pot-holes and caverns; a footpath snakes between miniature cliffs, with bridges giving views into the gorge; there's also a visitor centre.

Driving

The B6160 along Upper Wharfedale is a fine drive, with better views than from the narrow back road between Grassington and Kettlewell, and without any nerve-rackingly steep bits even keeping right on to West Burton. The side roads from Kettlewell over into Coverdale and past Hubberholme up to Hawes both have exhilarating views.

Over towards the E, the B6265 from Grassington to Pateley Bridge, once past the high-walled bends out of Grassington itself, is a good road with some memorable views (and passes the colourfully lit underground Stump Cross Caverns SE0863, well worth a look if you're passing; £2.50). The moorland road from the head of Nidderdale up to Masham is a splendid expedition.

Where to eat

Hetton SD9558 Angel (01756) 730263 Extremely popular dining pub with old-fashioned rambling rooms, consistently excellent imaginative food, very good service from hard-working friendly staff, well kept real ales, and over 300 wines; cl 3rd wk Jan; disabled access. £27.50|£4.50/£5.50.

Threshfield SD9763 OLD HALL (01756) 752441 Very busy pub handy for Dales walks, comfortably unfussy rooms, and huge helpings of good imaginative food relying on seasonal produce; no food pm Sun, Mon (exc bank hols); disabled access. £16|£2.50/£5.50

Settle SD8264 ROYAL OAK (01729) 822561 Wide choice of popular food in well kept low stone inn; ground floor is almost one huge room with a few walls dividing it into separate areas, dark oak panelling, and pleasantly relaxed atmosphere; cl pm 25 Dec; disabled access. £15|£2.50/£5.50.

Litton SD9074 QUEENS ARMS (01756) 770208 Welcoming 17th-c inn with good popular food, main bar with big collection of cigarette lighters, another room with more of a family atmosphere, and two coal fires; disabled access. £10/£4.95.

NORTH YORK MOORS

Attractive moors, valleys and villages, interesting cliffy coast; not that many places to visit, but plenty for a weekend or rather longer stay.

It's the valleys rather than the moors themselves which most visitors spend time in here: rich pastures, with red-tiled stone farmhouses, twisting rivers, quiet roads, and few villages. The higher moorland is generally very grand and empty, mile after mile of heather scoured by breath-snatching winds, where the few walkers have for company scatterings of hardy sheep and the occasional harsh cry of a grouse.

Though this area is not quite so rich in memorable walks as are the Dales, it does have an excellent choice – plenty to occupy anyone on a walking holiday. There are good drives, too. Even in high summer it's a good bit quieter than the Dales, and in low season very peaceful indeed. There is a splendid stretch of cliffy coast, with some delightful little fishing villages, the enjoyable working fishing port of Whitby, and the attractive traditional seaside resort of Scarborough – where the new Millennium centre is an entertaining jaunt through 1,000 years of history.

There are good places to stay in the valleys themselves: ideal for walks straight from the door. If you want to explore the area more widely, Helmsley, Pickering or one of the villages just off the A170 might be a better bet (including places just inside the next area, East Yorkshire). That road can get you around much more quickly than crossing from a village high in one valley to another. Of these two towns, Helmsley is probably the more attractive.

The ruins of Rievaulx Abbey are the area's crowning glory. There's a handful of other interesting places to visit, and a good few attractive villages.

Where to stay

Hackness SE9790 HACKNESS GRANGE Hackness, Scarborough YO13 0JW (01723) 882345 **£126**; 28 rms. Set in acres of grounds in the heart of the North York Moors National Park, this Victorian country house has efficient, friendly service, comfortable lounge and bar, fine food and open fire in restaurant, and indoor heated swimming pool, 9-hole pitch-and-putt, and hard tennis court; disabled access.

Helmsley SE6184 BLACK SWAN Market Pl, Helmsley YO6 5BJ (01439) 770466 £110; 44 well equipped and comfortable rms. Striking Georgian house and adjoining Tudor rectory with beamed and panelled hotel bar, attractive carved oak settles and Windsor armchairs, cosy and comfortable lounges with lots of character, and charming sheltered garden; disabled access.

Lastingham SE7391 LASTINGHAM GRANGE Lastingham, York YO6 6TH (01751) 417345 £109.95; 12 rms. Very attractive stone-walled country house in 10 acres of well kept gardens and fields with the moors beyond; homely, relaxed atmosphere in spacious lounge, open fire, fine breakfasts and dinners, extremely helpful service; marvellous walks; may close Dec–Feb.

Scalby TA0191 WREA HEAD Scalby, Scarborough YO13 0PP (01723) 378211 *£99; 21 individually decorated rms. Victorian country house in 14 acres of parkland and gardens with friendly staff, minstrels' gallery in oak-panelled hall and lounge, open fires, bow-windowed library, pretty flowers, and good food in airy restaurant; disabled access.

Whitby NZ9011 BAGDALE HALL 1 Bagdale, Whitby YO21 1QL (01947) 602958 *£78; 6 spacious rms with lounge area. Handsome medieval manor house with fine restaurant and bar lunches (best to book for Sunday lunch), open fires, beamed ceilings and stone-mullioned windows.

Dunsley NZ8611 DUNSLEY HALL Dunsley, Whitby YO21 3TL (01947) 893437 *£73; 7 spacious rms. Imposing hotel in 4 acres of grounds with croquet, hard tennis court, and 9-hole putting green; lots of oak panelling, comfortable furnishings, quietly relaxed atmosphere, billiard table, fitness room and indoor heated swimming pool; cl Christmas; disabled access.

Helmsley SE6184 FEVERSHAM ARMS 1 High St, Helmsley YO6 5AG (01439) 770766 £70; 18 comfortable rms. Pleasant, welcoming hotel in an acre of walled gardens with comfortable, cosy bars, and bar food inc superb seafood and marvellous cheeseboard served by smart waitresses; hard tennis court, sizeable outdoor heated swimming pool; disabled access.

Pickering SE7984 WHITE SWAN Market Pl, Pickering YO18 7AA (01751) 472288 £70; 13 rms. Inviting small and quiet plush hotel bar, friendly staff and locals, log fires, antiques in comfortable beamed residents' lounge, chip-free bar food, attractive restaurant with fine clarets and daily-changing food using the best local produce, and breakfasts with home-made marmalade.

Rosedale Abbey SE7396 BLACKSMITHS ARMS Rosedale Abbey, Pickering YO18 8EN (01751) 417331 *£70; 14 rms. Carefully extended and modernised old farmhouse in attractive surroundings at the foot of Rosedale, with friendly, traditionally furnished bar, open fires in cosy and comfortable lounges, and imaginative food in spacious and attractive dining room; lovely walks all round; disabled access.

Kirkbymoorside SE6986 GEORGE & DRAGON 17 Market Pl, Kirkbymoorside, York YO6 6AA (01751) 433334 £68; 19 rms in converted corn mill and ex-rectory at back of hotel. Handsome 17th-c coaching inn, very well run, with log fire in relaxed beamed bar, well kept real ales, a particularly fine choice of wines (the owner was originally a wine merchant) and whiskies, excellent food using the best local produce in elegant restaurant, pretty beamed residents' lounge, warmly friendly staff, and peaceful gardens; activity breaks, too; disabled access.

Rosedale Abbey SE7395 MILBURN ARMS Rosedale Abbey, Pickering YO18 8RA (01751) 417312 £66; 11 rms. Friendly 18th-c inn surrounded by fine steep moorland with log fire and books in comfortable drawing room, traditionally furnished beamed bar, very good English cooking in attractive restaurant, decent wine list, and helpful staff.

Goathland NZ8301 MALLYAN SPOUT Goathland, Mallyan Spout, Whitby YO22 5AN (01947) 86206 *£65; 24 rms. Warmly friendly creeper-covered Victorian hotel overlooking the moors on the edge of the sheep-grazed village green, with homely public rooms and a cosy restaurant; cl Christmas; children over 6 in restaurant in evening; limited disabled access.

Great Ayton NZ5611 AYTON HALL Low Green, Great Ayton, Middlesbrough, Cleveland TS9 6BW (01642) 723595 *£65; 12 rms. Handsome building in 6 acres of parkland, with elegant day rooms, paintings and antiques, cosy restaurant with interesting food and thoughtful wine list; archery, tennis, croquet and trapshooting; children over 11; disabled access.

Helmsley SE6184 CARLTON LODGE Bondgate, Helmsley YO6 5EY (01439) 770557 *£65; 12 rms. Personally run by convivial owners, most enjoyable food, log fire in comfortable lounge, garden; pets welcome away from public rooms; disabled access.

Rosedale Abbey SE7396 WHITE HORSE FARM HOTEL Rosedale Abbey, Pickering YO18 8SE (01751) 417239 £60; 15 rms. Friendly hotel in 11 acres of land with marvellous views, cosy beamed bar and log fire, comfortable lounge, generously served food, and decent range of wines and malt whiskies; excellent walks; cl 24–25 Dec.

Pickering SE7984 FOREST & VALE Malton Rd, Pickering YO18 7DL (01751) 472722 £59; 17 rms (the ones in the main building are nicest). Pleasant hotel with good service and food inc fresh fish from Whitby; an excellent base for exploring the area.

Sinnington SE7586 FOX & HOUNDS Sinnington, York YO6 6SQ (01751) 431577 *£55; 11 rms. Once a thriving coaching inn, this friendly place is in an attractive village with a pretty stream; open fire in cosy wood-panelled bar, comfortable residents' lounge, generous helpings of well prepared piping hot food in dining room, and helpful service; disabled access.

Helmsley SE6184 FEATHERS Market Pl, Helmsley YO6 5BH (01439) 770275 £53; 17 rms, 13 with own bthrm. Handsome and atmospheric old inn, with heavy beams and dark panelling, log fires, comfortable lounge bar, lots of wines, good-value well prepared food in bar and restaurant, well kept beers, and attractive back garden; cl Christmas and New Year; disabled access.

Blakey Ridge SE6897 LION Blakey Ridge, Pickering YO6 6LQ (01751) 417320 £51; 9 clean rms, most with own bthrm. Said to be the fourth highest inn in England, this has spectacular moorland views, characterful rambling bars, blazing fires, generous helpings of decent food served all day, good breakfasts and candlelit restaurant, 8 real ales, and genuinely friendly licensees and staff; fine walking country; cl 25 Dec; disabled access.

Cropton SE7588 NEW INN Cropton, Pickering YO18 8HH (01751) 417330 *£48; 8 rms. Comfortably modernised family-run village inn with interesting own-brew beers, small coffee lounge for residents, log fire in beamed bar, elegant little restaurant, and big helpings of good-value food; disabled access.

Egton Bridge NZ8105 HORSE SHOE Egton Bridge, Whitby YO21 1XE (01947) 85245 £46; 6 rms. Beautifully placed inn by River Esk (stepping stones big enough for children to sit on), lots of friendly wild birds, pleasant sheltered lawn, open fires, attractive and traditionally furnished bars, well cooked food in cottagey dining room, and decent wines; cl 25 Dec.

Chop Gate SE5699 HILL END FARM Chop Gate, Middlesbrough, Cleveland TS9 7JR (01439) 798278 *£36; 2 rms. Friendly 17th-c farmhouse with good farm cooking, comfortable lounge and dining room, and fine walks; on the farm is part of one of the last remaining ancient oak forests; cl Nov–Apr.

Egton Bridge NZ8105 POSTGATE Egton Bridge, Whitby YO21 1UX (01947) 85241 *£36; 7 rms, 1 with own bthrm. Relaxed and informal pub, super views looking down hill, decent daily-changing bar food inc several vegetarian dishes, well kept real ales, and featured in three series of TV *Heartbeat* series; fishing and riding can be arranged; very handy indeed for the quiet country station with trains to Whitby (connecting at Grosmont with the North Yorkshire Moors Railway).

Robin Hood's Bay NZ9505 COBLE Covet Hill, Robin Hood's Bay YO22 4SN (01947) 880042 £36; 2 rms, one with own bthrm. 17th-c ex-coastguard's cottage by beach with views over the bay from lounge and sun terrace, friendly, caring owners and huge first-class breakfasts (8 courses); good nearby walks.

Lastingham SE7391 BLACKSMITHS ARMS Lastingham, York YO6 6TL (01751) 417247 £35; 3 rms, shared bthrm. Cosy little village pub in lovely countryside near interesting ancient church, comfortable oak-beamed bar, top-class real ales brewed by their son, and decent food served all day; disabled access.

Staintondale SE9998 ISLAND FARM Staintondale, Scarborough YO13 0EB (01723) 870249 £34; 4 rms, showers. Comfortable modern farmhouse on working farm with fine views from spacious rooms, good home cooking, games room with toys and snooker, and all weather tennis court next to garden; cl Nov–Easter.

Aislaby NZ8608 COTE BANK FARM Egton Rd, Aislaby, Whitby YO21 1UG (01947) 895314 £32; 2 rms, shared bthrm. Comfortable 18th-c farmhouse with fine views, big garden, log fires, and good home cooking; lambing March/April; cl Christmas and maybe other times in winter; children over 5.

Cloughton TA0096 HAYBURN WYKE Cloughton, Scarborough YO13 0AU (01723) 870202 *£30; 4 well equipped rms. Rose-covered old hotel with rambling beamed interior, rough plastered ceilings, good straightforward food, friendly and efficient staff and well kept real ales; nr Hayburn Wyke cove; children over 10.

Fadmoor SE6789 PLOUGH Fadmoor, York YO6 6HY (01751) 431515 £28; 4 rms, shared bthrm. Hearty little pub in a stunning location and overlooking quiet village green, with spick-and-span bar, crackling open fire, simple old furnishings, cheery landlady, straightforward bar food (inc vegetarian dishes), and restaurant like a private dining room; children over 12.

To see and do

⏱🏛 **Brompton** SE9683 WORDSWORTH GALLERY (Gallows Hill) The former home of Mary Hutchinson, who married William Wordsworth at Brompton church in 1802. The medieval barn has an exhibition on the poet and Samuel Coleridge, as well as an exhibition of paintings and prints. Meals, snacks, shop, disabled access; cl 24-26 Dec; (01723) 863298; *£1 for Wordsworth exhibition.

🐄❀ 🐦 **Danby** NZ7008 THE MOORS CENTRE Surrounded with terraced riverside and woodland grounds, good exhibitions on the landscape and wildlife of the National Park, with audio-visual show, guided walks and events, adventure playground, and lots of useful information. Meals, snacks, shop, disabled access; cl wkdys Oct–Easter; (01287) 660540; free. The Duke of Wellington is useful for lunch.

✝ **Easby** NZ1800 EASBY ABBEY Extensive remains of the 12th-c Premonstratensian abbey, a pretty walk along the Swale from Richmond; disabled access; free.

🐄🏠🐝 **East Ayton** TA0085 HONEY FARM (Betton Farm Centre) Exhaustive exhibition on bees and honey-making, with sales of wax and honey-based products. Also animals, craft shops, farm shop and play area. Meals, snacks, shop, disabled access; (01723) 864001; *£1.50. The Copper Horse at Seamer has good food.

🏛 **Goathland** NZ8301 in the heart of the moors has a short walk from opposite the church to a wooded smooth-rocked gorge where the MALLYAN SPOUT waterfall is a fine sight. The hotel named after the waterfall does good food. The village is the setting for TV's *Heartbeat* (filming can be rather intrusive). A rather longer walk S from here, or reached direct by the narrow moorland lane S from Egton Bridge NZ8105, is WADE'S CAUSEWAY, a mile-long stretch of broad paved Roman road up over the moors, well restored and maintained.

🐦❀ **Hayburn Wyke** TA0097 From the very well sited hotel here steep Victorian woodland paths wind down to the cliff-sheltered cove; a clifftop path to the S gives fine views.

★🏠🐾🎋🏘❀♈ **Helmsley** SE6183 Lanes run straight up on to the moors from this attractive small market town. There's a large cobbled square (the busy market day is Fri), and enough antique shops and craft shops to please a visitor without seeming too touristy. A lively and bustling place, with a lot of class. It's dominated by the 12th-c CASTLE, ruined in 1644, and standing within enormous earthworks. Good for picnics. Shop; cl 1–2pm, winter Mon and Tues; £1.80. DUNCOMBE PARK Beautifully restored early 18th-c house, rebuilt after a fire at the turn of this century. The early 18th-c landscaped gardens, with grand terracing, are magnificent, covering 30 acres and set in 300 acres of memorable parkland. Meals, snacks, shop, disabled access; open Weds and Sun Apr and Oct, daily exc Mon and Tues May and Jun, then daily till Sept; (01439) 770213; *£4.50, gardens only *£2.75. You can wander through the estate (just granted nature reserve status) for £1. Besides the hotels and inns we recommend, the courtyard café outside the Edinburgh Woollen Mill does imaginative light lunches.

★ ☻ **Hutton le Hole** SE7090 is a very neat and pretty streamside village at the mouth of Farndale; sheep wander the streets. Its excellent FOLK MUSEUM is practically a village on its own, made up of various old buildings from the area re-erected in the 2-acre grounds, inc an Elizabethan manor house, gypsy caravan, and an Edwardian photographic studio. Inside are well displayed everyday articles going back to Roman times, inc a couple of intriguing witch-posts. Lots of demonstrations and events. Shop, disabled access; cl Nov–Mar; (01751) 417367; £2.50. The Crown here is useful for lunch.

✝ **Kirkdale** SE6886 has a Saxon church with unique Saxon sundial, and 7th-c Celtic crosses and carved stones.

★ ✝ ⌂ **Osmotherley** SE4598, perhaps more a small town than a village, is quietly attractive; the Three Tuns and Golden Lion have good food. MOUNT GRACE PRIORY Carthusian monks not only took a vow of silence but rarely emerged from their own individual cells. One of the cells at this ruined 14th-c priory has been fully restored, giving a good illustration of how the monks must have worked and lived. The ruins are better preserved than

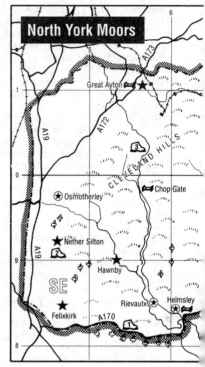

those of any other Carthusian establishment in England, and in spring an impressive display of daffodils makes it an especially attractive spot. An adjacent 17th-c manor house has an exhibition, and interesting arts and crafts connections. Snacks, shop, some disabled access; in winter cl 1–2pm and all Mon and Tues; (01609) 883494; £2. Just up the road at Ingleby Cross NZ4501, the ADVENTURE CENTRE hire out bikes, and can organise climbing, caving and canoeing; (01609) 882571.

★ ✝ ✳ ⌂ ⛰ ☻ **Pickering** SE7983 is another attractive small town, usually very quiet (busier Mon market day), with vivid medieval murals in the splendid tall-spired CHURCH. NORTH YORKSHIRE MOORS RAILWAY Steam train trips through some lovely countryside and nostalgically restored stations, a distance of 18 miles; the line was originally built by George Stephenson. The Grosmont end has various locomotives and antique

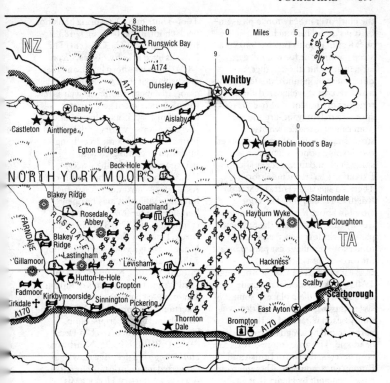

carriages (you can watch repairs), and you can stop off at Goathland (see above). Meals, snacks, shop, disabled access; cl Nov–Mar (exc Santa Specials, Dec wknds); (01751) 472508 for timetable; £7.90.
PICKERING CASTLE Ruins of 12th-c keep and later curtain walls and towers, with fine views from its imposing castle mound above the town. Shop, some disabled access; cl 1–2pm, winter Mon and Tues; £1.80. The BECK ISLE MUSEUM is a charmingly set 17th-c riverside house with a wonderful collection of local bygones, inc some fascinating old photographs. Shop, disabled access to ground floor; cl Nov–Mar; (01751) 473653; £1.75. The White Swan, Black Swan, Forest & Vale and Station Hotel all do decent food.
† ❋ ❀ ⌂ Rievaulx SE5785 RIEVAULX ABBEY Superbly atmospheric ruins of magnificent and once highly prosperous abbey, set among the wooded hills of Rye Dale. The nave, dating back to 1135, is one of the earliest built in England. Also among the spectacular three-tiered remains is a fine 13th c choir, and there's a visitor centre with displays on monastic life. The graceful colonnades, arches and lancet windows, lovely at any time, are extremely moving if you get there early or late on a wkdy out of season (when the absence of crowds adds a great deal to the site's appeal). Snacks, shop, some disabled access; cl winter Mon and Tues, 24–26 Dec, 1 Jan; (014396) 228; £2.20. There are dramatic views of the abbey from RIEVAULX TERRACE AND TEMPLES, a half-mile long grass-covered 18th-c terrace overlooking it. Each end is adorned with a classical temple; one a small Tuscan rotunda built to while away the hours in peaceful contemplation, the other, an elaborate Ionic creation, for hunting parties. An ideal spot for a picnic, with good frescoes and an exhibition on landscape design. Shop; cl Nov–Mar; £2.50; NT. Besides the many places in Helmsley not far off,

the Hare over in Scawton (a pleasant drive) is useful for lunch.

★ 🖰 **Robin Hood's Bay** NZ9505 is a steep picturesque fishing village, largely unspoilt (though there are quite a few shops and cafés for visitors now), its cottages clustered close together on the slopes above the rocky shore – a rich hunting-ground for pottering at low tide, when a surprising expanse of sand is exposed too. It was a popular haunt of smugglers, and the SMUGGLING EXPERIENCE has the whole story. There's a BIKE HIRE centre on Station Rd; (01947) 880488. The Olde Dolphin above the seafront does good freshly caught fish, and the Bay (with picture-window views) is good for food too. The village car park is up at the top – quite a climb.

🏭 ✳ 🏬 🏘 🎣 🖰 🈁 ♪ ! ✝ ⚓ **Scarborough** TA0388 has all the usual seaside attractions, and is a place of some style, its two great curves of firm sandy beach separated by the small harbour and by a high narrow headland. The once-impressive CASTLE is up here, on the site of British and Roman encampments. Thought to have been built by Henry II, it remained a royal palace of some importance until the reign of James I. Remains include the 13th-c barbican, medieval chapels and house, and the shell of the original 12th-c keep, and there are great coastal views from the walls. Shop, some disabled access; cl 24–26 Dec, 1 Jan; (01723) 372451; £1.50. Between the castle and the cliff edge are the remains of a Roman signal station, one of five such structures built in the 4th c to detect the approach of northern raiders. To the S is the older part of the resort, with antique tracked cliff lifts between prom and the pleasant streets of the upper town; a house associated with Richard III is here (though it now looks a little dilapidated), and there's a small craft centre in a former 14th-c inn. ROTUNDA MUSEUM (Vernon Rd) Georgian museum associated with William Smith, the 'father of English geology', now concentrating on local history, inc a Bronze Age skeleton and displays on the resort's Victorian heyday. Shop; cl Mon all yr, and

Tues–Thurs mid-Oct–spring bank hol (exc school hols); (01723) 374839; free. WOOD END (The Crescent) The Sitwells lived here for 60 years from 1870 (Edith was born here), and there are displays of their work and associated memorabilia, as well as the town's collection of geology and natural history. Lots of fossils, and Victorian conservatory with tropical plants – though not the free-flying birds that once mingled with partygoers; some disabled access. Details as above, and the same for the ART GALLERY next door, a striking Italianate villa; this may be open longer in winter for temporary exhibitions, (01723) 374753 to check. Down by the harbour, MILLENNIUM is a vivid journey through 1,000 years of the town's history, through Vikings, Normans and the Civil War to the early days of rail and Victorian sea bathing – very entertainingly done. Alan Ayckbourn contributed to the scripts. Shop, limited disabled access; cl 25 Dec; (01723) 501000; £3.75. Nearby the *Hatherleigh* is a deep-sea trawler converted into a little museum; free. AMAZING WORLD OF HOLOGRAMS (Foreshore Rd) Ideal for children, over 200 holograms that seem to come to life, from bodies in the bog through Viking helmets to film stars. Shop; open wknds Apr–Oct, daily late May–Sept; (01723) 859622; £1. Interesting CHURCHES include the medieval St Mary's, where Anne Brontë is buried, and the 19th-c St Martin's with elaborate work by Burne-Jones, William Morris and other Pre-Raphaelite artists. The SEA LIFE CENTRE (Scalby Mills) offers the same lively mixture we've described in several other resorts; cl 25 Dec; (01723) 376125; £4.25. Shows are still an essential ingredient in the Scarborough cocktail, from the more old-fashioned concerts to the theatre now linked to Alan Ayckbourn. One unique and entertainingly quaint tradition is the summer staging of miniaturised sea battles with all sorts of special effects among the ducks on the lake of Peasholm Park in the more seaside N part of the town; May–early Sept Mon and Thurs 3.30 pm.

Good views of the bay from the top of 500ft Oliver's Mount (and harbour views from the Golden Ball on the front).

🐗 **Staintondale** SE9998 SHIRE HORSE FARM Friendly little farm with good demonstrations and talks; as well as horses there are various rabbits, small animals and poultry, nature trails and lovely clifftop walks along part of the Cleveland Way. Meals, snacks, shop, disabled access; cl Mon (exc bank hols), Thurs, Sat, Oct–Mar; (01723) 870458; £3.50. The Hayburn Wyke Hotel and Bryherstones, both down off the Cloughton road, do good-value food.

★ **Staithes** NZ7818 Steep fishing village, unspoilt down by the shore, where little cottages and the storm-battered Cod & Lobster pose fetchingly against the staggering background of a great red-sandstone headland, a striking colour picture as the sun comes up.

★ † ♨ ❦ **Whitby** NZ8910 Famous as the port at which Count Dracula came ashore; Bram Stoker got the idea for the book in the fishermen's graveyard of the partly Norman CHURCH, 199 steps up from the harbour, with lovely woodwork. A famous scene in the novel takes place at WHITBY ABBEY, an impressive set of 13th-c ruins dramatically overlooking the harbour from their windswept clifftop setting. You can see the skeletal remains of the magnificent three-tiered choir and the north transept, and it's an evocative spot for a picnic. An earlier building had been the site of the Synod of Whitby, where the dating of Easter was thrashed out in 664. Shop; cl 24–26 Dec, 1 Jan; (01947) 603568; £1.50. The town is steep and away from the bright waterfront quite attractive, with picturesque old buildings (now often rather smart shops) and some quaint cobbled alleys in its original core E of the busy harbour, where excellent fresh fish is sold straight from the catch. Whitby's history is well illustrated in the delightfully old-fashioned and crowded MUSEUM (Pannett Park), which includes a good range of maritime exhibits (inc the only surviving part of Captain Cook's

original journal), Queen Victoria's nightdress, and the hand of a murderer used as a candle-holder by superstitious burglars. Shop, some disabled access; cl am Sun, pm Mon and Tues Oct–Apr; (01947) 602908; *£1. The CAPTAIN COOK MEMORIAL MUSEUM (Grape Lane) is more specifically devoted to the famous explorer, in the house where he lived as an apprentice in the shipping trade from 1746; rooms are furnished in period style with models, letters and drawings from Cook's later voyages. Shop; cl Nov–Mar, exc poss wknds in Mar and Nov – best to check first; (01947) 601900; *£1.80. There are more Cook places to visit over the border in Middlesbrough – see Northumbria chapter. Children probably won't be satisfied until they've visited the spooky DRACULA EXPERIENCE (Marine Parade), which vividly recreates scenes from the classic tale; cl winter wkdys; (01947) 601923; *£1.75. Besides good lunches at Bagdale Hall (see Where to stay), and excellent fish and chips from the Magpie Café, the Duke of York (Church St, at the bottom of the 199 steps) is useful for food.

❦ Classic **views** of the interlocking moor and valley landscapes are to be had from the graveyard of Gillamoor church SE6890; the lane at SE6188 a bit more than a mile N of Carlton, itself N of Helmsley; the hillside just S of Lastingham SE7290; the hillside at the top of the fearfully steep Rosedale Chimney road SE7294 heading S over Spaunton Moor from Rosedale Abbey; and the road on either side of Blakey Ridge SE6899. Sutton Bank SE5182 is the classic viewpoint for motorists.

This area has a number of decent **horse riding** centres, good for experts and beginners alike; the Moors Centre at Danby (see above) has the full list, and can also provide numbers for the various **cycle hire** centres dotted about the region.

★ Other **attractive villages** here, all with decent pubs, include Ainthorpe NZ7008, Beck Hole NZ8202 (Birch Hall is a unique cross between country tavern and village store; ideally visited along the former

railway track – see Walks, below),
Castleton NZ6908 high above the
Esk Valley, Cloughton Newlands
TA0196, Egton Bridge NZ8105
(pleasantly eccentric, twinned with a
fictional French village), Fadmoor
SE6789, Felixkirk SE4785, Great
Ayton NZ5611, Hawnby SE5489,
Lastingham SE7391, Levisham
SE8390, Nether Silton SE4692,
Rosedale Abbey SE7395 and
Runswick Bay NZ8217 (a very
pretty harbourless fishing village).
Thornton Dale SE8383 is delightful,
but we've had no pub
recommendation there.

Walks

The Cleveland Way, meticulously waymarked and signposted, is a great help in selecting and following there-and-back walks here. It follows the W, N and E margins of the Moors National Park, leaving it at one point to enter Cleveland (see also Northumbria section). Starting from Helmsley SE6184, it passes Rievaulx Abbey SE5785 (itself more dramatically viewed from approach routes down Rye Dale from the north). **Sutton Bank** SE5182 ⌂-1 is a steep escarpment with an enthralling view, and the most popular section of the Way here is S from the A170 along the level clifftop to the white horse hill figure SE5181. Immediately N of the A170 you can combine the path along the top of the slope with a venture down the nature trail into Garbutt Wood SE5374, a nature reserve abutting Gormire Lake SE5083, the only natural lake in the National Park. There's a lonely stretch with some road access over the **Hambleton Hills** SE5187 ⌂-2 to Osmotherley SE4597. N of **Chop Gate** SE5699 ⌂-3 (where the Buck does good food) is a fine section off the B1257, where the path westwards on the N slopes of the moors takes in rock outcrops.

Along the coast the Cleveland Way is consistently interesting – and so much more rewarding than the immediate hinterland that there-and-back walks keeping to the Way itself are more fun than trying to work out circular walks heading inland. The village of **Runswick Bay** NZ8217 ⌂-4 makes a pretty start point for the path to Staithes NZ7818, or you can begin closer from tiny Port Mulgrave NZ7197. A bus service is useful for the section linking Whitby NZ8910, Robin Hood's Bay NZ9505 and Scarborough TA0388. At the famous village of **Robin Hood's Bay** ⌂-5 the foreshore is a fascinating place for rock-pools, except at high tide; or you can walk along a fine section of cliffs to Ravenscar NZ9801, where a geological trail takes in old alum quarries; an abandoned railway provides an easy walkway back.

Off the Cleveland Way, Farndale and Rosedale have characteristic North York Moors scenery – lush green fields and red-roofed yellow-stone houses beneath the brooding moorland plateau. **Farndale** ⌂-6, the largest dale, is famous for its miles of wild daffodils in April, probably introduced and naturalised here many centuries ago. They're at their best around Low Mill SE6795, and any walk to enjoy them gives the chance of coming back down the ancient green lane of Rudland Rigg, for spectacular views. The friendly Feversham Arms at Church Houses SE6697, right next to the daffodil reserve, does very good value food. **Rosedale** ⌂-7 now seems to typify the quiet pastoral countryside of the area, though until 60 or 70 years ago it was a busy iron-working site. The old railway track that once served the quarries loops around the moor above, and makes an easily followed stroll. **Hutton le Hole** SE7090 ⌂-8 and Lastingham SE7391 are two charming villages, an hour or so apart on foot.

The E part of the National Park has large forest plantations; **Dalby Forest** SE8788 ⌂-9 has colour-coded trails. Around **Levisham** SE8390 ⌂-10 the scenery is open, with a track across the blustery moors and an attractive valley giving separate routes to and from the Hole of Horcum, just below the A169.

From **Grosmont** NZ8205 ⌂-11 you can walk a historic rail trail via Beck Hole along the abandoned line that preceded the current North Yorkshire Moors Railway route to Goathland NZ8301. From the Mallyan Spout Hotel in **Goathland** ⌂-12 a popular walk is to Mallyan Spout, a waterfall which tumbles into the side of a fine gorge. Within a walk of Goathland is **Wade's Causeway** NZ8312 ⌂-13, Britain's best-preserved stretch of Roman road (open to walkers only).

Driving

This is fine driving country, with relatively little traffic. High roads with good moorland views, though sometimes steep and narrow, include the one N from Hutton le Hole over Blakey Ridge to Castleton; the road straight up from Kirkbymoorside (a pleasantly old-fashioned small market town) forking left through Fadmoor to take you over the unpopulated wilds of Rudland Slack, looping round Cockayne and heading back to Helmsley; and the road branching off the B1257 N of Rievaulx Abbey, taking you through Hawnby and over to Osmotherley.

The attractive drive from Helmsley past Rievaulx Abbey to Old Byland and Cold Kirby brings you out by the top of Sutton Bank (for the outstanding view). If you turn left along the A170 and then take the next right turn down the steep road past the gliding club, you get a good view of the white horse cut into the hillside, and at Kilburn you can link with the drive we mention in the East Yorkshire section, through Coxwold, Byland Abbey and Ampleforth, to bring you back to Helmsley for a pleasant round trip.

Where to eat

Whitby NZ8911 is famous for its fish and chips, and the MAGPIE CAFÉ Pier Rd (01947) 602058, which overlooks the town and river, is said by some to have the best in England – where else could haddock taste so delicious? Lots of wonderfully evocative sepia photographs on the walls, cheerful service; cl from 6.30pm and from late Nov to Mar; children's menu. £11.40|£2.10/£4.95.

Apart from this and the other places we suggest in the text above, many of the places in the Where to stay section have good food.

EAST YORKSHIRE

Calm and untouristy – a civilised area for a quiet break.

This very civilised part of Yorkshire has in Coxwold one of England's prettiest villages (with Newburgh Priory well worth a visit), and in Castle Howard one of the country's most magnificent houses. Sutton Park and Nunnington Hall are also well worth a visit, as are the stricken remains of Byland Abbey and Kirkham Priory. Flamingo Land at Kirby Misperton is fun as a family outing, and Eden Camp just outside Malton is an unusual re-creation of World War II experiences. There's an interesting new visitor centre at Kilburn devoted to 'Mouseman' Thompson the furniture craftsman.

The countryside is altogether more muted than in those parts of North Yorkshire described above, and much less interesting for walkers, though the gentle generously wooded Howardian Hills between Coxwold and Malton present a series of quiet but attractive landscapes; more open wolds roll on between there and Flamborough Head. It's pleasant scenery to drive through.

Less well known than other parts of North Yorkshire, the area does have a quietly untouristy appeal, and some unshowy but attractive places to stay. It's easy to explore the Moors from here – in fact the boundary of the National Park dips south of the A170 through Kilburn, Ampleforth and Oswaldkirk to include Coxwold, Byland Abbey, Oldstead and Wass.

Where to stay

Hovingham SE6775 WORSLEY ARMS Hovingham, York YO6 4LA (01653) 628234 £98; 22 individually decorated bedrooms. Stone-built Georgian inn with comfortable, pretty sitting rooms, fresh flowers and open fires, carefully cooked food in elegant restaurant, and seats out by the stream.

Kilburn SE5179 FORRESTERS ARMS Kilburn, York YO6 4AH (01347) 868386 £58; 10 clean, bright rms. Friendly old coaching inn opposite pretty village gardens, sturdy but elegant furnishings made next door at Thompson furniture workshop, big log fire, and decent food in beamed bar and in restaurant; disabled access.

Harome SE6582 PHEASANT Harome, York YO6 5JG (01439) 771241 £57.50; 12 rms. Family-run hotel with relaxed, homely lounge and traditional bar with beams, inglenook fireplace and flagstones, good very popular food, efficient service, and indoor heated swimming pool; cl Christmas, Jan and Feb; children over 12; disabled access.

Wass SE5679 WOMBWELL ARMS Wass, York YO6 4BE (01347) 868280 £49; 3 individually furnished rms. Attractive, warmly welcoming small inn within the North York Moors National Park, with cosy central bar, good imaginative food and decent wines; cl early Jan for 10 days; children over 8.

Wharram le Street SE8666 RED HOUSE Wharram le Street, Malton YO17 9TL (01946) 768455 £48; 3 rms. Comfortable house with friendly owners, log fires in sitting rooms, good home cooking in dining room (using home-grown produce where possible), and lovely garden with tennis court; cl Christmas week.

Coxwold SE5377 FAUCONBERG ARMS Coxwold, York YO6 4AD (01347) 868214 *£40; 4 rms, 1 with shower. Civilised old stone inn in pretty village with big log fire, some handsome settles and gleaming copper in the 2 cosy and comfortably furnished rooms of the lounge bar, good food in restaurant and bar, an extensive wine list, and decent breakfasts.

Crayke SE5670 DURHAM OX Crayke, York YO6 4TE (01347) 821506 £35; 3 rms. Carefully run and warmly friendly village inn opposite church, marvellous views from top of hill, antique furnishings and panelling in bar, winter log fire and summer flowers, good bar food.

Ampleforth SE5878 CARR HOUSE FARM Shallowdale, Ampleforth, York YO6 4ED (01347) 868526 *£30; 2 rms. In peaceful undulating farmland and surrounded by an acre of garden, this 16th-c stone farmhouse has beams and oak panelling, flagstoned dining room with woodburning stove in inglenook fireplace, separate lounge; good breakfasts using home-made butter and preserves and fresh farm eggs; no smoking; cl Christmas and New Year; children over 7; no dogs.

To see and do

✝ **Byland Abbey** SE5579 The jagged ruins of this abbey, built for the Cistercians, date from the 12th and 13th c. Enough detail survives to show how fine it must have been: look out for the well preserved floor tiles and carved stone; cl winter Mon and Tues, some parts cl 1–2pm; (01347)

868614; £1.25. The nearby Abbey Inn is most enjoyable for lunch.

★ 🏰 ❀ ✝ 🎣 **Coxwold** SE5377 A neat and very attractive little stone-built village, very harmonious. Laurence Sterne's quaint SHANDY HALL has been well restored, the little study much as it must have been when he wrote *Tristram Shandy* here. Outside is a lovely walled garden. House open pm Weds and Sun Jun–Sept, though you can usually visit the gardens other days (exc Sat); (01347) 868465; *£2.50. Close by is the attractive 15th-c CHURCH of which Sterne was curate – it still has the box pews it had in his day. The Fauconberg Arms does good food. Just S, NEWBURGH PRIORY is a charming old house, partly Norman with Tudor and Georgian additions. One of the family married Oliver Cromwell's daughter, who rescued her father's headless corpse and had it reburied here; the room with the tomb is on the tour. Outside is a lovely 40-acre lakeside and riverside garden with a fine collection of dogwoods, splendid formal borders and lots of unusual plants; also miniature railway, children's adventure garden, woodland trail and 19th-c statuary walk. Plant sales, shop, meals and snacks, disabled access; grounds open pm Weds and Sun Apr–Jun; (01347) 868435; *£3, *£1.50 grounds only. Take some stale bread for the grateful waterfowl (even if you're just passing through – the lake's right by the road). There's a good working pottery.

🎣 **Filey** TA1180 is a much quieter seaside resort than Scarborough, its neighbour up the coast, with the main road dropping down a steep little valley between the church and the old town (and under a footbridge linking the two) to the beach, where fishermen still beach their boats. There's a small and attractively homely summer local MUSEUM in former medieval fishermen's cottages (Queen St; cl am and all Sat). The rock reef N of the town beyond the sands is interesting; to the S there are holiday camps, and inland the Royal Oak at Hunmanby has good-value food.

🎣 🏚 ! **Kilburn** SE5179 This quiet village is almost a place of pilgrimage to the Robert Thompson FURNITURE WORKSHOP, famous for the unobtrusive little mouse carved as a trademark that you'll see all over North Yorkshire, on church pews and in the better inns and pubs. There's a new visitor centre tracing the company history, and you can watch the craftsmen at work. Shop, disabled access; cl Mon (exc bank hols), Nov–Mar; (01347) 868222; £1.50. They make lovely, simple furniture – though not cheap (for a wider choice you might try the Old Mill at nearby Balk SE4881, where the craftsmen include ex-Thompson employees and prices seem lower). The oak they use can be seen all around. Near the church (with a memorial to Thompson carved by his own craftsmen) the Singing Bird does refreshments. Up above the village on Roulston Scar is a WHITE HORSE cut out of the turf in 1857 and unique in this part of the country.

🏇 😊 **Kirby Misperton** SE7779 FLAMINGO LAND ZOO AND FAMILY FUN PARK Huge adventure park with lots of rides and plenty of animals. Useful enough for children to let off steam. Meals, snacks, shop, disabled access; cl wkdys Oct, all Nov–Easter; (01653) 668287; £8.

✝ **Kirkham** SE7365 KIRKHAM PRIORY Remains of Augustinian priory in an attractive quiet spot by the River Derwent; finely sculpted lavatorium, graceful arcaded cloister, and handsome 13th-c gatehouse with some finely carved sculptures and shields. Shop, disabled access; cl 1–2pm, Oct–Mar; (01653) 618768; £1.25. The Stone Trough overlooking the ruins is good for lunch.

🏰 📷 ❀ 🦌 ♫ **Nr Malton** SE7170 CASTLE HOWARD (outside, to the W) Quite magnificent 18th-c palace designed by Sir John Vanbrugh, who up to then had no architectural experience whatsoever, but went on to create Blenheim Palace. The striking 300ft long façade is topped with a marvellous painted and gilded dome, an unforgettable sight beyond the lake as you approach from the north. Splendid apartments,

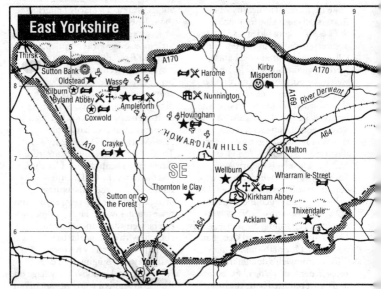

East Yorkshire

sculpture gallery and long gallery (192ft to be exact), magnificent chapel with stained glass by Burne-Jones, and beautiful paintings inc a Holbein portrait of Henry VIII, and works by Rubens, Reynolds and Gainsborough. The grounds are impressive but inviting, featuring the family mausoleum designed by Hawksmoor, the domed Temple of the Four Winds by Vanbrugh, and a beautiful rose garden; Ray Wood covers 30 acres and includes rare trees, rhododendrons and other shrubs. Also fantastic collection of period costume, and a good unobtrusive adventure playground. *Brideshead Revisited* was filmed here, and the TV cameras have been back again this last year. Meals, snacks, shop, disabled access; cl Nov–Mar; (01653) 648333; £6. EDEN CAMP SE7974 (just N of town, A64/A169) Elaborately recreated wartime scenes in buildings of former prisoner-of-war camp, very well done with sound, smells and even smoke effects. Covers a wide range of World War II experiences, from the rise of the Nazis to the blitz and Bomber Command ops room. There's a children's commando assault course, but it's the wartime generation that will probably get most out of the

place. You may have to queue for some of the huts on busy days. Meals and snacks in NAAFI, shop, disabled access; cl 24 Dec–13 Feb; (01653) 697777; £3. Malton itself is a comfortable market town with some interesting side streets, in prosperous farming and racehorse-training country. Sat is a busy market day (the lively livestock mart is on Tues and Fri). The Cornucopia (Commercial St, Norton) is a well run dining pub, and the Coach & Horses and Royal Oak do good generous food.

Nunnington SE6679 NUNNINGTON HALL Big 16th- to 17th-c house nicely set on the banks of the River Rye, with fine panelling in the hall and a magnificent staircase. A family home for nearly 400 years, perhaps the most intriguing feature is the unique Carlisle Collection of miniature rooms, each of them 1/8th life size. Meals, snacks, shop, limited disabled access; cl am, Mon (exc bank hols), Fri, Nov–Mar; £3.50, £1.60 garden only; NT. The Royal Oak is good for lunch, and the church has a fine effigy of a knight said to have rid the district of a Loathly Worm.

Sutton on the Forest SE5864 SUTTON PARK Friendly 1730s manor house with Chippendale and Sheraton

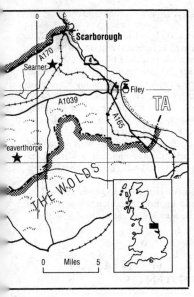

furnishings, and fine porcelain collection. The delightful grounds have terraced gardens, a Georgian ice house, lily pond, and pleasant woodland walks and nature trails. Snacks, shop, disabled access to grounds only; house open pm Easter wknd and bank hol Sun and Mon, gardens open daily Easter–Oct; (01347) 810249; £3.50. The New Inn at Huby has decent food.

★ **Attractive villages**, all with decent pubs, include Acklam SE7862, Ampleforth SE5879 (with its famous school and partly wooded moors), Crayke SE5670, Hovingham SE6775, Seamer TA0284, Weaverthorpe SE9771, Oldstead SE5380, Thixendale SE8461, Thornton le Clay SE6865 and Welburn SE7268.

Walks

The **Howardian Hills** ◻-1 protrude mildly from the surrounding plain, with a path along their N flanks giving intermittent views across to the North York Moors. Castle Howard SE7170 is of course the principal feature of the area, its vast estate threaded by a few public footpaths which gain glimpses of the great house and the landscaped parts of its grounds. From **Kirkham** SE7365 ◻-2 a path meanders S by a placid stretch of the River Derwent, to Howsham Bridge SE7362 and beyond.

The **Yorkshire Wolds** ◻-3 are quiet agricultural chalk country with few footpaths. The most useful are to be found on the well signposted long-distance Wolds Way from Hessle Haven TA0325 down in Humberside to Filey Brigg TA1381 on the coast, where it meets the inland Wolds Way. Thixendale SE6841 is perhaps the best starting point, with a characteristic dry valley to the S and some elevated land to the N, where the Way passes within sight of the abandoned medieval village of Wharram Percy SE8564.

The **coast** ◻-4 between Filey TA1180 and Scarborough TA0388 is followed by the Cleveland Way – an agreeable few hours' walk, although of less scenic significance than the cliffs further N, described in the North York Moors section. Oddly, the Way stops just short of Filey, at the headland of Filey Brigg, although there is nothing to prevent you from walking on into town.

Driving

Striding over this gently rolling countryside are some good long-legged back roads with attractive country views, particularly the one S from Hovingham through Sheriff Hutton and Flaxton, the estate road slicing S from Slingsby through the grounds of Castle Howard, and the old high road slightly W of S out of Norton, which runs down parallel to the A64 and joins the A166 near Gate Helmsley.

A very attractive slower road is the one which runs through Bagby (SE of Thirsk) through Kilburn to Coxwold, where a left turn takes you up to Byland Abbey, and on through Wass and Ampleforth to Oswaldkirk. This road gives good views of the prettily varied hills rising to the north.

Where to eat

Byland Abbey SE5579 ABBEY (01347) 868204 Beautifully placed pub opposite ruins of abbey, with imaginative food, well kept beers, and decent wines, an interesting series of rambling old rms, and big garden. £17|£2.50/£6.70.

Ampleforth SE5878 WHITE SWAN (01439) 788239 Big, neatly run modernised pub with wide choice of generously served food, popular Sun lunch, tempting wine list and very friendly staff; attractive village; cl 25 Dec. £17|£2.30/£5.50.

Nunnington SE6779 ROYAL OAK (01439) 788271 Friendly pub near Nunnington Hall with carefully chosen furnishings and enjoyable bar food with excellent daily specials; cl Mon; children over 8. £16|£2.50/£6.75.

Harome SE6582 STAR (01439) 70397 Civilised thatched pub with deeply polished dark rustic tables, cushioned old settles, lots to look at, rewarding bar food, evening restaurant, and garden; cl Mon and Tues; disabled access. £15|£2.95/£4.95.

Kirkham Abbey SE7466 STONE TROUGH (01653) 81713 Quaint beamed inn with small, cosy and interesting bars with log fires, good lunchtime bar food, old-fashioned restaurant with farmhouse atmosphere, seats outside with valley views; cl am Mon. £15|£2.50/£5.

HARROGATE, RIPON AND SURROUNDINGS

Comfortable and civilised, with some lovely houses and gardens.

This area has more for sightseers than any other part of North Yorkshire except for York itself (which is within very easy reach). Its particular high points are Fountains Abbey, one of Yorkshire's best-loved places, Ripley Castle, Newby Hall and Beningborough Hall, all with grand gardens. The most interesting gardens are those at Harlow Carr just outside Harrogate. Little known to visitors or even to locals, Markenfield Hall is a lovely place to look round. Ripon is an attractive and largely unspoilt market town with one of Britain's largest cathedrals, very well placed for several of the area's major attractions. Harrogate is an extremely civilised former spa resort, a pleasant place to spend a leisurely morning or afternoon; with its many hotels, good restaurants and relatively central position, it makes a good base for excursions further afield if you want the comforts of an up-market town around you. It has some of Yorkshire's smartest shops. Knaresborough is fun for a family outing. The countryside is less dramatic than neighbouring areas to the north, but there are pleasant places for strolls.

Where to stay

Nidd SE3061 NIDD HALL Nidd, Harrogate HG3 3BN (01423) 771598 £120; 59 spacious and individually decorated rms. Impressive Georgian manor house in 45 acres of landscaped grounds with fly fishing, punting on the lake, squash, tennis and leisure club facilities with indoor swimming pool; beautiful plasterwork, elaborate wrought-iron stairs, and fine red marble pillars in the entrance halls, lovely flowers, antiques and fine fireplaces in elegant drawing room and panelled library, and good, modern French cooking in graceful dining room; good for children with crèche/nannies/babysitting; disabled access.

Ripley SE2861 Boars Head Ripley, Harrogate HG3 1AY (01423) 771888 £105; 25 individually decorated rms. Beautiful old coaching inn with comfortable sofas in the attractively decorated lounges, long flagstoned bar, notable wines by the glass, good food in bar and restful dining room, and unobtrusive service; disabled access.

Bilbrough SE5346 Bilbrough Manor Bilbrough, York YO2 3PH (01937) 834002 *£85; 12 pretty rms. In a quiet village, this handsome country house has fine gardens, a comfortable wood-panelled lounge, log fires, library and bar, imaginative food, and courteous service; children over 10.

Markington SE2865 Hob Green Markington, Harrogate HG3 3PJ (01423) 770031 £80; 12 well equipped rms. Pretty gardens and over 800 acres of rolling countryside surround this stone hotel with its attractively decorated and comfortable lounge and garden room, and there are log fires, fresh flowers, a relaxed atmosphere, good food, and friendly service.

Harrogate SE3155 Old Swan Ripon Rd HG1 2SR (01423) 500055 £75; 135 rms. Close to the centre in quiet gardens, this fine hotel is very well run, with a friendly atmosphere, attractive day rooms, fresh flowers, and good food; disabled access.

Ripon SE3171 Ripon Spa Park St HG4 2BU (01765) 602172 £72; 40 rms. Neatly kept, friendly and comfortable Edwardian hotel with seven acres of gardens, yet only a short walk from the centre; attractive public rooms, and good food in bar and restaurant; disabled access.

Harrogate SE3155 Balmoral 16-18 Franklin Mount HG1 5EJ (01423) 508208 £62; 20 lovely rms, many with 4-posters. In lovely gardens but close to the centre, this popular hotel has a restful drawing room, cosy snug, interesting Oriental Bar, fine food in elegant restaurant, and helpful, friendly staff; children over 2 in restaurant; disabled access.

Masham SE2381 Kings Head Market Sq, Masham, Ripon HG4 4EF (01765) 689295 £58; 10 rms. Tall and handsome Georgian stone inn on market square in attractive small town; lots of flowers and hanging baskets, comfortable and neatly kept spacious lounge bar, and home-made food in bar and restaurant.

Harrogate SE3155 Alexa House 26 Ripon Rd HG1 2JJ (01423) 501988 £55; 13 rms, some in former stable block. Detached Victorian hotel with friendly staff, comfortable lounge, good home-cooking in big dining room, and marvellous breakfasts; good disabled access.

Harrogate SE3155 Russell Valley Drive HG2 0JN (01423) 509866 £50; 35 rms. Overlooking Valley Gardens, this pleasant Victorian hotel has a comfortable lounge, busy public bar, good food in oak-panelled restaurant, a relaxed atmosphere, and friendly service.

Aldborough SE4166 Ship Aldborough, Boroughbridge York YO5 9ER (01423) 322749 £40; 5 rms, showers. Friendly 14th-c pub near ancient church and Roman town, neat heavily beamed bar, warm coal fire, and good, popular bar food.

Masham SE2381 White Bear Masham, Ripon HG4 4EN (01765) 689319 £35; 2 rms, shared bthrm. Busy pub that's part of Theakstons old stone headquarters buildings with bric-a-brac in the traditionally furnished public bar, comfortable lounge, and decent bar food; cl 24-26 Dec, 30 Dec-1 Jan.

To see and do

Harrogate SE3155 This is an elegant and self-confident inland resort, a spa town which has kept a Victorian atmosphere despite now filling many of its handsome hotels with very up-to-date conference visitors. The layout of the town is very gracious and you couldn't ask for better shops, including many selling interesting antiques, and a surprising number of top-notch specialist shops. Though the darkish stone of the buildings does not itself do much to shrug off the gloom of a dour day, the town has always recognised that this is so, and fills almost every available space with colourful plant displays – even floral petticoats for lampposts.

The first thing a visitor notices is the great sweep of The Stray, open parkland which runs right along and through the south side of the centre. The elegant buildings of the compact central area sweep down from here to the pleasantly laid-out Valley Gardens, very Victorian, their curlicued central tea house run by a friendly Italian family. The relaxed tempo of the place, and the clean bracing climate (it stands 400ft up on the moors), have made it a popular retirement area.

✿ ♿ HARLOW CARR BOTANICAL GARDENS (W edge of town) Ornamental and woodland gardens over 68 acres, with streams, pools, rockeries, rhododendrons, spring bulbs and many interesting plants. Also a museum of gardening and a model village. Rarely busy, a place of real peace and fresh moorland air, and lovely out of season when it's virtually deserted and the excellent collection of heathers comes into its own. Meals, snacks, plant centre, disabled access; (01423) 565418; *£3.20 Mar-Oct, less Nov-Feb. The adjacent Harrogate Arms has good-value food.

♿ 🏠 ROYAL PUMP ROOM MUSEUM (Royal Parade) The central sulphur wells (there are other outlets all over the town) are housed here, enclosed by glass to control the smell. You can still order a free glass of the water at the original spa counter, now the ticket counter for the museum; remember that though it smells dreadful, it's good for you. The octagonal pump room building contains displays of 19th-c fine china and jewellery, as well as bath chairs and other impedimenta of the golden spa days; shop, disabled access; cl am Sun, 25–26 Dec, 1 Jan; (01423) 503340; £1. Next door the elegant ASSEMBLY ROOMS are kept much as they were, very genteel and palm-courtish; you can stroll around, sit down for musical coffee and cakes, or plunge into a (non-sulphurous) Turkish bath. The very first sulphur well was discovered in the 16th c and named the TEWIT WELL after the local word for the lapwings which led a local sporting gent to ride into what was then a smelly bog. It's up on The Stray, grandly encased in what looks like an Italianate mausoleum.

Besides the places mentioned in **Where to eat,** the Drum & Monkey (fish restaurant/wine bar, Montpellier Gardens), Hedleys (wine bar, Montpellier Parade), the Regency (off East Parade), and Bettys Tea Room (Parliament St), a very Yorkshire institution though founded by a Swiss, are all good for lunch or a snack; the café of the Theatre Royal is also a pleasant place.

Other things to see and do

🏛 **Aldborough** SE4066 ROMAN TOWN The northernmost civilian Roman town was on this site, its houses, courts, forum and temple surrounded by a 20ft-high, 9ft-thick wall. All that remains today are two pavements, the position of the wall and, in the museum, some of the finds from the site. Shop; cl Oct–Mar; (01423) 322768; *£1.20. The Ship is good for lunch.

🖼 🏠 ✿ **Beningbrough** SE5158 BENINGBROUGH HALL Stately early 18th-c baroque mansion, with a good collection from the National Portrait Gallery. Also fine carvings, big restored Victorian dairy, and a marvellous staircase with balusters carved in imitation of wrought iron. Lovely formal gardens include a conservatory and wilderness play area. Meals, snacks, shop, disabled access; cl Thurs, Fri (exc July and Aug), and Oct–Mar; £4.50, garden only £3; NT. The Dawnay Arms at nearby Newton on Ouse has good food.

✝ ✿ **Fountains Abbey** SE2768 FOUNTAINS ABBEY and STUDLEY ROYAL WATER GARDEN The largest monastic ruin in the country, this romantic

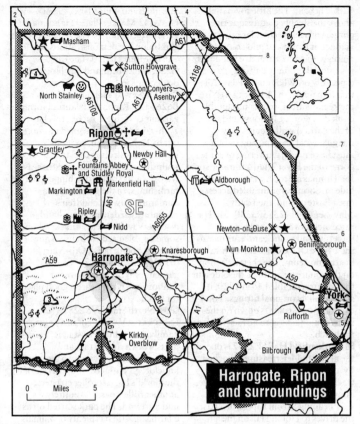

Harrogate, Ripon and surroundings

place was founded in 1132 by Cistercian monks, in a delightful riverside setting. Most of the remains are 12th c, but the proud main tower is 15th c; it's all beautifully floodlit Fri and Sat evenings from mid-Aug–mid-Oct. By the ruins are the lovely landscaped gardens begun by William Aislabie in 1768, which include ornamental temples and follies, formal water gardens, lakes aflutter with waterfowl, and 400 acres of deer park. The most beautiful approach is through the extraordinarily ornate Victorian CHURCH at the far end (open pm May–Sept only), and this 'back-door' entrance is the most tranquil too. An interesting modern visitor centre has been skilfully constructed so that it blends in and doesn't spoil the view. Meals and snacks, shop, good disabled access; cl Fri Nov–Jan, 24–25 Dec; £4, deer park free; NT.

The very prim and proper Sawley Arms in Sawley just W does good food.

★ ! ⌂ ☞ ♿ **Knaresborough** SE3557 In the 19th c quite a little tourist industry was concocted for the toffs from Harrogate around the alleged 16th-c prophecies of Mother Shipton. The cave she lived in is nicely set in 12 acres of riverside parkland, along with a limestone spring, the PETRIFYING WELL, which quickly coats teddy-bears and other unlikely objects in rock so that they can be sold as souvenirs; guided tours, with little local history museum. Snacks, shop, some disabled access; (01423) 864600; cl 25 Dec; *£4.25. From Abbey Rd you should be able to see the intriguing HOUSE IN THE ROCK, currently closed for renovation; a short walk down here brings you to St Robert's Cave, the riverside home of a

12th-c hermit. The little town itself above the steeply picturesque river gorge, with its spectacular railway viaduct, is a pleasant and colourful place, with some attractive buildings; it's a popular family day out, especially on Weds market day. All that remains of the 14th-c CASTLE are the keep (with museum and suitably dank dungeon), gatehouse and some of the curtain wall, but it's easy to imagine what an imposing sight it must have made, glowering over the gorge of the River Nidd a suitable spot for Thomas à Becket's murderers to hide in. Shop, some disabled access; open Easter wknd, then daily May–Sept; (01423) 503340; £1. The price includes a look at an underground tunnel, and entrance to the 14th-c OLD COURT, now a local history museum. The chemist's shop on the square is said to be the oldest in the country; established in 1720, it still has all its original fittings. You can hire ROWING BOATS down on the river. Blind Jacks is an attractive place for lunch.

🏛 **Markenfield Hall** SE2967 is one of the area's hidden treasures, reached by a longish walk along a riverside track S from Ripon, or its main drive, another track turning right off the A61 heading S from Ripon, just past the drives to Hollin Hall on the left. It's a secluded fortified and moated medieval manor house around a charming courtyard, with three lovely original rooms and splendid views from the battlements. Open Mon Apr–Oct, cl 12.30–2.15pm; *£1.

★ ↯⬩ **Masham** SE2280 (pronounced Mazzum) is a civilised small market town, dignified Georgian houses around its broad market square which comes to life on Weds. THEAKSTON BREWERY VISITOR CENTRE Next to the brewery, this explains the brewing process behind Theakstons beer, inc their Old Peculier (which adds a lovely flavour to cakes and puddings). There's a museum and video display. Shop; cl 1–2pm Nov-Dec, all day Tues, and mid-Dec–Easter; *£1. Tours of the brewery itself (*£2.50) should be booked in advance on (01765) 689544; you see more in the mornings; no under 10s. UREDALE GLASS (42 Market Place) Hand-made glassware. Cl Jan; (01765) 689780; glass-blowing demonstrations (not Sun or Mon) *£1.50. The Kings Head, White Bear and Bay Horse all do decent food.

⬩ 🏛 ⬩ **Newby Hall** SE3467 (off B6265 E of Ripon) In beautiful formal gardens covering 25 acres, this late 17th-c mansion, redesigned inside and out by Robert Adam, contains an important collection of classical sculpture and Gobelins tapestries, as well as a good range of Chippendale furnishings. In the grounds are a miniature railway, children's adventure garden and woodland discovery walk. Meals, snacks, shop, some disabled access; house cl am, Mon (exc bank hols), Oct–Mar; (01423) 322583; £5.20, £3.20 gardens only. The Ship over in Aldborough is the nearest good place for food.

☺ 🍴 **North Stainley** SE2876 LIGHTWATER VALLEY THEME PARK Family fun from the nostalgic pleasure of a steam train and traditional big-top circus to the white-knuckle, green-faced thrills of one of the world's biggest roller coasters; another rollercoaster is entirely underground. The park started off as a farm, and still has plenty of animals. Meals, snacks, shop, disabled access; open wknds and bank hols Apr–Oct, daily Jun–Aug; (01765) 635368; £8.95. The Bull in the pleasant riverside village of West Tanfield has popular food all day.

🏛 ⬩ **Norton Conyers** SE3176 (3½ miles NW of Ripon) The same family have lived in this late medieval house for 370 years, and the furniture and pictures reflect the fact that it's still very much a family home. James I, Charles I and James II all stayed here, while Charlotte Brontë used the building as one of her models for Thornfield Hall. Look out for the hoofprint on the stairs. Attractively planted 18th-c walled garden. Shop (with unusual plants and in season garden fruits); 1995 details were unconfirmed as we went to press: the house has been open pm Sun Apr–Oct, plus bank hols and daily last wk of July, and the garden daily exc Mon and Tues during the same period, but best to check first; (01765) 640333. The White Dog at Sutton Howgrave just N is good for lunch (not Mon).

❀ ▥ **Ripley** SE2860 RIPLEY CASTLE Beautiful castle, in the same family for an amazing 26 generations. Most of the current building dates from the 16th c, inc the tower, housing a collection of Royalist armour, and there's also a priest's hole, discovered by accident in 1964. For many the main attraction is the spendid gardens, the setting for the national hyacinth collection and (under glass) a fine tropical plant collection. Also birds-of-prey centre. Meals, snacks, shop, some disabled access; castle open wknds Apr–Oct, plus bank hols, Thurs and Fri Jun and Sept, and daily July and Aug, garden open Thurs–Sun in Mar, then daily to 23 Dec; (01423) 770152; castle and garden £3.75, gardens only £2.25. The attractive village, rebuilt in the 1820s, has a superb delicatessen. The Boars Head is a fine old place for lunch, and another good place a little way E is the Malt Shovel at Brearton SE3261.

✝ ♨ **Ripon** SE3171 Jointly with Bath, this has just been awarded the title of Britain's tidiest city. It's certainly pleasant to wander through. On Thurs colourful stalls fill the attractive and ancient market square (quite a few stalls too on Saturday, inc bric-a-brac); it's largely unspoilt, lined with specialist shops and old inns and hotels. At 9pm each night the Wakeman (a red-coated bugler)

blows a buffalo horn here, as one has done for centuries. Going from here down one of the town's engagingly narrow old streets you are rewarded by a magnificent view of the elegant Early English west front of the CATHEDRAL, spectacularly floodlit at night. It's one of the largest half-dozen in the country, and has plenty to see, inc very fine carving in both stone and wood, and a 7th-c crypt the oldest surviving part of any British cathedral building (and probably the oldest surviving crypt outside Italy). Shop, disabled access. A nicely chilling little PRISON MUSEUM looks at the history of the local police. Cl am exc Mon–Sat July and Aug, all Nov–Mar; *£1. The Water Rat (Bridge Lane) down by the River Skell has a charming view of the cathedral and generous food, and the Golden Lion just off the market square is useful too. Fountains Abbey and Markenfield Hall are within a walk from here, and Newby Hall and Norton Conyers are also quite close.

♨ **Rufforth** SE5351 MUSEUM OF MECHANICAL MUSIC (Bradley Grange) A collection of ornate European organs which play music from Brahms to the Beatles; fairground, street and cinema organs from 1870 to the present day. Snacks, shop, disabled access; open pm Sun Jun–Sept; (01904) 738773; £3.99. The Sun at Long Marston is good value.

★ **Attractive villages** with decent pubs in the area include Grantley SE2369, Kirkby Overblow SE3249, Newton on Ouse SE5160, Nun Monkton SE5058, Sutton Howgrave SE3279 and Ogden SE0730.

Walks

The grounds of **Studley Royal** SE2768 ⌂-1 are excellent for strolling, as is **Harlow Carr** SE2854 ⌂-2 on the edge of Harrogate. The moorland W of Harrogate has some possibilities for more stretching walks, for instance on **Stainburn Moor** SE2352 ⌂-3 from the car park by the woods along the side road W from Beckwithshaw, or on Denton Moor above the reservoirs S of Blubberhouses SE1655. Near the hamlet of Ilton SE1978 a no through road leads up to woodlands where you can walk to the **Druids Temple** ⌂-4, a scaled-down Stonehenge built by a landowner in the 1820s as work for local unemployed people.

Though this area has very little serious walking, it's within easy reach of both the Dales and the Moors; from Harrogate you can drive to Grassington or to Helmsley in about 45 mins.

Driving

This is not so rewarding for drives as the W, N and E of the county and for an excursion in the car you'd be best to head out there instead.

Where to eat

Harrogate SE3155 MILLERS 1 Montpellier Mews (01423) 530708 Attractive little restaurant with very good English and French cooking, lots of fish, a fine wine list, and good service; cl Sun, Mon. £23|£9.45.

Asenby SE3975 CRAB & LOBSTER (01845) 577286 Old thatched pub with a relaxed, informal but rather civilised atmosphere, interestingly furnished and cosy L-shaped with lots of bric-a-brac, really delicious food, and good wines by the glass; cl pm Sun. £20|£3.50/£8.50.

Harrogate SE3155 LA BERGERIE 15 Mount Parade (01423) 500089 Delightful unassuming French evening restaurant with freshly prepared, interesting food, and very good French staff; cl Sun; disabled access. £18.

Harrogate SE3155 TANNIN LEVEL 5 Raglan St (01423) 560595 Very good wine bar also serving continental breakfasts and early evening tapas; cl Sun; children allowed but not encouraged; limited disabled access. £18|£3.95/£7.50.

Harrogate SE3155 TIFFINS ON THE STRAY 11a Regent Parade (01423) 504041 Very good value vegetarian food (lovely puddings), take your own wine; cl Sun, Mon, 25 Dec. £18|£2.20/£2.75.

Harrogate SE3155 STUDELEY HOTEL Swan Rd (01423) 560425 Very good restaurant in homely hotel with generous helpings of good-value food, lots of chargrills; cl 25–26 Dec. £16|£1.90/£10.50.

Harrogate SE3155 GIANI'S Mount Parade (01423) 566453 Lively Italian restaurant with good pasta, pizzas and fresh fish; good with children; disabled access. £16/£4.50.

Sutton Howgrave SE3279 WHITE DOG (01765) 640404 Pretty village pub with comfortable beamed bar, good bar lunches; cl pms, Mon, 25 Dec, 1 Jan; children over 8. £15|£3.75/£6.

Harrogate SE3155 WILLIAM & VICTORIA Cold Bath Rd (01423) 521510 Wine bar with upstairs evening restaurant and serving hearty helpings of decent country cooking; cl Sun, Sat am; children over 12. £15|£2.20/£6.

Newton on Ouse SE5160 DAWNAY ARMS (01347) 848345 Attractive listed building with lots of beams and timbers in comfortable rooms, very good food in bar and restaurant, and moorings at bottom of garden; cl Mon am; disabled access. £15|£2.50/£4.50.

SOUTH AND WEST YORKSHIRE

The west has lots of interesting and unusual places to visit: good for a busy sightseeing weekend, with the moors for a quieter escape.

This has far more places to visit than the north and east, including outstanding free museums and lively 20th-c art collections. It makes an unusual, if not exactly restful, weekend break. Some of the big industrial cities are very rewarding. Bradford's film and photography museum is one of the most enjoyable museums in the country and it's free; the city also has many other points of interest.

Other places which stand out are Harewood House, Halifax (appealing cleaned-up mill town), Ilkley (attractive small spa town), the mining museum at Middlestown, Conisbrough Castle, the pioneering industrial village of Saltaire, Nostell Priory and Bramham Park.

Four less well known places are also extremely enjoyable: the postcard museum in Holmfirth, East Riddlesden Hall at Keighley, the Bagshaw Museum in Batley and the Colne Valley Museum at Golcar. The busy cities of Leeds and Sheffield both have a lot of things worth tracking down (including in Leeds an enjoyable new look at the past and future of pubs). Haworth makes the most of its Brontë connections, and the picturesque Keighley & Worth Valley Railway is fun for family outings. Hebden Bridge, interesting in itself, is a good base for both Bradford and Halifax. There's an incredibly good value subsidised train, with links also to Saltaire and Huddersfield (the Halifax–Huddersfield journey is fascinating for those who like trouble-up-mill scenery).

The west of the area is blessed with great moorland scenery coming right up to and indeed embracing the towns, and offering plenty of well above average walking, though perhaps not up to the exceptionally high standards of the Dales. It has a good few steeply attractive stone-built villages (and a remarkable number of pubs that seem to have been placed with a perfect eye for making the most of the countryside); but the real reason for coming to the area would be to make the most of its very considerable sightseeing possibilities, either with an eye to its rich industrial heritage, or to take in some of the stately homes and the like. In general, the west of the area scores hands down both for interest and for beauty over the east. With the present counties of South and West Yorkshire, we have included the bottom corner of North Yorkshire, below York itself and the A64.

Where to stay

Ilkley SE1147 ROMBALDS 11 West View, Wells Rd, Ilkley LS29 9JG (01943) 603201 £100; 15 rms. Part of a Georgian sandstone terrace and on the edge of the moor, this popular hotel offers good old-fashioned service from caring staff, a comfortable, attractively furnished lounge, and good, beautifully presented food; cl 27–30 Dec.

Halifax SE0826 HOLDSWORTH HOUSE Holdsworth, Halifax HX2 9TG (01422) 240024 *£95 inc £20 per person towards meal; 40 pretty, individually decorated rms. Lovely 17th-c house a few miles outside Halifax with antiques, fresh flowers and open fires in comfortable lounges, friendly, helpful staff, very fine oak-panelled dining room with imaginative food and carefully chosen wines, and garden; dogs welcome by prior arrangement; cl 25–30 Dec; disabled access.

Monk Fryston SE5029 MONK FRYSTON HALL Monk Fryston, Leeds LS25 5DU (01977) 682369 *£90; 28 comfortable rms. Grand manor house in attractive grounds with antiques and flowers in the oak-panelled bar and lounge, log fires, and friendly staff; disabled access.

Otley SE2045 CHEVIN LODGE Yorkgate, Otley LS21 3NU (01943) 467818 £74.50w; 50 rms. Built of Finnish logs; lots of walks through the 50 private acres of birchwood (free mountain bike too), and good restaurant food; tennis, fishing, and free membership of nearby leisure club: indoor swimming pool, gym and supervised crèche; disabled access.

Hebden Bridge SD9927 CARLTON Albert St, Hebden Bridge HX7 8ES (01422) 844400 *£69; 18 rms. Attractively modernised Victorian hotel with most day rooms on the first floor; comfortable, airy bar, good food in elegant restaurant, and a relaxed atmosphere.

Leeds SE3033 42 THE CALLS 42 The Calls, Leeds LS2 7EW (0113) 244 0099 £60w; 41 extremely attractive rms using original features such as old beams and an old winch, CD stereo with complementary library, satellite TV, and work desk. Stylish modern hotel in converted riverside grain mill with genuinely friendly staff; no restaurant but they have arrangements with several local restaurants; cl 24–30 Dec; limited disabled access.

Sheffield SK3687 CHARNWOOD Sharrow Lane S11 8AA (0114) 258 9411 £60; 22 comfortable, well equipped rms. Friendly extended Georgian house with peaceful lounges, conservatory, and extremely good food in both the Brasserie and elegant little Henfrey's restaurant; cl 24–26 Dec; disabled access.

Escrick SE6343 BLACK BULL Escrick, York YO4 6JP (01904) 728245 £48; 10 comfortable rms. Unchanging pub with cheerful fire, quickly served straightforward bar food and pleasant dining room.

Haworth SE0337 OLD WHITE LION Haworth, Keighley BD22 8DU (01535) 642313 £46; 14 comfortable rms. Warmly friendly 300-year-old inn with three bars, cosy restaurant with good vegetarian dishes, and oak-panelled residents' lounge; close to Brontë Museum, parsonage and church and the Keighley & Worth Valley Steam Railway.

Escrick SE6343 CHURCH COTTAGE Escrick, York YO4 6EX (01904) 728462 £40; 7 rms. Family-run guest house set next to the church in 2 acres of lawn and woodland with friendly owners, most attractively decorated rooms, and good breakfasts; disabled access.

Roydhouse SE2112 THREE ACRES Roydhouse, Shelley, Huddersfield HD8 8LR (01484) 602606 £40; 20 attractive rms. In lovely countryside, this extended 18th-c hotel has a welcoming atmosphere in its traditional bars, well kept real ales, and good food in two restaurants, using fresh local produce.

To see and do

🕭 **Batley** SE2424 BAGSHAW MUSEUM (Wilton Park) Beautiful Victorian Gothic mansion surrounded by pleasant lakeside park, with one of those excellent miscellaneous collections based on the curio-hunting of an individual enthusiast. All sorts of oddities from the byways of local history, natural history, and oriental arts. Shop, disabled access; cl am wknds; (01924) 472514; free. The Old Hall at Heckmondwike (B6117), once Joseph Priestley's home, is an interesting old place for lunch.

🕭🕴 🖻 🛱 **Bradford** SE1633 is the area's great surprise for the uninitiated. Though horribly knocked-about by heavy-handed civic designers in the 1960s and 1970s, many buildings survive from what was one of Britain's finest Victorian cities. These, in a solidly unifying northern stone, are a staggering monument to the days when its wools, woollens and worsteds ruled the world: gigantic and confidently Renaissance-style woollen and velvet mills, the imposing Wool Exchange, the opulent city-centre cliffs of heavily ornate merchants' warehouses in Little Germany behind the mostly 15th-c cathedral, and the florid exuberance of

the municipal buildings such as the Gothic city hall, the neo-classical St George's concert hall, the showily baroque Cartwright Hall (see below), even the great Undercliffe cemetery. The city's Asian immigrants have brought a vivid and visible dash of cultural diversity, and there's a feeling of underlying vigour and zest which make it exciting to visit. It has some excellent museums and galleries.

Standing out among these is the NATIONAL MUSEUM OF PHOTOGRAPHY, FILM AND TELEVISION (Princes View), one of the most well liked museums in the country, a remarkable place whose changing displays manage to be both entertaining and thought-provoking (you'll never take a newspaper photograph of a politician at face value again). It does get massively crowded at wknds. You can try reading the news, riding a magic carpet or having a go at vision mixing, but for many the highlight is the massive IMAX, the country's largest cinema screen, over five storeys high; carefully chosen films show it off to spectacular effect (it may be worth booking at busy times). Also the only cinema in the world to use the extended curved-screen Cinerama system (pm Sat only), various more conventional screenings, and an exhibition of favourite old TV programmes. Snacks, shop, disabled access; cl Mon (exc bank hols), 25–26 Dec; (01274) 727488; museum free, £3.80 IMAX, £6.20 IMAX and Cinerama. INDUSTRIAL MUSEUM (Moorside Rd, Eccleshill) Former spinning mill well illustrating the growth of the woollen and worsted textile industry. A tramway carries you up and down the Victorian street, which is complete with workers' cottages and working Victorian stables with shire horses. Also fully furnished mill owner's house, and a number of transport exhibits, inc locally made three- and four-wheeler cars. Meals, snacks, shop, disabled access; cl Mon (exc bank hols); (01274) 631756; free. COLOUR MUSEUM (Grattan Rd) Interesting and award-winning study of the use and perception of colour, with imaginative interactive displays on the effects of light and colour in general, and particularly the story of dyeing and textile printing. Shop, disabled access; cl am (exc Sat but cl then 12.30–2pm), all day Mon and Sun; (01274) 390955; £1.10. CARTWRIGHT HALL ART GALLERY (Lister Park) Dramatic baroque-style building in attractive floral park, housing the *Brown Boy* by Reynolds and a good representative selection of late 19th- and early 20th-c paintings. Snacks, shop, disabled access by prior arrangement; (01274) 493313; cl Mon exc bank hols; free. BOLLING HALL (Bowling Hall Rd, 1 m S) Classic Yorkshire manor house, dating mainly from the 17th c, but with some earlier (and later) parts, now home to the city's collection of local furniture and pictures. Fine panelling and plasterwork, and huge 15th-c heraldic stained-glass window representing great Yorkshire families. Shop, disabled access to ground floor; cl Mon (exc bank hols), 25–28 Dec, 1 Jan, Good Fri, and maybe 12.30–1.30; (01274) 723057; free. Useful places for a pub lunch include the Fountain (Heaton Rd), Rams Revenge or Shoulder of Mutton (both Kirkgate), but you might prefer one of the multitude of Indian, Pakistani or Bangladeshi restaurants (if people are eating with paratha bread or chapatis instead of forks, use your right hand not your left, for politeness). See also Shipley, below.

🌸 **Bolton Percy** SE5341 Behind its medieval gatehouse the 15th-c church has perhaps the most unusual CHURCHYARD in the country. Fifteen years ago local lecturer Roger Brook set about tackling its profusion of weeds, and since then has transformed it into a splendidly colourful garden, with more than a thousand different types of plant creeping around and over the headstones. Rather like a semi-wild cottage garden, it houses part of the National Collection of Dicentra. It's open all the time, but they have regular open days to find out more; (01904) 744213 for dates. The Crown is handy for something to eat.

🌸🏠 **Bramham** SE4141 BRAMHAM PARK The garden here is really quite beautiful, very much in the grand style: Versailles comes to Yorkshire. Long prospects of ornamental lakes, cascades, temples, statuary, grand hedges and stately trees and avenues surround a classical Queen Mary house of great distinction, with lovely period furnishings and paintings. Disabled access to grounds; open pm Sun, Tues, Weds and Thurs mid-Jun– early Sept, and gardens also open Easter and May bank hol wknds; (01937) 844265; house and gardens £3, gardens only £2. The Red Lion has good food.

🏰✟ **Conisbrough** SK5098 CONISBROUGH CASTLE Mightily impressive 12th-c castle with uniquely designed 90ft keep circular, with six buttresses and a curtain wall with solid round towers. They've recently added a roof and floors to re-create something of the original feel; a visitor centre underneath has a good exhibition. Snacks, developing craft shop, disabled access to visitor centre only; cl 25 Dec; (01709) 863329; £1.80. Sir Walter Scott set much of *Ivanhoe* here, writing the novel while staying at the Boat at Sprotbrough nearby; then a riverside farm, it's now a popular dining pub.

🏠♨ **Cusworth** SE5403 CUSWORTH HALL Excellent museum of South

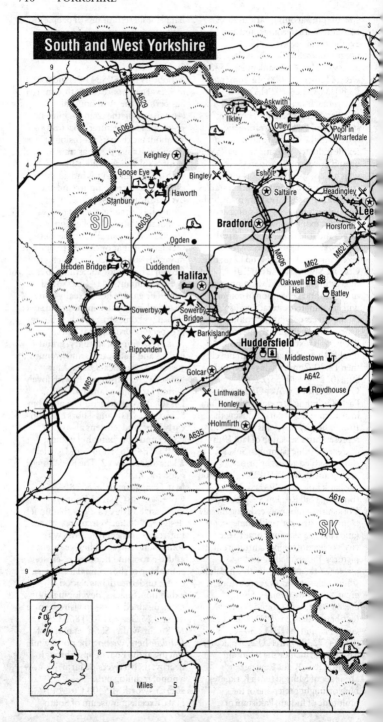

South and West Yorkshire

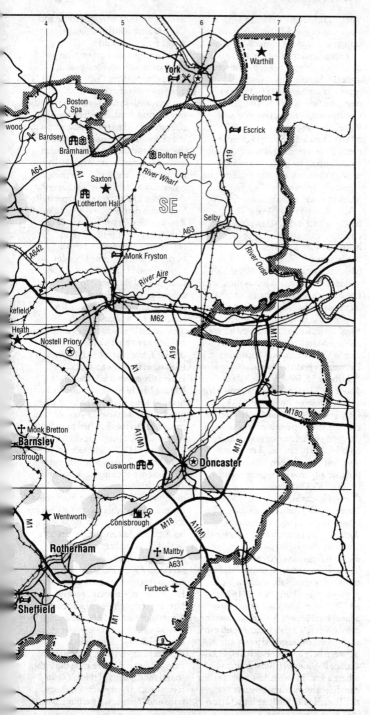

Yorkshire life, in an elegant 18th-c house, with good displays on mining, transport, costume and entertainment, and esp popular gallery of toys and childhood. Plenty to keep children amused. Snacks, shop, disabled access; cl am Sun; (01302) 782342; free. The Boat at Sprotbrough (see Conisbrough, above) is quite well placed for this, too.

♿🅿♨ **Doncaster** SE5803 doesn't really have a great deal to attract visitors apart from its race meetings, though there is some fine architecture, especially around the High St and Market Place, and a good antiques and junk market on Weds. The MUSEUM AND ART GALLERY is decent enough, with a good deal of natural history. Cl am Sun; free.

✈ **Elvington** SE7047 YORKSHIRE AIR MUSEUM Part of a World War II airfield and base preserved as it was then, with fine aircraft, an old control tower and plenty of other memorabilia inc engines, models and photographs. Meals, snacks, shop, disabled access; cl Nov–Mar; (01904) 608595; £3. The St Vincent Arms at Sutton upon Derwent is good for lunch.

✈ **Firbeck** SK5688 SOUTH YORKS AIRCRAFT MUSEUM (Home Farm) More aviation history, in former RAF Officers' Mess buildings. Relics from crashes, 20 aero engines, uniforms, a changing collection of planes and a couple of helicopters. Shop, some disabled access; open Sun and bank hols, or anytime by appointment; (01709) 812168; free.

♿🐾⚓ **Golcar** SE0915 COLNE VALLEY MUSEUM (Cliff Ash) Enthusiastic museum spread over three weavers' cottages, with hand weaving, spinning and clog-making in gaslit surroundings, and recreated 1850s living room. Shop, occasional craft festivals, some disabled access; open pm wknds and bank hols; (01484) 659762; 80p. The Scapehouse up on Scapegoat Hill (off A62) is popular for meals. There's a good year-round canal walk along the restored tow-path between here and Marsden SE0412 in *Last of the Summer Wine* country, where a small TUNNEL END MUSEUM has canalia, café and summer BOAT TRIPS; the Tunnel End pub here is useful for

food, as are the Carriage House and Olive Branch a little further off.

★ ⚓ ! ♿🅿 † ❋ **Halifax** SE0925 Another town with an impressive show of former textiles wealth, interesting to drive through when it's quiet on a summer evening or a Sunday, and surrounded by a splendid ring of moorland. The centre's been cleaned up and partly pedestrianised, which makes it pleasant to potter through, and there are a number of first-class attractions. Artistically the town is going through something of a renaissance, particularly around the enormous DEAN CLOUGH carpet mill, faced with demolition when it closed down some years ago, but now well restored and home to a thriving complex of galleries and small businesses; best are the Crossley Gallery and Henry Moore Studio, the latter a good showcase for contemporary sculpture. EUREKA! (Discovery Road) Good fun for children, for whom it's specially designed, a lively discovery centre with all sorts of hi-tech hands-on science displays, and themed exhibitions looking at how things work. Especially enjoyable is the Giant Mouth Machine which you can feed to find out what happens to food when you eat it, but wherever you go there's something to touch, smell or listen to. Meals, snacks, shop, disabled access; cl 25 Dec; (01422) 330069; £4.50. PIECE HALL (Centre) Magnificent Renaissance-looking galleried and arcaded building put up in 1775 by the merchants of Halifax as a market for their cloth. Now its merchants' rooms are filled with specialist shops selling books, antiques and bric-a-brac, as well as an art gallery and other exhibitions. Meals, snacks, disabled access; cl 25–26 Dec; free. The Italianate courtyard comes to life on Fri and Sat when there are 160 bustling stalls; there are a good few on Thurs too. Just off here, the CALDERDALE INDUSTRIAL MUSEUM (Central Works, Square Rd) comprehensively covers the area's many industries, recreating the sights, sounds and smells of the 1850s in reconstructed street scenes, shops, pubs and basement dwellings. Meals and snacks, shop, disabled access; cl Sun am, Mon (exc most bank hols); (01422) 358087; *£1.50. Close by, the medieval CHURCH has an extremely grand spire and fine carving. Look out for Old Tristram, the life-size painted carving of a beggar which was used to collect alms. Just out of the centre, set in a 90-acre park, SHIBDEN HALL AND FOLK MUSEUM (Listers Rd) is an excellently refurbished 15th-c house, each of its rooms illustrating a different period from its history. In the barn a folk museum has an interesting collection of horse-drawn vehicles, while around it is a reconstructed 19th-c village, with workshops, cottage and even a pub. For many this is a real Halifax highlight. Snacks, shop, limited disabled access; cl am Sun, Dec–Feb (exc Sun in Feb); (01422) 352246; £1.50. BANKFIELD MUSEUM (Ackroyd Park, Boothtown Rd) Collection of textiles and costume, as well as a regimental museum and a display on toys. Shop, disabled access on ground floor only; cl am Sun, Mon, 25–26 Dec, 1 Jan; (01422) 354823; free. The 250ft folly of WAINWRIGHT TOWER (off A646 just W) was originally a dyeworks chimney, and offers good views if you can manage all those steps. Usually open only bank hols – best to check with Industrial Museum (see above); 65p. The Shears (Paris Gates, Boys Lane) down steep lanes among the mill buildings is a pub that embraces much of Halifax's past and atmosphere.

🏛 ❋ ♥ ✝ 🐚 **Harewood** SE3144 HAREWOOD HOUSE The area's most magnificent stately home, inside and out. The splendidly palatial 18th-c exterior is back at its best now all the scaffolding is down, while restoration work inside has left the glorious Robert Adam plasterwork looking better than it has for probably 150 years. Fine Chippendale furnishings, exquisite Sèvres and Chinese porcelain, and paintings by Turner, El Greco, Bellini, Titian, and Gainsborough. Capability Brown designed the thousand-acre grounds, which have very pleasing lakeside and woodland walks, an outstanding collection of rhododendron species, and the famous landscaped bird gardens (some readers

feel you could spend half a day in just this part). Charles Berry's Terrace, also recently restored, has an excellent Gallery with contemporary art and crafts. Try to visit the 15th-c CHURCH, with a splendid array of tombs, and a curious tunnel under the wall of the churchyard, so that servants could arrive unseen by sensitive souls. There's a first class adventure playground. Meals, snacks, shop, helpful disabled access; cl Nov–Mar; (0113) 288 6331; £5.75 everything, £4.50 bird garden and grounds only, £2.50 grounds and terrace gallery only. Just N Wharfedale Grange have PICK-YOUR-OWN fruit. Two popular nearish places for lunch are the Bingley Arms at Bardsey and Shoulder of Mutton at Kirkby Overblow.

🐚🌊 **Haworth** SE0337 is a touristy village with plenty of craft shops, antique shops and tea shoppes catering for all the people drawn here by the Brontës (the steep cobbled main street does have quieter more atmospheric side alleys). Their former home the PARSONAGE MUSEUM has some 120,000 visitors a year (it was something of a tourist attraction even while Charlotte still lived here). The house is very carefully preserved, with period furnishings, very good changing exhibitions, and displays of the scribbling siblings' books, manuscripts and possessions. Shop; cl 9 Jan–3 Feb, 24–27 Dec; (01535) 642323; £3.60. For the most evocative views and atmosphere go up to the moors above town, very grand and not much different from when the Brontës knew them. MUSEUM OF CHILDHOOD Wide range of toys, dolls, trains and teddies; shop, disabled access (with help); (01535) 643593; cl wkdys Nov–Feb; *£1. The KEIGHLEY & WORTH VALLEY RAILWAY actually begins just N at Keighley (where you can connect with BR trains) but is based here. Run by enthusiastic volunteers, the line was built to serve the valley's mills, and passes through the heart of Brontë country. The Oxenhope terminus has a museum and restoration building, but the prettiest station is Oakworth (familiar to many from the film *The Railway Children*). Snacks, shop, disabled access; open daily Jun–early

Sept, Sun all year and most school hols; (01535) 647777 for timetable; £5.50 Day Rover ticket. The Fleece and Old Hall are useful for lunch; and see **Where to eat**, below.

★ ⌂⍟⌖☗✿! ♨ Hebden Bridge SD9927 Engaging small town deep in a valley below the moors, and stepped very steeply up the hillsides, with quite a lively subculture of art and craft shops. Sylvia Plath is buried in the churchyard in the ancient village of Heptonstall SD9728, a crippling climb above the town; it has a small museum, and Stubbings Wharf (Thistle Bottom) and the Robin Hood (A6033 towards Keighley) have good-value food. AUTOMOBILIA TRANSPORT MUSEUM (Billy Lane, Old Town) Austin and Morris cars, motorcycles and bicycles and other memorabilia from the humbler days of the motoring past, housed in three-storey former textile warehouse. You can arrange chauffered days out in some of the vehicles. Shop, disabled access; open pm Sun all year, plus pm Easter wk, bank hols, and Tues, Thurs and Fri May–Sept; (01422) 844775; *£2.20. MAUDE-WALKLEYS CLOG MILL (A646) makes an enormous number of different kinds of clog, from heavy-duty steel-toed industrial numbers to more fashionable frippery; you can see the range and watch them being made. Also craft and specialist shops. Meals, snacks, shop, disabled access; cl 25–26 Dec; free. WORLD OF THE HONEY BEE (Hebble End Mill) Bees at close quarters, with working hives, demonstrations, video, and free samples of over 30 different types of honey. Also Insect World exhibition. Wknd snacks, shop, some disabled access; cl wkdys Jan–Mar; (01422) 845557; £1. Next door are several working craftsmen, with demonstrations of skills inc glass-making, and in summer they do HORSE-DRAWN BARGE TRIPS along the canal basin; from £2.50. The hold of one barge has been converted into a VISITOR CENTRE with a real boatman's cabin (cl wkdys Oct–Mar). HEBDEN CRYPT (Valley Rd) Ideal for children, a creepy journey through myth, legend and horror – the gruesome exhibits are all too realistic. Snacks, shop; cl

Mon (exc bank and school hols), wkdys Dec–Easter; £2. HARDCASTLE CRAGS SD9630 is a pretty spot above the wooded river valley, for walks or picnic; the Nutclough House on the way up has decent food.

☗✝⍟ Holmfirth SE1408 Famed as the setting for TV's *Last of the Summer Wine*, with evocative little alleys, several good pubs (the Old Bridge is probably the best for lunch), and a handsome Georgian CHURCH. Bamforths, the postcard manufacturer, is based here, and the POSTCARD MUSEUM looks at their history (inc some interesting lantern slides and pioneering work with silent films), as well as that of the picture postcard in general. Shop, disabled access; cl am Sun, 25–26 Dec; (01484) 682231; £1. The Post Card pub nearby is handy for lunch.

⍟☗ Huddersfield SE1416 has a great sense of style in many of its buildings, especially around the station and central square, and much of the centre is closed to traffic. The ART GALLERY (Castle Hill, Almondbury) has a good view down over the town from its moorland setting, as does the Castle Hill Inn up here. The TOLSON MEMORIAL MUSEUM (Ravensknowle Park), housed in a former wool baron's mansion, has a good range of local history, inc a look at the cloth industry, and a collection of horse-drawn vehicles. Shop, disabled access; cl am Sun, 24–26 Dec, 1 Jan, Good Fri; free.

☗⍟⌂✝ Ilkley SE1147 owes its Victorian and Edwardian spaciousness and style to the mid-19th-c and later craze for hydropathic 'cures', which produced quite a rash of luxurious hydros using the town's pure moorland spring water. Their forerunner was the simple little bath-house built in mid-18th c around the ice-cold spring up on the moor just S of the town at WHITE WELLS; you can still follow the paths the infirm took by donkey. The group of characterful rocks known as the Cow & Calf up here also makes a pleasant short walk above the town. MANOR HOUSE GALLERY AND MUSEUM (Castle Yard) One of the few buildings in town to predate the 19th c, an Elizabethan manor house built on the site of a Roman fort, with local history displays. Part of the Roman wall can still be seen. Shop, disabled access ground floor only; cl Mon exc bank hols, Christmas, Good Fri; free. The CHURCH has three lovely Saxon crosses, and just beside it are more traces of the Roman fort. There are a good few prehistoric remains around the town, the best known of which is the Bronze Age SWASTIKA STONE, a symbol of eternity carved on a flat rock by a moorland path SE of the town, above wooded Hebers Ghyll; the stone is marked on the Ordnance Survey 1:50,000 map, at SE095469. Hebers Ghyll itself is a picturesque area of steep Victorian walkways, and the town makes a nice stop with its attractive gardens and interesting shops (you can see chocolate being made at Humphreys). Useful places for lunch include the Ilkley Moor Vaults (Stockel Rd/Stourton Rd) and Wheatley Arms (Ben Rhydding).

🎡🕯🍵👶 Keighley SE0641, pronounced 'Keithly', is a busy working town, but has a pleasant centre. The Grinning Rat on Church Green is useful for lunch. CLIFFE CASTLE MUSEUM AND GALLERY 19th-c mansion with French furniture from the Victoria & Albert Museum, as well as various local ephemera. Though quite close to the centre, it's set in a park well above the main road, with an aviary and greenhouses. Snacks in park, shop, disabled access ground floor only; cl Mon (exc bank hols), 25 Dec, Good Fri; free. EAST RIDDLESDEN HALL (Bradford Rd) is an interesting early 17th-c oak-panelled stone manor house with attractive plasterwork, period textiles and furniture, and formal walled garden. A huge medieval tithe barn in the grounds houses a collection of agricultural bygones, and there's still a medieval monastic fishpond. Meals, snacks, shop; cl am, Thurs (exc July and Aug), Fri, Nov–Mar; £3; NT. YORKSHIRE CAR COLLECTION (Grange St) Notable collection of gleaming vintage and classic cars, some once owned by the rich and famous (the rip in the hood of Mick Jagger's 1964 Ford Galaxie convertible is reputed

testimony to Marianne Faithfull's stiletto heel), and some that just bring a feeling of nostalgia. A new wing concentrates on American cars of the rock'n'roll era. Teas, shop, disabled access; cl pm Mon, winter wkdys, all Dec; (01535) 690499; *£3.50.

🎡❄🕯📷👶🚶♿👨‍👩‍👧✝🍺 Leeds SE3034 has an excellent and quite compact centre for the walker with freedom from traffic, lots of splendid covered arcades (Victorian, Edwardian and modern), and all sorts of interesting and engaging Victorian architectural details to spot (why did they put so many owls on their buildings?). Shoppers and theatre-goers are well catered for – the former in the exuberantly Venetian/Oriental glass-roofed MARKET, the biggest in Yorkshire, and the latter by the West Yorkshire Playhouse and The Grand (home of the excellent Opera North). The impressive 1860s CORN EXCHANGE is now filled with neat little specialist and designer shops, and has plenty of places for tea, coffee and so forth, as well as an excellent fresh Continental bread stall. There's a stamp market here on Sun and often a small jazz group at teatime. The imposing TOWN HALL is perhaps the high point of Leeds' essentially Victorian centre; and there are good gardens and open spaces. Down by the Waterfront, TETLEY BREWERY WHARF is a lively new centre looking at the history of the English pub, from a 14th-c monastic brewhouse to the Star & Crater, a bizarre prediction of what a pub might be like in the next century. Also period costumed characters, an interesting look at pub games and traditions, various crafts, shire horses, and an optional tour of the Tetley brewery itself (booking recommended or at least reserve a place as soon as you arrive). Plenty to do, with a good children's playground. Meals, snacks, shop, disabled access; cl Mon–Weds Oct–Mar; (0113) 243 1888; *£4.50. CITY ART GALLERY (The Headrow) Excellent collection of 20th-c British art, as well as English watercolours, craft centre, design gallery, and sculpture gallery, inc carefully chosen works by Henry Moore, who had his first exhibition here in 1941. Meals, snacks, shop, mostly disabled access; cl Sun, bank hols; free. Over a footbridge is the delightful HENRY MOORE INSTITUTE, with temporary exhibitions of sculpture from Roman times to the present, displayed in quite an unusual building (they don't actually show anything by Henry Moore). Shop, disabled access; cl Sun, bank hols; free. ARMLEY MILLS MUSEUM (Canal Rd) Once the largest woollen mill in the world, now a huge working museum, its floors given over to a massive display of textile machinery. Also reconstructions of a turn-of-the-century tailors' shop, buying room and clothing factory, presentations of the history of cinema projection, and demonstrations of static engines, steam locomotives and underground haulage. Snacks, shop, disabled access; cl Mon (exc bank hols), pm Sun, 25–26 Dec; (0113) 263 7861; £2. In summer you can take a canal BOAT TRIP from the city centre to here, booking necessary on (0113) 245 6195. The CITY MUSEUM (Claverley St) is quite a good one (cl Sun and Mon), while the University has an interesting little MUSEUM OF THE HISTORY OF EDUCATION, inc text and exercise books going back to the 17th c. Cl 12.30–1.30pm, wknds, bank hols and Tues following – may be best to book with Dr Foster, (0113) 233 4665; free. MIDDLETON COLLIERY RAILWAY, running from Turnstall Rd roundabout to Middleton Park, was the first railway to be authorised by Parliament. Later it was the first railway to succeed with steam locomotives, and in 1960 became the first standard-gauge line to be operated by enthusiasts. With a picnic area, fishing, nature trail and playgrounds as well as the trains, there's plenty for families here. Snacks, shop, disabled access; diesel trains pm Sat Apr–Sept, steam trains pm Sun Apr–Dec, bank hols, and Dec Sats; (0113) 271 0320; *£1.60. THWAITE MILLS (Stourton, 2 miles S of centre) This water-powered mill was the focus of a tiny island community perched between the River Calder – which drives the mill wheels – and the Aire & Calder Navigation. The Georgian mill-owner's house has been restored

and has displays on the site's history. Snacks, shop, disabled access; cl Mon (exc bank hols), 25–26 Dec, 1 Jan; (0113) 249 6453; £2. KIRKSTALL ABBEY (A65 towards Ilkley) The most complete example of a Cistercian abbey in the country, the ruins now standing among trees in a quiet suburban park. The massive arches of the Norman nave are impressive, and you can wander through several of the quite well preserved ancillary buildings. The 15th-c gatehouse has a very good social history museum. Shop, disabled access to ground floor only; cl am Sun, 25–26 Dec, 1 Jan; (0113) 275 5821; £2. MEANWOOD VALLEY URBAN FARM (Meanwood) Small working farm on regenerated waste land N of centre, with rare breeds and organic garden. Meals and snacks (not Mon), shop, good disabled access; (0113) 262 9759; *50p. TEMPLE NEWSAM HOUSE (5m E, S of A63) That trusty old faithful Capability Brown designed the wonderful 1,200 acres of landscaped parkland and gardens in which this house stands, an extraordinary asset for any city. The house itself dates from Tudor and Jacobean times, and contains the city's very good collections of decorative and fine art, as well as an exceptional assemblage of Chippendale furniture. Rare breeds in the grounds. Snacks, shop; cl Mon (exc bank hols), 25–26 Dec, 1 Jan; (0113) 264 7321; £2. In the centre, Whitelocks (Turks Head Yard, off Briggate) is a marvellous old city tavern, very much a Leeds institution. ♨ Lotherton Hall SE4436 (B1217 Garforth–Tadcaster) Edwardian house with displays ranging from oriental art to British fashion, as well as collections of paintings, silver and ceramics and some lovely furnishings. The grounds are being restored, and there's a bird garden. Snacks, shop, disabled access ground floor only; cl 12–1 pm, all day Mon, 25–26 Dec, 1 Jan; (0113) 281 3259; £2 house, grounds free. The White Swan at nearby Aberford is good for lunch. † Maltby SK5489 ROCHE ABBEY (off A634 SE) A fine gatehouse to the NW and the still-standing walls of the south and north transepts are all that's left of this 12th-c Cistercian abbey, but they make an impressive sight; cl Nov–Mar; *£1.25.

⛏ **Middlestown** SE2617 The YORKSHIRE MINING MUSEUM has deservedly won plenty of awards for its exploration of life as a coal miner. No simple reconstruction this – they take you 450ft underground, down one of Britain's oldest working mine shafts, where models and machinery have been set up to show the methods and working conditions of miners from the 1800s to the present. For the faint-hearted (and under 5s), on the surface there are pit ponies, 'paddy' train rides, steam winder, nature trail, and an adventure playground. Dress sensibly if you're going underground. Meals, snacks, shop, disabled access and excellent facilities; helpful to arrange it in advance; cl 25–26 Dec, 1 Jan; (01924) 848806; *£5.50. The Kaye Arms at Grange Moor does very good food.

† **Monk Bretton** SE3607 MONK BRETTON PRIORY Red sandstone remains of an important 12th-c Cluniac house, with gatehouse, church and other buildings, as well as some unusually well preserved drains. Shop; cl winter Mon and Tues; 80p. The ancient Mill of the Black Monks is pleasant at lunchtime (live music for young people most nights).

🏠 ✿ ♤ † ♗ **Nostell Priory** SE4017 Sumptuous Palladian mansion dating mainly from the 18th c, with an additional wing built by Adam in 1766. It has perhaps the best collection of Chippendale furniture anywhere, all specially designed for this house, and other highlights include the tapestry room, charming saloon, and a remarkably intricate 18th-c doll's house also said to have been furnished by Chippendale. The grounds are most attractive, with lakes, woodland walks, and a lovely rose garden. There's an interesting MEDIEVAL CHURCH near the entrance, and a craft centre in the stables. Meals, snacks, shop, disabled access; open pm wknds and bank hols Apr–Oct, plus pm Mon–Thurs July and Aug; £3.50 house and grounds, £2.20 grounds only; NT. The Spread Eagle has decent food.

🏠 ✿ **Oakwell Hall** SE2127 (signed off A651/A652 S of Birkenshaw) Moated Elizabethan manor house, altered in the 17th-c, and still furnished to give something of the atmosphere then; look out for the unusual dog gates at the foot of the staircase. Also period formal gardens, extensive country park with adventure playground, and lots of wknd events throughout the year. Snacks, shop, disabled access; cl am wknds, 24–27 Dec, 1–2 Jan; (01924) 474926; £1.

⛏ ♨ 🏠 🏠 🐄 **Sheffield** SK3587 is a large unpretty industrial city with a plain-looking centre, redeveloped extensively in post-war years. You really have to be a local to tap into the increasingly thriving and enjoyable cultural life of the place, but several places are rewarding to visit though needing a street map and quite a bit of journeying to get there. ABBEYDALE INDUSTRIAL HAMLET (Abbeydale Rd S) was one of the first industrial heritage sites made accessible to the public. The main feature is the 18th-c and early 19th-c water-powered scythe and steelworks, but there are also restored workers' and managers' houses, and on some days you can see workmen at their forges. Meals, snacks, shop, some disabled access; cl Mon exc bank hols; (0114) 236 7731; £2.50. KELHAM ISLAND INDUSTRIAL MUSEUM (around Alma St; and signed from centre) Lively exploration of Sheffield's industrial development, with all sorts of buildings, workshops and machinery collections (inc formidable working engines), and traditional cutlery craftsmen at work. Meals, snacks, shop, disabled access; has been cl Fri, Sat and three wks in Dec but this may change; (0114) 272 2106; £2.50. The Fat Cat here has good food. Out at Whiteley Woods (A625 towards Chapel en le Frith), the SHEPHERD WHEEL is an early cutlery grinding works established in 1584, using the same dangerous methods right up to the 1930s. Shop, disabled access; cl 12.30–1.30pm, Mon and Tues, 24–26 Dec, 1 Jan; free. More about the city's industrial heritage at the CITY MUSEUM (Weston Park), firmly traditional in its approach, but with some interesting collections, inc splendid displays of cutlery and antique Sheffield plate. Shop, disabled access; cl Mon, 25 Dec, 1 Jan; free. The pleasant park also has the first of Sheffield's three excellent ART GALLERIES, the MAPPIN featuring works by Renoir, Cézanne, Turner and even Walt Disney (open as City Museum); the other galleries are the GRAVES (Surrey St) with some fine decorative art, and the RUSKIN (Norfolk St), containing the collection of Victorian artist and writer John Ruskin, with an adjacent craft gallery. Both cl Sun; free. BISHOPS HOUSE (Meersbrook Park, S of centre) Striking 15th- and 16th-c yeoman's house, now a good varied museum of social history. Shop; cl Mon and Tues; (0114) 255 7701; £1. North of the centre at Tinsley the SHEFFIELD BUS MUSEUM has a diverse collection of buses and even pre-war milk floats, with related memorabilia and a big model railway. Shop, some disabled access; open pm wknds for restoration work, with special open days every couple of months when the displays are more lively; (0114) 255 3010; £1.

★ ♄ ▣ ♨ ! **Saltaire** SE1437 is the pioneering industrial village Joseph Salt developed in Shipley in the 1850s. Salt's beautifully thought-out classically designed village was so successful that even now it's a favoured place to live. It's well worth looking around, and you might want to try the antique CABLE RAILWAY. The 1853 GALLERY out here, named from the date when the magnificent mill it's housed in was built, is probably one of the largest private collections of art in the country, with around 300 paintings by David Hockney. Huge bookshop, disabled access; (01274) 531163; cl 25–26 Dec; free. Some good smart shops in the building too (inc one selling clothes made in the mill). Just up the road, the unique REED ORGAN AND HARMONIUM MUSEUM (Victoria Hall, Victoria Rd) has some eye-opening exhibits, inc one organ no bigger than a family bible. If you play the organ you may get the chance to try some of those on display. Shop; cl Fri, Sat, 2 wks at Christmas; (01274) 585601; £1.50. What was Sooty's World (Windmill Manor, Leeds Rd) is now an exhibition called FUREVER

FELINE, where animatronic cats stroll through pine-scented woodland scenes and talk in broad Yorkshire accents; useful for young children. Snacks, shop, disabled access; cl Fri in term time, 25–26 Dec, 1 Jan; *£3.75. There's a splendid flight of locks on the Leeds–Liverpool Canal here.

† ▣ ♨ ❀ **Wakefield** SE3320 has a number of handsome buildings, including its CATHEDRAL, much restored in Victorian times but with some fine 15th-c masonry and carvings (and a marvellous spire – the tallest in Yorkshire), its rare 14th-c BRIDGE CHAPEL over the River Calder, some Georgian and Regency houses most notably around Wood St and St Johns Sq, and its imposing civic buildings. ART GALLERY (Wentworth Terrace) Good collection of 20th-c painting and sculpture, internationally famous for its galleries devoted to two famous local sculptors Barbara Hepworth and Henry Moore. Shop; cl am Sun, 25–26 Dec, 1–2 Jan; free. YORKSHIRE SCULPTURE PARK (Bretton Hall College, West Bretton) Carefully and imaginatively displayed series of major contemporary sculpture set in fine 18th-c landscaped parkland. There are 16 works by Henry Moore in the adjacent country park. Meals, snacks, shop, disabled access; cl 25 Dec; (01924) 830302; free. The MUSEUM (Wood St) has a unique collection of preserved animals and exotic birds (cl am Sun), and there's a museum of psychiatry in the Stanley Royd Hospital, formerly a lunatic asylum (open Weds only, cl 1–2pm); both free. The Beer Engine (Westgate End) is fun for a light lunch on Friday or Saturday. Up at Heath there's an extraordinarily old-fashioned common with gipsy ponies alongside 18th-c mansions; the gaslit Kings Arms here is good.

✕ ❀ ➤ ⬩↥ **Worsbrough** SE3503 COUNTRY PARK, FARM AND MILL MUSEUM Hard to believe this peaceful country park was once a busy industrial area; the only sign of those days is the working corn mill, now a museum but still producing stoneground flour. The 200 acres also include nature trails, traditional and rare breeds, and several beehives, and there are lots of events throughout the year, esp on bank hols. Snacks, shop; mill cl Mon, Tues, Christmas wk; free.

★**Attractive or attractively placed villages** with decent pubs include Askwith SD1648, Barkisland SE0420, Boston Spa SE4345, Esholt SE1840, Luddenden SE0426 (the enormous Oats Royd Mill in the valley is a remarkable sight), Stanbury SE0037, Goose Eye SE0340, Heath SE3519, Honley SE1312, Ripponden SE0419 (medieval pack-horse bridge), Saxton SE4736 (where Lord Dacre is buried with his war horse), Sowerby SE0423, Sowerby Bridge SE0623 (the canal basin here always has a lot going on, and the Moorings is good for lunch), Warthill SE6755 and Wentworth SK3898.

Other useful **pubs in fine positions** or with good views include Dick Hudsons on the Otley Road at High Eldwick above Bingley SE1240, the Brown Cow by the open-access woods at Ireland Bridge (B6429) nearer Bingley, the Strines near Strines Reservoir above Bradfield SK2692, the Stanhope Arms on Windle Edge Lane nr Winscar Reservoir by Dunford Bridge SE1502, the New Inn at Eccup SE2842, the Scapehouse on Scapegoat Hill above Golcar SE0915, the Cow & Calf up Skew Hill Lane at Grenoside above Sheffield SK3293, the Malt Shovel at Harden SE0838, the Robin Hood at Pecket Well outside Hebden Bridge SD9928, the Cherry Tree on Bank End Lane at High Hoyland SE2710, the Fleece at Holme SE1006, the Buckstones on the A640 towards Denshaw high above Huddersfield SE1416, the Blacksmiths Arms on Heaton Moor Rd at Kirkheaton SE1818, the Shepherds Rest on Mankinholes Rd at Lumbutts SD9523, the Will's o' Nat's on Blackmoorfoot Rd at Meltham SE0910, the Mount Skip nr Midgley perched high over Hebden Bridge SE0027 (on the Calderdale Way footpath), the Hinchcliffe Arms at Cragg Vale, Mytholmroyd SE0126, the Hobbit up Hob Lane, Norland SE0723, the Grouse on Harehills Lane, Oldfield, nr Oakworth SE0038, the Causeway Foot on the Keighley Rd by Ogden Reservoir SE0631, the Waggon & Horses on the A6033 nr Oxenhope SE0335, the Pineberry on the A644 Keighley rd out of Queensbury SE1030, the Three Acres at Roydhouse near Shelley SE2112, the Clothiers Arms in Station Rd, Stocksmoor, nr Shepley SE1810, the White Horse at Slaithwaite SE0813, the Blue Ball nr Soyland SE0120, the Sportsmans Arms at Hawks Stones, Kebcote on Stansfield Moor SD9227, the Ring o' Bells on Hill Top Rd at Thornton SE0933, the Royal Oak on Turnshaw Rd, Ulley SK4687, the Freemasons Arms on Hopton Hall Lane at Upper Hopton SE1918, the Delvers on Cold Edge Rd at Wainstalls SE0428 and the Pack Horse at Widdop SD9333.

Walks

West Yorkshire has this area's best walking, particularly on the Pennine moors. The **Brontë country** ◠-1 around Haworth SE0337 is a favourite stamping-ground, with a good walk W through Penistone Hill Country Park SE2403 to the much-visited Brontë Waterfalls SD9935, and on through a remote valley to Withins SD9835, the original Wuthering Heights. Paths are plentiful hereabouts, although finding the way across fields frequently entails searching for unprominent stone stiles over the dry-stone walls. From **Hebden Bridge** SD9927 ◠-2, you can tackle a fearsomely steep cobbled lane up to Heptonstall SE9278 (you can get up there by car); from Heptonstall, a scenic path along the cliffs above the wooded valley of Colden Water SD9429 is the reward. Hardcastle Crags SD9630, a beauty spot to the N of Hebden Bridge, protrude above the trees that shelter Hebden Water. For views into adjacent Calderdale with the Rochdale Canal along its foot, take the Calderdale Way over **Norland Moor** SE0621 ◠-3, S of Sowerby Bridge SD0623 (road access close by).

Ilkley Moor △-4 S of Ilkley SE1147 has potential for satisfying high-level walks, while closer to Ilkley the Swastika Stone (see Ilkley in **To see and do**) makes an interesting objective beyond the pretty ravine of Heber's Ghyll SE0947. **The Chevin** SE2044 △-5 behind Otley SE2045, though not a high hill, gives a grand view of Wharfedale. Numerous reservoirs on the moors are served by footpaths, including **Ogden Reservoir** SE0630 △-6 N of Halifax and **Withens Clough Reservoir** SD9822 △-7 S of Hebden Bridge.

South Yorkshire does not have much good walking country, though the moors and reservoirs of the Pennines W of Sheffield have a certain rugged austerity. The high lands just touch the Peak District National Park: **Carl Wark** hill fort SK2561 △-8 is set handsomely in a great bowl fringed by gritstone outcrops. The **Anston Brook** △-9, accessible on foot from South Anston SK5183, flows through a wooded valley that interrupts the monotony of the flat farmlands SE of Rotherham.

Driving

West Yorkshire has some fine drives with interesting views often combining grand scenery with antique industrial settlements clinging to steep hillsides. Easy and relatively quiet main roads through attractive countryside include the A640 W of Huddersfield, the A6033 from Hebden Bridge to Haworth, the B6188 S of Mytholmroyd across the moors to join the A58, the B6113 above Ripponden and the nearby B6114 through Barkisland. Other interesting drives include the high road out of Haworth through Stanbury and up over the moors towards Nelson and Colne, the several moorland and valley roads around Goose Eye above Keighley (a very picturesque area, this), the old packhorse roads from Hebden Bridge into Lancashire (one up through Heptonstall and Widdop and the other through Blackshaw Head), and the back moorland roads between Guiseley and Otley around The Chevin. Further east, it's either too busy or too flat for driving to be much of a recreation.

Where to eat

Pool in Wharfedale SE2445 Pool Court Pool Bank; 9 miles to Leeds/Bradford/Harrogate (0113) 284 2288 Fine and beautifully kept Georgian house popular for miles around – with excellent fairly priced imaginative food, fine wines, and helpful friendly service; bedrooms; cl lunchtimes except by prior arrangement, Sun, bank hol Mon and 2 wks Christmas. £29.50.

Ripponden SE0419 Old Bridge (01422) 822295 Well kept medieval inn by pretty bridge over River Ryburn with interesting rooms, good wines and real ales, and very popular cold buffet wkday lunchtimes (best to book); charming evening restaurant just over the bridge; no bar food pm Sat, Sun (restaurant only then); no children; disabled access. £23 for 4 courses in restaurant.

Haworth SE0337 Weavers 15 West Lane (01535) 643822 Charming evening restaurant made up of weavers' cottages with most enjoyable hearty (not heavy) food, cheerful service, and lovely puddings; bedrooms; cl Sun, Mon, 2 wks Christmas, 2 wks July. £22.

Bardsey SE3643 Bingley Arms (01937) 572462 Ancient pub, decorated in keeping, full of interest and atmosphere, with very wide range of decent bar food, picturesque restaurant, and charming terrace. £16.50/£2.25/£5.50

Leeds SE3033 Leodis Victoria Mill (0113) 242 1010 Sister restaurant of the Paris in Horsforth, this attractive place on the ground floor of the old mill serves carefully cooked elegant Anglo-French food, and decent wines; cl Sun, Sat am; disabled access. £15.95.

Headingley SE2836 Salvos 115 Otley Rd (0113) 275 5017 Welcoming, family-run Italian restaurant with good food and cheerful service; cl Sun, 25–26 Dec. £15/£4.95.

Horsforth SE3033 Outside Inn (0113) 258 1410 Bustling friendly evening restaurant with thriving atmosphere, consistently good honest cooking, and welcoming service; cl Mon, 25–26 Dec; disabled access. £15.

Leeds SE3033 HANSAS GUJARATI VEGETARIAN RESTAURANT 72–74 North St (0113) 244 408 Very carefully prepared Indian vegetarian food from the state of Gujarat, helpful service, and a relaxed atmosphere; cl Sun, am Mon–Weds, 25 Dec. £15.

Horsforth SE3033 PARIS Town St (0113) 258 1885 Very popular, imaginative French food with an excellent value, early evening 3-course meal; first-class service; cl lunchtimes, 25–26 Dec, 1 Jan. £14.50.

Bingley SE1039 FISHERMANS Dowley Gap (01274) 564238 Carefully restored inn on River Aire (handy for the Five Rise Locks) with convivial atmosphere, and excellent value decent food; cl pm Sun, pm 25 Dec, disabled access. £11.75|£1.75/£4.50.

Linthwaite SE1014 BULLS HEAD (01484) 842715 Popular pub looking out over moors, with unassuming rooms, good daily-changing bar food served all day, and lovely puddings; partial disabled access. £11.50|£2.20/£4.75.

Help this year from: Maysie Thompson, Elizabeth and Anthony Watts, Stephen Barney, Anthony Barnes, Stuart Sutton, John and Joan Wyatt, Amanda Hodges, Juliet Williams, Andrew and Ruth Triggs, Michael and Jenny Back, Mark Bradley, Mrs A Du Croz, Pat Crabb, John and Joan Nash, David and Margaret Bloomfield, Frank Cummins, Jack Hill, Dave Braisted, M J Morgan, Jim and Maggie Cowell, Jan and Dave Booth, Michael Butler, CMW, JJW, I McCaskey, Frank Davidson, Brian Kneale, H Bramwell, Mike and Wendy Proctor, Geoffrey and Brenda Wilson, Lee Goulding, TBB, B B Pearce, Thomas Nott, Paul Cartledge, Brian Wainwright, Margaret Mason, David Thompson, H W Kennedy, Mayur Shah, WAH, Bronwen and Steve Wrigley, Ann and Frank Bowman, Norma and Keith Bloomfield, D L Parkhurst, David and Julie Glover, Dono and Carol Leaman, Bill Sykes, C H Stride, Bruce Bird, Peter and Lynn Brueton, Murray Dykes, A and M Dickinson, Wendy Arnold, Comus Elliott, GSB, Andrew Hazeldine, John Allsopp, Louise Knowles, Sarah Harvey, Paula Shillaw, Eileen Walker, Jim Farmer, G W H Kerby, Andrew Shore, Patrick Renouf, G P Wood, Lawrence Bacon, Jean Scott, Paul and Janet Waring, Ken Smith, Mark Undrill, Martyn and Mary Mullins, John and Christine Simpson, Catheryn and Richard Hicks, D M Caslaw, D Stokes, Elizabeth and Anthony Watts, Geoff and Angela Jaques, Gordon Theaker, Graham Reeve.

YORKSHIRE CALENDAR

Some of these dates were provisional as we went to press.

JANUARY

2 **Hubberholme** Land Letting at the George, 8pm: ancient form of auction determined by the length of a burning candle – the last bid gains the church lands grazing (01756) 760223

9 (Plough Monday) **Goathland** Plough Stots Service: church service, blessing and ancient long sword dance of Norse origin. Stots means bullock which name was transferred to the men who pulled the plough (01904) 704141

12 **York** Commemorative Service at York Minster: each NT property will bury a time capsule

FEBRUARY

10 **York** Jorvik Festival – *till Sat 25* (01904) 611944

25 **Ilkley** Complementary Medicine Festival at Kings Hall & Winter Garden – *till Sun 26* (01943) 609454

YORKSHIRE CALENDAR

FEBRUARY cont

28 **Scarborough** Shrovetide Skipping Festival at noon: 3/4 mile of Foreshore Rd closed to traffic for skipping in the road *till 5pm* (01723) 373333

MARCH

York L S Lowry: The Man and His Art at North City Art Gallery – *till 7 May* (01904) 623839

8 **Ilkley** Literature Festival – *till Sun 12* (01943) 601210

13 **Skipton** Music Festival – *till Sat 18* (01756) 793195

18 **Ilkley** British Society of Painters at Kings Hall & Winter Garden, possibly the largest art exhibition in Britain – *till Sun 26* (01943) 609454

APRIL

2 **Keighley** Riddlesden Revels at East Riddlesden Hall – *also first Sunday every month till Oct* (01535) 607075

12 **Harrogate** International Youth Music Festival – *till Weds 19* 0171-401 9941

17 **Ossett** World Coal Carrying Championships (01924) 273883

20 **Harrogate** Spring Flower Festival at Valley Gardens – *till Sun 23* (01423) 561049; **York** Academy of St Martin in the Fields Centenary Concert at York Minster

MAY

6 **Gawthorpe** Maypole, Feast and Procession (01924) 273883; **Leeds** International Music Festival – *till Sun 14* (0113) 245 2069

7 **Elphalborough** World Dock Pudding Championships at the Mytholmroyd Community Centre (01422) 883023; **Knaresborough** Yorkshire Festival of Transport at Allerton Hall – *till Mon 8* (01543) 450300

13 **Sheffield** Chamber Music Festival at the Crucible Studio Theatre – *till Sat 27* (01904) 645738

24 **Whitby** Upper Harbour Planting of the Penny Hedge (corruption of penance hedge) at 9am on the beach. Originated in 1159 when hunters did penance by building a hedge of stakes at the water's edge (01947) 602674

25 **Keld** Tan Hill Show at Tan Hill Inn (01833) 28246

26 **Swaledale, Wensleydale and Arkengarthdale** Swaledale Festival – *till 11 Jun* (01969) 22217

27 **Birstall** Re-enactment, 1695 at Oakwell Hall – *till Mon 29* (01924) 474926; **York** Busking Festival – *till Sun 28* (01904) 650355

28 **Ripon** English Civil War Society Muster at Fountains Abbey – *till Mon 29* (01765) 608888

29 **Helmsley** Country Fair at Duncombe Park (014393) 517

JUNE

4 **Leeds** Fireworks Concert at Harewood House (01625) 575681

8 **Bramham** International Horse Trials and Yorkshire Country Fair at Bramham Park – *till Sun 11* (01937) 844265

11 **Whitby** Festival – *till Mon 26* (01947) 820625

13 **Ripon** Open Air Shakespeare at Fountains Abbey – *till Mon 17* (01765) 608888

YORKSHIRE CALENDAR

JUNE cont

16 **Bradford** Festival – *till 8 July* (01274) 309199

17 **Leeds** Summer Heritage Festival – *till 2 July* (0113) 234 8080;
Otley Carnival (01943) 464204

18 **Nunnington** Yorkshire Music Afternoon at Nunnington Hall
(01439) 748283; **Walkington** Hay Ride, Waterworth Stackyard to
Bishopburton (01482) 866694

24 **Filey** Edwardian Festival – *till 2 July* (01723) 516142; **Thirsk** North
Yorkshire Country Show at Ryebeck Farm (01609) 773429;
Ripon Classical Concert with Fireworks at Fountains Abbey
(01765) 608888

25 **Ripon** Children's Concert at Fountains Abbey (01765) 608888;
Shipton by Beningbrough Victorian Picnic at Beningbrough Hall
(01904) 470666

30 **Cleckheaton** Folk Festival – *till 2 July* (01924) 404346

JULY

1 **Helmsley** Greater Yorkshire Traction Engine Club Steam Fair and Rally
at Duncombe Park (01439) 70213; **Whitby** Licensed Boatman's Angling
Festival – *till Mon 10* (01947) 602674

2 **Elsecar** Old Horse Party (01226) 746086; **Oxenhope** Straw Races
(01535) 644298

7 **Ripon** Music by Moonlight at Fountains Abbey – *till Sat 8* (01765)
608888; **York** Early Music Festival – *till Sun 16* (01904) 658338

8 **Huddersfield** Carnival at Greenhead Park (01484) 539552; **Ilkley**
Centenary of British Society of Miniaturists and British Watercolour
Society Exhibition at Kings Hall & Winter Garden – *till Sun 16*
(01943) 609454

9 **Skipton** Fireworks and Laser Concert at Broughton Hall (01625) 575681;
Whitby Blessing of the Boats at the Harbourside (01947) 602674

11 **Harrogate** Great Yorkshire Show at the Showground – *till Thurs 13*
(01423) 561536

15 **Masham** Steam Engine and Fair Organ Rally at Low Burton Hall –
till Sun 16 (01765) 689569

16 **Keighley** Period Garden Party at East Riddlesden Hall (01535) 607075

22 **Ryedale** Festival – *till 6 Aug* (01653) 600666

23 **Ripon** National Music Day at Fountains Abbey (01765) 608888

25 **Ryedale** Show at Welburn Park (01751) 431761

27 **Harrogate** International Festival – *till 10 Aug* (01423) 652303

29 **York** Celebration of Band Music (01904) 650355

AUGUST

1 **Egton Bridge** Old Gooseberry Show at St Heddas School
(01924) 384714

5 **Ripon** St Wilfrid's Procession (01765) 604579

6 **Ripley** Viennese Evening with Fireworks at Ripley Castle
(01625) 575681

8 **Bingley** Show at Myrtle Park (01274) 564400

12 **Halifax** Agricultural Show at Saville Park (01422) 355056

YORKSHIRE CALENDAR

AUGUST cont

16 **Danby** Agricultural Show (01287) 660594

19 **Whitby** Folk Week – *till Fri 25* (01482) 634742

23 **Egton** Show, a local favourite (01947) 895281

26 **Leyburn** Wensleydale Agricultural Show (01969) 40261; **Thongsbridge to Holmfirth** Torchlight Procession (01484) 640640; **West Witton** Burning of the Bartle (01969) 22034

27 **Ormesby** Steam Fair at Ormesby Hall – *till Mon 28* (01642) 324188

28 **Burniston** Horticultural and Agricultural Show at the Showground (01723) 366002; **Epworth** Show (01427) 873865

SEPTEMBER

2 **Keighley** and District Agricultural Show at Marley Fields (01535) 633852; **Sowerby Bridge** Rushbearing: colourful dramatic tradition from 17th-century when rushes were taken to the church for winter floor covering. Handsome rush cart is pulled along the lanes of the Ryburn Valley accompanied by Morris dancers and merriment (01422) 843831

3 **Leeds** Last Night of the Proms at Harewood House (01625) 575681; **Ripponden** Rushbearing – as above

9 **Castleton** and Danby Show (01287) 660409; **York** Festival of Traditional Dance – *till Sun 10* (01904) 650355

10 **Hardraw** Scar Brass Band Competition at the Green Dragon Inn (01904) 412383; **Sheffield** Transport Rally at Meadowhall Centre (0114) 248 9166

15 **Harrogate** Great autumn flower show at the Exhibition Halls – *till Sat 16* (01423) 561049

17 **Gomersal** Traditional Working Crafts Day at Red House (01274) 872165

21 **Stokesley** Show at the Showground (01642) 710630

23 **Ilkley** British Society of Painters at Kings Hall & Winter Garden, possibly the largest art exhibition in Britain – *till 1 Oct* (01943) 609454

29 **Bainbridge** Blowing the Forest Horn, every evening for people travelling across the moors, 700-year-old custom – *till 28 Feb*

30 **Masham** Sheep Fair and Bishop Blaise Procession (01765) 689300

OCTOBER

7 **Ripon** Yorkshire Three Choirs Festival at Ripon Cathedral – *till Tues 10* (0113) 247 6962

21 **Kirklees** One World Festival – *till Mon 30* (01484) 513808

NOVEMBER

4 **Embsay** Grand Bonfire, Firework Display and Steam Trains at Night at Embsay Steam Railway (01756) 794727

16 **Huddersfield** Comtemporary Music Festival – *till Sun 26* (01484) 425082

25 **Ilkley** British Watercolour Society Exhibition at Kings Hall & Winter Garden – *till 3 Dec* (01943) 609454

DECEMBER

24 **Haworth** Torchlight Procession and Carol Service (01535) 642329

LONDON

Exceptionally good sightseeing, shopping and shows; superb choice of restaurants, excellent places to stay (at high prices).

London ranks supreme for theatre, music and other entertainments, for the vast range of things you can find to do, see, visit, buy and eat, and for the ease of walking from one interesting thing to the next. It's let down by high restaurant and accommodation prices (to offset this, many places to visit are free). Like most big cities, it's impersonal, has noisy and smelly traffic problems in most of the centre (not in the City), and too much dirt and dilapidation (again, not in the City, nor in much of Westminster – and the parks and river are a real escape).

Almost all the things visitors might want to see are concentrated in the relatively small centre. We have divided this centre into a few general areas of a size to facilitate quite a bit of sightseeing in a day or so. As these central areas are so close together, you can very quickly get from one to the other – so the place you stay in needn't necessarily be in the area you want to explore. We have recommended only those hotels which we know to be comfortable and to have some individuality – places that would definitely add something to the enjoyment of your stay. If all you want is a bed for the night, there's an almost endless range of cheaper places, especially around Bloomsbury, Bayswater, South Kensington and Victoria.

As outer London does not appeal for a short break or weekend away, the only parts of it we have included are those which would really add something significant to a stay in the centre – Greenwich, Kew and Richmond, Hampton Court, Hampstead and Highgate. And we have singled out a few really rewarding places to visit in other districts.

There's a magnificent choice of restaurants, from the simplest to the most grandiose or most delicious (often not the same). Again, we've restricted our recommendations to a manageable number of places that have real character.

Unless you are familiar with London's roads or entirely confident about driving in a big city with too much traffic, poor local signposting and a lot of unpredictable drivers, don't come by car. For seeing much of London, a car is actually an encumbrance, because of the traffic and the expense of parking. The two exceptions to this general rule are that on a Sunday many of central London's roads are generally relatively quiet, with most street parking free; and that *very* early on a fine, late spring or summer morning – say, between 4 and 7 o'clock – it can be idyllic driving around the broad and empty streets seeing the stately buildings waking up in the early sunshine, without a single tourist to be seen around them.

London's 'tube', the underground railway, is the most straightforward way of getting around, and easy for even first-time visitors. The routes are all colour-coded, on the same system used in that master-piece of 1920s design, the pocket tube map (free from ticket offices); this is a big help in finding the platform you want, particularly in those busy stations that serve more than one line. In the text, we have grouped things to see and do under the heading of the most convenient tube station, using the ⊖ symbol. In the centre, the gap between stations is always much smaller than it looks on the tube map – so don't stick too rigidly to our divisions.

Except in dismally cold wet weather, most people find the buses more pleasant, and of course they let you sightsee as you go. It's worth checking out the lie of the land with a London Transport bus map (free), to see which routes are likely to be useful to you. The routes are all numbered, and each bus shows its route number. There are also several hop-on hop-off tour buses with commentary (some only at night).

A one-day travelcard is an excellent investment for the visitor, and you can even buy them in advance from newsagents. It's valid on buses, the tube and BR trains, for as many journeys as you want to make during the day (it does not cover the morning rush hour, or the night buses which run from about 11pm). A particular joy of this is that you can hop on and off buses for even quite short trips without bothering about the cost. If you're coming up to London by train, you can add a one-day travelcard to the rail fare at a big discount.

Taxis could scarcely be more convenient, but are expensive for just one or two people: anything except a very short trip will cost £5 or more.

For the theatre, a half-price ticket booth on Leicester Sq sells off surplus tickets for that day's performances: open around 12–2pm for matinée tickets, then from about 2.30pm for evenings – there's usually a queue so it's worth getting there earlier. Don't expect to find the blockbuster shows, but there's generally a decent choice.

THE WEST END

The area around Covent Garden, Soho, Piccadilly, Mayfair, Regent St and Oxford St is world-famous for its theatres, cinemas and interesting shops. Besides the great national galleries there are some intriguing, tucked-away, specialist museums. There's food to suit almost every pocket and taste: Chinatown has become a particularly vivid enclave, Neal St is a focus for vegetarian restaurants, there are staunchly old-fashioned institutions of Englishness like Rules or Simpson's, and you can find superbly imaginative, less conventional cooking. The shopping too is extraordinarily varied, from the daunting bustle of Oxford St, through the bookshops around Charing Cross Rd, the specialist food and cookery shops of Soho, and the elegant stores of Regent St and Piccadilly, to the ultra-smart clothes shops of South Molton St and Bond St. There are great opportunities for window-shopping in the small galleries and auction houses.

Where to stay

THE CONNAUGHT Carlos Pl W1Y 6AL 0171-499 7070; 90 lovely, individually decorated rms, inc 24 suites. A very special place with fine, old-fashioned values – there's no brochure, and prices are on application; elegant, restful day rooms filled with lovely flowers and antiques, fine panelling, exemplary service, and marvellous food in the two formal restaurants; disabled access.

BROWNS Albemarle St/Dover St W1A 4SW 0171-493 6020 £240; 118 comfortable, beautifully decorated rms (some at the back have a dull 'view' – say if this matters to you). Fine, very English hotel with country-house atmosphere, lovely panelling, deeply comfortable seats, flowers and antiques in the elegant public rooms, and a cosy bar; popular afternoon tea, and good food; disabled access.

CLARIDGES Brook St W1A 2JQ 0171-629 8860 £220w; 190 excellent rms. Grand hotel long used by royalty and heads of state, with liveried footmen, lift attendants and valets, elegant and comfortable day rooms, civilised, colonnaded foyer where the Hungarian Quartet plays; lovely formal restaurant with a mirrored mural and terrace, and a more intimate, smaller restaurant called the Causerie; dinner-dance Fri/Sat pm; complimentary golf at Wentworth and tennis at Vanderbilt Racquet Club; disabled access.

SAS PORTMAN 22 Portman Sq W1H 9FL 0171-486 5844 £211.75; 278 attractive and well equipped, modern rms. Efficiently run, smart, recently refurbished hotel with very friendly service, creative and imaginative cooking in the all-day restaurant, pleasant bar, and afternoon tea served by the lobby fireside; disabled access.

LANGHAM HILTON 1 Portland Pl W1N 3AA 0171-636 1000 £176w; 379 fine rms. Beautifully refurbished Victorian hotel opposite the BBC's Broadcasting House, with many original features, a champagne and caviar bar, clubby Chukkha Bar, very good service; health club with gym, steam room, sauna, solarium; disabled access.

LE MERIDIEN PICCADILLY 21 Piccadilly W1V 0BH 0171-734 8000 £159; 264 comfortable, well equipped rms. The very best in modern French hotel-keeping; attractive, quiet public rooms with professional and friendly service, popular afternoon tea, fine restaurant food, and free membership of the good health club downstairs; one child under 12 free in parents' room.

HAZLITTS 6 Frith St W1V 5TZ 0171-434 1771 £143.35; 23 rms with 18th- or 19th-c beds and free-standing Victorian baths with early brass shower mixer units. Behind a typically Soho façade of listed, early Georgian houses, this is a well kept and comfortably laid-out little hotel which could scarcely be handier for the West End; good, continental breakfasts served in your bedroom, and you can get snacks in the sitting room – lots of restaurants all around; kind, helpful service; cl Christmas.

ST GEORGE'S Langham Pl W1N 8QS 0171-580 0111 *£138; 86 light rms with marvellous views over London. Popular hotel, a stone's throw from Oxford Circus, with afternoon tea in both the bar and lounge, a fine rooftop restaurant and dinner-dance every Fri and Sat; disabled access.

CHESTERFIELD 35 Charles St W1X 8LX 0171-491 2622 *£130; 110 well equipped, pretty rms. Charming hotel with particularly courteous, helpful staff, afternoon tea in the wood-panelled library, a relaxed, club-style bar with resident pianist, and fine food in the attractive restaurant or light and airy terrace room.

CUMBERLAND Marble Arch W1A 4RF 0171-262 1234 £120; 896 comfortable, well equipped rms. Very well run, popular hotel with a modern, Art Deco bar, a fine choice of food in 4 restaurants (inc a Japanese one, traditional English, Chinese, and a brasserie), elegant lounge, and good service; disabled access.

DURRANTS George St W1H 6BJ 0171-935 8131 *£112.50; 96 well equipped rms, most with own bthrm; the quietest are at the back. Managed by the same family for over 70 years, this surprisingly quiet, privately owned central hotel, behind a delightful Georgian façade, has fine paintings and antiques, a clubby bar, and relaxing lounges; cosy, panelled restaurant with essentially English cooking, and helpful, pleasant staff; disabled access.

FIELDING 4 Broad Court WC2B 5QZ 0171-836 8305 £77; 26 rms, 24 with showers. Carefully renovated, well run, little 18th-c hotel opposite the Royal Opera House and charmingly lit at night by the preserved 19th-c gas lamps; cl 24–26 Dec.

To see and do

Charing Cross The tube station here is tucked away underneath TRAFALGAR SQUARE, which many people think of as the heart of central London. Named for the great naval victory of 1805, the square was designed by Nash and completed in 1841; the fountains were added a century later. The centrepiece, NELSON'S COLUMN, stretches up 185ft, its base guarded by four, huge, identical lions. Look out for the gifted roller-skaters who perform in the evenings around the base – and, of course, for the innumerable pigeons; Nelson now has a special coating to protect him from their droppings.

Right on the square, the NATIONAL GALLERY is quite magnificent. It houses the national collection of Western European painting, with around 2,000 pictures dating from the 13th to the 20th c. You'll probably enjoy it most if you're firm with yourself and restrict yourself to just a few of the galleries, rather than trying to rush round all of it. It's hard to pick out highlights, but don't miss the exciting Sainsbury Wing, which gives perfect lighting and viewing conditions for its treasure-trove of early Renaissance works. The gallery gets very busy, especially on a Sat, or at most times around the Impressionist works. Temporary exhibitions this year include Spanish Still Life (22 Feb–21 May), and a wide range of paintings normally displayed in National Trust properties, designed to tie in with the NT's centenary (from 22 Nov). Caravaggio's *Taking of Christ* (on loan from Dublin) can be seen between Feb and Apr. From the steps of the building, a neo-Classical affair opened in 1838, you get a splendid view of London – not just the buildings, but the people and buses at their most vibrant. Meals, snacks, shop, disabled access; cl am Sun, 24–26 Dec, 1 Jan, Good Fri, 1 May; 0171-839 3321; free.

Just around the corner is the NATIONAL PORTRAIT GALLERY (St Martin's Pl), grandly illustrating British history, with paintings of kings, queens and other notable characters arranged in chronological order from the top floor (medieval) to the present. It's been greatly extended, with more space for temporary shows and a new photography gallery. Their good exhibition on Christina Rossetti runs until mid-Feb. Shop, disabled access; cl am Sun, 24–26 Dec, 1 Jan, Good Fri, May Day; 0171-306 0055; free, small charge for some special exhibitions.

Plenty of theatres nr here, with a group based around this end of Charing Cross Rd and another up along the Strand. Marked out by the globe on top of the building, the Coliseum (St Martin's Lane) is the home of the English National Opera; you can usually get decently priced seats on the day, from 10am. Almost next door, the Chandos is a decent pub with food all day (upstairs is best), down past the post office, the underground Tappit Hen is an atmospheric wine bar, and there's no end of smart, little coffee shops and cafés near by. Another good place for music is the elegant church of ST MARTIN-IN-THE-FIELDS, with frequent lunchtime and evening concerts; 0171-930 0089 for programme. Unmistakable for its blue clock-dial – the only clock in this part of London that seems always to keep the right time – the church also has a busy coffee bar in its crypt, occasional exhibitions, and a very good afternoon craft market, useful for bargains. Every night the church is used as a shelter for the homeless, but even so as you make your way home from the theatre you're likely to see plenty of bodies huddled in shop doorways in these streets – a sadly common sight all over London but especially obvious around here.

🎭 🎨 🛍 ⊖ **Covent Garden** Partly pedestrianised, the former vegetable, fruit and flower market with its elegant buildings is now made over to smart café-bars, boutiques and stalls, such as those in the covered Piazza, selling good but expensive handmade clothes and craft items. There's also the Jubilee Market which specialises in different wares on different days. The many bars and restaurants are always lively at night, but again they're not cheap.

🔭 ! LONDON TRANSPORT MUSEUM (The Piazza) On the site of Covent Garden's former Flower Market, this has been wonderfully livened up in the last year or two. Now much more hands-on: you don't just see the collection of buses and trams, you hear and smell them, and can even try your hand at driving a computerised tube train. Plenty more touch-screen exhibits, as well as a good range of the splendid posters used by London Transport over the last century; during school hols they usually have costumed actors telling nostalgic transport tales. Meals, snacks, interesting shop, disabled access; cl 24–26 Dec; 0171-836 8557; £3.95.

👓 THEATRE MUSEUM (Tavistock St) Exhaustive look at events and personalities on the stage over the last few hundred years. Posters, puppets and props are among the permanent collection, which is astonishingly comprehensive, though arranged a little confusingly; it runs chronologically, but it's easy to find yourself going round backwards. The very good, and often lively, temporary displays leave the deepest impression. Shop, disabled access; cl Mon, 25–26 Dec; 0171-836 7891; £3.

! For the real thing you can tour the THEATRE ROYAL on Drury Lane, the oldest working theatre in the world. First opened in 1663 (Nell Gwynn was one of its earliest performers, and not just by royal appointment), but rebuilt several times over the next few centuries, it gives a fascinating glimpse behind the scenes, inc an intriguing hydraulic lift beneath the stage, still in use. Snacks, shop, disabled access; three tours a day (exc on Weds and Sat when only two because of matinee), 11am, 1pm (12.30 Weds and Sat), and 5.30pm, cl Sun; 0171-494 5091; £3.50.

✝ ! 🎭 ST PAUL'S CHURCH, also called the Actors' Church, is full of interesting memorials to performers. Pepys watched the first-ever Punch and Judy show here in 1662. Outside its back gate, facing the covered market, the theatrical tradition continues, with jugglers, clowns, mountebanks and unusual musicians performing on the cobbles. Nearby is the imposing OPERA HOUSE; good seats can cost anything up to £50 and more, though you can get much cheaper ones, and there are generally three or four dates in summer when major performances are relayed free to a giant screen on the Piazza. The box office (0171-240 1066) can tell you what's planned for this year, but be warned, these events are very popular and you'll have to get there early to bag a good spot.

🛍 One of the delights of this area is its range of unusual or specialist SHOPS. In the streets around the Piazza, Knutz (Russell St) has everything for the practical joker, from the old, black face soap to rather cheekier items, Suttons (Catherine St) have a bewildering variety of plant seeds, and Penhaligon's (Wellington St) sells lovely, old-fashioned toiletries. On the other side of the market, to the N of the tube station, interesting shops are set in a labyrinthine network of attractively rejuvenated alleys and streets; you will get lost, but wandering around is great fun, and they all lead back out into roughly the same area. Neal St is rewarding for its small craft and specialist shops, kitchen shops, and Neal's Yard, full of healthy living – it's delightful in summer, with its fresh paint and tubs of flowers. Floral St has elegant and expensive clothes and shoe shops (don't miss the Tintin shop – from cards to key-rings, paradise for the Tintin fan). No shortage of places to eat around here, but useful pubs for lunch or refreshment include the Marquis of Anglesea on Bow St, with a good-value upstairs restaurant, and the Lamb & Flag on Rose St, an attractive 300-year-old pub with decent snacks, its back room still much as Dickens described it.

🏧 ❂ **Leicester Sq** The tube station here is a favourite with Londoners stuck for a place to meet. Outside the Hippodrome exit especially, you'll see hordes of people milling around, anxiously looking for the friends they finally discover they've been standing next to for half an hour. All central London's attractions are within easy walking distance of here, with several of the more interesting theatres little more than five minutes' stroll. Around the edges of the bustling square, attractively cleaned up in recent years, are several huge cinemas, pricy but with excellent sound; you can see films more cheaply at the Prince Charles in Leicester Pl, leading off. The Swiss Centre on the far corner of the square sells exquisite chocolates and Swiss groceries; the well run Moon Under Water is much more reasonably priced than most pubs around here. Marked out by its dramatic, ornamental gate, CHINATOWN has developed its own character, inviting despite the locals' cool indifference to outsiders; the supermarkets and shops along pedestrianised Gerrard St and in neighbouring streets are fascinating, with their weird and wonderful vegetables, and odd-smelling dried meats and fish. Plenty of authentic Chinese restaurants, as well as less convincingly adapted telephone boxes.

Back by the tube station, this stretch of Charing Cross Rd is justifiably famous for its BOOKSHOPS, specialist and general, new and secondhand. Foyles is the biggest city bookstore, but trying to find what you want is time-consuming; Waterstones is very friendly and relaxed, with informed staff. Covent Garden Records at the famous address of 84 Charing Cross Rd is excellent for classical CDs. The side alleys between here and St Martin's Lane have good secondhand bookshops, several with specialisations such as the occult, antique children's books, or the theatre; Cecil Court is perhaps the best. The Salisbury on St Martin's Lane is a splendid Victorian pub, all velvet and cut glass (useful food counter). Not far away on Long Acre is Stanfords, the best map and guidebook shop in Britain, with helpful, knowledgeable staff, and books and maps covering all corners of the globe, as well as aspects of London you'd never even dreamed of. Leicester Sq is very handy for Soho, described below under Tottenham Court Rd.

❂ **Piccadilly Circus** Another lively hub of London life, with famous streets radiating off in every direction, each quite different in character: handsome Piccadilly roughly to the W, the theatres of bustling Shaftesbury Ave to the E, with smarter ones on Haymarket to the S, the coolly curving Regent St to the N – and, of course, the famous statue of Eros, where all the foreign students sit to be photographed.

🖼 ROYAL ACADEMY OF ARTS (Burlington House, Piccadilly) Quite magnificent building, with excellent, changing exhibitions for most of the year, then from Jun–Aug its famous (often notorious) Summer Exhibition of works by living artists great and small. Major exhibitions this year on Poussin (19 Jan–16 Apr), and often reproduced but rarely seen Impressionist and Post-Impressionist works from private Swiss collections (29 Jun–8 Oct). Meals, snacks, shop, disabled access by prior arrangement; cl 24–25 Dec, Good Fri; 0171-439 7438; admission charge varies – usually between £4 and £5.

♨ MUSEUM OF MANKIND (Burlington Gardens) Vast and interestingly displayed collections detailing the customs, art and material culture of inhabitants of the non-Western world. It generally consists of a series of changing exhibitions – go back each year and you'll rarely see the same things. This year's main exhibitions look at African arms, armour and pottery, and the Benin Empire. Meals, snacks, shop, disabled access; cl am Sun, Christmas, 1 Jan, Good Fri and 1st Mon in May; 0171-323 8043; free.

! ♨ ROCK CIRCUS (London Pavilion, Piccadilly Circus) Exuberant romp through the history of rock and roll, with wax figures and animated models of stars from Elvis to Bono, and a hi-tech musical accompaniment supplied via headsets. Snacks, shop, disabled access; cl 25 Dec – it's open most nights till 9 or even 10pm; 0171-734 8025; £6.95. The adjoining Trocadero is a vast, preserved building now redeveloped to include some rather gaudy shops, and the entertaining GUINNESS WORLD OF RECORDS which uses videos, life-sized models and the latest audio-technology to bring to life sporting and all sorts of other sometimes quite extraordinary world records; children especially should enjoy this. Shop, disabled access; cl 25 Dec; 0171-439 7331; £5.75. Though touristy, the Glassblower in Glasshouse St is handy for lunch.

📷 The streets around here are excellent for SHOPPING. On opposite sides of the traffic islands in Piccadilly Circus are Tower Records – three floors of pop, classical and jazz (open till midnight), and Lillywhites, the long-established sports clothes and equipment store. On Piccadilly, Simpson's has several floors of classic British clothes, for men and women (as well as rather unusual curved windows), while friendly Hatchards is a nicely old-fashioned bookshop where the staff are very good about turning vague requests into actual books. Almost next door, Fortnum's (Fortnum & Mason) has superior if expensive clothes, as well as the foods for which they're world-famous. Nearby, the Burlington Arcade is an elegant, Regency covered arcade of expensive but classy shops (excellent cashmere and knife/scissors shops, for instance), with a delightful set of rules, still enforced, that stop people whistling, singing or running in its confines. The Ritz hotel is gorgeously flamboyant inside: well worth the high price of having a frogged and liveried waiter bring you a cup of tea or a perfectly mixed whisky sour. Behind Piccadilly's S side is Jermyn St, where among other splendid but top-of-the-range shops you can buy fine cheeses at Paxton & Whitfields, briar pipes at Astleys, handmade shoes at Trickers, handmade shirts from Turnbull & Asser, flat hats at Bates, and old-fashioned toiletries at Floris. The Red Lion in Duke of York St, just off here, is a little gem of a pub, with

decent snacks (but very busy on wkdy lunchtimes). A landmark on Haymarket is one of the two branches of Burberrys the mac-makers (the other's in Regent St). Nr here the DESIGN CENTRE has changing exhibitions of modern British products that have won awards for a combination of beauty and efficiency; free.

📷 ⊖ Tottenham Court Rd is the handiest station for the most fashionable parts of SOHO, its coffee bars and cafés swarming with young people in the evenings. Many of Soho's Georgian terraces are rather run-down, with peepshows and naughty video shops stuffed into basements and ground floors, and too many taxis and cars using these narrow streets as rat-runs. But there are parts that have had much of their original, quiet charm restored, like Soho Sq and Meard St, and are still good for restaurants, or for shops connected with food or cooking. Old Compton St, central London's gayest st, has several interesting shops – Italian delicatessens (I Camisa is the best, with fabulous salamis), the Algerian Coffee Store which also sells lots of fruit teas, and two cheap but good wine and spirits shops. Milroys in Greek St has a wonderful collection of hundreds of different malt whiskies. Ferraris in Wardour St, the most traffic-plagued of Soho's streets, is excellent for kitchen equipment, particularly knives. Berwick St has a daily fruit and veg market – the lower half is more expensive but has better produce; at Simply Sausages down here you can watch them making some of their 43 different varieties of sausage, which include vegetarian and seafood flavours. The little Dog & Duck in Frith St and the Coach & Horses in Poland St (the *Private Eye* pub) are two of the nicest Soho locals; in Romilly St, another Coach & Horses is also on the well known, Soho characters' circuit, and Kettners, now part of the Pizza Express chain, is a very entertaining old building. The area as a whole forms a sort of square, with the tube stations at Leicester Sq, Piccadilly Circus and even Oxford Circus all just as convenient.

⚫ ⊖ **Oxford Circus** is at the heart of the city's busiest shopping area – busy and noisy Oxford St to the left and right, and altogether nicer Regent St to the S. OXFORD ST doesn't have a lot of character, but is full of good department stores such as Selfridges and John Lewis (the self-service restaurant is excellent for lunch), Marks & Spencer (two major outlets), BHS, Debenhams, the two giant music shops HMV and Virgin Megastore, as well as the usual high st shops. South Molton St and St Christopher's Pl, on either side of Oxford St, are full of designer clothes shops and smart cafés, and are fun to wander along; St Christopher's Pl also has quite an interesting antique market. REGENT ST is one of the grandest streets in the whole area, running down from the imposing yet rather bullying bulk of the BBC's Broadcasting House to its splendid curve towards Piccadilly Circus. Though there was great controversy when the original Regency buildings were demolished and replaced earlier this century, it now seems a harmonious st of considerable character. The fine shops here definitely enhance its appeal, even if all you want to do is browse. Liberty's is a splendid, Art Nouveau, timbered building full of gorgeous soft furnishings and clothes, Oriental and leather goods, jewellery and a good gift department. Other high points include Mappin & Webb for fine china, glass, and jewellery; Hamleys, a marvellous toy shop (not cheap, though); Aquascutum, great for expensive, English classic clothes; Garrard's the Royal jewellers; and Waterford/Wedgwood, for lovely china and glass in quite a wide range of prices. The Old Coffee House in Beak St around the corner from here, and the Red Lion in Kingly St, are useful for lunch. Carnaby St, tucked away behind, has some rather florid men's shops but is mainly full of small boutiques with trendy accessories, leather goods and tacky souvenirs; not really worth seeking out, apart from 1960s nostalgia, though some good street-fashion houses seem to be coming back here.

⚫ 🔲 ⊖ **Bond St** MAYFAIR W of Regent St and N of Piccadilly (and only the shortest of strolls from them; Green Park tube station, nr the S end of Bond St, is also handy) is mostly a quietly discreet area of elegant town houses, smart, well established hotels, and richly unobtrusive offices. It lets its hair down in SHEPHERD MARKET, a lively and colourful place, no longer a market but busy with cafés, good wine bars and pubs (the Bunch of Grapes and King's Arms), and little lanes to wander down. Despite their famous names, Berkeley Sq and Grosvenor Sq don't have any special appeal for visitors. Bond St with its continuation New Bond St is the area's main st for SHOPPING, though unless you want to spend a great deal of money on designer clothes and shoes, jewellery or Oriental rugs this is likely to be confined to the window. There are quite a few art and antique galleries, and a good indoor antique market (124 New Bond St). Asprey's is a remarkable place, with the most expensive fantasies created in rich and beautiful materials around the most everyday objects – if you've always wanted a diamond-studded, gold and titanium potato-peeler, this is where you're most likely to find it. Sotheby's auction rooms are fascinating to wander around. Other small and prestigious art galleries are dotted throughout Mayfair, particularly in nearby Dover St and Cork St; Grays antique market, off 58 Davies St, has hundreds of indoor stalls. South Audley St has Hobbs of Mayfair, a delicious, smart delicatessen, and Thomas Goode, a magnificent glass and china shop. Higgins in Duke St is the Queen's coffee-man. The best Mayfair pub is the Red Lion in Waverton St.

🔲 WALLACE COLLECTION (Hertford House, Manchester Sq – across Oxford St) Excellent art collection, beautifully displayed in an elegant, 18th-c house – once used as the Spanish Embassy. It's visually very seductive, with luscious paintings from the French school by Watteau, Boucher and Fragonard, great Canalettos, fine works by Rembrandt, Rubens and Van Dyck,

and works by British painters; also furniture – mostly 18th-c French, a notable assemblage of Sèvres porcelain, Italian majolica, and an amazing array of arms and armour, both Oriental and European; it's rarely busy. Shop, disabled access with prior warning; cl am Sun, 24–26 Dec, Good Fri, 1 Jan, May Day bank hol; 0171-935 0687; free.
! ▣ ✆ **Marble Arch** is useful for SPEAKER'S CORNER in Hyde Park, where every Sun morning you can still hear impassioned diatribes on all sorts of causes – or indeed on nothing at all. Also on Sun you can see what's probably the longest, free, open-air art exhibition in the world, with the work of 300 artists and craftsmen laid out along the park railings on Bayswater Rd; the Swan opposite gives a pleasant break. The HYDE PARK RIDING STABLES (Bathurst Mews) can organise horse-riding in the park; 0171-262 3791; £25 an hour. The tube station – with so many exits it's a real initiative test finding your way out – is also handy for Oxford St.

Where to eat

NICO AT NINETY 90 Park Lane W1 0171-409 1290 Nico Ladenis is one of the country's best-known chefs, and in this latest venture his legendary food is as sophisticated as ever; cl am Sat, Sun, 23 Dec–2 Jan; children over 7; disabled access. **£63 dinner, lunch £36.75**. There's also NICO CENTRAL 35 Great Portland St W1 0171-436 8846; cl am Sat, Sun, 23 Dec–2 Jan. **£33**; and SIMPLY NICO 48a Rochester Row SW1 0171-630 8061 – same closing hours. **£24.15**.

ALASTAIR LITTLE 49 Frith St W1 0171-734 5183 Beautifully presented, imaginative modern cooking in a very popular, unpretentious restaurant; fine wines; cl am Sat, Sun, bank hols. **£47.25**.

MIYAMA 38 Clarges St W1 0171-499 2443 Restful Japanese restaurant with carefully prepared, delicious food served by courteous, efficient staff in national costume – a favourite with Japanese over here; downstairs are private rooms, and a teppan-yaki counter; cl Christmas, New Year, bank hols; disabled access. **£38.85 dinner**; the set lunches are extremely good value at around **£19**.

GAY HUSSAR 2 Greek St W1 0171-437 0973 Hungarian restaurant still popular with literati and publishers even though most have moved out of Soho, with bags of atmosphere (downstairs has the most) and generous helpings of good, authentic food; cl Sun, bank hols. **£35**.

BISTROT BRUNO 63 Frith St W1 0171-734 4545 Extremely good, innovative food in a delightfully decorated restaurant – lots of reworking of traditional dishes and fine fresh fish; cl am Sat, Sun. **£28.50/£12.50**.

MON PLAISIR 21 Monmouth St WC2 0171-836 7243 Good-value, well prepared French food in this busy bistro, popular for pre-theatre meals; cl am Sat, all Sun, bank hols; partial disabled access. **£28**.

RULES 35 Maiden Lane WC2 0171-836 5314 Smart, very British, old restaurant – popular with the Establishment – serving extremely good English food inc fine game and oysters in season; cl 5 days over Christmas; disabled access. **£27, weekend 3-course lunch £15.95**.

SIMPSON'S 100 The Strand WC2 0171-836 9112 Marvellously old-fashioned place with traditional English cooking inc nursery puddings, and roasts carved as you want them at your table on silver-domed trolleys; all very decorous – the surroundings and atmosphere more memorable than the food; cl 25–26 Dec, 1 Jan, Good Fri; disabled access. **£25l£3.50/£10**.

FORTNUM & MASON 181 Piccadilly W1 0171-734 8040 On the corner of the famous store, with a separate entrance, the Fountain Restaurant with its attractive murals is spacious, airy and very civilised – the perfect place for tea (though they also do good breakfasts and brunch); cl Sun, bank hols; disabled access. **£20l£3.50/£6**.

CORK & BOTTLE 44–46 Cranbourn St WC2 0171-734 6592 Popular, basement wine bar, with good food inc interesting salads and unusual hot dishes;

cheerful service, and very well chosen wines – especially Australian; cl 25–26 Dec, 1 Jan. **£19**/£6.95.

TAPPIT HEN 5 William IV St WC2 0171-836 9839 Cosy and atmospheric little wine bar, very old-fashioned feeling, with decent snacks and good-value wines – excellent for a quick, pre-theatre, light supper (the smoked salmon sandwiches are lovely) or lunch; there's also a downstairs restaurant; cl Sat, Sun, bank hols. **£18**|£3/£5.

MUSEUM OF MANKIND CAFE, Café de Colombia, 6 Burlington Gardens W1 0171-287 8148 Smart, no-smoking café with freshly prepared food, inc fine coffee and morning/afternoon cakes; cl pm, am Sun; disabled access. **£17.50**/£6.95.

I VESPRI 33 Southampton St WC2 0171-379 7585 Comfortable and as thoroughly Italian as you'd want; cl Sun, bank hols; disabled access. **£14.70**|£2/£6.50.

GABYS 30 Charing Cross Rd WC2 0171-836 4233 Ideal for a quick snack before the theatre, with promptly served, perfect salt beef sandwiches and other good snacks, generous wine, too; very friendly and popular with actors. **£13.20**|£3/£4.80.

POONS 27 Lisle St WC2 0171-437 4549 WC2 Atmospheric, unlicensed and unmodernised Chinese restaurant with extremely good-value, tasty food; cl Good Fri, 24–26 Dec; **£12.60**|£1.75/£5.75. Other branches (more modern and expensive) at 4 Leicester St WC2 0171-437 1528 and 41 King St WC2 0171-240 1743.

CAFE IN THE CRYPT St Martin-in-the-Fields, Trafalgar Sq WC2 0171-839 4342 Good, freshly prepared food as well as a shop, art gallery (frequent exhibitions) and brass-rubbing centre; cl Sun, am Good Fri, 25–26 Dec, pm 1 Jan. **£12**|£2.55/£5.95.

BUNJIES COFFEE HOUSE 27 Litchfield St WC2 0171-240 1796 Cosy basement café with good vegetarian food; cl Sun. **£10**/£3.50.

FOOD FOR THOUGHT 31 Neal St WC2 0171-836 0239 Long-established and consistently good, unlicensed vegetarian restaurant, with a take-away service upstairs and communal eating at long tables downstairs – you can now also eat at tables outside; no corkage; cl pm Sun; 24 Dec–2 Jan. **£6.80**|£1.90/£2.80.

WESTMINSTER

Westminster, the site of the Court and the seat of government, has plenty to see related to the long and varied history of both monarchy and government. It's a pleasant area to walk around, much of it with only light traffic, and with few shops to add extra people to the wide pavements. Two parks bring a further feeling of space and grandeur.

Where to stay

GORING 15 Beeston Pl, Grosvenor Gardens, SW1W OJW 0171-396 9000 **£163**; 79 individually decorated rms. Built in 1910 by the grandfather of the present Mr Goring, this family-run and very English hotel has a particularly welcoming atmosphere (many of the staff have been there for years), very good modern cooking in the elegant restaurant, a comfortable lounge for afternoon tea, an airy cocktail bar, and a pretty garden; disabled access.

STAKIS ST ERMINS 2 Caxton St SW1H OQW 0171-222 7888 **£122**; 291 rms. Opulent Edwardian hotel with a handsome staircase, ornate plasterwork, antiques and elegant furniture in the luxurious day rooms, fine food in two restaurants, and helpful staff.

TOPSHAMS EBURY COURT 24–32 Ebury St SW1W 0LU 0171-730 8147 *****£115**; 42 cosy rms, most with own bthrm. Small, charmingly old-fashioned hotel made up of several town houses; friendly country house atmosphere, a new downstairs bar, attractive lounges, good food in the elegant restaurant, and decent wines; cl Christmas; disabled access.

ROYAL HORSEGUARDS THISTLE 2 Whitehall Court SW1 4HP 0171-839 3400 £112; 376 spacious rms. Comfortable, traditional hotel ideally placed for the area's sights and close to theatres, with elegant public rooms and a fine, marbled entrance; foyer, coffee shop, bar and restaurant; disabled access.

RUBENS 39–41 Buckingham Palace Rd SW1W OPS 0171-834 6600 £100w; 189 well equipped rms. Opposite Buckingham Palace and close to Victoria Station, this attractive hotel has comfortable day rooms that include an airy lounge with views of the Royal Mews, a restful library, and a cocktail bar with resident pianist.

To see and do

⛩🔲⊖ St James's Park BUCKINGHAM PALACE This is the third year that the public have been able to go inside the Palace, a move that's quickly proved popular; it's open for only eight weeks, but in 1994 during that period had 420,000 visitors. The main attraction is that this is where the Queen actually lives – her official London residence, where she meets other heads of state; the Royal Standard flies above it when she's home. But beyond that, while perhaps not ultimately the most satisfying of the royal palaces, it does pile a magnificent series of opulent sights into your walk through the state rooms. It's not a guided tour, and there aren't many clues to help you, so it's definitely worth buying the guide book and boning up on some of the things you're going to see before you go. The great inner courtyard is quite a surprise, in many ways more genuinely majestic and certainly more elegant than the familiar, more modern, classical façade. Once up the spectacular Grand Staircase you are into the throne room and other chambers of state where the predominant impression is of gold, red and splendour. The highlight comes next: the beautiful Picture Gallery, 150ft long and filled with paintings from the royal collection. The range of rooms following this, overlooking the garden (and perhaps a glimpse of a full-dressed footman walking corgis), were designed by Nash, and have plenty of interesting and even ironic touches. Theoretically you see all this at your own pace, but in practice you're likely to be carried along in the stream of other people, and you won't get much of a chance to linger. Tickets last year were sold each

day from a little booth on the corner of St James's Park, though as we went to press they hadn't decided how it would be organised for 1995, so best to check on 0171-493 3175; you may be able to buy tickets in advance. Busy shop, disabled access (and advanced booking for disabled); open Aug–Sept; £8.

The former chapel of the palace is now the QUEEN'S GALLERY, showing a changing selection of more of the magnificent paintings and other works of art from the royal collection. It's open every day exc Mon, Mar–22 Dec, cl am Sun; £3. The ROYAL MEWS lets you view the State Coaches, private driving carriages and even sleighs of the royal family, as well as the immaculately turned out Windsor greys and Cleveland bay carriage horses. Shop, disabled access; open pm Weds all year, plus pm Tues and Thurs Apr–Sept; £3. At the grand front palace gates, the guards still keep their unflinchingly solemn positions: you can watch the CHANGING OF THE GUARD every day (every other day in winter) at 11.30am – get there early to ensure a good view; the ceremony may be late or even cancelled in exceptionally wet weather.

❊⛩🔲 Walking through ST JAMES'S PARK is the best approach to the palace (you can get there more quickly, though less attractively, from Victoria). The oldest of the royal parks in London, it was drained and converted into a deer park by Henry VIII, redesigned in the style of Versailles by order of Charles II (who often went for walks through it), and then recreated by Nash for George IV this is the park which we see today, its relaxing lakeside environment particularly enjoyed by lunch-breaking office workers, with a brass band in summer. On Sun traffic is barred from its roads. Running all the way along the top of the park is THE MALL, the 3,412-ft-long ceremonial route laid out from 1660 by Charles II, with the palace at one end and the magnificent Admiralty Arch at the other. In between, as well as various grand buildings and government departments, are a couple of good, contemporary art galleries, with various changing exhibitions at the MALL GALLERIES (cl 22 Dec–4 Jan, 0171-930 6844 for exhibition information; *£2), and a wonderfully informal, little restaurant and bar at the ICA which, with exhibitions and cinemas too, is an excellent place to spend time 0171-930 0493; £1.50 day membership.

⌂ ⊖ Green Park ST JAMES'S PALACE Altogether more domestic-looking than Buckingham Palace (and much older), much of this palace is still given over to apartments for members of the royal family and their officials, so isn't open to the public. It does provide another good spot though for the CHANGING OF THE GUARD, with guardsmen leaving here at 11.15am to go the palace, and coming back at around 12.10. Charles I spent his last night here before walking across to Whitehall (see below) for his execution.

⌨ The area around St James's St and Pall Mall seems to have more gentlemen's clubs than anything else, but there is a good number of interesting, upmarket SHOPS too: handmade shoes at Lobb's, hats at Lock's, wonderful antiques at Spink's (King St), fishing equipment at Hardy's, and fine wines at Berry Bros & Rudd. This last is the only shop in London still to look both inside and out just as it did in the early 19th c, and they are very helpful even if you want just one humble bottle. Farlow's on Pall Mall have everything you might need for that expedition up the Limpopo or into the Gobi Desert. Christie's Auction Galleries are on King St (the friendly Red Lion, off here in Crown Passage, is useful for a snack), and there are some other top-of-the-market antique and book

shops nearby, up Duke St for instance.
❀ Walking up St James's St, most streets to the left will take you to GREEN PARK, the smallest of the parks in central London. It is not a formal garden but, watered by the Tyburn stream which runs below the park, does stay genuinely green in summer when London's other grassy spaces are getting dry and dusty.

✝ ⏾ ⊖ Westminster WESTMINSTER ABBEY There's been a church on this site since Saxon times, but it was Edward the Confessor who transformed it into the crowning place of English kings. Erected in the 13th c on the site of his original, it is surely one of the most impressive pieces of architecture to survive from the Middle Ages. Recent restoration and clean-ups have left it looking especially splendid at the moment, and certainly a quite different colour from the one visitors were used to. Although building took about 100 years, the original design was kept throughout, so that, with its huge rose window and flying buttresses, this church is closer in design to French Gothic architecture than any other English church. Hawksmoor designed the harmonious 18th-c addition of the W towers. Look out for the superb 13th-c sculpture and the arcading around the walls in the Chapel of St Faith. The church and its tranquil, much less visited cloisters are well worth dawdling over, but for many the main attractions are the royal chapels and loosely named Poets' Corner (it takes in historical and cultural figures from Chaucer to Handel), for which you have to pay. In addition to Edward the Confessor, pretty well every king and queen up to George II is buried here; the chapel for Henry VII is particularly impressive, and there are splendid tombs erected by James I for his mother Mary, Queen of Scots and his predecessor Elizabeth I. There's a brass rubbing centre in the cloisters. Shop, disabled access (but not to Henry VII chapel); royal chapels cl Sun, and between 2.45 and 3.45 Sat; church and cloisters free, chapels £4. If you're interested in history, the MUSEUM in the crypt underneath shouldn't be missed – it has effigies of many ancestors of the royal family made from their death masks, and often wearing their own clothes; £1. Adjacent ST MARGARET'S CHURCH is worth a look too; the official church of the House of Commons, it has some exceptional 16th-c Dutch stained glass, and Sir Walter Raleigh is buried here.

🏠☋ HOUSES OF PARLIAMENT (St Margaret St) These buildings are now of course the main seat of British government, but until Henry VIII moved to Whitehall Palace in 1529, the site was the main residence of the monarch. The medieval palace was destroyed by a catastrophic fire in 1834, but even today when they answer the phone they'll call it the Palace of Westminster. The present 19th-c building was designed by Charles Barry, though the Gothic detail which has given so much life to what would otherwise be rather a tiresomely deadpan, classical façade is by Pugin. One end of the extraordinary 940-ft structure finishes in a lofty Victorian tower (which flies the Union Jack when Parliament is in session), and the other in the clock tower which contains BIG BEN, the 3½-ton bell whose sonorous hourly rings are one of the best-known sounds in the world. Inside, over two miles of passages link the central hall and two chambers – the Houses of Lords and Commons to the N and S of the building respectively. To gain entrance to the Strangers' Galleries queue 5.30pm Mon–Thurs or 9.30am Fri – or arrange it first with your MP. A letter from your MP can also give access to what's called the Line of Route, going through both Houses and the Members' Lobby and Divisions Lobby, to Westminster Hall, from 1224–1882 the chief law court of the country. It witnessed such trials as those of Sir Thomas More and Charles I, and organising admission (not easy) is worth it even just to admire the magnificent hammerbeam roof, the earliest surviving example of its kind. There's an exhibition on Parliament's history across the road in the 14th-c JEWEL TOWER. Cl 24–26 Dec, 1 Jan; 0171-222 2219; £2.10. The Westminster

Arms in Storeys Gate across the square is the best pub nearby.

☋🏠 CABINET WAR ROOMS (King Charles St) Intriguing series of 21 rooms built to provide Sir Winston Churchill, the War Cabinet and his Chiefs of Staff with a safe place from which to plan their strategies during WWII. The Cabinet Room, Map Room and Prime Minister's Room were preserved intact from the end of the war, and the other rooms have been authentically restored since. Quite basic, the rooms are very evocative, with authentic sound effects adding to the atmosphere. Shop, disabled access; cl 24–26 Dec, 1 Jan; 0171-930 6961; £3.90. In the middle of Whitehall, the CENOTAPH, designed by Lutyens, is a more sombre reminder of this century's two world wars. Just along from here is DOWNING ST, where the Prime Minister lives at No 10 and the Chancellor of the Exchequer at No 11. You can't get past the gates, but you can at least have a passing look at its surprisingly modest buildings.

🏠🖼 BANQUETING HOUSE (Whitehall) This is the only surviving part of the Palace of Whitehall, designed by Inigo Jones and built in 1619; it was a royal residence until late that century. The severely classical hall is pretty much all there is to see, but an especially entertaining Walkman tour and good audio-visual exhibition maintain the interest for quite some time. The highlight is the wonderful ceiling painted by Rubens, commissioned by Charles I to glorify the Stuart monarchy. They've helpfully put mirrored tables underneath so you can study the detail without straining your neck; don't lean on these though – they're on wheels and liable to speed off like an errant supermarket trolley. Snacks, shop; cl Sun, 24–26 Dec, 1 Jan, Good Fri, and for some government functions; 0171-839 7569; *£2.90. Charles I was executed here, and it was also the site of his son's restoration. A survival of the kind of royal pageantry this area was once full of can be seen in the daily MOUNTING THE GUARD ceremony at Horse Guards Parade opposite, 11am Mon–Sat and 10am Sun. The partly

13th-c Silver Cross is an interesting old pub.

✝ ✿ ⊖ **Victoria** Not much to detain the visitor around here, but it is worth taking a detour from the glassy, governmental cliffs of Victoria St to the Byzantine splendour of the Roman Catholic WESTMINSTER CATHEDRAL, which offers the best views over central London from its tall tower (lift). Built in 1903, the red-brick building is an astonishing structure, very un-English, with handsome mosaics and marblework in its richly ornamental interior. Behind here in Vincent Sq, the Royal Horticultural Society have regular flower shows filled with beautifully arranged displays by specialist nurserymen; 0171-828 1744 for information. At other times their halls may be used for other exhibitions.

🅐 🏛 ⊖ **Pimlico** TATE GALLERY (Millbank) Designed in classical style to house the collection of Sir Henry Tate, the sugar refiner, and now containing the national collection of British art. It covers all important British artists for the past 450 years, with a large number of works by Turner and Constable, and plenty of contemporary sculpture. The collection has been enlarged this century to embrace foreign 20th-c art, especially French Impressionists and Post-Impressionists. Major exhibitions for 1995 look at the paintings of Willem de Koonig (16 Feb–7 May), the body in contemporary art (15 Jun–3 Sept), and painting in Tudor and Jacobean England (from 12 Oct). Meals, snacks, shop, disabled access; cl am Sun, 24–26 Dec, 1 Jan, Good Fri, May Day; 0171-821 7128; free (exc for major exhibitions). Though the Tate Gallery restaurant is a particularly good one, you might find the Morpeth Arms nearby useful, with its views of the stunning new MI6 building across the river.

Where to eat

EBURY WINE BAR 139 Ebury St SW1 0171-730 5447 Good imaginative food in this tiny, bustling wine bar. **£27.50**|£3.95/£7.95.

TATE GALLERY Millbank SW1 0171-834 6754 Smart and upmarket restaurant with a fine range of traditional dishes as well as some imaginative ones; good, classic wine list; cl Sun and pm, 24–26 Dec, 1 Jan, Good Fri, May Day; disabled access. **£26.50**/£7.85.

KEN LO'S MEMORIES OF CHINA 67 Ebury St SW1 0171-730 7734 Fine Chinese food in an attractively simple restaurant, with interesting set menus and courteous staff; cl am Sun, bank hols; disabled access. **£26.25**/£8.40.

FOOTSTOOL RESTAURANT St John's Smith Sq SW1 0171-222 2779 Converted church in this pleasant, political square, offering good, interesting food in the crypt; chamber music most evenings upstairs, also some lunchtimes; restaurant pm only (cl alternate Thurs); cl am wknd. **£21**/£6.30.

ICA The Mall SW1 0171-930 0493 Informal, serve-yourself restaurant with a short choice of good-value, honest food; cl pm, Christmas; disabled access; day membership £1.50. **£13.45**|£1.50/£4.95.

KNIGHTSBRIDGE, CHELSEA AND KENSINGTON

This area is one of contrasts – to the west are the looming Victorian façades of the various great museums, the splendid beauty of the former royal apartments of Kensington Palace, and the less visited charms of Leighton House and Linley Sambourne House, while to the south-east a placid network of clean-cut, subdued, Georgian terraced houses suddenly gives way to the ostentatious bustle of the King's Rd.

The shopping opportunities vary as widely – from the elegant materialism of Harrods to the hubbub of the Portobello Rd market, with a liberal dose of interesting and unusual antique shops.

Where to stay

BASIL STREET HOTEL 8 Basil St SW3 1AH 0171-581 3311 **£177**; 93 pleasant, decent-sized rms, most with own bthrm. Handy for Harrods and Hyde Park, this privately owned Edwardian hotel has a relaxed atmosphere, antiques, fine carpets and paintings in the public rooms, a panelled restaurant with reliably good food, a cellar wine bar, coffee shop and ladies' club; helpful, courteous service.

GORE 189 Queen's Gate SW7 5EX 0171-584 6601 **£160**; 54 individually decorated rms. In a tree-lined avenue and made up of two Victorian houses, this grand place is full of antiques and fine paintings, lovely furniture in walnut and mahogany, lots of big plants, a very informal and relaxed atmosphere, very good breakfasts and two bustling restaurants; cl 24–25 Dec.

NUMBER SIXTEEN 14–17 Sumner Pl SW7 3EG 0171-589 5232 **£145**; 36 individually decorated, pretty rms. Attractive terrace of early Victorian town houses with pretty flowering pots outside, particularly friendly, helpful staff, antiques and a restful atmosphere in the lounge (where there is an honesty bar) and drawing room, an open fire and fresh flowers, and a conservatory that opens on to a secluded walled garden; continental breakfasts served in own room; children over 12.

FENJA 69 Cadogan Gardens SW3 2RB 0171-589 7333 **£144**; 12 rms named after a famous writer or painter who lived nearby. Comfortable town house with fine paintings and prints, antiques and fresh flowers, an open fire in the drawing room, and a restful atmosphere; numerous restaurants nearby for meals (light meals can be served in room).

CONRAD Chelsea Harbour SW10 0XG 0171-823 3000 **£140w**; 160 suites with a spacious, light, living room area, current hardback novels, and free caviar where other hotels give you a couple of biscuits. American-owned, Europe's first purpose-built, luxury 'suite hotel' is tucked away in the quiet modern enclave of the Chelsea Harbour development and overlooks its small marina; good food served in the Brasserie (harbour views) or the Long Gallery, friendly service, an evening pianist, and a health club; disabled access.

L'HOTEL 28 Basil St SW3 1AT 071-589 6286 **£125**; 12 well equipped rms. Small, family-owned, French-style city hotel, close to Harrods and above the neatly kept, well run Metro wine bar where English and continental breakfasts are served, as well as good, modern French café food; friendly staff; disabled access.

HOTEL 167 167 Old Brompton Rd SW5 OAN 0171-373 0672 **£75**; 19 attractive, individually decorated rms. Lovely, little Victorian terraced house, with continental breakfasts being served in one's own room or the elegant, little dining room; light meals available.

LEXHAM 32–38 Lexham Gardens W8 5JU 0171-373 6571 **£62.50**; 66 rms, most with own bthrm. Good-value hotel run by the same family for nearly 40 years and set in a surprisingly peaceful square, with fine breakfasts in the restaurant overlooking the pleasant garden and friendly, hard-working staff; cl 22 Dec–2 Jan; disabled access.

To see and do

🏛 ✿ ⊖ **High St Kensington**
KENSINGTON PALACE (Kensington Gardens) A once-humble town house, remodelled by Sir Christopher Wren and then enlarged by William Kent, the birthplace of Queen Victoria and

principal, private, royal residence until the death of George II. It's now the London home of the Princess of Wales, Princess Margaret and Prince and Princess Michael of Kent. Some of the rooms are quite magnificent, with elaborate furnishings and decor, while others are interesting for their comparatively restrained understatement; a couple of the older ones could even be described as downright poky. Make sure you look up at the ceilings: some are exquisitely painted, inc an effective trompe-l'oeil dome (a couple of the patterns transfer very nicely to stationery in the gift shop). Also, pictures and furniture from the royal collection, and the court dress collection with changing displays of the many gorgeous costumes worn at royal ceremonies since 1750. The guides are very friendly and know their stuff. Snacks, shop, disabled access to ground floor only; cl 24–26 Dec, 1 Jan, Good Fri; 0171-937 9561; £4.50. Surrounding the palace, KENSINGTON GARDENS are well worth a wander, though less lush than neighbouring Hyde Park. There's a toy boats lake, playground, a fetching statue of Peter Pan, and a tree trunk carved with all sorts of little painted animals. On a sunny day you could be forgiven for thinking you'd stumbled on a beach club, as the grass is covered with prone bodies soaking up the radiation.

♨ ❀ COMMONWEALTH INSTITUTE (Kensington High St) An ambitious transformation, already under way, could when completed in 1996 make the institute one of London's most dynamic attractions, with a host of hi-tech interactive displays and a dazzling, audio-visual spectacular as the climax. In the meantime, you can still see their more traditional exhibitions on the life and culture of members of the Commonwealth – a bit dry, but astonishingly comprehensive, and fascinating if you allow enough time to explore properly. Meals, snacks, shop, disabled access; cl am Sun, 23–27 Dec, 1 Jan, Good Fri, May Day; 0171-603 4535; *£1. Behind it down Holland Walk, HOLLAND PARK is one of London's lesser-known open spaces, a wooded park with peacocks, summer open-air theatre and airy restaurant.

♨ ▣ LEIGHTON HOUSE (12 Holland Park Rd) This splendid 19th-c house is a uniquely opulent monument to high Victorian art, its lavish decor and collections assembled by the first owner, Lord Leighton, former president of the Royal Academy. The centrepiece Arab Hall has a fountain and an almost dazzling assemblage of Islamic tiles, and there's a fine collection of paintings by Millais, Burne-Jones, and Leighton himself; the gardens are open in summer. Cl Sun, bank hols; 0171-602 3316; free. Another interesting period house nearby is LINLEY SAMBOURNE HOUSE (18 Stafford Terrace), the 19th-c home of the celebrated *Punch* cartoonist. Unchanged since then, it's a fascinating example of a Victorian town house, with a fine collection of his work. Open Weds and pm Sun, Mar–Oct; 0181-994 1019; *£3.

♨ Kensington High St is good for SHOPPING, especially if you consider yourself young and fashionable: Hyper Hyper is smart and designerish, Kensington Market more bohemian to say the least; cl Sun. Decent food pubs in this area include the Britannia (Allen St), Scarsdale Arms (Edwardes Sq), Windsor Castle (Campden Hill Rd; excellent courtyard garden) and (a walk up Kensington Church St, which has some interesting antique shops) the Churchill Arms – surprisingly good Thai food.

♨ ▣ ♠ ✝ ❀ ⊖ **South Kensington**
VICTORIA & ALBERT MUSEUM (Cromwell Rd) Britain's national museum of art and design is one of the finest in the world; it was founded in 1851 by Prince Albert, and houses all manner of decorative arts, from all ages and countries. The galleries run to over 7 miles, so you should find superb examples of whatever interests you – on the way to find them passing tantalising collections devoted to subjects you didn't even know existed. Highlights include the spectacular new glass gallery (with touch-screen computer displays), the world's greatest collection of Constables, and a splendid collection of dresses from the 17th c on. This year they plan to open a new Raphael gallery, and temporary exhibitions will focus on Wedgwood (Jun–Sept), and Jain Art from India (from Nov). Meals, snacks (they do a good Sun brunch with jazz), shop, disabled access; cl am Mon, 24–26 Dec, 1 Jan;

0171-938 8500; £4.50 voluntary donation. Nearby the Roman Catholic BROMPTON ORATORY has a heavy magnificence, sombre despite the pallor of its marble. Beside it the gardens of HOLY TRINITY BROMPTON – London's most fashionable and certainly most lively church – lead you into a very peaceful corner of residential London, with a decent pub in Ennismore Mews (the Ennismore Arms, which does Sun lunches).

NATURAL HISTORY MUSEUM (Cromwell Rd) This elaborate Romanesque building is a vast place covering 4 acres, with a huge range of informative and entertaining displays and activities: you can find out exactly what you look like inside. See creepy-crawlies clambering all over the place, or meet a life-size blue whale. It's been very successfully jazzed up in recent years, and everyone who goes gets a real kick out of it. This was where people used to go to see the dinosaurs, and they're still at the forefront of that fad, with a hi-tech exhibition that even has robotic versions of the monsters. The Earth Galleries (entrance in Exhibition Rd), the largest exhibition on basic earth science in the world, include a piece of the moon and an earthquake simulator. Meals, snacks, shop, disabled access; cl 24–26 Dec, 1 Jan, Good Fri, May Day bank hol; 0171-938 9123; £5.

SCIENCE MUSEUM (Exhibition Rd) Like its neighbour the Natural History Museum, this is somewhere you shouldn't have any trouble getting children interested in. Over 600 working exhibits whizz you through all aspects of science and industry, with the highlight perhaps the very successful Launch Pad, a hi-tech, interactive gallery where you can have great fun carrying out your own experiments. Exhibits elsewhere range from Stephenson's *Rocket* to the Apollo 10 space capsule, with lively displays on food, flight and pharmaceuticals. Various temporary exhibitions, and special events like their all-night camp-ins – which enthral children. Meals, snacks, shop, disabled access; cl 24–26 Dec; 0171-938 8111; £4.50. If you plan a surfeit of museuming, you can get a cut-price collective ticket for all South Ken museums.

The ROYAL ALBERT HALL in Kensington Gore is the home of the summer Promenade Concerts and many other concerts throughout the year; finished in 1871, this huge, oval arena was built in honour of Prince Albert. Below the massive, metal and glass domed roof is a terracotta frieze which shows the progress of Man in the arts and sciences throughout the ages. Before modern technology got to grips with its acoustics, the hall used to be famous for its echo – it was said that this was the only hall where you could hear the works of modern composers twice. Across the road should be the ALBERT MEMORIAL, but, as ever, it was still rather pointlessly covered up as we went to press.

Knightsbridge HARRODS is a wonderful place to browse, and has most things anyone could want – there's even a personal shopper available to help you choose. But it's the food halls that visitors to London really enjoy; they're divided into fruit and veg, an interesting delicatessen, grocery, meat, poultry, fish (the display of fresh fish at the end of the room is legendary), bread and cakes, flowers, and wines – and the downstairs pantry is not as expensive as you might think. The Scotch House, almost opposite, is not cheap but does have lovely cashmeres, fine woollens, kilts and so forth; the Paxton's Head nearby is a useful dining pub, as is the King George IV tucked away just behind in Montpelier Sq. Harvey Nichols is a stylish department store, strong on classic English clothes and high fashion. Sloane St, stretching down from here, starts with a run of very expensive, chic clothes shops and jewellers. In the handsome terraces on the far side of Sloane St can be found the charming Grenadier (Wilton Row; no food in the bar, but a snug little restaurant) and the countryish Nag's Head (Kinnerton St).

Hyde Park Corner 340-acre HYDE PARK used to be a royal hunting park, and in 1851 was the site of the Great Exhibition. In the grounds of the park, nr the boating lake, is the SERPENTINE GALLERY, often with interesting exhibitions concentrating on younger contemporary artists – especially good for sculptural and allied arts; tel 0171-402 6075 to hear what's on. You can hire boats on the lake (from £5.50 an hour), or even swim in parts of it. At its bottom corner is the relentless torrent of traffic around Hyde Park Corner; the subway can bring you up nr the glittering neo-baroque gates erected in honour of the Queen Mother, or at the Duke of Wellington's elegant, former home APSLEY HOUSE. Designed by Robert Adam and containing some excellent paintings, this should reopen in Jun after a three-year restoration, though no firm details of dates and prices were available as we went to press; tel 0171-499 5676 to check.

🏠 ➔ **Sloane Sq** The heart of Chelsea, with Peter Jones, the mecca of the Sloanes, on the square itself (a sister department store of John Lewis, it's good value for money). Just around the corner, the Antelope in Eaton Terrace is a useful lunch stop. The bottom end of Sloane St has two interesting though expensive shops: Partridges, a fancy food shop, and the General Trading Company, with a fine collection of oddities, besides stylish kitchenware, soft furnishings, antiques, glass and so forth. Sloane Sq's most famous offshoot is the KING'S RD: not what it used to be, and a few places are now standing empty, though you can still find some really individual clothes and shoe shops, and three good antique markets (Chenil Galleries has some fine, specialist stalls; the other two go further down the price range but have interesting stuff). On you way along, refresh yourself at Henry J Beans (197 King's Rd; a rather trendy, American-style bar with good, quick snacks), La Bersagliera (a pleasantly clattery, matriarch-run pizza house just past Beaufort St) or the Sporting Page (Camera Pl/Limerston St). S from here, it's quite a short cut through to the Thames.

🏠 CARLYLE'S HOUSE (Cheyne Row) The home of the writer from 1834 till his death, with lots of letters and personal possessions, and an early piano played by Chopin. Cl Mon (exc bank hols), Tues, all Nov-Mar; £2.80; NT. The nearby King's Head & Eight Bells is almost villagey.

🏠 ❀ THE ROYAL HOSPITAL (Royal Hospital Rd) Christopher Wren's most glorious secular building, which still houses some 400 Chelsea Pensioners. Cl 12–2pm, am Sat, Sun (though you can go to the full dress service in the chapel at 11am on Sun, Christmas); free. The adjacent riverside Ranelagh Gardens are the site of the Chelsea Flower Show.

🏺 NATIONAL ARMY MUSEUM (Royal Hospital Rd) Surprisingly little visited but well and honestly presented – the history of the men of the British, Indian and Colonial armies from 1485, told with photographs, models, uniforms, prints and other mementos. The paintings include portraits by Gainsborough and Reynolds. They've recently opened a gallery on the Victorian army, and another housing the collections of the former Museum of the Women's Royal Army Corps. Snacks, shop, disabled access; cl 24–26 Dec, 1 Jan, Good Fri, May Day; 0171-730 0717; free.

❀ CHELSEA PHYSIC GARDEN (Royal Hospital Rd) If you're tired of the braying crowds of Chelsea, take refuge here. A real haven of peace – it was started in 1673 and forms the second-oldest botanic garden in the country. Its aim was to provide and study the plants used in medicine by the Society of Apothecaries, and by the late 18th c it was famous for its rare and unusual plants. It's still used for botanical and medicinal research, but is also full of lovely and unusual plants which thrive here in Thames-side London's warm microclimate, inc an ancient, fruiting olive tree. Snacks, shop, disabled access; open pm Weds and Sun Apr–Oct; 0171-352 5646; *£3.50. Where the road joins the river embankment, Old Church St, past the elegant Chelsea Old Church, takes you quickly to a good food pub – the Front Page.

🏠 The Pimlico Rd has an interesting collection of antique and other small SHOPS (and Peter's Restaurant, a very good-value, all-day, Italian-run café which has been a taxi-drivers' haunt for 20 years or more). The Orange Brewery here is a pub with an attached pie shop, and brews its own beers. Keep on along to Ebury Bridge for a classic photographic view of partly dismantled Battersea Power Station, beyond a sinuous network of railway lines.

🏠 ➔ **Fulham Broadway** is the best station for the clutch of good-value ANTIQUE SHOPS towards the bottom end of the Fulham Rd. You can quickly cut through to the interesting series of more specialised antique shops on the New King's Rd, some of which yield unexpected treasures: lovely old clocks, model ships (some 6ft long), garden furniture, and ornaments going back to the 16th c. Two shops specialise expensively but magnificently in mirrors, and there's also Christopher Wray's enormous lighting emporium which largely fuelled the vogue in Tiffany-style lamps and has almost any sort of lamp fitting you could possibly want. Not far from here, CHELSEA HARBOUR is an elaborate monument to the recession, a smart, waterside shopping centre almost like a ghost town, with untenanted shops and little action except for popular Deals Restaurant and the Canteen (see **Where to eat** section below), and the cheerfully, relaxed Matts café. Children like the glass-sided lifts which swoop up into the big dome. There's also a marina, where on Sun afternoons they often have jazz. The tube station is also handy for Chelsea Football Club, and the unfrequented, rather melancholy tranquillity of the somewhat overgrown BROMPTON CEMETERY. Nr here the Fox & Pheasant in Billing St makes a pleasant break.

Where to eat

TANTE CLAIRE 68 Royal Hospital Rd SW3 0171-352 6045 Exceptionally fine, modern French cooking in Pierre Koffmann's stylish restaurant – the lunchtime set menu is reasonably priced and very popular; courteous service, and some good-value, French country wines; jacket and tie are required; cl wknds, Christmas/New Year; children over 8. **£67 dinner, lunch £32**.

BIBENDUM 81 Fulham Rd SW3 0171-581 5817 Housed in the carefully renovated old Michelin building, this is a light, spacious and fashionable restaurant with excellent and enjoyable, robust French food – it's more elaborate in the evening; the downstairs oyster bar is very popular too; disabled access. **£60 dinner, lunch set menu £25**.

BLUE ELEPHANT 4–6 Fulham Broadway SW6 0171-385 6595 Luxurious Thai food eaten amongst waterfalls and exotic jungle greenery, with produce flown in weekly from Thailand; the set meals are better value; cl am Sat, 24–27 Dec; disabled access. **£35**.

BOMBAY BRASSERIE Courtfield Close, Courtfield Rd SW7 0171-370 4444 Big restaurant and conservatory with grand, colonial-style furnishings, very good Indian food using recipes from all over India (lots of vegetarian dishes), and courteous, helpful staff; it's cheaper at lunchtime when there's a buffet; cl 25–26 Dec; disabled access. **£32**.

CANTEEN Chelsea Harbour SW10 0171-351 7330 Airy and rather functional inside, but pleasantly so, and informal, with your money clearly going on food quality – which is excellent – instead of extra waiters or excessively plush surroundings; you may spot other trendy restaurateurs sitting chatting to the boss, Marco White; cl 4 days over Christmas. **£30/£10.50**.

CHUTNEY MARY 535 King's Rd SW10 0171-351 3113 Interesting Anglo-Indian food in a light conservatory and two dining rooms, also a bar; buffet only Sun; disabled access. **£30|£4.95/£8.95**.

BILL BENTLEYS Beauchamp Pl SW3 0171-589 5080 Though there's a decent upstairs fish restaurant, the nicest place is the crowded little bar, very popular with well-off local residents for good wine, highly individual service and choice nibbles such as fresh ham or oysters; cl Sun, bank hols. **£27.50/£5.50**.

MR WING 242 Old Brompton Rd SW5 0171-370 4450 Opulent, impressive surroundings with plants and an aquarium, and very good Chinese food; disabled access. £25/£6.95.

JULIE'S 137 Portland Rd W11 0171-727 7985 Well run and most attractively decorated, long-standing wine bar with lots of different sitting areas, antiques, lovely flowers and plants; good, imaginative food, and friendly service; cl 4 days Christmas; £24.70, set lunch £12.05.

SAN FREDIANO 62 Fulham Rd SW3 0171-584 8375 Consistently good (and very popular) Italian food with lots of interesting daily specials; cl Sun, bank hols. £24.70/£7.35.

WODKA 12 St Albans Grove W8 0171-937 6513 There's a choice of 13 vodkas to accompany the authentic Polish food at this simple, pleasant restaurant; cl am Sat, am Sun, bank hols. £22.50/£8.

DEALS Chelsea Harbour SW10 0171-352 5887 Bustling café-restaurant with good food ranging from hamburgers to sizzle platters and some Far Eastern touches (the Japanese vinaigrette is recommended and the prawns are delicious), generous glasses of decent house wine, nice cocktails, and very friendly service; best at lunchtime when it's less frenetic; great for children – especially Sun – when they have a magician going from table to table, plus a face-painter; cl Christmas; disabled access. £20/£5.75.

WINE GALLERY 49 Hollywood Rd SW10 0171-353 7572 Consistently good, nicely presented food, fairly priced wines, and helpful, friendly service; for fine-weather eating – an attractive, back courtyard with an enormous black cat; quieter at lunchtime; cl bank hols. £20|£3.50/£5.50.

LADBROKE ARMS 54 Ladbroke Rd W11 0171-727 6648 Unusually good, interesting food for a pub – proper home cooking inc traditional, Sunday family lunches; comfortable, with an open fire; cl pm 25 Dec; disabled access. £19|£2.50.

SCANDIES WINE BAR 4 Kynance Pl SW7 0171-589 3659 Relaxed wine bar with good food and friendly service; Sunday newspapers, and unlimited coffee; cl am Sat; disabled access. £18/£3.25.

ADAMS CAFE 77 Askew Rd W12 0181-743 0572 Decorated with lots of colourful Tunisian tiles, ceramics and plates, this daytime café turns into an evening Tunisian restaurant with Tunisian wine (sole importers to UK); cl Sun, bank hols, 2 wks Aug. £14/£6.

KALAMARES MICRO 66 Inverness Mews W2 0171-727 9122 (Not to be confused with its larger sister restaurant at No 76). Tiny, close-packed, authentically Greek restaurant (though all the waitresses seem to be Czech), with very good, cheap food and friendly service; unlicensed, take your own wine; cl Sun, am, and bank hols; £12.50/£5.50.

LUBA'S BISTRO 6 Yeoman's Row, off Brompton Rd SW3 0171-589 2950 Unlicensed, very long-standing, Russian evening restaurant in a converted stable; with gingham tablecloths, candles in bottles, friendly Russian or Polish waitresses, and good, generously served food. £12.

VICTORIA & ALBERT MUSEUM Museum Rd SW7 0171-581 2159 Tasty, good-value food in an airily spacious restaurant; newspapers to read and jazz brunches Sun morning; cl pm; disabled access. £7.50/£3.60.

THE CITY AND EAST END

This is the country's financial hub. Although the City's buildings are for the most part Victorian and Edwardian, the ground-plan follows the narrow, twisting streets and alleys of medieval times, and some churches and a handful of other buildings also date from the medieval or Tudor period. Around St Paul's and the Tower, the layout is more open – and far less affected by the City's human tides: most of the rest of the area is packed with worried financial workers during week-days, then when they leave goes into a catatonic trance in the evening and at weekends.

Originally, particular streets came to be associated with particular crafts and trades, and this is reflected in street names throughout the City – Carter Lane, Hosier Lane, Cloth Fair, Ropemaker St, Milk St, Silk St, Coopers Lane and so forth. The great City livery companies representing the various trades have effectively ruled the City for 800 years or more, with the right to appoint the Lord Mayor who heads the Corporation of London. This form of local government is quite different from that of any other town in Britain (and it certainly works – here, you won't find the dirt and dereliction that marks most other parts of London). Now, many of the Livery Companies have only a tenuous connection with the original crafts involved in their trades. But in a couple of places you can still see the old trades being carried on in much the same way as ever. The ancient Fishmongers Company still controls Billingsgate (West India Dock Rd, early morning Tues–Sat), and if you get up really early you can watch the Bummerees lugging huge carcasses around at Smithfield Market (Mon–Fri).

Though the halls of the City livery companies may have been rebuilt since they were first established in the Middle Ages, they still house some remarkable treasures. Some are open to visit, but only by prior arrangement: you'll have to book well ahead, through the City of London Information Centre, St Paul's Churchyard, EC4; 0171-332 1456.

The liveliest glimpse of East End life nowadays is to be had on Sunday mornings in Brick Lane market.

Where to stay

TOWER THISTLE St Katharine's Way E1 9LD 0171-481 2575 £110; 803 rms (ask for one with a view). In a marvellous location next to Tower Bridge and the Tower of London, this busy modern hotel has stylish public rooms, and several eating areas – the coffee shop (good views over Tower Bridge) doubles as an understated nightclub; disabled access.

To see and do

🏰 👶 ⊖ **Tower Hill** TOWER OF LONDON Picturesque, classic castle, the most notable building to survive the Great Fire of London. A lot of fun to look at even superficially, it dates back to the late 11th-c, though the site had been used as a defensive position by the Romans much earlier. Almost every period of English history has witnessed gruesome goings-on here, with not even the highest or mightiest safe from imprisonment or even execution: Walter Raleigh, Lady Jane Grey and two of Henry VIII's wives all spent their last days in the Tower.

From the reign of Charles II it housed the Royal Mint, but there's still ample evidence of its time as a prison (such as prisoners' graffiti on walls); it returned to its former role in both world wars. There's a mass of things to see here, inc enough armour and medieval weaponry to glut the most bloodthirsty small boy's appetite, the Crown Jewels, the Beefeaters and the ravens. You can also walk along the elevated battlements. Last year they opened a sparkling new Jewel House to show off the Crown Jewels, which it does much better than the old display; TV pictures show the detail more clearly than squinting in front can do, and on the busiest days those tempted to linger too long are gently drawn along by moving floorways. Also new is a reconstruction of the living quarters of Sir Walter Raleigh. Two towers that were part of Edward I's medieval palace are furnished in period style, and peopled with appropriately costumed guides re-creating 13th-c court life. You need a fair bit of time to see everything properly. Shop, some disabled access; cl 24–26 Dec, 1 Jan; 0171-488 5693; £7.95.

🏠❀☉ Distinctive TOWER BRIDGE gives wonderful views from its glass-covered walkway, 142ft above the Thames; hi-tech new displays also present the view at various other dates in the bridge's history. The bridge is unusual not just for its design, but because it's still fully operational; the *Times* newspaper shows when it's to be raised each day, and you can see some of the Victorian machinery that does all the work. A lively, state-of-the-art exhibition opened last year to celebrate the bridge's centenary, with multi-media shows designed to leave you feeling proud to be British. Shop, disabled access; cl 24–26 Dec, Good Fri; 0171-403 3761; £5.

🕭☺ TOWER HILL PAGEANT (Tower Hill Terrace) Entertaining dark ride through centuries of London's history, from the Romans right through to Docklands. There seems to be more to see than in other such places and the cars are quite ingeniously designed. At the end there's an exhibition of excavated finds from nearby. Shop, disabled access; cl 25 Dec; 0171-709 0081; £5.45. Tower Hill is also the best tube station for visiting St Katharine's Dock (see Docklands entry, below), and there's an appropriately castellated McDonalds outside.

✝☉ St Paul's ST PAUL'S CATHEDRAL looms out at you suddenly from among the crowded streets, despite the attempts of brasher, taller modern buildings to take over. Its huge dome is a pleasing shape after the stolid self-satisfaction of the Victorian and Edwardian masonry which still

dominates this area. Originally the cathedral was Gothic in style, with a towering 500-ft spire. It fell into disrepair and Wren was assigned to work on its renovation. He didn't relish the job (calling the battered building a heap of deformities) and no doubt was delighted when the Great Fire of London swept the old church away, allowing him to construct something entirely new. His mainly classical design is unlike any other cathedral in Britain, and it only took 35 years to build. The setting for various state occasions, it's full of interesting monuments – the one to John Donne was the only complete figure to be salvaged after the Great Fire. Look out for the wonderful carving on the exterior – some of which is by Grinling Gibbons, who also did the choir stalls. Other highlights include the Whispering Gallery, and the crypt, full of magnificent tombs and memorials to notable figures from British history. A new visitor centre should be completed by the end of the year. Shop, disabled access; cl Sun; 0171-236 4128; £3, £5 inc galleries. The City Pipe by the tube station is an enjoyable, weekday wine bar.

🏠☉ The 15th-c GUILDHALL (off Gresham St) is where the Court of Common Council, over which the Lord Mayor presides, administers the City of London. The Lord Mayor's Banquet is held in the great hall, hung with the banners and shields of the City's 90-odd livery companies. Underneath is the largest 15th-c crypt in the City, and there's also a clock museum with fascinating and intricate displays. The library contains an unrivalled collection of manuscripts and books relating to the City. Disabled access; cl Sun Oct–Apr, Christmas and for civic occasions; 0171-606 3030 ext 1460; guided tours, free.

🏠❀☉ Monument The MONUMENT (Monument St) is a 202-ft-high, fluted, doric-style column, designed by Wren and Hooke to mark the spot where the Great Fire of London began – in Pudding Lane exactly 202ft from its base. The views of the city from the top are tremendous, though there are 311 spiral steps up. Cl Sun Oct–Mar,

25–26 Dec, 1 Jan, Good Fri, May Day, maybe occasional other dates, so best to check first; 0171-626 2717; £1.

🏠👁⊖ **Bank** Some of the City's finest buildings are around here, though with most of them you'll have to content yourself with looking at just the outside. The neo-classical fortress that's the BANK OF ENGLAND (Bartholomew Lane) does still contain oodles of gold – though you can't see it, let alone get your hands on it. There's a small but interesting MUSEUM, which even shows how computerised currency speculators work. Disabled access; cl Sat, winter Suns 25–26 Dec, 1 Jan; free. Other handsome or interesting buildings include the neo-classical Custom House on Lower Thames St, Lloyds of London on Lime St, and the Renaissance-style Royal Exchange on Cornhill, with several proud columns in front. If you apply in writing in advance, you should be able to see inside the MANSION HOUSE (Bank), the official residence of the Lord Mayor of London. There's a suite of sumptuous 18th-c rooms, inc the fabulous Egyptian Hall. More lively is LEADENHALL MARKET (Whittington Ave, off Gracechurch St), a Victorian, iron and glass covered market, alive with Cockney humour yet quite smart, and filled with seafood, game, vegetables and fruit; cl afternoonish, wknds.

👁🏛⊖ **Barbican** MUSEUM OF LONDON (London Wall) No other city museum in the world is quite as comprehensive as this. London's development is told through chronological reconstructions and period clothes, music and various remains, from a medieval hen's egg to an early (and quite different) tube map – ever heard of the station called Post Office? There's a rather jolly, audio-visual presentation showing the spread of the Great Fire, and the 18th-, 19th- and 20th-c sections have almost too much to take in. It livens up considerably as it goes on, and you should allow plenty of time to explore it properly. Anyone with just a passing interest in history should find it compelling. They've just begun a seven-year redevelopment programme, and are tackling each gallery in turn; the prehistoric gallery should be ready

this summer. The museum adjoins a stretch of the original Roman wall. Meals, snacks, shop, disabled access; cl am Sun, Mon (exc bank hols) 24—26 Dec, 1 Jan; 0171-600 0807; *£3.50 – ticket valid for three months, and it certainly is the sort of place you want to come back to.

👁 NATIONAL POSTAL MUSEUM (King Edward St) Guaranteed to tickle any philatelist's fancy – a comprehensive collection of stamps from all over the world, as well as a history of the postal system. They have practically every stamp issued anywhere since 1840, and there's an unusual exhibition devoted to the letter box, a useful device introduced to Britain by post office surveyor (and novelist) Anthony Trollope. Shop, disabled access by prior arrangement; cl wknds and bank hols; 0171-239 5420; free.

🏠!▣ The Barbican could be called the north bank's equivalent to the South Bank arts centre – certainly its aesthetic equal. This complex includes cinemas, theatres, exhibition halls and galleries, and there is often free entertainment in the foyers. As we went to press, they did seem to be trying to make it easier for visitors to find their way around.

🏠!⊖ **Liverpool St** You can visit a quite remarkable house at number 18 FOLGATE ST – but be warned, this is no ordinary guided tour. It doesn't do the place justice to say that it's been furnished and decorated in period style – to all intents and purposes you really are back in the 18th c, with candles and gaslight flickering away, food and drink laid out on the table, even urine in the chamberpots. Dennis Severs the owner, who lives here, spends hours getting everything ready, and goes to extreme lengths to immerse people in the experience – it's not unusual to be locked in a cold, dark cellar, and he's been known to throw people out if he doesn't like them. Open 2–5pm the first Sun of each month; 0171-247 4013; £5, £30 for the more elaborate evening performances. In Liverpool St station, Hamilton Hall is an extraordinarily grand, ex-ballroom pub.

👁❀✝⊖ **Old St** GEFFRYE MUSEUM (Kingsland Rd) One of London's most friendly and interesting museums, yet little known; 18th-c almshouses converted to show the changing style of the English domestic interior. Displays go from lovely 17th-c oak panelling and furniture through elegant Georgian reconstructions and Victorian parlours to Art-Deco fashions. There's a notable herb garden, and they have an excellent programme of special events, talks and activities. Hugely enjoyable, and well worth tracking down. Snacks, shop, disabled access; cl Mon (exc bank hols), 24–26 Dec, 1 Jan, Good Fri; 0171-739 8368; free. WESLEY'S HOUSE (49 City Rd) The father of Methodism had his house and chapel built here in 1778, and they're still much as they were then, with plenty of his personal possessions. You can see Wesley's tomb, and the crypt has a museum on the history of Methodism. Shop, disabled access – limited in house, but good in museum; cl 25–26 Dec, limited opening Sun (when services); 0171-253 2262; *£3.

🏛🏠✿ **Farringdon** MUSEUM OF THE ORDER OF ST JOHN (St John's Lane) Housed in a 16th-c gatehouse and 12th-c crypt – silver, paintings and furniture belonging to the medieval Order, and displays relating to the history and work of its more modern offshoot, the St John's Ambulance. Shop, some disabled access; cl Sun, Christmas and Easter; 0171-253 6644; £2.50 suggested donation. Tours of the gatehouse and priory church on Tues, Fri and Sat at 11am and 2.30pm. The Eagle in Farringdon Rd has the best food of any London pub.

✿!✿ **Blackfriars** STORY OF TELECOMMUNICATIONS (145 Queen Victoria St) Run by BT, an engaging collection of just about every telephone there's ever been, from hugely complicated Victorian phones through gas-mask phones to fax machines. Most of the exhibits can be made to ring, buzz or bleep, and there's a film too. Shop, disabled access; 0171-248 7444; free. Nearby the Black Friar pub has sumptuous bronze and marble, Art Nouveau decoration.

!✿ **Aldgate East** Once the terror-stricken haunt of Jack the Ripper, Whitechapel is still one of London's poorest areas. BRICK LANE MARKET is London's biggest and most atmospheric st market – a riot of colour, smells and sound, inc some very entertaining market patter. There are plenty of bargains for early risers (and things to avoid – we've even seen someone specialising in secondhand felt-tip pens). The community is largely Asian, so much of the food and other wares are quite exotic. Open Sun 5am–2pm. COLUMBIA ST MARKET, a few streets N, entirely devoted to garden and house plants, has bargains as it closes around 1pm on Sun.

✿✿ **Bethnal Green** MUSEUM OF CHILDHOOD (Cambridge Heath Rd) This very special little museum houses the V & A's collection of toys, dolls, dolls' houses, games, puppets and children's costumes. Shop, disabled access with prior notice; cl am Sun, Fri, 25 Dec, Good Fri, May Day bank hol; 0181-980 2415; free.

✝ The City is full of striking **churches**, many of which have good lunchtime or evening concerts; among the more interesting ones are St Anne and St Agnes (Gresham St), particularly worth knowing for the Bach cantatas that may grace its Lutheran Sun services (0171-373 5566); St Bartholomew-the-Great (W Smithfield), partly Norman, with a 13th-c gateway into the market precincts, lunchtime recitals and choral evenings (0171-606 5171 for programme); and St Mary-le-Bow (Cheapside), with the famous Bow Bells and Thurs lunchtime early-music concerts (0171-248 5139).

🏛🏚🏗⚓ **Docklands** Once the heartland of Britain's trade-based empire, these 8½ square miles over the last decade became the largest redevelopment site in Europe – the old warehouses imaginatively converted into smart apartments and office blocks. 800-ft Canary Wharf is an all-too-obvious landmark; you can't go inside. Many of the buildings around it were designed to give a taste of the 21st c. While they're undoubtedly striking, there's sometimes a soullessness about the place that's positively eerie; on a weekend or holiday, Docklands is even more deserted than the rest of the City. It's reached and seen best by the

Docklands Light Railway which operates only on weekdays (the weekend replacement bus service is distinctly unscenic); the best bit is between West India Quay and Island Gardens, where you can get off and walk through the foot tunnel under the Thames to Greenwich. The London Docklands Visitor Centre, 3 Limeharbour, E14, 0171-512 1111, offers information, free maps and an audio-visual show. The earliest docks to be redeveloped are the most visitor-friendly: St Katharine's Dock (not far from Tower Hill), which has a lively marina, a quite cheerful pastiche of a Victorian pub, and lots going on, and Tobacco Dock, due to reopen this year as an American-style, factory shopping centre. Further E down the river is the gigantic, closeable Thames Flood Barrier, built to protect the city from freak tides; a Visitor Centre is on Unity Way, Woolwich SE18, 0181-854 1373. You can get boats down here from Westminster Pier (0181-854 5555, £5.70 return), and these now stop at Canary Wharf too.

Where to eat

The restaurants and wine bars in the City tend to be full at lunchtime with businessmen entertaining clients on expense accounts – and both service and price reflect this. Pubs and wine bars tend to empty at 2.20pm – a good time to go if you can hold out till then. At the weekend, the City is much quieter and a great many of the restaurants and pubs are shut. Balls Brothers and Davys wine bar chains are both reliably good for snacks or larger meals and decent wine.

Rouxl Britannia in Triton Court, 14 Finsbury Sq EC2 0171-256 6997 Run by the Roux brothers, this is a busy, rather cramped brasserie with very good food; cl pm and wknds. £28.50|£4.15/£7.

Olde Wine Shades 6 Martin Lane EC4 0171-626 6303 One of the few buildings to have escaped the Great Fire of 1666, and much as it was when Dickens used it as a tavern – heavy black beams, dignified alcoves, dark panelling and old-fashioned, high-backed settles; decent wine and good-value, traditional lunchtime snacks; packed with smart City types; cl pm and wknds; no children; jacket and tie are required. £16.50|£2.10/£3.30.

Blooms 90 Whitechapel High St E1 0171-247 6001 Strictly kosher Jewish restaurant with enjoyable food – most fun on Sun lunchtime when it's packed with Jewish families; cl pm Fri, all Sat and on Jewish hols. £13.23|£5.50/£7.70.

Hamilton Hall Bishopsgate EC2 0171-247 3579 Part of the new Liverpool St station development, with terrific, Victorian-baroque decor, lots of space, and a decent range of food all day; cl pm Sun, 25–26 Dec. £12/£4.15.

Besides those already mentioned, City pubs worth knowing include the Hand & Shears (Middle St EC1: very traditional Smithfield pub); Olde Mitre (Ely Pl, off Hatton Garden EC1: ancient-feeling enclave); and the Rising Sun (Rising Sun Court, Cloth Fair EC1).

BLOOMSBURY/HOLBORN/ REGENT'S PARK

The British Museum presides serenely over a civilised and genteel, if slightly faded area of Georgian squares, gardens and courts between the City and Westminster – legal and academic London. We have included with it the area over towards Marylebone, with Regent's Park (and the zoo) on its northern border; away from the shopping streets of Marylebone High St and Baker St this is largely residential, and the capital of private medicine and dentistry.

Where to stay

The hotels we have recommended for the West End make good bases too for this area, which is very easily reached from them. Bloomsbury does have a large number of hotels, especially for the more budget-conscious visitor, though many are on the tawdry side. Ones which can be recommended include the Academy (17 Gower St WC1E 6HG 0171-631 4115), the Morgan (24 Bloomsbury St WC1B 3QJ 0171-636 3735) – both handy for the British Museum – and the George (60 Cartwright Gardens WC1H 9EL 0171-387 6789).

To see and do

♨ 🏨 ⊖ **Russell Sq** BRITISH MUSEUM (Great Russell St) This monumental 19th-c building houses spectacular collections of priceless, man-made objects from all over the world, some of them over 3,000 years old. The range is staggering, in which just a few highlights are the Elgin Marbles, the log-book of Nelson's *Victory*, the wonderful and intriguing Egyptian galleries, the comprehensive galleries of Greek vases, the Oriental antiquities, and the Amaravati sculpture. There are also changing displays of historic books and documents (they often have a document of the month), administered by the British Library. Don't try to take it all in at once – decide what interests you most and stick to that, or your head will start reeling with the extent of this treasure-house before you've got even a tenth of the way through. Meals, snacks, shop, disabled access; cl am Sun, 25 Dec, 1 Jan, Good Fri, May Day; 0171-636 1555. Though it's normally free, you can avoid the crowds (worst at wknds) by paying £5 for the late-night opening on the first Tues of the month (not Jan). Just up Gower St, Dillons is a first-class, serious bookshop, and in Museum St, the Museum Tavern does decent food all day.

🏨 ♨ DICKENS' HOUSE Dickens lived at 48 Doughty St during his 20s, and during that period wrote the *Pickwick Papers*, *Oliver Twist* and *Nicholas Nickleby*. The drawing room has been reconstructed to appear as it was then, and there are a number of original manuscripts and first editions, pictures and personal possessions. His wife's sister died here in 1837, an event which the writer later used as the model for the death of Little Nell in *The Old Curiosity Shop*. Shop; cl Sun and Christmas week; 0171-405 2127; £2.

♨ ⊖ **Goodge St** POLLOCK'S TOY MUSEUM (1 Scala St) Housed in a rather charming setting, a wide range of playthings from all over the world and from all periods, almost as if lots of enthusiastic children had just left them scattered through these little rooms. Mechanical and optical toys, teddy bears, furniture, board games and theatres, and a proper toy shop downstairs. Disabled access to ground floor only; cl Sun and bank hols; 0171-636 3452; £2.

✤ 🏨 ♨ 🖪 ⊖ **Holborn** LINCOLN'S INN FIELDS A perfect example of the tranquil architecture of this area – a large, open space with trees and lawns surrounded by handsome houses; there are also tennis courts and summer band concerts – a pleasant place to spend a summer afternoon. SIR JOHN SOANE'S MUSEUM (13 Lincoln's Inn Fields) was built by the architect for his splendid collection of pictures, books and antiquities, inc an Egyptian sarcophagus. It's most eccentric, full of architectural tricks and mirrors, a complex natural-lighting system for the antiquities which cover most walls. There's a lovely picture by Turner, but the highlight is Hogarth's acid series on *The Rake's Progress* and *The Election*. When you've seen them, the guide swings open the hinged 'walls' and further treasures emerge, inc choice Piranesi drawings and a scale model of the Bank of England. Sir John was responsible for some of the most magnificent buildings in the City, and his collection of architectural drawings can be viewed by appointment. The guides are very friendly and helpful, the guidebook well worthwhile. Shop; cl Sun, Mon, 25–26 Dec, 1 Jan; 0171-405 2107; donations. The breakfast room of Soane's first house, no 12 next door, will be open for the first time from early this year.

Nearby, the Gothic ROYAL COURTS OF JUSTICE are impressive , and you can also stroll through the gardens of GRAY'S INN, said to have been laid out by Francis Bacon around 1600. This area really is legal London, and you'll usually find a lot of lawyers in the splendid Cittie of York (22 High Holborn), an enormous and very atmospheric basement pub with little private booths down one side. Another fine pub in this area is the opulent Victorian gin palace, the Princess Louise (208 High Holborn; good Thai food upstairs, not wknds). The 18th-c Seven Stars (Carey St) is delightful, and Dom Vitos Sandwich Bar on Kingsway has superb sandwiches, especially the avocado and crispy bacon.

🏛 ✛ **Temple** COURTAULD INSTITUTE GALLERIES (Somerset House, Strand) Outstanding collection of Impressionist and Post-Impressionist paintings, inc works by Monet, Renoir, Degas, Cézanne, Michelangelo, Rubens and Goya. The well restored rooms provide a suitably grand setting. Shop, disabled access; cl am Sun, 24–26 Dec, 1 Jan; 0171-873 2526; £3. Somerset House still has parts of the Public Records Office (the bulk of the files have moved to St Catherine's House on Kingsway), where you can have great fun rooting out skeletons in the family closet.

🏛 ✛ Of all the Inns of Court, the TEMPLE is perhaps the most impressive, and it boasts many famous literary figures among former members, inc Lamb, Thackeray and for a while Dr Johnson too. Most of the buildings date from after the reign of Elizabeth I or the Great Fire, but the name points to an older history: the land was owned by the Knights Templar from about 1160. MIDDLE TEMPLE HALL is a fine example of Tudor architecture, with a double hammerbeam roof and beautiful stained glass. There is a table made

from timber from Sir Francis Drake's ship the *Golden Hind* – he was a member of the Middle Temple – while a single oak tree from Windsor Forest supplied the wood for the 29-ft-long high table. Open 10am–12pm and 3–4pm Mon–Fri exc bank hols, during Aug, and over some vacations; 0171-353 4355; free. The Inner Temple has an unusual round church.

🏛 DR JOHNSON'S HOUSE (17 Gough Sq) is a perfect example of early 18th-c architecture, just as Dr Johnson himself was a perfect example of 18th-c barbed gentility. Between 1749 and 1759 he wrote his great *English Dictionary* here, and a first edition of this is on display, along with various memorabilia from his learned life. Shop; cl Sun and bank hols; 0171-353 3745; *£3. The passages and walkways around here are a good reminder of how London's streets used to be laid out; the 17th-c Olde Cheshire Cheese nearby is a splendid old place.

✛ 🔔 🏛 The church of ST BRIDE'S (Fleet St) is a Wren masterpiece, its splendid steeple the influence for today's traditional, three-tiered wedding cake; good Sun choir and frequent, short, lunchtime recitals (0171-353 1301 for programme). There's an interesting MUSEUM (cl am Sun, free) in the partly Roman crypt. Caxton set up his first printing press alongside, and ever since St Bride's has been the parish church for anyone involved in the press. This was especially handy in the days when adjoining Fleet St was the hub of newspaperland; today it's really just a passage between the law courts and the City – but look out for relics of the newspaper kingdoms such as the black-glass, former Daily Express Building.

! 🔔 ✛ **Baker St** MADAME TUSSAUD'S (Marylebone Rd) According to a recent survey 48 per cent of overseas visitors place this famous waxworks museum at the top of their list of things to do in London. Perhaps this is why the queues are generally so long and slow-moving – it's quite possible to spend more time in line than in the actual museum, so it's a good idea to book your ticket in advance. Some of the models are uncannily realistic, especially the more recent additions, but others are rather less successful (the royal family spring to mind). Children enjoy the grisly Chamber of Horrors (adults may find it slightly disturbing), as well as the entertaining new finale, the Spirit of London – a dark ride through a cheery interpretation of the city's history. In places rather witty, the ride is excellently put together but over a little quickly – rather like the museum as a whole, which some people may end up feeling is a bit overpriced. Meals, snacks, shop, disabled access; cl 25 Dec; 0171-935 6861; £7.95. As we went to press, the LONDON PLANETARIUM, next door, was just about to begin its first major transformation since opening in 1958. It will be closed until Easter, when it will reopen with a new, hi-tech star projector, and stunning-sounding, new displays and shows, inc a 3-D journey through the wonders of the universe; best to check with Madame Tussaud's for times and prices.

To many people the world over Baker St calls to mind only one thing – Conan Doyle's great detective. The famous address of 221b now has a SHERLOCK HOLMES MUSEUM, with various Holmes paraphernalia, and something of the atmosphere of the books re-created. Cl 25 Dec; 0171-935 8866; *£5.

 Great Portland St REGENT'S PARK Covering over 400 acres, this is the culmination of a glorious swathe of Regency terraces designed by John Nash, which can be seen almost all around it; the buildings of Park Crescent are among the finest. The park was originally intended to be the setting for a palace for the Prince Regent, after whom it was named: now it contains an open-air theatre where Shakespeare's plays are performed in the summer, the lovely Queen Mary's Rose Garden, a boating lake and, of course, LONDON ZOO (can also be reached from Regent's Park or Camden Town tube stations). The zoo has begun a 10-year redevelopment programme; you can already see a few changes. The collection of animals, birds, fish and insects has been slimmed down to concentrate on particularly endangered species or those which can be expected to breed here, from the tiniest creatures to elephants and gorillas. A particularly interesting feature is the Moonlight World in the Clore House where day and night are reversed so that you can watch nocturnal creatures such as vampire bats. The children's zoo is much bigger than it used to be, and animals can be handled here. Meals, snacks, shop, disabled access; cl 25 Dec; 0171-722 3333; *£6.95. The London Waterbus Company – one of several companies who now run CANAL BOAT TRIPS along the stretch of Regent's Canal between Little Venice and Camden Lock – make a stop for passengers who want to get off at the zoo; tel 0171-482 2550 for timetable and prices.

Where to eat

WAGAMAMA 4 Streatham St WC1 0171-323 9223 Attractive, simply furnished, Japanese basement restaurant with long tables and benches for communal eating; very friendly, cheerful service (using interesting, computerised order pads), a chatty, informal atmosphere, good, healthy food – raw salads, ramens (huge bowls of noodles with meat, vegetables and Japanese additions), rice dishes, sake, grape and plum wines, beer, and free green tea; exceptionally good value; cl Sun, Christmas, Easter Mon. £11.70/£4.

This area is only a short walk from the West End, so many of the restaurants we have mentioned in that section will be useful for this area too.

South of the River

The South Bank arts centre with its magnificent riverside site should be a magnet for visitors, but in fact the unappealing concrete blocks which house the complex are bleakly discouraging, and the hinterland too is unprepossessing. However, the South Bank walkways give marvellous views across the river – the best views of the Houses of Parliament are from the quiet, riverside walk between Westminster Bridge and the ancient palace of the Archbishop of Canterbury, by Lambeth Bridge. Dotted about the area are several places well worth visiting, including the Museum of the Moving Image, one of the most satisfying museums in the country, and the excellent Imperial War Museum. And besides the excellent shows and performances in the various halls and theatres of the South Bank complex, there is usually something going on in their foyers – including free entertainment.

Where to stay

Places on this side of the river are best visited from a base on the other side; somewhere in the West End or Westminster would be preferable.

To see and do

✲ ▣ ▣ ♨ ! ✆ **Waterloo** South Bank Centre These walkways, theatres, cinemas and galleries hide multifarious cultural treasures behind their hideous, stained concrete. There are sometimes open-air festivals between the attractions, with stalls of books, clothes and jewellery going down to the river, or free performances in the foyers of the various halls. The National Theatre, as well as the excellent productions in its three, different-sized auditoria, has interesting artistic exhibitions, guided tours behind the scenes, and good places to eat – often accompanied by live music in the foyer of the Olivier theatre. The National Film Theatre also has a nice little café, with many bookstalls set up in front of it. The Hayward Gallery specialises in world-class art exhibitions. The Royal Festival Hall often has free performances in the foyer, as well as a full programme of music and dance; it too has good cafés, inc a useful place for lunch. The Museum of the Moving Image, or MOMI as it's usually called, is also here, providing a romp through cinematic history which everyone really enjoys. Lively displays trace

moving pictures from magic lanterns to today's hi-tech, special effects. You can learn how to operate a television studio, read the news or fly like Superman, while older visitors should find the montage of old Pathé newsreels particularly nostalgic. The costumed actors work really hard with their performances. One of London's best attractions, and a visit can easily last several hours. Meals, snacks, shop, disabled access – contact reception when you get there. Cl 24–26 Dec; 0171-401 2636; £5.50.

✲ ♞ ♨ ! ✆ **London Bridge** The area around Bankside is very much on the up at the moment; there's quite a bit of redevelopment going on in the old buildings, and plenty more to come. Riverside promenades offer good Thames and City views – Wren is said to have watched the building of St Paul's from here, and Pepys certainly did watch London burning down in the Great Fire. One of the best cross-river views is from the modern Founders Arms. For centuries this was London's entertainment centre, full of theatres, bars and licensed brothels. The most famous of the theatres, Shakespeare's Globe Theatre, is being reconstructed on its original site, where it was open from 1599 to 1642 (when the Puritans closed it down). Problems with wood and various other snags have delayed completion of the late Sam Wanamaker's ambitious project, though it should be ready by April 1996. They hope to perform some of the plays the way they were done in the early 1600s – no spotlights, canned music or elaborate sets. In the meantime, it's fascinating watching the building progress. The adjacent BEAR GARDENS MUSEUM looks at the old and new Globes, with exhibitions on Elizabethan London and its theatre, and the life of Shakespeare. Shop, disabled access; museum cl 25 Dec; £4 museum, site free. The 17th-c George, in Borough High St, gives a good idea of how the area's buildings used to look back then; NT.

The CLINK EXHIBITION (Clink St) explores the less salubrious side of the area's history, on the site of the prison that gave its name to all others. Quite fascinating, the displays are very traditional in their approach, with lots to read and look at rather than to poke and push. An adults-only room is teasingly lit by a red light, though the sauce is more scholarly than Page Three. Included is one of the few working armourers in the country, making armour and chainmail on site – he'll rustle up a decent made-to-measure suit for around £1,000. Shop; cl 25–26 Dec, 1 Jan; 0171-403 5813; £2. Next door are the medieval remains of the Bishop of Winchester's palace, once said to be the biggest building in Europe, but now reduced to a single wall and an atmospheric rose window.

† SOUTHWARK CATHEDRAL, with some parts over 600 years older than the present, late 19th-c nave, is worth a passing look; interesting memorials to William Shakespeare (whose brother is buried here) and John Harvard, the founder of the American university. Meals, snacks, shop, disabled access; free. Across the busy main road, the church of St Thomas (St Thomas St) has a reconstructed OLD OPERATING THEATRE, and a museum looking at the history of surgery and herbal medicine. Cl Mon, 15 Dec–5 Jan; 0171-955 4791; *£2.

! LONDON DUNGEON (Tooley St) A more sensationalised look at London's seamy underside than you'll find at the Clink (see above), with witchcraft, torture, black magic and death all presented in ghoulishly life-like waxwork scenes. There's a new Jack the Ripper Experience. Very atmospheric, and genuinely historical in its own way – though perhaps getting a little pricey. Snacks, shop, disabled access; cl 24–26 Dec; 0171-403 0606; £6.50. Down the road, BRITAIN AT WAR is a splendidly put-together re-creation of Blitz-hit London, from reconstructed streets and air-raid shelters to a BBC Radio station and GI club. The special effects are suitably dramatic, with lots of smoke, smells and noise. Also, authentic period newsreels and front pages, a fully stocked shop and pub, and lots of fascinating little details. Shop, disabled access; cl 24–26 Dec; 0171-403 3171; £5. Off Tooley St, HAYS GALLERIA is an old dock attractively converted into a shopping arcade, with several places to eat inc a good, river-view pub, and a fascinating, whimsical, pirate-ship working sculpture by David Kemp.

❀ HMS BELFAST On the E side of London Bridge, opposite the Tower, docked permanently in the Pool of London, is the largest preserved cruiser ever built for the Royal Navy. Now its seven decks are a floating naval museum, with sound and light displays and various exhibitions. Anyone with even a passing interest in naval life and history should get a lot out of this, and there's plenty to see, from the ship's gun decks to its dental surgery. Snacks, shop, limited disabled access; cl 24–26 Dec; 0171-407 6434; *£4.

DESIGN MUSEUM (Butlers Wharf) Intriguing museum showing how design is used in the mass production of everyday objects, from cars and furniture to graphics and ceramics. Good temporary exhibitions. Meals, snacks, shop, disabled access; cl am wknds, 24–26 Dec, 1 Jan; 0171-403 6933; £4.50. Not far from here, the developing BRAMAH TEA AND COFFEE

MUSEUM (Clove Building) is an interesting look at two favourite commodities. Snacks, shop, disabled access; cl 25–26 Dec; 0171-378 0222; *£3. Nearby, the Anchor Tap (just off Shad Thames) is a handy refreshment stop.

👶 ♿ **Lambeth North** (or Westminster on the other side of the river) IMPERIAL WAR MUSEUM (Lambeth Rd) Recently brilliantly refurbished, this museum is now top-notch, using very up-to-date presentation techniques to give a vibrant and sometimes even nerve-racking exploration of all wars involving Britain and the Commonwealth since 1914. The Blitz Experience vividly recreates London's darkest days (a similar Trench Experience gives WWI the same treatment), and there's a chance to fly with the RAF on Operation Jericho (£1.30 extra). Also, interesting archive recordings of people's experiences of war. Their D-day exhibition should run until this summer. Meals, snacks, shop, disabled access; cl 24–26 Dec, 1 Jan; 0171-416 5000; £3.90, free after 4.30pm. It's housed in the former lunatic asylum known as Bedlam, the name a corruption of Bethlehem: the site was originally a hostel set up in the 13th-c by the bishop of that town. Almost facing each other further up Kennington Rd are two good tapas bars.

🏠 † ♿ LAMBETH PALACE (S end of Lambeth Bridge), the official residence of the Archbishop of Canterbury, has a charming, late 15th-c, red-brick exterior; though there are twice-weekly tours of the partly early medieval interior, they're fully booked for the next year and a half. The adjacent CHURCH OF ST MARY has the tombs of several archbishops, and Captain Bligh of the *Bounty* is buried here too. Just by the S gateway is the little MUSEUM OF GARDEN HISTORY founded in memory of John Tradescant, Charles I's gardener, with a small area planted with plants grown in his time. Tradescant himself is buried here. Snacks, shop; cl Sat and second Sun in Dec–first Sun in Mar; 0171-261 1891; free.

♿ FLORENCE NIGHTINGALE MUSEUM (St Thomas's Hospital, Lambeth Palace Rd) On the site of the first School of Nursing, a re–created hospital ward in the Crimea, and various artefacts and possessions of the Lady with the Lamp. Snacks, shop, disabled access; cl Mon, Christmas; 0171-620 0374; *£2.50.

❗ 👶 ♿ **Elephant & Castle** Get up very early on Fri for the bargains at BERMONDSEY MARKET (Bermondsey St/Long Lane): when the antique-dealers start arriving around 5am, other dealers literally pounce on the choice items while they're being set out, and by 8 or 9am things are more ordinary. It's probably the biggest primary source of antiques and bric-a-brac in London, and can be the most exciting. Take a torch in winter. CUMING MUSEUM (155 Walworth Rd) is of passing interest, with displays on Southwark history from Roman times, and more general collections, inc medieval charms and superstitions. Shop; cl Sun, Mon cl Christmas; 0171-701 1342; free.

Where to eat

RSJ 13a Coin St SE1 0171-928 4554 Relaxed and friendly restaurant with fine, modern British cooking and exceptional Loire wines in simple surroundings; handy for the South Bank shows; cl Sun, 4 days over Christmas. £24.35|£3.25|£11.30.

REBATO'S 169 South Lambeth Rd SW9 0171-735 6388 Busy, high-ceilinged tapas bar with friendly barman and waiters, and a good choice of tapas; also a Spanish restaurant; cl Sun, am Sat, bank hols, disabled access. £19.84|£4.40|£8.80.

PHUKET 246 Battersea Park Rd SW11 0171-223 5924 A bit of an expedition, but very good Thai food in a friendly and extremely unpretentious little restaurant, more café in style really – though the food is of far better quality than that; ask to sit upstairs; cl am, 24–26 Dec, 1 Jan. £16.53|£4/£6.10.

There's a clutch of useful tapas bars and the like up past the Imperial War

Museum, around the junction of Kennington Rd and Kennington Lane. Nr the Old Vic just S of Waterloo, La Barca (81 Lower Marsh St) is an enjoyably theatrical, Italian restaurant; and Caesar's (103 Waterloo Rd) is a decent, burger-style place. The café of the Young Vic (The Cut) does very good-value, light lunches, but you'll feel centuries old if you're out of your 20s. Decent pubs in this area include the ancient Anchor on Bankside, the Founders Arms on Bankside (spectacular views of St Paul's) and, above all, the George, off 77 Borough High St, the closest thing to an old-fashioned coaching inn left in London.

FURTHER AFIELD

We include here only those places which despite being away from the centre, appeal so much at least to some people that, for them, even a short stay in London would be incomplete without them. The most generally popular of these places are Greenwich and Kew.

Other parts of London do have many treasures tucked away, well worth Londoners themselves tracking down: prime among them the Whitechapel Gallery in Whitechapel High St, east of the City; out in west London, Osterley Park, Syon House, Chiswick Mall (18th-c Thames-side village), Chiswick Park (the first true example of English naturalistic landscaping, with Chiswick House, an early 18th-c partying pavilion), and maybe Hogarth's House; perhaps also, Portobello Rd market (classy antiques at the Notting Hill Gate end, junk, fruit and veg further down).

🏠🎯❗🎲⊖ **Camden Town** is these days a bohemian's idyll, with a very wide variety of unusual shops from radical bookshops to fashion workshops, from comic shops to one of London's best brassware and ironmongery shops. There are lots of restaurants and cafés too, and good delis serving the area's Italian and Greek communities; try the Parkway Deli for Italian, and Chris Milia (Pratt St) for Greek. What makes the area worth a visit is its weekend series of lively MARKETS, particularly the interesting craft, handmade fashion and other stalls around the attractively converted, former warehouses of Camden Lock. There's also a covered market on Camden High St, the Inverness St market for fruit and veg, and the Stables, where the best food stalls are to be found. Go and browse, but be warned that you may never again see such huge crowds. JEWISH MUSEUM (129 Albert St) Recently moved from Tavistock Sq to these more spacious premises, an excellent look at Jewish life, history and religion, with a particularly fine collection of ceremonial art, portraits and antiques, and various audio-visual programmes. Shop, disabled access; cl Fri, Sat, all bank and Jewish

hols; 0171-388 4525; *£2.50. The Princess of Wales up towards Primrose Hill (Chalcot Rd/Regent's Park Rd), does good bistro food.

🎯🏠✱◻🌸❄✚🎲❗⚓⇌ **Greenwich** The sort of place you can come back to time and time again; some of our contributors rate Greenwich more highly than anywhere else in the country, and the weekend market now has some excellent antiques, junk and secondhand books, also arts and crafts. Once a favoured residence of the royal family, Greenwich has a long and illustrious maritime heritage, still reflected in the museums, boats and grand old ships you can visit. Three of the best attractions, the Queen's House, National Maritime Museum and Royal Observatory, have just introduced a new joint ticket that covers all three for a bargain £4.95. You'll still pay this even if you can visit only one of them, but you don't have to do them all the same day; the new ticket represents a considerable saving on last year's prices. The QUEEN'S HOUSE (Romney Rd) stands on the site of the original, magnificent, royal palace; all that's left of that is the vaulted crypt beneath what's now called Queen Anne's Block. The new building was designed in the early 17th c by Inigo Jones for Anne of Denmark, and was finished for the wife of Charles I, Queen Henrietta Maria, who lived here for a while. The first Palladian-style villa in the country, it's recently been grandly (and expensively) refurbished to show how it was when first built. Sumptuous silks and furnishings, as well as a collection of Dutch seascapes; good Walkman commentary. Shop, disabled access; cl am Sun, 25–26 Dec; 0181-858 4422; *£4.95. It's the focal point of the glorious group of buildings that make up the ROYAL NAVAL COLLEGE, designed initially by Webb in the late 17th c, then augmented in succession by Wren, Vanbrugh, Hawksmoor and Ripley. There's an interesting chapel and a particularly notable painted hall. Shop; cl am, all Thurs, Good Fri, 25 Dec; 0181-858 2154; free. The view from across the river (there's a pedestrian tunnel under the Thames here) looks like an 18th-c print come to life. The NATIONAL MARITIME MUSEUM (Romney Rd) is good fun, telling the story of Britain and the sea, with plenty of boats, details of past royal fleets and vessels, great masterpieces of naval battles, and even Nelson's uniform. There's a new 20th-c gallery. The all-in ticket also covers entry to an exhibition on the wreck of the *Titanic,* which runs until Apr; in summer it will be replaced by a major new Nelson exhibition. Meals, snacks, shop, disabled access; dates and price as Queen's House.

GREENWICH PARK Wonderful views from this carefully landscaped park sloping down towards the river, which was laid out by Le Nôtre – whose love of symmetry is clear. A herd of deer graze in a smallish area of woodland and wild flowers known as the Wilderness, and there's the largest children's playground in any royal park. The park's chiefly famous for the OLD ROYAL OBSERVATORY, the original home of Greenwich Mean Time – standing as it does on zero meridian longitude. The brass line marking the meridian is still there set in the ground: putting one foot on either side is almost irresistible. The Wren-built observatory was founded by Charles II in 1675, and now houses a comprehensive collection of historic instruments for time-keeping, navigation and astronomy – recently spruced up, with good views from the top. Shop; details as Queen's House.

Sir Francis Chichester was the first to sail around the world single-handedly, and the yacht he did it in, GIPSY MOTH IV, is moored by Greenwich Pier, still with the equipment from the epic voyage. Cl 1–2pm, am Sun, Nov–Mar; 50p. You should be able to get boat trips from here up to Westminster (around £4). Nearby is the clipper CUTTY SARK, built in 1896 and the fastest of her time – she once sailed 363 nautical miles in a single day. On board, you can watch a video telling its story, and there's an impressive collection of ships' figureheads. Shop; cl am Sun, 24–26 Dec; 0181-858 3445; £3.25. The pub named after the vessel, nearby in Lassell St, is an attractive old place for lunch; other reliable Thames-view pubs here are the Trafalgar (Park Row) and Yacht (Crane St). FAN MUSEUM (12 Crooms Hill) Unique collection of around 2,000 fans and related items from all over the world. They even do fan-making classes. Shop, disabled access (with notice); cl am Sun, Mon, Christmas; 0181-858 7879; *£3. It's not far from here to Blackheath, a civilised place, good for a pleasant stroll, with the RANGER'S HOUSE a lovely stately home with fine furnishings, portraits and a collection of musical instruments. Cl winter Mon and Tues 24–26 Dec, 1 Jan; £1. 🏠✝⛲☸❋🎦⊖ **Hampstead** prides itself on its villagey atmosphere, and off the main streets its maze of twisting lanes is very picturesque. It's home to artistes of all kinds, and well heeled bohemians in general. Past inhabitants include Aldous Huxley, George Orwell, John Masefield and Katherine Mansfield. Down in Keats Grove (past the little Downshire Hill church, which has lovely, candlelit Christmas carol services), Keats and his lover and nurse Fanny Brawne lived in two fine Regency houses; KEATS' HOUSE now has interesting displays relating to his life, with manuscripts, letters and personal mementos (and maybe a recorded nightingale out in the garden on summer nights). Shop; cl 1–2pm, am Sun and winter wkdys, Christmas; 0171-435 2062; free. SIGMUND FREUD'S HOUSE (20 Maresfield Gardens) Extraordinary collection of antiques from various ancient cultures, as well as Freud's library, papers and indeed his desk and couch. The pioneering work of his daughter is also illustrated. Shop, some disabled access; open pm Weds–Sun; 0171-435 2002; £2.50. FENTON HOUSE (Windmill Hill) Fine William and Mary merchant's mansion, set in a walled garden, with Oriental, English and European china and an exceptional collection of early keyboard instruments. Their period-music concerts on some summer Weds evenings are well worth catching. Open pm Sat–Weds Apr–Oct, plus pm wknds in Mar; 0171-435 3471; £3; NT. The Flask in Flask Walk is a good pub (and a long-standing favourite of the local actors), as is the gaslit Holly Bush, prettily tucked away up Holly Mount. Particularly attractive areas include early Georgian Church Row, and Squires Mount (where the Regency-looking house at the end on the left, in fact built in the 1950s, belonged to Richard Burton and Elizabeth Taylor). Across the road from here is HAMPSTEAD HEATH, N London's best open space, with lakes, hilly prospects, and some wonderful views of the city skyline – Parliament Hill has a direction-finder pointing out various landmarks. Across the heath, KENWOOD achieved its present splendid proportions in the 18th c at the hands of Robert Adam. The house contains a fine collection of paintings, inc old masters and 18th- and 19th-c portraits by Reynolds and Gainsborough (English Heritage are working hard to re-acquire its original contents). The grounds are lovely and include Dr Johnson's summerhouse. In summer there are concerts out here, idyllic when it's fine, with the music drifting across the lake with its Japanese bridge, and sometimes a fireworks finale (virtually impossible

to park anywhere nr then). Meals, snacks, shop, disabled access; cl 24–25 Dec; 0181-348 1286; free. Nearby the ancient Spaniard's Inn is still as good as when Dickens made it famous in the *Pickwick Papers*.
🏠 ! ⊖ Highgate, on the far side of the heath (you can easily walk across from Hampstead), dates largely from the Victorian period and still keeps a villagey atmosphere, centred as it is around the High St. The village is dominated by Highgate School (which Betjeman attended and where T S Eliot taught). There are lots of pubs in this area, and some smart little cafés. The Grove, a row of very elegant Victorian houses, is home to such diverse musicians as Yehudi Menuhin and Sting. HIGHGATE CEMETERY (Swain's Lane) The most impressive of a series of landscaped and formal cemeteries started in the early decades of Victoria's reign on the outskirts of the city, and still in use. You'll find it hard to miss the tomb of Karl Marx – a monstrous head, frequently daubed with paint and slogans. It's more difficult to search out the graves of Christina Rossetti and George Eliot in the wonderfully atmospheric tangle of trees, shrubs and crumbling ivy-covered monuments. The E cemetery is open all year (exc 25–26 Dec), the W by guided tour only (not wkdys Dec–Feb), 0181-340 1834 for times; E cemetery *£1, W cemetery *£3.
🏠 🖼 ❄ ⛴ ⇌ Hampton Court
HAMPTON COURT is an amazing place, just as a royal palace should be. It was started by Cardinal Wolsey in the early 16th c and, as often happened, its splendour proved dangerous, pricking Henry VIII's jealousy so that Wolsey felt compelled to present the house to his king in an attempt to appease him. Successive monarchs have left their architectural marks: the hammerbeamed hall and kitchens were Henry's addition, the Fountain Court was designed by Wren for William and Mary, and much comes from the work of the Victorians (the chimneys mostly date from then). The rooms from each of these periods have managed to keep their distinctive styles, from the starkly imposing

Tudor kitchens (themselves taking up 50 rooms) to the elaborate grandeur of the Georgian chambers. The King's Staircase is wonderfully over the top, and the Picture Gallery has the finest Renaissance works from the royal collection. Look out too for the carvings by Grinling Gibbons and the cartoons by Mantegna in the Lower Orangery. One of the oldest parts, Henry VIII's Great Watching Chamber, has recently been restored after the 1986 fire to its original splendour. Meals, snacks, shop, disabled access; cl 25–26 Dec; 0181-781 9500; £7 – or if you really want to live like a king, you can hire a couple of the apartments here. HAMPTON COURT GARDENS are worth a visit in their own right, the elaborately landscaped grounds inc of course the famous maze. The annual flower show here is one of the world's biggest. The King's Arms, next to the Lion Gate, is good for lunch. BUSHEY PARK nearby is another royal park, formerly reserved for hunting. There are pleasant Thames-side walks around Hampton Court, and summer cruise boats from here back down to Westminster (0171-930 4721).

✿ ♨ 🏠 ⛱ ♿ ≋ Kew Bridge KEW GARDENS were started here in 1759 by George III's mother, and consisted of 9 acres landscaped by Capability Brown. By 1904, they had grown to cover 300 acres, with the foundations of the present wonderful collection firmly laid in the previous century by Sir Joseph Banks and the head gardener William Aiton. The glasshouses include the magnificent Princess of Wales range and the remarkable, restored Palm House; new this year is an Evolution House displaying plants from up to 400 million years ago. The gardens nr the entrance are largely formally arranged, and drift into attractively landscaped woodland, glades and tree collections further out. Look out for the many interesting buildings which have been constructed among all this greenery, for example the 163-ft-high Chinese Pagoda (too dodgy structurally to go inside now). There's also a gallery, and on some summer evenings, jazz concerts with

fireworks. A wonderful place you can come back to time and time again – always discovering something new. Meals, snacks, shop, disabled access; cl 25 Dec, 1 Jan; 0181-940 1171; £4. In the grounds too is KEW PALACE, built in 1631 and used by members of the royal family until Queen Charlotte's death in 1818. It's a Dutch-style, brick building that seems remarkably unroyal, and remains much as it was during George III's reign, with family paintings, furniture and tapestries. Shop; cl Oct–Apr; 0181-781 9500; £1.20. Kew was at that time one of the royal family's favourite residences, somewhere they could enjoy quiet times as a family. In the gardens they built a rusticated summerhouse, QUEEN CHARLOTTE'S COTTAGE, its interior designed to look like a tent. Open wknds and bank hols Apr–Sept; 70p, or joint ticket with Kew Palace £1.50. The Flower & Firkin at Kew BR station does decent, simple food.

Over the bridge from the gardens, by the tube station, the KEW BRIDGE STEAM MUSEUM (Green Dragon Lane) is housed in a splendid old pumping station, and has five Cornish beam engines, one of which you can walk through while it's working. Plenty of other engines and equipment too, as well as a miniature railway, and an interesting look at the development of London's water supply. Meals, snacks, shop; cl Christmas wk, Good Fri; 0181-568 4757; £2.70 wknds (when engines in steam), £1.50 wkdys. If you have the time, the MUSICAL MUSEUM (368 Brentford High St) is worth a look, with a fascinating collection of continuously playing, automatic musical instruments; great fun. Open pm wknds Apr–Oct, plus pm Weds, Thurs and Fri July and Aug; 0181-560 8108; £3.20. In summer you can come to Kew by cruise boat from Westminster – see the numbers we give for Hampton Court above and Richmond below.

🏠 ⛱ ✿ ♈ ♪ ≋ Richmond is an agreeable if much extended Thames village, with lots of fine 18th-c houses, especially around the green and up Richmond Hill. There are quite a few good dining pubs, inc the riverside

White Cross, and the White Swan (Old Palace Lane), Racing Page (Duke St) and Rose of York (Petersham Rd). The river along here is really attractive for strolls, and there are summer cruise boats from here back down to Westminster, stopping at Kew and Putney (more lovely riverside walks) on the way; 0171-930 2062. RICHMOND PARK is the most country-like of all London's parks, with great rolling spaces and wildlife (inc herds of deer), model boats on Adam's Pond, and fishing in the 18-acre Pen Ponds. There's a good, formal garden at Pembroke Lodge, and the Isabella Plantation's rhododendrons and azaleas are a must-see in season. Anyone with a car should make the extra effort to track down HAM HOUSE in Petersham (2 m, W), an outstanding Stuart mansion reopened again this year after a wonderful restoration. Open pm Sat–Weds Apr–Dec; *£4; NT. If you happen to be in Twickenham you can get a ferry across.

MORE SPECIALISED EXPEDITIONS

☎ ➌ **Angel** Camden Passage and the surrounding streets have a great collection of ANTIQUE SHOPS, well worth the expedition if that interests you. The nearby Island Queen (Noel Rd) does good food in its bar and upstairs restaurant.

✚ ! ➌ **Colindale** RAF MUSEUM (Grahame Park Way) The story of flight from early times, with 70 full-size aeroplanes, dramatic simulators, films and hands-on exhibits (you can have a go at the controls of a modern jet trainer), lively Battle of Britain Experience, and an interesting examination of the impact of flight on history and politics. Excellent for enthusiasts and flying-minded children, and warmly recommended by several of our contributors. Meals, snacks, shop, disabled access; cl 24–26 Dec, 1 Jan; 0181-205 9191; £5.20. If you're up this way and have time to spare, the newspaper section of the British Library (Colindale Ave) is fascinating – though you have to allow them time to find what you want.

➌ ♪ ➤ **Forest Hill** HORNIMAN MUSEUM (London Rd) Art Nouveau building with eclectic, mainly ethnographical collections inc a fine group of mummies, religious artefacts, and exotic folk art; also musical instruments, stuffed animals, and a very well laid out aquarium/ecosystem; children adore it. Snacks, shop, disabled access; cl am Sun, 23–26 Dec; free weekend talks/concerts; 0181-699 2339; free.

➌ ❀ ❁ ➌ **St John's Wood** LORD'S CRICKET GROUND Tours of the famous club and grounds, and the excellent MCC Museum, with an exhaustive collection of cricket memorabilia, inc the Ashes urn and 18th-c paintings of the game. As this is a private club, you can visit only by appointment, 0171-266 3825, though you can also see the museum if you're watching a cricket match during the season. Shop, disabled access by prior arrangement; £4.95. Down in Aberdeen Pl, Crockers is a remarkably opulent Victorian pub with decent food. On the far side of this sober residential area, take a stroll through PRIMROSE HILL, which was once part of the same hunting ground as Regent's Park. From the summit there are breathtaking views of the city.

➌ ☗ ➌ **Southfields** WIMBLEDON LAWN TENNIS MUSEUM (Church Rd) The only museum of its type, with trophies, pictures and other tennis memorabilia tracing the development of the game throughout this century. Also highlights of past Wimbledon championships, and a particularly interesting display on the changes in tennis fashions. You can see the famous Centre Court outside. Snacks, shop, disabled access; cl am Sun, Mon, during the championship fortnight and Christmas; 0181-946 6131; *£2.50. Incidentally, if you're in London during the Wimbledon fortnight it's always worth popping along to the club in the early evening around 5.30 or 6 – lots of people leave

then and they resell the seats cheaply.
🔲 🏵 ⊖ **Walthamstow Central**
WILLIAM MORRIS GALLERY (Lloyd
Park, Forest Rd) William Morris lived
here 1846–1858 and the house has an
excellent collection of his work:
fabrics, furnishings and wallpaper,
much of which is still fashionable
today. Upstairs are paintings and
work by the Pre-Raphaelites and
contemporaries, inc pictures by
Burne-Jones and Rossetti. The
attractive grounds (once the Morrises'
private garden) are ideal for picnics.
Shop, disabled access to ground floor
only – though this is where the main
exhibition is; cl 1–2pm, Mon and Sun
(exc open first Sun in month cl
12–2pm, Christmas); 0181-527
3782; free.
! ⊖ **Wembley Central** WEMBLEY
STADIUM (Empire Way) Tours of the
most famous football stadium in the
land, going from the dressing rooms
through the players' tunnel and on to
the pitch itself, with an audio-visual
show and displays of trophies and
related memorabilia. Meals, snacks,
shop, disabled access (with notice); cl
25–26 Dec, and during occasional
special events; 0181-902 8833; £5.95.
🔲 🏵 🏚 ⇌ **West Dulwich** DULWICH
PICTURE GALLERY (College Rd) The
country's oldest public picture gallery,
and though not large one of the best; a
good range of European Old Masters
with works by Poussin, Van Dyck,
Gainsborough and Rembrandt.
Surrounded by parks and fields, the
building itself is rather impressive.
Summer teas, shop, disabled access; cl
am Sun, Mon, 25–26 Dec; 0181-693
5254; *£2, free on Fri. The village still
is villagey, with imposing 18th-c
houses, duckpond and a good pub,
the Crown & Greyhound. Dulwich
Park is famously attractive at
rhododendron time.

Where to eat (North London)

ODETTES 130 Regent's Park Rd NW1 0171-586 5486 Slightly quaint, cellar
wine bar with lots of pictures on the walls, bags of character, and good food;
cl am Sat, pm Sun. £25, set lunch £10.

SEASHELL 49–51 Lisson Grove NW1 0171-723 8703 Take-away and straightforward restaurant selling excellent fresh fish and chips; disabled access; cl
Sun. £15.75.

EVERYMAN CAFE Hollybush Vale NW3 0171-431 2123 Sophisticated and busy,
but still relaxed, with an almost continental feel; cl 25 Dec. £15.20/£4.50.

Walks

Central London is fun to explore on foot, though the traffic and stop-start
rhythm can be wearying. One of the best overviews of the capital is had by
walking along the south bank of the Thames from Lambeth Bridge to Tower
Bridge, giving mostly traffic-free, panoramic views of the West End, St Paul's
Cathedral, the City, the Tower of London and finally Docklands. Unfortunately, you can't yet walk along the river E of HMS *Belfast* to Tower Bridge;
the path is blocked by a huge undeveloped building site, so you have to divert
into Tooley St – but can soon rejoin the river.

Quite a number of people lead guided walks. We have found Original London Walks (0171-624 3978) consistently good over the last few years, with a
choice of six or eight a day. Walks last about two hours, usually starting from
a tube station; you don't need to book, and the cost is around £4.

Out of the centre, London has idyllic verdant stretches around Kew and
Richmond. The Thames towpath can be combined with a walk in Richmond
Park and to Ham House. The towpath between Putney and Kew Bridge (you
have to cross the river a few times) has railway stations at either end, and you
can take in Chiswick Mall, Chiswick Park (a necessary diversion from the

river at a point where there is no towpath on the N bank), and Strand on the Green, as well as Kew Gardens.

Hampstead Heath, in the N, is an airy escape, with lots of paths, ponds, glades and hollows, and views of Central London from Parliament Hill. The Regent's Canal offers an excellent walk from Little Venice to Camden Lock, passing by Regent's Park and Primrose Hill (another good viewpoint).

The SE fringes of London give way to surprisingly rural North Downs countryside, still within the London borough of Bromley, around Knockholt, High Elms and Downe; paths are plentiful and well maintained. Only the view over S London from behind Knockholt church shows how close you are to the capital.

Help this year from: Thomas Nott, Brian Jones, John C Baker, Andy Thwaites, Gill Earle, Andrew Burton, Caroline Wright, Bob and Maggie Atherton, Wayne Brindle, Richard Waller, Walter Reid, Gordon, George Atkinson, Ian Phillips, Quentin Williamson, John Fazakerley, Dr J R G Beavon, Annie Rolfe, Susan and John Douglas, B Brown, Tony and Lynne Stark, Paul Bowden, David Dimock, Tim Heywood, Derek Patey, Comus Elliott, Don Kellaway, Angie Coles, Robert Gomme, Jenny and Brian Seller, E G Parish, S J Elliott, N and M Foster, Ralf Zeyssig.

LONDON CALENDAR

Some of these dates were provisional as we went to press.

JANUARY

1 **Parliament Sq** to **The Mall,** via **Whitehall, Trafalgar Sq, Lower Regent St, Piccadilly, Hyde Park Corner** and **Constitution Hill** London Parade 0181-566 8586

5 **Royal Academy of Arts** London Original Print Fair – *till Sun 8* 0171-439 7438; **Earls Court** International Boat Show – *till Sun 15* (01784) 473377

19 **Royal Academy of Arts** Poussin Exhibition – *till 9 Apr* 0171-439 7438

20 **King St** British Artists Celebrate the Centenary of the National Trust with sale of pictures in aid of the Foundation for Art at Christie's – *till 2 Feb* 0171-221 9230

25 **Piccadilly** World of Drawings and Watercolours at Park Lane Hotel – *till Sun 29* 0171-742 1611

29 **St James's Palace, The Mall, Horse Guards** to **Banqueting House,** Charles I Commemoration March: the King's Army (the Royalist Wing of the English Civil War Society) in 17th-c dress follow the route of Charles's last walk before his execution

FEBRUARY

2 **Alexandra Palace** Road Racing and Superbike Show – *till Sun 5* (01440) 707055

3 **Holborn** Blessing of the Throats at St Ethelreda Church

4 **Twickenham** Rugby Union: England v France 0181-892 8161

9 **Olympia** International Performance Motor Show – *till Sun 12* 0181-744 1585

14 **Olympia** Fine Art and Antique Fair – *till Sun 19* 0171-370 8188

16 **Olympia** Period Homes and Gardens Show – *till Sun 19* 0181-763 2233

23 **Olympia** Motor Racing Show – *till Sun 26* 0181-744 1585

28 **Lincoln's Inn Fields** Pancake Race

LONDON CALENDAR

MARCH

1 **St Paul's Cathedral** Cakes and Ale Sermon

4 **Alexandra Palace** Sailboat '95, The RYA National Dinghy Show – *till Sun 5* (01703) 629962

9 **Olympia** BBC Food Show – *till Sun 12* 0181-948 1666

11 **Westminster** RHS Orchid Show at Old Hall – *till Sun 12* 0171-834 4333

14 **Chelsea** Antique Fair at Chelsea Old Town Hall – *till Sun 19* (01444) 482514; **Westminster** RHS Competitions at RHS New Hall – *till Weds 15* 0171-834 4333

16 **Earls Court** Ideal Home Exhibition at Exhibition Centre – *till 9 Apr* (01895) 677677

18 **Twickenham** Rugby Union: England v Scotland 0181-892 8161

31 **Olympia** Dance World – *till 2 Apr* 0181-364 8680

APRIL

7 **Olympia** Bike '95 – *till Sun 9* (01225) 442244

11 **Westminster** RHS Show and Competition at RHS New and Old Halls – *till Weds 12* 0171-834 4333

13 **Olympia** International Spring Gardening Fair – *till Mon 17* 0171-782 6392

17 **Regent's Park** Harness Horse Parade; **Southwark** Chaucer Festival and start of Spring Pilgrimage from the Tower of London, crossing Tower Bridge to Southwark Cathedral before leaving for Canterbury (01227) 470379

MAY

2 **Westminster** RHS Competitions at the RHS New Hall – *till Weds 3* 0171-834 4333

6 **Twickenham** Rugby Union Cup Final 0181-892 8161

8 **Covent Garden** Festival – *till Sun 21* 0171-240 0930

16 **Westminster Cathedral** International Festival of Flowers with Music: celebrating the cathedral's 100th anniversary – *till Sat 20* (01638) 500577

23 **Chelsea** Flower Show at Royal Hospital – *till Fri 26* (members only 23–24) 0171-630 7422

JUNE

1 **Hampton Court** Music Festival – *till Sun 18* 0181-781 9507

2 **Greenwich** Festival – *till Sun 18* 0181 317-1085

7 **Horse Guards Parade** Beating Retreat – *till Thurs 8* 0171-414 2357; **Spitalfields** Festival at Christchurch Spitalfields – *till Weds 28* 0171-377 0287

8 **Olympia** Fine Art and Antique Fair – *till Sun 18* 0171-370 8188

10 **Whitehall** Trooping the Colour – the Queen's official birthday parade at Horse Guards Parade 0171-414 2357

12 **Covent Garden** Verdi Festival at the Royal Opera House – *till 15 July* 0171-240 1200

18 **London** to **Brighton** Bike Ride (01225) 480130

20 **City of London** Festival – *till 7 July* 0171-377 0540; **Westminster** RHS Ornamental Plant Competition at RHS New Hall – *till Weds 21* 0171-834 4333

24 **Westminster** and **City** Summer Chaucer Festival – *till Sat 22* (01227) 470379

LONDON CALENDAR

JUNE cont

26 **Wimbledon** Lawn Tennis Championships – *till 9 July* 0181-946 2244

JULY

4 **Hampton Court Palace** Flower Show – *till Sun 9* 0181-834 4333

9 **City of London** Festival – *till Weds 26* 0171-377 0540

11 **Honourable Artillery Company's Ground** Antique Fair at Armoury House, City Rd, – *till Sun 16* (01444) 482514

18 **Westminster** RHS Summer Fruit and Vegetable Competition at RHS New Hall – *till Weds 19* 0171-834 4333

21 **Royal Albert Hall** Henry Wood Promenade Concerts: centenary series – *till 16 Sept* 0171-765 4296

AUGUST

15 **Westminster** RHS Competitions at RHS New Hall – *till Weds 16* 0171-834 4333

18 **South Bank Centre** Folk Week – *till Fri 25* (01296) 394411

27 **Notting Hill** Carnival, Ladbroke Grove – *till Mon 28* 0181-964 0544

SEPTEMBER

1 **Rupert St** London Latin-American Film Festival at the Metro Cinema – *till Thurs 14* 0171-734 1506

12 **Chelsea** Antique Fair at Chelsea Old Town Hall – *till Sun 17* (01444) 482514

13 **Westminster** RHS Great Autumn Flower Show at RHS New and Old Halls – *till Weds 13* 0171-630 7422

26 **Wembley Arena** Horse of the Year Show – *till 1 Oct* (01203) 693088

28 **Soho** Jazz festival – *till 7 Oct* 0171-437 6437

OCTOBER

3 **Westminster** RHS Competitions at RHS New Hall – *till 1 Nov* 0171-630 7422

19 **Earls Court** London Motor Show Exhibition Centre – *till Sun 29* 0171-373 8141

22 **Trafalgar Sq** Trafalgar Service and Parade – 11am–1pm

30 **28 Cork St** British Society of Painters – *till 11 Nov* 0171-287 8408

NOVEMBER

1 **Royal Geographical Society** Kensington Gore, London International Environmental Film Festival – *till Sun 5* 0171-379 7390

5 **Hyde Park Corner** Start of the London to Brighton Veteran Car Run (01753) 681736

11 **City of London** Lord Mayor's Procession and Show from the Guildhall to the Royal Courts of Justice 0181-882 1083

12 **Whitehall** Remembrance Day Service and Parade 0171-414 2357

21 **Westminster** RHS Competitions at RHS New Hall – *till Weds 22* 0171-630 7422

DECEMBER

1 **Earls Court** World Darts Championships at Park International Hotel – *till Sat 2* 0181-883 5544

12 **Westminster** RHS Christmas Show at RHS New Hall – *till Weds 13* 0171-630 7422

31 **Trafalgar Sq** New Year's Eve Celebrations

SCOTLAND

Edinburgh has great appeal for a short city holiday; if the late summer Festival is not the main attraction for you, you'd probably enjoy the city more at a less crowded time of year. In the countryside, the deeply indented west coast from Strathclyde northwards has the broadest-based appeal, but almost every part of Scotland has some attraction for a short stay. Except in the north, there are a lot of places to visit – particularly castles, lived-in or ruined, but also some magnificent gardens (especially on the west coast, where they tend to be at their best in late May and June). Glasgow has possibilities for a lively and thought-provoking visit.

Much of Scotland is good for driving holidays; however, at the height of summer the most beautiful main roads do tend to attract too many other drivers for comfort. Though the Borders and the south-west corner of Scotland stay fairly quiet year-round, the west coast and Highlands are perhaps best visited in May and June.

Most of the castles and abbeys we list are owned by Historic Scotland; an Explorer ticket admits you free to all their properties, for £10 (one week) or £14 (two weeks); from tourist information centres, or in advance (0131) 244 3101.

For a short stay, the snag for many people in England is the sheer scale of the distances involved. As a rough guide, a three-hour drive will get anyone living north of Manchester or York well into the southern parts of Scotland. If you're coming from further south than that, the driving does become rather daunting. Trains and aeroplanes put much more of Scotland within reach for a short stay. There are direct flights from London and some regional airports to Edinburgh, Glasgow, Inverness and Aberdeen, with some local connections from there. The fastest trains do the London–Edinburgh run in around four hours, and there are sleepers from both London and Plymouth/Poole/Bristol. If you boarded the night sleeper for Inverness at nine o'clock in the evening in London, a hire car could get you on to Skye by about 11 o'clock the next morning.

SOUTH SCOTLAND

Edinburgh is excellent for a city break; lots to see and do elsewhere, with good quiet touring and walking in the Borders.

Edinburgh is a beautiful city, with many interesting places in a conveniently compact area – most of the main things to see are within an easy and pleasant walk of each other. There are some great things to see in Glasgow too, which has an edge of vitality that is very appealing.

The Borders scenery is grand without being austere, and pleasantly varied, with some of Scotland's best walking, and no end of little-visited ancient castles, romantic ruined abbeys, and other things to look at. The south-west corner of Scotland is one of the friendliest parts of Britain, particularly Galloway, and though it doesn't have quite such memorable scenery as the Borders, it has some interesting old monuments, attractive places to potter around in (particularly on the coast), and relatively few visitors. Ayrshire has some great golf courses and Scotland's most popular racecourse, but its main appeal might be to people wanting to follow the Robert Burns trail.

This part of Scotland has many great romantic castles such as those at Hermitage, Caerlaverock, Peebles and Castle Douglas; ruined abbeys such as those on Inchcolm (boats from South Queensferry) and at Glenluce and New Abbey; and rich gardens, prime among them those near Stranraer, at Port Logan, Stobo and Kirkbean, and at Brodick on Arran. There are many remarkably fine houses in the area, especially those we describe under Traquair, Selkirk, Thornhill, Duns and South Queensferry; Culzean Castle is a favourite Scottish family outing. The Newton Grange mining museum and the preserved printworks at Innerleithen are surprisingly interesting. Among new entries to the *Guide* this year, we'd particularly pick out the developing visitor attractions in New Lanark, the almost scholarly Teddy Melrose in Melrose and the entertaining sheepdog centre at Tweedhope.

Where to stay

Edinburgh NT2574 HOWARD 36 Great King St, Edinburgh EH3 6QH (0131) 557 3500 **£180**; 16 luxurious rms. Fine, civilised 18th-c hotel with comfortable, elegant public rooms, courteous, efficient service, and good food; cl between Christmas and New Year and 1st wk Jan; disabled access.

Gullane NT4882 GREYWALLS Duncar Rd, Gullane, East Lothian EH31 2EG (01620) 842144 **£160**; 22 individually decorated rms. Overlooking the Muirfield Golf Course, this beautiful Lutyens family-run house has antiques, open fires and flowers in its comfortable lounges and panelled library, very good food and fine wines in the restaurant, impeccable service, and lovely garden; cl Nov–Mar; disabled access.

Edinburgh NT2574 BALMORAL Princes St, Edinburgh EH2 2EQ (0131) 556 2414 ***£155**; 189 luxurious rms. Splendid Victorian hotel with wonderfully opulent entrance hall, elegant day rooms, lovely flowers, particularly friendly, helpful staff, and very good food in several restaurants; excellent leisure facilities; good disabled access.

Glasgow NS5865 ONE DEVONSHIRE GARDENS Glasgow G12 0UX (0141) 339 2001 **£140w**; 27 huge, opulent rms. Elegant hotel not far from city centre with luxurious Victorian furnishings in the public areas, fresh flowers, friendly staff, and fine modern cooking in the stylish restaurant; disabled access.

Maybole NS3009 LADYBURN Maybole, Ayrshire KA19 7SG (01655) 4585 **£140**; 8 rms. Quietly set family home in lovely wooded countryside with antiques, books and open fires in comfortable day rooms, and friendly staff; shooting and fishing can be arranged; self-catering flat also; cl 4 wks between Jan and Mar; no children; disabled access.

Kelso NT7334 SUNLAWS HOUSE Kelso, Roxburghshire TD5 8JZ (01573) 450331 ***£134**; 22 good rms. Splendid hotel in 200 acres of garden and parkland with relaxed and comfortable lounge, library and conservatory, open fires, hearty breakfasts and fine local produce used in the carefully prepared cooking; tennis, croquet, shooting, fishing, and falconry; disabled access.

Edinburgh NT2574 ROXBURGHE Charlotte Sq, Edinburgh EH2 4HG (0131) 225 3921 *£125; 75 rms. In an elegant square, this is a fine example of Adam architecture with quiet, elegant public rooms, enjoyable food in attractive restaurant, and good service; cl 25–26 Dec.

Gatehouse of Fleet NX5956 CALLY PALACE Gatehouse of Fleet, Castle Douglas, Kirkcudbrightshire DG7 2DL (01557) 814341 £124 inc dinner; 56 comfortable rms. 18th-c mansion in extensive grounds with lovely views, comfortable, rather splendid public rooms, and good food; leisure centre and 18-hole golf course; cl Jan and Feb; disabled access.

Auchencairn NX7951 COLLIN HOUSE Auchencairn, Castle Douglas, Kirkcudbrightshire DG7 1QN (01556) 640292 £120; 6 rms with period furniture. Attractive pink-washed stone house in 20 acres looking across to Hestan Island and the Solway Firth; fine views from the drawing room and dining room, relaxed sitting room, imaginative food and carefully chosen wines; cl 3/4 wks Jan/Feb; children over 10 in restaurant in evening (high tea for younger ones).

Dirleton NT5184 OPEN ARMS Dirleton, North Berwick, East Lothian EH39 5EG (01620) 850241 *£120; 7 comfortable, pretty rms. Run by the same family for over 45 years, this friendly hotel has a very comfortable lounge with log fire and nice little bar, and overlooks the ruins of Dirleton Castle; limited disabled access.

Edinburgh NT2574 CALEDONIAN Princes St, Edinburgh EH1 2AB (0131) 225 2433 £120w; 239 rms. On the site of the old Caledonian railway station, this is a grand place with spacious, elegant and comfortable public rooms, a fine sweeping staircase, marble pillars and chandeliers, and very good food in the stylish restaurant; disabled access.

Uphall NT0571 HOUSTOUN HOUSE Uphall, Broxburn, West Lothian EH52 6JS (01506) 853831 £115; 30 comfortable rms. 17th-c house in fine grounds with a quiet lounge, panelled dining rooms, cellar bar, and good food.

Portpatrick NX0054 KNOCKINAAM LODGE Portpatrick, Stranraer, Wigtownshire DG9 9AD (01776) 810471 £104; 10 individual rms. Lovely, very neatly kept little hotel with comfortable, pretty rooms, open fires, wonderful food, and friendly, caring service; the surroundings are dramatic and there are lots of fine cliff walks; cl Jan–mid-Mar; children over 12 in evening restaurant (high tea at 6); disabled access.

Bonnyrigg NT3065 DALHOUSIE CASTLE Bonnyrigg, Midlothian EH19 3JB (01875) 820153 £100; 24 rms, some of great character. Turreted red sandstone castle with some fine historic features such as the dungeon restaurant and oak-panelled library bar; children under 12 free if in parents' rm and meals half-price.

Peebles NT2540 CRINGLETIE HOUSE Peebles EH45 8PL (01721) 730233 £98; 13 pretty rms. Surrounded by 28 acres of garden and woodland and with fine views, this turreted baronial mansion, run by the same couple for over 20 years, is very welcoming and quiet, with delicious food using home-grown vegetables, extensive Scottish breakfasts, and excellent service; cl Jan and Feb.

Quothquan NS9939 SHIELDHILL Quothquan, Biggar, Lanarkshire ML12 6NA (01899) 20035 *£98; 11 pretty rms. Partly 13th-c hotel in a fine setting with comfortable oak-panelled lounge, open fires, library, particularly good food in the no smoking restaurant, and warm, friendly service; children over 10.

Brodick NS0136 AUCHRANNIE COUNTRY HOUSE Brodick, Island of Arran KA27 8BZ (01770) 302234 *£96; 28 attractive rms. Victorian country house hotel in 6 acres of grounds with indoor leisure complex (adult and children's swimming pools, too), several lounges, carefully prepared food in conservatory restaurant and more informal bistro, and a relaxed, friendly atmosphere; self-catering lodges; disabled access.

Kilwinning NS3043 MONTGREENAN MANSION HOUSE Montgreenan Estate, Kilwinning, Ayrshire KA13 7QZ (01294) 557733 £92; 21 rms. Grand Georgian-style mansion with a quiet, restful atmosphere, open fires and ornate plasterwork in elegant public rooms, friendly service, and extensive grounds with tennis, croquet and putting green.

Newton Stewart NX4165 KIRROUGHTREE Newton Stewart, Wigtownshire DG8 6AN (01671) 2141 £90; 17 spacious rms (many recently refurbished). Early 18th-c mansion in 8 acres of carefully landscaped gardens on edge of Galloway Forest Park; oak-panelled lounge with rococo furnishings, fresh flowers and French windows leading to terrace and croquet lawn, formal dining rooms (one is no smoking) with very good food, and friendly staff; leisure facilities available at sister hotel, the Cally Palace (see above) and fishing, shooting and stalking can be arranged; cl Jan and Feb; children over 10.

Rockcliffe NX8453 BARONS CRAIG Rockcliffe, Dalbeattie, Kirkcudbrightshire DG5 4QF (01556) 630225 £90; 22 rms, inc 4 family ones. 12 acres of gardens and woodland surround this imposing Victorian house with its relaxing lounges and fine views; lots of golf courses within easy reach; dogs welcome away from public rooms; cl end Oct–Easter; disabled access.

Selkirk NT4728 PHILIPBURN HOUSE Linglie Rd, Selkirk TD7 5LS (01750) 20747 £90; 16 pretty rms. A particularly good place for families, this very relaxing, family-run 18th-c hotel has Austrian-style furnishings, good food using the best local produce, an interesting wine list, and friendly service; fine walks in the surrounding grounds and woods, and swimming pool; disabled access.

Skelmorlie NS1967 MANOR PARK Skelmorlie, Ayrshire PA17 5HE (01475) 520832 £90; 22 rms. In 15 lovely acres of gardens with fine views, this country house has a spacious, quiet lounge and well stocked bar.

Auchencairn NX7951 BALCARY BAY Auchencairn, Castle Douglas, Kirkcudbrightshire DG7 1QZ (01556) 640217 £88; 17 rms with fine views. Charming hotel with wonderful views over the bay, neat grounds running down to the water, comfortable public rooms (one with log fire), friendly service, very good, enjoyable food, and lots of walks; cl mid-Nov–1st wk Mar.

Clarencefield NY0968 COMLONGON CASTLE Clarencefield, Dumfries DG1 TNA (0138 787) 283 £80; 11 rms. Country house with suits of armour in oak-panelled great hall, good food in Jacobean dining room, and relaxing drawing room, and right next door to a large border stronghold with dungeons, lofty battlements, archers' quarters and haunted long gallery – candlelit tour before dinner if you like; cl Jan and Feb.

Minnigaff NX4166 CREEBRIDGE HOUSE Minnigaff, Newton Stewart, Wigtownshire DG8 6NP (01671) 402121 £75; 20 rms. Attractive country-house hotel in 3 acres of gardens with relaxed, friendly atmosphere, open fire in comfortable drawing room, cheerful bar, and big choice of delicious food inc fine local fish and seafood; disabled access.

Lockerbie NY1381 DRYFESDALE HOTEL Lockerbie, Dumfriesshire DG11 2SF (01576) 202427 *£74; 15 rms, 6 on ground floor level. Relaxed and comfortable former manse with 5 acres of grounds, comfortable, homely lounge, good food in pleasant restaurant, and lovely surrounding countryside; cl 25–26 Dec; good disabled access.

Beattock NT0905 AUCHEN CASTLE Auchen, Beattock, Moffat, Dumfriesshire DG10 9SH (01683) 3407 £72; 25 pleasantly decorated rms, some in the lodge. Smart but friendly country-house hotel in lovely quiet spot with a trout-loch and spectacular hill views, good food, and peaceful, comfortable bar; cl Christmas and New Year.

Canonbie NY3976 RIVERSIDE Canonbie, Dumfriesshire DG14 0UX (01387) 371512 £72; 6 notably comfortable, well decorated rms. Peacefully civilised hotel with pleasant, no smoking restaurant, charming communicating bar rooms, excellent, imaginative food using organic or naturally fed produce, marvellous breakfasts with home-made breads, oatcakes and preserves, award-winning wines, good beers, and sympathetic service; fishing permits; cl 25 Dec, 1 Jan, 2 wks Nov, 2 wks Feb; children over 5.

Melrose NT5434 BURTS HOTEL Melrose, Roxburghshire TD6 9PN (01896) 822285 £72; 21 rms. Welcoming 18th-c inn in delightfully quiet village and close to ruined abbey; coal fire in bustling bar, residents' lounge, consistently popular, imaginative food, exceptional breakfasts, and a decent wine list; no accomm 24–26 Dec (open for meals then).

Edinburgh NT2574 DRUMMOND HOUSE 17 Drummond Pl, Edinburgh EH3 6PL (0131) 557 9189 *£70; 3 charming rms. Georgian town house in handsome square with antiques and fine rugs in elegant rooms, a warmly welcoming atmosphere, and good Scottish breakfasts; cl Christmas; children over 12.

Edinburgh NT2574 LODGE 6 Hampton Terrace, West Coates, Edinburgh EH12 5JD (0131) 337 3682 £70; 12 rms. Carefully restored and neatly kept little Georgian hotel with open fire and restful atmosphere in lounge, cosy cocktail bar, freshly cooked food in attractive dining room, and friendly, helpful owners; cl 14–27 Dec.

Portpatrick NX0054 CROWN Portpatrick, Stranraer, Wigtownshire DG9 8SX (01776) 810261 £70; 12 rms. Atmospheric harbourside inn with attractive bedrooms, rambling old-fashioned bar with interesting furnishings, airy 1930s-ish dining room, good food with an emphasis on local seafood, excellent breakfasts, carefully chosen wines.

Edinburgh NT2574 SIBBET HOUSE 26 Northumberland St, Edinburgh EH3 6LS (0131) 556 1078 £65; 3 pretty rms. Very well run Georgian hotel, full of interesting antiques and objects, with a relaxed atmosphere in the elegant drawing room, generous communal Scottish breakfasts, and charming owners; cl Christmas, New Year, Jan.

Gifford NT5368 TWEEDDALE ARMS Gifford, Haddington, East Lothian EH41 4QU (01620) 810240 £65; 16 rms. Civilised old inn in quiet village with comfortable sofas and chairs in tranquil lounge, gracious dining room, wide choice of good daily-changing food, and charming service; disabled access.

Kelso NT7334 EDNAM HOUSE Kelso, Roxburghshire TD5 7HT (01573) 24168 £65; 32 rms. Homely and relaxed family-run Georgian mansion with pleasantly old-fashioned rooms, helpful service, and 3 acres of gardens that run down to the banks of the River Tweed; cl Christmas.

Glasgow NS5865 BABBITY BOWSTER 16-18 Blackfriars St, Glasgow G1 1TE (0141) 552 5055 £64.50; 6 clean simple rms, showers. Warmly welcoming, rather continental place with decent breakfasts (served till late), attractively decorated airy bar, and a cheery first-floor restaurant, which hosts a gallery as well as a programme of musical and theatrical events.

Glasgow NS5865 RAB HA'S 83 Hutcheson St, Glasgow G1 1SH (0141) 552 2206 £60; 4 elegant rms. Sensitively converted and warmly friendly Georgian town house with delightfully informal ground floor bar, popular restaurant, and good service.

Innerleithen NT3336 TRAQUAIR ARMS Innerleithen, Peeblesshire EH44 6PD (01896) 830229 *£58; 10 comfortable rms. Very friendly pub with interesting choice of good food in attractive dining room, cosy lounge bar, friendly service, the superb local Traquair on handpump, and nice breakfasts; cl 25–26 Dec, 1–2 Jan.

Swinton NT8448 WHEATSHEAF Swinton, Duns, Berwickshire TD11 3JJ (01890) 860257 £58; 4 rms, showers. Warmly friendly inn with exceptionally good food (emphasis on fish), pleasantly decorated, relaxed main lounge plus small pubby area, separate locals' bar, and no smoking front conservatory; garden play area for children; cl middle 2 wks Feb, last wk Oct.

Tweedsmuir NT0924 CROOK INN Tweedsmuir, Biggar, Lanarkshire ML12 6QN (01899) 7272 *£52; 7 rms. Old drovers' inn on lonely road through grand hills with large, airy lounge, simply furnished back bar, sun lounge, various art-deco features, good food, and friendly service; attractive garden across the road, pétanque and putting in adjoining field, and glassblowing centre and Upper Tweed Heritage Centre in old stableblock (open daily); fishing permits.

Annan Water NT0712 COREHEAD FARM Annan Water, Moffat, Dumfriesshire DG10 9LT (01683) 20973 £48; 2 rms. Welcoming farmhouse on working hill sheep farm with woodburning stove in lounge, and good food using home-grown and local produce and their own naturally reared lamb and beef; excellent hill walking; children over 12; cl Nov–Mar.

Edinburgh NT2574 GREENWIDE 9 Royal Terrace, Edinburgh EH7 5AB (0131) 557 0022 £48; 13 individually decorated rms, most with own bthrm. Family-run hotel in Georgian terrace with friendly atmosphere, big lounge, hearty breakfasts, and quiet terraced garden; disabled access.

Melrose NT5434 DUNFERMLINE HOUSE Buccleuch St, Melrose, Roxburghshire TD6 9LB (01896) 822148 *£42; 5 rms. Neatly kept Victorian terraced house, close to Melrose Abbey ruins, with good breakfasts and friendly owners; cl 24–26 Dec.

Ettrick Valley NT3018 TUSHIELAW Ettrick Valley, Selkirk TD7 5HT (01750) 62205 *£38; 3 rms, one with own bath. Friendly little inn in lovely spot on Ettrick Water, imaginative restaurant food, intimate bar, fine views, own loch, and shooting and fishing (as well as birdwatching and walking).

Innerleithen NT3336 CADDON VIEW 14 Pirn Rd, Innerleithen, Peeblesshire EH44 6HH (01896) 830208 *£34; 5 well equipped rms, most with own bthrm. Warmly welcoming and relaxing grey stone Victorian villa with attractive candlelit dining room, really good, piping hot home-made food, comfortable lounge, and caring service; private parking; cl last 2 wks Jan; children under 3 free; disabled access.

Kirkcowan NX3260 CRAIGHLAW ARMS Kirkcowan, Newton Stewart, Wigtownshire DG8 OHQ (01671) 830283 £32; 3 clean, comfortable rms, shared bthrm. Carefully modernised old coachhouse in quiet village, with comfortable residents' lounge, imaginative choice of good home-cooked food including huge T-bone steaks, rod-caught salmon and wild brown trout; shooting and fishing; self-catering also.

Nenthorn NT6838 WHITEHILL FARM Nenthorn, Kelso, Roxburghshire TD5 7RZ (01573) 470203 £32; 4 rms, 3 with shared bthrm. Comfortable farmhouse on mixed farm with fine views, big garden, log fire in sitting room, and good home cooking; cl Christmas and New Year.

To see and do

Edinburgh NT2574 Part of Edinburgh's charm lies in the fact that in the 18th c the city authorities decided to develop it not by knocking down the crowded and outmoded narrow streets of largely medieval buildings in the Old Town and replacing them with new smart Georgian streets, but instead to create an entirely new part of the city, working from scratch. So the New Town, a masterpiece of spacious Georgian town planning that's a real pleasure to stroll through (especially since most of its grand stone buildings have been cleaned up), stretches out handsomely below the steep crag of Castle Rock and its medieval skyline. The whole city is dominated by the ancient silhouettes of Edinburgh Castle on its cliff and of the long erratic line of tall, narrow Old Town buildings stretched along beside it. Up here narrow streets and alleys with steep steps between them and courtyard closes leading off have a real flavour of the distant past, with a good many interesting ancient buildings (and a lot of the city's antiquarian bookshops and other interesting specialist shops). As in most cities, there's a hop-on hop-off tour bus, and the ticket gives discounts to some of the places to visit. Edinburgh does put on its best clothes and best events for its Festival; it's easier to see, and truer to itself, at other times of year. Lothian Regional Council have great plans for making the centre more pedestrian-friendly, especially the shopping side of Princes St; as we went to press details were still being finalised but it's likely that at least some of the proposals will be implemented on a trial basis early this year.

🏰 ✝ ❀ ♻ EDINBURGH CASTLE Perched on its hill above the city, the castle is a place of great magnetism; it's been a fortress since at least the 7th c, and recent excavations show there's been a settlement here for 4,000 years. The oldest building today is the beautiful St Margaret's Chapel in one of the courtyards, thought to have been built in the 12th c and little changed since. In 1314 the early buildings were destroyed to make the fortress useless to the invading English, so most of the castle is a series of later accretions. Highlights include the apartments of Mary, Queen of Scots; Mons Meg, the 15th-c Belgian cannon with which James II cowed the Black Douglases; and the Scottish Crown Jewels – centuries older than the English ones. Glorious views from the battlements, over the New Town, the Pentland Hills and the Firth of Forth to Fife beyond. Also worth a look are the Scottish National War Memorial built on the site of the castle's church, and the Scottish United Services Museum. Though you can wander around on your own, this is one place where the official guides are a great bonus – they leave from the drawbridge, several times a day. Shop, disabled access; cl 25–26 Dec, 1 Jan; £5. If you're around at lunchtime, look (and listen) for the firing of the One o' Clock Gun from the parapet.

🏠🖼️✣ PALACE OF HOLYROODHOUSE Imposing yet human-scale palace with its origins in the abbey of Holyrood, founded by David I. Once the court of Mary, Queen of Scots, it was used by Bonnie Prince Charlie during his occupation of Edinburgh, and is still a royal residence for part of the year. The oldest surviving part is James IV's tower, with Queen Mary's rooms on the second floor, where a plaque on the floor marks where her secretary Rizzio was murdered in front of her. The throne room and state rooms have period furniture, tapestries and paintings from the royal collection, and the picture gallery is interesting for its series of portraits of Scottish monarchs. The building has an almost domestic scale that makes it more inviting than many English palaces. By Easter this year they should have completed a number of improvements (bigger shop, new displays, better interpretation etc), and the gardens will be opened up for the first time. Shop, limited disabled access by prior arrangement; cl winter Sun, 2 wks mid–late May, 3 wks late Jun–early July and occasional other dates – it may be best to check first on (0131) 556 1096; *£4.

❗🏠🏰☕✝ Between the castle and the palace (for most people the two must-sees) is the ROYAL MILE, a largely medieval street around which you'll find a bewildering variety of interesting or historic houses and features, and quaint lanes leading off in all directions. Usefully, it's punctuated with cafés and bars in which to stop and work out your next move, starting with the old-world Ensign Ewart on the left as you leave the castle. We list the pick of the attractions as you'll find them heading down. Up at the top, the revolving lenses and mirrors of the 19th-c CAMERA OBSCURA create unique panoramas of the city as soon as the lights go down, with a good commentary; best on a sunny day. Also unusual exhibition of holography. Shop; cl 25 Dec, 1 Jan; (0131) 226 3709; *£3.20. Near here the SCOTCH WHISKY HERITAGE CENTRE entertainingly illustrates the story of the national drink, with a fun journey in a barrel-shaped car through well constructed sets and tableaux. Useful if you won't be visiting a real distillery; cl 25 Dec, 1 Jan; (0131) 220 0441; £3.80. GLADSTONE'S LAND Six-storeyed early 17th-c building, still with its arcaded front, and refurnished in period style to resemble the typical home of a rich merchant. The walls and ceilings have remarkable tempera paintings. Shop, limited disabled access; cl am Sun, Nov–Mar; £2.50; NTS. LADY STAIR'S HOUSE Named after its 18th-c occupant, this 17th-c house is home to the Writers Museum, a collection of manuscripts and objects associated with Robert Burns, Sir Walter Scott and Robert Louis Stevenson. Shop; cl Sun exc Festival, 25–26 Dec, 1–3 Jan; free. Scotland's High Kirk, ST GILES' CATHEDRAL is the city's most impressive ecclesiastical building, mainly 15th-c, but dating from around 1120. Topped with an ornate crown-like tower, it has monuments to famous Scots from Knox (minister here until his death) to R L Stevenson.

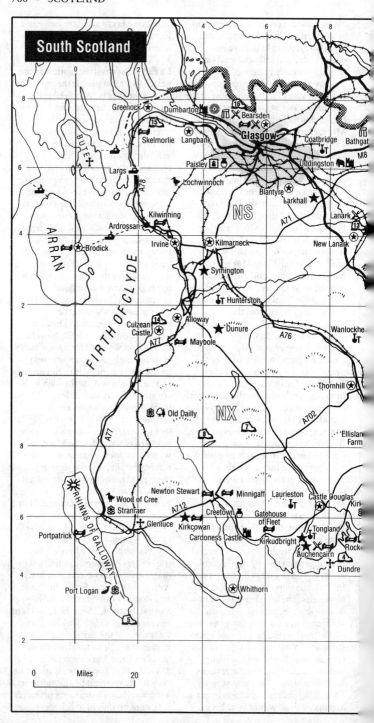

South Scotland

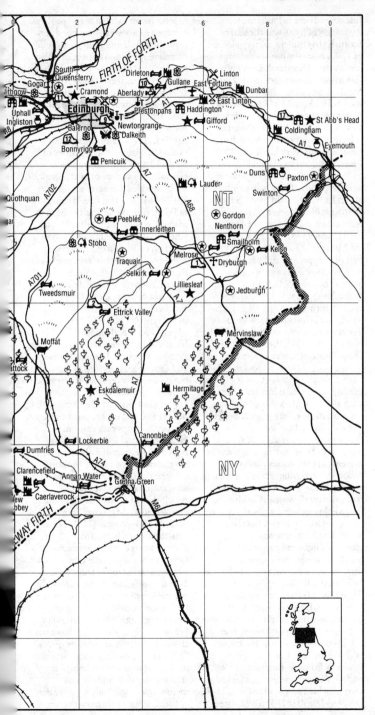

Just behind here in Parliament Sq, PARLIAMENT HOUSE was the seat of Scottish government until the Union of 1707, and now houses the supreme law courts of Scotland. Don't miss the fine hammerbeam roof in the Hall. Meals, snacks, disabled access; cl wknds; (0131) 225 2595; free. The oldest house on the Royal Mile is JOHN KNOX HOUSE where the great reformer is supposed to have died. Now looking every bit of its 500 years, it still has its original timber galleries, oak panelling and splendid painted ceiling. There's an exhibition about Knox's life and times. Snacks, shop, disabled access to ground floor only; cl Sun and 25 Dec–11 Jan; (0131) 556 9579; *£1.25. Opposite, the MUSEUM OF CHILDHOOD was the first of its type, and still one of the best, an outstanding collection of games, toys and dolls from all over the globe. Shop, disabled access; cl Sun exc pm during Festival; (0131) 529 4142; free. The elaborate CANONGATE TOLBOOTH is now an excellent social history exhibition, the People's Story. Shop, disabled access; cl Sun exc pm during Festival; free. Across the road, 16th-c HUNTLY HOUSE (Canongate) is the city's main local history museum, with all the exhibits thoughtfully – even artistically – arranged. Shop; cl Sun exc during Festival; free.

The main branch of the ROYAL MUSEUM OF SCOTLAND in Chambers St presents a tremendous variety of collections covering virtually anything you might care to poke around in, from all over the world. Children very much enjoy its intricate working scale models of early engines, but it has something for everyone – in a gloriously light and spacious Victorian building. Meals, snacks, shop, disabled access; cl am Sun, 25–26 Dec, 1–2 Jan; (0131) 225 7534; free.

NATIONAL GALLERY OF SCOTLAND (The Mound) Fine neo-classical building with an exceptional collection of paintings, with particularly fine examples of most European schools and periods as well as many great works by Ramsay, Raeburn, Wilkie and McTaggart; meals and snacks, shop, disabled access; cl am Sun, 25–26 Dec, 1–3 Jan; (0131) 356 8921; free

(exc for major exhibitions). The ROYAL SCOTTISH ACADEMY is in a second neo-classical temple alongside, with good changing exhibitions. Shop, disabled access; (0131) 225 6671 for what's on; £1.20 for annual exhibition Apr–July. On either side, like a broad moat for the castle (this was a loch before the New Town was built), are well tended gardens.

SCOTTISH NATIONAL PORTRAIT GALLERY (Queen St) The history of Scotland through a huge collection of portraits in a variety of media. Snacks, shop, disabled access; cl am Sun, 25–26 Dec, 1–3 Jan; free. It shares a building with the antiquities branch of the ROYAL MUSEUM OF SCOTLAND, where old-fashioned displays show a very rich collection of artefacts, jewellery and so forth from the Stone Age to the present; there's also a presentation on Stuart rule in Scotland. Snacks, shop, disabled access; cl am Sun.

SCOTTISH NATIONAL GALLERY OF MODERN ART (Belford Rd) Breathtaking collection inc works by Picasso, Magritte, Barbara Hepworth and Lichtenstein, as well as the national collection of Scottish modern art. Meals, snacks, shop, disabled access; cl am Sun, 25–26 Dec, 1–3 Jan; (0131) 556 8921; free, may be charges for special temporary exhibitions.

GEORGIAN HOUSE Archetypal period house, part of Robert Adam's magnificent terrace along the north side of Charlotte Sq. The rooms and servants' quarters have been refurbished in the style of 1800. Shop, disabled access to ground floor only; cl am Sun, Nov–Mar; £3; NTS. For a structured introduction to the New Town's smart terraces and clean-cut Georgian houses, try the CONSERVATION CENTRE near the top of Dundas St; cl 1–2pm; free. Close by, near Queen St, beyond a further strip of gardens, is a further Georgian area with some interesting shops. Hoggs in the alley behind stately Great King St has a wide choice of malt whiskies at low prices.

SCOTT MEMORIAL (Princes St) For many people this remarkably ornate structure is Edinburgh's most memorable single building after the castle. Terrific views from the top –

though it takes 287 steps to get there; cl Sun; £1.

✻ ! Dominating the eastern end of Princes St, CALTON HILL also has magnificent views over the city, best of all from the top of the 102 ft NELSON MONUMENT – if you can face the climb. Every day at 1pm the time ball drops as the gun from the castle goes off. Shop; cl am Sun (all day Sept–Apr) and Mon; £1. An observatory nearby houses the EDINBURGH EXPERIENCE, a half-hour 3-D history of the city (they provide special glasses); cl am (exc July–early Sept), Oct–Easter; *£2. An unusual sight up here is a romantic Doric colonnade, intended to be a full replica of the Parthenon (until the money ran out).

✤ ROYAL BOTANIC GARDEN (Inverleith Row) Founded as a physic garden in 1670 at Holyrood and then transplanted here (just N of the centre) in the early 19th c. Covering 72 acres, it has various splendid themed areas, with a woodland garden, peat garden, arboretum and the Glasshouse Experience, inc palm houses, fern house and aquatic house. They keep the most comprehensive rhododendron collection in the country, and grow many other rare Asiatic plants – particularly primulas and lilies and their more awkward relatives – to perfection. Guided tours leave from inside the West Gate at 11am and 2pm Apr–Sept. Meals, snacks, shop, disabled access; cl 25 Dec, 1 Jan; (0131) 552 7171; free.

✻ ROYAL OBSERVATORY (Blackford Hill) Good range of often lively astronomy displays, inc videos, computer games, and the biggest telescope in Scotland. Glorious views down over the city, and even as far as the Braid Hills. Shop, disabled access; cl am (exc wkdys Apr–Sept), 25 Dec, 1 Jan; (0131) 668 8405; £2.

🐘 EDINBURGH ZOO (Corstorphine Rd, 3m W on A8) One of the best zoos in Britain, especially praiseworthy for its penguin enclosure, the biggest in the world, with underwater viewing windows; don't miss the penguin parade every day at 2pm, Mar–Oct. Plenty other rare and odd-looking animals – check out some of the frogs.

They do evening guided tours May–Sept. Meals, snacks, shops (inc a special penguin and polar bear shop in summer), disabled access; (0131) 334 9171; £5.10.

✻ Out beyond Holyrood is the great saddle-back hill of ARTHUR'S SEAT in Holyrood Park, a pleasant place for wandering, with the largely unspoilt Duddingston village below it (the Sheep Heid here is a good pub).

🛍 There are lots of good shops dotted around town, especially on or near PRINCES ST – its tall, mainly Georgian buildings lining just the one side, giving an expansive view across the sunken gardens to the castle. Parallel with here is GEORGE ST, with some good superior shops, while Rose St, an alley between the two, has lots of pubs and cafés. More bars around the GRASSMARKET and LAWNMARKET, a lively area of the Old Town; Victoria St here has interesting shops.

To the W, the WATER OF LEITH is worth exploring, often very picturesque and ravine-like. By its banks, surprisingly close to Edinburgh's centre, is the quaint little Dean Village, unaffected by all the New Town building above it, and there's a fine series of Georgian crescents around Moray Place. Edinburgh's pubs and bars are a special delight, chatty places often of great character. Among the best for atmosphere are the Bow Bar (Victoria St), Bannerman's Bar (Cowgate), Café Royal and Guildford Arms (both W Register St), the Diggers (properly the Athletic Arms, Angle Park Terrace/Kilmarnock Rd), Kay's Bar (Jamaica St W), and Jolly Judge (James Court, off Lawnmarket); for food too, the Peacock (Lindsay Rd, Newhaven), Abbotsford, Kenilworth and Milnes (all Rose St), Starbank (Laverockbank Rd), Baille (Stockbridge), T G Willis (George St), Ocean Mist (a retired steam yacht in the Old Harbour at Leith) and Steadings (Biggar Rd – A702). The corner lobby bar of the Balmoral (see Where to stay) is a relaxing spot at the hub of the town. The Scottish Malt Whisky Society (Giles St, Leith), dedicated to cask-strength top-quality malt whiskies, has a downstairs bar/restaurant.

Glasgow NS5865 Glasgow has made huge strides in its crusade to convince a sceptical world that it has outgrown its former rather rough image. Besides excellent art galleries and interesting museums, it houses the Royal Scottish Orchestra (with a fine-sounding concert hall), the Scottish Opera and the Scottish Ballet. Its Mayfest is good, and, like the Edinburgh Festival, is developing entertaining fringes; other festivals take you virtually right through the year. There's a zing and vitality about the place that shows in the wealth of entertainment from street theatre and pub singers to big shows, the self-confidence and enormous civic pride of the people who live here, and even the huge modern development projects. Though there are many places to see and visit, a snag for visitors is that they are scattered around this sprawling city: the Burrell Collection, the most interesting place of all, is out in the suburbs.

🏠 🏛 The Merchant City area around George Sq and Buchanan St was built on a grid plan in the 19th c, and visually has something in common with New York Ciy – Americans are said to feel at home here. The proud and in their time innovative Victorian buildings have been cleaned back to their warm sandstone; Glasgow's smart shopping quarter, this is the most comfortable area to stroll around. The City Chambers (George Sq) is a spectacular monument to 1880s civic pride, marble everywhere; free tours. There are café-bars and bistros off Princes Sq, antique stalls in Victorian Village (Regent St). TENEMENT HOUSE (Buccleuch St) is a one-floor late 19th-c flat giving a vivid impression of life for many Glaswegians at the turn of the c. The same woman lived here from 1911 to 1965 and in that time scarcely changed a thing; its time-capsule quality was preserved by a subsequent owner, and then the flat, still with its original furnishings and fittings, was left to the NTS. Shop, disabled access; open pm Mar–Oct; £2; NTS. On the SE edge of this area, between Gallowgate and London Rd past the Tolbooth, the BARRAS (barrows) is an entertaining weekend flea-market. With around 800 stalls it's one of the biggest covered markets in the world, great for bargains or just passing time; try the plump fresh clappie doos (mussels). 🏠 ❀ Just SE of the centre the park of Glasgow Green includes the PEOPLE'S PALACE, a very enjoyable social history museum looking at the work and leisure of Glaswegians over the centuries, from Jacobite risings to Billy Connolly's boots. Shop, disabled access; cl 25 Dec, 1 Jan; (0141) 554 0223; free. The museum's café is housed in the adjacent WINTER GARDENS, a massive conservatory with huge tropical plants.

✝ 🏛 The oldest area, though not the most interesting, is just NE of the centre, around the 12th-c CATHEDRAL dedicated to St Mungo, the founder of the city. It's very well preserved, though most fittings date from the 19th c; best parts are the crypt, a gracefully vaulted affair built in the mid-13th c, and the Blackadder aisle. The spectacular Necropolis graveyard, one of Britain's finest cemeteries, is closed for restoration, but there's a fine overview from the cathedral. Nearby is Glasgow's oldest house, PROVAN'S LORDSHIP, used by the Prebend of Provan – a canon of the cathedral; it dates from 1471. It's been carefully restored and furnished according to several period styles. Shop; cl 25 Dec, 1 Jan; free. 🕭 🔳 NW of the centre, in the West End, Kelvingrove and the University quarter, there are some elegant streets, the main concentration of museums, and the botanic gardens (see below). HUNTERIAN MUSEUM (Hillhead St) Scotland's oldest museum, housing the University collections of ethnographic, palaeontological and anthropological material, along with lots of archaeology and minerals. Shop; cl Sun and public hols; free. The exhibitions were founded by Dr William Hunter, the 18th-c physician, who also bequeathed the core of fine paintings which form the basis of the adjacent HUNTERIAN ART GALLERY'S beautifully hung collection. A grand range of works by Whistler, interesting and well chosen contemporary British art and

sculpture, and a growing collection of
19th- and 20th-c paintings. Also an
amazing re-creation of the home of
Charles Rennie Mackintosh, the
designer/architect whose exuberant
yet very disciplined and clean-lined art
nouveau buildings stand out among
the more traditional solidity of much
of Glasgow. Snacks, shop, disabled
access with prior notice; cl Sun, public
hols; (0141) 330 5431; free.

⚑ 🏠 🔲 Sauchiehall St, one link
between this area and the centre is an
ordinary shopping street, but well
worth the walk for Mackintosh's
most famous building the GLASGOW
SCHOOL OF ART (Renfrew St, just off;
the tours are highly recommended,
(0141) 332 9797), and the
decoratively mirrored WILLOW TEA
ROOM (open till 5), furnished to his
designs, too. More space is devoted to
his work at the Glasgow Art Gallery
(see below) in the Glasgow Style
section, and you can buy works after
him at the Glasgow Style Gallery (Gt
Western Rd). The spacious and well
lit McLELLAN GALLERIES (Sauchiehall
St) have good changing exhibitions of
art. Shop, disabled access; cl between
shows; (0141) 331 1854; charge
varies according to exhibitions.

🔲 🥄 GLASGOW ART GALLERY AND
MUSEUM (Kelvingrove Park) Huge
Victorian building with amazingly
rich collection of paintings inc
familiar masterpieces from
Rembrandt's *Man in Armour* to
Dali's *Christ of St John of the Cross*.
Especially strong in works by the
French Impressionists, Post-
Impressionists, and Scottish artists
from the 17th c. Also sculpture, silver,
porcelain, armour, archaeology,
ethnography and natural history.
Meals, snacks, shop, disabled access;
cl 25 Dec, 1 Jan; free.

👣 The MUSEUM OF TRANSPORT (Kelvin
Hall, Bunhouse Rd) Comprehensive
collection of vehicles, from trams to
ships, very well displayed; the walk-
through car showroom is arranged as
if some were for sale, with original
prices displayed on the windscreens.
Also reconstructed 1938 sidestreet,
and even a subway station. Snacks,
shop, disabled access; cl 25–26 Dec,
1–2 Jan; (0141) 221 9600; free.

ﬧ The UNIVERSITY OF GLASGOW VISITOR
CENTRE (University Ave) Interactive
displays on the history and life of the
university (founded in 1451), with
tours around some of its grander
features, such as the Lion and Unicorn
Staircase, Bute and Randolph Halls
and Memorial Chapel. Snacks, shop,
disabled access; cl Sun exc pm
May–Sept, and 25–26 Dec, 1–2 Jan;
(0141) 330 5511; visitor centre free,
tours (11 am and 2 pm Weds, Fri and
Sat) £1.50. You can stay in some of
the university buildings during
vacations.

🌿 ﬧ The BOTANIC GARDENS (Queen
Margaret Drive, off Great Western Rd
on the edge of this area) slope gently
down to the River Kibble and are
famous for their fantastic glasshouses,
particularly the half-acre Kibble
Palace, with its soaring tree ferns
interspersed with Victorian sculpture.
Disabled access; main glasshouse cl
am; (0141) 334 2422; free.

🔲 🥄 🌿 Out in the suburbs, the
BURRELL COLLECTION (Pollok Country
Park, SW) is not to be missed, and
rarely gets too crowded. Splendidly
and imaginatively housed in a modern
building created to show its different
parts to perfection, the huge collection
– far too much to see at one go –
includes Egyptian alabaster, Chinese
jade, oriental rugs, remarkable
tapestries, medieval metalwork and
stained glass, even medieval doorways
and windows set into the walls, as
well as paintings by Degas, Manet and
Rembrandt among others. Meals and
snacks (well praised by readers), shop,
disabled access; (0141) 649 7151;
free, though you may have to pay for
parking. The treasures of nearby
POLLOK HOUSE include silver, ceramics
and porcelain, but it's the paintings
that really stand out, with a collection
of Spanish masters such as Goya and
El Greco cannily acquired in the days
when they were greatly undervalued.
Snacks, shop; cl 25 Dec, 1 Jan; (0141)
632 0274; free. Both of these are set in
361-acre POLLOK COUNTRY PARK, one
of the best of the several parks and
gardens you'll find around the centre,
with waterside and woodland trails,
guided Sun pm walks, rose garden,
advice for gardeners, shire horses,

and a herd of highland cattle; (0141) 632 9299.

❀ PROVAN HALL (Auchinlea Park, 4m E of centre). Virtually unchanged since the 16th c, it has a variety of formal and informal gardens inc a garden for the blind. Disabled access; cl wknds; free; NTS.

◧ ♨ ☺ HAGGS CASTLE (St Andrews Drive, S of centre) was built in the 1580s, and now is a museum specifically aimed at children, who are encouraged to explore the house and try to find out its history. Shop; cl 25 Dec, 1 Jan; (0141) 427 2725; free.

❀ GREENBANK GARDEN (Flenders Rd, Clarkston; some miles S off A726) aims to encourage and help owners of small gardens, so has lots of different shrubs and flowers to spark ideas. Also garden and greenhouse designed to meet the needs of disabled gardeners, with advice on specially designed tools. There's usually croquet tuition at 2.30pm the last Sun of the month, May–Sept. Tea room and shop (both cl wkdys Oct–Apr), disabled access; £2; NTS.

❀ ♨ ♧ ⌂ ☺ ♨ BELLAHOUSTON PARK (3 m SW) The Empire Exhibition of 1938 was held on these 171 acres, which now comprise a walled garden, sunken garden and sweeping lawns. An additional attraction is the Charles Rennie Mackintosh-designed house built here. Disabled access; free. Other good parks out towards the fringes

include ROUKEN GLEN PARK (Thornliebank, some miles SW), a place of great tranquil beauty, with a walled garden, gorgeous lawns, and woodland walks along the river to a waterfall at the head of the glen; and tree-lined VICTORIA PARK (Victoria Park Drive N, NW of centre) where the fossil remains in the Fossil Grove, some of them 230 million years old, were discovered by workmen digging a path in the late 19th c. Lots to do in LINN PARK (Cathcart/Castlemilk, some miles S) – riverside walks, nature trails, children's zoo, golf course, and collections of British ponies and highland cattle, as well as a ruined 14th-c castle, and an adventure playground for the disabled (prior arrangement preferred – (0141) 637 1147); visitor centre open pm wknds only; free. A walkway tracks along the Clyde now, its waterfront cleaned up. The veteran pleasure steamer *Waverley* makes some runs from here Jun–Aug – (0141) 221 8152 for times. Besides the restaurants we've mentioned, Glasgow is full of places to eat out in, formal and informal. The Horseshoe (Drury St) is a classic Glasgow pub, not at all daunting, and Babbity Bowster and Rab Ha's (see Where to stay) are very good. Other pubs and bars to try are the Griffin (Bath St), Bon Accord and Mitchells (both North St) and trendy Granary (Kilmarnock Rd, Shawlands).

Other things to see and do

◖▣ **Aberlady** NT4679 MYRETON MOTOR MUSEUM Wide-ranging collection of cars, motorbikes and military vehicles dating from 1900 or earlier, as well as period advertising, posters and enamel signs. Shop, disabled access; cl winter lunchtimes, 25 Dec–1 Jan; (01875) 870288; £2. This seaside town has good golf; the Green Craig on the seashore is useful for lunch and Kilspindie House Hotel does good lunches and high teas.

♓ ❀ ⌂ ♨ ▣ **Alloway** NS3318 LAND O' BURNS CENTRE Good introduction to both the poet and the area, with

various exhibitions, audio-visual display, and landscaped gardens. Meals, snacks, shop, disabled access; cl 25–26 Dec, 1–2 Jan; audio-visual show 50p. They can provide full details of the Burns Trail, upon which Alloway is a key stop: the writer was born in thatched BURNS COTTAGE in 1759. This has just been ambitiously restored inside and out, using up-to-date yet very unobtrusive technology to give a sensitive and realistic impression of how it was when the Burns family lived here; good collection of manuscripts and letters in adjacent museum. Not far away and included in the admission price is the BURNS MONUMENT, built in 1823 to a fine design by Thomas Hamilton Jr, adorned with characters from Burns' poems sculpted by James Thorn; this is a monument as monuments should be, very much alive. Summer snacks, shop, disabled access; cottage cl am Sun (exc Jun–Aug), all Sun Oct–Mar, monument cl all Oct-Mar; (01292) 441321; £2.20 (combined ticket). The MACLAURIN ART GALLERY (Rozelle Park, Monument Rd) has excellent changing displays of contemporary art and sculpture; free.

♨ 🏰 ❀ ♖ The island of **Arran** is just under an hour by ferry from Ardrossan NS2342 (two ferries a day in winter, more in season; a popular public-transport day trip from Glasgow), with summer ferries from Claonaig on Kintyre too. It has a marvellous variety of scenery from subtropical gardens to mountain deer forest. **Brodick** NS0136 here has a fine old CASTLE in lovely surroundings between the sea, hills and majestic mountain of Goat Fell NR9941. Parts of the castle are still obviously 13th-c, but there were extensions in 1652 and 1844. Very fierce-looking from the outside, but comfortably grand inside, it's full of fine treasures and furnishings, and is even a little homely in places. There are almost a hundred antlered heads on the walls of the main staircase. It's surrounded by magnificent formal gardens, with the highlight the woodland garden started in 1923 by the Duchess of Montrose, inc many lovely, rare, tender rhododendrons. Meals, snacks, shop, disabled access; cl Nov–Mar; castle open Easter wknd, then pm May–Sept, garden and country park open all year; £4, £2 garden and country park only; NTS. The Kingsley on the esplanade has decent home cooking, and the Ormidale Hotel has good-value food. The nearby ISLE OF ARRAN HERITAGE MUSEUM in an 18th-c croft farm has farming and shipping displays, a smithy where a blacksmith worked until the 1960s, and a cottage furnished as it would have been in the 1920s. Snacks, shop, disabled access; cl Sun, Nov–Mar; *£1.50. Arran has a good circular walk up and down Goat Fell, prominent for miles around, and you can follow the shore right around the N tip, the Cock of Arran.

❀ **Balerno** NT1666 MALLENY HOUSE GARDEN Charming gardens that are home to the national collection of 19th-c shrub roses (best in late Jun), as well as four clipped old yew trees – the survivors of a dozen planted in 1603. Disabled access; £1; NTS. The handsome Johnsburn House Hotel does good lunches.

🏛 ❀ Near **Bathgate** NS9871 CAIRNPAPPLE HILL (just E of Torpichen) One of the most important prehistoric sites in the country, a stone circle and series of successive burial cairns that seems to have been used for around 3,000 years from Neolithic times to the first c BC, and especially during the second millennium BC. Extraordinary views from this raw and atmospheric hilltop site, known locally as 'windy ways'; cl all winter; £1.

🏛 **Bearsden** NS5471 ROMAN BATH HOUSE Probably the best surviving visible Roman building in Scotland, built in the 2nd c for the garrison at Bearsden Fort, part of the Antonine Wall defences; free.

♖ 🏚 ⚱ ! **Biggar** NT0438 Several good museums here: the GLADSTONE COURT MUSEUM (N Back Rd) houses an entire reconstructed village street. Shop, disabled access; cl 12.30–2pm, am Sun, Nov–Easter; (01899) 21050; *£1.20. The adjacent GREENHILLS COVENANTERS HOUSE is a 17th-c farmhouse originally at Wiston but moved piece by piece and reassembled here, with rare breeds of sheep and poultry; cl am, mid-Oct–mid-May; *80p. MOAT PARK HERITAGE CENTRE Local history and geology. Shop, disabled access; cl am Sun, Nov–Mar; *£1.50. You can get a joint ticket for all three. The striking old GASWORKS building (Gasworks Rd), the only one of its type to survive, has displays on the coal-gas industry; open pm Jun–Sept; free. There's a PUPPET THEATRE just off the A702. When they're not doing shows they have backstage tours and a museum, so always something to see. Teas, shop, disabled access (tel first – they have to remove some seats in the theatre); cl winter Weds and Sun; (01899) 20631;

shows *£4, tour and museum *£2.50.

✺ ⚲ ❦ **Blantyre** NS6857 DAVID LIVINGSTONE CENTRE Birthplace of the famous explorer, with a museum on his life and work. An African Pavilion looks at the continent today, with contemporary crafts, and there's an adventure playground in the landscaped grounds. It's been livened up considerably in the last couple of years. Meals, snacks, shop, some disabled access; cl am Sun; (01698) 823140; £2.

♣ ✝ **Bute** The popular Glasgow holiday island is a half-hour ferry trip from Wemyss Bay/Skelmorlie NS1967; it has a mix of fresh air and ebullient summer entertainments. There's lovely open country in the north, and its southern tip has the remote windswept ruin of the MONASTERY OF ST BLANE, with a ruined Norman chapel in a delightful spot, a short way uphill from the road – just sheep and the occasional walker.

▥ ✈ **Caerlaverock** NX9968 13th-c CAERLAVEROCK CASTLE is protected not just by its moat but by the wild swampy marsh around it. It has an unusual triangular inner courtyard, and the elaborate projecting tops for dropping missiles on assailants were added to the towers in the 15th c. Shop, disabled access; *£2. The surrounding saltmarshes are a reserve of the WILDFOWL AND WETLANDS TRUST, with outstanding hide facilities and observation towers over its 100 acres. Countless wildfowl flock here, especially barnacle geese; between Oct and Apr there are generally around 13,000 of them, very dramatic when they're all in flight. Snacks, shop, some disabled access; cl 24–25 Dec; (0138 777) 200; £2.95 – as well as the usual concessions, they offer discounts to anyone turning up by bike, foot or public transport. The Nith at Glencaple has good-value food.

▥ **Cardoness Castle** NX5956 Well preserved 15th-c four-storey tower house, overlooking the Water of Fleet. Interesting fireplaces. Shop; cl winter wkdys; *£1.20. Gatehouse of Fleet has places to eat.

❦ ▥ ♣ **Castle Douglas** NX7560 THREAVE GARDEN (1m W off A75) is the National Trust for Scotland's

horticulture school, with plenty to see throughout the year in its walled garden and glasshouses. If you're there in spring, don't miss the massed display of over 200 varieties of daffodil. Meals, snacks, shop, disabled access; visitor centre cl Nov–Mar; £3; NTS. The Black Douglas, Archibald the Grim, built THREAVE CASTLE in the 14th c; four storeys high, it stands on an islet in the River Dee and you have to get a ferry across. Shop; cl am Sun, Oct–Mar; *£1.50 (inc ferry). The Royal Hotel has good-value food.

▥ **Clarencefield** NY0768 15th-c COMLONGON CASTLE is unusually well preserved, so much so that it's a popular spot for weddings. Interesting original features include the dungeons, kitchen, great hall and even privies; open Apr–Sept, by appointment only; (0138 787) 283; *£2.50.

⬇ **Coatbridge** NS7265 SUMMERLEE HERITAGE TRUST Ambitious centre looking at the local iron, steel and engineering industries, with the emphasis on how they affected the people and communities involved. Lots going on, spread over 25 acres of a former iron works, with working tramway, underground coalmine and miners' row-houses. The din from the working machines creates a real feeling of authenticity. Snacks, shop, disabled access; cl 25–26 Dec, 1–2 Jan; (01236) 431261; free.

▥ **Coldingham** NT9066 FAST CASTLE on the coast to the N isn't much more than a storm-battered pinnacle precariously tethered to the mainland cliffs by a dizzy walkway; free. Impressively defiant, the site was the model for Wolfs Crag in Scott's *The Bride of Lammermoor*.

✺ **Creetown** NX4758 GEM ROCK MUSEUM Enormous private collection of gemstones and minerals from around the world, some displayed in an atmospheric crystal cave. They also have an unusual fossilised dinosaur egg. Snacks, shop, disabled access; cl Thurs and Fri Dec, 2 wks over Christmas, wkdys Jan and Feb (exc by appointment); (01671) 820357; £2.25.

▥ ❦ ⚘ **Culzean Castle** NS3309 (pronounced 'Cullane') CULZEAN

CASTLE AND COUNTRY PARK A day here is one of the most popular outings in the region. The 18th-c mansion is one of great presence and brilliance, and the 563 acres of grounds are among the finest in Britain. Lushly planted and richly ornamental, Culzean was Scotland's first country park, and has bracing clifftop and shoreline walks, with woodlands and an 18th-c walled garden. The house was splendidly refashioned by Robert Adam, and it's been well restored recently to show off his work to full effect; particularly worth a look are the oval staircase and circular drawing room. Meals, snacks, shop, disabled access; house cl Nov–Mar, park open all year; £5.50 park and castle, £3 park only; NTS.

🦋 ❀ **Dalkeith** NT3367 EDINBURGH BUTTERFLY AND INSECT WORLD (Just N) Gloriously coloured exotic butterflies, as well as creatures like scorpions and tarantulas, bee garden, and new rain forest frog display. Set in a big garden centre, it's one of the biggest centres of its type in Europe. Shop, disabled access; cl Jan and Feb; (0131) 663 4932; £3.25.

🏰 ❀ **Dirleton** NT5184 DIRLETON CASTLE Grandly rebuilt after a siege in 1298, only to be destroyed again in 1650. It has a charming garden planted in the 16th c, with ancient yews and hedges around a bowling green; cl am Sun, 25–26 Dec, 1–2 Jan; *£2. The Castle Hotel and Open Arms in this pleasant golfing village are both useful for lunch.

✝ **Dryburgh** NT5932 DRYBURGH ABBEY Remarkably complete ruins of one of David I's monasteries, in a lovely setting among old cedars by the River Tweed – its graceful cloisters are very peaceful. Sir Walter Scott is buried here. Shop, some disabled access; cl 25–26 Dec, 1–2 Jan; *£2. The Buccleuch Arms at St Boswells is a civilised place for something to eat (sandwiches all day).

🏰 ❁ **Dumbarton** NS4075 DUMBARTON CASTLE Perched on a rock 240ft above the River Clyde, with dramatic views of the surrounding countryside. Most of what can be seen dates from the 18th and 19th c, though there are some earlier remains. Snacks, shop; cl Sun am, and winter

pm Thurs and Fri; *£1.50.

🏰 🏛 ✕ ! **Dumfries** NX9776 is another place with close Burns connections. The ROBERT BURNS CENTRE (Mill Rd) has an exhibition and audio-visual display about the poet, as well as an interesting scale model of the town at the time he wrote. Summer snacks, shop, disabled access; open daily exc am Sun in summer, then Oct–Mar cl 1–2pm, Sun and Mon; (01387) 64808; 80p for the audio-visual exhibition. BURNS HOUSE (Burns St) is where he lived for the three years before his death, and contains original letters and manuscripts, along with the chair in which he wrote his last poems and songs. Shop; cl 1–2pm, am Sun, and winter Sun and Mon; (01387) 55297; 70p. Neatly rounding off the tale is the BURNS MAUSOLEUM in St Michael's churchyard, in the form of a Greek temple and containing the tombs of Robert Burns, his on-and-off wife Jean Armour, and their five sons; you can usually make an appointment to visit at the Burns House. The GLOBE TAVERN (off High St) has two rooms still very much as they were when this was his regular haunt (Anna Park, the barmaid, bore his child). The town MUSEUM, housed in the tower of an 18th-c windmill, has a CAMERA OBSCURA; cl 1–2pm, am Sun, Oct–Mar; 80p. You can get a ticket that covers all these attractions for £1.60.

🏰 **Dunbar** NT6778 The harbour here is pretty, with some picturesque fragments of the medieval castle, and good walks nearby.

✝ **Dundrennan** NX7447 DUNDRENNAN ABBEY Ruined Cistercian abbey famous as the place Mary, Queen of Scots is thought to have spent her last night in Scotland. You can still see a lot of late Norman remains; cl winter; £1.20.

🏛 🏰 **Duns** NT8154 MANDERSTON Splendidly lavish house featuring the world's only silver staircase. It was built for the millionaire racecourse owner Sir James Miller, who told the architect to spare no expense. Other gloriously extravagant parts are the painted ceilings, and a ballroom decorated in Miller's racing colours. Vivid presentations of Edwardian life both above and below stairs, with stable block and marble dairy, fine formal gardens, and an unusual biscuit-tin museum. Teas, shop, disabled access; open pm Thurs and Sun, Apr–Oct and English bank hols in May and Aug; (01361) 83450; £5, £2.50 grounds only.

✠ **East Fortune** NT5579 MUSEUM OF FLIGHT Good range of aircraft, with 35 aeroplanes from a Spitfire to a Vulcan bomber, and displays on famous flyers and air traffic control. Snacks, shop, disabled access; cl Oct–Mar; (0162 088) 308; *£2.

🏰 ✗ **East Linton** NT5977 HAILES CASTLE Another brief stopping point for Mary, Queen of Scots, now in ruins, but lovely in spring, with wild flowers along the stream; free. PRESTON MILL is one of the oldest working water-driven oatmeal mills surviving in Scotland. It's a pretty spot, with an old dovecot nearby. Shop, limited disabled access; cl 1–2pm, am Sun, Oct exc pm wknds, all Nov–Mar; £1.80; NTS. The Drovers has very good food.

🏠👑🚜 **Ellisland Farm** NX9283 is where Robert Burns lived from 1788 to 1791 and tried unsuccessfully to introduce new farming methods. There are displays of material associated with the poet (who wrote *Tam o' Shanter* and *Auld Lang Syne* while living here), and cattle and sheep wander around much as they must have done then. Disabled access; cl 25 Dec; (01387) 74426; donations.

👑 **Eyemouth** NT9564 is an understated family holiday seaside town around a busy fishing port, with a decent beach, and a fascinating local MUSEUM commemorating the village's great fishing disaster of 1881. Shop, disabled access; cl am Sun (and pm Oct), Nov–Mar; *£1.50. The Contented Sole overlooking the harbour has good quick food.

✠ **Glenluce** NX1858 GLENLUCE ABBEY Ruined Cistercian abbey founded in the late 12th c, set in beautiful surroundings. Remains include a vaulted chapter house. Disabled access; cl am Sun, and winter wkdys; *£1.20.

❀ **Gogar** NT1672 SUNTRAP GARDEN AND ADVICE CENTRE (off A8 nr Edinburgh Airport) Splendidly informative as well as sumptuous to look at, with several different gardens (Italian, Japanese, rock, peat, herbaceous and woodland), and free advice and tips. Plant sales (wkdys only), disabled access; cl wknds Oct–Mar, 2 wks at Christmas; (01506) 854387; *£1. The Bridge at Ratho is a popular canalside family dining pub.

🏠▣❀❀ **Gordon** NT6439 MELLERSTAIN HOUSE William and Robert Adam both worked on this striking Georgian house, which has impressive plasterwork and furnishings, and paintings by Van Dyck and Gainsborough. Every house in Scotland seems to have something that belonged to Bonnie Prince Charlie – this one has his bagpipes. The terraced gardens and parkland are very pleasant, with fine views towards the distant hills. Snacks, shop, limited disabled access; cl am, all Sat, Oct–Easter; (01573) 410225; £3.50. The Gordon Arms has decent food.

👑▣✠ **Greenock** NS2776 is an industrial town spectacularly sited at the mouth of the Clyde. McLEAN MUSEUM AND ART GALLERY (Kelly St) Good local history, inc displays on James Watt who was born here, collections of model ships and engines, and exotic and very miscellaneous animals and artefacts brought from overseas by local travellers. Shop, disabled access to ground floor only; cl 12–1pm, all Sun; free. The CHURCH on the Esplanade (moved here from its original site in 1920) has stained glass by Burne-Jones and Rossetti.

❗ **Gretna Green** NY3268 It's now tourists rather than runaway couples that flock to the Old Blacksmith's Shop in this little Border village. More people come here than to just about any other Scottish attraction outside Edinburgh, despite the fact that there's really very little to see. An EXHIBITION CENTRE looks at the once thriving marriage business. Cl 25 Dec, 1 Jan; (01461) 388 224; £1.

🏠 **Haddington** NT5174 is a pretty market town; the comfortable George Hotel has above-average food. LENNOXLOVE The Duchess of Lennox (La Belle Stuart) gave this interesting old house its unusual name in memory of her dead husband. Among reminders of other members of her family are the casket and death mask of Mary, Queen of Scots. Also portraits, porcelain and furniture, and in the grounds the Cadzow herd of white park cattle, said to be descended from the sacrificial cattle of the Druids. Snacks, shop; open pm Weds, Sat and Sun May–Sept, plus Easter; (0162 082) 3720; *£3.

⛫ Hermitage NY5094 HERMITAGE CASTLE Almost perfect from the outside, the well restored but very forbidding remains of a 14th-c Border stronghold reeking of dire deeds. Shop; cl am Sun, wkdys Oct–Mar; *£1.20.

⚡ Hunterston NS4621 NUCLEAR POWER STATION Interesting visitor centre and tours of the power station itself. Snacks, shop, disabled access to visitor centre only; cl over Christmas and New Year; (0800) 838557; free.

♦ Ingliston NT1473 SCOTTISH AGRICULTURAL MUSEUM (Royal Highland Showground) Good exploration of the area's rural history, with old tools and equipment, and displays of domestic life. Snacks, shop, disabled access; cl 24 Dec–7 Jan; (0131) 333 2674; free.

🏛 Innerleithen NT3336 ROBERT SMAIL'S PRINTING WORKS (High St) Fully restored Victorian printer's shop, with water-powered press; you can try your hand at metal typesetting and hand-print your own bookmark. Shop, limited disabled access; cl 1–2pm, am Sun, all Nov–Mar; £2; NTS. The Traquair Arms at Traquair is the place to eat.

▣♦✾ Irvine NS3239 GLASGOW VENNEL MUSEUM AND BURNS HECKLING SHOP Art gallery and museum, and, behind, a reconstruction of the Heckling Shop where, as a young man, an unwilling Burns tried to learn the filthy trade of flax dressing. Happily for him, during a New Year's Eve party his aunt knocked over a candle and burned the building to ashes. Also a reconstruction of his lodgings. Disabled access; cl 1–2pm, am Sun, all Weds and winter Mon and Sun too; (01294) 75059; free. Down by the harbour, the SCOTTISH MARITIME MUSEUM has a good range of historic vessels and a restored

shipyard worker's flat. It's very much a working museum, with lots of restoration going on. Meals, snacks, shop, disabled access; cl Nov–Mar; (01294) 78283; *£1.75.

✝🏛♦⛫ Jedburgh NT6521 12th-c JEDBURGH ABBEY is the most complete of the ruined Border monasteries founded by David I, and is an impressive sight, despite its town setting. It was partly restored by the Victorians, who still used the roofless nave for services. The 86ft tower is imposing, and the west door is splendid. Snacks, shops, disabled access; cl am Sun; *£2.50. MARY, QUEEN OF SCOTS HOUSE (Queen St) Charming 16th-c fortified dwelling where Mary had to prolong her 1566 stay because of a near-mortal fever (she was later to say she wished she'd died here). There's a good interpretation of her life; look out for the left-handed spiral staircase which allowed the men of the Ker clan – traditionally all left-handed – to use their sword hands. Shop; cl Nov–Easter; (01835) 63331; £1.20. The former CASTLE JAIL (Castlegate), built in the 1820s on the site of the medieval castle, houses a local history museum. Shop, disabled access to ground floor only; cl Oct–Mar (01835) 63254; 80p. The Pheasant has good food. Just off the A68 S of town are the ruins of FERNIEHURST CASTLE.

✝♦🏛✤ Kelso NT7334 The greatest and wealthiest of the four famous Border abbeys was at Kelso, though today not much of the building remains. A nearby MUSEUM explains the abbey's history, and also has a reconstructed 19th-c marketplace. Shop; cl 12–1pm, am Sun, all Nov–Easter; *80p; NTS. FLOORS CASTLE (1 m N) Magnificent building designed by William Adam in 1721, much embellished the next century. Still the home of the Duke of Roxburghe, it's reputed to be Scotland's biggest inhabited house, with a window for every day of the year. Splendid collection of tapestries and French furniture, and wonderful walled garden (best July–Sept). Good home-made meals and snacks, shop, disabled access; open Easter wknd, then Sun-Thurs May, Jun and Sept, daily July and Aug, and Sun and Weds only in Oct; (01573) 223333; £3.40. Kelso is an attractive place to wander round, with lots of interesting events almost all year – its Sept ram sales are altogether more fun than you could imagine they'd be, with all sorts of agricultural side events. The Queen's Head is good for lunch.

🐾 👶 ♿ **Kilmarnock** NS4337 DEAN CASTLE The ancestral home of the Boyd family, now housing a wonderful collection of medieval arms and armour, musical instruments, tapestries, and a display of Burns' manuscripts. A good restoration means the 15th-c house and the 14th-c keep are shown almost in their original splendour. Snacks, shop; cl am, 25–26 Dec, 1–2 Jan; (01563) 22702; *£2. Surrounding the castle are 200 acres of woodland, with nature trails, deer park, riding and other activities.

❀ 👶 **Kirkbean** NX9859 ARBIGLAND GARDENS (off A710) Extensive woodland, formal and water gardens based around a lovely sandy bay. The US Admiral John Paul Jones worked here as a boy (his father was the gardener), and his birthplace nearby has been turned into a little museum. Snacks, shop, disabled access; cl am, Mon exc bank hols, Oct–Apr; (0138 788) 283; £2. The Steamboat at Carsethorne, with sea views, has good home cooking.

❀ ♿ 🏠 **Langbank** NS3673 FINLAYSTONE (1m W on A8) Some say the garden here is the finest in Scotland – formal and walled with woodland walks and adventure playgrounds. The house has connections with Robert Burns and John Knox (unlikely partners), as well as displays of dolls, Victorian flower books and Celtic art. Snacks (not winter wkdys), shop, disabled access; gardens open all year, house pm Sun Apr–Aug, or by arrangement; (01475) 540505; *£1.50.

⚓ **Largs** NX6755 is the pick of the traditional Clydeside resorts, with boats across the narrow strip of water to the island of Great Cumbrae. The pleasure steamer *Waverley* calls here in summer.

🐾 ♿ **Lauder** NT5347 THIRLESTANE CASTLE Charming old castle with interesting collection of old toys (some of which children can touch), and some of the best plasterwork in the country in the 17th-c state rooms. Also various nostalgic exhibitions, and new woodland walk. Snacks, shop; open pm Weds, Thurs and Sun May–Sept, daily (exc Sat) July and Aug; (01578) 722430; £3.50. The Eagle and Lauderdale Hotel are useful for lunch.

↕ **Laurieston** NX6864 The WEATHER CENTRE Fascinating guided tours of working weather centre, showing how the forecasts for some of Scotland's biggest newspapers are put together, using hi-tech instruments and satellite equipment. Tours at 10am, 12 and 2.30pm, Apr–Oct; (0164 45) 264; £3. The Laurie Arms is a useful stop.

🐾 🏠 **Linlithgow** NS9976 LINLITHGOW PALACE The birthplace of Mary, Queen of Scots; it burned down in 1746 and now makes a magnificently sombre ruin standing beside the loch. You can still see the chapel, great hall and a quad with a fountain. Shop, limited disabled access; cl am Sun; *£2. In the town a pleasant old tavern, the Four Marys, is named for her maids-in-waiting Mary Livingstone, Mary Fleming, Mary Beaton and Mary Seton, with relevant memorabilia. The HOUSE OF THE BINNS (4 m E) should reopen in May after quite a bit of restoration, inc a fresh coat of paint to the exterior that's cheered it up considerably. The home of the Dalyell family since the 17th c, it has some splendid plaster ceilings and a varied collection of furniture and porcelain. Disabled access; cl am, Fri, Oct–Apr; £3; NTS.

🕊 **Lochwinnoch** NS3559 RSPB NATURE CENTRE (on Large Rd) Bird reserve with fine views, good woodland and marsh nature trails, and several observation hides – one specially designed for disabled visitors. Wknd snacks, shop, disabled access; cl Christmas and New Year; (01505) 842663; *£2. The Mossend is a useful pub.

✝ 👶 ❀ 🏠 🏘 **Melrose** NT5434 The ruins of MELROSE ABBEY are among the finest in the country – and as Scott says, best in moonlight. Look out for the wonderful stonework on the 14th-c nave (and the pig playing the bagpipes). The heart of Robert the Bruce is buried somewhere in the church. Shop; disabled access; cl am Sun; *£2.50. The MUSEUM here is housed in a 16th-c abbey official's house, with material from the Trimontium Roman fort. Close by, PRIORWOOD GARDEN specialises in flowers suitable for drying, with a herb garden and display orchard illustrating apples through the ages. Shop; cl am Sun, 24 Dec–1 Apr; *50p; NTS. TEDDY MELROSE (The Wynd) Unusually comprehensive and informative teddy bear museum, reckoned by those in the know to be one of the best in the world. Even the coffee has won awards. Resident bear-maker on site. Snacks, shop, disabled access; cl Christmas wk; (01896) 822464; *£1.50. Also worth a look if you have time are the two dozen vintage cars of the MELROSE MOTOR MUSEUM by the Abbey; cl mid-Oct–Mar; (01896) 822624; £2. ABBOTSFORD HOUSE (3 m W) Set grandly on the River Tweed, this was the home of Sir Walter Scott until his death in 1832. You can still see his mammoth 9,000-volume library, and several of the historical oddities he liked to collect, inc Rob Roy's gun and Bonnie Prince Charlie's quaich (drinking cup). Snacks, shop, disabled access; cl am Sun, Nov–mid-Mar; (01896) 2043; £2.60. Besides the Burts Hotel, the Kings Arms is useful for lunch.

🐄 **Mervinslaw** NT6713 JEDFOREST DEER AND FARM PARK Working hill farm with deer as well as other animals, and several rare breeds. Good for children, and peaceful walks and trails nearby; cl Nov–Apr; (0183 54) 364; £2.30.

🐄 **Moffat** NT0805 still has some of the poise of its former days as a spa; the Black Bull, Star (Britain's narrowest hotel), Moffat House Hotel, Balmoral and Buccleuch Arms all do decent food. On the outskirts at the Moffat Fishery (Hamerlands Farm, Selkirk Rd) is the friendly TWEEDHOPE SHEEP DOG CENTRE, with demonstrations of working sheep dogs (11am and 3pm), and an exhibition. Teas, shop; cl wknds and

winter exc by appointment; (01683) 21471; *£2.

✝ ⛃ ✗ **New Abbey** NX9666 SWEETHEART ABBEY (on A710) One of the most romantic ruins in the area, with a lofty arched nave open to the sky, and a touching story attached. Shop, disabled access; cl winter pm Thurs and Fri; *£1. SHAMBELLIE HOUSE OF COSTUME (also on A710) Much extended in recent years, often dazzling displays of costume, thoughtfully arranged in appropriately furnished rooms. Snacks, shop; cl Nov–Mar; (0138 785) 375; £2. The pretty village also has a restored 18th-c CORN MILL. Shop; cl Thurs, and winter Fri; *£1.50.

★ ♍ ✞ ✗ 🏠 🕍 🐄 **New Lanark** NS8842 Founded in 1785 and now the subject of a major conservation programme, this is Scotland's best example of an industrial village, and has plenty to keep families amused for a good chunk of the day. Many of the old millworkers' buildings have been interestingly converted to modern accommodation, so it's very much a living village rather than a museum. The award-winning VISITOR CENTRE has an excellent dark-ride looking at life here in the 1820s (lots of special effects), as well as various other displays and working machinery. Snacks, shop, disabled access; cl 25±26 Dec, 1–2 Jan; (01555) 661345; *£2.95. The surrounding countryside is spectacular, with a short walk through a verdant gorge to the Falls of Clyde that used to power the mill. Also on the site are a nature reserve, craft workshops, period shop, classic car collection, and Scotland's biggest model railway.

⛏ **Newtongrange** NT3364 SCOTTISH MINING MUSEUM (Lady Victoria Colliery) Vivid re-creation of mining days, both at the pithead and back home, even in the tea rooms; the museum has been very well restored. Meals, snacks, shop, limited disabled access; cl Oct–Mar; (0131) 663 7519; £1.95.

❀ 🦋 **Old Dailly** NS2400 BARGANY GARDENS Fine ornamental trees, woodland walks winding through springtime glades of snowdrops, bluebells and daffodils, and a lily pond enveloped by azaleas and rhododendrons. Disabled access, cl Nov–Feb; (0146 587) 249; *£1, *£1.50 May and Jun.

☼⊡ **Paisley** NS4864 is of course not just a place but a pattern, so as well as a very wide range of 19th-c art, the appealing MUSEUM AND ART GALLERY (High St) has a marvellous collection of antique and more modern paisley shawls, along with the looms on which they were made. Shop; cl Sun and bank hols; (0141) 889 3151; free. Next door the COATS OBSERVATORY has good displays of astronomy, meteorology and space flight. Shop; cl am Mon, Tues, Thurs (when open till 8), all Sun and bank hols (0141) 889 2013; free. The Fox & Hounds over in Houston has a popular upstairs restaurant.

🏠⊡ 🏕 **Paxton** NT9352 PAXTON HOUSE (ON B6461) Built in 1758 by the lovestruck Patrick Billie, who hoped to marry a daughter of Frederick the Great; the marriage never took place, but the result was a splendid neo-Palladian mansion, designed and later embellished by the Adam family, and furnished by the Chippendales. The splendid gallery has paintings loaned from the National Gallery of Scotland, and among the other treasures is a frail pair of gloves given to Billie by his heroine. Also woodland and riverside walks, and adventure playground designed by the Territorial Army. Meals, snacks, shop, disabled access; cl Nov–Easter, house cl am; (01289) 386291; *£3.75.

★ 🏰☼❀✿⊡ **Peebles** NT2540 Attractive if sedate Border town, with quite a lot for visitors; the Tontine Hotel has reliable food. To the W is spectacularly set Neidpath Castle, converted from the original 14th-c tower in the late 16th and early 17th c. There's a rock-hewn well, small museum (children like the mummified rat), period kitchen, and a pit prison – not much chance of escape, some of the walls are 11ft thick. Super views from the parapets. Shop; cl Sun am, Nov–Easter, Oct open Tues only; (01721) 720333; £1.50. KAILZIE (2m SE) Extensive grounds with lovely old trees flanked by azaleas and rhododendrons, formal rose garden, walled garden, and small art gallery. Meals, snacks, shop, disabled access; best to check first in winter; (01721) 720007; £2.

🏛 **Penicuik** NT2360 EDINBURGH CRYSTAL VISITOR CENTRE (Eastfield) Demonstrations of glass-blowing, cutting, polishing, engraving and sand etching, and an exhibition on the crystal's history. Meals, snacks, shop, disabled access; tours Mon–Fri all year and wknds May–Sept (last wknd tour 2.45pm), cl 24–27 Dec, 1–2 Jan; (01968) 675128; *£2. They run a free minibus service from Waverley Bridge in Edinburgh (on the hour, Apr–Sept only).

❀ ✿ **Port Logan** NX0942 LOGAN BOTANIC GARDEN (off B7065) Another specialist garden of the Royal Botanic Garden of Edinburgh, containing a wide range of plants from the warm temperate regions of the southern hemisphere. Meals, snacks, shop, disabled access; cl Nov–mid-Mar; (01776) 860231; *£2. The village itself has a natural sea pool where fat fish will eat from your fingers; The Inn does good food.

⬇T **Prestonpans** NT3773 was the setting for Bonnie Prince Charlie's 1745 rout of the Hanoverians. The INDUSTRIAL HERITAGE MUSEUM is located on the oldest documented coal mining site in Britain. Reconstructed coal-face and colliery workshop, as well as displays on other local industries, from brick and pipe making to brewing and weaving. Lots going on (especially at wknds), with industrial steam locomotives put through their paces on the 1st Sun of each month. Snacks, shop, disabled access; cl Oct–Mar; (0131) 653 2904; free.

✳ The **Rhinns of Galloway** – the hammerhead of land in the extreme W of the area – is largely empty even in high summer, a very peaceful place, with cliffs (especially on the S point), rocks and small coves.

★ 🏠 **St Abbs** NT9167 on the E coast is a steep and pretty little seaside village by a sandy beach and the old fishing harbour, little used now. The cliffs of ST ABB'S HEAD are noisily crowded with breeding seabirds in late spring, with high breezy walks, and a LIGHTHOUSE which is often open for visits.

🏠 🏛 🖼 ❀ **Selkirk** NT4728 is good for bargain-hunting for the tweeds, woollens and cashmeres which are woven and knitted here; the Queen's Head has freshly cooked food. BOWHILL HOUSE (3 m W) has an outstanding collection of paintings, inc works by Canaletto, Van Dyck, Gainsborough and Claude, as well as impressive furnishings and porcelain, and memorabilia relating to Sir Walter Scott and Queen Victoria. Also restored Victorian kitchen, adventure playground, and surrounding country park. You can hire bicycles. Snacks, shop, disabled access; grounds open pm May–Aug (exc Fri), house pm July only; (01750) 20732; £3.50 park and house, £1 park only.

🏛 **Smailholm** NT6435 BORDER TOWER HOUSE (just S, signed off the B6404 NE of St Boswells) Classic 15th-c Border tower house, very well preserved – all 57ft of it. Display based on Sir Walter Scott's book *Minstrels of the Borders*, and an exhibition of dolls. Shop; cl 1–2pm, am Sun, Oct–Mar; *£1.50.

❅ 🏛 🖼 ❀ ♣ † **South Queensferry** NT1477 Notable for its views of the two great Forth bridges on either side, with piers to potter on; the Hawes Inn, famous from *Kidnapped*, is still going strong. Huge HOPETOUN HOUSE (2m W) is probably Scotland's best example of the work of William and Robert Adam. The magnificent reception rooms have a wonderful art collection with works by Canaletto and Gainsborough, while the superb and extensive grounds include a deer park and a flock of rare sheep. You can play croquet on the lawn, or climb up to the rooftop platform for wonderful views. Meals, snacks, shop, some disabled access; cl Oct–Easter; 0131-331 2451; £3.80, £2 grounds only. DALMENY HOUSE (3m E on B924) Despite its Tudor Gothic appearance this splendidly placed house dates only from the 19th c – there's a superb hammerbeamed roof, as well as fine furnishings, porcelain and portraits. Good walks in the grounds and on the shore. Snacks, disabled access; open May–Sept pm Sun, Mon, Tues only;

(0131) 331 1888; £3.20. It's a lovely half-hour seal-spotting ferry trip to INCHCOLM ABBEY, an Augustinian abbey founded by Alexander I, better preserved than any other in Scotland, with a fine 13th-c octagonal chapter house and a wall painting from the same period. Ferries at 11.45am, 1 and 3pm, summer only; (0131) 331 4857; £6.25 inc ferry.

❀ ♧ **Stobo** NT1635 DAWYCK BOTANIC GARDEN (on B712) is another specialist garden of the Royal Botanic Garden, particularly noted for its arboretum rich in mature conifers (inc a larch believed to have been planted in 1725), with notable Asiatic silver firs and many rarities. Other trees include the original of the fastigiate Dawyck beech, and a good collection of maples. Snacks, shop, disabled access; cl 22 Oct–15 Mar; (01721) 760254; *£2.

❀ **Stranraer** NX1059 CASTLE KENNEDY GARDENS Prettily set between two lochs (with lots of good walks around), these gardens were first laid out in the early 18th c, then after years of neglect were restored and developed in the 19th. They're particularly admired for their walled garden and flowering shrubs, especially the rhododendrons, azaleas and embothriums. Snacks, shop, limited disabled access; cl Oct–Mar; (01776) 702024; £2.

🏰 🖼 ♧ ♧ ♨ **Thornhill** NX8599 DRUMLANRIG CASTLE Spectacular and rather unusual pink sandstone castle built in the late 17th c, with a glory of fine panelling and furnishings (mainly Louis XIV), and splendid paintings by Leonardo, Holbein, Rembrandt and Murillo; you can see what's said to be Bonnie Prince Charlie's campaign kettle. Also craft workshops, peacocks wandering over the lawn, birds of prey, and extensive woodland walks. You can hire bikes, and there's a cycle museum. Snacks, shop, disabled access; cl am wknds, all Thurs, and castle all Sept–Apr (grounds cl Oct–Apr); (01848) 331682; £4.

♣ **Tongland** NX6953 TONGLAND TOUR Guided tours (approx every 1½ hours) of part of the Scottish Power Galloway hydro-electricity scheme, with a salmon-jumping ladder. Shop;

open mid-May–early Sept, not Sun; (01557) 30114 for tour times; free. The Selkirk Arms in Kirkcudbright is handy for lunch.

🏠 ! 🛏 ⚲ 🎫 ⚘ **Traquair** NT3235 TRAQUAIR HOUSE (on B709) One of the longest-inhabited and, for many, most romantic houses in the country; no less than 27 English and Scottish kings have stayed here. The Bear Gates have remained closed since 1745 when Bonnie Prince Charlie passed through them for the last time - they won't open again until the Stuarts regain their rightful place on the throne. An 18th-c brewery still produces tasty beers; you can try them between 2 and 4pm on Fri Jun–Sept. Traquair is particularly popular with our contributors – with a maze, antique and craft shops and an art gallery as well as the house and gardens there's plenty to see. Meals, snacks, shop, some disabled access; open pm Easter wk and May–Sept, am too in July and Aug; (01896) 830323; £3.50, £1.50 grounds only. The Traquair Arms is good.

🏠 🎠 **Uddingston** NS6960 GLASGOW ZOO (Calderpark) Growing open-plan zoo, specialising in cats and reptiles, with other rare mammals and birds, children's farm, wildlife garden, and wknd car boot sales. Meals, snacks, shop, disabled access; cl 25 Dec; (0141) 771 1185; £3.60. Nearby is picturesquely set BOTHWELL CASTLE, now ruined, but once the finest stone castle in the country; cl winter pm Thurs and Fri; *£1.50.

↓T Remote **Wanlockhead** NS8713 is Scotland's highest village. The MUSEUM OF LEAD MINING has guided tours of an 18th-c lead mine, and miners' cottages furnished in the styles of 1740 and 1890. A visitor centre displays a wide range of minerals, and you can even have a go at panning for gold. Meals and snacks, shop, limited disabled access; cl Nov–Mar; (01659) 74387; *£3.25.

🏛 ✝ ⚓ **Whithorn** NX4440 Scotland's first-recorded Christian settlement was established here by St Ninian 1,500 years ago, and soon became a place of pilgrimage. There have been a number of churches on the site since, the last of the line the ruined 13th-c

priory. Archaeologists have been hard at work here for some time, and you can generally watch the dig's progress during the summer. Information panels are kept up to date with what's going on, and a visitor centre has plenty of the finds, as well as a good audio-visual display. There's also an excellent museum, with some fine Celtic crosses. Shop, disabled access; museum and visitor centre cl Nov–Easter (though you can still wander round the priory ruins then); (01988) 500508; *£2.70. Down on the coast the Isle of Whithorn is a picturesque harbour with lots of yachtsmen: the Steam Packet has decent food.

↟ **Wood of Cree** NX4165 RSPB RESERVE One of the biggest and best examples of ancient woodland in southern Scotland, with all sorts of birds and wildlife among the trees and marshes; (01671) 2861; free.

The **coasts** have some fine stretches, with some attractive villages. On the W coast, the harbour towns of Isle of Whithorn NX4736 and Portpatrick NW9954 are attractive, usually with something going on down by the water, and Kippford NX8354 and Rockcliffe NX8453 are charming yachting places; there's a vast stretch of tidal sands backed by dunes just around the headland from Rockcliffe. All have useful pubs serving food.

★ **Other attractive villages** with decent pubs in the area include Auchencairn NX7951 (don't miss the lane down to Balcary Bay), Cramond NT1876, Dunure NS2515, Eskdalemuir NY2597 (it also has an unexpected Tibetan Buddhist temple and monastery), Gifford NT5368, Kirkcowan NX3260, Kirkcudbright NX6851 (particularly enjoyable), Larkhall NS7651, Lilliesleaf NT5325, and Symington NS3831. Some Clydeside pubs with decent food and good sea views include the Cardwell at Cardwell Bay in Gourock NS2477 and the Spinnaker there, and the Lookout in Troon Marina NS3230. Besides those we've mentioned as places to eat at or stay, inns where you can get a decent meal and which are particularly well placed for walkers, drivers or just

strollers in these parts include the
Murray Arms, Masons Arms and
Angel at Gatehouse of Fleet NX5956,
Golf Hotel at Gullane NT4882,
Breadalbane Hotel at Kildonan

NS0231, Border at Kirk Yetholm
NT8328, Selkirk Arms at
Kirkcudbright NX6851 and
Buccleuch Arms at St Boswells
NT5931.

Walks

The Border hills have plentiful solitary hill-walking. The Southern Upland Way
(coast to coast over S Scotland) is a good basis for day walks. Large distances
between places often make it hard to find focal points for walks. The **Eildon
Hills** ⌂-1 above Melrose NT5434 are splendidly compact, giving a very pleasing ridge walk along the top. The E shore of **St Marys Loch** NT2422 ⌂-2 is
tracked by the Southern Upland Way; the Tibbie Shiels Inn is a handy stop
here. A short drive to the S is a car park and starting point for a pretty walk up
a narrow glen to the spectacular Grey Mare's Tail waterfalls NY0195. You can
continue beyond them along Tail Burn to Loch Skeen NT1716.

The Dumfries and Galloway coast is long and unspoilt. Good peaceful
walks include going from Rockcliffe NX8453 E to **Castle Hill Point** NY9169
⌂-3 and beyond; or to **Balcary Point** NX8249 ⌂-4 on the W side of Auchencairn Bay; or around the **Mull of Galloway** NX1530 ⌂-5, Scotland's SW toe.
The summit of **Criffel** NX9562 ⌂-6, S of Dumfries, gives an astonishing view
of the English Lake District over the Solway Firth; the best access point is New
Abbey NX9666. The **Rhinns of Kells** ridge ⌂-7 has energetic hill walking
from Forrest Lodge NX5586 NW of New Galloway. Galloway Forest Park
has attractive trails around **Loch Trool** NX4179 ⌂-8, and a walk up Merrick
NX0054, the highest point in SW Scotland.

There is excellent walking close to Edinburgh. **Arthur's Seat** ⌂-9, the summit of Holyrood Park, is a mountain virtually in the city centre – a great vol-
canic mass giving a wonderful panorama over the city. The **Firth of Forth** ⌂-
10 has excellent shoreside walks along the sands from Aberlady NT4679 to
North Berwick NT5485, with stop-off possibilities at Dirleton NT5184 and
Gullane NT4882; a good bus service connects the shoreside villages between
North Berwick and Edinburgh, though the hinterland is dull.

W of the city, from the Cramond Brig Hotel on the A90, you can walk
along the wooded **River Almond** ⌂-11 to Cramond NT1876, cross the
Almond by ferry, then go along the shore past Dalmeny House, and finish
below the Forth Bridge at South Queensferry NT1477. There are frequent
buses back to the start, and to Edinburgh. The **Pentland Hills** NT1358 ⌂-12,
within easy reach of Edinburgh, are genuine uplands with some good high-
level walks and attractive reservoirs.

Just outside Lanark, the **Falls of Clyde** ⌂-13 are dramatic when the hydroelectric station upriver opens the sluices; a path snakes around river cliffs from
New Lanark NS8842. The **Culzean Castle** estate NS3309 ⌂-14 near Ayr is a
country park with an abundance of paths; woods, landscaped grounds, a lake,
and the adjacent coast add up to a worthwhile outing. Above Greenock
NS2776, the meandering **Greenock Cut** ⌂-15 (part of an elaborate abandoned water scheme for Greenock) allows a level walk around a hillside terrace giving views into the Highlands.

The country parks around Glasgow have lots of short walks: the one by
Mugdock NS5576 ⌂-16, N of the city, has two castle ruins, a view over Glas-
gow, and an attractive loch. Level walks can take in the early stages of the West
Highland Way, which starts at Milngavie NS5574 and takes glen routes to Fort
William (up in the area we discuss next), the scenery getting better all the way.

The best of the E coast is around **St Abb's Head** NT9169 ⌂-17 (walk from
Eyemouth or St Abbs).

Driving

The A70 and A702 heading SW from Edinburgh run through fine scenery, but both carry a fair amount of traffic. Another north–south trunk road out of Edinburgh, the busy A7, also has a lot of fine mountain and river scenery; but for pleasure the B709 which virtually parallels it is greatly preferable, taking you over the Moorfoot Hills and into desolate moorland, with attractive and altogether gentler interludes at Innerleithen, Traquair, Mountbenger in Yarrow (where the Gordon Arms is a very welcoming stop – and a haven for walkers), and the Tushielaw Hotel, then plunging on through grand hills to head S into Eskdale, with the River Esk bowling along beside the road. Another attractive alternative to the A7, at least S of Hawick, is he B6357/B6399 through peaceful Liddesdale, which more or less parallels it.

It is up in these southern hills that the finest drives are to be found. The B7009 which runs from the B709 at Tushielaw down the Ettrick Valley to the softer country around Selkirk is very rewarding; you can follow the River Ettrick in the opposite direction too, high into the forests around its headwaters. Another notable drive is the A708 between Selkirk and Moffat: fine hill scenery, the still waters of St Mary's Loch, and a view of at least part of the tremendous waterfall of the Grey Mare's Tail (worth getting out for a closer and more impressive view). From Moffat the A701 climbs up past the path to the Devil's Beef Tub (a huge crater where the border raiders hid cattle they'd rustled), then drops gently down through grand scenery along the valley of the upper River Tweed, among hills where the high sheep pastures shade into heather above.

On the E side of this area the Lammermuir Hills make for an attractive drive between Duns and Gifford, either along the riverside B6355 (more varied scenery), or on the more direct hill road through Longformacus (lonelier).

Over in the W the countryside is milder, though the A747 from Glenluce down to the Isle of Whithorn and the A715 down to Drummore and the Mull of Galloway are both pleasant coastal roads.

Where to eat

Glasgow NS5865 Rogano 11 Exchange Place (0141) 248 4055 Excellent restaurant decorated in splendidly sustained 1930s art deco style – emphasis on fish, though not exclusively so. £40. There's also an oyster bar (£15) with cocktails, and a very good value café open all day; cl am Sun, bank hols; disabled access.

Linlithgow NS9977 Champany (01506) 834532 Wonderful Aberdeen Angus beef as well as lovely fresh fish (they also have their own smoke-house), home-made ice-creams, and good wines; cheaper bistro-style meals in Champany Chop and Ale House next door; main restaurant cl Sun; children over 8; disabled access. £37.40/£17.50.

Glasgow NS5865 Ubiquitous Chip 12 Ashton Lane, Byres Rd (0141) 334 5007 Quintessentially Glasgow downstairs restaurant (no chips, hence the name) in Victorian coach house with friendly, efficient service, excellent modern Scottish food, outstanding wines, and no smoking areas; disabled access. £33. Upstairs is similar but less expensive.

East Linton NT5977 Drovers (01620) 860298 18th-c pub with attractively furnished bar, fresh interesting food inc local fish in upstairs restaurant, young enthusiastic staff; no children. £26/£10.50.

Bearsden NS5471 Fifty-Five BC 128 Drymen Rd (0141) 942 7272 Very good, interesting modern cooking using good local produce in attractive and stylish restaurant; friendly staff; cl Sun, 25–26 Dec, 1–2 Jan, disabled access. £25\£3.50/£4.50.

Edinburgh NT2574 L'Auberge 56 St Marys St (0131) 556 5888 Fine classic French cooking using the best local produce in comfortable, long-established restaurant. £24.

Edinburgh NT2574 Pierre Victoire 38–40 Grassmarket (0131) 226 2442 Bustling French restaurant with cheerful atmosphere, very good value food (especially at lunchtime), and decent little wine list; cl Sun. £20/£7.50.

Lanark NS8843 East India Company 32 Wellgate (01555) 663827 Simply but attractively decorated Indian restaurant with exceptionally good, carefully prepared food, and helpful, friendly service. £14/£4.50.

Edinburgh NT2574 Kalpna 2–3 St Patrick Sq 0131-667 9890 Extremely good Indian restaurant with carefully cooked and very fresh Gujerati vegetarian food and efficient service; cl Sun; disabled access. £12.50/£4.

Auchencairn NX7951 Smugglers Main St (01556) 640331 18th-c inn with comfortable, clean, bright, recently redecorated lounge bar and eating area serving good food inc outstanding puddings and cakes; disabled access. £12|£1.75/£4.30.

Glasgow NS5865 Horseshoe Bar 17 Drury St (0141) 221 3051 Excellent and unspoilt Victorian pub with horseshoe motif throughout, popular with lawyers and journalists, and amazingly cheap food; no bar food on Sun. £2.40 (3-course lunch)|40p/£1.

The West, Argyll and Loch Lomond

Mainland Scotland's finest scenery, especially on the coast, and some exceptional gardens.

Glorious scenery is the overriding reason for coming here, and the pick of it is on the west coast. It's not an area to come to for a lively time: drive, walk, potter around a great garden or two, unearth some prehistoric sights, go looking for seals or deer, and simply enjoy the glorious views; you might enjoy stopping at a new find for us, the bagpipe maker by Loch Lomond. It's great for exploring by car (though don't expect to go at any speed): the roads twist and turn around the intricate edges of the lochs and sea lochs, making endlessly varying combinations of water, trees and mountains. It's also got some of Scotland's most rewarding walking, and the West Highland Line steam train from Fort William takes you through some of the finest scenery.

May and June are the best months here, when the great gardens are at their best, the midges have not yet got into their stride, and the days are very long. Late September and October or even November can be lovely, with spells of good fine weather, the heather still a glorious colour on the hills, and the midges in retreat; but the days start to shorten dramatically. Many places close over the winter, when the days are too short to make much of the scenery.

Oban is a lively sea-town, and Dunoon has all you'd expect of a long-standing summer resort, but otherwise even Fort William is pretty quiet. The smaller places have a very relaxed and gentle pace of life: Inveraray is the most interesting. There are some very civilised hotels, and some very good value simpler places.

Where to stay

Port Appin NM9045 AIRDS HOTEL Port Appin, Appin, Argyll PA38 4DF (0163 173) 211 **£196 inc dinner**; 12 rms. Instantly relaxing 18th-c inn with lovely views of Loch Linnhe and the island of Lismore, blissfully comfortable day rooms, friendly and helpful service, and charming owners; the food is exceptional (as is the wine list) and there are lots of surrounding walks, with more on Lismore (small boat every two hours); cl mid-Jan–mid-Feb; dogs by arrangement.

Tiroran NM5834 TIRORAN HOUSE Island of Mull PA69 6ES (01681) 5232 **£180 inc dinner**; 9 rms. Carefully modernised sporting lodge in 15 acres of gardens and woodlands on the shores of Loch Scridain; comfortable, homely sitting room with family antiques and pretty flowers, log fires, and fine food using home-grown produce, meat from the estate, and island fish; cl early Oct–mid-May; children over 10.

Eriska NM9037 ISLE OF ERISKA HOTEL Ledaig, Eriska, Oban, Argyll PA37 1SD (01631) 72371 **£155**; 17 rms. In a wonderful position on a tiny island linked to the mainland by a bridge, this impressive hotel has undergone a major refurbishment and has added a leisure complex with indoor swimming pool, sauna, gym and so forth; very good food inc marvellous breakfasts, exceptionally good, professional service, lovely surrounding walks, and 9-hole pitch and putt course; cl Dec–Mar; children over 10 in evening restaurant (high tea provided); disabled access.

Oban NM8630 MANOR HOUSE Gallanach Rd, Oban, Argyll PA34 4LS (01631) 62087 **£132 inc dinner**; 11 rms. Small Georgian hotel with views across Oban Bay and grounds running down to the water; open fire and fresh flowers in comfortable lounge, cosy cocktail bar, very fresh local seafood in elegant restaurant, and a relaxed atmosphere; cl Jan; dogs welcome away from public rooms.

Kilninver NM8523 KNIPOCH Kilninver, Oban, Argyll PA34 4QT (01852) 6251 **£130**; 17 rms. Elegant and very well kept Georgian hotel in lovely countryside overlooking Loch Feochan; fine family portraits, log fires, fresh flowers and polished furniture in comfortable lounges and bars, carefully chosen wines and malt whiskies, and marvellous food inc their own smoked salmon; cl mid-Nov–mid-Feb.

Kilmore NM8824 GLENFEOCHAN HOUSE Kilmore, Oban, Argyll PA34 4QR (01631) 77273 ***£124**; 3 rms. Scottish Baronial home at the head of Loch Feochan in 350 acres inc a fine 6-acre garden open to the public, with elegant hall, staircase and drawing room, lots of fresh flowers, and excellent food; fishing; cl Nov–Mar; children over 10.

Crinan NR7894 CRINAN HOTEL Crinan, Lochgilphead, Strathclyde PA31 8SR (0154) 683 261 **£115**; 22 rms. Rather smart hotel by start of coast-to-coast canal, marvellous views from beautifully decorated cocktail bar and stylish formal top-floor restaurant, nautical decorations in lounge bar, lots of local fish and large wine list.

Tarbert NR8668 STONEFIELD CASTLE Tarbert, Argyll PA29 6YJ (01880) 820836 **£102 inc dinner**; 32 rms. With wonderful views and surrounding wooded grounds, this Scottish Baronial mansion has comfortable public rooms, and decent restaurant food; disabled access.

Strachur NN0901 CREGGANS Strachur, Cairndow, Argyll PA27 8BX (01369) 86279 ***£98**; 21 rms, 19 with own bthrm. Smart inn in extensive grounds overlooking sea loch and hills (deer-stalking, fishing and pony-trekking arranged), attractive lounge, conservatory and cocktail bar, lively locals' bar, particularly fine cooking and carefully chosen wines, coffee bar, and gift shop; disabled access.

Kilchrenan NN0322 ARDANAISEIG Kilchrenan, Taynuilt Argyll PA35 1HE (0186 63) 333 **£96**; 14 rms. Scottish Baronial house beside Loch Awe with stunning views, lovely gardens, delicious food using local supplies (especially seafood), quiet and comfortable drawing room and library, and friendly service; cl 30 Oct–1 Apr; children over 8.

Arduaine NM7910 Loch Melfort Arduaine, Oban, Argyll PA34 4XG (01852) 200233 £93; 27 rms, gorgeous sea views. Comfortable hotel popular in summer with passing yachtsmen (hotel's own moorings), nautical charts and marine glasses in airy, modern bar, own lobster pots and nets so emphasis on seafood, pleasant foreshore walks, lovely springtime woodland gardens.

Duror NM9854 Stewart Duror, Appin, Argyll PA38 4BW (0163 174) 268 £80; 19 rms in modern wing. Family-run Victorian country house with splendid views towards Loch Linnhe, five acres of splendid gardens (lovely in May/June), comfortable lounge with open fire, good food using local fish and game; own boat moorings and 31ft sloop; cl 15 Oct–Easter.

Kilchrenan NN0222 Taychreggan Kilchrenan, Taynuilt, Argyll PA35 1HQ (0186 63) 211 *£78; 15 rms. Civilised and extensively refurbished hotel with fine garden running down to Loch Awe, comfortable, airy bar with stuffed birds and fish, attractively served lunchtime bar food, polite efficient staff, good, freshly prepared food in no smoking dining room, careful wine list, 57 malt whiskies, and pretty inner courtyard; children over 12.

Fort William NN1074 Factors House Torlandy, Fort William, Inverness-shire PH33 6SN (01397) 705767 £75; 6 rms with fine views. Carefully run and warmly friendly little hotel beneath Ben Nevis, with good food, comfortable lounge, and fine walks; cl mid-Nov–mid-Mar; children over 6 in evening dining room.

Kilfinan NR9379 Kilfinan Hotel Kilfinan, Tighnabruaich, Argyll PA21 2AP (01700) 82201 £72; 11 rms. Friendly ex-coaching inn, popular locally, in fine scenery with sporting activities such as shooting, fishing and stalking; very good restaurant food, decent bar food, and log fires; cl Feb.

Onich NN0261 Allt-Nan-Ros Onich, Fort William, Inverness-shire PH33 6RY (01855) 3210 £71; 21 rms. Victorian shooting lodge with fine Scottish food, a friendly atmosphere, bright, airy rooms, and magnificent views across Loch Linnhe and the gardens; cl Nov–2 wks before Easter, disabled access.

Gigha Island NR6449 Isle of Gigha Hotel Argyll PA41 7AD (0158 35) 254 £68; 13 rms, most with own bthrm. Attractive, traditional family-run small hotel with lots of charm, a bustling bar (popular with yachtsmen and locals), neatly kept and comfortable residents' lounge, and fine local seafood in restaurant; cottages also; cl end Oct–beg Mar – but open New Year.

Tobermory NM5055 Tobermory Hotel 53 Main St, Tobermory, Island of Mull PA75 6NT (01688) 2091 £64; 17 rms. Friendly refurbished family-run hotel on the waterfront with flowers in the comfortable, homely lounges, warm relaxed atmosphere, and home cooking using fresh local produce; good disabled access.

Ardrishaig NR8485 Allt-na-Craig Tarbert Rd, Ardrishaig, Lochgilphead, Argyll PA30 8EP (01546) 603245 £56; 6 rms. Victorian mansion overlooking Loch Fyne with big lounge and dining area, log fire, and evening meals by request; cl Christmas and New Year; self-catering also.

Kilberry NR7164 Kilberry Inn Kilberry, Tarbert, Argyll PA29 6YD (01880) 3223 £50; 2 ground floor, no smoking rms. Homely and warmly welcoming inn on W coast of Knapdale with fine sea views, old-fashioned character, and outstanding country cooking – everything is home-made, from soups and breads to chutney and marmalade; cl mid-Oct–Easter (but open New Year); children over 8.

Connel Ferry NM9133 Falls of Lora Connel Ferry, Oban, Argyll PA37 1PB (01631) 71483 *£49; 30 comfortable, well modernised rms. Well kept Victorian hotel on edge of village and across road from Loch Etive, with several spacious communicating bar areas, good solidly comfortable modern furnishings, big watercolour landscapes, free-standing Scandinavian-style log fire, no smoking areas, and well presented food; cl 25 Dec, 1 Jan; disabled access.

Inveraray NN0908 George Inveraray, Argyll PA32 8TT (01499) 2111 £46; 14 rms. Friendly hotel with decent restaurant, stripped-stone bar, flagstones, exposed joists and log fire, and good choice of whiskies; cl 24–26 Dec, 1–3 Jan.

To see and do

❀ **Arduaine** NM8010 The seaside gardens here, a very sheltered spot with lovely views of the islets and islands, are almost subtropical, with many rarities beside the rhododendrons and magnolias which flourish so in this part of the world. Open daily; £2.00; NTS. The comfortable Loch Melfort Hotel, with great sea views, does good bar lunches.

⬩T **Auchindrain** NN0303 AUCHINDRAIN TOWNSHIP OPEN-AIR MUSEUM (on A83) The only communal tenancy township to have remained on its ancient site much in its original form. All the buildings have been excellently restored and simply furnished in period style, so you get a real feeling of stepping back into the past. Snacks, shop; cl Oct–Mar, and Sat in Apr; (01499) 5235; £2.40.

↗ **Barcaldine** NM9642 SEA LIFE CENTRE (on A828) Lively underwater centre (part of a chain with several in England and one in St Andrews), with hi-tech face-to-fish-face displays of native marine life, and playful seal puppies. Also nature trails and woodland adventure playground. Meals, snacks, shop, limited disabled access; cl wkdys Dec–mid-Feb; (0163 172) 386; £4.35. The Falls of Lora and Lochnell Arms down at Connel are reliable lunch stops.

❀ ◗ ❀ **Benmore** NS1385 YOUNGER BOTANIC GARDEN (on A815) An outstation of the Royal Botanic Garden in Edinburgh, with attractive woodland and glorious rhododendrons. Some enormously tall and magnificent conifers here, and a good many rarities. Nice views too. Meals, snacks, shop, disabled access; cl Nov–mid-Mar; (01369) 6261; *£2.

❀ ◗ ⚘ ⊞ **Cairndow** NN1810 ARDKINGLAS WOODLAND GARDEN On a hillside overlooking Loch Fyne, the pinetum here includes the tallest tree in Britain, a grand fir well over 200ft and still growing quickly, among a group of other noble trees. Also rhododendrons, azaleas and other exotic plants, and daffodils in spring.

Disabled access; donations. The same people run the TREE SHOP (about 2m N at the top of the loch), which specialises in specimen trees, indigenous Highland trees, and shrubs. Also lots of well crafted woodware (inc some lovely toys and puzzles); cl Jan; (0149 96) 263. Next door the Loch Fyne Oyster Bar is renowned for its fresh shellfish, which you can eat in the restaurant or buy in the shop.

★ ❀ ⚓ **Colintraive** NS0374 is an attractive village spread out along the shore of the sea loch, with lovely views across the narrow Kyles of Bute. There's a short ferry crossing to Rhubodach on Bute.

⬧ **Corpach** NN0977 TREASURES OF THE EARTH (Mallaig Rd) Award-winning collection of gemstones, crystals and minerals from around the world, imaginatively displayed in carefully lit rock cavities and caverns. Quite dazzling in places. Shop, disabled access; cl 25–26 Dec, Jan; (01397) 772283; *£2.50.

★ **Crinan** NR7894 The CRINAN CANAL was cut through the 9 miles at the top of the Kintyre peninsula at the end of the 18th c, to save coastal sailors many miles of dangerous waters; the end at Crinan is attractive, usually with one or two yachts or even a rare fishing boat waiting to enter the first lock, and the Crinan Hotel is a comfortable lunch stop.

⚓ ❀ **Dunoon** NS1776, brought in easy reach of Glasgow by frequent ferries, is a late Victorian resort with pleasant views from its fine long promenade; very busy in Aug.

⬧ ⬗ ⛫ **Fort William** NN1174 is a largely Victorian town that manages to combine its role as a regional centre with its other life as a holiday base, particularly for solid Ben Nevis which rises above it, and for the Caledonian Canal which leads on up into the Great Glen and across eventually to the North Sea. The cheerful WEST HIGHLAND MUSEUM (Cameron Sq) is very well organised, and especially good on Jacobite relics. The most interesting feature is a secret portrait of Prince Charlie that requires a curved mirror to decode it. Shop; cl Sun (exc pm July and Aug), and Mon Nov–Mar (when also cl every lunchtime); (01397) 702169; £1. The Alexandra Hotel and Nevis Bank Hotel are useful for food. In summer you can take steam train journeys on the WEST HIGHLAND LINE from here – it goes right up into the Highlands and the views are quite superb (see also North of Scotland section). On the NE edge of town (and usually under scaffolding) are the ruins of partly 13th-c INVERLOCHY CASTLE, site of the 1645 battle between Montrose and the Campbells; free.

♨ ✿ ♘ **Gigha Island** NR6449 3 miles offshore is linked by frequent ferries from Tayinloan on the A83 down the W coast of Kintyre, and is a perfect place for really getting away from it all. There's a small hotel, and rooms at the post office and other places, and you can hire bicycles to explore it properly. The island was bought in 1944 by Sir James Horlick, who created ACHAMORE GARDENS, a garden of woodlands filled with rhododendrons and azaleas, bringing over many of the plants from his home in Berkshire in laundry baskets. Lots of subtropical plants – the climate and soil are perfect for them. Meals, snacks, shop; *£2. Best to tel (0158 35) 254 for times of ferries out to the island. Try to see the strange old stones, some of which are supposed to have mysterious powers.

♿ **Glencoe** NN1058 The scenery around here is some of Scotland's most beautiful and wild. It's understandably popular with walkers and climbers, who share it with deer, wildcats and golden eagles. The area is most famous for the massacre of 1692 when billeted troops tried to murder all their MacDonald hosts. Close to where this happened, the GLENCOE VISITOR CENTRE (on A82) has the whole story, as well as useful local information. Snacks, shop, disabled access; cl mid-Oct–Mar; *50p; NTS. The Clachaig is popular for lunch.

♫ ✿ ❀ **Helensburgh** NS2982 THE HILL HOUSE (Upper Colquhoun St) In an area short of many great houses, this is a wonderful example of the work of Charles Rennie Mackintosh;

there's an exhibition about his life, and the gardens are being restored to their original form. Snacks, shop; cl am, Jan–Mar; £3; NTS. The dignified resort town, attractively placed on the Clyde, has some good views from its broad streets.

★ ✝ ♨ ♫ ♿ ♫ **Inveraray** NN0908 Beautifully placed and rather self-consciously elegant, this was built as an estate village in the 18th c. The bell tower of ALL SAINTS CHURCH has the world's second-heaviest ring of ten bells, installed as a Campbell War Memorial in 1931. Even if there's no one ringing the bells you should be able to hear a recording; cl 1–2pm, am Sun, all Oct–mid-May; £1 for tower, exhibition free. The CASTLE was built in 1743, long before the town became a magnet for visitors – in those days it was 40 miles to the nearest carriage road. Still the home of the Duke and Duchess of Argyll, it's filled with rich furnishings, tapestries and paintings. Particularly worth seeing are the great armoury hall and state rooms. Snacks, shop, some disabled access; cl 1–2pm (exc July and Aug), Fri, mid-Oct–Mar; (01499) 302203; *£3.50. INVERARAY JAIL (Church Sq) Probably the best prison museum in Britain, with costumed guides really bringing the place to life. You can watch a trial in the 1820 courtroom, try your hand at hard labour, and even experience the misery of being locked up in one of the sparse little cells. Not so long ago they won the European Museum of the Year award. Shop; cl 25 Dec, 1 Jan; (01499) 302381; £3.85. The Loch Fyne Hotel is pleasant for lunch, with stunning views. Nearby the ARGYLL WILDLIFE PARK (Dalchenna) has a collection of the sorts of animal traditionally found around these parts, from wild boars to wildcats – with some eminently tame wild creatures wandering around. Meals, snacks, shop, disabled access; open all year, though no facilities Nov–Mar; (01499) 302264; £3.60.

✝ ▥ **Kilmartin** NR8393 CHURCH is plain and Victorian but has a stunning 10th-c cross; the graveyard has interesting carved medieval tombstones. A short walk away are the well signed North, Mid and South

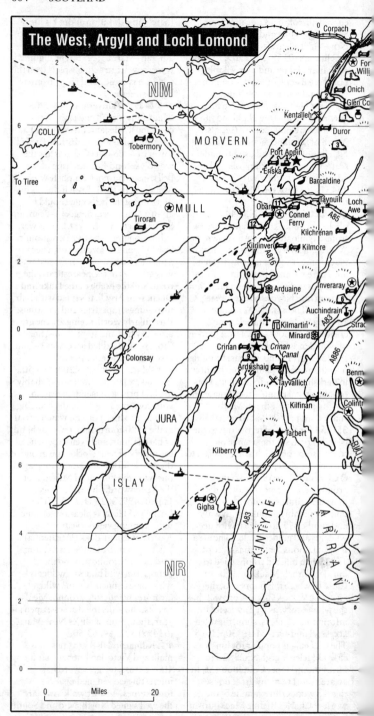

The West, Argyll and Loch Lomond

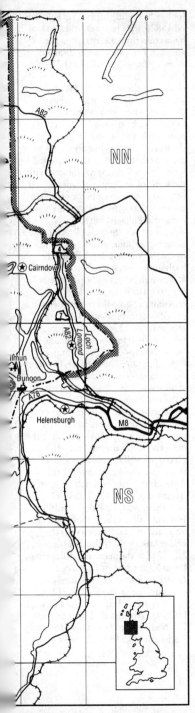

Cairns (impressive prehistoric monuments – you can climb into the North one via trap door and ladder, to see cup-and-ring carvings), and the Templewood stone circles. The simple Kilmartin Hotel is useful for lunch. DUNADD (3m S) This prehistoric hill fort was one of the ancient capitals of Dalriada from which the Celtic kingdom of Scotland was formed. Look out for the carvings nearby of a boar and a footprint, which probably mark the spot where early kings were invested with royal power.

Kilmun NS1781 has wonderful FOREST WALKS among rare conifers, an arboretum of great beauty, and some striking gum-trees.

Lochawe NN1227 CRUACHAN POWER STATION (3m W of village, off A85, nr Pass of Brander) Hydro-electric plant inside a vast cavern in the depths of Ben Cruachan, driven by water from a high-level reservoir on the mountain. Tours around the site are conducted in a minibus. Snacks, shop; cl Nov–Easter; (0186 62) 673; £1.80. The Glenorchy Lodge Hotel at Dalmally does good quick bar lunches.

Loch Lomond NS3957, in spite of being so close to Glasgow and on every coach company's hit list, does have a serene beauty that seems unspoilt by the visitors. Wee birdies sing and wild flowers spring – and the water is often calm enough to reflect the mountains. The best views are from the narrower N end, the quietest spots along the E shore. At the bottom end at **Balloch** NS3881, BALLOCH CASTLE COUNTRY PARK is a useful introduction to the area, with a visitor centre, woodland and meadow trails, walled garden, and fine views. Disabled access; cl Nov–Easter; (01389) 58216; free. Eight miles up the A82 from here is the rather jolly little THISTLE BAGPIPE WORKS, with demonstrations of bagpipe-making; cl 1 Jan; (01436) 860250; free. Cruises round the lake leave from Balloch, as well as from **Luss** NS3952, a good place to hire a boat for pottering about on the water. Past the N end of the loch, the Inverarnan Drovers Inn is an entertaining stop.

Minard NR9897 CRARAE GARDENS

(on A83) Lovely gardens noted for their rare ornamental shrubs and rhododendrons, azaleas and conifers, set in a beautiful gorge overlooking Loch Fyne. Snacks, shop and interesting plant sales (all summer only), limited disabled access; visitor centre cl Nov–Easter; (01546) 86614; *£2.50.

🕭🏠💀† **Mull** NM5834 For most people this island takes a bit of getting to for a weekend break, but if you are within reach its unspoilt coasts are certainly a dramatic lure. There's a good ferry service from Oban and Lochaline (and in summer from Kilchoan). A couple of castellated mansions, one going back to the 13th c and the other 19th-c, and a small museum in Tobermory, give some rainy-day scope. The interior is less interesting than the coast, with brackeny moors and conifer plantations over much of it, though there is some mountainous hill walking in the S. Offshore Iona, filled with a sense of spirituality as well as its tangible remains of ancient shrines, is lovely.

🏠🕭💀🌳🚩 **Oban** NM8630 is a bustling coastal town, a busy ferry port and also a popular place for holidaymakers, with a good cheerful atmosphere; the Oban Inn is fun, and the Lorne has decent food inc fresh local fish. Right on the waterfront, you can watch craftsmen at the GLASSWORKS making paperweights. Shop, disabled access; shop cl Sun (exc May–Sept), factory cl wknds; (01631) 63386; free. Besides the main ferries, there are boats to Lismore and (just a hop really) Kerrera. Four miles N (off A485) beautifully set DUNSTAFFNAGE CASTLE was once the prison of Flora MacDonald. It's now in ruins, but you can still see its gatehouse, round towers and 10ft-thick walls. A visitor centre was added last year. Snacks, shop; cl 12.30–1.30pm, am Sun, Oct–Mar; *£1.50. A little way south at Cologin, the countrified Barn which often has evening folk music is useful

for lunch. Slightly further S at Kilmore NM8824, the OBAN RARE-BREEDS FARM has a collection of very visitor-friendly animals. Teas, shop, some disabled access; cl Nov–Mar; (01631) 77608; £3.

★ 🚢 **Port Appin** NM9045 is an attractive little settlement, very peaceful, where you can pick wild blueberries by the roadside, catch a boat across to Lismore, or just sit by the water keeping your eyes open for the seals that are so common around here. This is *Kidnapped* country, with the scene of the Appin Murder not far off, and a monument marking where James of the Glens was wrongly hanged at Ballachulish to the N.

★ **Tarbert** NR8668 is a pleasant and quite picturesque harbourside small town; the Victoria overlooking the harbour has imaginative food.

🚩 **Taynuilt** NN0131 BONAWE IRON FURNACE The most complete remaining charcoal-fired ironworks in Britain, established in 1753 and worked until 1876. Iron produced here was used for the cannonballs for Nelson's ships. Shop; cl am Sun, all Oct–Mar; *£2. The Polfearn Hotel on the lochside does good food, and the station is a surprising location for a pub brewing its own beer.

Besides those we've mentioned in the text above, or as places to eat at or stay, inns where you can get a decent meal and which are particularly well placed for walkers, drivers or just strollers in these parts include the Ardentinny Hotel by Loch Long at Ardentinny NS1887, Galley of Lorne at Ardfern NM8004, Ballachulish Hotel at Ballachulish NN0858, Tigh an Truish at Clachan Seil near the bridge linking the little island of Seil NM7718 to the mainland, Kilchrenan Inn at Kilchrenan by Loch Awe NN0222, Portsonachan Hotel on the opposite side of that loch NN1227, Inverbeg Inn at Luss on Loch Lomond NS3593, Whistlefield Hotel by Loch Eck NS1493 and Loch Gair Hotel on Loch Gair NR9190.

Walks

For non-mountaineers the Highlands can be tantalising but problematic: compared to the uplands of England and Wales there are few obvious walking routes (OS maps show hardly any), and the scale of the scenery is often so vast that you need to walk for hours before the views change. The high peaks are mostly for the dedicated (and fit) enthusiast. An informal tradition of allowing general access exists on the mountains, but there are few rights of way, and areas are often closed for at least part of the grouse-shooting season (12 Aug–10 Dec), particularly its first few weeks, or the deer-stalking season (1 July–20 Oct for stags, 21 Oct–15 Feb for hinds).

There are attractive walks along many lochs, and around the complex coast and sea lochs. The area has a fair amount of forestry walks, sometimes taking in viewpoints and waterfalls. Many of the valleys (always called glens in Scotland) give good scope for walking: one fine walk is through semi-wooded terrain along the glen of the **River Leven** ⌂-1, from Kinlochleven NN1861 to the dam of the gigantic Blackwater Reservoir NN3059.

Glen Nevis NN1570 ⌂-2 near Fort William NN1174 is probably the best known valley, with splendid gorge scenery for an easy long mile to Steall Falls. Nearby Ben Nevis NN1671, though Britain's highest mountain, is one of the more easily managed summits, with a long, safe path up: expect big crowds in season. Munro-baggers (a 'Munro' is any 3,000ft peak – the nickname comes from Sir Hugh Munro, who tabulated them all) say it's far from being the best viewpoint mountain, though. The Pap of Glencoe NN1259 and the succession of peaks in the largely unwooded Mamore Forest NN1565 (access also from Glen Nevis) are more interesting; they don't require rock-climbing expertise, just reasonable fitness and plenty of time.

In **Glen Coe** NN1556 ⌂-3 you can discover the Lost Valley, a secret pasture-ground used by the MacDonalds for stolen cattle in times of clan warfare; it involves an ascent from the Meeting of the Three Waters NN1756. From **Altnafeadh** NN2256 ⌂-4 at the top of the glen, the West Highland Way takes a zigzag route N up the Devil's Staircase and through the mountains to Kinlochleven; another hill walk from Altnafeadh heads E up Beinn a' Chrôlaiste, one of Glen Coe's more manageable peaks. From Glen Coe, a squelchy walk along glens, with close-ups of mighty peaks for company, leads into **Glen Etive** NN1650 ⌂-5.

Around **Inveraray Castle** NN0908 ⌂-6 woodland trails include a view over Loch Fyne from Dunchuach Tower.

Loch Lomond, surprisingly, hasn't a lot of paths: the shoreline track, partly metalled, on the quieter E side, comes closest to the water. There's a good ascent of **Ben Lomond** NN3602 ⌂-7, the southernmost Munro, from Rowardennan NS3699 on this E side.

The **Caledonian Canal** ⌂-8 leading NE from Fort William NN1074 has straightforward towpath walks with mountain backdrops. The **Crinan Canal** ⌂-9 between Crinan and Lochgilphead provides a gentle stroll. Just N near **Kilmartin** NR8398 ⌂-10, tracks link a succession of ancient burial mounds.

Islands within reach of Oban have a few shoreside walks and the odd castle, eg **Lismore** ⌂-11 (also ferry from Port Appin) and **Kerrera** ⌂-12. There are a few good walks on **Mull**, though as usual not many defined paths.

Driving

W and N of Loch Lomond, almost every road is a delight, though none is quick except at quiet times. The roads that hug the shores of the sea lochs give particularly enchanting views, changing constantly – and have the great advantage over mountain roads that the weather has to be very bad indeed before the views lose all their charm. The circuit of the Mull of Kintyre makes a glorious drive, though very slow in summer. Other memorable moments here include the approach to Inveraray on the A83; the good A8003 down the Cowal Peninsula with great views over the Kyles of Bute to the island of Bute itself; the B8024 round the coast of the Knapdale Peninsula: just N of Oban, the view from the A85 of Dunstaffnage Castle moulded in rock on its wild promontory; and some miles N of here, the sight of Castle Stalker on its off-shore islet from the A828, one of Scotland's most romantic views. Inland, the B8074 up Glen Orchy is very pretty, with plenty of places to stop by the stream (much loved by midges in late summer). The A82 is a magnificent road, both through the awesome Pass of Glencoe and over the stern moorlands E and S of there.

Where to eat

Kentallen NN0057 ARDSHEAL HOUSE (01631) 74227 Particularly good food in attractive conservatory dining room of fine hotel set in 900 acres; very comfortable rooms, antiques, and relaxed atmosphere; lovely bedrooms; cl Mon–Thurs Nov–mid-Dec (open holidays), cl Jan, cl Mon–Thurs Feb and Mar; disabled access in dining room (not bedrooms). **£32 7 course dinner, £17 3 course lunch**/£6.

Kentallen NN0057 HOLLY TREE (01631) 74292 Super food in carefully con-verted railway station, cosy public rooms, lovely shoreside setting (best to book in winter); bedrooms; cl 2 wks end Nov; disabled access. **£30**|£1.75/£8.25.

Tayvallich NR7386 TAYVALLICH INN (01546) 7282 Simply refurbished pub overlooking yacht anchorage with emphasis on local seafood, though other decent dishes, too, dining conservatory (no smoking), and friendly service; cl Mon Nov–Mar. **£23**|£4.50/£5.50.

Fort William NN1074 ALEXANDRA The Parade (01397) 702241 Popular hotel in the town square with meals and snacks in the Great Food Stop (open all day) and the evening restaurant; disabled access. **£20.50 in restaurant**|£2/£4.99.

Many of the places in the **Where to stay** section, above, also offer extremely good food.

NORTH OF THE FORTH: CENTRAL HIGHLANDS AND EAST COAST

Memorable Highland and valley scenery, some sheltered coastal villages, plenty of sightseeing.

The area's best scenery is in the north: both Highland, and the more varied beauties of the valleys – the well known Spey, Dee and Don, and the lesser-known places such as the Angus glens of Glen Clova, Glen Esk and Glen Isla. The coast from Nairn to New Aberdour and Rosehearty and even right on round to Aberdeen is full of picturesque little coves, boiling seas around terrifying cliffy crags (Slains Castle and the nearby Bullers of Buchan are fine examples), unexpected sandy beaches and interesting small towns and villages: a part of Scot-land that's much underrated. On the southern fringes of the High-lands, Tayside has civilised towns such as Perth and on a much smaller scale Crieff, Pitlochry and Aberfeldy, with some tremendous forested valley scenery as well as its Highland hills. Further south, the countryside is a lot milder. Over in Fife it's largely agricultural, with quite a bit of industry dotted through it, but there are some attractive fishing villages, and splendid coastal golf courses. More centrally, the interesting town of Stirling does have the real moorland of Sheriff Muir nearby, as well as the Trossachs: a sort of Highlands in miniature, with lovely if small-scale landscapes of loch, river, forest, moor and mountain – but not the emptiness or the grandeur of the true Highlands.

Thoughout the area, there are a good many interesting places to visit – especially castles and great houses: Craigievar, Cawdor, Fyvie (near Turriff), Blair, Glamis, Crathes and Brodie are all outstanding castles, and Scone Palace and Falkland Palace are very rewarding. St Andrews, Perth, Stirling, Aberdeen, Dundee and the much smaller Anstruther and Culross are all worth considering for a day or half-day visit. Good family attractions include the Highland wildlife park at Kincraig, the Storybook Glen at Maryculter, the Bo'ness steam railway (other things there too), the safari/leisure park at Blair Drummond, and deer parks at Glengoulandie and Cupar. Of several distillery tours, the Glenturret one at Crieff is particularly enjoyable. Among new *Guide* entries this year, we'd particularly pick out the remarkable new Deep Sea World at North Queensferry, the entertaining Scottish Wool Centre at Aberfoyle, and the Wallace Monument in Stirling.

There's a fine choice of places to stay, and quite a good choice of places to eat – though they thin out as you head north.

Where to stay

Advie NJ1235 Tulchan Lodge Advie, Grantown on Spey, Morayshire PH26 3PW (01807) 510200 *£350 **full board**; 10 rms. Extremely civilised Edwardian sporting lodge with fishing on one of the best stretches of the Spey (each beat has its own ghillie and luxurious fishing cabin) and game shooting on 4,500 acres; fine paintings and antiques in gracious drawing room and comfortable panelled library. Good food, using much produce from the estate and kitchen gardens, served at one long candlelit table; billiards room, tennis; no children.

Auchterarder NN9413 Gleneagles Auchterarder, Perthshire PH3 1NF (01764) 662231 *£220; 234 individually decorated rms. Grand hotel in lovely surroundings with attractive gardens and outstanding leisure facilities: golf courses (inc a championship one designed by Jack Nicklaus), shooting, riding, fishing, a health spa, tennis, squash, bowling green, and croquet, and the British School of Falconry have a base here; comfortable, elegant high-ceilinged day rooms, several bars, professional but friendly service, live pianists, and good food using local produce (much is home-grown) in 3 main restaurants; disabled access.

Dunkeld NO0243 Kinnaird House Kinnaird Estate, Dunkeld, Perthshire PH8 0LB (01796) 482440 *£185; 9 spacious, individually decorated rms. 18th-c country-house hotel in 9,000-acre estate with very restful, civilised atmosphere in deeply comfortable, antique-filled rooms, lovely flowers, family mementos and pictures, log fires, good, creative food in no smoking dining room with its early 19th-c hand-painted frescoes, and very fine wine list, not cheap; excellent fishing on River Tay and 3 hill lochs, and shooting; cl Feb; children over 12; good disabled access.

Ballater NO3695 Tullich Lodge Ballater, Aberdeenshire AB35 5SB (01339) 755406 £160; 10 individually decorated rms. Characterful Baronial-style pink granite house, well run by the same owners for over 20 years, with fine views from handsome first-floor drawing room, chintzy little sitting room, open fire in informal bar (light lunches served here), and carefully prepared food using first-class ingredients in slightly formal panelled no smoking restaurant; high tea for children; good hill walking and lots of nearby golf courses; cl Dec–Mar.

Blairgowrie NO1745 KINLOCH HOUSE Blairgowrie, Perthshire PH10 6SG (01250) 884237 £152.50 inc dinner; 21 individually decorated rms. Creeper-covered 19th-c country house in 25 acres of parkland with highland cattle and fine views; relaxed lounges, comfortable bar, pretty conservatory with lots of plants, and fine choice of carefully prepared food in an elegant dining room; popular Sportsman's room with own entrance, drying facilities, gun cupboard, deep freeze, game larder and so forth; cl 15–29 Dec; disabled access.

Kinclaven by Stanley NO1436 BALLATHIE HOUSE Kinclaven by Stanley, Perth PH1 4QN (01250) 883268 *£150; 28 fine rms. Overlooking the River Tay, this turreted mansion has fresh flowers and log fires in the comfortable, carefully furnished day rooms, very good, interesting food in elegant dining room, and friendly service; disabled access.

Pitlochry NN9458 KILLIECRANKIE Pitlochry, Perthshire PH16 5LG (01796) 473220 £144 inc dinner; 10 spotlessly clean rms. Comfortable country hotel in spacious grounds with putting course and croquet lawn, splendid mountain views, mahogany-panelled bar with stuffed animals and fine wildlife paintings, spacious sitting room with books and games, a relaxed atmosphere, friendly owners and helpful staff, and excellent, well presented food in elegant restaurant; cl Jan and Feb.

Peat Inn NO4509 PEAT INN Peat Inn, Cupar, Fife KY15 5LH (01334) 840206 *£140; 8 luxurious rms. Famous restaurant with rooms: beams and white plaster walls, log fires and comfortable sofas, friendly service, fine, interesting food, and excellent wine list; cl 25 Dec, 1 Jan; disabled access.

Dunblane NN7801 CROMLIX HOUSE Kinbuck, Dunblane, Perthshire FK15 9JT (01786) 822125 *£135; 6 comfortable rms, 8 spacious suites. Walking, loch and river fishing or shooting are available on the 3,000 acres of land around this rather gracious country house; relaxing day rooms with fine antiques, furniture and family portaits, an informal atmosphere, very good food using estate game and local meats and fish, and courteous service; cl 2 wks Jan.

Auchterarder NN9413 AUCHTERARDER HOUSE Auchterarder, Perthshire PH3 1DZ (01764) 663646 £130; 15 individually furnished rms, some in turret, most with fine views. Baronial mansion with warm, homely atmosphere, lovely day rooms with open fires, lots of fresh flowers, fine panelling and antiques, good, imaginative food, and over 17 acres of grounds; children over 10; disabled access.

Newtonmore NN7199 ARD-NA-COILLE Kingussie Rd, Newtonmore, Inverness-shire PH20 1AY (01540) 673214 £130 inc dinner; 7 rms, those on first floor have fine views. Carefully run little Edwardian hotel in 2 acres of pine woodland with quiet country-house atmosphere, marvellous views of the Cairngorm Mountains from the public rooms, homely touches, attentive staff, extremely good 5-course set dinner, and thoughtful, very reasonably priced wine list; cl mid-Nov–end-Dec.

Scone NO1226 MURRAYSHALL HOUSE Scone, Perth PH2 7PH (01738) 551171 £130; 19 rms. Handsome mansion in 300 acres of parkland, very popular with golfers (it has its own course); comfortable, elegant public rooms, warm, friendly staff, relaxed atmosphere, imaginative food, and good wines; cl 23–28 Dec.

Ballater NO3695 CRAIGENDARROCH HOTEL Ballater, Aberdeenshire AB35 5XA (01339) 755858 *£125; 50 rms. In 29 acres and surrounded by lovely countryside, this popular hotel has lots of leisure facilities, comfortable public areas, friendly service, and very good food in 3 restaurants; good for children with crèche and Acorn Club; cl 5–6 Jan; disabled access.

Aberfeldy NN8549 FARLEYER HOUSE Aberfeldy, Perthshire PH15 2SE (01887) 820332 £120; 11 pretty rms. Charming country house with fine views over the Tay Valley, log fires, antiques and flowers in the library and drawing room, and excellent food in airy and elegant restaurant and Scottish bistro; use of nearby leisure club; disabled access.

Alloa NS8893 GEAN HOUSE Gean Park, Tullibody Rd, Alloa, Clackmannanshire FK10 2HS (01259) 219275 *£120; 7 luxury rms. Carefully restored mansion house in mature parkland with views of the Ochil Hills; elegant drawing room with inglenook fireplace, minstrels' gallery and marvellous windows, cosy library, and very good food in no smoking, walnut-panelled dining room overlooking the formal rose garden; disabled access.

Elgin NJ2162 MANSION HOUSE The Haugh, Elgin, Morayshire IV30 1AQ (01343) 548811 *£120; 22 rms. Relaxed and friendly Scottish Baronial mansion with prettily furnished public rooms, fresh flowers, lovely food inc fine breakfasts, and good wine list; country club facilities; disabled access.

Kildrummy NJ4617 KILDRUMMY CASTLE Kildrummy, Alford, Aberdeenshire AB33 8RA (01975) 571288 £118; 15 comfortable rms. Overlooking the ruins of the original 13th-c castle and set in lovely gardens, this castellated hotel has a fine oak-panelled Grand Hall, gracious drawing room, convivial bar, relaxing library, fresh flowers and open fires, good food using the best beef, game and fish, and welcoming, friendly staff; lots of fishing; cl Jan.

Stirling NS7993 STIRLING HIGHLAND Spittal St, Stirling FK8 1DU (01786) 475444 £110; 76 rms. Carefully converted former high school with castle views, lots of original features such as vaulted ceilings and wooden panelling in comfortable public areas, modern French cooking in elegant restaurant and Italian dishes in the bustling trattoria; health and leisure club; disabled access.

Callander NN6208 ROMAN CAMP Main St, Callander, Perthshire FK17 8BG (01877) 330003 £99; 14 pretty rms with garden views. Former hunting lodge rather like a small French chateau with characterful and comfortable lounge, restful library, open fires, an interesting little turret chapel, enjoyable food in elegant dining room, and 20 acres of grounds; disabled access; children over 5 in restaurant in evening.

Inverness NH6645 BUNCHREW HOUSE Bunchrew, Inverness IV3 6TA (01463) 234917 £98; 11 individually decorated rms. Warmly friendly 17th-c mansion on the shore of Beauly Firth with fine views and landscaped gardens, log fire in the elegant, panelled drawing room, and traditional cooking using local produce and locally caught game and venison.

Auchterhouse NO3337 OLD MANSION HOUSE Auchterhouse, Dundee, Angus DD3 0QN (01826) 26366 £95; 6 attractive rms. Carefully converted 16th-c Baronial house with fine entrance hall, comfortable day rooms, open fires, and very relaxed atmosphere; garden with outdoor swimming pool, croquet and tennis; cl 25–26 Dec, 1st wk Jan; children over 12 in evening dining room.

Nairn NH8856 CLIFTON HOUSE Viewfield St, Nairn IV12 4HW (01667) 53119 *£95; 12 individually decorated, comfortable rms. Lovely, civilised, flower-filled old family hotel (the present owner has lived in the house all his life and has been running it as a hotel since 1952), individually furnished with antiques, paintings and sculptures; extremely good food using local eggs, lovely fish, home-made jams and bread, late breakfasts, and exceptional wine list; during the winter they stage some 20 concerts, plays and recitals; cl mid-Dec–mid-Jan; pets welcome.

Whitebridge NH4413 KNOCKIE LODGE Whitebridge, Inverness IV1 2UP (01456) 486276 £95; 10 rms. Alone in the hills above Loch Ness with lovely views, this country house has been completely refurbished following a fire; a relaxed atmosphere and log and peat fires in spacious sitting room, caring, personal service, and very good food in candlelit dining room; fishing, deer stalking, hill walking and so forth; cl Oct–1 May; children over 10.

Cleish NT0998 NIVINGSTON HOUSE Cleish, Kinross KY13 7LS (01577) 850216 £90; 17 rms. Civilised small country-house hotel with relaxing bar and library, interesting food; sweeping lawn with distant hill views; cl 1st 2 wks Jan; disabled access.

Marnoch NJ5950 OLD MANSE OF MARNOCH Marnoch, Huntly, Aberdeenshire AB54 5RS (01466) 780873 £80; 5 light, well equipped rms. Georgian country house in 3 acres of gardens on the banks of the River Deveron, with antiques in comfortable sitting room, a friendly and informal atmosphere, imaginative 4-course set dinner in elegant dining room, a carefully chosen wine list, and superb breakfasts inc a marvellous range of teas and coffees.

Lundin Links NO4002 OLD MANOR Leven Rd, Lundin Links, Leven, Fife KY8 6AJ (01333) 320368 £79.50; 20 rms. Overlooking Lundin Links golf course, this neatly refurbished extended hotel has friendly staff and good local seafood in its two restaurants; dogs allowed; disabled access.

Dulnain Bridge NH9925 MUCKRACH LODGE Dulnain Bridge, Grantown on Spey, Morayshire PH26 3LY (01479) 851257 £78; 12 rms. 19th-c hunting lodge in 10 acres of grounds, with friendly and helpful owners and staff, comfortable, relaxed lounge, open fire, cosy little bar with decent lunchtime snacks, and conservatory restaurant; cl Nov; good disabled access.

Ardeonaig NN6635 ARDEONAIG Ardeonaig, Killin, Perthshire FK21 8SY (01567) 820400 *£77; 16 rms. Hotel in lovely setting with good food and pubby atmosphere in nice bar, and fishing (they have their own salmon fishing rights on Loch Tay, as well as fishing for trout and char; drying room, own harbour, boats, outboards and rod room), shooting and stalking can be arranged, their own pitch-and-putt course, lots of walks and pony-trekking; cl Nov and half Dec.

East Haugh NN9656 EAST HAUGH HOUSE East Haugh, Pitlochry, Perthshire PH16 5JS (01796) 473121 £70; 8 rms. Turreted stone house with lots of character, delightful conservatory bar, house party atmosphere, helpful, cheerful owners, and very good popular food inc local seafood and game in season; excellent shooting, stalking and salmon and trout fishing on surrounding local estates; may cl Christmas.

Spean Bridge NN2491 LETTERFINLAY LODGE Spean Bridge, Inverness-shire PH34 4DZ (01397) 712622 £70; 13 rms, 9 with own bthrm. Secluded and genteel family-run country house with picture window in extensive modern bar overlooking loch; elegantly panelled small cocktail bar, good, popular food, and friendly, attentive service; grounds run down through rhododendrons to the jetty and Loch Lochy; fishing can be arranged; cl Nov–Mar.

Kenmore NN7745 KENMORE Kenmore, Aberfeldy, Perthshire PH15 2NU (01887) 830205 £67; 38 rms. Scotland's oldest inn with relaxed atmosphere, friendly staff, open fires, good food in the no smoking restaurant, a poem in Burns' own handwriting on the plaster of one wall, river and loch fishing (salmon and trout), and own golf course; access to leisure centre; disabled access.

Crianlarich NN3825 ALLT-CHAORAIN COUNTRY HOUSE Crianlarich, Perthshire FK20 8RU (01838) 300283 *£66; 8 rms. Comfortable small hotel with homely atmosphere, log fire in lounge, honesty bar, sunroom with marvellous views, and good home-cooked food in wood-panelled dining room; lots of fishing, golf and walks nearby; cl 1 Nov–20 Mar; children over 9; disabled access.

Glendevon NN9904 TORMAUKIN Glendevon, Dollar, Clackmannanshire FK14 7JY (01259) 781252 £66; 10 rms, some in converted stable block. Comfortable, neatly kept inn in good walking country, loch and river fishing, lots of golf courses in reach; beamed dining room, softly lit bar, very good food (soup and coffee all day), fine breakfasts; cl 10 days Jan; disabled access.

Alyth NO2548 LANDS OF LOYAL Alyth, Blairgowrie, Perthshire PH11 8JQ (01828) 633151 £65; 14 rms. Mansion house in its own grounds with lovely panelled hall/lounge, roaring fire and staircase off to galleried bedroom floor; attractive dining rooms, delicious, innovative food, excellent local service, and fine views; good base for the area; cl 25–26 Dec.

Fochabers NJ3458 GORDON ARMS Fochabers, Morayshire IV32 7DH (01343) 820508 £65; 14 rms. Comfortable, traditional, small hotel with good food in restaurant and bars using fresh local produce, and fair choice of whiskies; can arrange stalking and fishing; disabled access.

Monymusk NJ6815 GRANT ARMS Monymusk, Inverurie, Aberdeenshire AB51 7HT (01467) 651226 £62; 15 rms, most with own bthrm. Smart old inn with decent food using local game and fish, dark-panelled lounge bar divided into 2 areas by a log fire in the stub wall, simpler public bar, and exclusive right to 15 miles of good trout and salmon fishing on the River Don; ghillie available; cl 1 Jan, disabled access.

Fintry NS6186 CULCREUCH CASTLE Fintry, Glasgow G63 0LW (01360) 860228 £59; 8 individually decorated rms with lovely views. Scotland's oldest inhabited castle, nearly 700 years old, in beautiful 1,600-acre parkland and surrounding hills and moors, with log fires and antiques in the public rooms, good freshly prepared food in candlelit panelled dining room, and a friendly, relaxed atmosphere; 8 modern Scandinavian holiday lodges, too.

Aberdeen NJ9305 FERRYHILL HOUSE 169 Bon Accord St, Aberdeen AB1 2UA (01224) 590867 £50w; 10 rms. Well run, small hotel with restaurant, wide choice of bar food, comfortable communicating spacious bar areas, very good choice of real ales and malt whiskies, and lots of tables on the neat, well sheltered lawns; cl 1 Jan.

Anstruther NO5704 SPINDRIFT Pittenweem Rd, Anstruther, Fife KY10 3DT (01333) 310573 *£50; 8 rms. Stone-built Victorian house, no smoking throughout, with honesty bar and log fire in comfortable lounge, a relaxed, friendly atmosphere, and freshly cooked food in dining room; cl Jan.

Ballater NO33695 GREEN INN 9 Victoria Rd, Ballater, Aberdeenshire AB35 5QQ (01339) 755701 £50; 3 pleasing rms. Friendly and attractively decorated restaurant with rooms serving delicious food using the best local produce inc interesting Scottish cheeses, and fine breakfasts; cl 2 wks Oct.

Balquhidder NN5320 MONACHYLE MHOR Balquhidder, Lochearnhead, Perthshire FK19 8PQ (01877) 384622 *£50; 6 rms with fine views overlooking Voil and Doine lochs. 18th-c farmhouse/hotel in 2,000-acre estate with prettily furnished rooms and good food using own game and herbs; private fishing and stalking for guests; children over 10.

Bridge of Cally NO1451 BRIDGE OF CALLY Bridge of Cally, Blairgowrie, Perthshire PH10 7JJ (01250) 886231 £50; 9 rms,. 6 with own bthrm. In an acre of grounds along the River Ardle, this former drovers' inn is a friendly, family-run place with good-value, home-made food using seasonal game in comfortable bar and restaurant; cl 25–26 Dec.

Kirkton of Glenisla NO2160 GLENISLA Blairgowrie, Perthshire PH11 8PH (01575) 582223 £50; 6 rms. Prettily placed 17th-c coaching inn, beautifully restored, with natural unpainted wood throughout, happily unmatched furniture, bar with open fire and two real ales, good bar suppers inc lovely Aberdeen Angus beef, and a cheerful, warm atmosphere – very much a local for the community; cl 24–26 Dec, disabled access.

Crail NO6108 GOLF Crail, Anstruther, Fife KY10 3TB (01333) 450206 £48; 5 neatly modernised rms. Village inn with plenty of atmosphere in bustling little public bar, coal fire in quieter lounge, home-made food inc high teas, and good breakfasts.

Dalcross NH7650 EASTER DALZIEL FARM Dalcross, Inverness IV1 2JL (01667) 462213 £34; 3 rms. Early Victorian farmhouse on 210 acres of family-run mixed farm (beef cattle and grain) with friendly, helpful owners, log fire in lounge, good Scottish breakfasts in big dining room and – when farm commitments allow – evening meal using own beef, lamb and veg; holiday cottages, too; cl Dec–Feb.

Carronbridge NS7483 LOCHEND FARM Carronbridge, Denny, Stirlingshire FK6 5JJ (01324) 822778 *£32; 2 rms, shared bthrm. 18th-c farmhouse in lovely position beside Loch Coulter on 750-acre upland sheep farm with sitting room, dining room and carefully prepared farmhouse cooking using own and local farm produce; cl Nov–Easter; no children.

To see and do

★ ❉ ⚐ 🏠 ▣ ✝ 💰 ! **Aberdeen**
NJ9305, Scotland's third-largest city, has a large and interesting HARBOUR, well worth pottering around (get up early one morning and visit the Fishmarket). The granite centre has wide, orderly streets not unlike Edinburgh's New Town in places, and parks. The MARITIME MUSEUM (Provost Ross's House, Shiprow) is in the town's third-oldest building (very striking), and has very good displays on the city's nautical heritage. When extensions are finished next year it will be six times as big as it is now. Shop, limited disabled access; cl Sun, 25-26 Dec, 1-2 Jan; free. SATROSPHERE (Justice Mill Lane) Lively hands-on science and technology centre – everything is there to be touched, and they have lots of changing displays and exhibitions. Great fun; snacks, shop, disabled access; cl Sun am, all day Tues (exc school hols), 25–26 Dec, 1–2 Jan; (01244) 213232; *£3. PROVOST SKENE'S HOUSE (Guestrow) Named after its most famous resident, a stately, well restored 16th-c house with recently refurbished period rooms, and remarkable painted ceilings. Meals, snacks, shop; cl Sun, 25–26 Dec, 1 Jan; free. Pretty much just around the corner, the ART GALLERY (Schoolhill) has a first-class collection of Scottish and English painting since the 16th c, and has always been particularly strong on contemporary works. Meals, snacks, shop, disabled access; cl Sun, 25–26 Dec, 1–2 Jan; free. The Ferryhill House Hotel (Bon Accord St), Royal Hotel (Bath St) and Athol (Kings Gate, W of centre) are useful for lunch, and the Prince of Wales (St Nicholas Lane) is the best proper pub in this part of Scotland. N of the centre, really too far to walk, the OLD TOWN above the River Don seems quite separate. It has some charming old streets to explore, and attractive buildings; its pedestrianised villagey High St is dominated by the University, especially the very Oxbridge-like King's College, founded in 1495. A VISITOR CENTRE outlines its history. Snacks (in barrel-vaulted former library), shop, disabled access; (01224) 273702; free. Its CHAPEL is one of the most complete examples of a medieval collegiate church in Britain. MARISCHAL COLLEGE (Broad St) was the later Protestant rival to King's, though the two were joined to form Aberdeen University in the last century. A splendid neo-Gothic structure, it has a decent MUSEUM; cl pm Sat, Sun; free. Also in this part is ST MACHAR'S CATHEDRAL, an austere mainly 15th-c church notable for its painted wooden heraldic ceiling. It's the only granite cathedral in the world. Just along from here the 19th-c CRUICKSHANK BOTANIC GARDEN (St Machar Dr) covers 11 acres with various smaller gardens – rock, water, rose and herbaceous – as well as trees and shrubs and a small terrace garden. Disabled access; cl wknds exc pm Sun May–Sept; (01224) 272704; free. Leafy Seaton Park is famous for its 14th-c Brig (or bridge) o' Balgownie.

★ **Aberfeldy** NN8549 is a nice quiet Highland shopping town, with a fine 18th-c stone bridge designed by William Adam. Weem, for a good lunch at the Ailean Chraggan, is close by.

🍺 🏠 ⚘ **Aberfoyle** NN5201 SCOTTISH WOOL CENTRE The story of Scottish wool from sheep to shop, entertainingly told by a live sheep show in the amphitheatre. They sell lots of woollen goods, and have demonstrations of crafts such as spinning and weaving. Baby lambs and goats for children, and a sheepdog training centre. Meals, snacks, disabled access; (01877) 38250; *£2.50.

👪 ⚐ **Alford** NJ5716 GRAMPIAN TRANSPORT MUSEUM Big collection of vintage vehicles, from horse-drawn sledges and carriages to motorcycles, cars and steamers. One of those places where there always seems to be plenty going on. Snacks (daily July and Aug, Sun only Jun and Sept), shop, disabled access; cl Nov–Mar; (019755) 62292; £2.50. More historic transport at the ALFORD VALLEY RAILWAY next door, a narrow-gauge passenger railway with trips in two one-mile sections, and a good static display at the station. Shop, disabled access; open pm wknds Apr–Sept, daily Jun–Aug – trains in steam peak wknds only; (0197 55) 62326; *£1.50. The Forbes Arms at Bridge of Alford has decent home cooking.

★ ☺ ✿ ♪ **Anstruther** NT5603 A pretty village with the nicely evocative SCOTTISH FISHERIES MUSEUM in a little cobbled courtyard by the harbour. Restored and model boats, aquarium, and an old fisherman's cottage in an expanding series of buildings built between the 16th and 19th c. Snacks, shop, disabled access; cl winter am Sun, 25–26 Dec, 1–2 Jan; (01333) 310628; £2.20. The Cellar and Craws Nest do good food.

✝ **Arbroath** NO6340 ARBROATH ABBEY Substantial remains of 12th-c abbey, connected to Thomas Becket and Robert the Bruce. The abbot's house is unusually complete; cl 25–26 Dec, 1–2 Jan; *£1.20.

🐾 **Aviemore** NH8912 is an uncompromisingly modern ski-resort village; the STRATHSPEY STEAM RAILWAY covers 5 miles of great scenery between here and Boat of Garten. Meals, snacks, shop, disabled access; usually open daily July–Sept (exc Sat Sept), plus other dates and wknds – best to ring for timetable; (01479) 810725; *£4.20. There are plenty of places to get something to eat in this sizable tourist development (the Olde Bridge is our current recommendation); it's a useful springboard for the Cairngorms and Glen More.

🏰 **Ballindalloch** NJ1636 GLENLIVET DISTILLERY Tours and tastings at the first Highland distillery to be licensed. Snacks, shop, limited disabled access; cl Sun, Nov–Feb; (01807) 590427; free. The Croft, a few miles south on the B9008, is good for lunch.

🏰 ✿ ♿ **Balmoral Castle** NO2588 is the royal family's Highland residence. Prince Albert bought the property four years after he and Queen Victoria had first rented it in 1848, and had a new castle built here by 1855. You can't go inside, but you can explore the wonderful gardens and woodlands, and there are various exhibitions. Snacks, shop, disabled access; open Mon–Sat May–July; (0133 97) 42334; *£2.50.

❀ **Benholm** NO8069 DAMSIDE GARDEN HERBS AND ARBORETUM Eight acres of variously themed herb gardens inc Celtic, Roman, monastic and Elizabethan. Meals, snacks, good shop, disabled access; cl Dec–Feb; (01561) 361496; *£1.

🏰 🏠 **Blair Atholl** NN8666 BLAIR CASTLE Nestling among forests and heather-clad hills, this is Scotland's most visited privately owned house, dating back to the 13th c, though largely renovated in the 18th. It's the home of the Duke of Atholl and his unique private army, shown off in their annual parade in May. Thirty-two rooms are open, with interesting collections of arms and armour, china, paintings and embroidery. A piper outside every day in summer adds to the atmosphere; meals. Snacks, shop, disabled access to ground floor only; cl Nov–Mar; (01796) 481207; *£5.

🐾 ☺ **Blair Drummond** NS7399 SAFARI AND LEISURE PARK Wild animals in natural surroundings, with an unusual aerial walkway above the big cats' reserve and a boat trip round the chimps' island. As well as often playful animals, there are rides, playgrounds and shows – it's set up very much as a family day out. They've recently added a zebra reserve. Meals, snacks, shop, disabled access; cl Oct–Mar; (01786) 841456; *£6. The Cross Keys at Kippen and Lion & Unicorn at Thornhill are quite handy for family lunches.

🏛 🏰 ☺ ♿ 🐾 🚂 **Bo'ness** NS9880 The KINNEIL ESTATE includes the interesting if not extensive remains of a ROMAN FORTLET, as well as a few later ruins and remains. The converted stables of adjacent KINNEIL HOUSE have a museum on the site's history, with an audio-visual display and lots of local pottery. You can still see the workshop where James Watt developed the steam engine, and there are pleasant woodland walks in the grounds. Shop, some disabled access; cl 12.30–1.30pm, Oct–Apr exc Sat; (01506) 824318; free. BO'NESS & KINNEIL RAILWAY Re-creation of the days of steam complete with relocated railway buildings and Scotland's largest collection of locomotives and rolling stock. The round trip is 7 miles long, and takes passengers to the woodlands of the Avon Gorge at Birkhill, where there are tours of an old CLAY MINE, its workings featuring fossilised trees embedded in the clay some 300 million years ago. Snacks, shop, disabled access to railway only; trains run wknds Apr–mid-Oct, daily July and Aug, though you can see the locomotives all year; (01506) 822298; *£5.50 mine and railway, *£3.60 train only.

ñ ☙ **Braemar** NO1491 One of the best known Highland villages, with a good VISITOR CENTRE showing useful films on the area's history and scenery (inc an interesting look at the building of Balmoral Castle), and of course on Braemar's famous Highland Gathering. Shop, disabled access; (0133 97) 41944; £1.90. BRAEMAR CASTLE nearby is a pleasant place to visit if in the area, and its charming exterior is highly unusual; cl Fri, Nov–Easter; *£1.90. The elegantly refurbished Fife Arms is useful for lunch.

☙ ▣ ♘ ⚘ **Brodie Castle** NH9757 Handsome gabled castle with extensive art collection featuring 17th-c paintings of the Dutch school, English watercolours and French Impressionists. Before the National Trust for Scotland took it over in 1980 it had been the seat of the same family since 1160. Outside are woodland walks and wildlife observation hides, and a beautiful collection of daffodils in spring. Snacks, shop, some disabled access; cl am Sun, mid-Oct–Mar; £3.50; NTS. Their occasional evenings of traditional Scottish music are enjoyed by readers. The nearest really good place for a meal is the Clifton Hotel in Nairn.

✝ ☙ **Burntisland** NT2386 Once famous for shipbuilding, now a popular little resort, with an unusual octagonal CHURCH, where the decision was made to produce the Authorised Version of the Bible in 1601. EDWARDIAN FAIR MUSEUM (High St, above library) Unusual museum recreating the sights and sounds of the town fair, with rides, stalls and sideshows all modelled on those in a

North of the Forth: Central Highlands and East Coast

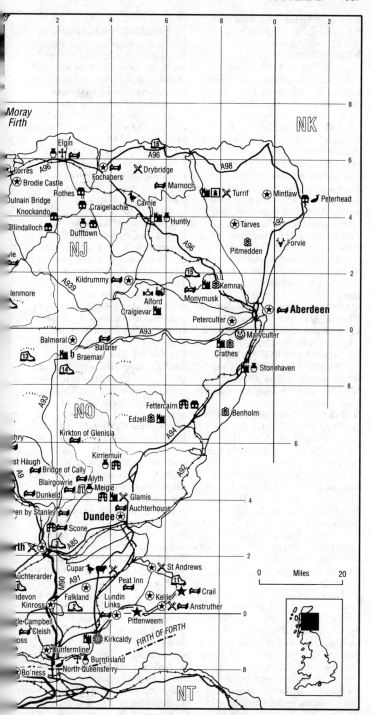

painting of the scene by a local artist; cl 1–2pm, all Sun and bank hols; (01592) 260732; free.

🦅 **Cairnie** NJ4844 NORTH EAST FALCONRY CENTRE Around 40 eagles, owls and falcons, with regular flying displays throughout the day. Snacks, shop, disabled access; cl Dec–Feb; (01466) 87344; *£3.50.

🍴 ⚘ ✕ 🏰 **Callander** NN6208 ROB ROY AND TROSSACHS VISITOR CENTRE (Ancaster Sq) The story of Scotland's most whitewashed rascal (or brave supporter of the downtrodden, depending on your point of view), well told with hi-tech displays. Also useful information on the beautiful surrounding countryside. Shop, disabled access; cl Jan and Feb; (01877) 330342; £2. The HEATHER CENTRE sells a vast range of heathers, plus alpines, herbs, shrubs and trees. Also miniature railway. Disabled access; cl 25 Dec, 1 Jan; (01877) 331188; free, 50p train. KILMAHOG WOOLLEN MILL (just N) Restored watermill, selling tweeds, tartans and other woollen gifts. Meals, snacks; cl 25–26 Dec, 1 Jan; (01877) 330268; free. Besides the nearby Myrtle (see Where to eat), the Byre at Brig o' Turk NN5306 out in the Trossachs is a very good dining pub.

🏛 ⚘ 🏌 **Castle Campbell** NS9698 Once known as Castle Gloom, this late 15th-c castle was burned by Cromwell's troops in the 1650s, but still has its courtyard, Great Hall and barrel roof, as well as splendid views from the tower; cl am Sun, and winter Thurs pm and all Fri; *£2. The most attractive approach is through the spectacular DOLLAR GLEN, 60 acres of wonderful woodland; take care, some of the paths are steep and narrow, and can be dangerous after rain. The Strathallan in Dollar has good food, especially fish.

🏛 🏠 🖼 🦌 **Cawdor** NH8450 CAWDOR CASTLE Home of the Thanes of Cawdor since the 14th c, this splendid old house is one of the most entertaining as well as interesting places to visit in the whole area. Look out especially for the tree inside a tower and the freshwater well inside the house, as well as the more usual fine tapestries, furnishings and paintings (inc Dali's odd interpretation of the Macbeth tale). The busy grounds have craft and wool shops, nature trails, and a little pitch-and-putt course. The castle was built here after William Calder had a dream telling him to build it on the spot where his donkey lay down to rest. Meals and snacks, shop, disabled access; cl Oct–Apr; (01667) 404615; £4, £2 grounds only. The nearby Cawdor Tavern is good for lunch.

🏛 **Clava Cairns** NH7748 A group of circular burial cairns from around 1600 BC surrounded by three concentric rings of great stones, on the banks of the River Nairn.

🏰 **Craigellachie** NJ2945 SPEYSIDE COOPERAGE CENTRE Working cooperage and visitor centre, with interesting exhibitions and a viewing area to watch the craftsmen at work. There's a reconstructed Victorian cooperage where life-size models speak in the local dialect. Shop (with wide range of wood goods), disabled access to exhibition only; cl Sun, winter Sat, 2 wks Christmas; (01340) 881303; *£1.70. Nearby is the distillery that produces the glorious sherry-casked Macallan, so it makes sense to combine the two. Guided tours wkdys 11am and 2pm, by appointment; (01340) 871471; free.

🏛 **Craigievar** NJ5509 (S of Alford) CRAIGIEVAR CASTLE Perhaps the most fairytale-romantic of the area's castles, this picturesque early 17th-c multiple tower dotted with erratically shaped windows soars to a mushrooming of corbels, turrets and crow-stepped gables, and inside the warren of narrow staircases takes you into a rich series of ornately beamed and plastered rooms. The National Trust for Scotland are worried that too many people come here, but if you do decide to visit (and it is worth while), try to avoid busy times, as it's not a place to absorb coach parties comfortably; house cl am, Oct–Apr, grounds open all year; £5; NTS.

🏛 ⚘ **Crathes** NO7596 CRATHES CASTLE Beautiful 16th-c tower house with wonderful interiors – especially its ceiling paintings, filled with wise old sayings in a mixture of Scots and English. Lots of charming original features, and royal associations going back to the early 14th c. Best of all are the surrounding gardens, inc a four-acre walled garden with a remarkable series of carefully toned colour borders, as well as nature trails, wild garden and interesting collection of unusual plants. Meals, snacks, shop, some disabled access; cl Nov–Mar; £4, garden only ticket available; NTS.

🏰 **Crieff** NN8621 GLENTURRET DISTILLERY Scotland's oldest distillery, dating from 1775 and using the pure water of the Turret Burn. The distillery cat Towser, who died in 1987, is still listed in the *Guinness Book of Records* as World Mousing Champion – challengers have 28,899 to beat. There's a particularly good visitor centre here. Good meals and snacks, shop, some disabled access; cl am Sun, all wknd Jan and Feb, 25–26 Dec, 1–2 Jan; (01764) 656565; *£2.90. The town perched on the edge of the Highlands is a pleasant stop.

🏳 **Culloden** NH7345 The bleak site of the gruesome massacre in which the 25-year-old Duke of Cumberland destroyed the Highland army of Bonnie Prince Charlie. On the moor a cairn marks this last bloody battle fought on mainland Britain. You can see the Graves of the Clans and the Wells of the Dead, as well as the Old Leanach Cottage around which the battle was fought, now refurbished in period style. Good audio-visual show. Meals, snacks, shop, disabled access; visitor centre cl Jan; £1.80; NTS. The Coach House (Stoneyfield, A92) does food.

★ 🏰🛏❀† **Culross** NO3714 is a fascinating small town on the Forth, virtually unchanged since the 16th and 17th c. Until the 1930s this was because no one could afford any improvements, and since then its red pantiled-roofed houses have been carefully restored and preserved by the National Trust for Scotland (they are still lived in). The laird's PALACE, the first building the Trust purchased here, has just reopened after a splendid restoration; fully furnished in period style, it has several new interpretative displays, and they're creating a 17th-c garden. Guides are good at pointing out those small but fascinating details. Snacks, shop, some disabled access; cl Nov–Easter; £3.50; NTS. The price includes a Walkman tour, and admission to the Trust's two other main properties here, the Town House, containing a good visitor centre, and the STUDY, with a Norwegian painted ceiling in the drawing room. You can see a good few other interesting buildings from the outside, as well as the remains of a 13th-c abbey.

🐗🦌 **Nr Cupar** NO3212 SCOTTISH DEER CENTRE (Just W on A91 at Bow of Fife) You can stroke the deer and even feed the young fawns here, and there are also nature and heritage trails, aerial walkways and observation platforms, an audio-visual show, adventure playground, and new falconry centre. Meals, snacks, shop, disabled access; cl Nov–Easter; (01337) 810391; £4. The Ostlers Close is good for lunch.

🏰🏠 **Doune** NN7201 DOUNE CASTLE A 14th-c stronghold with two fine restored towers on the banks of the River Teith. Strong associations with Bonnie Prince Charlie and Sir Walter Scott. Shop; cl am Sun and winter pm Thurs and all Fri; *£2. Close by, the DOUNE MOTOR MUSEUM has around 50 cars on display. Meals, snacks, shop, disabled access; cl Nov–Mar; (01786) 841203; £2.75. The village's bridge is said to have been built out of spite by James IV's tailor when the ferryman refused him a passage.

🏰🍺 **Dufftown** NJ3240 GLENFIDDICH DISTILLERY (1 m N) The only Highland distillery where you can follow the entire whisky production process from barley to bottle; most other distilleries bottle elsewhere. Tastings, shop, disabled access; cl winter wknds; (01340) 20373; free. Dufftown also has a useful museum.

† **Dunblane** NN7801 is a small town of ancient origin, with old buildings in its narrow streets, especially around the close of its elegant 13th-c CATHEDRAL. This incorporates a much older tower, and has a beautiful oval window that you can see only from outside. The Dunblane Hotel does prompt food.

❈▣🍺🏰❀♤◈☀ **Dundee** NO4030 is a bustling busy city,

though underneath the straightforward modern wrappings you can uncover signs of its distinguished heritage in a number of museums. Down at the DOCKS the Royal Research Ship *Discovery* was the first British purpose-built research vessel, commissioned for the ill-fated expedition by Scott to the Antarctic. It's been very well restored and livened up in the past couple of years, with the addition of an excellent visitor centre Discovery Point featuring hi-tech displays on the ship and the various people who used her. Shop, disabled access; cl 25 Dec, 1–2 Jan; (01382) 201245; £4. Nearby the 1824 frigate *Unicorn* is the oldest British-built warship still afloat, now containing a museum of naval life in her days in commission. Snacks, shop, limited disabled access; cl 25–26 Dec, 1–2 Jan; (01382) 200900; £3. Museums worth a look include the McMANUS GALLERIES MUSEUM (Albert Sq), with important works by 19th-c Scottish and English artists, and a splendid hall with vaulted ceiling and stained glass, and the BARRACK NATURAL HISTORY MUSEUM; both cl Sun, free. BROUGHTY CASTLE MUSEUM (Broughty Ferry) A 15th-c seaside castle rebuilt in the 19th c to defend the estuary, now a maritime museum. Plenty of harpoons and whaling exhibits – whaling used to be one of Dundee's major industries. Shop; cl 1–2pm, all Fri and Sun (exc pm summer); (01382) 76121; free. MILLS OBSERVATORY (Balgay Park) Britain's only full-time public observatory, housing exhibits on space research and astronomy, as well as a small planetarium (by prior arrangement only), and a splendid ten-inch refracting telescope; good audio-visual display. Shop; cl am Sat, all Sun, and till 3pm every day Oct–Mar (when open till 10 at night); (01382) 67138; free. CAMPERDOWN COUNTRY PARK Based around 19th-c Camperdown House, 400 acres of fine parkland with a variety of attractions, inc golf course, nature trails, woodland footpaths, and wildlife centre with indigenous animals from wolves to wildcats. Also adventure play area themed around the defeat of the Dutch at the 1797 Battle of Camperdown. Meals, snacks, shop, disabled access; (01382) 23141; free, £1.25 wildlife centre. CLAYPOTTS CASTLE (3m E of city centre) is a fine example of the tower house kind of castle; cl am Sun and all Oct–Mar; £1.20. The Royal Oak (Brook St), Mercantile (Commercial St) and Number 1 (Constitution Rd) all do cheap food, and in Broughty Ferry the Fisherman's Tavern and Ship (fantastic view upstairs) are good.

✝ ⚲ ✿ 🏠 ❀ **Dunfermline** NT0987 is quite a prosperous light-industry town with a distinguished distant past. ABBEY Remains of Benedictine abbey and later church buildings, pleasantly set in quiet precincts away from the busy centre. The foundations of the original 11th-c church are still under the more elaborate Norman nave, and the grave of King Robert the Bruce is marked by a modern brass in the choir stalls. The monastery guest house, once a royal palace, was the birthplace of Charles I. Shop, mostly disabled access; cl winter pm Thurs and Fri; *£1.50. The DISTRICT MUSEUM (Viewfield Terrace) includes an interesting explanation of the local manufacture of damask linen. Shop, disabled access to ground floor only; cl Sun and public hols; free. The ANDREW CARNEGIE MUSEUM (Moodie St) looks at a man who from humble origins here made a fortune in Pittsburgh steel, then gave away over $350 million in the days when a $ was a $ – all the while claiming he didn't believe in charity. They have handloom weaving demonstrations the first Fri of each month, May–Oct. Snacks summer wknds, shop, disabled access; cl am Sun, and am every day in winter; (01383) 724302; *£1.50. PITTENCRIEFF HOUSE MUSEUM (Pittencrieff Park) Fine 17th-c mansion in lovely rugged glen, with displays of local history and costume. Shop, disabled access to ground floor only; cl Tues, Nov–Apr; free. Make sure you wander through the surrounding park.

🏰 ❀ **Edzell** NO5969 EDZELL CASTLE Some unique features at this pretty old place – the walled garden planted here in 1604, and the charming series of heraldic and mythical sculptures that decorate the walls around it; these alternate with recesses for flowers and nests for birds. They claim to have captured on camera the castle's rather active ghost. Shop, disabled access; cl winter pmThurs and Fri; *£2.

✝ ✆ **Elgin** NJ2162 is a shopping town of some poise, with ancient buildings as well as its ruined 13th-c cathedral, and is handy for the north coast. Thunderton House has decent food. There's still quite a lot to see of the ruined CATHEDRAL, founded in 1224 and known as the Lantern of the North and the Glory of the Kingdom because of its extraordinary beauty and fine-traceried windows. The 15th-c nave has some ancient Celtic cross slabs with Pictish symbols. Shop; cl winter pm Thurs and Fri; *£1.20. The MUSEUM in the High St has a world-famous fossil collection; cl am Sun, Nov–Mar; (01343) 543675; £1. About 5m SW, nr Barnhill, PLUSCARDEN ABBEY NJ1458 is fascinating; built in the 13th c, it gradually fell to ruin, but was completely rebuilt this century by monks from Prinknash Abbey (see Gloucestershire chapter). There's a visitor centre illustrating its remarkable history; (0134 389) 257; free.

❀ ♧ ✿ ✆ ⊞ **Falkirk** NS8880 Just E of the town is CALLENDER PARK, a huge park with woodland walks, lots of summer activities, and CALLENDER HOUSE, a striking old house used briefly as a headquarters by Oliver Cromwell. Remodelled in the last century to look like a French chateau, it's now been opened up as a museum, with costumed guides interpreting its history. Meals, snacks, shop, disabled access; house cl winter Sun; house *£1.50, park free. Part of the Antonine Wall runs through the grounds, and 6m W of Falkirk at ROUGH CASTLE you can see one of its best preserved sections. Not too much is left of the Roman fort that once stood here, but you can still see the ramparts and ditches; free.

★ ✿ ❀ **Falkland** NO2507 is a very attractive village. FALKLAND PALACE Lovely Renaissance palace of the Stuart kings and queens, set below the Lomond Hills on the main street of the strollable little town. The rooms are beautifully decorated, especially the King's Bedchamber and the Chapel Royal. Not all is as old as it looks, but it doesn't really matter – accurate restoration work has created a comfortably cosy and genuinely lived-in feel. The French Renaissance architecture of the south range is particularly impressive. Pleasant gardens and grounds, with the 1539 tennis courts the oldest in the country. Shop; cl am Sun, Nov–Mar; £4, £2 garden only; NTS. Across the road the Town Hall has an exhibition on the history of the castle and royal burgh. The Covenanter Inn is useful for lunch.

✿ ✆ **Fettercairn** NO6475 FASQUE (just N) still belongs to the Gladstones, and the Prime Minister lived here from 1830-1851. The main rooms look as if they've scarcely been changed (let alone modernised) since he moved to Wales, and the servants' quarters are also an extraordinary period survival, complete with touching gallery of servants' portraits. Snacks, shop, disabled access; cl am, Fri, Oct–April; (01561) 340569; *£3. FETTERCAIRN DISTILLERY (Distillery Rd) One of Scotland's oldest licensed distilleries, with tours, tastings, and good audio-visual show. Shop, disabled access to visitor centre only; cl Sun, Oct–Apr; (01561) 340205. Fettercairn's square has a magnificent archway erected to commemorate a visit by Queen Victoria.

✆ ❀ ♧ ✆ **Fochabers** NJ3458 Just W of town the BAXTERS VISITOR CENTRE explores how the grocery shop set up by George and Margaret Baxter grew into a company whose food is now sold all over the world. Tours (not wknds), audio-visual show, landcaped gardens and woodland walk. Meals, snacks, good shops, disabled access; (01343) 820393; free. Fochabers itself has a very good FOLK MUSEUM (cl 1–2pm, *60p), and the Gordon Arms is a reliable food stop.

⊞ ✆ ✆ **Forres** NJ4265 SUENO'S STONE Mysterious 9th- or 10th-c stone that may have been erected to commemorate a forgotten battle. It's 20ft high, and is carved with a cross on one side and groups of warriors on the other. The FALCONER MUSEUM (Tolbooth St) has a good fossil collection. Cl winter lunchtimes, am Sun (exc Jun–Sept); free. DALLAS DHU (2m S) is a perfectly preserved Victorian distillery, which you can wander around on your own. It's been cleverly adapted using animatronic models to explain what's happening. Shop (with nearly 200 different types of whisky), disabled access; cl am Sun, and winter pm Thurs and all Fri (0131) 244 3101; *£2.

▓ **Fort George** NH7657 One of the finest examples of an 18th-c artillery building, one of three fortresses built after 1745, when the Hanoverians were taking no risks in keeping this area firmly under their thumb. Very big, with quite a bit to see. Snacks, shop, disabled access; cl am Sun, museum cl Sat; (01667) 462777; *£2.50. Just off from the fort in the Moray Firth you may be lucky enough to see one of the very few inshore schools of dolphins around the British coast.

✔ **Forvie** NK0228 FORVIE NATURE RESERVE The fifth largest sand dune system in Britain – and the one least disturbed by people, so lots of wildlife. From Apr to Aug you have to stick to the footpaths so as not to disturb the birds, but the rest of the year you can go where you like. Disabled access; visitor centre may be cl winter wkdys; (0136 887) 330; free.

▓ **Glamis** NO3848 GLAMIS CASTLE The family home of the Earls of Strathmore, and the childhood home of the Queen Mother – a splendid creation, utterly suitable as the setting for Shakespeare's murder of Duncan in *Macbeth*. Notable features include the chapel with its painted panels and ceiling, and the drawing room, and of course there are those stories about what's locked away in one of the towers. Meals, snacks, shop, some disabled access; cl Oct–Apr; (01307) 840393; £4.20. The Strathmore Arms is good for lunch.

▄ **Glengoulandie Deer Park** NN7652 Herds of red deer and other wild creatures kept in surroundings as close to their natural habitat as possible, yet keeping the animals within sight. Shop; cl Oct–May; (01887) 830261; £3 with car, £1 walking.

✔ **Glenmore** NH9808 CAIRNGORM REINDEER CENTRE Unique oppportunity to mingle with free-ranging reindeer in their natural surroundings, a pretty stretch of the Cairngorms; you can feed and stroke the animals. Guided walks leave the visitor centre every day at 11am (maybe 2.30 pm too in summer). The centre itself is open all day, with an interesting audio-visual display. Shop, disabled access to visitor centre only (though they usually have reindeer down here too); (01479) 861228; *£3.

▓ **Huntly** NJ5240 CASTLE The original medieval castle here was destroyed and rebuilt several times, once by Mary, Queen of Scots. Reconstructed for the last time in 1602, the ruins are worth a look for their ornate heraldic decorations. Shop; cl pm winter Thurs and Fri; *£2. In the square is a little local history museum.

▓ **Inverness** NH6645 is the biggest town up here, and the main shopping town for the whole of the N of Scotland (Melvens is a good book shop). It has an attractive riverside setting and is a handy centre without being at all touristy. Looking over the Moray Firth a few miles E, CASTLE STUART was built for the Earl of Moray in 1621 when his family, the Stuarts, ruled the United Kingdom; it was soon abandoned for nigh on three centuries, but has been restored to include decorations and furnishings that reflect its days of glory. So much celebration of Bonnie Prince Charlie is quite poignant just 3 miles from the scene of his final downfall. You can stay here by appointment. Shop; (01463) 790745; £3.

▓ **Kellie** NO5105 KELLIE CASTLE Fine example of 16th- and 17th-c domestic architecture, though parts date from the 14th c, with good collections of plasterwork, panelling and furniture. Also four acres of gardens, inc a Victorian walled garden and woodland area with adventure playground. Snacks, shop; house cl am, wkdys Apr, all Nov–Mar; £3, £1; garden only NTS.

▓ **Kemnay** NJ7212 CASTLE FRASER The architectural embellishments here are the work of two remarkably talented families of stonemasons, who helped to make it one of the grandest castles of Mar. The z-shaped building incorporates the remains of an earlier building, and there are excellent formal gardens. Snacks, shop; cl am (exc July and Aug), Oct–Apr (exc Easter wknd), grounds open all yr; (01330) 833463; £3.50; NTS.

▲ ❀ ⌂ Kildrummy NJ4516 KILDRUMMY CASTLE Now in ruins, though still with its original 13th-c round towers, hall and chapel, as well as some later remains; *£1.50. It provides a spectacular backdrop to the GARDENS, which are very beautiful indeed and of some botanical interest. There's an alpine garden in an old quarry, a water garden, walks in the woods and a video showing the changes in the garden through the seasons. Shop, disabled access; cl Nov–Mar; (0197 55) 71203; £2.

♄ Killiecrankie NN9162 Queen Victoria was just one of the people to have found this romantic spot beguiling, but it wasn't always so serene. In 1689 it was the site of a fierce battle when the Highlanders routed the troops of William III, and a VISITOR CENTRE tells the tale. Also displays on the area's natural history. Snacks, shop, disabled access; cl Nov–Apr; *£1; NTS. The Killiecrankie Hotel, with good food, is an attractive place.

🐾 Kincraig NH8305 HIGHLAND WILDLIFE PARK Drive-through safari past all sorts of animals native to the area such as reindeer, bears, wolves, wildcats and bison. Also walk-round area with aviaries, forest habitat, and pets' corner – all in lovely surroundings. Sheepdog demonstrations 2pm Sun, Tues and Thurs. Snacks, shop, disabled access; cl Nov–Mar; (01540) 651270; £11.70 for full car, £9.70 for car and 2 passengers.

☉ ⚘ ♄ Kingussie NH7501 (pronounced 'Kinoossie') The HIGHLAND FOLK MUSEUM (Duke St) was the first folk museum in Britain, originally opened on Iona in the 1930s. Still a good range of exhibits, inc craft demonstrations, displays of domestic life, and a reconstructed mill. Shop, disabled access; cl am Sun, and all winter wknds; (01540) 661307; *£2.50. The Royal is useful for lunch.

A couple of miles or so down the A96 just N of Newtonmore NN7199, the HIGHLAND FOLK PARK demonstrates the life and work of crofters at the turn of the century; you may be able to help with some of the seasonal activities, or feed the animals. Also a Museum of Highland Sport, which explains why so many of the area's golfers are left-handed. The park only opened last year, but they have ambitious plans for extending it; open July–Sept (exc Sun); (01540) 673351; £2.

⚓ ▲ ❀ Kinross NO1102 From the jetty ferries cross the loch to the island fortress LOCH LEVEN CASTLE, where Mary, Queen of Scots was imprisoned for a while; she managed to escape, but only after she had been persuaded to abdicate in favour of her infant son. Shop; limited disabled access; cl Oct–Mar; *£2. The loch itself is rather undramatic, but in the winter the evening flights and sounds of the thousands of ducks and geese here seem a mournful echo of those days. An RSPB RESERVE at the S end of the lake has good facilities for watching the birds; (01577) 862355; £2. KINROSS GARDENS Rather fine and formal, with yew trees, roses and herbaceous borders; cl Oct–Apr; (01577) 863467; *£2. The good Nivingston House at Cleish is not far.

▲ ❀ Kirkcaldy NT2791 (locally pronounced 'Kirkawdy' by the right wing and 'Kirkuddy' by the left) This busy resort and shopping town is not too interesting to visitors, but has some charming old wynds and houses in the eastern suburb of Dysart, which has its own picturesque little harbour. Between here and the main town is 15th-c RAVENSCRAIG CASTLE, perhaps most notable for its symmetrical shape. It was one of the first British castles designed to be defended by firearms, and has great views over the Firth of Forth; free.

🏠 ☉ Kirriemuir NO3954 BARRIE'S BIRTHPLACE The birthplace of the writer of *Peter Pan*: the upper floors are furnished in the style of the period, and next door are displays relating to his work, both literary and theatrical. Teas, shop, disabled access; cl am Sun, Oct–Apr (exc Easter wknd); £1.80; NTS.

🏰 **Knockando** NJ1842 TAMDHU DISTILLERY Half-hourly tours of nicely set distillery, housed in a former Victorian railway station. Tastings, shop; cl Sat (exc Jun–Sept), Sun, Nov–Apr; (0134 06) 221; £2.

☺ **Maryculter** NO8599 STORYBOOK GLEN Good for children, around 100 nursery rhymes and characters brought to life in 20 acres of beautiful Deeside countryside. Meals, snacks, shop, disabled access; cl winter wkdys; (01244) 732941; *£3.10. The Lairhillock at Netherley does good lunches.

🏰 **Marypark** NJ1938 GLENFARCLAS DISTILLERY Interesting displays of the production of one of the traditional top three malts, with tastings. Shop, limited disabled access; cl wknds exc Sat Jun–Sept, Christmas and New Year; (01807) 500257; *£2.50.

♂🏛 **Meigle** ND2844 MUSEUM Outstanding collection of Celtic Christian SCULPTURED STONES, all found in or around the churchyard. shop; cl Nov–Mar; *£1.20.

❀ ♘ ♄ **Mintlaw** NJ9847 ADEN COUNTRY PARK More than 200 acres of lovely woodland and farmland, criss-crossed with nature trails and with plenty of wildlife. The NE SCOTLAND AGRICULTURAL HERITAGE CENTRE here illustrates two centuries of farming history, with static displays and seasonal open-air demonstrations and tours. Meals, snacks, shop, disabled access; cl wkdys Apr and Oct, and all Nov–Mar; (01771) 622857; park free, heritage centre £1.

❀ ❀ **Muthill** NN8418 (pronounced 'mewtle') DRUMMOND CASTLE GARDENS Majestic formal gardens originally laid out in 1630 by John Drummond, 2nd Earl of Perth. Lovely views from the upper terrace, splendid early Victorian parterre, and centrepiece sundial designed and built by the master mason of King Charles I. Shop, limited disabled access; open pm May–Oct; (01764) 681257; *£3.

★ **Nairn** NH8856 is a quiet, relaxed and rather discreet old-fashioned resort on the N coast, with good sheltered beaches.

♪ **North Queensferry** NT1380 DEEP-SEA WORLD The most elaborate aquarium in the northern hemisphere;

moving walkways take you through an incredible transparent viewing tunnel as long as a football pitch, surrounded by a million gallons of water and sharks and exotic fish from all around the world. All done extremely well, and you can go round and round as often as you like. Also various touch and feel exhibits. Meals, snacks, shop, disabled access; cl 25 Dec; (01383) 411411; *£4.50.

♪♨🎖❀🏰⛵ **Perth** NO1123 is spaciously laid out along the broad River Tay; it has a popular craft centre in the Fair Maid's House, and an excellent specialist rhododendron nursery, Glendoick Gardens. There are a couple of decent museums and galleries, and Timothy's is good for lunch. BRANKLYN GARDEN (116 Dundee Rd) only covers about 2 acres but seems much bigger, thanks to a remarkable planting of interesting rhododendrons, small trees. Asiatic primulas, meconopsis, lilies and the like. Shop, limited disabled access; cl Nov–Feb; £2; NTS. CAITHNESS GLASS You can watch paperweight-making from a viewing gallery, and there's a collectors' museum and factory shop. Meals, snacks, disabled access; cl am Sun Nov–Mar, no glass-making wknds (exc July and Aug); (01738) 37373; free. Just W is HUNTINGTOWER CASTLE with an interesting painted ceiling (cl pm winter Thurs and Fri; *£1.50).

⛵🏠❀ **Peterculter** NJ7900 DRUM CASTLE still looks out over what's left of the medieval forest granted the family by Robert the Bruce. Mainly a much-altered Jacobean mansion, the house is based around a 13th-c keep, one of the three oldest tower houses in Scotland. There's a historic rose garden in the grounds. Snacks, shop, limited disabled access; cl am (exc July and Aug), wkdys Apr and Oct, all Nov–Mar; *£3.50; NTS. The Lairhillock Inn at Netherley a few miles S is good for lunch.

♪ 🏰 **Peterhead** NK1246 UGIE FISH HOUSE The oldest salmon fish house in Scotland, dating back 400 yrs; you can watch them smoking salmon (caught from the adjacent river in season), and they sell a good range of salmon and trout; cl 12–2pm, pm Sat, Sun; (01779) 76209; free.

🏠 ⛴ ♨ **Pitlochry** NN9458 has the comfortable feel of a place that's been an inland resort town for a good long time, and is beautifully set in fine countryside; a happy sort of place. EDRADOUR (2½ m E) is Scotland's smallest distillery, founded in 1825 and virtually unchanged since Victorian times. Guided tours, audio-visual show, tastings; shop; cl Sun, Nov–Feb (exc shop); (01796) 472095; free. The POWER STATION has exhibitions on the production of electricity, with access to the turbine viewing gallery. You can see the salmon as they pass upstream to their spawning grounds from the salmon ladder viewing chamber. Shop, disabled access; cl Nov–Mar; (01796) 473152; £1.50. Lovely woodland on the banks of man-made Loch Faskally with walks and nature trails.

❀ **Pitmedden** NJ8828 PITMEDDEN GARDEN Originally planted in the 17th c and pretty much unchanged since, with sundials, fountains and pavilions among the elaborate formal gardens. Snacks, shop, disabled access; cl Oct–Apr; £3; NTS.

† ♣ **Port of Menteith** NN5700 INCHMAHOME PRIORY Famous as the refuge of the infant Mary, Queen of Scots in 1543 (or, depending on your allegiances, as the burial-place of Robert Cunningham Grahame), this Augustinian priory was founded in 1238 on an island in the middle of the lake, and in spring and summer you can get a boat across. Robert the Bruce prayed here before the Battle of Bannockburn. Shop; cl all winter; *£2 inc ferry.

🏠 **Rothes** NJ2749 GLEN GRANT DISTILLERY Founded in 1840 by the brothers Grant, whose malt whisky was one of the first to be bottled and sold as a single malt. Guided tours and tastings; shop, disabled access; cl wknds (exc Sat July and Aug), Oct–Mar; (01340) 831413; free.

★ 🏰 † ♨ 🏖 🏌 **St Andrews** NO5116 is a civilised university town as well as a rather dignified seaside resort. It's outstanding for golfers, though summer visitors hoping to play on the hallowed greens of the Royal & Ancient Golf Club (the game's ruling authority) will have to tee up £50 despite having nowhere to change in; plans to build a new clubhouse for visitors are currently splitting the locals. The 13th-c CASTLE was the scene of Bishop Beaton's murder during a wave of anti-Catholic feeling in 1546. It was largely demolished in the 17th c to provide stone for the harbour, but some substantial ruins remain. Shop, disabled access; cl am Sun; *£2. The twin-towered remains of the Norman CATHEDRAL are impressive. In its time this was the largest cathedral in Scotland, but angry locals sacked it in the 16th c. Shop, disabled access; *£1.50. You can get a joint ticket with the castle for *£3. Beside it the very tall and narrow Romanesque ST RULES TOWER is part of the older church the cathedral was built to replace (perhaps pre-Conquest), and if you can face over 150 steps gives wonderful views from the top. There are a few interesting MUSEUMS on the city's history, some quite lively, and a number of fine buildings belonging to Scotland's oldest university – especially St Leonard's and St Mary's Colleges. South St is worth strolling along: attractive riggs or small courts and alleys off, the ancient West Port gateway at the end, and Holy Trinity Church where John Knox preached his first sermon in 1547. The GOLF MUSEUM (Bruce Embankment) fascinates anyone keen on the game, with interactive and audio-visual displays going right through its 500-year history. Assorted memorabilia include lots of glamorous golfing gear, as well as the most unlikely-looking old cleeks and so forth. The technology is incredibly up-to-date, with some of the most advanced features you're likely to come across in any museum. Shop, disabled access; cl Tues and Weds Nov–Apr, 25 Dec–1 Jan; (01334) 73306; *£3.50. SEA LIFE CENTRE (The Scores) Three resident seals, and lots of other examples of British native marine life, well displayed in realistic recreations of the sea bed. Lively touch displays, and a fun exhibition on monsters and mysteries of the deep. Meals, snacks, shop, disabled access; cl 25 Dec; (01334) 74786; £4.25. Besides the

Vine Leaf (see **Where to eat**), Ma Bell's (pleasant seafront views outside) and the St Andrews Wine Bar are useful for lunch, and the Grange a mile S has good food and wine.

🏠 **Scone** NO1126 (pronounced 'Scoon') SCONE PALACE was the seat of government in Scotland from Pictish times, though the current building is largely 16th-c behind an 18th-c castellated façade. It was the site of the Stone of Destiny – the famous coronation stone – until it was seized by the English in 1296, and indeed Scottish kings were crowned at Scone until 1651. Now there are good displays of porcelain, furniture, clocks and needlework, and the grounds are pleasant. Meals, snacks, shop, some disabled access; cl am Sun (exc July and Aug), mid-Oct–Good Fri; (01738) 552300; £4.20.

★ 🏰 🏠 ✝ ❀ 🍴 **Stirling** NS7993 Strategically placed on the Firth of Forth, this is a very unstuffy place, with the university students putting quite a bit of buzz into the atmosphere. STIRLING CASTLE provides magnificent views from its lofty hilltop site. It became very popular with the royal family in the 15th and 16th c, and most of the buildings date from that period. The finest features are the Chapel Royal built by James VI (and I of England), and the Renaissance palace built by James V. There's a very good visitor centre in a restored building next door. Snacks, shop; cl 25 Dec, 1–2 Jan; *£3.50. Dropping down the steep hill on which the castle stands is an attractive and interesting network of old streets, with a lot of character in their old-to-ancient buildings; MARY'S WALK is an interesting ruined Renaissance-style mansion, and the CHURCH of Holy Rood was where Mary, Queen of Scots and James VI were crowned as babies. The Settle Inn (St Mary's Wynd) is a useful and atmospheric pub. Just NE of town on top of Abbey Craig, the WALLACE MONUMENT is perhaps Stirling's most satisfying attraction, a huge 220ft Victorian tower with dramatic views from the top of its 246 spiralling steps. Each floor has lively audio-visual displays, one looking at Sir William Wallace,

another examining other Scottish heroes. Snacks, shop; cl wkdys Feb and Nov, all Dec and Jan; (01786) 472140; £2.35. the BANNOCKBURN HERITAGE CENTRE (2m S) has an audio-visual show on one of the country's most famous skirmishes; cl Nov–Mar; (01786) 812664; £1.80.

👌 🏰 **Stonehaven** NO8786 An old fishing town, with its more seasidey but discreet Victorian streets in the upper part; the harbourside Marine has good reasonably priced food. There's a good local history museum in the old TOLBOOTH on the Quay; cl 12–2pm, am Weds, Thurs, Sun, Oct–May; free. Just south on its precipitous sea-girt crag is the bleak and battered but still extensive and well preserved ruin of 14th-c DUNNOTTAR CASTLE. It sheltered the Scottish crown jewels during the Civil War, but has seen much darker episodes in its time. Shop; cl winter wknds, 25–26 Dec, 1 Jan; (01569) 62173; £2.

🏠 ❄ 🏡 🖼 🏰 **Tarves** NJ8634 Wonderfully grand HADDO HOUSE is renowned for its Choral Society and the concerts and operas they hold in the adjacent Hall; (01651) 851770 for what's on. Still very much a family home, the house was designed by William Adam, and refurbished in the 1880s in the Adam Revival style; the chapel has stained glass by Burne-Jones. Meals, snacks, shop, disabled access; house cl am (exc July and Aug), wkdys Oct, all Nov–Apr (exc Easter wknd), gardens open all year; £3.50; NTS. Surrounding the house is a 150-acre country park, with visitor centre, wildlife exhibition and guided walks, as well as a shop selling produce from the estate, and local goodies like salmon, venison, whisky and crafts. There's an interesting medieval tomb in Tarves churchyard. Nearby **Tolquhon** NJ8729 has a decidedly unstuffy little GALLERY of contemporary Scottish art and crafts (cl am Sun, Thurs), and the impressive remains of 15th-c TOLQUHON CASTLE (cl winter wkdys, *£1.50).

🏰 🖼 **Turriff** NJ7639 FYVIE CASTLE Each of the five towers of this magnificent palace was built in a different c by the family that lived here throughout; the oldest parts date back to the 13th c, and the whole building is one of the most fantastic examples of Scottish Baronial architecture. The wheel stair is one of the best in the country, and there are collections of armour, tapestry and notable paintings, inc works by Romney and Gainsborough. Snacks, shop, limited disabled access; cl am (exc Jun, July and Aug), mid-Oct–Easter; £3.50; NTS. The Towie Tavern does good food.

★ The East Neuk or east coast of Fife has pretty **fishing villages**, most notably Crail NO6108. Pittenweem NO5403 has some attractive crow-gabled houses (the gables in steps which seagulls rather than crows sit on here); all have decent pubs and inns. Of the area's abundance of LOCHS, **Loch Rannoch** NN6580 is among the quieter and more beautiful ones. **Loch Tay** NN6535 seems to change moment by moment as the clouds flit across the sky, and has a quiet road along its southern side; **Ben Lawers** NN6340 is an interesting spot, with alpine wild flowers not found elsewhere in Britain and a quite different feel from other Highland mountains; a steep road leads up the side. **Loch Ericht** NN5574 is very peaceful but does involve foot-slogging to make the most of it. **Loch Katrine** NN4510 is a lovely stretch of water that inspired Scott's *Lady of the Lake*, and has a Victorian steamer in summer. **Loch Voil** NN5020 further N is, like Loch Katrine, served by just a narrow back road, so fairly peaceful

even in summer; it's famous for having Rob Roy's grave at Balquhidder NN5320. **Loch Earn** NN6523 with a trunk road alongside is largely given over to water-skiing and that sort of thing. **Loch Ness** (see also Drumnadrochit in North of Scotland section, below) is of course the granddaddy of them all, and a place of great beauty; the calmest drive along it is the B862, though it leaves the loch shore more than the trunk road on the other side. Besides those we've mentioned as places to eat at or stay, inns where you can get a decent meal and which are particularly well placed for walkers, drivers or just strollers in these parts include the lochside St Fillans at Achray NN6924, Ship at Broughty Ferry NO4630, seaview Creel at Catterline NO8778, Loch Ericht Hotel at Dalwhinnie NN6384, Dores Hotel at Dores by Loch Ness NH5930, Anchor at Dunipace NS8083, Ship on the shore at Elie NO4900, Hungry Monk at Gartocharn NS4286, Old Mill at Killearn NS5285, Trossachs Hotel near Loch Achray NN5106, Corriegour Lodge near Altrua on Loch Lochy NN2390, Loch Tummel Hotel above Loch Tummel NN8460, Meikleour Inn at Meikleour NO1539 (handy for the 100-ft high beech hedge planted in 1746), Pennan Inn in the pretty seaside *Local Hero* village of Pennan NJ8465, Potarch Hotel at Potarch NO6097 and Sheriffmuir Inn on wild Sheriff Muir NN8202.

Walks

For general remarks about walking in the Highlands, see the Walks section of the West, Argyll and Loch Lomond.

This area is not quite so rewarding to the walker as the W coast, or the borders, but does have plenty of well above average walking. Some enjoyable strolls and easier walks include the **Knock of Crieff** NN8622 ◠-1, a wooded hill with a good viewpoint above Crieff; the **Lomond Hills** NO2206 ◠-2, a level walk from the car park by the road above Falkland NO2507 – not to be confused with Loch Lomond, this Fife upland gives views over most of SE Scotland; forest tracks and paths over **Kinnoull Hill** NO1322 ◠-3 above the River Tay just outside Perth NO1123; or the signposted circular walk into **Glen Lednock** NN7327 ◠-4 from Comrie NH4155.

The Trossachs NN5007, famously popular for their dense conifer forests, steep glens and beautifully framed lochs, are not brilliant for low-level walks unless you like forests; the route on to **Callander Crags** NN6308 ⌂-5 from Callander NN6307 is one of the best. However, they allow some good mountain walks comparable in difficulty to some of the fells of the English Lake District: **Ben Venue** NN4706 ⌂-6 and Ben Vorlich NN2912 ⌂-7 are among the best.

Glen Roy NN2985 ⌂-8 and its curious Parallel Roads (not actually roads but the tubmarks of a former glacier) can be seen from an easy track along its bottom, a spectacular 4-mile route from Brae Roy Lodge NN3392 (return the same way).

Loch Tay NN6838 ⌂-9 is dominated by the towering bulk of Ben Lawers NN6341, nearly 4,000ft but with a good track up. There are easier walks at the E end of the loch, from the attractive estate village of Kenmore NN7745 along the banks of the River Tay, or into the adjacent forest to a viewpoint over the loch.

The **Ochil Hills** NO0409 ⌂-10 are a range of green mountains which rise without preamble from the lowland plain – a striking textbook example of the Highland Fault. A path from Tillicoultry NS9197 up Mill Glen NS9198 takes you to Ben Cleuch NN9000, the highest point of the range. Don't miss the amazing short path around the base of Castle Campbell NS9699 above Dollar NS9698 – catwalks, rock overhangs, jungle-thick vegetation, and a swirling stream below.

On the Fife coast, the **Tentsmuir Sands** ⌂-11 give five miles of shore walking from Kinshalvy car park NO5024; you may see common and grey seals on the sandbanks, and there are shorter routes back through the forest. The S coastal path is now very difficult, particularly between St Andrews and Kingsbarns; the section from St Andrews to Rock and Spindle is all right but the path has become treacherous further on. It's also bad between Pittenweem and Elie.

A ski-lift from Glen More NH9807 above Aviemore is the easy way up to the summits of the **Cairngorms** ⌂-12, and there are manageable paths down. Loch an Eilean nestles beneath Cairn Gorm NJ0004, on the Aviemore side; a forest track encircles this delightful little loch, with its castle romantically placed on an isle.

From the **Linn of Dee** NO0689 ⌂-13 not far from Braemar are long glen walks into the Cairngorms along Glen Dee and the Lairig Ghru. From Braemar itself NO1491 you can follow a steep path up **Morrone** NO1388 ⌂-14, along a route used for a race in the Highland Gathering. **Bennachie** NJ6522 ⌂-15 on the E edge of the Grampians, nr Inverurie NJ7721, is not that high but has tremendous views over lowland Grampian; the gently rolling moorland top has several colour-coded Forestry Commission trails (the lower slopes are forested).

The **coast around Banff** NJ6864 ⌂-16 can be followed for some stretches (a bus service along the main road is a useful method of return), for instance from Portsoy NJ5866 to Findlater Castle NJ5467, a windswept ruin on the cliff-edge.

Driving

In and approaching the Highlands, the network of roads thins out, so you have to drive quite long distances to make satisfactory round tours: but this is the part where the drives are really memorable. Among a wealth of handsome roads, one fine route N, with exhilarating views much of the way, is the A823 through Glen Devon and Glen Eagles to join the A822 through Crieff and on up through the very pretty Sma' Glen, and then over the heather moors to fork left on the A826 to Aberfeldy. Around Aberfeldy many good drives include the run along Loch Tay (the very slow back road along the S side of the loch gives much better views of mighty Ben Lawers than the main road, though you don't then have the option of the very steep alpine detour up the gated road to Bridge of Balgie). The B846 N from Aberfeldy starts mildly though with good views of the lower slopes of volcano-looking Schiehallion, but after the turn left along Strath Tummel becomes a memorable drive along Loch Rannoch, before coming to a dead end above the trees among sweeping heather moors.

The A93 from Blairgowrie through Glenshee to Braemar and the Dee Valley is a glorious road with some tremendous mountain views, before you reach the richly wooded valley – also impressive, particularly in autumn. Right down to Banchory you can pick almost any spot to start a walk in lovely scenery, and part of the beauty of it is the way that majestic open moors are within such easy reach of the sheltered valley itself. It's a popular route, though, with quite a stream of slow summer traffic.

The steep A939 N of Ballater is one of the roads built by the Hanoverians after the 1745 rising, to tame the Highlands – and forges up over what still seems an untamably wild area, to Grantown on Spey.

As we've taken the Great Glen itself as our divide from the North, this area includes the B862 which runs down its SE side – the quieter of the two roads, unpocked by Nessie attractions, with places to stop by Loch Ness.

Off the B957 and A94 between Kirriemuir and Stonehaven little-travelled roads run up the Angus glens: not so dramatic as the better-known Highland glens, but very secluded, with a succession of pleasing views, attractive rivers, and occasional castle ruins. Glen Esk is perhaps the most rewarding, with an empty road running for miles alongside the North Esk up to black Loch Lee with its ancient church; but Glen Isla and Glen Clova run it close.

In the Central Region, around Stirling, there's a lot of potential for driving through attractive countryside without having to embark on such long runs as the Highlands often entail. The quiet road over Sheriff Muir is a surprisingly sudden foray into wild high moorland right on the edge of quite a busy conglomeration of urban areas, while to the west of the M9 the countryside is largely open and pleasant. The A821 through the Trossachs carries a lot of coach traffic in summer, as does the A81 and even the narrower B829 up Loch Ard to Loch Katrine.

There are no really memorable roads down in Fife, though the busy A92 along the coast between Inverkeithing and Kinghorn has some pleasant views across to Edinburgh, the B925 through Auchtertool is quite pleasant, the A909 climbing steeply out of Burntisland has an attractive passage as it passes the haunted Stenhouse Reservoir, and the A823 N from Dunfermline into the Cleish Hills is a good drive.

The M90 and A9 are strong spinal roads giving fast runs right up to Inverness; 3½ hours is a comfortable estimate from Edinburgh, though the A9 still has some single-carriageway stretches which are tiresome.

Where to eat

Aberfoyle NN5200 BRAEVAL MILL (01877) 382711 Converted mill with stone walls and flagstones, careful and extremely good food inc fine French cheeses, and helpful friendly staff; cl Mon, 1 wk Feb/June/Nov; children over 10; disabled access. £35.

Anstruther NO5603 CELLAR 24 East Green (01333) 310378 Characterful restaurant off little courtyard with beams, stone walls, open fires, wonderful fresh fish, and good wines; cl Sun, Mon, Christmas, 1 wk Nov; children over 8. £31/£5.25.

Cupar NO3714 OSTLERS CLOSE 25 Bonnygate (01334) 55574 Cosy, unpretentious restaurant with lovely food using local fresh produce, game and fish; good puddings and decent wines; cl Sun, Mon, 1st 2 wks June; children over 6 in evening; disabled access. £28/£8.

Kingussie NH7500 THE CROSS Tweed Mill Brae, Ardbroilach Rd (01540) 661166 Fine food based on local fish and game in old no smoking tweed mill beside a stream; very good wines; bedrooms; cl Tues, 1–27 Dec; children over 12. £27.50 4-course dinner, £15 3-course lunch.

Perth NO1123 NUMBER THIRTY THREE 33 George St (01738) 633771 Seafood restaurant with lighter meals served in the Oyster Bar and main meals eaten in the restaurant beyond – good puddings, too; cl 10 days over Christmas and New Year. £26/£5.

St Andrews NO5116 VINE LEAF 131 South St (01334) 77497 Though perhaps the alleyway outside is not an immediate enticement, the warmth of the welcome, attractively laid out tables, very good food, unobtrusive service and decent wines soon dispel any doubts; evenings only; cl Sun, Mon, 2 wks Jan, 2 wks Jun. £23.

Turriff NJ7250 TOWIE (01888) 4201 Good friendly atmosphere, stylish comfort, well presented, generous bar food, beautifully prepared food in no smoking restaurant, good choice of wines, and quietly efficient service; handy for Fyvie Castle and Delgatie Castle; disabled access. £22.50|£2.50/£5.

Drybridge NJ4362 OLD MONASTERY (01542) 832660 Lovely views from this former monastery as well as very good fish and game (fresh local produce), reasonably priced wines and friendly service, cl Sun, Mon, 1st 2 wks Nov, last 3 wks Jan; children over 8. £18.50/£5.50.

Weem NN8449 AILEAN CHRAGGAN (01887) 820346 Emphasis on well presented fish dishes in comfortable, friendly inn with lovely views; cl wkdys Jan/Feb. £16.50/£6.

Callander NN6208 MYRTLE (A84 just outside) (01877) 30919 Attractive old dining pub with two cosy, pretty restaurant rooms serving reasonably priced, well cooked and presented food and outstanding puddings; disabled access. £15/£5.50.

Glamis NO3846 STRATHMORE ARMS (01307) 840248 Picturesque, unspoilt village with simply decorated old inn, well presented delicious food inc wonderful puddings, roaring log fire in lounge, and good caring service; cl pm Mon Sept–Apr, 2 wks in winter; disabled access. £15|£3.50/£5.

NORTH OF SCOTLAND

Sensational west coast scenery, very comfortable places to stay.

The west coast has glorious sea, mountain and island scenery. Skye in particular is wonderful in good weather (the island really is a place where the success of a short stay depends on a spell of settled weather). The north coast is relatively wild and empty: addictive to some people, harsh and inhospitable to others. The east coast has good golf courses and long empty sandy beaches – perhaps more suitable for a quiet summer holiday than a weekend break, though Cromarty is a very attractive small town (its courthouse has an extraordinarily convincing reconstructed trial scene).

The few places to visit are best seen as an accompaniment to a holiday spent mainly enjoying the scenery. The highlights are Dunvegan Castle on Skye, Inverewe Gardens near Poolewe and Dunrobin Castle at Golspie; the Loch Ness Monster centre at Drumnadrochit is fun, and we found a new entry, the reindeer centre at Glenmore, most interesting.

There are some excellent places to stay – many of them so embracingly comfortable that when the weather does turn bad you might even be glad of an excuse not to go out.

The area is usually at its best between late May and early July, while the days are very long and before the midges have really got into their stride. The big snag is sheer distance: for most people, it takes too long to get up here for a short break.

Where to stay

Ullapool NH1294 ALTNAHARRIE Ullapool, Ross-shire IV26 2SS (01854) 83230 £250 inc dinner; 8 rms. On the shores of Loch Broom and reached by a 10 minute boat journey, this carefully restored house was originally built for drovers; 2 lounges with lots of books, open fire, a mix of Scandinavian and English furnishings, marvellously quiet, relaxing atmosphere, room service (they think tea-making facilities in rooms are a sign of neglect), truly magnificent food – 5 set courses with much of the food home-grown or caught locally – and very good wine list; no smoking; cl Nov–Easter; children over 8.

Arisaig NM6586 ARISAIG HOUSE Beasdale, Arisaig, Inverness-shire PH39 4NR (01687) 5622 £135; 14 most attractive rms with wonderful views, and 2 suites. Beautifully furnished and extremely comfortable hotel in attractive wooded and terraced grounds close to the shore; elegant drawing room, cosy morning room, lovely flowers, and very good, imaginative food using fresh local produce; billiards room, croquet; cl end Dec–Mar; children over 10.

Strontian NM8161 KILCAMB LODGE Strontian, Acharacle, Argyll PH36 4HY (01967) 402257 £128 inc dinner; 9 rms. Warmly friendly little hotel in 30 acres by Loch Sunart, with log fires in two lounges, carefully cooked food using fresh local ingredients, fine choice of malt whiskies in small bar, and a relaxed atmosphere; cl Nov–Mar.

Glenelg NG8119 GLENELG Glenelg, Kyle, Ross-shire IV40 8JR (01599) 522273 £110 inc dinner; 6 individually decorated and comfortable rms, all with fine views. Overlooking Skye across its own beach and sea loch, this carefully refurbished homely hotel has a relaxed bar, comfortable sofas and open fires, friendly staff, good food using local venison, local hill-bred lamb and lots of wonderfully fresh fish and seafood, and quite a few whiskies; the drive to the inn involves spectacular views from the steep road of Loch Duich; cl Oct–Easter (though open for house parties by arrangement); disabled access.

Harlosh NG2842 HARLOSH HOUSE Harlosh, Dunvegan, Island of Skye IV55 8ZG (01470) 521367 £96; 6 rms, 5 with own bthrm, and most with lovely views. One of the oldest buildings in NW Skye, this 18th-c house is on a small peninsula of land jutting out into Loch Bracadale; lochside gardens and lots of wildlife, a wonderfully quiet, homely lounge, home-made breads and imaginative cooking using fresh local produce in evening restaurant; cl Oct–Easter.

Ullapool NH1294 CEILIDH PLACE Ullapool, Ross-shire IV26 2TY (01854) 612103 £96; 13 rms, plus 10 in annexe across the road. White-painted hotel in quiet side street with attractive conservatory dining room, stylish café-bar with attractive modern prints and plants, good food, decent wines and cognacs, and a relaxed, friendly atmosphere; cl 2 wks Jan.

Achiltibuie NC0208 SUMMER ISLES Achiltibuie, Ullapool, Ross-shire IV26 2YG (01854) 622282 £92; 12 comfortable rms. Beautifully situated above the sea towards the end of a very long and lonely road, this warm, friendly and well furnished hotel has delicious set menus using fresh ingredients (in which it's largely self-sufficient), a choice of superb puddings and excellent array of uncommon cheeses; pretty watercolours and flowers; cl mid-Oct–Easter; children over 8.

Kyle of Lochalsh NG7627 LOCHALSH Ferry Rd, Kyle of Lochalsh, Ross-shire IV40 8AF (01599) 534202 £90; 40 rms. White-painted hotel with fine views over the sea to Skye, a comfortable lounge and cocktail bar (a fine choice of malt whiskies), and good food using fresh local seafood, venison and beef in pleasant restaurant; disabled access.

Skeabost NG4148 SKEABOST HOUSE Skeabost, Portree, Island of Skye IV51 9NP (01470) 532202 *£90; 26 rms, 5 in annexe in Garden House. Smart, friendly little hotel with lawn that runs down to Loch Snizort (good salmon fishing), spacious no smoking lounge (marvellous buffet table), new Victorian-style dining conservatory, lovely afternoon tea, log fires, high-ceilinged bar off stately hall, and billiards room; bog-and-water garden, 9-hole golf course; cl end Oct–Apr.

Shieldaig NG8154 TIGH AN EILEAN Shieldaig, Strathcarron, Ross-shire IV54 8XN (01520) 755251 £87; 11 rms. Attractive hotel in outstanding position, private fishing and sea fishing arranged, within easy reach of NTS Torridon Estate and Beinn Eighe nature reserve; pretty, comfortable residents' lounge with well stocked help-yourself bar and modern dining room with good-value local fish and game; cl Nov–Easter.

Scarista NG0996 SCARISTA HOUSE Scarista, Harris PA85 3HX (01859) 550238 £84; 8 rms, some in annexe. Marvellously wild countryside and empty beaches surround this isolated small hotel with its homely rooms and warm, friendly atmosphere; excellent for wildlife, walks and fishing; cl Oct–Mar; children over 8; dogs allowed; disabled access.

Isle Ornsay NG6912 KINLOCH LODGE Island of Skye IV43 8QY (01471) 833214 *£80; 10 rms. Surrounded by rugged mountain scenery at the head of Loch Na Dal, this charming little white stone hotel has a relaxed atmosphere in its comfortable and attractive drawing rooms, antiques, flowers, log fires, and portraits, and good, imaginative food; cl 1 Dec–28 Feb; children by arrangement.

Portree NG4843 ROSEDALE Beaumont Rd, Portree, Island of Skye IV51 9DB (01478) 613131 £80; 23 rms, many with harbour views. Built from 3 fishermen's cottages with lots of passages and stairs, this waterfront hotel has 2 traditional lounges, small first-floor restaurant with freshly cooked, popular food, lots of whiskies in the cocktail bar, helpful staff, harbourside garden and marvellous views; cl Oct–Apr.

Isle Ornsay NG6912 TIGH OSDA EILEAN IARMAIN Island of Skye IV43 8QR (01471) 833332 *£76; 12 individual rms, some in cottage opposite, and all with fine views. Sparkling white hotel with Gaelic-speaking staff and locals, big, cheerfully busy bar, pretty dining room with lovely sea views, and very good food; disabled access.

Scourie NC1544 EDDRACHILLES Badcall Bay, Scourie, Sutherland IV27 4TH (01971) 502080 *£74; 11 comfortable rms. Well run hotel in its own 320-acre estate overlooking Badcall Bay with wonderful island views; popular with nature-lovers – bird sanctuary nearby, seals, fishing and walking; cl Nov–Feb; children over 4.

Shiel Bridge NG9318 KINTAIL LODGE Shiel Bridge, Kyle, Ross-shire IV40 8HL (01599) 81275 £72; 12 good-value big rms. Pleasantly informal and fairly simple former shooting lodge on the shores of Loch Duich, with magnificent views, 4 acres of walled gardens, residents' lounge bar and comfortable sitting room, good well prepared food inc wild salmon, and fine collection of malt whiskies; cl 23 Dec–2 Jan.

Drumnadrochit NH5029 POLMAILY HOUSE Drumnadrochit, Inverness IV3 6XT (01456) 450343 £70; 10 light, pretty rms. Very relaxing and homely hotel in 18 acres of grounds with comfortable drawing room and library, open fires, and excellent food in the no smoking restaurant (wonderful packed lunches too); a good base for exploring the nearby glens – and a happy place for families, with swimming pool, tennis, croquet, ponies and pets; disabled access.

Plockton NG8033 HAVEN Plockton, Ross-shire IV52 8TW (01599) 84223 *£68; 13 rms. In a particularly lovely village, this homely little hotel has two comfortable lounges (one with an open fire), a conservatory, good home-cooked food using fresh local produce in attractive dining room, and a friendly, relaxed atmosphere; cl 18 Dec–10 Feb; children over 7.

Invermoriston NH4117 GLENMORISTON ARMS Invermoriston, Inverness IV3 6YA (01320) 351206 *£66; 8 good rms. Warmly friendly family-run hotel with cosy lounge, cheery stables bar (100 malt whiskies), good restaurant (book ahead), decent bar food, lots of malt whiskies, quick, friendly staff, and fishing and stalking by arrangement; not far from Loch Ness; cl 25 Dec.

Tongue NC5957 Ben Loyal Hotel Tongue, Lairg, Sutherland IV27 4XE (01847) 55216 £64; 18 rms, 6 in annexe, 12 with own bthrm. Very friendly and neatly modernised family hotel with lovely views over the bay (fine sunsets Jun/July), helpful staff, and fine food using fresh seasonal produce; fishing can be arranged for sea trout, salmon and brown trout, and lots of walks; cl Jan, early Feb; disabled access.

Kilchoan NM4863 Meall Mo Chridhe Country House Kilchoan, Acharacle, Argyll PH36 4LH (01972) 510238 £62.54; 3 warmly comfortable rms. Attractive 18th-c former manse in 45 acres with really lovely views over the Sound of Mull; log fire and sea views in homely lounge, very good food eaten at polished, candlelit dining table using fresh local and home-grown produce, their own free-range eggs, and home-made bread, scones and preserves (which they also sell in their small farm shop), and very friendly owners; take your own wine; handy summer car ferry Kilchoan–Tobermory; cl Nov–Feb; children over 12.

Ardvasar NG6203 Ardvasar Island of Skye IV45 8RT (01471) 844223 £58; 10 rms. Comfortably modernised 18th-c inn with spectacular views and run by obliging, friendly owners; nice residents' lounge and cocktail bar, popular locals' bar, open fire, good, fresh food inc local fish and shellfish and very good breakfasts; no accomm Dec–Mar.

Altnaharra NC5635 Altnaharra Altnaharra, Lairg, Sutherland IV27 4UE (01549) 411222 £56; 20 rms. Isolated 19th-c inn in fine countryside, very popular with keen fishermen with lots of facilities for them inc ghillies, tackle shop, rod racks, drying room, deep freezers; cl Oct–1 Mar; disabled access.

Garve NH3969 Inchbae Lodge Inchbae, Garve, Ross-shire IV23 2PH (01997) 5269 *£56; 12 rms, 6 in chalet. Friendly, family-run former hunting lodge in lovely Highland setting with comfortable, homely lounge, log fire, small bar, and good, imaginative restaurant food using fresh local produce; lots of wildlife, marvellous walks; cl 25–26 Dec; disabled access.

Melvich NC8765 Melvich Hotel Melvich, Thurso, Caithness KW14 7YJ (01641) 3206 £55; 14 rms, showers (and 4 bthrms in addition). Small, traditional hotel in lovely spot with homely furniture and peat fires in the civilised lounge, cosy bar, very relaxing atmosphere, friendly owners and staff, good food (especially local seafood and wild salmon), and fine views over Melvich Bay.

Drumnadrochit NH5029 Borlum Farmhouse Drumnadrochit, Inverness IV3 6XN (01456) 450358 £52; 5 rms. Traditional stone farmhouse with marvellous views over Loch Ness, warm, comfortably furnished sitting room with log fire, summer sitting room in glass conservatory, friendly atmosphere, and good Scottish breakfasts; BHS approved riding centre and can help with animals on farm; good provision for families; self-catering and caravan/camping also.

Mey ND2873 Castle Arms Mey, Thurso, Caithness KW14 8XH (0184 785) 244 £52; 8 good-value rms. Warm, friendly village inn in wide open countryside with marvellous restaurant food, wide range of good bar food, interesting whiskies, and welcoming staff; may cl am Oct–Easter; disabled access.

Raasay NG5641 (off Skye) Isle of Raasay Raasay, Kyle of Lochalsh, Ross-shire IV40 8PB (01478) 660222 £50; 12 rms. Victorian hotel with marvellous views over the Sound of Raasay to Skye and popular with walkers and bird-watchers; no petrol on the island; disabled access.

Lybster ND2436 Portland Arms Lybster, Caithness KW3 6BS (01593) 721208 £45w; 19 rms. Staunch old granite hotel with really friendly staff, attractive dining room, generous helpings of decent food, small, cosy panelled lounge bar, and plain locals' bar; shooting/fishing can be arranged.

Portree NG4843 Craiglockhart Beaumont Crescent, Portree, Island of Skye IV51 9DF (01478) 612233 *£44; 9 rms, some with own bthrm. Small family-run guesthouse overlooking harbour with fine views through picture windows in lounge and dining room and good breakfasts; cl Nov.

To see and do

❀ **Achiltibuie** NC0208
HYDROPONICUM Bizarre indoor garden of the future – without any soil. Fascinating guided tours show how plants such as figs, lemons and bananas grow quite happily using the nutrients from the soil, but not the soil itself. Good home-made meals and snacks, shop; open Apr–Sept, tours at 10am, 12, 2 and 5pm (more in summer); (01854) 622202; £3.50.

❀ ❀ ♤ **Balmacara** NG8127 Huge estate surrounding the Kyle of Lochalsh, with walks through breathtaking scenery. There are fantastic coastal views, and the stunning landscape is interspersed with lochs and impressive landmarks like the Five Sisters of Kintail and Beinn Fhada. The WOODLAND GARDENS of Lochalsh House are wonderful, with woodland walks, and lovely views towards Skye; £1; NTS. Guided walks are available from Balmacara on the Kyle to Plockton peninsula; PLOCKTON NG8033 itself is an idyllic waterside village, with palm trees along the village street, and the Plockton Hotel has good generous food.

♤ **Balnakiel** NC3969 is the most northwesterly part of mainland Britain, a wild and remote spot with spectacular scenery, and a little CRAFT VILLAGE, with workshops producing candles, country wines, pots and more; cl Sun, Nov–Mar; free.

♁ ✝ ✤ **Bettyhill** NC7062
STRATHNAVER MUSEUM Good exploration of the notorious Clearances of the Highlands, as well as Gaelic books and furnishings. Shop, some disabled access; cl 1–2pm, Sun, Nov–Mar; *£1.50. The museum is in the former village church, which has a pulpit dating from the late 12th c, and a finely carved 10th-c Celtic stone in the churchyard. Just S is a wonderful NATURE RESERVE, and the beach nearby is attractive.

♤ ♔ ❀ **Cape Wrath** NC2575 The stormy tip of coast is guarded by a lonely lighthouse. From Durness NC4067 near the beautiful sea loch Loch Eriboll you can make an adventurous summer expedition to here, by boat across the Kyle of Durness and then along a very long rough track to the lighthouse.

♙ ❀ **Dornie** NG8825 EILEAN DONAN CASTLE, Connected to the mainland by a causeway, and unforgettably beautiful. First built in 1220, destroyed in 1719 after being held by Jacobite troops, and then restored at the beginning of this century, it's perfectly positioned at the meeting point of Lochs Long, Duich and Alsh. Shop; cl winter; (01599) 85202; *£1.50. The Loch Duich Hotel does decent food.

! ♫ ♤ ♙ **Drumnadrochit** NH5029 is the best place to begin exploring LOCH NESS, a striking 24-mile loch with the largest volume of fresh water of any lake in the British Isles; up to 700ft deep in places, it's not hard to see why stories sprang up of what was hidden in its waters. The town's OFFICIAL LOCH NESS MONSTER EXHIBITION is a lively walk-through multi-media experience tracing the legend from its beginnings in Highland folklore to the scientific investigations of recent years. Also kilt-maker and glassblower. Meals, snacks, shop, disabled access; cl 25 Dec; (01456) 450473; £4. You can generally take BOAT TRIPS on the lake, some of them equipped with sonar for monster-spotting. Just SE of town on the western shore are the remains of 14th-c URQUHART CASTLE, once the biggest castle in Scotland. Shop; (0131) 244 34101; *£3.

♠ ♁ **Dunbeath** ND1630 LAIDHAY CROFT MUSEUM A 200-year-old thatched Caithness long house, with the living quarters, byre and stable furnished as they would have been 100 years ago. Snacks, disabled access; cl Dec–Feb; (0159 33) 244; *£1.

❀ **Duncansby Head** ND4073 is an attractive spot on a fine day, with cliff walks giving a good view of the spectacular Duncansby Stacks offshore. It's near John o' Groats ND3872, where the hotel on the harbour looking across to the Orkneys has decent food, and which gets its share of visitors under the mistaken impression that it's the most

northerly point on mainland Britain -
see next entry.

❀ **Dunnet Head** ND2076 really is the
furthest point north, also with views to
Orkney. A lovely spot on a clear early
summer's day, with spring flowers in
the close turf, and puffins pottering
around – but wild and unforgiving
when the weather changes.

➔ **Falls of Shin** NC5806 (B864 S of
Lairg) There's a good chance of seeing
SALMON LEAPING here in June or early
July, especially if there's been a dry
spell followed by rain so that the river
is in spate.

❀ **Gairloch** NG8076 GAIRLOCH
HERITAGE MUSEUM is perhaps the best
of the several heritage museums in the
Highlands, enthusiastically run, and
giving a good indication of life in the
area. Look out for the secret portrait
of Bonnie Prince Charlie which at first
looks like the meaningless daubings
of a child, but when revolved at
speed in a metal cylinder reveals his
likeness. Meals, snacks, shop,
disabled access; cl Sun, Oct–Mar;
(01445) 712287; *£1.50. The Old Inn
here is a useful stop.

⌂ **Glenfinnan** NM8980 Commanding
JACOBITE MONUMENT Built in 1815 to
commemorate the raising of the
standard for Bonnie Prince Charlie's
Highland rebellion at the head of Loch
Shiel. Good snacks, shop, limited
disabled access; cl 1–2pm, and facilities
cl Oct–Mar; £1; NTS.

❀❀❀◫⌂ **Golspie** NC8500
DUNROBIN CASTLE Splendid castle – a
gleaming turreted structure with views
out to sea and gardens modelled on
those at Versailles. The family home of
the Earls and Dukes of Sutherland
longer than anyone can remember, the
site was named after Earl Robin in the
13th c: he was responsible for the
original square keep. Drastically
renovated in the 19th c, it has fine
collections of furnishings and art, inc
several Canalettos, and a unique
collection of Pictish stones in the
former summerhouse. Snacks, shop; cl
am Sun, and all mid-Oct–Apr, though
gardens open all year; (01408)
633268; £3.50 (gardens free when
castle closed).

♄ ❀ **Helmsdale** ND0315 TIMESPAN
VISITOR CENTRE Lively reconstructions

of scenes in Highland history (with
sound effects), and a good audio-
visual display. Interesting herb garden
in the grounds. Snacks, shop, disabled
access; cl am Sun, all Nov–Easter;
(0143 12) 327; £2.75.

❀❀ **Kirkhill** NH5543 MONIACK
CASTLE The Highland Winery here is
quite an unusual enterprise, for two
reasons: it's rare to find a winery
producing country wines in Scotland,
and especially at an old castle like this,
the former fortress of the Lovat chiefs.
They also sell meat and game
preserves, and an interesting new
apricot, almond and banana jam.
Meals, snacks, shop; cl Sun; (01463)
831283; free.

❀ **Poolewe** NG8580 INVEREWE
Unmissable beautiful gardens full of
rare and subtropical plants, with a
magnificent background of mountain
scenery. The Atlantic Drift is
responsible for the special
microclimate which lets these unusual
plants flourish even though this is
further N than Moscow. Guided
walks with the gardener wkdys at
1pm, Apr–mid-Oct; meals, snacks,
shop, disabled access; visitor centre
and restaurant cl mid-Oct–Mar;
£2.80; NTS. Choppys has good well
priced food.

❀❀❀◫❀❀★ **Island of Skye**
NG4432 After Lewis, the biggest of
the islands off the Scottish coast,
linked to the mainland by boat from
the Kyle of Lochalsh, as it was in those
stormy days when Bonnie Prince
Charlie and Flora MacDonald made
the trip that has given the island its air
of romance ever since. Down in Sleat,
the southern peninsula (known as the
Garden of Skye), **Armadale** NC7865
has the CLAN DONALD CENTRE, a castle
built for Lord Macdonald in 1815; it
now houses the Museum of the Isles, a
good visitor centre looking at the
history of the clan. The surrounding
40 acres offer beautiful walks among
gardens and woodlands. Meals and
snacks (very good café), shop,
disabled access; cl Nov–Feb; (01471)
844305; £3.

Dramatic DUNVEGAN CASTLE
NG2548 has been the home of the
Chief of Macleod for 790 years. The
only stately home on the island, it has

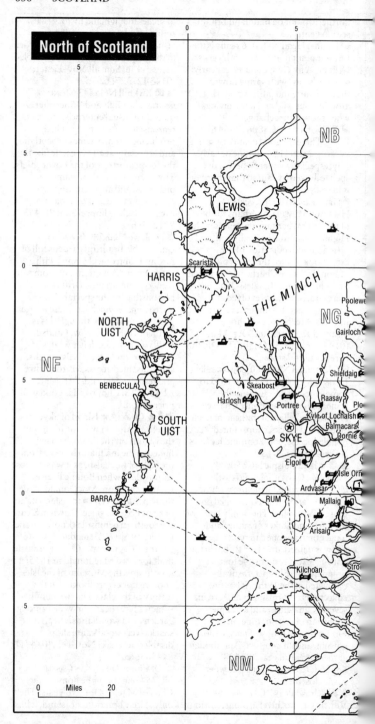

North of Scotland

NB

LEWIS

Scarista

HARRIS

THE MINCH

Poolewe

NORTH UIST

NG

Gairloch

NF

Shieldaig

BENBECULA

Skeabost

Raasay

Harlosh

Portree

Plo

Kyle of Lochalsh

SOUTH UIST

Balmacara

Dornie

SKYE

Elgol

Isle Orn

Ardvasar

Mallaig

BARRA

RUM

Arisaig

Kilchoan

Stro

NM

0   Miles   20

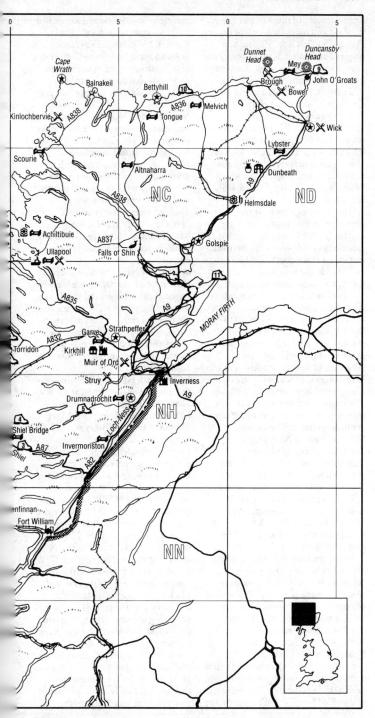

a good history of the clan and other displays and relics inc a lock of Bonnie Prince Charlie's hair. Staying here inspired Sir Walter Scott's *Lord of the Isles*. Meals, snacks, shop, disabled access; cl am Sun, Nov–Mar; (0147 022) 206; £4. As they're trying to develop the island as a place for winter breaks thanks to its mild climate, you may be able to go round the castle then if you give them a ring. It's beautifully set on the sea loch of Dunvegan, and there are BOAT TRIPS from the jetty to a nearby colony of brown and great grey Atlantic seals (Easter–Oct).

The coasts of Skye have plenty of opportunities for gentle pottering, and for finding quiet coves and bays, especially on the W coast, where for instance Tarskavaig NG5810 or Elgol NG5114 in the S, or Stein NG2556 in the N, are lovely spots to watch the sun go down. There are summer boat trips to the lonely and dramatic inlet of Loch Coruisk from Elgol: (01471) 866230 for times. The Trotternish peninsula in the NE has some quite extraordinary rock scenery; the Glenview Hotel at Culnaknock up here has good food, and in season the Flodigarry Hotel serves food all day. The jagged teeth of the Cuillin mountain range to the SE of the centre are unforgettable. The busiest harbour, **Portree** NG4843, is attractive and quite picturesque, though in summer tends to swarm with visitors; the harbourside Pier Hotel is right in the thick of the action.

Besides places mentioned in **Where to stay** and **Where to eat**, the Misty Isle at Dunvegan, Sligachan Inn at the junction of the A850 and A863 in the middle of the island, the Struan Grill at Struan and the Old Inn at Carbost all do decent food. Offshore, Raasay NG5641 is very peaceful, an ideal place for gentle pottering without lots of competition from other visitors – and for some quite stiff hill walks if that's what you prefer.

★ 🕭 ✍ Back on the mainland, **Strathpeffer** NH4858, originally a fashionable 19th-c spa resort, has quite a different feel from the rest of the area, with its rather continental appearance of dignified hotels and villas stepped up among its wooded slopes; some call it the Harrogate of the north. The restored Victorian railway station houses a good MUSEUM OF CHILDHOOD, along with several craft workshops. Shop; disabled access; cl am Sun, Nov–mid-Mar (exc by appointment); (01997) 421031; *£1.50.

♥ 🕭 **Torridon** NG8956 has stunning mountain scenery – some say the best in Scotland. The COUNTRYSIDE CENTRE is the gateway to a huge area of mountain nature reserve, and has good audio-visual displays on the scenery and wildlife, as well as a deer park and deer museum. Shop, disabled access; visitor centre cl am Sun, Oct–Apr; £1; NTS. Nearby at the Mains there are herds of red deer. The Kinlochewe Hotel (A896 E) has decent food.

⚓ **Ullapool** NH1294 is a good centre, with quite a busy harbour, a lot going on for a small place – and good eating (besides the places we've mentioned, the fish and chip restaurant is very good, with exceedingly presentable white wines, and the Ferry Boat is useful). You can get a ferry out to the Summer Isles.

🕭 🚌 🏛 **Wick** ND3551 The history of the town is well presented at the WICK HERITAGE CENTRE, in eight buildings by the harbour; cl Sun, Oct–May; (01955) 5393; *£1.50. You can buy factory seconds at the CAITHNESS GLASS FACTORY after following through the glass making process from start to finish. Meals, snacks, shop, disabled access; no glass making wknds; cl winter Sun; (01955) 2286; free. Just S of town, the CASTLE OF OLD WICK is a ruined four-storey square tower, probably dating from the 12th c.

🕭❉ A good way of seeing the scenery of the Highlands is by train: the WEST HIGHLAND LINE runs **steam trains** in summer between Fort William and Mallaig, and year-round normal trains. The views are terrific. One way of turning this into a round trip is to drive to Armadale on Skye, catch the morning ferry to Mallaig, the lunchtime (summer only) train to Fort William, sitting on the right-hand side facing the engine for the best views, then catch the early afternoon (again summer only) train back for the teatime crossing to Armadale. Another good train service is the cross-Highland line from Inverness to Kyle of Lochalsh, in 2½ hours – the last minutes of which are much the best. This is a part of the world where inns doing a decent bite to eat are very much at a premium, and a welcome sight indeed after miles of empty road. Besides those listed elsewhere, ones we can recommend for their positions include the seaside Applecross Inn at Applecross NG7144, Aultbea Inn at Aultbea NG8689, Aultguish Hotel NH3570 on the A835 nr Loch Glascarnoch, Badachro Inn at Badachro NG7773, Royal Hotel at Cromarty NH7867, Northern Sands at Dunnet ND2170, Lock at Fort Augustus NH3709, Old Inn at Gairloch NG8077, Cluanie in Glen Shiel NH0711, Kinlochewe Hotel at Kinlochewe NH0262, Kylesku Hotel at Kylesku NC2234 (the boatman here has taken readers for fascinating 4hr boat tours), Lewiston Arms at Lewiston NH5029, Loch Carron Hotel on Loch Carron NG9039, Glenuig Hotel at Lochailort NM7682, Invery Lodge Hotel overlooking Lochinver harbour NC0923 and Scrabster Inn at Scrabster ND0970. Almost all have bedrooms.

Walks

The Highlands offer ultra-tough mountain walking, but relatively few easier routes on defined paths (see general remarks in the **Walks** section of West Scotland, above); shorter circular walks are few and far between. Given good weather, full equipment and strong legs, the roadless country of **Knoydart** NG8000 ◁-1 on the W coast beckons: a real Highland wilderness. On this coast the areas of **Torridon** NG8956 ◁-2 and **Kintail** NG9917 ◁-3, including the Five Sisters of Kintail, are also wonderful for challenging walks, and there are a few outstanding easier ones, based, for example on Loch Torridon's shores. The **Falls of Glomach** NH0125 ◁-4 on Kintail is a tremendous waterfall in a wilderness setting.

Inland, **Glen Affric** NH1922 ◁-5, one of the most majestic glens, has a walking route along its floor. **Ben Eighe** NG9660 ◁-6 is one of the easier mountain ascents, with a well marked Mountain Trail making a circular route above Loch Maree.

Skye has lovely shoreside walks, such as from **Elgol** NG5213 ◁-7 to Loch na Creitheach NG5120 at the heart of the formidable Cuillin, a mecca for rock-climbers. The **Quiraing** NG4569 ◁-8 in the NE is a fascinating tumbled mass, with a surprisingly manageable path through it.

The E coast lacks the Highland drama but is blessed with a much drier climate: it's often nice to escape here from the W when the rain gets you down. **Duncansby Head** ND4073 ◁-9, the NE tip of Britain, offers an absorbing coastal walk S to see the 200ft-high Stacks of Duncansby, rock pinnacles now detached from the land. W of Thurso there's a pleasant stroll along the little road from the car park to the lighthouse on **Strathy Point** NC8269 ◁-10, at the end of a narrow peninsula. **Tarbat Ness** NH9487 ◁-11 juts out from the S side of Dornoch Firth; rather isolated, but worth the journey. You can walk around the peninsula here, from Portmahomack NH9184, past the lighthouse, and then along the S coast past a ruined castle to reach Rockfield NH9283.

Driving

On the W coast the roads give a glorious succession of intoxicating sea views, and as they often dip across country inland for short cuts, they alternate moorland and mountain scenery (the stretch between Loch Assynt and Ullapool is particularly wild), so you never get sated with the ocean and the rugged-shored sea lochs. There are so many beautiful views all along the coast road that it's difficult to rate any one stretch as finer than the rest; but two particularly memorable views are that of Plockton nestling along its sheltered inlet, from the side road just S of Stromeferry; and the famous view of Eilean Donan castle nr Dornie, E of the Kyle of Lochalsh.

When the main road leaves the coast for a cross-country short cut, there's usually a longer seaward detour. Such side roads are generally very slow – well worth taking, in a slightly pioneering spirit, if you're in no hurry whatsoever. One of the easiest and most rewarding of these detours is the A837 to the beautifully placed village of Lochinver. From here you can do an arduous circuit N to rejoin the main road, or head S into the unspoilt beauty of the Inverpolly nature reserve (again looping round to join the main road), or follow the dead-end road to Achiltibuie for an idyllic view of the Summer Isles. Another worthwhile coastal detour is the little road over to Loch Moidart from just N of Acharacle, for the views of the loch itself and of ruined Castle Tioram. For the more adventurous, there's a long, narrow road round the coast from Shieldaig to Applecross, which steely nerved souls can turn into a loop back to the main road by taking the staggeringly high and sharp-twisting Pass of the Cattle – Britain's highest pass.

Inland, the roads heading N through the centre, after leaving the healthy-feeling former spa valley of Strathpeffer, all strike through increasingly wild countryside. The A832 is fairly level to Achnasheen, then climbs through more mountainous scenery, with some sensational views; it meets the W coast road at Kinlochewe. The A835 is quite a good fast road up to Ullapool, the most civilised of all these routes, yet still with a good mix of forest, loch, river, moor and mountain. The A836 up to Bonar Bridge gives you a choice of three routes through highland wastes of moor, peat, lochs and lochans (little lochs), and bog – great if you want solitude. The A838 is the road for loch-lovers, scarcely leaving the side of one loch or another, twisting among the fine desolate peaks that tower over it (and sometimes making you wish you'd taken a gentler road) before it reaches the lumpier country of the NW coast.

The A831 looping NW of Drumnadrochit on Loch Ness is a good drive despite some rather gloomy stretches of conifer plantation; its main joy for drivers in search of great scenery is that at Cannich it gives access to a narrow road up Glen Cannich to Loch Mullardoch, a beautiful peaceful mountain valley; and to the one up Glen Affric, if anything even more beautiful. There's also a private gated track up Glen Strathfarrar which you may be able to get permission to use (ask at the Struy Inn about this).

To reach anywhere N of Kinlochewe by car from the south, incidentally, it's much quicker to go by Inverness than to make your way all the way up the W coast.

Where to eat

Muir of Ord NH5250 DOWER HOUSE (01463) 870096 Very good modern cooking in attractive hotel restaurant, fine wines, and friendly service; lovely gardens; cl 1 wk Oct, 25 Dec; disabled access; bedrooms. £30|£2.50/£5.

Bower ND2363 BOWER ½ m S of B876 (01955) 86292 Small, fairly simple country inn with good-value food in dining room, low ceilings, open fires, warship and submarine memorabilia, and friendly, informal service; may cl Mon–Thurs between Nov and Apr; £21|£2.75/£7.

Ullapool NH1294 MOREFIELD MOTEL (01854) 612161 Large helpings of exceptionally fresh fish and seafood (owners are ex-fishermen and divers), cooked enterprisingly, Aberdeen Angus steaks, daily roast beef, and vegetarian dishes in modern lounge and smart restaurant of basic hotel; cl Nov–Feb; disabled access. £18|£2/£4.50.

Kinlochbervie NC2156 OLD SCHOOL RESTAURANT (01971) 521383 Very good food in old school building with school-related items like photographs, maps, notebooks on tables; home-grown vegetables, local fish and venison, and good puddings; very good service; bedrooms in newish building; cl 25 Dec, 1 Jan; disabled access. £15|£1.65/£3.

Struy NH3939 STRUY INN (01463) 761219 Clean, pleasant and friendly small pub with very good, fairly priced food, and good range of malt whiskies; cl Mon, Tues, only open Thurs–Sun in winter; disabled access. £14|£1.75/£5.

Wick ND3652 LAMPLIGHTER 43 High St (01955) 3287 Extremely good food using local produce in small, cosy lunchtime restaurant (eve meals only summer Fri and Sat); friendly service; cl pm exc Thurs–Sat in summer, cl Oct; £12|£2.20/£4.50.

Brough ND2274 DUNNET HEAD TEAROOM/RESTAURANT (0184 785) 774 Small traditional, unpretentious cottage with good, reasonably priced food and snacks served all day by warmly friendly owners; good choice of vegetarian dishes, fresh salmon, local seafood, and local beef; take your own wine; cl Oct–Easter; children must be well behaved. 75p/£5.

Help this year from: Ralph A Raimi, J Roy Smylie, Ian Phillips, JJW, CMW, Christine and Malcolm Ingram, A J and J A Hartigan, Walter Reid, Martin and Jane Bailey, PC, JC, Ken Richards, Paul and Ursula Roberts, Derek and Maggie Washington, Roger and Sheila Thompson, Lee Goulding, Michael and Harriet Robinson, Neil Townend, M D Farman, L Grant, Richard Lewis, Mark Walker, Mr and Mrs G Hart, June and Tony Baldwin, Nigel Woolliscroft, Leith Stuart, Mark Hydes, Susan and John Douglas, Nigel and Sara Walker, June and Tony Baldwin, Eric and Jackie Robinson, Darren Ford, M E and G R Keene, Brian Bannatyne-Scott, Andrew and Helen Latchem, John and Elspeth Howell, Alan Wilcock, Christine Davidson, Joan and Tony Walker, SS, Paul and Ursula Randall, Thomas Nott, David Bloomfield, Geoffrey and Brenda Wilson, Jeanne and Tom Barnes, Margaret Kemp, Walter and Susan Rinaldi-Butcher, John Doig, Mrs Pat Crabb, Tim Galligan, Nick and Meriel Cox, Bill and Sylvia Trotter, Margaret and Fred Punter, Alan and Margaret Griffiths, Iain P Dinnes, Martyn Hart.

SCOTLAND CALENDAR

Some of these dates were provisional as we went to press.

JANUARY

1 **Stonehaven** Fireball Ceremony (01569) 762001

21 **Aviemore** Siberian Husky Club of GB Sled Dog Rally (01601) 28281

31 **Lerwick** Up-Helly-Aa (traditional Viking ceremony) – *till Feb 1*
(01595) 3768

FEBRUARY

1 **Glasgow** Scottish Boat, Caravan, Camping and Leisure Show at Scottish
Exhibition and Conference Centre – *till Sun 5* (0141) 248 3000

4 **Edinburgh** Rugby Union: Scotland v Ireland at Murrayfield (0131) 337 2346

MARCH

4 **Edinburgh** Rugby Union: Scotland v Wales at Murrayfield (0131) 337 2346

20 **Kingussie** Badenoch and Strathspey Music Festival – *till Fri 24*
(01540) 661797

30 **Edinburgh** Puppet and Animation Festival (0131) 556 9579

31 **Edinburgh** International Science Festival – *till April 17* (0131) 556 6446;
Gatehouse of Fleet Spring Festival of Music, Arts and Crafts – *till 2 April*
(01557) 814030

APRIL

3 **Fort William** International Festival of Film and TV in the Celtic Counties
at the Aird Centre – *till Fri 7* (01463) 226189

6 **Aberdeen** Scottish Connection Festival – the best of all things Scottish –
till Sun 16 (01224) 484661

8 **Melrose** Rugby Sevens (01896) 822993

28 **Girvan** Traditional Folk Festival – *till Sun 30* (01563) 44855; **Glasgow**
Mayfest – *till 20 May* (0141) 552 8000; **Pitlochry** Festival – *till 7 Oct*
(01796) 473054

MAY

1 **Borders** River Tweed Festival – *till Weds 31* (01750) 20555

19 **Strichen** Buchan Heritage Festival – *till Sun 21* (01771) 653761

22 **Edinburgh** Scottish International Children's Festival (0131) 554 6297

25 **Stromness** Orkney Traditional Folk Festival (01856) 851331

26 **Dumfries** and Galloway Arts Festival – *till 4 June* (01387) 60447;
Newport on Tay Scottish Open Carriage Driving Championships
(01334) 85707

27 **Bathgate** and West Lothian Highland Games (01506) 54507; **Blackford**
Highland Games (01764) 682314; **Innerleithen** Celebration of Scottish
Beer – *till Sun 28* (01896) 830323

28 **Blair Atholl** International Highland Games (01796) 481355

29 **Holy Loch and Loch Long** Shore Carnival (01369) 84228

JUNE

2 **Tarbert** Mod Na Hearadh – Gaelic Music Festival (01859) 502385

3 **Strathmiglo** Highland Games (01337) 860467

Scotland Calendar

JUNE cont

4 **Kilmarnock** and Loudoun Burns Day (01563) 21140; **Markinch** Highland Games (01592) 759038

8 **Lanark** Lanimer Day (01555) 663251

10 **Dumfries** Guid Nychburris Festival – *till Sat 18* (01387) 54805; **Oban** Kilmore and Kilbride Highland Games (01631) 77241

11 **Aberdeen** Kildrummy Castle Rally (01224) 823402; **Forfar** Highland Games (01307) 465605

16 **Edinburgh** Leith Jazz Festival – *till Sun 18* (0131) 553 5566

18 **Aberdeen** Highland Games (01224) 522475; **Ratho** Scottish Open Canal Jump Competition (0131) 333 1320

22 **Ingliston** Royal Highland Show at the Royal Highland Showground – *till Sun 25* (0131) 333 2444

24 **Aberdeen** Steam Engine Festival – *till Sun 25* (01224) 626300; **Ceres** Highland Games (01334) 828877

25 **Coatbridge** Historic Vehicle Festival (01236) 431261; **Leven** Veteran and Vintage Car Rally (01333) 429464; **Perth** Coronation Pageant (01738) 552300

30 **Dingwall** Highland Traditional Music Festival – *till 2 July* (01349) 883341; **Glasgow** International Jazz Festival – *till 9 July* (0141) 552 3572

JULY

1 **Annan** Riding of the Marches (01461) 202708; **Barra** Festival – *till Fri 14* (01871) 810667; **Perth** Game Conservancy Scottish Fair – *till Sun 2* (01620) 850577

5 **Auchterarder** Scottish Open Golf at Gleneagles Hotel golf club – *till Sat 8* (01783) 21111

8 **Dingwall** Highland Games (01349) 862024; **Jedburgh** Border Games (01835) 863677

15 **Elgin** Highland Games (01343) 842578; **Forfar** Scottish Transport Extravaganza (01307) 462496; **Leith** Cutty Sark Tall Ships Race – *till Tues 18* (01705) 586367

16 **Stonehaven** Highland Games (01569) 762001

17 **Aberdeen** International Football Festival – *till Sat 22* (01224) 276276

18 **Inveraray** Traditional Highland Games (01499) 2342

20 **St Andrews** Golf Open Championship at the Old Course – *till Sun 23* (01334) 472112

21 **Inverness** Highland Games (01463) 724262; **Taynuilt** Highland Games (01866) 2431

23 **Island of Bute** Folk Festival – *till Wed 26* (01700) 504734

24 **Inverness** Tattoo – *till Sat 29* (01463) 235571; **Plockton** Regatta – *till 5 Aug* (01599) 544421; **Portree** Skye Folk Festival – *till Sat 29* (01478) 612506

28 **Langholm** Common Riding (01387) 380428; **West coast** West Highland Yachting Week – *till 4 Aug* (01631) 63309

30 **by Aviemore** Rothiemurehus International Highland Games (01479) 810858; **St Andrews** Highland Games (01334) 476305

Scotland Calendar

AUGUST

2 **Aberdeen** International Youth Festival – *till Sat 12* 0181-946 2995;
Portree Island of Skye Highland Games (01478) 612540

3 **Muir of Ord** Black Isle Show (01463) 233957

4 **Edinburgh** Military Tattoo at Edinburgh Castle – *till Sat 26* (0131) 225 1188

5 **Edinburgh** International Jazz Festival – *till Sat 12* (0131) 557 1642

7 **St Andrews** Lammas Fair and Market – *till Sat 8* (01334) 53722

10 **Fortrose** St Boniface Fair (01381) 620954

12 **Edinburgh** International Film Festival at Filmhouse – *till Sun 27*
(0131) 228 4051 and Book Festival at Charlotte Square Gardens –
till Mon 28 (0131) 228 5444; **Glasgow** World Pipe Band
Championships (0141) 221 5414

13 **Edinburgh** International Festival and Fringe Festival (world's largest
festival of the arts) – *till 2 Sept* (0131) 226 4001

17 **Kilmartin** National Sheepdog Trials – *till Sat 19* (01234) 352672

19 **Glenfinnan** Highland Games – the NTS celebrates 250 years since
Bonnie Prince Charlie raised his standard here and 50 years since these
games were first held to mark his arrival and the 'rising of the clans'
(01463) 232034; **Machrihanish** Surf Rodeo (01880) 820255

20 **Golspie** Vintage Motor Rally (01408) 633808

24 **Oban** Argyllshire Highland Gathering (01631) 562671

25 **Dunoon** Cowal Highland Gathering – *till Sat 26* (01369) 3206

26 **Peebles** Arts Festival – *till Sept 10* (01721) 720371

31 **Edinburgh** Glenlivet Fireworks Concert (0131) 226 4001

SEPTEMBER

1 **Kirriemuir** Traditional Music Festival – *till Sun 3* (01575) 540261

2 **Braemar** Royal Highland Gathering at Princess Royal and Duke
Memorial Park (01339) 755377

3 **Blairgowrie** Highland Games (01250) 872043

16 **Leuchars** RAF Leuchars Battle of Britain Airshow (01334) 839000

30 **Motherwell** Music Festival – *till Oct 7* (01698) 266166

OCTOBER

12 **Aberdeen** Alternative Festival – *till Sat 21* (01224) 635822

13 **Borders** Festival throughout the Scottish Borders – *till Sun 29* (01896) 4751;
Tobermory Tour of Mull Car Rally – *till Sun 15* (01704) 575597

20 **Edinburgh** and **Glasgow** French film festival at Edinburgh Film House
and Glasgow Film Theatre – *till Mon 30* (0131) 228 6382

31 **Edinburgh** Scottish International Storytelling Festival – *till Nov 11*
(0131) 556 9579

DECEMBER

23 **Grantown on Spey** Torchlight Procession (01479) 872126

31 **Biggar** Ne'erday Bonfire (01899) 20661; **Comrie** Flambeaux Procession
– *till Jan 1*; **Edinburgh** Hogmanay Celebrations (0131) 557 1700

WALES

Wales combines in its relatively small area an abundance of natural beauty with a good range of interesting places to visit. These vary from romantic ruined abbeys and a profusion of medieval castles to lively mining museums, mainly slate in North Wales, coal in South Wales: these are increasingly family rather than just adult attractions. There are just a few grand houses and gardens.

North Wales has the best mix of glorious scenery with plenty of other things to do, is excellent for walking, and gets the lion's share of summer visitors; it includes the Snowdonia National Park with the highest mountains in Wales or England. West Wales has the most spectacular coastline (the Pembrokeshire Coast National Park), with some lovely walks along it; once you've got there, the far west is a civilised place for a relaxing break. Mid-Wales has fewer touristy things for visitors to do – and for many that is a special attraction – but it does have grand scenery, some very pleasant, small towns, certainly plenty to fill a weekend or longer stay, and a really unspoilt feel: it includes the Brecon Beacons National Park, the empty and lonely Cambrian Mountains (two, wonderful, high-level drives here), and the 'Welsh lake district' of the Elan Valley reservoirs. South Wales might appeal if you want to delve into the industrial past (or if you find castles irresistible); areas of fine scenery here include parts of the Gower peninsula and the gorge of the lower Wye Valley, graced by Tintern Abbey.

Weather is a problem here: there tends to be a lot of it, and though the Welsh coast preserves a gloomy magnificence in poor weather, the upland areas are more or less a write-off then.

We have mentioned a handful of the Roman and prehistoric sites in which the area abounds. You can get more information from CADW (Welsh Historic Monuments Commission) (01222) 465511, which is also responsible for the care of the great majority of the historic castles and other monuments here: if you plan to visit many of their sites, a week's or fortnight's Explorer ticket from tourist information centres or CADW direct is good value as it admits to all.

NORTH WALES

Great variety of beautiful scenery, lots to do, some excellent places to stay in.

This area has the highest British mountains outside Scotland – great expanses of hill and mountain including dramatic Snowdonia and in the centre, the Berwyn Hills which (unlike Snowdon) stay lonely year-round. It also has countryside which charms in a quite different way: the intricate and rather intimate landscapes of Clwyd, the rich Vale of

Conwy, the deserted, sandy shores of the Lleyn Peninsula, and the peace of Anglesey – twice the size of the Isle of Wight with just half the population.

A wide choice of places to visit and things to do includes a surprising abundance of picturesque railway lines. Among other places, highlights include Erddig at Wrexham, Caernarfon and Conwy castles, the great garden of Bodnant at Tal y Cafn, the interesting and lively slate-mining activities particularly around Blaenau Ffestiniog, the fantasy-village of Portmeirion, and, for families, the zoo in its lovely setting at Colwyn Bay, and the sea zoo at Brynsiencyn on Anglesey. Our favourites among new additions here this year are the Greenwood Centre at Bethel, Bryn Bras Gardens at Llanrug and the Butterfly Palace (Europe's largest) at Menai Bridge. Betws-y-Coed is always a popular spot, and Llandudno, Beaumaris on Anglesey and Llangollen are all attractive towns with plenty to see.

There are long beaches on many of the coasts, with the traditional resorts of Prestatyn, Rhyl, Colwyn Bay and the more stylish Llandudno on the north coast, and places like Barmouth on the west coast.

One drawback is that people in North Wales do strike some visitors as unfriendly. Another is that in poor weather the views do close in; there is more likelihood of cloud and rain here than in, say, the Yorkshire Dales.

There's a good choice of places to stay, and quite a reasonable choice of places at which to eat out.

Where to stay

Talsarnau SH6236 MAES-Y-NEUADD Talsarnau, Gwynedd LL47 6YA (01766) 780200 **£147 inc dinner**; 16 luxurious rms. Looking out across Snowdonia National Park, this extended, 14th-c, attractive mansion is set in 8 acres of landscaped hillside; flowers and plants, antiques, and open fires, a peaceful atmosphere, very good food, and charming staff; children over 7 in evening restaurant; disabled access.

Llandudno SH7883 BODYSGALLEN HALL Llandudno, Gwynedd LL30 1RS (01492) 584466 **£139.90**; 28 deeply comfortable rms, 19 in hotel. Fine, 17th-c house in its own parkland, with mullioned windows, oak panelling, lovely entrance hall and a first-floor drawing room, open fires, very good, imaginative food, and an 18th-c walled rose garden and knot garden; children over 8; disabled access.

Portmeirion SH5937 PORTMEIRION HOTEL Penrhyndeudraeth, Porthmadog, Gwynedd LL48 6ER (01766) 770228 **£119 in hotel** (14 rms), **£85 in village** (17 rms). On the edge of an estuary and surrounded by beaches and woods (and traffic-free), this is a remarkable place; the hotel down by the water is quite luxurious – elegant rooms with marble, gilt, and rich, colourful fabrics; behind and in the steeply landscaped grounds above it is a well dispersed, very colourful Italianate village, luscious to look at, inc all sorts of characterful cottage bedrooms tucked into the hillside; very romantic when the day visitors have left; lots to do; cl 1 Jan–3 Feb. See Portmeirion entry in **To see and do** section below.

Conwy SH7777 CASTLE High St, Conwy, Gwynedd LL32 8DB (01492) 592324 **£116 inc dinner**; 29 rms. Historic town with this early 16th-c inn, one of the most characterful in the Forte chain; good food in the pretty restaurant, proper pubby bar (popular with locals), friendly, helpful staff, decent breakfast, and car parking.

Capel Coch SH4682 TRE-YSGAWEN HALL Capel Coch, Llangefni, Isle of Anglesey LL77 7UR (01248) 750750 £109.50; 20 luxurious rms. Handsome, Victorian stone mansion with landscaped gardens, a plushly comfortable bar, carefully decorated lounge, friendly staff and fine food in the conservatory-style restaurant; clay-pigeon shooting; disabled access.

Caernarfon SH4862 SEIONT MANOR Llanrug, Caernarfon, Gwynedd LL55 2AQ (01286) 673366 *£96.50; 28 luxurious rms. Fine hotel built from the original farmstead of a Georgian manor house and standing in 150 acres of mature parkland; open fires and comfortable sofas in the lounge, a restful atmosphere in the library and drawing room, imaginative food in the four interconnecting areas of the restaurant, and leisure suite with swimming pool, gym, sauna and solarium.

Llandrillo SJ0337 TYDDYN LLAN Llandrillo, Corwen, Clwyd LL21 0ST (0149 084) 264 £88; 10 pretty rms. Restful, Georgian house with fresh flowers and antiques in the elegantly furnished and comfortable public rooms, charming staff, very good, inventive food and 3 acres of lovely gardens; fishing on 4 miles of River Dee (ghillies available) and fine forest walks (guides are available); cl first 2 wks Feb.

Penmaenpool SH6918 GEORGE III Penmaenpool, Dolgellau, Gwynedd LL40 1YD (01341) 422525 *£88; 12 rms, some in an award-winning, converted railway station. Cosy 17th-c inn on the Mawddach estuary, with good lunchtime food, an imaginative evening restaurant, nice lounge with a log fire, beamed and partly panelled bar (real ales), fine nearby walks, and free salmon and trout fishing permits for residents; disabled access.

Llansanffraid Glan Conwy SH7878 OLD RECTORY Llansanffraid, Gwynedd LL28 5LF (01429) 580611 £84; 6 deeply comfortable rms. Sophisticated Georgian house in pleasant gardens, with fine views over Conwy estuary, Conwy Castle and Snowdonia; delightful public rooms with flowers, antiques and family photos, and after introductions over cocktails, the delicious food can either be eaten together or at separate tables; marvellous wine list, good Welsh breakfasts, and warm, friendly staff; cl 14 Dec–1 Feb; children over 5 or under 9 months.

Llanarmon D C SJ1633 WEST ARMS Llanarmon D C, Llangollen, Clwyd LL20 7LD (0169 176) 665 £80; 12 rms. Charming and civilised old place with heavy beams and timbers, log fires in inglenook fireplaces, a lounge bar interestingly furnished with antique settles, sofas in the old-fashioned entrance hall, comfortable locals' bar, good food, and a friendly, quiet atmosphere; the lawn runs down to the River Ceiriog (fishing for residents); cl end Jan for 2 wks; disabled access.

Llangollen SJ2142 BRYN HOWEL Llangollen, Clwyd LL20 7UW (01978) 860331 £79; 38 rms. Extended Victorian mansion in the lovely Vale of Llangollen, with comfortable lounges, a panelled bar and small cocktail bar, open fires, and good food using home-grown herbs and fresh local produce in the restaurant; neat grounds, sauna and solarium, and salmon and trout fishing on private waters of the River Dee.

Betws-y-Coed SH7956 ROYAL OAK Betws-y-Coed, Gwynedd LL24 0AY (01690) 710219 £78; 27 recently refurbished rms. Pleasant hotel with civilised bar and lounge areas, open fires, leather chairs and a relaxed atmosphere; wonderfully fresh fish and seasonal game in the restaurant, and a popular grill room.

Capel Garmon SH8255 TAN-Y-FOEL COUNTRY HOUSE Capel Garmon, Betws-y-Coed, Gwynedd LL26 0RE (01690) 710507 £76; 9 spotlessly clean rms. Just a couple of miles from Betws-y-Coed, this charming, partly 16th-c, no-smoking manor house is in an almost traffic-free area with mature gardens and marvellous surrounding countryside of Conwy Valley and Snowdonia; lounge with a log fire in winter, conservatory in summer, warm, friendly, relaxing atmosphere and good food using the freshest produce, inc local lamb and home-made bread; swimming pool (Jun–Oct); cl Christmas; children over 9; no pets.

Beaumaris SH6076 OLDE BULLS HEAD Castle St Beaumaris, Anglesey, Gwynedd LL58 8AP (01248) 810329 £73; 11 rms with antiques and brass bedsteads. Partly 15th-c pub, nr the castle, with snug alcoves, low beams and an open fire in the quaint, rambling bar, interesting decorations, popular bar food, very good restaurant food (especially fish), fine wines, and cheery service; the entrance to the pretty courtyard is closed by the biggest, single-hinged door in Britain; cl 25–26 Dec, 1 Jan; children over 7 in dining room.

Llanwddyn SJ0219 LAKE VYRNWY Llanwddyn, Oswestry, Powys SY10 0LY (0169 173) 692 £72.50; 38 rms, the ones overlooking the lake are the nicest. With particularly helpful, courteous staff, this large, Tudor-style mansion has lots of sporting activities (especially fishing) and is set in 24,000 acres of woodland; log fires and sporting prints in the comfortable and elegant public rooms, a relaxed atmosphere, fine views from its hillside high over the lake, and good food using home-made preserves, chutneys, mustards and vinegars and home-grown produce from their own kitchen garden; nice teas, too.

Llanfyllin SJ1419 BODFACH HALL Llanfyllin, Powys SY22 5HS (01691) 648272 *£68; 9 quiet rms. Elegant house in 4 acres of mature garden, with a restful, friendly atmosphere, residents' drawing room, spacious lounge bar, simple food in the oak-panelled dining room, and very good service; cl Nov–Feb.

Abersoch SH3128 PORTH TOCYN Bwlch Tocyn, Abersoch, Pwllheli, Gwynedd LL53 7BU (01758) 713303 £64; 17 attractive rms. On a headland with fine views, this is a lovely place to stay – with a refreshingly sensible and helpful approach to families, though it is not solely a family hotel; very friendly, hard-working owners and staff, several cosy interconnecting sitting rooms with antiques and fresh flowers, most enjoyable traditional cooking in the restaurant (lots of options such as light lunches, high teas for children, and imaginative Sun lunches), and a happy atmosphere; lots of space outside, heated swimming pool in summer, hard tennis court; cl mid-Nov–wk before Easter; disabled access.

Llanarmon D C SJ1633 HAND Llanarmon, D C, Llangollen, Clwyd LL20 7LD (0169 176) 666 £64; 12 rms. Very civilised country inn surrounded by outstanding scenery, with a comfortably furnished lounge, log fire, fine restaurant food, good-value bar food, and quick, friendly service; hard tennis court; disabled access.

Betws-y-Coed SH7956 TY GWYN Betws-y-Coed, Gwynedd LL24 0SG (01690) 710383 £52; 13 lovely rms, most with own bthrm. Welcoming, 17th-c coaching inn with interesting old prints, furniture and bric-a-brac (owners own the antique shop next door), nice food, and friendly service; pleasant setting overlooking the river and a very good base for the area; discounts for children sharing parents' rm; dogs welcome; disabled access.

Llangollen SJ2142 BRITANNIA (Horseshoe Pass; A542, N) Llangollen, Clwyd LL20 8DW (01978) 860144 £50; 5 clean and pretty rms, all with four-posters. Picturesque inn based on a 15th-c core, though much extended and comfortably modernised, with traditional, 17th-c, Welsh elm furniture, generous helpings of decent food in the dining area and two bars, pleasant staff, lovely views and an attractive garden; cl 25 Dec.

Maentwrog SH6741 GRAPES Maentwrog, Blaenau Ffestiniog, Gwynedd LL41 4HN (0176 685) 208 £50; 6 rms. Bustling, family-run, 17th-c coaching inn with interesting lamps, guns and blowlamps, old pine furniture, and stripped stone walls in the relaxed, friendly bars; hearty, wholesome bar food, big breakfasts, and good views from the terrace and garden.

Llanrwst SH8061 PRIORY Maenan, Llanwrst, Gwynedd LL26 0UL (01492) 660247 £49; 12 rms. Stately Victorian hotel with a battlemented tower, an elegant lounge, welcoming bar, log fires, good food, Welsh singing Sat evenings, and lovely gardens; 11 acres of woodland across the road, and close to fishing and Bodnant Gardens.

Beddgelert SH5948 SYGUN FAWR COUNTRY HOUSE Beddgelert, Caernarfon,

Gwynedd LL55 4NE (01766) 890258 £48; 7 rms. Marvellous views of the Gwynant Valley and Snowdon range from this secluded, 17th-c hotel; comfortable sitting room, and home cooking in the candlelit, traditionally furnished dining room; lots of walks; cl 1 Jan–1 Feb.

Llannefydd SH9770 Hawk and Buckle Llannefydd, Denbigh, Clwyd LL16 5ED (0174 579) 249 £48; 10 modern rms, lovely views. Pleasant, 17th-c stone inn, 700ft up in the hills with remarkable views; a decent choice of food using fresh local produce, a neatly kept beamed and knocked-through lounge bar, and a good base for exploring the area – by horse, car or on foot; cl 25 Dec; children over 8.

Erbistock SJ3542 Boat Erbistock, Wrexham, Clwyd LL13 0DL (01978) 780143 £45; 1 rm with a small lounge and breakfast area and river views. Popular dining pub, busy in summer, with decent food, a pleasant, small, flagstoned bar, beamed dining room and big eating annexe, and a pretty, partly terraced garden by the River Dee – enchanting on a quiet summer's day; cl 25–26 Dec, 1 Jan.

Llanerchymedd SH4284 Llwydiarth Fawr Farm Llanerchymedd, Gwynedd LL71 8DF (01248) 470321 £45; 3 rms in main house, 6 cottage suites in grounds. Handsome Georgian farmhouse on an 850-acre, cattle and sheep farm, with a particularly warm, homely atmosphere and welcome, comfortable lounge with antiques, log fire, books and lovely views, a second room for guests with another log fire, very good, home-made food using farm and other fresh local produce; terrace, a lake for private fishing, nature walks, and birdwatching; cl Christmas.

Capel Garmon SH8155 White Horse Capel Garmon, Llanrwst, Gwynedd LL26 0RW (01690) 710271 *£44; 7 rms. Comfortable, homely inn with a friendly atmosphere, very good, home-made food in both the bar and little restaurant, marvellous breakfasts, magnificent views and delightful countryside; children over 10.

Llanrwst SH8061 Cae'r Berllan Betws Rd, Llanrwst, Gwynedd LL26 0PP £44; 2 rms with antique beds and fine views. Listed, 16th-c manor house in 2½ acres of lovely gardens surrounded by the Conwy Valley, with lots of atmosphere, massive old beams and oak partitioning, and good, imaginative food using home-grown and local produce (they think of themselves as a restaurant with rooms – open to non-residents Weds–Sat, booking essential); cl Nov, Jan and Feb (open Dec).

Llangollen SJ2142 Abbey Grange Llangollen, Clwyd LL20 8NN (01978) 860753 £42; 8 comfortable rms. Cosily converted, former quarrymaster's house in a beautiful spot with superb views, nr Valle Crucis Abbey; decent food, good wine list, and efficient, courteous service.

Maentwrog SH6741 Plas Tan y Bwlch Maentwrog, Blaenau Ffestiniog, Gwynedd LL41 3YU (01766) 85324 *£42; 35 rms, 12 with own bthrm. Converted Victorian mansion (now the Snowdonia National Park Study Centre) with lovely valley views, satisfying, sturdy, self-service food, and attractive walks in own grounds; cl 2 wks over Christmas.

Tremeirchion SJ0873 Bach-y-Graig Tremeirchion, St Asaph, Clwyd LL17 0UH (01745) 730627 *£38; 3 rms, 2 with brass beds. Wales's first brick-built house with a date-stone of 1567, this is set in a 200-acre dairy farm at the foot of the Clwydian range; an inglenook fireplace in the big lounge, home-cooking using home-produced beef and lamb and own free-range eggs, and a warm welcome; can join in farm activities or walk along their woodland trail; cl Christmas/New Year.

Llanerchymedd SH4284 Tre'r Ddol Farm Llanerchymedd, Isle of Anglesey, Gwynedd LL71 7AR (01248) 470278 *£36; 3 rms with original features. Neatly kept, 400-year-old farmhouse on a working mixed farm of 200 acres; with an original staircase, log fire in the cosy lounge, a homely, relaxed atmosphere and good farmhouse cooking; can help with day-to-day farm work, free riding for children, and birdwatching; cl Christmas.

Tudweiliog SH2437 Lion Tudweiliog, Pwllheli, Gwynedd LL53 8ND (01758) 770244 £36; 5 rms, 2 with own bthrm. Extended, 300-year-old village pub with excellent-value, home-made food in the comfortable bar and dining rooms, a welcome for families, garden with play area, lovely views, and a 10-minute walk to the beach; cl 22–28 Dec.

Welshpool SJ2207 Moat Farm Welshpool, Powys SY21 8SE (01938) 553179 £36; 3 rms. Attractive, 17th-c farmhouse in big gardens on a dairy farm, with a quiet, comfortable lounge, lovely beamed dining room with good home-cooking, and pool table; cl Nov–Mar.

Ffordd-las SJ0771 Berllan Bach Ffordd-las, Llandyrnog, Denbigh, Clwyd LL16 4LT (01824) 790732 £35; 3 rms with French windows onto individual patios. Carefully converted cottage and barns at the foot of the hills in the lovely Vale of Clwyd, with a woodburning stove in the comfortable sitting room, and good food in the dining conservatory; marvellous walks, well behaved dogs welcome; disabled access.

Llanfihangel-yng-Nywynfa SJ0814 Cyfie Farm Llanfihangel-yng-Nywynfa, Llanfyllin, Powys SY22 5JE (01691) 648451 £35; 3 rms with lovely views. Carefully restored, 17th-c, Welsh stone longhouse on 178 acres of stock cattle and sheep farm (guests are welcome to take an interest in the lambs, shearing and dipping and hay-gathering); timbered and beamed rooms with fine family furniture, log fire in the residents' lounge, hearty farmhouse cooking in an attractive, conservatory dining room, and a relaxed, friendly atmosphere.

Brynsiencyn SH4867 Plas Trefarthen Brynsiencyn, Llanfairpwllgwyngyll, Gwynedd LL61 6SZ (01248) 430379 £34; 8 rms, most with own bthrm. Happy and comfortable family house with panoramic views of Caernarfon Castle and the Snowdonia mountain range; a guest lounge, full-size snooker table, table tennis, and home-cooked food using produce grown on the farm; Mrs Roberts is a well known soprano soloist for Welsh choirs.

Hanmer SJ4639 Buck Farm Hanmer, Whitchurch Shrops SY14 7LX (0194 874) 339 £34; 4 rms, shared bthrm. 16th-c, half-timbered farmhouse in rolling dairy country, with a well stocked library and very good, imaginative food using only fresh produce, often organic; lots to do in the area; no smoking.

Saron SH4659 Pengwern Saron, Caernarfon, Gwynedd LL54 5UH (01286) 830717 £34; 3 rms. In 130 acres of land which runs down to Foryd Bay, this spacious farmhouse has marvellous views of Snowdonia and provides delicious food, using home-produced beef and lamb, in the attractive dining room; cl Dec/Jan.

Gellilydan SH6839 Tyddyn Du Farm Gellilydan, Ffestiniog, Gwynedd LL41 4RB (01766) 85281 *£32; 4 rms with views of hills and mountains, 1 in private cottage suite. 400-year-old farmhouse on a working farm in the heart of Snowdonia National Park, with beams and exposed stonework, big inglenook fireplace in the residents' lounge, and wholesome, home-made food using own free-range eggs; can help with the lambs, goats, ducks, sheep and pony; fine walks; cl Christmas.

Llanrhaeadr-ym-Mochnant SJ1326 Plas-Yn-Llan Llanrhaeadr-ym-Mochnant, Oswestry, Shrops SY10 0JN (01691) 780236 £32; 4 rms, shared bthrm. Creeper-clad, former coaching inn with a woodburning stove and beams in the dining room, residents' TV lounge and library, good food using local produce, and a big, secluded garden.

Pwllheli SH3835 Yoke House Farm Pwllheli, Gwynedd LL53 5TY (01758) 612621 £32; 2 rms, shared bthrm. Warmly welcoming Georgian farmhouse on a 290-acre working farm; can watch milking, calf-feeding and there's a nature trail; cl Oct–Apr; children over 11.

Fron-goch SH9139 Fferm Fron-Goch Fron-goch, Bala, Gwynedd LL23 7NT (01678) 520483 £30; 3 rms. Traditional stone farmhouse with a history going back to the 14th c, on 600 acres of working farm in the lovely, unspoilt countryside of the Snowdonia National Park; beams, log fire, antiques and old paintings, a friendly atmosphere and good breakfasts; children over 9.

To see and do

🏛 **Aberffraw** SH3270 BARCLODIAD Y GAWRES Some 5,000 years old, this 20-ft underground passage tomb at the top of the cliff is notable for the patterns carved by the entrance and in the side chambers, which you make out with a good torch; it's sealed, but you can ask for a key at the Wayside Café in Llanfaelog, about a mile away. Hard to believe now, but Aberffraw was once the Welsh capital, and the native Gwynedd princes held court here from the 9th to the 13th c. There are some lovely unspoilt coves and beaches nearby.

✝ ❀ ♨ 🏛 🖼 👜 ❀ **Bangor** SH5771 Quiet university town with a pedestrianised high st and a yacht harbour that adds a lively touch in summer. A CATHEDRAL was founded here 70 years before the one at Canterbury; the present building is restored 13th to 15th c, and has an interesting 16th-c carving of Christ bound and seated on a rock, as well as some fine Victorian stained glass. The Bible Garden outside contains only plants which are mentioned in the Scriptures. Opposite is a little museum of rural Welsh life, and the Nelson, nr the harbour, has decent food. PENRHYN CASTLE (1 m, E) Splendid, neo-Norman fantasy built by a slate magnate in the 19th c: the interior is in suitably grand style, with quite remarkable – and often bizarre – panelling, decoration and furnishings. The cathedral-like great hall is heated by the Roman method of hot air under the floor, and one of the beds weighs over a ton – it's made out of slate. An unexpectedly rich collection of paintings includes works by Rembrandt and Canaletto. In the stableyard is a museum devoted to the industrial railways which have left Wales with such a legacy of quaint, narrow-gauge lines; the unique exhibits include very early locomotives. Also a walled garden, adventure playground, and pleasant walks with good views. Meals, snacks, shop, disabled access; cl am (exc July and Aug), Tues, Nov–Mar; £4.40, garden only £2; NT.

★ 🏛 🏰 ♨ ♪ ✝ **Beaumaris** SH6076 The most attractive town on Anglesey, with a good deal of character, several old buildings, a busy waterfront, and a 15th-c church. CASTLE One of the most impressive and complete of the castles built by Edward I, despite the struggle over it with Owen Glyndwr in the early 1400s, and the plundering of its lead, timber and stone in later ages. Beautifully symmetrical, it took from 1295 to 1312 to build (though the money ran out before it could be finished). Shop, good disabled access; cl 24–26 Dec, 1 Jan; (01248) 810361; £1.50. Opposite the castle, the COURTHOUSE is a unique Victorian survival. You can stand in the dock and imagine you're just about to be sentenced. Open Easter, wknds in May and daily Jun–Sept, exc when court in session; £1.35. Down the road, the GAOL paints a vivid picture of the harshness of the 19th-c prison system, with its treadmill, dank, pokey cells, and the route to the scaffold for condemned prisoners. Shop, limited disabled access; open as courthouse above, or by appointment, (01248) 810291; £2.30, joint with courthouse £2.80. MARINE WORLD (on the sea front) Lively displays of the sea life of the Menai Straits, with quite an unusual combination of creatures. Snacks, shop, disabled access; cl 25 Dec; (01248) 810072; £1.95. The CHURCH of St Mary and St Nicholas, which has a robust square tower, houses the stone coffin of Joan, daughter of King John and wife of the Welsh leader Llewellyn the Great. The Olde Bull's Head is excellent for lunch.

★ ♪T ❀ **Beddgelert** SH5948 A quiet village, which dreamed up the myth that it was the resting place of Llewellyn's faithful mastiff over a hundred years ago and has been living on it ever since. SYGUN COPPER MINE Interesting tours through often spectacular, underground mine workings, with magnificent stalactites and stalagmites and traces of gold and silver in the copper ore veins. When you come up at the end you're greeted by a wonderful view of the

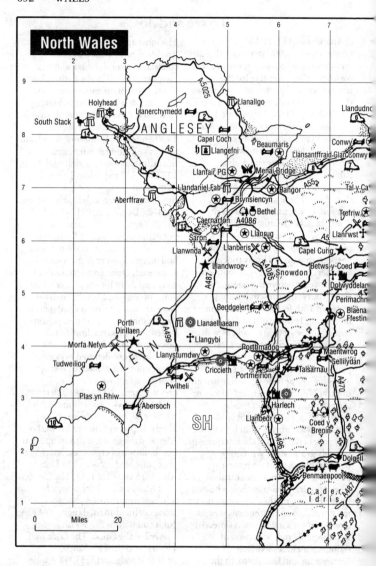

North Wales

mountains. Also, a good audio-visual presentation, and a display of artefacts found during excavations. Snacks, shop, some disabled access; cl 25 Dec; (01766) 86584; £3.90. The Prince Llewelyn is good for lunch.
⏏ ⚘ **Bethel** SH5365 GREENWOOD CENTRE An unexpected delight – a lively look at trees and wood from trunks and rainforests to wooden Ethiopian pillows. You can handle most of the exhibits, and there's 17 acres of woodland to explore. Most of the exhibition is indoors, so is ideal for rainy days, but worth popping into at any time. Teas, shop, disabled access; ring for winter opening; (01248) 671493; £2.75. The Vaynol Arms at Pentir has decent food.
★ ⚘ ⏚ **Betws-y-Coed** SH7956 19th-c resort village in a beautiful wooded gorge at the head of the Vale of Conwy, on the road to Bangor (and thence Ireland) as well as to Snowdon.

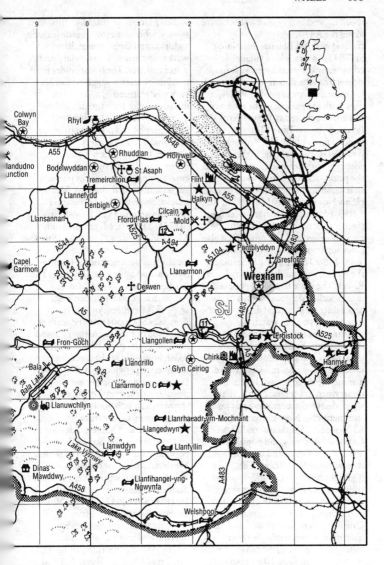

Surrounded by picturesque woodland and river walks, this village has over a century of catering to visitors behind it. The raging Swallow Falls and Fairy Glen, just W of the village itself, are deservedly regarded as some of the area's finest beauty spots. There are also a number of interesting bridges nearby, as well as the bizarre-looking Ugly House, which looks like a series of boulders thrown haphazardly together. CONWY VALLEY RAILWAY

MUSEUM (Old Goods Yard) Good look at the narrow- and standard-gauge railways of N Wales, with railway stock and other memorabilia, model railway layouts, a steam-hauled model railway in the 4-acre grounds, and a 15-inch-gauge tramway to take visitors to the woods. Snacks, shop, disabled access; cl winter wkdys; (01690) 710568; site free, £1 museum. The Ty Gwyn has good food, and the Waterloo is useful too. The next entry is just a short drive along the A470.

🏠 ❀ ⬆ ⬆ ☼ ☺ ! **Blaenau Ffestiniog** SH7045 is a straggle of village completely dwarfed by the vast spoil slopes from the slate mines all around it – once the slate capital of Wales, now with the passing of the industry like a living museum. PUMPED STORAGE POWER STATION (Tan y Grisiau) Guided tours of the first hydroelectric pumped storage scheme in the country, with dramatic views towards the peaks of Snowdonia. Meals, snacks, shop, limited disabled access; cl Sat, Nov–Easter; (01766) 830310; £2.50. From the information centre there's an attractive drive up into the mountains to Stwlan Dam, which also gives super views. GLODDFA GANOL SLATE MINE The largest slate mine in the world, with guided tours by Land-Rover. The mine has been reopened, and as well as demonstrations of the art of slate splitting and displays of the machinery, you can watch the blasting operations from the safety of the museum. You can go right down into the workings too, and there's a little narrow-gauge railway. Above ground are three period, furnished, quarrymen's cottages. Meals, snacks, shop, disabled access; cl wknds (exc summer hols), Nov–Easter; (01776) 830664; £3.75. LLECHWEDD SLATE CAVERNS Very busy and popular, always developing and bang up-to-date with the latest ideas. The highlight has to be the underground train journeys through the caverns, with dramatic sound and light effects and a choice of two different routes. One way re-creates the world of the Victorian miner, while the other (along Britain's steepest railway) ends with a walk through 10 atmospheric chambers, each with its own sound and light show. Plenty on the surface too, with a railway museum, slate mill and complete Victorian village. Meals, snacks, shop, some disabled access; cl 25–26 Dec, 1 Jan; (01766) 830306; single tour £4.75, both £7.25, surface attractions free. The very friendly Grapes at Maentwrog is fairly handy for lunch.

❀ ♪ 🐦 🏠 ☼ ✝ **Bodelwyddan** SH9974 BODELWYDDAN CASTLE The walled gardens surrounding this showy, white-limestone castle include a glorious melange of woodland walks, flowering plants, aviary and water features. The house (older than its 19th-c exterior suggests) has been very well restored as a Victorian mansion, with furniture from the Victoria & Albert Museum, and photographs and portraits from the National Portrait Gallery. Plenty for children to enjoy, inc a woodland adventure playground, and entertaining exhibitions of puzzles, games and optical illusions. Meals, snacks, shop, disabled access; cl Fri (exc July and Aug), all Nov–Mar; (01745) 584060; £4, grounds only £1.50. In the village itself, the 19th-c Marble Church, built entirely of locally quarried limestone, is an unusual and quite splendid sight. The Farmer's Arms at The Waen, St Asaph, has good home-cooking.

♪ 🐦 ☼ 🏛 **Brynsiencyn** SH4867 ANGLESEY SEA ZOO (Just S) Excellent collection of marine creatures found around Anglesey and the N Wales coast, housed in tanks specially designed to provide as unrestricted and natural an environment as possible. Also, a walk-through shipwreck, touch pools for picking up live specimens, adventure playground, and home-made fudge and ice-cream. This is now the most popular wildlife attraction in Wales. Meals, snacks (their oysters are guaranteed to contain a pearl), shop, disabled access; cl 19–26 Dec, 1–6 Jan; (01248) 430411; £3.95. Nearby the FOEL FARM PARK is a friendly working farm with daily sheep-milking and more home-made ice-cream. Also tractor rides, walks and rare breeds. Snacks, shop, disabled access; cl Nov–Easter; (01248) 430646; £2.95. Another farm here, Gwydryn Hir, lets you PICK YOUR OWN fruit, veg and flowers while taking in the view of Snowdonia. Open Jun–Oct; (01248) 430344. A couple of miles NW of the village, by the back road towards Llangaffo, is what looks like a Stone Age hut, but is actually a burial chamber from which the covering earth has been eroded over the millennia. The Mermaid at Foel

Ferry is quite useful for lunch.

🏰 ♨ 🏚 ✝ **Caernarfon** SH4862 still has lengths of its 13th-c town walls, crowding in its quaintly narrow streets (quaint, that is, unless you're trying to drive through them). CASTLE The largest of Edward I's Welsh castles, built after the defeat of Llewellyn the Last, and still quite spectacular. Finished in 1328, it's unusual both for its octagonal towers and for the bands of colour decorating the walls. Edward's son was born here and presented to the people, setting the precedent for future Princes of Wales; there's an exhibition on this, along with an audio-visual display and regimental museum. Shop; cl am Sun in winter, 24–26 Dec, 1 Jan; (01286) 677617; *£3.50. In the sq outside, around the statue of former MP David Lloyd George, they still have a busy Sat market. The castle walls were thought to be partly modelled on the walls of Constantinople – reflecting the tradition that Constantine the Great was born at nearby SEGONTIUM, a Roman fort dating from AD78. Excavations have exposed the remains of various rebuildings during its three centuries of importance, and there's a museum with some of the finds. Shop, disabled access; cl am Sun, 24–26 Dec, 1 Jan, Good Fri; (01286) 675625; free. The harbour is busy with yachts in summer, and you can go over a restored, steam-powered dredger moored here. AIR WORLD (Airport) Lively displays of helicopters, aeroplanes and a trainer, encouraging people to climb aboard. Also a great many model aeroplanes, and pleasure sky trips. Meals, snacks, shop, disabled access; cl 24 Dec–4 Jan; (01286) 830800; £3.50. The Black Boy and Palace Vaults do decent food.

🏰 ❀ **Chirk** SJ2368 The quiet little town, important as a staging post on the former road to Ireland, has something of a bypassed-by-time feel now; the Hand and Bridge are quite useful for lunch. A little to the W, right by a well preserved stretch of the earthworks of Offa's Dyke, is CHIRK CASTLE, one of the lucky few of Edward I's castles to survive as an occupied home rather than fall to ruin. This year they're celebrating the 700th anniversary of the start of its construction, and the recently restored exterior still remains much as it was then, with its high walls and drum towers. Lots of alterations inside over the years – most of the medieval-looking decorations were by Pugin in the 19th c, the elegant stone staircase dates from the 18th c, and the Long Gallery is 17th c. Meals, snacks, shop, some disabled access; cl am, Mon, Sat (though this may change to Tues this year – best to check), Nov–Mar; (01691) 777701; £4; NT. The formal gardens are magnificent.

🔔 ✔ **Coed y Brenin** SH7326 The name means King's Forest, and it was so called to commemorate the Silver Jubilee of King George. There are some beautifully varied sights and landscapes, as well as wildlife observation hides, and over 50 miles of walks. THE FOREST PARK AND VISITOR CENTRE at Maesgwn is an excellent introduction. Snacks, shop, disabled access; cl Nov–Easter; (01341) 422289; free. You can hire bikes from here.

☺ 🐦 ❀ ❄ 🔔 **Colwyn Bay** SH8678 Busy, summer seaside resort with all that's wanted for a family beach holiday, though not as nice as Llandudno just along the coast (see entry below). The quieter end at Rhos-on-Sea has a PUPPET THEATRE. Cl winter exc school hols; (01492) 548166 for programme and prices. WELSH MOUNTAIN ZOO and Flagstaff Gardens Lots of exotic animals in natural-looking habitats, but what really distinguishes this zoo from any other is the setting overlooking Colwyn Bay; the views are quite magnificent. The 37 acres of gardens and woodland in which the zoo is set attract plenty of local wildlife. Meals, snacks, shop, disabled access; cl 25 Dec; (01492) 532938; *£4.95. The Mountain View at Mochdre has good-value food.

★ 🏰 ❀ 🏚 ♪ ⛵ **Conwy** SH7777 Cheerful old town dominated by its CASTLE (Castle St), one of the best-known castles in Wales and one of the most important examples of military architecture in the whole of Europe.

Built for Edward I in 1283–89, it's very well preserved, still looking exactly as a medieval fortress should, despite the ravages it suffered in the Civil War and beyond. There's an exhibition on Edward and the other castles he built, as well as a scale model of the castle and the town in the early 14th c. The tops of the turrets offer fine panoramic views; the most dramatic views of the castle itself are from the other side of the estuary. Shop; cl 24–26 Dec; (01492) 592358; £2.90. The castle was the key part of the town's elaborate defensive system – 21 (originally 22) towers linked by walls some 30ft high, still the most complete town wall in Wales. You can walk along some parts, looking down over the narrow little streets that still follow their medieval layout. The bridges spanning the river are also worth a second glance – the suspension bridge was built by Telford in 1826, and the tubular bridge by Stephenson in 1848. The only house which dates from the 14th c, surviving the turbulence of events in this frontier town, is ABERCONWY HOUSE, once the home of a prosperous merchant. Rooms are furnished in period style and there's an interesting audio-visual presentation. Shop; cl Tues, Nov–Mar; £1.80; NT. The elaborate Tudor mansion PLAS MAWR (High St) is currently undergoing extensive restoration, and it will be some time before it's completely ready. Last summer though, the Royal Cambrian Academy (who have art demonstrations next door) did open up a few of the rooms, so if you're passing it may be worth having a look to see if they're doing the same this year. Nicely placed on the quayside is Britain's SMALLEST HOUSE, 6ft wide and its front wall only 10ft high. Squeezed into the two rooms (one up, one down) are all the comforts of home, or at least most – there's no lavatatory. It's furnished in the style of a mid-Victorian Welsh cottage. Shop, disabled access; cl Good Fri, Nov–Mar; * 50p. There's a little aquarium nearby, and you can usually go on summer boat trips. The Castle Hotel (High St) is a civilised place for lunch. New roadways nearby have

eased what was an appalling traffic jam through Conwy – you may still be held up, particularly going through one of the craggy, old town gates.

† **Corwen** SJ0843 has a couple of rather special churches nearby. One mile N, 17th-c RUG CHAPEL looks uninspiring from the outside, but inside is a riot of colour – almost every available piece of woodwork covered with cheery patterns and paintwork; £1.50. A mile or so down the road (and covered by the same ticket), LANGAR CHURCH was built in the 13th c, and has some remarkable paintings of the seven deadly sins.

▥ ※ Criccieth SH5038 Restrained resort with a good sheltered, sandy beach. CRICCIETH CASTLE The remains of this 13th-c castle stand on a rocky, mounded peninsula above the little town, affording superb views over Tremadog Bay. Parts of the inner walls are well preserved, and there's an impressive gatehouse. A very good exhibition, including a cartoon video, looks at Gerald of Wales and other Welsh princes and castles. Shop, disabled access; cl wkdys and am Sun in winter, 24–26 Dec, 1 Jan; (01766) 522227; £2. The Prince of Wales is a reliable food pub.

▥ † ♿ Denbigh SJ0566 CASTLE The gatehouse of this ruined castle is still impressive, with its trio of towers and a superb archway; the figure on the summit is believed to represent Edward I. The castle was started in 1282, as were the town walls which describe almost a complete circuit. Among the remains are one of the gateways and Leicester's church, the remnants of an ambitious church built by the Earl of Leicester, favourite of Elizabeth I. Cl Oct–Apr; £1.50. A museum on the High St has interesting finds from nearby Bronze Age sites. The Cerrigllwydion Arms at nearby Llanynys, to the SE, has good food.

† **Derwen** SJ0751 The medieval CHURCH here has an elaborately carved rood screen and loft, with some old wall paintings and an excellent Celtic cross in the churchyard.

▦ Dinas Mawddwy SH8513 MEIRION MILL The village, among riverside woods below the mountains on the S fringes of Snowdonia, provides a charming setting for this working woollen mill, in the grounds of the old Mawddwy railway station. Snacks, shop (lots of locally made goods), disabled access; cl Dec–Feb; (01650) 531311; free. Nearby is a picturesque packhorse bridge, and the friendly Red Lion has decent food.

☖ ✝ Dolwyddelan SH7352 DOLWYDDELAN CASTLE Picturesquely set on a lightly wooded crag, these old ruins were reputedly the birthplace of Llewellyn the Great. You can still see a restored keep of around 1200 and a 13th-c curtain wall. Cl am Sun, 24–26 Dec, 1 Jan; £1.50. The village church is attractive.

☖ Flint SJ2472 CASTLE Parts of the walls and corner towers survive, but the most impressive remnant of this 13th-c castle is the great tower or donjon, which is separated by the moat. Overlooking the River Dee, it was the first of those built by Edward I to subdue the natives, and has a role in Shakespeare's *Richard II*. Cl am Sun in winter, 25–26 Dec, 1 Jan; free. The Britannia in nearby Halkyn is good for lunch, with fine views.

⌁ ❀ ⚘ ★ Glyn Ceiriog SJ2038 CHWAREL WYNNE MINE Set in beautiful surroundings, an 18th-c slate mine with entertaining half-hour guided tours of the underground workings. The 12-acre landscaped grounds have won several awards, and there are nature trails and walks through the adjacent old woodland. Snacks, shop (selling alpines and evergreens in season), disabled access; cl Nov–Mar; (01691) 718343; *£2.50. The Woolpack, right by the slate tramway in the attractively unspoilt village, is good for lunch, and the valley's remote landscape is popular with walkers.

✝ Gresford SJ3555 The village CHURCH has some wonderful, medieval stained glass, and its bells are often described as one of the Seven Wonders of Wales. A yew tree outside is reputed to be 1,400 years old.

☖ ❀ Harlech SH5831 CASTLE Splendid-looking structure built in 1283–90 by Edward I, its rugged glory the massive, twin-towered gatehouse, now housing an exhibition on the site's history. It was starved into capitulation by Owen Glyndwr in 1404, and later dogged defence inspired the song *Men of Harlech*. Before the sea retreated there was a sheer drop into the water on one side, but it now stands above dunes, with wonderful views of Snowdonia from the battlements. Shop; cl am Sun in winter, 24–26 Dec, 1 Jan; (01766) 780552; £2.90. The village around it has all that the crowds of summer visitors to the castle and the good beach could want. The riverside Victoria at Llanbedr does decent food.

⌂ ❀ Holyhead SH2582 is a long-established fishing town on little Holy Island, now an unassuming resort with some burial chambers and ancient sites not far away (see also South Stack entry below). The Victorian breakwater protecting the harbour is Britain's longest; a maritime museum – (01407) 762816 – explores its seafaring heritage. Across the old Four-Mile Bridge at Valley the Bull has good-value food.

! ♭ ☖ ⌂ ☖ Holywell SJ1876 ST WINEFRIDE'S WELL has the holy spring that turned the spot into a centre of pilgrimage – it's supposed to have healing powers. The neighbouring GREENFIELD VALLEY HERITAGE PARK has a farm museum, and an increasing number of buildings rescued from their original sites and rebuilt here. These include a 17th-c cottage, Victorian farmhouse, and a school, all furnished in period style. Also the remains of a Cistercian abbey and a good few relics of the Industrial Revolution. Snacks, shop, disabled access; cl winter exc pm Sun; (01352) 714172; £1.20. Pleasant walks from here through the valley to the coast.

⌂ ❀ Llanaelhaearn SH3744 Off the B4417, just up the hill from here, a signed path leads to the TRE'R CEIRI HILL FORT, occupied from the Bronze Age through to the Dark Ages; a massive stone wall, lots of hut foundations, and fine views. At Morfa Nefyn nearby, the Bryncynan and (overlooking a lovely sandy bay) Cliff Hotel do good lunches.

⌂ Llanallgo SH4985 DIN LLUGWY ANCIENT VILLAGE The remains of a 4th-c village: a pentagonal stone wall surrounds two circular and seven rectangular buildings; free. The Parciau Arms at Marianglas is the best place for a meal.

⊥т ♪ ♧ᴸLlanbedr SH5826 Maes Artro village Imaginatively converted, wartime RAF camp with lots to do: an original air-raid shelter complete with light and sound effects, a 'Village of Yesteryear', log fort playground, marine aquarium, and nature trails through the woodland. Snacks, shop, disabled access; cl Oct–Easter; (01341) 23467; £2.75. The Victoria here is useful for lunch.

🐄🐷❋♧🏠🏔🐾 Llanberis SH5760 is full of B & Bs, small hotels, shops and cafés for the summer visitors here for Snowdon. There are a number of craft shops dotted along the High St, and the Dolbadarn Hotel has a pony trekking centre, with beginners' rides to the lower slopes of the mountain. Cl Oct–Easter; (01286) 870277.

Snowdon Mountain Railway The easiest way to climb Snowdon, on Britain's only public rack-and-pinion railway, operated by vintage, Swiss steam and modern diesel locomotives. It follows the route of an old pony track and takes passengers up over 3,000ft right to the summit – glorious breathtaking views which, on a good day, might include the Isle of Man and the Wicklow Mountains. It's without a doubt one of the most spectacular train journeys in the country. Trains leave when there are more than a couple of dozen people on board – so if there aren't many people about you may have to wait for it to start, and if there are you may have to queue (there is a sort of booking service). When trains are running to the summit, you can visit the highest postbox in Britain. Remember as your head may quite literally be up in the clouds it can be chilly, so wrap up well. Meals, snacks, shop, disabled access (with notice); open mid-Mar–Oct, though always best to ring first, (01286) 870223; £12.80 return. See Walks section below for other ways to enjoy the splendid scenery of Snowdon.

Lake Railway Four-mile trips along the shore of Llyn Padarn, using steam locomotives dating from 1889 to 1948. Ideal for those who want the steamtrain experience but don't want to spend too long getting it. Meals, snacks, shop, disabled access, but no wheelchairs on the train; cl Nov–Feb; (01286) 870549 for timetable; £3.60. The station is set in a super lakeside park, with walks through ancient woodland, also home to the Welsh Slate Museum – until it closed in 1969 one of the biggest quarries in the country. The quarry workshop has been preserved largely in its original state – complete with working craftsmen and machinery, inc the foundry and the Dinorwic waterwheel, one of the largest in the world. Shop, disabled access; cl Oct–Easter (though they may let you see the site if passing); (01286) 870360; £1.50. Power of Wales Purpose-built centre which serves as a prelude to a tour of the Dinorwic power station, with a hi-tech presentation on the theme of 'power' in Wales, taking in Druids, Romans, Owen Glyndwr, and, of course, the pumped storage generating station itself. After the film, a coach whisks you off for a tour of the spectacular station (one of Europe's biggest), deep in the mountain. Snacks, shop, disabled access (24 hours' notice for wheelchairs in the power station); cl wknds Dec–Jan; 01286 870636; *£5. Snowdon Honey Farm Demonstrations of honey-making, videos on beekeeping, and lots of bees safely behind glass. Teas, shop, some disabled access; cl wkdys Nov–Easter; (01286) 870218; £2.50.

Dolbadarn Castle Overlooking Llyn Peris at the foot of the Llanberis Pass (A4086), this castle was built in the early 13th c by Llewellyn the Great – it has a fine round keep. Cl am Sun winter; £1. Just N of town is a modern working pottery. Cl Christmas wk; (01286) 872529; free. Another good spot for Snowdon walks is the Pen-y-Gwryd at Nant Gwynant to the E; also a pleasant place for lunch.

🏛Llandaniel Fab SH5070 Bryn Celli Ddu Restored, Neolithic, passage burial chamber built over a previous stone circle, at the end of a long tunnel, with a carved stone over a burial pit; locked, but the key at a

nearby farmhouse; free. Take a torch.
★ ☺ ♪ ❀ ✝ ⊟ ᕫ Llandudno SH7881
The main holiday town in the area,
and though it does have a well
sheltered, long curve of good, pebbly
beach, a promenade and a reasonable
range of resort entertainments, it
doesn't feel at all brash. This is largely
because from the beginning it was laid
out to follow a careful 19th-c design
which has preserved a unified
character and a sense of style and
spaciousness ever since. There are
charming little shops and boutiques, a
well restored pier (from where you
can fish), and cable cars as well as the
famous tramway up the massive
Great Orme headland which protects
the main beach – there's a quieter but
more exposed beach on the far side.
Climbing up to the summit yourself is
much more fun (a couple of cafés en
route have views to justify stopping),
and when you get there, there's a
12th-c church and a visitor centre
with local geology. Up here the GREAT
ORME MINES go back 4,000 years –
they're the only prehistoric mine
workings open to the public, and the
biggest such site so far discovered.
Displays of finds, an audio-visual
exhibition, and guided underground
walks through the cavernous, former
copper workings themselves. Teas,
shop, disabled access (not
underground); cl Dec and Jan;
(01492) 870447; *£3.80. Back in
town, the RABBIT HOLE is a rather jolly
exhibition devoted to *Alice in
Wonderland*; the real Alice holidayed
in Llandudno as a child. Shop,
disabled access; cl winter Suns, 2 wks
Nov; *£2.30. The CONWY VALLEY
RAILWAY, a BR line from here to
Blaenau Ffestiniog, runs through
magnificent scenery and has several
useful stops en route. The Queen's
Head at Glanwydden, off the Colwyn
Bay road, does very good food.
❀ ᕫ 🎦 ⊛ ❀ Llanfairpwllgwyngyllgog-
erychwyrndrobwllllantysiliogogogoch
SH5372 Excellent views of
Snowdonia and the Menai Strait from
the top of the Marquess of Anglesey's
column, built in 1816 to
commemorate the military
achievements of Wellington's second
in command at the Battle of Waterloo;

60p. Fine mountain views, too, from
his creeper-covered, former home
PLAS NEWYDD, a couple of miles from
the village; an elegant 18th-c mansion
best known for its mural by Rex
Whistler. There are a number of other
works by the painter as well, along
with a military museum showing
relics from Waterloo. Also, a good
spring garden with rhododendrons.
Meals, snacks, shop, some disabled
access; cl am, Sat, Oct (exc Fri and
Sun), Nov–Mar; £3.80; NT. Locals
generally shorten their village's
remarkable name to Llanfair PG, or
Llanfairpwll. The nearby village of
Penmynydd was the ancient home of
the Tudor family. The Liverpool
Arms at Menai Bridge is the nearest
good place for lunch.
♭ 🏛 Llangefni SH4676 Right in the
centre of Anglesey, with a big, open-
air market every Thurs. ORIEL YNYS
MON Gallery with imaginative
displays on the history of the island, as
well as a collection of wildlife
paintings by C F Tunnicliffe. Snacks,
shop, disabled access; cl Mon (exc
bank hols); (01248) 724444; £2.
✝ 🏰 ❀ ᕫ ⚑ ✹ ⚓ Llangollen SJ2141 is
not special in itself despite a good few
solid and gracious, Georgian and
Victorian villas; what makes it
attractive is its charming valley setting
above the River Dee; it has discreet
hotels that cater for the generally
older people to whom the area most
appeals – though comes vividly alive
during the Eisteddfod. VALLE CRUCIS
ABBEY (A542, N) Substantial remains
of the early 13th-c abbey church, and
some beautifully carved grave slabs.
Shop, limited disabled access; cl am
Sun, 24–26 Dec, 1 Jan; £1.50. The
ruins stand at the bottom of the
Horseshoe Pass, a nerve-rackingly
steep mountain drive offering superb
views; the Britannia, just above the
abbey, has decent food and
exceptional views. PLAS NEWYDD Lady
Eleanor Butler and Sarah Ponsonby,
the 'ladies of Llangollen', lived here
from 1780 to 1831. The beautiful,
half-timbered house has stained glass,
leather wall coverings and the
domestic paraphernalia of the period.
Shop, disabled access to ground floor
only; cl Nov–Mar; £1.70. LLANGOLLEN

RAILWAY Until it closed in 1968 this 5-mile stretch was part of the Great Western Railway; now restored, with steam and diesel trains from the pleasantly preserved station to the village of Glyndyfrdwy up the Dee (the Bedwyn Arms in a lovely setting above the river does food). By Easter they hope to have extended the line a little further. There's a special coach for the disabled (you have to book). Snacks, shop; cl 25 Dec – trains don't usually run Jan–Mar, (01978) 860951 for timetable; £5 full return fare, less for a shorter trip, and 50p for just the old station. CANAL EXHIBITION CENTRE (The Wharf) Interesting and imaginative displays on the history of canals in Wales, with a useful audio-visual display. Meals, snacks, shop, disabled access; cl Weds in Apr, Thurs and Fri in Oct, all Nov–Mar; (01978) 860702; £1. They organise HORSE-DRAWN BOAT TRIPS along the Vale of Llangollen; £2. The Pontcysyllte aqueduct (off A5/A539, E) is very spectacular to cross – by boat or on foot. The Abbey Grange Hotel and the Sun Trevor, high over the valley at nearby Trevor Uchaf, are good for lunch.

✝ Llangybi SH4241 ST CYBI'S WELL Known to the Welsh as Fynnon Gybi, this has been reckoned to have healing properties for over a thousand years. St Cybi was a 6th-c Cornish saint, known as a healer of the sick. Look out for the corbelled beehive vaulting inside the roofless stone structure, which is Irish in style.

❁ ❧ ❁ Llanrug SH5462 BRYN BRAS Lovely gardens and grounds covering 32 acres around a striking, 19th-c, Romanesque castle. Spacious lawns, walled knot garden, hill and woodland walks, and good views to Snowdon. You can stay in quite luxurious suites in the castle (all year). Good teas (on the lawn), shop; open pm Tues–Fri and bank hols (exc summer hols) from spring bank hol–mid-Sept; (01286) 870210; *£3.50. The village itself is not specially appealing but the Glyntwrog is useful for food.

★ ✝ Llanrwst SH8061 Pretty little town with an old stone bridge over the Conwy river, said to be the work of Inigo Jones. GWYDIR CHAPEL, added by the influential Wynn family to the parish church in the 17th c, has a stone coffin reputedly that of Llewellyn the Great, as well as a magnificent rood screen from the ruins of Maenan Abbey. The Wynns also constructed the nearby GWYDIR UCHAF CHAPEL, with intriguing ceiling paintings. The Priory Hotel (A470, N) is useful for lunch.

❧ ❁ Llanuwchllyn SH8730 BALA LAKE RAILWAY Some of the carriages on trains using this delightful 4½-mile route are open to the elements, which seems to make the views of the lake and mountains more vivid. The locomotives were once used to haul slate in the N Wales quarries. Meals, snacks, shop, disabled access (but no facilities); cl occasionally Mon and Fri in Apr and Sept, all Nov–Mar; (016784) 666; £4.80. The Olde Bull's Head in Bala is quite useful for lunch.

⌂ ♨ ❧ ☛ Llanystumdwy SH4738 LLOYD GEORGE MEMORIAL MUSEUM Audio-visual displays and memorabilia relating to the life of Lloyd George, whose family moved here from Manchester when he was a boy. They lived in nearby Highgate Cottage, which has been restored to the way it was then, and has a neat Victorian garden. Shop, disabled access; cl am wknds, Nov–Easter, exc by appointment; (01766) 522071; £2.10. It's a short stroll from here to the site where he's buried. Just up the hill, children should enjoy the RABBIT FARM, which as well as around 700 rabbits has other animals and pony rides. (01766) 523136; cl Nov–Easter; £2.

✿ Menai Bridge SH5572 takes its name from Thomas Telford's magnificent suspension bridge linking Anglesey to the mainland, the first such iron bridge in the world. BUTTERFLY PALACE Exotic butterflies from all corners of the globe, as well as a bird house, insectarium, reptile house, and an adventure playground. Meals, snacks, shop, disabled access; cl Jan and Feb; (01248) 712474; £3.25. The waterside Liverpool Arms has good-value, fresh food.

✝ Mold SJ2464 has a richly decorated parish CHURCH, built to commemorate the victory of Henry Tudor at Bosworth Field in 1485. The We Three Loggerheads in a lovely setting out on the Ruthin road has good food. ✗ ✿ ⋒ **Penmachno** SH7950 PENMACHNO WOOLLEN MILL Timeless watermill powered by the River Machno, with local weavers explaining and demonstrating the history and craft of the cottage weaving industry. The setting is lovely. Snacks, good shop; cl 25 Dec; (01690) 710545; free. TY'N Y COED Fully furnished, 19th-c farmhouse showing the traditional way of life in this area. Open pm Thurs, Fri and Sun Apr–Sept; £1.50; NT. TY MAWR (Wybrnant, on forest rd, W of village) Picturesque, lonely, thick-walled medieval cottage, birthplace of Bishop William Morgan who first translated the Bible into Welsh (see St Asaph entry below). It's been restored to how it was in the 16th c. Shop, disabled access; open pm Thurs–Sun Apr–Sept, plus pm Fri and Sun Oct; *£1.50; NT.

∀ ☛ **Penmaenpool** SH6918 has a small nature reserve, and a very useful nature information centre which will direct you to promising places throughout this whole area, which has good walks. About a mile away, Abergwynant Farm (on the A493) has a PONY TREKKING CENTRE which will take beginners out for an hour over scenic routes; you can stay here too. (01341) 422377; from £7.50. The George III is a pleasant place for lunch.

⋒ ❀ ⋒ **Plas yn Rhiw** SH2532 PLAS YN RHIW Charming if unassuming little manor house, worth a visit for the gardens and woodland, inc a waterfall, snowdrop wood and subtropical specimens. Shop, limited disabled access; cl am, Sat, Nov–Apr; £2.30; NT. The setting is lovely, overlooking one of the area's wildest coasts. The Glyn-y-Weddw at Llanbedrog is quite handy for lunch.

⛟ ☛ ⋒ **Porthmadog** SH5638 is quite a busy shopping town of low, slate-roofed houses, with a spacious harbour. The famous narrow-gauge FFESTINIOG RAILWAY was opened in 1836 to carry slate from Blaenau Ffestiniog to Porthmadog by gravity.

Shut down in 1946, it reopened in 1955 and has gradually been extended to climb the 13¼ miles to Blaenau Ffestiniog. Meals, snacks, shop, some disabled access; cl wkdys Nov–Feb (exc school hols); fares vary up to £11.60. The adjacent FFESTINIOG RAILWAY MUSEUM tells the story of the railway, with exhibits inc a four-wheeled hearse converted from an old quarryman's coach, a slate wagon, and one of the original steam locos from 1863; opening times as railway. The railway links with the British Rail Cambrian Coast Line, hugging the coast from Pwllheli to Machynlleth, with many stops along the way. Overshadowed by its more famous neighbour in size but certainly not in spirit is the WELSH HIGHLAND RAILWAY (opposite the BR station), an enthusiastically restored line with big plans for expansion; their eventual aim is to run up to Caernarfon. The current 35-minute round trip includes a stop at their locomotive storage sheds. Snacks, shop; trains daily summer hols and most Suns Apr–Oct, (01766) 513402 for timetable; *£1.25. POTTERY (Snowdon Mill) You can watch pottery being made here and even make a piece yourself. Also displays on the history of pottery and a mural illustrating the town's history. Shop, very good disabled access; cl wknds exc July, Aug and bank hols, check for winter opening; (01766) 512137; 50p, £2.50 for activities. The Ship has decent food, as does the Golden Fleece in nearby Tremadog.

★ ⋒ ❀ ⋒ ! ❈ **Portmeirion** SH5937 On the steep, wooded shores of an inlet from Tremadog Bay, this fairy-tale holiday village, designed by Welsh architect Sir Clough Williams Ellis, is set in 175 acres of lush, coastal cliff and woodland gardens. Quite charming, it's an Italianate folly – pastel-washed cottages interlaced with grottoes, cobbled squares, also a bell tower, castle, lighthouse, and long, picturesque flights of steps zigzagging down to the water, which at low tide dries to miles of sand. The central hotel building has a library which was originally in the Great Exhibition of 1851 in London.

Enveloping the village are the 60 acres of Gwyllt gardens, with fine displays of rhododendrons, azaleas, hydrangeas and subtropical flora; good, wild woodlands, too. You have to pay a toll to enter the village, but once in can see the house where Noel Coward wrote *Blithe Spirit* and the locations for the cult TV series *The Prisoner*, while children can play in the playground, on a make-believe schooner apparently moored by the hotel, or, tide permitting, on the beach. A lovely relaxing place, quite unlike anywhere else. Meals, snacks, shops; (01766) 770228; £3, less Nov–Mar. The ancestral home of Williams Ellis was PLAS BRONDANW at nearby Llanfrothen SH6142, which has an architectural garden he designed to please the eye and give the best possible views; (01766) 771136; £1.50.

Prestatyn SJ0783 Bustling seaside resort standing at one end of the 168-mile route of Offa's Dyke, marked by a stone pillar above the main beach.

🏰 🏠 ❀ ✝ **Rhuddlan** SJ0878 Once a busy port, now a sleepy little town with a fine old CASTLE adapted by Edward I from an earlier Norman structure. It was from here that the King organised the administration of Wales. Overlooking the river, it's a pretty spot. Cl Oct–Apr; £1.50. Slightly E on the road to Dyserth, BODRHYDDAN HALL has been the home of the Constable of Rhuddlan Castle for centuries. It's got a lovely doll's-house front, and some wonderfully elaborate fireplaces in the drawing room, as well as a formal French garden and an interesting well-house built by Inigo Jones. Teas, disabled access to ground floor only; open pm Tues and Thurs Jun–Sept; (01745) 590414; *£2. Follow the road through to Dyserth and there's a partly 13th-c parish church (with Jesse window), and a plunging 60ft waterfall. The 16th-c Blue Lion at Cwm has decent food.

👤 🎣 **Rhyl** SJ0181 is an often rather brash seaside resort, but if you're passing with children, the Knight's Cavern, a lively interpretation of Welsh history, should amuse them. There's also one of the SEA LIFE CENTRES that we've described elsewhere, with a dramatic Shark Encounter as well as the usual, walk-through underwater tunnel. Meals, snacks, shop, disabled access; cl 25 Dec; (01745) 344660; £4.25.

✝ 👤 **St Asaph** SJ0475 Tiny little city with the smallest CATHEDRAL in Britain, founded in 537. A column in the grounds commemorates its most famous cleric – Bishop Morgan (see Penmachno entry above) and his work translating the Bible into Welsh. There's also a little museum with finds from the site. The Farmer's Arms (The Waen) does proper food.

🦅 🏛 **South Stack** SH2082 The spectacular cliffs nr the lighthouse are full of seabird breeding colonies, and there's a 780-acre RSPB RESERVE, where you may be able to see guillemots, razorbills and puffins (especially around May, Jun and July). Lots of colourful wild flowers too, and maybe the odd seal. The visitor centre has closed-circuit TV pictures of nesting birds; guided walks leave here at 2pm Tues and Sat May–Aug. Visitor centre cl mid-Sept–Easter; (01407) 764973; free. Nearby is a large group of the foundations of HUT CIRCLES, probably around 2,000 years old, still with some visible traces of stone sleeping slabs.

❀ **Tal y Cafn** SH8072 BODNANT GARDEN Started in 1875 but improved in 1900 (and indeed ever since, in the hands of the green-fingered family which has owned them), these gardens are among Britain's greatest. Part of the 80-acre grounds have a beautiful woodland garden in a sheltered valley, notable for its rhododendrons and azaleas, while below the house are five terraces in the Italian style, with a canal pool and an open-air stage on the lowest. Many fine rare plants inc unusual trees and shrubs. Meals, snacks, shop, disabled access (but it is steep in places); cl Nov–mid-Mar; £3.60; NT. The Ferry and Tal-y-Cafn Inn are useful for lunch, and also in this lovely valley are the ancient Groes Inn at Tyn-y-Groes, and the Olde Bull in a delightful setting on the hillside opposite at Llanbedr-y-Cennin, both with good food.

🏠 ❀ 👤 ✝ **Trefriw** SH7863 TREFRIW WOOLLEN MILL The same family have run this woollen mill for 135 years; two hydroelectric turbines are driven by the fast-flowing Afon Crafnant, and there's a weaver's garden growing plants traditionally used by textile craft-workers (best Jun–Sept). They have weaving demonstrations in the turbine house wkdys all year (even Nov–Easter when the mill itself is closed), as well as most Sats and summer Suns. Maybe spinning demonstrations too in summer, so worth checking first to see exactly what's going on. Snacks, shop (selling tapestries and tweeds made here), disabled access; (01492) 640462; free. Trefriw used to be a spa, and you can still see the WELLS on the northern outskirts of the village. The village also has a 14th-c church; the Black Lion and Lodge at Tal y Bont both have good home-cooking.

✝ 🏠 ✿ ↧ ♄ **Wrexham** SJ3248 is an industrial town; the 15th-c CHURCH is worth a look, with its magnificent steeple. ERDDIG (just S of town) Superb late 17th-c house, especially interesting for the way you can explore the life of those 'upstairs' and 'downstairs' just as thoroughly; the gallery of servants' portraits is especially touching. Enlarged and improved in the early 18th c, the house is filled with splendid original furnishings, inc a magnificent state bed in Chinese silk. Restored outbuildings include a laundry, bakehouse, estate smithy and sawmill, and the surrounding parkland is very pleasant to stroll through. It's one of the most attractive places to visit in all of Wales. Meals, snacks, shop, disabled access with prior notice; cl Thurs and Fri, and Nov–Easter; *£5 all inclusive, belowstairs tour *£3; NT. BERSHAM

INDUSTRIAL HERITAGE CENTRE (Bersham, 2 m, W) Well re-created, 18th-c ironworks, along with a good overview of other local industries, and demonstrations of various traditional skills. Snacks, shop, limited disabled access; heritage centre cl am wknds, ironworks cl am and Oct–Easter; (01978) 261529; £1. The Boat at Erbistock on the Dee, a few miles S of Erddig, has been good for lunch.

★ **Attractive villages** in the area, all with decent pubs but in general tending to appeal for their surroundings more than for the beauty of their buildings, include Capel Curig SH7258 (pleasant walks here), Cilcain SJ1865, Erbistock SJ3542, Halkyn SJ2172, Hanmer SJ4639, Llanarmon DC SJ1633, Llandwrog SH4456, Llangedwyn SJ1924 in the Tanat Valley, Llansannan SH9466, Pontblyddyn SJ2761 and Porth Dinllaen SH2741 (an idyllic seaside spot, but you have to walk to it). Other pubs and inns in scenic areas or with notable views include the Porth Tocyn Hotel, above the sea at Abersoch SH3128, Sportsman's Arms up on the A543, S of Bylchau SH9863, White Horse at Capel Garmon SH8155, Grouse at Carrog SJ1144, T'yn-y-Groes at Ganllwyd SH7224, Eagle & Child in the hilltop village of Gwaenysgor SJ0881, the Druid at Llanferres SJ1961 (doing well under new management), Cross Foxes on the Dee at Overton Bridge SJ3643, the Ship, by acres of sand on the shore of Red Wharf Bay SH5281, Cwellyn Arms at Rhyd-ddu SH5753 (big playground), White Eagle on Holy Island at Rhoscolyn SH2676 and Caerffynon Hall at Talsarnau SH6236.

Walks

This area has plenty of fine walking, both gentle and taxing – somewhere to justify a walking holiday.

Snowdonia's main mountain group soars dramatically, many of its peaks having easily identifiable shapes (if you can see them at all through the mist). **Snowdon** SH6054 △-1, the highest mountain in England or Wales, has a number of ways up ranging from the easy path alongside the mountain railway to the enthralling Horseshoe Route, which makes its way along knifeedge ridges; the Pyg Track and Watkin Path are among the favourites. For a taster of the mountain without actually going up it, follow the start of the

Miner's Track (from the Pen-y-pass car park on the A4086), which really is a track as far as Glaslyn, the last of four lakes passed. Recommended lower-level rambles include the **reservoirs** N of Capel Curig SH4682 ⌂-2, the nature trail around **Llyn Idwal** SH6459 ⌂-3 (a superbly sited lake beneath Glyder Fach), the **Aberglaslyn Pass** SH5947 ⌂-4 S of Beddgelert, and the signposted **Precipice Walk** SH7321 ⌂-5 N of Dolgellau SH7318. There's a pleasant riverside stroll along the old railway track by the Afon Llugwy, W from Betws-y-Coed SH7956, and you can walk along the shores of Bala Lake SH9134.

Much of the coast is built up or ribboned by roads. Notable exceptions giving good walks are **Great Orme Head** SH7683 ⌂-6 (quaintly reachable by a steep tram from Llandudno), **Conwy Mountain** SH7577 ⌂-7 (not a real mountain but with views of Anglesey worthy of mountain status), and **Lavan Sands** SH6376 ⌂-8, nr Aber SH6573. The very unspoilt **Lleyn Peninsula** ⌂-9 has an 1,849ft mountain, Yr Eifl SH3644 (the Rivals), close to the coast. The **peninsula tip** ⌂-10 has some nice coastal walks starting W from Aberdaron SH1726, and E of here is the spectacular bay of Hell's Mouth SH2626 (decent pub food at the Sun in Llanengan).

Castell Dinas Bran SJ2243 ⌂-11 in Clwyd is the place to head for from Llangollen SJ2142. The hill fort site commands views over the vale and is close by the Panorama Walk (actually a surfaced minor road). **Moel Fammau** SJ1663 ⌂-12 is the highest point of the Clwydian range, a bulging massif with clearly marked paths; walk up from the car park through colour-coded forest trails or over open land, for views of much of Snowdonia, the edge of the Peak District and the Wirral.

Anglesey is too flat to offer much interest inland, but its lovely beaches, as at **Newborough Warren** SH4263 ⌂-13, are satisfying enough. Paths intermittently follow the indented coastline around Amlwch SH4493. **Holyhead Mountain** SH2182 ⌂-14 is a dramatic hill at the W tip of Holy Island.

Driving

This area, criss-crossed with roads that are excellent for country drives, has superb possibilities for a touring holiday or for day and half-day outings. The main routes attract a great many touring visitors, by car, coach and caravan, so in high season you will find quite a lot of traffic on these main roads, and quite a lot of touristy things by the roadside. But it's easy to forge off into lovely areas which get less attention, and outside high summer even the trunk roads through the area settle down into an altogether more relaxed pace of life. In poor weather the higher routes do get quickly swathed in mist.

Around Snowdon, the A4086, A498 and A4805 are all very splendid. The roads through the rich Vale of Conwy are not to be missed, with broad hill views all around. The A5 across the area must rank as the most scenic of all single-figure trunk roads, though the scenery, combining mountains with rivers and grand fir forests, is even better on the A470 trunk road (not too busy except in high summer) S from Betws-y-Coed to Dolgellau. (On this road, if you're heading S, as you come to the end of the Trawsfynydd lake on your right and cross the river bridge, the second left turn takes you along a lane which in about 2½ miles gives access to an enormously tall standing stone out on the moor quite nr the road.)

The A499 down into the quiet landscapes of the Lleyn Peninsula, and the B4417 continuing along its N coast, is a more scenic route than the A497 on its S side.

The A494 up to Bala is a striking valley road, with high mountains above it. Lake Vyrnwy has more character than Bala Lake, even though it's a reservoir and the pine-forested landscape around it is largely an artificial creation of the 1880s. The hotel here has decent food and great views. Good B roads lead to it, and there's a fiercely steep back road through dramatic passes between its W end and Dinas Mawddwy – a rewarding, adventurous drive for the steely-nerved.

The A487 between Dolgellau and Machynlleth has some attractive scenery, particularly around Corris; the dead-end side road up past Corris itself takes you into a charming, peaceful valley.

Though it's a there-and-back drive, when the high mountain snows are melting in spring or after heavy rain it's worth taking the back road from Llanrhaeadr-ym-Mochnant up to Tan-y-Pistyll to see the remarkably high waterfall of Pistyll Rhaeadr. Another road into equally quiet but higher country is the B4501 up around Llyn Brenig.

The area around Llangollen has some fine drives; the A542 N has some memorable mountain views, and to the S, the B4500 from Chirk to Llanarmon DC and beyond takes you into extremely tranquil countryside, a beautifully secluded valley. The roads around the Clwydian Hills, inc the B5429 and even the trunk A494 between Mold and Ruthin, are filled with pleasant views.

The A496/A493 coast roads are for the most part undramatic; the best parts are around the Mawddach estuary, and along the tidal flats of the Dovey estuary around Aberdovey. Above here, the back road cutting off the Aberdovey 'corner' of the A493 runs prettily through the so-called Happy Valley, below high hills.

Driving on Anglesey is not memorable in its own right.

Reasonably good roads mean that from Llandudno in the N, say, one can get to almost any part of even this large area in little more than 1½ hours. The A55 across the N coast has improved dramatically in the last few years, and is now largely dual carriageway all the way to Bangor.

Where to eat

Pwllheli SH3735 Plas Bodegroes (01758) 612363 Lovely, Georgian manor house surrounded by tree-filled grounds, with comfortably restful rooms, good food using superb, fresh local produce and a very fine wine list; bedrooms; cl Mon, Nov–Feb; disabled access in restaurant only. **£36 for 5 courses.**

Llanberis SH5760 Y Bistro 43–45 High St (01286) 871278 Friendly, no-smoking restaurant with good local produce used in the Welsh cooking – fine fish; cl Sun and Mon in winter. **£26.50.**

Llandudno Junction SH8180 Queens Head (01492) 546570 Busy but comfortable pub, lots of very nice seafood, excellent, home-made puddings, good daily specials, interesting evening extras, and decent wines; cl 25 Dec; children over 7. **£17.75|£3/£5.30.**

Morfa Nefyn SH2840 Bryncynan Gwynedd (01758) 720879 Comfortable and friendly country pub which is buzzing in summer, quiet in winter (nice log fires); quickly served bar food from soup through fish pie and summer seafood to steaks, and good restaurant food; cl Sun, 25 Dec. **£16/£6.50.**

Mold SJ1962 We Three Loggerheads (01352) 810337 Carefully and interestingly refurbished old pub on two levels, with a wide choice of very imaginative and well presented bar food, decent wines, and well kept real ales; cl pm 25 Dec. **£16|£2.95/£5.20.**

Bala SH9236 Neuadd-Y-Cyfnod (Old School Restaurant) High St (01678) 521269 Relaxed and informal restaurant with huge helpings of good-value food (morning coffee, lunch, tea and dinner), pleasant service, and attractive furnishings; cl Nov–Mar (open from Easter); disabled access. **£12|£1.75/£3.95.**

Llanwnda SH4758 Goat (01286) 830256 Old-fashioned, genuinely Welsh pub with an excellent, help-yourself, cold lunchtime buffet Easter–Sept – £5 eat as much as you like.

WEST WALES

Fine, unspoilt coast and interesting places to potter around: great for a quiet, relaxing break.

The best of the scenery here is on the coast, which has many extremely attractive stretches and plenty of first-class walking in the Pembrokeshire Coast National Park. In the south this is very gentle, with level cliffs, intricate estuaries and some lovely sandy beaches as around the civilised small resort of Tenby – formerly a well fortified, medieval town. In the west and north it's much more rugged, with dolphins this last summer as well as seals, and particularly appealing between St David's and Strumble Head near Fishguard (largely unspoilt, full of rocky coves and exhilarating cliff walks), around St Brides Bay (low cliffs flanking surfing beaches), by the picturesque fishing villages of Solva and Little Haven, and in the wild places around Marloes. The Park also includes the blustery Prescelly Hills and the secluded Gwaun Valley.

St David's is the most interesting place to visit, with its cathedral a real surprise in such rural surroundings, and a good few things to look at nearby. Kidwelly, Carew and Pembroke are the most impressive of the many castles. Though there is not a large number of other places to visit, and virtually no bright-lights attractions, there's plenty to fill a short stay, with highlights including boat trips to the offshore islands (seabirds and seals), the ancient gold mines at Pumsaint, the woodland garden at Amroth and (new to this edition of the *Guide*) the farmhouse cheese-maker near Castle Morris. It's quite a good area for families, with particular attractions at Narberth and St Florence.

On the whole, the inland scenery here, though unspoilt, is less interesting than the coast – mainly pastoral farmland – so there aren't the dramatic scenic drives of North and Mid-Wales, but there is a reasonable amount of pleasant, gentle motoring. The best parts are around Brechfa and Abergorlech.

Prices in this area are comparatively low – good value for money; decent food has to be searched out.

Where to stay

Penally SS1199 PENALLY ABBEY Penally, Tenby, Dyfed SA70 7PY (01834) 843033 £84; 12 pretty rms, many with 4-poster beds, and 4 in coach house. Gothic-style, country-house hotel in 5 acres of gardens and woodlands with fine views across the golf course and Carmarthen Bay; open fire in the comfortable lounge, tiny bar, conservatory, very good food in the elegant, candlelit restaurant, delicious breakfasts, small indoor swimming pool, snooker, and croquet; children over 7 in restaurant; disabled access.

St David's SM7525 WARPOOL COURT St David's, Haverfordwest, Dyfed SA62 6BN (01437) 720300 £79; 25 rms. Originally built as St David's Cathedral School in the 1860s and bordering National Trust land, this popular hotel enjoys lovely views over St Brides Bay; Ada Williams' collection of lovely, hand-painted tiles can be seen in the comfortable public rooms, food in the spacious, elegant restaurant is imaginative, and staff are helpful and friendly; quiet gardens, heated summer swimming pool, tennis, excercise room, table tennis, pool, croquet, and free golf at St David's golf club; cl Jan.

Broad Haven SM8614 DRUIDSTONE Broad Haven, Haverfordwest, Dyfed SA62 3NE (01437) 781221 *£60; 9 rms sharing bthrms (and 4 holiday cottages, 2 with wheelchair access). Alone on the coast, above an effectively private beach with exhilarating cliff walks, this roomy and very informal, friendly hotel with something of a folk-club and 'outward bound' feel at times, is extremely winning and relaxing if you take to its unique combination of good, wholesome and often memorably inventive food, slightly fend-for-yourself approach amid elderly furniture, and glorious seaside surroundings. All sorts of unusual sporting activities inc sand-yachting. Restaurant cl pm Sun; restricted opening times 6 wks each side of Christmas – phone for details; don't go on spec – strongly advised to book for accommodation and meals, as often fully booked; disabled access (see above).

Crugybar SN6537 GLANRANNELL PARK Crugybar, Llanwrda, Dyfed SA19 8SA (01558) 685230 *£56; 8 rms. Surrounded by lawns and overlooking a small private lake in 23 acres of parkland, this peaceful hotel has two comfortable lounges and a small library, a well stocked bar, good food using fresh local produce when possible, and friendly, helpful staff; lots of wildlife, pony-trekking, and fishing; cl 30 Oct–1 Apr.

Newport SN0539 CNAPAN East St, Newport, Dyfed SA42 0WF (01239) 820575 £46; 5 rms. Attractively furnished and homely, little family-run hotel with very friendly owners, decent food (lots of vegetarian dishes), and a relaxed atmosphere; lovely countryside and coastal walks nearby; cl 24–26 Dec, Feb; in winter, except for residents, the restaurant's open only at wknds.

Pontfaen SN0134 TREGYNON COUNTRY FARMHOUSE Pontfaen, Gwaun Valley, Fishguard, Dyfed SA65 9TU (01239) 820531 £46; 8 rms. Peacefully set, 16th-c farmhouse on the edge of a valley in lovely, unspoilt countryside with lots of wildlife and walks, big inglenook fireplace in the beamed lounge, a friendly welcome, and very good, imaginative additive-free food using their own and produce from neighbouring farms, home-smoked meats and home-made preserves; cl 2 wks in winter; disabled access.

Carew SN0403 OLD STABLE COTTAGE Carew, Tenby, Dyfed SA70 8SL (01646) 651889 £45; 3 rms. Originally a stable and carthouse for the castle, this attractive place has an inglenook fireplace and an original bread oven, a games room, conservatory overlooking the garden, and good, Aga-cooked food; cl Dec–Feb; children over 10.

Nevern SN0840 TREWERN ARMS Nevern, Newport, Dyfed SA42 0NB (01239) 820395 £45; 9 rms. Welcoming, creeper-clad, old inn in a pleasant riverside hamlet nr the interesting pilgrims' church; with a very warm welcome, interestingly decorated, slate-floored bar, good, generously served food, and well kept real ales.

Fishguard SM9537 MANOR HOUSE Fishguard, Dyfed SA65 9HG (01348) 873260 £42; 7 comfortable rms, most with own bthrm. Georgian house with fine views of the harbour, a well planned basement restaurant with a good choice of international, home-made food using fresh local produce; cl 24–28 Dec.

Fishguard SM9537 GILFACH GOCH FARM Fishguard, Dyfed SA65 9SR (01348) 873871 £40; 6 rms, 3 with own bthrm. Traditional and carefully modernised, 18th-c Welsh stone farmhouse on a 10-acre smallholding with sheep, donkeys, a Vietnamese pot-bellied pig, dogs, cats, and fowl; lovely views, log fires, a homely lounge, good country cooking using many home-produced ingredients, and a safe garden for children; no smoking; cl Nov–Easter.

Pen-y-Cwm SM8423 LOCHMEYLER FARM Pen-y-Cwm, Llandeloy, Haverfordwest, Dyfed SA62 6LL (01348) 837724 *£40; 10 rms. Attractive, 16th-c farmhouse on a 220-acre working dairy farm; two lounges (one is no smoking), log fires, traditional farmhouse cooking in the pleasant dining room, and a mature garden; can walk around the farm trails; children over 10; disabled access.

Spittal SM9723 Lower Haythog Spittal, Haverfordwest, Dyfed SA62 5QL (01437) 731279 £40; 7 rms. Centuries-old farmhouse on a working dairy farm set in 250 acres of unspoilt countryside; with a comfortable lounge, log fires, books and games, traditional breakfasts, good cooking in the dining room, and friendly owners; swing and slide in the garden, trout ponds in the woods; cl Christmas; disabled access.

Brechfa SN5230 Forest Arms Brechfa, Carmarthen, Dyfed SA32 7RA (01267) 202339 £36; 4 comfortable, good-value rms, shared bthrm. Simply renovated and spotless, stone-built village inn with generous home-cooking, an unusually big inglenook fireplace in the flagstoned bar, quick, cheerful, family service, lovely walking and wildlife around.

Rhydlewis SN3447 Broniwan Rhydlewis, Llandysul, Dyfed SA44 5PF (01239) 851261 *£33; 3 pretty rms, 2 with own bthrm. Grey stone house with pine-panelled windows, on a small farm surrounded by beech and pine trees, with fine views of the Prescelly Hills in the distance; lots of wildlife, sandy coast within 10 minutes' drive, you can help with calves, hens, and cows; also, a stone barn with games, table tennis and books; woodburning stove in the comfortable sitting room, a separate dining room, and good, naturally produced food from the garden and farm (inc vegetarian dishes); no smoking; children over 5.

To see and do

❀ ♤ **Amroth** SN1508 has a lovely beach; the New Inn facing it has good home-cooking inc local seafood. Colby Woodland Garden Beautiful woodland gardens in a sheltered valley – very pleasant and colourful, especially in autumn. A walled garden with Gothic gazebo is open from Apr. Snacks, shop, limited disabled access; cl Nov–Mar; £2.50; NT.

☛ **Begelly** SN1107 Folly Farm Busy, working dairy farm, with the chance to milk a cow – or watch the more modern methods in the milking parlour. They make sure everyone gets a chance to bottle-feed some of the friendly animals. Snacks, shop, disabled access; cl Nov–Easter; (01834) 812731; £3. There's good fresh fish at the Royal Oak down in the quiet, extended, seaside village of Saundersfoot, which has a lighthouse on the spit sheltering the harbour.

✝ ❀ **Bosherston** SR9694 St Govan's Chapel Simple, recently reroofed, 14th-c ruin, included for its exciting position halfway down the sea cliffs, down rough rock steps; the former holy well just below has now dried up. The Lily Ponds, here since monastic times and an easy walk from the village car park, are a fine sight when in bloom in summer; free, NT. The St Govan's pub is useful for lunch.

▟ ✖ **Carew** SN0403 Carew Castle and Tidal Mill This magnificent Norman castle was the setting for the Great Tournament of 1507. Its ivy-clad, SE tower is especially handsome. The mill is one of just three restored tidal mills in Britain, with records dating back to 1558, and has an exhibition on the story of milling. Shop, limited disabled access; cl Nov–Mar; (01646) 651782; £2 both, £1.40 each. By the good Carew Inn nearby is the Carew Cross, an impressive 13ft Celtic cross dating from the 11th c.

▟ ⌂ ♨ ❀ ➤ **Carmarthen** SN4120 Busy, regional market town, according to legend the birthplace of Merlin: an old tree once stood in the centre and the saying was 'When Merlin's oak shall tumble down, then shall fall Carmarthen town'. Nothing gets in the way of modern road-planners and down came the tree – it's preserved in a glass case, but some still say modern additions to the town have fulfilled the prophecy. There are the remains of a 13th-c castle, and on Priory St, an unusual, 2nd-c Roman amphitheatre. Just out of town at Abergwili SN4321, a former palace of the Bishop of St David's is now the good CARMARTHEN MUSEUM, in 7 acres of attractive grounds. Shop, disabled access to ground floor only; cl Sun, 24 Dec–1 Jan, Good Fri; (01267) 231691; 50p. The Cresselly Arms, along the A40 E, at Pont ar Gothi is nice for lunch. About 3 miles N at Bronwydd, the GWILI RAILWAY does short steamtrain trips along a scenic standard-gauge branch line of the old Great Western Railway. Also miniature railway and vintage signal box. Snacks, shop, disabled access; trains daily in summer, most Suns and some Weds Apr–Oct; (01267) 732176; *£2.80.

▥ ❀ **Castell Henllys** SN1139 (signed off the A487, E of Newport – where the Llwyngwair Arms surprises with its authentic Indian food) Iron Age hill fort in beautiful countryside overlooking the River Gwaun, with an interesting reconstruction of three, big, conical roundhouses. Also a forge, smithy, primitive looms and herb garden. Snacks, shop, some disabled access; cl Nov–Mar; (01239) 97319; *£2.

🐑 🐄 **Castle Morris** SM9031 LLANGLOFFAN FARMHOUSE CHEESE (Llangloffan Farm, just N) A range of delicious, traditional, farmhouse hard cheeses are handmade here, and you can watch them do it. Before Mr Downey set up the farm (run entirely on organic principles) he was a viola player in the Halle orchestra; his award-winning cheeses now go all over the world. Snacks, shop; cheese-making 10am–12.30pm Mon, Weds, Thurs, and Sat Apr–Oct, plus Tues and Fri May–Sept, farm shop open daily exc Sun; (013485) 241; £1.75. The excellent-value, fish restaurant at Letterston is handy.

🏰 ❀ ✚ ♨ **Cilgerran** SN1943 CASTLE Picturesquely placed on a crag above the River Teifi, this twin-towered Plantagenet fortress has good views from its towers and high walls, though, as usual, you have to go up a spiral staircase to see them. Shop (not Sat); cl am Sun in winter; *£1.50. WELSH WILDLIFE CENTRE Covering 350 acres, this is one of the richest areas of wetland in the district; the reedbed is the second biggest in Wales. You'll probably see more towards dusk, but

even then some bashful creatures might not emerge; a video shows the species you may have missed. Have a look at the rather innovative new building they put up last year. Meals, snacks, shop, disabled access; (01239) 621600; *£1.75. The ancient Pendre is useful for lunch.

⬇ **Dre-Fach Felindre** SN3538 MUSEUM OF THE WELSH WOOLLEN INDUSTRY Part of the National Museum of Wales, a fascinating working museum with textile machinery and tools dating back to the 18th c. Also displays on the industry from the Middle Ages, factory trails, and demonstrations of fabric-making – you may be able to try your hand at spinning. Snacks, shop, some disabled access; cl 25 Dec; (01559) 370929; *£1. There are decent places to eat in Newcastle Emlyn.

🏠 **Fishguard** SM9537 has an old fishing harbour surrounded by appropriately small streets of terraced cottages (the Ship here has lots of atmosphere), and an entirely separate, big commercial harbour used by the Irish ferries. In between, the upper town has some attractive old buildings and is pleasant to saunter through; the Royal Oak (The Sq) has decent food. You can drive or walk up on to the high headland which protects the harbour; its cliffs are quite grand, particularly where the seas boil through the narrow neck cutting off the rock on which Strumble Head lighthouse stands – down on the rocks there you quite often see seals even in the spring, though they're more common in late summer.

🏰 ⬇ **Kidwelly** SN4006 KIDWELLY CASTLE When this impressive castle was built in the 12th c the sea used to wash against the steep slope below it. Four massive towers, the tremendous gatehouse and much of the outer walls still remain, with steps up to the battlements and turrets. From the walls, the narrow, medieval st layout of Kidwelly itself is very obvious. Shop, some disabled access; cl am Sun in winter; (01554) 890104; *£2. The nearby INDUSTRIAL MUSEUM looks at two great Welsh industries, coal- and tin-mining. The original tinplate-working buildings are still here, and there's an exhibition of coal-mining

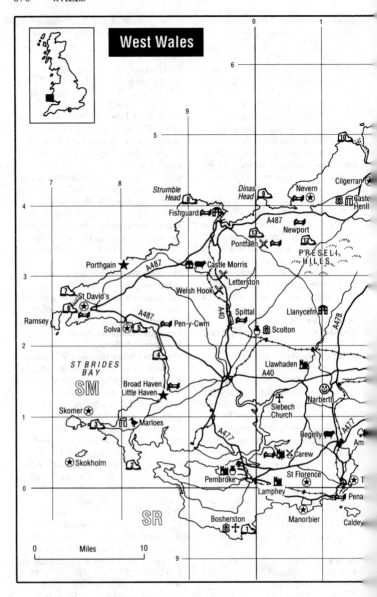

West Wales

Strumble Head 8

Fishguard

A487

Porthgain ★ A487 Castle Morris

Welsh Hook

St David's

Ramsey

Solva A487 Pen-y-Cwm

ST BRIDES BAY

SM

Broad Haven
Little Haven ★

Skomer ★

Skokholm ★

Marloes

Dinas Head 9 Nevern Cilgerran

Caste
Henll

A487 Newport

Pontfaen 13 12 PRESELI
HILLS

Letterston

Spittal Llanycefn A478

Scolton

Llawhaden
A40

Slebech
Church Narberth

Begelly A477 Am

Carew

Pembroke St Florence T

Lamphey Pena

Bosherston Manorbier Caldey

0 Miles 10

SR

with pithead gear and a winding engine. Snacks, shop, disabled access; cl am wknds (exc summer and bank hols); (01554) 891078; £1. The riverside Gwenllian Court Hotel has decent food.

Lamphey SN0100 LAMPHEY PALACE Ruined 13th-c palace once belonging to the Bishops of St David's. Shop,

disabled access; cl Oct–Apr; £1.50.

Laugharne SN2910 (pronounced 'Larn') DYLAN THOMAS'S BOAT HOUSE Wales's most prolific recent poet lived here while he was writing *Under Milk Wood*, and there are still some of his family photographs and furniture; also, an exhibition and art gallery. The writing

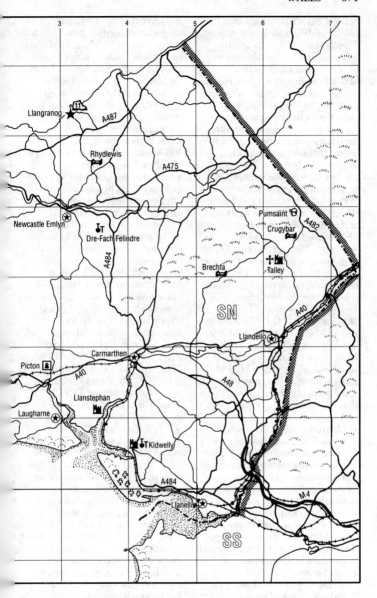

shed he used for so many poems is nearby. Snacks, shop; cl Sat in winter; (01994) 427420; £1.10. The ruined CASTLE he described as 'brown as owls' is a massive, battlemented compilation of styles from the 12th to 16th c, giving views of the estuary; it should be reopening this summer. ★ 🏰 ♨ **Llandeilo** SN6222 is an

attractive sloping town; the Plough at Rhosmaen just N is a favourite local dining pub. DINEFWR CASTLE (20 minutes' walk from the riverside lodge at the S edge of town; follow the Dyfed Wildlife Trust path) You can't go inside this isolated, largely 13th-c castle, on a wooded hill overlooking the Capability Brown parkland beyond, but it's a fine sight from the outside and the walk is very pleasant. There's absolutely no trace of the medieval town which is known to have stood outside the walls.

■☃⛵ **Llanelli** SN5000 PARC HOWARD ART GALLERY AND MUSEUM Set in pleasant parkland, the largest collection of the distinctive local pottery in existence, as well as other local history, and pictures by local artist J Dickson Innes. Snacks; cl 1–2pm, wknds exc pm summer, 25–26 Dec; free. The Stepney (Park St) is handy for lunch. WILDFOWL AND WETLANDS TRUST (3 m, E) Set beside Wales's main estuary for wildfowl and waders, with plenty of observation hides and special walkways. Many of the birds will feed from your hand, and at their summer duckery you can hear ducklings calling from inside their eggs. Meals, snacks, shop, disabled access; cl 25 Dec; (01554) 741087; £3.30.

▥ **Llanstephan** SN3510 LLANSTEPHAN CASTLE Majestically overlooking the Tywi estuary and Carmarthen Bay from an isolated ridge high over the water, this sprawling 11th to 13th-c ruin has an impressive gatehouse with a fine, vaulted ceiling. You can still see the slots for drenching intruders with boiling fat or lead; free.

▦ **Llanycefn** SN0923 PENRHOS COTTAGE There can't have been many housing problems around here if local tradition is to be believed; apparently anyone who built a house overnight on common land was entitled to claim it, and this old cottage was such a one, frantically constructed by friends and family. It gives an interesting insight into traditional country life. Shop, disabled access; cl 1–2pm, am Sun, all Mon, and all Oct–mid-May exc Easter Sun and Mon; (01437) 731328; *20p. The Bush nearby at Llandissilio is useful for lunch.

▥ **Llawhaden** SN0617 LLAWHADEN CASTLE 12th-c castle surrounded by a deep moat, with the remains of the 13th- and 14th-c bishop's hall, kitchen and bakehouse; free. The post office nearby sells guides and postcards.

▥★✻ **Manorbier** SS0697 MANORBIER CASTLE Still in the hands of the family who have owned it for over

300 years, this impressive, partly 12th-c fortress looking down to the beach has massive, medieval outer walls and an early round tower, with a 13th-c chapel and other buildings, and more modern constructions within the walls. Shop; cl Oct–Apr; (01834) 871394; £1.50. The quiet village is attractive, and there's a striking view of the castle from the church. The Castle Inn is useful for lunch.

⛵▦ **Marloes** SM7908 DEER PARK Not actually a deer park, but a wild, cliffy headland a couple of miles W, joined to the mainland by quite a narrow isthmus showing steep Iron Age defences; a place to watch birds (choughs breed here) and maybe seals on the offshore rocks. The Lobster Pot in Marloes is a useful informal family pub.

☺ **Narberth** SN0615 OAKWOOD ADVENTURE AND LEISURE PARK Lively theme park in 80 acres of landscaped countryside, with lots of rides and attractions, boats on the lake and a theatre. Meals, snacks, shop, disabled access; cl wkdys in Oct (exc half-term), Nov–mid-Mar; (01834) 891373; £7.45. More family activities next door at the CANASTON CENTRE, inc a reconstruction of TV's *Crystal Maze*. The Coach & Horses does good, cheap snacks.

★✝▦✻ **Nevern** SN0840 is an interesting, old, riverside village with a medieval bridge over the Nyfer. The CHURCH has a tall, 10th-c, carved Celtic cross and other carved stones, some with Viking patterns, in the graveyard, where the massive yew trees are reputed to weep tears of blood if the priest is not Welsh-speaking. The Trewern Arms is good for lunch. Some miles SE, towards Brynberian, is PENTRE IFAN BURIAL CHAMBER SN0937, one of the most impressive ancient monuments in Wales: a striking, former long barrow, with the enormous capstone still held up by three of the four surviving great upright megaliths – the former earth covering has all gone, leaving the stones alone on the ridge, which has great views over the Nyfer valley.

★✗☃✿ **Newcastle Emlyn** SN3042 has an attractive main st leading down to an ancient bridge; the Bunch of

Grapes and Pelican do decent food. Also a sawmill, museum, craft shops and trout ponds. Meals, snacks, shop, some disabled access; cl Nov–Easter; (01239) 710810; £2.

★ ⚲ Pembroke SM9801 PEMBROKE CASTLE The birthplace of Henry VII and thus the Tudor dynasty, this impressive 13th-c castle is largely intact, and its endless passages, tunnels and stairways are great fun to explore. The 75ft tower is one of the finest in Britain; good visitor centre. Snacks, shop, disabled access; cl 25–26 Dec, 1 Jan; (01646) 684585; £2 (guided tours, Jun–Aug exc Sat, 50p extra). Just across the road, the MUSEUM OF THE HOME (Westgate Hill) is an intriguing private collection of all sorts of everyday objects from the past 300 years, in a pleasant domestic setting. No under-5s; open Mon–Thurs May–Sept; (01646) 681200; *£1.20. The Pembroke Ferry by the water, at the foot of the bridge over the estuary, does good, fresh fish, and the Waterman's Arms, also nicely sited with lovely castle views, is good value.

▣ Picton Castle SN2717 GRAHAM SUTHERLAND GALLERY Big collection of Sutherland's incredible paintings, many reflecting his self-declared obsession with Wales. Part of the National Museum of Wales, with regular special events and exhibitions. Meals, snacks, shop, disabled access; cl 12.30–1.30pm, Mon (exc bank hols), Oct–Mar; (01437) 751296; *£1.

੪ ! Pumsaint SN6640 DOLAUCOTHI GOLD MINES 2,000 years of gold-mining are the focus of this unique mine, used since Roman times; tours of both the Roman adits and the deeper 1930s' workings complete with miners' lamps and helmets; good visitor centre. Snacks, shop; cl Nov–Mar, underground tours late May–late Sept; (015585) 359; *£4.80 for full tour, *£3 just site.

★ † ⚲ ✦ ☞ ☺ ♣ ✈ ❀ ⑪ St David's SM7525 The cathedral here can boast a longer continuous settlement than any other in Britain, but thanks to the relative isolation of the place it's stayed undeveloped and today is little more than a village. CATHEDRAL The Norman building on the site of an earlier Celtic monastery had largely collapsed by the 15th c and elaborate repairs had to be made; the new roof is an impressive, lace-like, oak affair, and oak features in most of the rest of the church; there's a fine collection of Celtic sculptured crosses. Cl am Sun; shop, disabled access; £1 suggested donation. Lots of colourful flowers in spring. BISHOP'S PALACE Impressive ruins of what was clearly the very grand main residence of the bishops. Plenty of quadrangles, stairways and splendid arcaded walls, with all sorts of intricate and often entertaining details (like the carvings below the arcaded parapets); there's a good exhibition on the history of the site. Very atmospheric and tranquil, particularly out of season when you may have it largely to yourself. Shop, limited disabled access; cl am winter Suns, 25–26 Dec, 1 Jan; (01437) 720517; £1.50. OCEANARIUM Excellent insight into sea and shore life; highlights include the shark tank and the rock pool, where you can see a variety of marine creatures. Meals, snacks, shop, limited disabled access; (01437) 720453; £2.25. ST DAVID'S FARM PARK (NE edge of town) Big collection of rare breeds, as well as rides on either a tractor or one of their shire horses. Meals, snacks, shop, disabled access; cl Nov–Mar; (01437) 721601; best to ring for prices. ADVENTURE DAYS can organise well supervised abseiling, canoeing, rock-climbing and other activities – ideal for off-loading active children for the day; cl Sun, 25–26 Dec, 1 Jan; (01437) 721611; various charges.

In summer there are BOAT TRIPS to rocky Ramsey Island, where seabirds nest in great numbers. About ½ mile away is the reputed birthplace of St Non, the mother of St David; there are lovely sea views from the very scant ruins of the chapel here, signed down a track from the useful St Non's Hotel, with a holy well nearby. The area is extremely rich in ANCIENT SITES, such as the Neolithic burial chambers up by St David's Head or over towards Solva, and the ramparts of the coastal hill forts right on the point of St David's Head and overlooking Caerfai Bay, just S of the town. It's a good place for coastal walks – always something interesting to see, whether it's a prehistoric monument or a bird you can't quite make out. The Old Cross Hotel nr the cathedral is a civilised place for lunch, and the Farmer's Arms is cheap and cheerful.

🐾 ⛲ ✿ 🌿 ♪ **St Florence** SM0801 MANOR HOUSE WILDLIFE AND LEISURE PARK Over 25 acres of wooded grounds and gardens with exotic birds, reptiles and fish, a pets' corner, playground, model railway and twice-daily falconry displays (not Sat). Meals, snacks, shop, disabled access; cl Oct–Easter; (01646) 651201; £3.50. The Old Parsonage Farm does quick, family food.

♨ ✿ **Scolton** SM9822 SCOLTON MANOR MUSEUM Early Victorian mansion showing the history and natural history of the Pembrokeshire area, with several rooms furnished in turn of the century style. The 60 acres of grounds have fine trees and shrubs. Snacks, shop, disabled access; cl Mon (exc bank hols), Nov–Mar; (01437) 731328; 50p.

✝ **Slebech Church** SN0313 (off the A40, 5 miles E of Haverfordwest) Gloriously isolated, ruined 12th-c church, formerly a temple of the Knights Hospitaller, by the tidal waters of the East Cleddau. Though there is a track from the main road, it's more enjoyable to turn down the A4075, take the next right turn and park by the mill, walk over the bridge and down the track through the woods above the river. In Haverfordwest, George's (Market St) does good food.

★ ✳ 🏚 **Solva** SM8024 One of the prettiest villages on the coast, with a great deal of character. On the opposite bank from the harbour, a high crag (enclosed by the ramparts of an Iron Age fort) gives pretty views of the attractive little fishing village and the coast. The Ship, Harbour House and Cambrian Arms all do decent food.

✝ 🏚 **Talley** SN6332 TALLEY ABBEY Ruins of a once magnificent, 12th-c abbey, still looking good, especially the two pointed archways. Cl am winter Suns; £1.

★ 🏚 ♨ 🖼 🏰 ✝ ♨ 🏚 **Tenby** SN1300 is a pleasantly restrained, family seaside resort, with sheltered beaches and

rock coves. It's a walled town – the splendidly preserved, 13th-c wall still with many of its towers left, as well as a magnificent, 14th-c, arched barbican gateway; a moat used to run the whole length of what is now a tree-lined st. There are some 13th-c remains of the castle on the headland above the yachting harbour – sections of wall, watchtowers, and gateway. Within the castle site is a decent local history and geology MUSEUM, with interesting finds from several of West Wales's prehistoric sites. Also an art gallery with a collection of Augustus and Gwen John. Shop; cl winter wknds; (01834) 842809; *£1. TUDOR MERCHANT'S HOUSE (Quay Hill) Fine example of gabled, 15th-c architecture, a good, Flemish chimney and the remains of frescoes on three walls. Shop; cl Sat, Nov–Mar; £1.60; NT. St Mary's is an interesting, 13th-c CHURCH with a huge steeple and a plaque commemorating a local invention that many of us use every day – the equals sign. From the harbour there are summer boat trips to CALDY ISLAND (May–Sept wkdys, £5), still a monastic island, where the Cistercian monks have cream and honey for sale, as well as more durable crafts. Besides the modern abbey, there's a 13th-c church with a simple, cobbled floor – still in use – on one side of the small cloister of the original priory; these ancient priory buildings (which you can see from outside but not enter) give a better sense of the past than almost anywhere else in West Wales. Much older, back on the mainland, is HOYLES MOUTH CAVE (off the A4139, just SW, Trefloyne Lane towards St Florence; short path through the wood, on the left after 500 yards). Running more than 100ft back into the hillside, this spooky place has yielded Ice Age mammoth bones, as well as human tools dating back over 10,000 years. Take a torch; don't go in winter, which would disturb the hibernating bats. The Lamb and the Coach & Horses are useful for lunch.

⚓ ✙ 🌿 🖼 Particularly worth a visit are the three islands of **Skomer** SM7209, **Skokholm** SM7305 and, much further out to sea, **Grassholme** SM5909, all of which can be reached by boats run by the National Parks. Skomer has 720 acres of spectacular wild scenery with countless birds and flowers, as well as seals playing on the shore – maybe common seals briefly in Jun or July, more likely grey seals and their pups in Sept and Oct; it's also remarkable for the easily traced remains of the Iron Age settlement here – there's a well laid-out trail. It's currently popular with birdwatchers thanks to the presence of several breeding pairs of short-eared owls. Grassholme is notable for its 30,000 pairs of gannets: on a clear, sunny morning even from the coast you can see it's white with them. Skokholm has Britain's first bird observatory. Sailing times from Dale Sailing Co, tel (01646) 601636. In Dale SM8005, where the boats usually leave from, the Griffin overlooking the anchorage is handy for lunch.

★ Three other **seaside villages** well worth visiting, all with decent pubs right by the sea, are Little Haven SM8512, Llangranog SN3054 (nice family beach backed by cliffs) and Porthgain SM8132. The line of colourwashed houses facing the harbour at Aberaeron SN4462 is very pretty, and the Harbourmaster here is a useful stop. Pubs and inns doing food elsewhere that are noteworthy for their fine positions include the Black Lion at Abergorlech SN5833 (lots of good walks nearby), Forest Arms at Brechfa SN5230, Cresselly Arms by the water at Cresswell Quay SN0406, Denant Mill at Dreenhill SM9214 (includes a Goan restaurant), Sailor's Safety by the sea below Dinas Head SN0139 and the Stanley Arms, on the Cleddau estuary opposite Picton Castle, at Landshipping SN0111.

Walks

The best of the area's walks are along sections of the Pembrokeshire Coastal Path, which snakes around the intricate Pembrokeshire seaboard. In the S, the lily ponds at **Bosherston** SR9694 △-1 merit a diversion off the path. The **Dale peninsula** SM8103 △-2, at the entrance to the huge, natural harbour of Milford Haven, has gentle, level-topped terrain looking down on the shipping activities, reducing the giant oil tankers to a pleasantly toy-like scale. With the **Marloes peninsula** △-3 SM7708 to the W, similarly gentle above its cliffs, it supplies memorable walkers' routes that need only minimal inland walking to complete the circuit – from Marloes peninsula, Skomer Island is in sight.

There are some attractive, sandy-floored rock coves to explore at low tide around **Little Haven** SM8512 △-4 and the Druidstone Hotel SM8616 to the N, with a good cliff walk northwards to the long sweep of sand and surf at Newgale Sands SM8421 (food all day at the Duke of Edinburgh). The fishing village of **Solva** SM8024 △-5 occupies a narrow, precipitous creek – very picturesque: there's a pleasant, interesting, shortish path E from here to Dinas Fawr SM8022, the opposite headland.

From the cathedral city of **St David's** SM7525 △-6, paths lead S to St Non's chapel on the coast; W, St Justinian SM7225 (there is yet another chapel here) looks over Ramsey Island. **St David's Head** SM7227 △-7 is noticeably more rugged – spectacular in autumn with both heather and gorse out; from the top of Carn Ledi, the moorland hill close by the coastal path, you can often see Ireland.

Strumble Head SM8941 △-8 typifies the rocky, big-dipper coastline of northern Pembrokeshire; there is a car park nr the lighthouse. **Dinas Head** SN0041 △-9 is a nice, miniature headland which takes about an hour to tour.

Cemaes Head SN1350 △-10, in Cardigan Bay, gives good views over the mouth of the Teifi estuary and out over the Irish Sea. Cardiganshire lacks a coastal path for much of the way, but the fishing village of **Llangranog** SN3054 △-11 offers a pleasant stroll to a headland to the N.

Inland, the **Prescelly Hills** or Mynydd Preseli SN1032 △-12 provide enjoyable walks, with some interesting views, on largely unspoilt moors capped by ancient cairns and other antiquities. The lusher **Gwaun Valley** ⌒-13 offers pretty walks along the wooded river either upstream or downstream of Pontfaen SN0234.

Driving

The most memorable scenery for drivers in this area is well inland, along the attractive B4310 through Brechfa and Abergorlech; particularly between these two villages, the countryside is reminiscent of alpine or Pyrenean foothills, with a mix of forest, valley, river and mountain views. Meeting this road at Llansawel is another good, varied hill road, the B4337, which links with the B4302 along the Dulais Valley from Llandeilo. More or less along the boundary of what we've described as West Wales is the A482 from Llanwrda to Lampeter (not quick, but a nice hill road), and on to Aberaeron.

On the coast between St David's and Fishguard, the slow road through Llanrhian, Trevine and Abercastle gives some lovely sea views. Inland from Fishguard, the B4313 runs up into the lonely Prescelly Hills with some far views, and the left turn on to the B4329 down to Eglyswrw is an attractive, little-travelled road, also with some decent views. The little back road off the B4313 running through the Cwm Gwaun valley is quite delightful: intricate, rather lush pastoral scenery with lots of ancient woodland. If you're travelling from Newport to Cardigan, the B4582 is a good short cut.

Nr Cardigan, an attractive drive off the A478 S takes you through Cilgerran, then bears left towards Llechryd: turn right just before the Llechryd bridge to follow the River Teifi, then cross the B4332 at Penrhiw to run almost due S on very narrow country roads to the B4299 at Trelech. A very different sort of road in much the same area is the surprisingly fast one all the way from the E end of Whitland on the A40, following the ridge route up to Tegryn (the highest village in the former county of Pembrokeshire), and on through Boncath on the B4332 to meet the A478 a little S of Cardigan.

Along the southern coast to the SW corner there's little memorable driving, as the country's either too flat or too hedged to give many views. However, the little back roads twisting round the complex estuary inland from Pembroke are pleasant for pottering (especially around Carew and Cresswell Quay). At the mouth of Milford Haven, the roads down to Dale Point and St Ann's Head, off the B4327, are worth taking if you're in the area, as are the coastal lanes around Little Haven and Broad Haven, running up above the surfing beaches from Nolton Haven to Newgale on the A487.

Where to eat

Pontfaen SN0134 Gelli Fawr Country House (01239) 820343 Outstanding food served in very generous helpings; must book and best to phone for winter closing dates; comfortable bedrooms too; disabled access. £23.50|£2.95/£4.95.

Welsh Hook SM9327 Stone Hall (01348) 840212 Imaginative French food and fine wines in the beamed restaurant of this 14th-c house; characterful bar, lovely grounds, and bedrooms; cl Mon Oct–March. £19.45.

Letterston SM9429 Something Cooking (A40, 5 miles S of Fishguard) (01348) 840621 Cheerful and enthusiastically run fish restaurant with truly outstanding fresh fish, served by neat, uniformed waitresses – very reasonable prices, too; cl Sun, 24 Dec for one wk. £11.50/£3.75.

MID-WALES

**The quietest part of Wales, with splendid, unspoilt scenery;
limited but interesting choice of places to visit.**

If not quite up to the very best that Snowdonia and the West Wales
coast can offer, this area does have spectacular scenery and well
above-average walking, with plenty of it. Its advantage over those
other two areas is that in summer it's much less visited, sparsely populated, with far more sheep than people. Towns are small, friendly
and mostly untouristy: it's one of the best parts of Britain for a really
quiet break. There is no proliferation of off-the-shelf amusements –
the most colourful events tend to be village fêtes and livestock auctions – but the area does have a handful of particularly interesting
places to visit: Powis Castle at Welshpool; the unique Centre for
Alternative Technology near Machynlleth; Hay-on-Wye, with its millions of secondhand and antiquarian books; the showcaves at Abercraf;
and the lively, silver-lead mine museum near Ponterwyd, close to the
beauty spot of Devil's Bridge. The castles which dominate the other
parts of Wales peter out here – this area was simply too wild for the
invaders to reckon with, but there are a couple of good, scenic steam
railways, from Aberystwyth and from Llanfair Caerinion.

For drivers as well as for walkers, there's lots to discover here. Little-
used, former drovers' roads gingerly penetrate the huge tracts of forest and moorland around the Llyn Brianne reservoir, the Cambrian
Mountains and the reservoirs above the Elan Valley, giving access
both to the hardier walkers and to those who stay firmly in their cars.
Other kinder ranges of hills tempt out more people, most notably the
western Black Mountain, the Brecon Beacons and the eastern Black
Mountains, as well as the range stretching all the way up the borders
from Brecon to the Kerry hills and beyond.

A change of mood down in the valleys centres on a string of inland
spas or former spa towns surrounded by hills, dignified and slightly
old-fashioned in the style of many such places on the Continent. Llandrindod Wells is the most prominent, but Builth Wells and the much
smaller Llanwrtyd Wells share the same character; Llanidloes (with
its Elizabethan, timbered market hall, unique for Wales) and
Presteigne are also attractive small towns with some interesting buildings. The area's river valleys are among the finest in Wales: the
friendly Usk, the rather more imposing upper Wye, and above
Aberystwyth, the beautiful Vale of Rheidol.

There is a good choice of places to stay, in all parts of the price spectrum.

Where to stay

Llyswen SO1337 LLANGOED HALL Llyswen, Brecon, Powys LD3 0YP (01874)
754525 **£140**; 23 very pretty rms with luxurious touches. Fine, partly 16th-c
house, beautifully converted into a first-class hotel with a lovely, house-party

atmosphere; handsome hall, elegant and spacious public rooms with antiques, fresh flowers and views over the grounds, imaginative modern cooking, and very good Welsh breakfasts; marvellous surrounding countryside; children over 8.

Eglwysfach SN6996 YNYSHIR HALL Eglwysfach, Machynlleth, Powys SY20 8TA (01654) 781209 £95; 8 rms. Carefully run, old manor house in landscaped gardens adjoining the Ynyshir bird reserve, with antiques, log fires and paintings in the light and airy public rooms, extremely good food using home-grown vegetables, and thoughtful service; children over 9.

Presteigne SO3265 RADNORSHIRE ARMS, Presteigne, Powys LD8 2BE (01544) 267406 £92; 16 rms. Rambling, handsomely timbered, 17th-c, Forte hotel with elegantly moulded beams and fine, dark panelling in the lounge bar; polite, attentive service, and decent food and wines.

Llandrindod Wells SO0561 METROPOLE Temple St, Llandrindod Wells, Powys LD1 5DY (01597) 823700 £77; 122 rms. Run by the same family for over a hundred years, this big hotel has spacious and comfortable public rooms, good traditional cooking using fresh local produce, and a leisure complex with swimming pool, exercise machines, sauna and so forth; disabled access.

Montgomery SO2296 DRAGON Market Sq, Montgomery, Powys SY15 6AA (01686) 668359 *£69; 15 rms. Attractive, black and white timbered, small hotel with a pleasant, grey-stone tiled hall, comfortable residents' lounge, beamed bar, good food using local produce in the restaurant, and welcoming licensees; indoor swimming pool.

Aberdovey SN6296 PENHELIG ARMS, Aberdovey, Gwynedd LL35 0LT (01654) 767215 *£68; 10 comfortable rms. Carefully refurbished building in a fine position overlooking the sea, with a cosy bar, pleasant dining room, open fires, good food (especially local fish), and an extensive wine list; lovely views of the Dyfy Estuary; no accomm 25–26 Dec.

Crickhowell SO2118 GLIFFAES COUNTRY HOUSE Crickhowell, Powys NP8 1RH (01874) 730371 *£66; 22 rms. Run by the same family for over 40 years with an enjoyably informal and relaxed atmosphere, a comfortable, big sitting room, elegant drawing room, conservatory, good cooking, and cheerful staff; wonderfully quiet, peaceful surroundings in its own 29 acres (lovely rare trees), fishing on two stretches, hard tennis court, golf practice net and a putting and croquet lawn; cl 5 Jan–24 Feb.

Llangurig SN8482 GLANSEVERN ARMS Llangurig, Llanidloes, Powys SY18 6SY (0155 15) 240 £60; 8 rms. Welcoming inn, 1,050ft up among the hills and forests of the upper Wye Valley, with good food using local produce in the restaurant, log fires, cosy bar, and lots of books in the lounge; 1 mile of private fishing on the River Wye; cl 20–31 Dec.

Llyswen SO1337 GRIFFIN Llyswen, Brecon, Powys LD3 0UR (01874) 754241 *£60; 8 rms, 7 with own bthrm. Old-fashioned and warmly welcoming inn with imaginative food in the no-smoking restaurant (brook trout and salmon caught by the family, local game in season), an interesting, comfortable bar with a huge inglenook, and helpful service; fishing and shooting courses; cl 25–26 Dec.

Aberdovey SN6296 BODFOR Sea Front, Aberdovey, Gwynedd LL36 0EA (01654) 767475 *£54; 16 rms with showers and most with sea views. Small, family-run, Victorian hotel on the sea front, with a bar, comfortable lounge, good restaurant food, and helpful service; cl 22 Dec–3 Jan.

Crickhowell SO2118 BEAR Crickhowell, Powys NP8 1BW (01873) 810408 £52; 23 rms, the back ones are the best. Particularly friendly coaching inn with a good, civilised atmosphere, excellent food (Welsh specialities as well), some fine wines and ports; lots of antiques, deeply comfortable seats, and a roaring log fire in the heavily beamed lounge; pretty, flower-filled courtyard; disabled access; dogs welcome.

Beulah SN9151 TROUT Beulah, Llanwrtyd Wells, Powys LD5 4UU (01591) 620235 £50; 5 comfortable rms. Neatly kept and attractively refurbished inn with friendly owners, front lounge bar and restaurant area, popular main bar with a log fire, and a small dining room.

Llanwrtyd Wells SN8746 Cwmirfon Lodge Llanwrtyd Wells, Powys LD5 4TN (0159 13) 217 *£48; 2 comfortable rms. Former sporting lodge in 3 acres of grounds adjoining Forestry Commission land, with a woodburning stove in the drawing room, an attractive dining room with open fire, very good food, and an extremely friendly atmosphere; cl Christmas; no children; self-catering also.

Newbridge-on-Wye SO0158 New Inn Newbridge-on-Wye, Llandrindod Wells, Powys LD1 6HY (01597) 860211 £48; 7 rms. Friendly, well modernised, old village inn, nicely set in the upper Wye Valley; generous lunchtime hot dishes, a good evening restaurant, spacious, carpeted back lounge, a public bar, and welcoming licensees; cl pm 25 Dec.

Hay-on-Wye SO2342 Old Black Lion Hay-on-Wye, Hereford, Powys HR3 5AD (01497) 820841 £41.90; 10 rms. Ancient town inn with good food in both the restaurant and bar (inc vegetarian), low beams and black panelling, and close to fishing (private salmon- and trout-fishing) and riding; children over 5; limited disabled access.

Aberhafesp SO0692 Dyffryn Aberhafesp, Newtown, Powys SY16 3JD (01585) 206412 £40; 3 rms. Carefully restored, half-timbered barn on a 100-acre sheep and beef cattle farm, with a residents' lounge overlooking the stream, traditional cooking in the dining room, and friendly owners; children's play area and nature trail.

Guilsfield SJ2212 Lower Trelydan Guilsfield, Welshpool, Powys SY21 9PH (01938) 553105 £36; 3 rms. Charming, black and white farmhouse on a working beef cattle and sheep farm; lovely, heavily beamed ceilings, fine antiques and comfortable seating, a cosy licensed bar, warm and friendly atmosphere, and delicious farmhouse cooking; pretty garden.

Carno SN9697 Aleppo Merchant Carno, Caersws, Powys SY17 5LL (01686) 420210 *£35; 5 rms, shared bthrm. Warm, friendly and reliable 17th-c inn with a comfortably modernised, beamed lounge bar, an open fire in the small adjoining lounge, a fair choice of well liked food inc vegetarian and Indian dishes, and well kept real ales; children over 12.

Cwmdu SO1823 Farmers Arms Cwmdu, Crickhowell, Powys NP8 1RU (01874) 730464 £35; 2 rms. Welcoming cottagey pub with a coal fire in the flagstoned bar, comfortable lounge, decent bar food, pleasant staff, and tables in the big garden; handy for the Black Mountains; cl 24–26 Dec.

Rhayader SN9768 Beili Neuadd Rhayader, Powys LD6 5NS (01597) 810211 *£35; 3 rms. Charming, partly 16th-c, stone-built farmhouse in a quiet position, with log fires in the renovated rooms; fishing, pony-trekking and guided walks nearby; cl Christmas; children over 10.

Trecastle SN8829 Castle Trecastle, Brecon, Powys LD3 8UH (01874) 636354 £35; 10 comfortable rms. Neatly kept and recently refurbished Georgian inn, with friendly owners and lovely food in both the restaurant and bar; good value.

Churchstoke SO2794 Drewin Farm Churchstoke, Montgomery, Powys SY15 6TW (01588) 620325 £34; 2 rms, 1 with own bthrm. Attractive, 17th-c farmhouse with lovely views, a warm welcome, comfortable lounge, dining room and games room with snooker table in a converted granary; Offa's Dyke footpath runs through the mixed farm of sheep, cattle and crops; cl Dec–Feb.

Felinfach SO0833 Trehenry Farm Felinfach, Brecon, Powys LD3 0LN (01874) 754312 £34; 3 rms. 18th-c farmhouse on a 200-acre farm with lovely views of the Black Mountains and Brecon Beacons; inglenook fireplaces, beams, TV lounge, good food, and a large garden; self-catering also; cl Christmas.

Newtown SO1191 Lower Gwestydd Newtown, Powys SY16 3AY (01686) 626718 £32; 3 rms. Traditional, 17th-c, black and white half-timbered house in lovely countryside and on 200 acres of mainly sheep and arable farmland; comfortable lounge and dining room, and good food using their own chickens, home-grown fruit and veg, and Welsh lamb; you can wander around the farm; cl Christmas.

Gladestry SO2355 ROYAL OAK Gladestry, Kington, Powys HR5 3NR (0154 422) 669 £30; 3 spotless, well equipped rms, shared bthrm. Unpretentious, beamed and flagstoned inn on Offa's Dyke, quiet and relaxing, with welcoming licensees; good, home-cooked bar food, a refurbished lounge, separate bar, picnic-table sets in the lovely, secluded garden behind; nice breakfasts; cl 25 Dec. **Pennal** SH7000 GOGARTH HALL FARM Pennal, Machynlleth Powys SY20 9LB (01654) 791235 £28; 2 rms. 17th-c house on a working farm of suckler cows and sheep, with marvellous views of the Dovey estuary; a dining room and lounge, and guests are welcome to walk around the farm; baby-sitting available; self-catering also.

To see and do

★ **Aberdovey** SN6296 Attractive, restrained resort with very pleasant, sheltered beaches but none of the crowds or tat they usually bring. Legend has it there's a lost city beneath the sea, inundated by the crashing waves in a great storm 1,500 years ago. Sometimes at night, imaginative people can hear the mournful tolling of its bells. Besides the Penhelig Arms Hotel, the Britannia does good food and has great views.

▣☗➤◨ **Aberystwyth** SN5881 Lowkey resort, scarcely changed in 20 years, with long shingle beaches and a sedate cliff railway to the large camera obscura high above town. Quite a scholarly town too, with a university, and the NATIONAL LIBRARY OF WALES (Penglais Hill), which has exhibitions of fine, early Welsh and Celtic manuscripts and art. Cl Sun, bank hols and first full wk Oct; free. Also a good museum, and one of the very few of Edward I's castles in this part of Wales. Its main attraction for families is the VALE OF RHEIDOL RAILWAY, with steamtrains for several miles along the picturesque twists of the Rheidol Valley to the dramatic beauty-spot gorge of Devil's Bridge (see entry below). Snacks, disabled access; trains run most days Easter–Oct, though not Fri Sept, or Tues–Thurs in Oct; (tel 01970) 625819 for timetable; £9.80.

⛪✝☗ **Brecon** SO0428 Characterful small town, with some fine old buildings around its town sq and narrow streets, and a bustling livestock market on Tues and Fri. The striking Norman Priory was grandly restored in the 19th c and became a cathedral in 1923. Also the rather sad remnants of a castle, and a couple of decent little museums, the best of which, the BRECKNOCK MUSEUM (Captain's Walk), contains the town's excellently preserved assize court. Cl 1–2pm, winter Suns; free. The George (George St) has good-value food. Some of the highest peaks in the area are a short drive away, and there's a useful National Parks Visitor Centre, just S in the BRECON BEACONS MOUNTAIN CENTRE.

☗➤ **Carreg Cennen Castle** SN6619 (nr Trapp, SE of Llandeilo) Few castles can boast as excellent a setting as these old ruins, dramatically dominating their limestone crag high above the river, and overlooking the unspoilt countryside towards the Black Mountains as they have for centuries. Rebuilt in the 13th c (and again in the 19th – you can easily distinguish the new stonework), the castle has a mysterious passage in the side of the cliff, and there's a working farm with rare breeds. Readers like coming here, several saying the people who look after it are charming. Meals, snacks, shop, some disabled access; cl 25 Dec; (01558) 822291; *£2. The Cennen Arms nearby has good simple food.

☗☺➤☗✽♤! **Craig-y-nos** SN8315 DAN YR OGOF SHOWCAVES (Just N, on the A4067) Fascinating series of caves, well lit to bring out the extraordinary rock formations. The Cathedral Cave is the largest single chamber open to the public in any British showcave, while 3,000 years ago Bone Cave was lived in by humans. There's also a dinosaur park, Iron Age farm, new shire horse centre, artificial ski-slope, museum, and audio-visual displays, so lots to see. Meals, snacks, shop; cl Nov–Mar; (01639) 730284; £5.50. Down the road, CRAIG-Y-NOS COUNTRY PARK is ideal for a picnic or a stroll – 40 acres of woodland, lake and meadow, landscaped and developed in the last century by the opera singer Adelina Patti. The visitor centre has a good range of activities (inc interactive and computer displays), and they've recently added a wild flower maze. Shop, disabled access; cl 25 Dec; (01639) 730395; 50p parking charge. The Ancient Briton at Pen-y-Cae is handy for lunch.

♠ **Devil's Bridge** SN7376 Pretty bridges and a dramatic waterfall, tucked away in an atmospheric wooded gorge. The oldest bridge gave this beauty spot its name, when it was built by the Devil in order to trap an old woman into giving him her soul; she outwitted him. Wordsworth was inspired to write a sonnet after a visit here (see also **Driving** section below). The entertaining Halfway Inn at Pisgah, on the A4120 to Aberystwyth, is good for lunch.

※ ♥ ⌂ ♣ **Elan Valley** SN9365 These four lakes are the best and most famous of the many man-made reservoirs in Wales. Even the dams look good, and there are splendid views; several of our readers really enjoy coming here. It's an excellent spot for birdwatching, especially in summer, and among the many species you may see red kites. The VISITOR CENTRE in Elan village is the best place to start, with an audio-visual show and various walks and displays. Cl Nov–Easter; (01597) 810880; free. Outside is a statue of Shelley, who lived in a house now lost beneath the water. At nearby Rhayader SN9768, the Bear and the Castle are good food stops, and you can tour the workshops of WELSH ROYAL CRYSTAL (cl 25 Dec, 1 Jan, no glass-making wknds; £2). There are excellent views from the farm trail at GIGRIN FARM (South Rd, just out of town), where this year they'll also be opening a red kite centre with hides; (01597) 810243; *£2.

🚂 **Fairbourne** SH6114 FAIRBOURNE AND BARMOUTH STEAM RAILWAY Running the 2½ miles to the end of the peninsula and the ferry for Barmouth, this started life in 1890 as a horse-drawn railway which was used to carry building materials for the seaside resort of Fairbourne. Meals, snacks, shop; cl Oct–Easter; tel (01341) 250362 for timetable; £3.35. The Fairbourne Hotel is quite useful for lunch, as is the attractively set George III along the estuary at Penmaenpool.

★ **Hay-on-Wye** SO2342 is a pleasant small town which has become a world centre for secondhand and antiquarian books. There is a growing number of antique shops too, as well as a rather jolly puzzle and teddy-bear shop on Broad St. Hay Bluff nearby has lovely walks, and it's within easy reach of the Black Mountains, the Golden Valley over the English border, and the attractive, unspoilt countryside just over the Gwent border that we've mentioned in the South Wales section. Besides the fine Old Black Lion, the Kilvert Court, (01497) 821042, can be recommended both for food and as a place to stay.

† **Llanbister** SO1173 The CHURCH here is interesting, with a chimney instead of the usual tower, and there's an even better one a mile away at Llananno, with an astonishingly elaborate rood screen that wouldn't be out of place in a cathedral.

★ ⌂ ※ ♨ **Llandrindod Wells** SO0561 is a civilised, inland resort, a largely intact gem of the railway age, with imposing buildings on broad avenues and terraces, wrought-iron frills everywhere, elegant flower displays and Victorian parks, antique shop fronts and little canopies along the shopping streets. It was clearly a resort for temperance – though there are places to drink, they're tucked discreetly away. The former spa pump room has been reopened, and there's a very old-fashioned boating lake, as well as a charming town MUSEUM (Temple St) (in winter cl pm Sat and Sun; (01597) 824513 free). The atmospheric old Llanerch has good home-cooking, and the altogether smarter Metropole Hotel generally does some food all day.

🚂 **Llanfair Caereinion** SJ1006 WELSHPOOL & LLANFAIR LIGHT RAILWAY Colonial and Austrian steam locomotives are among the wide variety of engines that run along this

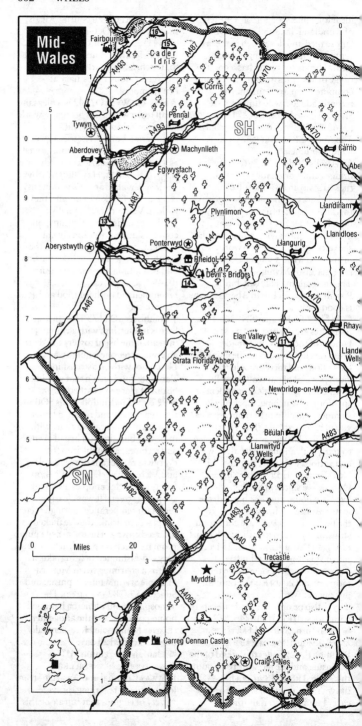

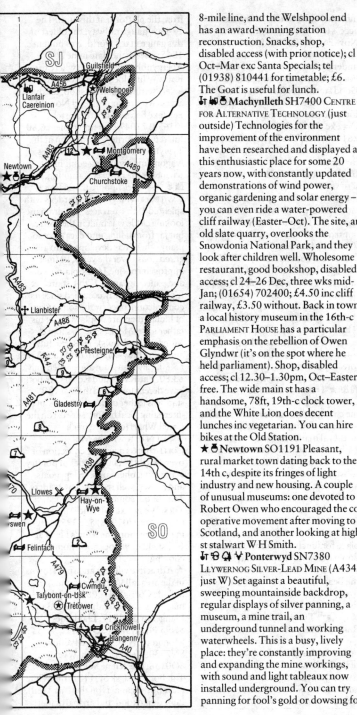

8-mile line, and the Welshpool end has an award-winning station reconstruction. Snacks, shop, disabled access (with prior notice); cl Oct–Mar exc Santa Specials; tel (01938) 810441 for timetable; £6. The Goat is useful for lunch.

↓T 🏠♿ **Machynlleth** SH7400 CENTRE FOR ALTERNATIVE TECHNOLOGY (just outside) Technologies for the improvement of the environment have been researched and displayed at this enthusiastic place for some 20 years now, with constantly updated demonstrations of wind power, organic gardening and solar energy – you can even ride a water-powered cliff railway (Easter–Oct). The site, an old slate quarry, overlooks the Snowdonia National Park, and they look after children well. Wholesome restaurant, good bookshop, disabled access; cl 24–26 Dec, three wks mid-Jan; (01654) 702400; £4.50 inc cliff railway, £3.50 without. Back in town, a local history museum in the 16th-c PARLIAMENT HOUSE has a particular emphasis on the rebellion of Owen Glyndwr (it's on the spot where he held parliament). Shop, disabled access; cl 12.30–1.30pm, Oct–Easter; free. The wide main st has a handsome, 78ft, 19th-c clock tower, and the White Lion does decent lunches inc vegetarian. You can hire bikes at the Old Station.

★ ♿ **Newtown** SO1191 Pleasant, rural market town dating back to the 14th c, despite its fringes of light industry and new housing. A couple of unusual museums: one devoted to Robert Owen who encouraged the co-operative movement after moving to Scotland, and another looking at high st stalwart W H Smith.

↓T 🏠 ♿ ✦ **Ponterwyd** SN7380 LLYWERNOG SILVER-LEAD MINE (A434, just W) Set against a beautiful, sweeping mountainside backdrop, regular displays of silver panning, a museum, a mine trail, an underground tunnel and working waterwheels. This is a busy, lively place: they're constantly improving and expanding the mine workings, with sound and light tableaux now installed underground. You can try panning for fool's gold or dowsing for mineral veins. Snacks, shop, disabled access (exc underground); cl mid-Nov–Easter; (01970) 890620; *£2.95 museum and site, *£3.05 inc underground. BWLCH NANT-YR-ARIAN FOREST VISITOR CENTRE (Llanafan) Good starting point for exploring the forest, with walks and a few activities for children. Shop, disabled access; cl Oct exc wknds–Easter; (01974) 261404; free. The Dyffryn Castell, in the spectacular valley to the E, is nice for lunch.

☎ ✒ **Rheidol** SN7178 HYDROELECTRIC SCHEME Guided tours of the power station with an unexpected fish farm. Good nature trails, scenic lakes and reservoirs, trout fishing. Snacks, limited disabled access; cl Nov–Mar; (01970) 84667; £1.70.

✝ 📷 **Strata Florida Abbey** SN7566 Though there's little left of this once-important centre of learning, except the ruined church and cloister, the surroundings are lovely. It's thought that the 14th-c poet Dafyd ap Gwilym is buried here. Teas, shop, disabled access; cl am Sun, Oct–Mar; £1.50. The road continues through the pine forest up into the mountains, eventually reaching the Llyn Brianne reservoir.

🏰 📷 ★ **Tretower** SO1821 TRETOWER COURT AND CASTLE vividly illustrate the change from castle to less fortified accommodation over the ages. The medieval manor house dates from the 14th c, though it has been developed over the centuries; beside it is the substantial ruin of an 11th-c motte and bailey, with 9ft-thick walls and a three-storey tower. Shop, limited disabled access; cl am Sun, 24–26 Dec, 1 Jan; (01874) 730279; £2. The Nantyffin Cider Mill is a good, handy place for lunch. Crickhowell, further down the road, is a pleasant, village-sized 'town', with an excellent inn in the Bear, and a fine ancient bridge over the Usk (which the decent Bridge End Inn overlooks).

🛥 ❋ ♤ ⛵ **Tywyn** SH5800 TALYLLYN RAILWAY This railway journey affords glorious views, climbing from the little seaside resort up the steep sides of the Fathew Valley and stopping for passengers to admire Dolgoch Falls and visit the Nant Gwernol Forest (there's a waterfall two minutes away

from the platform at this end). The 27-inch-gauge railway, the oldest of this gauge in the world, was built in 1865 to serve the slate mine at Abergynolwyn SH6807 (where the Railway Inn does decent food in a lovely setting). Snacks, shop, disabled access with prior notice; cl Nov–14 Feb (exc before Christmas); tel (01654) 710472 for timetable; £6.80 full return journey. A museum at the Tywyn Station shows locomotives, wagons and signalling equipment whenever the railway is running.

📷 ❋ ♤ ⛵ **Welshpool** SJ2106 POWIS CASTLE Set in magnificent gardens with splendid 18th-c terraces, this dramatic-looking castle was built in the 13th c, but far from falling into decay like so many others, has developed into a grand house over the years, its finer improvements inc 16th-c plasterwork and panelling, and a 17th-c staircase. It's been constantly occupied since its construction, once by the son of Clive of India – there are displays about his father's life. Meals, snacks, shop; cl Mon (exc bank hols), Tues (exc July and Aug), Nov–Mar; (01938) 554336; £5.80, Clive museum and garden only £3.80. The Raven and Royal Oak both have decent food, and the main BR station is rather unusual. There's an interesting local history MUSEUM on the Canal Wharf (cl Weds; free).

Just N of town, the MOORS COLLECTION is a private collection of over 140 different varieties of poultry, waterfowl, pheasants, sheep, goats and horses, well regarded by readers. Teas, shop, some disabled access; cl Tues, Weds (exc July and Aug), mid-Oct–Easter; (01938) 553395; £2. Out in this direction, the King's Head at Guilsfield now does good home-cooking.

★ **Attractive villages and small towns** in the area, all with decent pubs, include Corris SH7608 (everything made of slate), Llandinam SO0388, Llangenny SO2417, Llanidloes SN9584, Llyswen SO1337, Montgomery SO2296, Myddfai SN7730, Newbridge-on-Wye SO0158, Presteigne SO3265 and Talybont-on-Usk SO1122 (the White Hart by the canal is on the Taff Trail). Pubs doing food that are particularly worth noting for their positions include the Farmer's Arms at Cwmdu SO1823, Dolfor Inn at Dolfor SO1187, White Swan at Llanfrynach SO0725, Coach & Horses above the canal at Llangynidr SO1519 (lovely walks), Stables Hotel at Neuadd Fawr SO2322 (good hill walking), Harp at Old Radnor SO2559 (another nice base for walks) and the canalside Royal Oak at Pencelli SO0925.

✝ **Fine churches** can be found at Old Radnor SO2559 (handsome screen and roof, Britain's oldest organ-case and font) and Presteigne SO3265. But the speciality of the area is unspoilt and humble rustic churches in beautiful settings, such as Aberedw SO0847, Bleddfa SO2168 (the reopened Hundred House is a good base for walkers), Disserth SO0358, Llanbadarn-y-garreg SO1148, Maesyronnen Chapel SO1740 NW of Hay, and Rhulen SO1349.

Walks

The **Brecon Beacons** ⌂-1 proper are a pair of graceful pointed summits connected by a short ridge that seems to be visible from most of South Wales, and that gives a magnificent high-level walk along the crest, which has massive drops on the northern side. Pen y Fan SO0121 (2,906ft) is the highest Welsh summit outside Snowdonia, and the main E–W upland spine effectively stretches about 5 miles. The most popular route up from Pont ar Daf SN9819, from the A470 to the W, is straightforward enough, although there has been some serious footpath erosion, but the N approaches are more exciting and surprisingly little walked.

The **Black Mountains** ⌂-2, making up the eastern part of the Brecon Beacons National Park, are a range of finger-shaped ridges bordering on to Herefordshire (and shared with South Wales), with steep-sided valleys in between. Most of the best views are from the Offa's Dyke Path along the E flanks: the land eastwards slopes abruptly down to low-lying, agricultural Herefordshire, and views far into England give you a feeling of true border country. Circular walks here tend to be long and hefty, often with two major ascents to get you up on to the different ridges, but the scenic Gospel Pass road from Hay-on-Wye SO2342 lets you drive up to within reasonable striking distance of Hay Bluff SO2436 (2,200ft). Twmpa SO2234 (2,263ft) is better known by its intriguing English name of Lord Hereford's Knob; though it's not itself on the Offa's Dyke Path, it is nearby, and you can combine it with Hay Bluff in a longer walk. Llanthony Abbey, with a pub, makes a beautiful objective in the valley below, where diligent map-reading is needed for a cross-fields route from Cwmyoy SO2923, with extensions on to the Offa's Dyke Path on the ridge to complete a satisfying circuit.

Confusingly, the westernmost range in the National Park is called **Black Mountain** SN7417 ⌂-3. Much of the high terrain is a long way from the road, so this part is more the preserve of the committed long-distance walker. The craggy ridge known as Carmarthen Fan protrudes dramatically above the moors and provides the high point of a long but rewarding walk from the N.

The southern parts of the Brecon Beacons National Park, within easy reach of South Wales, have gentler walking, in the form of forest walks in the large conifer plantations there, where waterfalls and a series of attractive reservoirs are the main features.

The lusher swathes of the **Usk Valley** ⌂-4 can be enjoyed by walks along the towpath of the 33-mile Monmouthshire & Brecon canal.

A series of mighty **waterfalls** ⌂-5 with few rivals in Britain grace the deep, wooded gorges of the Nedd, Hepste and Mellte, just inside the southern Park boundary. An easy path from Pontneddfechan SN9007, nr Glyn Neath, leads along the River Nedd, while Porth yr Ogof car park SN9212, nr Ystradfellte, is convenient for the Mellte. Dire warning notices ward you off getting too close to the edge (it is certainly hazardously slippery), but you can accompany the river most of the way to its junction with the Hepste. Here, a path actually crosses the river by going behind the curtain of Sgwd yr Eira waterfall – a rock ledge holds you in safely, but it's an excitingly damp experience.

The Offa's Dyke Path again provides the major attraction further N, in the former county of Radnorshire. On its coast-to-coast route over the Welsh Marches it takes in some very attractive, hill-farm country between Hay-on-Wye and Knighton SO2872, inc **Hergest Ridge** △-6 (described in the Herefordshire chapter, but easily reached from this side) and some well preserved stretches of Offa's 9th-c boundary marker between Knighton and Kington SO2956.

Away from Offa's Dyke, Radnorshire is less well known than it deserves to be, with old drovers' tracks providing some enjoyable escapist walking, and a reasonable network of field paths. There are few major objectives, but it is all very pleasant: the best bets include the **River Wye** △-7 around Aberedw SO0847 and Boughrood SO1339; the **hills** △-8 between Aberedw, Glascwm SO1553 and Gladestry SO2355 (where the Royal Oak is on the Offa's Dyke Path); and the upland massif of **Radnor Forest** △-9 (open country for the most part, with conifers on the northern slopes), where walks include New Radnor SO2160 to the modest summit of the quaintly named Whimble SO2062, and from the A44 between Llanfihangel-nant-Melan SO1858 and New Radnor to Water-break-its-neck waterfall SO1860 (don't miss the path at the top of the fall).

From Llandrindod Wells SO0561, a sedate walk around the town's lake can extend into an expedition E of **Cefnllys Castle** SO0861 △-10, an impressively sited hill fort with a lonely church below, close to Shaky Bridge (no longer shaky); a nature trail here takes you along the banks of the River Ithon.

W of Rhayader, some high-level trackways afford magnificent views over the Cambrian Mountains and the adjacent **Elan Valley** SN9768 △-11; lower-level options start from the Elan Valley visitor centre and neighbouring reservoirs, and include forest walks and strolls along the old railway track by the water's edge.

The former county of Montgomeryshire consists of the quintessential, sheep-grazed lands of rural Wales. Much of it lacks high objectives for walkers, with few major peaks and fair distances between villages, but **Montgomery** SO2296 △-12, with its castle perched above, is rewarding for a short exploration on foot, and the windswept (often boggy) uplands of Plynlimon and the Cambrian Mountains, though not endowed with the friendliest of climates, can be extremely exhilarating.

On the **coast** △-13, you can do a one-way walk along the straight stretch between Aberystwyth SN5881 and Borth SN6189, using the train service between the two for the other half of the round trip. Similarly, walks in or above the pretty **Vale of Rheidol** △-14, between Aberystwyth and the Devil's Bridge SN7376, can be aided by the private railway between the two. The most dramatic parts here are around Devil's Bridge.

Cader Idris SH7113 △-15, a great peak in the S of the National Park, offers various ways up its friendly slopes. The **estuary walk** △-16 along the old railway track beside the Mawddach estuary, between Penmaenpool SH6918 and Fairbourne SH6114, gives wonderful views; you can detour to the Arthog waterfalls SH6414, on the lower slopes of Cader Idris.

Driving

One of the most scenic roads in the area is the main A44 across to Aberystwyth, particularly where it climbs high beside the upper Wye past Rhayader, around Pant Mawr, and then over the watershed into the gauntly swooping valley around Dyffryn Castell. Just past here at Ponterwyd, a left turn on to the A4120, passing the Devil's Bridge beauty spot, gives the best views of the Vale of Rheidol as you approach Aberystwyth.

The B4574 from Devil's Bridge takes you through conifer plantations to a quiet road up a very narrow river gorge past Cwmystwyth. This broadens out into the Elan Valley, with a series of attractively landcaped reservoirs. This is one of the nicest parts of Wales for country drives, and can also be reached by the B4518, up past buzzard crags from Rhayader.

From Llanwrtyd Wells, a slow back road follows the Irfon Valley into the hills, hemmed in by conifer plantations for part of the way, but it does take you into a huge area of otherwise untracked, mountainous country deep in central Wales, and eventually right over to Tregaron, with a worthwhile southerly detour to see the Llyn Brianne reservoir. There are some very steep and twisty sections on this road. For the fainter-hearted, the altogether easier but busier A483 between Llanwrtyd Wells and Llandovery passes through some fine scenery.

Along the Usk between Crickhowell and Brecon, the B4558 on the S side of the river is a pleasant, quiet road through lovely scenery. From Talybont, a narrow road goes steeply up into the Brecon Beacons with its outcrops of rock beckoning you over the empty moorlands; the main roads over the Beacons from Brecon and from Sennybridge give a good feel of this expansive area too.

A nice stretch of coast road is the main A487 between Aberaeron and Aberystwyth, which runs on high enough ground to show Ireland as a shadow on the horizon; as does the B4572 just N of Aberystwyth.

Right over in the E, pleasant roads into good scenery include the B4560 from the South Wales valleys up through Bwlch and Llangorse to Talgarth, and the B4594 up over the hills through Painscastle, Newcastle and Gladestry, forking left up to Old Radnor with its lovely views over the Radnor Forest, and then on by the B4362 to Presteigne, or perhaps the B4357 on to Knighton.

Where to eat

Llowes SO1941 RADNOR ARMS (01497) 847460 Small, modest and very old, with a log fire in the bar, a neat, little cottagey dining room, and tables in the imaginatively planted garden; very wide choice of notably good food (tempting puddings), a congenial atmosphere, and friendly staff; cl pm Sun, Mon (exc bank hols). £16.50|£3/£6.

Craig-y-Nos SN8315 COACH HOUSE (01639) 730767 Originally the stables to the castle, this is a carefully converted restaurant with Victorian features, attractive pine furniture, decent food inc Welsh teas, friendly, and efficient service; also a craft shop where you can watch potters, saddlers and textile artists at work; cl Tues, and in winter it's best to phone beforehand. £12|£1.60/£5.40. Many of the places listed in the **Where to stay** section above serve very good food, too.

SOUTH WALES

The best part of Wales for sightseeing, with some fine scenery.

There are more sights to see and interesting places to visit in this part of Wales than in any other – particularly industrial heritage attractions at Porth, Blaenavon and Cardiff, the opulent Castell Coch at Tongwynlais, the scenic Brecon Mountain Railway out of Merthyr Tydfil (which itself is well worth exploring), the gardens at St Nicholas, a good number of spectacular medieval castles (with the one at Caerphilly prime among them), the idyllic ruined priory at Llanthony, Tintern abbey in the lower Wye Valley between Monmouth and

Chepstow, the Roman remains at Caerleon, showy Tredegar House in Newport and the hawking centre in Barry. Cardiff, though not a desirable town to stay in, has lots to see on a day visit, including a first-class museum and art gallery, and an enjoyable hands-on science centre too lively to be called a museum. The zoo at Cilfrew is attractive, and the Rhondda Heritage Park, with several exciting new features this year, is much enjoyed by families now. The ambitious garden village being developed at Victoria Park near Ebbw Vale (a new entry this year) is very interesting. Monmouth and Chepstow are small towns of great character.

Though the area has no really outstanding scenery, it has some most attractive unspoilt countryside, for example around the further edges of the Gower peninsula (almost like a mini-Pembrokeshire), the cliffs at Nash Point near St Donats, the hills on the edge of the Brecon Beacons above the former mining valleys (which themselves are more appealing than many might think, with a strong sense of place), the fine gorge of the lower Wye Valley (magnificent in autumn) and the edge of the Black Mountains (which are discussed in the Mid-Wales section). Overall, a short stay here will appeal most to people – including children – who will enjoy finding out at least a little about the area's remarkable past. Coupling some of the interesting memorials of that past with the quieter delights of some of its better countryside could make for a memorable stay.

Where to stay

Whitebrook SO5306 CROWN AT WHITEBROOK Whitebrook, Monmouth, Gwent NP5 4TX (01600) 860254 **£120 inc dinner**; 12 neat rms. Small modernised hotel with 17th-c heart in beautiful Wye Valley, with friendly, caring service, a relaxed atmosphere, comfortable lounge and bar; excellent, original French cooking and fine wines in small cosy restaurant, and very good breakfasts; cl 25–26 Dec.

Govilon SO2613 LLANWENARTH HOUSE Govilon, Abergavenny, Gwent NP7 9SF (01873) 830289 **£70**; 4 spacious, comfortable rms. Fine family-run 16th-c manor house in quiet grounds within Brecon Beacons National Park, with gracious sitting room, log fires, antiques and fresh flowers; fine food using local game and fish and home-produced meat, poultry and garden veg in elegant candlelit dining room, and friendly, helpful staff; lots to do nearby; croquet; cl mid-Jan–1st wknd Mar; children over 10; disabled access.

Monmouth SO5113 RIVERSIDE Cinderhill St, Monmouth, Gwent NP5 3EY (01600) 715577 ***£68**; 17 rms. Comfortable, refurbished bustling hotel near the River Monnow and 13th-c fortified gatehouse, with good-value bar meals, an extensive menu in restaurant, conservatory, and a warm welcome; disabled access.

Monmouth SO5113 KINGS HEAD Agincourt Sq, Monmouth, Gwent NP5 3DY (01600) 712177 **£65**; 28 rms, most with own bthrm. Attractive black and white 17th-c coaching inn with friendly staff, beamed bar with log fire and elegant cocktail bar, fresh flowers, good food, and private car park; disabled access.

Abergavenny SO3014 LLANWENARTH ARMS Brecon Rd, Abergavenny, Gwent NP8 1EP (01873) 810550 ***£59**; 18 attractive rms in adjacent wing with lovely views. Welcoming, extended hotel with 16th-c heart in marvellous position on the bank of the River Usk with salmon and trout fishing; two bars,

Victorian conservatory, a warm welcome (especially for families), wide choice of home-made food in bar and restaurant, and terrace; disabled access.

Tintern Parva SO5301 Parva Farmhouse Tintern Parva, Chepstow, Gwent NP6 6SQ (01291) 689411 £58; 9 comfortable rms. Friendly stone farmhouse, rebuilt in mid-17th c, with leather chesterfields, woodburning stove and honesty bar in large beamed lounge, books (no TV downstairs), and very good food and wine (inc wine using home-grown grapes) in cosy redecorated restaurant; 50 yds from River Wye and lovely surrounding countryside.

Oxwich SS5286 Oxwich Bay Oxwich Bay, Swansea SA3 1LS (01792) 390329 £53; 13 rms. Comfortable hotel on edge of beach with dedicated, friendly staff, food served all day, restaurant/lounge bar with panoramic views, and a welcome for families; lovely area; cl 24–25 Dec.

Little Mill SO3203 Pentwyn Farm Little Mill, Pontypool, Gwent NP4 0HQ (0495) 785249 *£36; 4 rms. Most attractive pink-washed 16th-c longhouse on mixed farm of 120 acres; open fire in big sitting room, lots of books and games, good country cooking around large table in beamed dining room, large garden with swimming pool, table tennis in barn, and rough shooting in woods; cl Christmas; children over 4.

To see and do

⇊↑ **Aberdulais** SS7799 Aberdulais Falls Since the 16th c these have been used to power a range of industries from copper-smelting to tin-plate. Renovations on the turbine house are now complete, and the antique water-wheel is once again generating electricity. Wknd snacks, shop, disabled access (right to the top of the falls thanks to a lift powered by the electricity generated on site). Cl 24 Dec–1 Jan; (01639) 636674; £2.70, slightly less in winter; NT.

✝ ◫ ♿ **Abergavenny** SO2914 has some attractive ancient buildings in Nevill St and particularly Market St. There's a busy Tues and Fri market. The church has a remarkable collection of memorials. The remains of the 12th- and 14th-c castle include the walls, towers and rebuilt gatehouse; the early 19th-c keep and an adjoining house now contain a local history museum. Shop; cl 1–2pm, Sun (exc pm in summer), 24–26 Dec, 1 Jan; (01873) 854282; £1. A good Museum of Childhood and the Home on Market St includes a doll from the *Titanic*. Snacks, shop, disabled access; cl 25 Dec; (01873) 850063; *£2. The Hen & Chickens and Greyhound have good-value food, while just outside Abergavenny the King of Prussia (B4598 SE), Horse & Jockey (old Raglan rd) and Llanwenarth Arms (Brecon rd) are also good.

➤ **Barry** ST1268 Lively seaside resort which, along with its jutting-out peninsula Barry Island, grew as a centre for the coal industry. Remains of 13th-c castle, and usual fairground attractions for children. Welsh Hawking Centre (Weycock Rd) Cheery centre with over 200 birds of prey. Regular flying demonstrations, and a variety of animals for children to fuss. Snacks, shop, some disabled access; cl 25 Dec; (01446) 734687; £3. Nearby, the Star in Dinas Powis is good for lunch.

⇊↑ **Blaenavon** SO2508 Big Pit Mining Museum Sample the life of a miner by donning a safety helmet and descending 300ft in the cage into the Big Pit, which closed as a working coal mine in 1980. Also a reconstructed miner's cottage, and an exhibition in the old pithead baths. Good fun – but make sure you dress sensibly. Meals, snacks, shop, disabled access with prior warning; cl most of Dec-Feb; (01495) 790311; £4.95. Nearby are some pretty much perfectly preserved 18th-c ironworks. Cl am Sun; £1.

◫ ⚘ ❀ **Bridgend** SS9079 Newcastle Ruined 12th-c castle with surviving rectangular tower, richly carved Norman gateway and massive curtain walls; collect key from nearby corner shop. The prosperous industrial town below isn't much of a place for visitors, but nearby Merthyr Mawr SS8877, with its interesting warren of high sandhills, is attractive, as are Southerndown and Ogmore (see below). The ruined PRIORY at Ewenny is one of the finest fortified religious buildings in Britain, and there's a working POTTERY close by (cl 1–2pm, Sun exc pm summer; free). Slightly N of Bridgend, BRYNGARW COUNTRY PARK is an unexpectedly tranquil refuge from the M4, with woodland walks, formal gardens, ornamental lakes and a Japanese garden; snacks, shop, disabled access; cl 25–26 Dec; (01656) 725155; free.

🏛🕒**Caerleon** ST3490 FORTRESS BATHS, AMPHITHEATRE AND BARRACKS One of the best examples of an amphitheatre in the country, alongside a similarly well preserved bath house, now under cover. Also the foundations of barrack lines and parts of the ramparts, and the remains of the cookhouse and latrines. Cl am winter Sun, 25–26 Dec, 1 Jan; £1.50. The adjacent ROMAN LEGIONARY MUSEUM gives some idea of the daily life of the garrison, with plenty of finds from the site and elsewhere. Shop, disabled access; cl am Sun, 24–26 Dec, 1 Jan, Good Fri; (01633) 423134; £1.50. You can get a joint ticket for the Museum and the Baths. The Tourist Information Centre on the High St has a little art gallery and various craft workshops; the Wheatsheaf out at Llanhennock ST3592 has good-value snacks.

🏰**Caerphilly** ST1587 Oddly strung-out small town, dominated by the CASTLE, the largest in Wales, with extensive land and water defences. Rising sheer from its broad outer moat, it's a proper picture-book castle, pleasing for this reason to the most casual visitor. It also enthrals serious students of castle architecture, as it's a remarkably complex design of concentric defences. Watch out for the incredible leaning tower, which looks like it's going to topple over any second. Cl am winter Suns; (01222) 465511; £2. The ancient Courthouse overlooking the castle has a good quick carvery (they also make and sell Caerphilly cheese), while the thatched Travellers Rest is good value.

🏛**Caerwent** ST4791 ROMAN WALLS These massive walls, still some 15ft high in places, enclosed the large site of Venta Silurum – over 40 acres, enough for a sizeable town, though none of that's left now; free. The Carpenters Arms up in the attractive village of Shirenewton does good-value food.

🏰🕒**Caldicot** ST4888 The 12th–14th-c CASTLE was restored as a family home in the 1880s, and lived in until 20 years ago – since when it's been a local museum. It's surrounded by a country park. Snacks, shop, limited disabled access; cl am Sun, Nov–Feb, lunchtimes in Mar; (01291) 420241; *£1.20.

🏰🕒⚓❀!**Cardiff** ST1876 The civic centre has a range of grand 20th-c white stone civic or governmental buildings around a formal park. The old city centre is closer to Cardiff Castle (see below), which has Capability Brown's 18th-c landscaped park between it and the river. In the centre, parts are pedestrianised (for example around the fine church of St John the Baptist), and there are many covered shopping arcades, Victorian and modern. CARDIFF CASTLE Despite their fairy-tale medieval appearance, the main buildings are largely 19th c, when the Marquess of Bute employed William Burges to rebuild and restore the place, adding richly romantic wall paintings, tapestries and carvings. Some parts are much older, and in the grounds there's even a piece of a 10ft-thick wall which formed part of a Roman fort here. The Norman keep survives, and there's a 13th-c tower – they look like proper castle architecture, perched on a little mound. Snacks, shop; cl 25–26 Dec, 1 Jan; (01222) 822083; £3.30 for full guided tour, £2.20 grounds only. The later towers are now a couple of regimental museums. NATIONAL MUSEUM OF WALES (Cathays Park) Considerably enlivened recently and now truly of national interest, with interactive displays and exhibitions on subjects as diverse as ceramics, coins and prehistoric sea monsters. The East Wing has an impressive collection of paintings, with notable French Impressionists, and there's an excellent section on the evolution of the Welsh landscape. Meals, snacks, shop, disabled access; cl am Sun, Mon exc bank hols, 25 Dec; (01222)

344111; £2.50. WELSH INDUSTRIAL AND MARITIME MUSEUM (Bute St) Exhaustive exploration of Welsh industrial and maritime development, spread over five former dockland buildings. One gallery houses ancient trams, cars and so forth, another various industrial engines (many of which may clank, whirr, thud or grind noisily into life), another locomotives, full size or model, yet another ships and shipping, and there's more outside. Shop, disabled access; cl Mon (exc bank hols), 24–26 Dec, 1 Jan; (01222) 481919; £1.50. TECHNIQUEST (Stuart St) Fun as well as interest at this hands-on high-tech science centre, with some fascinating displays – even a realistic dragon conjured up by laser. They've just moved across the road to a new site by the docks, doubling the exhibition space and making it the biggest science centre in Britain. New features include a planetarium and science theatre. All exceptionally well done, and an excellent family excursion. Snacks, shop, disabled access; cl Mon during term-time, 24–26 Dec; (01222) 460211; £3. These last two attractions are at the heart of the Cardiff Bay Development Area, an ambitious rejuvenation of the Inner Harbour and Docklands. There's also an incredible space-age-looking VISITOR CENTRE explaining the project, and a slightly incongruous Norwegian timbered church; the dockland's New Sea Lock (Harrowby St) may be Cardiff's most unspoilt pub, the smarter Wharf (Atlantic Wharf) is right on the water's edge. Llandaff is a mile or two out from the centre, where the CATHEDRAL has been rebuilt several times; it includes some delightful medieval masonry, Pre-Raphaelite works, a marvellous modern timber roof, and a central concrete arch that you may think a mistake. The nearby green has an attractive collection of buildings around it. WELSH FOLK MUSEUM (St Fagans, 4m W) Excellent 100-acre open-air museum, with a variety of reconstructed buildings from castles to cottages illustrating styles and living conditions throughout the ages. Buildings have come from all over Wales, and there are some remarkable exhibits, inc a homely gas-lit Edwardian farmhouse and an entire Celtic village. Also crafts and lots of seasonal events – there's plenty to fascinate here. It's part of the National Museum of Wales. Meals, snacks, shop, disabled access; cl Sun Nov–Mar, 25–26 Dec, 1 Jan; (01222) 569441; *£4. In Cardiff centre the Cottage and Philharmonic both in St Mary's St and Golden Cross in Custom House St are quite useful for lunch.

⚑ ♿ Chepstow ST5393 is a steep but civilised small town, still with its battlemented 13th-c town gate. CHEPSTOW CASTLE The first recorded Norman stone castle, proudly standing on an easily defended spot above the Wye, overlooks the harbour. You can still peep out through the variety of slots for weapons cut into the massive walls and towers. The huge gatehouse with its portcullis grooves and ancient gates is splendid. There's an exhibition on siege warfare and the English Civil War, and you can try on a period helmet. Shop, disabled access; cl am Sun in winter, 24–26 Dec, 1 Jan; £2.90. STUART CRYSTAL have a museum and workshop opposite, and there's a working pottery on Lower Church St (cl 1–2pm). There's a good local history MUSEUM on Bridge St. Cl 1–2pm, am Sun; £1. The civilised Bridge and Castle View are both good for lunch.

✔ ! Cilfrew SN7700 PENSCYNOR WILDLIFE PARK Lots of animals in a charming setting, inc meerkats, parrots, tropical birds and 25 species of monkey. You can feed rainbow trout or take a ride in the chairlift to the clifftop – coming down again on an exciting bobsleigh ride. Meals, snacks, shop, disabled access; cl 25 Dec; (01639) 642189; £4.

⚑ Coity SS9281 COITY CASTLE The Hall, chapel and remains of a square keep are preserved on this site, which was used as a stronghold from the 12th to the 16th c; key available locally, see notice on gate; free. The Six Bells opposite is useful for lunch.

⚒ Crynant SN7904 CEFN COED COLLIERY MUSEUM The story of mining in the Dulais Valley on the site of a former colliery. It still has a steam

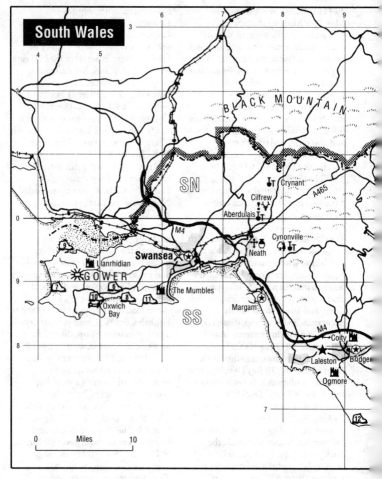

winding-engine, though the winding gear is now run by electricity. Also a simulated underground mining gallery, boilerhouse and compressor house. Summer snacks, shop, disabled access; cl 25 Dec–2 Jan; (01639) 750556; £1.25. Just up the valley at Seven Sisters is a WORKING SAWMILL with wood-working demonstrations. The same site also has a miners lamp museum, and a Wild West town (with cowboy gunfights) for children. Meals, snacks, shop, disabled access; open wknds Apr–1st wknd in Sept, daily summer and bank hols; (01639) 701443; £1.95.

🐏 🐑 **Cwmbran** ST2995

GREENMEADOW COMMUNITY FARM (1m W) Founded to protect one of the encroaching new town's last green areas, this friendly farm has a wide range of animals – traditional, rare and cuddly – as well as a deer enclosure, bluebell wood, and various craft workshops. Meals, snacks, shop, disabled access; cl 25 Dec; (01633) 862202; £2.25. Up towards Pontypool the canalside Open Hearth (Griffithstown) has good food.

🐂 🚂 **Cynonville** SS8294 AFAN FOREST PARK 9,000 tranquil acres of forest, with lots of trails for walking or cycling (you can hire mountain bikes in summer), visitor centre, and the WELSH MINERS MUSEUM, vividly illustrating life as a miner with coal faces, pit gear and

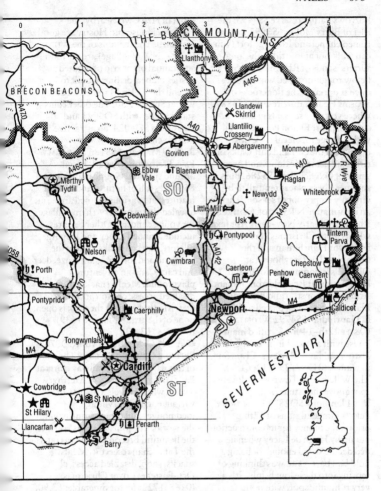

mining equipment among the displays. Meals, snacks, shop, disabled access; park cl only 25–26 Dec, museum cl wkdys Nov–May; (01639) 850564; 50p museum, park free, though £1 parking charge wknds and bank hols Apr–Aug.

❀ **Ebbw Vale** SO1609 VICTORIA PARK (Victoria, 2m S on A4046) The site of the 1992 Garden Festival, still full of the lakes, gardens, wetlands and woodland from then. Much of the site is being developed as an ambitious garden village, with houses, shops and businesses gradually being constructed over parts of the landscaped grounds, though the bulk of these will remain untouched; it's

fascinating watching the project's progress. A Visitor Centre has the full story. Pleasant walks and trails, interesting exhibitions, and some quite extraordinary sculptures, one made from 30,000 individually modelled clay bricks. Snacks, shop, disabled access; centre cl 25 Dec; (01495) 350010; free.

❈ **The Gower** This peninsula stretching W of Swansea has quite a bit of off-putting ribbon development along the roads entering it, but it's well worth persevering as the further parts are full of interest around the coast: the long glistening cockle sands below Llanrhidian SS4992; the dunes and marshy slacks of the Whiteford

Burrows nature reserve SS4495; the islet of Burry Holms SS3992 with its ruined chapel and Iron Age fort (you can walk out at low tide); the long surfers' sands of Rhossili Bay SS3990 below rough-cropped windswept open moorland; the tidal rocks of Worms Head nature reserve SS3887 where you may see seals in late summer; Port Eynon Point SS4884 with its huge medieval rock-dove dovecot in the cliff and cliff walks on either side; and the dunes and broad sands of Oxwich Bay SS5286. Busy in summer, these places tend all to be virtually empty out of season. There's an informative NT VISITOR CENTRE at Rhossili. Cl early Nov–early Apr (exc wknds up to Christmas). See entries below for Llanrhidian and the Mumbles. The Greyhound at Oldwalls is popular for food, and King Arthur at Reynoldston, Joiners Arms at Bishopston and Britannia at Llanmadoc are well placed too.

🏰 Llanrhidian SS4792 WEOBLEY CASTLE 12th–14th-c fortified manor house with an exhibition on the area's history, and superb views. Cl am Sun in winter; (01792) 390012; £1.50. The Welcome to Town is in a lovely spot above the estuary.

🏰 † Llanthony SO2827 LLANTHONY PRIORY Graceful ruins of 12th-c priory, the money for its construction put up by Hugh de Lacey when he decided he'd had enough of being a bold bad baron and was thinking of retiring into these lonely hills. It's a very romantic spot, with nothing much but the noise of the sheep to disturb the peace. You can still see the west towers, north nave arcade and south transept, covering a variety of architectural styles. Always open, free. The very ancient crypt bar below the Abbey Hotel, right among the priory buildings, is useful for a snack lunch – a most unusual place. On the way up the valley, turn off to see medieval CWMYOY CHURCH SO2923: repeated landslips have left the whole church twisted, and its tower leans at an angle that makes the Tower of Pisa look positively sober.

🏰 Llantilio Crosseny SO3915 is attractive, and there's a lovely view of the 13th-c church from the former

moat of Hen Cwrt nearby; the Halfway House and Hostry are good for lunch. The remains of the WHITE CASTLE (NW of village) are the most substantial of the trio of moated castles Hubert de Burgh built to defend the Welsh Marches. Cl am winter Suns; £1.50. The other ruins stand at Skenfrith SO4621 and Grosmont SO4024, an attractive hillside village.

🏰 🎢 ☺ Margam SS8186 MARGAM PARK Pretty country park based around splendid Gothic mansion, its 850 acres full of natural and historic features and various themed areas, inc a scaled-down nursery-rhyme village for young children. Other features include a ruined abbey and Iron Age hill fort, marked walks among the parkland and forests, giant maze, deer and cattle, and an adventure playground. Meals, snacks, shop, disabled access; cl Mon and Tues Oct–Mar (when only the park is open, none of the attractions); (01639) 871131; *£3.10.

🏰🎢🚂♿🎢 Merthyr Tydfil SO0707 BRECON MOUNTAIN RAILWAY The route of this narrow-gauge railway starts at Pant Station, 3 miles N of Merthyr Tydfil, where there's a display of various engines inc vintage locomotives and others from around the world. The journey takes you into the beautiful Brecon Beacons as far as the Taf Fechan reservoir. Meals, snacks, shop, disabled access; cl Oct–Easter exc over Christmas; (01685) 722988 for timetable; £3.90. On a disused railway line, the Dowlais Viaduct is a striking sight, well worth a detour. CYFARTHFA CASTLE (Cyfarthfa Park) Impressive early 19th-c castellated Gothic mansion, set in beautiful gardens dating from the same period. It was built for the owner of what were then the largest ironworks in Britain. Recently restored to their full Regency glory, the state rooms contain a museum with displays on Egyptology and archaeology. Snacks, shop, disabled access; cl am Sun, and Sat too in winter, when also cl 1–2pm; (01685) 723112; *80p. JOSEPH PARRY'S COTTAGE (Chapel Row) The composer of *Myfanwy* was born here, and the ground floor has been restored and decorated in the style of the 1840s. Also displays about the industrial and social history of the area in those prosperous 19th-c days. Shop, limited disabled access; cl am, Nov–Easter; (01685) 73117; 60p. YNYSFACH ENGINE HOUSE Models, photographs and an excellent audio-visual programme recount the history of the local iron industry. The displays are housed where once stood the beam-engine of the Ynysfach Iron Works. Snacks, shop; cl am wknds (all day winter), 25 Dec; (01685) 721858; *£1.15. The interesting Red Lion up at Penderyn is useful for lunch and not that far off, and the Glan Taff down the road in Treharris (off the road and over the bridge) is useful too. GARWNANT FOREST CENTRE SN9913 (5m NW, off A470) Looking out over the Llwyn-On reservoir on the S edge of the National Park, carefully restored old farm buildings with displays on forestry, wildlife and conservation, and information on nature trails and cycle routes through the forest. Snacks, shop, disabled access; centre cl am wknds, Oct–Easter, though the park is open all year; (01639) 710221; free.

★ ☠ ♿ **Monmouth** SO5102 is an attractive market town of considerable character; below the remains of the 12th-c castle where Henry V was born, and the 17th-c Great Castle House (built with enormous blocks of masonry in its precincts), the main Agincourt Square is surrounded by handsome buildings, inc the imposing central Shire Hall with its arcaded market floor. The town nestles in the crook formed by the River Wye and the River Monnow, with a splendid 13th-c gatehouse bridge over the Monnow. The NELSON MUSEUM AND LOCAL HISTORY CENTRE (Priory St) has a tremendous collection relating to Nelson – china, books, prints, letters, glass, medals and best of all his fighting sword. Nelson has nothing to do with Monmouth, but the collection was originally put together by Lady Llangattock who lived nearby. Shop, disabled access; cl 1–2pm, 24–26 Dec, 1 Jan; (01600)

713519; £1. The Punch House is the most enjoyable place here for lunch, and the King's Head Hotel and, at the other end of town, Riverside Hotel are also good.

☠ **Mumbles** SS6188 OYSTERMOUTH CASTLE Very complete ruins of the de Breose family castle, in a small park overlooking the bay. The gatehouse, chapel and great hall date from the 13th to 14th c; 80p. Mumbles is a pleasantly unspoilt resort, and the White Rose does good-value food.

✝ ♿ **Neath** SS7597 NEATH ABBEY The remains of a Cistercian abbey founded in 1130 by Richard de Grainville. Disabled access; cl am Sun, 25–26 Dec; free. The BOROUGH MUSEUM (Gwyn Hall, Orchard St) has a good range of local history, inc finds from a nearby Roman fort. Shop, disabled access; cl Sun, Mon (exc bank hols); (01639) 645741; free.

🏠♿ **Nelson** ST1195 LLANCAIACH FAWR This is the sort of stately home children won't mind visiting – they can try on armour, have a go at crushing herbs in the kitchen, or dress up in period clothes in the nursery. The Elizabethan manor house has been transformed into a living history museum, its Civil War days brought vividly to life by costumed guides who rarely step out of character – they even speak in 17th-c style. Meals, snacks, shop, disabled access; cl 25–26 Dec, 1 Jan; (01443) 412248; £3.50.

♿🏠🌸⚘ **Newport** ST3189 is industrial. The MUSEUM AND ART GALLERY on John Frost Square has good varied collections ranging from Roman finds to teapots. Shop, mostly disabled access; cl Sun and bank hols; (01633) 840064; free. TREDEGAR HOUSE (SW edge of town) Magnificent 17th-c house and gardens set in 90-acre landscaped park. The Morgans, later Lords Tredegar, lived here for five centuries, and the activities of the household, below and above stairs, are well illustrated in the 30 or so rooms on show. In the grounds are carriage rides, self-guided trails and craft workshops, as well as boating and an adventure playfarm. Meals, snacks, shop, disabled access; cl Mon, Tues, Oct wkdys, Nov–Mar; (01633) 816069; £3.50. Past here on the

B4239 the Lighthouse at St Brides
Wentlooge has good food upstairs,
and great Severn views.

☗ Ogmore SS8675 OGMORE CASTLE
Three-storeyed 12th-c keep with a
preserved hooded fireplace, a dry
moat surrounding the inner ward and
a surviving 40ft west wall. The setting
of this ruin is attractive: odd that this
impressive fortress was only built to
defend the row of stepping stones
which still cross the river; free. The
Pelican is good for lunch, and the
cheery Three Golden Cups along the
road at Southerndown gives sea views
to Devon on a clear day. Just past it
there's a car park by the interestingly
preserved remains of the seaside
gardens of entirely demolished
Dunraven Castle SS8873, with walks
by the cliffs over the sands and rock
pools, and around to the fragmentary
remains of an Iron Age promontory
hill fort above the sea.

ヮ▣ Penarth ST1871 COSMESTON
MEDIEVAL VILLAGE (just S) Living
museum of medieval life,
reconstructed on the site of an actual
village which was deserted during the
14th c. Hens and sheep wander round
between the cottages. Snacks, shop,
disabled access; cl Dec; (01222)
708686; £1. It's set in the Cosmeston
Lakes Country Park with lakes,
woodland and wildlife. TURNER HOUSE
Small gallery with temporary
exhibitions from the National
Museum of Wales. Shop, disabled
access to ground floor only; cl
12.45–2pm, am Sun, Mon (exc bank
hols), and between exhibitions; 50p.
Down by the sea S of the town at
Swanbridge the Captain's Wife has
just been reopened as a comfortable
family dining pub.

☗ Penhow ST4290 PENHOW CASTLE
The oldest lived-in castle in Wales,
with tours of the restored rooms
taking you from the 12th-c ramparts
and Norman bedchamber through the
15th-c Great Hall with its minstrels'
gallery to the Victorian housekeeper's
room. There's a choice of several good
Walkman tours, some concentrating
on a particular topic, such as the
musical or domestic history of the
building. You can stay here; snacks,
shop; cl Mon (exc bank hols), Tues,

Oct–Easter exc Weds and occasional
Suns – best to check first; (01633)
400800; £2.95.

ヮ ♘ Pontypool SO2800 VALLEY
INHERITANCE (Dare Country Park) The
story of a South Wales valley, with
exhibitions, displays and films housed
in this Georgian stable block of
Pontypool Park House. Snacks, shop,
disabled access; cl am Sun, all Jan;
(01495) 752036; *£1.20. The
surrounding country park has
pleasant wood and moorland walks.
The Open Hearth just below the canal
at Griffithstown is good for lunch.

ヮ! Porth ST0491 RHONDDA HERITAGE
PARK Based in the last colliery
buildings in the area, a very good
developing centre with lively multi-
media exhibitions recreating the days
when coal was king. Sights, sounds
and smells from the life and work of
the miners, and an excellent new
underground tour showing what it
was like to work a shift; the noise and
heat are uncannily realistic. It ends
with an exciting dark ride back to the
surface. Unusual features include the
gallery with art by locals, a section on
the role of women, and an authentic
Valley chapel. Good themed play area
for children. Meals, snacks, shop,
disabled access; cl Mon Oct–Mar,
25–26 Dec; (01443) 682036; *£4.95.

☗ Raglan SO4107 RAGLAN CASTLE
Quite magnificent ruins of 15th-c
castle, particularly notable for its
Yellow Tower of Gwent. Its intricate
history is displayed in the closet tower
and two rooms of the gatehouse. Cl
am winter Sun; *£2. The friendly Ship
has decent food.

ⵀ St Hilary ST0173 BEAUPRÉ CASTLE
Well preserved ruined Elizabethan
courtyard mansion with an
extraordinarily elaborate three-storey
Italianate porch; free. The Bush is
good for lunch.

❀ ♘ St Nicholas ST0972 DYFFRYN
GARDENS Small themed gardens and
seasonal bedding displays help break
up the 50 acres of rare plants and
shrubs which make up these lovely
gardens. Also extensive plant houses,
inc a large temperate house and a
succulent house, and an arboretum.
Meals, snacks, shop, disabled access;
information centre cl Nov–Mar;

(01222) 591966; *£2. There's an open-air theatre here in summer.

🏰 ✤ ⬆ 🅿 🔆 **Swansea** SS6592, largely post-industrial and commercial, has few buildings of any age or great appeal to visitors. Long sandy beaches have made it something of a family summer resort. Among some high spots is the 1934 GUILDHALL, containing the Brangwyn Hall with its 16 huge British Empire murals painted by Sir Frank Brangwyn for the House of Lords – Wales's gain, as they were judged too controversial. There are some castle ruins (which one is not allowed into but can see from outside), inc a striking 14th-c first-floor arcade. MARITIME AND INDUSTRIAL MUSEUM (Museum Sq, Maritime Quarter) In the heart of the revitalised docks, an excellent collection that's now one of the most-visited attractions in the area. Highlights include the collection of historic ships – the biggest and most varied collection of floating maritime exhibits in Wales (Apr–Oct) – and a complete working woollen mill. Lots of thought is put into the displays. Shop, disabled access; cl Mon (exc bank hols), 25–26 Dec, 1 Jan; (01792) 650351; free. GLYNN VIVIAN ART GALLERY AND MUSEUM (Alexandra Rd) Good changing exhibitions, with permanent displays of porcelain from Swansea's all-too-brief but brilliant period of production between 1814 and 1824, and paintings, drawings and sculptures by British, French and, above all, Welsh artists – especially the locally born Ceri Richards. Shop, some disabled access; cl Mon (exc bank hols); (01792) 655006; free. PLANTASIA (Parc Tawe) Tropical and desert plants in big futuristic landscaped glasshouse, also aviary. Snacks, shop, disabled access; (01792) 474555; cl Mon, 25–26 Dec; *£1. The Hanbury in Kingsway is popular for lunch.

✝ 🌿 **Tintern** SO5200 TINTERN ABBEY Remarkably well preserved, these 14th-c ruins were considered an essential spot for 18th-c artists and poets to visit, lying as they do in a lovely part of the steeply wooded Wye Valley. Wordsworth was just one of them to find inspiration here. The arches and windows still bear witness to the fact that it was once the richest abbey in Wales. Shop, disabled access; cl 24–26 Dec, 1 Jan; (01291) 689251; £2. The ABBEY MILL nearby has been converted into a craft centre, with a decent coffee shop; cl winter Mon and Tues. A VISITOR CENTRE at Tintern Old Station can help you make the most of the surrounding hills and woodland.

🏰 **Tongwynlais** ST1382 CASTELL COCH This spectacular triangular hillside landmark, designed in 1875 by William Burges for the Marquis of Bute, is actually based on a 13th-c castle in spite of its improbable appearance, something by Disney out of Wagner – red sandstone, conical towers, drawbridge and portcullis. Though never finished, it's a very successful pastiche, and inside is just as impressive: an astonishly elaborate mock-medieval idyll of gilt, gorgeous colours, statues, murals and carvings – especially remarkable is the bedroom of Lady Bute, decorated on the theme of Sleeping Beauty. Shop, disabled access to ground floor only; cl am winter Suns, 24–26 Dec, 1 Jan; (01222) 810101; £2.

★ **Attractive villages or small towns**, all with decent pubs, include Bedwellty SO1600, Cowbridge SS9974, Laleston SS8879, St Hilary ST0173 and Usk SO3801, which also has a decent rural life museum in an old barn. Pubs or inns elsewhere which are particularly useful for their attractive surroundings or views include the Lamb & Flag out on the Brecon road from Abergavenny SO2515, Bridgend by the canal at Gilwern SO2414, Old Glais at Glais SN7000, Prince of Wales at Kenfig SS8383, Old House at Llangynwyd SS8588, Greyhound at Llantrisant ST3997, Brynfynnon at Llanwonno ST0295, Plough & Harrow at Monknash SS9270, Rowan Tree at Nelson ST1195 and Halfway House at Talycoed SO4115.

✝ **Churches:** Patrishow in the Black Mountains not far from Llanthony is remarkable, with a musicians' gallery and a mural of a figure of Death wielding a shovel; Bettws Newydd SO3605, largely unaltered from the 15th c, also has a gallery and fine screen.

Walks

Part of Gwent's boundary with England is made up of the picturesque Lower Wye gorge. The **Wye Valley Walk** ⌂-1 connects Chepstow ST5394 with Tintern SO5301 – there are only occasional views down to the river, but the short detour up steps to the Wynd Cliff viewpoint ST5297 gets an extensive panorama. Further good sections of the gorge can be walked from **Monmouth** SO5113 ⌂-2 to Fairview Rock SO5514, a lofty crag near the Biblins suspension bridge; a level track supplies an easy riverside route.

The industrial valleys have rather scrappy moorland and patches of conifer plantations rising high above the towns; it's not a pretty scene, but its gruff sense of place appeals to some. There are some interesting examples of post-mining land reclamation, including **Parc Cwm Darran** ⌂-3 in the Rhymney Valley near Bargoed ST1499, which now provides a wide variety of natural habitats for wildlife and plants, with scenery ranging from the valley floor through forest areas to upland moors with superb views of the Brecon Beacons; and the **Afon Lwyd Valley** ⌂-4 between Cwmbran New Town ST2995 and Blaenavon SO2509. The abrupt transition from here into the empty wildness of the Brecon Beacons National Park (described under Mid-Wales but very easily reached from here) is startling. The Black Mountains, too, are discussed under Mid-Wales, though the valleys stretching up into them from Gwent, for instance past **Llanthony** SO2827 ⌂-5, offer some of the best approaches.

The Gower Peninsula encapsulates on a small scale many different types of Welsh landscape, once beyond the creeping urbanisation W of Swansea. It rises to rounded moorland hills such as **Cefn Bryn** SS4989 ⌂-6 and **Rhossili Down** SS4190 ⌂-7, which offer breathtaking views of both – or all three – coasts. From Rhossili you can also take in Mewslade Bay SS4187, where the sands are enclosed by limestone cliffs. From **Penmaen** SS5388 ⌂-8 (NT car park near the church) a good walk follows the lane to Threecliff Bay, then heads W along the coast as far as Nicholaston Farm to end with the mild ascent of Cefn Bryn ridge. **Whiteford Burrows** SS4495 ⌂-9 (pine trees and sand dunes), **Oxwich Bay** SS5196 ⌂-10 (more dunes, presided over by Oxwich Point on its W side), and tiny **Brandy Cove** SS5887 ⌂-11 (walk down the wooded Bishopston Valley to get there) are among other highlights. The N coast is attractive only at its western extreme.

Closer to Cardiff, the curious striped cliffs of the Glamorgan coast look over the Bristol Channel to Exmoor. **Nash Point** SS9168 ⌂-12 is the best access point, as it is worth getting to shore level to see the cliffs in their full glory.

Driving

The NW corner of Gwent has some of this area's most attractive drives, through lonely and unspoilt hill country. A delightful run is from Llanfihangel Crucorney a few miles N of Abergavenny up the Vale of Ewyas into these sheep-dotted hills, passing Llanthony Priory and on to Hay-on-Wye in Mid-Wales. Near the bottom of this charming valley, the side road to Crickhowell (also in Mid-Wales) is another pleasant drive. Gwent also has a fine stretch of the Wye Valley, and the slow A466 following the river between Chepstow and Monmouth, passing Tintern and dodging across into Gloucestershire, has lovely scenery, particularly in autumn; this is the most dramatic if not the most lonely of the Gwent valleys, twisting through high hills.

Other parts of Gwent are less striking, though still pleasant for country drives. N of Monmouth, the B4347 up to Grosmont is a pleasant drive through quiet rolling farmland with a succession of gentle views, typical of this area. The views are generally more interesting in the N, where the hills add a touch of grandeur, than in the S. The B4521 and B4233 across the heart of the area, and the B4598 from Abergavenny to Usk, share this pastoral mood, and the many side roads which straggle off into this farmland bring you into very rustic territory. The B4235 from Chepstow to Usk has some good views over this Gwent countryside, framed by distant hills. Almost paralleling it is a road between Usk and Caerwent through the high country of Caerwent, for the most part pretty, though a mile or two winds through dense conifer plantations.

The roads up the narrow former mining valleys of Glamorgan are interesting for the way the brick houses are so steeply terraced along the sides, and also for the way that side roads take you so quickly into higher untouched mountain pastures. In this part the hills between the valleys are increasingly blanketed with conifer plantations. One pleasant road that winds around the edges of the forest, with good valley views, as well as taking you into it is the hill road off the A4233 above Ferndale, zigzagging very steeply up towards St Gwynno Forest around Llanwonno. Another busier road with a good mix of forest and valley views is the A4061/A4107 between Rhondda and Cwmafan. Up the Rhondda Valley, once past Treherbert the A4061 linking at Hirwaun with the A4059 is an attractive road to Brecon in Mid-Wales, as is the quite busy A470 from Merthyr Tydfil.

On the coast, the B4524 from Ewenny past Ogmore gives a good view of ruined Ogmore Castle, the extensive Merthyr Mawr sand dunes, and then past Ogmore by Sea some brief but fine sea and coast views – best from the side road in Southerndown down to the beachside Dunraven car park. From the W exit roundabout at junction 46 of the M4 (first left off the A48 back towards Neath), the back road to Ammanford is quite good, up over high lonely sheep pastures. Around the Gower, the B4295 and then the coast road through Old-walls to Cheriton give good views out over the Loughor cockle flats.

Besides the M4 itself, the M50 to Ross-on-Wye gives a good connection with the M5, and from Ross the A40 is a good dual carriageway, through attractive scenery, to Abergavenny. Three good N/S dual carriageways which also help to open up the area are the A449 between Newport and Raglan, the A4042 from Newport up past Pontypool, and the A470 from Cardiff up towards Merthyr Tydfil. These good communications put most parts of the area within an hour or so of the Severn Bridge, and if the traffic's flowing freely you can, for example, get to Abergavenny from Birmingham in about 1½ hours.

Where to eat

Llandewi Skirrid SO3416 WALNUT TREE (01873) 852797 Comfortable, stylish dining pub run by the same licensees for over 25 years, with outstanding, imaginative – though not cheap – food (wonderful puddings and fine cheeses), attractive choice of wines (particularly strong on Italian ones), and efficient, friendly service; cl Sun, Mon, 2 wks Feb; disabled access. £32|£5.50/£11.50.

Cardiff ST1877 HAPPY GATHERING (01222) 397531 Very good Chinese food; cl 24–26 Dec. £18.75|£8.

Swansea SS6187 ROOTS 2 Woodville Rd (01792) 366006 Fresh, home-made vegetarian food in simple restaurant/café (most choice in evening), relaxed atmosphere, friendly staff; bring your own wine; Fridays are reserved for non-smokers, other days there is a no-smoking area; cl Sun, Mon, 25 Dec. £17.50|£1.60/£4.75.

Cardiff ST1877 LUCIANOS Park Lane (01222) 382367 Good Italian food warmly recommended by contributors; cl Sun, bank hols. £3.50.

Llancarfan ST0570 FOX & HOUNDS (01446) 781297 Comfortably modernised, friendly old pub in lovely village with rambling bar, open fire, popular restaurant, tasty food, good coffee, and helpful service; no food winter pm Sun. £1.50/£4.50.

Help this year from: D C Head, Ron and Pat Grace, Guy Sankey, Tom and Jeanne Barnes, John Oddey, Mavis Linstrum, Michael and Jenny Back, G Hallett, Mr and Mrs Bryn Gardner, D Evans, A A Turnbull, Dr and Mrs A K Clarke, Ian Phillips, S Watkins, P A Taylor, Mr and Mrs B Hobden, Barbara Ann Mayer, Patrick Freeman, R T and J C Moggridge, C H Stride, Andrew Lindell, Dave Braisted, Derek and Cerys Williams, Nick Haslewood, Mary Ann Cameron, John and Joan Nash, Joan and Michel Hooper-Immins, L G Milligan, Ian Clay, Dr Bill Baker, P J Howell, Nigel Woolliscroft, Philip Putwain, D W Jones-Williams, P G Topp, W F C Phillips, A A Turnbull, G Richardson, Simon and Louise Chappell, Mrs D M Everard, Peter and Audrey Dowsett, John MacLean, E G Parish, Linda and Brian Davis, Mark Bradley, Lorrie and Mick Marchington, M G Lavery, Pete Baker, Gwynne Harper, M E Hughes, Mike Dickerson, S Watkin, Basil Minson, Steve Thomas, G Roberts, DG, Neil and Elaine Piper, Paul McPherson, Eric and Jackie Robinson, Brian and Jill Bond, T A Smith, Roy Bromell, Mike Dickerson, Lyn Juffernholz, Alan Ruttley, Jay Voss, Anne Morris, Neal Marsden, Ian Jones, James Skinner, Robert Huddleston, Graham Reeve, Wyn Churchill.

WALES CALENDAR

Some of these dates were provisional as we went to press.

JANUARY

1 **Swansea** UK year of Literature and Writing – *till 31 Dec* (01792) 645939;
Newport Museum and Art Gallery: L S Lowry – The Man and His Art –
till Sat 21 (01633) 840064

13 **Llanwrtyd Wells** Saturnalia – Celebrating the Old Roman Festival
(015913) 236

14 **Aberystwyth** New Contemporaries at Jenny Fell Arts Centre – *till Weds 25,
also 16 Feb–11 March* (01970) 622889

MARCH

10 **LLanwrtyd Wells** Folk Weekend – *till Sun 12* (015913) 635

18 **Cardiff** Arms Park, Rugby Union: Wales v Ireland (01222) 390111

24 **Port Talbot** Welsh Beautiful Homes and Gardens Exhibition – *till Sun 26*
(01202) 604306

APRIL

14 **Tondu** Welsh International Rugby Festival – *till Mon 17*
(01656) 767577

15 **Llanelwedd** Working Breeds of Wales Dog Show at the Showground
(01639) 823078

17 **Llanelwedd** Fishing Fair at the Showground (01982) 553563

28 **Narbeth** Lansker Walking Festival – *till 6 May* (01834) 860965

29 **Llanelwedd** Wales and Border Counties Game and Country Fair at the
Showground – *till Sun 30* (01386) 48974

MAY

6 **Bodedern** and District Festival with Wakes, stagecoach, moral play
and concerts – *till Fri 12* (01407) 740858; **Corwen** Verdi's Requiem
as part of the Dee and Clwyd Festival of Choral Music (016784) 638;
Haverfordwest Pembrokeshire YFC County Rally at the County
Showground (01437) 762639; **Llandudno** Extravaganza – *till Mon 8*
(01492) 871031; **Llanelwedd** Glanusk Stallion Show at the
Showground (01892) 553563; **Porthmadog** Steam Gala with
military flavour and visiting WW1 locomotives from France and UK
(01766) 512340; **Wrexham Maelor** Arts Festival – *till Sat 27*
(01978) 292681

11 **Newtown** Mid-Wales May festival – *till Sun 14* (01686) 688102;
Cardiff Singer of the world competition at St David's Hall, The Hayes –
till Sat 17 (01222) 572888

19 **Llangollen** International Festival of Jazz – *till Sun 21* (0151) 339 3367

20 **Llanelwedd** Royal Welsh International Antique and Collectors Fair at
the Showground – *till Sun 21* (01636) 702326

25 **Llantilio Crossenny** Festival of Music and Drama with chamber music,
opera and orchestral works – *till Sun 28* (01873) 840352

26 **Hay-on-Wye** Hay Festival – *till 4 Jun* (01497) 821299;
Llanfair Clydogau Spring Fair with world, folk and local music,
dance and music workshops. All under canvas – *till Mon 29*
(0157 045) 379

WALES CALENDAR

MAY cont

27 **Beaumaris** Festival – *till 4 Jun* (01248) 750057 Ext 110; **Cardiff** Jazz Festival – *till Mon 29* (01222) 340591; **Llanelwedd** Welsh Motorcycle Extravaganza at the Showground – *till Sun 28* (01934) 626159; **St David's** Cathedral Festival – *till 3 Jun* (01437) 720804; **St Donat's** Crafts in Action at St Donat's Castle – *till Sun 28* (01446) 794848

JUNE

3 **Cardiff** Annual Festival of Male Voice Praise at St David's Hall (01222) 371236; **St Asaph** Fireworks and Laser Concert at Bodelwyddan Castle (01625) 575681

10 **Cardiff** Singer of the World Competition at St David's Hall – *till Sat 17* (01222) 371236; **Chepstow** Horse Trials – *till Sun 11* (01291) 622419; **Llanwrtyd Wells** Man v Horse v Mountain Bike, £15,000 prize if runner wins, currently 4 min gap (01591) 610236; **Rhydyfelin** Aberystwyth Agricultural Show at Tanycastell Park (01970) 820030

12 **Margam** Passion Play at Margam Park – *till Sat 17, also Mon 19–Weds 24* (01639) 813578

17 **Criccieth** Festival – *till Mon 26* (01766) 810584

18 **nr Wrexham** Water Music at Erddig (01978) 777701

23 **Cardiff** Festival of Welsh Folk Dancing – *till Sun 25* (01222) 825078

24 **Llanfairpwll** Midsummer Concert at Plas Newydd (01248) 714795; **St Athan** RAF St Athan At Home Day (01978) 798651

30 **St Donat's** Welsh International Festival of Storytelling at St Donat's Arts Centre – *till 2 July* (01446) 792 151; **Tal-y-Cafn** Garden Entertainment Evening with Concert at Bodnant Garden (01492) 860123; **Trefriw** North Wales Bluegrass Festival – *till 2 July* (01492) 580454

JULY

1 **Machen** Agricultural Show at Mill Farm (01633) 440278

4 **Llangollen** International Music Eisteddfod including choir of the world competition at Eisteddfod Field – *till Sun 9* (01978) 860236

5 **Stepaside** Country Fair at Colby Woodland Garden – *till Fri 7* (01834) 811885

7 **Cardiff** Hot Air Balloon Festival at Cardiff Castle – *till Sun 9* (01222) 590580

8 **Powis Castle** Mid-Wales Festival of Transport – *till Sun 9* (01938) 553680

13 **Cardiff** Welsh Proms at St David's Hall, The Hayes – *till Sat 22* (01222) 342611

14 **Aberystwyth** International Potters Festival at the Arts Centre, Penglais Hill – *till Sun 16* (01970) 622882

22 **Wales** National Youth Orchestra of Wales 50th anniversary, venue to be announced – *till 11 Aug* (01222) 571260; **Aberystwyth** International Music Festival and summer school at Arts Centre, Penglais Hill – *till 4 Aug* (01970) 622889; **Fishguard** Music Festival – *till Sat 29* (01348) 873612; **Pumsaint** Gold Panning Championships at Dolaucothi Gold Mines – *till Sun 23* (01558) 650359

23 **Chirk** 700th Outdoor Anniversary Concert with Fireworks at Chirk Castle (01691) 777701

24 **Conwy** Festival – *till Sun 30* (01492) 592650; **Llanelwedd** Royal Welsh Show at Royal Welsh Showground – *till Thurs 27* (01982) 553683

29 **Abertillery** World Sevens (Rugby) – *till Sun 30* (01495) 350555

WALES CALENDAR

AUGUST

2 **Aberaeron** Sheepdog Trials (01545) 570534; **Narbeth** West Wales Children's Festival – *till Sat 5* (01834) 860268

3 **Pennal** National Sheepdog Trials – *till Sat 5* (01234) 352672

5 **Colwyn** Royal National Eisteddfod of Wales – *till Sat 12* (01222) 763777

7 **Cardiff** International Festival of Street Entertainment – *till Sat 12* (01222) 751235

10 **Nantyci** United Counties Show at the Showground – *till Fri 11* (01267) 232141

11 **Brecon** Jazz Festival – *till Sun 13* (01874) 625557; **Cardiff** Big Weekend and the Lord Mayor's Parade – *till Sun 13*

12 **Vale of Glamorgan** and **Cardiff** Festival – *till Sun 20* (01446) 794848

15 **nr Gwalchmai** Anglesey County Show at the Showground – *till Weds 16* (01407) 720072

16 **Blaenannerch** Dyfed Air Day at the Airfield (01267) 231812

19 **Llandrindod Wells** Victorian festival in the town – *till Sun 27* (01597) 823441

20 **Heol Penrallt** Gwyl Machynlleth Festival at the Tabernacle Cultural Centre – *till Sun 27* (01654) 703355

26 **Llanfairpwll** Enterprise Neptune 30th Anniversary Concert at Plas Newydd (01248) 714795

28 **Llanwrtyd Wells** World Bog Snorkling Championship and the Mountain Bike Bog Leaping Point to Point (01591) 610236

29 **Llanarthney** Sheepdog Trials at Wernbongam Farm (01267) 290282

SEPTEMBER

7 **Barmouth** Arts Festival in conjunction with the National Trust Centenary – *till Fri 15* (01341) 280845

9 **Cardiff** Festival of Music – *till 8 Oct* (01222) 342611; **Gwernesney** Usk Show (01291) 672379

14 **Holywell** International Sheepdog Trials – *till Sat 16* (01234) 352672; **Mostyn** International Sheepdog Trials – *till Sat 16*

15 **Tenby** Arts Festival – *till Sat 23* (01834) 843774

17 **North Wales** Music Festival – *till 23 Sept* (01600) 716419; **Newport** Vintage Car Rally (01633) 895145

25 **Swansea** Festival of Music and the Arts – *till 5 Nov* (01792) 302432

27 **Aberystwyth** Children's Art Festival – *till Sat 30* (01970) 622889

OCTOBER

2 **Laugharne** Big Court Night at the Town Hall; probably the last place in Britain where the Portreeve, Corporation and Grand Jury still function – new Portreeve elected in trad ceremony

20 **Fishguard** Spirit of Youth Festival – *till Sat 28* (01348) 873867

29 **Snowdonia** Marathon (01492) 860123

NOVEMBER

10 **Aberystwyth** Welsh International Film Festival – *till Sun 19* (01970) 617995

DECEMBER

5 **Llanelwedd** Royal Welsh Agricultural Winter Fair at the Showground (01982) 553683

31 **Llanwrtyd Wells** New Year Walk In – torchlit walk (015913) 2356; **Mountain Ash** Guto Nyth Bran – torchlit midnight road race

NATIONAL CALENDAR

This year the **Festival of Arts and Culture 1995** is celebrated around the country with a year long programme of classical events, rock concerts, talks and performances incorporating the country's largest and best festivals and many smaller local offerings. The **National Trust Centenary** is marked by a tremendous range of events throughout the year with many open-air fireworks concerts and plays, and memorial services in cathedrals throughout the country. Swansea will be transformed for the **UK Year of Literature and Writing** by a host of changing themes and mini-festivals. This year is also 50 years since the end of World War II, the tercentenary of the death of Henry Purcell and 250 years since Bonnie Prince Charlie led the Jacobite uprising.

JANUARY

Marazion, Cornwall Charter Anniversary – *till Dec*; **Newlyn, Cornwall** series of major exhibitions to mark the Centennial Year of Newlyn Art Gallery – *till Dec*

1 **London** Parade from Parliament Square; **Mawnan Smith, Cornwall** Trebah Icicle Charity Swim; **Stonehaven, Scotland** Fireball Ceremony; **Swansea, Wales** UK Year of Literature and Writing – *till 31 Dec*

2 **Hubberholme, Yorks** Land Letting at the George, 8pm – ancient form of auction

5 **Earls Court, London** International Boat Show – *till Sun 15*

6 **Guildford, Surrey** Wassailing – Twelfth night pub tour by Morris men; **Haxey, Humber** Haxey Hood Colourful Ancient Game created in 13th-c

9 (Plough Monday) **Goathland, Yorks** Plough Stots Service – church service, blessing and ancient long sword dance of Norse origin

12 **York** NT Commemorative Service at York Minster, each NT property will bury a time capsule

17 (old Twelfth Night) **Carhampton, Somerset** Wassailing the Apple Trees

18 **Birmingham** LAPADA Antiques and Fine Art Fair at the National Exhibition Centre (NEC) – *till Sun 22*

26 **Norwich** London Mime Exhibition – *till Fri 27* at the Arts Centre

28 **Durham** Wildlife Photographer of the Year at Durham Light Infantry Museum and Durham Art Gallery – *till 26 Feb*; **Liverpool** Chinese New Year Celebrations – *till 5 Feb*; **Nantwich, Cheshire** Holly Holy Day, celebration of the battle of Namptwyche

29 **London** Charles I Commemoration March from St James's Palace – the King's Army (the Royalist Wing of the English Civil War Society) in 17th-c dress follow the route of Charles' last walk before his execution

31 **Lerwick, Scotland** Up-Helly-Aa – *till Feb 1*

FEBRUARY

4 **Aylesbury, Bucks** Chess Congress at the Civic Centre – *till Sun 5*

5 **Newcastle upon Tyne** Chinese New Year in Chinatown

FEBRUARY cont

6 **Bournemouth, Dorset** International Festival of Food and Wine – *till Thurs 9*; **St Ives, Cornwall** Hurling of the Silver Ball and Feast Monday Celebrations throughout the town

10 **York** Jorvik festival – *till Sat 25*

11 **Dorchester** Wildlife Photographer of the Year Exhibition at the Dorset County Museum – *till 18 Mar*

22 **Birmingham** Forties Festival – *till mid-April*

24 **Grasmere, Cumbria** Wordsworth Book Collectors Weekend at Dove Cottage – *till Sun 26*

25 **Bedford** Bedfordshire Music Festival at the Corn Exchange – *till Sat 4*

28 (Shrove Tuesday) **Ashbourne, Derbys** Shrovetide Football Game; **Atherstone, Midlands** Shrovetide Football; **Corfe Castle, Dorset** Marblers' and Stonecutters' Day – amusing traditional event; **Lichfield, Staffs** Shrovetide Fair; **Scarborough, Yorks** Shrovetide Skipping Festival at noon; **St Ives, Cornwall** Hurling of the Silver Ball

MARCH

2 **Norwich** Blues Festival at the Arts Centre – *till Sat 4*

3 **Clacton, Essex** Real Ale and Jazz Festival – *till Sun 5*; **Guildford, Surrey** International Music Festival – *till Sun 26*

4 **Canterbury, Kent** NT Centenary Concert in the Cathedral; **Truro** Cornwall Brass Band Association Annual Contest in City Hall

6 **Dover, Kent** Film Festival – *till Fri 10*; **Liverpool** Festival of Music – *till Fri 10*

7 **Birmingham** World Figure Skating Championships at the NEC – *till Sun 12*

8 **Ilkley, Yorks** Literature Festival – *till Sun 12*

9 **Birmingham** Great British Innovation and Inventions Fair and the International Inventions Fair at the NEC – *till Sun 12*, also Individual Homes Exhibition

13 **Skipton, Yorks** Music Festival – *till Sat 18*

14 **Cheltenham, Glos** Gold Cup Meeting at the Racecourse nr Prestbury – *till Fri 17*

16 **Birmingham** Crufts Dog Show at the NEC – *till Sun 19*; **Earls Court, London** Ideal Home Exhibition – *till 9 April*

18 **Alwalton, Cambs** National Shire Horse Show at the East of England Showground; **Aylesbury, Bucks** Festival of the Arts – *till 22 April* with closing concert *on 30 April*; **Ilkley, Yorks** British Society of Painters at Kings Hall and Winter Garden, possibly the largest art exhibition in Britain – *till Sun 26*; **Stoke Heath, Midlands** Hands-on Science Weekend at Avoncroft Museum of Buildings – *till Sun 19*

24 **Port Talbot, Wales** Welsh Beautiful Homes and Gardens Exhibition – *till Sun 26*

31 **Edinburgh** International Science Festival – *till April 17*

APRIL

1 **Putney, London** to **Mortlake** Oxford v Cambridge University Boat Race; **Sulgrave, Midlands** Living History 1645 (English Civil War) at Sulgrave Manor – *till Sun 9*

APRIL cont

4 **Birmingham** British International Antiques Fair at the NEC – *till Sun 9*; **Gloucester** Blues Festival – *till Sun 16*

8 **Salisbury, Wilts** Concert: War Requiem at Salisbury Cathedral

12 **Harrogate, Yorks** International Youth Music Festival – *till Weds 19*

13 **Olympia, London** International Spring Gardening Fair – *till Mon 17*

14 **Bristol, Somerset** Harveys Wine Museum 30th Anniversary and 200th Anniversary of Harveys in Bristol – *till 24 Dec*; **Goulceby, Lincs** Redhill Good Friday Service, cross-bearing parishioners lead procession up hill and re-enact erection of the crosses; **Hull, Humber** Church Arts and Organ Festival – *till Mon 17*; **Ironbridge, Shrops** 'An Ironmaster's Home' – opening of Dale House at Blists Hill Open-Air Museum; **Lancaster** Maritime Festival – *till Mon 17*; **Long Melford, Suffolk** Historical Re-creation at Kentwell Hall – *till Mon 17*; **Worcester** Civil War Festival and Encampment at the Commandery – *till Sun 23*

15 **Bacup, Lancs** Britannia Coconut Dancers from 9am; **Llanelwedd, Wales** Working Breeds of Wales Dog Show at the Showground

16 **Knebworth, Herts** American Civil War Battle Re-enactment – *till Mon 17* at Knebworth Park; **West Stow, Suffolk** Saxon Market at West Stow Country Park and Anglo Saxon Village – *till Mon 17*

17 **Ossett, Yorks** World Coal Carrying Championships; **Southwark, London** Chaucer Festival and start of Spring Pilgrimage from the Tower of London, crossing Tower Bridge to Southwark Cathedral before leaving for Canterbury

21 **Kendal, Cumbria** Northern International Festival of Mime, Dance and Visual Theatre at the Brewery Arts Centre – *till 1 May*; **Morpeth, Northumbria** Northumbrian Gathering – *till Sun 23*; **Newton Abbot, Devon** Maltings Beer Festival at Tuckers Maltings – *till Sun 23*

22 **Canterbury, Kent** Medieval Fair, Costumed Cavalcade and Chaucer Commemoration Service; **Stratford-upon-Avon, Midlands** Shakespeare Birthday Celebrations in the town centre

23 **Gloucester** St George's Day Celebrations with Mummers and Morris dancers

25 **Thundersley, Essex** European Beer Festival at Runnymede Hall – *till Sat 29*

27 **Malvern, Hereford & Worcs** Wales Championship Dog Show at the Three Counties Showground – *till Sun 30*

28 **Bath, Somerset** Spring Flower Show at Royal Victoria Park – *till Sun 30*; **Girvan, Scotland** Traditional Folk Festival – *till Sun 30*; **Hastings, Sussex** Jack in the Green Morris Dancing Festival – *till 1 May*; **Newquay, Cornwall** Great Cornwall Balloon Festival on the Sea Front – *till 1 May*; **Pitlochry, Scotland** Festival – *till 7 Oct*

29 **Bodiam, Kent** Medieval Fair at the Castle – *till Sun 30*; **High Wycombe, Bucks** Arts Festival – *till 28 May*; **Long Melford, Suffolk** Historical Re-creation at Kentwell Hall – *till Weds 30*; **Sulgrave, Midlands** American Indian Encampment at Sulgrave Manor – *till May 1*; **Weymouth, Dorset** International Beach Kite Festival – *till Sun 30*

30 **Minehead, Somerset** Hobby Horse Parade – *till 3 May*

MAY

1 **Arreton, IoW** Living History at Arreton Manor – *till Fri 19*; **Berwick-upon-Tweed, Northumbria** Riding the Bounds; **Hertford** Music Festival – *till Weds 31*; **Newport, IoW** May Day Ceilidh and Morris men at Longstone, Mottistone Down; **Padstow, Cornwall** Obby Oss Celebrations; **Rochester, Kent** Sweeps Festival Procession

4 **Badminton, Somerset** Horse trials – *till Sun 7*; **Merseyside, Lancs** VE Day Celebrations – *till Tues 9*

5 **Brighton, Sussex** Festival – *till Sun 28*; also Horse Driving Trials at Stanmer Park – *till Sun 7*; **Malvern, Hereford & Worcs** Spring Gardening Show at the Three Counties Showground – *till Sun 7*; **Weymouth, Dorset** VE Day Celebrations and Commemorations – *till Mon 8*; **Winthorpe** Nottinghamshire County Show at Newark Showground – *till Sat 6*

6 **Birmingham** BBC Top Gear Classic and Sportscar Show at the NEC – *till Mon 8*; **Guildford, Surrey** May Day Ceremony Morris Men dance at dawn on the Downs, dancing throughout the day in the town; **Helston, Cornwall** Furry Dance, spring street festival; **Hever, Kent** Day of Dance at Hever Castle; **Knutsford, Cheshire** Royal May Day; **Leeds, Yorks** International Music Festival – *till Sun 14*; **Long Melford, Suffolk** Historic Re-creation at Kentwell Hall – *till Sun 7*; **Rochester, Kent** Sweeps Festival – *till Mon 8*; **Spalding, Lincs** Flower Parade – *till Mon 8*; **nr Wareham, Dorset** Corfe Castle Medieval Weekend – *till Mon 8*

7 **Amesbury, Wilts** Sarsen Trail Walk and Marathon which crosses Salisbury Plain (normally closed to the public); **Bodiam, Sussex** Medieval Fair at Bodiam Castle – *till Mon 8*; **Dover, Kent** Festival – *till Sun 21* with VE Day Celebrations *on Mon 8*; **Elphalborough, Yorks** World Dock Pudding Championships; **Loughborough** Leicestershire County Show at Dishley Grange – *till Mon 8*; **Randwick, Glos** Cheese Rolling; **Winchester, Hants** VE Service in Winchester Cathedral

8 **Cerne Abbas, Dorset** Wessex Morris Men dance on Giant Hill at 7am; **Chatham, Kent** VE Day Celebrations at the Historic Dockyard; **Covent Garden, London** Festival – *till Sun 21*; **Ironbridge, Shrops** Glory Days – VE Day commemoration at Blists Hill Open-Air Museum; **Normanby, Humber** Victorian Day at Normanby Hall; **Winchester, Hants** VE Day Street Party

10 **St Mellion, Cornwall** International Open at St Mellion Golf and Country Club – *till Sun 14*; **Windsor, Berks** Royal Windsor Horse Show at Home Park – *till Sun 14*

11 **Beverley, Humber** Early Music Festival – *till Sun 14*; **Cardiff, Wales** Singer of the World Competition at St David's Hall – *till Sat 17*

12 **Birmingham** Readers and Writers Festival – *till Sat 20*; **Solihull, Midlands** Festival – *till Sat 20*

13 **Battle, Sussex** Festival – *till Sat 27*; **Boston, Lincs** Taverner Festival (450th anniversary) – *till Sun 21*; **Bournemouth, Dorset** International Festival – *till Sun 28*; **Chelmsford, Essex** Cathedral Festival – *till Sat 20*; **Chester** Lord Mayor's Show and Festival of Transport in the town centre and at the Roodee – *till Sun 14*; **Epping, Essex** Fighter Meet at North Weald Air Field – *till Sun 14*; **Felixstowe, Suffolk** Folk Festival – *till Tues 16*; **Knebworth** Hertfordshire Garden Show at Knebworth Park – *till Sun 14*; **Marbury, Cheshire** Merry Days – *till Sun 14*; **Randwick, Glos** Rap; **Salisbury, Wilts** Festival – *till Sat 27*; **Sheffield, Yorks** Chamber Music Festival at the Crucible Studio Theatre – *till Sat 27*

14 **Ingham, Suffolk** South Suffolk Show at Ampton Park

18 **Clyst St Mary** Devon County Show at Westpoint Showground – *till Sat 20*

19 **Bath, Somerset** International Festival – *till 4 Jun*; **Chester** Beating the Retreat in the Castle Square; **Keswick, Cumbria** Jazz Festival – *till Sun 21*; **Llangollen, Wales** International Festival of Jazz – *till Sun 21*; **Plymouth, Cornwall** Lord Mayor's Day Parade; **Shrewsbury, Shrops** Shropshire and West Midland Agricultural Show at the Showground – *till Sat 20*; **Strichen, Scotland** Buchan Heritage Festival – *till Sun 21*

20 **Dorchester** VE Parade; **Llanelwedd, Wales** Royal Welsh International Antique and Collectors Fair at the Showground – *till Sun 21*; **Malvern, Hereford & Worcs** Festival – *till 4 Jun*; **Tintagel, Cornwall** Festival of Music and the Arts – *till Mon 29*

21 **Berwick-upon-Tweed, Northumbria** Border Marches Festival; **Ramsgate, Kent** Spring Festival of Arts and Architecture – *till 4 Jun*; **Worcester** NT Centenary Service at the Cathedral

22 **Edinburgh** Scottish International Children's Festival; **Glyndebourne, Sussex** Opera Season – *till 27 Aug*

23 **Chelsea, London** Flower Show at Royal Hospital – *till Fri 26* (members only 23-24)

24 **Bromsgrove, Hereford & Worcs** Court Leet and Court Baron – procession through town from 10.30am, carnival from 2pm; **Leicester** Early Music Festival at St Mary de Castro – *till Sat 10*; **Stafford** County Show at the County Showground – *till Thurs 25*

25 **Bisley, Glos** Well Blessings; **Firle, Sussex** Charleston Festival at Charleston Farmhouse – *till Mon 29*; **Llantilio Crossenny, Wales** Festival of Music and Drama – *till Sun 28*; **Stromness, Scotland** Orkney Traditional Folk Festival; **Tilford, Surrey** Bach Festival at All Saints Church – *till Sat 27*; **Tissington, Derbys** Well Dressing – *till Weds 31*; **Windsor, Berks** Windsor International Horse Trials at Great Windsor Park – *till Sun 28*

26 **Chippenham, Wilts** Folk Festival – *till Mon 29*; **Combe Martin, Cornwall** Hunting of the Earl of Rone – *till Mon 29*; **Dumfries, Scotland** and Galloway Arts Festival – *till 4 Jun*; **Hay-on-Wye, Wales** Hay Festival – *till 4 Jun*; **Llanfair Clydogau, Wales** Spring Fair (all under canvas) – *till Mon 29*; **Long Melford, Suffolk** Historic Re-creation at Kentwell Hall – *till Mon 29*; **Newport on Tay, Scotland** Scottish Open Carriage Driving Championships; **Virginia Water, Surrey** PGA Golf Championship at Wentworth – *till Mon 29*

27 **Bathgate, Scotland** and West Lothian Highland Games; **Beaumaris, Wales** Festival – *till 4 Jun*; **Birstall, Yorks** Re-enactment, 1695 at Oakwell Hall – *till Mon 29*; **Blackford, Scotland** Highland Games; **Broad Oak, Sussex** Heathfield and District Agricultural Show; **Cardiff, Wales** Jazz Festival – *till Mon 29*; **Endon, Staffs** Well Dressing; **Hever, Kent** Merry England Weekend at Hever Castle; **Innerleithen, Scotland** Celebration of Scottish Beer – *till Sun 28*; **Llanelwedd, Wales** Welsh Motorcycle Extravaganza at the Showground – *till Sun 28*; **Liverpool** Show at Wavertree; **Redbourn** Hertfordshire County Show – *till Sun 28*; **St David's, Wales** Cathedral Festival – *till 3 Jun*; **Worcester** Oak Apple Festival at the Commandery – *till Mon 29*; **Worcester** Regatta; **York** Busking Festival – *till Sun 28*

MAY cont

28 **Blair Atholl, Scotland** International Highland Games; **Felbrigg, Norfolk** Folk Music Festival at Felbrigg Hall; **Great Leighs** Essex Motor Show at the Showground – *till Mon 29*; **Northampton** British Falconry and Raptor Fair and Northamptonshire Game Fair at Althorp House – *till Mon 29*; **Ripon, Yorks** English Civil War Society Muster at Fountains Abbey – *till Mon 29*; **Southend-on-Sea, Essex** Airshow at Western Esplanade – *till Mon 29*; **Woodstock, Oxon** Grand Charity Cricket Match at Blenheim Palace

29 **Brockworth, Glos** Coopers Hill Cheese Rolling from 6pm; **Castleton, Derbys** Garland Ceremony commemorating the escape of Charles II from the Roundheads; **Corbridge** Northumberland County Show at Tynedale Park; **Elvaston** Derbyshire County Show at Elvaston Castle; **Guildford** Surrey County Show at Stoke Park; **Lichfield, Staffs** Court of Arraye and Bowers Procession; **Long Ashton, Somerset** North Somerset Show at Ashton Court Estate; **Oxford** Lord Mayor's Parade and Show at South Park; **Porthcurno, Cornwall** Minack Theatre Summer Festival – *till 16 Sept*

30 **Chippenham, Wilts** Western Golf Open at Bowood Golf and Country Club – *till 1 Jun*

31 **Ipswich** Suffolk Show at Suffolk Showground – *till 1 Jun*

JUNE

1 **Hampton Court, London** Music Festival – *till Sun 18*; **Neston, Cheshire** Ladies Day; **Rochester, Kent** Dickens Festival – *till Sun 4*

2 **Bridgnorth, Shrops** English Haydn Festival – *till Sat 10*; **Chipping Campden, Glos** Robert Dover's Games; **Greenwich, London** Festival – *till Sun 18*; **Thaxted, Essex** National Morris Dancing Festival – *till Sun 4*

3 **Alwalton, Cambs** Steam and Vintage Spectacular at the East of England Showground – *till Sun 4*; **Cardiff, Wales** Annual Festival of Male Voice Praise at St David's Hall; **Chipping Campden, Glos** Scuttlebrook Wake; **Dunster, Somerset** Civil War Garrison at Dunster Castle – *till Sun 4*; **Hull, Humber** Lord Mayor's Parade and Gala; **Leeds, Kent** Balloon and Vintage Car Fiesta at Leeds Castle – *till Sun 4*; **Leominster, Hereford & Worcs** Festival – *till Sun 11*; **Lincoln** Water Festival – *till Sun 4*; **Liverpool** Lord Mayor's Parade; **Market Deeping, Lincs** Agricultural Show – *till Sun 4*; **St Asaph, Wales** Fireworks and Laser Concert at Bodelwyddan Castle; **Ventnor, IoW** Smuggling Pageant – *till Weds 7*

4 **Horse Guards Parade, London** Beating Retreat – *till Thurs 8*; **Uttoxeter, Staffs** Midland Counties Show at the Racecourse

8 **Appleby, Cumbria** Horse Fair; gypsies gather from all over Europe – *till Weds 14*; **Ardingly, Sussex** South of England Agricultural Show at the Showground – *till Sat 10*; **Bramham, Yorks** International Horse Trials and Yorkshire Country Fair at Bramham Park – *till Sun 11*; **Olympia, London** Fine Art and Antiques Fair – *till Sun 18* ; **Southampton, Hants** Film Festival – *till Weds 22*; **Wadebridge** Royal Cornwall Show at the Royal Cornwall Showground – *till Sat 10*

9 **Lichfield, Staffs** Jazz Festival at Lichfield Arts Centre – *till Sun 11*; **Liverpool** Festival of Comedy – *till Weds 21*, also Africa Oye – *till Sat 17* with free festival at Birkenhead Park *on Sat 10*; **Snape, Suffolk** Aldeburgh Festival of Music and Arts – *till Sun 25*

JUNE cont

10 **Ashford in the Water, Derbys** Well Dressing; **Cardiff, Wales** Singer of the World Competition at St David's Hall – *till Sat 17*; **Chepstow, Wales** Horse Trials – *till Sun 11*; **Llanwrtyd Wells, Wales** Man v Horse v Mountain Bike; **Whitehall, London** Trooping the Colour

11 **Aberdeen, Scotland** Kildrummy Castle Rally; **Bridgnorth, Shrops** Open-Air Opera Gala with Fireworks at Dudmaston Hall; **Singleton, Sussex** Heavy Horses at the Weald and Downland Open-Air Museum; **Whitby, Yorks** Festival – *till Mon 26*

12 **Covent Garden, London** Verdi Festival at the Royal Opera House – *till 15 July*; **Margam, Wales** Passion Play at Margam Park – *till Sat 17* also *Mon 19–Weds 24*; **Penzance, Cornwall** Golowan Week – *till Sun 25*, including Sea and Sail Festival from Fri 23 and Mazey Day on Sat 24; **Windsor, Berks** Garter Ceremony at St George's Chapel after procession from Windsor Castle (limited tickets in advance)

13 **Ascot, Berks** Racecourse, Royal Ascot – *till Fri 16*; **Malvern, Hereford & Worcs** Three Counties Show at the Three Counties Showground – *till Thurs 15*

14 **Birmingham** BBC Gardeners' World Live at the NEC – *till Sun 18*

16 **Beverley, Humber** Folk Festival – *till Sun 18*; **Bradford, Yorks** Festival – *till 8 July*; **Cambo, Northumbria** Outdoor Concert with Lasers and Fireworks at Wallington; **Edinburgh** Leith Jazz Festival – *till Sun 18*; **Great Bookham, Surrey** Son et Lumiere – The History of Polesden Lacey at Polesden Lacey – *till Sun 18*; **Great Leighs** Essex County Show at the Showground – *till Sun 18*; **Lichfield, Staffs** Folk Festival at Lichfield Arts Centre – *till Sun 18*

17 **Abington, Oxon** Election of the Mayor of Ock Street (tradition since 1700); **Derby** Festival – *till Sun 25*; **Leeds, Yorks** Summer Heritage Festival – *till 2 July*; **Leicester** International Music Festival – *till Sun 25*; **Liverpool** Mozart's Requiem at the Metropolitan Cathedral; **Milford, Staffs** Afternoon of Scottish Dance at Shugborough; **Northampton** Battle of Naseby at Holdenby House – *till Sun 18*; **Ovingham, Northumbria** Goose Fair; **Sandling, Kent** Midsummer Folk Festival at the Museum of Kent Life – *till Sun 18*; **Stourton, Wilts** Viennese Symphony Concert with Fireworks and Lasers at Stourhead House and Gardens

18 **Aberdeen, Scotland** Highland Games; **Grimsby, Humber** Brass Band Festival at the Town Hall; **Halton, Bucks** RAF Halton Air Show; **Hanley, Staffs** Exhibition at the City Museum and Art Gallery to mark the bicentenary of the death of Josiah Wedgwood – *till 1 Oct*; **Kirkby Lonsdale, Cumbria** Brass Band Contest; **Long Melford, Suffolk** Historical Re-creation at Kentwell Hall – *every wknd till 16July*; **Ratho, Scotland** Scottish Open Canal Jump Competition; **Shifnal, Shrops** Cosford Air Show; **Whiteparish, Wilts** Salisbury and South Wiltshire Agricultural Show

19 **Eastbourne, Sussex** International Ladies Lawn Tennis Championship at Devonshire Park; **Singleton, Sussex** Midsummer Marvels at the Weald and Downland Open-Air Museum – *till Fri 23*

20 **City of London** Festival – *till 7 July*; **Sevenoaks, Kent** Summer Festival – *till Thurs 29*; **Tabley** Cheshire County Show at the County Showground – *till Weds 21*

21 **Grange de Lings** Lincolnshire Show at the Lincolnshire Showground – *till Thurs 22*; **Stonehenge, Wilts** Druid Summer Solstice Ceremony from midnight of 20th

JUNE cont

22 **Ingliston, Scotland** Royal Highland Show at the Royal Highland Showground – *till Sun 25*; **Lichfield, Staffs** Real Ale, Jazz and Blues Festival at Lichfield Arts Centre – *till Sun 25*

23 **Cardiff, Wales** Festival of Welsh Folk Dancing – *till Sun 25*; **Shrewsbury, Shrops** International Music Festival – *till 3 July*; **Truro, Cornwall** Three Spires Festival at Truro Cathedral – *till 8 July*

24 **Canterbury, Kent** Chaucer Festival – *till 22 July*; **Chieveley, Berks** Garden and Leisure Show at Newbury Showground – *till Sun 25*; **Cirencester, Glos** Festival of Music and the Arts – *till 8 July*; **Crawley, Sussex** Festival – *till 8 July*; **East Molesey, Surrey** Metropolitan Police Horse Show and Tournament at the Metropolitan Police Mounted Branch at Imber Court – *till Sun 25*; **Glastonbury, Somerset** Pilgrimage to the Abbey (Church of England); **Hope, Staffs** Wakes and Well Dressing; **Leeds, Kent** Open-Air Concert at Leeds Castle; **Ludlow, Shrops** Festival – *till Sun 9*; **Reading, Berks** Waterfest; **Ripon, Yorks** Classical Concert with Fireworks at Fountains Abbey; **St Athan, Wales** RAF St Athan At Home Day; **Thirsk, Yorks** North Yorkshire Country Show at Ryebeck Farm; **Westminster and City, London** Summer Chaucer Festival – *till Sat 22*

25 **Alnwick** Fair – costumed re-enactments – *till 1 July*; **Bury St Edmunds, Suffolk** Hidden Gardens, over 20 private gardens open in the historic town centre; **Glastonbury, Somerset** Pilgrimage to the Abbey (Roman Catholic); **Perth, Scotland** Coronation Pageant; **Ripon, Yorks** Children's Concert at Fountains Abbey

28 **Henley-on-Thames, Oxon** Henley Royal Regatta – *till 2 July*; **Norwich** Royal Norfolk Show at the Showground – *till Thurs 29*

29 **Ludlow, Shrops** Jazz and Fringe Festival at the Bull Hotel – *till 9 July*

30 **Dingwall, Scotland** Highland Traditional Music Festival – *till 2 July*; **Exeter, Devon** Festival – *till 16 July*; **Glasgow** International Jazz Festival – *till 9 July*; **Sandringham, Norfolk** Country Weekend and Horse Driving Trials – *till 2 July*; **St Donats, Wales** Welsh International Festival of Storytelling at St Donats Arts Centre – *till 2 July*; **Trefriw, Wales** North Wales Bluegrass Festival – *till 2 July*; **Windsor, Berks** Royal Windsor Rose and Horticultural Show at Windsor Castle, Home Park Private – *till 2 July*

JULY

1 **Ambleside, Cumbria** Rushbearing; **Annan, Scotland** Riding of the Marches; **Bracknell, Berks** Festival – *till Sun 2*; **Cheltenham, Glos** International Festival of Music – *till Sun 16*; **Dover, Kent** Carnival; **Guildford, Surrey** Festival – *till Sun 16*; **Harwich, Essex** Festival – *till Sun 9*; **Hull, Humber** Festival inc buskers competition – *till Mon 31*; **Leeds, Kent** Open-Air Concert at Leeds Castle; **Musgrave, Cumbria** Rushbearing; **Petworth, Sussex** Festival at Petworth Park – *till Sun 9*; **Southend-on-Sea, Essex** Punch and Judy Festival – *till Sun 2*; **Sulgrave, Midlands** Living History 1580 (Elizabethan England) at Sulgrave Manor – *till Sun 9*; **Warwick, Midlands** and **Leamington** Festival – *till Sun 16*; **Worcester** Carnival

2 **Chichester, Sussex** Festivities – *till Tues 18*; **Great Bookham, Surrey** Promenade Concert and Fireworks at Polesden Lacey; **Newquay, Cornwall** 1900 week – *till Fri 7*

JULY cont

3 **Kenilworth, Midlands** Royal International Agricultural Show at the National Agricultural Centre (NAC), Stoneleigh Park – *till Thurs 6*

4 **Hampton Court Palace, London** Flower Show – *till Sun 9*; **Llangollen, Wales** International Music Eisteddfod inc choir of the world competition – *till Sun 9*

5 **Stafford** Festival – *till Sun 16*

6 **Bowness on Windermere, Cumbria** Lake Windermere Festival – *till Sun 9*

7 **Cardiff, Wales** Hot Air Balloon Festival at Cardiff Castle – *till Sun 9*; **Grimsby, Humber** International Jazz Festival at King George V Stadium – *till Sun 9*; **Hereford** Summer Festival – *till Sun 16*; **Lichfield, Staffs** Festival and Fringe at Lichfield Arts Centre – *till Sun 16*; **West Wycombe, Bucks** Battle of Trafalgar at West Wycombe Park; **Winchester, Hants** Hat Fair: Festival of Street Theatre – *till Sun 9*; **York** Early Music Festival – *till Sun 16*

8 **Buckingham** Summer Festival – *till Fri 14*; **Durham** Miners Gala; **Horndean** Hampshire Country Fair and Sheep Dog Trials at Queen Elizabeth Country Park; **Ilkley, Yorks** Centenary of British Society of Miniaturists and British Watercolour Society Exhibition at Kings Hall and Winter Garden – *till Sun 16*; **Norwich** Lord Mayor's Street Procession; **Stratford-upon-Avon, Midlands** Festival – *till Sat 22*; **Warminster, Wilts** Outdoor Concert with Fireworks at Longleat House; **Wigan, Lancs** Jazz Festival – *till Sun 9*; **Wirral, Lancs** Show – *till Sun 9*

9 **City of London, London** Festival – *till Weds 26*; **Marlborough, Wilts** Festival – *till Sun 23*; **Shrewsbury, Shrops** World Music and Cajun Day at the Castle

11 **Harrogate, Yorks** Great Yorkshire Show at the Showground – *till Thurs 13*

12 **Breamore, Hants** Hampshire Celebrates VE Day at Breamore House – *till Thurs 13*; **Buxton, Derbys** Festival, inc Well Dressing and Carnival – *till Sun 30*; **Reading, Berks** WOMAD Festival at Rivermead – *till Sun 23*

13 **Cambridge** Film Festival – *till Sun 30*; **Cardiff, Wales** Welsh Proms at St David's Hall, The Hayes – *till Sat 22*; **Detling** Kent County Show at the Showground – *till Sat 15*

14 **Aberystwyth, Wales** International Potters Festival at the Arts Centre, Penglais Hill – *till Sun 16*; **Ivy Hatch, Kent** NT Centenary Concert at Ightham Mote – *till Sat 15*; **Northampton** Show at Abington Park – *till Sun 16*; **Radley, Oxon** Fireworks Concert at Radley College – *till Sun 16*, also *Fri 21 – Sun 23*; **Redcar, Northumbria** International Folk Music, Dance and Song Festival at the Redcar Bowl – *till Sun 16*; **Towcester, Midlands** British Grand Prix at Silverstone Circuit – *till Sun 16*

15 **Bishop Auckland, Northumbria** Early Music Festival at Auckland Castle – *till Sun 16*; **Carlisle, Cumbria** Cumberland Show; **Chester-le-Street** Durham County Show at Clondyke Garden Centre – *till Sun 16*; **Corby, Midlands** Highland Gathering at West Glebe Park; **Hadleigh, Suffolk** East Anglian Summer Music Festival – *till 6 Aug*; **Ilchester, Somerset** International Air Day at RNAS Yeovilton; **King's Lynn, Norfolk** Festival – *till Sat 29*; **Lamberhurst, Sussex** Fireworks and Laser Concert at Bewl Water; **Leith, Scotland** Cutty Sark Tall Ships Race – *till Tues 18*; **Oundle, Midlands** International Festival – *till Sun 23*; **Reigate, Surrey** Summer Music with firework finale concert – *till Sun 30*; **Southend-on-Sea, Essex** '999' Emergency Services Seafront Spectacular on Western Esplanade – *till Sun 16*

JULY cont

16 **Ashbourne, Derbys** Highland Gathering; **Middlesbrough, Northumbria** Mela (Asian Day) at Central Gardens; **Tolpuddle, Dorset** Martyrs Rally, annual trade union rally

18 **Alwalton, Cambs** East of England Show at East of England Showground – *till Thurs 20*

20 **Chichester, Sussex** Southern Cathedrals Festival at Chichester Cathedral – *till Sun 23*; **Lamberhurst, Kent** Open-Air Opera at Scotney Castle – *till Sun 23*, also *from Thurs 27 – Sat 29*; **Reading, Berks** Real Ale and Jazz Festival – *till Sat 22*; **St Andrews, Scotland** Golf Open Championship at the Old Course – *till Sun 23*

21 **Chester** Summer Music Festival – *till Sat 29*; **Chorley, Lancs** Royal Lancashire Show at Astley Park – *till Sun 23*; **Inverness, Scotland** Highland Games; **Northwood** Royal Isle of Wight Agricultural Society County Show at the Northwood Showground; **Royal Albert Hall, London** Henry Wood Promenade Concerts (centenary series) – *till 16 Sept*; **Warminster, Wilts** Wiltshire Balloon Festival at Longleat House – *till Sun 23*; **Wenlock Edge, Shrops** Festival at the Edge (international storytelling festival) at the Wenlock Edge Inn – *till Sun 23*

22 **Aberystwyth, Wales** International Music Festival and Summer School – *till 4 Aug*; **Cheltenham, Glos** Cricket Festival – *till Sun 30*; **Church Stretton, Shrops** and South Shropshire Arts Festival – *till 5 Aug*; **Gloucester** Festival and Carnival – *till 5 Aug*, also Museums Week and Cricket Festival – *till Sun 30*; **Lyme Regis, Dorset** Lifeboat Week inc the Red Arrows – *till Sat 30*; **Middlesbrough, Northumbria** Cleveland County Show at Stewart Park; **Milford, Staffs** Firework and Laser Concert at Shugborough; **Rochester, Chatham and Strood, Kent** Medway Arts Festival – *till Sun 30*; **Tewkesbury, Glos** Festival – *till Sun 30*; **Tiverton, Devon** Mid-Devon Show

23 **Chirk, Wales** 700th Outdoor Anniversary Concert with Fireworks at Chirk Castle; **Dartmouth, Devon** Town Week – *till Sun 30*; **Hull, Humber** Brass Band Competition and Concert; **Isle of Bute, Scotland** Folk Festival – *till Weds 26*; **Singleton, Sussex** Rare and Traditional Breeds Show at the Weald and Downland Open-Air Museum

24 **Conwy, Wales** Festival – *till Sun 30*; **Llanelwedd** Royal Welsh Show at Royal Welsh Showground – *till Thurs 27*; **Inverness, Scotland** Tattoo – *till Sat 29*; **Portree, Scotland** Skye Folk Festival – *till Sat 29*

25 **Brockenhurst, Hants** New Forest and Hampshire County Show at New Park Farm – *till Thurs 27*; **Goodwood, Sussex** Glorious Goodwood at the Racecourse – *till Sat 29*

26 **Nantwich** and South Cheshire Show at Dorfold Hall Park

27 **Harrogate, Yorks** International Festival – *till 10 Aug*; **Lamberhurst, Kent** Open-Air Opera at Scotney Castle – *till Sat 29*

28 **Flookburgh** Cumbria Steam Gathering – *till Sun 30*; **Horringer, Suffolk** Centenary Spectacular Open-Air Concert at Ickworth House – *till Sat 29*

29 **Bradford-on-Tone, Somerset** Craft and Cider Country Fayre at Sheppey's Cider Farm – *till Sun 30*; **Cowes, IoW** Week – *till 6 Aug*; **Stamford, Lincs** Fireworks and Laser Symphony Concert at Burghley House; **Tunbridge Wells, Kent** Georgian Festivities on the Pantiles – *till 6 Aug*; **Weston-super-Mare, Somerset** Helidays – helicopter fly-ins, static displays and pleasure flights – *till Sun 30*; **Woodstock, Oxon** Fireworks Concert at Blenheim Palace – *till Sun 30*; **York** Celebration of Band Music

JULY cont

30 **by Aviemore, Scotland** Rothiemurehus International Highland Games; **Knebworth, Herts** Fireworks and Laser Symphony Concert at Knebworth Park; **St Andrews, Scotland** Highland Games

31 **Salcombe, Devon** Town Regatta – *till 5 Aug*

AUGUST

1 **Snape, Suffolk** Proms at Snape Maltings – *till Thurs 31*

2 **Ambleside, Cumbria** Lake District Summer Music Festival – *till Weds 16*; **Landkey, Devon** North Devon Show at Plym's Farm; **Portree, Scotland** Isle of Skye Highland Games

3 **Pennal, Wales** National Sheepdog Trials – *till Sat 5*

4 **Bowness-on-Windermere, Cumbria** Classic Motor Boat Rally at Windermere Steam Boat Museum – *till Sun 6*; **Edinburgh** Military Tattoo at Edinburgh Castle – *till Sat 26*; **Portsmouth, Hants** and Southsea Show at Southsea Common – *till Sun 6*; **Sidmouth, Devon** International Festival of Folk Arts – *till Fri 11*; **Southend-on-Sea, Essex** Jazz Festival – *till Sun 6*; **Warwick, Midlands** Folk Festival – *till Sat 5*

5 **Alnwick, Northumbria** International Music Festival – *till Sat 12*; **Colwyn, Wales** Royal National Eisteddfod of Wales – *till Sat 12*; **Crawley, Surrey** International Festival of Arts at the Hawth – *till Sun 6*; **Edinburgh** International Jazz Festival – *till Sat 12*; **Garstang, Lancs** Agricultural Show; **Hastings, Sussex** Old Town Week inc open days at private houses – *till Sun 13*; **Leicester** Caribbean Carnival at Victoria Park; **Ross-on-Wye, Hereford & Worcs** Carnival; **Sunderland, Northumbria** International Air Show – *till Sun 6*; **Woodstock, Oxon** Flower Show at Blenheim Palace – *till Sun 6*; **Yarmouth, IoW** Carnival – *till procession on Sat 12*

6 **Dorchester** South Dorset Fayre at Came Park; **Falmouth, Cornwall** Regatta Week – *till Sat 12*; **Skendleby** Lincolnshire Sheepdog Trials at Lodge Farm; **Sulgrave, Midlands** Outdoor Theatre at Sulgrave Manor – *till Mon 7*

7 **Cardiff, Wales** International Festival of Street Entertainment – *till Sat 12*

8 **Hull, Humber** Jazz Festival on the Waterfront – *till Sun 13*

9 **Cowes, IoW** Festival – *till Mon 28*

10 **Ings, Cumbria** Lake District Sheep Dog Trials at Hill Top Farm; **Nantyci, Wales** United Counties Show at the Showground – *till Fri 11*; **Yardley Gobion, Midlands** National Sheepdog Trials – *till Sat 12*

11 **Brecon, Wales** Jazz Festival – *till Sun 13*; **Cardiff** Big Weekend and the Lord Mayor's Parade – *till Sun 13*; **Cropredy, Oxon** Folk, Rock Festival with Fairport Convention – *till Sat 12*; **Marlborough, Wilts** Wiltshire Artists Annual Exhibition at St Peter's Church: sale of about 275 works by 60 artists – *till Sat 19*; **Minchinhampton, Glos** British Open Horse Trials Championship at Gatcombe Park – *till Sun 13*; **Southend-on-Sea, Essex** Carnival Week – *till Sat 19*; **Weymouth, Dorset** VJ Day Celebrations and Commemorations – final end of WWII – *till Weds 16*

12 **Billingham, Northumbria** International Folklore Festival – *till Sat 19*; **Breamore, Hants** Hampshire Celebrates Victory at Breamore House – *till Sun 13*; **Calne, Wilts** Open-Air Fireworks and Laser Symphony Concert at Bowood House and Gardens; **Cambo, Northumbria** Open-Air Classics with Fireworks at Wallington; **Edinburgh** International

AUGUST cont

Film Festival at Filmhouse – *till Sun 27*, also Book Festival at Charlotte Sq Gardens – *till Mon 28*; **Glasgow** World Pipe Band Championships; **Halifax, Yorks** Agricultural Show at Saville Park; **Horringer, Suffolk** Mozart and Salieri in the Open Air at Ickworth House; **Long Ashton, Somerset** International Bristol Balloon Fiesta at Ashton Court Estate – *till Mon 14*; **Rye, Sussex** Medieval Week – *till Sun 13*; **Vale of Glamorgan, Wales** and **Cardiff** Festival – *till Sun 20*; **Worcester** Elizabethan Festival at the Commandery – *till Sun 20*

13 **Arreton, IoW** Pageant at Arreton Manor; **Edinburgh** International Festival and Fringe Festival (world's largest festival of the arts) – *till 2 Sept*; **Macclesfield, Cheshire** Rushbearing Ceremony at Macclesfield Forest Chapel; **Northampton** Fireworks and Laser Concert at Althorp House

14 **Torbay, Devon** Royal Regatta – *till Fri 18*

15 **nr Gwalchmai, Wales** Anglesey County Show at the Showground – *till Weds 16*

16 **Blaenannerch, Wales** Dyfed Air Day at the Airfield; **Hythe, Kent** Venetian Fete – floating carnival viewed from Royal Military Canal; **Weymouth, Dorset** Carnival and Firework Festival

17 **Grasmere, Cumbria** Traditional Sports inc Lakeland wrestling; **Kilmartin, Scotland** National Sheepdog Trials – *till Sat 19*; **Weston-under-Lizard, Staffs** Heart of England Music Festival at Weston Park – *till Sun 20*

18 **Blickling, Norfolk** Fireworks and Laser Concert at Blickling – *till Sat 19*; **Northampton** Hot Air Balloon Festival at Northampton Racecourse – *till Sun 20*; **Oakham, Leics** International Bird Watching Fair – *till Sun 20*; **South Bank Centre, London** Folk Week – *till Fri 25*; **nr Wimborne Minster, Dorset** Beating the Retreat at Kingston Lacy

19 **Detling, Kent** Steam and Transport Rally at the Showground – *till Sun 20*; **Gloucester** Cathedral, Three Choirs Festival – *till Sat 26*; **Shepton Mallet, Somerset** County and Agricultural Show at the Royal Bath and West Showground – *till Sun 20*; **Whitby, Yorks** Folk Week – *till Fri 25*; **Woburn, Beds** De Havilland Moth Club Annual Fly-in at Woburn Abbey – *till Sun 20*

20 **Alfriston, Sussex** Festival – *till Mon 28*; **Eastbourne, Sussex** Airbourne 95 on the seafront – *till Birdman Competition on Sun 20*; **Fowey, Cornwall** Royal Regatta and Carnival – *till Sat 26*; **Morecambe and Lancaster** Folklore Fiesta – *till Weds 23*

23 **Motcombe, Dorset** Gillingham and Shaftesbury Show at Motcombe Turnpike Showground; **Priddy, Somerset** Sheep Fair

24 **Dartmouth, Devon** Royal Regatta – *till Sat 26*; **Oban, Scotland** Argyllshire Highland Gathering

25 **Arundel, Sussex** Festival – *till 3 Sept*; **Lancaster** Georgian Legacy Festival – *till Mon 28*; **Liverpool** Beatles Festival – *till Tues 29*; **Long Melford, Suffolk** Historical Re-creation at Kentwell Hall – *till Mon 28*; **Reading, Berks** Rock Festival – *till Sun 27*; **Wadebridge** Cornwall Folk Festival throughout the town – *till Mon 28*

26 **Bude, Cornwall** Jazz Festival throughout the town – *till 2 Sept*; **Clacton-on-Sea, Essex** Jazz Festival – *till Mon 28*; **Egham, Surrey** Royal Show at Runnymede – *till Sun 27*; **Elsham, Humber** Folkdance Festival at Elsham Hall Country and Wildlife Park – *till Mon 28*; **Eyam, Derbys** Well

AUGUST cont

Dressings; **Leyburn, Yorks** Wensleydale Agricultural Show; **Peebles, Scotland** Arts Festival – *till 10 Sept*; **Plymouth, Devon** Navy Days at HM Naval Base – *till Mon 28*; **Rochester, Kent** Norman Rochester – *till Mon 28*; **West Witton, Yorks** Burning of the Bartle

27 **Leicester** International Air Display at the Airport; **Leicester** Show at Abbey Park – *till Mon 28*; **Notting Hill, London** Carnival, Ladbroke Grove – *till Mon 28*; **Stithians, Cornwall** Cornish Game and Country Fayre at the Showground, Kennal Farm; **Sulgrave, Midlands** Living History 1780 (Georgian England) at Sulgrave Manor – *till Mon 30*; **West Stow, Suffolk** Saxon Summer Market at West Stow Country Park and Anglo Saxon Village – *till Mon 28*

28 **Bourton-on-the-Water, Glos** Football in the River Windrush; **Dartington, Devon** Literature Festival at Dartington Hall Gardens – *till 4 Sept*; **Liverpool** Matthew Street Festival – free festival with music, street performers and carnival atmosphere; **Newcastle upon Tyne** Free Festival

29 **St Albans, Herts** National Miniature Rose Show at The Royal National Rose Society, Chiswell Green – *till Weds 30*

30 **Tarrant Hinton, Dorset** Great Dorset Steam Fair at the Showground – *till 3 Sept*

31 **Alwalton, Cambs** British Show Ponies Society at the East of England Showground – *till 2 Sept*; **Edinburgh** Glenlivet Fireworks Concert; **Hull, Humber** International Sea Shanty Festival – *till 3 Sept*; **Stamford, Lincs** Burghley Horse Trials at Burghley Park – *till Sun 3*

SEPTEMBER

1 **Alcester, Midlands** Last Night of the Proms at Ragley Hall; **Kirriemuir, Scotland** Traditional Music Festival – *till Sun 3*; **Rupert Street, London** Latin American Film Festival at the Metro Cinema – *till Thurs 14*

2 **Braemar, Scotland** Royal Highland Gathering at Princess Royal and Duke Memorial Park; **Canterbury, Kent** Hop Hoodening at the Cathedral – Hop Picking Festival; **Dorchester, Dorset** Agricultural Show at Came Park; **Faversham, Kent** English Hop Festival – *till Sun 3*; **Goudhurst, Kent** Finchcocks Festival, *every wknd till 1 Oct*; **Keighley, Yorks** and District Agricultural Show at Marley Fields; **Long Ashton, Somerset** International Kite Festival at Ashton Court Estate – *till Sun 3*; **Montacute, Somerset** Band of the Royal Marines, Joust, Laser Show and Ox Roast at Montacute House – *till Sun 3*; **Newquay, Cornwall** Festival – *till Sat 9*; **Sowerby Bridge, Yorks** Rushbearing; **Uckfield, Sussex** Torchlight Procession and Fireworks; **nr Wareham, Dorset** Corfe Castle Medieval Weekend – *till Sun 3*; **Worcester** Re-encactment of 'The Escape of Charles II' during the Battle of Worcester – *till Sun 3*

3 **Ripponden, Yorks** Rushbearing; **Spencers Wood, Berks** Wokingham and Reading Agricultural Show

6 **Plymouth, Devon** 375th Anniversary of the Sailing of the *Mayflower*

7 **Barmouth, Wales** Arts Festival in conjunction with the NT Centenary – *till Fri 15*; **Weedon** Buckinghamshire County Show at the County Showground

8 **Crewe and Nantwich, Cheshire** Folk Festival – *till Sun 10*; **Toddington** South Bedfordshire County Show at the South Bedfordshire County Showground – *till Sun 9*

SEPTEMBER cont

9 **Berwick-upon-Tweed, Northumbria** Military Tattoo at Berwick Barracks – *till Sun 10*; **Cardiff, Wales** Festival of Music – *till 8 Oct*; **Lichfield, Staffs** Sheriff's Ride; **Shepton Mallet, Somerset** Countryside Cavalcade at the Royal Bath and West Showground – *till Sun 10*; **Sulgrave, Midlands** American Civil War Re-enactment at Sulgrave Manor – *till Sun 10*; **Seaham, Northumbria** East Durham Show at the Showground – *till Sun 10*; **Stow-on-the-Wold, Glos** Day of Dance; **York** Festival of Traditional Dance – *till Sun 10*

10 **Hardraw, Yorks** Scar Brass Band Competition; **Newcastle upon Tyne** Science Festival at Newcastle University – *till Fri 15*; **Norwich** Town and Country at the Showground; **Sutton Cheney, Leics** Re-enactment of the Battle of Bosworth at Bosworth Field

11 **Abbots Bromley, Staffs** Ancient Horn Dance

13 **Westminster, London** RHS Great Autumn Flower Show – *till Weds 13*

14 **Crooklands, Cumbria** Westmorland County Show at Lane Farm; **Holywell, Wales** International Sheepdog Trials – *till Sat 16*; **Woodstock, Oxon** Blenheim International Horse Trials – *till Sun 17*

15 **Harrogate, Yorks** Great Autumn Flower Show – *till Sat 16*; **Winchester, Hants** Celebration of the Arts – *till Sun 24*

16 **Chieveley, Berks** Newbury and Royal County of Berkshire Show at the Newbury Showground – *till Sun 17*; **Egremont, Cumbria** Crab Fair including world gurning championships; **Ipswich, Suffolk** County and Agricultural Show at the Suffolk Showground – *till Sun 17*; **Leuchars, Scotland** RAF Leuchars Battle of Britain Airshow; **Southampton, Hants** International Boat Show – *till Sun 24*

17 **Hadleigh, Suffolk** British Horse Society Horse Trials at Chelsworth Park

21 **Thame, Bucks** Agricultural Show

22 **Shrewsbury, Shrops** International Ballooning Fiesta at Attingham Park – *till Sun 24*

23 **Ilkley, Yorks** British Society of Painters – *till 1 Oct*; **Long Melford, Suffolk** Historical Re-creation at Kentwell Hall – *till Sun 24*; **Pewsey, Wilts** Illuminated Carnival Procession; **Wooburn Green, Marlow, High Wycombe, Bourne End, Bucks** Wooburn Festival – *till 14 Oct*

24 **Aylesbury, Bucks** Charter Day – a Stuart Day; **Urswick, Cumbria** Rushbearing

25 **Folkestone** Kent Literature Festival – *till 1 Oct*; **Swansea, Wales** Festival of Music and the Arts – *till 5 Nov*

26 **Chester** National Waterways Festival; **Wembley Arena, London** Horse of the Year Show – *till 1 Oct*

27 **Aberystwyth, Wales** Children's Art Festival – *till Sat 30*

28 **Soho, London** Jazz Festival – *till 7 Oct*

29 **Chiddingly, Sussex** Festival – *till 8 Oct*; **Malvern, Hereford & Worcs** Jazz Festival at the Winter Gardens Complex – *till 1 Oct*

OCTOBER

5 **Norwich** Norfolk and Norwich Festival – *till Sun 15*; **Nottingham** Goose Fair – *till Sat 7*

6 **Cheltenham, Glos** Festival of Literature – *till Sat 14*; **Hull, Humber** Comedy Festival – *till 2 Dec* and Fair – *till Sat 14*

OCTOBER cont

7 **Canterbury, Kent** Festival – *till Sat 21*; **Stroud, Glos** Arts Festival – *till Sat 21*; **Ripon, Yorks** Yorkshire Three Choirs Festival at Ripon Cathedral – *till Tues 10*

12 **Aberdeen, Scotland** Alternative Festival – *till Sat 21*

13 **Borders, Scotland** Festival throughout the Scottish Borders – *till Sun 29*

14 **Exeter, Devon** Carnival

19 **Earls Court Exhibition Centre, London** Motor Show – *till Sun 29*

20 **Edinburgh** and **Glasgow** French Film Festival at Edinburgh Film House and Glasgow Film Theatre – *till Mon 30*; **Lancaster** Literature Festival – *till Sun 29*

21 **Corfe Castle, Dorset** Civil War Garrison Weekend – *till Sun 22*; **Singleton, Sussex** Steam Threshing and Ploughing at the Weald and Downland Open-Air Museum – *till Sun 22*; **Taunton, Somerset** Illuminated Carnival and Cider Barrel Rolling Race; **Trafalgar Square, London** Trafalgar Service and Parade

23 **Norwich** CAMRA Beer Festival at St Andrew's Hall

27 **Birmingham** International Motorcycle Show at the NEC – *till Sun 5*

31 **Edinburgh** Scottish International Storytelling Festival – *till 11 Nov*

NOVEMBER

2 **Bridgwater, Somerset** Guy Fawkes Carnival, one of Europe's most spectacular illuminated parades

3 **Kendal, Cumbria** Jazz and Blues Festival at the Brewery Arts Centre – *till Sun 19*

4 **Battle, Sussex** Fireworks with effigy; **Embsay, Yorks** Grand Bonfire, Firework Display and Steam Trains at Night at Embsay Steam Railway; **Lewes, Sussex** Torchlight Procession and Fireworks, the best of Britain's bonfire celebrations; **Lancaster** Fireworks Spectacular at Castle Hill; **Leeds, Kent** Grand Firework Spectacular at Leeds Castle; **North Petherton, Somerset** Guy Fawkes Carnival (as Bridgwater above); **Ottery St Mary, Devon** Rolling of the Tar Barrels

5 **Fleetwood, Lancs** Firework Display and Birdman Competition at Fleetwood Pier; **Hyde Park Corner, London** start of the London to Brighton Veteran Car Run; **Shebbear, Devon** Turning the Devil's Boulder

6 **Burnham-on-Sea, Somerset** Guy Fawkes Carnival (as Bridgwater above)

8 **Mansion House to Guildhall, London** Installation of the Lord Mayor; **Shepton Mallet, Somerset** Guy Fawkes Carnival (as Bridgwater above)

9 **Hull, Humber** Literature Festival – *till Mon 20*

10 **Aberystwyth, Wales** Welsh International Film Festival – *till Sun 19*; **Wells, Somerset** Guy Fawkes Carnival (as Bridgwater above)

11 St Martin's Day **Bletchley, Bucks** Firing the Poppers; **City of London** Lord Mayor's Procession and Show from the Guildhall to the Royal Courts of Justice; **Glastonbury, Somerset** Guy Fawkes Carnival (as Bridgwater above)

12 **Whitehall, London** Remembrance Day Service and Parade

13 **Weston-super-Mare, Somerset** Guy Fawkes Carnival (as Bridgwater above)

NOVEMBER cont

16 **Huddersfield, Yorks** Comtemporary Music Festival – *till Sun 26*; **Santon Bridge, Cumbria** Biggest Liar in the World Competition

23 **Birmingham** Good Food, Cooking and Kitchen Show at the NEC – *till Sun 26*

25 **Ilkley, Yorks** British Watercolour Society Exhibition at Kings Hall and Winter Garden – *till 3 Dec*

26 **Bristol, Somerset** Advent Sunday at the Lord Mayor's Chapel, College Green

27 **Derby** Bonnie Prince Charlie 250th Anniversary – *till 10 Dec*

DECEMBER

1 **Birmingham** Clothes Show Live at the NEC – *till Weds 6*

7 **Warwick, Midlands** Victorian Street Fair and Christmas Lights Switch On

26 **Crookham Village, Hants** Mummers Play at midday; **Folkestone, Kent** Boxing Day Dip at East Cliff Sands; **Gloucester** Mummers and Morris Dancers in the Cathedral Precincts and New Inn Courtyard at midday; **Sunderland, Northumbria** Boxing Day Dip

31 **Allendale, Northumbria** Baal Festival; **Biggar, Scotland** Ne'erday Bonfire; **Comrie** Flambeaux Procession – *till 1 Jan*; **Edinburgh** Hogmanay Celebrations; **Llanwrtyd Wells, Wales** New Year Walk In – torchlight walk

Self-sufficient hotels

The hotels, inns and other places listed here have plenty to do on the premises or in their grounds – enough for most people to be happy to stay put there all day:

Berkshire
Streatley, Swan Diplomat
Windsor, Oakley Court

Buckinghamshire
Aylesbury, Hartwell House
Marlow, Compleat Angler
Taplow, Cliveden

Cambridgeshire
Flitwick, Flitwick Manor
Needingwath, Pike and Eel
Six Mile Bottom, Swynford
　　Paddocks
Wansford, Haycock

Cheshire
Macclesfield, Sutton Hall Hotel
Nantwich, Rookery Hall
Sandiway, Nunsmere Hall

Cornwall
Carne Beach, Nare
Gerrans Bay, Pendower Beach
　　House
Looe, Talland Bay
Mawnan Smith, Meudan
Mawnan Smith, Nansidwell Country
　　House
Mullion, Polurrian
Newlyn, Higher Faugan
St Keyne, Old Rectory

Isles of Scilly
Tresco, Island

Cumbria
Brampton, Farlam Hall
Crook, Gilpin Lodge
Derwent Water, Lodore Swiss
Grasmere, Michael's Nook
Grasmere, White Moss House
Grasmere, Wordsworth
Pooley Bridge, Sharrow Bay
Rydal, Glen Rothay
Seatoller, Seatoller House
Watermillock, Old Church
Windermere, Langdale Chase

Derbyshire
Ashbourne, Callow Hall
Bakewell, Hassop Hall
Barslow, Cavendish
Matlock, Riber Hall

Devon
Burgh Island, Burgh Island
Chagford, Gidleigh Park
Chittlehamholt, Highbullen
Clawton, Court Barn
Dulverton, Ashwick Country
　　House
Dulverton, Tarr Steps
East Portlemouth, Gara Rock
Gittisham, Combe House
Goveton, Buckland-tout-Saints
Higher Bulstone, Bulstone
Lewdown, Lewtrenchard Manor
Marlborough, Soar Mill Cove
Salcombe, Tides Reach
South Molton, Whitechapel
　　Manor
Torquay, Imperial
Whimple, Woodhayes

Gloucester
Buckland, Buckland Manor
Charingworth, Charingworth Manor
Cheltenham, Greenway
Clearwell, Clearwell Castle
Lower Slaughter, Lower Slaughter
　　Manor
Tetbury, Calcot Manor
Upper Slaughter, Lords of the Manor
Westonbirt, Hare and Hounds

Hampshire
Hurstbourne Tarrant, Esseborne
　　Manor
Lymington, Passford House
New Milton, Chewton Glen

Hereford & Worcester
Bromsgrove, Grafton Manor
Ledbury, Hope End Country House

Lancashire
Whitewell, Inn at Whitewell

Leicestershire, Lincolnshire and Nottinghamshire
Leics
Oakham, Hambleton Hall
Packington, Springs Hydro
Stapleford, Stapleford Park
Lincs
Stamford, George
Notts
Bestwood Country Park, Bestwood Lodge

Midlands
Ansty, Ansty Hall
Leamington Spa, Mallory Court
Stratford-upon-Avon, Welcombe
Sutton Coldfield, New Hall
Wishaw, Belfry

Norfolk
Grimston, Congham Hall
Hethersett, Park Farm

Northumbria
Cornhill-on-Tweed, Tillmouth Park
Easington, Grinkle Park
Longframlington, Embleton Hall

Oxfordshire
Great Milton, Manoir aux Quat' Saisons
Horton cum Studley, Studley Priory
Wallingford, Shillingford Bridge
Weston on the Green, Weston Manor

Somerset and Avon
Freshford, Homewood Park
Hunstrete, Hunstrete House
Kilve, Meadow House
Ston Easton, Ston Easton Park
Thornbury, Thornbury Castle

Suffolk
Hintlesham, Hintlesham Hall
Woodbridge, Seckford Hall

Surrey
Bagshot, Pennyhill Park

Sussex
Alfriston, Deans Place
Amberley, Amberley Castle
Climping, Bailiffscourt
East Grinstead, Gravetye Manor
Rusper, Ghyll Manor
Uckfield, Horsted Place

Wiltshire
Colerne, Lucknam Park

Easton Grey, Whatley Manor
Ford, White Hart
Warminster, Bishopstrow House

Yorkshire
Bilbrough, Bilbrough Manor
Bolton Abbey, Devonshire Arms
Dunsley, Dunsley Hall
Hackness, Hackness Grange
Nidd, Nidd Hall
Otley, Chevin Lodge
Sedbusk, Stone House
York, Middlethorpe Hall

Scotland
South
Edinburgh, Balmoral
Gatehouse of Fleet, Cally Palace
Gullane, Greywalls
Kelso, Sunlaws House
Kilwinning, Mountgreenan Mansion House
West
Port Appin, The Airds
Strachur, Creggans
Kilfinan, Kilfinan Hotel
North of the Forth
Advie, Tulchan Lodge
Auchterarder, Gleneagles
Auchterhouse, Old Mansion House
Ballater, Craigendarroch Hotel
Balquhidder, Monachyle Mhor
Blairgowrie, Kinloch House
Dunblane, Cromlix House
Dunkeld, Kinnaird House
East Haugh, East Haugh House
Kenmore, Kenmore
Killiecrankie, Pitlochry
Monymusk, Grant Arms
Scone, Murryshall House
North
Altnaharra, Altnaharra
Isle Ornsay, Kinloch Ledge
Skeabost, Skeabost House

Wales
North
Llandrillo, Tyddyn Llan
Llandudno, Bodysgallen Hall
Llanwddyn, Lake Vyrnwy
Portmeirion, Portmeirion
Talsarneau, Maes-y-Neuadd
Mid
Eglwysfach, Ynyshir Hall
West
Broad Haven, Druidstone
Crugybar, Glanrannell Park

Waterside hotels

The hotels and other places to stay listed here are right beside the sea, a sizeable river, canal, lake or loch that contributes significantly to their attraction:

Berkshire
Hungerford, Marshgate Cottage
Kintbury, Dundas Arms
Streatley, Swan Diplomat
Windsor, Oakley Court

Buckinghamshire
Marlow, Compleat Angler
Taplow, Cliveden

Cambridgeshire and Bedfordshire
Huntingdon, George
Needingworth, Pike & Eel

Cheshire
Sandiway, Nunsmere Hall

Cornwall
Bodinnick, Old Ferry
Calstock, Danescombe Valley
Carne Beach, Nare
Constantine Bay, Treglos
Crafthole, Finnygook
Fowey, Fowey Hotel
Fowey, Marina
Gerrans Bay, Pendower Beach House
Gillan, Tregildry
Golant, Cormorant
Gunwalloe, Halzephron
Lamorna Cove, Lamorna Cove
Little Petherick, Old Mill Country
    House
Looe, Talland Bay
Mawnan Smith, Meudon
Mawnan Smith, Nansidwell Country
    House
Mullion, Polurrian
Padstow, Old Custom House
Port Isaac, Port Gaverne
Portloe, Lugger
Portloe, Seal Cottage
Portscatho, Roseland House
Sennen, Old Success
Sennen, State House
St Ives, Garrack
St Mawes, Rising Sun
Trelights, Long Cross

Isles of Scilly
Pelistry Bay, Carnwethers
St Mary's, Tregarthens
Tresco, Island

Cumbria
Alston, Lovelady Shield
Ambleside, Wateredge
Dent, Sportsmans
Grasmere, Oak Bank
Grasmere, White Moss House
Mungrisdale, Mill Hotel
Pooley Bridge, Sharrow Bay
Silloth, Skinburness
Thirlmere, Dale Head Hall
Watermillock, Leeming House
Watermillock, Old Church
Windermere, Holbeck Ghyll Country
    House
Windermere, Langdale Chase

Derbyshire and Staffordshire
Ashford in the Water, Riverside
    Country House

Devon
Ashprington, Watermans Arms
Burgh Island, Burgh Island
Chagford, Mill End
Dartmouth, Royal Castle
East Portlemouth, Gara Rock
Exebridge, Anchor
Lifton, Arundell Arms
Lynmouth, Rising Sun
Malborough, Soar Mill Cove
Meeth, Giffords Hele
Salcombe, Tides Reach
Torquay, Imperial

Dorset
Poole, Haven
Wareham, Priory

Essex
Burnham on Crouch, White Harte
Dedham, Maison Talbooth
West Mersea, Victory

Gloucestershire
Bibury, Swan

Hampshire
Lee on the Solent, Belle Vue

Hereford & Worcester
Symonds Yat, Saracens Head

Isle of Wight
Yarmouth, Bugle
Yarmouth, George

Humberside
Hull, Forte Crest

Lancashire
Bilsborrow, Guy's Thatched Hamlet
Blackpool, Imperial
Whitewell, Inn at Whitewell

Leicestershire, Lincolnshire, Nottinghamshire
Leics
Empingham, White Horse
Oakham, Hambleton Hall

Norfolk
Blakeney, Blakeney Hotel

Northumberland
Chollerford, George
Seahouses, Olde Ship

Oxfordshire
Henley, Red Lion
Moulsford, Beetle & Wedge
Wallingford, Shillingford Bridge

Shropshire
Llanfair Waterdine, Red Lion
Shrewsbury, Mytton Hall

Somerset and Avon
Somerton, Lynch Country House

Suffolk
Aldeburgh, White Lion
Needham Market, Pipps Ford

Sussex
Bognor Regis, Royal Norfolk
Brighton, Grand
Eastbourne, Grand
Eastbourne, Seacroft
Wadhurst, Newbarn
Wisborough Green, Old Wharf

Wiltshire
Rowde, Lower Foxhangers Farm
Salisbury, Old Mill
Salisbury, Rose & Crown
Warminster, Bishopstrow House

Yorkshire
Burnsall, Red Lion
Egton Bridge, Horse Shoe

London
Conrad, SW10
Tower Thistle, E1

Scotland
South
Auchencairn, Balcary Bay
Ettrick Valley, Tushielaw
Kelso, Ednam House
Portpatrick, Crown
Portpatrick, Knockinaam Lodge
West
Arduaine, Loch Melfort
Crinan, Crinan Hotel
Duror, Stewart
Eriska, Isle of Eriska Hotel
Kilchrenan, Ardanaiseig
Kilchrenan, Taychreggan
Kilmore, Glenfeochan House
Kilninver, Knipoch
Oban, Manor House
Onich, Allt-Nan-Ros
Port Appin, The Airds
Strachur, Creggans
Tiroran, Tiroran House
Tobermory, Tobermory
North of the Forth
Bridge of Cally, Bridge of Cally
Carronbridge, Lochend Farm
Inverness, Bunchrew House
Kenmore, Kenmore
Kyle of Lochalsh, Lochalsh
Spean Bridge, Letterfinlay Lodge
North
Achiltibuie, Summer Isles
Arisaig, Arisaig House
Dornie Loch, Duich
Glenelg, Glenelg
Melvich, Melvich Hotel
Scourie, Eddrachilles
Shieldaig, Tigh an Eilean
Strontian, Kilcamb Lodge
Tongue, Ben Loyal Hotel
Ullapool, Altnaharrie
Skye
Isle Ornsay, Kinloch Lodge
Skeabost, Skeabost House
Sleat, Ord House

Wales
North
Aberdovey, Bodfor
Aberdovey, Penhelig Arms
Betwys-y-Coed, Ty Gwyn
Erbistock, Boat
Llangollen, Bryn Howel
Llanwddyn, Lake Vyrnwy
Portmeirion, Portmeirion

Mid
Penmaenpool, George III
West
Broad Haven, Druidstone

South
Abergavenny, Llanwenarth Arms
Monmouth, Riverside
Oxwich Bay, Oxwich Bay

Hotels well placed for walks

The hotels, inns and other places we list here are placed where you can go for a good longish walk, straight from the door:

Bucks
Aylesbury, Hartwell House
Fawley, Walnut Tree
Hambleden, Stag & Huntsman
Taplow, Cliveden

Cheshire
Higher Burwardsley, Pheasant

Cornwall
Botallack, Manor Farm
Buryas Bridge, Rose Farm
Carne Beach, Nare
Constantine Bay, Treglos
Gerrans Bay, Pendower Beach House
Lamorna Cove, Lamorna Cove
Mawnan Smith, Meudon
Mawnan Smith, Nansidwell Country House
Mullion, Polurrian
Pendeen, Trewellard Manor Farm
Port Isaac, Port Gaverne
Portloe, Lugger
Portloe, Seal Cottage
Portscatho, Roseland House
Sennen, Old Success
Sennen, State House
Trelights, Longcross
Trenale, Trebrea Lodge

Isles of Scilly
Pelistry Bay, Carnwethers
Tresco, Island

Cumbria
Alston, Middle Bayles Farm
Barbon, Barbon Inn
Bassenthwaite Lake, Pheasant
Bowland Bridge, Hare & Hounds
Brampton, Farlam Hall
Brandlingill, Low Hall
Crook, Wild Boar
Dent, Sportsmans
Derwent Water, Lodore Swiss
Dockray, Royal
Elterwater, Britannia Inn
Eskdale Green, Bower House

Far Sawrey, Sawrey
Garrigill, George & Dragon
Grasmere, Michael's Nook
Grasmere, Swan
Grasmere, White Moss House
Grasmere, Wordsworth
Grizedale, Grizedale Lodge
Hawkshead, Highfield House
Hawkshead, Summer Hill
Ireby, Overwater Hall
Kirkcambeck, Cracrop Farm
Langdale, Langdale
Langdale, Old Dungeon Ghyll
Little Langdale, Three Shires
Lorton, New House Farm
Mungrisdale, Mill Hotel
Pooley Bridge, Sharrow Bay
Ravenstonedale, Fat Lamb
Seatoller, Seatoller House
Spark Bridge, Bridgefield House
Torver, Church House
Torver, Old Rectory
Troutbeck, Mortal Man
Wasdale Head, Wasdale Head
Winton, Bay Horse
Witherslack, Old Vicarage

Derbyshire and Staffordshire
Butterton, Black Lion
Castleton, Castle
Castleton, Olde Nags Head
Dovedale, Peveril of the Peak
Great Longstone, Barn
Greendale, Old Furnace Farm
Hathersage, George
Hathersage, Highlow Hall
Hope, Poachers Arms
Monsal Head, Monsal Head Hotel
Rowland, Holly Cottage

Devon
Bossington, Orchard Guest House
Bovey Tracey, Edgemoor Hotel
Chagford, Gidleigh Park
Chittlehamholt, Highbullen
Countisbury, Exmoor Sandpiper
Croyde, Whiteleaf

Dulverton, Highercombe
Dulverton, Tarr Steps
East Portlemouth, Gara Rock
Exford, White Horse
Haytor Vale, Rock
Heddons Mouth, Heddons Gate
Holne, Church House
Knowstone, Masons Arms
Lydford, Castle
Lynmouth, Rising Sun
Lynton, Hewitt's
Lynton, Lynton Cottage
Malborough, Soar Mill Cove
Meeth, Giffords Hele
Moretonhampstead, Great
  Sloncombe Farm
Oakford, Newhouse FarmWest
  Buckland, Huxtable Farm
Porlock, Ship
Porlock, West Porlock House
Preston, Sampsons Farm
Salcombe, Tides Reach
Selworthy, Hindon Farm
Slapton, Tower

Gloucestershire
Buckland, Buckland Manor
Clearwell, Clearwell Castle
Clearwell, Wyndham Arms
Great Rissington, Lamb
North Nibley, New Inn
St Briavels, George
Viney Hill, Lower Viney Country
  Guest House

Hampshire
Beaulieu, Montagu Arms
Eastleigh, Park Farm

Hereford & Worcester
Chaddesley Corbett, Brockencote
  Hall
Frith Common, Hunt House Farm
Great Malvern, Foley Arms
Kinnersley, Upper Newton
  Farmhouse
Leysters, Hills Farm
Ruckhall Common, Ancient Camp
Symonds Yat, Saracens Head
Woolhope, Butchers Arms

Kent
Ashford, Eastwell Manor
Chartham, Thruxted Oast
Groombridge, Crown
Headcorn, Bletchenden Manor Farm
Pluckley, Elvey Farm
Sissinghurst, Sissinghurst Castle Farm

St Margarets At Cliffe, Cliffe Tavern
  Hotel
Teston, Court Lodge
Warren Street, Harrow

Lancashire
Ashworth Valley, Leaches Farm
Chipping, Carr Side Farm
Darwen, Old Rosins
Gibbon Bridge, Gibbon Bridge
  Country House
Slaidburn, Parrock Head Farm
Waddington, Backford Cottage
Waddington, Peter Barn
Whitewell, Inn at Whitewell

**Leicestershire, Lincolnshire,
  Nottinghamshire,**
Leics
Empingham, White Horse
Oakham, Hambleton Hall
Stapleford, Stapleford Park
Notts
Bestwood Country Park, Bestwood
  Lodge

Norfolk
Winterton on Sea, Fishermans Return
Titchwell, Manor Hotel
Thornham, Lifeboat
Grimston, Congham Hall
South Lopham, Malting Farm

Northumberland and Durham
Bamburgh, Lord Crewe Arms
Cornhill on Tweed, Tillmouth Park
Cotherstone, Fox & Hounds
High Force, High Force Hotel
Middleton in Teesdale, Teesdale
Newton by the Sea, Joiners Arms
Romaldkirk, Rose & Crown
Tarset, Earls Lodge

Oxfordshire
Asthall, Maytime
Checkenden, Highwayman
Minster Lovell, Hill Grove Farm
Minster Lovell, Old Swan
Uffington, Craven
Woodstock, Feathers

Shropshire
Church Stretton, Long Mynd
Church Stretton, Mynd House
Clun, New House Farm
Hopesay, Old Rectory
Llanfair Waterdine, Red Lion
Strefford, Strefford Hall Farm

Wenlock Edge, Wenlock Edge Inn
Woolstaston, Rectory

Somerset and Avon
Dulverton, Ashwick House
Dulverton, Tarr Steps
Dunster, Luttrell Arms
Emborough, Redhill Farm
Exford, White Horse
Hunstrete, Hunstrete House
Isle Brewers, Bushfurlong Farm
Kilve, Meadow House
Lower Vellow, Curdon Mill
Middlecombe, Periton Park
Pinksmoor, Pinksmoor Millhouse
Roadwater, Wood Advent Farm
Stanton Drew, Valley Farm
West Bagborough, Rising Sun
Wiveliscombe, Deepleigh

Suffolk
Aldeburgh, White Lion
Hintlesham, College Farm
Southwold, Crown
Southwold, Swan
Westleton, Crown

Surrey
Albury, Drummond Arms
Bagshot, Pennyhill Park

Sussex
Alfriston, Deans Place
Alfriston, Star
Amberley, Amberley Castle
Battle, Netherfield Place
Bosham, Kenwood
Bosham, Millstream
Ditchling, Bull
Fittleworth, Swan
Fletching, Griffin
Poynings, Manor Farm
Shipley, Goffsland Farm
Storrington, Abingworth Hall
Telham, Little Hemingfold
  Farmhouse
Turners Hill, Alexander House
Winchelsea, New Inn

Wiltshire
Alderton, Manor Farm
Ebbesbourne Wake, Horseshoes
Gastard, Boyds Farm
Rowde, Lower Foxhangers Farm
West Grafton, Rose Garth

Yorkshire
Ampleforth, Carr House Farm
Arncliffe, Falcon
Askrigg, Kings Arms
Austwick, Game Cock
Bainbridge, Rose & Crown
Blakey Ridge, Lion
Bolton Abbey, Devonshire Arms
Buckden, Buck
Burnsall, Red Lion
Chapel le Dale, Old Hill
Cloughton, Hayburn Wyke
Cray, White Lion
Danby Wiske, White Swan
Egton Bridge, Horse Shoe
Egton Bridge, Postgate
Fadmoor, Plough
Feizor, Scar Close Farm
Goathland, Mallyan Spout
Grassington, Black Horse
Hackness, Hackness Grange
Hawes, Cocketts
Kilnsey, Tennant Arms
Lastingham, Blacksmiths Arms
Lastingham, Lastingham Grange
Malham, Buck
Markington, Hob Green
Middlesmoor, Crown
Otley, Chevin Lodge
Ramsgill, Yorke Arms
Richmond, Whashton Springs
  Farm
Robin Hood's Bay, Coble
Rosedale Abbey, Blacksmiths
  Arms
Rosedale Abbey, Milburn Arms
Rosedale Abbey, White Horse
Sedbusk, Stone House
Settle, Falcon Manor
Simonstone, Simonstone Hall
Stainforth, Craven Heifer
Starbotton, Fox & Hounds
Wath in Nidderdale, Sportsmans
  Arms
West Burton, Fox & Hounds
Wigglesworth, Plough

Scotland
South
Auchencairn, Balcary Bay
Beattock, Auchen Castle
Ettrick Valley, Tushielaw
Lockerbie, Dryfesdale Hotel
Minnigaff, Creebridge House
Nenthorn, Whitehill Farm
Portpatrick, Knockinaam Lodge
Quothquan, Shieldhill
Rockcliffe, Barons Craig
Selkirk, Philipburn House
Tweedsmuir, Crook Inn

West
Arduaine, Loch Melfort
Eriska, Isle of Eriska Hotel
Kilberry, Kilberry Inn
Kilchrenan, Ardanaiseig
Kilchrenan, Taychreggan
Kilfinan, Kilfinan Hotel
Kilmore, Glenfeochan House
Onich, Allt-Nan-Ros
Port Appin, The Airds
Strachur, Creggans
Tarbert, Stonefield Castle
North of the Forth
Advie, Tulchan Lodge
Ardeonaig, Ardeonaig
Auchterarder, Gleneagles
Ballater, Craigendarroch Hotel
Ballater, Tullich Lodge
Balquhidder, Monachyle Mhor
Carronbridge, Lochend Farm
Crianlarich, Allt-Chaorain Country
  House
Dalcross, Easter Dalziel Farm
Dulnain Bridge, Muckrach Lodge
Dunblane, Cromlix House
Dunkeld, Kinnaird House
East Haugh, East Haugh House
Fintry, Culcreuch Castle
Glendevon, Tormaukin
Kenmore, Kenmore
Kirkton of Glenisla, Glenisla
Pitlochry, Killiecrankie
Scone, Murrayshall House
Spean Bridge, Letterfinlay Lodge
Whitebridge, Knockie Lodge
North
Achiltibuie, Summer Isles
Altnaharra, Altnaharra
Ardvasar, Ardvasar
Arisaig, Arisaig House
Culnaknock, Glenview
Dornie Loch, Duich
Drumnadrochit, Borlum
  Farmhouse
Drumnadrochit, Polmaily House
Glenelg, Glenelg
Invermoriston, Glenmoriston
  Arms
Isle Ornsay, Kinloch Lodge
Isle Ornsay, Tigh Osda Eilean
  Iarmain
Kilchoan, Meall Mo Chridhe
Melvich, Melvich Hotel
Mey, Castle Arms
Portree, Rosedale
Raasay, Isle of Raasay
Scourie, Eddrachilles
Shiel Bridge, Kintail Lodge

Shieldaig, Tigh an Eilean
Skeabost, Skeabost House
Sleat, Ord House
Tongue, Ben Loyal Hotel
Ullapool, Altnaharrie

Wales
North
Abersoch, Porth Tocyn
Beddgelert, Sygun Fawr Country
  House
Betws-y-Coed, Royal Oak
Betws-y-Coed, Ty Gwyn
Brynsienecyn, Plas Trefarthen
Capel Garmon, Tan-y-Foel Country
  House
Capel Garmon, White Horse
Ffordd-las, Berllan Bach
Frongoch, Fferm Fron-Goch
Gellilydan, Tyddyn Du
Hanmer, Buck Farm
Llanarmon DC, Hand
Llanarmon DC, West Arms
Llandrillo, Tyddyn Llan
Llanerchymedd, Llwydiarth Fawr
  Farm
Llanerchymedd, Tre'r Ddol Farm
Llanfyllin, Bodfach Hall
Llangollen, Abbey Grange
Llangollen, Britannia
Llanwddyn, Lake Vyrnwy
Maentwrog, Plas Tan y Bwlch
Portmeirion, Portmeirion
Pwllheli, Yoke House Farm
Tremeirchion, Bach-y-Graig
Mid
Cwmdu, Farmers Arms
Eglwysfach, Ynyshir Hall
Gladestry, Royal Oak
Llangurig, Glansevern Arms
Llanwrtyd Wells, Cwmirfon
  Lodge
Llyswen, Llangoed Hall
Newport, Cnapan
Newtown, Lower Gwestydd
Old Radnor, Harp
Penmaenpool, George III
Pennal, Gogarth Hall Farm
Pontfaen, Tregynon Country
  Farmhouse
Rhayader, Beili Neuadd
Rhydlewis, Broniwan
West
Brechfa, Forest Arms
Broad Haven, Druidstone
Newport, Cnapan
South
Llanthony, Half Moon

Well placed hotels

The hotels, inns and other places listed below are placed very conveniently for sightseeing – there are interesting things nearby which you can get to on foot:

Cambridgeshire
Cambridge, Kirkwood House

Cheshire
Chester, Chester Grosvenor

Devon
Dartmouth, Royal Castle
Exeter, Royal Clarence
Exeter, St Olaves Court
Exeter, White Hart

Dorset
Bournemouth, Langtry Manor
Dorchester, Kings Arms
Poole, Mansion House

Hampshire
Winchester, Royal
Winchester, Wykeham Arms
Portsmouth, Sally Port

Hertfordshire
St Albans, White Hart

Humberside
Hull, Forte Crest

Kent
Canterbury, Cathedral Gate
Canterbury, Thanington

Lancashire
Blackpool, Imperial
Lancaster, Post House

Leicestershire, Lincolnshire and Nottinghamshire
Lincs
Lincoln, D'Isney Place
Lincoln, Edward King House
Lincoln, White Hart
Stamford, George

Midlands
Stratford-upon-Avon, Arden Thistle
Stratford-upon-Avon, Carlton
Stratford-upon-Avon, Coach House
Stratford-upon-Avon, Melita
Stratford-upon-Avon, Shakespeare
Stratford-upon-Avon, Stratford House
Stratford-upon-Avon, Welcombe

Northumbria
Durham, Royal County

Oxfordshire
Oxford, Old Parsonage
Oxford, Randolph

Somerset and Avon
Bath, Brocks
Bath, Dorian House
Bath, Haydon House
Bath, Priory
Bath, Queensberry
Bath, Royal Crescent

Sussex
Brighton, Topps
Chichester, Bedford
Chichester, Suffolk House
Rye, George
Rye, Jeakes House

Wiltshire
Salisbury, Farthings
Salisbury, Old Mill
Salisbury, Red Lion
Salisbury, Rose and Crown

Yorkshire
Harrogate, Balmoral
Harrogate, Hazlewood
Harrogate, Old Swan
Harrogate, Russell
York, 4 South Parade
York, Grange
York, Holmwood House
York, Middlethorpe Hall
York, Viking

Scotland
Edinburgh, Balmoral
Edinburgh, Caledonian
Edinburgh, Howard
Edinburgh, Roxburghe
Glasgow, Babbity Bowster
Glasgow, One Devonshire Gardens
Glasgow, Rab Ha's

Hotels with good food

In the hotels, inns and other places listed below, the quality of the food is high enough to make it a significant part of the pleasure of staying here:

Berkshire
Hampstead Marshall, White Hart
Kintbury, Dundas Arms
Pangbourne, Copper
Windsor, Oakley Court
Yattendon, Royal Oak

Buckinghamshire
Aston Clinton, Bell
Aylesbury, Hartwell House
Fawley, Walnut Tree
Marlow, Compleat Angler
Taplow, Cliveden
Winslow, Bell

Cambridgeshire
Cambridge, Cambridge Lodge
Eltisley, Leeds Arms
Flitwick, Flitwick Manor
Huntingdon, Old Bridge
Stilton, Bell
Wansford, Haycock

Cheshire
Bickley Moss, Cholmondely Arms
Brereton Green, Bears Head
Chester, Crabwell Manor
Chester, Grosvenor
Knutsford, Long View
Nantwich, Rookery Hall

Cornwall
Calstock, Danescombe Valley
Carne Beach, Nare
Fowey, Marina
Gerrans Bay, Pendover Beach House
Golant, Cormorant
Mawnan Smith, Nansidwell Country House
Padstow, Old Custom House
Pelynt, Jubilee
Port Isaac, Port Gaverne
Portloe, Lugger
Sennen, Old Success
St Ives, Garrack
Tregadillet, Eliot Arms
Treleigh, Inn For All Seasons

Isles of Scilly
Tresco, Island

Cumbria
Alston, Lovelady Shield
Ambleside, Rothay Manor
Barbon, Barbon Inn
Brackenthwaite, Pickett Howe
Cartmel, Uplands
Crosby on Eden, Crosby Lodge
Eskdale Green, Bower House
Grasmere, Michael's Nook
Grizedale, Grizedale Lodge
Ireby, Overwater Hall
Lorton, New House Farm
Lupton, Lupton Tower
Mungrisdale, Mill
Pooley Bridge, Sharrow Bay
Seatoller, Seatoller House
Spark Bridge, Bridgefield House
Watermillock, Leeming House
Watermillock, Old Church
Windermere, Miller House
Witherslack, Old Vicarage

Derbyshire
Ashbourne, Callow Hall
Ashford in the Water, Ashford Hotel
Ashford in the Water, Riverside Country House
Baslow, Cavendish
Baslow, Fischer's Baslow Hall
Biggin-by-Hartington, Biggin Hall
Buxton, Westminster Hotel
Grindleford, Maynard Arms
Hope, Poachers Arms
Matlock, Riber Hall
Monsal Head, Monsal Head
Rowland, Holly Cottage
Rowsley, Peacock
Shottle, Dannah Farm
Staffordshire
Alrewas, Claymar

Devon
Bishops Tawton, Halmpstone
Chagford, Gidleigh Park
Chittlehamholt, Highbullen
Croyde, Whiteleaf
Dartmouth, Royal Castle
Dulverton, Ashwick Country House
Exeter, White Hart
Gittisham, Combe House
Goveton, Buckland-tout-Saints
Gulworthy, Horn of Plenty
Haytor, Bel Alp House
Haytor Vale, Rock

Knowstone, Knowstone Court
Lewdown, Lewtrenchard Manor
Marlborough, Soar Mill Cove
Porlock, West Porlock House
Rousdon, Dower House
Salcombe, Tides Reach
South Molton, Whitechapel Manor
Stockland, Kings Arms
West Buckland, Huxtable Farm
Whimple, Woodhayes

Essex
Dedham, Maison Tollbooth
West Mersea, Blackwater

Gloucestershire
Bibury, Bibury Court
Bibury, Swan
Bledington, Kings Head
Charingworth, Charingworth Manor
Cheltenham, Greenway
Cirencester, Fleece
Clearwell, Wyndham Arms
Corse Lawn, Corse Lawn House
Lower Slaughter, Lower Slaughter
    House
Shurdington, Greenway
Tetbury, Calcot Manor
Tetbury, Close
Upper Slaughter, Lords of the Manor

Hampshire
Copythorne, Old Well
Hayling Island, Cockle Warren
    Cottage
Hurstbourne Tarrant, Esseborne
    Manor
Lymington, Stanwell House
Middle Wallop, Fifehead Manor
New Milton, Chewton Glen
Sparsholt, Lainston House
Winchester, Wykeham Arms

Hereford & Worcester
Abberley, Elms
Brimfield, Roebuck
Broadway, Collin House
Broadway, Lygon Arms
Bromsgrove, Grafton Manor
Chaddesley Corbett, Brockencote
    Hall
Evesham, Evesham
Harvington, Mill
Kington, Penrhos Court
Ledbury, Evesham
Ledbury, Hope End Country House
Symonds Yat, Saracens Head
Ullingswick, The Steppes

Isle of Wight
Seaview, Seaview

Kent
Ashford, Eastwell Manor
Faverhsam, Frith Farm House
Pluckley, Dering Arms
Shipbourne, Chaser
Snorden, Chequers
St Margarets at Cliffe, Walletts Court

Lancashire
Bury, Normandie
Cowan Bridge, Hipping Hall
Gibbon Bridge, Gibbon Bridge
    Country House
Manchester, Victoria & Albert
Slaidburn, Parrock Head Farm
Waddington, Peter Barn

**Leicestershire, Lincolnshire and
    Nottinghamshire**
Leics
Empingham, White Horse
Market Harborough, Three Swans
Medbourne, Nevill Arms
Oakham, Hambleton Hall
Stapleford, Stapleford Park
Stretton, Ram Jam Inn
Lincs
Barkston, Barkston House
Dyke, Wishing Well
Stamford, George
Notts
Drakholes, Griffin

Midlands
Culworth, Fulford House
Hockley Heath, Nuthurst Grange
Leamington Spa, Mallory Court
Stratford-upon-Avon, Stratford
    House
Sutton Coldfield, New Hall

Norfolk
Erpingham, Saracens Head
Great Snoring, Old Rectory
Grimston, Congham Hall
South Lopham, Malting Farm
Swaffham, Strattons

Northumbria
Chatton, Percy Arms
Easington, Grinkle Park
Longframlington, Embleton Hall
Middleton in Teesdale, Teesdale
Romaldkirk, Rose & Crown
Tow Law, Greenwell Farm

Warkworth, Warkworth Country
  House
Wylam, Laburnam House

Oxford
Burford, Angel
Charlbury, Bell
Chedlington, Manor
Clanfield, Plough
Great Milton, Manoir aux Quat'
  Saisons
Henley, Red Lion
Kingham, Mill House
Moulsford, Beetle & Wedge
Shipton-under-Wychwood, Lamb
Stonor, Stonor Arms
Woodstock, Feathers

Shropshire
Church Stretton, Mynd House
Hodnet, Bear
Hopesay, Old Rectory
Ludlow, Dinham Hall
Much Wenlock, Talbot
Norton, Hundred House
Wenlock Edge, Wenlock Edge Inn
Worfield, Old Vicarage

Somerset and Avon
Ansford, Bonds Hotel
Bath, Haydon House
Bath, Royal Crescent
Bradford on Avon, Bradford Old
  Windmill
Croscombe, Bull Terrier
Freshford, Homewood Park
Glastonbury, Number 3
Hunstrete, Hunstrete House
Kilve, Hood Arms
Langley Marsh, Langley House
Lower Vellow, Curdon Mill
Stoke St Gregory, Rose & Crown
Ston Easton, Ston Easton Park
Thornbury, Thornbury Castle
Vellow, Curdon Mill

Suffolk
Campsea Ashe, Old Rectory
Lavenham, Angel
Lavenham, Swan
Needham Market, Pipps Ford
Southwold, Crown

Surrey
Bagshott, Pennyhill Park

Sussex
Amberley, Amberley Castle

Amberley, Amberley Castle
Battle, Netherfield Place
Chichester, Suffolk House
East Grinstead, Gravelye Manor
Eastbourne, Grand
Hartfield, Bolebroke Mill
Lower Beeding, South Lodge
Seddlescombe, Brick Wall
Seddlescombe, Brickwall
Telham, Little Hemingfold
  Farmhouse
Turners Hill, Alexander House
Uckfield, Horsted Place

Wiltshire
Bradford-on-Avon, Woolley Grange
Burbage, Old Vicarage
Castle Combe, Manor House
Colerne, Lucknam Park
Corsley, Lane End Cottage
Ford, White Hart
Heytesbury, Angel
Hindon, Lamb
Horningsham, Bath Arms
Nettleton, Fosse Farmhouse
Teffont Evias, Howards House
Warminster, Bishopstrow House

Yorkshire
Askrigg, Kings Arms
Elslack, Tempest Arms
Kirkbymoorside, George & Dragon
Nidd, Nidd Hall
Pickhill, Nags Head
Richmond, Whashton Springs
  Farm
Sedbusk, Stone House
Sheffield, Charnwood
Shipton by Beningbrough, Sidings
Thornton Watlass, Buck
Wath in Nidderdale, Sportsmans
  Arms
York, 4 South Parade
York, Grange
York, Holmwood House
York, Middlethorpe Hall

Scotland
South
Auchencairn, Balcony Bay
Auchencairn, Collin House
Beattock, Auchen Castle
Canonbie, Riverside
Edinburgh, Balmoral
Edinburgh, Caledonian
Ettrick Valley, Tushielaw
Glasgow, One Devonshire
  Gardens

Gullane, Greywalls
Innerleithen, Caddon View
Kirkcowan, Craighlaw Arms
Melrose, Burts Hotel
Newton Stewart, Kirroughtree
Peebles, Cringletie House
Portpatrick, Crown
Portpatrick, Knockinaam Lodge
Quothquan, Shieldhill
Selkirk, Philipburn House
Swinton, Wheatsheaf
Tweedsmuir, Crook Inn
West
Arduaine, Loch Melfort
Eriska, Isle of Eriska
Kilberry, Kilberry
Kilchrenan, Ardanaiseig
Kilfinan, Kilfinan Hotel
Kilmore, Glenfeochan House
Kilninver, Knipoch
Port Appin, The Airds
Tiroran, Tiroran House
North of Forth
Aberfeldy, Farleyer House
Advie, Tulchan Lodge
Alyth, Lands of Loyal
Auchterarder, Auchterarder
    House
Ballater, Tullich Lodge
Blairgowrie, Kinloch House
Dunblane, Cromlix House
Dunkeld, Kinnaird House
East Haugh, East Haugh House
Elgin, Mansion House
Fintry, Culcreuch Castle
Glendevan, Tormaukin
Kinclaven by Stanley, Ballathie
    House
Nairn, Clifton House
Newtonmore, Ard-na-Coille
Peat Inn, Peat Inn
Pitlochry, Killiecrankie
Scone, Murrayshall House
Whitebridge, Knockie Lodge
North
Achiltibuie, Summer Isles
Arisaig, Arisaig House
Culnaknock, Glenview

Drumnadrochit, Polmaily House
Garve, Inchbae Lodge
Glenelg, Glenelg
Harlosh, Harlosh House
Isle Ornsay, Kinloch Lodge
Kilchoan, Meall Mo Chridhe
Mey, Castle Arms
Skeabost, Skeabost House
Sleat, Ord House
Ullapool, Altnaharrie
Wales
North
Abersoch, Porth Tocyn
Betws-y-Coed, Royal Oak
Capel Garmon, Tan-y-Foel Country
    House
Capel Garmon, White Horse
Conwy, Old Rectory
Hanmer, Buck Farm
Llanarmon DC, Hand
Llandrillo, Tuddyn Llan
Llandudno, Bodysgallen Hall
Llanerchymedd, Llwydiarth Fawr
    Farm
Llanrwst, Cae'r Berllan
Llansantffraid Glan Conwy, Old
    Rectory
Llanwddyn, Lake Vyrnwy
Penally, Penally Abbey
Talsarneau, Maes-y-Neuadd
South
Govilon, Llanwenarth House
Oxwich Bay, Oxwich Bay
Tintern Parva, Parva Farmhouse
Whitebrook, Crown at
    Whitebrook
Mid
Crickhowell, Bear
Eglwysfach, Ynyshir Hall
Llyswen, Griffin
Llyswen, Llangoed Hall
Newtown, Lower Gwestydd
Penmaenpool, George III
West
Broad Haven, Druidstone
Pontfaen, Tregynon Country
    Farmhouse
Rhydlewis, Broniwan

Hotels in secluded places

These hotels, inns and other places to stay are either secluded in their own grounds or in a very quiet spot, with attractive surroundings:

Buckinghamshire
Taplow, Cliveden

Cambridgeshire
Needingworth, Pike & Eel

Cheshire
Higher Burwardsley, Pheasant

Cornwall
Botallack, Manor Farm
Buryas Bridge, Rose Farm
Carne Beach, Nare
Constantine Bay, Treglos
Gerrans Bay, Pendower Beach House
Looe, Talland Bay
Mawnan Smith, Meudon
Mawnan Smith, Nansidwell Country House
Mullion, Polurrian
Port Isaac, Port Gaverne

Isles of Scilly
Tresco, Island

Cumbria,
Alston, Lovelady Shield
Brackenthwaite, Pickett Howe
Brandlingill, Low Hall
Cockermouth, High Stanger Farm
Dockray, Royal Ullswater
Garrigill, George & Dragon
Grasmere, Michael's Nook
Grasmere, White Moss House
Grizedale, Grizedale Lodge
Hawkshead, Highfield House
Ireby, Overwater Hall
Langdale, Old Dungeon Ghyll
Pooley Bridge, Sharrow Bay
Seatoller, Seatoller House
Spark Bridge, Bridgefield House
Talkin, Hullerbank
Torver, Old Rectory
Wasdale Head, Wasdale Head
Windermere, Miller Howe
Witherslack, Old Vicarage

Derbyshire and Staffordshire
Ashbourne, Callow Hall
Bakewell, Hassop Hall
Monsal Head, Monsal Head Hotel
Rowland, Holly Cottage
Shottle, Dannah Farm

Staffs
Greendale, Old Furnace Farm

Devon
Aveton Gifford, Court Barton Farmhouse
Branscombe, Look Out
Burgh Island, Burgh Island
Chagford, Gidleigh Park
Chagford, Mill End
Chittlehamholt, Highbullen
Dulverton, Ashwick Country House
Dulverton, Tarr Steps
East Portlemouth, Gara Rock
Gittisham, Combe House
Lewdown, Lewtrenchard Manor
Lynton, Hewitt's
Malborough, Soar Mill Cove
Morchard Bishop, Wigham
Moretonhampstead, Great Sloncombe Farm
Oakford, Newhouse Farm
Salcombe, Tides Reach
West Buckland, Huxtable Farm

Dorset
Chedington, Chedington Court
Evershot, Summer Lodge
Halstock, Halstock Mill

Gloucestershire
Buckland, Buckland Manor

Hereford & Worcester
Chaddesley Corbett, Brockencote Hall
Frith Common, Hunt House Farm
Ledbury, Hope End Country House
Leysters, Hills Farm
Malvern Wells, Cottage in the Wood
Ruckhall Common, Ancient Camp

Lancs
Chipping, Carr Side Farm
Slaidburn, Parrock Head Farm
Whitewell, Inn at Whitewell

Leicestershire
Oakham, Hambleton Hall
Stapleford, Stapleford Park

Northumbria

Northumberland

Cornhill on Tweed, Tillmouth Park
Edlingham, Lumbylaw Farm
Longframlington, Embleton Hall
Tarset, Earls Lodge

Durham

Easington, Grinkle Park
High Force, High Force Hotel
Tow Law, Greenwell Farm

Shropshire

Clun, New House Farm
Gretton, Court Farm
Hopesay, Old Rectory
Strefford, Strefford Hall Farm

Somerset

Dulverton, Tarr Steps
Emborough, Redhill Farm
Hunstrete, Hunstrete House
Lower Vellow, Curdon Mill
Middlecombe, Periton Park
Roadwater, Wood Advent Farm

Surrey

Bagshot, Pennyhill Park

Sussex

Battle, Netherfield Place
East Grinstead, Gravetye Manor
Poynings, Manor Farm
Rusper, Ghyll Manor
Rusper, Rusper House
Shipley, Goffsland Farm
Telham, Little Hemingfold
  Farmhouse
Turners Hill, Alexander House

Wiltshire

Castle Combe, Manor House
Rowde, Lower Foxhangers Farm
Stourton, Spread Eagle

Yorkshire

Ampleforth, Carr House Farm
Arncliffe, Falcon
Bolton Abbey, Devonshire Arms
  Country House
Chop Gate, Hill End Farm
Cloughton, Hayburn Wyke
Feizor, Scar Close Farm
Hackness, Hackness Grange
Lastingham, Lastingham Grange
Markington, Hob Green
Middlesmoor, Crown
Otley, Chevin Lodge
Richmond, Whashton Springs Farm

Rosedale Abbey, White Horse
Sedbusk, Stone House
Wath in Nidderdale, Sportsmans
  Arms

Scotland

South

Auchencairn, Balcary Bay
Auchencairn, Collin House
Beattock, Auchen Castle
Gatehouse of Fleet, Cally Palace
Kelso, Sunlaws House
Peebles, Cringletie House
Portpatrick, Knockinaam Lodge
Quothquan, Shieldhill
Rockcliffe, Barons Craig

West

Arduaine, Loch Melfort
Duror, Stewart
Eriska, Isle of Eriska Hotel
Isle of Gigha, Isle of Gigha Hotel
Kilchrenan, Ardanaiseig
Kilchrenan, Taychreggan
Kilmore, Glenfeochan House
Onich, Allt-Nan-Ros
Port Appin, The Airds
Strachur, Creggans
Tarbert, Stonefield Castle
Tiroran, Tiroran House

North of the Forth

Aberfeldy, Farleyer House
Advie, Tulchan Lodge
Ardeonaig, Ardeonaig
Auchterarder, Gleneagles
Ballater, Craigendarroch Hotel
Balquhidder, Monachyle Mhor
Blairgowrie, Kinloch House
Callander, Roman Camp
Carronbridge, Lochend Farm
Cleish, Nivingston House
Dalcross, Easter Dalziel Farm
Dulnain Bridge, Muckrach Lodge
Dunblane, Cromlix House
Dunkeld, Kinnaird House
Fintry, Culcreuch Castle
Inverness, Bunchrew House
Kinclaven by Stanely, Ballathie
  House
Kirkton of Glenisla, Glenisla
Pitlochry, Killiecrankie
Scone, Murrayshall House
Spean Bridge, Letterfinlay Lodge
Whitebridge, Knockie Lodge

North

Achiltibuie, Summer Isles
Arisaig, Arisaig House
Dornie Loch, Duich
Drumnadrochit, Borlum Farmhouse

Garve, Inchbae Lodge
Glenelg, Glenelg
Kilchoan, Meall Mo Chridhe
Melvich, Melvich Hotel
Scarista, Scarista House
Scourie, Eddrachilles
Shieldaig, Tigh an Eilean
Ullapool, Altnaharrie
Skye
Culnaknock, Glenview
Harlosh, Harlosh House
Isle Ornsay, Kinloch Lodge
Isle Ornsay, Tigh Osda Eilean
  Iarmain
Raasay, Isle of Raasay
Skeabost, Skeabost House
Sleat, Ord House

Wales
North
Beddgelert, Sygun Fawr Country
  House
Capel Garmon, Tan-y-Foel Country
  House
Conwy, Old Rectory
Gellilydan, Tyddyn Du
Hanmer, Buck Farm
Llanarmon DC, Hand
Llanarmon DC, West Arms
Llandrillo, Tyddyn Llan

Llanerchymedd, Llwydiarth Fawr
  Farm
Llanwddyn, Lake Vyrnwy
Maentwrog, Plas Tan y Bwlch
Portmeirion, Portmeirion
Pwllheli, Yoke House Farm
Tremeirchion, Bach-y-Graig
Mid
Churchstoke, Drewin Farm
Crickhowell, Gliffaes Country House
Eglwysfach, Ynyshir Hall
Llangurig, Glansevern Arms
Llanwrtyd Wells, Cwmirfon Lodge
Llyswen, Llangoed Hall
Newtown, Lower Gwestydd
Old Radnor, Harp
Pennal, Gogarth Hall Farm
Rhayader, Beili Neuadd
West
Broad Haven, Druidstone
Crugybar, Glanrannell Park
Pen-y-Cwm, Lochmeyler Farm
Pontfaen, Tregynon Country
  Farmhouse
Rhydlewis, Broniwan
South
Govilon, Llanwenarth House
Little Mill, Pentwyn Farm
Llanthony, Half Moon
Tintern Parva, Parva Farmhouse

Report forms

Please report to us: you can use the card in the middle of the book, tear-out forms on the following pages, or just plain paper – whichever's easiest for you. We need to know what you think of the places mentioned in this edition – especially, whether you think we should add to or change our descriptions of them. We need to know about other places worthy of inclusion. We need to know about ones that should not be included. We try to answer all letters, and readers who send us reports will be offered a discount on the price of the next edition that benefits from their help.

If you are recommending a new entry, the more detail you can put into your description, the better. This'll help not just us but also your fellow-readers gauge its appeal. A description of its character and even furnishings is a tremendous boon. Imagine you're writing about it for the *Guide* itself, and put in the sorts of things you'd want to know yourself before deciding whether to choose it.

The atmosphere and character of a holiday hotel or simpler place to stay, or of a restaurant, are very important to us – why it would, or would not, appeal to people who don't know it. And, of course, the quality and type of its food matter a lot, too, so please tell us about that as well. A full address and telephone number is an enormous help.

We'd also very much like you to let us know of places you've enjoyed visiting – anything from a little village to a stately home, from a shop selling unusual things to a factory visit, from an outstanding plant nursery to a hot-air balloon festival, from a hidden-away country church to a cathedral, from a peaceful wood or a nature reserve or a stretch of unspoilt coastal cliff to a theme park or a zoo or a pleasure beach. We're also particularly interested in enjoyable walks and drives. Whatever it is, if you've enjoyed it, please tell us about it.

There are several different forms on the following pages: one for endorsement of existing entries; forms for more detailed descriptions of places to visit, and hotels/restaurants; and finally, one for your overall favourite nominations.

When you go to a hotel, restaurant, or anywhere else, don't tell them you're a reporter for *The Good Weekend Guide*; we do make clear that all inspections are anonymous, and if you declare yourself as a reporter you risk getting special treatment – for better or for worse!

When you write to *The Good Weekend Guide,* FREEPOST TN1569, WADHURST, E Sussex TN5 7BR, you don't need a stamp in the UK. We'll gladly send you more forms (free) if you wish. The information you send us will be stored in our computer files.

Though we try to answer letters, we do have other work to do, besides producing this *Guide.* So please understand if there's a delay. And from June well into autumn, when we are fully extended getting the next edition to the printers, we put all letters and reports aside, not answering them until the rush is over (and after our post-press-day autumn holiday). The end of May is pretty much the cut-off date for reasoned consideration of reports for the next edition – and the earlier the better, if they're suggestions of new entries.

We'll assume we can print your name or initials as a recommender unless you tell us otherwise.

I have been to the following hotels/restaurants/attractions/places in
The 1995 Good Weekend Guide **in the last few months, found them
as described, and confirm that they deserve continued inclusion:**

Your own name and address *(block capitals please)*

Place to visit / Event

Its name:

Address:

Postcode: Telephone:

_____

Description/why it appeals

_____

Special tips

PLEASE GIVE YOUR NAME AND ADDRESS ON THE BACK OF THIS FORM

Your own name and address *(block capitals please)*

Please tick this box if you would like more forms ☐

Please return to:
        The Good Weekend Guide
        FREEPOST TN1569
        WADHURST
        E Sussex
        TN5 7BR

Place to eat at or stay in

Its name:

Address:

Postcode: Telephone:

What is this? (eg hotel, restaurant, B&B, inn, farmhouse)

Description/why it appeals *NB please describe character, food, service, and if relevant mention views, surroundings, walks direct from establishment, nearby attractions etc*

Your own name and address *(block capitals please)*

Please tick this box if you would like more forms ☐

Please return to:
 The Good Weekend Guide
 FREEPOST TN1569
 WADHURST
 E Sussex
 TN5 7BR

The Good Weekend Guide: Your Top Nominations

Please list for us your personal choices as special recommendations, in each or any of the following categories. In each category you can give UP TO THREE CHOICES, in order – starting with your first choice.

BEST AREA ALL ROUND, FOR A WEEKEND OR SHORT BREAK

BEST TOWN OR CITY, FOR A SHORT BREAK

AREA WITH MOST FRIENDLY PEOPLE

NICEST PLACE TO STAY (hotel, inn, B&B, farmhouse, etc)

BEST MEAL OUT

ATTRACTION OR PLACE YOU'VE MOST ENJOYED VISITING

EVENT / FESTIVAL YOU'VE MOST ENJOYED

PRETTIEST VILLAGE YOU'VE SEEN

PLEASE GIVE YOUR NAME AND ADDRESS ON THE BACK OF THIS FORM

Your own name and address *(block capitals please)*

Please tick this box if you would like more forms ☐

Please return to:
        The Good Weekend Guide
        FREEPOST TN1569
        WADHURST
        E Sussex
        TN5 7BR

Place to visit / Event

Its name:

Address:

Postcode: Telephone:

___

Description/why it appeals

___

Special tips

PLEASE GIVE YOUR NAME AND ADDRESS ON THE BACK OF THIS

Your own name and address *(block capitals please)*

Please tick this box if you would like more forms ☐

Please return to:

The Good Weekend Guide
FREEPOST TN1569
WADHURST
E Sussex
TN5 7BR

ORM